ROUTLEDGE HANDBOOK OF CIVIL SOCIETY IN ASIA

The *Routledge Handbook of Civil Society in Asia* is an interdisciplinary resource, covering one of the most dynamically expanding sectors in contemporary Asia. Originally a product of Western thinking, civil society represents a particular set of relationships between the state and either society or the individual. Each culture, however, molds its own version of civil society, reflecting its most important values and traditions.

This handbook provides a comprehensive survey of the directions and nuances of civil society, featuring contributions by leading specialists on Asian society from the fields of political science, sociology, anthropology, and other disciplines. Comprising thirty-five essays on critical topics and issues, it is divided into two main sections:

Part I covers country specific reviews, including Japan, China, South Korea, India, and Singapore.

Part II offers a series of thematic chapters, such as democratization, social enterprise, civic activism, and the media.

As an analysis of Asian social, cultural, and political phenomena from the perspective of civil society in the post-World War II era, this book will be useful to students and scholars of Asian Studies, Asian Politics, and Comparative Politics.

Akihiro Ogawa is Professor of Japanese Studies at the Asia Institute of the University of Melbourne.

ROUTLEDGE HANDBOOK OF CIVIL SOCIETY IN ASIA

Edited by Akihiro Ogawa

LONDON AND NEW YORK

First published 2018
by Routledge
2 Park Square, Milton Park, Abingdon, Oxon OX14 4RN

and by Routledge
711 Third Avenue, New York, NY 10017

Routledge is an imprint of the Taylor & Francis Group, an informa business

British Library Cataloguing in Publication Data
A catalogue record for this book is available from the British Library

Library of Congress Cataloging in Publication Data
A catalog record for this book has been requested

ISBN: 978-1-138-65595-9 (hbk)
ISBN: 978-1-315-10085-2 (ebk)

Typeset in Bembo
by Wearset Ltd, Boldon, Tyne and Wear

Dedicated to all of the civil society people we met in the field

CONTENTS

List of illustrations   *x*

Notes on contributors   *xi*

Foreword by Jeff Kingston   *xx*

Acknowledgments   *xxiii*

Introduction   1
Akihiro Ogawa

PART I
Country review   **15**

1   Japan   17
    Simon Avenell

2   South Korea   33
    Yooil Bae

3   China   49
    Anthony J. Spires

4   Hong Kong   66
    Alvin Y. So

5   Taiwan   79
    Anru Lee

6   Mongolia   95
    Dulam Bumochir

Contents

7 The Philippines
Jorge V. Tigno
110

8 Vietnam
Jörg Wischermann and Dang Thi Viet Phuong
129

9 Malaysia
Gaik Cheng Khoo
143

10 Singapore
Gillian Koh and Debbie Soon
160

11 Indonesia
Vedi R. Hadiz
175

12 Cambodia
Astrid Norén-Nilsson
191

13 Laos
Gretchen Kunze
204

14 Thailand
Bencharat Sae Chua
215

15 Burma (Myanmar)
Stephen McCarthy
227

16 India
Pradeep Taneja and Salim Lakha
236

17 Pakistan
Nadeem Malik
248

18 Bangladesh
M. Anwar Hossen
264

19 Nepal
Mukta S. Tamang
278

20 Bhutan
Michiyo Kiwako Okuma Nyström
293

21 Sri Lanka
Udan Fernando
311

PART II
Thematic review   **325**

22 Democratization   327
Apichai W. Shipper

23 Authoritarian rule   344
Jörg Wischermann

24 The third sector   362
Ruth Phillips

25 Social enterprises   376
Rosario Laratta

26 Philanthropy   390
Masayuki Deguchi

27 Development   407
Chika Watanabe

28 Media   420
Claudia Astarita

29 Human rights   435
Jennifer Chan

30 Family   456
Allison Alexy

31 Queer   469
Claire Maree

32 Youth activism   477
Ian Rowen

33 Migration   488
Daniel Kremers and Stefan Rother

34 Base protest   505
Yuko Kawato

35 Sustainability and climate governance   520
Janelle Knox-Hayes

Index   *537*

ILLUSTRATIONS

Figures

2.1 Approval rating of government institutions in South Korea, 2003–2014 39
2.2 Growth of registered NGOs in South Korea in the 2000s 40
2.3 Patterns of social group participation in South Korea 41
23.1 Civil society roles 355

Tables

7.1 Registration/accreditation of non-governmental entities in the Philippines 121
20.1 Example of traditional local resource management institutions in Bhutan 297
22.1 Indexes of demography, income, democracy, and civil society in Asia 328
35.1 Interview subject list 533

Map

Map of Asia xxiv

CONTRIBUTORS

Allison Alexy is an Assistant Professor in the Department of Asian Languages and Cultures at the University of Michigan, Ann Arbor. Her research explores intimacy, family norms, and law in contemporary Japan. She is finishing a book, *Divorce and the Romance of Independence in Contemporary Japan*, and has completed research about international child custody disputes and abductions involving Japanese citizens. Alexy has co-edited two books: *Home and Family in Japan: Continuity and Transformation* (with Richard Ronald, Routledge, 2010) and *Intimate Japan* (with Emma E. Cook, forthcoming). Her research has been supported by the Fulbright IIE Fellowship, the Japan Foundation, and an Abe Fellowship administered by the Social Science Research Council.

Claudia Astarita is a Fellow at the Asia Institute, the University of Melbourne. She regularly contributes articles on Asian political, economic, and social issues to several newspapers and magazines such as *Corriere della Sera*, *Panorama*, and *South China Morning Post*. She obtained her PhD in Asian Studies from the University of Hong Kong in early 2010. Her main research interests include China's political and economic development, Chinese and Indian foreign policies, East Asian regionalism and regional economic integration, Asian civil society, and the role of media and memory (both official and unofficial) in reshaping historical narratives in Asia.

Simon Avenell is an Associate Professor and Associate Dean at the Australian National University (ANU) College of Asia and the Pacific. He received his PhD in History at the University of California, Berkeley, in 2003. Prior to ANU, he spent nine years at the National University of Singapore. His research interests include civil society, environmentalism, transnational activism, and political thought in contemporary Japan. His publications include *Making Japanese Citizens: Civil Society and the Mythology of the Shimin in Postwar Japan* (2010); "Antinuclear Radicals: Scientific Experts and Antinuclear Activism in Japan," in *Science, Technology, and Society* 21(1), 2016; and *Transnational Japan in the Global Environmental Movement* (2017).

Yooil Bae is an Associate of Asian Urbanism Cluster at the Asia Research Institute, National University of Singapore. He publishes on comparative politics and policy, state–society relationships, urban political economy, and environmental politics in East Asia in journals, including *International Journal of Urban and Regional Research*, *Pacific Review*, *Democratization*, and *Cities*. He is the co-author of a book, *Mega-Events and Mega-Ambitions: South Korea's Rise and the Strategic Use of the Big Four Events* (2017).

Dulam Bumochir is a Professor of Anthropology in the Department of Anthropology and Archaeology of the National University of Mongolia, and a Research Associate in the Department of Anthropology of the University College London (UCL). His PhD is in Philology from the Mongolian Academy of Sciences (2000), and Anthropology from the University of Cambridge (2006). His research area is broad; he started his career exploring folk and shamanic practices, rituals, and chants. In 2000, he expanded his research to a new field in Qinghai, China, focusing on sincerity, performance, and power of respect in the social production of ethnic identity, politics, and state amongst minority Mongol pastoralists. Currently, he examines environment and nationalism in Mongolia. He elaborates "environment" to be a neoliberal asset and political instrument widely engaged in multiple local, national, and global discourses.

Jennifer Chan is an Associate Professor in the Faculty of Education at the University of British Columbia in Vancouver, Canada. She graduated from Stanford University with a PhD in International Comparative Education. She is the author of *Politics in the Corridor of Dying: AIDS Activism and Global Health Governance* (2015) and *Gender and Human Rights Politics in Japan: Global Norms and Domestic Networks* (2004). She is also the editor of *Another Japan is Possible: New Social Movements and Global Citizenship Education* (2008). She has published widely in *Critique Internationale, Comparative Education, International Feminist Journal of Politics, Recherche Feministes, International Review of Education,* and *Globalisation, Societies and Education.* Her research interests lie in international human rights law and social movements, civil society, anti-racism and multiculturalism, gender, global health governance, and global justice movement.

Bencharat Sae Chua is a Lecturer at the Institute of Human Rights and Peace Studies, Mahidol University, Thailand. Her research interests focus on understanding human rights claims and discourses in the context of contentions over the meanings of democracy and citizenship. With her background of working with developmental NGOs before joining academics, she is interested in the roles of social movements and civil society in Thailand and Southeast Asia, in particular.

Dang Thi Viet Phuong is a sociologist at the Institute of Sociology, Vietnam Academy of Social Sciences (VASS). She is Deputy Head of the Department of Social Security and Social Work. Her fields of interest are the development of civil society, problems of social welfare, and rural development. Dang has been involved in several international research projects exploring the development of civil society in Vietnam since 2000. Her most recent publications include *The Collective Life: The Sociology of Voluntary Associations in North Vietnamese Rural Areas* (2015).

Masayuki Deguchi is a Professor at the National Museum of Ethnology (MINPAKU) and Graduate University for Advanced Studies (SOKENDAI), Japan. He has rich experiences not only of academics but also of third sector organizations and government. He was appointed Commissioner, Public Interest Corporation Commission (Japan's Charity Commission), by the prime minister upon obtaining the consent of both houses of the Diet (2007–2013), and also served as a member of the Governmental Tax Commission (2003–2009). From 2005 to 2006, he was President of the International Society for the Third Sector Research (ISTR).

Udan Fernando obtained his PhD from the University of Amsterdam in International Development Cooperation. His thesis focused on the politics of aid regarding the Dutch aid system and Sri Lankan NGOs. Fernando's specialization has previously been Law, Economics, Management, and Labor Studies. Throughout his career, from Head of the Development Commission of the National Christian Council of Sri Lanka (1989–1995), to Executive Director of Paltra (gte) Ltd (1996–2001), Guest Researcher at the University of Amsterdam (2002–2007), and Senior Consultant of Context International, Netherlands (2008–2012), he has focused on development cooperation and aid policy in Sri Lanka, Europe, East and West Africa, and Southeast Asia. Recent assignments include co-authoring the National Human Development Report (UNDP, 2014) and the position paper on "Sri Lankan Civil Society and International Donors for Oxfam" (2015), and contributing to a UN publication titled "New MIC in the Block: Middle Income Country Status and Civil Society in Sri Lanka" (2016). Fernando is currently the Executive Director of the Centre for Poverty Analysis (CEPA), a Sri Lankan think-tank.

Vedi R. Hadiz, before joining the University of Melbourne's Asia Institute in 2016 as Professor and Convenor of Asian Studies, was Professor of Asian Societies and Politics at Murdoch University's Asia Research Centre, and Director of its Indonesia Research Program. An Indonesian national, he was an Australian Research Council Future Fellow in 2010–2014. Hadiz received his PhD from Murdoch University in 1996 where he was a Research Fellow until he went to the National University of Singapore in 2000. At NUS, he was an Associate Professor in the Department of Sociology until returning to Murdoch in 2010. His research interests revolve around issues related to political sociology and political economy, especially those related to the contradictions of development in Indonesia and Southeast Asia broadly, and more recently, in the Middle East. His latest book is titled *Islamic Populism in Indonesia and the Middle East* (2016).

M. Anwar Hossen is a Professor in the Sociology Department, University of Dhaka, Bangladesh, and a co-editor of *Bandung: Journal of the Global South*. He has eighteen years' experience in teaching and research at four universities in Bangladesh and Canada. Hossen has extensively published articles with Brill, Routledge, and Springer, and in the *Social Science Review*. His new book *Water Policy and Governance in South Asia: Empowering Rural Communities* was published by Routledge in early 2017. He received the Nehru Humanitarian Award, and the International Development Research Center award. Currently, his research focuses on water governance, civil society, climate change, and agricultural communities in South Asia.

Yuko Kawato is a Research Fellow at the Asia Centre, a think-tank in Paris, France. She obtained her PhD in Political Science from the University of Washington. Her expertise is in Japan's civil society and foreign policy. Her publications include *Protests Against U.S. Military Base Policy in Asia: Persuasion and Its Limits* (Stanford University Press, 2015); a book chapter on civil society in Jeff Kingston (Ed.), *Natural Disaster and Nuclear Crisis in Japan: Response and Recovery After 3/11* (with Robert Pekkanen and Yutaka Tsujinaka, Routledge, 2012); and articles on Japan's civil society and foreign policy in Asia Centre's *Japan Analysis*.

Gaik Cheng Khoo is an Associate Professor at the University of Nottingham Malaysia Campus where she teaches film and cultural studies. She is interested in cosmopolitanism, citizenship, and questions of belonging and identity as manifested in film, food, and space. Her current research focuses on Korean migrants in Malaysia. Her recent publications include a book co-authored with Jean Duruz, *Eating Together: Food Space and Identity in Malaysia and Singapore* (2014; 2015); a book co-edited with Julian Lee, *Malaysia's New Ethnoscapes and Ways of Belonging* (Routledge, 2015); and numerous journal articles and book chapters on independent film-making in Malaysia and Singapore. Her forthcoming publications focus on the taste and cultural sustainability of Penang hawker food, and on Bersih, the Malaysian Coalition for Free and Fair Elections. Khoo is the founder of the Association of Southeast Asian Cinemas, a region-based biannual international conference going into its tenth manifestation in 2017.

Jeff Kingston is Director of Asian Studies at Temple University, Japan. He has edited *Press Freedom in Contemporary Japan* (Routledge, 2017), *Asian Nationalisms Reconsidered* (Routledge, 2016), *Critical Issues in Contemporary Japan* (Routledge, 2014), and *Natural Disaster and Nuclear Crisis* (Routledge, 2012), and is author of *Nationalism in Asia: A History Since 1945* (2017), *Contemporary Japan* (2013), and *Japan's Quiet Transformation* (Routledge, 2004). In addition to various book chapters and scholarly articles, he writes *Counterpoint*, a weekly column for the *Japan Times*.

Janelle Knox-Hayes is the Lister Brothers Associate Professor of Economic Geography and Planning in the Department of Urban Studies and Planning, MIT. Her research focuses on the ways in which social and environmental systems are governed under changing temporal and spatial scales as a consequence of globalization. Her latest project examines how social values shape sustainable development in the Arctic. She is an author and co-author of multiple journal articles and two books, including *Saving for Retirement* (with Gordon L. Clark and Kendra Strauss, 2012), and *The Culture of Markets: The Political Economy of Climate Governance* (2016). She is also the book review editor of the *Journal of Economic Geography*, and editor for the *Cambridge Journal of Regions, Economy and Society*.

Gillian Koh is Deputy Director (Research) and Head of the Politics and Governance Cluster at the Institute of Policy Studies of the National University of Singapore. Her areas of research and published work are in electoral politics, state–society relations, and the development of civil society in Singapore, and her recent publications includes a co-edited book *Civil Society and the State in Singapore* (2017). Koh received her PhD in Sociological Studies from the University of Sheffield, UK. She has been with the Institute of Policy Studies since 1996.

Daniel Kremers is a Senior Research Fellow at the German Institute for Japanese Studies (DIJ) in Tokyo. He received his PhD in Japanese Studies from Martin-Luther-University Halle-Wittenberg, Germany. He studied Japanese Studies, Political Science, and Journalism at Leipzig University, and as an exchange student visited the Graduate School of Political Science (GSPS) and the Graduate School of Asia Pacific Studies (GSAPS) at Waseda University, Tokyo. His dissertation investigated the influence of advocacy and lobbying by labor unions, NGOs, employer associations, and parties on Japan's immigration policy in a case study on the Technical Intern Training Program (TITP). His current research focuses on the use of renewable energies in local communities and its effects on the equity and resilience of societies. Together with film-maker Tilman König, Kremers co-produced and co-directed the documentary *Sour Strawberries—Japan's hidden "guest workers."*

Gretchen Kunze has nearly two decades of experience in international development, particularly in the areas of governance, civic engagement, and access to justice, and has spent over fourteen years living and working in Asia. She is currently based in Yangon as the Myanmar Country Representative for World Learning, where she leads their Institute for Political and Civic Engagement. Kunze oversaw programs in Laos for over seven years and lived in Vientiane from 2009 to 2013 as Country Representative for The Asia Foundation. Previously, she was the

Deputy Country Representative for Thailand and Laos and was based in Bangkok. She has written numerous articles on Laos and has also lived and worked in Mongolia, Japan, Sweden, and the USA.

Salim Lakha is an Honorary Senior Fellow in the School of Social and Political Sciences at the University of Melbourne. He was formerly the Coordinator of the Development Studies Program at the University of Melbourne and in 2011, a Visiting Senior Research Fellow at the Asia Research Institute, National University of Singapore. Lakha's specialization is India, and his research interests include social protection, decentralization, governance and development, international migration, and transnational identities. He is currently engaged in a collaborative research project that examines the role of social audit as an accountability tool under the Mahatma Gandhi National Rural Employment Guarantee Scheme (MGNREGS), introduced by the Government of India in 2005. It is a rights-based scheme aimed at promoting the security of livelihood, inclusive growth, and social accountability. The broader aim of the research is to explore whether MGNREGS is contributing to poverty alleviation and a deepening of democracy. This research is funded by the Australia India Institute, University of Melbourne.

Rosario Laratta is a Professor of Political Science and Social Policy at the International College of Liberal Arts, Yamanashi Gakuin University, Japan. He obtained a PhD and MA in Political Sociology from the University of Warwick, UK, and an MA in Public Policy from Bocconi University, Italy. Laratta is the author and editor of many books such as *Nonprofit Organizations in England and Japan: Examining Advocacy, Accountability, and Ethical Climate* (2012) and *Empirical Policy Research—Letting the Data Speak for Themselves* (2013). His most recent publication includes an edited book *Social Enterprise—Context-Dependent Dynamics in a Global Perspective* (2016).

Anru Lee is a faculty member in the Anthropology Department, John Jay College of Criminal Justice, the City University of New York. Her research focuses on the Asia-Pacific region and issues of capitalism, modernity, gender and sexuality, and urban anthropology. Lee is the author of *In the Name of Harmony and Prosperity: Labor and Gender Politics in Taiwan's Economic Restructuring* (SUNY, 2004) and is co-editor of *Women in the New Taiwan: Gender Roles and Gender Consciousness in a Changing Society* (ME Sharpe, 2004). Her current project investigates urban public transit systems as related to issues of technology, governance, and citizenship. Her most recent fieldwork looks at the Mass Rapid Transit (MRT) systems in Taipei and Kaohsiung, the two largest cities in Taiwan, in the context of the country's struggle for cultural and national identity.

Stephen McCarthy is a Research Fellow and Senior Lecturer in Southeast Asian Politics at the Griffith Asia Institute and the School of Government and International Relations, Griffith University, Australia. He has published widely in international journals including *Pacific Review*, *Democratization*, *Environmental Politics*, and *International Political Science Review*. He is the author of *The Political Theory of Tyranny in Singapore and Burma* (Routledge, 2006).

Nadeem Malik has been the Director of the Development Studies Program of the University of Melbourne from 2009 to 2014. He did his PhD in Development Studies from the University of Melbourne. Prior to the current academic appointment, he worked in the development sector as a researcher and a trainer for twenty years. Malik's major areas of specialization are third world development, globalization, gender and development, governance, civil society and the state, and project management.

Claire Maree is a Senior Lecturer in Japanese at the Asia Institute, University of Melbourne. Her research spans the areas of critical language studies, gender/sexuality and language studies, media studies, and queer studies. Maree is current sole chief investigator (CI) for the research project "Writing Identity onto the Screen: Subtitles and Captions in Japanese Media" (Australian Research Council Discovery Project150102964). She is also Lead CI on a team project with colleagues from Australia and Japan: "Thirty Years of Talk: A Panel Study of Kobe Women's Interview Discourse" (Australian Research Council Discovery Project 170102598). Her major publications include '*Onē-kotoba' Ron* [On '*Onē-kotoba*' (*Language of Queens*)] (2013) and *Hatsuwasha no gengo sutoratejī toshite no negoshiēshon kōi* [*Negotiation as a Linguistic Strategy of Speakers*] (2007). She contributes articles to journals such as *The Asia-Pacific Journal*, *Media International Australia*, *Nihon Joseigakkai-shi*, *Women's Studies*, *Intersections*, *Gendai Shisō*, and *Sexualities*.

Astrid Norén-Nilsson is an Associate Senior Lecturer in the Study of Modern South-East Asia at the Centre for East and South-East Asian Studies, Lund University, Sweden. She holds a PhD in Politics and International Studies from the University of Cambridge (2013) and carried out postdoctoral research at the Royal Netherlands Institute of Southeast Asian and Caribbean Studies (KITLV), Leiden, The Netherlands (2013–15). She is the author of *Cambodia's Second Kingdom: Nation, Imagination, and Democracy* (2016) and has published extensively in a variety of journals, including *Pacific Affairs*, *Journal of Southeast Asian Studies*, *SOJOURN: Journal of Social Issues in Southeast Asia*, *Jane's Intelligence Review*, and *Peace Review: A Journal of Social Justice*.

Michiyo Kiwako Okuma Nyström holds a PhD in International Education from Stockholm University. Kiwako worked as a researcher at the Institute of International Education (2003–2009) and at the Center for Pacific Asia Studies (2006–2008), both at Stockholm University. She has broad interests in social anthropological studies and sociology of education. She has conducted her research in a village of indigenous people in Canada, and in a village in The Gambia. She has also conducted studies on education in rural communities in Sweden, Japan, and Bhutan with qualitative research methodology. Currently, she is working as an independent researcher and is interested in social changes in Bhutan and Gross National Happiness, which challenges the conventional interpretations of development.

Akihiro Ogawa is Professor of Japanese Studies at the University of Melbourne's Asia Institute. He completed a PhD in Anthropology in 2004 at Cornell University, followed by two years of postdoctoral work at Harvard University's Program on US–Japan Relations and Department of Anthropology. He then taught at Stockholm University, Sweden, from 2007 to 2015. His major research interest is in contemporary Japanese society, focusing on civil society. He is the author of two books: the award-winning *The Failure of Civil Society?: The Third Sector and the State in Contemporary Japan* (SUNY, 2009) and *Lifelong Learning in Neoliberal Japan: Risk, Knowledge, and Community* (SUNY, 2015). He writes extensively on politics, social movements, peace, and education.

Ruth Phillips is Associate Dean (Postgraduate Research) and an Associate Professor in the Faculty of Education and Social Work at the University of Sydney. Her background is in social policy and political science; she has supervised postgraduate students conducting research on the third sector, particularly in Southeast and East Asia where she has expertise in the third sector and welfare states and a personal research focus on the role of feminism and women's activism in the third sector. Phillips has been an active member of the International Society for Third Sector Research (ISTR) for sixteen years, is now a board member, and has been a member of Australian and New Zealand Third Sector Research (ANZTSR) for twelve years. She was co-editor of *Third Sector Review* (2010–2014). She has published research papers in *VOLUNTAS: International Journal of Voluntary and Nonprofit Organizations*, *Third Sector Review*, *Non-Profit Management and Leadership Journal*, *Critical Social Policy*, and *Feminist Review*, as well as a number of book chapters.

Stefan Rother is a Researcher and Lecturer at the Department of Political Science, University of Freiburg, Germany. His research focus is on international migration, global governance, social movements, regional integration, and non-/post-Western theories of international relations. He was a Fellow at the Freiburg Institute for Advanced Studies (FRIAS) and researcher and editorial manager of the *International Quarterly for Asian Studies* at the Arnold Bergstraesser Institute for Socio-Cultural Research. In 2012, he completed his doctorate at the University of Freiburg. He has conducted extensive fieldwork in Southeast Asia, and participant observation at global governance fora and civil society parallel and counter-events at the UN, ILO, ASEAN, and WTO-level. His latest monograph is *Democratization through Migration? Political Remittances and Participation of Philippine Return Migrants* (with Christl Kessler, 2016).

Ian Rowen is an Assistant Professor of Geography at Nanyang Technological University in Singapore and Associate Researcher at the French Centre for Research on Contemporary China in Taipei. A Fulbright Scholar in 2013–2014, he conducted participant observation on the Taiwan Sunflower Movement and Hong Kong Umbrella Movement. He holds a PhD in Geography from the University of Colorado and has been a visiting scholar at Fudan University, China, and the University of Tübingen, Germany, and a Postdoctoral Fellow at Academia Sinica, Taiwan. He has written about regional politics, social movements, and tourism for *The Journal of Asian Studies*, *International Journal of Transitional Justice*, *Annals of the American Association of Geographers*, *Annals of Tourism Research*, *Asian Anthropology*, *Journal of Archaeology and Anthropology*, the BBC, *Guardian*, and other publications.

Apichai W. Shipper is Adjunct Associate Professor in the Asian Studies Program at Georgetown University and Asia Regional Chair at the Foreign Service Institute of the US Department of State. He is the author of *Fighting for Foreigners: Immigration and Its Impact on Japanese Democracy* (Cornell University Press, 2008), and the guest editor of a Special Issue (2010) in *Pacific Affairs* on "Citizenship and Migration." He currently serves on the Cornell Alumni Board for Diversity (Mosaic), and on the Executive Committee of *Pacific Affairs*.

Alvin Y. So is a sociologist who taught at the University of Hawaii before his present affiliation with the Division of Social Science at Hong Kong University of Science and Technology. His research interests include development, class and class conflict, social movements, and Greater China (mainland China, Hong Kong, and Taiwan). His recent publications include *The Global Rise of China* (with Yin-Wah Chu, Polity Press, 2015), *Class and Class Conflict in Post-Socialist China* (World Scientific, 2013), *Handbook of Contemporary China* (co-edited with William Tay, 2012), and *Hong Kong's Embattled Democracy: A Societal Analysis* (1999).

Debbie Soon is a Research Associate at the Institute of Policy Studies (IPS) of the National University of Singapore. Her research interests are in the study of political identities, ideologies, and political communication. Her published work includes co-authored chapters on migration, identity, and civil society issues. She received her Master's degree in Sociology from the University of Essex, UK.

Anthony J. Spires is an Associate Professor of Sociology and Director of the Centre for Social Innovation Studies at The Chinese University of Hong Kong. He holds a PhD in Sociology from Yale University. Spires' research focuses on the development of civil society in China. Recent publications include an analysis of the political survival strategies of China's grassroots, an assessment of grant-making to China by US foundations, and a survey of Chinese domestic foundations. He serves as a Consulting Editor for the *American Journal of Sociology* and is a frequent reviewer for other publications. He is currently working on a book about democratic culture, youth, and civil society in China.

Mukta S. Tamang is an anthropologist teaching at the Central Department of Anthropology at Tribhuvan University, Nepal. His major areas of work include indigenous people's issues, history and identity, participatory approaches, human rights, and social inclusion. He has several scholarly publications to his credit dealing with social, cultural, political, and developmental issues. He completed his PhD at Cornell University and is currently a Research Fellow at the New School for Social Research in New York City. He has also served as Visiting Fellow at Jawaharlal Nehru University, India, and at Goldsmiths, University of London.

Pradeep Taneja lectures in Asian politics and international relations at the University of Melbourne, where he is also a Fellow of the Australia India Institute and an Associate of the Centre for Contemporary Chinese Studies. He spent many years studying or working in China, including as a consultant on an Australian foreign aid project. His primary areas of research are Chinese and Indian foreign policies and political economies. Taneja is currently working on a book about the rise of China from an Indian perspective. He is frequently interviewed by Australian and foreign media on the developments in the Asia-Pacific region.

Jorge V. Tigno is a Professor at the Department of Political Science at the University of the Philippines—Diliman. He has a doctorate in Public Administration from the UP National College of Public Administration and Governance (NCPAG). His research interests are in the areas of Asian labor migration and comparative immigration policies, democratic consolidation and transitions in Southeast Asia, NGOs and state–civil society relations in the Philippines, and electoral and political reforms in developing states.

Chika Watanabe is a Lecturer (Assistant Professor) in Social Anthropology at the University of Manchester, UK. Her research and teaching interests revolve around issues of development, humanitarianism, NGOs, religion and secularity, ethics and morality, and disasters. She has published and has forthcoming essays in journals such as *Cultural Anthropology*, *American Anthropologist*, and *Gastronomica*. She is currently working on a book manuscript titled *Becoming One: Nonreligion and the Moral Imaginations of a Japanese NGO in Myanmar*.

Jörg Wischermann is an Associate Research Fellow at the GIGA Institute of Asian Studies, Hamburg/Berlin. He served as academic head of the project "Civil Society Organisations as Supporters of Authoritarian Rule? A Cross-Regional Comparison (Vietnam, Algeria, and Mozambique)" (2013–2016). From 2008 to 2010, he was academic head of the project "Civil Society and Governance in Vietnam," funded by the German Research Council. From 1999 to 2003, he was a Research Fellow at the Otto Suhr Institute for Political Science, Free University of Berlin, responsible for the project "The Relationship between 'Civic Organizations' and 'Governmental Organizations' in the Vietnamese Transition Period," funded by the Volkswagen Foundation. His recent publications include "Vietnamese Civic Organizations: Supporters of or Obstacles to Further Democratisation?" in *Journal of Current Southeast Asian Affairs* (September 2016) and "Do Associations Support Authoritarian Rule? Tentative Answers from Algeria, Mozambique, and Vietnam" in *GIGA Working Paper* No. 295 (December 2016).

FOREWORD

Jeff Kingston

The expansion of civil society throughout Asia over recent decades is a sign of the times and is having a significant effect on people's lives, their relations with the state, on the institutions of the state, and on prevailing norms and values. The ambit of civil society extends from welfare services, the environment, refugees, legal services, and politics to counseling, trafficking, entrepreneurship, education, and beyond. There is no shortage of needs and public demands for what civil society actors engage in, yet funding woes, regulatory hurdles, and wary and intolerant governments impose significant constraints. Illiberal democracies and authoritarian governments are targeting foreign funding of civil society because they fear and oppose the spread of Western values, ideologies, and practices. These suspicions are fueled by concerns that civil society is undermining and discrediting the state by engaging in advocacy for causes and people, who have been marginalized or mistreated by government officials and policies. By empowering people, civil society challenges and subverts the state's monopoly of power, while providing services the state is not delivering may raise awkward questions for those who govern.

There are two major trends influencing the twenty-first century operating environment for civil society in Asia: the spread of neo-liberal economic policies and the rise and consolidation of illiberal democracies. Neo-liberal economic reforms are embraced to varying degrees, but share the goal of paring back the role of the state, cutting taxes, and reducing government budgets. The impact on vulnerable people in society can be catastrophic as services and subsides aimed at mitigating poverty, improving living standards, and addressing health and educational problems are slashed. Such reforms create a niche for civil society as it responds to what effectively is an outsourcing of government services. In these areas, we find that the state is generally more tolerant of civil society organizations because they tackle problems that the government doesn't, but the potential for political mischief ensures vigilant monitoring in more authoritarian polities

Problematically, neoliberal reforms tend to accentuate disparities and polarize society. Across the globe we are witnessing the dispossessed and marginalized respond to the broken promises of globalization and the gathering uncertainties and gloomy omens for the less privileged. Pankaj Mishra in *The Age of Anger* (2017) captures the *Zeitgeist* of our age as the appeal of the neoliberal democratic model has faded because it is not delivering for the many while ubiquitous images of the good life taunt them with what they can never have. Envy, disappointment, and anxiety are alienating and arousing people against what is seen as a rigged system designed to keep them down. The Internet enables widespread awareness of what some can attain, but also brings a disturbing realization that very few get such opportunities. Thwarted dreams and aspirations create a hothouse of discontent that fuels populist politics and breeds radicalism.

The other significant trend shaping the civil society ecosystem in Asia is the spread of illiberal democracies and the persistence of authoritarian governance. Illiberal democracies hold elections, often feature prolonged one-party rule, nominally uphold their constitutions and embrace the rule of law, but draw on authoritarian convictions and practices to ensure that democracy is kept on a short leash. Cronyism, corruption, and opacity are defining features of illiberal democracy and in this age of anger, repression is the favored means of retaining power and quelling opposition. The grass-roots wildfire of frustration sparked by neoliberal reforms and heightened disparities have drawn an illiberal political response from the ruling classes. There is no single model of illiberal democracy, but in general, they stifle political debate, engage in media censorship, resort to intimidation, and limit space for political contestation. They breed intolerance, encourage bigotry, engage in "Othering" minorities, and create a hostile climate for civil society. This is because civil society arouses citizens and disseminates liberal values antithetical to reactionary agendas. In Asia, the winds of illiberalism are gathering momentum, shrinking the space for civil society at a time when it is more needed than ever due to neoliberal reforms.

Illiberal democracies also encourage uncivil society, spawning hate-mongering groups that are often connected with and used by powerful political forces. The rise of conservative religious organizations, some of them extremist and prone to intimidation and violence, is a transnational phenomenon in South and Southeast Asia evident in India, Sri Lanka, Pakistan, Bangladesh, Myanmar, Malaysia, Indonesia, and the Philippines. Moderate religious organizations appear to have lost considerable influence to less tolerant groups and merchants of hate who are mainstreaming their agenda, one that combines stricter observance with religious chauvinism. This spread of uncivil society enables elites to project their power down to the grass-roots level by invoking populist issues in ways that have a chilling effect on liberal civil society.

Governments across Asia remain ambivalent about civil society, seeing them as a combination of political threat, partner, and talisman of globalization. Yet even in illiberal democracies, there is a desire to appear modern and overcome pariah status by connecting with global norms, and civil society can be a bridge to do so. But partnering is usually on the state's terms. Throughout the region, civil society is coming under closer government scrutiny and tighter regulatory monitoring because the state doesn't quite trust civil society actors and wants to know what they are doing and at whose behest.

The emergence of a vibrant civil society in many Asian societies is not an onward and upward process, depending not only on sustained citizens' support and participation, but also on shifting political winds. In some cases, partnership between the state and civil society has flourished, helping to mitigate various socio-economic problems. For example, in terms of natural disasters, in the 2000s civil society has played a key role in disaster relief and recovery and is contributing significantly to promoting disaster resilience in vulnerable communities. Their vital role is recognized by states across the region and as such, they have gained social legitimacy.

This Handbook of case studies and thematic analysis confirms the vibrancy of civil society in Asia, how in many respects they have become mainstreamed and viewed as essential, but it also highlights the challenges they face. While the flowering of civil society in Asia is undeniable, the gains made are fragile and vulnerable to adverse political developments. Even in nations that have navigated democratic transitions, civil society is not always what it seems as some organizations that enjoy the support of international donors are controlled by local elites representing legacy power networks antithetical to liberal agendas. Moreover, the political sensitivities of authorities means that there are no-go zones and taboo topics where civil society activism is not welcome or can only operate under duress and within tightly circumscribed bounds. Contributors describe how civil society has managed to carve out space even in authoritarian societies, but activities and impact are circumscribed to avoid undesired consequences. China, for example, is allowing environmental activism even as it incarcerates journalists, lawyers, and other activists who venture into sensitive political issues, involving repression, human rights, nepotism, and corruption. All across Asia, as the following chapters attest, civil society is flexibly navigating an evolving space where hazards and needs abound.

Reference

Mishra, Pankaj. 2017. *The Age of Anger: A History of the Present*. New York: Farrar, Straus & Giroux.

ACKNOWLEDGMENTS

First of all, on behalf of all of the authors contributing chapters to this volume, we greatly appreciate all of the research contact and collaboration we had with civil society groups. We learned a lot during our field research from their knowledge and behaviors, which inspired our research imagination.

My thanks go to the generous support from the Japan Foundation Grant for Intellectual Exchange Conference (No. 28 RIE-RC-1010293), which made it possible for many authors to come to the *Civil Society in Asia: International Conference in Melbourne* on February 2 and 3, 2017. Grants from the University of Melbourne's Asia Institute were also helpful.

Claudia Astaria was the chief conference coordinator, and she did fabulous and very efficient work. Special thanks also goes to three of you—Simon Avenell, Jörg Wischermann, and Jenifer Chan, as chairs for each discussion group, who helped facilitate the conference discussion with me. I should mention that our doctoral students at Melbourne played an active role in helping the group discussions as well as the whole discussion. I thank Akina Mikami, Stefan Fuchs, Asha Ross, Adam Eldridge, Maki Yoshida, Edward Hyatt, and Sonja Petrovic.

Jeff Kingston raised the idea of organizing the above-mentioned conference to me, and all of us realized getting together in person indeed would mean a lot. I met Jeff almost thirty years ago, and studied many Asian history subjects with him. Since then, he always stimulates my intellectual curiosity and expands my capacity for ways of thinking. This book is a culmination of my learning on Asian society and politics.

The editorial work for this book was massive. The book idea originally came to me in July 2015. While moving myself from Europe (Stockholm/London) to Australia, I wrote the book proposal and contacted more than forty scholars who are internationally active in producing Asian civil society scholarship. Thank you all for agreeing to write chapters. I greatly appreciate your contributions. The research network we have been building up through this book project is our valuable asset.

I appreciate editorial assistance from Maki Yoshida and Asha Ross at the last stage.

Debbie and Hannah, thank you for your patience when I was working on this book. It was hard, but it is finally done (or, I suppose more accurately, the starting point has been completed. This is solid groundwork for the future).

Akihiro Ogawa, PhD

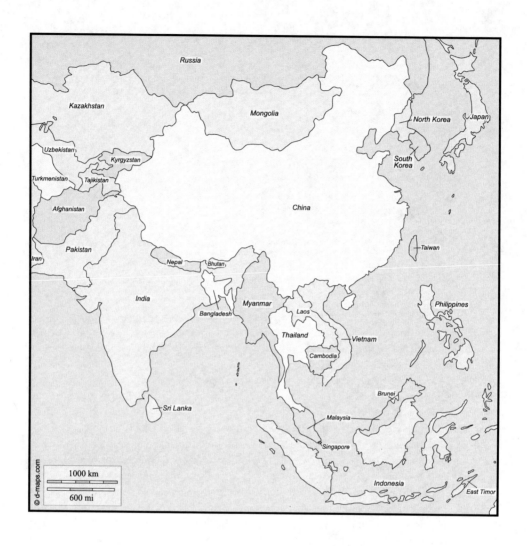

INTRODUCTION

Akihiro Ogawa

Today, civil society is one of the most dynamically expanding sectors in Asia. Civil society is a public sphere that broadly refers to the non-state institutions and associations critical to sustaining democratic participation. It originally emerged from Western history. As an anthropologist, I argue that civil society is an ethnocentric idea representing a particular set of relationships between the state and individuals in the West. Most of the existing scholarship on civil society has been narrowly circumscribed by modern Western modes of liberal individualism (e.g., Edwards 2011).

Over time, however, the concept spread to other cultures. Each society molds its own version of civil society, reflecting social relationships that have been historically forged by specific experiences. These may extol a range of values, which may include individual liberty, public solidarity, pluralism, and nonviolence, all of which sustain a vibrant civic culture. However, like in the West, civil society in Asia may also include social interests that are highly politically exclusionary and illiberal. This volume is the start of an interdisciplinary effort to analyze civil society and its internal dynamics, in the context of different cultures and histories, to obtain a more holistic understanding of Asian civil society.

The authors of this Handbook primarily focus on one question: what are the distinctive characteristics of Asian civil society? However, the intention is not to simplify the nature of Asian civil society. Instead, we consider the diverse representations of forms and patterns framed within civil society. We use "civil society" as an analytical lens through which to address cultural, social, political, and historical contestations and transformations, primarily in the post-World War II era, in an interdisciplinary manner. The authors represent a range of disciplines and include political scientists, sociologists, anthropologists, historians, economists, and geographers.

The Handbook is comprehensive in nature as it presents twenty-one country studies in East, Southeast, and South Asia, with an additional fourteen thematic reviews, including democratization, authoritarian rule, the third sector, media, human rights, gender, youth activism, and climate governance. Throughout the Handbook, contributors elucidate beliefs and practices advocated and nurtured by local civil society groups and individuals at the grass-roots level in Asian societies.

Importantly, the Handbook tries to present local voices as much as possible. As the Editor, I intentionally picked, as far as possible, local scholars and practitioners who could write in English, simply because their voices are under-represented in the international scholarship on Asian civil society. I also included scholars and practitioners from North America, Europe, and Australia, who have conducted long-term engaged field research in Asian societies and who are themselves deeply immersed in local people's daily lives. Amongst the total of forty contributors to this book project, the majority (twenty-four) are Asians, and rest (sixteen) are Westerners. This Handbook, thus, creates a unique, balanced discussion space about Asian civil society.

Western scholars have, indeed, been dominant in the existing scholarship on civil society, since the concept's revival in the 1990s. The concept has been primarily discussed in the post-Cold-War context, mostly referring to the emergence of civil society in Eastern Europe. The phenomenon was also described by Lester Salamon (1994: 109) as "a global associational revolution," which has seen the upsurge of civil society organizations (CSOs), such as non-governmental organizations (NGOs) and non-profit organizations (NPOs). Since the 1990s, there has been a remarkable growth in the sheer number of works on civil society. But in my view, this scholarship is highly idealized, presenting abstract theoretical formulations of high-level political institutions based on experiences in the West. The authors of this Handbook share the concern that there are too few grounded analyses of grass-roots practices and values in Asian civil society in the existing scholarship.

One of the most important recent works exclusively focusing on Asian civil society is *Civil Society and Political Changes in Asia: Expanding and Contracting Democratic Space*, an edited volume by Muthiah Alagappa published in 2004. That volume analyzed civil society primarily in the context of fostering a democratic political culture in twelve Asian countries. Since then, we have been witnessing solid, continuing, and mostly healthy new developments of civil society in Asia. The research interests shared by this Handbook's authors lie less in the structural or political role of civil society (although these are within our range of analysis) and more in exploring and documenting everyday practices, cultural values, and beliefs at the local level. Our research objective is not to argue over what civil society *is*, but rather to discover what civil society *does*. In the chapters that follow, each author documents their own experiences and observations, and thereby updates our knowledge on Asian civil society.

Three frameworks for understanding Asian civil society

The Handbook captures three distinctive frameworks for understanding civil society in contemporary Asia: (1) the dynamism of state–society relations; (2) the emerging civil society under authoritarian rule; and (3) social movements—transnational activism and networking for integrating grass-roots people in Asian societies.

State–society relations

The authors examine the dynamism of state–society relations, which is a key to analyzing important aspects of Asian civil society. The relations reflect both aspects: how the state molds civil society and civil society groups and actors interact with the state. Amongst the thirty-five chapters, nine country reviews and six thematic chapters contribute to our understanding of this perspective.

The three country review chapters concerning East Asia (Japan, South Korea, and Taiwan) present an interesting overview of civil society developments through the lens of state and society relations. Simon Avenell (Chapter 1) highlights the 1990s, when civil society captured the imagination of civil society, a process that developed since the early post-World War II period. It was, indeed, around the 1990s that civil society (*shimin shakai*) and such ideas as volunteering (*borantia katsudō*), NGOs, NPOs, community building (*machizukuri*), and citizens' activities (*shimin katsudō*) became topics of broad scholarly, media, and public attention, both in Japan and amongst foreign observers of the country. State–society relations in Japan were highlighted during the Kobe earthquake in 1995, when an influx of disaster volunteers demonstrated the untapped potential: this triggered the national government to institutionalize volunteerism under the NPO Law of 1998. Avenell's analysis considers long-term historical transformations, international influences, and numerous immediate regulatory, political, and social developments that helped to propel civil society into the limelight.

Yooil Bae (Chapter 2) discusses civil society developments in South Korea. It is generally perceived that robust civil society activism was a driving force behind the 1980s democratization movement, and key to propelling a further flowering since then. Under two progressive civilian administrations, civil society flourished. However, several new conditions since the late 2000s, such as the rise of conservative groups, the emergence of conservative administrations, and weak mediating institutions have made South Korean citizens dissatisfied with the process of communicating their demands to the state. Consequently, regardless of democratic developments, Bae argues that state–society relationships in South Korea mainly occur outside the existing political structure. The notion of "strong state and contentious society" persists. To unravel the intertwined developments of civil society and democracy in South Korea, this chapter traces the historical trajectory of state–society relations, exploring the institutional and contextual elements responsible for the emergence of the new mode of mass protests and candlelight vigils leading to the impeachment of President Park Geun-hye in 2017.

Anru Lee (Chapter 5) documents a traditional state–local relationship in Taiwan through an anthropological lens. Lee focuses on "community-building" (*shequ yingzao*), one of the most potent and widely employed terms in Taiwan's public sphere in recent decades. She reviews how the course and discourse of community-building both reflects the development of civil society and shapes the contours of civic activism in post-authoritarian Taiwan. Since the 1990s, community organizing has become a process for building a vibrant civil society and, in turn, represents the ideal that people are inspired to pursue. As illustrated in Lee's examples, many of these community empowerment projects are aimed at fundamental transformations of Taiwan's civil society by focusing on changing cultural values and social relations at the grass-roots level. However, the process of community-building in Taiwan also highlights that the practice of civil society must confront pervasive and ongoing changes in the framework of state–local interactions. Furthermore, as Taiwan is increasingly incorporated into the global economy, economic development started as a means to, but ultimately became the goal of, community-building. Taiwan highlights the importance of understanding community building as a constant struggle and process rather than an achieved goal.

Jorge V. Tigno (Chapter 7) provides critical observations on state–society relations in the Philippines. Despite widespread acclaim for Philippine civil society as the organized power of the people, it is unclear whether CSOs are actually able to achieve a significant degree of democratic consolidation for the country. Tigno argues that the CSO community in the Philippines continues to be vibrant and diverse, and has proliferated as a platform for citizen engagement since the 1980s. However, while they are essential to the democratization process, he points out that it remains to be seen whether CSOs will be sufficient to effect genuine and lasting democratic consolidation. He describes the historical roots of CSOs by situating their emergence in the context of faith-based mutual aid societies, and the contemporary context of the anti-Marcos dictatorship struggle of the 1970s and 1980s. Tigno claims that while such organized elements of civil society have certainly been a force to reckon with, the strengthening of the country's democratic institutions remains unfinished business.

Five country review chapters from South Asia (India, Pakistan, Bangladesh, Nepal, and Bhutan) contribute to our further understanding of Asian civil society through the lens of state–society relations. Pradeep Taneja and Salim Lakha (Chapter 16) highlight some of the characteristics of Indian civil society: focusing on the past two decades, they examine several episodes in which civil society organizations played an important role in effecting changes to government policies or laws. They present three case studies to identify commonalities or trends that define key features of civil society in India. The cases examined are: the right to information campaign; the enactment of the Mahatma Gandhi National Rural Employment Guarantee Scheme; and the 2011 anti-corruption movement of Anna Hazare. These case studies reveal that civil society activism in India can, under receptive political conditions, lead to meaningful change that benefits, or has the potential to benefit, large numbers of people in the country, responding to their grievances and aspirations. The chapter also notes the growing mistrust of civil society organizations and their harassment by the conservative Narendra Modi government that came to power in 2014.

Nadeem Malik (Chapter 17) provides a critical profile analysis of Pakistani civil society actors; his chapters focus on local actors—including NGOs, trade unions, and various bar councils and bar associations—and their relationships with the state and democracy. Malik argues that foreign-funded NGOs are often engaged in unsustainable projects, as donor priorities continually change, requiring the NGOs to either discontinue projects or close entirely. Trade unions are appallingly weak and incapable of effectively fighting for workers' rights in a society dominated by feudal lords, business elites, the military, and anti-labor regimes. In addition, the media face challenges, as religious extremism, intimidation, coercion, bribery, threats, and pressure from the government, the military, and intelligence services inhibit a free press and endanger journalists. As a result, the media finds it difficult to promote accountability and transparency. Finally, the Lawyers' Movement in Pakistan has been unable to forge lasting ties with civil society, making it more difficult to realize the rule of law. These adverse circumstances inhibit the strengthening of democracy and compromise the judiciary's independence.

Meanwhile, M. Anwar Hossen (Chapter 18) explores the grass-roots voices presented by civil society in Bangladesh. Hossen argues that civil society conveys community voices to both the state and international agencies in seeking to address local concerns and promote human rights. In Bangladesh, civil society is concentrated in NGOs, which work as pressure groups to incorporate marginalized community voices, often related to environmental concerns and human rights, into government deliberations. However, civil society does not always perform its tasks properly, as its representatives need to conform to the agendas of the global power structure in order to obtain funding. By aligning with this external power structure, NGO's effectively represent and convey the voices of local people. In this chapter, Hossen draws our attention to the issue of agenda setting and how this influences civil society.

Mukta S. Tamang (Chapter 19) introduces Nepali civil society, arguing that the notion of citizenship and civil society emerged and evolved in Nepal in conjunction with the evolving concept of state. In Nepal, civil society is referred to as *nagarik samaj* or "citizen's society" in contemporary discourse. Beginning with resistance to the patrimonial feudal state of oligarchy and autocracy, Nepal continues to struggle toward inclusive democracy. In this process, civil society took shape and continually transforms itself into newer forms. Tamang argues that civil society in Nepal should be analyzed in the context of the changing nature of the state and struggle for democracy therein. Despite a myriad of limitations, civil society engagement has contributed to making both state and society more open, as part of the democratic struggle. He assesses the ways civil society has contributed to or hindered the possibilities of an open, tolerant, and accountable society, and fostering democracy in the country. Tamang suggests that realizing civil society in Nepal is part of a larger democratic movement involving a struggle for the historically marginalized to become fuller citizens with equal rights.

Michiyo Kiwako Okuma Nyström (Chapter 20) examines the role of Bhutan's civil society against the background of the unique development philosophy—"Gross National Happiness (GNH)"—pushed by the state since the 1970s, and now permeating all levels of Bhutan's socio-political structure. She claims that the close collaboration between the government and CSOs is one of the characteristics of civil society in Bhutan. The government recognizes CSOs' competencies in such areas as sustainable rural development and nature conservation. In this chapter, she first introduces the socio-cultural, political, and economic contexts of civil society in Bhutan. Second, she presents three cases of informal organizations and institutions in civil society in Bhutan that have faced changes. Those cases are analyzed from the perspectives of emerging new thoughts, institutionalization of the informal, and encountering different types of knowledge.

Apichai Shipper's chapter on democratization (Chapter 22) explores how CSOs have impacted democratic transitions in Asia including Thailand, the Philippines, South Korea, Myanmar, Mongolia, Taiwan, and Indonesia. He examines to what extent CSOs have contributed to deepening consolidation and retrenchment of democratization. These societal actors continued to contribute to democratic deepening in newly democratized Korea and Taiwan, as well as in the more developed democracy of Japan. At the same time, he also argues that some civil society groups function to reinforce the status quo and can hinder democratization by propagating hate speech and/or inciting violence against minority groups. Of particular importance for the direction of democratization is the interplay between state and societal actors—it is not simply the emergence of an autonomous bourgeoisie. Therefore, this analysis does not assume a zero-sum relationship between state and society: a strong civil society can result in democratic transitions, deepening, and retrenchment, depending on the nature of state–societal interactions.

This Handbook also includes three chapters related to the development of the third sector in Asia. Ruth Phillips (Chapter 24) provides an overview of the third sector, a term that refers to "intermediate organizations" that interact with the state (first sector) and the market (second sector). Phillips discusses how the third sector is located in Asia, while exploring the scope of third sector research in Asia, focusing on local researchers from a range of countries. She also examines the rise of social enterprises, the core relationship between the third sector and the state, and the relationship between third sector organizations' functions, such as advocacy and welfare service delivery, and democratization and citizenship.

Building upon Phillips' chapter, Rosario Laratta (Chapter 25) provides detailed analysis of social enterprises, specifically focusing on Work Integration Social Enterprises (WISEs), the most diffused type of social enterprises in Asia. WISEs provide employment for disadvantaged people and aim to integrate disadvantaged groups of people into society by providing them with work opportunities. Hokkaido WISEs in Japan have represented a sustainable business model of working with disadvantaged people for more than two decades. By drawing on the recent work of Japanese social enterprises, Laratta explores both the organizational goals and support structures of those organizations. Three major factors account for the sustainability and growth of this model: a system of cooperative banks that promote the activities of social enterprises; a willingness to promote cross-sector partnerships in the local community; and democratic operational governance based on transparency and cooperation. The Hokkaido WISE model sets an inspiring example for other Asian civil societies of what is possible when mentally disabled people are properly trained in a supportive environment.

Masayuki Deguchi (Chapter 26) focuses on philanthropy as a form of social relationship developed by third sector organizations. Although the broadest definition of philanthropy is privately providing and volunteering for public purposes, Asian researchers often associate it with the West, especially the United States. This chapter focuses on philanthropy as a US concept and how the concept has resonated in Asia. Deguchi picks three forms of concept carrier for philanthropy. The first is corporate philanthropy: Japan not only imported the concept of philanthropy from the USA but also learned directly in the USA in the 1980s. The second form of carrier relates to the fact that many Chinese and Indian citizens live in the USA. They conduct philanthropic activities and influence their home countries through diaspora philanthropy. The third carrier is the local offices of big US Foundations across Asia. They exported the concept of philanthropy directly to Asia. In addition to these three approaches, this chapter also discusses how philanthropic organizations are networked, explores new trends in philanthropy, and discusses future issues that will shape philanthropic activity.

Finally, there are two chapters that offer fresh and interesting perspectives on state–society relations in Asian civil society. According to Chika Watanabe (Chapter 27), scholars and observers of Asia have long argued that civil society in the region tends to be dominated by a top-down topology of state–society relations. Similarly, ideologies of development in Asian countries have been described in terms of growth-oriented and state-led development. While these views are not entirely wrong, they preclude consideration of the more complex and multifaceted relations that coalesce around development actors as nodes of people's aspirations for a better world. In this chapter, she proposes that examining development NGOs through a methodological focus on actors and personal relationships, blind to the categories of "the state" and "civil society," can illuminate political processes that might be overlooked in orthodox analyses. Specifically, Watanabe focuses on the individual relations that intersected at one of the oldest NGOs in Japan, and reveals how conservative and powerful politicians, religious leaders, and aid officials came together to shape early conceptions of development aid. She suggests that the rethinking of state–society relations, in the field of Japanese development aid, can offer alternative analytical tools to understand "emerging donors" in Asia, beyond the assumption of top-down imaginations.

Claudia Astarita's chapter on the media (Chapter 28) is another innovative perspective on state–society relations in Asian civil society scholarship. When new media started revealing their potential in terms of global outreach and accessibility, the Internet was promoted as a powerful defender of civil societies. In this chapter, Astarita argues that the media can become a double-edged sword for civil societies. Building on two Asian case studies (India and China), this chapter argues that the urgency of regulating the media and the massive flow of information they spread are crucial to strengthening the positive dimensions of media–civil society relations. The restoration of integrity, defined as the promotion of values such as truthfulness and accuracy, emerges as the key variable to achieve this aim.

Authoritarian rule

To deepen our understanding of civil society in contemporary Asia, examining the influence of authoritarianism is crucial. Amongst the twenty-one country review chapters, ten chapters provide detailed analysis of various forms of civil society and CSOs at the grass-roots level under authoritarian regimes. The country chapters include China and Hong Kong, as well as Southeast Asian countries: Vietnam, Malaysia, Singapore, Indonesia, Cambodia, Laos, Thailand, and Burma (Myanmar). The authors examine how authoritarian spaces shape civil society, and explain the complicated dynamics.

Anthony J. Spires (Chapter 3) examines Chinese civil society. Chinese leaders are clearly intent on retaining control over society through whatever means possible. Exactly how control over society is pursued, particularly over burgeoning, independent societal forces, is the question that has animated most studies of civil society in China for the last twenty-five years. Spires addresses this question, but also draws special attention to the agency of grass-roots actors themselves. He divides the chapter into three parts. First, he discusses the debate over how to conceptualize civil society in China, tracing interest in government-led efforts to establish and control "government-organized non-governmental organizations" (GONGOs) in the 1990s, and connecting that to emerging studies of bottom-up "grass-roots NGOs" that began to blossom after the turn of the millennium. Second, he examines the ways in which the Chinese state has sought to govern civil society through an evolving legal and regulatory framework, despite its recurring use of extra-legal repression. The concluding section explores areas of research that hold promise for deepening our understanding of Chinese civil society.

Alvin Y. So (Chapter 4) adds another perspective on Chinese civil society from Hong Kong. So argues that Hong Kong is a hybrid "liberal authoritarian" regime that combines a fairly high level of civil liberty with a limited electoral franchise. Inevitably, this liberal authoritarian regime has profoundly impacted the nature of civil society in Hong Kong. In addition, since 1997, Hong Kong has been transformed from a British colony into a Special Administrative Region (SAR) of China. He argues that the complicated national integration process has led to the emergence of uncivil society organizations and protests in Hong Kong. This chapter ends by discussing how these organizations have been posing a challenge to the traditional civil society organizations in contemporary Hong Kong.

Jörg Wischermann and Dang Thi Viet Phuong (Chapter 8) jointly illustrate the forms and substance of civil society in Vietnam. After overviewing the rules and regulations that govern the establishment and operation of CSOs, Wischermann and Dang characterize local politicians' views on civil society, followed by societal actors' views of civil society and CSOs. They describe who, from a socio-demographic perspective, these civil society actors are, and in which policy fields CSOs work. They then delineate how the relationships between CSOs and the state have developed over time, and the roles CSOs play within the Vietnamese political system. Finally, they address the newly and controversially discussed question of whether Vietnamese CSOs are supporters of, or obstacles to, processes of democratization in their country. In concluding, they compare one of the most important findings—the understanding of civil society and CSOs from the perspective of the Vietnamese actors—to the view of actors from other Asian countries on this topic.

Gaik Cheng Khoo (Chapter 9) explores Malaysian civil society, which comprises individuals (e.g., public intellectuals, students, and volunteers), charity and welfare organizations, civic associations, trade unions, political-minded religious organizations, NGOs, and Islamic as well as international NGOs. While the majority are apolitical, Khoo argues that they are divided along ethnic, linguistic, and religious lines. Malaysia's ethnic pluralism is becoming an increasing source of contention for conservative groups in the push to preserve Malay ethnic rights and assert Islamic Shariah as the law of the land, replacing the secular Constitution. This has led to the rise of constitutional patriots who invoke the Constitution to protect the rights of ethnic and religious minorities and to restore the integrity of secular institutions in light of massive corruption. Her chapter provides a historical overview of civil society in Malaysia, arguing that due to the introduction of increasingly authoritarian laws and pessimism about reform since Najib Razak became prime minister in 2009, volunteerism is increasing as citizens reap the satisfaction of more immediate results from their actions than from attending street rallies. To this end, Khoo focuses on the work of activist citizens who favor rights and the rule of law in constructing a civil sphere.

Gillian Koh and Debbie Soon (Chapter 10) examine civil society in Singapore, which is often considered to be an electoral authoritarian regime—a remarkable exception in the developed world, where economic development seems not to have been accompanied by political liberalization and democratization. Citing the development of civic activism in the areas of migration; religion, secularism, and morality; and conservation, Koh and Soon demonstrate the energies that animate civil society in Singapore. Some groups partner the Singaporean state, while others resist the state and yet both types have shaped public policy. There are those that have chosen non-confrontational strategies, playing a long game in their bid to secure social and legislative change. Koh and Soon highlight intra-civil society conflict and cooperation to illustrate the rising complexity, and discuss how Singaporean civil society groups have extended their activism into regional and international environments. They argue that the Internet provides the impetus for further development of civil society, making public education and the strengthening of the democratic ethos more pertinent than ever to ensure that the public and the governing regime welcome social and political diversity.

Vedi R. Hadiz (Chapter 11) insightfully analyzes Indonesia's "uncivil" society. In Indonesia, uncivil society comprises heterogeneous social interests, including those prone to mobilizing various kinds of discriminatory politics as instruments in social conflicts, only now within a democratic political context. While these interests are by no means hegemonic, Hadiz argues that they do influence social conflicts and electoral politics, undermining democratic, liberal, and pluralist values. We see this in the proliferation of paramilitary organizations, which recruit especially from amongst poor youths and engage in violence and intimidation, targeting vulnerable elements in society, often in the service of oligarchs. These organizations help to steer Indonesian democracy in an increasingly conservative and illiberal direction. The rights of religious and sexual minorities and women are not upheld, despite the presence of political parties, parliaments, a robust media, regular free elections, and other freedoms attained since democratization at the end of the twentieth century.

Astrid Norén-Nilsson (Chapter 12) argues that Cambodian civil society is young and fragile, and has been heavily dependent on international aid and reconstruction. These characteristics have largely shaped how civil society is defined domestically. Both popular understandings and scholarship typically perceive civil society to be formed by associational activities, and employ it as a lens for studying formal organizations, human rights groups, and trade unions. Norén-Nilsson examines competing understandings of Cambodian civil society through four prisms: civil society and the state; the role of the international donor community; civil society and transitional justice; and the re-emergence of historical civil society. She concludes that despite a proliferation of grass-roots social movements fighting for access to natural resources, there is little knowledge about their activities, membership, and relations to the development community and to the state.

Gretchen Kunze (Chapter 13), based on her long-term experiences as a practitioner, points out that while civil society organizations do exist in Laos, the one-party Communist state is considered amongst the world's most restrictive countries with respect to civil society. Despite its significant development challenges, in this stable, peaceful country with gradual but consistent economic growth, there is no sign of governmental change on the horizon. In this chapter, Kunze explains the current context of the country, recent developments in its civil society sector, the impact of international intervention and foreign direct investment on civil society, and the prospects for the future of Lao civil society. She posits that, given the country's political and economic circumstances and how they are intertwined with foreign direct investment from China, with its restricted civil society, there is little incentive and, therefore, little expectation for the restrictive environment to change significantly. Some form of civil society will continue to exist and constructively contribute to the nation's development, though, for its own preservation, it will operate in lockstep with the government, limited to complementing and furthering the state's policies and plans for national development, rather than being an overt activist force.

Bencharat Sae Chua (Chapter 14) claims that recent political conflicts in Thailand raise questions about civil society's contribution to democracy. In justifying the military coup in 2014, numerous Thai civil society actors called for the rejection of representative democracy, replacing politicians with seemingly morally superior people. This rejection of electoral democracy raises the need to revisit both the concepts and practices of civil society and democracy in Thailand. Chua analyses the role and nature of Thai civil society by tracing its development in the context of the country's democratization. She argues that Thai civil society has been evolving in close connection with the state, in terms of both its operations and ideology. In many instances, this leads civil society to advance oligarchic control and domination.

Stephen McCarthy (Chapter 15) gives an updated account on civil society in Burma (Myanmar). Military rule has had a transformational impact on civil society in the Asia-Pacific region. Yet modern and traditional civil society can still exist under authoritarian conditions, although the latter may threaten the state's dominance of political society in a militarized regime. McCarthy examines the nature of civil and political society in Burma, a country that has recently emerged from direct military rule. He considers the military's changing role, and how it has taken steps to safeguard its role in political society. In particular, he examines how the maintenance of their political role requires the co-optation or neutralization of important elements in traditional civil society. In transitional political environments, new freedoms can create a sense of openness in society, however, unrestrained freedom also challenges conservative military thinking. While Burma continues its transition away from direct military rule, understanding how militaries preserve their influence and respond to new challenges informs our understanding of authoritarian resilience in the region and the limits to democratic reforms.

Finally, in the thematic review section, Jörg Wischermann (Chapter 23) offers insights into various ways of understanding, conceptualizing, and examining empirically authoritarian regimes and authoritarianism, civil society, and CSOs, and their relationships with the authoritarian state. To this end, the chapter first delves into various ways of understanding, defining, and classifying authoritarian regimes and authoritarianism. It then describes, in detail, the most important theoretical problems inherent in using a simplified, schematic, and realm-based understanding of civil society. Thereafter, alternative ways of conceptualizing civil society and CSOs under authoritarian rule are examined. Employing case studies conducted in Vietnam, Wischermann refers to an actor- and action-centered understanding of civil society; to concepts based on functionalist and relational assumptions; and, finally, to a Gramsci-inspired perspective on civil society.

Social movements

Social movements are a dynamic aspect in Asian civil society. This Handbook includes the most up-to-date accounts on social movements in contemporary Asia. Nine chapters—two country review chapters and seven thematic reviews—discuss various activisms in which grass-roots people are at the forefront. The chapters portray the dynamism we should consider in the integration between local and global, traditional and modern, and how legitimacy is constructed in the specific context of social movements, beyond references to the state.

Dulam Bumochir (Chapter 6) documents the development of Mongolian civil society since the collapse of the Soviet Union, focusing on environmental movements through his ethnographic research. Bumochir first explores the constitutions of Mongolia approved in 1924, 1940, and 1960, and argues that Euro-American philosophical and legal concepts of civil society, if not practiced, have certainly been introduced and legitimized in the country since 1924. Since 1990, certain groups and individuals have possessed words and concepts such as "democracy" and "civil society." He argues that nationalist environmental protestors distinguish themselves from those individuals, groups, and NGOs, and reveal a reluctance to be identified with civil society. This is mainly because, in contrast to nationalist environmental protestors, pro-democratic and civil society groups import internationalized concepts, protocols, acts, and regulations, while the protestors invoke Mongolian history and tradition. This contrast suggests that civil society or NGOs are "import machines," bringing in not only different concepts of civil society, but also a whole range of Western values and norms presented as worthy goals for modern Mongolians to embrace. As such, NGOs function as vehicles for cultural imperialism.

Udan Fernando (Chapter 21) closely examines the so-called "*venasa*" (change), a political transformation that occurred in the 2015 elections when the authoritarian and repressive Mahinda Rajapaksa regime was ousted at the ballot box. Particular attention is given to the run up to the Presidential Election held in January 2015 and the General Election in August of the same year. Positioned in a review of the scholarship on Sri Lankan civil society, its history and orientation since the mid-1990s, Fernando includes a commentary on civil society's interface with the government. The purpose of such a close scrutiny is to understand the changing character of civil society during that period, and how it has configured itself vis-à-vis a changing political landscape since 2009, which coincides with the end of the civil war between the minority Tamils and the majority Sinhalese state. The chapter draws on the author's long-standing focus on civil society scholarship, as well as his engagement in a variety of civil society organizations, movements, and networks.

These two country case studies are followed by thematic chapters showcasing the various types of ongoing social movements in Asian societies. Jennifer Chan (Chapter 29) introduces the major developments and scholarship on human rights in Asia during three historical periods since 1989. Chan uses specific examples of civil society actors in five major clusters of rights: political liberalization; accountability for past abuses; minority rights; socio-economic rights; and women's human rights. She examines these examples in terms of four themes: grass-roots mobilization of rights discourses and advocacy education; intersectionality; the post-structuralist turn and rights as competing narratives; and beyond the state and the civil society-strengthening imperative. The chapter concludes by noting several key challenges concerning human rights and civil society in Asia, including democratic reforms, the "multicultural challenge," Internet surveillance, counter-terrorism, and the China in Africa question.

Allison Alexy (Chapter 30) considers family, tracing and locating the dynamism of civil society scholarship within her own ethnographic work about parental abduction and activism in contemporary Japan. Most common definitions of "civil society" posit it as fundamentally exterior to family life, an intimate sphere. In the scholarly literature, family is frequently used to define the outer edge of civil society, suggesting that family lives and civil society are non-overlapping, separate spheres. In this chapter, Alexy argues that, despite such common definitional exclusions, in practice, civil society and family membership intertwine to a substantial degree. Primarily drawing on scholarship about Asia, she posits that this interrelationship occurs through three overlapping dynamics: first, family membership regularly motivates or is used to legitimize civil society participation; second, many civil society groups are organized specifically around family issues and concerns; third, some states rely on families to provide services that might otherwise be expected from civil society. By paying attention to these overlaps, Alexy claims that we can better situate the processes that pull people into civic engagement.

Claire Maree's chapter on queer (Chapter 31) highlights an important trend: Asia is witnessing a surge in the visibility of and organization around LGBTI (Lesbian, Gay, Bisexual, Transgender, and Intersex) and SOGI (sexual orientation and gender identity) related rights and advocacy. The United National Development Programme (UNDP) and the United States Agency for International Development (USAID)'s "Being LGBT in Asia" initiative, for example, has produced country reports that outline "A Participatory Review and Analysis of the Legal and Social Environment for Lesbian, Gay, Bisexual and Transgender (LGBT) Persons and Civil Society." As work by queer theorists has shown, however, engagement with civil society and citizenship from queer theory perspectives necessitates critical examination of the intersections of empire, globalization, neoliberalism, sovereignty, terrorism, and compulsory able-bodiedness. For example, Maree draws on ongoing collaborative work on the critical deployment of queer theories from the contested locale of "Japan" and "Asia" to engage with civil society. She argues for increased critical readings of the representations of queer lives, and discussion of the contexts that both shape and trouble localized demands for rights.

Following up on a series of rights activism, the Handbook considers one of the most impactful activisms recently observed in East Asia. Ian Rowen (Chapter 32) focuses on youth activism, tracing youth connections, collaborations, and contestations within and between particular societies and polities. Rowen situates the histories of Asian youth activism in a national and transnational context. The first part presents an analytic overview of youth activism in various (post-)colonial and (post-)authoritarian contexts. The second part moves to the specific 2014 cases of the Taiwan Sunflower Student Movements and the Hong Kong Umbrella Movement, the most significant recent social movements in the Chinese-speaking world. Considering these in combination with his analysis of the Japanese SEALDs (Students Emergency Action for Liberal Democracy–s) actions in 2015–2016, Rowen examines continuities and ruptures between past patterns and new and unfolding modes of activism.

Migration is another emerging field for civil society. Daniel Kremers and Stefan Rother (Chapter 33) argue that Asia is a region of intense and varied transnational migration. Transnational migrants in the low-skilled employment sector constitute a particularly vulnerable group in the countries where they reside as they are often excluded from fundamental rights and government services. This poses significant challenges and opportunities for civil society in promoting the rights of migrants. Migrant interest organizations (MIOs) in Asia are as diverse as the circumstances and needs of migrants of varying nationality, gender, educational background, ethnicity, and age. Since most migrants move to seek better employment opportunities and income, organizations addressing labor-related issues play a central role. After presenting a typology of MIOs and providing an overview of the relevant literature, the chapter discusses case studies from Japan and Hong Kong. Kremers and Rother show how, in Japan, support and advocacy for mostly female migrants working in adult entertainment and foreign technical interns is strongly rooted in the labor movement and Catholic organizations, and is done on behalf of the migrants. In contrast, transnational advocacy for domestic workers in Hong Kong is mainly based on the self-organization and political mobilization of overseas Filipino workers (OFWs) and Indonesian migrants, and is linked to regional and global networks.

Meanwhile, Yuko Kawato (Chapter 34) observes a continuing activism in Asia: anti-US base protest. Since the end of World War II, protests against US military basing and related policies have continued in the Philippines, Japan, and South Korea. The protests have covered diverse issues, such as base closure, base construction through land expropriation, jurisdiction, and custody when American military personnel commit crimes, and environmental problems in and around military bases. These protests have demanded changes in policies that violate valued norms such as pacifism, anti-militarism, sovereignty, human rights, anti-nuclear, and environmental concerns. Kawato examines the influence of these demands, based on so-called "normative arguments," on base policies. Drawing on research about persuasion in social psychology and norms in international relations theory, she presents the conditions under which protesters' normative arguments can and cannot persuade policy makers to change base policy. When protesters persuade policy makers who operate within enabling domestic institutional contexts, base policies change in fundamental ways. She also explains how protests can still generate political or military incentives for policy makers to adjust policy when persuasion fails. When policy makers decide not to change policy, they can offer symbolic concessions to appear norm-abiding, to save face, and/or to secure a smoother implementation of policies that protesters oppose.

The Handbook concludes with a chapter titled "Sustainability and Climate Governance" by Janelle Knox-Hayes (Chapter 35). She documents a unique activism mobilized by Japanese business-interest CSOs. Climate change is one of the greatest challenges facing society in the twenty-first century. As such, civil society plays a central role in the creation and implementation of climate policy. One of its important functions is to translate global, technocratic imperatives into local political economies. Knox-Hayes examines the role of business civil society actors in the formation and execution of climate policy in Japan, focusing specifically on a business federation—the Keidanren—and the role of its political economic culture. She finds that efforts by Japanese policy makers to implement globally prescribed markets did not fit with the Japanese political economic culture and were, therefore, successfully opposed and reformulated in collaboration with civil society.

Although there is no chapter specifically focused on gender, multiple chapters incorporate gender analysis. Gender is an overarching topic across the Handbook, relating to other variables in our analyses. In addition to the three chapters by Alexy, Chan, and Maree, the subsection titled "Advocacy and Gender" in Bumochir's chapter on Mongolian civil society (Chapter 6) introduces the story of a woman who established an NGO focused on human rights and labor union movements. Also, Phillips' chapter on the third sector (Chapter 24) clarifies the role of women in third sector organizations in Asia, and she documents very lively and diverse groups of organizations dedicated to addressing gender inequality and women's participation in the region. Furthermore, Kremers and Rother (Chapter 33) consider female migrants from the Philippines working as maids in Hong Kong.

Envisioning future research

This Handbook presents the most up-to-date accounts of Asian civil society scholarship. While reviewing the existing scholarship, our contributors are also mindful about the possibilities of expanding research on Asian civil society in the near future. Here, I note the conversations amongst the authors who gathered to share their research on February 2 and 3, 2017 at the "Civil Society in Asia: International Conference in Melbourne."

First, the current country-based studies can be extended to transnational and global contexts. For example, one group focused on transnational environment and justice. They refer to fragments about the trajectory of historical and spatial civic connection that stem from the Fukushima disaster in March 2011, specifically in relation to the social change that occurred before and after the three nuclear meltdowns. They are interested in the many civil society voices heard around Fukushima, and elsewhere in Asia, including India, Vietnam, and Taiwan, where Japan tries to export nuclear power technology. Across Asia, people are raising their voices against nuclear energy due to safety and environmental anxieties. We also discussed further examining the impact of liberal democracy in Asia, and liberal legal frameworks, and how they are affecting the operating environment for CSOs. Finally, in terms of transnational research, it is important to assess the impact of transnational civil society networking on domestic civil society.

This point brings us to a related concern. Some countries are generally under-represented in Asian civil society scholarship (and this Handbook)—for example, the Central Asian nations of Kazakhstan, Uzbekistan, Tajikistan, Kyrgyzstan, and Turkmenistan. This area showcases the nexus of authoritarian rule, Islamic politics, and the legacies of Soviet communist rule and is subject to extensive ongoing interventions and influence by Moscow. Given the area's strategic importance due to large oil and gas reserves, and the potential for cross-border terrorism, how civil society evolves there may have significant consequences. Much is made of the rising Asia story, but some scholars are skeptical about the future, pointing to demographic problems, resource constraints, and flash points of conflict. We are interested in how a civil society will influence such trajectories in the region and to what extent they can lessen tensions between nations.

Second, comparative studies based on thematic analysis are crucial to understanding the significance of what is observed in country case studies to identify cross-national commonalities and divergences informed by deep understanding of the relevant context. For example, in focusing on authoritarian regimes under military rule which are undergoing democratic transitions, the evolving situation in Burma (Myanmar) can be better understood in relation to post-military politics in Indonesia. Furthermore, comparative studies can even be extended to cross-regional comparisons: for example, there is much to be learned by comparing the emergence of religious extremism in South Asia (India, Sri Lanka, and Bangladesh), Southeast Asia (Burma, Indonesia, Thailand, and the Philippines), and China. Meanwhile, Asian specialists might benefit from thematic comparison of experiences in other continents. For example, when exploring the Chinese influence on civil society in Laos, we can compare with counterparts in Africa, where China has recently been establishing a strong presence. Alternatively, when investigating post-military transitions, we could consider Burma (Myanmar), Indonesia, and many Latin American examples.

Third, there is a need for more critical understanding of the media's role in, and influence over, civil society. There is an extensive literature on the democratizing potential of the media and social media—such as Facebook, Twitter, and YouTube—but there is no systematic up-to-date study of its impact on civil society in Asia. There has also been insufficient attention to mainstream media's role in disseminating and mainstreaming new norms and values and shaping the discourse on civil society. Meanwhile, we should examine some of the positive impacts of social media in terms of fostering active participation and new forms of civic engagement. Does novel digital connectivity foster novel civic affiliation? One of the new projects conducted by two participants in this Handbook project, Claudia Astarita and Akihiro Ogawa, explores new cognitive frameworks and paradigms to decode how the media influenced the narration of post-World War II events in Germany, Italy, and Japan; how this interpretation impacted on the rhetoric of formal apology, peace, and stability; and how this process can be adjusted to spread new civil society values and perspectives consistent with promoting reconciliation. This project, titled "Embedding the Apology in the Media: How Civil Society Contributes to Reconciliation," is funded by the Toyota Foundation Research Grant Program (Joint Research Grant) from 2017 to 2019 (D16-R-0167). Meanwhile, there are also new risks and the key question arises of whether the media can maintain its bearings in this age of fake news, alternative facts, and political polarization. To date, little research has been conducted on the ways that it does not support democratic values and polarizes civil discourse, and is subject to censorship and self-censorship in ways that undermine its role as the fourth estate. And there are growing concerns about the role of social media for surveillance purposes. It is therefore important to assess how these factors influence civil society and the values that support it.

Finally, we want to bring intersectionality into our assessments of civil society. Intersectionality is a concept often used to analyze oppressive institutions and norms that breed racism, xenophobia, sexism, homophobia, etc. and how they are interconnected and thus cannot be examined separately. One issue raised at the conference was the absence of "class" in discussing civil society in this Handbook. We recognize the need to elucidate how class relates to our research. How do members of civil society groups (and their donors) recognize class in crafting agendas and policies? Does civil society represent a particular class and reproduce inequality? Is it problematic that civil society is disproportionately a middle-class project and does this make it blind to the needs of other classes? Across the region, our contributors identify the need to study the intersectionality of class, race, and gender in civil society and what specific challenges this presents. We have made a small start here by noting differences between Asian and Western civil society constructs, and indeed within Asia, regarding the meaning of intersectionality. For example, these issues are analyzed in Chan's chapter on human rights (Chapter 29), while Alexy's chapter on family (Chapter 30) observes that Western scholars on civil society have long described how the public sphere relies on gendered dichotomies that contrast male and female roles and attributes in ways that reinforce such constructs. Additionally, Maree's chapter on queer (Chapter 31) analyzes LGBT intersectionality at the grass-roots level in Asia. Perhaps this small start can create momentum in this field of civil society inquiry, and hope that readers and researchers will be informed and inspired by this Handbook.

References

Alagappa, Muthiah, ed. 2004. *Civil Society and Political Changes in Asia: Expanding and Contracting Democratic Space*. Stanford, CA: Stanford University Press.
Edwards, Michael. 2011. *The Oxford Handbook of Civil Society*. Oxford: Oxford University Press.
Salamon, Lester M. 1994. The Rise of the Nonprofit Sector. *Foreign Affairs* 73(4): 109–122.

PART I

Country review

1

JAPAN

Simon Avenell

Japanese civil society: theories, history, and prospects

The 1990s was a watershed in the imagination and development of civil society in contemporary Japan, much in the same way the 1970s proved definitive for civil society in Latin America and Eastern Europe. It was around this time that civil society (*shimin shakai*) and ideas like volunteering (*borantia katsudō*), NGO (non-governmental organization), NPO (non-profit organization), community building (*machizukuri*), and citizens' activities (*shimin katsudō*) became topics of broad scholarly, media, and public attention in Japan and amongst foreign observers. A major earthquake in Kobe City in 1995 combined with long-term historical transformations, international influences, and a number of immediate regulatory, political, and social developments helped to propel civil society into the limelight. This chapter examines Japanese civil society from four perspectives. First, it gives a brief overview of the composition of the sector; second, it discusses key scholarly debates on Japanese civil society; third, it briefly surveys the historical development of the sector and; fourth, it introduces a new direction in research.

The composition of civil society in Japan

If we define civil society as "the sphere of uncoerced human association between the individual and the state, in which people undertake collective action for normative and substantive purposes, relatively independent of government and the market," then Japanese civil society qualifies strongly on all counts (Edwards 2011: 4). Similar to other advanced industrialized nations, in Japan, we find a vibrant non-profit sector, a large and diverse array of voluntary grass-roots associations, many contentious social movements addressing pressing social and political issues, a budding realm of social enterprises and social entrepreneurship, and a maturing arena of internationally active non-governmental organizations. This section considers some of these major groups in Japanese civil society.

Amongst the oldest and most widespread groups populating Japanese civil society are neighborhood associations (NHAs), which number around 300,000 nationwide. Robert Pekkanen defines NHAs as: "voluntary groups whose membership is drawn from a small, geographically delimited, and exclusive residential area (a neighborhood) and whose activities are multiple and are centered on that same area" (2006: 87). NHAs usually comprise around 100 households and engage in a variety of activities including cleaning, maintaining roads, organizing local festivals, celebrations and ceremonies, providing support for the elderly, and managing garbage collection (See Kawato, Pekkanen, and Yamamoto 2015; Pekkanen 2006: 85–129; Pekkanen, Tsujinaka, and Yamamoto 2014). Established in the Meiji period (1868–1912), NHAs have traditionally had a close relationship with the state, especially local governments. During the Pacific War, they were absorbed into the national mobilization regime only to be disbanded by the Allied Occupation (1945–1952) and then legalized and reconstituted as voluntary independent organizations in 1952. Although urbanization and generational change are impacting their significance, NHAs remain a central part of associational life in Japan today. They provide fertile material for scholars of Japanese civil society and state–society relations because of their somewhat ambiguous character, which straddles the boundaries of state and civil society (Pekkanen et al. 2014: 5–6). Indeed, NHAs are an appropriate point of entry into the study of civil society in Japan because they signpost the important role of the state in shaping associational life in the country.

Along with NHAs, Public Interest Legal Persons (PILPs) comprise another significant slice of the civil society sector in Japan.[1] PILPs are incorporated and regulated under Article 34 of the Japanese Civil Code and include, for example, foundations, medical legal persons, social welfare legal persons, school legal persons, and religious legal persons. PILPs, like NHAs, straddle the boundaries of state and society. Thanks to subcontracting, subsidies, and staffing, some PILPs are almost indistinguishable from government agencies. PILPs have also been subjected to strict oversight from state authorities. Qualifying for and maintaining the PILP status entails meeting the standards of "public interest" defined by the relevant bureaucratic authorities. In effect, officials have been able to use this "public interest" requirement to hand pick the groups that conform to their needs and preferences. Only with the passing of the Law for the Promotion of Specified Nonprofit Activities (NPO Law) in 1998 did it become much easier for many civic groups to become incorporated as NPOs without having to meet the stringent and arguably subjective requirements for PILPs under the Civil Code.

NPOs incorporated under the new 1998 law arguably epitomize the movement away from bureaucratic oversight toward greater autonomy in Japanese civil society over the past two decades or so. As of September 2016, 51,260 organizations had attained NPO status and a further 972 qualified as so-called "approved" (nintei) NPOs whose donors receive tax concessions for donations (Cabinet Office of Japan, 2016a). NPOs can engage in one or more of the twenty activities set out under the new law, such as disaster relief, international cooperation, community building, tourism, environmental protection, consumer protection, peace and human rights, and gender equality (Cabinet Office of Japan, 2016b). Groups involved in health and welfare, education, children's well-being, community building, and NPO support are the most numerous. According to Akihiro Ogawa (2014: 54), NPOs can be grouped into two distinct categories. The most prevalent are those providing services or acting as subcontractors for local governments while smaller groups can be categorized as "social enterprises" that are formulating their own creative solutions to pressing issues, such as childcare, food safety, and the environment (Ogawa 2014: 54–55). Even amongst this newest category of civil society organizations (CSOs), the tension between state influence and organizational autonomy persists.

Apart from the above entities, Japanese civil society is home to a plethora of other groups including consumer advocacy groups, consumer cooperatives, environmental preservation and anti-industrial pollution groups, women's organizations, minority advocacy groups (Ainu, resident Koreans, Burakumin), anti-military base movements (especially in Okinawa), pacifist and anti-war groups, anti-nuclear power and anti-atomic weapons groups, self-help groups, and alternative movements (e.g., organic farming, recycling), internationally active non-governmental organizations, disaster response and recovery groups, and more recently, self-advocacy groups of homeless persons and so-called "freeters." Recent years have also witnessed the rise of anti-foreigner and xenophobic movements, as well as groups demanding the return of the Japanese abducted by North Korea. Although sometimes not included in civil society, religious organizations, labor unions, business organizations, and agricultural cooperatives also contribute to associational life through engagement in issues beyond belief, work, and the market. I discuss some of these groups in detail below.

Overall, the number of civil society organizations in Japan has increased steadily in the post-World War II era (Kawato *et al.* 2015: 1259; Tsujinaka 2003). Moreover, the types of groups that are emerging appear to be different from before, with self-consciously independent (from the state) groups becoming more prominent. As Yutaka Tsujinaka (2003: 99, 114) points out, although Japanese civil society has been traditionally dominated by groups building social capital or providing services, recently, we see more groups actively trying to influence policy making and implementation.

Approaches to the study of civil society in Japan

Research on civil society in Japan can be usefully categorized in terms of the emphasis it gives to the state. At one end of this spectrum is research evidencing how the state and its regulatory instruments have powerfully shaped civil society in Japan; at the other end is research that, while recognizing this powerful institutional factor, points to long-term structural transformations, the agency of civil society actors, and international factors. For clarity, I suggest three broad approaches in research to date: state–institutional, historical, evolutionary, and civil society advocacy. In practice, most researchers, while stressing one factor, also recognize the multiplicity of variables shaping the sector.

Statist–institutional approach: The dominant approach in research on Japanese civil society to date has been the statist–institutional approach that, in a nutshell, argues that the state—more than any other factor—has deeply shaped the historical development of civil society in Japan. Political scientist Susan Pharr delineated this perspective most lucidly in a seminal volume, *The State of Civil Society in Japan*, stating that the "most striking feature of Japan's civil society over the past century" is "the degree to which the state has taken an activist stance toward civic life, monitoring it, penetrating it, and seeking to steer it with a wide range of distinct policy tools targeted by group or sector" (2003: 325). Concretely, groundbreaking work by Pekkanen has shown how the Japanese state's use of legal instruments such as the Civil Code has resulted in a civil society "with many small groups offering rich forms of 'social capital' but few large professionalized advocacy groups capable of influencing policy making" (2006: 7). This Pekkanen (2006) calls Japan's "dual civil society," characterized by countless "members" but few "advocates." Working from an anthropological perspective, Akihiro Ogawa (2004, 2009) argues that the Japanese state nurtures volunteer subjectivity as part of its neoliberal agenda. Ogawa is critical of the 1998 NPO Law, suggesting that it has partially become a "tool" for the state to "pursue a policy of welfare service retrenchment by empowering the nonprofit sector" (2004: 93). The government is arguably "taking advantage" of the recent popularity of volunteering to "streamline" the "framework of public administration" (Ogawa 2004: 93).

Such entanglement between the state and civic groups is not new. The historian Sheldon Garon (1997, 2003) has convincingly shown how, through partnerships (albeit unequal) with civic groups, the Japanese state has avoided costly social programs and nurtured values with respect to saving, hygiene, morals, and social welfare. For example, Garon (1997) shows how women's groups supported state initiatives to promote saving and religious organizations assisted in welfare relief to the poor, orphans, and wayward youth. Garon speaks of the "intertwining of civil society and state" and stresses that the capacity of the Japanese state to manage society depended a great deal on "the active participation of groups in civil society" (2003: 48). Indeed, "had Japan possessed a less vigorous civil society, its state would have remained an ineffective autocratic regime, unable to manufacture consent" (Garon 2003: 61).

This is not to say that the Japanese state has absolutely dominated civil society. Research also reveals how civic groups have shaped the state's responses and how some groups even subverted state institutions. Daniel Aldrich (2008: 10), for instance, convincingly shows how state officials tailored strategies to placate civil society groups that threatened to veto public works projects such as airports and nuclear power plants. As he explains, "there is a strong correlation between sustained, intense opposition and the use of preference-altering policy instruments that seek to capture the hearts of local citizens" (Aldrich 2008: 10). On top of this, Aldrich also notes how officials deliberately chose sites for nuclear power plants with low population density, high rates of depopulation, and weak local organizations (Aldrich 2008: 11). Aldrich shows that areas with low social capital were less likely to mount a successful resistance.

From a different angle, Karen Nakamura shows how a civic group, the Japanese Federation of the Deaf (JFD), managed to reap the "rewards of cooperating with the state while avoiding the pitfalls of cooptation and loss of autonomy" (Nakamura 2002: 33). In the case of the JFD, this strategy involved "leaving the national organization politically independent," yet "financially constrained," while allowing "prefectural associations to incorporate" as PILPs, giving them access to "government funds" but tying "their hands politically" (Nakamura 2002: 18). As Nakamura observes, "the relationship between power and resistance is complex and intertwined" (2002: 33).

Before moving on from the statist–institutional approach, one more perspective warrants mention for the interesting question it raises about state influence over civil society in Japan. Based on her work on volunteering, Mary Alice Haddad (2007) argues that the "embedded" and cooperative relationship many civic groups have with the state may actually be related to a norm in Japan that the government must take responsibility for handling social issues. This norm arguably "encourage[s] involvement in volunteer organizations that have close, embedded relationships with the government" (Haddad 2007: 6). From this perspective, state involvement in civil society happens partially because citizens expect it.

Historical evolutionary approach: The path-breaking empirical and theoretical work of the political scientist Yutaka Tsujinaka (2002, 2003) shifts attention from the state to the longer-term historical transformations in civil society in Japan. Surveying modern Japanese history, Tsujinaka identifies "waves of democratization," which were accompanied by relatively more intensive formation of associations. "The path to modernization has not been completely linear: there have been several booms and waves of vitalization among civil society organizations in Japan" (Tsujinaka 2003: 84). Tsujinaka (2003: 98–99) notes a shift in the types of groups that are formed in each cycle or wave, with a transition from the producer sector to the social service sector, and finally, most recently, the advocacy sector. In the pre-war era, Tsujinaka (2010) identifies two associational waves: one after the Meiji Restoration in the 1870s and 1880s, which was marked by the formation of around 2,000 associations and another in the interwar period (1918–1937). After the wartime co-optation of civic groups, Tsujinaka proposes four important phases of civil society development in the post-war era: 1945–1957, during which the "number of associations sharply increased" with the "focal point being the labor unions"; 1957–1975, when there was "an overall movement towards developmentalism, and business/economic associations and labor unions made up a substantial number of total associational formations," although "social movements such as citizens' and residents' movements" also proliferated; 1975–1996, when "there was a shift from citizens' and residents' movements to citizen participation which coordinated its efforts with the public administration" (2010). There was also a growth in the number of international NGOs, especially after the Indochinese refugee crisis in the late 1970s. Finally, the fourth phase, a post-1996 wave, which witnessed the emergence of many new social service and advocacy-oriented groups, as well as an overall deterioration in the financial situation and participation figures of associations. Based on these waves of associationalism, Tsujinaka suggests a "maturation" and "pluralization" of civil society in Japan (with a caveat that participation has declined since the mid-1990s) (2003: 109–110, 115).

While Tsujinaka points to long-term macro-structural transformations in civil society, others emphasize more recent political, demographic, and economic factors in explaining the emergence of civil society. Many suggest that the decline of Japan's developmentalist model of governance, the so-called "developmental state" (Johnson 1982) around the early 1990s, provided an opportunity for the emergence of civil society. In other words, civil society's rise came about in response to "institutional fatigue" (Amenomori 2003: 1), government officials' "fall from grace" due to scandal, and economic stagnation (Takao 2007: 18), and/or "a maturation of industrialization that weakened the need for a developmental system" (Hirata 2002: 26). In a slight variation of such explanations, some argue that the very success of the development state in advancing Japan "to a new level of affluence" quite unintentionally resulted in "the increasing prominence of civil society organizations" (Pekkanen 2004: 363, 375). Furthermore, as I discuss below, when considering the evolution of this sector in Japan of late, we also need to consider factors such as demographic change (especially aging) and the diffusion of international norms supportive of civil society.

Civil society advocacy approach: A third approach to the study of civil society in Japan draws attention to activists, think-tanks, politicians, and others, who began to advocate for the development of civil society in Japan beginning around the late 1980s. I call this the "civil society advocacy approach" because the focus in such research is on the agency of (primarily) non-state actors in raising the profile and legitimacy of the sector. Once again, like historical evolution approaches, research here generally recognizes the powerful shaping role of the state as well as the influence of macro-structural socio-economic and political transformations, but it also calls attention to the active initiatives from below. Research by Koichi Hasegawa, Chika Shinohara, and Jeffrey Broadbent (2007: 183), for instance, argue that initiatives by NGO leaders, scholars, social elites, and the media in the early 1990s produced a "social expectation" toward civil society. This social expectation helped to fuel the movement for the NPO Law, passed in 1998. Hasegawa and colleagues (2007) build on Tsujinaka's evolutionary explanation by proposing a mechanism—namely, civil society advocacy—for the emergence of civil society in Japan. Moreover, while Hasegawa and colleagues focus on the role of civil society advocates in the early 1990s, other research (Avenell 2010; Takada 1998; Yamamoto 1999) suggests a longer trajectory of civil society advocacy dating back to the 1970s and 1980s, when leading groups began to question the prevalent modes of contention and protest and search for sustainable, socially constructive models of activism.

In the context of theoretical debates about civil society in Japan, it is also worth mentioning that Japanese intellectuals in the 1950s and 1960s were amongst the first worldwide to resurrect the term "civil society" in a positive sense (Carver *et al.* 2000: 544; Yamaguchi 2004; Yoshida 2005). Until very recently, studies of civil society have traced its contemporary reemergence within political discourse to the democratic movements of Eastern Europe and Latin America in the 1970s. But in the 1950s and 1960s, Japanese scholars such as Uchida Yoshihiko, Hirata Kiyoaki, and Matsushita Keiichi had already begun to reformulate the idea as both a positive and aspirational concept (Avenell 2011: 319). This project grew out of an earlier project amongst liberal modernizationist intellectuals such as Ōtsuka Hisao, Maruyama Masao, and Kawashima Takeyoshi, who believed that although Japan had achieved industrial modernity, its people lacked the ethos of modern democratic political subjects. As Andrew Barshay explains, for Uchida and others, "civil society ... was the very instrument of positive social transformation" and "could not possibly be the mere ideological reflex of bourgeois hegemony because that hegemony had never formed" (2003: 68–69). Indeed, I have argued that the appeal of civil society for these Japanese intellectuals mirrored its appeal elsewhere later in the 1970s:

> a viscerally felt dissatisfaction with actually existing socialism and socialist theory, a growing concern about the impact of late capitalism on liberal democracy, political consciousness, and identity, and a repugnance for the totalizing proclivities of modern political and economic institutions.
>
> *(Avenell 2011: 313)*

Although this debate would fade out of memory until quite recently, it reminds us that the contemporary revival of civil society in Japan and elsewhere might also be understood as part of a global historical transformation. I return to this international aspect of Japanese civil society below.

History and development of civil society in Japan

Although research on the category of Japanese civil society only began in earnest around the 1990s, the "substance of civil society" has a much deeper history (Tsujinaka 2010). Determining how far back to go, of course, is partially a definitional issue. Because civil society is most often defined in terms of what it is not (i.e., the state, the market, the family, and the individual), studying it in pre-modern times when the boundaries of the "state" and "society" are fuzzy can be problematic. Nevertheless, if perceived more simply as associational activities independent of the "authorities" and not aimed at influencing or seizing authority or controlling economic resources, then Japan clearly has a history of associationalism traceable to at least the sixteenth century, when we can find examples of Buddhist temples providing charitable relief, associations of merchants, and peasant uprisings (Kawato *et al.* 2015: 1262). During Japan's Tokugawa (or Edo) period (1603–1868), an era of quasi-centralization, samurai teaching academies, merchant associations, networks of wealthy farmers, and various mutual aid associations flourished (Deguchi 2000: 18–19; Iokibe 1999: 53–56). The most commonly cited example from this time is the Kaitokudō, an educational academy supported by wealthy merchants in the city of Osaka, 1724–1869 (Deguchi 2000: 18; Najita 1987). Toward the latter part of this era, we also witness a rise in peasant protests, urban disturbances, and status-crossing networks (Vlastos 1990). In a fascinating study on the many aesthetic networks of the period, Eiko Ikegami (2005) describes the emergence of "bonds of civility" amongst samurai, merchants, and artists as they gathered together for artistic pursuits (e.g., the Japanese tea ceremony), which crossed traditional status divides. According to Ikegami, although Edo Japan,

> did not develop a civic associational domain that fit the Western notion of civil society ... if we define *civility* as the cultural grammar of sociability that governs interactional public spaces, then the widespread practices and sophisticated characteristics of Toku-gawa sociability would certainly be deserving of the term civility.
>
> *(Ikegami 2005: 19)*

In a sense, Ikegami suggests that some of the values and practices of progressive civil society were in place at this time, even though civil society was then not possible as a legitimate political space.

The ensuing Meiji period (1868–1912) heralded sweeping changes, including the abolition of social statuses, new freedom of movement, urbanization, and the inflow of ideas—like liberalism—from the West. As noted above, Tsujinaka (2010) identifies a wave of associational organizing in the first two decades of this period (1870s–1880s). Because of their access to new ideas from abroad, elite intellectuals were amongst the first to organize civic groups. The most famous was Meirokusha, a learned society formed by some of the most influential public commentators and intellectuals of the time, such as Fukuzawa Yukichi, Katō Hiroyuki, and Nishimura Shigeki. This group set itself the task of introducing Western ideas of civilization and enlightenment to Japan through public presentations and the group's magazine, *Meiroku Zasshi*.

While this first wave of modern associationalism was unfolding in the Meiji period, some of the key regulatory instruments that the Japanese state would use to control and shape civil society were also installed. Most importantly, the Meiji Civil Code with its requirement that all incorporated PILPs be officially vetted and monitored in terms of "public interest" provisions was promulgated in 1896. As Masayuki Deguchi points out, "underlying this legal provision [was] the idea that the state has a monopoly over matters of the public interest, based in turn on the idea that public interest activities are the province of the state" (2000: 20). Six years earlier, in 1890, the *Constitution of the Empire of Japan* (the Meiji Constitution) came into force. Imperial sovereignty under this instrument meant that, at least formally, most power lay in the hands of the Emperor, while his subjects enjoyed limited rights that could be (and indeed were) curtailed by subsequent legislation. Thus, from the beginning of Japan's modernization, we witness an expansion in associational life accompanied by state initiatives to proactively manage this space.

Such tendencies continued into the era of Taishō democracy (1905–1932).[2] In terms of association formation, this period witnessed intensive labor organizing, the rise of tenant unions, the establishment of pioneering women's groups such as the New Women's Association (Shinfujin Kyōkai, 1919), and mass civic protest in the Hibiya Riot (1905) and the Rice Riots (1918). Makoto Iokibe (1999: 75) identifies an "associational revolution" between 1913 and the Manchurian Incident of 1931 involving business groups such as the Japan Chamber of Commerce and Industry, the socialist Japan Fabian Society; minority groups such as the National Levelers Association (Suiheisha) for former outcastes; and even international exchange groups such as the Pacific Society. According to Iokibe, the "proliferation of nonprofit" and "value-promotion" groups was "phenomenal" at the time, but none "put down the sturdy roots" necessary to resist "ultranationalism and militarism" after 1931 (1999: 75).

Throughout this period of Taishō democracy, many groups such as women's groups and religious organizations worked closely with the state in "moral suasion" campaigns (Garon 1997). In some cases, the state–civic group relationship became so close as to make such groups indistinguishable from state agencies. The Red Cross Society, established by Sano Tsunetami in 1877, for example, was so generously supported by the Japanese Empress "that it acquired the characteristics of a government body" (Deguchi 2000: 19). Similarly, the Holy Spirit Group (Seirei), a barracks-style hospital established by Christians in 1930, only became financially viable with a "special grant" from the Emperor, which not only solved its financial woes but also brought great social legitimacy to the group, which it would not have garnered otherwise (Deguchi 2000: 18–19). The state also used less subtle instruments to manage civil society during the early twentieth century. The *Public Order and Police Law* of 1900 targeted labor organizations by restricting freedoms of speech and assembly, and was proactively utilized to stifle "dangerous" political ideas. Moreover, in 1925 the infamous *Peace Preservation Law* came into effect. This law was specifically aimed at suppressing and eradicating leftist activism in the country and it marked the beginning of a period of intensive state suppression of civil society, which would culminate in the almost complete loss of civic autonomy vis-à-vis the state under the wartime Imperial Rule Assistance Association (IRAA) established in 1940.

The Allied Occupation of Japan (1946–1952) marked the beginning of a new wave of civic group formation as the illiberal institutional and social structures of the war and pre-war years were systematically dismantled (although not completely eradicated). As Garon puts it, "for a society long accustomed to active associational life and a lively public sphere, defeat and occupation served as potent catalysts" (2003: 57). Drawing on rights of speech, assembly, and association under the American-authored post-war constitution, these years witnessed a rise in labor and consumer activism, the reformation of disbanded religions (Soka Gakkai), and the creation of women's groups (the Women's Democratic Club, the Housewives Association) and minority advocacy groups (the Buraku Liberation League). NHAs, which had been dismantled as undemocratic organizations by the occupation authorities, were allowed to re-form as voluntary, independent organizations as soon as the occupation ended in 1952 and quickly became the mainstay of civil society thereafter. Anti-Atomic bomb movements also formed in the mid-1950s. Following the irradiation of a Japanese fishing vessel, the *Lucky Dragon Number 5*, after an American atomic weapon test at Bikini Atoll in the South Pacific in 1954, Japanese citizens (women in particular) began an opposition signature campaign. In the following year, the Japan Council Against Atomic and Hydrogen Bombs (Gensuikyō) was formed as the peak anti-nuclear organization in the country, although internal ideological divisions during the Cold War led to a division in 1965 when socialists and labor groups split to form the Japan Congress Against A- and H-Bombs (Gensuikin).

The period from around the late 1950s to the early 1970s was one of intensive, contentious, and sometimes violent civic activism and student radicalism. In terms of mass movements, the massive demonstrations against the renewal of the USA–Japan security treaty in 1959–1960 brought together a great diversity of labor unions, political parties, religious organizations, student groups, professional associations (i.e., scientists, lawyers), academics and public intellectuals, and many unaffiliated citizens who spontaneously formed their own groups (Avenell 2010; Sasaki-Uemura 2001). This so-called "Anpo Struggle" witnessed the largest public demonstrations in post-war Japan, but its defeat, coupled with the trouncing of militant unionism at the Mitsui Miike Coal Mine in 1960, marked the end of mass street protests for many decades. Student protests exploded again in the late 1960s, but were eventually crushed by the strong hand of the state against the backdrop of growing public abhorrence for student radicalism (Oguma 2009).

Although the influence of students and organized labor began to wane after the 1960s, independent grass-roots citizen activism greatly expanded. The pioneering "citizen movements" (*shimin undo*) of the 1960s were the Voices of the Voiceless Association (Koe naki Koe no Kai) started by leftist scholars, artists, and ordinary citizens in the heat of the 1960 security treaty crisis, and *Beheiren*, the Citizens Committee for Peace in Vietnam, established in 1965 with the outbreak of hostilities during the Vietnam War. Both of these movements had strong pacifist, anti-war, and anti-US ideologies and both prided themselves on holding a stanch "autonomy" from the established organs of the left (Avenell 2010; Havens 1987; Michiba 2005). Their legacy continues today in groups such as the Article 9 Association (Kyūjō no Kai), a group committed to maintaining Article 9 of the Japanese constitution, which renounces war and commits Japan to pacifism (Ogawa 2014: 58).

An industrial pollution nightmare caused by breakneck economic growth from 1955 to 1973 stimulated a parallel wave of anti-pollution and anti-development residents' and victims' movements (Avenell 2006, 2012a; Broadbent 1998; McKean 1981). The earliest mobilizations comprised pollution victims and their advocates, for example, victims of mercury poisoning from Minamata Bay and air pollution victims from Yokkaichi City (George 2001; McKean 1981). They were supported by pioneering pollution victims' advocacy groups such as the Research Committee on Pollution (Kōgai Kenkyū Iinkai) established by leftist economists, engineers, natural scientists, and lawyers (Avenell 2012b). In an attempt to pre-empt industrial pollution in their communities, citizens also began to form prevention movements; the most notable was in 1964 in Shizuoka Prefecture, where groups successfully resisted the construction of a petrochemical factory (Lewis 1980). Similar prevention movements mobilized (unsuccessfully) in Yokohama (opposing a new freight line) and Chiba (opposing a new international airport). By the early 1970s, pressure from these movements (numbering over 3,000 nationwide) became so intense that the ruling conservative Liberal Democratic Party, fearful of an electoral backlash, passed some of the most stringent environmental protection regulations in the world targeting the so-called Pollution Diet of 1970. Achieving this political response was undoubtedly one of the greatest victories for Japanese civil society in the modern history of the country, which was made even more impressive by the court victories of industrial pollution victims around the same time (Gresser, Fujikura, and Morishima 1981: 29–51).

Of course, we need to recognize that neither the anti-war pacifist citizens' movements nor the environmental movements of the time managed to carve out a space for themselves in mainstream politics, partly due to effective "damage control" by the conservative politicians and bureaucrats, and also due to these groups' localist and independent outlook, which was often at odds with the organizational politics of the socialist and communist parties. Quite different from West Germany, for example, where the environmental movement charted a path into party politics and government, the period after the peak of anti-pollution protests from the early 1970s through the 1990s has often been described as an "ice age" of contentious civic activism in Japan (Maruyama 1985: 61). In many respects, this is true; widespread protest certainly waned but contentious activism did not disappear altogether. Moreover, a range of fascinating new civil society initiatives began to take root during this period, providing the foundation for some of the important developments in Japanese civil society in the 1990s.

Throughout the 1970s and 1980s, protest movements mobilized against diverse problems such as nuclear power plants, bullet train lines, and US military bases (especially in Okinawa). In 1975, for instance, scientists and other anti-nuclear activists established the Citizens' Nuclear Information Center (CNIC) which, under the guidance of nuclear chemist Takagi Jinzaburō, served as one of the few watchdogs of the nuclear power industry in Japan (Avenell 2016). Such initiatives were few, however. Many activists who had cut their teeth in the citizen and student movements of the 1960s and early 1970s now turned their energies to so-called "alternative" movements such as organic farming, recycling, consumer cooperatives, and movements for the disabled (Avenell 2010). Pioneering movements in this new wave of "proposal-style" citizens' movements included the Association to Preserve the Earth (organic produce), the Japan Recycling Movement Citizens' Association (1977), the Dandelion House (empowering the disabled) (1973), the Seikatsu Club (consumer cooperative) (1965), and Peace Boat (international youth exchange) (1983). Leaders of these movements called on participants to abandon the "accusatory" and "oppositional" approach of earlier movements in favor of a constructive form of activism capable of proposing an alternative lifestyle to mainstream Japanese society (Avenell 2009; Takada 1998: 167). Their movements reached a crescendo in the mid-1980s with the publication of a pioneering directory of 1,300 new civic groups and an ocean voyage in

1986—the so-called "Banana Boat" cruise—involving 510 activists from 170 of the new movements. The 1980s cruise and directory represented one of the earliest attempts to build a solid network amongst grass-roots civic groups.

State officials also continued to play a role in the development of Japanese civil society during the 1970s and 1980s, most notably in the sphere of volunteering. The first Oil Shock of 1973 coupled with new concerns about an aging society and social welfare paved the way for discussions about "small government" and "a reconsideration of welfare" at the time. Although the Japanese state had long supported institutionalized forms of volunteering such as the ubiquitous district welfare commissioners (*minsei-iin*), civil liberties commissioners (*jinken yōgo iin*), and NHAs, during this period, the ministries involved in health and welfare and education, in particular, began to develop policies for the promotion and spread of volunteering nationwide. In terms of infrastructure, the government began to establish volunteer centers in local social welfare councils for the registration and management of volunteers and they allocated funds for policies to nurture volunteering amongst women and the youth. The language used by officials also began to resemble that used by the new proposal movements, with policy statements regularly referring to "self-realization," "self-autonomy," and "creative" activism (Avenell 2010). Not surprisingly, volunteer groups providing services to the bedridden and elderly increased dramatically.

Beginning with the Banana Boat cruise in 1986, from the mid-1980s onward, Japanese civic groups devoted more attention to building networks and strengthening the infrastructure of civil society in Japan (Takada 1998: 165). These initiatives became more formalized in the early 1990s through groups such as the Japan Networkers Conference, which engaged in discussions about the poor financial condition of many civic groups and invited experts from the USA and elsewhere to discuss the regulatory framework for civil society in their countries. Similar initiatives of the time included the NPO Research Forum established in Osaka in 1993, the National Institute for Research Advancement's (NIRA) influential 1994 report on the state of "citizens' public interest activities," and the establishment in 1994 of C's: The Association to Establish a System to Support Civic Activities. C's brought together around twenty-four civic groups committed to the passing of new legislation, making it easier for groups to incorporate and encouraging donations through tax breaks (Yamamoto 1999: 107). The Japanese corporate sector was also involved in these initiatives. The Toyota Foundation, for instance, provided financial support for the networking conferences of the late 1980s and early 1990s. Moreover, in 1989, the Japanese Business Federation (Keidanren) established its "1% Club," whose member organizations commit to donate 1 percent of their yearly recurring profits or disposable incomes to social causes. Local governments also become involved by establishing "community building centers" (*machizukuri sentā*) and passing municipal ordinances to support civic activities (Takada 1998: 172).

In the midst of these movements for building the infrastructure of civil society, in 1995, Kobe City and surrounding areas were hit by a massive earthquake. While the national government dithered in response, grass-roots volunteer groups, NHAs, local officials, and even organized crime syndicates provided immediate relief on the ground. Thousands of youth from around the nation converged on Kobe to assist in one of the most impressive outpourings of volunteerism in modern Japanese history. Building on this energy, thereafter, the movement for a new law to support civic activities intensified, resulting ultimately in the passing of the NPO Law in 1998. As Pekkenan observes, "even had the Hanshin Awaji earthquake not occurred, many critics claim that an NPO Law would have been passed within a decade anyway." But "the response to the earthquake was key … in hastening and highlighting these changes. The visibility of volunteers accelerated significantly a process already underway" (2003: 69).

Ironically enough, another major earthquake (and tsunami) on March 11, 2011 stimulated an impressive disaster response by civic groups and a brief outburst of anti-nuclear protest. Drawing on their experience in Kobe, veteran volunteers and disaster response groups took the lead in coordinating volunteers and providing emergency services in the affected regions (Avenell 2012c). Remarkably different from Kobe, the Japanese government also quickly embraced disaster response groups, sending officials to frequent government-NGO liaison meetings and even appointing leading activists to official disaster-response positions. The reactor meltdowns and explosions at the Fukushima Daiichi Plant stimulated a flurry of protest throughout Japan, especially in Tokyo. In September 2011, anti-nuclear power rallies in the city attracted numbers unseen since the heady days of the Anpo protests of 1960. However, these protests proved ephemeral and despite apparent widespread opposition to nuclear power, by 2016, some reactors came back online. Just what this means for civil society in Japan is unclear. The successful disaster response and the largely unsuccessful anti-nuclear power protests suggest that Japanese civil society may not have changed much: a space strong in social capital yet critically weak in advocacy in spite of the supposedly transformative changes of the 1990s. Coupled with the ambiguous messages from the earthquake and Fukushima disaster, in recent years, we have seen the rise of anti-foreigner and xenophobic movements. Moreover, mobilizations for the return of Japanese nationals abducted by North Korea garner great support from conservative politicians, the far right, and many ordinary citizens, but movements for marginalized groups such as unemployed (and underemployed) youth, the homeless, immigrants, and foreign workers struggle for public recognition and political traction.

Directions in the study of Japanese civil society

The rising prominence of Japanese civil society over the past two to three decades has been accompanied by an increase and a qualitative diversification of research on the sector. This final section presents a brief overview of the author's recent work on international factors in the study of Japanese civil society. As discussed above, the bulk of scholarship on Japanese civil society to date has focused on developments at the national level and below, with marked attention to the role of the state. Nevertheless, researchers have become increasingly sensitive to the impact of international factors, especially international norm diffusion. Tadashi Yamamoto (1999: 99) and Robert Pekkanen (2004: 376) both note how Japanese corporations learned about practices of corporate social responsibility (CSR) and philanthropy through their operations in Europe and North America, where such activity was expected. International norms supportive of NGOs also influenced Japanese governmental approaches to the sector. Kim Reimann (2003) persuasively shows how the "emergence of a new international norm in the 1980s and 1990s regarding the role of [international development] NGOs as partners to the state" offered "new opportunities" for Japanese groups interested in this area. This "push from the outside" encouraged Japanese officials to reconsider and reformulate their policies and attitudes toward international development NGOs (Reimann 2003: 301). The most significant policy change according to Reimann (2003: 302) was the creation of funding schemes in various ministries for IDNGO projects in developing countries.

Japanese civic groups also learned from involvement abroad. Keiko Hirata (2002: 73) explains how globalization promoted "new values and norms" and brought about a "skill revolution" amongst activists. Going abroad offered "new models of behavior and organization for Japanese NGOs that helped them achieve their goals" (Reimann 2002: 181). Attendance at international events such as United Nations (UN) conferences appears to have been particularly important in terms of learning. It is no coincidence that Japanese groups' networking and civil society

27

advocacy initiatives in the late 1980s and early 1990s coincided with increased Japanese NGO participation at landmark UN conferences. Beginning with the UN Conference on Environment and Development (1992), which Yamamoto (1999: 99) describes as a "watershed moment" for Japanese civic groups, in the years leading up to the passing of the NPO Law (1998), Japanese NGOs attended the UN Conference on Human Rights (Vienna, 1993), the International Conference on Population and Development (Cairo, 1994), the World Conference for Social Development (Copenhagen 1995), the Fourth World Conference on Women (Beijing 1995), and the Third Conference of the Parties to the Framework Convention on Climate Change (COP3, 1997). Japanese NGOs such as the Kiko Forum active at COP3 benefited greatly from financial and logistical support from their German counterparts, the Klima Forum. In turn, the Kiko Forum and other internationally active Japanese NGOs became models for the sector as a whole.

My own recent research (Avenell 2013, 2017) on the Japanese environmental movement suggests that international and transnational elements have been playing a role in the development of Japanese civil society for a long time. As early as the late 1960s, Japanese anti-pollution activists such as the engineer Ui Jun traveled to Europe and North America to learn about activism in those regions, as well as to transmit news about Japanese industrial pollution and protests. Japanese pollution victims participated in the NGO forums at the landmark United Nations Conference on the Human Environment (UNCHE) in Stockholm in 1972 amidst great media fanfare. In the early 1970s, Japanese groups joined counterpart groups in Thailand and South Korea to oppose the relocation of polluting Japanese industries to these countries, while leading mercury poisoning experts, such as the physician Harada Masazumi, traveled to Canada and Indonesia to conduct tests on communities whose waterways had been contaminated with mercury. In the 1980s, anti-nuclear activists in Japan joined activists in Pacific Islands to oppose the planned ocean dumping of Japanese nuclear waste. Such transnational connections intensified throughout the 1990s as Japanese groups became involved in a myriad of international issues such as deforestation, stratospheric ozone depletion, and global warming.

The 1970s and 1980s appear to have been a particularly formative era in Japanese civic groups' transnational involvement. Apart from pollution and the environment, Japanese groups became involved in gender issues, human rights, minority issues, peace and anti-war activism, and grass-roots economic development. Groups such as the Independent Lectures on Pollution (1969–1985) and Beheiren (1965–1974) were pioneers in forging overseas connections. Later, groups included the Pacific Asia Resource Center (PARC) established by former anti-Vietnam War activists in 1973 as a hub for civic activism and human rights advocacy throughout the region. Takagi Jinzaburō's anti-nuclear power group, the CNIC, also became active transnationally through its English-language newsletter *Nuke Info Tokyo*. In response to the spread of so-called *kiseng* sex tourism in South Korea and other areas of Asia, in 1973, the journalist Matsui Yayori and other Japanese women established the Women's Association to Oppose Kiseng Tourism (Michiba 2011: 118, 120). Japanese NGOs also became involved in development projects. The Shalpa Neer group, for instance, was formed in 1972 to provide financial and other forms of assistance to communities in Bangladesh, while in 1973 Takami Toshihiro established the Asian Rural Institute to train leaders from developing countries in methods of sustainable agriculture. The Indochina refugee crisis of the late 1970s was an early "watershed" in the development of transnationally active Japanese NGOs. Many of Japan's leading NGOs such as the Japan International Volunteer Center (1980) and Shanti Volunteer Association (1980) cut their teeth in the heat of this crisis. These transnational, regional, international, and global aspects of Japanese civil society are still largely under-researched and, hence, offer fertile ground for furthering our understanding this sector. Like the Japanese nation, Japan's civil society has not developed in a vacuum. Given this, we might ask how the forces of regionalization, internationalization, and globalization have shaped Japanese civil society and vice versa. What have Japanese NGOs learned through overseas involvement and how has this learning been injected back into domestic civil society? Conversely, how have Japanese groups contributed to the shaping of civil societies in other countries, regionally and globally?

Notes

1 Some NHAs are incorporated.
2 The Taishō period ran from 1912 to 1926.

Suggested readings

Kawato, Yuko, Robert J. Pekkanen, and Hidehiro Yamamoto. 2015. Civil Society in Japan. In *The SAGE Handbook of Modern Japanese Studies*. James D. Babb, ed. Pp. 1259–1371. London: SAGE.
Ogawa, Akihiro. 2014. Civil Society: Past, Present, and Future. In *Critical Issues in Contemporary Japan*. Jeff Kingston, ed. Pp. 52–63. London and New York: Routledge.
Schwartz, Frank J., and Susan J. Pharr, eds. 2003. *The State of Civil Society in Japan*. Cambridge: Cambridge University Press.
Pekkanen, Robert. 2006. *Japan's Dual Civil Society: Members Without Advocates*. Stanford, CA: Stanford University Press.
Garon, Sheldon. 1997. *Molding Japanese Minds: The State in Everyday Life*. Princeton, NJ: Princeton University Press.

Websites

Cabinet Office NPO Homepage, www.npo-homepage.go.jp/.
The Cabinet Office NPO Homepage aims to provide information on the NPO incorporation, procedures, event information, volunteer organizations, conferences, and statistics on NPOs in Japan.
Japan NPO Center, www.jnpoc.ne.jp/en/.
The Japan NPO Center is an organization for the non-profit sector, with the aim to strengthen the social, political, and economic support base for voluntary non-profit organizations in Japan.

References

Aldrich, Daniel. 2008. *Site Fights: Divisive Facilities and Civil Society in Japan and the West*. Ithaca, NY: Cornell University Press.
Amenomori, Takayoshi. 2003. The Notion of Civil Society in Contemporary Japan: Mere Fashion or a Reflection of Structural Change?. Paper presented at the Third ISTR Asia and the Pacific Regional Conference, Beijing, China, October 24–26.
Avenell, Simon. 2006. Regional Egoism as the Public Good: Residents' Movements in Japan during the 1960s and 1970s. *Japan Forum* 18(1): 89–113.
Avenell, Simon. 2009. Civil Society and the New Civic Movements in Japan: Convergence, Collaboration, and Transformation. *The Journal of Japanese Studies* 35(2): 247–283.
Avenell, Simon. 2010. *Making Japanese Citizens: Civil Society and the Mythology of the Shimin in Postwar Japan*. Berkeley, CA: University of California Press.
Avenell, Simon. 2011. Japan and the Global Revival of the "Civil Society" Idea: Contemporaneity and the Retreat of Criticality. *Japan Forum* 23(3): 311–338.
Avenell, Simon. 2012a. Japan's Long Environmental Sixties and the Birth of a Green Leviathan. *Japanese Studies* 32 (3): 423–444.
Avenell, Simon. 2012b. From Fearsome Pollution to Fukushima: Environmental Activism and the Nuclear Blind Spot in Contemporary Japan. *Environmental History* 17 (2): 244–276.
Avenell, Simon. 2012c. From Kobe to Tohoku: The Potential and the Peril of a Volunteer Infrastructure. In *Natural Disaster and Nuclear Crisis in Japan: Response and Recovery after Japan's 3/11*. Jeff Kingston, ed. Pp. 53–77. London and New York: Routledge.

Avenell, Simon. 2013. The Borderless Archipelago: Toward a Transnational History of Japanese Environmentalism. *Environment and History* (19): 397–425.

Avenell, Simon. 2016. Antinuclear Radicals: Scientific Experts and Antinuclear Activism in Japan. *Science, Technology, and Society: An International Journal* 21(1) 2016: 88–109.

Avenell, Simon. 2017. *Transnational Japan in the Global Environmental Movement*. Honolulu, HI: University of Hawai'i Press.

Barshay, Andrew. 2003. Capitalism and Civil Society in Postwar Japan: Perspectives from Intellectual History. In *The State of Civil Society in Japan*. Frank J. Schwartz and Susan J. Pharr, eds. Pp. 63–80. Cambridge: Cambridge University Press.

Broadbent, Jeffrey. 1998. *Environmental Politics in Japan: Networks of Power and Protest*. Cambridge: Cambridge University Press.

Cabinet Office of Japan. 2016a. Tokutei Hieiri Katsudō Hōjin no Ninteisū no Suii [Variations in Numbers of Approvals of Specified Non-Profit Activities Legal Persons]. Electronic document, www.npo-homepage.go.jp/about/toukei-info/ninshou-seni, accessed November 12, 2016 (in Japanese).

Cabinet Office of Japan. 2016b. Tokutei Hieiri Katsudō Hōjin no Katsudō Bun'ya nit suite (Heisei 28 nen 9 gatsu 30 nichi genzai) [Areas of Activity of Specified Non-Profit Activities Legal Persons] (As at September 30, 2016). Electronic document, www.npo-homepage.go.jp/about/toukei-info/ninshou-bunyabetsu, accessed November 12, 2016 (in Japanese).

Carver, Terrell, Shin Chiba, Reiji Matsumoto, James Martin, Bob Jessop, Fumio Iida, and Atsushi Sugita. 2000. "Civil Society" in Contemporary Japanese Politics: Implications for Contemporary Political Research. *European Journal of Political Research* 37: 541–555.

Deguchi, Masayuki. 2000. Not For Profit: A Brief History of Japanese Nonprofit Organizations. *Look Japan* 45(526): 18–20.

Edwards, Michael. 2011. Introduction: Civil Society and the Geometry of Human Relations. In *The Oxford Handbook of Civil Society*. Michael Edwards, ed. Pp. 3–13. New York: Oxford University Press.

Garon, Sheldon. 1997. *Molding Japanese Minds: The State in Everyday Life*. Princeton, NJ: Princeton University Press.

Garon, Sheldon. 2003. From Meiji to Heisei: The State and Civil Society in Japan. In *The State of Civil Society in Japan*. Frank J. Schwartz and Susan J. Pharr, eds. Pp. 42–62. Cambridge: Cambridge University Press.

George, Timothy S. 2001. *Minamata: Pollution and the Struggle for Democracy in Postwar Japan*. Cambridge, MA: Harvard University Press.

Gresser, Julian, Koichiro Fujikura, and Akio Morishima. 1981. *Environmental Law in Japan*. London and Cambridge: MIT Press.

Haddad, Mary Alice. 2007. *Politics and Volunteering in Japan: A Global Perspective*. New York: Cambridge University Press.

Hasegawa, Koichi, Chika Shinohara, and Jeffrey P. Broadbent. 2007. The Effects of "Social Expectation" on the Development of Civil Society in Japan. *Journal of Civil Society* 3(28): 179–203.

Havens, Thomas R. H. 1987. *Fire Across the Sea: The Vietnam War and Japan 1965–1975*. Princeton, NJ: Princeton University Press.

Hirata, Keiko. 2002. *Civil Society in Japan: The Growing Role of NGO's in Tokyo's Aid Development Policy*. New York: Palgrave Macmillan.

Ikegami, Eiko. 2005. *Bonds of Civility: Aesthetic Networks and the Political Origins of Japanese Culture*. New York: Cambridge University Press.

Iokibe, Makoto. 1999. Japan's Civil Society: An Historical Overview. In *Deciding the Public Good: Governance and Civil Society in Japan*. Yamamoto Tadashi, ed. Pp. 51–96. Tokyo: Japan Center for International Exchange.

Johnson, Chalmers. 1982. *MITI and the Japanese Miracle*. Stanford, CA: Stanford University Press.

Kawato, Yuko, Robert J. Pekkanen, and Hidehiro Yamamoto. 2015. Civil Society in Japan. In *The SAGE Handbook of Modern Japanese Studies*. James D. Babb, ed. Pp. 1259–1371. London: Sage.

Lewis, Jack. 1980. Civic Protest in Mishima: Citizens' Movements and the Politics of the Environment in Contemporary Japan. In *Political Opposition and Local Politics in Japan*. Kurt Steiner, Ellis S. Krauss, and Scott Flanagan, eds. Pp. 274–313. Princeton, NJ: Princeton University Press.

Maruyama, Hisashi. 1985. *Minikomi no Dōjidaishi* [Grass-roots Publications in Historical Context]. Tokyo: Heibonsha (in Japanese).

McKean, Margaret. 1981. *Environmental Protest and Citizen Politics in Japan*. Berkeley, CA: University of California Press.

Michiba, Chikanobu. 2005. *Senryō to Heiwa: Sengo to iu Keiken* [*Occupation and Peace: The Post-war Experience*]. Tokyo: Seidosha (in Japanese).

Michiba, Chikanobu. 2011. Posuto-Betonamu Sensōki ni okeru Ajia Rentai Undō: "Uchinaru Ajia" to "Ajia no naka no Nihon" no aida de [Asian Solidarity Movements in the Post-Vietnam War Era: Between the "Asia Within" and "Japan in Asia"]. In *Iwanami Kōza: Higashi Ajia Kingendai Tsūshi Dai8kan: Betonamu Sensō no Jidai 1960–1975nen* [*Iwanami Lectures: A General History of Modern and Contemporary East Asia Volume 8: The Vietnam War Era 1960–1975*]. Wada Haruki, Gotō Ken'ichi, Kibata Yōichi, Yamamuro Shin'ichi, Cho Kyeungdal, Nakano Satoshi, and Kawashima Shin, eds. Pp. 97–127. Tokyo: Iwanami Shoten (in Japanese).

Najita, Tetsuo. 1987. *Visions of Virtue in Tokugawa Japan: the Kaitokudō Merchant Academy of Osaka*. Chicago, IL: University of Chicago Press.

Nakamura, Karen. 2002. Resistance and Co-optation: the Japanese Federation of the Deaf and its Relations with State Power. *Social Science Japan Journal* 5(1): 17–35.

NIRA (Sōgō Kenkyū Kaihatsu Kikō). 1994. *Shimin Kōeki Katsudō Kihon Seibi ni kansuru Chōsa Kenkyū* [*Research Report on the Support System for Citizens' Public Interest Activities*]. Tokyo: Sōgō Kenkyū Kaihatsu Kikō (in Japanese).

Ogawa, Akihiro. 2004. Invited by the State: Institutionalizing Volunteer Subjectivity in Contemporary Japan. *Asian Anthropology* 3: 71–96.

Ogawa, Akihiro. 2009. *The Failure of Civil Society?: The Third Sector and the State in Contemporary Japan*. Albany, NY: State University of New York Press.

Ogawa, Akihiro. 2014. Civil Society: Past, Present, and Future. In *Critical Issues in Contemporary Japan*. Jeff Kingston, ed. Pp. 52–63. London and New York: Routledge.

Oguma, Eiji. 2009. *1968* vols. 1 and 2. Tokyo: Shin'yōsha (in Japanese).

Pekkanen, Robert J. 2003. The Politics of Regulating the Non-Profit Sector. In *The Voluntary and Non-Profit Sector in Japan: The Challenge of Change*. Stephen P. Osborne, ed. Pp. 53–75. London and New York: RoutledgeCurzon.

Pekkanen, Robert J. 2004. After the Developmental State: Civil Society in Japan. *Journal of East Asian Studies* 4: 363–388.

Pekkanen, Robert J. 2006. *Japan's Dual Civil Society: Members Without Advocates*. Stanford, CA: Stanford University Press.

Pekkanen, Robert J., Yutaka Tsujinaka, and Hidehiro Yamamoto. 2014. *Neighborhood Associations and Local Governance in Japan*. Abingdon and New York: Routledge.

Pharr, Susan J. 2003. Conclusion: Targeting by an Activist State: Japan as a Civil Society Model. In *The State of Civil Society in Japan*. Frank J. Schwartz and Susan J. Pharr, eds. Pp. 316–336. Cambridge: Cambridge University Press.

Reimann, Kim D. 2002. Building Networks from the Outside In: Japanese NGOs and the Kyoto Climate Change Conference 2002. In *Globalization and Resistance: Transnational Dimensions of Social Movements*. Jackie Smith and Hank Johnston, eds. Pp. 173–87. Lanham, MD: Rowman & Littlefield.

Reimann, Kim D. 2003. Building Global Civil Society from the Outside In? Japanese International Development NGOs, the State, and International Norms. In *The State of Civil Society in Japan*. Frank J. Schwartz and Susan J. Pharr, eds. Pp. 298–315. Cambridge: Cambridge University Press.

Sasaki-Uemura, Wesley. 2001. *Organizing the Spontaneous: Citizen Protest in Postwar Japan*. Honolulu, HI: University of Hawai'i Press.

Takada, Akihiko. 1998. Gendai Shimin Shakai ni okeru Shimin Undō no Henyō: Nettowākingu no Dōnyū kara "Shimin Katsudō"—NPO e [The Transformation of Citizens' Movements in Contemporary Civil Society: From the Introduction of Networking to "Citizens" Activities—NPOs]. In *Gendai Shimin Shakai to Aidentiti: 21 Seiki no Shimin Shakai to Kyōdōsei—Riron to Tenbō* [*Contemporary Civil Society and Identity: 21st Century Civil Society and Cooperation—Theories and Prospects*]. Aoi Kazuo, Takahashi Akira, and Jōji Kōkichi, eds. Pp. 160–185. Tokyo: Azusa Shuppansha (in Japanese).

Takao, Yasuo. 2007. *Reinventing Japan: From Merchant Nation to Civic Nation*. New York: Palgrave Macmillan.

Tsujinaka, Yutaka. 2002. *Gendai Nihon no Shimin Shakai—Rieki Dantai* (Gendai no Shimin Shakai—Rieki Dantai Kenkyū Sōsho [1]) [*Civil Society in Contemporary Japan—Interest Groups* (Contemporary Civil Society—Interest Group Research Series)]. Tokyo: Bokutakusha (in Japanese).

Tsujinaka, Yutaka. 2003. From Developmentalism to Maturity: Japan's Civil Society Organizations in Comparative Perspective. In *The State of Civil Society in Japan*. Frank J. Schwartz and Susan J. Pharr, eds. Pp. 83–115. Cambridge: Cambridge University Press.

Tsujinaka, Yutaka. 2010. Civil Society in Japan. *Inter Faculty* 1. Electronic document, https://journal.hass. tsukuba.ac.jp/interfaculty/issue/view/1, accessed February 12, 2016.

Vlastos, Stephen. 1990. *Peasant Protests and Uprisings in Tokugawa Japan*. Berkeley, CA: University of California Press.

Yamaguchi, Yasushi. 2004. *Shimin Shakai Ron: Rekishiteki Isan to Shintenkai* [*On Civil Society: Historical Legacies and New Developments*]. Tokyo: Yuhikaku (in Japanese).

Yamamoto, Tadashi. 1999. Emergence of Japan's Civil Society and Its Future Challenges. In *Deciding the Public Good: Governance and Civil Society in Japan*. Yamamoto Tadashi, ed. Pp. 97–124. Tokyo: Japan Center for International Exchange.

Yoshida, Masatoshi. 2005. *Shimin Shakai Ron: Sono Riron to Rekishi* [*On Civil Society: Theory and History*]. Tokyo: Ōtsuki Shoten (in Japanese).

2

SOUTH KOREA

Yooil Bae

Civil society in South Korea at a crossroad

Evolution of civil society in South Korea can be divided into the periods "before" and "after" democratization in the late 1980s. The concept of civil society in South Korea emerged in the process of democratization struggle through various forms of mobilization, such as student, labor, human rights, and other types of movements against the authoritarian regime; civil society was understood as representing "public good" or "civic virtue" (Choi 2005). The common target of these movements was only democratization. However, under the rule of the authoritarian state, for this "anti-state" civil society in Korea it was difficult to find a mode of grass-roots civic organizations and participation as in old Western democracies. Citizens' movements for democracy under the military regime often tended to be elite-centric, contentious, and narrowly focused (Bae, Shin, and Lee 2011; Lee and Arrington 2008).

Unlike the pre-democratization era, the 1990s and the 2000s set new conditions for the transformation of civil society in Korea. The scope, goals, and approaches of civil society movements and organizations changed further during this period, because of the changed conditions and environment. After democratization, weakening of the centralized and strong state created conditions for wider grass-roots civic participation and modifications of civil society's goals and "modus operandi" (Fioramonti and Fiori 2010). Second, unprecedented changes in the environment, such as globalization, decentralization, and multiculturalism affected the diversification of the modes of activities and goals of civil society organizations. In the post-democratization period (1987 onward), Korean civil society has achieved much wider and inclusive participation and has expanded the scope of interests to various political and social issues, such as anti-nuclear, women's participation, electoral reform, anti-corruption, consumer protection, environmental protection, and so forth (Kalinowski 2008; Lim 2000; Oh 2012). Korea has witnessed an explosive growth in the number of civil society organizations, from about 4,000 in the mid-1990s to 30,000 in 2015 (Ock 2015).

Given the widespread recognition of the notable growth of civil society in South Korea, however, whether a vibrant civil society and mass participation in the post-democratization period have actually created "cultural and social" as well as institutional building blocks to deepen democracy is still an open question.[1] It is generally perceived that robust civil society activism in Korea was a driving force for the grand democratization of 1987 and further development of democracy. Yet, if we understand that the dimensions of civil society are self-governing and intermediary organizations (institutions) within "public space" linking the general public and the strong state, it might be difficult to say that civil society in Korea has been faithful to its role as the linkage. Contrary to prevailing views, old conservative values, such as growth-first ideology, Cold War order (against North Korea), and chaebol-oriented economy (corporate interests) have been strengthened and reproduced, as the conservative mass media has had negative effects on citizens' push for more socio-economic rights.[2] The right-wing conservative organizations ("New Right") in the 2000s grew in prominence and power during the Kim Dae-jung (1998–2003) and Roh Moo-hyun (2003–2008) administrations and challenged the administrations' policy to engage with North Korea. The changes in the Korea–US Alliance have also led to ideological polarization of civil society (Kim 2012: 57). In addition, Korea's underdeveloped mediating institutions—that is, political parties and interest groups—have made social groups dissatisfied with the magnitude and quality of dialogue with the state. In turn, as Jennifer Oh (2012: 537) aptly puts it, the main mode of state–society relationships in Korea "still occurs outside the existing political structure," even after more than two decades of democracy. The notion of a "strong state and contentious society" still continues, as shown in the anti-US Beef protest (2008) and the million-strong candlelight vigil against the Park Geun-hye government (2016).

This chapter argues that civil society has played an important role in carrying important and sensitive political and socio-economic agendas to the fore in Korea, but its inability to monitor and influence the government processes eventually led to massive mobilization of general citizens lately. To unravel this complicated development trajectory of civil society and democracy in South Korea, the rest of this chapter is organized as follows. The first section briefly examines civil society development in Korea "before and after" democratization. The second section explores important features of civil society and their relationship to the political arena in present-day Korea. The last section illustrates the state–society relationships and modes of communication on important policy and political issues such as the anti-US Beef protest and the anti-Park Geun-hye protest.

Development of civil society in South Korea: change and continuity

The origin of Korean civil society in the modern period can be traced back to the resistance of the elements of civil society against Japanese colonial rule (1910–1945). Civil society was mobilized for the anti-Japanese movement and became the early form of contentious civil society politics, and then in the second half of the 1900s, it was the target of strong oppression and surveillance by the Japanese colonial government (Koo 1993). On the other hand, from the early twentieth century onward, a modern type of association, with interests in social issues such as education, enlightenment, women, self-governing, and so forth, began to be formed by Confucian literati, intellectuals, and religious leaders (Song 2013). Until the early 1960s, however, most of the associations did not have the ability to self-govern and were service oriented, devoted to saving the poor (Kim 2004: 82).

Despite a striking resemblance between social mobilization and associations during the Japanese rule and modern civil society in Korea, it has been commonly shared that the immediate origin of civil society is anti-government sentiments and democratic activism against the three authoritarian regimes of Syngman Rhee (1948–1960), Park Chung-hee (1963–1979), and Chun Doo-hwan (1981–1987). Korea as a newly independent nation state with a liberal democratic political system was ushered in 1948. After Koreans paid a dear price to defend the country from the destructive communist attack during the Korean War (1950–1953), they expected that the newly introduced democracy would be put in place. Since the regime employed suppressive measures toward progressive civil society, the "elements" of civil society, including labor groups and student groups during the Rhee regime, remained relatively "quiescent" (Kim 2000).[3] Yet, as the constitutional amendment for the permanent rule of Rhee and massive election fraud were ratified and carried out by the ruling Liberal Party in the latter part of the 1950s, the disobedience movement began with the mobilization of college students against the Rhee regime and a broader spectrum of people, including intellectuals, university professors, and religious leaders, turned up in the street protest marches later in April 1960. As a result, the Rhee regime was overthrown by the April Revolution, but the contentious and rebellious mode of civic society activism still continued under the interim democratic government (the Second Republic).

However, Korean citizens' strong desire for democracy could not last that long, due to the new democratic government's inability and unwillingness to accommodate pro-democracy demands from the bottom. Students and other civil society organizations had profound suspicions about the successive democratic governments (1960–1961) and wanted to preserve the spirit of the April Revolution. They were deeply disappointed by some of the undemocratic practices of the new government and decided to continue their pro-democracy struggle against the new regime (Kim 2000: 44–45). Since there was no leading group except students, forging an anti-state alliance amongst different types of interests and organizations was also difficult. In the end, the short period of democratic transition was crushed by a military coup in May 1961.

Under the control of the military regime for more than two decades (1961–1987), the democratic spirit and achievements of student activism in the April Revolution were by and large negated by the military coup and the authoritarian rule. Members of the military coup (1960) claimed that they had staged the coup to save the nation from the communists and to rebuild democratic politics and the national economy (Han 2011). Over time, however, military governments began to undermine or ignore democratic principles, and therefore civil society groups had to continue their pro-democracy protests.[4] Until the passage of the *Yushin* Constitution (1972) that imposed an unvarnished dictatorship, civil society during this period was somewhat visible and significant in several incidents. In particular, there were a number of anti-government protests mainly by student groups, dissident intellectuals, and opposition politicians against the Park regime's Korea–Japan normalization policy (June 1965) and the decision to send Korean troops to the Vietnam War (August 1965). Toward the early 1970s, other civil society actors, including laborers, journalists, university professors, and so forth also joined pro-democracy movements. However, despite relatively active and continuous civil society activism against the authoritarian regime, other civil society groups during this period (1961–1972) remained largely dormant and were effectively controlled by the Park regime by the enforcement of martial law, closing universities, and other suppressive measures. Somewhat large-scale uprisings were rather "intermittent," lacking greater mass participation (Kim 2000).

Most of the 1970s is remembered by many as "the dark age for Korean democracy," as Park put the seventh amendment of the constitution into effect (the *Yushin* Constitution), which gave excessively concentrated political power in one man's hand by abolishing the presidential term limit, allowing appointments of one-third of National Assemblymen, and promulgating extraordinary measures (Kil 2001: 48–49). The Korean Central Intelligence Agency (KCIA) was also effectively installed to undertake repressive measures for controlling student movements and labor unionism. The omnipresence of the national security agenda (anti-communist campaign) and espionage scandals effectively tamed and threatened civil society under the *Yushin* system and Park's successor, Chun Doo-hwan (1980–1987), continued to rule the country with an iron hand (Park 2015).

To summarize, throughout the authoritarian period from the 1950s to the mid-1980s, multiple generations of pro-democracy activists—in particular, students, religious leaders, laborers, and dissident intellectuals—emerged and slowly grew to claim the democracy they had desired. Nevertheless, bitter and often conflicting relationships between the pro-democracy advocates and the authoritarian government led to several deadly incidents and the torture of civilian activists. Other than student groups and dissident intellectuals, a large part of civil society was still dormant and inadequately effective in forging a stronger alliance amongst civil society organizations. Substantial economic growth under the authoritarian regime also worked negatively for the grand democratization movement, as the white-collar workers and the middle class did not take a clear stance on civil society activism (Fioramonti and Fiori 2010: 89). All in all, although the slow and intermittent development of civil society during the Park regime and the earlier Chun regime became the crucial basis of a sustained movement for democracy, civil society was largely quenched.

Civil society and the transition to democracy

After the sudden demise of the Park regime in October 1979, citizens of South Korea expected the democratization process to begin, but again, they were alarmed over the possibility of the re-emergence of a new military regime. Angered students calling for the withdrawal of suppressive policies and the launch of democratic government waged street demonstrations again. In response, the so-called "new military" seized political power through a military coup in December 1979, pressured the interim government to proclaim martial law and mobilized special forces, which eventually caused a large number of casualties and several hundred deaths in Gwang-ju in May 1980 (Yeo 2013). During the earlier period, the Chun regime (1981–1987) certainly inherited the authoritarian legacy of the previous Park government and constrained the political activities of opposition politicians, mass media, and civil society.

Although the Chun regime thoroughly suppressed the democratization movement and civil society, several conditions and structural features opened up a window of opportunity for civil society in late 1983. The Chun regime's political liberalization policy ("the appeasement policy") relaxed the grip on people and allowed some of his repressive tactics to be reduced. The improvements in economic performance during the early 1980s made the Chun regime feel confident about using softer control with less oppressive measures (Min, Shin, Lee, and Yoon 2008). In addition, the regime needed to uplift the image of South Korea under global scrutiny in order to cover its lack of political legitimacy and successfully host the 1986 Asian Games and 1988 Seoul Olympics (Heo and Roehrig 2010: 36–38). Ironically, the regime's complacency in social control and institutions gave an impetus to the "resurrection" of civil society and the explosive growth of the democratization movement by lifting political bans on campus activities, releasing student protesters and political prisoners, and restoring legislative politics. The liberalization triggered the reformation of people's movement groups amongst students, labor unions, and religious groups, which eventually came together to form an umbrella alliance for democratization, the People's Movement Coalition for Democracy and Reunification (PMCDR) in 1985. By 1987, this alliance expanded to include almost all major sectors and groups, including the middle and white-collar classes, and more importantly, it supported the opposition leaders to pressure the Chun government into accepting a democratic revision of the constitution (Yeo 2013).[5] This further intensified the democratization movement in terms of its magnitude and eventually led to "the June Democratic Uprising" and the end of authoritarian rule in 1987.

Overall, pro-democracy movements by various civil society groups came of age under the authoritarian regime from 1960–1987, but they played a crucial role in democratization. The most notable characteristic of Korean civil society during this period was its contentious nature against the authoritarian regime. Regardless of the military regime's control against the people's aspiration for democracy and surveillance of the society, violent eruption of civil society and social forces eventually overturned the regime (Kim 2000; Koo 1993; Oh 2012; Ryoo 2009). Second, students, religious groups, and dissident intellectuals took the initiative and other groups, as well as general citizens, offered support for the pro-democracy movement. But until the late 1980s, civil society organizations were secretly mobilized, with occasional and intermittent explosive actions due to the suppressive government policies (Lim 2000). Last, civil society and independent social organizations that emerged during the authoritarian regime were developed in the struggle against dictatorship. Democracy was the only shared goal amongst diverse social organizations. Therefore, other expectations such as inequality and economic justice were not fully addressed in the democratization movement, and this conflict in the conceptions of "substantive" democracy later proved to be an issue during the process of democratization.[6] Since the movement organizers were in agreement with one another on the goal of democratization and the breakdown of the authoritarian regime, ideology and class-consciousness played a less significant role (Kim 2000). Therefore, though democracy and the breakdown of the military regime were achieved to some extent, the outcome was not satisfactory for all sectors of the society.

Civil society after democratization

Civil society, in the process of democratization in Korea, played critical roles in multiple junctures of the democratic movement by compelling the authoritarian regime to yield political power to democratic forces and mobilizing people nationwide. As Korea began to democratize politically, organized labor and civic organizations sought to create a public platform to resist the monopoly of capital and the dominance of the state. From the 1980s onward, there was an outburst of the general public's desire for various public policy agendas that had been suppressed during the authoritarian government. The rise of citizens' movements emphasized substantial changes in somewhat progressive policy agendas, such as labor rights, human rights, and social-economic well-being, as well as citizens' expanded participation in public policy debates. But at the same time, civil society activism was seriously challenged due to the growth of conservative civic organizations, the emergence of new conditions such as the financial crisis (1997), and the weak intermediary organizations in democratic politics. These challenges have eventually led civil society movements to mass protests that have been frequently labeled "candlelight vigil protests." The following sections elaborate the rise and decline of civic activism in the post-democratization period in Korea.

Rise of new citizens' movement group under the civilian governments

Looking at the process of the democratization movement until 1987, the civil society organizations in Korea allied together for the shared goal of democratization, but ironically, cohesion within civil society was absent after democratization. It has been argued that civil society that once played an important role in democratization is generally demobilized and marginalized after the transition. In fact, after the restoration of democratic elections and institutions under the Roh Tae-woo administration (1988–1993), politics in Korea increasingly revolved around political parties and presidential/national assembly elections. However, civil society activism in Korea continued its vibrant role in post-democratization politics in many ways. Different types of civic organizations and social interest groups burgeoned and became prominent in expanding citizens' rights and building pluralistic and autonomous public space equivalent to that of democratic countries in the Western world. In particular, the most notable strands in civil society activism since 1988 were the continuation of the traditional people's movement (*minjung undong*) and the emergence of the new citizens' movement (*simin undong*).

The traditional people's movement groups, which were previously united for democratization under the umbrella organization PMCDR, lost their common target for a while but strived to find a new role in post-democratization politics. The main players in these traditional groups were mainly blue-collar workers, students, anti-government activists, peasants, and the urban poor (Kim 2013). After the transition, this group evolved into several national-level organizations, such as the National Council of University Student Representatives (*Chondaehyop*, 1989) and the Korea Confederation of Trade Unions (*Minju Nochong*, 1990), and continued movements against the state. These groups sustained the "democratization movement after democratization," labeling the Roh Tae-woo regime as pseudo-democracy and often resorted to old movement tactics, illegal and violent measures (Kim 2013: 63). For them, the battle for democracy was not over, as the Roh regime arrested some dissidents in the name of national security, crushed several labor strikes in the name of losing international competitiveness, and mobilized conservative politicians by merging three political parties in the early 1990s (Cumings 2005: 394–395).

However, regardless of the continuous activism and the growth in organizational capacity, a number of people's movement groups gradually shifted their respective orientations toward a softer style and policy advocacy through somewhat peaceful campaigning and non-violent activism (Kim 2000). On the one hand, the general public increasingly distanced itself from the claims and practical tactics of the people's movement groups that were class based, violent, and conflictual in the past (Kim 2013). On the other hand, the traditional people's movement seemed irrelevant to the reform politics after democratization, because of several political-economic reforms implemented by the Roh administration and the newly elected Kim Young-sam administration (1993–1998). Compared to the past, Roh reduced civilian repression substantially and showed a receptive attitude toward political opponents (Kim 2013). Despite several attempts to frustrate decentralization, local elections were restored under his government (Bae and Kim 2013). In particular, the unprecedented political and socio-economic reforms implemented by the Kim administration, as well as the normalization of its relationships with civil society organizations, stunned people's movement groups, particularly radical groups (Kim 2000).[7] As a result, some of the people's movement groups attempted to repackage themselves as moderate citizens' movement groups.

Since the early 1990s, new civic movement organizations—that is, citizens' movement groups—supported by the middle-class, white-collar professionals, intellectuals, and so forth began to garner publicity and popularity for slogans and campaign strategies for policy-related issues, such as electoral reform (fair election), economic justice, environment, consumer rights, gender equality, and so forth. The growing popularity and public trust in citizens' movement groups were further strengthened, as institutional politics during the first decade of post-democratization underwent a serious crisis. In democratized countries, intermediary organizations such as interest groups and political parties in general play a crucial role in communicating citizens' voice to the state and the political world. Yet, neither interest groups nor political parties in Korea successfully fulfilled the role of representing citizens (Fioramonti and Fiori 2010; Oh 2012). It was the general view that interest groups sought their self-interests at the expense of the society as a whole (Oh 2012: 539). At the same time, political parties' political ideology was very weak and they were not good at channeling citizens' demands to the state, as their policy capacity and ideological orientations were also weak (Lee 2009: 37). In such circumstances, citizens' movement groups that aimed at broader political and socio-economic reform gained a notable reputation and occasionally proposed substantive policy proposals to the National Assembly (Bae and Kim 2013). As Figure 2.1 supports, they gained nationwide support and were often reported to be the most trusted social institutions in the 1990s and 2000s (Shin 2006).

A notable trend throughout the 1990s and the 2000s was the rise of several "general purpose" civil society organizations that sought to reconcile the two major camps: the traditional radical people's movement groups and moderate citizens' movement groups. These organizations were often sizable networks of civic engagement that allowed for civil society to influence policy decisions and became critical partners for political parties (Lee and Arrington 2008). Examples were mega-sized civic organizations, including the "big three": the People's Solidarity for Participatory Democracy (PSPD), the Citizen's Coalition for Economic Justice (CCEJ), and the Korean Federation of Environmental Movements (KFEM), which were founded and became the most powerful social actors in the early and mid-1990s (Cho 2000). They engaged in legislative politics for enacting various reform programs and often supported the ruling parties for promoting progressive agendas. In 2000, for example, PSPD and more than 400 civil society organizations formed the Citizens' Alliance for the General Elections (CAGE) at the time of the National Assembly election and made a list of unfit candidates who were corrupt or violated laws (Lim 2000: 19).[8] The CCEJ, which was founded in 1989, originally intended to work on economic justice issues, including poverty reduction, business–labor relations, and improving socio-economic inequality. Yet it steadily expanded its policy capacity and interests to cover a

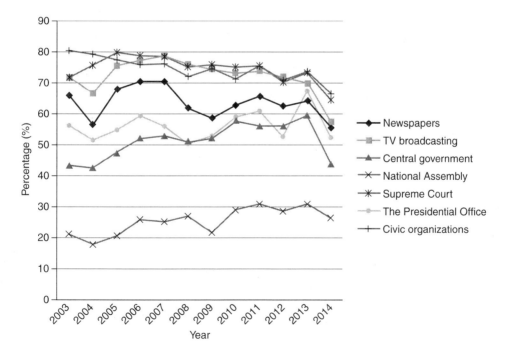

Figure 2.1 Approval rating of government institutions, 2003–2014.

Source: Korea Social Science Data Archive, Korean General Social Survey, 2003–2014.

Note
The approval rating is the combination of "excellent" and "very good."

broader range of issues and contributed to several reforms such as decentralization reform (Bae and Kim 2013: 272). As such, throughout the 1990s and the 2000s, the moderate and general-purpose civic organizations experienced tremendous growth in terms of membership, financial resources, and influence on politics and society.

The other trend of civil society during this period was the emergence of a favorable institutional environment for civil society activism. Two civilian presidents—Kim Dae-jung and Roh Moo-hyun—displayed a deeper understanding of and interest in civil society activism and promoted activists' participation in government policy-making. In both administrations, civil society actors, as well as intellectuals and professionals armed with specialized knowledge, extensively participated in government advisory committees and often provided important policy alternatives and feedback to the civilian government (Bae and Kim 2013). Hyuk-Rae Kim (2013: 66) claimed that more than 200 PSPD members experienced high-ranked government positions and a number of civil society leaders such as Kim Myung-ja and Lee Jae-young often took ministerial positions. Furthermore, the Kim Dae-jung administration enacted the Non-profit Organization Aid Law (2000) and provided financial support to registered (national or local) civic organizations. This financial subsidy for non-governmental organizations (NGOs) further strengthened their organizational capacity and enhanced the chances for general citizens to pursue public interests through civic organizations (Kim 2013: 65). As Figure 2.2 shows, the growth of registered NGOs since 2000—in particular, local-level NGOs—has been explosive. Korea's exceptional level of information and communication technology (ICT) and favorable mass media coverage has also furthered the growth of civil society.

Despite this success in the 1990s and the 2000s, it might be very difficult to label Korean civil society politics as a "Tocquevillian participatory civil society" that promotes mutual trust and

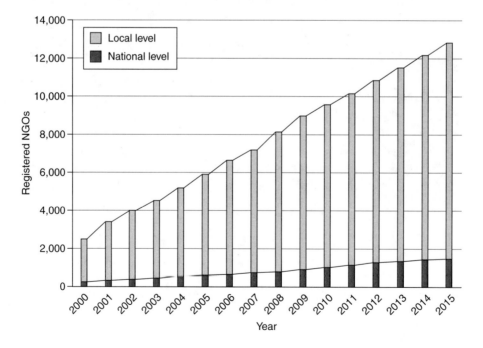

Figure 2.2 Growth of registered NGOs in the 2000s.

Source: Ministry of the Interior, A Report on the Status of Nonprofit Organization Register, 2000–2015. Retrieved from www.index.go.kr.

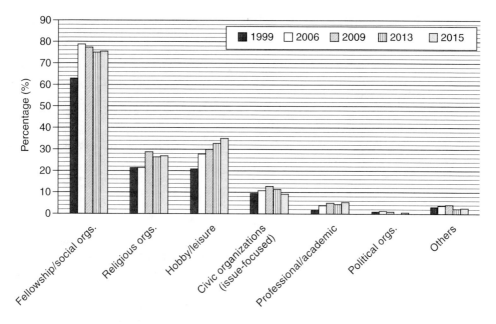

Figure 2.3 Patterns of social group participation in South Korea.

Source: Korea Statistical Information Service, Korea Social Survey, 1999–2015.

reciprocity, and strengthens a much wider participatory democracy. The building of institutional arrangements for the promotion of civil society has been rather successful, yet the quality of participation of the general public in politics and socio-economic discourses through civil society is questionable. According to a social survey (Figure 2.3), people over fifteen years of age were asked whether they have participated in any form of social organizations and the rate of positive response (percent) increased from 23.1 percent (1999) to 50 percent (2013). Yet an overwhelming majority of them has participated in fellowship/social groups such as meetings of school alumni associations or hobby-/leisure-related organizations. The general public's participation in social groups that can influence politics and policy-making has been fairly low and only a small percentage of civic groups have engaged in political affairs (Yeo 2013). Some important socio-economic agendas such as labor rights were often abandoned in favor of non-political, non-violent, and elite-oriented civic organizations. In the second half of the 2000s, with the re-emergence of the conservative regime (2008 onward), the collaborative relationship between the state and civil society has deteriorated and failed to address several important issues.

Challenges to civil society activism in contemporary Korea

Although most observers of Korea agree that civil society in Korea has been reinvigorated and has made remarkable progress toward consolidation of democracy since 1987, it has faced several challenges. In addition to the above-mentioned characteristics of Korean civil society—that is, non-political, non-violent, and elite-oriented—a number of structural conditions have resulted in a polarized civil society (left vs. right), alienating many ordinary citizens. As the middle class became major participants of civil society organizations, a number of class- and ideology-based issues, such as labor and economic inequality, have gained little attention (Choi 2005: 236).

Above all, the re-emergence of the conservative regime since 2008 has remapped the landscape of civil society politics in Korea.

The division between the conservative and the progressive in Korea is artificial at times, but the re-emergence of the conservative has had a negative impact on civil society politics in many respects. The government's preferential treatment and resource allocation for civil society organizations has been done selectively for the conservative groups that have been selectively supportive of or closer to the regime. For instance, the Ministry of Public Administration and Safety, which reviews the qualifications of non-profit organizations for financial assistance based on the Nonprofit Organization Aid Law, often selectively provided grants to pro-conservative civil society organizations (Kim 2012: 58).[9] These conservative organizations, which became prevalent in many political debates, were often supported by major conservative mass media and contributed to the securitization of political issues.

Ironically, the expansion of right-wing conservative civil society coincided with the promotion of civil society under the two civilian administrations. The conservative organizations that took over "the spirit of the Cold War era" revolved around the Kim Dae-jung administration's engagement policy toward North Korea. The progressive agenda toward North Korea by the Kim administration and liberal civic organizations also promoted counter-mobilization of the "anti-Sunshine Policy" group (conservative), and from this point onward, the ideological polarization of civil society continued under successive administrations (Kim 2012).[10] Jang-Jip Choi (2005) claimed that the ideology of authoritarianism and the Cold War system was repackaged and reproduced as conservative political ideology through conservative mass media, such as *Chosun Ilbo*, *Dong-A Ilbo*, and *JoongAng Ilbo*. Labor unionism, engagement policy toward North Korea, chaebol reform, economic justice, and other similar issues, which might dismantle the legacy of authoritarian developmentalism and vested interests, were painted in negative hues. For example, these groups, including war veterans, conservative Christian groups, and North Korean defectors, have valued the traditional security alliance with the US against current and former communist groups, frequently organized pro-US protests denouncing anti-American demonstrators as "North Korea sympathizers" ("*jongbuk*"), and rallied near Seoul Plaza near the City Hall (Yeo 2013).

The limited role of civil society in economic globalization and justice issues has also been a serious challenge to the movement. In fact, many general-purpose civic organizations such as the PSPD and CCEJ have paid serious attention to these issues. After the Asian Financial Crisis of 1997, the Kim Dae-jung administration organized a tripartite commission (labor–management–government) to deal with several issues related to employment. Yet civic organizations' and labor unions' participation in the committee was more nominal than functional. They failed to oppose the introduction of non-regular labor force that bifurcated the workforce into protected and unprotected laborers and failed to enhance social safety nets (Hundt 2015: 478). In the case of the regulation of large-scale retail stores (2010, super supermarkets, SSM), to protect small- and medium-scale retail stores and traditional markets in Korea, the PSPD and civic advocates wanted stricter regulation of business days/hours to protect "street" retailers, but the proposal was substantially frustrated by the government and big business (Yoon 2016). Overall, neoliberalism ironically enhanced the state's position in restructuring the national economy and weakened the voices of civil society groups in the process of neoliberal reform and free trade agreements.

Last but not the least, the development of ICT and the wide use of social media today have contributed to a more spontaneous and horizontal mobilization of general citizens, but Korea's exceptionally well-developed ICT and infrastructure has brought about somewhat mixed results. On the one hand, an entirely new structure of communication and mobilization via the Internet has provided various avenues for citizens' political actions. On the other hand, however, information technology in Korea has mobilized unorganized citizens and younger generations behind a "veil of anonymity" in more or less individualized and fragmented ways, which poses a serious threat to collective civil society activism (Shin 2013). The civic activism via information technology has also resulted in unnecessary competition over policies and political issues amongst civic groups, which means more attention to issues in the limelight than the pressing ones (Kim 2013).

In sum, the new scenario for civil society activism, such as the re-emergence of conservative politics, the wave of globalization, and the unintended consequences of the development of information technology, coincided with the "institutionalized incompetence" of political society and general-purpose civil society, resulting in a new form of social movement in Korea, derisively called candlelight vigils. This relatively new form of activism, which diversified the mode of civic movement, was derived from the participation of a large number of politically polarized and fragmented citizens who were dissatisfied with the existing structure of civil society politics and weak political parties.

Mass mobilization and the "culture" of candlelight vigil protests

Mass mobilization, a heritage from the anti-authoritarian movements, has remained dominant in Korean politics and was reproduced as the culture of protest in most of the 2000s. There have been several hundred mass protests with tens of thousands of participants annually over various political and socio-economic issues. The first mass protest that signaled the shift in civil society activism from a citizens' movement to mass mobilization or culture of candlelight vigil was the Koreans' protest against the "unfair" USA–ROK Korea Status of Forces Agreement (SOFA) in 2002, when two middle-school girls were fatally struck by an armored United States Forces Korea (USFK) vehicle and the accused were found not guilty in a US court. The candlelight vigil called for a sincere and official apology from the George W. Bush administration and the revision of SOFA; it was followed by many similar mass mobilizations over various political and socio-economic issues.

The candlelight vigil and mass mobilization have become very serious and systematized since the protest in 2008, when the Lee Myeong-bak administration decided to import US beef that was possibly contaminated by bovine spongiform encephalopathy (BSE), commonly known as mad cow disease. On April 19, 2008, the Lee administration signed the US beef import agreement with the United States government and after ten days, a television show, titled "PD Notebook," dubiously claimed that BSE-infected downer cows were randomly slaughtered and the Korean government would import all parts of cows without much control and inspection power in the next four years. Regardless of the truth about the deal with the US government and the safety of US beef, this show provoked the general public's anger and led to the anti-US beef protest that drew hundreds of thousands of Koreans, including teenage students, parents pushing strollers, and non-organized citizens in downtown Seoul.[11] While the protest lasted several months, several hundred people were detained every day. As time passed by, each of the Lee administration's policies, from the Grand Canal project and the privatization policy, to foreign policy and North Korean policy, came under fire (Veale 2008). President Lee, who came to power with the largest margin of victory in modern Korean history, was caught by the protest and his popularity dropped substantially over the decision.

The 2008 candlelight vigils were followed by various mass protests, and the most notable is the protest against the Park Geun-hye (2013–present) administration. After it was revealed in November 2016 that Park's long-time friend, Choi Soon-sil, bestrides state affairs and was involved in several corruption scandals in November 2016, a very large number of Koreans, often estimated to be close to or exceeding a million, have poured into downtown Seoul to call for Park's resignation (or impeachment) and close investigation of the scandals. For several weeks from November 2016, there were volcanic-levels of outrage across the country and Park's approval rating dropped to the lowest level (0 to 5 percent) in the country's history. The crowds have been impressively organized and their strong march to the Blue House (President's Office) was convivial and peaceful.

These recent mass protests and candlelight vigils have provided a number of new insights into civil society in South Korea. First, since the early 2000s, the movements have gradually become more spontaneous and less organized (Kim 2012). There have been protest "organizers" and leaders who are usually members of civil society organizations, but most of the participants mobilized and gathered by themselves. New ICTs such as social media have been effectively utilized for self-mobilization, but general participants in the movements often refuse to unilaterally follow the leadership of civic organizers (Shin 2013: 254). Second, in the age of the IT revolution, Korean civil society is heavily armed with information and knowledge about policy matters and often disseminates reliable and convincing data and information to the general public. In the case of the anti-US beef movement, civil society groups had complete access to the available information and could verify any data regarding the safety of American meat products. Civil society's information power in the 2000s, that often coincided with a high tide against the conservative government, frequently caused political polarization and unresolvable policy debates (Hong 2010). Oh says, "Importantly, mass mobilizations are increasingly occurring in a context of a politically informed population" (2012: 536). Third and relatedly, the rise of conservative organizations has led to the polarization of political ideology and this has pushed each side to forge political coalitions for the pursuit of their goals. At the same time, coalitions amongst different groups for a particular policy or political issue have become easier. Last, nontraditional participants in civil society, such as youths, students, parent groups, white-collar workers, and so forth have become major participants of the "culture" of candlelight vigils and often share their experiences or disseminate pictures via social media such as Facebook and Twitter (Kim 2012). They are also accustomed to singing "protest songs" (*minjung gayo*) and organizing cultural events as "rituals" at protest sites. In a similar vein, it has become relatively easier for general citizens to tap into day-to-day policy issues and agendas, while traditional civic and non-profit organizations steadily lose their influence and grow apart from citizens.

Conclusion

Since the democratization of South Korea, civil society has undergone many changes over the past three decades and keeps evolving in ways that have not been experienced before. For a while after the democratization, civil society experienced explosive growth in numbers and the scope of activities, and became important in monitoring governmental and political activities and proposals for alternative policies. Favorable institutional arrangements and environment during the progressive and civilian administrations also enhanced civil society's growth in size and strength. Under the strong executive power of government, mediating organizations such as interest groups and political parties were not successful in carrying citizens' desires to the government's agenda-setting process, but in the end, civil society has had to play the mediating role. At the same time, the emergence of the conservative regime in the late 2000s has been concurrent with the rise of conservative civic organizations. Political polarization between civil society and the right-wing conservative groups over various policy issues has made problem-solving in "institutional politics" very difficult. In this situation, regardless of the development of democracy, civil society has still worked outside the political system and the hitherto structured "contentious" state–society relationship has continued in Korea.

The recent development of social movements in the form of mass protests and candlelight vigils indicates that Korea is entering a new phase of citizen politics. While traditional people's movements and new citizens' movements gradually lose their influence and social trust, mass protests and candlelight vigils have provided a new public sphere where everyone can express concerns over various issues, ranging from everyday policy problems to the turnover of the government. These unorganized, leaderless, non-violent, and voluntary candlelight vigils have created a new avenue for citizen participation and associational life, but at the same time, the possible consequences of this politics of mass participation are still largely unknown and uncertain. The polarization of politics and the forging of coalitions behind the scenes possibly pose a great threat to institutional politics and public authority.

Notes

1 Mass society theorists and neo-Tocquevillian scholars have posited that vibrant civic community and affluent associational life enrich citizens' social lives, generate reciprocity, build social trust, and eventually contribute to healthier democracy. For example, see Barber (1995), Fukuyama (1995), and Putman (1995: 67).

2 For example, Choi (2005: 233) claimed that "labor-exclusionary developmentalism" combined with neoliberalism substantially weakened the "representativeness" of civil society and also democratic consolidation in Korea. Originally, people called for "economic justice" or "economic democratization" during the heat of the democratization movement in the 1980s but the once-fizzled-out issue has re-emerged as the core public debate on substantive democracy after two decades (Kim 2012: 54–55).

3 Until the late 1950s, the major elements of civil society—such as labor workers, university students, peasants, and so forth—were tightly controlled and marginalized due to severe repression (Kim 2000: 28–30).

4 Park Chung-hee and the engineers of the coup made vague promises to relinquish power to civilian and democratic leadership when the right time came, but the turnover process was not carried out for several years (Kang 2001: 82). Instead, Park created the Democratic Republican Party and won the 1963 presidential election.

5 During most of the authoritarian regime, the middle class and the white-collar groups—that is, urban professionals, intellectuals, the self-employed, and so forth—were not active participants in the democratization movement. Their joining provided a greater impetus for a wider mass campaign in the grand democratization in 1987 (Ryoo 2009: 27).

6 Due to different perceptions of democracy, the seriousness and urgency of forming a united front by different elements of civil society suppressed discrepancies in what people believed democracy should be (Kim 2000). Class identities of different ideological strands of the left began to be shaped during this period, but democratization became the top priority (Yeo 2013).

7 Those reforms included anti-corruption bills (real-name banking system, public officials' ethics act), anti-authoritarianism (removal of private military clubs and reorganizing intelligence agencies), electoral reforms (campaign fund reform), and so forth (Diamond and Shin 2000).

8 Many civil society organizations and non-governmental organizations (NGOs) complained about the election of corrupt politicians who were involved in election fraud, the former authoritarian government, and the usage of regionalism sentiment in the 1996 National Assembly election. They initiated the "fair election" movement and in the 2000 general election, they formed this coalition to issue a blacklist of "unfit" candidates. In terms of the number of participating organizations and scale, CAGE was the largest clean election movement that made concerted efforts to encompass all regions of Korea in the 2000 election (Han 2012: 70).

9 According to the law, the government was not supposed to grant financial aid to civil society organizations pursuing political issues, but during the Lee Myeong-bak administration, several billion Korean won were granted to conservative groups, including New Right Korea, engaging in national security issues (Yoon 2016: 63).

10 "New Right Korea," which packaged itself as a "patriot camp" (*aeguk jinyeong*), was the first and foremost organized civic organization dedicated to the conservative political-economic ideology advocating free-market capitalism, a security alliance with the traditional allies such as the USA, and hardline policies toward North Korea. This group was initially launched in 2004 in reaction to the Roh Moohyun administration's engagement policy toward North Korea (Ahn 2006).

11 The candlelight vigils in 2008 over US beef eventually led to violent protests against the Lee administration. After the close investigation of the content of PD Notebook's report, it turned out that the general public had been misinformed in many respects, but in the end, most of the cabinet members in the Lee administration resigned (Howard 2009).

Suggested readings

Kim, Sunhyuk. 2000. *The Politics of Democratization in Korea: The Role of Civil Society*. Pittsburgh, PA: University of Pittsburgh Press.

Shin, Gi-Wook, and Paul Chang. 2011. *South Korean Social Movements: From Democracy to Civil Society*. New York: Routledge.

Yoon, Jiso. 2016. *Advocacy and Policymaking in South Korea: How the Legacy of State and Society Relationships Shapes Contemporary Public Policy*. Albany, NY: SUNY Press.

Websites

Citizens' Coalition for Economic Justice (CCEJ), www.ccej.or.kr.

The CCEJ is a union of people from different socio-economic backgrounds with the aim to combat economic and social injustice through the organized power of citizens, using legal and nonviolent methods to establish realistic alternatives and solutions.

Korea Social Science Data Archive (KOSSDA), www.kossda.or.kr/eng/.

KOSSDA is a nonprofit organization with the aim to acquire, preserve, and disseminate Korean social science data and literature; this information is available in an archive on the website.

People's Solidarity for Participatory Democracy, www.peoplepower21.org/English.

People's Solidarity for Participatory Democracy is a non-governmental organization based in Seoul, with the aim to promote participation in the government decision-making process; this is in an effort to establish transparency and accountability.

References

Ahn, Byong-Jick. 2006. South Korea's "New Right." *The Wall Street Journal*, June 7. Electronic document, www.wsj.com/articles/SB114962716222173009, accessed January 2, 2017.

Bae, Yooil, Dong-Ae Shin, and Yong Wook Lee. 2011. Making and Unmaking of Transnational Environmental Cooperation: The Case of Reclamation Projects in Japan and Korea. *The Pacific Review* 24(2): 201–223.

Bae, Yooil, and Sunhyuk Kim. 2013. Civil Society and Local Activism in South Korea's Local Democratization. *Democratization* 20(2): 260–286.

Barber, Benjamin. 1995. *Jihad vs. McWorld: How the Planet is both Falling Apart and Coming Together—and What This Means for Democracy*. New York: New York Times Books.

Cho, Hee Yeon. 2000. Democratic Transition and Changes in Korean NGOs. *Korea Journal* 40(2): 275–304.

Choi, Jang Jip. 2005. *Democracy after Democratization: Conservative Origins and Crisis of Korean Democracy*. Seoul: Humanitas.

Cumings, Bruce. 2005. *Korea's Place in the Sun: A Modern History*. New York: Norton.

Diamond, Larry, and Doh Chull Shin. 2000. Introduction: Institutional Reform and Democratic Consolidation in Korea. In *Institutional Reform and Democratic Consolidation in Korea*. Larry Diamond and Doh Chull Shin, eds. Pp. 1–41. Stanford, CA: Hoover Institution Press.

Fioramonti, Lorenzo, and Antonio Fiori. 2010. The Changing Role of Civil Society in Democratization: Evidence from South Africa (1990–2009) and South Korea (1987–2009). *African and Asian Studies* 9: 83–104.

Fukuyama, Francis. 1995. *Trust: The Social Virtues and the Creation of Prosperity*. New York: Free Press.

Han, Yong-Sup. 2011. The May Sixteenth Military Coup. In *The Park Chung Hee Era: The Transformation of South Korea*. Byung-Kook Kim and Ezra Vogel, eds. Pp. 35–57. Cambridge, MA: Harvard University Press.

Han, Jong-woo. 2012. *Networked Information Technologies, Elections, and Politics: Korea and the United States*. Lanham, MD: Lexington Books.

Heo, Uk, and Terence Roehrig. 2010. *South Korea Since 1980*. Cambridge: Cambridge University Press.

Hong, Sung-gi. 2010. A Look at the Changes in Debate Structure in Korea through the Candlelight Vigils. *Korea Journal* 50(3): 100–127.

Howard, Ian. 2009. Korean Media Bias and Government Intervention in Media. *SAIS US-Korea 2009 Yearbook*. Electronic document, http://uskoreainstitute.org/wp-content/uploads/2010/05/2009_Yearbook_Howard.pdf, accessed January 9, 2017.

Hundt, David. 2015. Neoliberalism, the Developmental State and Civil Society in Korea. *Asian Studies Review* 39(3): 466–482.

Kalinowski, Thomas. 2008. State–Civil Society Synergy and Cooptation: The Case of the Minority Shareholder Movement in Korea. *Korea Observer* 39(3): 339–367.

Kang, David C. 2001. Institutional Foundations of Korean Politics. In *Understanding Korean Politics: An Introduction*. Soong Hoom Kil and Chung-in Moon, eds. Pp. 71–106. Albany, NY: State University of New York Press.

Kil, Soong Hoom. 2001. Development of Korean Politics: A Historical Profile. In *Understanding Korean Politics: An Introduction*. Soong Hoom Kil and Chung-in Moon, eds. Pp. 33–70. Albany, NY: State University of New York Press.

Kim, Hyuk-Rae. 2013. *State-Centric to Contested Social Governance in Korea: Shifting Power*. New York: Routledge.

Kim, Inchoon. 2004. Voluntary Associations, Social Capital, and Civil Society in Comparative Perspective: South Korea and Sweden. *Global Economic Review* 33(4): 75–96.

Kim, Sunhyuk. 2000. *The Politics of Democratization in Korea: The Role of Civil Society*. Pittsburgh, PA: Pittsburgh University Press.

Kim, Sunhyuk. 2012. "Contentious Democracy" in South Korea: An Active Civil Society and Ineffectual Political Parties. *Taiwan Journal of Democracy* 8(2): 51–61.

Koo, Hagen. 1993. *Strong State and Contentious Society*. In *State and Society in Contemporary Korea*. Hagen Koo, ed. Pp. 231–249. Ithaca, NY: Cornell University Press.

Lee, Sook-Jong, and Celeste Arrington. 2008. The Politics of NGOs and Democratic Governance in South Korea and Japan. *Pacific Focus* 23(1): 75–96.

Lee, Yoonkyung. 2009. Democracies without Parties? Political Parties and Social Movements for Democratic Representation in Korea. *Korea Observer* 40(1): 27–52.

Lim, Hy-Sop. 2000. Historical Development of Civil Social Movements in Korea: Trajectories and Issues. *Korea Journal* 40(3): 5–25.

Min, Joon-Ki, Myeongsun Shin, Jeongbok Lee, and Seongyi Yoon. 2008. *The Politics of Korea: Institution, Process and Development*. Seoul: Nanam.

Ock, Hyunju. 2015. Korea's Civil Society at a Crossroads. *The Korea Herald*, August 16. Electronic Document, www.koreaherald.com/view.php?ud=20150816000370, accessed December 19, 2016.

Oh, Jennifer S. 2012. Strong State and Strong Civil Society in Contemporary South Korea. *Asian Survey* 52(3): 528–549.

Park, Paul Y. 2015. *Protest Dialectics: State Repression and South Korea's Democracy Movement, 1970–1979*. Stanford, CA: Stanford University Press.

Putnam, Robert D. 1995. Bowling Alone: America's Declining Social Capital. *Journal of Democracy* 6: 65–78.

Ryoo, Woongjae. 2009. The Public Sphere and the Rise of South Korean Civil Society. *Journal of Contemporary Asia* 39(1): 23–35.

Shin, Jin-Wook. 2013. Individualisation of Civil Society in the Context of the Information Age: The Case of South Korea. *International Social Science Journal* 64: 249–261.

Shin, Kwang-Yeong. 2006. The Citizens' Movement in Korea. *Korea Journal* 46(2): 5–34.

Song, Ho Geun. 2013. *The Birth of Citizen in Modern Korea: Modernization of Chosun and Changes of Perception of Public Sphere*. Seoul: Mineumsa.

Veale, Jennifer. 2008. South Koreans' Beef over Beef. *Time*, June 10. Electronic document, http://content.time.com/time/world/article/0,8599,1813235,00.html, accessed January 9, 2017.

Yeo, Andrew. 2013. South Korean Civil Society: Implications for the U.S.–ROK Alliance. Electronic document, www.cfr.org/south-korea/south-korean-civil-society-implications-us-rok-alliance/p31091, accessed December 29, 2016.

Yoon, Jiso. 2016. *Advocacy and Policymaking in South Korea: How the Legacy of State and Society Relationships Shapes Contemporary Public Policy*. Albany, NY: State University of New York Press.

3

CHINA

Anthony J. Spires

The state and the field

The study of civil society in contemporary China has been approached almost exclusively through the lens of state–society relations. The "opening and reform" initiated by Deng Xiaoping began China's spectacular economic ascent in the 1980s; however, on the whole, it has led to little political reform. The Chinese Communist Party (CCP) remains in control, and whether we describe the country as an authoritarian state or as "post-totalitarian" (Chan 2005), it is clear that the CCP leaders are intent on maintaining their control over society through any means possible. *How* control over society is pursued, particularly control over burgeoning, independent societal forces, is the question that has engaged most studies on civil society in China for the last twenty-five years. In this chapter, I address this question but also highlight the agency of grass-roots actors to argue that they are not mere passive players in a game whose rules are established by the state.[1]

This chapter is divided into three main parts. First, I discuss the debate over the conceptualization of civil society in China by tracing the interest in government-led efforts to establish and control "government-organized non-governmental organizations" (GONGOs) in the 1990s and connecting it to emerging studies on the bottom-up "grass-roots" non-governmental organizations (NGOs) that began to blossom after the turn of the millennium. Second, I consider the ways in which the Chinese state has—despite its recurring use of extra-legal repression—aimed to govern civil society through an evolving legal and regulatory framework that culminated in the passage of a Charity Law and a Law on International Nongovernmental Organizations (INGOs) in 2016. In the third and concluding section, I point out areas of research that hold promise for deepening our understanding of Chinese civil society.[2]

Changing and challenging conceptualizations[3]

Corporatism and the search for an autonomous civil society in China

The scholarly search for civil society in China began in earnest in the immediate aftermath of the violent suppression of protests at Tiananmen Square in June 1989. Motivated by the explosive social unrest made visible by the demonstrations, in 1993, the journal *Modern China* brought together historians and social scientists to explore the applicability of the civil society concept and the significance of emergent non-governmental organizations (NGOs) in China (Chamberlain 1993; Huang 1993; Madsen 1993; Rankin 1993; Rowe 1993; Wakeman 1993). In the same year, Craig Calhoun, a witness to the Tiananmen Square events, urged that discussions of civil society's history and potential rise in China should focus less on "the mere presence of institutions outside the realm of the state" and more on "whether those extra state institutions have substantial capacity to alter patterns of integration or the overall exercise of power" (Calhoun 1993: 278).

These publications nurtured a sense of urgency in the social sciences about what civil society in China looks like, whether it exists, and—if it does exist—what it means for the country's social and political development. Yet, the line between the state and the "non-governmental" in China has not been easy to distinguish. Even before China's economic reforms began in earnest in the early 1980s, the Chinese government had established several "mass organizations" that it would later claim to be the equivalent of the civil society associations that are central to social and political life in the United States and other democracies. The All-China Federation of Trade Unions (ACFTU), the All-China Women's Federation (ACWF), the Communist Youth League (CYL), and other mass organizations were established under the strict control of the Maoist party state. Such groups were intended to be the special representatives of their various constituencies and to operate as "transmission belts," assisting in the work of the government by bringing the needs of society to the attention of the leadership while conveying state policies and ideology to the masses.

Despite the Chinese state's desire to remain in control of associational life, in the lead-up to the 1995 United Nations' Fourth World Conference on Women, China was forced to grapple with the issue of what "real" non-governmental organizations entail. Beijing had strongly lobbied to host the event, but because the United Nations charter guarantees NGOs the right to participate in an advisory capacity, China had to prepare for an influx of international NGOs looking to attend a parallel NGO forum. Thus, the Chinese authorities had to contend with the question of whether China had its own NGOs that could attend such an event or whether it would be isolated from this part of the international community. The sociologist Naihua Zhang relates how at an international preparatory meeting held in Manila in 1993,

> the vigorous, spontaneous interaction and exchange among the participating NGOs was a challenging and eye-opening experience for the Chinese delegations. The ACWF delegations also found themselves at the center of a debate over the validity of the ACWF's presence at the conference as some participants charged that it was not a "real NGO."
>
> *(Zhang 2001: 159)*

In response to this criticism, Zhang writes, "the Chinese government formally termed the ACWF 'China's largest NGO that aims at raising the status of women'" in a proclamation aimed at an international audience; however, this new description did not change its domestic identity (Zhang 2001: 159).

Given the violent suppression of a (potentially) nascent civil society that initially generated extensive interest, it is somewhat surprising that, until recently, published studies of associations in contemporary China have focused predominantly on GONGOs (Chan and Qiu 1999; Foster 2001, 2002; Ma 2006; Pearson 1994; Unger and Chan 1995; Whiting 1991).[4] While many scholars have focused on issues of autonomy and influence, most have also generally assumed or concluded that China's authoritarian state is strong enough to effectively eliminate the space for viable autonomous organizations (Brook and Frolic 1997; Chan 2005; Ma 2002, 2006; Stalley and Yang 2006; Unger 1996; Wang and He 2004; White, Howell, and Shang 1996; Zhang 2001).

Still, scholarly interest in GONGOs is well warranted. Since the early 1990s, China has established a panoply of GONGOs, including sports associations, business associations, academic associations, and groups dedicated (at least in name) to other fields of activity. Elizabeth Economy (2004) points to various motives for this phenomenon, including finding resting spots for retired cadres and redundant staff who were left jobless during the government downsizings of 1998 and 2003. According to official statistics, at the end of 2015, there were over 662,000 registered "NGOs" in China (Ministry of Civil Affairs of the People's Republic of China, 2016), and most of them are widely assumed to be GONGOs.[5] The Chinese government has been quite happy to present these organizations as "NGOs" to foreigners in order to attract foreign funding and boost the legitimacy of its GONGOs in the eyes of the world (Economy 2004; Zhang 2001; Zhao 2006). Nonetheless, within China, the government has chosen to equate the English term "NGO" with the Chinese terms *minjian zuzhi* (people's sphere organization) or, since 2008, *shehui zuzhi* (social organization). For domestic NGOs, at least, these renderings are politically preferable to the literal translation of "non-governmental organization" (*fei zhengfu zuzhi*) because the prefix "non" (*fei*) can be interpreted in Chinese as "anti" (*fan*).

Consistent with the analysis of authoritarianism put forth by Philippe Schmitter (1974) and affirmed by Wolfgang Streeck and Lane Kenworthy (2005), scholars have identified China's GONGOs as examples of state-led "corporatism" in which the state recognizes only one sectoral organization and aims to use that organization to maintain communication with that sector of society (Chan 1993; Wu 2002; Yu 2007).[6] Bringing the concept of corporatism to bear on the analyses of China, Jonathan Unger and Anita Chan underscore the fact that in a corporatist system "the state determines which organizations will be recognized as legitimate" (2008: 49) and argue that "China is *more* corporatist … than any other nation that we know of, in that all associations not only must be officially registered but also must first have a Party or state-related *sponsor* in order to register" (Unger and Chan 2008: 55). The prominent Chinese scholar and democratic theorist Keping Yu has promoted a similar view, arguing that "China has already formed a civil society," but that "like China's market economy and democratic politics, it displays its own special characteristics," first of which is that "Chinese civil society is a typical government-directed type of civil society" (2007: 20). Such perspectives and studies have advanced our understanding of how an authoritarian government can act to shepherd potential citizen groupings into politically palatable organizations under its own control. At the same time, this line of research has increased our understanding of the struggles over power and autonomy between these GONGOs and various government agencies (Economy 2004; Foster 2002).

Grass-roots NGOs and the emergence of bottom-up civil society

Although the corporatist nature of civil society growth in China seems to have led to a consensus that autonomy is limited, many studies are rooted in a Tocquevillean tradition that expects associations to have a democratizing effect on the state (Foster 2001). Such democratic premises are evident in the work of scholars who have suggested that groups closely aligned to the government may also push forward the development of civil society and open the political system to more voices (Hsu and Hasmath 2014; Teets 2014).[7] Rather than viewing the requirement to have a supervisory agency as an enervating control mechanism, the former head of the Ford Foundation's Beijing office (and political scientist) Tony Saich (2000) suggested that registered

NGOs can operate within the constraints of the regulations in a fairly efficacious, but not completely independent manner. Saich, as others, argued that such organizations benefit from the legitimacy and protection extended by their sponsoring agency and may also be granted greater access to policy makers.

Despite the proliferation of GONGOs since the early 1990s, over the past fifteen years, we have also observed the emergence of grass-roots NGOs that do not fit easily within the corporatist framework. These unofficial, "bottom-up" grass-roots NGOs (*caogen zuzhi*) lie outside the vertical control mechanisms that the party has tried to impose and are formed by Chinese citizens without the government's initiative or approval in social spaces where the government is absent, impotent, or unwilling to act. Typically, they provide some sort of social service in fields such as HIV/AIDS, labor rights, environmental protection, and education. Some also engage in explicit advocacy, although many blur the distinction between advocacy and social service delivery. Of course, the extreme political sensitivity of true civil society associations in China and in any authoritarian state should not be underestimated. Since NGOs potentially provide alternative spaces for political organizing and mobilization, they are viewed by some members in China's government as a serious threat.

People in grass-roots NGOs commonly seek to emphasize their differences in comparison with GONGOs—"those government-run groups" or groups "with a government background." Grass-roots NGOs, in common estimation, are not government creations, nor spin-offs of government agencies looking to push cadres into early retirement or create an NGO "hat" for officials to wear when traveling overseas. By and large, they receive neither funding nor tangible assets (such as free office space) from government agencies. They are run by local Chinese people, who are not answerable to the headquarters in another country. They may receive funding from foreign governments or foundations, or locally from their founders, volunteers, or members. They may be organized by social elites or by people without a high-school education. They may operate under top-down power structures and clear hierarchies, or they may show a high degree of internal democracy. They may comprise staff, volunteers, members, or a combination of the three. Last, they may be legally registered with the government as NGOs or businesses, or they may not register with the government in any form. As in other authoritarian regimes, unregistered groups run the political risk of being branded "illegal organizations," while those registered as businesses risk being shut down for fraudulently presenting themselves as non-profitable to their funders and the public.

Given the challenges faced by independent associations, along with the government's efforts to create its own officially approved GONGOs, how do ostensibly illegal grass-roots organizations survive in China's authoritarian state? For NGOs with close government ties, personal relationships or "*guanxi*" have played a key role in NGO strategies to win support from the government (Zhao 2004). Carolyn Hsu's study of seven early-wave Chinese NGOs, which were mostly started and staffed by people with previous state-sector work experience, found that "all of their leaders insisted that cultivating good relationships with state agencies was the key strategy for securing organizational resources because of the state's capacity to permit or constrain access to even non-state resources" (Hsu 2010: 267). Jingen Zhang and Wenjia Zhuang (2008), in a case study of a housing complex association, found that a strategy of "informal politics" was the only pathway through which a grass-roots organization could interact with and hope to affect the government, given the lack of formal structures for NGOs to participate in China's current political structure. Likewise, Andreas Fulda, Yanyan Li, and Qinghua Song (2012) found that grass-roots groups were increasingly pursuing trust relationships with government actors, and seeking out "first-in-command" cadres in order to build a collaboration that would yield tangible benefits for both the state and NGO actors. The situation varies greatly across regions and issue areas, as well, requiring adroit "reading" of the local political climate and the personalities of relevant government officials involved. Groups working on environmental issues, HIV-AIDS, and LGBT rights have met with unpredictable levels of support or obstruction from local officials when seeking legal registration and funding (Hildebrandt 2013).

Drawing on interviews and participant-observation in China, I have argued (Spires 2011) that grass-roots NGOs survive in China due to the fragmented nature of the Chinese state and the ways in which media censorship works to keep information local. Chinese grass-roots NGOs have survived only insofar as they refrain from making democratic claims and address the social needs that might fuel grievances against the state. For its part, the state tolerates such groups as long as particular state agents can claim credit for any good works while avoiding blame for any problems. Thus, grass-roots NGOs and China's authoritarian state can coexist in a "contingent symbiosis" that—far from leading to an inevitable democratization—allows illegal groups to operate openly while relieving the state of some of its social welfare obligations. Subsequent studies, in particular a three-province survey of grass-roots NGOs (Spires, Tao, and Chan 2014), provide support for this coexistence thesis. By comparing 263 NGOs across issue areas (including HIV, education, environment, and labor rights) and regions (Beijing, Guangdong, and Yunnan), my colleagues and I found that grass-roots groups were tapping into high levels of human resources—volunteers, boards of directors, and informal government ties—even in the absence of official government approval for their activities.

Regulating civil society

Given the rapid increase in registered NGO numbers over the past twenty-five years—from just over 4,000 groups in 1989 to more than 600,000 in 2015—one might be tempted to conclude that China has experienced an "associational revolution" akin to that identified by Lester Salamon and Helmut Anheier (1997) in other areas of the world. However, prior to the Charity Law of 2016, government regulations required that all NGOs, in order to be registered, must first find a professional supervisory unit (PSU) within the government—an arrangement designed to allow the government to regulate, organize, and monitor NGOs better. This requirement has been widely perceived as the biggest legal obstacle to grass-roots groups that wish to become registered NGOs.[8]

The Chinese state's official regulatory framework governing civil society has evolved alongside the transformation of civil society since 1989. Prior to the promulgation of the Charity Law, extant regulations made it extremely challenging for most grass-roots civil society groups to register as "proper" NGOs. While many groups could find informal support from government agencies, few government officials were willing to risk their professional reputations and future by agreeing to serve as a formal supervisory agency for NGOs. Without legal status as an NGO, basic organizational tasks, like opening a bank account or signing a lease for office space, present obstacles to establishing a formal organization. Even where these have been accomplished through some means, fundraising efforts have depended on personal trust in the NGO's founder and the power of the group's mission and vision since unregistered groups (and even some registered ones) cannot provide tax deductions to donors. The media was banned from reporting on "illegal organizations" in 2005, which meant that most grass-roots groups could only be covered under the guise of "good individuals" doing good work, and not as organizations per se. The term "civil society" (*gongmin shehui*) was itself banned from the media several years later, thus limiting the popularization of the concept beyond academia. Moreover, in 2011, a former high-ranking official published an article in an official party-approved journal claiming civil society to be a "trap" laid by Western forces that were hostile to China (Zhou

2011). In 2013, news spread on the Chinese social media platform, *Weibo*, that university professors were forbidden to talk about seven sensitive issues in class, including universal values, media freedom, and civil society, thus making the latter a taboo term even in the classroom.

At the time of writing (late 2016), we are on the cusp of a potentially dramatic new era in regulation for Chinese civil society. Starting around 2010, in some larger cities like Guangzhou, Shanghai, and Beijing, restrictions were eased on organizations working on "charitable" activities that local governments deemed acceptable. Slowly, some groups engaged in education work, environmental work, or volunteering on particular issues were allowed to register directly under the Ministry of Civil Affairs without needing an additional supervisory agency to vouch for them. While this was a major sign that a "loosening" of controls might be on the horizon, groups engaged in fields deemed politically sensitive, like labor rights and LGBT issues, have continued to be marginalized and are not allowed to register as legal NGOs.

Charity Law of 2016

The Charity Law, which took effect in September 2016, heralds a major shift in the way China regulates domestic civil society organizations.[9] Under public discussion since at least 2014, the single biggest change brought by this new law is that "charitable organizations" (*cishan zuzhi*) are no longer required to find a supervisory agency as their sponsor. If they fulfill all other legal requirements, they can register directly under the Ministry of Civil Affairs. Since the additional supervisory agency requirement was widely seen as the main obstacle to legalization under the older rules, the promise of the new law is that the energies and goodwill of 1.4 billion people will be unleashed and civil society will flourish. Significantly, the law also offers the possibility of legal fundraising for those groups that, once registered, operate "normally" for two years. We can only presume that the term "normally" means not breaking any laws. These two changes could dramatically transform the possibilities for civil society in China.

However, the Charity Law offers a specific definition of "charitable activities" that worries some NGOs engaged in advocacy and, at the same time, fails to mention explicitly areas of work that some NGOs consider as their main mission. Amongst the areas explicitly included are helping the poor, the needy, orphans, those who are ill, the elderly, and the disabled. The provision of relief during times of natural disaster, promoting sports, preventing pollution, and "other public interest activities" are also listed. On the other hand, labor rights promotion is not mentioned at all, nor are legal aid clinics and other activities that involve promoting the rule of law. In a series of focus groups that I ran in early 2016, during an open comment period on a draft of the law, a number of LGBT groups voiced their concern that the law's proscriptions against harming "societal morality" (*shehui gongde*) would be used to prevent their advocacy of LGBT rights, awareness-raising on LGBT issues, and community building. Other groups worried that the law's proscription against harming "national security" would be used as an excuse to exclude them from registering because the authority to define "national security" lies with the government, and the term is frequently invoked to suppress NGO activity.[10]

In the same focus groups, involving over fifty grass-roots NGO staff in five cities across China, one crucial obstacle to the law's implementation became apparent as discussions unfolded. Many participants were skeptical that the law would be implemented according to its spirit at the local government level. A number of groups expressed concern that they would not be recognized as a "charitable organization" by local officials, who, they believed, hold a narrow definition of "charity." Indeed, many of the participants did not initially see how the law was related to their own groups. "People giving out rice at a temple" and "rich people giving away money" were two characterizations of "charity" (*cishan*) that NGO leaders offered. The law also refers to "public interest" (*gongyi*) activities, a term which many grass-roots groups have adopted for themselves in recent years. But, in the text of the law, "public interest" is used in ways that made focus group participants suspect that the law's drafters did not understand the work of NGOs or the distinction between working for the public good and doing "charity." Thus, the NGOs' lack of faith in local officials and a belief that they would apply the most conservative definition of charity possible limited these groups' desire to register under the new law. Out of more than fifty participants, fewer than five expressed interest in pursuing registration after the law takes effect; they preferred to stick with the status quo rather than risk adding more challenges to their work.

International Nongovernmental Organization Law of 2016

From the 1980s, as China began to re-open to the world, international NGOs and foreign grantmakers played an instrumental role in stimulating the development of domestic civil society in China. The Ford Foundation, amongst others, provided financial and technical support to people who would later establish prominent Chinese NGOs. The international connections and ideas that flowed into China were also important in exposing future Chinese activists to the norms and values of global civil society. For the past three decades, however, most INGOs working in China have inhabited a legal "gray zone." In the absence of a clear legal framework, INGOs have managed their China programs with a hotchpotch of formal and informal arrangements. In recent years, twenty-nine foreign philanthropic foundations did successfully register with the Ministry of Civil Affairs under the 2004 Regulations on Foundations, however, they represent only a small portion of the total population of the active foreign grantmakers in China.

The legal framework governing INGO activities in Mainland China changed dramatically on April 28, 2016 when the National People's Congress passed an INGO Law (also translated as the "Foreign NGO Law" or "Overseas NGO Law"). This new law aims to regulate all activities within Mainland China undertaken by foreign-based, non-profit, non-governmental organizations, including NGOs based in Hong Kong, Macau, and Taiwan. Rather than authorizing the Ministry of Civil Affairs to regulate such groups—it has arguably had the most contact with and the deepest understanding of INGOs—this new law frames INGO activities as an issue of national security, assigning registration and governance authority to the Ministry of Public Security.

In recent years, a central fear of the Chinese state vis-à-vis its own citizens is that Chinese people are being corrupted by "Western ideas," such as multi-party democracy, human rights, and "civil society." "Universal values" are a bogeyman that the Chinese Communist Party trots out regularly, depicting them as a trap laid by evil foreign forces seeking to overthrow the Chinese state and bring down the Party. To counter such influences, Party leaders have called on universities, the media, and the government-led Chinese Youth League to re-double their efforts toward "correct" value inculcation and stamping out any views that risk misleading vulnerable young minds. Ominous warnings about US-funded "color revolutions" that will land Chinese in the same dire situation as Syrian refugees are now circulating via official state media.

It is against this backdrop that the new INGO Law should be understood. While state media and official proclamations emphasize the fact that foreign NGOs are welcome in China, the law itself is written in a way that imposes major barriers to the entry of new groups and, very likely, will drive out INGOs that currently work in China. The biggest obstacle will be a familiar one: as with grass-roots NGOs prior to the Charity Law, the INGO Law requires foreign organizations to first find a "professional supervisory unit" (PSU) from within the government bureaucracy to sponsor their presence and activities in China. On the surface, this may not seem so challenging, as for the past few decades many INGOs have operated programs or made grants to Chinese grantees with the knowledge and cooperation of government officials, even in the absence of a clear legal framework permitting such activities. Such arrangements seemed to suffice for all intents and purposes until the political winds shifted in 2014. That summer, between June and July, the Ministry of National Security launched a nationwide investigation of INGOs, talking with INGO staff as well as government agencies and academic institutions that had partnerships with foreign NGOs and foundations. Grass-roots groups were also investigated and asked to file reports detailing their foreign contacts.

In focus groups and interviews leading up to the INGO Law's official promulgation in 2016, an almost universal concern raised by INGO leaders was the law's requirement to seek official sponsorship from a PSU before registering with the Ministry of Public Security.[11] In many cases, despite having worked closely with government partners for years or even decades, many INGOs cited their partners' reluctance to serve as a PSU as the main obstacle in continuing their work in China under the new law. Their concern was that potential PSU heads see political risk—both for their own individual careers and their agency's reputation—as outweighing any potential benefit they may gain from continued cooperation. In the absence of incentives or guarantees from the central government, many INGOs believed that they would be unable to find a PSU. Since late July 2016, of over twenty INGOs who said they had approached a potential PSU, only one was optimistic about their long-term partner's willingness to serve as a PSU. In another case, approaching four different potential PSUs had yielded answers including, "We need to wait to see if we will be on the PSU list," "We need to wait on details," and "We are not sure if we'll be qualified." These were similar to the responses reported by other INGOs. Despite the possibilities implied by such responses, almost all of the INGOs that sought promises of support were pessimistic about their chances of succeeding in obtaining sponsorship from a qualified PSU.

Another concern voiced by a number of groups was the law's proscriptions against engaging in "political activities." Since a number of high-profile INGOs have worked with Chinese government ministries on, for example, criminal law reform, education reform, and environmental regulations, their leadership wonders whether these will be interpreted as "political" and, thus, be banned once the new law takes effect. Additionally, the burden on small volunteer-based NGOs, including many from Hong Kong, may be too great to sustain their activities under the new law. Many such groups have few government contacts and only know officials at the village or township level where they conduct small-scale projects or extra-curricular education activities. For these groups, pursuing higher-level political patronage seems intimidating, if not impossible. Time will tell, of course, what strategies can be devised and how tightly the new law will be implemented. At the time of writing (mid-December, 2016), with only two weeks to go before the law is implemented, the Ministry of Public Security has yet to release a list of approved supervisory agencies, leaving many INGOs in limbo regarding the way forward.

Recurring repression

Despite the promises of a more favorable legal structure, repression of civil society is a recurring phenomenon in China. As in other authoritarian states, the Chinese party state is constantly on guard against the formation of independent groups that might challenge its authority. Both individuals and organizations are potential targets, and in the last few years, numerous examples attest to the Chinese government's continuing anxiety about threats to its rule.[12] In early 2014, the lawyer Xu Zhiyong and other "New Citizen Movement" activists were put on trial for disturbing public order after organizing "citizen dinners" to discuss current social and political issues. In early 2015, the case of the "feminist five" drew international attention when five young women were detained for planning to hold public advocacy actions against sexual violence. In late 2015, labor rights activists Zeng Feiyang, Tang Huanxing, Zhu Xiaomei, and He Xiaobo, amongst others, were arrested and charged with various crimes.

International NGOs have not been exempted from repression, although in comparison to domestic groups, the authorities have generally been less hands-on due to the fear of creating an "incident" that could harm China's international reputation. In one news-making case in early 2016, however, Peter Dahlin, a Swedish resident of Beijing, who led a group promoting legal education and defense work, was detained for suspected endangering of state security and was forced to apologize for harming the Chinese nation on television before being deported. Coming after the nationwide investigation of INGOs in 2014 and just as the INGO Law was being publicly floated, this was most likely a case of "killing the chicken to scare the monkeys," or making an example of a "bad" INGO in order to caution others against getting out of line. Other INGO staff have also reported being "invited to tea"—a euphemism for being questioned—by state security authorities interested in learning more about INGO activities and sources of funding. Prior to 2015, such questioning was generally limited to the PRC national staff working at INGOs. However, with the rise of the INGO Law to the legislative agenda, by late 2016, a number of foreign staff had also received and accepted such "invitations."

Recent developments and future research

Civil society in China is in a state of flux. From the rise of GONGOs in the 1990s to the emergence of grass-roots groups just after the turn of the century, the field has evolved more rapidly than observers have been able to capture. There is always a scholarly lag in making sense of what happens on the ground, and in studies on China, this is perhaps more pronounced due to the country's economic and social dynamism. In this section, I aim to highlight a few recent developments that present exciting new opportunities for future inquiry.

Volunteering

Voluntary association and volunteering are two different animals. The former, as insightfully described by Tocqueville, can bring out the best and the worst in human sociability. But civil society's threat to authoritarian regimes is perhaps best understood through this broad category of activity; it spans a huge range of purposes and implications, from cults (as the Falungong was branded in 1999), business interests, singing groups, hiking clubs, church groups, and teams of volunteer teachers to political party formations. Most such groups have no express political goals, but it is their potential to form a political alternative to the ruling CCP that makes them of such concern to Beijing.

In contrast to the political implications of voluntary association, volunteering as an activity—for whatever purpose—is far less understood as an aspect of contemporary Chinese society. Even the few studies on the 2008 Sichuan earthquake response that mention the outpouring of support from volunteers have mostly considered NGOs and their professionalized staff as the key focus of investigation, and they have been mostly concerned with the relationship between these groups and the state (Teets 2009). While we can see the outpouring of support as a watershed year for volunteering in China, we know little about the diversity of volunteers' motivations or the impact of encounters between urban, educated youth and the poor, rural, and dispossessed people who are frequently the targets of their efforts.

Yet the story to be told is not only about *self-organized* volunteering. As Outi Luova (2011) explains, in the wake of the 1989 protests, China's Ministry of Civil Affairs fixed upon volunteering as a way to reduce social tensions and address the new social needs brought by economic reform and restructuring. The government regularly engages in a "Learn from Lei Feng" campaign to teach children and encourage everyone to follow the example of a now legendary model of self-sacrifice from the CCP's early days. Similarly, in the lead-up to the 2008 Beijing Olympics, the government's volunteer recruitment efforts aimed to mold model citizens by promoting discourses of glory and greatness that would give face to the Chinese nation (Chong 2011). Ying Xu (2012) documents how, in recent years, the Communist Youth League (CYL) has worked tirelessly to develop youth volunteering as one of its key purposes, thereby promoting its own institutional legitimacy and survival. In 2013, the CYL celebrated twenty years of organized volunteering, proclaiming that nationwide it had established volunteer associations in all provinces, including in almost 3,000 cities and 2,000 universities. Moreover, it boasted over 130,000 volunteer service sites and had registered more than 40 million volunteers. Collectively, in 2012 alone, CYL volunteers had reportedly performed more than 690 million hours of volunteer service.[13] Yet, how these volunteer activities are received by the young people they seek to mobilize is not well understood. My own recent study of youth-based volunteer associations in southern China has found a strong aversion to such government-led activities, with young people drawing a strong contrast between volunteering with "sincerity" in one's heart versus government-led efforts that are only "for show."[14] How this plays out nationwide is unclear, especially in areas where the local culture of self-organized volunteering may be relatively weak.

Philanthropy

Private philanthropy received a shot in the arm with the promulgation of the 2004 Regulations on Foundations, which provided the basic structure for setting up a private foundation in China. With the massive amounts of private wealth accumulated in the past twenty years, China's billionaires have grown to at least 400 individuals and families in 2016, up almost 20 percent from 2015, and more than double the 168 tallied in 2014.[15] While not all of these are establishing private philanthropies, both corporate and family foundations are now emerging as a growing force in Chinese civil society. According to the Beijing-based China Foundation Center—an information clearinghouse modeled on the US-based Foundation Center—at the end of 2010, there were 1,096 private foundations registered in China, but by the end of 2015, there were 3,324 such organizations, a more than a threefold increase within just five years (Ma, Cheng, and Guo 2016: 52).

While the sector's rapid growth is widely recognized, grantmakers' motivations, goals, and backgrounds are not well understood. In a recent nationwide survey, Weijun Lai *et al.* (2015) found that the largest group of private foundations were funded not by entrepreneurs but by government-background non-profits aiming not at supporting grass-roots NGOs but at fundraising for (government-run) universities. Business people in China, as a whole, have been reluctant for their giving to clash with state priorities, choosing "safer" issues such as health and education and often channeling any charitable funds through GONGOs set up as foundations. As such a new phenomenon, and with little transparency in the sector, it remains to be seen whether private, institutionalized philanthropy will support the diversity of purposes embraced and pursued by grass-roots NGOs or simply work to further government goals.

Funding and the depoliticizing of civil society?

Another recent development in Chinese civil society yet to be adequately understood is the new state policy of government "purchasing of services" from NGOs. This type of outsourcing, of course, is well known in other places and has, in China's case, been learned most directly from study tours and studies of Hong Kong, the USA, and the UK. Dating from at least the year 2000, when several districts of Shanghai started outsourcing elder-care services, government agencies in large cities such as Shenzhen, Guangzhou, and Beijing regularly put out calls for bids on government projects (Ma 2015). Ranging from projects like after-school educational programs for children to the provision of specialized health services, these programs offer large sums of money to groups deemed "qualified" to apply. The city of Guangzhou has spent an estimated 1.7 billion RMB (roughly US$250 million) on such outsourcing in the past decade. Almost always restricted to the delivery of social services, however, it seems that seldom, if ever, is government funding available for research and explicit advocacy efforts by NGOs. Being unable to register as proper NGOs, for example, prevents most labor rights organizations from participating in outsourcing programs and promoting their rights agenda.

This phenomenon raises many unanswered questions. Do such funding relationships lead to mission creep? Is government funding inducing a new wave of GONGOs, which are created solely for the purpose of obtaining such funds (as described to me by one official)? Alternatively, are groups able to accept government funding for some projects while maintaining a critical stance toward government policy and raising other funds from other sources? (Chaves, Stephens, and Galaskiewicz 2004; Peng 2016). One recent study of protest actions in China argues that the Chinese state practices a kind of "bargained authoritarianism," wherein the state preserves stability "by depoliticizing state–society confrontation and by allowing aggrieved citizens a certain degree of political leverage and relatively expansive opportunities to obtain material concessions and symbolic rewards from the state" (Lee and Zhang 2013: 1503–1504). Following this line of analysis, NGOs pushing the boundary may be bought off by the Chinese state or, perhaps more commonly, social discontent and disruption—both organized and not-so-formally organized—may be quelled by showering money on key protest leaders. Newfound wealth has indeed brought many new tricks to state maintenance of authoritarian rule. How these changes will facilitate or constrain civil society, however, cannot yet be ascertained from the few studies produced to date.

In addition to government outsourcing of social services, another related phenomenon is government sponsorship of "incubators" (*shehui zuzhi fuhua jidi*) or "charity parks" (*gongyi yuanqu*) in various cities. Shanghai's Pudong Charity Services Park, for example, officially opened in 2009 in an old handkerchief factory and housed twenty-six "social organizations" as of 2012 (Ji 2012). Funded by the local district government, the idea of this park—and others like it in Shenzhen, Guangzhou, and elsewhere—is to promote "innovation, cooperation, and growth" for local organizations (Ji 2012: 61). Scholars have only begun noticing the rapid emergence of these officially sponsored spaces for "social innovation" (a term recently embraced in official propaganda). Incubators typically facilitate the flow of government funds and provide office space and trainings to resident organizations. But, as with purchasing of services, this development begs questions about the management of such spaces, the autonomy of resident "social organizations," the selection criteria and processes that determine which groups are invited to join, and the surveillance of civil society activities.

Increased funding from government sources also challenges our earlier definitions of a "grass-roots NGO." Around the years 2006 in Shanghai and 2007 in Guangdong, the local government began promoting the development of social work as a profession and, to further that goal, began the first large-scale outsourcing programs. With a surge in new "social work organizations" (*shegong zuzhi*), earlier conceptualizations of "grass-roots groups" as those without government support and without a government background must be revisited. Now that government funding, for its preferred issues, is flowing freely, it may be that some groups are emerging and almost immediately obtaining government funds. Whereas this was politically difficult to imagine at an earlier stage, if not unheard of, in this new era we need to rethink how we distinguish between GONGOs and those "bottom-up" groups that most clearly fit the "pure" definition of civil society organizations. The earlier unidimensional definition lacked scholarly rigor. Yet, it may be possible for new Chinese NGOs to emerge, accept government funds, and still run independently of government influence. This is a question for analysis at the organizational level as well as one that holds significance for understanding the sector overall. Its answer(s) will inform our understandings of civil society's political implications and of how the Chinese state exerts (or fails to exert) control over potentially independent associations. It may turn out that government funding serves to capture societal energies as they emerge and to co-opt or depoliticize civil society. But, as Mark Chaves *et al.* (2004) found in a study of non-profits in the USA, increased government funding might not actually inhibit advocacy work. In the case of China, this is still an open question.

Back to the roots—democracy and civil society

As noted in this chapter's introduction, the study of civil society in China has largely focused on state–society relations and involved an active search for the democratic stirrings of an independent associational life. Despite periodic crackdowns and persistent repression—and the possibility that government funding will work to co-opt NGOs—there is evidence that civil society is engaging in a kind of quiet advocacy role in a number of fields by giving voice to those outside formal structures of power and authority, and impacting decisions, if not broad policies, that impact their lives.

Diana Fu (2016), for example, finds in a detailed study of "underground" labor NGOs that despite great pressure from authorities, in the face of rights abuses and unfair treatment such organizations promote a "disguised collective action." In her examples, "claimants are coached to deploy a repertoire of atomized actions that targets the bureaucratic mandate to maintain social stability and also appeals to officials' moral authority," helping to "secure concessions for participants while allowing activists to strike a middle ground between challenging authorities and organizational survival" (Fu 2016: 1). In a more above-ground example of online organizing, initiated by an anti-domestic violence feminist organization, Angela Leggett (2016) describes how activists challenged "status quo marginalization of domestic violence in the public sphere and facilitate[d] discussion around formal and informal institutional reform, thereby influencing social attitudes and potentially also policy and law making" (Leggett 2016:1). Similarly, Carsten Vala's (2012) study of Protestant churches argues that collective action to change church registration policies is not only helping the churches but also working to lessen state domination of society more broadly.

As Tocquevilleans have argued, civil society can constitute a site of training in which participants hone an appreciation for democratic institutions and learn the skills and habits of democracy. In the case of China, the legal scholar Eva Pils suggests, "political pressure on—and sometimes repression of—civil society is met by the strengthening and diversification of resources to resist pressure, and often contributes to rising consciousness of the institutional safeguards needed for a genuine civil society" (Pils 2012: 2). Yet, since participation in contemporary NGOs, whether as staff or volunteers, is a relatively new phenomenon in China, and because such activities are increasingly challenged by political restrictions, the field is in dire need of in-depth and long-term studies that seek to assess the impact of participation on the individuals involved. Do voluntary associations in China, as Tocquevillean analyses might lead us to expect, teach the skills and habits of democracy? And, given the recurring repression and challenges of doing such work in an authoritarian regime, does long-term participation lead to radicalization of activists and/or a heightened awareness of the possibilities and limitations of state-allowed civic engagement?

Conclusion

Taking action within civil society in China can be extremely challenging since it requires both passion and a willingness to take risks that are near impossible to calculate rationally. For researchers, as well, attempting to observe, measure, understand, and convey to others the situation of civil society in China (while respecting our basic ethical obligations to not harm our research subjects) is a task rife with obstacles. Nonetheless, with the "regularization" of civil society that may be born from the 2016 Charity Law and the INGO Law, the prospects for large-scale survey research on Chinese civil society are greatly improved. Likewise, as some civil society organizations are brought out of the shadows and into the academic spotlight, micro-level qualitative research should also yield deeper insights into the impacts of internal dynamics and external pressures on the sector's development. With the rise of private philanthropy, volunteering, the spread of the "NGO" as an organizational form, and the possibility of more consistent regulation by the state, we can also anticipate the consolidation of a coherent organizational field (DiMaggio and Powell 1983) that offers itself as a more amenable object of study. If an update to this overview is written in ten years' time, hopefully, it will be more about what we *do* know than what we do not.

Notes

1 There are other areas of civil society that have attracted well-deserved attention and careful study. The co-evolution of the Internet and civil society has been documented by Yang (2003a; 2003b) and Tai (2006). Likewise, issues of basic rights and rights-oriented protest have been encapsulated by O'Brien and Li's (2006) concept of "rightful resistance." These studies expand the scope of theoretical concerns and the implications of civil society development. In this chapter, however, I focus attention on the organizational actors that are integral to civil society studies.

2 One recurring theme throughout the chapter is that what we do not know about civil society in China far outweighs what we do know. This is, to be sure, due to the difficulties of conducting research on such a politically sensitive topic in an authoritarian state. Unfortunately, these challenges are numerous and cannot be elucidated satisfactorily here.

3 This section draws on and updates the literature reviewed in Spires (2011).

4 For a sample of the few early contrary views against the consensus depictions of Chinese NGOs as "bridges" to the state (Unger 1996) or of GONGOs that are embedded within government agencies (Wu 2002), see Bentley (2004), Chan, Qiu, and Zhu (2005), and Zhang and Baum (2004).

5 Prior to the 2016 Charity Law, regulations set out by China's Ministry of Civil Affairs (MOCA) established three categories of *minjian zuzhi*: membership-based "social organizations" (*shehui tuanti*); private non-commercial enterprises (*minban feiqiye danwei*) or non-profit social-service organizations; and philanthropic foundations (*jijinhui*).

6 Kang and Han (2008) have called for a modification of this general understanding. They argue that the government's official approach has been one of "graduated controls" in which different types of organizations are subjected to varying degrees of governmental supervision.

7 Due to the general restrictions on survey research and the political sensitivity of civil society, to date there has been no comprehensive national survey of registered organizations. However, it is a common consensus amongst Chinese government officials, academics, and NGO participants that GONGOs have comprised the overwhelming majority of registered groups.

8 Other obstacles included fundraising restrictions and a limit on the geographical area within which the NGO is permitted to operate.
9 Chinese and English versions of the law are available at: http://anthonyjspires.com. Earlier, in 2013, a central government document, drawing on local experiments like the one in Guangdong, declared that direct registration should be opened up to business associations, scientific societies, charitable groups, and community service organizations; however, the implementation was not uniform.
10 For grass-roots NGOs' feedback on the Draft Law, see: http://anthonyjspires.com.
11 For a full report of the INGOs' concerns regarding the Law, visit: http://anthonyjspires.com.
12 Yuen (2015) offers a comprehensive and insightful analysis of the recent repression.
13 "Qingnian zhiyuanzhe xingdong 20 nian zhuce zhiyuanzhe chao 4000 wan." *People's Daily* [*Renmin Ribao*], December 3, 2013. Electronic document, http://cpc.people.com.cn/n/2013/1203/c363174–23723505.html, accessed February 2, 2015.
14 See Spires (unpublished) and Peng (2016).
15 Flannery, Russell. Inside The 2016 Forbes List Of China's 400 Richest People: Wang Jianlin Repeats At No. 1. *Forbes*, Electronic document, www.forbes.com/sites/russellflannery/2016/10/26/inside-the-2016-forbes-list-of-china-400-richest-people-wang-jianlin-repeats-at-no-1/#6bcdd1684321, accessed November 22, 2016.

Suggested readings

Gallagher, Mary. 2004. China: The Limits of Civil Society in a Late Leninist State. In *Civil Society and Political Change in Asia: Expanding and Contracting Democratic Space*. Muthiah Alagappa, ed. Pp. 419–452. Stanford, CA: Stanford University Press.
Gao, Xiaoxian. 2010. From the Heyang Model to the Shaanxi Model: Action Research on Women's Participation in Village Governance. *The China Quarterly* 204: 870–898.
Gold, Thomas B. 1990. The Resurgence of Civil Society in China. *Journal of Democracy* 1(1): 18–31.
Howell, Jude. 2011. Civil Society in China. In *The Oxford Handbook of Civil Society*. Michael Edwards, ed. Pp. 159–170. New York: Oxford University Press.
Lora-Wainwright, Anna. 2013. The Inadequate Life: Rural Industrial Pollution and Lay Epidemiology in China. *The China Quarterly* 214: 302–320.
McCormick, Barrett L., Su Shaozhi, and Xiao Xiaoming. 1992. The 1989 Democracy Movement: A Review of the Prospects for Civil Society in China. *Pacific Affairs* 65(2): 182–201.
White, Gordon. 1993. Prospects for Civil Society in China: A Case Study of Xiaoshan City. *The Australian Journal of Chinese Affairs* 29: 63–87.

Websites

China Change, https://chinachange.org/.
China Change is a website with a focus on news relating to civil society and human rights' activities in China, with the purpose to provide a link between China and the rest of the world.

China Development Brief, http://chinadevelopmentbrief.cn/.
China Development Brief is a non-profit organization working to provide access to media, research, services and networking to NGOs, Foundations, businesses, researchers, and policy makers, with the purpose to empower China's civil society.

China Foundation Center, http://en.foundationcenter.org.cn/.
The China Foundation Center is a registered public charity, working to deliver critical information with the objective of establishing transparency in philanthropic markets in China.

NGOCN (in Chinese), www.ngocn.net/.
NGOCN is a public service network providing information on industry and recruitment, and news relating to industry-related activity, social development, and public interest topics.

References

Bentley, Julia Greenwood. 2004. Survival Strategies for Civil Society Organizations in China. *The International Journal of Not-for-Profit Law* 2(2). Electronic document, www.icnl.org/research/journal/vol.6iss2/art_1.htm, accessed November 29, 2016.

Brook, Timothy, and B. Michael Frolic. 1997. *Civil Society in China*. Armonk, NY: M. E. Sharpe.

Calhoun, Craig. 1993. Civil Society and the Public Sphere. *Public Culture* (Winter) 5(2): 267–280.

Chamberlain, Heath B. 1993. On the Search for Civil Society in China. *Modern China* 19(2): 199–215.

Chan, Anita. 1993. Revolution or Corporatism?: Workers and Trade Unions in Post-Mao China. *The Australian Journal of Chinese Affairs* 29: 31–61.

Chan, Kin-man. 2005. The Development of NGOs under a Post-Totalitarian Regime: The Case of China. In *Civil Life, Globalization, and Political Change in Asia: Organizing Between Family and State*. Robert Wellner, ed. Pp. 20–41. New York: Routledge.

Chan, Kin-man, Haixiong Qiu, and Jianggang Zhu. 2005. Chinese NGOs Strive to Survive. In *Social Transformations in Chinese Societies*. Chan, Kwok-bun, Tak-sing Cheung, and Yanjie Bian, eds. Pp. 131–159. Leiden and Boston, MA: Brill.

Chan, Kin-man, and Haixiong Qiu. 1999. Shetuan, Shehui Ziben ji Zhengjing Fazhan [Social Organizations, Social Capital, and Political and Economic Development]. *Shehuixue Yanjiu* [*Sociological Research*] 4: 64–74 (in Chinese).

Chaves, Mark, Laura Stephens, and Joseph Galaskiewicz. 2004. Does Government Funding Suppress Non-profits' Political Activity? *American Sociological Review* 69(2): 292–316.

Chong, Gladys P. L. 2011. Volunteers as the "New" Model Citizens: Governing Citizens through Soft Power. *China Information* 25(1): 33–59.

DiMaggio, Paul J., and Walter W. Powell. 1983. The Iron Cage Revisited: Institutional Isomorphism and Collective Rationality in Organizational Fields. *American Sociology Review* 48(2): 147–160.

Economy, Elizabeth C. 2004. *The River Runs Black: the Environmental Challenge to China's Future*. Ithaca, NY: Cornell University Press.

Flannery, Russell. Inside The 2016 Forbes List of China's 400 Richest People: Wang Jianlin Repeats At No. 1. *Forbes*. Electronic document, www.forbes.com/sites/russellflannery/2016/10/26/inside-the-2016-forbes-list-of-china-400-richest-people-wang-jianlin-repeats-at-no-1/#6bcdd1684321, accessed November 22, 2016.

Foster, Kenneth W. 2001. Associations in the Embrace of an Authoritarian State: State Domination of Society? *Studies in Comparative International Development* 35(4): 85–109.

Foster, Kenneth W. 2002. Embedded within State Agency: Business Association in Yantai. *The China Journal* 47: 41–65.

Fu, Diana. 2016. Disguised Collective Action in China. *Comparative Political Studies*. Electronic document, http://cps.sagepub.com/cgi/doi/10.1177/0010414015626437, accessed May 10, 2016.

Fulda, Andreas, Yanyan Li, and Qinghua Song. 2012. New Strategies of Civil Society in China: A Case Study of the Network Governance Approach. *Journal of Contemporary China* 21(76): 675–693.

Hildebrandt, Timothy. 2013. *Social Organizations and the Authoritarian State in China*. Cambridge: Cambridge University Press.

Hsu, Carolyn. 2010. Beyond Civil Society: An Organizational Perspective on State–NGO Relations in the People's Republic of China. *Journal of Civil Society* 6(3): 259–77.

Hsu, Jennifer Y. J., and Reza Hasmath. 2014. The Local Corporatist State and NGO Relations in China. *Journal of Contemporary China* 23(87): 516–34.

Huang, Philip, C. C. 1993. "Public Sphere"/"Civil Society" in China?: The Third Realm between State and Society. *Modern China* 19(2): 216–240.

Ji, Zhongxian. 2012. Yuanqu moshi: Shehui zuzhi fazhan de yizhong xin lujing—yi Pudong gongyi fuwu yuan wei li [Park Models: A New Pathway to Social Organization Development: Taking Pudong Charity Service Park as an Example]. *Jiangsu Xingzheng Xueyuan Xuebao* [*Jiangsu Administrative College Journal*] 1: 61–64 + 67 (in Chinese).

Kang, Xiaoguang, and Heng Han. 2008. Graduated Controls: The State–Society Relationship in Contemporary China. *Modern China* 34(1): 36–55.

Lai, Weijun, Jiangang Zhu, Lin Tao, and Anthony Spires. 2015. Bounded by the State: Government Priorities and the Development of Private Philanthropic Foundations in China. *The China Quarterly* 224: 1083–1092.

Lee, Ching Kwan, and Yonghong Zhang. 2013. The Power of Instability: Unraveling the Micro-Foundations of Bargained Authoritarianism in China. *American Journal of Sociology* 118(6): 1475–1508.

Leggett, Angela. 2016. Online Civic Engagement and the Anti-Domestic Violence Movement in China: Shifting Norms and Influencing Law. *VOLUNTAS: International Journal of Voluntary and Nonprofit Organizations* (February 5): 1–27.

Luova, Outi. 2011. Community Volunteers' Associations in Contemporary Tianjin: Multipurpose Partners of the Party-State. *Journal of Contemporary China* 72: 772–794.

Ma, Qing. 2015. Zhongguo zhengfu goumai fuwu de lishi, chengguo yu tiaozhan [The Chinese Government's History of Purchasing of Services: Results and Challenges]. *Shenyang Gongye Daxue Xuebao Shehui Kexue Ban* [*Journal of Shenyang University of Technology (Social Science Edition)*] 8(4): 295–298 (in Chinese).

Ma, Qiusha. 2002. The Governance of NGOs in China since 1978: How Much Autonomy?. *Nonprofit and Voluntary Sector Quarterly* 31(3): 305–328.

Ma, Qiusha. 2006. *Non-Governmental Organizations in Contemporary China Paving the Way to Civil Society?*. London and New York: Routledge.

Ma, Xin, Gang Cheng, and Changyan Guo. 2016. Chinese Foundation Development in 2015. In *Annual Report on China's Philanthropy Development (2016)*. Tuan Yang, ed. Pp. 51–70. Beijing: Social Science Academic Press.

Madsen, Richard. 1993. The Public Sphere, Civil Society and Moral Community: A Research Agenda for Contemporary China Studies. *Modern China* 19(2): 183–198.

O'Brien, Kevin J. and Lianjiang Li. 2006. *Rightful Resistance in Rural China*. New York: Cambridge University Press.

Pearson, Margaret M. 1994. The Janus Face of Business Associations in China: Socialist Corporatism in Foreign Enterprises. *The Australian Journal of Chinese Affairs* 31: 25–46.

Peng, Qiaoyang. 2016. *Grassroots NGOs and their Strategic Alliances with the Chinese State: A Case Study in Guangzhou*. MPhil thesis, University of Hong Kong.

People's Daily [Renmin Ribao]. 2013.Qingnian zhiyuanzhe xingdong 20 nian zhuce zhiyuanzhe chao 4000 wan [20 Years of Youth Volunteers in Action: Registered Volunteers Exceed 40 million]. *People's Daily* [*Renmin Ribao*], December 3. Electronic document, http://cpc.people.com.cn/n/2013/1203/c363174-23723505.html, accessed February 2, 2015.

Pils, Eva. 2012. Discussing "Civil Society" and "Liberal Communities" in China. *China Perspectives* 3: 2–7.

Rankin, Mary Backus. 1993. Some Observations on a Chinese Public Sphere. *Modern China* 19(2). 158–182.

Rowe, William T. 1993. The Problem of "Civil Society" in Late Imperial China. *Modern China* 19(2): 139–157.

Saich, Tony. 2000. Negotiating the State: The Development of Social Organizations in China. *The China Quarterly* 161: 124–141.

Salamon, Lester M., and Helmut K. Anheier. 1997. The Civil Society Sector. *Society* 34(2): 60–65.

Schmitter, Philippe C. 1974. Still the Century of Corporatism?. *The Review of Politics* 36(1): 85–131.

Spires, Anthony J. (unpublished). Chinese Youth and Alternative Narratives of Volunteering. Unpublished manuscript.

Spires, Anthony J. 2011. Contingent Symbiosis and Civil Society in an Authoritarian State: Understanding the Survival of China's Grassroots NGOs. *American Journal of Sociology* 117(1): 1–45.

Spires, Anthony J., Lin Tao, and Kin-man Chan. 2014. Societal Support for China's Grass-Roots NGOs: Evidence from Yunnan, Guangdong and Beijing. *The China Journal* 71: 65–90.

Stalley, Phillip, and Dongning Yang. 2006. An Emerging Environmental Movement in China? *The China Quarterly* 186: 333–356.

Streeck, Wolfgang, and Lane Kenworthy. 2005. Theories and Practices of Neo-Corporatism. In *A Handbook of Political Sociology: States, Civil Societies and Globalization*. Thomas Janoski, Robert R. Alford, Alexander M. Hicks, and Mildred A. Schwartz, eds. Pp. 441–460. New York: Cambridge University Press.

Tai, Zixue. 2006. *The Internet in China: Cyberspace and Civil Society*. Abingdon: Routledge.

Teets, Jessica C. 2009. Post-Earthquake Relief and Reconstruction Efforts: The Emergence of Civil Society in China? *The China Quarterly* 198: 330–347.

Teets, Jessica C. 2014. *Civil Society Under Authoritarianism: The China Model*. Cambridge: Cambridge University Press.

Unger, Jonathan. 1996. Bridges: Private Business, the Chinese Government and the Rise of New Associations. *The China Quarterly* 147: 795–819.

Unger, Jonathan, and Anita Chan. 1995. China, Corporatism, and the East Asian Model. *The Australian Journal of Chinese Affairs* 33: 29–53.

Unger, Jonathan, and Anita Chan. 2008. Associations in a Bind: The Emergence of Political Corporatism. In *Associations and the Chinese State: Contested Spaces*. Jonathan Unger, ed. Pp. 48–68. Armonk, NY: M. E. Sharpe.

Vala, Carsten T. 2012. Protestant Christianity and Civil Society in Authoritarian China. *China Perspectives* 3: 43–52.

Wakeman, Frederic Jr. 1993. The Civil Society and Public Sphere Debate: Western Reflections on Chinese Political Culture. *Modern China* 19(2): 108–138.

Wang, Shaoguang, and Jianyu He. 2004. Associational Revolution in China: Mapping the Landscapes. *Korean Observer* 35(3): 485–533.

White, Gordon, Jude A. Howell, and Xiaoyuan Shang. 1996. *In Search of Civil Society: Market Reform and Social Change in Contemporary China*. Oxford: Clarendon Press.

Whiting, Susan H. 1991. The Politics of NGO Development in China. *VOLUNTAS: International Journal of Voluntary and Nonprofit Organizations* 2(2): 16–48.

Wu, Fengshi. 2002. New Partners or Old Brothers? GONGOs in Transitional Environmental Advocacy in China. *China Environment Series* 5: 45–58.

Xu, Ying. 2012. Chinese Communist Youth League, Political Capital and the Legitimising of Volunteering in China. *International Journal of Adolescence and Youth* 17(2–3): 95–112.

Yang, Guobin. 2003a. The Co-Evolution of the Internet and Civil Society in China. *Asian Survey* 43(3): 405–422.

Yang, Guobin. 2003b. The Internet and Civil Society in China: A Preliminary Assessment. *Journal of Contemporary China* 12(36): 453–475.

Yu, Keping. 2007. Zhongguo Gongminshehui Yanjiu de Ruogan Wenti [A Few Issues in Chinese Civil Society Research]. *Journal of the Party School of the Central Committee of the Communist Party of China* 11(6): 14–22 (in Chinese).

Yuen, Samson. 2015. Friend or Foe? The Diminishing Space for China's Civil Society. *China Perspectives* 3: 51–56.

Zhang, Jingen, and Wenjia Zhuang. 2008. Fei zhengshi zhengzhi: Yige caogen NGO de xingdong celüe—yi Guangzhou yezhu weiyuanhui lianyihui choubei weiyuanhui wei li [Informal Politics: One Grass-Roots NGO's Action Strategy—Taking the Preparatory Committee of the Guangzhou Residents' Committee Alliance as an Example]. *Shehuixue Yanjiu* [*Sociological Research*] 2: 133–150 + 245 (in Chinese).

Zhang, Naihua. 2001. In Search for "Authentic" NGOs: The NGO Discourse and Women's Organizations in China. In *Chinese Women Organizing: Cadres, Feminists, Muslims, Queers*. Ping-Chun Hsiung, Maria Jaschok, and Cecilia Milwertz, eds. Pp. 159–179. Oxford and New York: Berg.

Zhang, Xin, and Richard Baum. 2004. Civil Society and the Autonomy of a Rural NGOs. *The China Journal* 52: 97–107.

Zhao, Liqing. 2006. Ruhe Kandai Zai Zhongguo de Waiguo Feizhengfuzuzhi [How to View Foreign Non-Governmental Organizations in China]. *Study Times*, August 21. Electronic document, www.studytimes.com.cn/txt/200608/21/content_7094045.htm, accessed November 1, 2016 (in Chinese).

Zhao, Xiumei. 2004. Zhongguo NGO dui zhengfu de celüe: Yige chubu kaocha [Chinese NGOs' Strategies Toward Government: A Preliminary Investigation]. *Kaifang Shidai* [*Open Times*] 6: 5–23 (in Chinese).

Zhou, Benshun. 2011. *Zou Zhongguo tese shehui guanli chuangxin zhi lu* [*Walk the Road of an Innovative Social Management with Chinese Characteristics*]. Qiushi 10. Electronic document, www.qstheory.cn/zxdk/2011/2011010/201105/t20110513_80501.htm, accessed May 1, 2016 (in Chinese).

4

HONG KONG

Alvin Y. So

Vibrant civil society in Hong Kong

Hong Kong was a British colony for over a century. Because of Hong Kong's peculiar geopolitics in the period after World War II, Hong Kong was turned into a modern city in the second half of the twentieth century. In 1997, China resumed the sovereignty over Hong Kong, and Hong Kong became a special administrative region of China. All these historical processes, needless to stress, have left a profound impact on the nature of civil society in Hong Kong. This chapter argues that the existing literature has failed to capture the unique characteristics of Hong Kong's civil society, and researchers need to develop a new embeddedness approach to examine the nature and historical development of Hong Kong's civil society. Before this chapter begins the analysis, it is necessary to explain briefly what we mean by civil society and how civil society is defined in Hong Kong literature.

"Civil society," for Gordon White, is the sociologically counterpart of "the market" in the economic sphere and of "democracy" in the political sphere. Civil society functions as a counter-image of the state, as an "embodiment of social virtue confronting political vice, the realm of freedom versus the realm of coercion, of participation versus hierarchy, pluralism versus conformity, spontaneity versus manipulation, purity versus corruption" (2004: 6–7). Similarly, Larry Diamond comments that: "as a realm of organized social life that is open, voluntary, self-generating, and autonomous from the state, and bound by a set of shared rules, civil society stands between the state and the private sector" (1999: 221).

In Hong Kong, civil society is defined as "the arena, outside of the family, the government, and the market, where people associate to advance common interests" (HKCSI 2006: iv). As such, civil society is a very imprecise concept: it largely describes the things that it does not belong to (such as, it is outside the state, the market, and the family). However, it states little about what civil society does and how it accomplishes its goals. In addition, Ngok Ma (2007, emphasis added by the author) remarks that the concept of *civil society* is often confused with the concept of *political society*. Whereas political society is the arena in which actors compete to assume power within the state, in a democracy, that would include political parties, elections, and legislature, civil society associations are outside the state and they merely seek to influence the government policies relevant to their interests without seeking to gain state power or win elections. Of course, the boundary between a political society and a civil society is highly dynamic and subject to change depending on the historical specific state–society relations. Unless a civil society is completely apolitical, it has the potential for being transformed into a political society if it wants to successfully accomplish its goals.

In Hong Kong Studies, research on civil society in Hong Kong has been limited. The following review is based on the three sets of reports below:

1   The first report was produced by the Central Policy Unit (CPU) of the Hong Kong government, which commissioned a Hong Kong-wide survey of the third sector. The CPU (2004) found that the third sector in Hong Kong had a population of 16,662 organizations that spanned fourteen categories: education and research; professional, industry, business, and trade unions; district- and community-based organizations; civic and advocacy organizations; law and legal services; politics; welfare services; health services; environment; sports; arts and culture; religion; philanthropic intermediaries; and international and cross-boundary activities.

   This survey also found that welfare service oriented and community-based organizations constituted the bulk of third sector organizations, while advocacy or political groups made up a tiny 1.3 percent of all associations. The 16,662 civil society organizations (across the fourteen categories) reported in this survey point to a sizable and vibrant civil society in Hong Kong, but the 1.3 percent of advocacy or political groups shows a somewhat underdeveloped political society. Thus, Wai-man Lam and Irene Tong (2007: 143) remark that these figures show that Hong Kong might be a classic case of political liberalization (guaranteeing civil liberties) without democratization.

2   The second report was produced in 2006 by the *Hong Kong Civil Society Index* (HKCSI) research project. HKCSI was a part of the CIVICUS (also known as the World Wide Alliance for Citizen Participation), an international NGO aimed at charting the development of civil society worldwide. HKCSI conducted: (a) a civil society organization survey; (b) in-depth interviews with representatives of selected stakeholder organizations spanning fourteen categories of civic organizations; (c) a media review in which two newspapers and one broader medium were monitored; (d) three policy impact case studies of the budgetary process, youth employment, and the legislation of Article 23; (e) a corporate social responsibility study, which comprised a study of the activities of social responsibility performed by ten of the largest listed companies in Hong Kong; and (f) a secondary data analysis and literature review.

   In addition, based on the criteria used across countries by the CIVICUS, HKCSI generated a *Civil Society Diamond* in which civil society was scored along four dimensions, namely, the *structure* of civil society, the *environment* in which civil society operates, the *values* upheld by civil society actors, and the *impact* of the activities pursued by the actors. The preliminary findings of the HKCSI (2006) showed that Hong Kong civil society scored lowest on the dimension of structure, which was 1.2 on a 3-point scale with "0" being the lowest mark and "3" the highest. Hong Kong civil society was found to be weak on "the depth of citizen participation" and "level of organization." The score on the dimension of environment was 1.5, and both "values" and "impact" attained a score of 1.9. Thus, although Hong Kong civil society was found to be weak in the dimension of structure, it scored higher in "values" and "impacts." Hong Kong civil society organizations did not have adequate resources and manpower, and people's level of involvement in civil society organizations (CSOs) is low and shallow. CSOs also had little horizontal integration; the alliance formed amongst them was usually ad hoc and unstable. However, CSOs were found to be quite active in promoting the values of democracy, equality, justice, tolerance, and democracy. They were found to be quite effective in educating citizens, in articulating the liberal, democratic values; and in lobbying the government for service provision and empowering citizens, although its impact in these areas was still restricted.

3   The third series of the report was produced by the Centre for Civil Society and Governance (CCSG) at the University of Hong Kong. In the *Social Service Sector* report, CCSG (2009) found that 90 percent of social services in Hong Kong are offered by civil society organizations that are largely subsidized by the government, but the new funding formulae (called the "Lump Sum Grant System") has brought about problems in finance, staff morale, and the service quality of social service organizations. The report also found that social service organizations have stable financial resources and well-trained professionals, but insufficient manpower for advocacy; their cooperative network within and outside the sector is also fairly fragmented.

In the *Natural and Built Environment Conservation Sector* report, CCSG (2010) also found that most conservation groups (CGs) were young and small, by conventional measures, with an average age of 10.5 years and two-thirds of them were established after 2002. Only half of them had the resources to hire full-time staff; they mostly relied on donations from the general public, membership fees, services, and sales for funding, and they received little government-related funding or commercial donations. The report comments that given the small overall capacity of CGs, their record of advocacy mobilization has been rather impressive. About 55 percent of CGs reported participation in a total of ninety-seven policy advocacy activities (including protests, signature campaigns, press conferences, and submissions to the government) in the previous twelve months.

In the *International Non-governmental Organizations* (INGOs) report, CCSG (2015) examined a database of 215 legally established INGOs. It found that as Asia's travel and information hub, Hong Kong offers INGOs the advantages of freedom of association, a predictable and well-functioning regulatory environment, and ease of fundraising. It argues that Hong Kong is a good place for INGOs to raise funds, thanks to the generosity of local residents and a high concentration of multinational corporations and local businesses. This INGOs report found that a typical INGO in Hong Kong would likely be a company established around the year 2000, possessing six–seven full time staff and a yearly income below HK$1 million. Its main focus would be the delivery of services outside Hong Kong rather than service or advocacy work for the local community. It would have a formal board governance structure, a set of public accountability mechanisms, mechanisms for obtaining feedback from stakeholders, and a means of evaluating their performance and maintaining their service quality.

In sum, the literature has provided a lot of valuable information on civil society in Hong Kong. They reported that Hong Kong civil society was sizeable with 16,662 civil society organizations across fourteen sectors. Civil society was active and vibrant, but had little impact on the policy of the Hong Kong government. However, the above literature tends to be more descriptive than analytical, and it fails to capture the distinctive characteristics of the civil society in Hong Kong because it examines civil society in isolation from the larger structural context. It forgets that civil society cannot be analyzed in a vacuum because civil society is embedded in a polity and an economy. Thus, civil society is inevitably shaped by the existing political and economic structures and contradictions.

Distinctive characteristics of civil society in Hong Kong

To capture the distinctive characteristics of the civil society, researchers must bring back the nature of the polity and economy where civil society is embedded. What then is the nature of polity and economy in contemporary Hong Kong? From a comparative perspective, Brian Fong (2013) argues that since the handover of sovereignty in 1997, Hong Kong has evolved into a hybrid regime that can be labeled as liberal authoritarian featuring a limited electoral franchise and strong civil liberties as well as an increasingly active civil society. This liberal authoritarian hybrid regime has a long history. When Hong Kong became a British colony in 1842, the British administration entrenched a liberal authoritarian regime in the city state. As a colony, political powers were concentrated in the hands of the colonial state headed by the governor, and the people of Hong Kong were denied the rights to choose their own government through democratic elections. Nevertheless, a fairly high level of civil liberties was in place for many decades.

After China resumed the sovereignty of Hong Kong in 1997, Hong Kong became a special administrative region (SAR) of China, and the colonial government was transformed into the HKSAR government. The change from British to Chinese rule, however, has not changed the nature of the liberal authoritarian regime because various civil liberties are guaranteed under the Basic Law (the mini-constitution) governing Hong Kong. On the other hand, although democratization has been underway since the mid-1980s, Hong Kong is far from having developed into a full-fledged democracy because of its limited franchise (So 1999). Nowadays, half of the seats in the Legislative Council are chosen by popular election, but the Chief Executive, who replaced the colonial governor as government head after 1997, remains hand-picked by an election committee controlled by Beijing and cannot be held accountable by the Hong Kong people. Thus, Hong Kong's experience is unique: post-colonial Hong Kong is a liberal authoritarian hybrid regime with a high degree of civil liberties, but some limited elements of democratic elections. Like other hybrid regimes, Hong Kong falls short of modern standards of liberal democracies, yet is not totally authoritarian.

How does this hybrid regime shape the civil society in post-colonial Hong Kong? First of all, Ngok Ma (2008) points out that the high level of civil liberties in Hong Kong reduces the pressure for a unified opposition in a Solidarity-like manner. Although the democrats and liberal CSOs face encroachment on their autonomy and freedom at times, they are almost never prosecuted and enjoy a reasonable degree of freedom of speech, association, and action. The CSOs have seen little urgency in forming one single territory-wide organization to resist oppression. The lack of perceived urgency also has driven them to insist on their own autonomy and self-identity, instead of uniting into one single opposition with institutional reform as their goal. This explains why Hong Kong's civil society is weak in structure and networking. It has low levels of horizontal linkage and organization institutionalization, which means that liberal CSOs cannot accumulate enough resources to enhance their mobilization and bargaining power vis-à-vis their incumbents.

In addition, a high level of civil liberties and ample freedom allows Hong Kong people to join protests and movements with a relatively low risk of facing arrest or political persecution, which has helped to foster the development of civil society in Hong Kong. However, ample freedom has also led the average person to be less dissatisfied with the hybrid regime, because they do not feel oppressed and they do not have a sense of urgency that the system must be transformed. This contradiction helps to explain the rapid rise and fall of civil protests in Hong Kong. If the CSOs or the general public perceives a great threat to their interests or lifestyle, they can easily be mobilized into protest action. However, as fear subsides, they quickly go back to their old routines and the movement dissipates.

Furthermore, since Hong Kong people have experienced a high level of civil liberties for over a century, civil liberties have become a core value of Hong Kong. CSOs are committed to maintaining the autonomy of the public sphere and the movements which aim to preserve civil liberties (like the July 1, 2003 protests, which attracted an estimated 500,000 people to the protest site) have drawn the largest turnouts over the past two decades. Thus, the *Civil Society Index Report* (HKCSI 2006) found that CSO's efforts contribute significantly to upholding civil rights and freedoms in society. Ma also remarks:

> The ideological inclination toward *ethical civil society* that drove the liberal CSOs to focus on maintaining autonomy of the public sphere, making them less compromising and more identity-conscious, and causing them to refrain from forming a pragmatic political movement that was intent on the seizure of political power.
>
> *(Ma 2008: 173, emphasis added by the author)*

To a certain extent, this inclination toward ethical civil society is an expression of the growing influence of the new middle class of educated professionals, who are interested in pursuing post-materialistic values (like freedom, autonomy) and lifestyle.

Finally, this hybrid regime has induced a particular mode of civil protest in Hong Kong. Although civil society organizations experienced numerous protests over the past forty years, Hong Kong protests have been labeled as "polite politics" (Ho 2000) because they were peaceful and rational, and followed existing rules and regulations set up by the police. The protesters did not disrupt social life or resort to violence, and their large-scale protests (e.g., the annual June 4 commemoration and July 1 demonstration) were highly regulated and predictable.

Emergence of "uncivil society" organizations and protests in Hong Kong

However, a new form of uncivil society organization and protest has emerged in Hong Kong in the mid-2010s. These nascent uncivil society organizations include "Hong Kong First," "Hong Kong Resurgence," "Civic Passion," and "Proletariat Political Institute" (Sautman and Yan 2015). I use the label of "uncivil society" because these nascent organizations and protests are quite different from the previous civil society organizations (CSOs) and protests in the following ways.

First, previous CSOs aimed to "rebuild local communities," to "preserve local heritages (such as Star Ferry and Queen's Pier) and promoted the liberal values of tolerance, non-discrimination, rational dialogue, and mutual respect; they tolerated immigrants and tourists in Hong Kong, and they wanted to provide adequate social services to meet the basic needs of the newcomers. In contrast, the nascent uncivil society organizations are against immigrants and tourists from Mainland China. They label mainland immigrants as "locust" because they accuse mainland immigrants of consuming the precious resources (like apartments in public housing, school places, hospital beds, and daily necessities like baby formula) from the local Hong Kong people. To a certain extent, these nascent uncivil society organizations are similar to the conservative, right-wing anti-immigrant organizations in contemporary Europe.

In addition, nascent anti-mainland protests are distinguished by their mode of protest. Whereas previous civil protests were quite peaceful and orderly, recent anti-mainland protests could be labeled as "militant" because they often involve clashes and violent confrontation with mainlanders, counter-demonstrators, and the police. In early 2015, for example, anti-mainland protesters staged weekly rallies against parallel traders (who trade across the border) in rural Hong Kong—the areas most affected by the growing influx of Chinese shoppers. Because parallel traders didn't bear a mark on their foreheads, the protesters wound up targeting anybody who was seen with bulky baggage on the street. The lucky ones were heckled and mobbed, while the less fortunate had their possessions searched or thrown about. Still others, like the elderly busker who happened to be passing through with a large amplifier in a cart bag, was mistaken for a mainlander and was roughed up by protesters. As a result, the anti-mainland protests in 2015 usually provoked clashes not only with mainlander parallel traders, but also with mainland tourists, counter-demonstrators, and the Hong Kong police. They often forced the nearby shops and markets to close during their protests. In the protest in Yuen Long, for example, the police had to use pepper sprays to separate the protesters from the counter-demonstrators. A woman was reportedly injured. A total of thirty-three people were arrested.

> Moreover, this new mode of anti-mainland protests also differs in its location and social composition. Whereas the previous wave of civil protests took place in urban Hong Kong (like the Central and Admiralty), this new wave of anti-mainland protests takes place in rural Hong Kong (the New Territory). Whereas the participants of the previous wave of civil protests were mostly college-educated middle class professionals, participants of this new mode of anti-movement protests often come from the grassroots working-class population living in public housing estates.
>
> *(Yuen 2015)*

Furthermore, this new wave of anti-mainland protests was distinguished by its mode of mobilization. Whereas the previous wave of civil protests relied on civil society organizations to mobilize their participants, this new wave of anti-mainland protests relied on "e-mobilization" to mobilize their supporters. Usually an announcement on Facebook was sufficient to jump-start the protest. This recent wave could be labeled as "disorganized" protests because protest organizers usually did not know how many people would show up at a particular protest site, and they had little control over their protesters' behavior.

Finally, this new wave of anti-mainland protest was distinguished by its poor public image in the Hong Kong mass media. Whereas previous civil protests were reported favorably in the mass media because they defended the core liberal values of Hong Kong, the recent anti-mainland protests received negative reports from reporters, who often labeled the protests as "xenophobic" and condemned the protesters as troublemakers. Reporters from the mass media also accused them of engaging in "uncivilized behavior" like insulting the tourists, kicking the tourists' luggage; as well as stereotyping mainlanders as "locusts" (FlorCruz 2014; Siu, Lo, and Cheung 2015).

In short, the nascent uncivil society organizations and protests were distinguished by the following traits: (1) anti-immigrant values and discrimination and intolerance toward the Mainland Chinese; (2) militant and irrational strategy used for protests which often lead to clashes and violence; and (3) "xenophobic" image reported in the Hong Kong mass media. In this respect, uncivil society can be conceptualized as a counter-image of the civil society, and as an embodiment of negative values against liberalism and rationality; of coercion versus freedom; of hierarchy versus participation; of conformity versus pluralism; of manipulation versus spontaneity; and of tolerance versus discrimination.

What then explains the emergence of these uncivil society organizations and protests in Hong Kong over recent years? In order to understand the historical formation of uncivil society in 2010, we need to consider national reunification with a new lens and examine the sociopolitical changes of Hong Kong since the handover in 1997.

Process of national reunification

Over the past two centuries, even though Hong Kong was turned into a British colony and completely cut off from communist China after 1949, the people of Hong Kong always identified themselves as Chinese and embraced Chinese nationalism from an ethno-cultural angle (So 2015). Thus, it is quite surprising that an anti-mainland movement (and many uncivil society organizations) suddenly erupted in Hong Kong several years ago, even though the colony had been transformed into a special administrative region (SAR) of China since 1997. What went wrong with Hong Kong's reunification process at the dawn of the twenty-first century? This chapter argues that the uncivil society organizations and protests in Hong Kong are a product of the complex socio-economic transformations, which were triggered by the process of national integration with Mainland China, namely, the influx of immigrants and tourists, the growing social inequalities, the emergence of a "localist" discourse and the formation of new *localist* organizations, and the setback of the democracy movement.

Influx of immigrants and tourists

As Ngok Ma (2015) explains, the "One Country, Two Systems" model sought to insert mechanisms of separation between Mainland China and Hong Kong after the handover. However, the increase in mainland–Hong Kong integration and the influx of mainland immigrants and tourists since 2003 have made this separation difficult. For immigrants, each day, 150 mainlanders received a one-way entry permit to legally reside in Hong Kong after 1997. Many of them are wives and children of Hong Kong residents. This amounts to about 55,000 mainland immigrants every year or 0.55 million mainland immigrants every decade. For tourists, meanwhile, before the 1997 handover, mainlanders had to visit Hong Kong on official tours and go through a complicated application process, which sometimes took months to process. A new Individual Traveller's Scheme (ITS) was introduced in 2003. Mainlanders in nine Chinese provinces can visit Hong Kong independently without joining an official tour. ITS was meant to boost tourism and consumption in Hong Kong, which was still suffering from the 2003 SARS (Severe Acute Respiratory Syndrome) epidemic. ITS was quickly expanded to include mainland cites, thus, leading to a rapid increase of mainland tourists to Hong Kong. In 2004, the number of individual tourists from Mainland China was only 4.3 million, but the number of tourists soon jumped tenfold to 47 million in 2014. This massive influx of tourists and immigrants has sparked new social tensions in the Hong Kong society (Ma 2015).

A huge amount of hot money followed mainland immigration and tourism and pushed property prices to record levels. Many Hong Kong workers and middle-class professionals complained that they could not afford to buy homes due to the mainlander housing bubble. In addition, when mainland spenders arrived in droves to purchase luxury goods (e.g., jewelry and branded items), major shopping malls saw a mushrooming of high-end boutiques catering to this influx of nouveau riche wealth and consumption habits, thus, driving up the rent and knocking small local shops out of business. Mainland visitors were also interested in other basic necessities (e.g., drugs and milk powder), believing that Hong Kong had better quality control. When Mainland China was plagued by the tainted baby milk scandal in 2008, mainland visitors descended on Hong Kong's supermarkets and drug stores causing a temporary shortage (Ma 2015).

Hong Kongers complained that they were subsidizing the costs for mainland tourists (in terms of crowding in public transport, heavy traffic, and long lines at bus stops, etc.), while only the large chain stores were reaping the financial benefits from tourism. Chiefly, their worries were focused on the rising housing prices, and particularly the cost of housing and the rising rent over the past few years. Hong Kongers said they were forced to pay higher "tourist prices" for local restaurants and other goods as a result of the influx of mainland tourists. In addition, Hong Kongers accused mainland tourists of violating certain codes of civility that they had taken for granted. Mainland tourists, they say, jump lines, defecate in the street, and talk loudly in public places. Furthermore, Hong Kongers complained that stores catered only to the needs of mainland tourists who flood their local neighborhoods. Thus, Hong Kongers advocated the preservation of local communities, lifestyles, and values in response to the devastating onslaught of mainland tourists. Furthermore, the competition for scarce resources aggravated hostility against mainlanders. For years, pregnant women were allowed to give birth in Hong Kong hospitals, regardless of their nationality, after paying a surcharge. The child would automatically acquire Hong Kong permanent residence status, even if neither of the parents was a Hong Kong resident. After the Individual Visitor Scheme was introduced in 2003, tens of thousands of mainland mothers came to Hong Kong to give birth, and take advantage of the better medical facilities, thus, making their children eligible for all the welfare benefits accorded to permanent residents in Hong Kong. In 2011, there were 35,736 children born of non-Hong Kong parents, which led to an outcry about the invasion of mainlanders, who would drain public resources in the future (Ma 2015: 47–48).

Growing social inequalities

In the first decade of the twenty-first century, Hong Kong workers have been facing the problem of a declining number of manufacturing jobs (which were relocated across the border in Mainland China) combined with a massive influx of new immigrants. The neoliberal policies of the Hong Kong SAR government, such as cutting the welfare budget, eliminating long-term civil servant positions for new hires, and privatizing public utilities, has further aggravated the social inequalities and poverty in Hong Kong. As a result, Hong Kong became one of the most unequal places in the world. Hong Kong's Gini coefficient rose to a dangerous level of 0.537 in 2011, which is the highest point since the beginning of the records in 1971 (Sautman and Yan 2015). Lai-shan Sze (2007) observed that the living conditions of those at the bottom has been deteriorating over the last decade, and the income and wealth gap between the haves and the have-nots has widened. Similarly, Tai Lok Lui points out that:

> issues concerning poverty, growing income inequalities, and the emergence of the so-called "working poor" have become public concerns. … Social tensions are growing. Increasingly, people are becoming anxious, self-protective, and insecure in the face of growing competition for scarce resources.
>
> *(Tai Lok Lui 2007: 222)*

In sum, the livelihood of the Hong Kong people is threatened by the growing social inequality, the declining social mobility in Hong Kong, and the influx of mainland immigrants and tourists.

Emergence of localist discourse and localist organizations

In 2006 and 2007, a new group called "Local Action" started a series of local cultural heritage protests, trying to prevent the Hong Kong government from demolishing historical sites, such as the Star Ferry Terminal and Queen's Pier. Local Action has articulated a new *localist* discourse that the Star Ferry Terminal and Queen's Pier are public places full of rich collective memory. Local Action wants to "reclaim the public space" from the developers, to promote people's participation in community and social planning, and to nurture community autonomy. Thus, the grassroots can preserve the local lifestyle and reinforce their sense of belonging that helps to identify Hong Kong as their home (So 2008).

To a certain extent, Local Action's "localist" discourse is the harbinger of a new wave of anti-mainland protests, and many new localist organizations, declaring that their mission is to protect Hong Kong's resources and way of life from the mainland invasion, have sprung up over the past few years. These new political organizations include: "Hong Kong First," "Hong Kong Resurgence," "Hong Kong Autonomy Movement," "Population Policy Concern Group," "North District Parallel Imports Concern Group," "Civic Passion," "Indigenous Democratic Front," "People Power," and "Proletariat Political Institute" (Sautman and Yan 2015).

These new political organizations were small and highly autonomous. Since the organizations were small, independent, and diverse, they tended to rely on the Internet or social media platforms, such as Facebook, YouTube, and bulletin blogs, to mobilize their participants. These localist organizations neither planned for the future nor had a long-term coherent strategy. Instead, they are prompt in taking spontaneous, creative, and discontinuous action. Each participant or each subgroup could choose its own mode of demonstration, and they seldom coordinated with each other to wage a large-scale collective action.

Setback of the democracy movement

Although Local Action has articulated a localist discourse, it is still a civil society organization and belongs in the traditional democracy camp as when it first emerged in Hong Kong in the 2000s because it advocates peaceful democratic protest and it wants to promote grass-roots democracy at the community level. Like other civil society organizations in the pan-democratic groups, it still hopes to democratize the Hong Kong government and turn the HKSAR into a government for the Hong Kong people.

The recent setback of the democracy movement, however, has shown that the democracy path is a dead-end street. The failure of the seventy-nine-day Occupy Hong Kong Movement in 2014 has further convinced the protesters that they can't trust the Hong Kong government anymore, while peaceful protests and rational dialogue with Hong Kong government officials cannot solve their grievances. Thus, they need to take a more militant stand to defend Hong Kong's autonomy in order to protect Hong Kong's interests and way of life. For example, Joshua Wong (2015), a student leader of the Umbrella Movement, comments that Hong Kongers should not only focus on universal suffrage, but should also fight for the city's right to self-determination. Wong argues that Hong Kongers should launch a movement for self-determination, before the expiration of the "One Country, Two Systems" policy in 2047, to attain the right to determine their city's future.

Thus far, I have identified the complex interplay amongst the influx of tourists and immigrants, the increase of social inequality, the emergence of a localist discourse, the formation of localist organizations, and the setback of democracy movements as the underlying socio-political factors that sparked the emergence of uncivil society organizations and protests. As such, what is the implication of these nascent uncivil organizations and protests for Hong Kong? How would they shape the political development of Hong Kong in the near future?

Political implications

Needless to stress, this new wave of uncivil organizations and protests has exerted a profound impact on the politics of Hong Kong, namely, it challenges the legitimacy of traditional civil society organizations, deepens the socio-political polarization in Hong Kong society, and threatens the prospects for national reunification in Greater China.

Challenging the legitimacy of traditional civil society organizations

The traditional civil society is facing a strong challenge from the uncivil social organizations and protests. For the post-1990s generation, the rational, peaceful, liberal-democratic strategy of protest is becoming outdated. The younger generation believes that, given the failure of the Umbrella Movement in 2014, Hong Kongers should try a more militant mode of protest to defend the interests and autonomy of Hong Kong. However, the recent election of the Legislative Council (Legco) in September 2016 showed that militant uncivil society organizations like Civic Passion have not yet captured the hearts of the Hong Kong people, as this organization succeeded in winning only one seat in the legislature. On the other hand, at least half a dozen leaders from the traditional civil movement camp won their seats in the Legco election. Thus, although the uncivil society organizations appear to be highly influential amongst the younger generation and grass-roots population in Hong Kong, they still have not emerged as a dominant political force in Hong Kong politics (Lian 2016; Yung 2016).

Deepening the socio-political polarization in Hong Kong's society

Although Hong Kong society is quite polarized as a result of the growing social inequality in the twenty-first century, the emergency of this new wave of uncivil organizations and protests has further deepened the socio-political polarization process in the democratic camp. Anti-mainland protesters openly stereotype the previous civil society protesters as "left rubbers" or the "Greater China sympathizers," and critique the latter's peaceful, liberal, and non-violent method as outdated and ineffective. Instead of paying attention to the democracy movement in Mainland China, anti-mainland protesters argue that the civil society protesters should focus on local matters in Hong Kong. In other words, the civil society protesters (including pan-democrats) should, following the path of anti-mainland protesters, put forward the slogan "Hong Kong First" or "Hong Kong Priority." To the civil society protesters, the new anti-mainland protesters are obviously a divisive force that will weaken the democracy movement. Thus, some frustrated civil society protesters also agree with the pro-establishment organizations which label the anti-mainland protesters as "rightists," "racists," or "fascists."

In addition, this new wave of anti-mainland protests has triggered the pro-establishment forces to set up their own brand of uncivil society and set up their own patriotic movement organizations. For instance, during the Umbrella Movement (or called Occupy Central Movement) in 2014, establishment forces set up an "Anti-Occupy Central" movement, which was backed strategically by the police, mafia, and pro-Beijing mass media in order to intimidate and harass civil society protesters on the street. In this respect, Hong Kong society is increasingly divided into two big camps: anti-mainland groups versus pro-mainland group. Every policy (immigration, housing, education, population, welfare, etc.) is interpreted based on this spectrum between anti- and pro-mainland. This socio-political polarization in Hong Kong society allows little political space for any traditional civil society organizations to take a middle position.

As a result, Hong Kong politics is increasing torn between the two poles of anti-mainland versus pro-mainland and between the two poles of civil society organizations and protests versus uncivil society organizations and protests.

Threatening the prospects for national reunification in Greater China

At present, uncivil society organizations of anti-mainland protesters are still conducted on a small scale. Uncivil organizations have limited resources; they receive little support from the Hong Kong population except the grass-roots population; their protest actions are scattered, and they are not united in the coordination of their protests. However, if they were further provoked by the pro-Beijing patriotic organizations, if the Hong Kong government continues to ignore the grievances of the grass-roots population (such as the ever-rising property prices, the baby formula shortage, and the worsening of lifestyle for the grass-roots population), and if Beijing continues its hardliner policy toward Hong Kong, it is possible that anti-mainland protests could quickly grow into a robust Hong Kong nationalist movement and develop more linkages with the independence movement in Taiwan. In this scenario, the small uncivil society organizations and movements have the potential to threaten the national reunification project in Greater China.

Suggested readings

Fong, Brian C. H. 2013. State–Society Conflicts under Hong Kong's Hybrid Regime. *Asian Survey* 53(5): 854–882.

Lam, Wai-man, and Irene L. K. Tong. 2007. Civil Society and NGOs. In *Contemporary Hong Kong Politics: Governance in the Post-1997 Era*. Wai-man Lam, Percy Luen-tim Lui, and Ian Holliday, eds. Pp. 135–154. Hong Kong: Hong Kong University Press.

Lee, Eliza Wing-yee. 2012. Civil Society Organizations and Local Governance in Hong Kong. In *Repositioning the Hong Kong Government*. Stephen Wing-Kai Chiu and Siu-Lun Wong, eds. Pp. 147–164. Hong Kong: Hong Kong University Press.

Ma, Ngok. 2007. *Political Development in Hong Kong: State, Political Society, and Civil Society*. Hong Kong: Hong Kong University Press.

Ma, Ngok. 2008. Civil Society and Democratization in Hong Kong: Paradox and Duality. *Taiwan Journal of Democracy* 4(2): 155–175.

So, Alvin. Y. 1999. *Hong Kong Embattled Democracy: A Societal Analysis*. Baltimore, MD: Johns Hopkins University Press.

Websites

Center for Civil Society and Governance, http://web.hku.hk/~ccsg.
The objectives of the Center for Civil Society and Governance include establishing a clear understanding of the state of civil society in Hong Kong, understanding the consequences of activity in CSOs, and developing practical measures to strengthen civil society and its emphasis on accountability, transparency, and accessibility.

Civic Exchange, www.civic-exchange.org.
An independent think-tank undertaking research into creating a sustainable Hong Kong.

Study on the Third Sector Landscape in Hong Kong, www.cpu.gov.hk/doc/en/research_reports/3rd_content.pdf.
This is a report providing information related to the third sector in Hong Kong, including history, research methodology, insight into organizations, and its relationship to the environment, arts and culture, sport, religion, and health.

References

CCSG (Centre for Civil Society and Governance). 2009. *Serving Alone: The Social Service Sector in Hong Kong: Annual Report on the Civil Society in Hong Kong 2009.* Hong Kong: Department of Politics and Public Administration.

CCSG (Centre for Civil Society and Governance). 2010. *The Natural and Built Environment Conservation Sector: Annual Report on the Civil Society in Hong Kong 2010.* Hong Kong: Department of Politics and Public Administration.

CCSG (Centre for Civil Society and Governance). 2015. *At the Gateway to Asia: An International & Cross-Boundary Non-Governmental Organizations in Hong Kong: Report on the Capacity of Civil Society Organizations, 2014–2015.* Hong Kong: Department of Politics and Public Administration.

CPU (Central Policy Unit). 2004. *Study of the Third Sector Landscape in Hong Kong.* Hong Kong: Government Printer.

Diamond, Larry. 1999. *Developing Democracy: Towards Consolidation.* Baltimore, MD: Johns Hopkins University Press.

FlorCruz, Michelle. 2014. Anti-Locust Protest in Hong Kong Call for Restrictions on Chinese Mainland Tourists. *International Business Times*, February 19. Electronic document, www.ibtimes.com/anti-locust-protests-hong-kong-call-restrictions-chinese-mainland-tourists-1556457, accessed September 29, 2015.

Fong, Brian C. H. 2013. State–Society Conflicts under Hong Kong's Hybrid Regime. *Asian Survey* 53(5): 854–882.

HKCSI (Hong Kong Civil Society Index). 2006. *Civil Society Index: Report.* Electronic document, www.google.com.hk/webhp?source=search_app#q=Civil+society+index+Hong+Kong, accessed September 11, 2016.

Ho, Kwok Leung. 2000. *Polite Politics: A Sociological Analysis of an Urban Protest in Hong Kong.* Aldershot: Ashgate.

Lam, Wai-man, and Irene Tong. 2007. Civil Society and NGOs. In *Contemporary Hong Kong Politics: Governance in the Post-1997 Era.* Wai-man Lam, Percy Luen-tim Lui, and Ian Holliday, eds. Pp. 135–154. Hong Kong: Hong Kong University Press.

Lian, Yi-Zheng. 2016. Can Beijing stop Hong Kong's Separatists? *New York Times*, September 12. Electronic document, www.nytimes.com/2016/09/13/opinion/can-beijing-stop-hong-kongs-separatists.html, accessed September 12, 2016.

Lui, Tai Lok. 2007. Class Relations After 1997. In *Starting From 1997: Civil Society's First Ten Years.* Ray Yep, ed. Pp. 222–231. Hong Kong: SynergyNet.

Ma, Ngok. 2007. *Political Development in Hong Kong: State, Political Society, and Civil Society.* Hong Kong: Hong Kong University Press.

Ma, Ngok. 2008. Civil Society and Democratization in Hong Kong: Paradox and Duality. *Taiwan Journal of Democracy* 4(2): 155–175.

Ma, Ngok. 2015. The Rise of Anti-China Sentiments in Hong Kong and the 2012 Legislative Council Election. *The China Review* 15(1): 39–66.

Sautman, Barry, and Hairong Yan. 2015. Localists and "Locusts" in Hong Kong: Creating a Yellow-Red Peril Discourse. *Maryland Series in Contemporary Asian Studies* 221(2): 1–94.

Siu, Phila, Clifford Lo, and Tony Cheung. 2015. Hong Kong Security Chief Blasts Anti-Mainlander Protests after Suspected Traders "Abused and Kicked." *South China Morning Post*, March 10. Electronic document, www.scmp.com/news/hong-kong/article/1733503/parallel-trading-protest-hong-kongs-government-house-will-face-police?page=all, accessed September 29, 2015.

So, Alvin Y. 1999. *Hong Kong Embattled Democracy: A Societal Analysis.* Baltimore, MD: Johns Hopkins University Press.

So, Alvin Y. 2008. Social Conflict in Hong Kong after 1997: The Emergence of a Post-Modern Mode of Social Movement? In *China's Hong Kong Transformed.* Ming K. Chan, ed. Pp. 233–249. Hong Kong: City University Press.

So, Alvin Y. 2015. The Making of Nationalism in Hong Kong. In *Asian Nationalism Reconsidered.* Jeff Kingston, ed. Pp. 135–146. New York: Routledge.

Sze, Lai-shan. 2007. Poverty in an Affluent Society. In *Starting From 1997: Civil Society's First Ten Years.* Ray Yep, ed. Pp. 232–278. Hong Kong: SynergyNet.

White, Gordon. 2004. Civil Society, Democratization and Development: Clearing the Analytical Ground. In *Civil Society in Democratization.* Peter Burnell and Peter Calvert, eds. Pp. 6–21. London: Frank Cass.

Wong, Joshua. 2015. Self-Determination is the Only Solution in Hong Kong. *Time*, September 24. Electronic document, http://time.com/4042269/hong-kong-self-determination-occupy-umbrella-revolution/, accessed September 28, 2015.

Yuen, Yeuk-laam. 2015. Anti-Mainland Traders Stage Third Violent Protest in Hong Kong. *Global Times*, March 2. Electronic document, www.globaltimes.cn/content/909614.shtml, accessed September 29, 2015.

Yung, Chester. 2016. Hong Kong Elections: New Parties Pick Up Seats. *The Wall Street Journal*, September 5. Electronic document, www.wsj.com/articles/pro-democracy-camp-in-hong-kong-faces-test-1472 873577, accessed September 26, 2016.

5

TAIWAN

Anru Lee

Community-building, civil society, and civic activism in Taiwan: promises and predicaments

This chapter focuses on "community-building" (*shequ yingzao* [社區營造]), one of the most potent and widely employed terms in Taiwan's public sphere in recent decades, and reviews how the course and discourse of community-building reflects the development of civil society and shapes the contour of civic activism in post-authoritarian Taiwan. Much has been written about Taiwan's civil society through surging social movements, political rallies, and street demonstrations since the 1980s (e.g., Ho 2010; Ho and Lin 2011; Hsiao 1990), epitomized by the 2014 Sunflower Movement—the twenty-four-day occupation of Taiwan's Congress that embodied the collective endeavor of different constituencies of civil society, including student activists, leading non-government organizations (NGOs) on labor, gender, environmental, welfare, and human rights issues, and more fundamentally, the general public/concerned citizens (Rowen 2015 and Chapter 32 in this volume; Wang 2017). In this chapter, however, I focus on community-building. The reason for my choice is twofold. First of all, in contrast to social movements that tend to be loud, noisy, and with relatively well-defined objectives and immediate urgency, community-building is a "quiet revolution." Community-building is mundane. The progress of community-building projects can be slow, with twists and turns, and the effect can be ambiguous without clearly outlined goals or easily identified accomplishments. Yet, precisely because of its propinquity to everyday life, community-building reveals the quotidian dynamics and struggle within a community on issues such as consensus-building and public affairs management significant to the ongoing development of civil society. This enables us to explore how the emergence and operation of civil society comes about in complicated local formations. Furthermore, community-building concerns not merely the community as if it were a self-sufficient entity. Rather, the course of community-building reflects the way a community is embedded within a larger political-economic context. Community-building as a strategy to strengthen Taiwan's civil society is therefore susceptible to the influence of various external factors. Specifically, a close examination of the contour of community-building brings to light the equivocal relationship between the state and civil society, in the sense that the Taiwan government has been and continues to be the primary source of funding for local community projects. The fact that communities are spatially grounded entities also helps to show the impact of current economic globalization. Local projects under the auspices of community-building have frequently been implemented as projects of economic revitalization through cultural means. While this may be considered by many as essential to the survival of deindustrialized communities (particularly in rural areas) in Taiwan's post-industrial economy, it nonetheless undermines the political potency central to the original intention of community-building.

To substantiate the points made above, this chapter is divided into a few sections. I start with the background of why "community"—or the rebuilding of community or the building of a new kind of community—is considered by grass-roots activists (and, later, government officials) as imperative in Taiwan's struggle for an effective civil society. Also addressed in this section is how this renewed interest in "community" was transformed into actions, for which two different types of community-building-cum-civic activism are examined. This is followed by a discussion of the government-led Integrated Community-Building Program (社區總體營造) in the mid-1990s. Examples of community projects under the Integrated Community-Building Program will be discussed to evaluate both the effectiveness of community-building as an agent of civil society and the paradox embedded in community-building as an approach to both political empowerment and economic advancement. The third section picks up the economic dimension of community-building, and discusses the predicament faced by community-building movements after the 2000s, when place-making became a major strategy of economic revival in the countryside and of boosting global economic competitiveness in cities.

Community-building as a grass-roots movement

In the years immediately after the lift of martial law, a "community study" fervor was witnessed in Taiwan in the 1990s (Huang 1995; Lü 2002). Whether in local or national radio shows or amongst public television broadcasts, community-related topics were an essential part of the programming. Major newspapers also expanded their reporting on neighborhood stories, local cultural-historical societies, and community activities. From grass-roots radicals for democracy to defenders of status quo, and from ordinary housewives' endeavors for their local concerns to politicians attempting to win popular support, regardless of one's political belief or moral standing, "community" was in the center of their discourses and it was the cause that everybody was claiming to fight for. On the surface, this dovetails with the trend of community movement, particularly in capitalist advanced countries in Europe and North America since the 1990s. In these countries, a new governance structure emphasizing community mobilization and civic activism has been deployed as a mechanism for urban regeneration and social reconstruction to make up for the failed or insufficient government policies against a neoliberal economy (Jessop 2002). In Taiwan, however, the rise of the community movement was much less the result of a declined welfare state, because the welfare state was not a reality (Lin and Chiu 2014: 86). Rather, the phenomenon of the community movement was inspired by two seemingly opposing forces: community mobilization based on local history and identity by political and social movement veterans seeking alternative sites for long-term, grass-roots organizing, on the one hand, and the promotion of the state in the attempt to build a renewed national identity, as well as a new kind of citizens, on the other (Huang 1995). Yet, why was "community" deemed so central in the concern of both the state and grass-roots activists? What similar or different meanings were conveyed by "community" in each of these conceptualizations? And, fundamentally, what is the connection between civil society and "community" or "community-building" in the context of Taiwan?

At the root of Western definitions of civil society is the dichotomous separation between the state and society. On the level of day-to-day practice, it points to a new kind of social organization—self-organized voluntary associations based on horizontal ties of trust—that is no longer based on primary social bonds such as kinship and that is also independent from the state. These voluntary associations then constitute a public sphere "where individuals and groups interact to influence the publicly shared understanding that governs interrelationships in collective life" (Weller 1999) and where citizens are free to pursue their collective identities and interests. While broad-based horizontal institutions intermediate between the family and the state, such as temple organizations or business associations, have been widely observed in modern Taiwanese history (Skoggard 2016), it is doubtful whether such institutions have contributed to an independent local public sphere, especially under the tight political control of the Nationalist (Kuomintang or KMT) government (Weller 1999).[1] The KMT regime effectively depoliticized self-organized voluntary groups throughout most of the post-World War II era until the political liberalization in the 1980s.

This history of state–society relations has had clear consequences for the meaning and characteristic of the political subjectivity specific to civil society. Directly, the authoritarian nature of the state was the prime object against which grass-roots organizing found its cause and focus. Furthermore, the legitimacy of the KMT regime rested not only on the political and legal structure but also on the cultural ideology that supported this structure. In its effort to establish governing legitimacy on Taiwan after its defeat in the Chinese Civil War in 1949, the exiled KMT (led by Chiang Kai-shek at the time) propagated the concept of cultural China to serve not only as the basis of national identity but also of the government/bureaucratic structure (Chun 1994, 1996). Accordingly, local culture became "both a capacity for resisting the oppression from above and a venue for incubating political subjectivity within the state" (Jung 2016: 514). The political liberalization after the late 1980s made it permissible to conceptualize a nationscape based on the land actually inhabited by the population of Taiwan and governed by the national government on Taiwan, instead of being based on an imagined, KMT-promulgated, unified China. In this political context, community-building as a means to (re)inscribe local meaning and identity and to (re)integrate space, place, and political life was—and continues to be—deemed crucial by grass-roots activists to the process of political democratization (Chuang 2013: 121). Furthermore, central to the idea of community-building in Taiwan is the acknowledgement of past political inequality amongst various cultural and ethnic groups. Community-building is therefore a part of the socio-political movement that seeks to create a new political legitimacy and social justice based on equality (L. Wang 2004).

Two examples of community organizing exemplify this early wave of community movement: the Hsin Kang Cultural Movement and the Meinung Anti-Dam Movement. Resonating with the evolution of social movements in Taiwan, these two movements were instigated by people who left their hometowns to pursue a college education in metropolitan Taipei but, after graduation, forwent a career in Taipei and came home because of their deep commitment to the well-being of their birthplaces. Each of these movements has its own roots of origin, but both have developed into prominent advocacy groups that have had a great impact on local development and inspire emulation from community advocates nationwide.

The Hsin Kang Cultural Movement

Home to one of the most prominent Matus temples and an important site of annual pilgrimage in Taiwan, the Hsin Kang Township of Chiayi County became a pioneer of community movement in the late 1980s. The Hsin Kang Cultural Movement was initiated by Dr. Chen Jin-huang as an attempt at cultural revival to fill the vacuum created after the loosening of state political control. Similar to many grass-roots activists at the time, Dr. Chen reckoned that there existed a poverty of culture, caused by the prolonged implementation of martial law that provided the KMT regime its legitimacy based on a faraway territory. People were led to ignore the land they were inhabiting and look down on the way of life grounded on this land. As a result, traditional art and culture bred and nurtured in this soil, including temple architecture and festivals, music, and even the rice, fruits, and agricultural produce, were disregarded. Yet, in their place came vulgar popular cultural practices such as strippers performing at funerals and temple festivals and an illegal lottery called "Everybody is happy." The lift of martial law was therefore a moment of political-ideological loss—and in his practice, Dr. Chen heard many complaints of palpitations, insomnia, irritability, and depression from his patients. Yet, this ideological loss also presented an opportunity to refocus on one's immediate environment and cultural heritage (Yang 2010). In October 1987, three months after martial law was suspended and the citizens' right to assemble and congregate guaranteed by Taiwan's constitution was reinstalled, Dr. Chen invited the choreographer Lin Hwai-min—likely the most famous native son of Hsin Kang—and his world-renowned Cloud Gate Dance Theater to come home and perform on a makeshift stage at the local high school's auditorium. That night, Hsin Kang residents crowded the auditorium, coming with their friends and families, and sitting or standing casually, just like they would have done if they were attending a performance at the courtyard of their famed Matsu Temple.

Holding a performance at a local temple courtyard is a time-honored custom in reverence of the local god and the community whose safety and integrity that he/she protects. Dr. Chen's collaboration with Lin's Cloud Gate was therefore meant to awaken the communal spirit, as well as to (re)introduce quality cultural activities, once a regular part of local daily life for the Hsin Kang people. It also marked the birth of the Hsin Kang Foundation of Culture and Education, one of the earliest grass-roots-instigated, community-based non-profit organizations.[2] Just like Cloud Gate that is best known for its infusion of indigenous cultural elements with the Western modern dance genre, active members of the Hsin Kang Foundation also seek to extend traditional associations and social relations into new areas of community life and public affairs. Since early on, a key to the success of the Hsin Kang Foundation has been its ability to work with pre-existing (and long-standing) organizations, including youth and women's groups, senior citizens' groups, and especially temple-affiliated associations that are frequently overlooked by community movement advocates elsewhere in Taiwan as they are considered to be lacking in modern, rational, or progressive streaks (W-P. Lin 2016). By working closely with these established local organizations, the Hsin Kang Foundation embraces activism not only in areas such as culture/art and history/memory, but also in child education and environmental protection (H. Lin 2011). The foundation's attempt was to elevate people's cultural level and to improve the quality of life. It pushed the limit of community work and changed the conventional understanding of community advocacy.

Quickly, the "Hsin Kang Experience" was widely reported on the news media, and it became a highly desirable community-development model. The Hsin Kang Foundation, situated in the Hsin Kang Township, was also invited by the Council for Cultural Affairs (now the Ministry of Culture) to be part of the National Art Festival. A main directive of the National Art Festival was to showcase locally initiated art performances and cultural activities. This annual festival later became a prelude to the state-supported Integrated Community-Building Program. While the recognition from the central government and the funding that came with the recognition were by and large welcome, doubts and concerns were gradually raised by some community activists of the Hsin Kang Foundation. Specially, they questioned the purpose of taking part in government-sponsored "community" festivals or activities, as these festivals or activities were often aimed at attracting domestic or even international tourists/visitors for primarily economic reasons. As a result, much of the local time, labor, and energy was consumed but very little of it went to benefit the local population and/or local causes directly (H. Lin 2011: 387).

This critique points to two fundamental factors that shape community movements in Taiwan: the continual and active role of the state in setting community development agendas and providing funding accordingly, on the one hand, and the increasingly dominant global economic concern that weighs heavily on the minds of the government and local residents (if not necessarily advocates). These, in turn, not only impact the current state of Taiwan's civil society, but also challenge our general understanding of the concept of civil society. I will return to these issues later in this chapter.

The Meinung Anti-Dam/People's Movement

One major goal of community activism in the post-martial law era was to refocus the citizens' concern and affection on the land they inhabit, from which a renewed collective identity and public ownership could be hoped to develop. Given the affinity between land and ecology, environmentalism or environmental protection naturally emerged as a significant part of the discourse of many of the community movements (Lee 2007). An environmental cause also gives grass-roots activists a focus for their praxis that has immediate impact on their local communities. The Meinung Anti-Dam/People's Movement presents a prime example of this.

Located in southern Taiwan, Meinung is a small Hakka town with an agricultural economy based on tobacco production. As such, Meinung has long had a strong and distinct cultural identity as an agrarian Hakka community. The Meinung Anti-Dam/People's Movement began when a group of returning student activists came home after the Wild Lily Student Movement[3] and redirected their activism to local environmental issues in 1990. Originally, these student activists focused on the protection of endangered Blue-Winged Pitta—or "Birds of Eight Colors" (八色鳥) as they are known in Taiwan—and their compromised habitat as a way of highlighting the destruction of Meinung's natural environment. These efforts quickly led to a strong critique of the Taiwan government's detrimental developmental policy. Specifically, the planned dam construction near Meinung, aimed at supplying water to the region's growing heavy industries, prompted a series of protests (Yang 2010: 107–108).

The Anti-Dam Movement started with a small circle of young intellectuals and schoolteachers, but it gradually developed into a broad coalition of residents and organizations. In 1994, the movement organizers officially formed the Meinung People's Association with the aim of expanding the Anti-Dam Movement through grass-roots and community-based actions.[4] Subsequently, the movement was construed as a struggle for survival of the distinctive Hakka culture, and the strong Hakka identity became an important component in mobilizing the community. The cultural production of the movement was also extended to include other community-building and environmental education efforts, such as surveying the overall geological and hydrological conditions of southern Taiwan, promoting knowledge about the agrarian way of life based on tobacco production, and creating protest music from traditional Hakka mountain songs and musical instruments (Yang 2010: 108). A Yellow Butterfly Festival (which has become an annual event since 1995) was also created. The proposed Meinung Dam would flood 6.4 square kilometers of widespread forest that provides a unique habitat for Yellow Butterflies and a wide variety of wildlife species—hence the name "Yellow Butterfly Valley" (黃蝶谷). Because the dam would inundate the entire valley, protecting the valley to safeguard the wildlife habitat became another rallying point for the activists. The Yellow Butterfly Festival, intended to promote the awareness for the valley, thus took on a distinctively cultural flavor, while being imbued with ecological values (Hou 2000: 18).

From "Good mountain and good water to leave future generations, good men and good women against the dam" to "Let's sing the mountain songs," the change in slogans also indicated the transformation of the Anti-Dam movement into a broader social, cultural, and environmental movement.[5] Furthermore, it is fundamentally a youth Hakka movement, initiated by a small number of returning college graduates but ultimately carried forward by young people both in and outside Meinung. In recent years, this youth passion found its way to a deeper and more lasting cause. Since 2000, core members of the Meinung People's Association have been engaging earnestly in the operation and curriculum development of their local Chi(shan)-Mei(nung) Community College, wherein they propagate a rural way of life rooted in the daily routine of production, labor, and leisure, and put in practice public discussion and participation in organic agriculture or other ecological issues pertaining to environmental sustainability (Yang 2010: 108). They emphasized the importance of grass-roots democracy and local subjectivity, as ways to respond to the developmental forces both from the Taiwan state and the global market. The involvement in community colleges actually indicated the next phase of civic activism, not just in Meinung but also across the whole of Taiwan (Ku 2005; Yang 2010).

Community-building as state directive

Political changes that occurred during and after the 1990s gave rise to community empowerment projects, which enabled communities to be the new players between the state and society. This, in turn, had an impact on further political development. Grass-roots activists, however, were not the only force highlighting the centrality of "community" and "community-building" in socio-political transformation. Under President Lee Teng-hui's call for Taiwan as "a collective of a shared life" (*shengming gongtong ti* [生命共同體]), the Taiwan government also quickly adopted community-building as a means to forge a new consensus on national identity, as well as to build a new kind of citizenship in the 1990s (Chuang 2005; L. Huang 1995).[6]

Broadly speaking, state-sponsored community development is not a new phenomenon in Taiwan. After the promotion by the United Nations as a strategy to advance the living standard in developing countries, community development was on the Taiwan government's agenda as early as the 1960s. Yet, at that time, community development was under the charge of the Ministry of the Interior, the main mission of which was to improve the physical environment (such as construction of roads, gutters, and community center buildings). It was about public works/infrastructure upgrading but not about prompting community coherence or consensus (Liu 2008: 316–317). The "community" in this context was defined by physical space, and community development was essentially a top-down, government-led operation.

A different government approach toward "community" began to appear in the mid-1990s, when the Council for Cultural Affairs (CCA; now the Ministry of Culture) championed an Integrated Community-Building Program. Enacted in 1994, the Integrated Community-Building Program was a state-sponsored community development project that urged local governments to incorporate grass-roots initiatives into their public policy and channeled funds directly to support locally instigated cultural activities (Lü 2002). Similar to grass-roots initiatives, an immediate goal of the Integrated Community-Building Program was to look for local characters in local history. This place-grounded identity was then expected to form the basis of a collective consciousness, which would enable community residents to work together toward common goals. In the words of Chen Chi-nan, a Yale-trained anthropologist and the architect of the Integrated Community-Building Program, who later served as the CCA Minister,

Community empowerment represents a shift of thinking mode. Starting from making a new person to making a new society and a new country, it is a quiet revolution. Community empowerment emphasizes the spirit of participation of citizens … let the communities take the lead and propose their future by showing concern for their local environment, and then the provision from government budgets will follow.[7]

The CCA soon launched four anchor projects under the umbrella Integrated Community-Building Program—"Building Public Spaces for Performance and Exhibition," "Preserving and Renovating Traditional Cultural Spaces," "Building Local Museums," and "Developing Community Cultural Activities"—and the central government of Taiwan budgeted 12.6 billion New Taiwan Dollars (about US$382 million) for the planning and implementation of these initiatives (Huang and Hsu 2011: 136). At this stage, the emphasis of the Integrated Community-Building Program was placed on "indigenization" or "rediscovering local histories," from which various forms of government-funded community activism or community-based projects flourished (Lü 2002; Tseng 2013). Community became a place where the innovative top-down (state) and bottom-up (society) forces encountered each other (Huang and Hsu 2011: 136). Quickly, however, the CCA took its cue from the Machizukuri (community-building) Movement in Japan and added "Revitalizing Local Cultural Industries" to the Integrated Community-Building agenda. This was partly propelled by the government's need for a focus point to rally for community building, especially in the countryside. The Machizukuri Movement, which is frequently applied for rural economic revitalization by inspiring/mobilizing local people to participate in value-added craft productions, innovative cultural industries, and tourism, seemed to provide an ideal model to emulate, as rural areas in Taiwan are deeply affected by similar forces of economic globalization and liberalization (Huang and Hsu 2011: 136–137). As a result, economic outputs generated by community cultures became a major concern of government-sponsored community projects (C. Wang *et al.* 2011). The revival of local historical-cultural heritage was no longer merely for self-esteem but for upgrading the place; it was turned into a venue of money making. Politically, however, it was also expected that such a community-based economy would revitalize the solidarity and reciprocity amongst local populations with shared concerns—hence, the advance of civic engagement in public and communal affairs (Huang and Hsu 2011: 140–141).

A full prescription of community empowerment as the remedy for local economies—and, vice versa, local economic revitalization as an approach to community empowerment—did not happen until central Taiwan was hit by a major earthquake on September 21, 1999, which claimed nearly 3,000 lives and took down tens of thousands of houses. As part of the government's disaster relief effort, the CCA soon incorporated the reconstruction work into the Integrated Community-Building Program, and engaged a large number of professionals—including architects, planners, social workers, and community organizers—for a wide range of services. These professionals introduced new practices such as ecotourism and organic farming into some of the rural communities hard hit by the earthquake, which were subsequently emulated by other cities and townships (Huang and Hsu 2011: 137).[8] The tragic event of the earthquake hence also became an occasion to present—and test—the strength of community organizing in Taiwan. Amongst these post-earthquake reconstruction endeavors, the Tau-Mi Ecological Community, the first of its kind in Taiwan, is considered to be one of the most successful and now serves as a model example of community development.

The (Re)construction of the Tau-Mi Ecological Community

The experience of the Tau-Mi Ecological Community, the Taiwanese anthropologist Shaw-wu Jung suggests, is "the result of the people making sense of their subjectivities as political agents as well as recipients of the government's privileges [particularly in terms of funding], a result of at once a historical-cultural growth and a rational-ethical creation" (2012: 35). This characterization, I would argue, is not limited to post-earthquake community reconstruction, but depicts Taiwan's community movement in relation to the state.

Today's Tau-mi is famous for its fresh air and rich natural environment. However, this has not always been the case. Before the September 21 earthquake in 1999 destroyed most of its farmlands, Tau-mi was an agricultural village in decline and it was losing its population to urban areas with a more promising job market. An unintended consequence of this economic and demographic marginality was that the village had come to be surrounded by a vast span of undeveloped wetland, which functions as a repository of diverse ecological resources (Jung 2016: 516). A study conducted by the nearby Endemic Species Research Center, a government-affiliated research facility, reported that Tau-mi has nineteen of the roughly twenty-nine amphibian species recorded on Taiwan. It is also home to seven kinds of dragonfly and several protected reptiles. This rich biodiversity inspired community activists from the New Homeland Foundation, a nationally renowned organization for its efforts to preserve and promote local cultures that was enlisted to assist the reconstruction effort, to develop the idea of community-based ecotourism. The New Homeland activists were excited about the prospect. For them, community-based ecotourism provided a viable economic strategy for which every local person was a stakeholder, while, at the same time, it would create a new public virtue of environmental sustainability and a new vision for the village to be the custodian of a biodiverse ecosystem. Ecotourism also fits the global discourse on climate change that has taken a strong hold in Taiwan, in which "eco" everything is a new fashion in the popular culture (Jung 2016: 517). As the post-industrial urbanization created a strong market for domestic tourism, rural villages turned orchards and farms into places where city residents could go and spend some leisure time doing bird (or small wildlife) watching, picking fruits and vegetables, or picnicking (Jung 2016: 519). Ecotourism seemed to present an ideal solution to everybody in the Tau-mi reconstruction.

To put the idea of ecotourism in practice, a village self-organizing association was established with the help of the New Homeland Foundation. This association was to give the community as a whole more control over the development and management of its ecosystem, as the community would share most of the profits obtained from tourism (Jung 2016: 517). Training classes were given to interested villagers to broaden their knowledge about local flora and fauna. These training sessions were not only to heighten the residents' awareness about their unique natural environment but, more crucially, to prepare them to become certified local guides for eco-tours in the village (New Homeland Foundation 2004: 17). Since 1999, Tau-mi has been undergoing major changes to transform itself into an eco- and tourist-friendly space. Low-impact living, water treatment plants, permaculture, and ecological buildings were introduced. Environmentally harmful betel-nut cultivation was abandoned, and in its place came cedar trees. Local agricultural production has been attuned to tourism and educational purposes. The wetlands are now reserved for producing and maintaining a stock of frogs and fireflies—the trademarks of Tau-mi as an eco-village (Jung 2016: 517–518). All of these transformations have won praise from the media and the public and attracted a considerable amount of tourists. Today, tourism and real estate are the two dominant industries in the village, whose hills are now occupied by many Western-style bed-and-breakfast hotels originally started by local villagers but increasingly bought out or established by outside owners and investors.

Civil society and Taiwan's state–society dynamics

The new identity of Tau-mi as a place rich with cultural and natural resources has also changed local residents' notion about their own village. Even though the government (through the Integrated Community-Building Program funding) continues to play a strong role in Tau-mi's reconstruction effort, ecotourism indeed provides a vehicle for local civic organizing and participation. People are genuinely engaged in village affairs, and frequently voice their opinions at the village association's meetings—something unthinkable merely a decade ago. The Tau-mi example, therefore, raises a fundamental question about state–society relationship in the practice of civil society. It sheds light on the fact that civil society is not necessarily constituted against the state, but rather a product of historical conditions embedded in the ever-changing sociopolitical dynamics of a particularly locality.

Revealed in the case of Tau-mi is the impact of the decades-long authoritarian legacy on the trajectory of civil society in Taiwan as a newly democratized society. The authoritarian state of Taiwan was far reaching into many aspects of local society, and it maintained its ruling legitimacy through intricate webs of social networks (Mattlin 2011). Local politicians/factions were co-opted by the state with extensive local patronage arrangements. Subsidy upon subsidy was given to local communities as a means to ensure their support of—or compliance with—the government. This history of state–society relationship has a profound impact on the nature of political subjectivity specific to civil society. Immediately, the expansive control of the authoritarian state has made it hard for any post-martial law civic organizing to be entirely independent from the state. The government continues to hold much power over local, community, or non-profit associations through laws and regulations (Ku 2012: 25–43). Consequently, while post-authoritarian citizenship in Taiwan has been increasingly characterized by the citizens' claims on rights, the claims often call for the active involvement—if not direction intervention—of the government. The effectiveness of the state continues to be assessed by its ability and willingness to respond to the citizens' requests. The community-building in Tau-mi thus illustrates the inadequacy of conceptualizing civil society formation as a zero-sum game between the state and society. Rather, it should be considered as a co-production between them (Ho 2012).[9]

The Tau-mi case raises an important issue vis-à-vis the market as well. Initially, local residents came together to work on the reconstruction effort based on their shared communal bonds. Over time, the emphasis on tourist consumption as a central reconstruction strategy gradually turned the community into a business under which villagers began to define their friends and neighbors as business partners. Furthermore, the forces of commodification inevitably led to greater class and economic differences, especially with the influx of outsider investments. As a result, paradoxically, the more the villagers are encouraged to participate in village affairs, the more community-building becomes entrepreneurial in nature (Jung 2016: 522).

Urban community-building as place-making in the global context

Initially, a major distinction existed between community building in rural and urban Taiwan. In the countryside where both manufacturing industries and agriculture are in decline, local economic development is the most important goal of community empowerment. In cities, however, community organizing is often prompted by concerns over the breakdown of communities engendered by Taiwan's rapid urbanization or forces of globalization. Since the 1980s, one has observed urban social mobilization over causes such as fighting for quality supply of collective consumption, contesting against NIMBY facilities, and resisting government land acquisition under the decree of eminent domain, or cleaning up illegal squatter settlements (S. Huang

2012). The root of the mobilization was not necessarily cultural in nature. However, when community-building that emphasized local cultural and identity formation grew into a widely accepted public discourse, culture also became the cause of many urban community movements—at least strategically—after the 1990s. This is in and of itself practical, given the larger socio-political context of Taiwan, in which culture provides a highly emotional and legitimate reason for citizen struggles. Yet, along with the transformation of the basis of urban social movements came the soaring international competition between cities (Jou, Hansen, and Wu 2011; Jou, Clark, and Chen 2016). Facing this new stage of global economic development, municipal administrations in Taiwan often support, cooperate, or comply with community organizing, not because it is a right thing to do, but because "culture" has become a valuable commodity (C. Wang 2010). City governments have sought to reutilize historical buildings or cultural assets to boost local economies and revitalize declined neighborhoods. This often has the effect of raising local real estate prices, leading to the outcome of gentrification. Subsequently, the goal of urban community movements conflates with the government's place-making effort, to the extent that cultural production of space for economic purposes constantly takes precedence over civic concerns and citizens' public engagement (W-I. Lin 2015). This predicament is exemplified by the two cases of community organizing in Wan-hua District of Taipei City discussed below.

Culture, heritage, and citizens' movements: Dali and Bopiliao in Wan-hua, Taipei

The "Dali Community" (大理社區) was not an administrative designation, but only came into existence as a result of civic mobilization in the late 1990s. Wan-hua District—or Monga, as it is historically known—where the Dali Community is located, was one of the earliest developed areas in Taipei in the eighteenth century. However, the lack in public investment in the next century or so made Wan-hua one of the stagnant districts in Taipei in the late twentieth century. As the city center shifted to other parts of Taipei, Wan-hua no longer carried the past glamor, but came to be known as a place of urban deterioration, drawing populations such as gangsters, prostitutes, or the homeless, deemed unfavorable by the general public. When the construction plan of an electrical substation was revealed in the early 1990s, residents adjacent to the planned facility organized and protested. As a result, the plan to build an electrical substation was stopped and the "Dali Community" began to take shape. Later, Dali residents organized another major rally when the government announced that land in the neighborhood owned by Taiwan Sugar Corporation (a semi-state enterprise) would be developed into a large nursing home through public-private partnership. Several concerns prompted the residents' resistance: the decision that would favor certain private investors was made without the input of local people; and such a decision would further exacerbate the negative image of the community as a place of an aging population and declining economy. Also, a large nursing home would bring in several hundred more occupants to an already crowded neighborhood that lacked sufficient public amenities. What the local community wanted was the government's reinvestment in public facilities that could be used by all residents on a daily basis (Hsia *et al.* 2002). Yet, this objection was understood as being motivated by "anti-social welfare" selfishness by the government and reported as such by the media respectively. Only when the community, with the help of urban planning academics from National Taiwan University, reshaped their focus and reframed their resistance as a struggle to preserve the historical memory of Taiwan's sugar industry, did they transcend their concerns and gain more support for their cause.

The government responded accordingly. The land of Taiwan Sugar on which the nursing home was planned was transformed into a community park. The warehouse and train platform used for sugar cane transportation on the land were designated as historical architectures and preserved on their original site. Ultimately, the historical relations between the Dali Community, Taiwan Sugar Corporation, and Taiwan's sugar industry were articulated through the community movement and commemorated in the newly established community park (Hsia *et al.* 2002). This seemed to be a win–win solution, as the revitalized historical memory advocated by the progressive academics was embodied in the much-needed public space demanded by the community.[10]

Nevertheless, the government was planning for more. In the late 2000s, the Taipei City government allocated more money to upgrade the community park into a Tangbu Culture Park—primarily a space for Taiwanese traditional performing arts—and invited Ming Hwa Yuan Arts & Cultural Groups, a renowned Taiwanese Opera troupe, to be resident at the park.[11] This move dovetailed with the city's master plan to develop Taipei into a "creative city." The invigorated cultural image of the neighborhood seemed to provide a perfect foundation upon which new and creative ideas could be developed—and traditional cultural elements could be reinvented—into viable cultural assets (Lin and Chiu 2014: 102). Consequently, the community park ceases to be a public space enjoyed by people in the area and becomes a space for tourism and cultural industry. Yet, the evolving nature of the community park does not seem to be opposed by local residents, as the "creative city" projects a positive image of progress and economic prospects longed for by the people in this struggling neighborhood (Lin and Chiu 2014: 103).

Likewise, the Bopiliao movement—also in Wan-hua District—started as an anti-demolition protest against the municipal government's land acquisition project for the expansion of a nearby elementary school. The affected land was reserved for the school expansion by the Japanese colonial government in the early twentieth century. Since then, however, the city had grown substantially and private citizens had squatted on the land for both commercial and residential purposes. After gaining support from progressive academics, the Bopiliao movement turned to advocating historical preservation. Similar to the Dali community movement, the significance of Bopiliao in Taipei's early pioneering history was emphasized. Culture was used as a strategy to resist the official urban planning, turning an anti-acquisition protest into a movement for heritage production (C. Wang 2013: 677). The community-based Association for the Promotion of Historical Preservation of Bopiliao actively engaged in historical inquiry, oral history interviews, and collecting old photographs and other information to assert the historical-cultural values of the area. To avoid the impression of obstructing school expansion due to private interests, a land trust concept was also suggested, so that the local residents could be endowed with the right to engage in heritage management (Chen 2003). In the end, the Taipei City government did stop the demolition and preserve part of the historical buildings advocated by the community association. However, the city government also removed the resident squatters according to the original plan but renamed the area "the Bopiliao Historic District." Today, Bopiliao is becoming a major tourist attraction and it is a popular destination for period film or television production in Taipei City (L. Huang 2014).

"Local currency system" as an alternative: the examples of Gardens City and Beitou

Yet, community empowerment is a reflexive process (W. Wang 2011). While the increasing commodification of culture poses a challenge to the prospect of community-building in urban areas (just like in the countryside), grass-roots activists also work hard to find alternatives not based on the logic of capital accumulation for future community development (Hou 2013).

The introduction of a "local currency system" (LCS) in some communities in metropolitan Taipei presents such an endeavor.

LCSs are local currency systems driven by local circuits of consumption, exchange, and production in primarily developed economies such as the United Kingdom (Lee *et al.* 2004: 595). Some Taiwanese community activists are eager advocates for LCSs because their existence provides the (admittedly limited) possibilities of local socio-economic self-determination and organization. Gardens City—a residential neighborhood in New Taipei City—is one of the communities currently practicing a local currency system. Residents in Gardens City use "Flower Currencies" to trade assorted errands, such as help with children, cutting hair, cleaning water towers, repairing computers, or teaching English or Taiwanese. The Flower Currency system is not merely about economic transactions but also about local solutions to an ever-encroaching global economy. More importantly, it is about creating trust and social capital through circulating needs and services amongst community members, which, ultimately and hopefully, would lead to the (re)construction of social relations central to community empowerment in Gardens City (W. Wang 2011: 20–21).[12]

Another LCS example is the Time Bank shared amongst various community organizations in the Beitou District of Taipei City. Similar to the "Flower Currency" system, the Time Bank is a mechanism through which services or objects are exchanged, based on the principle of reciprocity—and social networks and capital can be created—amongst members in the community. In Beitou, however, the Time Bank is not the first attempt toward community building, but the latest step of a decades-long process of community empowerment. Beitou, like Wan-hua, is an old district of Taipei with a long and prominent history. It has been a popular hot springs resort area since the Japanese colonial period in the late nineteenth century. Starting with a series of historical preservation movements in 1995, grass-roots activists have been working non-stop toward creating a vibrant community movement in Beitou. Through their efforts, the Beitou Hot Springs Public Bath, in danger of being demolished, was successfully preserved in 1998. This was a significant accomplishment of community organizing, not simply because the Public Bath was an important symbol of public life in historic Beitou. The continuous operation of such a public amenity offers citizens a budget place to enjoy Beitou's famed hot springs amid the pricy hotels and resorts in this rapidly gentrifying area. The small streams and ditches around the public bath also provide a natural gathering place when people sit down to dip their feet and chat. Step by step, active residents in Beitou formed a Peitou [Beitou] Cultural Foundation, drafted a Beitou Community Charter, engaged in public policy planning and deliberations, founded a Beitou Community College, established a Beitou Public Assembly Hall, organized "Beitou-ology" panel discussions, and held Citizens' Forums for Community Empowerment.[13] The Time Bank is the most recent endeavor, for which the Beitou Cultural Foundation is raising funds and trying to join forces with community groups elsewhere to create a Taiwanese Alliance of Time Banks (W. Wang 2011: 21–22).

Conclusion

After a decade of intense street confrontations, social movements in the form of protests and demonstrations started to ease in Taiwan in the early 1990s. This does not suggest the demise of civil society, however. Rather, it indicates a new phase of civic activism, as many social movement activists began to devote themselves to community organizing. Social forces did not vanish but have been transformed. Community involvement has become a process for building a vibrant civil society and, in turn, the ideal that embodies civil society, which people are inspired to uphold (Jung 2012: 25). Since the lifting of martial law in the late 1980s, Taiwan has experienced an exponential growth of non-profit, civic associations with diverse areas of focus, such as ecology, urban design and built environment, health and wellness, economy, education, religion, history, and culture. Many (if not all) of these associations have an active interest in public affairs engagement amongst their memberships (Ku 2012). Furthermore, through the support of the Integrated Community-Building Program and subsequent government campaigns, various social movement organizations have also transformed themselves into legitimate players in the national arena and at the policy level (Ho 2012: 411).

Community mobilization and revitalization is deepening the process of democratization in Taiwan. As shown in the examples presented above, many of the community empowerment projects are aimed at fundamental transformations of Taiwan's civil society by focusing on changing cultural values and social relations at the very grass-roots level. At the center of this revitalization movement is locality and local residents, who are often overlooked by institutionalized social movements that lack the capacity to incorporate these elements into their organizations (Chuang 2005: 400). However, also revealed in the examples given in this chapter is the complex relationship between the state and society. The course of community-building in Taiwan highlights the fact that the practice of civil society must confront the pervasive and ongoing changes in the framework of state–local interactions (Jung 2012: 22). Furthermore, as Taiwan is increasingly incorporated into the global economic process, economic development that was started as a means, ultimately, has become the goal of community-building. Community-building is, therefore, a constant struggle. It should be understood as a process, not merely as a consequence.

Notes

1 Looking forward, Weller (1999) maintains that, although such groups do not conform to the concept of civil society in its usual sense, they may be developed into alternative vehicles for political transformation; they could be mobilized into means to a democratic political culture.

2 For details, see the Hsin Kang Foundation of Culture and Education website, www.hkfce.org.tw/.

3 The Wild Lily Student Movement was a student protest for democracy in 1990. It constituted a six-day sit-in demonstration on the Chiang Kai-shek Memorial Square in Taipei, which successfully pressured the then-President Lee Teng-hui to accelerate democratic institutional reforms, including terminating the Period of Mobilization for the Suppression of Communist Rebellion (which gave legitimacy to Taiwan's prolonged martial law), dissolving the National Assembly, changing the way members of the Legislative Yuan were elected, and, ultimately, realizing the direct election of the president.

4 For details, see the Meinung People's Association Facebook Page, www.facebook.com/mpa1994.

5 The slogans (in Chinese) are, respectively, "好山好水留子孫, 好男好女反水庫," and "我等就來唱山歌."

6 Lee Teng-hui was the first Republic of China president of Taiwanese descent. His presidency, which covered the years from 1988 to 2000, played a critical role in reshaping Taiwan's state apparatus, both substantially and symbolically, in the post-martial law era.

7 The original texts came from Chen Chi-nan (1999) "Talking about the Sustainability of Taiwan from the Community Empowerment," in *The Handbook of Good Neighbors* (Taiwan, Tainan: Rural–Urban Foundation). The translation is from Huang and Hsu (2011: 135).

8 Once again, the CCA learned from the Japanese experience of engaging NGOs in the reconstruction after the Hanshin earthquake. The fact that a Paper Church designed by the Japanese architect Shigeru Ban, which once stood in the Hanshin Earthquake Reconstruction Area, now stands in Tao-mi attests to the close ties between Japanese and Taiwanese community activists and professionals (Huang and Hsu 2011: 138). For details, see the New Homeland Foundation website, www.homeland.org.tw.

9 Nevertheless, whether the call for state involvement in community self-organizing is a transitional phenomenon pertaining to a newly democratized society like Taiwan or a lasting phenomenon remains to be seen.

10 This is by no means to indicate that there was only consensus but not conflict within the community or between the community and planning professionals. Scholarly works on community-building, such

as those cited in this chapter, all show that the process of community-building is also a process of consensus building. This is certainly the case of the Dali community movement, in which the function of the community park has been continually debated amongst all parties of interest.

11 For details, see the Taipei City Department of Cultural Affairs website, http://english.culture.gov. taipei/ct.asp?xItem=42756808&ctNode=30860&mp=119002.
12 For details, see the Gardens City Facebook page, https://zh-tw.facebook.com/gardenscity.
13 For details, see the Peitou Cultural Foundation website, www.ptcf.org.tw.

Suggested readings

Ho Ming-sho, and Hsiu-hsin Lin, eds. 2011. *Shehui Yundong de Niandai: Ershi Nian Lia De Taiwan Gongmin Shehui* [*The Era of Social Movements: Civil Society in Taiwan in the Past Two Decades*]. Taipei: Qunxue (in Chinese).

Hou, Jeffrey, ed. 2013. *Fanzao Chengshi: Taiwan Feidianxing Chengshi Guihua* [*City Remaking*]. Taipei: Zuoan (in Chinese).

Huang, Liling, and Jinn-yuh Hsu. 2011. From Cultural Building, Economic Revitalization to Local Partnership? The Changing Nature of Community Mobilization in Taiwan. *International Planning Studies* 16(2): 127–146.

Lü, Hsin-yi. 2002. *The Politics of Locality: Making a Nation of Communities in Taiwan*. London and New York: Routledge.

References

Chen, Fu-wei. 2003. Shuo Yige Bopiliao de Gushi: Fenxi Bengjie de Dushi Baocun Lunshu [To Tell a Story About Bopiliao: Analyzing the Collapsed Urban Conservation Discourse]. MA thesis, National Tsing Hua University (in Chinese).

Chuang, Ya-chung. 2005. Place, Identity, and Social Movements: Shequ and Neighborhood Organizing in Taipei City. *Positions: East Asia Cultures Critique* 13(2): 379–410.

Chuang, Ya-chung. 2013. *Democracy on Trial: Social Movements and Cultural Politics in Post-authoritarian Taiwan*. Hong Kong: The Chinese University Press.

Chun, Allen. 1994. From Nationalism to Nationalizing: Cultural Imagination and State Formation in Postwar Taiwan. *The Australian Journal of Chinese Affairs* 31: 49–69.

Chun, Allen. 1996. Discourses of Identity in the Changing Spaces of Public Culture in Taiwan, Hong Kong, and Singapore. *Theory, Culture & Society* 13(1): 51–75.

Ho, Ming-sho. 2010. Understanding the Trajectory of Social Movements in Taiwan, 1980–2010. *Journal of Current Chinese Affairs* 39(3): 3–22.

Ho, Ming-sho. 2012. Sponsoring Civil Society: State and Community Movement in Taiwan. *Sociological Inquiry* 82(3): 404–423.

Ho, Ming-sho, and Hsiu-hsin Lin, eds. 2011. *Shehui Yundong de Niandai: Ershi Nian Lia de Taiwan Gongmin Shehui* [*The Era of Social Movements: Civil Society in Taiwan in the Past Two Decades*]. Taipei: Qunxue (in Chinese).

Hou, Jeffrey. 2000. Cultural Production of Environmental Activism: Two Cases in Southern Taiwan. Paper presented at the Fifth Annual Conference on the History and Culture of Taiwan, UCLA, October 12–15.

Hou, Jeffrey, ed. 2013. *Fanzao Chengshi: Taiwan Feidianxing Chengshi Guihua* [*City Remaking*]. Taipei: Zuoan (in Chinese).

Hsia, Chu-joe, Lucie Cheng, Hsing-chun Chen, and Po-fen Tai. 2002. Chaoxiang Shimin Chengshi: Taipei Dalijie Shequ Yundong [Toward a Citizens' City: The Dali Community Movement of Taipei]. *Taiwan: A Radical Quarterly in Social Studies* 46: 141–172 (in Chinese).

Hsiao, Michael Hsin-huang. 1990. Emerging Social Movements and the Rise of a Demanding Civil Society in Taiwan. *The Australian Journal of Chinese Affairs* 24: 163–180.

Huang, Liling. 1995. Xinguojia Jianguo Zhong Shequ Jiaose de Zhuanbian: Shequ Gongtongti de Lunshu Fenxi [Changing Roles of Community Amid the Construction of a New Nation State]. MA thesis, National Taiwan University (in Chinese).

Huang, Liling. 2014. The Uneasy Partnership and Contested Meanings of Urban Form: Examining the Policies of Urban Regeneration in Bangka, Taipei. In *Globalization and New Intra-Urban Dynamics in*

Asian Cities. Natacha Aveline-Dubachh, Sue-ching Jou, and Hsin-huang Michael Hsiao, eds. Pp. 65–99. Taipei: National Taiwan University Press.

Huang, Liling, and Jinn-yuh Hsu. 2011. From Cultural Building, Economic Revitalization to Local Partnership?: The Changing Nature of Community Mobilization in Taiwan. *International Planning Studies* 16(2): 127–146.

Huang, Sun Quan. 2012. *Luse Tuituji: Jiuling Niandai Taibei de Weijian, Gongyuan, Ziran Fangdichan Yu Zhiduhua Dijing* [*Green Bulldozer: The Squatters, Parks, Nature Estate and Institutionalized Landscape in 1990s Taipei*]. Taipei: Pozhoubao (in Chinese).

Jessop, Bob. 2002. *The Future of the Capitalist State*. Cambridge: Polity Press.

Jou, Sue-ching, Eric Clark, and Hsiao-wei Chen. 2016. Gentrification and Revanchist Urbanism in Taipei? *Urban Studies* 53(3): 560–576.

Jou, Sue-ching, Anders Lund Hansen, and Hsin-ling Wu. 2011. Accumulation by Dispossession and Neoliberal Urban Planning: "Landing" the Mega-Projects in Taipei. In *Contradictions of Neoliberal Planning: Cities, Policies, and Politics*. Tuna Tasan-Kok and Guy Baeten, eds. Pp. 151–171. New York: Springer.

Jung, Shaw-wu. 2012. Building Civil Society on Rubble: Citizenship and the Politics of Culture in Taiwan. *Critique of Anthropology* 32(1): 20–42.

Jung, Shaw-wu. 2016. Landscapes and Governance: Practicing Citizenship in the Construction of an Eco-village in Taiwan. *Citizenship Studies* 20(3–4): 510–526.

Ku, Chung-hwa. 2005. *Jiedu Shehuili: Taiwan de Xuexi Shehui Yu Gongmin Shehui* [*Reading Social Force: Learning Society and Civil Society in Taiwan*]. Taipei: Zuoan (in Chinese).

Ku, Chung-hwa. 2012. *Gongmin Shehui, Zhuozhuang* [*Civil Society*]. Taipei: Kaixue wenhua (in Chinese).

Lee, Anru. 2007. Southern Green Revolution: Urban Environmental Activism in Kaohsiung, Taiwan. *City and Society* 19(1): 114–138.

Lee, Roger, Andrew Leyshon, Theresa Aldridge, Jane Tooke, Colin Williams, and Nigel Thrift. 2004. Making Geographies and Histories?: Constructing Local Circuits of Value. *Environment and Planning D: Society and Space* 22(4): 595–617.

Lin, Hsiu-hsin. 2011. Xingang shequ yundong [The Hsin Kang Social Movement]. In *Shehui Yundong de Niandai* [*The Age of Social Movements*]. Ming-sho Ho and Hsiu-hsin Lin, eds. Pp. 374–410. Taipei: Qunxue (in Chinese).

Lin, Wei-ping. 2016. Why Build a Temple?: The Materialization of New Community Ideals in the Demilitarized Islands between China and Taiwan. *Material Religion* DOI: 10.1080/17432200. 2016.1237050.

Lin, Wen-I. 2015. Wenhui Chuangyi Daoxiang Dushi Zaisheng, "Xin" Dushi Zhili de Shijian Ji Quehan: Yi Dihua Jiequ Weili [Cultural Creativity-Led Regeneration, Exercise of "New" Urban Governance and Its Discontents: A Case Study of Dihua Neighborhood in Taipei]. *Dushi Yu Jihua* [*Journal of City and Planning*] 42(4): 423–454 (in Chinese).

Lin, Wen-i, and Shu-yi Chiu. 2014. Houzhengzhi de Shequ Dongyuan Yu Gongshi Jiangou: Yige Taibei Shequ Wenhua Jiangou de Anli [Community Activation and Consensus Building in the Post-Political Condition: A Case Study of Community Culture Construction in Taipei]. *Dili Xuebao* [*Journal of Geographical Science*] 72: 85–109 (in Chinese).

Liu Li-wei. 2008. Shequ Yingzao de Fansi [Reflections on Community Empowerment: Consideration of Urban–Rural Differences, Perspectives of Urban Development, and Exploration of the Bottom-Up Concept]. *Dushi Yu Jihua* [*Journal of City and Planning*] 35(4): 313–338 (in Chinese).

Lü, Hsin-yi. 2002. *The Politics of Locality: Making a Nation of Communities in Taiwan*. London and New York: Routledge.

Mattlin, Mikael. 2011. *Politicized Society: The Long Shadow of Taiwan's One-party Legacy*. Copenhagen: NIAS Press.

New Homeland Foundation. 2004. *Stories of Tau-Mi Village*. Nantou: County Cultural Center.

Rowen, Ian. 2015. Inside Taiwan's Sunflower Movement: Twenty-Four Days in a Student-Occupied Parliament, and the Future of the Region. *Journal of Asian Studies* 74(1): 5–21.

Skoggard, Ian. 2016. *The Indigenous Dynamic in Taiwan's Postwar Development: Religious and Historical Roots of Entrepreneurship*. New York and London: Routledge.

Tseng Shu-cheng. 2013. *Taiwan de Shequ Yingzao* [*Community-Building in Taiwan*]. Taipei: Yuantsu wenhua (in Chinese).

Wang, Chih-Hung. 2010. Dushi Shehui Yundong de Xianxing Wenhua Zhuanxiang? 1990 Niandai Qijin de Taibei Jingyan [The Manifest Cultural Turn for Urban Social Movements? Taipei Experience, 1990s-2000s]. *Jianzhu Yu Chengxiang Xuebao* [*Journal of Building and Planning*] 16: 39–64 (in Chinese).

Wang, Chih-hung. 2013. Heritage Formation and Cultural Governance: The Production of Bopiliao Historic District, Taipei. *International Journal of Heritage Studies* 19(7): 679–691.

Wang, Chih-hung, Yi-ling Chen, Su-yue Li, Yu-hsien Su, Ping-lin Li, Chia-yi Li, Pei-ling Chao, Chi-yu Kuo, Tsai-lun Cheng, and Li-ben Chang. 2011. *Wenhua Zhili Yu Kongjian Zhengzhi* [*Cultural Governance and the Politics of Space*]. Taipei: Qunxue (in Chinese).

Wang, Chih-ming. 2017. The Future that Belongs to Us: Affective Politics, Neoliberalism and the Sunflower Movement. *International Journal of Cultural Studies* DOI: 10.1177/1367877916683824.

Wang, Li-jung. 2004. Multiculturalism in Taiwan. *International Journal of Cultural Policy* 10(3): 301–318.

Wang, Wen-cheng. 2011. Fanshenxing de Shequ Yingzao: Shijianxing de Dilixue Xiangxiang [Reflexive Community Empowerment: Geographical Imagination of Practice]. *Dushi Yu Jihua* [*Journal of City and Planning*] 38(1): 1–29 (in Chinese).

Weller, Robert. 1999. *Alternate Civility: Democracy and Culture in China and Taiwan*. Boulder, CO: Westview.

Yang, Hung-jen. 2010. Yi Shequ Weiming [In the Name of Community]. In *Zhixu Binfen de Niandai, 1990–2010* [*An Era of Multiple Orders, 1990–2010*]. Jieh-min Wu, Yun Fan, and Er-der Ku, eds. Pp. 87–98. Taipei: Zuoan (in Chinese).

6

MONGOLIA

Dulam Bumochir[1]

Import machine

The Mongolian terms *ardchilal* (democracy) and *irgenii niigem* (civil society) have become key terminologies in public and political life for portraying relationships of the state, government, administration, legacy, and policy on one side and national and international non-state, donor, development, aid, environment, conservation, and human rights organizations, associations, societies, unions (broadly implying people), and the society on the other. The word *ardchilal* literally means "people-ization" and *irgenii niigem* literally means "civil or citizens' society" and, yet, there is no consistent definition and understanding regarding the content and application of these words and people constantly discuss, debate, and argue what they really mean when using these words (cf. Chuluunjav 1997). The excessive employment and manifold application of the words make it necessary to deal with these words in order to understand and maybe to take part in social and political dialogues; they also create doubt, uncertainty, obscuration, hesitation, and confusion, both about the content of these words and about the people who employ and "own" (I will return to the issue of "owning democracy" later) these terms, namely, the Democratic Party of Mongolia. This is not a unique picture in the study of democracy and civil society in the wider world. This situation can be best explained in relation to the Western roots of these words and their exportation to the rest of the world.

Civil society, both as a philosophical concept and as a social organization, developed originally in the West in the eighteenth, nineteenth, and early twentieth centuries (Cohen and Arato 1992: 83–174; Ferguson [1767] 1995; Gramsci 1971; Hall 1995: 3–7; Hann 1996: 3–6; Hegel [1821] 1991; Keane 1988: 35–67; Lewis 2002: 569–573; Nord 2000: xiii–xxxii; Seligman 1992: 15–99; Tocqueville [1835] 1994; Torsello 2012: 29–33). Then, "civil society" "withered" (Keane 1988: 5) and remained "forgotten" (Lewis 2002: 573) in Europe for a while, until the middle of the twentieth century when civil society started to "return" (Bell 1989: 56) to, "revive" (Cohen and Arato 1992: 15–18; Lewis 2002: 573; Torsello 2012: 33–35) in, "awaken" (Bermeo 2000: 237) in, and "re-emerge" (Lewis 2002: 573) in different parts of Europe, which was a "renaissance of civil society" (Keane 1988: 1–2; Seligman 1992: 2). However, in the non-West, civil society was not "returning"; instead, the West was exporting it (Amarsanaa, Baas-ansuren, and Zolzaya 2013: 5; Comaroff and Comaroff 1999: 5; Hall 1995: 22, 25; Hann 1996: 2; Sampson 1996: 119; Torsello 2012: 28). The Western export does not end with bringing "civil society" to the non-West. John A. Hall (1995: 22), Robert Jenkins (2001: 252), David Lewis (2002: 577–578), Steven Sampson (1996: 122), Janine Wedel (1992: 323), and many others show how civil society organizations served as an "ingredient" and as an instrument of capitalist northern countries in establishing and developing a universal culture of democracy. In this way, those "civil society" organizations continue to import more of the West. Following those who argue that civil society is a Western export and operate to introduce Western democracy and liberalism, I argue that civil society is a Western exported import machine. Civil society as a machine reorganizes society by importing Western fundamental philosophical principles and concepts of liberalism, democracy, market, governance, and state. This is always done by introducing, advocating, capacity building, lobbying, implanting, and formalizing the so-called global, universal, and international laws, acts, conventions, ethics, structures, and standards that contribute to maintaining liberalism and democracy.

To develop this argument of an import machine, I follow James Ferguson's (1994) discussion on international development projects in Africa and borrow his key term "anti-politics machine"; I modify it as "import machine" to explain what civil society does. Unlike Ferguson's "anti-politics," my interest is not in the "suspension of politics" (Ferguson 1994: 180) but in the "import." The development projects in Africa (Ferguson's "anti-politics machine") and "civil society" in Mongolia are both transnational apparatuses (or "machines") and import Western culture to different extents.[2] What interests me are the "civil society organizations" in Mongolia—if not all, then most of them—that import Western concepts and practices in the name of international, universal, and global democracy and liberalism. This is not new since "we expect democracy to be married to civil practices" and the "key meanings of civil society are effectively present in the concepts of democracy and liberalism" (Hall 1995: 2, 26).

Detailed ethnography shows that environmental protestors often reject the name "civil society," although they are often addressed as and considered to be civil society by the media and public discourses in Mongolia. They attempt to present and develop an alternative form of citizens' activism that is original and historic to Mongolia and cannot be mistaken for the Western exported form of civil society. This is mainly because most of the "civil society" non-governmental organizations (NGOs) in Mongolia import foreign culture, rather than encouraging, promoting, preserving, and reinforcing the nation's traditional culture. A Western-style civil society contributes to the construction of an alternative national identity that is modern, contemporary, liberal, and democratic. However, those who hesitate to employ the word "civil society" are not against "civil society" and "democracy." They simply view the words and concepts such as "democracy" and "civil society" as being possessed and limited by other groups, individuals, and institutions developing and formalizing Western exported standards and constructing the new image of democratic Mongolia. The Western-style "civil society organizations" (*irgenii niigmiin baiguullaga*) and Democratic Party worked to introduce and develop the understanding of "civil society,"[3] using the name "civil society" by copying the so-called Western style. Therefore, many think that terms such as "democracy" and "civil society" signify the achievements of the Democratic Party and pro-democracy NGOs and organizations. This signification creates certain limits in the use of these terms and concepts and makes nationalist environmental protestors decide not to employ the terms. Hence, I argue that the Democratic Party and Western-style civil society organizations possess and own terms such as "democracy" and "civil society," which prevents nationalist groups and organizations from employing those terms.

While there is increasing engagement, employment, and dramatic expansion of civil society in Mongolia (for the Freedom House survey scale of Mongolian democracy and civil society, see Addleton 2013: 56), very little attention has been paid to the study of civil society, both in

English and in Mongolian, with the exception of a few important works. One of the first is the CIVICUS Civil Society Index report for Mongolia. From 2004 to 2005, the Center for Citizens' Alliance, a Mongolian NGO that functioned as the International Civil Society Forum for Democracy Secretariat, undertook the assessment of the state of civil society in Mongolia using the Civil Society Index (CSI) methodology, which was developed by the international civil society network CIVICUS: World Alliance for Citizen Participation (Center for Citizens' Alliance 2006: 7). While the above work introduces Mongolia's civil society in its entirety and develops a big picture rich in information and data, it lacks a great deal of scholarly engagement and discourse. There is a lack of dialogue between the works of civil society practitioners and scholars in the field of philosophy, sociology, political science, sociology, and law who show an interest in the study of civil society. In 2012, the Institute of Philosophy, Sociology and Law, Mongolian Academy of Sciences, organized a conference under the title "Formation of civil society in Mongolia." The proceeding of the conference (Amarsanaa *et al.* 2013) is the main scholarly handbook of Mongolian civil society. The papers published in the proceeding mostly acknowledge Western philosophy and classic discourses of civil society to discuss the formation of civil society in Mongolia since the 1990s. In this way, both the works allude to either Western practices or philosophy in assessing the formation and state of Mongolia's civil society and reveal challenges and weaknesses needing further achievements. There are other works that do not discuss civil society organizations but focus on movements, activisms, and protests.[4] The Japanese scholar Muneyuki Murai (2012) worked in Mongolia and followed the citizens' movements and political discourses that occurred from the end of 2003 to the end of 2008 and consistently produced reviews, which were later translated into Mongolian and published as a book. The articles on protest movements published by Byambajav Dalaibuyan (2012, 2015), David Sneath (2010), and Caroline Upton (2012, 2013) demonstrate collective identity, identity politics, homeland consciousness, mechanisms of rural protests, local resistance against mining, as the authors' perceptions of grassroots, the network and collaboration between urban and rural movement organizations, etc. None of the above literatures discuss the pre-democratic history and concept of "civil society" in Mongolia and its conflict between local (grass-roots) and global (Western) trajectories in Mongolia. In addition, narratives in the field of democracy indirectly discuss the civil society of Mongolia. I discuss such narratives in detail below.

Owning democracy

Following Mongolian historians, namely, Chuluun Dashdavaa (2003: 56), Sodnomdarjaa Otgonjargal (2003: 159–161), and Bazar Shirendev ([1969] 1999: 337), who claim that the 1921 revolution was a "bourgeois democratic revolution" (*khöröngötnii ardchilsan khuvisgal*), I argue that the origin of Mongolia's Western democracy dates back to the 1920s, not to the 1990s. To contribute to the argument, in the following section, I discuss the articles in the first (1924), second (1940), and third (1960) constitutions of Mongolia, which have been legitimizing democracy since the early 1920s.

It is commonly opined that Mongolia's democracy emerged from the transformation of the so-called "democratic movement" (*ardchilsan khödölgöön*) or "democratic revolution" (*ardchilsan khuvisgal*) in the late 1980s and early 1990s (Fish 1998: 127; Fritz 2008: 770–779; Kaplonski 2004: 48–71; Nordby 1992: 175; Sanders 1992: 520; Severinghaus 1994: 75). For instance, Steven Fish makes the bold statement that "until 1990s Mongolia had no tradition of democracy" (1998: 127). This common idea applies not only to democracy but also to civil society (cf. Center for Citizens' Alliance 2006: 26; Dashpurev 2013: 41, 43; Undarya 2013: 68). Contrary to common opinion, Paula Sabloff (2002: 26) argues that Mongolia's democracy pre-dates the 1989 democratic revolution by 800 years—to the political culture of Chinggis Khan. I do not fully agree with her argument that Chinggis Khan operated a democratic political culture. On the contrary, Andrew F. March poses an interesting question: "Who is managing Genghis [Chinggis] Khan's legacy in Mongolia? How are pro-democracy Mongols claiming Genghis [Chinggis] Khan as a symbol versus Mongols who would use him for an authoritarian solution to the ills of market transition?" (March 2003: 65). For our purposes here, Chinggis Khan is noteworthy because he became essential to the Mongolian understanding of democracy, not because he was democratic, as Sabloff argues, but because contemporary democrats attempt to possess and practice its power over the political concepts left unoccupied by the Revolutionary Party. During the Soviet regime, Chinggis Khan was dismissed by the Revolutionary Party, as was Western democracy. The Revolutionary Party possessed the ideas of "revolution" and "independence" that they brought to Mongolia in 1921. The Democratic Party continued this practice of the Revolutionary Party to own certain achievements and concepts that were important in the history of the Mongols. After 1990, Mongolian democrats took up the abandoned spheres such as the Imperial history of the Mongols, Chinggis Khan, and Western democracy and utilized them to construct their identity, sphere, scope, and mission and a Mongolian understanding of democracy.

In 2012, when the Democratic Party won majority seats in the parliamentary election and occupied the government, they made changes to national holidays; in particular, they cancelled a public holiday that celebrates the first constitution and establishment of the Mongolian People's Republic on November 26, 1924. The media termed the act as the "first constitution debased by democracy"[5] and revealed the democrats' reluctance to recognize the importance of the first constitution, while its contents could be considered the philosophical roots of Western democracy and the "arrival of modern political thoughts of Mongolia."[6] The debasement was not simply against the first constitution but more precisely against the pronouncement of democracy as it appeared before the current democratic leaders. The first constitution can issue an official recognition to the founders of the old Revolutionary Party as the people who started democracy in Mongolia in the early 1920s.

The mission statement at the beginning of the 1992 constitution declares that the people of Mongolia shall build a "humane, civil, and democratic society" (*khümüünleg, irgenii, ardchilsan niigem*), which is clearly the first appearance of the combined word *irgenii niigem* ("civil society") in Mongolia. In the following sections, I argue that this statement and the constitution as a whole are not completely new. Alan J. K. Sanders (1992) analyzes all the four constitutions of Mongolia, of 1924, 1940, 1960, and 1992. Unfortunately, he fails to notice all the articles and statements that pronounced democracy in the previous constitutions and declares the new constitution of 1992 as a "blueprint for democracy." In fact, we find that many of the "humane" and "democratic" features were legitimized in Mongolia long before 1992. The earliest legitimization of the basic features of "civil society," "human right," and "democracy" was the first constitution of the Mongolian People's Republic (MPR), which was approved and declared on November 26, 1924. The first chapter of the constitution "reveals and declares freedom of 'genuine people'" (*jinkhene ardyn erkh chölöög iltgen tunkhaglakh ni*), which can be seen as a form of civil society in early Soviet Mongolia. Further, Article 2 in the first chapter demonstrates the *jinkhene ard*, literally meaning "genuine people," in contrast to *khuuchny ezerkheg khargis* (which means "old tyrannical autocrats" or "foreign and domestic tyrannical autocrats") in Article 5, whose regime needs to be abolished in order to protect the "genuine people." Article 2 also declares the new regime meeting the *yos* etiquette of *jinkhene ard*. There are more "civil society" elements in Articles 6 to 11. For instance, Article 6 declares the freedom of belief and religion; Article 7 permits the freedom of speech, freedom to critique, and freedom to publish; Article 8 allows the organization of public meetings and celebrations; Article 9 speaks of starting an *evlel* "association" and *khorshoo* "companies"; Article 10 emphasizes free education; and Article 11 restricts discrimination based on ethnicity, faith, and gender. Finally, Chapter 7 is dedicated to the declaration of equal rights to vote and be elected. Both Chapter 10 in the amended version of the 1940 constitution and Chapter 7 in the 1960 version further preserved almost all these contents, since its first declaration in 1924, until 1992. In 1960, Article 82 in Chapter 7 issues the right to consolidate (*evlelden negdeh*), and start a political party (*uls töriin nam*) and any other public and/or civil organizations (*olon niitiin baiguullaga*). The article also reveals an older version of the above-mentioned 1992 mission statement that the people of the Mongolian People's Republic shall build a "humane, democratic, and socialist society" (*khümüüünleg, ardchilsan, socialist niigem*). The only difference from the same statement in the 1992 constitution is the removal of the word "socialist," which is replaced with the word "civil." This is a mark of the transformation from Soviet socialism to Western democracy. In this way, the so-called blueprint of Mongolian democracy for Sanders is actually a continuity of the former constitution established in 1924.

Based on the above analysis of legislation, which acknowledges democracy, I argue that by the early 1920s, Mongolia had already formalized the basic concepts and legal environment of civil society and democracy. This is because in the early 1920s, the bourgeois revolutionary leaders copied the model of Great Britain and the West to draft the first Constitution of Mongolia (Otgonjargal 2003: 161). These concepts were not formalized in the same way that Mongolia has been doing it since the 1990s, by way of advocating American democracy (cf. Addleton 2013: 38–39). In fact, this was done in different ways under the control of Soviet socialism (*niigem juram*) and totalitarian governance by addressing liberation (*erkh chölöö*) from the above-mentioned colonial occupations (*gadaadyn khargisuud*), "feudal" (*feudal*) and "capitalist" (*khöröngötön*) exploitations (*möljlög*), despotism (*khargislal*), and "class struggle and warfare." Therefore, according to the communist ideology, "freedom," "human rights," and "democracy" mean being free from "feudalism," "capitalism," and "colonialism" (for different freedoms, cf. High 2013; Humphrey 2007). After the 1990s, Mongolia experienced a different type of "freedom" from totalitarian oppression and Soviet occupation by conveying the ideas of Western democracy, free market economy, capitalism, and neoliberalism. Here, I am not arguing that Mongolia had a Western understanding of "civil society" and "democracy" that was fully accepted and practiced since the 1920s, especially when the term *jinkhene ard* ("genuine people") indicated the oppressed working class versus bourgeoisie or "black" (aristocrats) and "yellow" (high-ranking lamas) denoted feudal overlords. Instead, I draw the conclusion that the basic elements of and legal environment necessary to develop "civil society," such as human rights, freedom, equality, non-discrimination, and permission to organize meetings and start associations and political parties, were already legitimized by the constitution prior to 1992. This actually meets the definition of civil society used in the 2006 CSI report of Mongolia "as an arena, rather than a set of organizations" (Center for Citizens' Alliance 2006: 14). If "civil society" is an "arena," rather than organizations, then it is a social and political environment complex having numerous elements, features, and segments, consisting of parts including what I call the basics of civil society, which appeared in the first constitution.

Here, what matters the most after 1990 is the influence and occupation of American democracy, which became the most important criterion in the scope of democracy and civil society in Mongolia. Therefore, for many, what Mongolia had prior to 1990 can be easily considered as not "democracy," especially for *ardchilalynkhan* ("democrats" referring to the Democratic Party) those promoting American democracy. They utilize and employ democracy in the very construction of the party's identity and political principles. In the previous two decades, their claim for the "ownership" of democracy in Mongolia constructed an understanding that Mongolians were not free; had no human rights, democracy, or civil society; and experienced only tyranny prior to 1990. *Ardchilalynkhan* (democrats) claim that all those concepts were brought about by the "democratic movement" (*ardchilsan khödölgöön*) and the Democratic Party. The scope of democracy constructed by the democrats in Mongolia, I hope, explains why the history of democracy and civil society in Mongolia always starts not from the 1920s but from the 1990s. The scope rigidly suggests that "democracy" is a Western culture, not a Soviet one, as is the concept of civil society.

The following materials help me argue that protest movements exist with or without the Western, modern, and constructed term "civil society." As I briefly mentioned earlier, the contemporary politics of democrats owning Mongolia's "democracy"—including civil society—restricts the wider application and acknowledgement of "civil society," and the term is reduced to a certain period of time and group of people in Mongolia. Further, in addition to the perceived "ownership" of democracy, the Democratic Party's failures in ruling the national government from 2012 to 2016 caused widespread public discontent and made *ardchilalynkhan* (democrats) together with the term *ardchilal* (democracy) completely unfashionable. Because such failures are intensely attached to the framework of the constructed concept of "democracy" in Mongolia—and strictly apply to a particular period of time and people—the members of later protest movements and groups are reluctant to acknowledge not only the term "democracy" but also "civil society." Civil society is very much attached to donor and aid organizations and the pro-democratic and pro-American civil society NGOs that first introduced Western-style civil society to Mongolia (cf. Amarsanaa *et al.* 2013: 6; Baasansuren and Bold-Erdene 2013: 48; Chuluunbaatar 2013: 137; Chuluunbaatar and Gan-Ulzii 2013: 28). Therefore, the employment of the term "civil society" misrepresents, misleads, and obscures their intentions and principles by creating an impression that they are incorporated with the democrats and pro-American democracy NGOs. Instead, they try to incorporate their identity with the previous revolutionary historical protest movements of Mongolia.

Escape from "civil society"

This section focuses on the historicization of protest movements. More precisely, instead of making a direct correspondence to the "democratic movements" (*ardchilsan khödölgöön*) of the late 1980s and early 1990s, the so-called civil or citizens' movement (*irgenii khödölgöön*) members, participants, and organizers, whose roles are examined in detail in this chapter, explain the meaning and purpose of their movements with respect to the historical protests that took place in Mongolia in the late nineteenth and early twentieth centuries. Unlike those in the early 1990s, the protest movements of the 2000s were not associated with the term "democratic movements." A new term, *irgenii khödölgöön* (meaning "citizens' movement"), emerged and became an important part of the understanding of civil society in the previous decade, even while many of the environmental protestors started escaping from the Western-style civil society and were seeking an alternative identity. Those who did not desire to be mistaken for the Western-style civil society historicized their inspiration and linked themselves to the protest movements that occurred in the late nineteenth and early twentieth centuries.

Darkhad shaman Ch. Chinbat, from north Mongolia, was the first shaman to publicly protest against mining in the mid-2000s. I had not seen Chinbat for many years—since the late 1990s—until early 2007, when I saw him on television campaigning in a press conference against "Mongol Gazar" (Mongol Land), one of the largest Mongolian gold-mining companies. He was very concerned about the environment and the shamanic shrines in the Darkhad Depression

(Darkhadyn Khotgor or Shishgediin Khotgor), a large valley known as the Darkhad people's homeland in Khövsgöl *aimag*, in the north of Mongolia. He discovered a cadastral map where the land in the Depression was divided into pieces and given away for licensed mining. He was addressing the point that land is sacred and cannot be owned by any companies or people for exploitation because shamanic spirits own the land (cf. Pedersen 2011: 169). This is the reason why Darkhads set up small wooden sheds and placed a diseased shaman's costumes and instruments across the Depression, which is called *kheeriin ongodyn asar* (also *jatar* and *ambaar*), literally meaning the "tent of wilderness spirit." Chinbat claimed that land belongs to those ancestral spirits who became the masters (*ezen* and pl. *ezed*) of the land clearly marked by their shrines. Indeed, Darkhads and their homeland are famous for their "powerful," "authentic," and "well-preserved" shamanic practices, including curses. Chinbat openly threatened those planning to exploit the land by confirming that "shamans are capable of doing many things." When I interviewed him much later, in December 2015, I had a chance to find out more about his campaign. His protest started from his spirit's call (*ongodyn duudlaga*), which sent him the following poetic intuitions to protect his homeland:

Khoid taigyn nutgiig chin	Your north taiga homeland
Khuiten gartanguud khorolloo	Has been poisoned by the cold handed
Ar taigyn nutgiig chin	Your back taiga homeland
Azar setgeltenguud buzarlalaa	Has been impurified by the evil-hearted
Aliv khuu min bosooroi!	Come on son, get up!
Övdög toigoo teniilgeere	Stretch your knee and kneecap
Öödöögöö bushuu khööröörei	Take off urgently to the upward [sky]
Örgön khangaigaa tuularai	Traverse the wide Khangai [mountain]
Örgön zondoo ochooroi	Come to your great mass [people]
Örgön Shishgid chin chamaig ügüilj baina	Your wide Shishged is longing for you!

Not long after receiving this message, Chinbat discovered some news regarding Parliament Member D. Idvekhiten and the announcement about issuing mining licenses in the Darkhad Depression, which made him eager to find the cadastral map of the region, where he found the shocking depiction of his homeland being divided (*khircheed khircheed*) for dozens of mining companies. This made him realize why those large trucks carrying equipment were heading to the Darkhad Depression, approaching the pass called Öliin Khalzan Davaa, which is the only route by which vehicles can enter the Depression. The trucks belonged to Mongol Gazar, a Mongolian gold-mining company. They were on their way to the Öliin Khalzan Davaa pass to start the extraction of a gold deposit near Sharyn Nuur Lake. Chinbat decided to organize a press conference to reveal information on the mining licenses and appeal to the local people to campaign against the extraction. In the press conference, which was broadcast by various television news programs, he told the local Darkhads, "you are living on land of others" (*ta nar khünii gazar deer amidarch baigaa yum baina*). He was in Ulaanbaatar and did not manage to come to the pass, however, he contacted local people, who had seen him on the news, and they immediately campaigned against the mining company and did not let the trucks into the Depression. The local people of Ulaan-Uul *sum* threw stones at the mining company vehicles and made them leave the pass. When I asked Chinbat for more information on the matter, he immediately made a phone call to his friend Battsogt. After a short telephone conversation, Chinbat said that this was his friend from the Ulaan-Uul *sum* subdistrict, who had been the *sum* governor at the time of Chinbat's appeal to local people to campaign against mining companies. Battsogt was his main contact in Ulaan-Uul, who organized and participated in the strike in person.

His campaign continued in 2008 by recruiting more shamans and spirits through a worship of local *ovoo* to protect the Depression from exploitation by mining companies. After his telephone conversation with Battsogt, Chinbat continued his talk about the cleaning and re-establishment of the *ovoo* sacrificial stone cairns on the pass in the following year, around June 20, 2008. The ceremony was not dedicated to the *ovoo* on the pass alone; instead, in this event, Chinbat appealed to all the Darkhad shamans to join the ceremony to evoke and raise all the local spirits to unite and protect the Depression. Using all means of media and his personal contacts, he appealed to the shamans to invoke their spirits on the same day and at the same time, at 7.30 am, wherever they were. On the morning of the worship, he kept receiving telephone calls from different shamans and lay people who wanted to inform him and his colleagues about the processes of worships occurring all around the Depression and elsewhere. According to his estimation, approximately 300 people—including many shamans—joined his spiritual campaign.

When I asked him specifically against whom he was protesting, he replied, "I mainly blamed the state (*tör*) and those state rulers (*töriin udirdlaga*) for enabling such things." He continued telling me about the Darkhads' fight for their territory (*gazar*) and homeland (*nutag*) against the Qing rule. Darkhads used to have patrols (*kharuuluud*) stationed along their southern border, which adjoined central Mongolia and was heavily occupied by the Qing government. He claims that local oral history tells them that many of the patrols consisted of shamans, and non-shaman patrols were receiving shamanic assistances. Patrols used to inform the shamans about the trips made by Qing representatives (Manj Amban), who were appointed to reside and rule the Depression, and shamans used to conduct rituals to stop them on the way by creating different obstacles (such as breaking their carts and transports). With this story, Chinbat points out that Darkhad shamans were historically the protectors of their territory (*gazar*) and homeland (*nutag*), and he is simply *continuing* this tradition rather than learning it from somewhere else. He also made a direct link to the "gold patrols" (*altny kharuul*) that protected Mongol land from Chinese illegal gold miners, who roamed Mongolia during the Qing rule. He claimed that he read somewhere about the Mongol "gold patrols," and he found them to be similar to the above-mentioned Darkhad patrols that he learned about from his elders.[7]

In the media, Chinbat and his protest were addressed as a "citizens' movement" (*irgenii khödölgöön*). When we started talking about his protest movement with respect to the "citizens' movement" (*irgenii khödölgöön*) and "civil society organizations" (*irgenii niigmiin baiguullaga*), he expressed his reluctance to associate himself with the term "civil society." According to his thinking, his protest is entirely different from the contemporary concept of civil society that has developed in Mongolia since the 1990s. Moreover, he corrected himself by saying that he is not against civil society and democracy and revealed his hesitation to be part of any politicized social groups, trends, and factions such as the Democratic Party. Instead, it is a lot safer for him to present himself and his protest in relation to what Darkhad shamans have historically done. In other words, according to his self-representation, the Western concept of civil society is completely foreign to and absent from his activities, while local shamanic history is intrinsic to them.

Chinbat is not the only person to make a link between current protest movements and similar historical precedents. I talked to many others, who brought up similar analogies. For example, the identification card of the *Gal Ündesten Kholboo* (Fire Nation Association) says, "you my brothers and multifarious citizens are the savior spirit (*sülden*) of the country and state existence," a statement that is claimed to be a "teaching of Chinggis Khan." Not only protestors but also politicians (cf. Batsuuri 2016) and scholars (Murai 2012: 444) develop the same historical associations. The same concern and escape from foreign advocacy is also raised by

Ts. Munkhbayar, the founder and leader of *Ongi golynkhon khödölgöön* (the Ongi River Movement [ORM]). His solution was to transform the movement into a grass-roots and self-funded movement, which I discuss below.

Advocacy and gender

In 2005, a female founding member of the ORM, N. Bayarsaikhan, decided to start a different environmental NGO, *Khil khyazgaargüi alkham* (Steps Without Borders), which focused more on human rights; she currently chairs the organization. At the same time, the ORM expanded and started a larger union movement called *Mongol nutag minu evsel* (My Mongol Homeland), uniting river movements from fourteen different *aimag* provinces. In an interview with Bayarsaikhan, she made a clear division between two different types of environmental NGOs: one is *baiguullaga* (organizations), while the other is *khödölgöön* (movement/activism). The former comprises office-based work and is good at producing paperwork—which is what she is doing now—while the latter tends to operate outdoors and is good at showing physical resistance—which is what her colleague Ts. Munkhbayar and others such as *Bosoo Khökh Mongol* (Standing Blue Mongol) and *Gal Ündesten Kholboo* (Fire Nation Association) are currently doing. In this way, this section demonstrates a division between two types of NGOs, both of which are understood as civil society. Their differences do not lie in the division between the indoor and outdoor or the clerical and physical; however, according to Ts. Munkhbayar's concern, it is more to do with foreign advocacy and funding, which also reveals a strong gender division. In fact, this is not entirely new but is something that has existed since the beginning of "civil society" in Mongolia in the 1990s. The Civil Society Index report for Mongolia describes it as follows:

> The adoption of the democratic constitution in 1992 and the holding of the first free and fair parliamentary elections in the same year provided further impetus for the emergence of a new type of citizen's organization: Western-style issue-oriented, office-based, more professionalized advocacy and oversight non-governmental organizations (NGOs) aimed at influencing public policy and holding the government accountable. Some of the most active NGOs were pro-democracy and pro-development organizations, which were formed and led by women affiliated with opposition parties. The development of NGOs in the 1990s was supported financially, technically and ideologically by a number of foreign and international organizations, such as The Asia Foundation (USA), Konrad Adenauer Foundation (Germany), USAID, UNDP, NED, AusAID and the Global Fund for Women.
>
> *(Center for Citizens' Alliance 2006: 27)*

In contrast to the above description of active "civil society organizations" (*irgenii niigmiin baiguullaga*), environmental movement protestors do not in many ways fit into any of the descriptions outlined above. They are usually not Western style; not office based; not professional advocacy; not pro-democracy or pro-democrats; not pro-development; not exclusively supported and financed by foreign and international organizations; and, finally, in most of the cases, not led by women. Instead, the environmental protest movements that I am addressing are historic, traditional, nationalist, and street- and outdoor-based events dominated by male members from the countryside and having much hesitation with respect to accepting foreign and international funds.

The ORM is one of the largest, oldest, and most well-known environmental protest movements that emerged during the late 1990s and early 2000s. Some *sum* subdistrict governors and chairs of citizens' representatives met in the local government from eight *sums* of three different *aimag* provinces along River Ongi and first began to discuss the problems of herders migrating across these *sums*. The discussion developed to reveal the reasons for the herders' migration. They discovered that the migration was due to the disappearance of River Ongi, and Lake Ulaan (Ulaan Nuur) in Ömnögovi *aimag*, which was the main water source for more than 60,000 people. They went to see the beginning of the river in Uyanga *sum* of Övörkhangai *aimag* and discovered that three concrete walls closed the river for mining exploitation. Erel, a Mongolian mining company, had constructed the walls (cf. Bayarsaikhan and Amarsanaa 2007: 17). Not long after they appeared in public, a German NGO, the Konrad Adenauer Foundation, contacted the ORM and offered all sorts of support, such as funding and seminars on democracy, civil society, state, and environmental movement (cf. Bayarsaikhan and Amarsanaa 2007: 27–33, 46–52). Funds for travel, field trips, visits, workshops, and more were generously offered continually from one project to another, requiring them to submit future project proposals even before finishing the current projects (cf. Addleton 2013: 39–40, 64–65). Then, in the mid-2000s, the The Asia Foundation (TAF) also offered funding to promote their activity, and a similar collaboration continued until after Ts. Munkhbayar received the Goldman Prize[8] in 2007. Now, the organization and policy of the movement are completely different. Seven out of the eight board members of the ORM are herders, and they are planning full self-funding in the future.

At the end of November 2015, when my colleague Byambabaatar and I first arranged to meet Ts. Munkhbayar in Ulaanbaatar, the first question he asked us, as soon as we showed him our informed consent, was about the funding for our research. When we mentioned the European Research Council grant, he neither looked fully convinced by our explanation nor revealed any suspicion. His main point was that international donor organizations and funding can have different hidden agendas and possibly contribute to the creation of a database, which can be later used against the interest of local people and the nation. According to him, the same happened to his collaboration with the TAF. The TAF enthusiastically offered support and sponsorship to the ORM, and even submitted Munkhbayar's nomination for the Goldman Prize (cf. Snow 2011). Unfortunately, according to Munkhbayar, he discovered much later that the organization had a history of being involved with US intelligence (the Central Intelligence Agency). From this experience, Munkhbayar learned that receiving funding from anyone anywhere—not just international donors—is a potential risk to advocacy.

There is increasing concern, problematization, and suspicion toward foreign and international funding, including suspicions of implicit "agenda" and "advocacy," which do not mesh well with the protestors' purposes. These suspicions about funding agencies can taint the reputations of the protestors, calling into question their motive and reputations: are they being paid to accomplish certain tasks or are they genuinely committed to protecting the environment, etc.? In Mongolia, the understanding of "advocacy" is entangled in multiple suspicions of money-making and money laundering; serving the interests of foreigners, international corporations, and politicians; and establishing political careers and positions. In this way, funding and advocacy are problematized to different extents and in different ways. Nationalist protestors who do not prioritize "Western style," "professional advocacy," "pro-democracy," and "pro-development" problematize advocacy more than others. With funding and "advocacy" come great risks of misrepresentation of local "civil society" organizations and protest movements; they can be made (or seen) to be an instrument or tool for larger international and national political institutions and agents, and the protestors' original interests and intentions can be multiplied, split, and obscured.

Therefore, Ts. Munkhbayar considers that the best way to operate any protest movement is to fund its activities with a politically secure financial source. To accomplish such vital and immediate requirements, he and his colleagues together with local herders decided to plant berries (sea buckthorn) along River Ongi. First, it is hoped that this will support the water level of the river. Second, according to the legislation permits, any land with cultivated trees and bushes can be privatized by those who cultivate it; local herders can actually own land along the river, which prevents the loss of local pasture around the river to mining companies. Third, they can actually profit from the berries by selling them and the movement can be self-funded in the future using the income from the berries. Munkhbayar also considers this idea solely local—it makes no use of foreign initiatives or advocacy. He told us that his mother used to plant berries on the side of the river in the 1980s. After years of resistance and activism, he decided to try his mothers' way by encouraging local herders to plant berry trees and bushes along the river and own the land. In other words, Munkhbayar and local herders are now engaged in a contest to own land legally in order to protect the environment. When we came to see him in Saikhan-Ovoo *sum*, Dundgovi *aimag*, he showed us his mothers' garden with sea buckthorn trees near the *sum* settlement on the side of River Ongi and several other similar gardens along the river.

Planting berry trees is not the only solution initiated by him to self-fund the movement. He also started a herd for the movement, which was a relatively new initiative compared to the planting of the trees. At the board meeting of the ORM in November 2015, he officially presented his idea to create a herd to fund the movement. The easiest and quickest way to make it happen was by collecting donations from local herders. In the meeting, there were members representing five different *sum* subdistricts along the river. Everyone in the meeting found it a very good idea in order to make the movement financially sustainable and protect it from external advocacy. Munkhbayar told us that he was surprised to see the members reacting quickly: within a week's time, every *sum* decided to contribute 100 sheep, which added up to 250 outside his yurt. Two young men, both herders and members of the movement, decided to help by voluntarily taking care of the river movement herd.

Munkhbayar's initiative and attempt to self-fund is now completely different from how Bayarsaikhan describes the earlier stages of environmental movements and their informal policy on funding "to accept any funding and concern on how to spend it." This is because, as he admits, when Ts. Munkhbayar started his protest in the early 2000s, he had no idea of the concept of civil society, differences between "imported" and "grassroots," and the consequences of foreign advocacy. Therefore, he received extensive support from different international donor organizations, namely, the Konrad Adenauer Foundation (Germany) and TAF, as we saw earlier. In contrast to the previous stages of the development of environmental movements in Mongolia, the recent ethnography of the ORM helps me argue that we are experiencing a new age of environmental movement, an attempt to divorce itself from foreign donors and Western advocacy. The difference is now apparent between the two types of NGOs: one is often addressed as a "civil society organization" (*irgenii niigmiin baiguullaga*) and the other as a "citizen's movement" (*irgenii khödölgöön*). This is not only about the organization, structure, different operations, and funding sources of NGOs but also very much about their grassrootedness vis-à-vis foreign advocacy. The consequences of Western implantation sparked the separation and caused the ORM to accept a more grass-roots approach (cf. Upton 2012: 244), which I discuss in the conclusion.

Conclusion

In the current state of civil society in Mongolia, I suggest that it is important to not mistake the nationalist environmental protestors for the Western advocacy civil society NGOs. Although there is no clear boundary or difference between the two, they are certainly not the same.

However, the clear difference is as follows: the Western advocacy NGOs accept while environmental protestors escape from the Western concept of civil society.

Byambajav Dalaibuyan writes about river movements, focusing on Munkhbayar. Basing on the experiences of Munkhbayar, Dalaibuyan concludes, "most local movement organizations are increasingly transforming into advocacy organizations rather than community-based organizations that the donors anticipated" (2015: 97). This is largely true for most civil society organizations but not anymore for the ORM and the other environmental protestors I worked with. The materials used by Dalaibuyan are no longer valid and relevant to explain those who escape from civil society. The ethnography of this chapter helps me to argue against Dalaibuyan and suggest the opposite. As I repeatedly state, the above environmental protestors escape from advocacy and are reluctant to be associated with the name "civil society" because, for them, civil society is a foreign advocacy that imports Western concepts and practices. This is what Anna Tsing (2005) calls the "friction" of local–global collaboration. She argues that their collaboration does not mean that the local and global have common interests, but rather it maintains difference and friction at its heart (Tsing 2005: 246, 248–249, 264). Therefore, the underlying "friction" in the collaboration creates new interests and identities, which are created by local environmental protestors while escaping from the global civil society.

The demonstration of civil society in the sense of a Western exported import machine also explains why nationalist environmental protestors escape from it. The nature of their principles intensely maintain images of a traditional way of life and nationalistic sentiments based on homeland and environment, which are the "enemies" of "civil society" in the work by John A. Hall. There are five enemies of "civil society." The third one listed by him is a form of nationalism of a single nation, whether real or constructed, to its own state, which subverts the state, and its characteristic practices make it oppose civil society. More precisely, he referred to ethnic nationalism as leading to incivility in society (Hall 1995: 12–13). The environmental protestors in Mongolia employ "ethnic nationalism," rather than "civic nationalism" (cf. Brubaker 1999). This explains well the reason why environmental protestors escape from the concept of civil society. In fact, it is not just about their escape, but the Western concept of civil society fails to embrace them by not favoring ethnic nationalism. The import of Western interests and advocacy conflicts with nationalistic interests. Even though there is a clear conflict, environmental protestors do not identify themselves as "enemies," as it is mentioned in Hall's work, or an opposition to civil society. Again, like Tsing's "friction," which is "not a synonym for resistance" (2005: 6), although environmental protestors escape from and hesitate to accept the civil society exported from the West, they often collaborate with and support all other national and international "civil society organizations," when they have the same interests.

Notes

1 I acknowledge the contribution of a European Research Council grant (project number 515115) to the Department of Anthropology, University College London, and Civil Society Scholar Award of the Open Society Foundation for supporting this research.
2 I agree that there is a machine in development and civil society that does both of them (anti-politics and import) or none of them.
3 In an interview during the fieldwork in November 2015, G. Urantsooj, founder and chair of the Centre for Human Rights and Development, also said that her first consistent understanding of civil society came from attending trainings and workshops that were organized by international organizations such as the Soros Foundation and Open Society Institute in the late 1990s. Further, she said that local NGOs were the first to develop and disseminate their understanding of "civil society" in Mongolia.

4 Tamir Chultemsuren, a lecturer at the Department of Sociology and Social Work, National University of Mongolia, is developing a PhD thesis on the political protests of contemporary Mongolia. I thank Tamir for sharing his opinion on civil society and letting me read a draft of his thesis.

5 www.bataar.mn/10016822, accessed March 1, 2017.

6 Personal communication with David Sneath, February 2, 2016, Cambridge, United Kingdom.

7 E. Jigmeddorj presented a paper titled "Mongolchuudyn baigali khamgaalakh ulamjlal: Altny kharuu-lyn jisheegeer" ["Mongolians Tradition of Protecting Nature: On the Example of Gold Patrol"] at the 36th International conference on Mongolian Studies of the Korean Association for Mongolian Studies held in Seoul, Korea, in 2015.

8 The Goldman Prize is a prestigious environmental prize. In 1989, Richard N. Goldman (1920–2010) and his wife Rhoda H. Goldman (1924–1996) established the Goldman Environmental Prize. The prize honors the achievements and leadership of grass-roots environmental activists worldwide.

Suggested readings

Amarsanaa, Jügnee, D. Baasansuren, and M. Zolzaya, eds. 2013. *Mongol dakhi irgenii niigmiin tölövshil* [*The Formation of Civil Society in Mongolia*]. Ulaanbaatar: Admon.

Center for Citizens' Alliance. 2006. *State of Civil Society in Mongolia (2004–2005)*.

Chuluunjav, D., ed. 1996. *Irgenii niigmiin onol praktikiin zarim asuudal: Shine ündsen khuuli, irgenii niigem* [*Some Practical and Theoretical Questions of Civil Society*]. Ulaanbaatar: Admon (in Mongolian).

CIVICUS Civil Society Index Report for Mongolia. Electronic document, www.civicus.org/new/media/CSI_Mongolia_Country_Report.pdf, accessed June 16, 2016.

Dalaibuyan, Byambajav. 2015. The River Movements' Struggle in Mongolia. *Social Movement Studies* 14(1): 92–97.

Sneath, David. 2010. Political Mobilization and the Construction of Collective Identity in Mongolia. *Central Asian Survey* 29(3): 251–267.

Upton, Caroline. 2013. The New Politics of Pastoralism: Identity, Justice and Global Activism. *Geoforum* 54: 207–216.

Websites

Citizens' Council of Mongolian Environment, http://mecc.mn/p/359.
An organization dedicated to the conservation and protection of Mongolia's natural environment.

Fire Nation Association, http://gal-undesten.blogspot.co.uk/p/blog-page.html.
A civil society advocate, who uses traditional aspects of Mongolian culture in an effort to raise awareness and power protests against actions taken by the government that are deemed anti-democratic.

Konrad-Adenauer-Stiftung Mongolia, www.kas.de/mongolei/mn/about/.
The Konrad-Adenauer-Foundation website promotes its basic principle as a foundation of freedom, justice, and solidarity, concerned with defending democracy in Mongolia.

Monfemnet National Network, www.monfemnet.org.
A non-profit, non-governmental organization dedicated to protecting human rights, women's gender equality, and democracy in Mongolia.

National Center Against Violence, www.safefuture.mn.
A non-governmental organization (working in conjunction with international embassies) dedicated to building development programs and engaging the community to stand against violence in many forms, standing against injustice and moving toward social equality.

National Human Rights Commission of Mongolia (NHRCM), www.mn-nhrc.org.
The NHRCM was admitted as a full member institution at the Asia-Pacific Forum of National Human Rights Institutions (APF) in 2001; it promotes the respect and protection of human rights and freedoms.

References

Addleton, Jonathan S. 2013. *Mongolia and the United States*. Hong Kong: Hong Kong University Press.

Amarsanaa, Jügnee, D. Baasansuren, and M. Zolzaya, eds. 2013. *Mongol dakhi irgenii niigmiin tölövshil* [*The Formation of Civil Society in Mongolia*]. Ulaanbaatar: Admon.

Baasansuren, D., and D. Bold-Erdene. 2013. Irgenii niigem dekh sonirkholyn büleg ba uls töriin nam [Interest Groups and Political Parties in the Civil Society]. In *Mongol dakhi irgenii niigmiin tölövshil* [*The Formation of Civil Society in Mongolia*]. J. Amarsanaa, D. Baasansuren, and M. Zolzaya, eds. Pp. 5–18. Ulaanbaatar: Admon (in Mongolian).

Batsuuri, Haltar. 2016. Manjiin üyed 10 saya, önöödör 400 saya khoninii örtei bid! [Our Debt: 10 Million Sheep During the Manchu Period, 400 Million Today!]. Electronic document, www.batsuuri.com/манжийн-үед-10-сая-өнөөдөр-400-сая-хонины-өр/, accessed June 16, 2016 (in Mongolian).

Bayarsaikhan, Namsrai, and S. Amarsanaa. 2007. *Töriig tsochooson ongiinkhon* [*People of Ongi who Alarmed the State*]. Ulaanbaatar: Od Press (in Mongolian).

Bell, Daniel. 1989. American Exceptionalism Revisited: Role of Civil Society. *The Public Interest* 95: 38–56.

Bermeo, N. 2000. Civil Society after Democracy: Some Conclusions. In *Civil Society before Democracy: Lessons from Nineteenth-Century Europe*. Nancy Bermeo and Philip Nord, eds. Pp. 237–261. New York: Rowman and Littlefield.

Brubaker, Rogers. 1999. The Manichean Myth: Rethinking the Distinction between "Civic" and "Ethnic" Nationalism. In *Nation and National Identity: The European Experience in Perspective*. Hanspeter Kriesi, Klaus Armingeon, Hannes Slegrist, and Andreas Wimmer, eds. Pp. 55–73. Zurich: Rüegger (in Mongolian).

Center for Citizens' Alliance. 2006. *State of Civil Society in Mongolia (2004–2005)*. CIVICUS Civil Society Index Report for Mongolia. Electronic document, www.civicus.org/new/media/CSI_Mongolia_Country_Report.pdf, accessed June 16, 2016.

Chuluunbaatar, G. 2013. Orchin üyiin iregnii niigmiin ünet züil, shalguur üzüülelt [Criteria and Value of Contemporary Civil Society]. In *Mongol dakhi irgenii niigmiin tölövshil* [*The Formation of Civil Society in Mongolia*]. J. Amarsanaa, D. Baasansuren, and M. Zolzaya, eds. Pp. 118–146. Ulaanbaatar: Admon (in Mongolian).

Chuluunbaatar, G., and Ch. Gan-Ulzii. 2013. Irgenii niigmiin sudalgaany philosophi arga züin asuudald [Philosophical and Methodological Questions in the Study of Civil Society]. In *Mongol dakhi irgenii niigmiin tölövshil* [*The Formation of Civil Society in Mongolia*]. J. Amarsanaa, D. Baasansuren, and M. Zolzaya, eds. Pp. 18–31. Ulaanbaatar: Admon (in Mongolian).

Chuluunjav, D. 1997 Orshil [Introduction]. In *Irgenii niigmiin onol praktikiin zarim asuudal: Shine ündsen khuuli, irgenii niigem* [*Some Practical and Theoretical Questions of Civil Society*]. D. Chuluunjav, ed. Pp. 6–15. Ulaanbaatar: Admon (in Mongolian).

Cohen, Jean L., and Andrew Arato. 1992. *Civil Society and Political Theory*. Cambridge, MA: MIT Press.

Comaroff, John, and Jean Comaroff. 1999. Introduction. In *Civil Society and Political Imagination in Africa: Critical Perspectives*. John L. Comaroff and Jean Comaroff, eds. Pp. 1–44. Chicago, IL: University of Chicago Press.

Dalaibuyan, Byambajav. 2012. Mobilizing against Dispossession: Gold Mining and a Local Resistance Movement in Mongolia. *Journal of the Center for Northern Humanities* 14: 13–32.

Dalaibuyan, Byambajav. 2015. The River Movements' Struggle in Mongolia. *Social Movement Studies* 14(1): 92–97.

Dashdavaa, Chuluun. 2003. *Ulaan tüükh* [*Red History*]. Ulaanbaatar (in Mongolian).

Dashpurev, P. 2013. Mongol dakhi iregnii niigem ba uls töriin bodlogo [Civil Society and Political Strategy in Mongolia]. In *Mongol dakhi irgenii niigmiin tölövshil* [*The Formation of Civil Society in Mongolia*]. J. Amarsanaa, D. Baasansuren, and M. Zolzaya, eds. Pp. 40–118. Ulaanbaatar: Admon (in Mongolian).

Ferguson, Adam. [1767] 1995. *An Essay on the History of Civil Society*. Cambridge: Cambridge University Press.

Ferguson, James. 1994. Anti-Politics Machine. *The Ecologist* 24(5): 176–181.

Fish, Steven M. 1998. Mongolia: Democracy without Prerequisites. *Journal of Democracy* 9(3): 127–141.

Fritz, Verena. 2008. Mongolia: The Rise and Travails of a Deviant Democracy. *Democratization* 15(4): 766–788.

Gramsci, Antonio. 1971. *Selections from the Prison Notebooks*. London: Lawrence and Wishart.

Hall, John A. 1995. In Search of Civil Society. In *Civil Society: Theory, History, Comparison*. John A. Hall, ed. Pp. 1–32. London: Polity.

Hann, Chris. 1996. Introduction: Political Society and Civil Anthropology. In *Civil Society: Challenging Western Models*. Chris Hann and Elizabeth Dunn, eds. Pp. 1–25. London: Routledge.

Hegel, G. W. F. [1821] 1991. *Elements of the Philosophy of Right*. Cambridge: Cambridge University Press.

High, Mette. 2013. Cosmologies of Freedom and Buddhist Self-Transformation in the Mongolian Gold Rush. *Journal of the Royal Anthropological Institute* 19(4): 753–770.

Humphrey, Caroline. 2007. Alternative Freedoms. *Proceedings of the American Philosophical Society* 151(1): 1–10.

Jenkins, Robert. 2001. Mistaking "Governance" for "Politics": Foreign Aid, Democracy, and the Construction of Civil Society. In *Civil Society: History and Possibilities*. Sudipta Kaviraj and Sunil Khilnani, eds. Pp. 251–268. Cambridge: Cambridge University Press.

Kaplonski, Christopher. 2004. *Truth, History and Politics in Mongolia: The Memories of Heroes*. London: RoutledgeCurzon.

Keane, John. 1988. Despotism and Democracy: The Origins and Development of the Distinction between Civil Society and the State 1750–1850. In *Civil Society and the State: New European Perspectives*. John Keane, ed. Pp. 35–73. London: Verso.

Lewis, David. 2002. Civil Society in African Contexts: Reflections on the Usefulness of a Concept. *Development and Change* 33(4): 569–586.

March, Andrew F. 2003. Citizen Genghis: On Explaining Mongolian Democracy through "Political Culture". *Central Asian Survey* 22(1): 61–66.

Murai, Muneyuki. 2012. *Irgenii 'khödölgöönii örnöl ba tögsgöl 2004–2008* [Start and End of Civil Movements 2004–2008]. Ulaanbaatar: Erdenezul (in Mongolian).

Nord, Philiph. 2000. Introduction. In *Civil Society before Democracy: Lessons from Nineteenth-Century Europe*. Nancy Bermeo and Philip Nord, eds. Pp. xiii–3. New York: Rowman and Littlefield.

Nordby, Judith. 1992. Democratic Mongolia, 1991: Problems and Prospects. *Journal of Communist Studies* 8(1): 175–179.

Otgonjargal, Sodnomdarjaa. 2003. *New Perspectives on the History of the Twentieth Century Mongolia*. Ulaanbaatar: Admon (in Mongolian).

Pedersen, Morten Axel. 2011. *Not Quite Shamans: Spirit Worlds and Political Lives in Northern Mongolia*. Ithaca, NY: Cornell University Press.

Sabloff, Paula L. W. 2002. Why Mongolia? The Political Culture of an Emerging Democracy. *Central Asian Survey* 21(1): 19–36.

Sampson, Steven. 1996. The Social Life of Project: Importing Civil Society to Albania. In *Civil Society: Challenging Western Models*. Chris Hann and Elizabeth Dunn, eds. Pp. 119–141. London: Routledge.

Sanders, Alan J. K. 1992. Mongolia's New Constitution: Blueprint for Democracy. *Asian Survey* 32(6): 506–520.

Seligman, Adam. 1992. *The Idea of Civil Society*. New York: The Free Press.

Severinghaus, Sheldon R. 1994. Mongolia in 1994: Strengthening Democracy. *Asian Survey* 35(1): 70–75.

Shirendev, Bazar. [1969] 1999. *Mongol ardyn khuvisgalyn tüükh* [History of People's Revolution of Mongolia]. Ulaanbaatar (in Mongolian).

Sneath, David. 2010. Political Mobilization and the Construction of Collective Identity in Mongolia. *Central Asian Survey* 29(3): 251–267.

Snow, Keith Harmon. 2011. Goldman Prizewinner Shoots up Foreign Mining Firms in Mongolia. In *dissidentvoice.org*. Electronic document, http://dissidentvoice.org/2011/03/goldman-prizewinner-shoots-up-foreign-mining-firms-in-mongolia/, accessed February 8, 2017.

Tocqueville, Alexis de. [1835] 1994. *Democracy in America*. London: Everyman.

Torsello, Davide. 2012. *The New Environmentalism: Civil Society and Corruption in the Enlarged EU*. Aldershot: Ashgate.

Tsing, Anna Lowenhaupt. 2005. *Friction: An Ethnography of Global Connection*. Princeton, NJ: Princeton University Press.

Undarya, T. 2013. State of Civil Society Development in Mongolia. *Mongolian Journal of International Affairs* 18: 58–63.

Upton, Caroline. 2012. Mining, Resistance and Pastoral Livelihoods in Contemporary Mongolia. In *Change in Democratic Mongolia: Social Relations, Health, Mobile Pastoralism, and Mining*. Julian Dierkes, ed. Pp. 223–249. Leiden: Brill.

Upton, Caroline. 2013. The New Politics of Pastoralism: Identity, Justice and Global Activism. *Geoforum* 54: 207–216.

Wedel, Janine R., ed. 1992. *The Unplanned Society: Poland during and after Communism*. New York: Columbia University Press.

7

THE PHILIPPINES

Jorge V. Tigno

Organized people power

Civil society has had a remarkable impact on democracies everywhere in the last half century, but its repercussions are most striking in the developing world, where democratic institutions are still taking root. In many parts of the world today, civil society has become the sine qua non of the democratization process itself (Diamond 1994; Mercer 2002). While its organized elements have claimed a stake in a multitude of development issues and concerns globally over the last three to four decades, from protecting the environment to promoting rural development, civil society's more significant contributions have been observed to lie in the domain of politics (Bratton 1989). Certainly, the number of civil society organizations (CSOs) has not only grown exponentially in many countries, but has also provided a vital platform for citizen engagement, as well as becoming a motivating force for political development (Alagappa 2004; Clarke 1998; Mercer 2002; Thapa 2012).

The 1980s ushered in a new era for civil society in the Philippines (Domingo 2013). It was during this period that more open and popular civil society movements emerged against the authoritarian rule by Ferdinand Marcos. The strong clamor for the removal of Marcos came to be known as people power and "EDSA" has come to symbolize that type of power of the people against dictatorial rule. The acronym stands for the main thoroughfare (Epifanio de los Santos Avenue) in Metropolitan Manila which was occupied by a large number of Filipinos in late February 1986 calling for the ouster of Marcos. Within days of people taking over EDSA, Marcos fled the country and sought exile in Hawaii, courtesy of the United States. While some analysts celebrate the courage of the Filipinos in the face of tyranny, other, more religious groups have hailed the "EDSA" event as a kind of miracle and an act of divine intervention. The Philippine Left would see "EDSA" as largely symbolic of the actions of a liberal segment of the bourgeoisie and one that effectively glossed over and marginalized the protracted armed struggle against Marcos. Whatever the interpretation, civil society groups saw an opening in the post-EDSA political space that they could now access, that had not been there before. The open, participatory, and progressive character of Philippine civil society today traces its roots to EDSA and the subsequent restoration of formal liberal democratic structures and mechanisms in the 1980s. In the aftermath of the uprising against authoritarian rule in 1986, CSOs in the country have increasingly and openly played a significant role in popular empowerment strategies for good governance, political accountability, and sustainable development.

But more than thirty years down the road, the Philippines is still a long way from effectively consolidating and institutionalizing its democratic mechanisms and processes. The post-1986 democratic political system has been described as "unconsolidated" (Schmitter 1992), "shallow and flawed" (Putzel 1999: 214), and "patrimonial" (Hutchcroft 1998), dominated by oligarchs and extended families (Hutchcroft 1991), as well as entrenched local bosses (Sidel 1999). Despite the claimed appreciation (albeit romanticized view) attached to Philippine civil society, that is, as a force for good and for everything that democracy stands for, it remains a question where it has taken the country in the last four decades. The Philippine case appears to defy the conventional logic that, in the words of two prominent civil society scholars, a "robust civil society" can "help consolidate and deepen democracy" (Stephan and Linz 1996: 18). Despite having a pervasive, strong, and empowering civil society, the Philippine political system continues to be weak, clientelistic, ineffective, and prone to elite capture.

Although civil society in the country has evolved into a generally dispersed and diverse community, its historically close association with "the power of the people" is perhaps undeniably its most common and strongest feature. Indeed, scholars on the Philippines acknowledge the critical role played by civil society in establishing and shaping the bedrock of democracy in the country (Clarke 1998, 2013; Hedman 2006; Silliman and Noble 1998; Thapa 2012; Wurfel 2004).

While they may be essential to the democratization process, it remains to be seen whether CSOs are also sufficient to bring about genuine and lasting democratic consolidation and institutionalization in the country (Thapa 2012; Wurfel 2004). Although they are able to mediate social relations to some extent and have the potential to undermine traditional hierarchical and patronage-based political structures, the voluntary groups found in the Philippines have yet to have such an effective and lasting impact on the country's socio-political landscape in terms of bringing about the genuine and sustained empowerment of the people. Much of this is due, ironically, to their diversity and pervasiveness, which in some ways are their "strengths" as a community. Their diversity has also led to their lack of coherence and cohesiveness. Their expansion and proliferation may be a good thing, but it can also be a source of their weakness. Internal contestations and conflicts persisting within and between these organized elements of people power specific to the manner and objectives of their struggles can lead to doubts as to their assumed coherence and homogeneity as a group. Likewise, it also mitigates the extent of their contribution to the institutionalization of democratic governance altogether, notwithstanding their strong potential to foster a more accountable and effective government in promoting public welfare (Clarke 1998; Mercer 2002; Wurfel 2004).

Organized elements of civil society in the Philippines are either non-governmental organizations (NGOs) and/or people's organizations (POs). During the late 1980s up to the 1990s, they were also called "cause-oriented groups"; their leaders are sometimes called "street parliamentarians" for their propensity to voice social issues and take their struggles out to the streets (Domingo 2013; Nelson 1988: 20; see Geronimo 2016). At times, they are also referred to as "the third sector" or "the non-profit sector" by some scholars (Cariño 2002; Domingo 2013). Broadly, NGOs refer to "private, non-profit, professional organisations with a distinctive legal character, concerned with public welfare goals," while POs are "local, non-profit membership-based associations that organise and mobilise their constituents in support of collective welfare goals" (Clarke 1998: 2–3). Claire Mercer (2002) further adds that NGOs are associations run by an employed staff (often composed of urban professionals) and are able to generate funds for their operations from (local and foreign) donors. Such NGOs are to be differentiated from grassroots organizations (GROs) that are smaller in size and are able to operate largely from voluntary work but are still dependent on external or even NGO funding support (Mercer 2002). In the

Philippines, however, the term POs is used more than GROs, because the latter has been popularly attached to a different line of work altogether—GROs is a colloquial term that stands for "guest relations officers" or people who typically work in the entertainment services sector. It is also used in the popular discourse as a euphemism for prostitutes.

Given the fact that the two possess numerous common elements, it is easy to conflate NGOs with POs, since they are both entities involved in a wide range of (non-state) development and pro-poor/pro-people initiatives. In many cases, "NGOs" have become the catch-all term for all forms of collective or communitarian voluntary initiatives that are not part of government, the private business sector, and the family. Interestingly, although NGOs and POs are often used interchangeably in the Philippines, both continue to be seen as forces integral to civil society and crucial to mobilizing resources and people toward a greater sense of democratic and accountable governance (Domingo 2013). For the purposes of this chapter, CSOs is used interchangeably with NGOs, and POs are subsumed under both terms.

This chapter offers an overview of the nature and character of CSOs in the Philippines as they are operationalized in the activities and pursuits of NGOs and POs. It attempts to answer a number of basic questions about the emergence, persistence, and expansion of these organized segments of civil society, as well as the directions they are taking and the challenges they are likely facing today. What factors would explain their emergence in Philippine society and their entry into politics? How can their proliferation be explained? What issues and challenges confront Philippine civil society and CSOs?

The chapter will provide a basic description of the historical roots of CSOs in the country by situating their emergence and proliferation in: (a) the historical context of the emergence of faith-based mutual aid societies; and (b) the contemporary context of the anti-dictatorship struggle of the 1970s and the 1980s. As well, the chapter will describe the constitutional framework for the existence and proliferation of CSOs in the country. Finally, the chapter will attempt to point out some of the key challenges facing the sector today.

The chapter argues that while such organized elements of civil society have certainly been a force to reckon with for the state and the market, it remains to be seen whether CSOs have collectively fostered the strengthening and consolidation of the country's democratic institutions. The notion that civil society groups can be a progressive force is certainly a fascinating one. However, in critically examining the state of civil society in the Philippines, the NGOs and POs that now dominate the country's socio-political landscape may actually pose a threat to (rather than foster) the establishment of more effective democratic institutions.

Historical beginnings and critical conjunctures

The CSOs that dominate the Philippine social and political landscape today emerged and proliferated due to certain junctures in the country's history. The phenomenal wave of NGOs in the Philippines that began in the 1980s emerged from a long line of community-based, self-help, and voluntary organizations dating as far back as the late sixteenth century (Bankoff 2007; Cariño 2002; Clarke 1998). Although they were not as common and pervasive as the NGOs of today, civic and philanthropic associations were allowed by the Spanish colonial authorities to be established at the local levels. Some were organized as lay religious confraternities (brotherhoods) or sodalities (the *cofradias* as these were called), while others were established as local self-help professional guilds or *gremios* that became the forerunners of the cooperatives and trade unions of today (Sibal 1996). The more prominent of these *cofradias* included the *Hermanidad de la Misericordia* organized in 1594, the *Congregacion de la Santisima Virgen* established in 1600, and the *Venerable Orden Tercera de San Francisco* created in 1729 (Ikehata 1990: 111–112). All these faith-based associations undertook various charitable and economic activities and were supported by the religious and secular colonial authorities of the period (Bankoff 2007). As a longstanding agrarian and subsistence farming area, poverty and economic uncertainties were commonplace in the Philippines. The members of the *cofradias* performed certain acts of charity, like visiting and caring for the sick and dying, things that the Spanish friars could not do in all cases, given the fact that there were too few of them in the islands at the time. Under such conditions, these formal and informal but largely voluntary and charitable associations were a godsend for the poor in that these organizations allowed them "to withstand the magnitude and frequency of [their] misfortunes" (Bankoff 2007: 330). Moreover, although they were primarily religious lay people, the members of these *cofradias* also became dedicated adherents of traditional social values like *bayanihan* (collective mutual assistance), *kapatiran* (brotherhood), and *damayan* (mutual aid in times of crisis).

The *cofradias* were, in many cases, informal but deeply embedded associations that had an extensive presence throughout the archipelago during the Spanish colonial period. It was not uncommon for towns and satellite settlements to have one or more active *cofradias* (Barrion 1961; Bankoff 2007). Although they were supposed to operate with formal authorization from the colonial administration, especially the governor-general and the diocese, in practice, many did not do so prior to the eighteenth century (Barrion 1961). Some of these *cofradias* though were viewed with suspicion and seen as a threat by the colonial authorities, simply because they involved the natives. However, Spanish Catholicism, combined with Filipino folk beliefs, has a way of consolidating and strengthening grass-roots protest actions, allowing them to endure over time (see Ileto 1979). A case in point is the *Cofradia de San Jose*, a confraternity founded by Apolinario de la Cruz (popularly known as *Hermano Pule*) in 1832. When the official recognition he sought from the Spanish and Catholic authorities for his folk association was denied (for racist reasons), *Hermano Pule* rallied thousands of his followers and revolted against the colonial authorities. The Spanish authorities violently suppressed the association, leading to the arrest and death of thousands of the *cofradia*'s followers, including Hermano Pule himself (see Lee 1971). Despite the difficulties they experienced at the hands of the colonial authorities, many *cofradias* thrived and endured due to the much-needed service and support system they were able to deliver to the poor.

> The evidence suggests, in fact, that these *cofradias* were more than simply a means of expressing religious faith, and that they acted in the way of mutual support and as benefit associations on behalf of their members in times of misfortune or travail, providing needed labour, material assistance and even money. Moreover, their membership was extensive, sometimes exceeding several hundred persons, and was especially strong among female members of the community.
>
> *(Bankoff 2007: 331)*

By the early part of the twentieth century, larger and more formally organized associations began to emerge in the Philippines. The American administration encouraged local rural and agricultural credit cooperatives, as well as mutual benefit associations, the establishment of which was seen as an integral part of America's strategy to spread democratic values, counter the influence of the Church, encourage self-reliance, and promote overall political stability for the country (Bankoff 2007; Clarke 1998). In 1906, the formal legal framework for civic associations and other charities had been established through the Philippine Corporate Law. Mutual benefit associations in the country persisted and proliferated throughout the first half of the twentieth century under the Americans. Citing figures at the time, Greg Bankoff (2007) points out that membership in agricultural credit cooperatives between 1918 and 1923 increased almost three-fold from 29,259 to 77,479 persons, covering 547 associations in forty-two provinces throughout the archipelago (Bankoff 2007: 334).

By the 1960s and the 1970s, civil society in the Philippines had evolved into a more vibrant but more politically radicalized landscape of groups and movements of workers and students against the *ancien régime*.

> Membership of the progressive or development-oriented organizations that subsequently emerged as a result of these political events was mainly confined to Roman Catholic Church workers, the union movement and urban middle-class intellectuals, but an increasing concern with education, community-based primary care, gender issues, the promotion and protection of civil and political rights and the provision of material support for the activities of grassroots organizations soon expanded both their appeal and their involvement.
>
> *(Bankoff 2007: 344)*

Under martial rule, Ferdinand Marcos severely restricted and prohibited the activities of non-governmental groups (such as trade unions and student organizations) that advocated the anti-dictatorship cause and encouraged those that were in support of the authoritarian system (Sibal 1996). Marcos embarked on a project to craft a strong state and a disciplined and orderly society. The strongman ruled by decree, with little or no open opposition or real accountability. A critical civil society was seen as a threat to the nation and the dictatorship. Those organizations that could not be co-opted were outlawed. In some cases, Marcos established his own alternative civic organizations that operated in quasi-official fashion. For instance, in place of the radical student organization in the pre-martial law period called the *Kabataan Makabayan* or KM (literally, the nationalist youth), Marcos established the *Kabataang Barangay* or KB (village youth) that promoted the ideals of authoritarian discipline and respect for the leader. The KM had become an underground organization. Not surprisingly, the first KB chairman was none other than Maria Imelda Josefa Romualdez Marcos or Imee, the eldest daughter of the dictator and now governor of the province of Ilocos Norte, a known Marcos bailiwick.

As Marcos tightened his grip on the economy and society, so did the agencies of government become overconfident, inept, and corrupt. The rampant inefficiencies of and corruption in the government created the need for an alternative system that allowed for independent NGOs and POs to flourish and provide much-needed services to the people that government agencies could not. Initially, these CSO initiatives were constrained to operate in a clandestine manner. Their very existence challenged the mantle of benevolent autocracy that Marcos came to represent. Predictably, many of these organizations were opposed to authoritarian rule and everything that the Marcos regime stood for. A few were even accused of providing financial and logistical support to the movement that advocated armed opposition to the regime, the National Democratic Front (NDF), as well as the Communist Party of the Philippines (CPP) and its armed wing, the New People's Army (NPA). This prompted the regime to clamp down on organized people's initiatives. The main CSOs that were allowed to operate (albeit still suspect) were those that were sanctioned by the Catholic and Christian Churches. These faith-based organizations and networks were engaged in community-based anti-poverty and other social development concerns, particularly in the rural areas. The Catholic Church in the Philippines, like its counterpart in many countries in Latin America, had been revitalized by the encyclicals of the Second Vatican Council of the 1960s that emphasized that the Church concern itself with the real injustices and miseries of the people. Indeed, in a Catholic-majority country like the Philippines, the Church has become a focal point not only for the people's discontent, but also of their radical struggle to overcome it and it is this social action feature of the Church organization that had not become a major irritant for the Marcos regime (Youngblood 1978).

> In the Philippine context, prominent Roman Catholic theologians have identified the task of liberation as a struggle to overcome the "structural injustices operative in liberal capitalism." The social structures and institutions of capitalism, they argue, have injustice built into them. While stopping short of advocating a revolutionary alternative, the Church is presented as the champion of drastic reform.
>
> *(Shoesmith 1979: 247)*

Another turning point for Philippine civil society was reached in the early 1980s. While there has been a weakening worldwide of traditional mechanisms for popular participation and mediation since the 1980s, such as political parties and trade unions, this global phenomenon does not seem to explain the emergence and proliferation of NGOs and POs in the Philippines. Mainstream electoral political parties and trade unions have historically been weak and ineffective in the country to begin with. The "associational revolution," as Gerard Clarke (1998) puts it, took place in the Philippines especially beginning in the 1980s as a result of various significant socio-political events and forces.

Politically oriented NGOs began to proliferate in the country by the 1980s. Following the assassination in 1983 of Benigno Aquino, a staunch leader of the anti-Marcos movement, and the ouster of the dictator himself in 1986, there was an explosion in the number of motivated NGOs and POs in the country "fuelled in part by the huge amounts of foreign aid that flowed into the country to fund reconstruction and to stabilize democratic institutions" (Bankoff 2007: 344; Wurfel 2004). The period between 1989 and 1992 shows the highest growth rate in the number of NGOs and POs in the country (Clarke 1998: 71). Between 1984 and 1995, the number of registered NGOs grew nearly threefold, from 23,800 to over 70,000 (Clarke 1998: 71).

But even as civil society groups in the Philippines began to occupy a more prominent and open space in the society and politics during and after the EDSA people power revolt, ironically, they "had a remarkably small impact on policy and politics in the Aquino administration" (Wurfel 2004: 216). Although NGOs were heavily involved in the crafting of the 1987 constitution, essentially the post-Marcos period simply restored the traditional (pre-dictatorship) political set-up that had been temporarily disturbed by Marcos. On the surface, the system had the appearance of a thriving and vibrant democracy—regular elections, term limits on politicians, and competing electoral political parties. Beneath it all, however, the clientelistic and elitist system remained. It is even likely that NGOs were used by traditional politicians to gain some degree of popular legitimacy and regain the power they had lost during the period of autocratic rule under Marcos.

By the early 2000s, NGOs in the Philippines had become a diverse and heavily empowered sector operating in an environment that openly supported and encouraged them. In 2001, people power once again came to the fore in the movement to oust (and later defend) a discredited president. Faced with corruption allegations, Joseph "Erap" Estrada, a populist president elected in 1998, had been impeached, but the final outcome of the impeachment trial in the Senate had been pre-empted by popular calls for his ouster. In the midst of mounting calls (dubbed the second people power or EDSA Dos) for his removal, Estrada voluntarily left the presidential palace in January 2001. Shortly after, however, the supporters of Estrada rallied to his side and attempted an EDSA Tres, but this failed, as their political and financial resources dwindled. A kind of "people power fatigue" had set in at this point, as some observers have attempted to explain the fizzling support for EDSA Tres and other succeeding political events (Poole 2009). Faced with growing allegations of corruption and bribery herself, Gloria Macapagal Arroyo, Estrada's vice-president and successor, became extremely unpopular. An opinion poll in late 2007 considered Arroyo "the most corrupt" Philippine president in history, more than Ferdinand Marcos and Joseph Estrada (Flores 2007). Yet even with such allegations against her and her administration, Arroyo did not encounter the same kind of convulsive people power that Estrada and Marcos faced.

The civil society that emerged in the Philippines beginning in the socio-political upheaval of 1986 is a diverse and active community nurtured by an open and tolerant society that it had helped create. It is a community with a historically high level of overall popular legitimacy and acceptability, which is able to engage in a wide range of advocacies locally as well as nationally. The socio-economic need that these NGOs were able to fill (which the government could not in many cases) at the local and rural levels was also undeniable. However, without a common overarching structure, the majority of civil society organizations have gradually slipped toward working within the established political system and entrenched patronage networks, weakening their potential as a force for democratic consolidation (Thapa 2012: 14). The historically progressive and democratic role played by civil society has been stymied by the dominance of patronage politics.

In historical terms, Philippine civil society has evolved into an open virtual space for self-organization and voluntary action, occupied by diverse entities, groups, and organizations, "some more enduring and autonomous than others" (Franco 2004: 97) and some more progressive, revolutionary, and democratic than others. The growth of CSOs at certain historical junctures can be explained in terms of the vacuum that these organizations needed to fill up, combined with the officiating role of the state to either constrict or encourage their propagation by way of policy action (Clarke 2013), as will be evident in the following section.

The present constitutional mandate

While civil society is a terrain for non-state initiatives, its character and operations are nevertheless affected by state policy. Historically, in the case of the Philippines, government policy toward civil society has oscillated, "veering from liberal support ... to outright hostility" (Clarke 2013: 60), although the important role of CSOs in society is now enshrined in the 1987 Constitution.

With the end of Marcos' authoritarianism in 1986 came the period when civil society flourished, leading to a vibrant terrain that endures up to now. Numerous CSO that took part in and even led the struggle against the dictatorship also took part in the political reconstruction afterwards. Not surprisingly, when Corazon Aquino created the Constitutional Commission in early 1986 to draft the country's post-Marcos constitution, many of those appointed commissioners came from civil society groups associated with the anti-Marcos and anti-martial law movement. The process of crafting the 1987 Constitution effectively institutionalized people power, first, by allowing for popular participation in the process of crafting the constitution (via public hearings and consultations) and, second, by providing mechanisms for the representation of the largely marginalized and poor segment of the population in virtually all political institutions. Indeed, the pro-people and pro-poor tenor of the deliberations amongst the members of the commission at the time was undeniable. The country's constitutional foundations had been established on the so-called principle of preferential treatment for the poor and the oppressed. Commissioner Edmundo Garcia (himself coming from the NGO community) stated at the start of the deliberations within the Commission that the constitution which the body intended to produce was to have a peculiar bias in favor of the marginalized and poor, as well as the organized segments of the people.

> So I want to make this clear. I think we should lay our cards on the table. In this sense, although this is a constitution for all the people, still it must be biased for the poor or the majority in this land ... (1) That the powers of government must be limited; (2) That the freedom of all, especially of those who have less in life, must be guaranteed; ... (3) That economic equality must be encouraged and defended; (4) That popular participation must be insured; and (5) That people's organizations must be recognized.
>
> *(Garcia in Republic of the Philippines 1986a: 63)*

Given the overwhelming role played by grass-roots organizations (especially the POs) to oust a dictator, a great deal of confidence was expressed during the commission deliberations on the capacity of people's organizations to deliver a more progressive form of politics. Such was the sentiment voiced by Commissioner Felicitas Aquino.

> It is my firm resolve that the people's organizations, the cause-oriented groups, are now in a position politically and logistically to successfully launch organic leaders who would transcend parochial interests and be able to capture popular imagination for national leadership ... [to] lead us to an era of new people's politics.
>
> *(Aquino in Republic of the Philippines 1986b: 71)*

As a result, a "party-list" system was also enshrined in the Constitution. This new political arrangement allowed representatives from marginalized groups and sectors (such as "labor, peasant, urban poor, indigenous cultural communities, youth, and such other sectors as may be provided by law, except the religious sector") to be elected as party-list representatives in the House of Representatives (Republic of the Philippines 1987, Article 6, Section 5). In 1995, Republic Act 7941 was passed that allowed for:

> the election of representatives to the House of Representatives through a party-list system of registered national, regional and sectoral parties or organizations or coalitions ... belonging to the marginalized and underrepresented sectors, organizations and parties, and who lack well-defined political constituencies but who could contribute to the formulation and enactment of appropriate legislation that will benefit the nation as a whole.
>
> *(Republic of the Philippines 1995, Section 2)*

There were other attempts in the course of the deliberations of the Commission, particularly on the part of former NGO leaders and street parliamentarians, to "institutionalize" or even "constitutionalize" people power as a basic principle in the Constitution (Republic of the Philippines 1986a, 1986b).

One way that people power had been "institutionalized" is found in the popular initiative provision of the 1987 Constitution that allows for the people to initiate national and local legislation as later provided by Congress.

> The Congress shall, as early as possible, provide for a system of initiative and referendum, and the exceptions therefrom, whereby the people can directly propose and

enact laws or approve or reject any act or law or part thereof passed by the Congress or local legislative body after the registration of a petition therefor signed by at least ten per centum of the total number of registered voters, of which every legislative district must be represented by at least three per centum of the registered voters thereof.

(Republic of the Philippines 1987, Article 6, Section 32)

However, while such a people's initiative law is already incorporated in the Local Government Code of 1991, as will be discussed further, Congress has yet to pass a law to allow for a people's initiative mechanism for national legislation.

The same is the case for constitutional amendments. Although the 1987 Constitution does provide for the people to initiate constitutional amendments, Congress still needs to enact the necessary law to operationalize this.

Amendments to this Constitution may likewise be directly proposed by the people through initiative upon a petition of at least twelve per centum of the total number of registered voters, of which every legislative district must be represented by at least three per centum of the registered voters therein ... The Congress shall provide for the implementation of the exercise of this right.

(Republic of the Philippines 1987, Article 17, Section 2)

As the backbone of Philippine civil society, the protection and promotion of NGOs and sectoral associations is also enshrined in the 1987 Constitution.

The State shall encourage non-governmental, community-based, or sectoral organizations that promote the welfare of the nation.

(Republic of the Philippines 1987, Article 2, Section 23)

Early on, the members of the commission recognized and acknowledged the vibrancy and political necessity of the country's civil society community. Commissioner Florangel Rosario Braid acknowledged that incorporating non-governmental entities in the constitution would follow a growing trend, not only in the Philippines but also throughout the world, concerning organized efforts to promote volunteerism and participatory governance.

This provision recognizes a philosophy that is prevalent now even in our country as well as in many other countries of the world—that volunteerism and participation of nongovernmental organizations should be encouraged ... [G]overnment-led development has failed to reduce disparities, has failed to trickle down resources to the majority and that the next decade should be a decade where volunteerism, community-based and nongovernment agencies, independent organizations will be given their due support.

(Rosario Braid in Republic of the Philippines 1986c: 903)

However, Commissioner Rosario Braid also clarified that the term "nongovernmental" does not just incorporate a sense of independence from government but also "acknowledges private enterprise and privatization," although she does also conflate these terms with "private initiatives" (Rosario Braid in Republic of the Philippines 1986c: 903).

At the same time, the Constitution not only defines but also empowers POs to undertake initiatives to protect and enable the people in pursuit of their welfare, as well as in promoting the public interest. In doing so, the Constitution effectively limits the powers of the State in that it is now required by law to undertake consultations with such people's organizations.

> The State shall respect the role of independent people's organizations to enable the people to pursue and protect, within the democratic framework, their legitimate and collective interests and aspirations through peaceful and lawful means.
>
> People's organizations are *bona fide* associations of citizens with demonstrated capacity to promote the public interest and with identifiable leadership, membership, and structure.
>
> The right of the people and their organizations to effective and reasonable participation at all levels of social, political, and economic decision-making shall not be abridged. The State shall, by law, facilitate the establishment of adequate consultation mechanisms.
>
> *(Republic of the Philippines 1987, Article 13, Sections 15 and 16)*

Indeed, the people's organizations were seen by many in the Constitutional Commission to play an important role in bringing about "social justice" in partnership with government. As pointed out by Commissioner Ponciano Bennagen, POs have a complementary role as well as an oversight function vis-à-vis the government.

> [There are] two major actors in the realization of social justice: On the one hand, we have the executive, legislative, and judicial structures of government, and on the other, we have the people's organizations. ... [F]ormal structures ... would allow the achievement of social justice. People's organizations would complement these formal structures by providing certain informal structures within which they can exert pressure on the various structures of government to be more responsive.
>
> *(Bennagen in Republic of the Philippines 1986b: 651)*

Armed with their new constitutional mandate, civil society groups are seen to play a more active and open role in policy advocacy, as well as in calls for greater transparency and accountability in government. Since the 1990s, the operations of these CSOs have become increasingly been incorporated in national laws. The 1991 Local Government Code (LGC) or Republic Act Number 7160 makes it,

> the policy of the State to require all national agencies and offices to conduct periodic consultations with appropriate local government units, nongovernmental and people's organizations, and other concerned sectors of the community before any project or program is implemented in their respective jurisdictions.
>
> *(Republic of the Philippines 1991, Book 1, Section 2)*

It is not uncommon to find similar provisions in other national laws.

The Local Government Code likewise mandates local governments to "promote the establishment and operation of people's and nongovernmental organizations to become active partners in the pursuit of local autonomy" (Book 1, Section 34). Local NGO and PO representation in numerous special boards is guaranteed in the LGC. NGOs and POs have achieved significant headway in community-building, as well as providing much-needed basic services in many localities throughout the country, although it still remains to be seen whether their inclusion in the local governance process can be sustained over the long term (see Tigno 1997).

With their integration into the formal mechanisms of the Philippine political system, it now became necessary for the NGOs themselves to be registered, monitored, and to some extent have their activities regulated by the state. Since the state now mandated that NGOs be included in the official governance mechanisms (at both the national and local levels), it now became necessary to determine who could be accredited/registered as such non-governmental entities. Historically, non-governmental activities have been the subject of monitoring, control, and regulation by the state, which looked upon these CSOs with suspicion. However, the post-Marcos period was different in that it now mandated the inclusion of such NGOs in the formal mechanisms of governance. As such, the proliferation of these non-state and largely voluntary organizations during the 1990s can also be explained in terms of the extent to which the state allowed for the accreditation of such institutions during the period, as seen in Table 7.1. It was during this decade that official policies became more "NGO-sensitive" and a slew of government agencies sought their participation, assistance, and advice on matters of government development policies.

The advent of a strong civil society movement in the Philippines during the anti-dictatorship struggle provided the conditions that would eventually mandate the important role of NGOs and POs in rebuilding the democratic system in the country. Armed with such a mandate (from the Constitution, no less) a more inclusive and open environment in the post-1986 period had now allowed NGOs to take part in the formal (official) mechanisms of governance. No longer were they at the margins, even though they continued to claim to represent the marginalized. However, their formal inclusion into the government establishment necessitated the creation of certain systems through which they could be accredited or recognized as genuine representatives of the marginalized sectors of society. The slew of government accreditation systems that emerged, especially between the late 1980s and throughout the 1990s, provided the avenue for the propagation and proliferation of NGOs and POs in the country.

Locating and mapping civil society

In general, civil society is the "complex and dynamic ensemble of legally protected nongovernmental institutions that tend to be non-violent, self-organizing, self-reflexive, and permanently in tension with each other and with state institutions that 'frame,' constrict, and enable their activities" (Keane 1998: 6). Given the historical and institutional contexts of the country, contemporary civil society in the Philippines is seen in a more progressive (albeit, radical) light as an arena where "oppression is challenged and emancipation is nurtured" (Clarke 2013: 16). It is a space where its inhabitants (CSOs) attach a strong degree of preferential treatment for the poor, marginalized, and oppressed. The proponents of this view look upon the state and the market (the purveyors of oppression and enslavement) as anathema to civil society. The late Philippines expert David Wurfel (2004) also contends that NGOs are but a segment of that larger space.

> "Civil society" is here meant to include all social, cultural, religious, and non-profit economic organizations outside government but operating within the framework of law. NGOs, organized for social action, community development, livelihood improvement and other purposes, are only a segment of that wider term.
>
> *(Wurfel 2004: 215)*

As pointed out at the beginning, this chapter situates CSOs within the specific activities of NGOs and POs. Philippine NGOs typically claim to speak on behalf of civil society and in opposition to government policies and programs, and much of their collective impact is felt in

Table 7.1 Registration/accreditation of non-governmental entities in the Philippines

CSOs	Regulating agency	Legal basis
Social Welfare Entities	Department of Social Welfare and Development (DSWD)	Regulating the Practice of Social Work and Social Work Agencies (RA 4373) 1965
Labor Organizations and Unions and Rural Workers Organizations	Department of Labor and Employment (DOLE)	Labor Code of the Philippines (PD 442) 1974
Non-stock and Non-profit Corporations	Securities and Exchange Commission (SEC)	Corporation Code of the Philippines (BP 68) 1980
Parent–Teacher Associations	Department of Education (DEPED)	Education Act (BP 232) 1982
Citizens' Electoral Watchdogs	Commission on Elections (COMELEC)	Omnibus Election Code (BP 881) 1985
Agrarian Reform Communities	Department of Agrarian Reform (DAR)	Comprehensive Agrarian Reform Act (RA 6657) 1988 and DAR Order Number 11–89
Cooperatives	Cooperative Development Authority (CDA)	Cooperative Development Authority Act (RA 6939) 1990
NGOs in the Local Development Council	Department of Interior and Local Government (DILG) and LGUs	Local Government Code (RA 7160) 1991
Higher Education Institutions	Commission on Higher Education (CHED)	Higher Education Act (RA 7722) 1994
Trade and Guild Associations	Technical Education and Skills Development Authority (TESDA)	TESDA Act (RA 7796) 1994
Youth Organizations	National Youth Commission (NYC)	Youth in Nation Building Act (RA 8044) 1995
Health Care Providers	Philippine Health Insurance Corporation (PHIC)	National Health Insurance Act (RA 7875) 1995
Farmers Cooperatives and Extension Service Providers	Department of Agriculture (DA)	Agriculture and Fisheries Modernization Act (RA 8435) 1997 and DA Order Number 12 (2012)
Indigenous Peoples Organizations	National Commission on Indigenous Peoples (NCIP)	Indigenous Peoples Rights Act (RA 8371) 1997
Donee Institutions	Bureau of Internal Revenue (BIR)	BIR Regulations 1998
POs in Forest Management	Department of Environment and Natural Resources (DENR)	DENR Administrative Order 99–36 and 99–53
NGOs and Voluntary Organizations	National Council on Disability Affairs (NCDA)	Magna Carta for Persons with Disabilities (RA 9442) 2007
Homeowners' Associations	Housing and Land Use Regulatory Board (HLURB)	Magna Carta for Homeowners and Homeowners' Associations (RA 9904) 2010
Organizations of Basic Sectors	National Anti-Poverty Commission (NAPC)	Presidential Administrative Order 21 (2011)
Mutual Benefit Associations	Insurance Commission (IC)	Insurance Code (RA 10607) 2013

Source: based on Tables 1 and 2 in Domingo (2013: 6, 8–11).

the area of policy advocacy (Clarke 1998 and 2013). Their strong point is primarily "in providing alternative mechanisms and strategies in responding to the social, economic, and political demands of the citizenry, especially the less fortunate, marginalized, and *voiceless*" (Domingo 2013: 2).

Also, in the Philippines, a distinction is made between non-governmental entities that are profit oriented and those that are not. The Corporation Code of the Philippines sets a distinction between "stock" and "non-stock" corporations. As provided for in the Corporation Code, a non-stock corporation is an organization that does not provide for the distribution of any dividend income to its members or officers and any profit accrued is to be used only to further the goals of the organization (Republic of the Philippines 1980, Section 87). A stock corporation is an entity authorized "to distribute to the holders of such shares dividends or allotments of the surplus profits on the basis of the shares held" (Republic of the Philippines 1980, Section 3). This distinction sets out the parameters between "non-profit" NGOs and profit-oriented business entities and organizations (Clarke 2013: 70). Civil society constitutes the realm of voluntary and non-profit activities and initiatives.

Karina Constantino-David (1997) makes a distinction between profit and non-profit groups that operate outside the state and for the welfare of those in the margins. However, Constantino-David goes beyond this initial dichotomy of non-state entities by making a further distinction across non-profit and non-government groups to the extent of illustrating the nuanced complexity and organizational sophistication of civil society in the Philippines. Constantino-David (1997) defined NGOs as "all organizations that intersect with the domain of the state but are not part of the state apparatus [as] civil society entities" and that they are identified as such based on "the fact that they contest state power, individually or in concert, by attempting to transform unequal power relations" (Constantino-David 1997: 22). In other words, civil society becomes the space to challenge the power and authority of the state and make it more accountable to the people. She also makes a broad distinction between individuals (calling them non-government individuals or NGIs), mass membership-based peoples' organizations (POs), institutions (known as NGOs), and ideological forces and movements.

NGIs are persons who operate outside an organizational structure and are given legitimacy by the state, but play an important role in strengthening non-state interventions. POs are broadly subdivided into professional, academic, and civic organizations (PACOs), government-run/-initiated POs (GRIPOs), and genuine, autonomous people's organizations (GUAPOs). NGOs are also subdivided into development, justice, and advocacy NGOs (DJANGOs), traditional NGOs (TANGOs), funding agency NGOs (FUNDANGOs), mutant NGOs (MUNGOs) such as government-run/-initiated NGOs (GRINGOs), business-organized NGOs (BONGOs), and NGO entrepreneurs (COME NGOs) that take advantage of the availability of funds from donor development agencies. Ideological forces such as the Bagong Alyansang Makabayan (BAYAN) and the Moro National Liberation Front (MNLF), amongst others, articulate ideological positions and paradigms as an alternative response to the programs of the government. A number of GUAPOs and DJANGOs are said to be influenced by these ideological forces. At the time that this mapping was first articulated, it may have been a useful tool to identify how and why certain NGOs and POs alliances are formed. However, the utility of such a mapping remains to be seen in light of the fact that many of the terms used to name these organizations are highly normative. Moreover, such a mapping conflates the organizations with the space that they occupy (civil society).

No full and precise count of CSOs exists in the Philippines today. At best, one finds a wide range of numbers from different scholars and coordinating agencies. According to Wurfel (2004), the number of officially registered non-stock and non-profit organizations in the country could easily reach 60,000 in the early 2000s, although "this number includes private schools and hospitals, professional associations, and other private, non-profit institutions, none of which are usually regarded as NGOs" (Wurfel 2004: 215). Gerard Clarke (2013) lists no less than eighteen organizational typologies of Philippine CSOs, from trade unions, to cooperatives, to religious organizations and people's organizations (See Clarke 2013: 214–215).

A compilation undertaken by Phillip Tuaño (2011) estimates the number of NGOs in the country anywhere from a low of 15,000 (Brillantes 1995) and 20,000 (Aldaba 1993) to a high of 497,000 (Cariño 2002). The Securities and Exchange Commission (SEC) is said to have around 107,000 registered non-stock and non-profit corporations in 2009 (Tuaño 2011). The estimates vary greatly due to differences in definitions. Ledivina Cariño (2002) counts all CSOs (NGOs and POs), while Alex Brillantes (1995) and Tuaño (2011) only count NGOs, and the SEC statistics include all non-stock and non-profit corporations.

However, what seems to be evident from these estimates is that the numbers of such organizations have been growing over the years. The legalization of CSOs in the Philippines has produced a burgeoning NGO "cottage industry," where such entities can be easily established. NGOs may have proliferated throughout the world, but the Philippines is said to have the highest in Asia on a per capita basis (Wurfel 2004: 215). It may well be "the NGO capital of the world" with a "dizzying alphabet soup of groups, organizations, alliances, coalitions that spring up every few months or so, or when a public interest issue hits public consciousness" (Jimenez-David 2011).

A more recent and less conceptual mapping survey than the one undertaken by Constantino-David was done by the Local Government Academy (LGA) under the Department of Interior and Local Government (DILG), in partnership with the Philippine Partnership for the Development of Human Resources in Rural Areas (PhilDHRRA), a rural development network, in 2011 (LGA 2011). Nearly 3,500 organizations were surveyed and profiled, operating in sixty-nine provinces throughout the country and covering six types of CSOs: NGOs, POs, cooperatives, social movements, civic organizations, and professional/industry associations. Nearly half of the CSOs profiled are cooperatives. Almost one-fourth are POs. Interestingly, the study distinguishes between POs and cooperatives that are also mass-membership-based organizations. Most of the organizations surveyed were rural- and community-based, which can be attributed perhaps to the fact that the partner NGO is heavily involved in rural development undertakings. Almost half are small-scale operations with an annual budget of less than PhP150,000 (roughly equivalent to US$3,000 at current rates), although other organizations have considerably higher financial resources.

Philippine NGOs have recently landed in the headlines for quite different reasons, giving them a bad reputation. In 2013, investigators from the Commission on Audit (COA) uncovered efforts to defraud the government on the part of certain NGOs in collusion with corrupt politicians. Using their so-called Priority Development Assistance Fund (PDAF, which is a euphemism for pork barrel funds), some politicians were able to channel government funds into ghost projects supposedly undertaken by NGOs in the countryside. Dozens of NGOs were able to defraud the government of around PhP10 billion (around US$200 million at current rates) by way of bogus public works, agricultural assistance, and other social development projects, including scholarships to fictitious students. These NGOs "broke all rules" concerning the allocation and disbursement of public funds (Bernal 2014), leading to popular resentment and suspicion toward these kinds of organizations. The accused "mastermind" of this scheme, Janet Lim-Napoles, a businesswoman prominent in social circles in the country, and two senators, have been arrested and are still in prison.

Conclusions: the political importance of CSOs in the Philippines

Forming CSOs helps to challenge social apathy, to bolster group confidence, and to generate community resolve. Civil society groups help "people make claims on government and to secure their entitlements or rights" as well as "to ward off predatory elites such as loan sharks, property developers, or rack landlords" (Clarke 2013: 2).

The formation and development of Philippine civil society can be seen as an ongoing process, with significant consequences for and in the larger processes of democratization and democratic consolidation (Clarke 2013; Coronel Ferrer 1997; Domingo 2013). One cannot underestimate the important role played by CSOs in bringing about the transition out of authoritarianism toward more popular forms of governance. Indeed, Philippine civil society groups have widened the avenue for democratic (i.e., popular) participation in governance in the country. However, it can also be argued that "there is no necessary connection between civil society and democratic change" and that CSOs "have both expanded and contracted democratic space" (Alagappa 2004: 10). Although they have made significant strides in taking part in efforts to promote transparent and accountable government, the capacity of civil society groups to participate in official governance remains constrained (Eaton 2003). The absence of democratic consolidation is caused by the competing logics of restoring the old-style democratic regime and the heightened importance attached to civil society.

> [T]he transition to democracy in 1986 represented both the restoration of traditional political society and the transformation of civil society into a vibrant actor in the Philippines. The simultaneous processes of restoration and transformation set the stage for deep conflicts between actors in political society and civil society, and this conflict has had enormous consequences for the pace and extent of democratization.
>
> *(Eaton 2003: 470)*

It can be stated as well that the democratic role of Philippine civil society has been largely stifled or stymied and even co-opted by the restored (and now entrenched) traditional political system (Eaton 2003). The kind of informal (i.e., voluntary) politics that CSOs are known for either has not taken sustainable roots in the Philippines or has been institutionally hijacked by patronage politics.

Civil society in the Philippines has been described as "robust and vibrant" (Arugay 2005: 80). A civil society index developed by CIVICUS and applied to the Philippines gives the country a "respectable" rating (CODE-NGO and CIVICUS 2011). The enthusiasm and energy of the people that organize and maintain these organizations, especially in terms of how they attempt to engage, critique, and collaborate with government, seems to know no boundaries.

The groups and initiatives that thrive in Philippine civil society have been said to differ in many ways—the nature of their operations (e.g., service-oriented or motivated by policy advocacy); their level and character of organization (e.g., mass-membership-based or professional staff-based; Church-initiated/-based or based in academe or business); and their ideological perspectives (Coronel Ferrer 1997: 2). The extent of underdevelopment and mismanagement in government has certainly not discouraged many civil society groups from coming out and thriving in the last three to four decades.

Philippine CSOs are often perceived as a relatively homogenous set. This perception is aided by two characteristics. They are composed largely of NGOs that are run by partly voluntary but mainly paid staff, and nearly all of them can be found in urban areas like Metro Manila. It is understandable that these staff-based CSOs are concentrated in urban centers like Metro Manila, since many of them are primarily engaged in policy advocacy on a wide array of issues, ranging from human rights to environmental protection.

However, not all Philippine NGOs and POs are created equal. Some label themselves as more progressive than others. As a result, conflicts, rivalries, and competition can persist between them as well as with government. Yet NGOs and POs can be enablers of both the people and the state. They can operate and do things in areas where states and markets cannot and are unable. They can foster volunteerism, combat apathy, and strengthen citizenship confidence. These NGOs and POs thrive in an environment that is open and inclusive.

Philippine civil society has also been described as "fractious," characterized by "intra-civil society political conflict and fragmentation," porous to an "elite-dominated political society" and "competing visions of democracy" (Franco 2004: 97; see Coronel Ferrer 1997). There is still some uncertainty in the ways that Philippine civil society can potentially be a motive force for transforming the country's socio-political landscape, especially vis-à-vis the inability of the state to impose its will upon the larger society. It still remains to be seen whether civil society in the Philippines can actually be a force for democratic consolidation in the country (Thapa 2012). Indeed, as pointed out by Muthiah Alagappa—"civil society is a necessary but not sufficient condition for democratic development" (Alagappa 2004: 11).

Civil society in the Philippines has had a rather checkered political accomplishment in historical terms. The organized elements of civil society were clearly instrumental in the overthrow of the Marcos dictatorship and in bolstering support for Corazon Aquino throughout several coup attempts, as well as in the removal of Estrada in the midst of corruption allegations. However, they were not as successful in bringing an end to the Arroyo administration, despite the clamor for its end amid widespread allegations of electoral impropriety.

As they become more and more prominent in the social and political landscape of the country, NGOs and POs would need to slowly abandon their self-ascribed authority and allow themselves to be subjected to the same degree of scrutiny as those officials in government, if they are to be considered true partners in development. Gerard Clarke (1998) points out that if they intend to take part in the already open political sphere and demand accountability of government, they should also be able to subject themselves to the same degree of scrutiny to remove any doubts that still linger, particularly in the wake of the Lim-Napoles scandal.

Civil society groups have been largely associated with serious efforts to counter the traditional politics of patronage. Indeed, their appearance in the Philippine landscape may have signaled the beginning of the end of "trapo" politics. The term "trapo" is an abbreviated fusion of traditional politician but also refers to a dish rag or floor rag in Filipino. However, observers were also quick to point out that the political system that emerged post-EDSA 1986 was no different from the old-style democratic system led by an oligarchic political class (Anderson 1988; Coronel *et al.* 2004; McCoy 2009; Wurfel 1988). Since 1986, a number of NGO leaders and activists have sought and/or accepted positions in government. Many have been disillusioned, while others thrive. Nevertheless, it remains to be seen whether new actors from within the NGO community can effectively challenge traditional politicians in ways that can bring about the institutionalization of more democratic, effective, and accountable governance norms, mechanisms, and practices (Eaton 2003). In effect, NGOs may have inadvertently served to restore (or even further entrench and legitimize) the pre-Martial Law political system, even as many of its well-intentioned leaders attempted to distinguish themselves from the old-style political elites.

Suggested readings

Cariño, Ledivinia, ed. 2002. *Between the State and the Market: The Nonprofit Sector and Civil Society in the Philippines*. Manila: NJP Printmakers.

Clarke, Gerard. 2013. *Civil Society in the Philippines; Theoretical, Methodological, and Policy Debates*. Abingdon and New York: Routledge.

Coronel Ferrer, Miriam, ed. 1997. *Philippine Democracy Agenda: Civil Society Making Civil Society*. Quezon City: Third World Studies Center, University of the Philippines.

Hedman, Eva-Lotta. 2006. *In the Name of Civil Society; From Free Election Movements to People Power in the Philippines*. Honolulu, HI: University of Hawai'i Press.

Local Government Academy (LGA). 2011. *Diversity and Discovery: Mapping Civil Society Organizations in the Philippines*. Pasig City: Department of Interior and Local Government.

Miranda, Felipe, ed. 1997. *Democratization: Philippine Perspectives*. Quezon City: University of the Philippines Press.

Miranda, Felipe, and Temario Rivera, eds. 2016. *Chasing the Wind; Assessing Philippine Democracy*. Quezon City: Commission on Human Rights and UNDP.

Silliman, Sidney G., and Lela Noble, eds. 1998. *Organizing for Democracy: NGOs, Civil Society and the Philippine State*. Honolulu, HI: University of Hawai'i Press.

References

Alagappa, Muthiah, ed. 2004. *Civil Society and Political Change in Asia; Expanding and Contracting Democratic Space*. Stanford, CA: Stanford University Press.

Aldaba, Fernando.1993. The Role of NGOs in Social Transformation. *Philippine Politics and Society* 1(2): 2–54.

Anderson, Benedict. 1988. Cacique Democracy in the Philippines: Origins and Dreams. *New Left Review* 169(1): 3–33.

Arugay, Aries. 2005. The Accountability Deficit in the Philippines: Implications and Prospects for Democratic Consolidation. *Philippine Political Science Journal* 26(49): 63–88.

Bankoff, Greg. 2007. Dangers to Going it Alone: Social Capital and the Origins of Community Resilience in the Philippines. *Continuity and Change* 22(2): 327–355.

Barrion, Caridad. 1961. *Religious Life of the Laity in Eighteenth-Century Philippines: As Reflected in the Decrees of the Council of Manila of 1771 and the Synod of Calasiao of 1773*. Manila: University of Santo Tomas Press.

Bernal, Buena. 2014. COA Witness: Napoles Broke All Rules. Rappler News. Electronic document, www.rappler.com/nation/65642-coa-witness-napoles-ngos, accessed August 10, 2016.

Bratton, Michael. 1989. The Politics of Government-NGO Relations in Africa. *World Development* 17(4): 569–587.

Brillantes, Alex Jr. 1995. NGOs as Alternative Delivery Systems: The Philippine Experience. In *Alternative Delivery Systems for Public Services: Health Care, NGOs, Credit, Cooperatives*. Romeo Ocampo and Oscar Alfonso, eds. Pp. 114–127. Quezon City: Association of Development Research and Training Institutes of Asia and the Pacific (ADIPA).

Cariño, Ledivina, ed. 2002. *Between the State and the Market: The Nonprofit Sector and Civil Society in the Philippines*. Manila: NJP Printmakers.

Caucus of Development NGOs (CODE-NGO) and CIVICUS: World Alliance for Citizen Participation (CIVICUS). 2011. *Civil Society Index: Philippines; An Assessment of Philippine Civil Society*. Quezon City: CODE-NGO. Electronic document,www.ombudsman.gov.ph/UNDP4/wp-content/uploads/2013/03/CSI-Report_Bookv.pdf, accessed August 8, 2016.

Clarke, Gerard. 1998. *The Politics of NGOs in Southeast Asia; Participation and Protest in the Philippines*. London and New York: Routledge.

Clarke, Gerard. 2013. *Civil Society in the Philippines; Theoretical, Methodological, and Policy Debates*. Abingdon and New York: Routledge.

Constantino-David, Karina. 1997. Intra-Civil Society Relations. In *Philippine Democracy Agenda: Civil Society Making Civil Society*. Miriam Coronel Ferrer, ed. Pp. 21–50. Quezon City: Third World Studies Center.

Coronel, Sheila, Yvonne Chua, Boomba Cruz, and Luz Rimban. 2004. *The Rulemakers: How the Wealthy and Well-Born Dominate Congress*. Quezon City: Philippine Center for Investigative Journalism (PCIJ).

Coronel Ferrer, Miriam, ed. 1997. *Philippine Democracy Agenda: Civil Society Making Civil Society*. Quezon City: Third World Studies Center.

Diamond, Larry. 1994. Rethinking Civil Society: Toward Democratic Consolidation. *Journal of Democracy* 5(3): 4–17.

Domingo, Ma. Oliva. 2013. The Legal Framework for the Philippine Third Sector: Progressive or Regressive? Paper presented at the 8th Asia Pacific Regional Conference of the International Society for Third Sector Research (ISTR), October 24–26, 2013, Seoul. Electronic document, http://ncpag.upd.edu.ph/wp-content/uploads/2014/03/ISTR-2013-PAPER-FINAL.pdf, accessed November 10, 2016.

Eaton, Kent. 2003. Restoration or Transformation? "Trapos" Versus NGOs in the Democratization of the Philippines. *The Journal of Asian Studies* 62(2): 469–496.

Flores, Helen. 2007. Poll: GMA Most Corrupt RP Leader. *The Philippine Star* Global. December 12. Electronic document, www.philstar.com:8080/headlines/32762/poll-gma-most-corrupt-rp-leader, accessed December 10, 2016.

Franco, Jennifer. 2004. The Philippines; Fractious Civil Society and Competing Visions of Democracy. In *Civil Society and Political Change in Asia; Expanding and Contracting Democratic Space*. Muthiah Alagappa, ed. Pp. 97–137. Stanford, CA: Stanford University Press.

Geronimo, Jee. 2016. Martial Law Speak: Words that Defined the Anti-Marcos Movement. *Rappler Philippines*. Electronic document, www.rappler.com/nation/123550-martial-law-activists-lingo-edsa, accessed December 10, 2016.

Hedman, Eva-Lotta. 2006. *In the Name of Civil Society: From Free Election Movements to People Power in the Philippines*. Honolulu, HI: University of Hawai'i Press.

Hutchcroft, Paul. 1991. Review: Oligarchs and Cronies in the Philippine State: The Politics of Patrimonial Plunder. *World Politics* 43(3): 414–450.

Hutchcroft, Paul. 1998. *Booty Capitalism: The Politics of Banking in the Philippines*. Ithaca, NY: Cornell University Press.

Ileto, Reynaldo. 1979. *Pasyon and Revolution: Popular Movements in the Philippines 1840–1910*. Quezon City: Ateneo de Manila University Press.

Ikehata, Setsuko. 1990. Popular Catholicism in the Nineteenth-Century Philippines: The Case of the Cofradia de San Jose. In *Reading Southeast Asia: Translation of Contemporary Japanese Scholarship on Southeast Asia*, Vol. 1. Takashi Shiraishi, ed. Pp. 109–188. Ithaca, NY: Cornell University Southeast Asia Program.

Jimenez-David, Rina. 2011. The NGO Capital of the World.Inquirer.net. June 11. Electronic document, http://opinion.inquirer.net/6139/the-ngo-capital-of-the-world, accessed August 10, 2016.

Keane, John. 1998. *Civil Society: Old Images, New Visions*. Cambridge: Polity Press.

Lee, David. 1971. Some Reflections about the Cofradia de San Juan Jose as a Philippine Religious Uprising. *Asian Studies Journal of Critical Perspectives on Asia* 9(2): 126–143.

Local Government Academy (LGA). 2011. *Diversity and Discovery: Mapping Civil Society Organizations in the Philippines*. Pasig City: Department of Interior and Local Government.

McCoy, Alfred, ed. 2009. *An Anarchy of Families; State and Family in the Philippines*. Madison, WI and Quezon City: University of Wisconsin Press and Ateneo de Manila University Press.

Mercer, Claire. 2002. NGOs, Civil Society and Democratization: A Critical Review of the Literature. *Progress in Development Studies* 2(1): 5–22.

Nelson, Anne. 1988. In the Grotto of the Pink Sisters. *Mother Jones Magazine* 13(1): 18–24.

Poole, Peter. 2009. *Politics and Society in Southeast Asia*. Jefferson, NC and London: McFarland and Company, Inc. Publishers.

Putzel, James. 1999. Survival of an Imperfect Democracy in the Philippines. *Democratization* 6(1): 198–223.

Republic of the Philippines. 1980. *The Corporation Code of the Philippines, Batas Pambansa 68*. Manila.

Republic of the Philippines. 1986a. *Proceedings and Debates of the Constitutional Commission Volume 1*. Prepared by the Editorial/Publication Unit under the supervision of Hon. Flerida Ruth Romero, Secretary-General. Quezon City: The Constitutional Commission of 1986. Electronic document, https://archive.org/details/record-of-constitutional-commission-volume-1, accessed November 11, 2016.

Republic of the Philippines. 1986b. *Proceedings and Debates of the Constitutional Commission Volume 2*. Prepared by the Editorial/Publication Unit under the supervision of Hon. Flerida Ruth Romero, Secretary-General. Quezon City: The Constitutional Commission of 1986. Electronic document, https://archive.org/details/record-of-the-constitutional-commission-volume-2, accessed November 11, 2016.

Republic of the Philippines. 1986c. *Proceedings and Debates of the Constitutional Commission Volume 4.* Prepared by the Editorial/Publication Unit under the supervision of Hon. Flerida Ruth Romero, Secretary-General. Quezon City: The Constitutional Commission of 1986. Electronic document, https://archive.org/details/record-of-the-constitutional-commission-volume-4, accessed November 12, 2016.

Republic of the Philippines. 1987. *The Philippine Constitution.* Manila.

Republic of the Philippines. 1991. *Republic Act 7160—An Act Providing for a Local Government Code of 1991.* Manila.

Republic of the Philippines. 1995. *Republic Act 7941—An Act Providing for the election of Party-List Representatives Through the Party-List System, and Appropriating Funds Therefor.* Manila.

Schmitter, Philippe. 1992. The Consolidation of Democracy and Representation of Social Groups. *American Behavioral Scientist* 35(4–5): 422–449.

Shoesmith, Dennis. 1979. Church and Martial Law in the Philippines: The Continuing Debate. *Southeast Asian Affairs,* 246–257.

Sibal, Jorge. 1996. A Century of the Philippine Cooperative Movement. University of Wisconsin Center for Cooperatives. Electronic document, www.uwcc.wisc.edu/info/abroad/sibal.html, accessed December 10, 2016.

Sidel, John. 1999. *Capital, Coercion, and Crime: Bossism in the Philippines.* Stanford, CA: Stanford University.

Silliman, Sidney G., and Lela Noble, eds. 1998. *Organizing for Democracy: NGOs, Civil Society and the Philippine State.* Honolulu, HI: University of Hawai'i Press.

Stepan, Alfred, and Juan J. Linz. 1996. Toward Consolidated Democracies. *Journal of Democracy* 7(2): 14–33.

Thapa, Basan. 2012. Ambivalent Civil Society in Democratic Consolidation—The Case of Local Chambers of Commerce and Industry in the Visayas and Northern Mindanao. MA thesis, Potsdam University. Electronic document, http://basantathapa.de/wp-content/uploads/2014/08/THAPA-MA-Ambivalent-civil-society-in-democratic-consolidation.pdf, accessed August 8, 2016.

Tigno, Jorge V. 1997. People Empowerment: Looking into NGOs, POs and Selected Organizations. In *Democratization: Philippine Perspectives.* Felipe B. Miranda, ed. Pp. 83–113. Quezon City: University of the Philippines Press.

Tuaño, Phillip. 2011. Philippine Non-Government Organizations (NGOs): Contributions, Capacities, Challenges. In *Civil Society Organizations in the Philippines, A Mapping and Strategic Assessment.* Lydia Yu Jose, ed. Pp. 9–46. Quezon City: Civil Society Resource Institute.

Wurfel, David. 1988. *Filipino Politics: Development and Decay.* Ithaca, NY: Cornell University Press.

Wurfel, David. 2004. Civil Society and Democratization in the Philippine. In *Growth and Governance in Asia.* Yoichiro Sato, ed. Honolulu: Asia-Pacific Center for Security Studies. Electronic document, www.apcss.org/Publications/Edited%20Volumes/GrowthGovernance_files/GrowthGovernance.htm, accessed October 10, 2016.

Youngblood, Robert. 1978. Church Opposition to Martial Law in the Philippines. *Asian Survey* 18(5): 505–520.

8

VIETNAM

Jörg Wischermann and Dang Thi Viet Phuong

Against all odds: civil society in Vietnam

Vietnam is a one-party state. Since re-unification in 1975–1976, the Communist Party of Vietnam (CPV) has ruled the country alone and has not tolerated any organized opposition. In name, Vietnam is a socialist republic. Epitomizing the socialist orientation is the state sector, which, according to the 2013 constitution, plays the leading role in the economy. Another essential characteristic of this "socialist orientation" is the mechanisms and principles defining the functioning of the state apparatus. Here, the Marxist-Leninist mechanism of "democratic centralism," which is enshrined in the 2013 constitution, stands out.[1] The policy of renovation (*Đổi Mới*), approved at the Sixth Party Congress in 1986, is largely confined to economic reforms. To date, there has been no transition to a more democratic and pluralistic form of rule (for an opposing view, see Nguyen 2016).

Against such a background, commonly believed to be unconducive to the germination and development of civil society and civil society organizations (CSOs), and in complex interaction with the deep and sustained societal change toward a market economy (which set in during the early 1980s and was accompanied by the CPV's official approval of *Đổi Mới* in 1986), Vietnam witnessed the development and spread of many new formal and informal associations (see for example Beaulieu 1994; Sidel 1995; Wischermann and Nguyen 2003: 190–195). In addition, the politics of "socialization" (*xã hội hóa*), as the CPV called it, might have played a supportive role in a "mushrooming" of the various kinds of associations that took place between the mid-1990s and 2010.[2]

As of December 2014, Vietnam officially has 52,565 associations. Amongst these, 483 are operating nationwide and 8,792 are, in official terms, associations with "specific characteristics," which are mostly, but not exclusively, professional organizations (Government Report No. 502/TTr-CP, October 13, 2015). This official number does not include the tens of thousands of non-governmental organizations (NGOs) and Farmers' Organizations (for the latter, see Fforde and Huan 2001). This data suggests that in Vietnam some hundred thousand associations exist. And all these organizations exist within or side by side with an authoritarian political regime.[3]

Though relating to different strands of theoretical considerations on what constitutes civil society and civil society organizations, existing research suggests that there *is* civil society and there are civil society organizations in Vietnam. This broad agreement, shared by foreign and local scholars, foreign and local politicians and development practitioners alike, echoes most Vietnamese civil society actors' views, who see their organizations representing civil society. They understand civil society organizations as promoting and protecting the interests of their members, clientele, and/or beneficiaries, and as entertaining various forms of dialogue with the authorities. This understanding is founded on a basically descriptive understanding of civil society. It lacks any explicit reference to liberal norms and to processes of democratization. After a long period of negation, at least some segments of those in power seem to perceive civil society and civil society organizations as useful, not least for the delivery of public welfare services and for the purpose of "societal control" (Bui 2013: 77).

In this chapter, we illustrate the forms and substance of civil society and civil society organizations in Vietnam. First, we offer a brief overview of the rules and regulations that are decisive for the foundation and operation of associations,[4] then we briefly characterize the local politicians' views on civil society followed by the societal actors' views of civil society and civil society organizations, and after that, we describe who, from a socio-demographic perspective, these civil society actors are and in which policy fields civil society organizations work. Then we will delineate how the relationships between the civil society organizations and the state have developed and which roles civil society organizations play within the Vietnamese political system. Finally, we address the newly and controversially discussed question of whether Vietnamese civil society organizations are supporters of or obstacles to the processes of democratization in their country. In conclusion, we compare one of the most important findings, viz. the understanding of civil society and civil society organizations from the perspective of the Vietnamese actors, to the views of actors from other Asian countries on this topic.

In all sections of this chapter, we compile what is known about civil society and civil society organizations in Vietnam and focus on, wherever possible, the actors' views. In most sections, we refer to or even base the description and analysis on results from our own research (Wischermann 2003, 2010, 2011, 2013; Wischermann and Nguyen 2003; Wischermann *et al.* 2015; Wischermann *et al.* 2016a; Wischermann *et al.* 2016b). As regards the types of CSOs, we use a typology that has served well in three surveys (1999–2003; 2008–2010; 2013–2016). We differentiate between mass organizations, professionals' organizations, NGOs, business organizations, and faith-based organizations.[5]

Rules and regulations decisive for the foundation and operation of associations

All Vietnamese constitutions since 1945 have recognized the right to freedom of association and assembly as one of the five basic rights of the respective state's citizens. This basic right in the Democratic Republic of Vietnam (vulgo North-Vietnam, the legal predecessor of the Socialist Republic of Vietnam, founded in 1976) was concretized by two laws issued in 1957: the law on the freedom of assembly (No. 101-SL/L003/1957) and the law on the right of association (No. 102-SL/L004/1957). These two laws are still in effect and they are the highest legal basis regulating the operation of associations in Vietnam.

In the decade after the official start of *Đổi Mới* in 1986, the CPV and state have issued many legal documents related to the organization and management of associations. Here we would like to mention Decree 35-HĐBT ("*Hội đồng bộ trưởng*" or "Councils of Ministers"), issued in 1992, addressing the activities in the area of science and technology, which is important since it allowed individuals to establish social organizations specifically in these policy areas. The Civil Code, issued in 1995, was a legal response to the need to establish legal entities. This collection of laws also confirms the right of an individual to form associations, thereby, making the establishment and running of an association more an activity of the citizens rather than an activity of the state. At least indirectly related to the enactment of these legal documents, we observe a "mushrooming" of associations in the late 1990s in the North, whereas in the South of Vietnam we observe a "foundation boom" of various types of associations preceding the enactments of those legal documents in the early and mid-1990s.[6]

In the early 1990s, the National Assembly began to draft and discuss a law to replace the Law no. 102/1957 on associations. Various Draft Laws on associations have been discussed since then. Until now (2016), sixteen drafts have been brought to the National Assembly for discussion and vote. In its autumn session of 2016, the National Assembly postponed the discussion of the 16th Draft Law on Associations partly due to controversies amongst the Deputies and partly due to civil society organizations' pressure to suspend the vote.

In 2003, the Government issued Decree 88/2003 on the organization, operation, and state management of associations. This decree does not apply to organizations such as the Viet Nam Fatherland Front, Viet Nam General Confederation of Labor, Ho Chi Minh Communist Youth Union, Viet Nam Farmers' Association, Viet Nam Veterans Association, Viet Nam Women's Union, or religious congregations. In ranking, these organizations enjoy the most prominent position amongst associations in Vietnam: They have a special legal status and the state pays for, at least, a part of their staff's salaries and other organizational expenses. Decree 88/2003 defines associations as:

> voluntary organizations of citizens, organizations of Vietnamese of the same professions, the same hobbies, the same social strata, for the common purposes of gathering and uniting members, regular activities, non-profit-making, aiming to protect members' legitimate rights and interests, to support one another for efficient activities, contribute to the country's socioeconomic development.
>
> *(Decree 88/2003)*

The establishment of such an association must be approved by "responsible authorities" (*cơ quan nhà nước có thẩm quyền*).[7]

Shortly after its enactment, Decree No. 88 was criticized because of its complicated requirements as regards setting up an association, the number of necessary members for that, the association's internal regulations, and the state's possibility to interfere severely in these affairs, etc. It is significant that the decree is based on an "ask-and-give" mechanism: Founders of associations must ask the respective responsible authority to allow them to set up associations. In accordance with the constitutional guarantee of the right to freedom of association, the state should just register the establishment of an association. The decree did not meet the earlier criteria set up by the CPV, which had asked for a much more simple and less complicated legal document.

In 2010, the prime minister issued Decree No. 45 that replaced Decree 88/2003. Two years later, this decree was further amended and supplemented (Decree 33/2012/ND-CP). Decree 45/2010 left unchanged the way in which Decree 88/2003 had defined associations, the establishment of such an organization, and the "ask-and-give" mechanism that regulates the relationship between founders of an association and the respective authorities. Obviously, the new decree aimed at intensifying the state's control of associations since the regulations in the organization, operation, and state management of associations have been tightened. Along with continuing efforts to amend the Draft Law on Associations, there is an ongoing debate on a decree to supplement Decrees 45/2010 and 33/2012, following Decision 858/QD-BNV, dated July 30, 2013, of the Minister of Home Affairs on approving the proposal of replacing Decrees 45/2010 and 33/2012.

Civil society and civil society organizations: from the views of the CPV and the state

In accordance with specifics of authoritarian rule (for example, leaving societal actors in uncertainty about the ruler's thoughts and intentions) and related to principles of Marxist-Leninist provenience, a large part of the politics in Vietnam and inside the CPV remains difficult to decipher. It is in this context that we cannot say for sure how the debate on civil society went inside the party. However, there are at least indications that after the re-unification of the country (1976), the CPV strictly negated the necessity and development of something like civil society;[8] that during the 1970s and 1980s, the Communist Party saw and used mass organizations "as a school of socialism and communism for all social strata, as an invaluable collaborator of the state, as the link connecting the CPV and the masses" (as the Central Party's 4th meeting, tenure 5, June/1983 indicated, cited in Dang 2015: 47); and finally, that from the 1980s until the early "noughties," the CPV saw civil society and civil society organizations as protagonists of schemes of "peaceful evolution," put forward by the US administration and other "enemies of socialism."[9] Even after the CPV removed their aim of establishing a "proletarian dictatorship" from the program (1990) and the country's constitution (1992), at least until the early noughties, state planners saw, for example, poverty alleviation "as the duty of the state and a problem which would be solved mainly by state-administered programs at a given time: 'The operation of social organizations is just temporarily urgent!'" (Wischermann 2003: 886) Thus, for quite a long time, the idea that the state should limit its operations, to what it can do best or what others in the society refuse to do, was alien to Vietnamese officials (Marr 1994: 9).

However, mirroring societal changes, indicated by the development of a variety of new types of civil society organizations, and thinking about the potential political fallout of this development and new modes of governance, in 2007 Tran Ngoc Hien, a theoretician of the CPV, "called for renewed and bold thinking by allowing civil society as the *third cornerstone* alongside the market economy and the law-based state to lay the full foundation for the political and economic system in Vietnam" (cited in Bui 2013: 79; emphasis by the author). This suggests that inside the CPV, cadres thought of changes in terms of governance structures, since following the official line in Vietnam only mass organizations, controlled by the CPV, are called the "third pillar" of Vietnam's political system (the other two are the Communist Party and the state it controls). Furthermore, we are tempted to read into the leading theoretician's suggestions that the intention of these internal party thinkers might have been to broaden the base of the CPV's rule by means of including a carefully selected variety of civil society organizations. The decision to create "special associations" somewhat later (Decree 68/2010/QD-TTg, November 1, 2010), selected by the prime minister and equipped with specific rights and privileges, might be seen as a case in point. But there are also strong indications that such new thinking did not aim at changing the privileged role of mass organizations or a certain number of professional and other organizations that were closely related to and under the control of the CPV. Here, the expenses to run the mass organizations and the "special associations," equal to 0.35 percent of the GDP, are a case in point (as of 2014; the calculation is based on the total estimated budget for the mass organizations, see Nguyen, Nguyen, and Vu 2015: 175). Such expenses for a number of civil society organizations make sense, because the party wants to subsidize these organizations to help secure its control.

Even today (2016), "*xã hội dân sự*" (or civil society) is still a term which the party and state officials use rarely and reluctantly, and if they use it, it is not in a clearly defined sense. Nevertheless, the Vietnamese government, to a certain extent, recognizes, endorses, or tolerates services that CSOs render to the public (Bui 2013: 77). Under rare circumstances, politicians closely related to the CPV even bow to the pressure from civil society, civil society organizations, and social movements (Bui 2016: 99–103).

Civil society: from the actors' perspective

Up to now, there has been only one survey on civil society organizations (Wischermann 2010) that is representative for at least those in Hanoi and Ho Chi Minh City, and in which the actors were asked about their understanding of civil society and civil society organizations. However, earlier studies (e.g., Kerkvliet , Nguyen, and Bach 2008), and also subsequent explorations (such as Bui 2013; Taylor *et al.* 2012) arrived at similar results using different methods. Findings from the survey of Jörg Wischermann (2010) and his Vietnamese colleagues show that 45 percent of the respondents are of the opinion that civil society is represented in civil society organizations, that is, unions and associations. These promote and protect the interests of their members, clientele, and/or beneficiaries; they entertain a formal dialogue with local authorities/government; they may serve as a bridge between state and people (position 1). Named second-most (27 percent) is a notion of civil society that is very well known from Eastern and Western Europe, but also from Latin America and Africa: Civil society is "the most democratic society." However, the state's and government's roles as regards development and management of civil society may vary from country to country (position 2). Only 12 percent thought of civil society as a distinct sphere between state, economy, and family (position 3). This is a classic, basically essentialist understanding of civil society that carries a litany of political and ethical aspirations and implications.

Whereas one may read a strong impetus toward political change and democracy into position 2, the majority's position 1 puts "society first" and focuses on societal change, societal self-help, solidarity, and the like. It lacks most, if not all, normative underpinnings that both other concepts have. As used here, the understanding of civil society as an ensemble of civil society organizations is basically descriptive and lacks almost any explicit reference to the processes of democratization. In contrast, actors who are in favor of the second position aim at having a stronger say in the processes of policy-forming and decision-making, a bigger say in holding officials accountable, and the like.[10] Thus, this understanding is powerful in terms of politics and is oriented toward various types of political reforms.

A few years later, Hai Thiem Bui (2013) confirmed that a basically descriptive understanding of civil society, a view not based on normative standards of liberal provenience, was still typical for most Vietnamese civil society organizations:

> In the Vietnamese context civil society is broadly understood as a sphere of associative actions to articulate common interests and demands of citizens, to protect their rights, and to meet their needs vis-à-vis the state by seeking to engage with governance to negotiate ideas, norms, values, and practices of the state.
>
> *(Bui 2013: 80–81)*

Who are the actors of the Vietnamese civil society?

Findings from the survey of Wischermann and his Vietnamese colleagues, from 2008–2010 (Wischermann 2010), show that in general civil society organizations' representatives are well educated: 53 percent hold a university degree, and almost a fifth hold a doctoral degree (18 percent). More than two-thirds of the interviewed representatives are forty-nine years or older;

the largest peer group consists of those who were born between 1955 and 1960 (21 percent). CSOs in both cities are male-dominated with more than two-thirds of the leading personnel being men (68 percent). In Ho Chi Minh City, the gender ratio is a bit more balanced than in Hanoi. It is only within the peer group of those between forty-nine and fifty-four years old that more women than men are chairpersons, directors, etc. of civil society organizations (56 percent vs. 44 percent). It is noticeable that men dominate the professional organizations, the business organizations, and the mass organizations. Only in NGOs, the gender ratio is slightly more balanced (60 percent vs. 40 percent). Amongst the Hanoi-based business and professional organizations, there is literally no female representative (Wischermann 2010: 16).

According to Irene Norlund's CIVICUS survey (2006), "most leaders of Vietnamese NGOs are former government employees or academics. They are primarily either retired or young and have a (foreign) university education background" (Norlund 2006: 49). Later on, William Taylor *et al.* (2012) present more differentiated findings. They find that NGOs and NGO-like organizations in Hanoi and Ho Chi Minh City are run by young actors and led by, in part, less experienced actors. However,

> CSO staff in Hanoi generally have higher qualifications than their southern counterparts, with more Ph.D. and masters degree holders. While female staff members outnumber their male colleagues across the board, the gender gap is particularly wide in Ho Chi Minh-City.
>
> *(Taylor et al. 2012: 13)*

They explain these differences by referring to the different nature of NGOs and NGO-like civil society organizations in the two cities:

> More of the organizations in Hanoi function as research institutes requiring higher levels of education, whereas the NGOs surveyed in the south are dominated by charitable work and community intervention. The activities they carry out require more practical facilitators and social workers, professions that tend to draw more women than men.
>
> *(Taylor et al. 2012: 13f)*

Taylor *et al.* (2012) observe a new generation of NGOs emerging, which were led by younger, well-educated professionals with a strong commitment to social equality and justice. A number of former International NGO (INGO) workers left their organizations to start their own (Taylor *et al.* 2012: 15).

Civil society organizations: fields of activities

Civil society organizations in Vietnam are addressing a wide range of issues such as poverty reduction, gender-based violence, environmental problems, and not least, the issues of empowerment and democratization. Examining the role of mass organizations, Shozo Sakata (2006) finds that these organizations contribute significantly to poverty reduction. In particular, mass organizations inform and help poor people at the local level to obtain microcredits (Sakata 2006: 57, 72). In a similar vein, Norlund (2006) stresses the impact of civil society organizations on poverty alleviation and as regards the empowerment of citizens. Moreover, she finds that all types of civil society organizations are active and successful at informing and educating citizens on public issues (Norlund 2006: 99f.).

According to a survey representative for civil society organizations in Hanoi and Ho Chi Minh City (Wischermann 2010), the five most frequent fields of activities are: social work (35.7 percent), health (22.3 percent), promotion of economic development (21.3 percent), education (19.0 percent), and community development (17.0 percent).[11] Taylor *et al.* (2012) stress differences, in terms of the activities, between NGOs based in Hanoi and those working in Ho Chi Minh City. Hanoian NGOs focus on research, policy analysis, and technical assistance, whereas the organizations in Ho Chi Minh City tend to concentrate on concrete social issues and the provision of services to disadvantaged populations. They explain this difference by referring to the longer history of social work as a field of study and practice in the south "as does the greater involvement of faith-based organizations in non-profit and charity work in HCMC" (Taylor *et al.* 2012: 17).[12]

Differences regarding the NGOs' activities that were observed in the 1990s and early noughties to a certain degree and extent still exist today (2016). At least the Northerners' preference for policy advocacy and the formulation and implementation of policies is still to be observed. However, to explain this difference one does not need to refer to different political and socio-cultural traditions. In general, the political center is Hanoi, and although Ho Chi Minh City may be an economic hub, it is far away from the political center. Moreover, politicians in Hanoi are difficult to reach—this holds true for northern NGOs, but all the more so for those from the south.

Besides those differences in the activities and approach, Taylor *et al.* (2012) make an important point when they refer to the influence of international donors on the agenda of Hanoi-based NGOs (Taylor *et al.* 2012: 17–18). Not least, due to such influence in the capital and elsewhere, many civil society organizations are involved in activities addressing the problem of climate change. Civil society organizations and various networks are implementing a variety of projects with a focus on mitigation, adaptation, or capacity-building at the community level. Besides, policy advocacy and to a lesser extent community and media advocacy activities have been carried out by networks of NGOs and cross-sectoral alliances involving government and donor representatives (Wells-Dang 2012). Laura Faludi (2016) observes a similar phenomenon when she describes how international donors backed, if not promoted, the support of NGOs in Hanoi and Ho Chi Minh City and their engagement for the rights of LGBT and marriage equality (Faludi 2016: 90–91).

As for political involvement, since the early years of this century,

> there has been a concerted effort to form explicitly political organizations dedicated to the promotion of democracy, human rights and religious freedom. An unprecedented number of political organizations have been formed. […] These groups are considered illegal by the state and therefore have no standing in Vietnam's one-party system.
>
> *(Thayer 2009: 11)*

Most recently, in addition to registered organizations, many individual civil campaigns and activities have been organized, such as the "no plastic" (aiming at educating people to use plastic bags less often), the "6,700 trees" (protest against the replacement of thousands of century-old trees in Hanoi, see Vu 2017), the "stop nuclear power" and the "save Son Doong cave" campaign.

> Although these initiatives barely end up as formally registered organizations, they have created new space for people to participate in solving the problems of society without the government's permission. These developments cause positive changes in the decision-making process and give CS in Vietnam a face.
>
> *(Ha 2014)*

Roles of civil society organizations

Roles of civil society organizations in general and their relationships with the state

In an exploratory study, Wischermann *et al.* (2015) found that the most important roles that interviewed civil society organizations' representatives in Hanoi and Ho Chi Minh City name are those of "advocate" (though not one who applies a confrontational style), "service provider," and the role of a "bridge between state and society." Only a few civil society organizations see themselves as performing the role of a "watchdog" or carrying out "lobbying" activities (Wischermann *et al.* 2015: 4).

The latter indicates the strong impact various forms of authoritarian state power have on civil society organizations, which in turn seem to be hesitant to choose roles that might imply conflicts with the authorities. However, most recently (August 25, 2016), civil society organizations assembled in Hanoi and discussed an understanding of advocacy and lobbying, which would include forms of opposition to laws decided, decrees announced, and policies which authorities intend to implement.

Nevertheless, various studies suggest that working *with* and *not against* the government is still prevalent. This holds true, although data from one of the rare analyses allowing us to compare civil society organizations and state relationships at the end of the 1990s and in 2009 (Wischermann 2010; Wischermann and Nguyen 2003) lead to the conclusion that conflicts between civil society organizations and the state have increased. More concretely, in 2009, round about one-third, compared to up to two-thirds in the study from 2000, of all representatives indicates that these relationships are "easy." In general, the proportion of those indicating problems arising out of the relationship between those organizations, encountered at least case- or time-wise, has nearly doubled between 2000 and 2009. Wischermann (2010), however, assesses this as kind of a normalization process, not as a process of increasing tensions between civil society organizations and the state (Wischermann 2010: 31–33). Furthermore, Wischermann (2010) ascertains that the relationships between civil society organizations and governmental organizations are more relaxed in Ho Chi Minh City than in Hanoi (Wischermann 2010: 30).

In 2008, Ben Tria Kerkvliet *et al.* (2008) came to similar results. They stress that civil society organizations, in the eyes of the actors, play roles which are complimentary to the state. First, civil society organizations advise the state to get the views of and consult with citizens and organizations in society: "Lobbying, in particularly, can be good when it conveys people's under-standings and views to influence authorities to make better policies" (Kerkvliet *et al.* 2008: 20). Second, civil society organizations help to "carry out government programs, as well as doing things the state does not. Thereby, civil society groups provide services that are beneficial to the state and society" (Kerkvliet *et al.* 2008: 21).

A couple of years later, in their analysis of the relationships between local NGOs and the state, Taylor *et al.* (2012) conclude that: "establishing close relationships with the authorities at different levels is vital to most organizations' strategies and a determining factor in the success of their program activities" (Taylor *et al.* 2012: 23). The authors explain these findings with the strong impact that the political environment has on the relationships between Hanoi- and Ho Chi Minh City-based NGOs and the authorities. The lack of a clear legal framework "creates an uncertain operating environment and reinforces the importance of personal networks in getting things done rather than a set of transparent procedures applicable to all NGOs" (Taylor *et al.* 2012: 22).

In sum, what we can observe is that Vietnamese civil society organizations are not opposed to the state or, at least, not opposed to the state based on principles. They are working with the central and/or local state. However, such co-operation happens in various ways and does not exclude tensions or even conflicts between both unequal partners. Moreover, civil society organizations perform various roles, which are beneficial to the clientele civil society organizations cater to, but also to the local and central state. Finally, civil society organizations still face many challenges as regards the interaction with the state, not only but also because of a still missing Law on Associations and the lack of transparent and enforceable rules and regulations.

Civil society organizations: supporters or obstacles in the processes of democratization?

This question constitutes a relatively new subject that Vietnamese and foreign researchers are addressing. In a recent study, Wischermann *et al.* (2016a; 2016b) ask whether civil society organizations are supporters of authoritarian regimes. They explore the roles that civil society and civil society organizations play in three "post-socialist" countries (Algeria, Mozambique, Vietnam).

In their survey, Wischermann and his colleagues analyze the interdependent and reciprocal relations between civil society organizations and the different forms of state power with respect to one specific issue and in three policy fields (decision-making in civil society organizations, welfare policy concerning HIV/AIDS; economic policy concerning small- and medium-sized enterprises; policies concerning gender equality and the rights of women and sexual minorities) to assess the relations between civil society organizations and the state's infrastructural and discursive power.[13]

In what follows, we summarize the most important Vietnam-related results from the study of Wischermann *et al.* (2016a) as regards the roles civil society organizations play as supporters or obstacles in the processes of democratization:

1   In terms of their internal structure, Vietnamese civil society organizations succumb to this form of authoritarian state power ("infrastructural power") and many of them adopt the state's and/or the state ruling party's organizational principles (such as "democratic centralism"). The state's and the ruling party's interference in the internal processes of civil society organizations is widely accepted. Thus, authoritarian and authoritarianism-promoting, state-determined structures are accepted, if not enforced. As a result, in terms of intra-organizational decision-making processes, most Vietnamese civil society organizations are hierarchically structured, if not organized in an authoritarian way. In the sense of Tocqueville, they are not "schools of democracy." There are exceptions to this rule, namely some NGOs, but the authors assume them to be a tiny minority.

2   Most Vietnamese civil society organizations that are engaged in the welfare provision sector, either willingly or unwillingly, help to foster the foundations of authoritarianism. This means that whether they intend to or not, these organizations help to negate citizens' individual and collective self-determination and autonomy. Thus, they could be considered as obstacles to democratization. NGOs very cautiously undertake steps that might help the development of democracy-promoting effects. They, however, place so many restrictions on themselves that they can be, at best, considered as potential supporters of further democratization.

3   In the field of economic policy, especially the promotion of small- and medium-sized enterprises (SMEs), the research team found that some business organizations and certain

professional organizations have been co-opted by the Vietnamese state.[14] These organizations are not agents of democratization. Although they help to change various economic policies and although their activities produce some democracy-promoting effects, overall these organizations help to secure existing power structures and those in power. They are obstacles to democratization.

4   Finally, Wischermann *et al.* (2016a) explored the roles of one mass organization and various NGOs in the field of gender equality, women's rights, and rights of sexual minorities. Their analysis suggests that this mass organization is an obstacle to further democratization. Although the mass organization's positions and activities help to develop some democracy-promoting effects, these effects are eclipsed by this organization's fundamental understanding of gender, its position of principle regarding the rights of sexual minorities, and its role as a mass organization under the leadership of and within the system of rule of the CPV. By contrast, some NGOs active in this policy field can be considered supporters of further democratization.

Wischermann *et al.* (2016a) conclude that there is no simple and straightforward answer to the leading question, and there is no one type of Vietnamese civil society organization that, without further qualification, can be called a supporter of *or* an obstacle to democratization. However, there are indications for the validity of the assumption that Vietnamese NGOs, in some policy fields, have the potential to or already play the role of agents of democratic change.

Conclusion

In the sections above, we have presented an overview on the mostly restrictive rules with which those in power try to regulate the foundation and operation of civil society organizations of various sorts. We have further described the diverging views of local politicians on civil society and societal actors' understanding of civil society and civil society organizations. We then got a closer look at the founders and representatives of civil society organizations; the broad array of activities civil society organizations pursue; the roles civil society organizations play and their varying relationships with the state. Finally, we described the roles civil society organizations play as regards processes of democratization or preservation of Vietnam's authoritarian political regime.

From the view of the actors on what civil society is about and what civil society organizations are, we found that from most civil society actors' perspectives, civil society basically is represented in the ensemble of civil society organizations—a view prevalent in Asia as found by Muthiah Alagappa (2004). More precisely, most Vietnamese civil society actors' understanding of civil society focuses on societal change, societal self-help, solidarity, and the like; it is basically descriptive, lacks most if not all normative underpinnings, and does not explicitly refer to processes of democratization. Nevertheless, this understanding includes that civil society organizations engage with the state in that civil society organizations "articulate common interests and demands of citizens, to protect their rights, and to meet their needs vis-à-vis the state by seeking to engage with governance to negotiate ideas, norms, values, and practices" (Bui 2013: 93).

In conclusion, we thus see that Vietnamese civil society and civil society organizations as not very different, if at all, from their Asian counterparts and are playing similar roles. Following Arun Patnaik (2012), civil society and civil society organizations fulfill "positive" and "negative" functions: Like civil society organizations in other Asian countries, some Vietnamese civil society organizations help to foster processes of democratization, others help to preserve the existing regime, and some are doing both.

In conclusion, we argue that if there is no difference in principles betw̲ civil society and civil society organizations and those from other countries in ̲ because of the functions of civil society and civil society organizations in capitalist soc̲ help to maintain and/or change the existing power positions of various classes and social gr̲ and the power relations between them.

Notes

1 Democratic centralism is a leadership principle for communist parties developed by W. I. Lenin. According to this principle: (a) the state and party are structured in a hierarchical and centralized manner; (b) the party and state leadership is elected from the bottom up, but the selection of electoral candidates is top-down; (c) decisions made by higher-level bodies for the lower levels are binding; and (d) minorities must subordinate themselves to the majority and a tight party discipline. The questioning of decisions that have already been made is seen as a sign of disloyalty. A form of authoritarian central- ism has developed from the principle of democratic centralism.

2 After drastic cuts in public services and welfare schemes, the state and the CPV welcome services, especially in the fields of public health and education even when it is rendered by local NGOs.

3 The theoretical implications of the question, debated widely amongst various scholars analyzing the situation in Vietnam and other countries, as to whether "real" civil society and civil society organiza- tions can and do exist in authoritarian countries, are discussed in the Chapter 23: Authoritarian Rule.

4 Since the Vietnamese government does not officially recognize civil society and civil society organiza- tions, the rules and regulations address associations in general and those of various types.

5 Thus, we include organizations which are in general closely affiliated with and under the control of the VCP (see Wischermann *et al.* 2015: 14–17, 19–20). This is because, in the opinion of most actors engaged in those organizations, their associations are societal and not state organizations (though closely affiliated with and providing useful services for the state). For the VCP, these organizations are prim- arily societal organizations and useful for the state the party dominates because they link party and state with the society.

6 For an explanation of these differences, see Sidel (1995: 293–299) and Wischermann and Nguyen (2003: 190–195, 225–227).

7 According to Article 15, Decree 88/2003, the Ministry of Home Affairs allows the establishment, divi- sion, separation, merger, consolidation, and dissolution, and approves the charters of associations oper- ating nationwide or inter-provincially; at the provincial level, the presidents of the People's Committee grant such permissions to associations operating within their respective provinces.

8 The resolution of the Fourth Party Congress in 1976 and the newly adopted party statute made it clear that the CPV intended to lead the way toward a rather orthodox version of socialism. This "left no space whatsoever for concepts such as civil society" (Marr 1994: 3).

9 For a description of seminars held, booklets issued, and book-length essays written focusing on "Anti- peaceful Evolutionism" in the 1990s, see Marr (1994: 3–10).

10 Note that representatives of mass organizations (50 percent) and representatives of professional organi- zations (28 percent) are in favor of that view (position 2). Only 22 percent of the representatives of NGOs and business organizations share this view (Wischermann 2010: 19).

11 Here, we draw on unpublished results from the survey of Wischermann *et al.*: "Civil Society Action and Governance in Vietnam" (2008–2010), funded by the German Research Council (KO 3513/3–1).

12 The difference in terms of activities and approaches taken between NGOs working in the north and the south of Vietnam has been described in detail by Sidel (1995: 294, 297–299) and Wischermann (2003: 874–877).

13 The theoretical assumptions of this project are outlined in Chapter 23: Authoritarian Rule.

14 According to Selznick (1949) "(c)ooptation (is) … the process of absorbing new elements into the leadership or policy-determining structure of an organization as a means of averting threats to its stability or existence" (Selznick 1949: 13).

Suggested readings

Alagappa, Muthiah, ed. 2004. *Civil Society and Political Change in Asia*. Stanford, CA: Stanford University Press.

Bui, Hai Thiem. 2013. The Development of Civil Society and Dynamics of Governance in Vietnam's One Party Rule. *Global Change, Peace & Security* 25(1): 77–93.

Marr, David. 1994. The Vietnam Communist Party and Civil Society. Paper presented at the Vietnam Update conference: Doi Moi, The State and Civil Society, Australian National University, November 10–11.

Wischermann, Jörg. 2003. Vietnam in the Era of Doi Moi. Issue-Oriented Organizations and Their Relationship to the Government. *Asian Survey* XLIII (6): 867–889.

Wischermann, Jörg, Bui The Cuong, Dang Thi Viet Phuong. 2016. Vietnamese Civic Organisations: Supporters of or Obstacles to Further Democratisation? Results from an Empirical Study. *Journal of Current Southeast Asian Affairs* 35(2): 57–88.

Websites

The Institute for Studies of Society, Economics and Environment, http://isee.org.vn/en.

A science and technology organization working toward equality for all minority groups in Vietnam through conferences, policy advocacy, education, and community initiatives.

People's Participation Working Group, http://ppwgvietnam.info/en.

An informal network to create a forum between organizations and professionals to exchange information on issues relating to grass-roots democracy and civil society in Vietnam, and to coordinate groups acting for the same purpose.

The United Nations (Country Team in Viet Nam), http://un.org.vn/en.html.

This site consists of links to all UN agencies, funds and programs within and relating to Viet Nam.

Wake It Up, www.wakeitup.net/.

A non-governmental organization based in Hanoi, Vietnam with the mission statement: "to help gather social power to solve social issues."

References

Alagappa, Muthiah, ed. 2004. *Civil Society and Political Change in Asia*. Stanford, CA: Stanford University Press.

Beaulieu, Carole. 1994. Is it an NGO? Is it Civil Society?: Is it Pluralism Wriggling about?. *Institute of Current World Affairs*. Electronic document, www.icwa.org/wp-content/uploads/2015/09/CB-26.pdf, accessed September 23, 2016.

Bui, Hai Thiem. 2013. The Development of Civil Society and Dynamics of Governance in Vietnam's One Party Rule. *Global Change, Peace & Security* 25(1): 77–93.

Bui, Hai Thiem. 2016. The Influence of Social Media in Vietnam's Elite Politics. *Journal of Southeast Asian Affairs* 35(2): 89–112.

Dang, Thi Viet Phuong. 2015. *The Collective Life. The Sociology of Voluntary Associations in North Vietnamese Rural Areas*. Hanoi: Vietnam National University Press.

Faludi, Laura. 2016. *The Vietnamese LGBT Movement and the Media. Framing and re-Framing Homosexuality in Vietnamese Public and Media Discourses*. Wissenschaftliche Hausarbeit zur Erlangung des akademischen Grades eines Masters of Arts der Universität Hamburg [Magisterial Thesis, University of Hamburg].

Fforde, Adam, and Nguyen Dinh Huan. 2001. *Vietnamese Rural Society and its Institutions; Results of a Study of Cooperative Groups and Cooperatives in Three Provinces*. Electronic document, www.academia.edu/475955/Vietnamese_rural_society_and_its_institutions_Results_of_a_study_of_cooperative_groups_and_cooperatives_in_three_Provinces, accessed September 23, 2016.

Ha, Thi Quynh Nga. 2014. Climate Change and Energy in Vietnam: Is the Door Open for Civil Society?. Friedrich-Ebert Stiftung. Electronic document, www.fes-sustainability.org/de/nachhaltigkeit-und-demokratie/climate-change-and-energy-vietnam, accessed September 23, 2016.

Kerkvliet, Ben Tria, Quang A. Nguyen, and Sinh Tan Bach. 2008. *Forms of Engagement Between State Agencies and Civil Society Organizations in Vietnam. Study Report.* Electronic document, http://ngocentre.org.vn/files/docs/Forms_of_Engagement_FINAL_COMPLETE.pdf, accessed September 23, 2016.

Marr, David. 1994. The Vietnam Communist Party and Civil Society. Paper presented at the Vietnam Update conference: Doi Moi, The State and Civil Society, Australian National University, November 10–11.

Nguyen, Hong Hai. 2016. *Political Dynamics of Grassroots Democracy in Vietnam.* New York: Palgrave Macmillan.

Nguyen, Duc Thanh, Khac Giang Nguyen, and Cuong Sy Vu. 2015. Social and Economic Costs of State-sponsored Mass Organisations in Vietnam Hanoi. Hanoi: Hong Duc Publisher.

Norlund, Irene, ed. 2006. *The Emerging Civil Society. An Initial Assessment of Civil Society in Vietnam.* Hanoi: Vietnam Institute of Development Studies. Electronic document, www.vids.org.vn/vn/Attach/20065222515_CSI_VN_Final_report.pdf, accessed December 15, 2016.

Patnaik, Arun K. 2012. The Contemporary Significance of Gramsci's Critique of Civil Society. *Working USA* 15: 577–588.

Sakata, Shozo. 2006. Changing Roles of Mass Organizations in Poverty Reduction in Vietnam. In *Actors for Poverty Reduction in Vietnam.* Vu Tuan Anh and Shozo Sakata, eds. Pp. 49–79. Chiba: Institute of Developing Economies (printed in Hanoi).

Selznick, Philip. 1949. *TVA and the Grass Roots. A Study in the Sociology of Formal Organization.* Berkeley, CA: University of California Press.

Sidel, Mark. 1995. The Emergence of a Nonprofit Sector and Philanthropy in the Socialist Republic of Vietnam. In *Emerging Civil Society in the Asia Pacific Community.* Tadashi Yamamoto, ed. Pp. 293–304. Singapore: Institute of Southeast Asian Studies.

Taylor, William, Thu Hang Nguyen, Quang Pham Tu, and Tuyet Thi Ngoc Huynh. 2012. *Civil Society in Vietnam: A Comparative Study of Civil Society Organizations in Hanoi and Ho Chi Minh City.* Hanoi: The Asia Foundation. Electronic document, https://asiafoundation.org/resources/pdfs/CivilSocietyReportFINALweb.pdf, accessed September 23, 2016.

Thayer, Carlyle A. 2009. Vietnam and the Challenge of Political Civil Society. *Contemporary Southeast Asia* 31(1): 1–27.

Vu, Ngoc Anh. 2017. *Grassroots Environmental Activism in an Authoritarian Context: The Trees Movement in Vietnam. VOLUNTAS: International Journal of Voluntary and Nonprofit Organizations.* DOI: 10.1007/s11266-017-9829-1.

Wells-Dang, Andrew. 2012. Civil Society and Climate Change in Vietnam. Actors, Roles, and Possibilities, PACT, Vietnam Country Office (May 2012). Electronic document, www.vesdi.org.vn/images/download/Pact%20Civil%20Society%20and%20Climate%20Change%20report%20final.doc, accessed September 23, 2016.

Wells-Dang, Andrew. 2012. Civil Society and Climate Change in Vietnam. Actors, Roles, and Possibilities, PACT, Vietnam Country Office (May 2012). Electronic document, www.vesdi.org.vn/images/download/Pact%20Civil%20Society%20and%20Climate%20Change%20report%20final.doc, accessed September 23, 2016.

Wischermann, Jörg. 2003. Vietnam in the Era of Doi Moi. Issue-Oriented Organizations and Their Relationship to the Government. *Asian Survey* 43(6): 867–889.

Wischermann, Jörg. 2010. Civil Society Action and Governance in Vietnam. Selected Findings from an Empirical Survey. *Journal of Current Southeast Asian Affairs* 2: 3–40, Electronic document, www.giga-hamburg.de/en/publication/civil-society-action-and-governance-in-vietnam-selected-findings-from-an-empirical, accessed December 27, 2016.

Wischermann, Jörg. 2011. Governance and Civil Society Action in Vietnam: Changing the Rules from Within—Potentials and Limits. *Asian Politics and Policies* 3(3): 383–411.

Wischermann, Jörg. 2013. Civic Organizations in Vietnam's One-Party State: Supporters of Authoritarian Rule? *GIGA Working Paper* No. 228 July 2013. Hamburg: GIGA, Electronic document, www.giga-hamburg.de/en/publication/civic-organizations-in-vietnams-one-party-state-supporters-of-authoritarian-rule, accessed December 27, 2016.

Wischermann, Jörg, The Cuong Bui, and Phuong Thi Viet Dang. 2016a. Vietnamese Civic Organisations: Supporters of or Obstacles to Further Democratisation? Results from an Empirical Survey. *Journal of Current Southeast Asian Affairs* 35(2): 57–88.

Wischermann, Jörg, Bettina Bunk, Jasmin Lorch, and Patrick Köllner. 2016b. Do Associations Support Authoritarian Rule? Tentative Answers from Algeria, Mozambique, and Vietnam. *GIGA Working Paper*

No. 295, November 2016. Hamburg: GIGA. Electronic document, www.giga-hamburg.de/en/publication/do-associations-support-authoritarian-rule-algeria-mozambique-vietnam, accessed December 27, 2016.

Wischermann, Jörg, The Cuong Bui, Vinh Quang Nguyen, Phuong Thi Viet Dang, and Chau Thi Minh Nguyen. 2015. Under the State's Thumb: Results from an Empirical Survey of Civil Organizations in Vietnam. *GIGA Working Paper* No. 276, July 2015. Hamburg: GIGA, Electronic document, www.giga-hamburg.de/en/publication/results-from-an-empirical-survey-of-civic-organizations-in-of-civic-organizations-in-vietnam, accessed December 27, 2016.

Wischermann, Jörg, and Quang Vinh Nguyen. 2003. The Relationship between Civic and Governmental Organizations in Vietnam: Selected Finding. In *Getting Organized in Vietnam: Moving in and around the Socialist State*. Benedict J. Tria Kerkvliet, Russell Hiang-Khng Heng, and David Koh Wee Hock, eds. Pp. 185–233. Singapore: Institute of Southeast Asian Studies Singapore.

9

MALAYSIA

Gaik Cheng Khoo

Civil society, activist citizens, and the civil sphere

Malaysia, in practice, is an electoral authoritarian regime (Case 2009) that exercises authoritarian powers of repression, despite inheriting the colonial legacy of a constitutional monarchy and a parliamentary system at its Independence in 1957. That said, it has "a long and lively tradition of opposition politics and associational activity" (Weiss 2003a: 59). Generally, "civil society" is usually mentioned as a barometer of democracy in articles about the state of politics in Malaysia since Tun Dr. Mahathir Mohamed's prime ministership (1981–2003), with the majority of articles concentrating on advocacy-oriented non-governmental organizations (NGOs). The most prolific research with regard to social movements and politics has been conducted by the political scientist Meredith Weiss (Weiss and Hassan 2003; Weiss 2003a, 2003b, 2004a, 2004b, 2006, 2011). Weiss describes the unique nature of Malaysian civil society in that it includes sectarian organizations. More broadly, NGOs in Malaysia include:

> any group of citizens engaged in collective action for self-help or issue advocacy outside the aegis of the state, even if lacking a mass base, hardly democratic and supporting some links with political society (elements from government and opposition parties and state institutions).
>
> *(Weiss 2003a: 62)*

Under Malaysian law, NGOs are registered societies. Sometimes regarded as a "third force" (Iskandar 2016; Pasuni 2011), civil society involves: "citizens acting collectively in a public sphere to express their interests, passions, and ideas, exchange information, achieve mutual goals, make demands on the state and hold state officials accountable" (Diamond 1994: 5 in Van Rooy 1998: 20). Within this parameter, Lee Hock Guan's survey on civil society in Malaysia covers the main NGOs, along the themes of race and identity politics, gender, environment, and human rights up until 2011. The state largely prioritizes national security over its citizens' rights to freedoms of speech, expression, peaceful assembly, and association (Lee 2011: 73; Lim 1995: 166), which are enshrined in Article 10 of the Federal Constitution. Writing half a decade later, Lee's point remains salient: ethno-religious divisions within civil society will continue to be a problem because conservative Muslim and Malay rights groups support the government's ideology and practice of Malay-Muslim dominance at the expense of ethnic and religious minorities for the groups ultimately want Malaysia to be an Islamic state.

Most studies on civil society in Malaysia come under globalization, development, democracy, media (George 2006; Tan 2008), and politics. Scholars focus on its relationship with oppositional politics (Hewison and Rodan 1996) and its potential influence on political reform (Weiss 2003a), the expansion of the political sphere and broadening of democracy (Weiss 2012), social movements (Ang 2014; Govindasamy 2014; Khoo 2015; Lee 2010; Liow 2009; Ng, Maznah, and Tan 2006; Weiss and Hassan 2003; Weiss 2011) and diverse NGO activities connected to the protection of civil and individual human rights and collective goods such as the environment (Ramakrishna 2003), urban heritage (Goh 2014; Kelly 2004), refugees and foreign workers, lesbian, gay, bisexual, and transgender (LGBT) rights (Lee 2013), and indigenous peoples.

Broadly speaking, Malaysian civil society consists of thousands of groups and individuals (public intellectuals), civic associations, trade unions, students, volunteers, politically minded religious organizations, local NGOs, and Islamic and international NGOs of varying sizes. Other groups are charity and welfare organizations that are apolitical and thus are seldom discussed in studies on Malaysian civil society. Due to the largely reactive character of Malaysian civil society, these apolitical groups might behave politically when a particular cause arises. Not all work for the common good, nor are all strictly autonomous from the state or market. Instead, civil society can also provide input to shape and influence government policy (women's groups or consumer associations like the Federation of Malaysian Consumers Associations [FOMCA]) or, like Perkasa and Pekida, advance the agenda and right-wing ideology of the ruling party United Malays National Organisation (UMNO) in advocating for Malay dominance.[1] Such conservative groups, nevertheless, contribute to the broadening of democracy as they test the limits of liberal democracy with their drive for "uncivil outcomes" through threats of violence by staging counter-protests (Van Rooy 1998: 18). Even their rhetoric of merely preserving Article 153 about the special position of Malays refers back to the Constitution, although they have likely misinterpreted privilege (which can be withdrawn) as right (which everyone has regardless of ethnicity) (Kua 2012). Some organizations receive support from corporations for environmental sustainability and community investment under the corporate social responsibility policy; some obtain funding from international NGOs, state governments (held by opposition parties), local think-tanks, and foreign embassies (e.g., the annual Freedom Film Festival organized by the Centre for the People's Communications, KOMAS); and others obtain support from welfare-oriented groups that seek support from state institutions (at the federal level) and political parties.[2]

Malaysia comprises a multi-ethnic society with a Malay Muslim majority (the Chinese population has fallen to 24 percent and the Indian to 7 percent). Hence, affirmative action for the majority, comprising Malays, under the New Economic Policy 1971–1990 and ensuing five-year national plans continue to, more or less, uphold ethnic Malay dominance in all fields. The racialization and racism that are infused into Malaysian society have equally divided its civil society (Weiss 2003b: 41), especially from the mid-2000s onward, which culminated in the Lina Joy apostasy case and ban on *The Catholic Herald* for using the word "Allah" to refer to "God" (Manirajan, Koon, and Tan 2015).

Such racism and diminution of ethnic and religious minority rights through a gradual syaria-hization of laws are the results of a powerful mix of Islamization and the ideology of Malay ethnic hegemony. In an earlier essay, I argued that this phenomenon gave rise to constitutional patriotism in the mid-2000s, when vocal civil society actors attempted to reclaim the secular liberal foundations of Malaysian pluralism as enshrined in the Constitution (Khoo 2014).

However, since the Constitution not only protects the rights of ethnic and religious minorities but also sets up the rule of law, it could be said that civil society evoked a discourse of constitutional patriotism in earlier times whenever illiberal changes were proposed or made to the Constitution and whenever the rule of law was transgressed to diminish democracy. See, for example, the Aliran founder Chandra Muzaffar's numerous articles against Mahathir's attempts to curb the constitutional power of the rulers and concentrate political powers in the Executive (Chandra 1986, 1989). In short, constitutional patriots are those Malaysian individuals, activists, and NGOs who believe that the Constitution stands for justice, equality, and fairness to Malaysians of all ethnic backgrounds and recognizes their rights to practice their differences. In other words, constitutional patriots are cosmopolitan in accepting and embracing cultural differences and in holding on to the idea of unity in diversity. Cosmopolitans emphasize issues that are common to all and ideally transcend ethnic, class, and gender divisions: ending corruption, having in place efficient governance, ensuring electoral justice, and observing the rule of law.

Rather than discussing the main advocacy NGOs, like other authors, I prefer to draw attention to civic empowerment and on-the-ground engagement by "activist citizens" who, through their "acts of citizenship," emerge "not as beings already defined [by pre-existing scripts] but as beings acting and reacting with others" (Isin 2008: 39). In effect, what occurs amongst the attendees at Bersih[3] rallies and in anti-racism music videos is the formation of a public sphere as people come together to act as a collective force (Khoo 2014, 2015). Further, here, I want to cross over from merely mapping out the landscape of Malaysian civil society (its NGOs) to a discussion on what galvanizes its public sphere. By "public sphere," I mean the processes that transform apathetic citizens into active citizens who engage, through informed ways, in critical discourses on social issues that are geared toward influencing state policy. One such cosmopolitan is Syed Azmi Alhabshi, a volunteerist social activist. I choose to discuss him as a counterweight to the numerous conservative Islamic NGOs, large and small, because he is a moderate Muslim public figure whose non-partisan acts of charity and exemplary nature provide a means to think about the effects of individual action within civil society. While he does not overtly reference the Constitution, his civic actions and activities are aligned with the cosmopolitan ethos of constitutional patriotism. However, first, this chapter will briefly outline the developments in Malaysian civil society as it reacts to conditions under various prime ministers. I will then conclude by discussing how, in response to "uncivil groups" in Malaysian civil society, progressive actors, who favor rights and the rule of law as vested in the Constitution, desire and work toward constructing a "civil sphere" (Alexander 2006).

History

Ethnic- and faith-based associations involved in welfare and service provision were around in the beginning of the twentieth century during colonial times (Lee 2011: 75). They were the forerunners of modern civil society. However, the more political aspect of civil society can be traced to the 1920s, when the English term "politics" entered the discourse of a nascent anti-colonial consciousness amongst Malay nationalists and Chinese progressive groups (Milner 1991: 119 in Weiss 2003a: 60). Some of the most repressive laws existing today were introduced under the British to control secret societies (Weiss 2003b: 31) and curb the spread of communism after the war. Subsequent post-colonial governments, instead of abolishing them, conveniently used them to curb dissent from their political opponents and critics and "intimidate and neutralize" civil society (Lee 2011: 74): the Police Act (1967), the 1948 Sedition Act, the Internal Security Act (ISA), which allowed for detention without trial (1960; repealed in July 2012, see Fritz and Flaherty 2002), the Official Secrets Act (1971), which discourages transparency and accountability, and regulation to control civil society through the Trade Unions Act (1959), and the Societies Act (1966).⁴ In the aftermath of the 1969 race riots, the Printing Presses Act of 1948 was amended in 1971 to allow the withdrawal of licenses. Student activism, which had been lively since the 1930s and actively anti-colonial in 1949, continued into the 1960s, when students were involved in politics off campus. The University Malaya Student Union (UMSU), which was at the forefront of student activism, toured the country, holding public rallies in the lead up to the 1969 election. Thus, their power was curbed by the University and University Colleges Act (UUCA) in 1971, which denied students political and economic autonomy to organize student affairs on campus. More importantly, an amendment in 1975 prohibited students from being the members of political parties or expressing sympathy or opposition to political parties. Student activism thus peaked in the mid-1970s, with students at the forefront of the 1974 farmers' protest in Baling, Kedah (where young Anwar Ibrahim spoke and was arrested).⁵ It is only recently, since October 2011, when this specific provision in Section 15 of the UUCA was found unconstitutional for contravening the freedom of expression enshrined in Article 10 of the Constitution, that student activism has been on the rise. A new generation of vocal student leaders was arrested, brought to court for participating in rallies and protests for electoral reforms, charged for sedition, and even suspended from university (Lim 2013; Oliver 2015). Overseas, Malaysian student groups have historically and currently also been actively engaged in discourses over issues at home. A new group calling themselves Malaysian Progressives, and based in the United Kingdom and Australia, aims for political reform and student empowerment.⁶ Several have graduated and returned home to form NGOs friendly to the Opposition, like INVOKE. According to its website, "INVOKE is made up of ordinary Malaysians who yearn for an end to 59 years of corruption, mismanagement & injustice" (INVOKE Malaysia 2016).

After the 1969 race riots, which saw the detention of 117 individuals under the ISA (Funston 2001: 177), Malaysian civil society turned toward issues confronting the developing world: environmental and consumer protection, as well as growing religious consciousness (Lee 2011). The 1970s in Malaysia saw the establishment of environmental and consumer protection groups, the Consumer Association of Penang (CAP), Federation of Malaysian Consumers Association (FOMCA), Sahabat Alam Malaysia (SAM), Environmental Protection Society of Malaysia (EPSM), and World Wildlife Fund Malaysia, and progressive intellectuals based in Penang formed Aliran (1977), which did much to promote broader democratization and set agendas regarding "marginalized communities and the provision of 'public goods'" (Lee 2011; Weiss 2004b: 111). In that way, Aliran together with the Malaysian Bar Council might be considered early constitutional patriots.

Islamic resurgence and missionary activities in the early 1970s saw the establishment of Muslim NGOs: Angkatan Belia Islam Malaysia (1972), the Malaysian Islamic Youth Movement whose leader Anwar Ibrahim was invited to join, and subsequently joined, Mahathir's government in the 1980s (a strategic move for UMNO to gain Islamic credentials in the political battle for Malay votes with the Pan-Malaysian Islamic Party [PAS]), and al-Arqam, a well-organized, economically independent religious sect that was banned in 1994 and whose five key members were arrested under the ISA. Concurrently, Christians became politically conscious, as they had strong links with the Malaysian left resulting from the influence of liberation theology (Lee 2011). Later, in 1985, the Christian Federation of Malaysia was formed. An umbrella group, it included the Catholic Bishops' Conference of Malaysia, the Protestant and Oriental Orthodox Council of Churches of Malaysia, and the Evangelicals in the National Evangelical Christian Fellowship (Welsh 2013: 282). In the 1980s of the Mahathir era, Christian groups were not openly critical, except for the Catholic Bishops, who issued a statement against Operation Lalang, whereby over a hundred social activists and opposition figures were arrested and detained under the ISA ostensibly for fears of causing another race riot.[7]

Mahathir era (1981–2003)

Mahathir's era, while heralding rapid modernization and development, was marked by increasing authoritarianism. Operation Lalang (1987) was launched in the midst of internal party struggles when Mahathir won the leadership of his party by a narrow margin. Following this, crackdowns deployed to mask the weakness of or internal fragmentation within UMNO became a textbook procedure: after all, in 2007, declassified documents had revealed that the "race" riot of May 13, 1969 was actually a *coup d'état* engineered to topple Prime Minister Tunku Abdul Rahman (Kua 2007). Passed in 1960 to continue the fight against the communists (despite the end of the Emergency period), the ISA was used against religious "deviants" and political opponents, most notably in 1998 against Deputy Prime Minister Anwar Ibrahim. The crackdown did not stop there: the licenses of three newspapers were revoked, many freedoms were curtailed, and legislation was amended to restrict freedom. The Police Act required police permits for all political meetings and public gatherings with more than five people, and the Printing Presses and Publications Act (1984), which had replaced the Printing Presses Act (1971) and removed judicial review and appeal to the king, was amended in 1987 to introduce annual license renewals for newspapers, leading to a system of self-censorship and press control as the Minister of Home Affairs retained absolute discretion to grant permits for newspapers. Mahathir also weakened the powers of the judiciary, as well as those of the traditional rulers/royalty, to concentrate power in the Executive. From 1986 to 1988, Mahathir held three top offices: as Prime Minister, the Minister of Home Affairs, and the Minister of Justice. Ironically, while deploying repressive laws introduced during the colonial era, he was simultaneously critical of Western liberal discourse, regarding civil liberties (especially the respect for individual human rights) as a Western imposition and citing how it contravened "Asian Values" and was a secondary consideration to economic stability. Critics point to these processes that weakened the liberal institutions as having paved the way for the gross excesses committed under Najib Razak's government.

Even if the repressive laws succeeded in instilling fear in mainstream society regarding expressing their discontent beyond the ballot box, the crackdown reinforced the importance of human rights as being something fundamentally worth protecting: the first Prime Minister of Malaysia Tunku Abdul Rahman, who strongly criticized the 1987 crackdown, supported civil society's move to establish the National Human Rights Society (Hakam) as early as 1988, but it was only registered in 1991. A more independent NGO started by ex-Ops Lalang political detainees is Suaram (1989) and, much later, in 1999, the government formed the Human Rights Commission of Malaysia, Suhakam, in line with the United Nations High Commissioner for Refugees (UNHCR) principles.[8] However, Suhakam has been criticized for being ineffective and not independent enough since its commissioners are government appointees (Liu 2015: 297–98).

Within the restrictive parameters of religion and patriarchy, women's NGOs functioned through subtle negotiation, rather than direct confrontation, in order to seek cooperation from state actors (like the Ministry of Women and Family) and prevent being accused of functioning as the agents of foreign powers, which might cause their demands to be easily dismissed. If women's groups were involved in the welfare and education of women and issues such as equal pay and maternity leave in the 1970s, the 1980s and 1990s saw local women's advocacy groups being affected by transnational women's movements and funding in terms of the kinds of foci (sexual and domestic violence against women; violence in the media; and, later, sex trafficking) and types of discourses and language deployed, that is, human rights and governance (Martinez 2003). The All Women's Action Society Malaysia (AWAM) (established in 1985), Women's Aid Organisation, and Women's Centre for Change in Penang, all started in the early 1980s to help victims of domestic violence. They came under a Joint Action Group Against Violence Against Women (JAG) that campaigned for eleven years to pass and then implement the Domestic Violence Act of 1994. In 1989, a group of professional urban liberal Muslim feminists formed Sisters in Islam (SIS) to campaign for the rights of Muslim women due to increasing enactment of gender discriminatory policies and laws in the syariah framework (Lee 2011: 79). They were frustrated with how Muslim women were disadvantaged by the dual legal system in Malaysia that decided Muslim women could not enjoy feminist gains in family law in the civil courts since they came under syariah law. Although their supporters are limited to the urban and educated, SIS is important as it is the only progressive Muslim women's organization that is sufficiently courageous to confront conservative religious leaders and Islamic NGOs using arguments grounded in Islamic theology.

What contributed to the growth of civil society in Malaysia from the late 1990s onward? Even though civil society was very much weakened by Operation Lalang in 1987, two key phenomena played a huge role in precipitating the expansion of civil society: the first was the Reformasi movement in 1998 in the aftermath of the then Deputy Prime Minister Anwar Ibrahim being sacked, arrested, and then beaten up while in police custody (Bowie 2004). Triggered by a combination of several factors—urbanization centered in the big cities, a burgeoning educated middle class, the financial crisis, and inspiration from the popular toppling of Suharto in neighboring Indonesia—Reformasi was important for fostering inter-ethnic solidarity amongst Malaysians and bringing back mass street demonstrations and civil disobedience to protest corruption, cronyism, and authoritarianism (Weiss 2003a: 63). The second was the growth of the Internet, which the then Prime Minister Mahathir Mohamed agreed not to censor as part of the conditions to encourage foreign information technology (IT) companies to set up and invest in the MultiMedia Super Corridor. Indeed, the early Internet played a crucial role in offering alternative and anti-Barisan Nasional views during Reformasi, with key pro-Anwar individuals going on to become renegade bloggers in the ensuing millennium. Reformasi's legacy came in the shape of the birth of an opposition party, KeAdilan (the Justice Party), led by Anwar Ibrahim (and his wife Wan Azizah while Anwar was imprisoned under dubious charges) and, more surreptitiously, the radicalization of a whole new generation of activists, some of whom joined the Opposition in the 2008 elections.[9] It would go on to play an even greater role, leading up to the 2008 general elections and the contest between civil society and the government (Leong 2013: 11, 87).

Abdullah Badawi era (2003–2009): the rise of constitutional patriotism

As the son of a famous religious teacher, Mahathir's chosen successor Abdullah Badawi commanded respect for his clean image, consultative style, and openness to all ethnic communities. Given the benefit of the doubt by voters, who were relieved that the Mahathir era was over, and Abdullah's promise to drive out corruption, the ruling National Front or Barisan Nasional (BN) won by a landslide in the 2004 elections. Under Abdullah, civil society flourished and expanded, though the greater freedom of expression in the media and on the streets was not only limited to progressive groups but also saw an increase in vocal right-wing Malay and Muslim NGOs that regarded the alliance of ethnic minority interest groups (like the Malaysian Consultative Council of Buddhism, Christianity, Hinduism and Sikhism [MCCBCHS]), liberal elements of civil society, and lawyers (represented by the activist Bar Council) as a threat to Islam and Malay hegemony. Abdullah's period was the height of constitutional patriotic discourse for civil society (Khoo 2014). Mahathir's 2001 announcement that Malaysia is an Islamic state, despite vocal criticism expressed by the Bar Council, the Opposition, and progressive NGOs, empowered Islamic authorities and government officials to contravene the rights of ethnic and sexual minorities and liberal Muslims, especially Muslim women through the moral policing of women's bodies, with police enforcement and direct statements from Malay politicians threatening race riots any time ethnic minorities express that they too have rights. Instigated by several legal cases involving covert religious conversions to Islam and the battle for custody of the children of inter-faith couples in which civil court judges retreated by giving power to the syariah court, the lawyers were concerned about the erosion of fundamental liberties set out in the Constitution and formed a coalition to educate Malaysians about their constitutional rights and defend the freedom to profess and practice one's faith under Article 11 (Lee 2010). A series of cases, including the apostasy case of Lina Joy and the ban on the use of the word "Allah," which was used in the Malay-language section of the *Catholic Herald* to refer to God, dominated headlines and fueled religious tensions. The Article 11 coalition faced pressure and silencing tactics from PEMBELA, a coalition of seventy Muslim NGOs and clerics that was formed to defend the sanctity of syariah law and oppose apostasy. Such right-wing Islamic groups disrupted and shut down forums with police cooperation and were so controversial that Abdullah announced a gag order with respect to discussions about the Constitution and freedom of religion (Lee 2010: 92).

The year 2007 marked a turning point for civil society (and politics), as it was the year of public rallies not seen since Reformasi: first, in September, lawyers marched to the administrative capital, Putrajaya, to protest corruption in the judiciary; then, Bersih, the Coalition for Free and Fair Elections focusing on electoral reform (reacting to massive fraud during the 2004 Sarawak elections), held a march attended by 30,000–40,000 people to deliver a memorandum to the king. In November, the Hindu Rights Action Force (Hindraf) organized a protest march against alleged discriminatory policies, ranging from the destruction of Hindu temples to make way for development and "body-snatchings"[10] to the plight of the plantation Tamils; 30,000–50,000 Indians showed up to submit a 100,000-signature memorandum to the British High Commission in Kuala Lumpur to appoint a Queen's Counsel to represent them in a class action lawsuit against the United Kingdom government for abandoning them to "the mercy of a majority Malay-Muslim government that ha[d] violated [their] rights as minority Indians" (Amrith 2013: 282). The police greeted both Hindraf and Bersih rallies with roadblocks, tear gas, water cannons, and arrests; the Hindraf organizers were subsequently put under the ISA, and the movement was banned. If anything, arguably, the heavy-handed clampdown on peaceful marchers may have provoked citizen outrage and emboldened some Malaysians who were, otherwise, passive and apolitical bystanders to participate in future demonstrations (see Welsh 2013: 287–288). Indeed, a new non-partisan Bersih committee was formed, calling itself Bersih 2.0, and it held a second rally in 2011 that attracted 50,000. Moreover, the movement went global as overseas Malaysians organized Bersih rallies in thirty-two cities.[11] These mega-events as symptoms of public discontent played a role in the BN's loss of two-thirds majority in the 2008 elections and Abdullah's fall from power. Despite all his promises and good intentions to clean up corruption, improve race relations, and establish effective governance, Abdullah failed to take action or speak up against the more violent rhetoric of groups that verged on hate speech and could conceivably be deemed seditious; moreover, he did not manage to establish an Independent Police Complaints and Misconduct Commission to investigate custodial deaths.[12]

Najib Razak era (2009–present): kleptocracy, hypocrisy, and hyper-racist discourse

Immediately after the 2012 election results were announced, in which BN's popular vote count slipped to 49 percent and the incumbent won by a diminished majority, Prime Minister Najib Razak labeled the results a "Chinese tsunami," harkening back to the results of the 2008 elections, which the press had labeled "a political tsunami." This racist scapegoating of Chinese Malaysians spurred civil society and the Opposition to organize an anti-racist "Black 505 Rally" at Kelana Jaya Stadium, which was attended by 120,000 protestors. It also contradicted the national unity and "people first" message embodied in Najib's "1Malaysia" campaign, long considered by those outside BN as a hollow slogan. At the time of writing, the racist discourse and Othering of non-Muslims and non-Malays is intense and carries the weight of a distinct Islamization that impinges on the liberties of non-believers and liberal Muslims. In response to this right-wing extremism, twenty-five distinguished former civil servants became social activists and formed the G25-Malaysia. According to their website, they are:

> committed to pursue a just, democratic, peaceful, tolerant, harmonious, moderate and progressive multi-racial, multi cultural, multi religious Malaysia through Islamic principles of *Wassatiyah* (moderation) and *Maqasid Syariah* (well-being of the people) that affirms justice, compassion, mercy, equity.[13]

While incorporating Islamic discourse in their mission statement, the group is clearly politically moderate and considers the Constitution and Rukun Negara (which supports multiculturalism) sacrosanct. In short, they want to keep intact secularism, liberalism, and pluralism, as enshrined in the Constitution (Oorjitham 2016). While this NGO undeniably consists of respectable elites only, their senior positions within the civil service (and undoubtedly BN) are likely to carry more weight and influence policy and decision-making compared to those taking more "radical" stances, like the Islamic Renaissance Front, which is an intellectual movement and think-tank that is "committed to liberating the Muslim mind from rigid orthodoxy and conservatism."[14]

Under Najib, civil liberties were even more severely curbed than under Mahathir and the perception of corruption was worse (Carvalho 2016). Marred by what *Guardian* Editorial (2016) calls "The World's Biggest Financial Scandal," in which over US$1 billion was transferred into his personal accounts from 1MDB, a state investment fund, and various unpopular policies (the introduction of 6 percent GST, forced return of university student loans, lifting of food subsidies, and rising costs of living), Najib went after his critics by using a combination of surveillance, censorship, and outright bans, exploiting legal loopholes and rewriting the law. Despite promising to abolish the country's sedition laws, "In 2015 alone, Amnesty International reported at least 91 individuals were arrested, charged or investigated for sedition—almost five times as many as during the law's first 50 years of existence" (Teoh 2016). They include Opposition politicians, academics, journalists, cartoonists, students, and even ordinary people who expressed contempt for the regime. More insidiously, the ISA, although finally repealed, was replaced with the even more restrictive Peaceful Assembly Act (introduced in 2012); the Security Offences (Special Measures) Act (SOSMA); and the National Security Council, which allows the "authorities to carry out warrantless arrests, search and seize property, and impose curfews at will" (Amnesty International 2016). The Criminal Procedure Code was also amended to make an array of offenses "non-bailable," amongst other proposals (Koh 2016). Other repressive tools at his disposal include the Prevention of Terrorism Act (POTA) 2015 (Syahir n.d.). On another front, disillusionment with the Opposition-controlled state governments regarding the allocation of development projects and deforestation leading to new environmental problems and threats to local heritage invited much criticism from residents associations, heritage conservationists, environmentalists, and ordinary citizens (e.g., the Penang Forum).

Challenges

Within this current restrictive framework, how can civil society survive and thrive? Historically, Reformasi and the 2008 general election results have shown that for civil society to effect change, it has to work with the Opposition (Weiss 2003a). This feeling is manifested in the support of individual Bersih committee members (albeit with some reservations by others within the steering committee who are critical of Mahathir) for the ex-Prime Minister's petition, The Citizens' Declaration, requesting Najib's removal from office by peaceful and legal means as a way to "Save Malaysia" (*The Coverage* 2016). Backed by former UMNO politicians, who were critical of Najib's role in the 1MDB crisis and were sacked by Najib, including Mahathir's son, Opposition stalwarts, and newly minted NGOs like Challenger—Change Led by the Young Generation, the petition garnered over 1 million signatures. However, disillusioned with an Opposition substantially weakened by ideological factionalism, infighting, and a loss of progressive leadership (the imprisonment of Anwar Ibrahim again for sodomy and the death of PAS' spiritual leader Nik Aziz),[15] Malaysians find solace in immersing themselves in non-partisan civil society projects of their own like volunteerism and charity work, which can yield short-term or immediate positive results. A non-partisan civil society is more likely to gain traction from cynical members of the public who perceive politicians as being self-interested. In that sense, the work of non-partisan cosmopolitan (by this I mean one who is open to the cultures of others) humanitarian volunteers is notably important to break down racial barriers, for example, United Sikhs flying out to deliver aid to indigenous Temiar trapped by the flood in February 2015 (United Sikhs 2015); the Malaysian Global Progressives, which is mentioned above; and my case study of Syed Azmi Alhabshi, described below.

Case study: Syed Azmi Alhabshi and millennial volunteerism

It bears saying that religious and racial extremism provokes a shift toward the middle ground and the simultaneous rise of moderates and non-governmental independents (NGIs), "outspoken individuals who function as institutions unto themselves," who emerge from the "new" middle classes (Weiss 2003b: 62). One such NGI is the 30-something-year-old Syed Azmi. He is a co-founder of Free Market, where people freely give away things, and Suspended Meals, in which customers can pay for two meals, one of which will be given free to another restaurant patron in need. He is involved in numerous awareness and charity events and community projects to help the homeless, the poor, the aged, flood victims, and refugees by setting up soup kitchens and providing free education (Boo 2015). I argue that everyday individual acts of civility and ethics that are motivated by kindness and Muslim charity can be interpreted as reacting against an increasingly divisive, un-cosmopolitan political discourse and an individualist outlook that is the consequence of long-term racialization and Othering by those espousing an intolerant Wahhabi-style Islam. In that sense, such everyday practices and informal sociality are inherently political, what more when shared on his Facebook page, where he has over 112,000 Facebook followers.[16] His Facebook page brings attention to little-discussed, but prevalent, taboo subjects like child sexual abuse[17] and, thus, stretches the boundaries of democracy and discourse via the creation of public spheres. On the site, information is exchanged to educate and empower the public. For example, a mother of two daughters, aged three and six, felt sufficiently empowered to lodge a police report on behalf of her children against her husband, the sole breadwinner of the family, after reading Syed Azmi's posts on the issue in early September 2016.[18] Syed Azmi then provided some financial support together with a few donors who had read about this family from his posts. In that sense, the site acts as a contact point for supporting offline activities and actions. Cases and stories are shared, and there is dialogical exchange between him and his followers offering moral support to the causes he is involved in or that he endorses and posts on his wall. As a concerned citizen, he also went to parliament together with the women's NGO JAG to narrate the reality of sexual abuse cases with the aim of strengthening child protection laws.

Asked in an interview on Business FM Radio 89.9 (2016) if he thinks that the death threats he received from conservative Muslims for organizing the "I Want to Touch a Dog"[19] event were due to creeping Islamization, he avoids blaming Islamization and, instead says that it is a question of the lack of civility:

> I don't know if to call it Islamization but the way people react is harsh, cruel and rude … totally obnoxious and it's more like a small group of people who cannot accept to agree to disagree or accept having a polite courteous discussion. I have a problem with people like that.

(Business FM 89.9 2016)

The NGI's sidestepping of criticizing Islamization is logical given that the ever-humble English-speaking Syed Azmi, while living a modern urban life, is also deeply spiritual and leads in his words and deeds. Based on the proliferation of Islamic NGOs in the past two decades, it is a wise move to avoid pinpointing Islamization in the way that some "liberal" Muslims do. He believes that Islam is about how we treat others and, by posting his experiences and encounters with Others, demonstrates the rational, independent thinking aspect of Islam that advocates self-governance. Rather than imposing his views on others, he says, "I want other people to do the things that they think is [sic] right for them to do" (Business FM 89.9 2016). In other words, it is not about how Islam governs people through social prohibition, but more about finding a moral compass within the self—and then acting upon it.

The problem Syed Azmi identifies above is that those interactions violate the rules of civility, which should be "an exchange in which both parties make one another feel good about the encounter," its point being decreasing the hostility toward others in the conduct of everyday life (Sennett 2013: 120, 124). Civility is missing in Malaysian civil society when it includes groups like the Red Shirts Movement that stage counter-rallies to Bersih and threaten violence against Chinese Malaysians and, separately, the chair of Bersih 2.0 for simply asking Malaysians to exercise their freedom to peacefully assemble on the streets to demand Najib's resignation. These groups appear as Najib's proxies and defend him against accusations of theft in relation to the 1MDB scandal. Their partisan stance toward the main political party and the near guarantee of impunity for their actions suggest that under such circumstances, democracy cannot thrive as "only a civil society that is truly *civil* supports democracy" (Aspinall 2004: 90 in Ford 2013: 11).

In that sense, Jeffrey Alexander's call for a new concept of civil society as the "civil sphere" is apropos. The civil sphere is "a world of values and institutions that generates the capacity for social criticism and democratic integration at the same time" (Alexander 2006: 4). Such a sphere hinges on "solidarity, empathy for those we do not know but whom we respect out of principle because we are committed to a common secular faith" (Alexander 2006: 4). The foundations of this civil sphere underwrite the formation of NGIs like Syed Azmi and NGOs like G25 and

Harmoni (Persatuan Promosi Harmoni Malaysia), of which the latter was formed to "provide a platform for the voices of the moderate-majority to be heard" (Tan 2015). Harmoni together with other Muslim NGOs issued a joint statement saying that the Red Shirts do not represent the voice of Malay Muslims and requesting that the Red Shirts rally planned for Malaysia Day on September 16, 2015 be called off (FMT Reporters 2015).[20] This insistence on respecting the pluralism enshrined in the secular Constitution marks (within Malaysian civil society) the boundary between constitutional patriots who literally play by the rules, who are proponents of a civil sphere, and those whose actions are uncivil in their assertion of the discourse of Malay ethnic dominance. In dealing rationally with the question of difference, constitutional patriots like Wong Chin-Huat also would conceivably subscribe to the civil sphere (Khoo 2014: 336). Wong asks:

> Are people who oppose us or our ideas all stupid or bad? Can we understand then disagree, rather than disagree without understanding? Can we accept that people are bound to have differences—in politics or otherwise—because of their values, experiences and circumstances? Can we refute only ideas with facts and logic, and not negate people with hatred and arrogance? The answers to these questions are vital, because it will decide if we can attain democracy.
>
> Democracy is never about living with people who agree with us. It is about coexisting, competing and cooperating with people who disagree with us. Democracy requires some basic decency and reciprocity.
>
> *(Wong 2016)*

Sennett, writing about the politics of cooperation, would agree. Rather than opponents closing off from each other and becoming stuck in a room of mirrors, he proposes looking outward: "Looking outward makes for a better social bond than imagining others are reflected in ourselves, or as though society itself was constructed as a room of mirrors. But looking outward is a skill [that] people have to learn" (Sennett 2013: 278); perhaps, this is especially more so within "civil" society.

This chapter has characterized Malaysian civil society as reactive in describing how community or activist groups identify and fill in gaps caused by the state in terms of inadequate or failed provision of services and care. I have framed some of these civil society actors as constitutional patriots who believe in the rule of law and in strengthening secular institutions, even if they may not be overtly political. As political change is increasingly seen as remote, Malaysians may be transferring their efforts to volunteerism in the belief that: "the smallest act in the most limited circumstances bears the seed of the same boundlessness, because one deed, and sometimes one word, suffices to change every constellation" (Arendt 1998: 190). Arendt's words belie an optimism about activism and civil society and in people like Syed Azmi, who show how everyday acts of kindness can ultimately be political in that they suggest a possibility of being and acting together (Sennett 2013). In fact, in a multicultural society straining to keep the strands of democracy together, being and acting together across class, race, nationality, and political and ideological beliefs is a crucial strategy for civil society to blossom, as has been demonstrated by successful coalition work in the past—by the Consumers Association of Penang—and presently— by Bersih 2.0. Without this, Malaysia would be a culturally poorer nation.

Unfortunately, the recent examples of civil society activism that support a secular inclusive vision of democracy are also limited to the actions and beliefs of a relatively small minority of middle-class well-meaning Malaysians. They form new groups (BEBAS meaning "freedom") in response to Bills like Act 335 that would enhance "Shariah punishments of 30 years' jail,

RM100,000 fine and 100 lashes from the current limits of three years' jail, a RM5,000 fine and six strokes of the rotan [cane]" (Zurairi 2017). The effectiveness of such groups is curbed by their lack of contact with the Malay grassroots, who are captivated by the communalism of UMNO, which appeals to them in the name of promoting equality in an authoritarian one-party state. Within such stubborn structural determinations, political change is also hampered by a weak opposition, personal and communal patronage and political stagnation to which mass rallies calling for the PM to step down have proven ineffective (Wong 2017). Seen in this light, NGOs seeking to make changes that do not challenge the state directly will be relatively more successful.

Notes

1 Perkasa or *Persatuan Pribumi Perkasa* (Malay for "Mighty Native Organization") is a Malay supremacist NGO formed by the ex-UMNO politician Ibrahim Ali in the aftermath of the Malaysian general elections in 2008 when the BN lost the Indian and Chinese voters. Pekida (established in the 1970s, the Association of Islamic Welfare and Proselytization of Malaysia) is another Malay supremacist NGO believed to be associated with the shadowy Tiga Line (Three Lines), a militant group with ties to UMNO. Lemière characterizes the relationship between Pekida and UMNO as "connivance militancy": "a secret political arrangement by which a formal political actor (i.e. political party, a government or a politician) subcontracts legal and/or illegal political actions serving its interests—ranging from advocacy to demonstrations and violence—to groups of individuals" (Lemière 2014: 93).
2 Yayasan Chow Kit, which provides a twenty-four-hour drop-in center and schooling for at-risk children in the working-class neighborhood of Chow Kit in Kuala Lumpur, receives funding from the Ministry for the Development of Women, Family and Society and other strategic partners. See Yayasan Chow Kit (n.d.).
3 Bersih in Malay meaning "clean," formed as a coalition of over twenty-five NGOs and five opposition political parties whose mandate is free and fair elections in 2006. Bersih 2.0 has held several mass rallies and continues to put pressure on the electoral commission to perform its job in a neutral manner.
4 For a comprehensive brief, see Rock (2016: 58–60).
5 For a concise review on each of the Acts discussed above, see Funston (2001: 177–179).
6 Malaysian Progressives United Kingdom (2016) *Making Students Matter*. Electronic document, www. malaysianprogressivesuk.com/; and Malaysian Progressives in Australia (2014) *Welcome to Malaysian Progressives Webpage*. Electronic document, www.mpozaustralia.org/, both accessed January 27, 2017.
7 But critics believe that Operation Lalang (*lalang* means "weed"), which began on October 27, 1987, was a crackdown meant to control Mahathir's political opponents. One hundred and six people were arrested under the draconian Internal Security Act, including members of parliament, politicians, unionists, NGO activists, intellectuals, religious leaders and educationists. Publishing licenses for two weekly and two daily newspapers were withdrawn and amendments made to the Police Act to curtail freedom of assembly.
8 The initiative was developed when Malaysia was elected to the UNHCR 1993–1995. Interestingly, and perhaps not coincidentally, the Malaysian Chair of the UNHCR in 1995 was Dato Musa Hitam, former deputy Prime Minister to Mahathir who turned against the latter in the divided UMNO in 1987.
9 See Weiss (2004b) for a more comprehensive view on civil society during the Mahathir years.
10 Such cases occurred when the family of a recently deceased non-Muslim showed up to claim the body but was told that the deceased had converted to Islam without their knowledge and, hence, would be buried as a Muslim.
11 Bersih rallies were organized in thirty-two cities, see www.bersih.org/rallies/bersih2/.
12 There were a total of 231 deaths in police custody between the year 2000 and May 2013 (Leong 2014).
13 See G25-Malaysia's website, www.g25malaysia.org/about-us.
14 See Islamic Renaissance Front, http://irfront.net/about-irf/introduction/.
15 The New Hope Alliance (Pakatan Harapan) was formed in September 2015 to replace the defunct Pakatan Rakyat. It consists of the Justice Party; Democratic Action Party; and newly formed Parti Amanah Negara (PAN), a splinter party of PAS.

16 Syed Azmi (AmiKimmy) Facebook page. Electronic document, www.facebook.com/syed.azmi.
148?fref=ts, accessed January 27, 2017.

17 This issue had surfaced only a few months before (in June), with the arrest of the British pedophile
Richard Huckle for abusing 200 children in Malaysia (Holmes 2016).

18 See September 6, 2016 posting on Syed Azmi (AmiKimmy) Facebook page. Electronic document,
www.facebook.com/syed.azmi.148?fref=ts, accessed January 27, 2017.

19 In Malaysia, many Muslims consider dogs unclean and, therefore, haram. Syed Azmi received thou
sands of death threats and hateful messages for organizing this event to allow Muslims to pet dogs.

20 Unfortunately, their voices were unheeded as the rally proceeded (see Teoh 2015).

Suggested readings

Koh, Jun Lin. 2016. Your Kini Guide to the Criminal Procedure Code Amendments. *Malaysiakini*, May
25. Electronic document, www.malaysiakini.com/news/342838, accessed September 27, 2016.

Lee, Hock Guan. 2011. Civil Society in Malaysia. In *An ASEAN Community for All: Exploring the Scope for
Civil Society Engagement*. Terence Chong and Stefanie Elies, eds. Pp. 73–85. Singapore: Friedrich Stiftung.

Weiss, Meredith L. 2003a. Civil Society and Political Reform in Malaysia. In *Civil Society in Asia: In Search
of Democracy and Development in Bangladesh*. David C. Schak and Wayne Hudson, eds. Pp. 59–72. Burlington, VT: Ashgate.

Weiss, Meredith L. 2003b. Malaysian NGOs: History, Legal Framework and Characteristics. In *Social
Movements in Malaysia: From Moral Communities to NGOs*. Meredith L. Weiss and Saliha Hassan, eds.
Pp. 17–44 New York: Routledge.

Welsh, Bridget. 2013. Enabling and Empowering Malaysians. In *Awakening: The Abdullah Badawi Years in
Malaysia*. Bridget Welsh and James U. H. Chin, eds. Pp. 272–293. Petaling Jaya: Strategic Information
and Research Development Centre.

Websites

BERSIH 2.0 (The Coalition for Clean and Fair Elections), www.bersih.org.
Previously known as NET, the Coalition for Clean and Fair Elections became Bersih 2.0 in 2010; it comprises civil society organizations dedicated to ensuring clean and fair elections, and effectively monitoring
the political situation in Malaysia.

G25, www.g25malaysia.org/about-us.
G25 is a committee working toward a "multi-racial, multi-cultural, multi-religious Malaysia" through
moderation and respect, and the upholding of the Federal Constitution.

INVOKE, www.invokemalaysia.org/about/.
INVOKE is a team devoted to helping progressive and pro-reform candidates gain political power in
Malaysia, through community organizing and a significant volunteer and donation program.

Islamic Renaissance Front, http://irfront.net/about-irf/introduction/.
A think-tank based in Kuala Lumpur, promoting Muslim intellectual discourse to engage in the promotion
of democracy, liberty and social justice and "the revival and reform of Islamic thought."

Sisters In Islam, www.sistersinislam.org.my/.
Sisters in Islam is working to promote awareness of gender equality issues in Islam, to eliminate discrimination against women and to empower women to become leaders in justice and change.

Suaram, www.suaram.net/.
A non-governmental organization working since 1989 for the promotion of human rights in Malaysia,
with a focus currently on the right to trial, right to justice, documentation and monitoring, and refugee
protection.

Syed Azmi Facebook page, www.facebook.com/syed.azmi.148?fref=nf.
Syed Azmi's Facebook page, which shows his work as Head of Volunteers at NGOHub, and videos and
posts relating to his work in Malaysia including the promotion of child welfare issues.

References

Alexander, Jeffrey C. 2006. *The Civil Sphere*. Oxford: Oxford University Press.

Amnesty International. 2016. Malaysia: National Security Council Act Gives Authorities Unchecked and Abusive Powers. Amnesty.org, August 1. Electronic document, www.amnesty.org/en/latest/news/2016/08/malaysia-national-security-act-abusive-powers/, accessed December 22, 2016.

Amrith, Sunil. 2013. *Crossing the Bay of Bengal: The Furies of Nature and the Fortunes of Migrants*. Cambridge, MA: Harvard University Press.

Ang, Ming Chee. 2014. *Institutions and Social Mobilization: The Chinese Education Movement in Malaysia, 1951–2011*. Singapore: Institute of Southeast Asian Studies.

Arendt, Hannah. 1998. *The Human Condition*. 2nd Edn. Chicago, IL: University of Chicago Press.

Aspinall, Edward. 2004. Indonesia: Transformation of Civil Society and Democratic Breakthrough. In *Civil Society and Political Change in Asia: Expanding and Contracting Democratic Space*. Muthiah Alagappa, ed. Pp. 25–60. Stanford, CA: Stanford University Press.

Boo, Su-Lyn. 2015. 10 Things about: Syed Azmi, the Passionate Do-Gooder. *The Malay Mail*, November 16. Electronic document, www.themalaymailonline.com/malaysia/article/10-things-about-syed-azmi-the-passionate-do-gooder, accessed September 27, 2016.

Bowie, Alasdair. 2004. Civil Society and Democratization in Malaysia. In *Growth and Governance in Asia*. Yoichiro Sato, ed. Pp. 193–201. Honolulu, HI: Asia Pacific Center for Security Studies.

Business FM 89.9. 2016. Walking the Talk with Syed Azmi Alhabshi and Maryam Lee, Project Dialog. Radio podcast, September 9, www.bfm.my/bg-syed-azmi-alhabshi-and-maryam-lee-walking-the-talk.html, accessed December 22, 2016.

Carvalho, Martin. 2016. Malaysia Slides Four Points Down Global Corruption Perception Index. *The Star*, January 27. Electronic document, www.thestar.com.my/news/nation/2016/01/27/malaysia-slides-four-down-global-corruption-perception-index/, accessed September 27, 2016.

Case, William. 2009. Electoral Authoritarianism in Malaysia: Trajectory Shift. *The Pacific Review* 22(3): 311–333.

Chandra, Muzaffar. 1986. *Freedom in Fetters: An Analysis of the State of Democracy in Malaysia*. Penang: Aliran.

Chandra, Muzaffar. 1989. *Challenges and Choices in Malaysian Politics and Society*. Penang: Aliran.

The Coverage. 2016. Selamatkan Malaysia Citizens' Declaration To Seek The Removal of Najib. thecoverage.my, March 5. Electronic document, http://thecoverage.my/news/malaysia-citizens-declaration-to-seek-the-removal-of-najib/, accessed December 23, 2016.

Diamond, Larry. 1994. Rethinking Civil Society: Toward Democratic Consolidation. *Journal of Democracy* 5(3): 4–17.

FMT Reporters. 2015. Stop *Himpunan Maruah Melayu* on Sept 16. *Free Malaysia Today*, September 7. Electronic document, www.freemalaysiatoday.com/category/nation/2015/09/07/stop-himpunan-maruah-melayu-on-sept-16/, accessed September 27, 2016.

Ford, Michele, 2013. Social Activism in Southeast Asia: An introduction. In *Social Activism in Southeast Asia*. Michele Ford, ed. Pp. 1–21. New York: Routledge.

Fritz, Nicole, and Martin Flaherty. 2002. Unjust Order: Malaysia's Internal Security Act. *Fordham International Law Journal* 26(5): 1345–1437.

Funston, John. 2001. Malaysia: Developmental State Challenged. In *Government & Politics in Southeast Asia*. John Funston, ed. Pp. 160–202. Singapore: Institute of Southeast Asian Studies.

George, Cherian. 2006. *Contentious Journalism and the Internet: Towards Democratic Discourse in Malaysia and Singapore*. Seattle, WA: University of Washington Press.

Goh, Daniel. 2014. Between History and Heritage: Post-Colonialism, Globalisation, and the Remaking of Malacca, Penang, and Singapore. *TRaNS: Trans-Regional and -National Studies of Southeast Asia* 2: 79–101.

Govindasamy, Anantha R. 2014. Social Movements in Contemporary Malaysia: The Cases of BERSIH, HINDRAF and Perkasa. In *Routledge Handbook of Contemporary Malaysia*. Meredith Weiss, ed. Pp. 116–126. New York and London: Routledge.

Guardian Editorial. 2016. The Guardian View on Malaysian Politics: A Scandal Meriting the World's Attention. *Guardian*, July 28. Electronic document, www.theguardian.com/commentisfree/2016/jul/28/the-guardian-view-on-malaysian-politics-a-scandal-meriting-the-worlds-attention, accessed December 22, 2016.

Hewison, Kevin, and Garry Rodan. 1996. The Ebb and Flow of Civil Society and the Decline of the Left in Southeast Asia. In *Political Oppositions in Industrialising Asia*. Garry Rodan, ed. Pp. 40–94. London and New York: Routledge.

Holmes, Oliver. 2016. British Pedophile Inquiry: Malaysia "Repeatedly" Pressed UK for Data on Abuser. *Guardian*, June 3. Electronic document, www.theguardian.com/world/2016/jun/03/british-paedophile-richard-huckle-malaysia-repeatedly-press-uk-police-victims, accessed September 27, 2016.

INVOKE Malaysia. 2016. *INVOKE homepage*. Electronic document, www.invokemalaysia.org/, accessed January 27, 2017.

Isin, Engin. 2008. Theorizing Acts of Citizenship. In *Acts of Citizenship*. Engin. F. Isin and Greg M. Nielsen, eds. Pp. 15–43. London: Zed Books.

Iskandar, Shakira. 2016. Has the Civil Society Betrayed the Rakyat?. *The Malay Mail Online*, March 10. Electronic document, www.themalaymailonline.com/what-you-think/article/has-the-civil-society-betrayed-the-rakyat-shakira-iskandar, accessed September 27, 2016.

Kelly, Phillip F. 2004. Developing Dissent in Industrializing Localities: Civil Society in Penang and Batam. In *Challenging Authoritarianism in Southeast Asia: Comparing Indonesia and Malaysia*. Ariel Heryanto and Sumit K. Mandal, eds. Pp. 33–46. London: Routledge.

Khoo, Gaik Cheng. 2014. The Rise of Constitutional Patriotism in Malaysian Civil Society. *Asian Studies Review* 38(3): 325–344.

Khoo, Gaik Cheng. 2015. *Bersih dan Ubah*: Citizenship Rights, Intergenerational Togetherness and Multi-cultural Unity in Malaysia. In *Worlding Multiculturalisms: The Politics of Inter-Asian Dwelling*. Daniel P. S. Goh, ed. Pp. 109–126. London: Routledge.

Koh, Jun Lin. 2016. Your Kini Guide to the Criminal Procedure Code amendments. *Malaysiakini*, May 25. Electronic document, www.malaysiakini.com/news/342838, accessed September 27, 2016.

Kua, Kia Soong. 2007. *May 13: Declassified Documents on the Malaysian Riots of 1969*. Malaysia: Suaram Komunikasi.

Kua, Kia Soong. 2012. The Difference Between Rights and Privileges. *Free Malaysia Today*, December 6. Electronic document, www.freemalaysiatoday.com/category/opinion/2012/12/06/the-difference-between-rights-and-privileges/, accessed September 27, 2016.

Lee, Hock Guan. 2011. Civil Society in Malaysia. In *An ASEAN Community for All: Exploring the Scope for Civil Society Engagement*. Terence Chong and Stefanie Elies, eds. Pp. 73–85. Singapore: Friedrich Stiftung.

Lee, Julian C. H. 2010. *Islamization and Activism in Malaysia*. Singapore: Institute of Southeast Asian Studies.

Lee, Julian C.H. 2013. Sexuality Rights Activism in Malaysia: The Case of Seksualiti Merdeka. In *Social Activism in Southeast Asia*. Michele Ford, ed. Pp. 170–186. Abingdon: Routledge.

Lemière, Sophie. 2014. Gangsta and Politics in Malaysia. In *Misplaced Democracy: Malaysian Politics and People*. Sophie Lemière, ed. Pp. 91–108. Petaling Jaya: Strategic Institute of Research Development.

Leong, Christopher. 2014. Opening Remarks, Public Forum on Police Accountability in Malaysia. Kuala Lumpur, August 16. Electronic document, www.malaysianbar.org.my/speeches/opening_remarks_by_christopher_leong_president_malaysian_bar_at_the_public_forum_on_police_accountability_in_malaysia_kuala_lumpur_16_aug_2014.html, accessed September 27, 2016.

Leong, Susan. 2013. *New Media and the Nation in Malaysia*. New York: Routledge.

Lim, Ida. 2013. Future of Student Activism in Malaysia, as Seen by its Leaders. *The Malay Mail*, September 9. Electronic document, www.themalaymailonline.com/malaysia/article/future-of-student-activism-in-malaysia-as-seen-by-its-leaders#sthash.awCFM5ZA.dpuf, accessed September 27, 2016.

Lim, Teck Ghee. 1995. Nongovernmental Organizations in Malaysia and Regional Networking. In *Emerging Civil Society in the Asia Pacific Community*. Tadashi Yamamoto, ed. Pp. 165–182. Singapore: Institute of Southeast Asian Studies, Japan Centre for International Exchange and The Asia Pacific Philanthropy Consortium.

Liow, J. Chinyong. 2009. *Piety and Politics: Islamism in Contemporary Malaysia*. New York: Oxford University Press.

Liu, John. 2015. Civil Liberties in Contemporary Malaysia: Progress, Regression and the Resurgence of "Asian Values." In *Routledge Book of Contemporary Malaysia*. Meredith Weiss, ed. Pp. 290–301. New York: Routledge.

Manirajan Ramasamy, Chong Pooi Koon, and Andrea Tan. 2015. Malaysia Catholics Can't Use Allah as Religious Strife Rises. *Bloomberg*, January 21. Electronic document, www.bloomberg.com/news/articles/2015-01-21/malaysia-s-top-court-bans-catholic-use-of-allah-in-newspaper, accessed September 27, 2016.

Martinez, Patricia. 2003. Complex Configurations: The Women's Agenda for Change and The Women's Candidacy Initiative. In *Social Movements in Malaysia: From Moral Communities to NGOs*. Meredith L. Weiss and Saliha Hassan, eds. Pp. 75–96. New York: Routledge.

Milner, Anthony. 1991. Inventing Politics: The Case of Malaysia. *Past & Present: A Journal of Historical Studies* 132 (August): 104–29.

Ng, Cecilia, Maznah Mohamad, and Tan Beng Hui. 2006. *Feminism and the Women's Movement in Malaysia: An Unsung (R)evolution*. New York: Routledge.

Oliver, Scott. 2015. Could Malaysia's New Wave of Bold Student Activists be on the Verge of an Uprising? February 20. Electronic document, www.vice.com/en_uk/read/could-malaysias-new-wave-of-bold-student-student-activists-be-on-the-verge-of-an-uprising-290, accessed September 16, 2016.

Oorjitham, Santha. 2016. Torchbearers for Founding Fathers. *The Star*, September 4. Electronic document, www.g25malaysia.org/single-post/2016/09/04/Torchbearers-for-founding-fathers, accessed September 27, 2016.

Pasuni, Afif. 2011. The "Third Force" in Malaysia: Finding Relevance in an Emerging Duopoly. *S. Rajaratnam School of International Studies Commentary*. 120, August 15. Electronic document, www.hpu.edu/CHSS/History/PapersCommentariesStudies/RSISCommentaryThirdForceInMalaysia.pdf, accessed September 27, 2016.

Ramakrishna, Sundari. 2003. The Environmental Movement in Malaysia. In *Social Movements in Malaysia: From Moral Communities to NGOs*. Meredith L. Weiss and Saliha Hassan, eds. Pp. 115–139. New York: Routledge.

Rock, Michael T. 2016. *Dictators, Democrats, and Development in Southeast Asia: Implications for the Rest*. New York: Oxford University Press.

Sennett, Richard. 2013. *Together: The Rituals, Pleasures and Politics of Cooperation*. London: Penguin.

Syahir Ashri. n.d. 9 Things to Know About the Prevention of Terrorism Act. Poskod.my. Electronic document, http://poskod.my/cheat-sheets/9-things-know-prevention-terrorism-act/, accessed December 22, 2016.

Tan, Jun E. 2008. *Blogging and Democratization in Malaysia: A New Civil Society in the Making*. Petaling Jaya, Selangor: Strategic Information and Research Development Centre.

Tan, Nicole L. K. 2015. I Dream of a Better Malaysia. Letters. *Malaysiakini*, December 19. Electronic document, www.malaysiakini.com/letters/323923, accessed September 27, 2016.

Teoh, Bob. 2016. Restoring Press Freedom in Malaysia. *Malaysiakini*, May 3. Electronic document, www.malaysiakini.com/news/340059, accessed August 31, 2016.

Teoh, Shannon. 2015. "Red Shirt" Rally Brings Out Malaysians' Insecurities. *Straits Times*, September 30. Electronic document, www.straitstimes.com/opinion/red-shirt-rally-brings-out-malaysians-insecurities, accessed September 27, 2016.

United Sikhs. 2015. *HELP the Temiar Natives of Malaysia TODAY!* Press release. Electronic document, http://unitedsikhs.org/PressReleases/PRSRLS-03-02-15-01.html, accessed 27 January 2017.

Van Rooy, Alison. 1998. Civil Society as Idea: An Analytical Hatstand? In *Civil Society and the Aid Industry*. Alison Van Rooy, ed. Pp. 6–30. London: Earthscan.

Weiss, Meredith L. 2003a. Civil Society and Political Reform in Malaysia. In *Civil Society in Asia: In Search of Democracy and Development in Bangladesh*. David C. Schak and Wayne Hudson, eds. Pp. 59–72. Burlington, VT: Ashgate.

Weiss, Meredith L. 2003b. Malaysian NGOs: History, Legal Framework and Characteristics. In *Social Movements in Malaysia: From Moral Communities to NGOs*. Meredith L. Weiss and Saliha Hassan, eds. Pp. 17–44. New York: Routledge.

Weiss, Meredith L. 2004a. Construction of Counterhegemonic Narratives and Agendas. In *Civil Society and Political Change in Asia: Expanding and Contracting Democratic Space*. Muthiah Alagappa, ed. Pp. 259–291. Stanford, CA: Stanford University Press.

Weiss, Meredith L. 2004b. Mahathir's Unintended Legacy: Civil Society. In *Reflections: The Mahathir Years*. Bridget Welsh, ed. Pp. 110–118. Washington, DC: Southeast Asia Studies Program, SAIS.

Weiss, Meredith L. 2006. *Protest and Possibilities: Civil Society and Coalitions for Political Change in Malaysia*. Stanford, CA: Stanford University Press.

Weiss, Meredith L. 2011. *Student Activism in Malaysia: Crucible, Mirror, Sideshow*. Ithaca, NY: Cornell South East Asia Program.

Weiss, Meredith L. 2012. Malaysia: More Transformed than Transformational. In *Student Activism in Asia Between Protest and Powerlessness*. Meredith L. Weiss and Edward Aspinall, eds. Pp. 205–228. Minneapolis, MN: University of Minnesota Press.

Weiss, Meredith L., and Saliha Hassan eds. 2003. *Social Movements in Malaysia: From Moral Communities to NGOs*. New York: Routledge.

Welsh, Bridget. 2013. Enabling and Empowering Malaysians. In *Awakening: The Abdullah Badawi Years in Malaysia*. Bridget Welsh and James U. H. Chin, eds. Pp. 272–293. Petaling Jaya: Strategic Information and Research Development Centre.

Wong, Chin Huat. 2016. Of Karpal Singh and Haron Din. Comment. *Malaysiakini*, September 17. Electronic document, www.malaysiakini.com/news/356003#ixzz4KV9zwIBm, accessed September 24, 2016.

Wong, Chin Huat. 2017. A Malaysian Trilogy. *New York Times* Op-Ed. February 2. Electronic document, https://mobile.nytimes.com/2017/02/02/opinion/a-malaysian-trilogy.html?_r=0&referer=https%3A%2F%2Fwww.google.com%2F, accessed February 14, 2017.

Yayasan Chow Kit. n.d. *Every Child Matters*. Electronic document, www.yck.org.my/, accessed 26 August, 2016.

Zurairi A.R. 2017. Activist Group to Counter PAS Rally with Anti-Shariah Bill Gathering on Feb 18. *The Malay Mail*, January 18. Electronic document, www.themalaymailonline.com/malaysia/article/activist-group-to-counter-pas-rally-with-anti-shariah-bill-gathering-on-feb#sthash.XZEPFvS9.dpuf, accessed February 14, 2017.

10

SINGAPORE

Gillian Koh and Debbie Soon

Contestation, conflict, and cooperation with the state

Singapore is often considered by scholars to be an electoral authoritarian regime—a remarkable exception in the developed world—where economic development seems not to have been accompanied by political liberalization and democratization (Diamond 2002, 2013). The question that follows is, if civil society does indeed exist, what then of its form and substance? More critically, looking again at the substantive existing realities as they have evolved over the past fifty years of one-party dominance since Independence, is Diamond's characterization of Singapore's political system still fair? This chapter provides a brief survey of Singaporean civil society since independence to suggest how the quality of democracy has evolved on the ground. This begins with a quick introduction to that citizen sector, before turning to how scholars have analyzed it, and a review of more recent evidence of developments in civil society to answer the question above.

Evolution of civil society in Singapore

Civil society in Singapore spans a broad variety of activities, be they in the form of resistance to dominant narratives, ideologies, and practices that stem from the state or mainstream society, or as an expression of post-material desires and demands, especially of younger as well as more affluent segments of society. The deeply political forms of civil society include the conservation movement, gay rights and broader human rights-based activism, free-media advocates, public intellectuals, and the independent local theater space.

It may surprise some, but certainly not those tracking civil society development over the past decades, that Singapore's theater groups have had a deep history of challenging state laws, policies, and governing narratives. This has been at times to the players' peril, but it is also an area where there has been an evolution in state engagement with theater and a liberalization of that space.

To provide a flavor of that evolution, we delve into the "story" of independent theater—those forms and companies that explore the social dilemmas of the day and question society's or the state's approach to them. Our illustration focuses on the less scripted and at that time, experimental formats of Forum Theatre and Performance Art.

In 1993, two plays by local and independent drama company, The Necessary Stage (TNS), called *Mixed Blessings* and *MCP*, explored themes of mixed-race romantic relationships, and the stereotype of heads of households who hold chauvinistic attitudes, respectively. These are plays that invite members of the audience to role-play characters they watched, in order to bring a different and more desirable outcome to the story portrayed. The TNS plays resulted in much unease amongst policy makers, as audiences took to them to spontaneously offer visceral responses to gender and race relations (Morelos 1999). Academic accounts explain that the situation was inflamed when national broadsheet, *The Straits Times*, sensationalized the coverage of the two plays. The state withdrew funding for Forum Theatre and imposed a deposit of SG$10,000 (about US$7,000) for such performances as a safeguard, so that they could carry on without incident (Chong 2011c).

The reception to Performance Art was similar—when artiste Josef Ng snipped his pubic hair with his back to the audience as a symbolic protest of the police entrapment of gays in the wee hours of January 1, 1994, there was outrage amongst the public and government authorities. The broader context is that the law criminalizes sex between men. Ng was fined SG$1,000 (about US$700) for what was deemed as an obscene act and banned from performing it. As with Forum Theatre, state support for Performance Art ceased (K. Tan 2017).

Since then, the space has opened up to allow local artiste Loo Zihan to re-enact Ng's performance as part of an annual arts festival at the M1 Singapore Fringe Festival 2012. Theatre groups like TNS and another company, Drama Box, now regularly perform Forum Theatre on topics like domestic violence, migrant worker rights, end-of-life issues, and terrorism. The companies even work with government agencies to create critical works when it is clear that there are mutual interests in shifting public attitudes and the artists know they are not compromising their independence and autonomy. On other occasions, where there are concerns about public sensitivities, a system has gradually evolved to allow for audience advisories (Drama Box 2016; The Necessary Stage 2014). While there are other artistic players who are skeptical of such developments, it is clear that a level of mutual trust has emerged over time between the government and its agencies that oversee artistic production, like the Media Development Authority (which, amongst other things, regulated artistic content until its recent reincarnation as the Infocomm Media Development Authority) and companies like TNS (A. Tan 2017).

The Founder and Artistic Director of TNS, Alvin Tan, has described the interaction of independent artists with the Singaporean state using the different points on a compass as a metaphor. The two sides can choose to be in opposition with each other like the North Pole is to the South Pole, but there are other positions on a compass like East, West, North-East, and South-East and as Tan put it, "we can also choose not to stay fixed in any position. TNS chose the latter approach" (A. Tan 2017).

The second group of civil society interests is post-material, and usually involves individuals or groups, who look beyond their self to broader interests, including animal welfare. Again, to illustrate the evolution of this sector, in the early part of this millennium, the Cat Welfare Society was denied registration as a society until it changed its name from "Cat Project" (Lim 2000). The group wanted the name "Cat Project" for its emphasis on its sterilization program. However, according to anecdotal accounts, the authorities said that the group had to have the word "society" in its name to be officially registered as one (Dawn 2007). The suspicion has always been, however, that the humane approach of sterilizing stray cats in public housing estates put the group at loggerheads with the government's impulse to cull. After all, the same reason that residents are not allowed to keep cats as pets in their flats applies to the stray population in densely populated public residential estates—the cats are difficult to confine in one place and the caterwauling presents unacceptable noise pollution.

Today, we see that animal welfare groups, like the leading Animal Concerns Research and Education Society (ACRES), have found room to engage not only in public education on the treatment of animals, but also in calling out trade in endangered wildlife, in addition to providing services to the government to address animal welfare and abuse. ACRES was also a part of a broader initiative called the Animal Welfare Legislation Review Committee that brought together multiple stakeholders to craft a modern and more progressive Animal and Bird (Amendment) Bill, which was passed in Parliament in November 2014 (Ng 2016) to enhance animal welfare, especially through the regulation of the pet trade. ACRES and other animal welfare groups are successful in partnering with the government and offering their expertise and peer pressure to shape public policy (Wong 2013). And as for cats in the public housing apartments, there has been a government-sanctioned pilot scheme to allow them in two such estates, the first of which began in October 2012. The status is due for final reckoning in 2017 (Khew 2015).

With a flavor of the changes that have taken place in civil society in Singapore, the next section reviews how developments in the sector have been interpreted in scholarly political and sociological literature.

The operating conditions for civil society

As described by scholars listed in the previous section, civil society groups have faced restrictions in their activism in Singapore, but it is also fair to say that there has been greater liberalization of the space in recent times. These limits can be divided into two categories: hard laws and soft political restraints. Legally, even as the Singapore Constitution provides for freedoms of association, assembly, and speech, these are limited by other legislation that prioritizes public order and security (Constitution of the Republic of Singapore: Articles [1] and [2]; Tan 2011a). As it concerns the freedom of association, civil society groups are primarily governed by the Societies Act (Cap. 311), which from 2004, states that groups of ten or more persons can be automatically registered, except where their mission deals with race, language, religion, political, and civil rights, if they have foreign links, or promote martial arts. These cases will have to go through the normal review process (Ministry of Home Affairs 2004). There are then limits and requirements that accompany the acceptance of funding for civil society organizations. In this, groups that the state has gazetted as political associations cannot accept more than SG$5,000 (about US$3,500) in anonymous donations and are also prohibited from receiving foreign donations (Political Donations Act, Cap. 236).

The freedom to assemble is proscribed by the 2009 Public Order Act (Cap. 257. A), which considers a single person as an assembly. Indoor public talks do not require a police license from 2004, if no foreign organizers or speakers are involved. More recently, it was clarified that foreign sponsorship of political events like the Pink Dot Picnic (discussed later) is disallowed. Singaporeans can make public speeches or hold demonstrations at one location—the Speakers' Corner at Hong Lim Park, established in 2000, provided that they do not touch on the topics of race or religion. They simply have to register their intent with the National Parks Board, the agency that regulates public parks like that one, beforehand.

Other laws on expression and speech include the Sedition Act (Cap. 290), which provides the state with legal means to take action against individuals who are deemed to have stirred up ill will against it, between Singapore citizens and residents, or amongst the various ethnic, religious groups or classes of Singaporeans. There is also the Newspaper and Printing Presses Act (Cap. 206), which enforces a compulsory licensing system for establishing newspapers and a system of management shares in specific relation to running newspaper companies (Tay 2003). Such management shares can only be held with the approval of the government ministry that regulates the Act. It allows holders the equivalent of 200 votes for each share on any resolution relating to the appointment or dismissal of a director or any member of the staff in the company when compared to the single vote that holders of the ordinary shares have. The Public Entertainments and Meetings Act (Cap. 257) makes it compulsory for anyone intending to put up a public performance to receive a license beforehand.

There are also soft political and moral restraints that set the "norms" for acceptable political speech. Government leaders castigate activists or public intellectuals that have crossed the line if they engaged in character assassination of those from their ranks. There have been occasions when they have, in their personal capacity, sued the speakers for defamation. Another principle is that consistent political commentary will invite political leaders to ask that the speakers join a formal political party and properly declare their political and partisan interests; academia and civil society do not provide sanctuaries for what are deemed to be partisan, political activities (Barr 2008; Tan 2009).

Theorizing civil society

While scholars may have argued previously that Singapore is a hybrid regime of an electoral authoritarian state (Diamond 2002), they are likely to recognize that political development has progressed to a stage where it is a competitive authoritarian regime (Diamond 2012; Ortmann 2012). This is attributed to a higher level of political pluralism and contestation that has emerged and manifested in partisan politics and also the livening-up of civil society and independent, alternative media over recent years.

Emerging out of the conflict tradition are those who view civil society as being necessarily a reflection of class conflict. Scholars like Garry Rodan (1996) take a political economy view of state–society relations, noting that successful economic development has led to the rise of the growing middle class, where interests either rise up to challenge the state or become co-opted into political institutions of the establishment. Beng Huat Chua (1995) sees the state responding to competing civil society interests through the use of the narrative of "Asian communitarianism." Its emphasis on social order is a reflection of the state's attempt to reinforce a hegemonic ideological consensus that staves off the effects of changing social reality. Through "communitarianism," the state cautions against an excess of individualism and the importance of embracing shared interests of the nation and society.

Building on this are scholars who take the Hegelian model as epitomizing the way the state frames its relationship with citizens and civil society. Chong explains how the state places itself above the fray of sectoral interests and conflict; it presents itself as safeguarding the higher-order national interest and seeks to maintain an ideological consensus for popular support (Chong 2006; Lee 2004). Scholars diverge on their views on how effective this has been, with Chua (1995) describing the state striving to maintain hegemonic consensus in the mid-1990s and Chong (2006) finding a more fluid relationship that is open to contestation from the ground in the mid-2000s. Terence Lee (2005) argues that the state employs the use of "gestural politics," where the boundaries for participation are loosened in official rhetoric, but particular limits to civil society activity still abound. Rodan sees, more subtly, a variegated landscape where different sectors and civic actors enjoy different levels of autonomy from the state (Jayasuriya and Rodan 2007; Rodan 2013).

Scholars from the Western liberal democratic, liberal communitarian, and social capital traditions take a more benign view of the evolution of state–civil society relations. The role of the liberal state lies in ensuring that individuals can pursue their self interests and, by extension, group interests (Alagappa 2004; Kumar 1993; Scalet and Schmidtz 2002). Chan (2014) spells out how a better-educated and globalized professional class does manifest more liberal political tendencies. Robert Putnam has argued that healthy associational activity can result in pro-social outcomes when "social capital" or reciprocal and trust-based relational ties between peers are formed (Putnam 2007; Putnam, Leonardi, and Nanetti 1993). Maria Francesch-Huidobro (2008) and Tay Keong Tan (2008) in their case studies present important findings on how social capital has been generated within the green movement and between that and policy makers.

Other scholars provide perspectives on the mechanics of how civil society groups interact with the state. Chua has argued that civil society groups span a continuum in terms of their relations with the state. On one end are "junior partners" to the state that operate within its ideological framework in, say, the social welfare sector. On the other end are groups that challenge and resist the dominant narratives of the state (Chua 2003a). These, mapping to Rodan's notion of rising middle-class interests, include theater groups, as discussed in the introduction, and groups in the space of human rights activism and conservation.

Chua (2003b), Suzaina Kadir (2004), and Gillian Koh and Giok Ling Ooi (2004) add flesh to the variegated experiences between civil society and the state with case studies of specific interactions between the state and parts of civil society. Kadir argued in her survey in the early 2000s that: "Groups that embrace a public issue and seek to assert consistent pressure on certain government policies via interest advocacy have been more successful than those that advocate particularistic (ethnic/religious) issues." Chua homes in on some of those areas in his 2003 article, noting that while the activism in theater and the ethnic-based groups were not quashed aggressively through legal force "until the political sphere is democratized through competitive politics, all civil-society activities will exist at the suffering [sic] of the politically hegemonic PAP government" (Chua 2003b: 36). Kadir also states, "Civil society in Singapore cannot bring about fundamental or even substantial political change. It can only urge the state to trim the banyan tree further, thereby opening up space and light for civil society to thrive" (2004: 350). Most Singaporean scholars discussing the existing forms of civil society therefore draw a clear distinction between political and civil society and do not see the ground-up civic energy translating into democratic transition and consolidation unless and until the course of electoral politics changes. We see more interactive effects between the two not-unrelated spaces of political and civic activism.

More recent scholarship has engaged in alternative narratives of specific historical occasions where they argue the state suppressed civil society, as in the case of the Marxist Conspiracy of 1987, when twenty-two civic activists were put in detention without trial for allegedly instigating social upheaval in relation to foreign workers (Barr and Trocki 2008; Lim and Lee 2016).

Another area of scholarship relates to the legal frameworks by which civil society operates. The law, as legal scholar Simon Tay has put it, "can limit or enable civil society." This is not only in the content of laws, but, perhaps even more importantly, in the process of law making itself and "'interpretation' of the law." (Tay 2003: 186). Tay proposed, in the early 2000s, how room for civic activism could be expanded and this has been updated by Kevin Tan (2017). Tan argues that many of the legal impediments to a more active civil society stem from the government's fear of subversive political activity. He adds, however, that recommendations to repeal the Sedition Act and for provisions in the Penal Code to deal with threats to social harmony are not as important as for the government to "climb the learning curve of dealing with alternative voices quickly." He explains that it is a steep curve, because Singaporean leaders are "conditioned to think of people who disagree with them as troublemakers," rather than recognize that civil society comprises not only the helping hands of those who provide social services—those "junior partners" in Chua's lexicon, but "helping heads" too. The latter group that the state is ambivalent about, Tan argues, may be the same creative force that it needs to power the economy, which the state by its dictum says requires social and political harmony to thrive.

The facts are that the PAP is a democratic socialist movement, that Singapore has experienced successful capitalist development and finally, that Singapore as an open and globalized city state has been and will be an unequal society. The PAP's commitment to redistributive policies and a progressive fiscal system has meant that it has kept class conflict or what it calls the "politics of envy" at bay, because it has been conscious of it, even if that consciousness has waxed and waned over the fifty-year period. The ideological constructs of "Asian communitarianism" and "meritocracy," as well as its posture as the guardian of national interests, have kept civil society somewhat more confined to dealing with the post-material interests of civic and human rights, conservation, and the welfare of migrant workers. However, it should be noted that the protests against foreign labor and immigration that emerged from 2011 to 2013 and will be discussed later, were jolts from civil society, active citizens, and political parties to more carefully attend to broader and material interests of Singaporeans, when it was felt that the regime had neglected these. But, by and large, the PAP State has itself been informed by the conflict tradition and re-calibrated its policies to take heed of dissent. There is, most certainly, the emergence of that middle class that also cares about what transcends the dollars and cents of economic development, and wishes for a less capitalist-oriented state. This is seen in the interest in cultural diversity, the conservation of the built and green heritage, and the humane treatment of workers and animals for its own sake. It is in that sense that both theories of modernization and liberal democracy on the one hand, and the Marxian tradition of dialectical materialism, on the other, seem to play out. The long and short of it is that the PAP State has the choice of adaptation to political and social diversity or a reversion to demand for political conformity and control. What will be clear is that the former strategy has been adopted much more than the latter in recent years, which translates to a non-linear yet gradual transition to democratic consolidation in the country. We will illustrate this in the next section.

Making sense of civil society and its ground energies

The three areas we have selected to focus on are migration; religion, secularism, and morality; and conservation. We take three angles to the analysis. First, we ask where they stand vis-à-vis the state; second, we also look at the interaction within civil society; third, we look at whether there is an international nexus in the activism at the end of the section.

Migration

As mentioned briefly earlier, three decades ago, twenty-two social and lay workers, some of whom volunteered with the Geylang Catholic Center for Foreign Workers, were arrested for what the government termed a "Marxist Conspiracy" (Lyons 2004; Piper 2006). While the group was accused of a nascent Marxist plot to overthrow the state through its activism amongst foreign workers, critical accounts argue that this was the government's manner of dealing with dissenting voices and a reaction to the prospect of how an alternative center of power could mobilise itself (Barr 2008; Wijeysingha 2012). The arrests created a climate where advocacy work regarding migrant workers seemed perilous (Piper 2006). Today, however, there are groups that actively promote migrant worker welfare and rights, even as they were understandably cautious about engaging the state initially (Gee 2016).

The most obvious case of groups that partner the state include the Migrant Worker Centre (MWC), set up by the National Trades Union Congress, and the Singapore National Employers

Federation, which have close ties to the government—what Chua would term "junior partners of the state." There is also the Archdiocesan Commission for the Pastoral Care of Migrants and Itinerant People, which is a Catholic organization that provides for the social welfare needs of migrants in Singapore. Groups on the other end of the spectrum that wear their independence as a badge of honor include Transient Workers Count Too (TWC2) and the Humanitarian Organization of Migrant Economics (HOME) (Mathews and Soon 2015).

The latter set of organizations has been strategic in their approach. The past president and current head of research of TWC2, John Gee, shares that by "giving practical form to individual human rights standards, [TWC2] … made more progress than if [it] … had simply reiterated demands for Singapore to sign this convention or that treaty" (Gee 2016: 58). The practice of providing constructive policy suggestions rather than outright criticism to the government has helped TWC2 make inroads in addressing migrant worker welfare (Gee 2016).

In shedding light on the mechanics of how change happens in this sector, Chanranpal Bal (2015) contends that there is a need to examine the production politics of migrant worker activism to understand how groups leverage the opportunities presented on the ground to advocate better outcomes for migrant workers. In this, he argues that a critical mass of cases of worker desertion had provided migrant worker advocacy groups like TWC2 and HOME with the platform to engage in discussions with government bodies like the Ministry of Manpower on addressing worker welfare. These sessions serve as opportunities for groups like TWC2 and HOME to argue their case and sensitize government representatives to issues on the ground, which typically have to do with unsafe and unfair employment practices. These can be seen as steps by the government to ensure that Singapore is still attractive to migrant labor and in the long term, good for business interests rather than bad for it—this is the paradigm shift that has been effected. Through the advocacy of migrant worker groups like TWC2 and HOME, the government made it illegal in July 2008 for employers to collect kickbacks when securing employment of workers (Ministry of Manpower 2009), and from April 2016, it became compulsory for employers to issue itemized pay slips, as well as key employment terms, to employees (Ministry of Manpower 2016). The government has also set and enforced minimum accommodation and worker safety standards over the years.

Groups in the migrant worker welfare advocacy space have had a collaborative relationship. The Solidarity for Migrant Workers coalition, comprising TWC2, HOME, and Migrant Voices was established to pool resources for effective advocacy (Ortmann 2015), a result of which was legislation introduced in 2013 to establish the right of foreign domestic workers to a day of leave from work every week (Day Off 2016).

A state that is pro-business and knows that stable and healthy labor relations even amongst the foreign workforce are important, and civil society that is willing to explore other modalities of interacting based on an understanding of how trust and reciprocity work, have resulted in positive outcomes. This can be explained by both the conflict and liberal communitarian theorizing discussed earlier.

At an even higher stake is public support for the foreign labor and immigration policies of the government. A series of mass protests that were held in 2013 on its *Population White Paper* was a reflection of the public wariness about the effect of those policies—resource competition in transport, housing, and education; wage depression in the low-wage, low-skilled segment of the labor market where the majority of foreigners work; and cultural change, given that one-third of the total population are not Singaporean residents. Thus, the protestors voiced their discomfort with the government's announced population planning parameter of 6.9 million in three rallies in 2013 (Koh and Soon 2015). The state's response, even before the protests, but certainly after it, was to promise a tightening of the level of foreign workforce growth, which has material impact on economic growth (unless the general level of productivity and innovation can rise) (Lee 2013). While the material impulses of the protests can be explained by conflict theory, it is understood that the PAP state's responses are in good part explained by the electoral losses the ruling party suffered in the preceding general election of May 2011, where the population issue was a hot button issue. This was the same in a by-election at the start of 2013 just before the White Paper was released. Others may point to the state anticipating the limits of growth through the strategy of force-feeding the economy with foreign labor in its economic blueprint issued by the Economic Strategies Committee and operationalized in the national budget in 2010 (Economic Strategies Committee 2010). The "chastisement" of voters at the polls will have reinforced the need to calibrate workforce and economic strategy to give greater focus to the direct socio-economic and cultural concerns of Singaporeans who were raised well before May 2011. A footnote to this case study is, of course, the rise of anti-foreigner rhetoric, the negative side of civic activism, a point that we will return to at the end of this chapter.

Religion, secularism, and morality

A fair bit of literature has emerged in recent years on civil society activism in the space of religion, secularism, and morality. Returning to Chua's framework, historically, groups in the religious space have been extensions of state institutions in providing social welfare services (Mathews 2009a, 2009b) and of course, cultural and spiritual ballast to society, reinforcing the notion of an Asian communitarian ideal. In addition, the state has, over the years, reinforced the need to keep politics out of religion and has policed that actively.

However, in recent years, religious groups and individuals have been more vocal on issues of morality, namely, on the issues of gambling and gay rights. In this, religious groups see themselves as a voice of conscience to a state they suspect of being too pragmatic in shaping Singapore into the image of a thriving creative hub and an attractive home to global talent (Chang 2012; Chong 2011a; Lee 2005). With regard to the casinos, the state introduced strong social safeguards against problem gambling and entry for Singaporeans into the gambling facilities at integrated resorts with its decision to legalize casinos in 2005, having taken into account the discomfort expressed by such groups (Lee 2005).

As for gay rights, we see the manifestation of the clash of values in intra-civil society conflict through the specific case of the "AWARE Saga." In March 2009, a group of new members of the Association of Women for Action, Research and Education (AWARE), a non-government organization dedicated to advocacy on gender rights, took over the reins of leadership through due process at an annual general meeting. When the old guard at AWARE brought this to light in the mainstream media, journalists made the case that the new leaders were linked to the same church and for all intents and purposes generated articles to suggest that the new group was steeplejacking AWARE. On the other side, these new leaders said that they were dedicated to returning the organization to its original mission and also that in the course of taking over, had found evidence that AWARE had been portraying homosexuality as being "normal" in the sexuality education classes it had been commissioned to run in public schools. In the event, the new leaders were ousted at an extraordinary general meeting in early May that year (Chong 2011b).

Supporters for the normalization of homosexuality rode on the momentum from the AWARE Saga to launch a public campaign called the "Pink Dot Picnic" although the conceptualization of the latter pre-dated the former (Chua 2014). It invites people who support the idea that all Singaporeans deserve "the freedom to love" to don pink outfits and gather at Speakers' Corner for a picnic. The first was held in May 2009 and the movement is now called Pink

Dot.sg. By 2014, it had gained sufficient momentum to precipitate a push back from some religious conservatives. That year, a group of Christian leaders applied to the police to organize a "Red Dot Family Festival" or "#FamFest" on the same day but at a different location, which was denied, ostensibly because their proposed location was inappropriate for such activity. The date of the Pink Dot that year also coincided with the beginning of the fasting month for Muslims. Muslim leader Ustaz Noor Deros called on his followers to don white clothing in what has been known as the Wear White movement to symbolize a call to return to purity, and a rejection of the liberal values expressed by Pink Dot. Those who proposed the abortive FamFest then encouraged their followers to join the Wear White movement at the worship services that week (Koh and Soon 2015).

Clearly, these are all symptoms of referred pain from the broader struggle around gay rights in Singapore. Activists seeking the decriminalizing of gay sex between consenting men have, over years of struggle, taken a pragmatic approach to engaging the state in an act of "strategic adaptation" (Chua 2012). In this, "[a]ctivists adjust their tactics according to changes in formal law and cultural norms, and push the limits of those norms while simultaneously adhering to them" (Chua 2012: 714). Pink Dot stands as a prime example of this, where the key message of the event is presented in a non-threatening manner, rather than the outright assertion of rights in the way that has played out in many Western liberal democracies (Chua 2012, 2014).

We see in this situation of conflict between the space of religion, secularism, and morality, groups appealing to the state to step in as a neutral arbiter. This played out very clearly in the AWARE Saga, where members of the liberal-ousted leadership appealed to members of Parliament to weigh in. Nonetheless, the state's position, stated only after the acute crisis was over, was to stay above the fray; to maintain that the controversy remained within what it considered acceptable bounds. This was while activists from both sides slugged it out, especially since there was not going to be any change in legislation. The government has often said it would not take the lead on this agenda, as it would let the majority in society set the pace for change (Singapore Parliament Reports 2007). The government did intervene minimally during the AWARE Saga when the Internal Security Division questioned a Christian pastor for calling on his flock to take sides and thereby crossed the line of mixing religion with politics (Ghani and Koh 2011). We see the elements of the Hegelian state at play here, standing above sectoral interests. The advocacy and support for the cause, however, clearly appeals to liberal democratic notions of liberty and equality.

Conservation

Another sphere of active resistance against the state is in green and heritage conservation. Unlike the intra-civil society conflict that we witnessed with religious and pro-LGBT groups, this is one area we see collaboration around efforts to save the Bukit Brown Cemetery and the Green Rail Corridor. The former is considered a repository of national memories where pioneers of the nation rest, as well as rich animal and plant life. As such, groups like the Nature Society (Singapore) (NSS) and the Singapore Heritage Society (SHS) had appraised that value in SHS' publication entitled *Spaces of the Dead: A Case from the Living* (Tan 2011b). Other informal groups have organized walking tours to raise awareness of the site's value. When the state announced that a four-lane dual carriageway would be constructed through Bukit Brown and that graves would be exhumed to widen a road on one of its borders in September 2011, green and brown groups stood ready to oppose those moves. While dialogue sessions were convened between civil society and the government, it emerged that there had been a mismatch of expectations—the government said it merely wished to inform activists of its plans, while the activists wished to have the government explore alternative arrangements so that Bukit Brown would be fully preserved. The nature and heritage groups were able to secure slight modifications to the government's plans to their dissatisfaction—an "eco-bridge" which would allow fauna to pass under it; a smaller number of graves exhumed than originally intended (Koh and Soon 2015).

The Green Rail Corridor is a unique, continuous stretch of land where the defunct Malayan Railway (KTM) once ran from the north to the south of the island. The NSS had been appraising its value and published its findings and recommendations in the document, *The Green Corridor A Proposal to Keep the Railway Lands as a Continuous Green Corridor* (Tham 2010), having known that the southern Tanjong Pagar terminus would be closed in 2011 and that KTM train services into Singapore would be terminated altogether. The proposal particularly cautioned against parceling out the Green Corridor, with its rich flora, fauna, and heritage, for commercial interests. Through the consultations, the state communicated that it had to balance competing needs for the land and the episode ended with the release of the Urban Redevelopment Authority's (URA) Land Use Plan (2013). Although the plans did not state that the whole of the corridor would be preserved, it referred to the Rail Corridor in terms not dissimilar to what conservation groups proposed and said that the Rail Corridor "will offer inviting routes for joggers and cyclists, and improve access to recreational and heritage sites" (Koh and Soon 2015; URA 2013).

Green groups, such as the NSS, have been particularly successful in their evidence-based approach to advocacy. The other instances of this were the moratorium on redeveloping Lower Peirce Reservoir (which is set in Singapore's oldest secondary rainforest) into a golf course and the saving of bio-rich mudflats of Chek Jawa off Pulau Ubin, a tiny island beyond the east coast of Singapore (Geh 2008; Teh and Raju 2010). Francesch-Huidobro's detailed study of civic activism and state engagement in green conservation leads her to conclude that the processes were "far from consultative and open," even though the state had become more consultative and had grown its policy networks to include concerned citizens. She found that the organizations operating in it were "co-opted and subordinated by the state," even though both sides were "opening-up" to each other. Writing in 2008, she speculated that civil society would grow further, given the liberalization promised by Singapore's third Prime Minister, Lee Hsien Loong. In the transitional era when the study was conducted, she described the model of governance as "disciplined governance"—with the analogy of the relationship that a freed slave would have with his former owner. Since then, however, we have demonstrated with more recent developments that an increasingly liberal populace and a pragmatic civil society are finding, at times, a liberalizing state on the other side of the table.

So as not to suggest that Singapore civil society is entirely parochial and driven merely by its own steam, it must be acknowledged that some groups do engage with regional and international counterparts—TWC2 and HOME are part of the Migrant Forum in Asia (Lyons 2009); the Singapore Anti-Death Penalty Campaign, as well as the Think Centre, are part of the Anti-Death Penalty Asia Network (ADPAN), an international coalition spearheaded by Amnesty International. Coalition-building also takes place where activists in AWARE, TWC2, HOME, and disability and gay groups work together to craft submissions to the United Nations Universal Periodic Review (Ortmann 2015). Their knowledge of developments in the international arena has also helped them shape their local campaigns. Given the networking, information sharing, and mobilization of resources that modern-day information technology allows, it is quite possible that there will be more collaboration within and beyond the country's shores, but in ways that do not raise suspicions of foreign interference in domestic politics that the state would not tolerate.

Whither civil society

The brief review of contemporary developments in civil society in Singapore suggests a more pragmatic, problem-solving orientation, rather than an ideological, rights-based, and adversarial approach it takes in engaging the state. These have played out on a range of policy issues and sectors—both the material as well as post-material interests. The state has responded sometimes with changes in public policy and sometimes to explain the status quo. The conditions for the operation of civil society have also been liberalized over the past two decades, even if not in a linear fashion. It would not be fair to suggest that TNS, TWC2, and NSS, for instance, have been "co-opted."

There has been a greater level of conflict and cooperation within civil society as well. Much of this has been facilitated by the Internet and new media, for obvious reasons. This is especially the case where certain forms of civil society are controversial or illegal, which then poses a limit on which groups can meet offline. The Internet has been instrumental in facilitating the growth of the LGBT lobby, and providing a safe space to gather, at a time when the state was conducting raids at gay pubs in the offline world (Chua 2012). It is also on those issues of gay rights or on foreigners in Singapore, expressed online, where we see ugly and uncivil conflict. Carol Soon and Hichang Cho (2014) report in their study of political bloggers in Singapore that many formed connections through Internet forums. As Soon and Cho have stated about the Internet, "Changes in political opportunity structures, in part due to technology adoption and in part a result of authorities' evolving mindsets towards media regulation, have created loopholes through which interest groups recruit and mobilize supporters" (Soon and Cho 2014: 538).

There are instances too when bloggers have met with state action, having been found guilty of defaming government leaders, scandalizing the judiciary, or publishing falsehoods that create ill-will amongst different people's groups in Singapore.

Going by the trends discussed in the chapter, the future of civil society is likely to see even more complex relations emerge. This is where groups within civil society may cooperate with each other; others may exist to oppose others. This is also where some groups may choose to oppose the state at some junctures and then cooperate with it at other times. This is why Tan's metaphor of the compass is useful as long as we remember that the groups tend to be clear about their core interest. This is pragmatic civil society at work.

Such trends also suggest that there is a need to strengthen the ethos of democratic discourse going forward. A study conducted by Bin Abdul Aziz Johannis *et al.* (2016) invited civil society representatives from different sides of the fence to dialogue on divisive issues like homosexuality, abortion, and the death penalty. Participants in the study agreed that there is a language and there are modalities that even the most fierce combatants and committed advocates should avoid so as not to undermine the liberal and democratic ethos in discussing or negotiating the interests involved.

The further maturation of Singapore's civil society will hinge on how Singaporeans dialogue with those whose views may be very different from their own, in both the online and real world spaces, and how the government chooses also to dialogue with those it would have, in a different era, considered "troublemakers." Scholars should continue to find Singapore a fascinating case for work on democratic theory and civil society for many years to come.

Suggested readings

Chong, Terence. 2006. Embodying Society's Best: Hegel and the Singapore State. *Journal of Contemporary Asia* 36(3): 283–304.
Chua, Beng Huat. 1995. *Communitarian Ideology and Democracy in Singapore*. London: Routledge.

Koh, Gillian, and Giok Ling Ooi, eds. 2003. *State–Society Relations in Singapore*. Singapore: Eastern Universities Press.

Koh, Gillian, and Debbie Soon. 2016. *Singapore Chronicles: Civil Society*. Singapore: Straits Times Press.

Lim, Jason, and Terence Lee, eds. 2016. *Singapore: Negotiating State and Society, 1965–2015*. London and New York: Routledge.

Koh, Gillian, ed. 2016. *Commentary* 25: 61–68. Electronic document, www.nuss.org.sg/publication/1466159004_commentary2016%20-%20final.pdf, accessed October 3, 2016.

Ortmann, Stephan. 2012. Policy Advocacy in a Competitive Authoritarian Regime: The Growth of Civil Society and Agenda Setting in Singapore. *Administration and Society* 44(6S): 13–25.

Ortmann, Stephan. 2015. Political Change and Civil Society Coalitions in Singapore. *Government and Opposition* 50(1): 119–139.

Rodan, Garry. 1996. State–Society Relations and Political Opposition in Singapore. In *Political Oppositions in Industrialising Asia*. Garry Rodan, ed. Pp. 95–127. London: Routledge.

Soon, Carol, and Gillian Koh, eds. 2017. *Civil Society and the State in Singapore*. Singapore: World Scientific Publishing.

References

Alagappa, Muthiah. 2004. Civil Society and Political Change: An Analytical Framework. In *Civil Society and Political Change in Asia: Expanding and Contracting Democratic Space*. Muthiah Alagappa, ed. Pp. 25–57. Stanford, CA: Stanford University Press.

Bal, Chanranpal S. 2015. Production Politics and Migrant Labour Advocacy in Singapore. *Journal of Contemporary Asia* 45(2): 219–242.

Barr, Michael D. 2008. Singapore's Catholic Social Activists: Alleged Marxist Conspirators. In *Paths Not Taken: Political Pluralism in Post-War Singapore*. Michael D. Barr and Carl A. Trocki, eds. Pp. 228–247. Singapore: NUS Press.

Barr, Michael D., and Carl A. Trocki, eds. 2008. *Paths Not Taken: Political Pluralism in Post-War Singapore*. Singapore: NUS Press.

Chan, Heng Chee. 2014. Governance in Singapore: History and Legacy. In *Singapore Perspectives 2013: Governance*. Gillian Koh, ed. Pp. 7–16. Singapore: World Scientific Publishing.

Chang, Peter T. C. 2012. Singapore's Cultural Experimentation: Gay Rights, Stem Cells, Casinos and the Evangelical Response. *Religion, State and Society* 40(2): 192–211.

Chong, Terence. 2006. Embodying Society's Best: Hegel and the Singapore State. *Journal of Contemporary Asia* 36(3): 283–304.

Chong, Terence. 2011a. Filling the Moral Void: The Christian Right in Singapore. *Journal of Contemporary Asia* 41(4): 566–583.

Chong, Terence. 2011b. Introduction. In *The Aware Saga: Civil Society and Public Morality in Singapore*. Terence Chong, ed. Pp. 1–13. Singapore: NUS Press.

Chong, Terence. 2011c. *The Theatre and the State in Singapore: Orthodoxy and Resistance*. London and New York: Routledge.

Chua, Beng Huat. 1995. *Communitarian Ideology and Democracy in Singapore*. London: Routledge.

Chua, Beng Huat. 2003a. The Relative Autonomies of the State and Civil Society In *State–Society Relations in Singapore*. Gillian Koh and Giok Ling Ooi, eds. Pp. 62–76. Singapore: Eastern Universities Press.

Chua, Beng Huat. 2003b. Non-Transformative Politics: Civil Society in Singapore. In *Civil Society in Asia: In Search of Democracy and Development in Bangladesh*. David C. Schak and Wayne Hudson, eds. Pp. 20–39. Burlington, VT: Ashgate.

Chua, Lynette J. 2012. Pragmatic Resistance, Law and Social Movements in Authoritarian States: The Case of Gay Collective Action in Singapore. *Law and Society Review* 46(4): 713–748.

Chua, Lynette J. 2014. *Mobilizing Gay Singapore: Rights and Resistance in an Authoritarian State*. Singapore: NUS Press.

Constitution of the Republic of Singapore. 2015. Singapore Statutes Online. Electronic document, http://statutes.agc.gov.sg/, accessed September 27, 2016.

Day Off. 2016. For a Regular Day Off for Domestic Workers in Singapore. Electronic document, www.dayoff.sg/, accessed September 26, 2016.

Dawn. 2007. Working with the Cat Welfare Society [Web log post]. December 27. Electronic document, http://catwelfare.blogspot.sg/, accessed October 13, 2016.

Diamond, Larry. 2002. Thinking about Hybrid Regimes. *Journal of Democracy* 13(2): 21–35.

Diamond, Larry. 2012. The Coming Wave. *Journal of Democracy* 23(1): 5–13.

Diamond, Larry. 2013. Introduction. In *Democracy in East* Asia: *A New Century*. Larry Diamond, Marc F. Plattner, and Yun-Han Chu, eds. Pp. ix–xxx. Baltimore, MD: Johns Hopkins University Press.

Drama Box. 2016. Scenes: Forum Theatre. Electronic document, http://dramabox.org/eng/productions-community-festival2015.html, accessed September 26, 2016.

Economic Strategies Committee. 2010. *Report of the Economic Strategies Committee*. Electronic document, www.mof.gov.sg/Portals/0/MOF%20For/Businesses/ESC%20Recommendations/ESC%20Full%20 Report.pdf, accessed February 19, 2017.

Francesch-Huidobro, Maria. 2008. *Governance, Politics and the Environment*. Singapore: Institute of Southeast Asian Studies.

Gee, John. 2016. Transient Workers Count Too's Singaporean Way with Advocacy on Migrant Workers. *Commentary* 25: 54–60. Electronic document, www.nuss.org.sg/publication/1466159004_ commentary2016%20-%20final.pdf, accessed October 3, 2016.

Geh, Min. 2008. Growing Green Space. *Social Space* 1: 84–89. Electronic document, https://centres.smu.edu.sg/lien/files/2013/10/GehMinGreenSpace.pdf, accessed September 26, 2016.

Ghani, Azhar, and Gillian Koh. 2011. The Politics of (Non-)Interference from the Singapore State. In *The AWARE Saga: Civil Society and Public Morality in Singapore*. Terence Chong, ed. Pp. 36–50. Singapore: NUS Press.

Jayasuriya, Kanishka, and Garry Rodan. 2007. Beyond Hybrid Regimes: More Participation, Less Contestation in Southeast Asia. *Democratization* 14(5): 773–794.

Johannis, Bin Abdul Aziz, Gillian Koh, Mathew Mathews, and Tan Min-Wei. 2016. SG50 and Beyond: Protecting the Public Space in the New Era of Singaporean Pluralism. *Institute of Policy Studies Working Papers 25*. Electronic document, http://lkyspp.nus.edu.sg/ips/wp-content/uploads/sites/2/2016/08/ IPS-Working-Paper_No25_SG50-and-Beyond_0508161.pdf, accessed September 26, 2016.

Kadir, Suzaina. 2004. Engagement and Autonomy with the Political Status Quo. In *Civil Society and Political Change in Asia*. Muthiah Alagappa, ed. Pp. 324–354. Stanford, CA: Stanford University Press.

Khew, Carolyn. 2015. Chong Pang's Cat Project Gets 2-Year Extension, Expansion Plans. *The Straits Times*, January 11. Electronic document, https://global-factiva-com.libproxy1.nus.edu.sg, accessed February 19, 2017.

Koh, Gillian, and Giok Ling Ooi. 2004. Relationship between State and Society in Singapore. Clarifying the Conceptions, Assessing the Ground. In *Civil Society in Southeast Asia*. Hock Guan Lee, ed. Pp. 167–197. Singapore: Institute of Southeast Asian Studies.

Koh, Gillian, and Debbie Soon. 2015. Developing Civil Society in Singapore. In *50 Years of Social Issues in Singapore*. David Chan, ed. Pp. 205–228. Singapore: World Scientific Publishing.

Kumar, Krishan. 1993. Civil Society: An Inquiry into the Usefulness of an Historical Term. *British Journal of Sociology* 44(3): 375–395.

Lee, Hock Guan. 2004. Introduction: Civil Society in Southeast Asia. In *Civil Society in Southeast Asia*. Hock Guan Lee, ed. Pp. 1–26. Singapore: Institute of Southeast Asian Studies.

Lee, Hsien Loong. 2005. Statement by Prime Minister Lee Hsien Loong on the Integrated Resort on Monday, April 18, 2005 at Parliament House. Ministry of Trade and Industry. Electronic document, www.mti.gov.sg/MTIInsights/Documents/Ministerial%20Statement%20-%20PM%2018apr05.pdf, accessed September 25, 2016.

Lee, Hsien Loong. 2013. A Sustainable Population for a Dynamic Singapore. Singapore Parliament Reports No. 12, Session 1, Vol. 90, Sitting No. 6, 8 February. Electronic document, www.parliament.gov.sg/ publications-singapore-official-reports, accessed October 6, 2016.

Lee, Terence. 2005. Gestural Politics: Civil Society in "New" Singapore. *Journal of Social Issues in Southeast Asia* 20(2): 132–154.

Lim, Jason, and Terence Lee. 2016. *Singapore: Negotiating State and Society, 1965–2015*. London and New York: Routledge.

Lim, Lydia. 2000. How Uncivil, Really, is the Societies Act?. *The Straits Times*, January 22. Electronic document, https://global-factiva-com.libproxy1.nus.edu.sg, accessed September 30, 2016.

Lyons, Lenore. 2004. Organizing for Domestic Worker Rights in Singapore: The Limits of Transnationalism. In *Feminist Politics, Activism and Vision: Local and Global Challenges*. Lucian Ricciutelli, Angela Rose Miles, and Margaret McFadden, eds. Pp. 149–168. London and Inanna Publications and Education, Toronto: Zed Publications.

Lyons, Lenore. 2009. Transcending the Border: Transnational Imperatives in Singapore's Migrant Worker Rights Movement. *Critical Asian Studies* 41(1): 89–112.

M1 Singapore Fringe Festival. 2012. Art and Faith: Cane. Electronic document, www.singaporefringe.com/fringe2012/cane.html, accessed September 26, 2016.

Mathews, Mathew. 2009a. Accommodating Relationships: The Church and State in Singapore. In *Christianity and the State in Asia: Complicity and Conflict*. Julius Bautista and Francis G. L Khek, eds. Pp. 184–200. London and New York: Routledge.

Mathews, Mathew. 2009b. Christianity in Singapore: The Voice of Moral Conscience to the State. *Journal of Contemporary Religion* 24(1): 53–65

Mathews, Mathew, and Debbie Soon. 2015. Immigration and the Role of Civil Society in Singapore. In *Asia on the Move: Regional Migration and the Role of Civil Society*. Mely Caballero-Anthony and Toshihiro Menju, eds. Pp. 65–81. Tokyo: Japan Center for International Exchange.

Ministry of Home Affairs. 2004. Press Release for Automatic Registration of Societies. August 27. Electronic document, www.nas.gov.sg/archivesonline/speeches/view-html?filename=2004082797.htm, accessed September 26, 2016.

Ministry of Manpower. 2009. Can Report to the Authorities if Employers are Receiving Kickbacks. September 12 and 17. Electronic document, www.mom.gov.sg/newsroom/press-replies/2009/can-report-to-the-authorities-if-employers-are-rec, accessed September 23, 2016.

Ministry of Manpower. 2016. Amendments to the Employment Act. Electronic document, www.mom.gov.sg/employment-practices/employment-act/amendments-to-the-act, accessed September 23, 2016.

Morelos, Ronaldo. 1999. *Symbols and Power in Theatre of the Oppressed*. Appendix E. Dissertation, https://minerva-access.unimelb.edu.au/handle/11343/38881, accessed February 19, 2017.

The Necessary Stage. 2014. Good People. Electronic document, www.necessary.org/index.php/main-season/good-people, accessed September 26, 2016.

Newspaper and Printing Presses Act, Cap. 206. Singapore Statutes Online. Electronic document, http://statutes.agc.gov.sg/, accessed September 27, 2016.

Ng, Louis. 2016. Developing the Singapore Soul: ACRES and Animal Welfare. *Commentary* 25: 61–68. Electronic document, www.nuss.org.sg/publication/1466159004_commentary2016%20-%20final.pdf, accessed October 5, 2016.

Ortmann, Stephan. 2012. Policy Advocacy in a Competitive Authoritarian Regime: The Growth of Civil Society and Agenda Setting in Singapore. *Administration and Society* 44(6S): 13–25.

Ortmann, Stephan. 2015. Political Change and Civil Society Coalitions in Singapore. *Government and Opposition* 50(1): 119–139.

Political Donations Act, Cap. 236. Singapore Statutes Online. Electronic document, http://statutes.agc.gov.sg/, accessed September 27, 2016.

Piper, Nicola. 2006. Migrant Worker Activism in Singapore and Malaysia: Freedom of Association and the Role of the State. *Asian and Pacific Migration Journal* 15(3): 359–379.

Public Order Act, Cap. 257. Singapore Statutes Online. Electronic document, http://statutes.agc.gov.sg/, accessed September 27, 2016.

Public Entertainments and Meetings Act, Cap. 257. Singapore Statutes Online. Electronic document, http://statutes.agc.gov.sg/, accessed September 27, 2016.

Putnam, Robert D. 2007. E Pluribus Unum: Diversity and Community in the Twenty-first Century—The 2006 Johan Skytte Prize Lecture. *Scandinavian Political Studies* 30(2): 137–174.

Putnam, Robert D., Robert Leonardi, and Raffaella Nanetti. 1993. *Making Democracy Work: Civic Traditions in Modern Italy*. Princeton, NJ: Princeton University Press.

Rodan, Garry. 1996. State–Society Relations and Political Opposition in Singapore. In *Political Oppositions in Industrialising Asia*. Garry Rodan, ed. Pp. 95–127. London: Routledge.

Rodan, Garry. 2013. Southeast Asian Activism and Limits to Independent Political Space. In *Social Activism in Southeast Asia*. Michaele Ford, ed. Pp. 22–39. London: Routledge.

Scalet, Steven, and David Schmidtz. 2002. State, Civil Society and Classical Liberalism. In *Civil Society and Government*. Nancy L. Rosenblum and Robert C. Post, eds. Pp. 26–47. Princeton, NJ: Princeton University Press.

Sedition Act, Cap. 290. Singapore Statutes Online. Electronic document, http://statutes.agc.gov.sg/, accessed September 27, 2016.

Singapore Parliament Reports. 2007. Penal Code (Amendment) Bill. October 23. Electronic document, http://sprs.parl.gov.sg/, accessed September 27, 2016.

Soon, Carol, and Hichang Cho. 2014. OMGs! Offline-based Movement Organizations, Online-based Movement Organizations and Network Mobilization: A Case Study of Political Bloggers in Singapore. *Information, Communication and Society* 17(5): 537–559.

Societies Act, Cap. 311. Singapore Statutes Online. Electronic document, http://statutes.agc.gov.sg/, accessed September 27, 2016.

Tan, Alvin. 2017. Quiet Riot for New Possibilities. In *Civil Society and the State in Singapore*. Carol Soon and Gillian Koh, eds. Pp. 49–67. Singapore: World Scientific Publishing.

Tan, Kenneth P. T. 2009. Who's Afraid of Catherine Lim?: The State in Patriarchal Singapore. *Asian Studies Review* 33(1): 43–62.

Tan, Kevin. 2011a. *An Introduction to Singapore's Constitution*. Singapore: Talisman.

Tan, Kevin, ed. 2011b. *Spaces of the Dead: A Case from the Living*. Singapore: Ethos Books.

Tan, Kevin. 2017. Growing Civil Society in Singapore: The Future Legislative Landscape. In *Civil Society and the State in Singapore*. Carol Soon and Gillian Koh, eds. Pp. 241–279. Singapore: World Scientific Publishing.

Tan, Tay Keong. 2008. Social Capital and State–Civil Society Relations in Singapore. *Institute of Policy Studies Working Papers 9*. Electronic document, http://lkyspp.nus.edu.sg/ips/wp-content/uploads/sites/2/2013/06/wp9.pdf, accessed September 27, 2016.

Tay, Simon. 2003. Civil Society and the Law: Three Dimensions for Change in the 21st Century. In *State–Society Relations in Singapore*. Gillian Koh and Giok Ling Ooi, eds. Pp. 170–189. Singapore: Eastern Universities Press.

Teh, Tiong Sa, and Durairaju Kumaran Raju. 2010. Conserving Marine Biodiversity and Role of Individuals: A Case Study of Chek Jawa, Pulau Ubin, Singapore. Paper presented at a seminar on Growth, Equity and Environment: Missing Link between Academic Research and Policy Matters in Marine Park Areas, Faculty of Economics and Administration, University of Malaya, Kuala Lumpur, Malaysia, April 15. Electronic document, http://wildshores.blogspot.sg/2010/08/individuals-and-marine-conservation.html#.V-iBQ_l96Ul, accessed September 26, 2016.

Tham, Wai H., ed. 2010. *The Green Corridor A Proposal to Keep the Railway Lands as a Continuous Green Corridor*. Electronic document, https://nss.org.sg/documents/TheGreenCorridor101103.pdf, accessed September 26, 2016.

URA (Urban Redevelopment Authority). 2013. *A High Quality Living Environment for all Singaporeans: Land Use Plan to Support Singapore's Future Population*. January. Electronic document, www.mnd.gov.sg/landuseplan/e-book/index.html#/4/, accessed September 26, 2016.

Wijeysingha, Vincent. June 2, 2012. Dr. Vincent Wijeysingha: Lies of the "Marxist conspiracy." In *Ex Chersonesus Aurea* [*Web Log Post*]. Electronic document, http://exchersonesusaurea.blogspot.sg/2012/06/dr-vincent-wijeysingha-lies-of-marxist.html, accessed September 23, 2016.

Wong, Tessa. 2013. Louis Ng: "Pushing the Govt into a Corner will backfire." *The Straits Times*, October 19. Electronic document, https://global-factiva-com.libproxy1.nus.edu.sg, accessed April 10, 2016.

11

INDONESIA

Vedi R. Hadiz

Civil society after authoritarianism

After nearly two decades of post-authoritarianism, Indonesian civil society still does not serve as an effectual reservoir of organized social interests able to robustly put forward an agenda of liberal reform and social pluralism. In fact, it is argued here that civil society in Indonesia comprises heterogeneous social interests, including those that are prone to mobilizing intolerance and various forms of discrimination as an instrument in salient social conflicts that now take place in a democratic political context. While these interests are by no means hegemonic, they do influence how social conflicts take place as the ideas and values that emanate from them become mainstreamed to a considerable extent. From this point of view, the Indonesian case shows some similarities to that of India (Sahoo 2013), where socially and politically exclusivist tendencies—in the form of Hindutva—have been able to make good use of democratic political processes through the utilization, in that case, of idioms related to Hindu nationalism.[1]

The chapter pays special attention to the emergence of what may be called "uncivil groups," many of which take the form of paramilitary organizations. Like all civil society entities, these are rooted in the development of autonomous and voluntary associations. They also extend specific sets of interests and values onto arenas of political contestation, although with the effect of reinforcing the illiberal and exclusionary tendencies of Indonesian democracy, rather than its more liberal and socially inclusive ones. I suggest that it is important to consider such groups in discussions on contemporary Indonesian civil society. As Gordon White points out, it is possible to envisage civil society as encompassing "decidedly 'uncivil' entities like the Mafia, 'primordial' nationalist, ethnic or religious fundamentalist organizations, as well as 'modern' entities such as trade unions, chambers of commerce and professional associations" (1994: 377).

Adopting such a viewpoint seems appropriate in addressing the Indonesian case, as this chapter makes clear. How the presence of such groups helps to shape Indonesian democracy and its civil society requires examination, especially with regard to the broader context within which competition over access to the levers of power and resources now takes place. Following on previous work, it is suggested that such competition has been dominated by social alliances that are led by the kinds of social interests that were nurtured under the prior authoritarian era but have now reconstituted themselves within the institutional framework of Indonesia's quite vibrant and highly competitive democracy (Robison and Hadiz 2004).

The chapter proceeds by scrutinizing the theoretical debates on civil society generally as it relates to Indonesia, and then addresses the specific case of the post-authoritarian era. In the process, it revisits some older debates on Indonesian civil society and places them in the contemporary context of a post-authoritarian Indonesia that has been lauded for its achievements in such matters as introducing free elections and the freedoms of association and expression. It asks why in spite of such democratization, the politics of intolerance and social exclusion seems to be on the rise, emanating from civil society itself. This tendency has been apparent in the form of attacks on members of religious minorities, the remnants of a long-vanquished Indonesian communist tradition, members of the lesbian, gay, bisexual, and transgender (LGBT) community, and even on women and the freedoms they had enjoyed without much dispute in previous times (Topsfield and Rompies 2016). The work of various scholars, including those writing predominantly in the Indonesian language, are used to pinpoint the intersections between the Indonesian and more general debates and to highlight how the Indonesian case can help inform more theoretical discussions on civil society and its possible political effects.

The contending perspectives

The concept of civil society was first used in Indonesian scholarly and political debates not long after it began to feature heavily in a new international literature on development and democracy at around the end of the Cold War. Thus, White had observed more than two decades ago that:

> Together with the market and democracy, "civil society" is one of the "magic trio" of developmental panaceas which emerged in the 1980s and now dominate conventional prescriptions for the ills of the 1990s. As the third element of a comprehensive reaction against the developmental states of the 1960s and 1970s, civil society is a sociological counterpart of the market in the economic sphere and to democracy in the political sphere.
>
> *(White 1994: 375)*

It is therefore not a coincidence that "civil society" gained prominence in Indonesia when it did. An impetus was, of course, such developments as the fall of the Iron Curtain in Eastern Europe; another was the internal political conflict that characterized the New Order regime of Soeharto, which, in hindsight, was then already moving into the last decade of its more than thirty-year period of rule. Of course, there was some expectation that the development of an educated urban middle class, in particular, as a product of economic modernization, would produce civil society movements that could raise consciousness of issues related to social and political rights. However, as Richard Robison (1996) pointed out, much of that Indonesian middle class was politically conservative, developing a stake in the social stability ensured by the authoritarian state and fearing the threat to their property and social position that lower-class movements might instigate.

Broadly speaking, nevertheless, the concept civil society was harnessed to political projects that fostered political opposition to Soeharto's New Order regime by encouraging independent grass-roots organization. Especially amongst non-governmental organizations (NGOs) and a small number of dissident intellectuals, it enabled criticism of both its rigid authoritarianism and corruption-ridden developmental path. Conversely, however, others attempted to latch on to the civil society debate as part of an effort to contain or even domesticate such opposition. They did so by highlighting the capacity of reform within the regime to allow for greater public participation, while also emphasizing communitarian-like interpretations of civil society that negated the need for the overthrow of New Order authoritarianism.

Muhammad A. S. Hikam (1996) was one of the most well-known Indonesian scholars of Indonesian politics to focus on the concept of civil society during this period. His work was, by his own characterization, highly eclectic theoretically and contained elements of both Tocquevillian and Gramscian tendencies in thinking about civil society—the former emphasizes the innately positive effects of autonomous and voluntary associations, while the latter underscores the need to counterbalance what he saw as the hegemony of the state. However, other influences were also evident in his work, ranging from Habermasian sociology to broadly communitarian ideas. In this regard, his work was quite representative of the thinking of the Indonesian liberal intelligentsia in the late New Order period—which sought various sources of intellectual validation for their pursuit of gradual political liberalization, if not democratization, and yet confronted many entrenched barriers posed by an authoritarian regime that at the time seemed quite impregnable.

It is worth quoting Hikam at some length at this juncture:

> The understanding of *civil society* that I use in this book is eclectic, although its main reference is the understanding used by de Tocqueville. *Civil society* can be defined as *the spheres of social life that are organized and characterized, among others, by voluntarism, self-generation, and self-support, as well as a high level of autonomy in relation to the state and bonds with norms and legal values to which its citizenry complies.* As political space, *civil society* is a sphere that guarantees autonomous behavior, action, and reflection that is not constrained by the conditions of material life and not absorbed by the formal network of political institutions. Implied is the existence of a *free public sphere*, where the citizenry can undertake free communicative transactions.
>
> *(Hikam 1996: 3, translation by the author, emphasis in the original)*

He then continues with the following observation in relation to Indonesia, especially the role of intellectuals in its civil society:

> What about the intellectuals that Gramsci had hoped would become the vanguard of *civil society* development? In my opinion, the development of intellectual life in Indonesia is troubling when we see the paucity of alternative ideas that emanate from it. The current *trend* seems to be for intellectuals to feel secure when they are close to centers of power. They make the excuse that transformation can take place more effectively when they are inside them. This is a tragedy for the tradition of free intellectuals that existed in the generation of the independence movement or among religious leaders in the past.
>
> *(Hikam 1996: 7)*

Hence, although Hikam was optimistic about the democratizing potential of civil society as a matter of principle, he appeared less consistently sanguine about the Indonesian case that he encountered while conducting his study. This is not surprising because Indonesian civil society was severely disorganized under New Order rule, which was predicated in large part upon the systematic and pervasive demobilization of grass-roots political activity.

In fact, the legacy of this systemic disorganization has been difficult to shake off (Robison and Hadiz 2004), in spite of the unraveling of the New Order nearly two decades ago. For this reason, Indonesia's labor movement, for example, although at times boisterous, has had little influence from the beginning of the democratic era in forging alliances within civil society based on a project of extending rights (Hadiz 2001a) that would empower the working class, in spite of advances on wage-related issues. Indonesia's intellectuals—specifically those inclined toward liberal reform—continue to have very little in terms of a social base and remain largely confined to newspaper opinion pages and occasional appearances on television. Most of them who are politically engaged continue to gravitate toward the state bureaucracy and technocracy, and many have taken up positions within elite predatory alliances, including at the local level of politics, providing intellectual legitimation—and much more in some cases—for several unsavory political practices (Kusman 2015). Not surprisingly, it has been suggested that the legacy of the New Order also accounts for the fact that Indonesian civil society contains within itself an assortment of social interests that contradict the values of democratic pluralism and that may be both illiberal and prone to the use of violence (Hadiz 2001b), given that these were nurtured under the New Order's authoritarian rule. Ian Wilson's (2015) study of organizations that trade on intimidation and violence seems to suggest that these observations continue to be applicable (also see Ryter 2005). How is such a situation in Indonesia to be explained within the theoretical debates on civil society more generally?

As is well known, the theoretical approaches to civil society are varied. They could be categorized as "liberal pluralist," "communitarian," "Marxist," and "Habermasian" in their respective orientations. The liberal pluralist position, which is perhaps the most influential in the literature, owes much to the Tocquevillian tradition, which considers civility as emanating from the pervasiveness of activity based on autonomous and voluntary association. In many ways, the literature on "social capital" as purveyed by Robert Putnam (1993) follows on from this tradition, especially in its insistence that associational and other collectively undertaken activities are the key facets of functioning democratic societies. For Putnam, "features of social organizations, such as trust, norms, and networks" constitute "a community's stock of social capital" (1993: 175) and, thus, an abundance of the latter produces a sort of "civic context" that, in turn, enables better government (1993: 182). As is the case for the liberal tradition of thinking on civil society more generally, the main idea put forward is that dense networks of civic associations ensure that democratic institutions work more effectively.

A second approach, though internally diverse, can be called "communitarian." It has an assortment of intellectual forbearers and can be traced to traditions that vary from European organic-statism and Durkheimian sociology, all the way to, amongst others, Jewish and Muslim philosophy and Christian idealist and corporatist thinking and, finally, a reconstituted Confucianism in Asia. However, its common emphasis is on the organic links between state and society that cultivate values that would prevent social disintegration and could strengthen social solidarity instead. One of its major proponents is Amitai Etzioni, who suggests that:

> *free individuals require a community*, which backs them up against encroachment by the state and sustains morality by drawing on the gentle prodding of kin, friends, neighbors, and other community members, rather than building on government controls or fear of authorities.
>
> *(Etzioni 1993: 15, emphasis in the original)*

Different kinds of communitarians will seek out this morality from dissimilar cultural sources. For some of the proponents of "Asian Values" in parts of Northeast and Southeast Asia, for example, they are to be found specifically in Confucian values (albeit inevitably reinterpreted for the world of modern capitalism) (Fox 1997). In Indonesia, the state ideology of Pancasila has served as one purported source, replete with its pre-colonial feudal influences, while for others one must look at the religion of Islam for the necessary cultural underpinnings.

A third approach, the "Marxian" one, is best represented by, though not confined to, the work of the twentieth-century theorist and activist Antonio Gramsci and his followers to the present day. These have tended to look at civil society as an arena of hegemonic and counter-hegemonic competition linked to compliance of a capitalist social order and resistance to it. Gramsci himself identified two "superstructural 'levels' in his analysis. The first of these he called 'civil society,' which for him was 'the ensemble of organisms commonly called 'private' '" (1971: 12). The second level he called "political society" or "the state." According to Gramsci, these "two levels correspond on the one hand to the functions of 'hegemony' which the dominant group exercises throughout society and on the other hand to that of 'direct domination' or command exercised through the state and 'juridical' government" (1971: 12). As mentioned earlier, for Gramsci, intellectuals played a major part in the exercise of hegemony, and in the case of organic intellectuals tied to the proletarian movement, in launching counter-hegemonic projects. For some Southeast Asianists working on civil society issues, Gramsci's works have been a launch pad for their critiques of Tocquevillian views that tend to reify it as a coherent and unified entity (Hedman 2005; Thompson 2011). In the same vein, Gramscian understandings of hegemony could be utilized in critiques of communitarian views about the common sources of moral values in societies.

Yet another approach may be associated with the wide-ranging project associated with Jürgen Habermas (1989). Though Habermas' intellectual roots were in the Marxian critical sociology of the Frankfurt School, his conception of civil society was to be decidedly influenced by a political liberalism that privileged a "public sphere" where rational communication by individuals on common affairs purportedly took place. For Habermas, this was a characteristic especially of European coffee shops and salons where people could discuss ideas free of the distorting effect of "public opinion" created by the mass media. In this regard, the opinion of Craig Calhoun provides an important cautionary note to the adoption of Habermasian perspectives in analyses of civil society in experiences like those of Indonesia:

> Habermas idealized eighteenth-century English parliamentarianism, newspapers, and coffee house conversation. He presented the public sphere as a realm of civil society in which private citizens could communicate openly about matters of public concern, transcending their particular statuses and addressing the state without becoming part of it.
>
> *(Calhoun 2011: 219–220)*

Given the above discussion, it is important to be cognizant of the different ways in which civil society has been conceived when discussing it in the Indonesian context. The danger is to use the same terms in debate with others but to somehow have the different meanings attached to them obscured by the readiness to assume a common vocabulary of civil society. In spite of this danger, White has usefully identified in his essay where the usages of civil society have tended to converge, even while accounting for varied intellectual genealogies and, therefore, analytical points of emphases. He suggested that there was consensus that civil society could be conceived of as:

> an intermediate associational realm between state and family populated by organisations which are separate from the state, enjoy autonomy in relation to the state and are formed voluntarily by members of society to protect or extend their interests or values.
>
> *(White 1994: 379)*

It appears that this kind of core definition could still be utilized in spite of some problems that might be associated especially with versions of the communitarian view that see moral values linking state and society more or less organically. However, if we were to accept that civil society groups serve to extend the interests and values of their members, then it appears that— even if they are not formally political vehicles—their activities would have political *effects*. From such a point of view, conceiving complete autonomy from the state might also present issues in empirical analysis, given that activities that have major political effects would tend to intersect, in some shape of form, with those of the state.

At this point, it may be useful to introduce the contribution to the literature on Asian politics and development by the so-called "Murdoch School," to which this present chapter traces its own intellectual roots, as it pertains to debates about civil society.[2] Authors like Garry Rodan and Kevin Hewison (1996) had recognized the growing prominence of civil society as a concept in the literature on Asian politics from the 1990s. Their intervention especially infused the concerns of Marxian political economy and political sociology by addressing civil society as an arena of competition between different sets of social interests that are not equally endowed in terms of power and resources (Rodan 1996: 4). At its core, their contribution extended a critique of cultural essentialist treatments of Asian politics, which had led to once fashionable arguments about the so-called Asian Values (Mahbubani 1993). Within such arguments, a culturally but implausibly homogenized "Asia" was often portrayed as being inherently inclined toward the values associated with strong leadership and consensus, rather than toward democratic processes entailing a measure of conflict in decision-making and governance more generally. For the advocates of the Murdoch School, such a tendency has always been less about cultural immutability than about historically configured and entrenched systems of power that have impeded the growth of liberal and social democratic political tendencies.

Moreover, they recognized that even if the space for civil society has expanded together with Asian social transformations, it might have done so especially because of the successful struggles of anti-democratic groups within it (Rodan 1996: 5). As a logical consequence, a related position—as amongst others expounded by Alagappa (2004)—that there is no necessary link between civil society and the advance of democratization can be readily accepted, as well. In fact, the reverse may be true (Alagappa 2004: xi) in some contexts—in that the growth of certain civil society groups may have anti-democratic political effects, which was also Rodan's position.

For Rodan and Hewison (1996), therefore, as in the present chapter, what is important is the specific constellation of social interests and power that reside within civil society and, inevitably, its relationships with the state. The relative weakness of political liberalism—and of more radical politics—in many Asian countries may be traced, from this sort of analytical framework, to several factors. These are the legacies of post-colonial state formation, the outcomes of social conflict during the Cold War (which saw the destruction of the Left in much of Asia), and to the sort of political disciplining related to the onslaughts of neoliberal globalization that marginalized liberal/social democratic and more radical critiques. It is these social and historical developments that are the causes of the relative weakness of liberal-pluralist and other reformist streams in Asian civil society, rather than an ingrained cultural propensity to contain or resist them.

In other words, the political effects of civil society and its development are not predetermined. What these may be in specific cases requires empirical investigation that takes into account issues of historical legacies, social structures, how social alliances express particular kinds of constellations of power and interest, and the modes of competition over power and tangible resources.

Indonesian debates

The Indonesian literature on civil society has intersected in various ways with the broader debates on civil society, as already alluded to in the prior mention of the work by Hikam. The views of Indonesian scholars like him have been shaped both by immersion in the broader debates on the nature and role of civil society and historically specific Indonesian experiences. In particular, civil society was relevant to questions about how and where a democratic movement or tendency could emerge in Indonesia in the authoritarian era and, more recently, to those about the continuing weakness of liberal reformist impulses in spite of nearly two decades of democracy.

Verena Beittinger-Lee (2005: 98–100) has gone over the different ways in which it is possible to categorize Indonesian scholarship on civil society, though she opts to divide it into just two camps. The first camp she identifies, and associates with Hikam and others, stresses the universality and Indonesian applicability of the concept of civil society, though its members have never agreed upon the exact translation of the term (favorites include *masyarakat sipil*— which is closer to "civilian society"—and *masyarakat warga* and *masyarakat kewargaan*—which are closer in literal meaning to "society of citizens"). The second camp, according to Beittinger-Lee, seeks to establish a specifically Islamic bent on the concept. Favoring the term *masyarakat madani*—which has Islamic overtones—they connect the idea of civil society with the ostensibly egalitarian morality of seventh-century Muslims. In many ways, their view—though full of internal contradictions due to a principled rejection of class-based politics—served as a counterpoint to those who see civil society development as necessarily accompanying the rise of a Western-style market economy and all its cultural trappings.

No matter how one chooses to categorize the Indonesian scholarship, it is clear that from the late 1980s and throughout the 1990s—and on to the present democratic period—the concept of civil society has been a mainstay in the lexicon of liberal reformers, who may not be numerous or politically powerful but remain well represented in the media and in public discussions. This is seen in the employment by NGOs—typically run by urban and educated middle-class reformists—of the concept of civil society in various position papers and in their propaganda material throughout this period (e.g., CESDA 1996). It should be noted, however, that international development organizations were also quick to jump onto the civil society bandwagon. Thus, a World Bank (2000) report depicting the institution's own civil society "turn" extolled the virtues of a well-developed civil society in not only ensuring public participation but also in inculcating the values necessary for the functioning of the market amongst the citizenry. According to this World Bank report, civil society is a "dynamic web" that consists of "not-for-profit organizations and special interest groups, either formal or informal, working to improve the lives of their constituents" (World Bank 2000). Yet, there is little recognition by the World Bank that civil society may include mutually antagonistic social interests and some of them are much more powerful than others.

In some ways, the interest of international development organizations in the concept of civil society—and, therefore, civil society capacity building—contributed to its political domestication, and not just in Indonesia. As in other developing countries, the democratizing vision of Indonesian NGOs, no matter how always incoherently presented, had to somehow meet with the more technocratic visions of their international donors, who were influenced by the shifting ideas in the international development community, as initiated by the World Bank. The ultimate result was arguably the partial absorption of the struggles of these NGOs into the technocratic blueprint of reform. In the end, this brought the NGOs to support the agendas of "good governance" as they became developmental orthodoxy—paradoxically—while often maintaining a rhetoric that was critical of neoliberal globalization and its anti-egalitarian consequences.

However, besides the aforementioned Hikam, another scholar of Indonesian civil society was the late Mansour Fakih, who should be quoted at some length also. According to Fakih, who was a well-respected NGO activist, "the main battle is political and ideological, namely against the modernization/developmentalism hegemony." For him, this kind of hegemony could be "defined as an organizing principle or world view, diffused by agencies and institutions, which exerts ideological control ... into every area of daily life" (1991: 11). Citing Gramsci specifically, Fakih pushed forward the idea that the core mission of NGOs in Indonesia was to act "as a counter-hegemonic institution" that must "strengthen civil society by facilitating 'critical consciousness'" (Fakih 1991: 11).

Indeed, Gramscian thinking had made inroads into sections of the Indonesian NGO movement by the 1980s and 1990s, partly because it offered a "back way" to reference Marxian analysis—under conditions where the conveyance of its ideas remained heavily restricted. Not only was communism outlawed following the anti-communist massacres in Indonesia in the 1960s, but the teaching of "Marxism-Leninism" was also banned—as it continues to be today—under a decree by the Indonesian supra-parliament, the People's Consultative Council, or MPR. However, Fakih probably did not realize yet that the very concept of civil society was in the process of being at least partially appropriated, and therefore domesticated, by the likes of the World Bank, as it became integrated to neoliberal reform agendas (Hadiz 2010). Such appropriation would effectively leave little room for Gramscian challenges.

However, another means through which the idea of civil society was domesticated in Indonesia has been through the insertion of it into the debates of certain political idioms and symbols associated with the Islamic religion. That this took place has been alluded to earlier in this chapter, and this accounts for the second "camp" identified by Beittinger-Lee (2009). The adherents of this more communitarian view of civil society had in common with the Tocquevillians, in spite of their differing cultural orientations, the inclination to gloss over the diversity and mutually antagonistic nature of social interests within civil society in favor of a conception of internal harmony—in this case, especially amongst the *ummah* or "community of believers." Indeed, the favored translation of civil society for them, *masyarakat madani*, denoted the form of societal organization that was developed by none other than the Prophet Mohammad in the town of Medina during his self-exile from Mecca.

It was no coincidence that this religious turn in the civil society debates in Indonesia took place in the context of specific kinds of developments within the New Order regime. Due to intra-regime conflict (particularly between the president and the military; Honna 2003: 11), a new association was constructed in the 1990s called ICMI (Association of Indonesian Islamic Intellectuals), with the support of Soeharto and his protégé and future successor, the technocrat-engineer B. J. Habibie (Hefner 2000). Geared to enlist the support of the increasingly religiously conscious, self-confident, and upwardly mobile urban middle class, ICMI became a vehicle that clearly espoused a position of gradual reform from within the regime and staved off calls for radical change from outside.

The by-product of this sort of development was the kind of writing on civil society produced by Mahasin (1996), yet another noted middle-class NGO activist and mild critic of the New Order. Mahasin mused about the historical *ummah* that was led by the Prophet Mohammad himself as a kind of "civil society" that had existed prior to the experiences that produced the entity in Europe that is usually associated with the label. What this sort of conception allowed for was a way of thinking about modernity and "civility" rooted in social mores that were imagined to be distinctly Islamic, independent of the experiences of the Enlightenment and the struggles over capitalist transitions in the West.

However, this sort of thinking suffered from a romanticization of the *ummah* that was an interesting mirror image of liberal views that idealized civil society as it appeared in the West— whether in the form of Habermas' European coffee shops or Putnam's yearning for a time in American history when the stock of social capital would be maintained by team bowling. In reality, the social differentiation brought about by economic modernization under the New Order meant that the *ummah* increasingly encompassed the sections of the society that had unequal levels of access to power and resources. Nevertheless, it was somewhat easy for Muslim middle-class intellectuals of the time to take a view that ignored this with the advent of ICMI, which seemed to be opening up such access to them like never before, at least until the demise of the New Order. It is revealing, for instance, that no real effort was ever exerted by the proponents of ICMI to organize the urban and rural poor, of which Indonesia had an abundance, most of whom would be at least nominally Muslim.

Uncivility and democratic politics

It has been pointed out that, whether belonging to Beittinger-Lee's first or second camps, Indonesian thinkers on civil society have tended to commit the common error of conceiving it as an internally homogenous entity. Even the Gramscian critique of Fakih did not give much thought to how, if NGOs were to take up the counter-hegemonic role he had assigned to them, they would be engaged in inevitable conflict with the sections of civil society that did not share the values he believed they should extol. He also did not problematize the social bases of such a counter-hegemonic project and the consequences of the almost total absence of effective leftist and other radical organized political forces to get behind it.[3]

In actuality, the Indonesian experience casts doubt not only on views about relative homogeneity within civil society, but also on the veracity of the almost quintessentially liberal idea that civil society development would necessarily move in a direction that was liberalizing and pluralizing. Thus, the aspect of civil society as an arena within which social conflict takes place is useful to underscore in analyzing the Indonesian case, while also recognizing that such conflict takes place in an environment of power imbalances. Within this environment, "uncivil" voluntary associations that pursue their interests and objectives through the use of tactics including violence and intimidation have been produced. Many have taken part, at least indirectly, in predatory alliances that have come to colonize Indonesia's democratic institutions (Hadiz 2010; Robison and Hadiz 2004), dominated by social interests that had been previously nurtured under authoritarianism and that count the use of violent tactics amongst their political armory. What is perhaps of special concern is that such tactics have continuously been honed under conditions of what is widely regarded as having been a successful democratization process over the previous two decades.

From a comparative perspective, though, the Indonesian experience is not especially startling. Sheri Berman's (1997) work on civil society in Germany during the Weimar Republic in the 1920s until the rise to power of Nazism convincingly shows that civil society can give birth to violent, anti-democratic groups. In a slightly later work, she suggested that civil society in parts of the Arab world was actually not sustaining political liberalism but incubating a form of "illiberal radicalism," pointing to the activities of Islamic charity organizations and so on (Berman 2003: 258). As mentioned earlier, the rise of Hindutva in India championed by politically exclusionary organizations like the National Patriotic Organization (RSS), which is a paramilitary entity linked closely to the Bharatiya Janata Party (BJP) and historically influenced by European fascism (Teltumbde 2006), provides another example. The work of Sarbeswar Sahoo (2013) even shows how the ideology of Hindutva has affected the objectives of some sections of the

NGO community that ostensibly work to improve the welfare of tribal groups who lie outside the traditional Hindu caste system. One NGO he studied in Rajasthan stated that one of its aims was to convince the tribal peoples that they and the Hindus "both belong to the same blood" and that another aim was to "stop religious conversion" (Sahoo 2013: 145), the latter denoting the RSS' and BJP's extreme hostility toward India's Muslim population.

In Indonesia, some of the associations that are inclined toward violence, intimidation, and social exclusion can be dated to around the beginning of the democratic era, while others go back to before the advent of the New Order, like the Pemuda Pancasila (PP). The highly scrutinized newer organizations today, such as the Islamic Defenders Front (FPI) (Wilson 2015; Woodward *et al.* 2014) and Forum Betawi Rempug (FBR; Betawi Brotherhood Forum) (Wilson 2015), have become well known for their role in a number of violent incidents. They have been noted especially for their actions against religious and other vulnerable minorities, all undertaken on the pretext of upholding their version of Islamic morality and thereby securing a niche for them in contests over power and resources. Both espouse an Islamic identity and make claims of speaking for an *ummah* that, in its self-narrative, has been historically marginalized since the colonial times. This is so even if the FBR also claims to "speak for" the "Betawi" population of Jakarta, a predominantly Muslim ethnic group within the capital that asserts "native" status, although it had actually emerged from a mix of various ethnic communities since the city was established as Batavia by Dutch colonialists in the seventeenth century (Noor 2012). Less scrutinized, but no less "uncivil," are organizations like the Laskar Bali (Bachelard 2014), a paramilitary organization on the predominantly Hindu island of Bali that has deployed the Hindu/Balinese identity to validate its participation in matters such as violent land grabs and in local politics (Nordholt 2007).

The FPI, which has branches in many Indonesian cities, was formed in the direct aftermath of the fall of the New Order in 1998. Led by a religious scholar and activist of Middle Eastern descent known as Habieb Rizieq, it has been at the forefront of ideological calls for the establishment of an Islamic state. This does not mean, however, that the FPI has not been entangled in elite alliances at the national and local levels that are ensconced in the institutions of the present state, having enjoyed close ties with sections of the Indonesian military and police forces (Bush 2015: 247). Most recently, it has played a leading role in instigating the mass rejection of the election bid of Jakarta's governor Basuki Tjahaja Purnama, more popularly known as "Ahok." A member of the traditionally politically vulnerable ethnic Chinese and Christian minorities, Ahok was accused of having committed blasphemy by way of making some purportedly disrespectful comments on Islamic teachings (Wijaya 2016). The FPI's prior "career highlights" include a violent attack on an assembly of religious freedom activists in Jakarta in 2008 and the killing of several members of the minority Ahmadiyyah sect across various parts of the provinces of West Java and Banten in several attacks in 2011 (Pasandaran 2013).

FBR, for its own part, has unswervingly deployed a critique of the state that it depicts as having socially and economically marginalized Betawi Muslims in their own city. Over a large part of the democratic period, it has transformed itself from a loose amalgamation of street gangs into a well-directed organization that links such gangs to a larger support base amongst the urban poor, while simultaneously developing strategic ties to political and economic elites (Wilson 2015: 91). At a basic level, these downward and upward alliances appear to be aimed at continually enlarging the FBR's share of Jakarta's vast and lucrative protection rackets.

In spite of their involvement in violent and, often criminal, activity, these "Islamic" and highly sectarian organizations commonly proclaim having the role of inculcating religious morality in the society (Beittinger-Lee 2009: 190). They point especially to the mostly underprivileged youths that they recruit, who might otherwise have ended up in a quagmire of various vices—including those involving the drugs and alcohol prohibited by Islamic morality. With regard to upholding such morality, the FPI, in particular, has been known for its so-called "sweeping" exercises, which are ostensibly aimed at closing down dens of immoral activity. These have regularly included nightclubs, karaoke bars, and massage parlors (Wilson 2005)—though such actions may be linked to turf wars with other organizations providing protection to such establishments.

Of course, it is possible to view the role played by such organizations as representing the mere "excesses" in Indonesia's democratization process, where uncontrollable developments perhaps inevitably take place. However, this view would be both simplistic and misleading as the origins of the newer "vigilante" organizations primarily lie at the tail end of the New Order rule, or at least the period when regimists were still struggling to cope with an unprecedented wave of demands for reform in 1998–1999—in the context of deep economic crisis. It is arguable that they were the products of attempts to develop a narrative that depicted the regime's pillars as accommodating the interests of Islam—in spite of a history of suppression of Islamic politics in the 1970s and 1980s (Solahuddin 2011) and a range of their opponents being foreign lackeys. Thus, an organization called Pam-Swakarsa was unleashed during this period, partly manned by thugs in Islamic garb, mainly to fight off anti-regime demonstrators while trying to save the beleaguered short presidency of B. J. Habibie (Wilson 2014: 253). Some of those involved in the Pam-Swakarsa initiative would later on become active in paramilitary groups that espouse an Islamic identity.

While many of these developments were focused in Jakarta, they took place in some provincial cities as well, where outbreaks of unrest had also occurred at the end of the Soeharto period and the very beginning of the new period of democracy that began after Soeharto's resignation from the presidency in May 1998. In the Central Java city of Solo, for example, where the current Indonesian president, Joko Widodo, began his business and political career, fixers like Mudrick Sangidoe played a central role in the birth of paramilitaries espousing an Islamic political identity (Sidel 2007: 64–66), although they were initially in alliance with more secular forces. Not long afterward, such Islamic paramilitaries became involved in turf wars with rival "secular-nationalist" paramilitary organizations (Hadiz 2016: 112)—with which they also compete for the loyalty of masses of the urban poor who join for the uniforms and the jobs, formal and informal, that are allocated to the members. Most such jobs have to do with the provision of private security. It is significant that for many of the growing lumpenproletariat of Indonesia's cities, these paramilitaries provide sources of income, as well as valuable support networks, in a country where the social welfare system is highly undeveloped.

Today, a range of "Islamic" paramilitaries exist in Indonesia alongside the FPI and FBR, which, though operating outside of the official institutions of politics, play a distinct role in contests over power and resources, including at the local level (Mudhoffir forthcoming) and as more or less professional organizers of mass demonstrations. Nevertheless, there is a long tradition of paramilitary organizations in Indonesia that focus on recruiting lower-class youths. On the one hand, they could be historically linked to the tradition of the *lasykar* or *laskar*, which were informal fighting forces that struggled on the side of the fledging Republic of Indonesia against the Dutch colonial power in the independence war of 1945–1949 (Cribb 1991). Because of this history, today's paramilitary organizations seek to take advantage of the lingering romantic ideas about the role of youths in the nation's early history, even if such organizations have no direct ties to those early "independence heroes."

On the other hand, a better comparison would be with the "youth organizations" that ran criminal enterprises conspiring with the police and military during the New Order. The most notorious amongst these was the PP (Ryter 1998), which in spite of losing some of its luster—due to the rise of competitors—remains well established with long-standing national and local chapters. During its heyday in the New Order authoritarian period, the PP practically served as the private bodyguards of the New Order oligarchy due to the existence of personal links between leading members and the top politico-bureaucratic and business families (Lintner 2002: 284; Wilson 2015: 52–53). Equally importantly, the PP continues to wield power over a range of criminal enterprises, including gambling, prostitution, drug distribution, and protection rackets. It was once and continues to be involved, as well, in outwardly more legitimate activities like debt collection, street parking fee collection, and providing security for factories, markets, shopping malls, discotheques, and movie theaters (See Ryter 2002).

Loren Ryter's PhD thesis (2002), which has unfortunately never been rewritten for publication, knowledgeably traced the genesis of the PP in anti-communist youth groups that began to form in North Sumatra before the advent of the New Order. As shown in the recent Academy Award-nominated film *The Act of Killing* (2012), one of the grudges that these youths held against the Indonesian Communist Party (PKI) originated in the latter's support of policies for curbing the showing of Hollywood films, in the context of the Cold War, in local cinemas. Encouraged by the military, which was already long embroiled in conflict with the PKI, local street youths established the PP for the highly un-ideological reason that the curb on imported Hollywood films was bad for their livelihood as ticket scalpers.

From such origins, the PP grew to become a national organization, with its headquarters in Jakarta, which staked a claim as an organization that represented the interests of Indonesia's youths, especially the less economically privileged ones. It also claimed to inculcate nationalist morality and loyalty to the state amongst such youths. It did not have a monopoly on these claims, however, as numerous "youth/gangster" organizations also emerged at the time, including the once greatly feared Ikatan Pemuda Karya (IPK). In North Sumatra, the birthplace of the PP, the IPK was in fact the most powerful of such organizations for many decades (Hadiz 2006: 234), including the first decade or so of the democratic period, until the death of its patriarch and founder, Olo Panggabean, in 2009.

Today, the PP's branches continue to be a prominent feature in the underworld of large cities like the national capital city of Jakarta; Surabaya, the capital of East Java province; and Medan, Surabaya's counterpart in North Sumatra. At the same time, some of its leading members have become so "legit" that they have taken up such positions as members of local parliaments or district heads (Hadiz 2010: 116–117). In fact, organizations like the PP have also been involved in the democratic era in local conflicts over power and resources, becoming part of social alliances competing over the spoils of power and also being prominent in the settling of labor and land disputes, usually in favor of the powerful (Beittinger-Lee 2009: 165; Hadiz 2001b: 128). Interestingly, the PP and IPK, as well as their rivals amongst a range of other youth/gangster organizations, including "Islamic" ones, have universally claimed that they deliver an important service to society (Bakker 2016) by providing employment, training in various skills (including the martial arts), and a sense of belonging to a community for otherwise disenfranchised youths.

However, the impact of these organizations is not confined to the outcomes of the specific cases of conflict in which they become involved. It may be said that the sort of values and ideas that they uphold to validate their role in Indonesian politics and society—that is, to purportedly safeguard its morality, and especially that of its youth—is affecting the trajectory of Indonesian democracy itself. With the capacity to mobilize support especially amongst the urban poor, take direct action against targets, and exercise violence and intimidation, these organizations are valuable allies to predatory elites that dominate Indonesia's democratic institutions in their competition with each other. The main result of their entanglement in these alliances, and the consequent public dissemination of their views on a host of social and political issues, helps to steer Indonesian democracy toward a more distinctly conservative and illiberal direction. It is the kind of democracy where the rights of religious and sexual minorities, other vulnerable groups, and large numbers of women are not protected and upheld, in spite of the ostensible presence of political parties, parliaments, a robust media, regular free elections, and freedom to organize and associate.

Conclusion

The chapter focuses on what might be called "uncivil" tendencies within Indonesian civil society and links their presence to broader theoretical debates on the nature of civil society. The point of the exercise has been to show that unlike especially Tocquevillian viewpoints, certain civil society developments may have political effects that are distinctly in contradiction to the affirmation of democratic, liberal, and pluralist values. In the Indonesian case, we see this in the proliferation of organizations such as paramilitaries, which recruit especially from poor youths and have practiced a kind of politics that has prominently involved violence and intimidation, especially against the more vulnerable elements of the society and often in the service of the powerful. They do this even as they make claims of contributing to the social welfare of these youths and providing them with the sort of social networks that may help them develop a sense of attachment to society.

The Indonesian case also affirms theoretical understandings of civil society that underline the various and typically mutually antagonistic social interests within it. It shows that the political effects of civil society development cannot be predetermined but are largely contingent on the existing balance of social forces, which must be understood according to specific historical and social contexts. It critiques liberal (and also communitarian and, to an extent, Habermasian) understandings of civil society that often gloss over the differences within civil society or highlight only their pluralizing tendencies.

Notes

1 The main difference is that Hindutva has won power in India, while the exponents of socially exclusivist forms of Islam have never come close to winning power in Indonesia. However, we also see similar tendencies in advanced liberal democracies. For example, in Australia, the re-emergence of the extreme right in the form of "Hansonism" is testament to the mainstreaming of the racist exclusionary policies and political values associated with it, especially through their adoption, and therefore validation, by established politicians and media pundits (Wilson 2016). Further—as in the conversion of formerly Democratic strongholds to the bastions of support of Donald Trump in the American presidential elections of 2016—we see across Western Europe the shift of support to right-wing political movements from the sections of society that had been support bases for social democratic political tendencies.

2 A good exemplar of its approach can be found in Rodan, Hewison, and Robison (2001).

3 A partial exception was the student-led leftist organization, the People's Democratic Party (PRD), which was quelled in the late New Order.

Suggested readings

Budiman, Arief, ed. 1990. *State and Civil Society in Indonesia*. Clayton, VIC: Centre of Southeast Asian Studies, Monash University.

Edwards, Michael, ed. 2011. *The Oxford Handbook of Civil Society*. Oxford: Oxford University Press.

Gellner, Ernest. 1996. *Condition of Liberty: Civil Society and Its Rivals*. New York: Penguin Books.

Hadiwinata, Bob. 2003. *The Politics of NGOs in Indonesia: Developing Democracy and Managing a Movement.* New York: Routledge.

Nyman, Mikaela. 2006. *Democratising Indonesia: the Challenges of Civil Society in the Era of Reformasi.* Copenhagen: NIAS.

Websites

Betawi Brotherhood Forum (Tangerang City Regional Coordinator), http://fbr-korwil-tangerang.blogspot.com.au/.

A controversial organization in Indonesia, portrayed through the media to be violent and radical; contrasting depictions explain it to be a means for survival in a region with high unemployment and socioeconomic inequality.

Front Pembela Islam—Islamic Defenders Front, www.fpi.or.id/.

An organization in Indonesia for the promotion of sharia law, associated with many violent acts in the name of Islam.

Ikatan Pemuda Karya—Youth Association Work (CPI), http://ikatanpemudakarya.org/.

A youth-oriented organization based in Indonesia, committed to those who struggle to find work.

Laskar Bali gang, http://pasukanlaskarbali.blogspot.com.au/.

A gang associated with significant violence in Indonesia.

Islam "Mega-Bintang," http://ormasmegabintang.blogspot.com.au/.

Supporters of Indonesian Democratic Party of Struggle (PDI-P) leader Megawati Sukarnoputri, in coalition with the Islamic party PPP (United Development Party), formed a "coalition of the oppressed," which became known as the Mega-Bintang.

Pancasila Youth (Pemuda Pancasila), www.pemuda-pancasila.or.id/.

An Indonesian paramilitary organization, known for playing a significant role in supporting Soeharto's military coup in 1965.

References

Alagappa, Muthiah. 2004. Preface. In *Civil Society and Political Change in Asia: Expanding and Contracting Democratic Space.* Muthiah Alagappa, ed. Pp. ix–xiii. Stanford, CA: Stanford University Press.

Bachelard, Michael. 2014. The Dark Side of the Sun. *The Sydney Morning Herald*, August 9.

Bakker, Laurens. 2016. Militias, Security and Citizenship in Indonesia. In *Social, Economic and Political Studies of the Middle East and Asia.* Dale Eickelman, ed. Pp. 125–154. Leiden: Koninklijke Brill.

Beittinger-Lee, Verena. 2005. Civil Society in Indonesia: Concepts and Realities. In *Democratisation in Indonesia After the Fall of Suharto.* Ingrid Wessel, ed. Pp. 93–103. Berlin: Logos Verlag.

Beittinger-Lee, Verena. 2009. *(Un)Civil Society and Political Change in Indonesia: A Contested Arena.* New York: Routledge.

Berman, Sheri. 1997. Civil Society and the Collapse of the Weimar Republic. *World Politics* 49(3): 401–429.

Berman, Sheri. 2003. Islam, Revolution, and Civil Society. *Perspectives on Politics* 1: 257–272.

Bush, Robin. 2015. Religious Politics and Minority Rights During the Yudhoyono Presidency. In *The Yudhoyono Presidency: Indonesia's Decade of Stability and Stagnation.* Edward Aspinall, Marcus Mietzner, and Dirk Tomsa, eds. Pp. 239–257. Singapore: ISEAS.

Calhoun, Craig. 2011. Civil Society and the Public Sphere. In *the Oxford Handbook of Civil Society.* Michael Edwards, ed. Pp. 311–332. New York: Oxford University Press.

CESDA. 1996. *Indonesian NGO Agenda.* Jakarta: CESDA-LP3ES.

Cribb, Robert. 1991. *Gangsters and Revolutionaries: The Jakarta's People Militia and the Indonesian Revolution 1945–1949.* Sydney: Allen & Unwin.

Etzioni, Amitai. 1993. *The Spirit of Community: Rights Responsibilities, and the Communication Agenda.* New York: Crown Publishers.

Fakih, Mansour. 1991. *NGOs in Indonesia: Issues in Hegemony and Social Change.* Hills South, Amherst: Center for International Education.

Fox, Russell. 1997. Confucian and Communitarian Responses to Liberal Democracy. *The Review of Politics* 59(3): 561–592.

Gramsci, Antonio. 1971. *Selections from the Prison Notebooks.* Quintin Hoare and Geoffrey Nowell Smith, trans. New York: International Publishers.

Habermas, Jürgen. 1989. *Structural Transformation of the Public Sphere*. Thomas Burger and Frederick Lawrence, trans. Cambridge, MA: MIT Press.

Hadiz, Vedi R. 2001a. New Organising Vehicles in Indonesia: Origins and Prospects. In *Organising Labour in Globalising Asia*. Jane Hutchison and Andrew Brown, eds. Pp. 108–126. London: Routledge.

Hadiz, Vedi R. 2001b. Mirroring the Past or Reflecting the Future? Class and Religious Pluralism in Indonesian Labor. In *the Politics of Multiculturalism: Pluralism and Citizenship in Malaysia, Singapore, and Indonesia*. Robert Hefner, ed. Pp. 268–290. Honolulu, HI: University of Hawai'i Press.

Hadiz, Vedi R. 2006. Indonesian Local Party Politics: A Site of Resistance to Neoliberal Reform. In *Neoliberalism and Conflict in Asia after 9/11*. Garry Rodan and Kevin Hewison, eds. Pp. 224–244. Abingdon: Routledge.

Hadiz, Vedi R. 2010. *Localising Power in Post-Authoritarian Indonesia: A Southeast Asia Perspective*. Stanford, CA: Stanford University Press.

Hadiz, Vedi R. 2016. *Islamic Populism in Indonesia and the Middle East*. Cambridge: Cambridge University Press.

Hedman, Eva-Lotta. 2005. Global Civil Society in One Country? Class Formation and Business Activism in the Philippines. In *Southeast Asian Responses to Globalization: Restructuring Governance and Deepening Democracy*. Francis Kok Wah Loh and Öjendal Joakim, eds. Pp. 138–172. Copenhagen: Nordic Institute of Asian Studies.

Hefner, Robert. 2000. *Civil Islam: Muslims and Democratization in Indonesia*. Princeton, NJ: Princeton University Press.

Hikam, Muhammad A. S. 1996. *Demokrasi dan Civil Society* [*Democracy and Civil Society*]. 2nd Edn. Jakarta: LP3ES (in Indonesian).

Honna, Jun. 2003. *Military Politics and Democratization in Indonesia*. London: Routledge.

Kusman, Airlangga Pribadi. 2015. *The Politics of Good Governance in Post-Authoritarian East Java: Intellectuals and Local Power in Indonesia*. PhD thesis, Murdoch University.

Lintner, Bertil. 2002. *Blood Brothers: The Criminal Underworld of Asia*. New York: Palgrave Macmillan.

Mahasin, Aswab. 1996. Empowering Civil Society: the NGO Agenda. In *the Indonesian NGO Agenda*. Rustam Ibrahim, ed. Pp. 1–9. Jakarta: CESDA-LP3ES.

Mahbubani, Kishore. 1993. The Dangers of Decadence: What the Rest Can Teach the West. *Foreign Affairs* 72(4): 10–14.

Mudhoffir, Abdil Mughis. Forthcoming. Islamic Militias and Capitalist Development in Post-Authoritarian Indonesia. *Journal of Contemporary Asia*.

Noor, Farish. 2012. The Forum Betawi Rempug (FBR) of Jakarta: An Ethnic-Cultural Solidarity Movement in a Globalising Indonesia. *RSIS Working Paper* 242: 1–17.

Nordholt, Henk. 2007. *Bali: An Open Fortress, 1995–2005*. Singapore: NUS Press.

Pasandaran, Camelia. 2013. FPI Forces Ahmadiyah Mosque to Close in West Java. *The Jakarta Globe*. Electronic document, www.jakartaglobe.beritasatu.com/featured-2/fpi-forces-ahmadiyah-mosque-to-close-in-west-java/, accessed October 31, 2016.

Putnam, Robert. 1993. *Making Democracy Work: Civic Traditions in Modern Italy*. Princeton, NJ: Princeton University Press.

Rodan, Garry, Kevin Hewison, and Richard Robison, eds. 2001. *The Political Economy of South-East Asia: Conflict, Crises and Change*. Oxford: Oxford University Press.

Robison, Richard. 1996. The Middle Class and the Bourgeoisie in Indonesia. In *the New Rich in Asia*. Richard Robison and David S. G. Goodman, eds. Pp. 79–104. London: Routledge.

Robison, Richard, and Vedi R. Hadiz 2004. *Reorganising Power in Indonesia: The Politics of Oligarchy in an Age of Markets*. New York: RoutledgeCurzon.

Rodan, Garry. 1996. Theorising Political Opposition in East and Southeast Asia. In *Political Oppositions in Industrialising Asia*. Garry Rodan, ed. Pp. 1–37. London: Routledge.

Rodan, Garry, and Kevin Hewison. 1996. The Ebb and Flow of Civil Society and the Decline of the Left in Southeast Asia. In *Political Oppositions in Industrialising Asia*. Garry Rodan, ed. Pp. 40–71. London: Routledge.

Ryter, Loren. 1998. Pemuda Pancasila: The Last Loyalist Free Men of Suharto's Order?. *Indonesia* 66: 44–73.

Ryter, Loren. 2002. *Youth Gangs and the State in Indonesia*. PhD thesis, University of Washington.

Ryter, Loren. 2005. Reformasi Gangsters. *Inside Indonesia* 82: 22–23.

Sahoo, Sarbeswar. 2013. *Civil Society and Democratization in India: Institutions, Ideologies and Interests*. Abingdon: Routledge.

Sidel, John. 2007. *Riot, Pogroms, Jihad: Religious Violence in Indonesia.* Singapore: NUS Press.

Solahuddin. 2011. *NII sampai JI: Salafi Jihadisme di Indonesia* [*NII to JI, Salafy Jihadism in Indonesia*]. Jakarta: Komunitas Bambu (in Indonesian).

Teltumbde, Anand. 2006. The Hindu Fundamentalist Politics in India. In *Empire and Neoliberalism in Asia.* Vedi Hadiz, ed. Pp. 247–261. London: Routledge.

The Act of Killing. 2012. Film. Denmark: Joshua Oppenheimer.

Thompson, Mark. 2011. Moore Meets Gramsci and Burke in Southeast Asia: New Democracies and "Civil" Societies. In *the Crisis of Democratic Governance in Southeast Asia.* Aurel Croissant and Marco Bünte, eds. Pp. 57–74. New York: Palgrave Macmillan.

Topsfield, Jewel, and Karuni Rompies. 2016. A Moral Hazard: Indonesia at Flashpoint over Gay Rights. *Sydney Morning Herald*, February 20. Electronic document, www.theherald.com.au/story/3739828/a-moral-hazard-indonesia-at-flashpoint-over-gay-rights/?cs=12, accessed October 31, 2016.

White, Gordon. 1994. Civil Society, Democratization and Development (I): Clearing the Analytical Ground. *Democratization* 1(2): 375–390.

Wijaya, Callistasia Anggun. 2016. MUI Accuses Ahok of Religious Defamation. *The Jakarta Post*, October 12. Electronic document, www.thejakartapost.com/news/2016/10/12/mui-accuses-ahok-of-religious-defamation.html, accessed October 31, 2016.

Wilson, Ian. 2005. Continuity and Change: The Changing Contours of Organized Violence in Post–New Order Indonesia. *Critical Asian Studies* 38(2): 265–297.

Wilson, Ian. 2014. Morality Racketeering: Vigilantism and Populist Islamic Militancy in Indonesia. In *Between Dissent and Power: The Transformation of Islamic Politics in the Middle East and Asia.* Khoo Boo Teik, Vedi Hadiz, and Yoshihiro Nakanishi, eds. Pp. 248–274. Basingstoke: Palgrave Macmillan.

Wilson, Ian. 2015. *The Politics of Protection Rackets in Post-New Order Indonesia: Coercive Capital, Authority and Street Politics.* London: Routledge.

Wilson, Jason. 2016. "How Conservatives Made Hanson's Ideas Part of the Political Furniture," *Guardian*, October 4. Electronic document, www.theguardian.com/commentisfree/2016/oct/04/how-conservatives-made-hansons-ideas-part-of-the-political-furniture, accessed October 31, 2016.

Woodward, Mark, Mariani Yahya, Inayah Rohmaniyah, Diana Murtaugh Coleman, Chris Lundry, and Ali Amin. 2014. The Islamic Defenders Front: Demonization, Violence and the State in Indonesia. *Contemporary Islam* 8(2): 153–171.

World Bank. 2000. *World Development Report 1999/2000: Entering the 21st Century.* Oxford: Oxford University Press.

12

CAMBODIA

Astrid Norén-Nilsson

The shifting landscape of Cambodian civil society

Cambodian civil society is young and fragile and has been heavily dependent on international aid and reconstruction. These characteristics have largely shaped how civil society is defined and understood domestically, though there are now signs that local characteristics increasingly permeate a growing associational realm. The emergence of civil society can be traced to the post-conflict reconstruction period that followed the 1991 Paris Peace Accords, which put an end to more than two decades of civil war and conflict. The early phase of reconstruction was marked by external interventions (Downie and Kingsbury 2001). International non-governmental organizations (NGOs) were established in the capital, Phnom Penh, followed quickly by a proliferation of domestic NGOs and civil society organizations (CSOs). By the latter half of the 1990s, international NGOs had begun to establish themselves in rural areas, and many Cambodian NGOs/CSOs had emerged. Civil society's discourse surrounding international development was then transmitted to Cambodian NGOs (Öjendal 2014).

By the early 2000s, local community-based organizations (CBOs) were widely established and are now ubiquitous (Kim and Öjendal 2012). Their agendas were typically defined by just a few individuals, often including local officials, and often set up by foreign NGOs or Cambodian CSOs with foreign support. These CBOs can consequently be understood as a hybrid phenomenon, bringing together local, state, and foreign development interests (Öjendal 2014). Recently, local organizations, such as savings groups, have emerged across Cambodia. This suggests that although donors managed to build civil society only to a limited extent by concentrating on a small group of NGOs, their involvement has nonetheless triggered genuine grass-roots civil society action (Ou and Kim 2013).

Over the 2000s, a drying up of international aid (Ou and Kim 2014) combined with new and restrictive policies resulted in a decline in the activity levels of NGOs. Joakim Öjendal (2014) notes that there has been a huge expansion in the NGO sector since the early 1990s, but makes the assessment that Cambodia lags far behind other developmental contexts such as those of India or the Philippines. Confirmed official figures for the number of NGOs are not available. In 2012, about 3,000 NGOs were estimated to be registered with the Ministry of Interior, and 350–400 of these were thought to be operational (Dosch 2012). The World Bank estimates that there are more than 8,000 CBOs, close to 2000 NGOs, around 400 labor unions, and a great number of "other" organizations including village-based "traditional associations" in Cambodia (Öjendal 2014). Trade unions are civil society-like groups. Most organized workers are employed in the garments sector, which has the highest union density in any industry in any country in Asia (Nuon and Serrano 2010). In 2010, it was estimated that about 60 percent of the approximately 294,470 garment workers were unionized (ILO 2010).

This chapter, rather than attempting to comprehensively cover the many areas of activity within this changeful civil society sphere, sets out to survey trends in the conceptualization of Cambodian civil society by focusing on a few determinants shaping how civil society is defined, understood, practiced, and argued in the Cambodian context. I will proceed as follows: The first section outlines the various concerns involved in defining Cambodian civil society. Next, contending models of the relationship between Cambodian civil society and the state will be discussed. Thereafter, I will turn to the role of the international donor community in shaping Cambodian civil society. Finally, different perspectives on the re-emergence of historical civil society—whether so named or not—are assessed. In the conclusion, it will be argued that a research agenda in the future would do well to focus on the various forms of current grass-roots social movements that have proliferated in Cambodia, but remain outside the scope of much research on civil society.

Defining Cambodian civil society

Recent scholarship has explored how civil society has been conceptualized in Cambodia, rather than departing from the endogenous development of civil society theory. Gabi Waibel, Judith Ehlert, and Hart Feuer (2014) brought together an interdisciplinary group of researchers who explored "the ways in which the concept of civil society was applied in their primarily empirical work" (Feuer, Trong, and Ehlert 2014: 253). They concluded that civil society is typically employed as a lens for studying associational activity in a given domain. It was also found that the civil society lens was employed because of personal choices related to the orientation of the researcher, rather than arising from the subject matter itself.

The context of international aid and reconstruction with pertaining definitions of civil society has set the tone for popular Cambodian conceptions of civil society. Öjendal (2014) found development and advocacy activities emanating from the international aid and reconstruction agenda to be hegemonic in discussions of civil society. Consequently, those conducting research on Cambodia using a civil society framework tend to focus on formal organizations, human rights groups, and other typical forms of civil society such as unions. Development aid is understood to have brought more Western conceptions of civil society to Cambodia, as compared to neighboring countries like Vietnam. Associations and organizations are popularly understood to make up civil society (Ou and Kim 2014). Andrew Wells-Dangs (2014) finds that this focus on NGOs makes Cambodian civil society appear more dynamic than it is, and argues instead for a perspective focusing on networks of NGOs, individual activists, and local communities, which "offers a locally relevant path through the definitional pitfalls of civil society." According to Wells-Dangs (2014: 62), popular discourses on civil society carry connotations of grass-roots resistance.

There is an ongoing debate on how scholars should operationalize the concept of civil society. Waibel (2014) argues that Cambodian social actors themselves should define which state—society relationships and activities are important and that researchers should look at processes that embody and promote civil society's interests when investigating civil society. According to Waibel, outside researchers have imposed normative categories, predetermining which groups or organizations are to be included or excluded from civil society, and this has left out many areas of civil society action.

Waibel *et al.* (2014) take their cues from the emphasis on the necessity of conducting anthropological research to grasp local meanings, which has been a prominent trend in earlier and contemporary scholarship on civil society in Southeast Asia, following scholars such as Chris Hann and Elizabeth Dunn (1996). Consequently, Waibel *et al.* seek to expand the Eurocentric conceptual and empirical understandings of civil society by situating its functions within certain contexts. Their volume examines the contestation of the terminology and meaning of civil society by assessing contemporary discourses on and manifestations of civil society in Cambodia and Vietnam.

Öjendal (2014) understands today's Cambodian civil society to be a product of particular dilemmas that emerged in the post-conflict reconstruction phase. He notes that civil society is an uneasy concept when situated within a culture and history marked by an autonomous elite that is distanced from the populace by steep hierarchies, and by an absence of formation of associations beyond those of kinship. Öjendal argues that two different paradigms—the historically and culturally defined perceptions of civil society, poised against a normatively laden and imported modern/liberal conception thereof—have produced contradictions in emerging civil society through a series of evolutionary phases.

Sivhuoch Ou and Sedara Kim (2014) point to how the standard term for civil society—*sangkum civil*—a concept that has been widely circulated in Cambodia since the early 1990s, is wholly imported. In Khmer, only the word *sangkum* (society) is commonly used. NGOs, which the term *sangkum civil* typically refers to, are commonly known in Khmer as *angka*; a concept which evokes both the murderous Pol Pot regime and emerging development practitioners enjoying access to resources, good employment, membership of a class distinct from the private sector and the state, salaries, and education. Despite the novelty of *sangkum civil* as a concept, it is embedded in a cultural and linguistic context reaching further back.

A number of studies identify a dynamic in which historical and cultural images and practices within Cambodian civil society are mutually adapting, resulting in a rapid transformation of Cambodian civil society (Hughes and Un 2011; Öjendal and Kim 2012). Despite Cambodian civil society being typically cast as historically docile, power has become increasingly diluted, giving rise to new tensions with the state (Öjendal and Kim 2006).

Civil society and the state

With the expansion of civil society in the 1990s, NGOs came to fulfill a large share of typically state functions. Formal mechanisms now exist, through which NGOs—often in collaboration with UN agencies, multilateral funding institutions, and Western government donors—engage with the Cambodian government on matters of national development and policy implementation. While the Cambodian government values the resources and services NGOs provide—such as agricultural development, medical services, and poverty alleviation—Prime Minister Hun Sen and the ruling Cambodian People's Party (CPP) have been critical of NGOs that focus on governance and human rights issues. Moreover, youth organizations and trade unions are seen as possible powerhouses and subject to intense co-option by state interests. Since the mid-2000s, the state has increasingly reduced the liberties of NGOs and tightened regulations (Heder 2005). In August 2015, the controversial "Law on NGOs and Associations" was passed. The law has been widely criticized (including by the United Nations and international NGOs) for restricting civil society's right to freedom of association and expression by potentially enabling the government to shut down organizations that criticize it. Following unrest in the garment sector before and during the aftermath of 2013 national elections, the Law on Unions of Enterprises (Trade Union Law) was passed in April 2016. The government has stated that the law is to promote the well-being of unions, but labor leaders and human rights NGOs have charged that it protects government-backed unions while undermining independent trade unions. The current decline in foreign aid has facilitated recent state restriction of civil society space.

A frequently proposed model sets out a competitive relationship between the Cambodian state and civil society. As Ly Thim (2014) points out, civil society is perceived by the state as a challenge to its monopoly on power. According to Hart Feuer *et al.* (2014), although the state views civil society as a partner in service delivery and policy, the government is increasingly aware of the everyday politics entailed in civil society activities. It, therefore, seeks to control civil society politically by having the state shape and restrict the environment in which associational activity can emerge.

Another common model proposes that there is a mutual relationship between state and civil society. Contributors to Waibel *et al.* (2014) typically found "government engagements—or the lack thereof—as an aspect of engendering and envisioning civil society rather than a linear oppositional force" (Waibel 2014: 12). This model is in line with broader scholarship on Asia: Muthiah Alagappa (2004) concluded that in Asia, CSOs do not fundamentally challenge the state but seek to achieve their objectives by utilizing the room to maneuver that the state provides. For Caroline Hughes (2009a), in Cambodia (as in many other states in Asia), the elite patronage of civil society activities sometimes blurs the line between state sponsorship and autonomous actions. Clientelist networks between elite coalitions and societal actors involve formally autonomous civil society associations in political competition, forming an "uncivil society" that fragments and co-opts civil society.

According to David Norman (2014), civil society is increasingly being transformed into a technocratic model so as to serve as a supporting mechanism for an efficient market and accountable state in line with the neoliberal new policy agenda. In this model, CSOs are "an integral cog in contemporary neoliberal donor strategies" intended to reform the state's political and economic architecture (Norman 2014: 242). In spite of the organizational independence of civil society from the state and market, state and market coordination mechanisms permeate civil society under good governance frameworks. Öjendal (2014) convincingly identifies a new dynamic of power between the state and civil society that emerged over the course of the 2000s. It is defined by: 1) democratic decentralization; 2) an increased local presence of NGOs/CSOs; 3) a shrinking of the development-oriented, externally funded civil society; and 4) a shift in the balance of power to benefit domestic Cambodian interests over outside ones. Decentralized authorities are more open to working with local NGOs, which has resulted in an increased local presence of NGOs/CSOs and a new-found, mutual search for new relations (Kim and Öjendal 2012; Öjendal and Kim 2012). NGOs adapt to the shrinking of externally funded civil society by commercialization and private sector engagement, pursuing private consultancy, or scaling down. Associational civil society is growing. First, professional, well-funded NGOs are typically supported and influenced by international counterparts and lack broad membership. Second, there are home-grown and self-reliant CSOs, which have limited spread and budget but work with culturally appropriate methods, and which cooperate closely with local authorities. Third, there are CBOs that respond to local needs. These are set up under directives from local governments and often include village and commune officials, and so possess parastatal characteristics (Öjendal 2014). With the current gradual decline in foreign aid, the state is now attempting to impose more systematic controls on the growing civil society that has come to fill the intermediate sphere, which, historically, was an empty space.

The role of the international donor community

Most of Cambodia's CSOs rely on outside funding sources. Between 2003 and 2008, official development assistance (ODA) averaged US$600 million a year, coming from thirty-nine bilateral and multilateral donors (Ek and Sok 2008; cited in Dosch 2012). With the increase of aid from China and South Korea, disbursements of external assistance have progressively increased, reaching US$1.46 billion in 2013. Between 2004 and 2013, the year-on-year compound increase amounted to 11.4 percent (Courtnadge 2014; information extracted from Cambodia ODA & NGO Databases). The aid per capita ratio nearly doubled between 2000 and 2010, paralleling the doubling of ODA provision during this period. In 2014, per capita aid stood at US$52, making Cambodia the second most aid-dependent country in Southeast Asia after Laos (US$71) (World Bank Indicators Database). Only about one-tenth of total ODA is disbursed by non-state actors, but foreign donors typically prefer to partner with Cambodian NGOs. In recent years, there has been an increase in concessional loan financing and in grant support from NGOs (Courtnadge 2014).

International donor involvement in Cambodia has been extensively analyzed in the scholarly literature. Given the heavy reliance on external funding by NGOs, much of this literature examines the ways in which the international donor community shapes Cambodian civil society and the consequences for its functioning. Charting the emergence of 'civil society' since 1991, Caroline Hughes (2003) argued that the political economy of international support exacerbated Khmer cultural predispositions to supporting a civil society that comprised organizations that were centralized, hierarchical, and heavily emphasized the didactic transmission of foreign knowledge while professionally mediating between grass-roots organizations and the government. The close orientation of these organizations toward international priorities forestalled a role as vectors of cultural change that might have promoted democratization. Caroline Hughes (2007) finds that international agencies, despite professing support for civil society, have championed a neoliberal agenda that promotes atomizing modes of participation so as to demobilize and depoliticize contentious local groups. Consequently, the state has been able to repress radical leaders and diminish space for public participation. Hughes (2009b) also finds that one effect of the reliance on external funding is a divide between social collectives that have funding and those that do not. Hughes maintains that international actors showed little interest in the new forms of collective action initiated by Cambodians in the 1990s. Civil society activities have been influenced by "pre-set, internationally sanctioned disciplinary boundaries" (Hughes 2009b: 127) that are thus policed by competitive and selective external funding. Aid donors promote a politic that is confining, breaks down non-state authority structures, and focuses on individual action rather than building up the public sphere and fostering collective action.

Norman (2014) similarly argues that donor involvement has co-opted Cambodian civil society under a broader neoliberal umbrella. Externally driven donor pressures have resulted in the construction of particular neoliberal spaces in which CSOs function as donors' technical implementation mechanisms by performing the two key roles of professional service providers (NGOs being elevated into the role of public service providers) and democratic watchdogs (civil society used as a mechanism for democratic oversight). A particular model of civil society, in which economistic and administrative modes of participation are core values of civil society participation, is thus cultivated.

NGO accountability has been found to typically be directed upward (to donors) rather than downward (to beneficiaries). Seima Khlok, Ouch Phoumim, and Nil Vanna (2003) found that NGOs typically aim to please donors rather than respond to the demands of the beneficiaries. Yukiko Yonekura (1999) similarly found that NGOs represent target beneficiaries quite poorly.

NGOs have also been found to be detached from the populace at large, and are marked by low levels of public participation (SPM 2003, 2006) and a lack of grass-roots links (Khlok *et al.* 2003; Malena and Chhim 2009; Un 2004).

The governance structure of NGOs is typically found to be problematic due to undemocratic and hierarchical elements. Using secondary data and qualitative interview results from about twenty NGOs, INGOs, and research institutes, Ou and Kim (2014) found that externally supported NGOs are more accountable to donors than they are to beneficiaries; that they identify with their professional status rather than with their duty to beneficiaries; that they are detached from the grassroots; and that they lack democratic structures. NGO dependence on foreign aid has led to a co-optation of civil society by donors' agendas and an erosion of NGOs' independent social base. The net result is that democratic principles have failed to find anchorage in the way NGOs operate, which means that they are overly directed by considerations of hierarchy, class cleavages, patronage, nepotism, and autocracy, so that NGOs form but an illusion of civil society.

Aid dependence is also found to have weakened Cambodian civil society both by distorting government incentives for good governance and in the international community's lack of resolve in promoting democratic change. Sophal Ear (2012) finds that the international community has contributed funding to organizations that make Cambodia's democracy more liberal, but that, regrettably, funding has not built up civil society beyond elections, and that there has been little pressure on the government to reform. International aid has been directed toward elections and politically oriented CS groups, representing short-term stabilization efforts that should be discarded to fulfill long-term transformative goals that socially embed democratic processes. Dependence on external funding also makes local NGOs vulnerable to shifts in policy or funding priorities, and thus prevents long-term planning.

Joern Dosch (2012) examines the consequences of aid dependence for the ownership of Cambodian civil society. His central question is whether "donors set the development agenda according to their own interests and ideologies, which are then duly followed and implemented by local NGOs," or if "NGOs have the upper hand in designing program and project activities in line with their specific concepts and needs"—a question which he examines in the context of Cambodia's peace-building process.

Building on sixty-eight interviews and group discussions with NGO workers, donor organizations, diplomats, academics, journalists, and government officials in 2010 and 2011, Dosch (2012) finds that, most commonly, it is the donor organization that commissions an NGO to implement a project in line with the donor's interests and strategies. Donors have initiated a justice-driven approach to peace, by inserting the notion of transitional justice as the main pillar of the current peace-building process. Externally funded NGOs are the main actors in building the related institutional frameworks. Dosch (2012) concludes that the aid dependence on NGOs has resulted in a predominantly donor-driven peace-building process in which NGOs follow the interests and agenda of donors, rather than beneficiaries.

A rare case study of civil society's contribution to transitional justice processes in Cambodia is offered by Christoph Sperfeldt (2012), who explores the roles of local civil society actors around the externally funded, internationalized criminal court, the Extraordinary Chambers in the Courts of Cambodia (ECCC). Around ten to fifteen local NGOs have engaged at different times with the ECCC process, most notably in the areas of victim participation and outreach. Sperfeldt finds that relatively strong and proactive local civil society organizations support and complement the work of the ECCC.

Re-emergence of historical civil society

Cambodian post-conflict reconstruction has entailed the re-emergence of historical societal institutions. In an influential account, William Collins (1998) found indigenous civil society to be flourishing in the Cambodian countryside, reflecting the preservation of traditional social and cultural organizations, associations and activities. Cambodian society has historically been marked by mobility, fluidity, and loose organization in small entities. Ethnic Khmer villages are not socially cohesive (Ovesen, Trankell, and Öjendal 1996) and although they do possess some traditional cooperative measures, collective action is rare (Ros, Tem, and Thompson 2011). Historically, associations did not form. Historical Cambodian civil society is, rather, to be found in the religious realm, in patron–client relations, or in kinship-based relations (Ebihara 1968; Ledgerwood 2002; Ovesen *et al.* 1996). The recent resurgence and new directions of these phenomena are considered by some scholarship as a revival of historical civil society, yet the bulk of scholarship on these topics avoids situating these within debates on civil society.

Cambodian Buddhism

Cambodian Buddhism has had a pervasive influence in shaping Cambodia, both socially and politically. In 1989, state policies toward religion were liberalized and the period since has been marked by religious innovation. A range of phenomena have reappeared, including spirit mediums and monks bestowing blessings with water; these have become increasingly socially significant in the period after 1989 (Marston 2004). Scholarship has, therefore, assessed the ability of religion to re-forge communal bonds—one aspect of civil society.

Detailed ethnographies of the reconstruction of village Buddhism has generally avoided the language of civil society, but nonetheless, they provide adequate and empirically based assessments of the level of social cohesion promoted by contemporary local level Buddhism. Judy Ledgerwood (2008) found the Buddhist act of merit-making to be a key focus of village-based Buddhist practice in rural Kandal province in 2003, just as it was during earlier research carried out in the area in 1960 (Ebihara 1968). She argues that the reciprocal relations of giving and receiving, around which the act of merit-making is centered, "literally bind the community together" (Ledgerwood 2008: 159). Still, this glue has been diluted: Ledgerwood finds that, while being Khmer previously also equated being Buddhist, it is now possible to imagine otherwise (Ledgerwood 2008: 161). Satoru Kobayashi (2008) explores the state of village Buddhism in today's rural Cambodia as it is reflected in the reconstruction of Buddhist temples. Examining the networking activities that temple reconstruction involves, Kobayashi identifies tension and conflict amongst participants—despite the fact that local Buddhist leaders emphasize a sense of popular unity. Kobayashi concludes that the:

> Buddhist temple in present day Cambodia is a much more complex place than the "harmonious center of rural life" it has often been described as. Whilst the shared ideology of merit-making facilitates cooperative activity, questions of identity frequently lead to competition and conflict.
>
> *(Kobayashi 2008: 189)*

Many pagoda-based associational activities are not recognized as part of civil society by development agents and the state, but they nonetheless play a critical role in communal relations (Ehlert 2014). There is a scholarly consensus that the re-establishment of pagodas is an expression of rural efforts to recreate moral order. Alexandra Kent (2007) explores such efforts through the re-establishment of pagodas and the consecration of their boundaries and situates these dynamics in the context of an increasing politicization of the local, Buddhist world.

One line of inquiry concerns the ability of organized Buddhism to act as a "third realm." The Cambodian sangha is politicized, as groups of the sangha are aligned with rival political parties: the dominant *Mahanikay* Order is loyal to the incumbent Cambodian People's Party and the smaller *Thommayut* Order traditionally supports royalists (Harris 2001). The embroilment in party politics complicates the ability of the sangha to function as a proper check on the government.

Some have looked to NGO movements linked to Buddhism to challenge the state. Ian Harris (2005) discusses how foreign NGOs in the 1990s exerted a profound effect on the development of Buddhism in Cambodia by their funding of institutional Buddhism. External financial support prioritized forms of Buddhism that were moving in a socially engaged, modernist direction (Harris 2005). International development agencies and NGOs, such as the German-based Konrad Adenauer Foundation (KAF) and the German Technical Cooperation Agency (GTZ), sponsored Engaged Buddhism in Cambodia, including the Buddhism for Development (BFD) organization, as well as environmental Buddhist movements (Harris 2005). Socially engaged Buddhism has taken a clear stance on social activism and has accomplished a great deal in generating grass-roots support.

The Dhammyatra peace marches stand out because of the ways in which they have garnered popular support over a long period of time and united disparate groups of Cambodians. The marches began in Cambodia in 1992, and initially brought together Cambodians who were returning from refugee camps and those residing in the country. Kathryn Poethig conceives of Engaged Buddhism in Asia "part of a trend toward an increasingly global civil society in which political moralities are transmitted by transnational religious movements" (2004: 199). She takes the integration of engaged Buddhism into Cambodia's religious and political landscape as proof of its adaptability to a maturing civil society. For Poethig, the Dhammayatra marches have further strengthened Cambodia's civil society through encouraging initiatives from monks and *tun ji* participating in the walks, the educational component of the walks (on matters such as landmines, domestic violence, and deforestation), and contributing to the practice and philosophy of nonviolence in Cambodia's civil society by training a generation of peace activists. This training has since been replicated by other peace-based local and international NGOs in Cambodia (Poethig 2004: 208–209).

However, views on the accomplishments of Buddhist-based NGOs are mixed today. John Marston (2009) outlines what he refers to as an emerging civil society: organizations which appear to challenge the state. Marston finds that although a few new organizations have found a niche for themselves, religiously based NGOs do not seem to be growing, nor are significant new NGOs formed along these lines. Marston ascribes this state of affairs to an internal failure of the NGO structure to "connect" with grass-roots Cambodia, so that religiously affiliated NGOs appear to be "inserted" into Cambodian society. Hybrid ideologies, such as those attempting to meld human rights with Buddhism, are sometimes an incongruous result. Consequently, NGOs have taken on an increasingly lay orientation for the sake of their survival. This suggests that the two forms of civil society—the associational civil society with development objectives and with the structure of an NGO, and that of Buddhism—do not credibly merge to present a unified challenge to the state.

If not in NGOs, Marston has repeatedly located the potential for genuine social mobilization in movements around monks, which flourished dramatically after 1989. Marston (2004) examines the small cult of *Tapas*, considering it and other religious projects in the 1990s to be a process of exploring the degree to which ideas of nation, democracy, and Cambodian sovereignty really do provide agency. Marston (2009) finds that movements arising around dissident monks have genuinely captured the imaginations of grass-roots Cambodians. Such movements have worked within the social institutions of Cambodian Buddhism while critiquing it. For Marston, such movements, therefore, evidence that Buddhist movements can indeed challenge the social order (Marston 2009) and carry the civil society mantle more convincingly.

Family, kinship, and patronage networks

The nuclear household has traditionally been the basic unit of Cambodian social life. Anthropological and sociological scholarship has sketched a sort of Khmer peasant individualism, marked by the implementation of private land holdings, the sacredness of private property, and absence of communal land that has counteracted village organization, leading Jan Ovesen *et al.* (1996) to propose that "Every household is an island." Recent work finds that a lack of solidarity and collective action in rural areas persists (Ros *et al.* 2011).

Though there is little to bridge communities, household networks are formed through kinship (defined by blood and marriage), friendship, reciprocity, or proximity (Heuveline 2016). Recent studies find relatively strong social capital in terms of bonding amongst relatives (CDRI 2012; Kim 2011). Yet, the absence of elders after the Khmer Rouge regime of Democratic Kampuchea (1975–1979), as bearers and transmitters of the moral and social order, has been interpreted as a structural void in society, producing a form of "communal existential uncertainty" (Zucker 2008: 195–197).

A culture of patronage permeates Cambodian society. Kinship and associated patronages remain central to village reciprocity (Ledgerwood and Vijghen 2002: 143). Each individual has a place in a *khsae* (patron–client network) and is backed by a *khnong* (patron). Whereas patronage was historically based on local landholdings, it now revolves around money, business, and political connections. Emerging in the late 1980s, today's governance system is neo-patrimonial: informal patrimonial power based on traditional patron–client power dynamics mixed with formal, legal-rational bureaucratic power (Pak, Horn, and Eng 2007: 57). Persistent patron–client relations shape the realm of formal associations. Louise Coventry (2017) finds that CBOs are likely to emerge under the sponsorship of local patrons, to continue relying on patron–client relations, and to engage in mutual assistance and service delivery, rather than in advocacy that could upset existing power relations. Patron–client relations contribute to a situation in which NGOs have taken up the civil society space to the detriment of smaller CBOs.

Conclusion

As suggested by the above literature review, social movements are not typically considered part of Cambodian civil society—indeed, it would appear that there has been nothing to fit that label (Henke 2011: 298). However, by recording sporadic and fragmented resistance movements, social movement analysis can have more applicability than a liberal conception of civil society (Hughes 2001). The associations typically conceived of as originating from civil society have engendered collective non-state action motivated by personal interests and grievances. In 2003, Hughes found that the major contribution of NGOs has been to encourage the emergence of "a panoply of small-scale, interest-based movements lobbying government over issues of policy" (2003: 141). Particularly since the late 1990s, these movements offered opportunities for a new form of citizen mobilization, representing the best hope for democratic revitalization. At the moment of writing, recently emerged natural resource management activist networks appear to have assumed this role. Writing in 2011, Henke attributes to them a "social-movement-like-quality" and makes the assessment that "the development of these networks has occurred in the last two years" but that "they have so far remained under the radar of academic and most other Cambodia watchers" (2011: 299). For Henke, the tentative emergence of a social movement for the common people means that this poses a real civil society challenge to the state, contrary to the NGO-ization of civil society that supports state dominance (2011: 308).

In the years since such forms of mobilization have proliferated—many of them growing into what should arguably be understood as grass-roots social movements. Very little is known regarding the various forms of these current grass-roots social movements fighting for access to and control of natural resources in Cambodia, in terms of the partnerships from which they are created, their supporters, and the influence of the aid industry. Fundamental knowledge of their activities, their membership, leadership and support base, and the conditions under which these movements operate, is lacking. Moreover, little is known about the expectations of the general populace regarding natural resource access and control. Finally, there is little knowledge of the strategies employed by the incumbent government to either co-opt or direct social movements.

With this in mind, the SOMANARE (SOcial Movements, Access to NAtural REsources) Research project (2016–2020) has since been established. It brings together an interdisciplinary group of researchers (including the author) representing perspectives from anthropology, agronomy, political science, development studies, and geography. The first objective of the research is to study social conflicts over resource access and control by engaging with a political ecology perspective. The second objective is to understand the dynamics of the efforts by the Cambodian state in employing new forms of governmentality to control natural resources for the benefit of privileged elites. Research for the project pays particular attention to the dimension of "glocalization" (i.e., "the global in the local") when assessing the tools and strategies used or imagined by different segments of the population in response to top-down interventions by the state, aid agencies, and transnational and national corporations. The project seeks to establish an adequate methodology for mapping the emergence and the nature of social movements in rural Cambodia, delineating their various characteristics, agents, obstacles, challenges, and likely results. This dynamic field of action represents a new turn in the shifting landscape of Cambodian civil society. It opens the door for the development of a richer civil society in both empirical and conceptual terms, providing particularly fertile ground for future research.

Suggested readings

Henke, Roger. 2011. NGOs, People's Movements, and Natural Resource Management. In *Cambodia's Economic Transformation*. Caroline Hughes and Kheang Un, eds. Pp. 288–309. Copenhagen: NIAS Press.

Hughes, Caroline. 2003. Promoting Democracy: NGOs and "Civil Society." In *The Political Economy of Cambodia's Transition, 1991–2001*. London: RoutledgeCurzon.

Ou, Sivhuoch, and Sedata Kim. 2013. 20 Years' Strengthening of Cambodian Civil Society: Time for Reflection. *Working Paper Series* No. 85. Phnom Penh: CDRI (Cambodia Development Research Institute).

Waibel, Gabi, Judith Ehlert, and Hart N. Feuer, eds. 2014. *Southeast Asia and the Civil Society Gaze: Scoping a Contested Concept in Cambodia and Vietnam*. Abingdon and New York: Routledge.

Website

Council for the Development of Cambodia, http://cdc.khmer.biz/.
Database maintained on behalf of all ministries and agencies of the Royal Government of Cambodia, working to connect NGOs, development partners, and visitors for aid management in Cambodia.

References

Alagappa, Muthiah. 2004. The Nonstate Public Sphere in Asia: Dynamic Growth, Industrialization Lag. In *Civil Society and Political Change in Asia: Expanding and Contracting Democratic Space*. Muthiah Alagappa, ed. Pp. 1–21. Stanford, CA: Stanford University Press.

CDRI (Cambodia Development Research Institute). 2012. *Survey Report on Social Capital and Sustainable Development in Cambodia*. Phnom Penh: Cambodia Development Research Institute.

Collins, William. 1998. *Grassroots Civil Society in Cambodia*. Phnom Penh: Center for Advanced Study.

Courtnadge, Philip. 2014. Cambodia. New York and Paris: Global Partnership for Effective Development Co-operation.

Coventry, Louise. 2017. Civil Society in Cambodia: Challenges and Contestations. In *The Handbook of Contemporary Cambodia*. Katherine Brickell and Simon Springer, eds. Pp. 53–63. London and New York: Routledge.

Dosch, Joern. 2012. The Role of Civil Society in Cambodia's Peace-Building Process. *Asian Survey* 52(6): 1067–1088.

Downie, Sue, and Damien Kingsbury. 2001. Political Development and the Re-Emergence of Civil Society in Cambodia. *Contemporary Southeast Asia* 23(1): 43–64.

Ear, Sophal. 2012. *Aid Dependence in Cambodia: How Foreign Assistance Undermines Democracy*. New York: Columbia University Press.

Ebihara, May. 1968. Svay, a Khmer Village in Cambodia. PhD thesis, Columbia University.

Ehlert, Judith. 2014. Proto Civil Society: Pagodas and the Socio-Religious Space in Rural Cambodia. In *Southeast Asia and the Civil Society Gaze: Scoping a Contested Concept in Cambodia and Vietnam*. Gabi Waibel, Judith Ehlert, and Hart N. Feuer, eds. Pp. 203–217. Abingdon and New York: Routledge.

Ek, Chanboreth, and Sok Hach. 2008. Aid Effectiveness in Cambodia. *Wolfensohn Center for Development Working Paper* 7. Washington, DC: Brookings.

Feuer, Hart, Phuong Le Trong, and Judith Ehlert. 2014. Conclusion: The Civil Society Gaze. In *Southeast Asia and the Civil Society Gaze: Scoping a Contested Concept in Cambodia and Vietnam*. Gabi Waibel, Judith Ehlert, and Hart N. Feuer, eds. Pp. 253–264. Abingdon and New York: Routledge.

Hann, Chris, and Elizabeth Dunn. 1996. Introduction: Political Society and Civil Anthropology. In *Civil Society: Challenging Western Models*. Chris Hann and Elizabeth Dunn, eds. Pp. 1–26. London and New York: Routledge.

Harris, Ian. 2001. Buddhist Sangha Groupings in Cambodia. *Buddhist Studies Review* 18(1): 73–106.

Harris, Ian. 2005. *Cambodian Buddhism: History and Practice*. Honolulu, HI: University of Hawai'i Press.

Heder, Steve. 2005. Hun Sen's Consolidation: Death or Beginning of Reform? *Southeast Asian Affairs* (May 2005): 111–113.

Henke, Roger. 2011. NGOs, People's Movements, and Natural Resource Management. In *Cambodia's Economic Transformation*. Caroline Hughes and Kheang Un, eds. Pp. 288–309. Copenhagen: NIAS Press.

Heuveline, Patrick. 2016. Households and Family Processes. In *The Handbook of Contemporary Cambodia*. Katherine Brickell and Simon Springer, eds. Pp. 336–345. London and New York: Routledge.

Hughes, Caroline. 2001. Mystics and Militants: Democratic Reform in Cambodia. *International Politics* 38(1): 47–64.

Hughes, Caroline. 2003. *The Political Economy of Cambodia's Transition, 1991–2001*. London and New York: RoutledgeCurzon.

Hughes, Caroline. 2007. Transnational Networks, International Organizations and Political Participation in Cambodia: Human Rights, Labour Rights and Common Rights. *Democratization* 14(5): 834–852.

Hughes, Caroline. 2009a. Civil Society in Southeast Asia. In *Contemporary Southeast Asia*. 2nd Edn. Mark Beeson, ed. Pp. 125–142. New York: Palgrave Macmillan.

Hughes, Caroline. 2009b. *Dependent Communities: Aid and Politics in Cambodia and East Timor*. Ithaca, NY: Cornell University Press.

Hughes, Caroline, and Kheang Un, eds. 2011. *Cambodia's Economic Transformation*. Copenhagen: NIAS Press.

ILO. 2010. *23rd Synthesis Report on Working Conditions in Cambodia's Garment Sector*. Phnom Penh: ILO Better Factories Project.

Kent, Alexandra. 2007. Purchasing Power and Pagodas: The Sīma Monastic Boundary and Consumer Politics in Cambodia. *Journal of Southeast Asian Studies* 38(2): 335–354.

Khlok, Seima, Ouch Phoumim, and Nil Vanna. 2003. *Margin to Mainstream. An Assessment of Community Based Organizations in Cambodia*. Washington, DC: World Bank.

Kim, Sedara. 2011. Reciprocity: Informal Patterns of Social Interaction in a Cambodian Village. In *Anthropology and Community in Cambodia: Reflections on the Work of May Ebihara*. John Marston, ed. Pp. 153–170. Clayton, VIC: Monash University Press.

Kim, Sedara, and Joakim Öjendal. 2012. Accountability and Local Politics in Natural Resource Management. In *Cambodia's Economic Transformation*. Caroline Hughes and Kheang Un, eds. Pp. 266–87. Copenhagen: NIAS Press.

Kobayashi, Satoru. 2008. Reconstructing Buddhist Temple Buildings: An Analysis of Village Buddhism after the Era of Turmoil. In *People of Virtue: Reconfiguring Religion, Power, and Moral Order in Cambodia*. Alexandra Kent and David Chandler, eds. Pp. 169–94. Copenhagen: NIAS Press.

Ledgerwood, Judy. 2002. *Cambodia Emerges from the Past: Eight Essays*. Dekalb, IL: Southeast Asia Publications, Centre for Southeast Asian Studies, Northern Illinois University.

Ledgerwood, Judy. 2008. Buddhist Practice in Rural Kandal Province, 1960 and 2003—An Essay in Honor of May M. Ebihara. In *People of Virtue: Reconfiguring Religion, Power, and Moral Order in Cambodia*. Alexandra Kent and David Chandler, eds. Pp. 147–168. Copenhagen: NIAS Press.

Ledgerwood, Judy, and John Vijghen. 2002. *Decision Making in Rural Khmer Villages*. Dekalb, IL: Centre for Southeast Asian Studies, Northern Illinois University.

Malena, Carmen, and Kristina Chhim. 2009. *Linking Citizens and the State: An Assessment of Civil Society Contributions to Good Governance in Cambodia*. Washington DC: World Bank.

Marston, John. 2004. Clay into Stone: A Modern-Day Tapas. In *History, Buddhism, and New Religious Movements in Cambodia*. Marston John Amos and Elizabeth Guthrie, eds. Pp. 170–192. Honolulu, HI: University of Hawai'i Press.

Marston, John. 2009. Cambodian Religion Since 1989. In *Beyond Democracy in Cambodia: Political Reconstruction in a Post-Conflict Society*. Joakim Öjendal and Mona Lilja, eds. Pp. 224–249. Copenhagen: NIAS.

Norman, David J. 2014. From Shouting to Counting: Civil Society and Good Governance Reform in Cambodia. *Pacific Review* 27(2): 241–264.

Nuon, Veasna, and Melisa Serrano. 2010. *Building Unions in Cambodia: History, Challenges, Strategies*. Singapore: Friedrich Ebert Stiftung Office for Regional Cooperation in Asia.

Öjendal, Joakim. 2014. In Search of a Civil Society: Re-Negotiating State–Society Relations in Cambodia. In *Southeast Asia and the Civil Society Gaze: Scoping a Contested Concept in Cambodia and Vietnam*. Gabi Waibel, Judith Ehlert, and Hart N. Feuer, eds. Pp. 21–38. Abingdon and New York: Routledge.

Öjendal, Joakim, and Sedara Kim. 2006. "Korob Kaud Klach": In Search of Agency in Rural Cambodia. *Journal of Southeast Asian Studies* 37(3): 507–526.

Öjendal, Joakim, and Sedara Kim. 2012. *Is Your Ground as Common as Mine?: A Critical Review of the Role of Civil Society in Local Governance in Cambodia*. Phnom Penh: The Asia Foundation, Mimeo.

Ou, Sivhuoch, and Sedata Kim. 2013. 20 Years' Strengthening of Cambodian Civil Society: Time for Reflection. *Working Paper Series* No. 85. Phnom Penh: CDRI (Cambodia Development Research Institute).

Ou, Sivhuoch, and Sedara Kim. 2014. NGOs and the Illusion of a Cambodian Civil Society. In *Southeast Asia and the Civil Society Gaze: Scoping a Contested Concept in Cambodia and Vietnam*. Gabi Waibel, Judith Ehlert, and Hart N. Feuer, eds. Pp. 187–202. Abingdon and New York: Routledge.

Ovesen, Jan, Inga-Britt Trankell, and Joakim Ojendal. 1996. *When Every Household is an Island: Social Organization and Power Structures in Rural Cambodia*. Uppsala: Dept. of Cultural Anthropology, Uppsala University; Stockholm: Sida.

Pak, Kimchoeun, Vuthy Horn, and Netra Eng. 2007. *Accountability and Neo-Patrimonialism in Cambodia. A Critical Literature Review*. Phnom Penh: Cambodia Development Research Institute.

Poethig, Kathryn. 2004. Locating the Transnational in Cambodia's Dhammayatra. In *History, Buddhism, and New Religious Movements in Cambodia*. Marston John Amos and Elizabeth Guthrie, eds. Pp. 197–212. Honolulu, HI: University of Hawai'i Press.

Ros, Bandeth, Ly Tem, and Anna Thompson. 2011. Catchment Governance and Cooperation Dilemmas: A Case Study from Cambodia. *Working Paper* 61. Phnom Penh: CDRI (CDRI (Cambodia Development Research Institute).

Sperfeldt, Christoph. 2012. Cambodian Civil Society and the Khmer Rouge Tribunal. *International Journal of Transitional Justice* 6(1): 1–12.

SPM Consultants. 2003. *Civil Society and Democracy in Cambodia: Changing Roles and Trends. The Fifth Report of the SIDA Advisory Team on Democratic Governance*. Stockholm and Phnom Penh: SPM Consultants.

SPM Consultants. 2006. *Civil Society and Uncivilized Politics: Trends and Roles of Cambodian Civil Society and Possibility for SIDA Support. The Eighth Report of the SIDA Advisory Team on Democratic Governance.* Stockholm and Phnom Penh: SPM Consultants.

Thim, Ly. 2014. Mobilizing Against Hydropower Projects: Multi-Scale Dimensions of Civil Society Action in a Transboundary Setting. In *Southeast Asia and the Civil Society Gaze: Scoping a Contested Concept in Cambodia and Vietnam.* Gabi Waibel, Judith Ehlert, and Hart N. Feuer, eds. Pp. 153–167. Abingdon and New York: Routledge.

Un, Kheang. 2004. *Democratization Without Consolidation: The Case of Cambodia, 1993–2004.* PhD thesis, Northern Illinois University.

Waibel, Gabi. 2014 Grasping Discourses, Researching Practices: Investigating Civil Society in Vietnam and Cambodia. In *Southeast Asia and the Civil Society Gaze: Scoping a Contested Concept in Cambodia and Vietnam.* Gabi Waibel, Judith Ehlert, and Hart N. Feuer, eds. Pp. 1–17. Abingdon and New York: Routledge.

Waibel, Gabi, Judith Ehlert, and Hart N. Feuer, eds. 2014. *Southeast Asia and the Civil Society Gaze.* Abingdon and New York: Routledge.

Wells-Dang, Andrew. 2014. Civil Society Networks in Cambodia and Vietnam: A Comparative Analysis. In *Southeast Asia and the Civil Society Gaze: Scoping a Contested Concept in Cambodia and Vietnam.* Gabi Waibel, Judith Ehlert, and Hart N. Feuer, eds. Pp. 61–76. Abingdon and New York: Routledge.

World Bank Indicators Database. Electronic document, http://data.worldbank.org/indicator/DT.ODA.ODAT.PC.ZS?view=chart, accessed 10 December 2016.

Yonekura, Yukiko. 1999. *The Emergence of Civil Society in Cambodia: Its Role in the Democratization Process.* PhD thesis, University of Sussex.

Zucker, Eve. 2008. The Absence of Elders: Chaos and Moral Order in the Aftermath of the Khmer Rouge. In *People of Virtue: Reconfiguring Religion, Power, and Moral Order in Cambodia.* Alexandra Kent and David Chandler, eds. Pp. 195–212. Copenhagen: NIAS.

13

LAOS

Gretchen Kunze

Keeping civil society quiet in Laos

In 2016, President Barack Obama became the first sitting US president to visit the Lao People's Democratic Republic (Laos). Laos was the chair of the Association of Southeast Asian Nations (ASEAN) in 2016, and, therefore, it hosted the annual summit of the regional body's national leaders. A few weeks earlier, the ASEAN People's Forum/ASEAN Civil Society Conference (APF/ACSC—the regular accompanying event for civil society leaders from the region), which also should have been hosted by Laos, was held in Timor Leste, after the Lao government claimed that it did not have the funds to host this meeting and it could not ensure the safety of its participants. This was the first time in the history of these meetings, since their first iteration in 2005, that the chairing ASEAN country did not also host the APF/ACSC. "Civil society in Laos remains under a hostile spotlight from the government, and UN rights officials have noted that there are few places in the world where they have encountered greater fear and intimidation among community organizations and NGOs," said Walden Bello, a former member of the Philippines Congress and Vice-Chair of ASEAN Parliamentarians for Human Rights (APHR; APHR 2016).

Laos is considered amongst the world's most restrictive countries with respect to civil society. In this chapter, I will explain the current context of the country, recent developments in the civil society sector, the impact of international intervention and foreign direct investment on civil society, and the prospects for its future. I posit that, given the country's political and economic circumstances and how they are intertwined with foreign direct investment, there is little likelihood for the restrictive environment to change, and although some kind of civil society will continue to exist and constructively contribute to the nation's development, it will be limited to complementing the state's policies and plans rather than being an activist force. Instead of conducting a broad survey of the various social structures that exist in Laos today that can arguably be included in a comprehensive discussion of civil society, this chapter will focus on what can be considered as "formalized" or "professional" civil society organizations that are locally known as non-profit associations (NPAs). Henceforth, references to civil society organizations (CSOs) will primarily consider NPAs.

Scholarship and research on Laos

In Southeast Asia, where national and international scholars have produced an extensive array of academic works on every imaginable topic, Laos remains an anomaly. Lao scholars are few, and the resulting research is scarce and can be largely attributed to a handful of researchers, as pointed out by N. J. Enfield (2010). In this tightly controlled one-party state, political information and reliable data are difficult to access and any topic that is perceived as challenging the government or political system, even in the spirit of academic study, is highly sensitive. Rigorous anthropological, linguistic, scientific, historical, cultural, and other studies do appear (Evans 1988, 2002; Kunze 2010; Pholsena 2006; Stuart-Fox 1986; see also www.laostudies.org); however, the paucity of information is especially apparent in the realm of political science in general and, particularly, civil society. The late Grant Evans explicitly raised this issue during his keynote speech at the Third Annual Lao Studies Conference in Khon Kaen, Thailand in July 2010. Furthermore, as there are no independent media outlets in Laos, journalistic investigation is also sparse, barring a small number of writers, who are mostly based outside of the country and often use unnamed sources. For those with interest and perseverance, Laos remains a fascinating subject for further academic exploration.

In this context of minimal academic research, international organizations, including the World Bank, the Asian Development Bank, the United Nations Democracy Programme, and international non-governmental organizations (INGOs), with their long-term presence in the country, have filled a part of the gap by producing timely and useful information on Lao civil society. Perhaps the most comprehensive recent overview on civil society in Laos was written by Rik Delnoye (2010) as part of a working paper series for the Swiss Agency for Development and Cooperation in 2010, titled "Survey on Civil Society Development in the Lao PDR: Current Practices and Potential for Future Growth." This work not only provides an analysis of the new developments in the government's engagement with civil society at that time, but also presents the views of the stakeholders on what these steps meant and what roles the various stakeholders, including donors, could play to contribute effectively to the anticipated growth of the sector.

The publication was produced at a critical point for civil society in Laos, with the passage of new legislation regarding the official establishment and registration of local CSOs. While it appeared possible that civil society could be facing an unprecedented opportunity in Laos, given the broader situation in the country this cautious optimism was kept in check by the political context. Delnoye (2010: 26–29) presents a hopeful overview of the actions taken by the government at that time, but it is useful to keep in mind that, in fact, Laos was not experiencing a significant change in its government or widespread reform. Rather, the developments were a potentially modest step toward openness for civil society within the existing political system instead of an abrupt and broad change enabling civil society to operate freely. The situation raised the new question of what a Lao civil society would look like within the country's political circumstances. As Delnoye explains, "Specifically in the Lao context there is a need to conceptually reframe civil society discussions and broaden the empirical base on civil society's role and added value" (2010: 16).

The answer to this question about civil society's characteristics in Laos is still developing. It is central to any analysis of the "efficacy" or "success" of the sector; yet the realistic objective of building this sector remains unclear. Going beyond academic analysis, Delnoye contributes to this inquiry by examining the perspectives on and rationale for the existence of civil society through interviews with various stakeholders, including the Government of Lao (GOL), Lao civil society actors, donors, INGOs, and others. Unsurprisingly, he identifies stark differences in the perspectives of these categories of stakeholders. During the interviews, GOL representatives expressed support of the sector primarily to further the government's development goals and complement their work to provide services to the Lao people (see Delnoye 2010: 45–47). INGOs and donors, while recognizing the extensive benefits of this function, viewed this as only a part of the sector's role, with a distinct interest in the CSOs that contribute to increasing citizen voice and pluralism. Delnoye cites one particularly illustrative response: "We expect our NPA partners to take up a more daring role in terms of lobby and advocacy. We, and I guess the majority of INGOs, are not interested in funding pure service delivery by NPAs" (Delnoye 2010: 47). This leaves the local organizations in the middle. Despite their own goals and visions, they recognize the need to remain aligned with government interests to be permitted to exist and function. At the same time, they are dependent on donor funding and, thus, they must also be responsive to their objectives, and somehow manage to balance the expectations and parameters on both sides. NPAs expressed the importance of moving slowly to avoid creating problems in their positive relationships with the government that are essential for them to be able to continue their work (Delnoye 2010: 49). In light of the current developments in Laos discussed later in this chapter, this caution was and remains critical.

Laos government and society

Laos is one of the handful of one-party countries in the world that still describes itself as Marxist-Leninist. In 1975, the Communist forces overthrew the monarchy and began the single-party Lao People's Democratic Republic, an event that is today referred to as "the change in government." Unlike some of its neighbors, the Communist government in Laos did not enact a radical collectivization process or impose a dramatic transformation in pursuit of a utopian society. It did, however, close itself off from all but Communist Bloc countries. Most of today's government officials, academics, and other professionals who attended university in the 1980s and earlier did so in the Soviet Union, Cuba, or Eastern Europe. Moreover, the overwhelming majority of senior Party officials, until today, were educated in either China or Vietnam rather than in Western democracies.

Laos was fighting its own civil war for decades prior to 1975, and was also embroiled in the USA–Vietnam war. A large section of the infamous Ho Chi Minh trail, which was used by the Vietnamese communists to transport soldiers and supplies between North and South Vietnam, ran through eastern Laos. Furthermore, Laos maintained numerous communist strongholds as part of its own civil war, particularly in the northeast of the country. As a consequence, Laos is the most bombed per capita country in the world. Unexploded ordinance (UXO) remains an issue today, and continues to kill and injure people every year. The poorest areas of the country at the present time coincide with the areas that were most heavily bombed during that period.

The economy declined further following the change in government within a broader region experiencing increasing economic growth. Laos eventually opted to change its economic course and re-engage internationally, while continuing to adhere to its political structure. In 1986, Laos began opening its economy through a reform program known as the New Economic Mechanism. In 1997, Laos joined the Association of Southeast Asian Nations, and in 2011, it opened a stock market in Vientiane as a symbolic move toward capitalism. In 2013, after fifteen years of negotiations, Laos became the 158th member of the World Trade Organization.

Laos remains a one-party communist state that is controlled by the Lao People's Revolutionary Party, which is the only legally permitted party in the country. As compared to its neighbors, particularly to the west and south, officials are proud to highlight that Laos has one of the most stable political regimes in Southeast Asia. There is no substantial opposition group, much less an insurgent force, and no threat of a change in power in the near future. All significant government decisions are made by the eleven-member Politburo and the sixty-one-member Central Committee of the Lao People's Revolutionary Party. The National Assembly, which consists of 132 seats, is elected every five years. In recent years, the National Assembly has been more active in debating legislation, but its decisions are still in line with Party agendas.

In the name of maintaining stability, the government does not tolerate dissent, and political rallies, protests, and uprisings are virtually non-existent. The media is state-run and tightly controlled. From time to time, there are rumors of civic action or citizen protest around issues, such as labor disputes or forced relocation due to infrastructure projects supported by the government, but due to the government's control over the media, the details are usually unsubstantiated and are not widely known other than through informal means. The nation's human rights record has been criticized internationally, but its closed nature restricts the reporting or fact-finding that could concretely affirm many of the allegations.

Laos faces numerous development challenges, but poverty levels have declined significantly in recent years and growth in GDP is predicted to remain strong. The growth has benefited the population unevenly, and for the first time the country is facing dramatic inequality between its rural and urban populations. Outside the capital of Vientiane and a few other cities, many people continue to live without electricity or access to basic facilities. Adequate health care, sanitation, and education all remain serious problems, and most of the country still relies on subsistence agriculture.

While the country has been opening up economically in recent years, with its economy largely dependent upon foreign direct investment from its mentor countries Vietnam and China, as well as Thailand, there has been limited effective international pressure to reform (in contrast, for example, to neighboring Vietnam with its growing Western investment and ties necessitating some movement toward certain Western norms). Transparency International ranks Laos amongst the most corrupt countries in the world (2016).

Laos has no significant manufacturing industry. Its domestic market is still small, the workforce largely untrained, and its landlocked position makes export challenging and expensive. Tourism and natural resources (hydropower potential, mining, and timber) are significant to the economy. Laos is optimistic about its economic future that is largely based on the anticipated returns from the controversial US$1.3 billion Nam Theun 2 Dam scheme, which was inaugurated in 2010 and is intended to generate electricity that will be exported to Thailand. A number of other big hydropower projects are also planned. Thirty-five percent of the Mekong River runs through Laos. This is the largest percentage of the river in any one of the five Lower Mekong Countries (LMCs). Nam Theun 2 is drawing extreme criticism, as it will be the first hydropower dam on the main branch of the Mekong, and critics assert that there has not been nearly enough consultation or research into its effects on the river and Laos' downstream neighbors. This is causing rare public condemnation from other LMC governments, namely, downstream Cambodia and Vietnam, who are worried that the dam will have severe and potentially irreversible effects on agriculture, livelihood, and food security. In spite of the international controversy, construction has begun, and the issue remains contentious. Within Laos, the media presents only positive prospects for the dam's impact.

Though the statistics are questionable, it has been estimated that 35 percent of the population consists of minority groups, which are traditionally and significantly less influential and more impoverished than the majority population of Lao Loum, or lowland Lao. The country's rugged terrain makes it time-consuming and difficult to reach remote villages that are often most in need of services. The majority of the roads are unpaved (and tend to wash out during the monsoons). Many villages throughout the country do not have access to roads at all and can only be reached by small boats or on footpaths, which can mean a journey of two days to the nearest town. Under these circumstances, any kind of intervention—from administering immunizations against diseases to organizing basic literacy campaigns—can be daunting. In Northern Laos lies the area called the Golden Triangle, which is known for its poppy cultivation for narcotic production. With significant foreign assistance from the United Nations, the USA, and other donors, the cultivation has been almost stopped, however, there have been reports and rumors that some small levels of production have recurred in recent years.

State of civil society

Considering formal structured groups, civil society in Laos is amongst the most limited in the world. Most of the public are not familiar with the idea of civil society, nor do they have a notion of the work done by civil society other than humanitarian projects that are largely conducted by INGOs. Since its founding, the state has disseminated information and policies, delivered basic social services, and consulted the public through the Party-led mass organizations. Mass organizations are large membership-based groups that provide some service delivery and public education. There are four mass organizations in Laos: the Lao Women's Union, the Lao Front for National Construction, the Lao People's Revolutionary Youth Union, and the Federation of Lao Trade Unions. The Lao Women's Union has been the most successful in attracting international partners due to the interest of international donors in women's issues and because the other mass organizations have had difficulty with management and meeting donors' requirements.

With hundreds of thousands of members, well-organized communication and outreach structures, and presence throughout the country, including in the most remote villages, these mass organizations have played roles that are traditionally performed by civil society organizations in other countries and political contexts. Yet it is important to remember that they are a part of the Party structure and report to the state rather than the public or their members. While they can be extremely effective in functions such as spreading information and propaganda, as part of the Party, their mandate is to reinforce the aims of the Party; they are not independent drivers of change and do not advocate for policy or political stances that oppose the Party's objectives. Their public campaigns address topics along the lines of disease control, hygiene, domestic violence, or moral precepts such as respecting elders or honoring Lao culture.

Buddhist temples also play a prominent role in daily life, and about 50 percent of the country is Buddhist. All religious organizations and clergy fall under the purview of the Lao Front. Temples may operate schools or periodically provide humanitarian assistance contributions, but they are generally not involved in broad development work and are not activists, as seen in some other Asian countries such as Thailand or Myanmar.

Although neither widely known nor utilized, under Article 44 of the Lao Constitution civil society groups in the official form of "associations" are legally permitted. Article 44 states:

> Lao citizens have the right and freedom of speech, press and assembly, and have the right to set up associations and to stage demonstrations which are not contrary to the laws.[1]

Despite the fact that civil society associations are technically legal in Laos, prior to the late 2000s, the process of opening and maintaining them was largely undefined and ad hoc. There were no standard procedures for their establishment, roles, and functions, and no clear oversight by a single designated government agency. To establish an association, official approval from an appropriate ministry or mass organization was required, but the decision regarding which ministry to approach would likely be based on personal relations or recommendations. The process itself varied over time and across offices.

Over the past decade, the GOL has taken steps to reduce these ambiguities. The progress toward creating a defined legal mandate began with the drafting of a Decree on Associations in 2006, and continued with the subsequent Decree on Foundations and legislation concerning the development and oversight of business associations. For example, in April 2009, the Prime Minister's Office approved the Decree on Associations (Decree Number 115/PM) with the stated aim to increase the number of associations, streamline the registration process, and improve oversight. The Decree, which took effect in November 2009, defines an "association" as being a "non-profit civil organization set up on a voluntary basis and operating on a permanent basis to protect the rights and legitimate interest of the association, its members or communities." The "types of associations" that have been listed include economic associations; professional, technical, and creative associations; social welfare associations; and others (see Lao People's Democratic Republic 2009). This decree was unprecedented in its attempt to systematize and codify the registration process for civil society associations and consolidate their oversight under one government body, the Civil Society Division within the Public Administration and Civil Service Authority (PACSA).

It is relevant to note that these local organizations are called NPAs, or non-profit associations. The term "non-governmental" organization (NGO) is perceived to give the impression of being in opposition to the government and is, therefore, considered inappropriate. The impetus for formalizing the status of NPAs is largely seen as originating in the National Socio-Economic Development Plan 2006–2010, which expressed a commitment to "enable the provision of basic social and essential economic services, ensure security and facilitate the participation and empowerment of the poor in economic, social, political and other arenas to reduce poverty on a sustainable basis" (Lao People's Democratic Republic 2006: 5). By some estimates, the government recognized the role local associations could play in national development and the ways in which they can help the government to meet its goals. Moreover, the government acknowledged that in order to receive foreign funding, organizations often have to be legally recognized by the country in which they operate. As Laos continued to build its international presence and linkages, it was important to allow some presence of civil society in order to appear legitimate by international norms.

The passage of the decree was originally met largely with optimism by proponents of the development of a civil society sector in Laos.[2] CSOs submitted paperwork to PACSA to formally register and international donors sought ways to support this nascent sector. Lao and international groups collaborated to create the nation's only civil society center, the Learning House for Development, that offers office space, shared resources (such as a copy machine), and facilities to hold meetings.

Since that time, however, much of the early optimism has waned. Beyond the first two waves of applicants, the government has not approved the registration of many new NPAs, thus leaving these organizations in a legal gray zone where they have provided documentation to establish their existence but they do not have the legal approval to carry out their work. Partly due to the difficulty of registration, the quoted number of Lao associations varies greatly, depending on the source of information. Some speculate that 100 to 300 associations exist throughout the country, while international organizations generally accept that there are probably fewer than fifty associations capable of effectively operating with any level of impact. Regardless of their legal status and barring a few exceptions, the majority of these associations are still in the initial stages of organizational development and often lack basic capabilities that are needed to operate, such as identifying opportunities and applying for funding, meeting the standard financial and audit requirements of funders, developing management plans, and designing programs beyond short-term projects or events. Most Lao citizens are unaware that associations exist, and much less what role they can or do play.

The sector's activities continue to be extensively modest and the under tight scrutiny and control of the government. NPAs remain largely focused on service delivery provision to address the nation's development needs, seldom pursue any type of advocacy or activism, and do not closely engage in coalitions with foreign activist networks; all these activities would not be tolerated by the Lao government. There is extreme sensitivity around phrases such as human rights, advocacy, campaigns, and other ideas that can be perceived as placing citizens against the government or its policies. So as not to run afoul of the government, NPAs do not seek reform overtly, engage in any protests, or make "demands," and any form of political dissent, anti-hydropower sentiment, and human and property rights issues are generally given a wide berth. Lao CSO leaders are acutely aware of the sensitivity toward these issues and are accustomed to working within the implicit government-sanctioned boundaries and, if they are working with INGO partners or Western donors, navigating between partner/donor expectations and political limitations. Self-censorship is followed by the Lao NPAs and international partners to avoid drawing negative government attention or repercussions. Due to these restrictions, there are proponents for moving some of the focus on developing civil society organizations to those in rural areas. In rural areas, the organizations often face less government scrutiny, and, correspondingly, can function more freely, however, they are nascent and often dependent on one or two people. Therefore, it is unlikely that they will develop into organizations of large impact in the near future. Although they undoubtedly have a positive effect on their respective villages and communities, it would be unrealistic to view them as broad instruments of social change.

"Where is Sombath?"[3]

Perhaps the most significant stifling of Lao civil society in recent years was the disappearance of a prominent Lao NPA leader, which is widely believed to be an act of the GOL. The disappearance in 2012 of the internationally acclaimed civil society leader Sombath Somphone continues to shadow all CSO activity. The sentiment of many Lao people is that, "if this could happen to someone as well known as Sombath, then it could easily happen to me."[4] Some organizations curtailed their activities and some NPA leaders left the country for a period after the disappearance.

Somphone is the founder and director of the Participatory Development Training Center (PADETC), a civil society organization based in Vientiane that focuses on ecologically sustainable development, self-reliance, and youth training, particularly amongst the rural poor. In 2005, he won the Ramon Magsaysay Award for Community Leadership, often called the Nobel Peace Prize of Asia. He retired from his position as PADETC Director in June 2012 to spend time with his family, meditate, and write. At that time, he had just conducted a survey amongst rural populations to measure "happiness" and "sufferings" throughout Laos's provinces with support from the United Nations Development Programme (UNDP) and cooperation from the local authorities and Lao mass organizations. The findings of this consultation were that Lao people wanted good governance, sustainable livelihood and social well-being, good health and adequate education, and protection of natural resources, and that the government was not adequately providing for or safeguarding these areas (Pham and Somphone 2012). This was a bold statement to make to the government, and particularly because the UNDP recommended that the GOL consider this a statement from the people.[5]

New Mandala, www.newmandala.org/category/laos/.
Hosted by ANU, New Mandala provides information especially devoted to politics and society in Southeast Asia.

Sombath Somphone, www.sombath.org.
A site dedicated to raising awareness about the work and disappearance of Sombath Somphone, an internationally acclaimed community development worker in Laos.

Google Group, LaoFAB.org.
A forum focused on sharing information related to farming, agriculture, and business in Laos.

Vientiane Times, www.vientianetimes.com.
Site of the most widely-read English language daily newspaper in Laos.

References

APHR (ASEAN Parliamentarians for Human Rights). 2016. Tackle Human Rights Abuses in Laos. Electronic document, http://aseanmp.org/2016/08/31/tackle-human-rights-abuses-laos/, accessed January 10, 2016.

Delnoye, Rik. 2010. Survey on Civil Society Development in the Lao PDR: Current Practices and Potential for Future Growth. *Working Paper Series*. Vientiane: Swiss Agency for Development and Cooperation.

Diamond, Larry. 1994. Rethinking Civil Society: Toward Democratic Consolidation. *Journal of Democracy* 5(3): 4–17.

Enfield, N. J. 2010. Language and Culture in Laos: An Agenda for Research. *The Journal of Lao Studies* 1(1): 48–54.

Evans, Grant. 1988. *The Politics of Ritual and Remembrance: Laos Since 1975*. Honolulu, HI: University of Hawai'i Press.

Evans, Grant. 2002. *A Short History of Laos: The Land In between*. Crows Nest, NSW: Allen & Unwin.

Kunze, Gretchen. 2010. New Decree Opens Way for Civil Society in Laos. The Asia Foundation. In *Asia: Weekly Insights and Analysis*. Electronic document, http://asiafoundation.org/2010/06/02/new-decree-opens-way-for-civil-society-in-laos/, accessed January 3, 2017.

Kunze, Gretchen. 2012. Nascent Civil Society in Lao PDR in the Shadow of China's Economic Presence. In *Global Civil Society: Shifting Powers in a Shifting World*. Heidi Moksnes and Mia Melin, eds. Pp. 154–158. Uppsala: Uppsala University.

Lao People's Democratic Republic. 2006. National Socio-Economic Development Plan 2006–2011. Electronic document, http://moe.gov.la/laoesdf/Background_Docs/Eng/NSEDP_Eng.pdf, accessed September 10, 2016.

Lao People's Democratic Republic. 2009. Guidelines and Manual on Decree on Associations. Vientiane, December 2009.

Phouthonesy, Ekaphone. 2010. China Surpasses Thailand as Biggest Investor in Laos. *Vientiane Times*, July 16.

Pholsena, Vatthana. 2006. *Postwar Laos: The Politics of Culture, History, and Identity*. Ithaca, NY: Cornell University Press.

Pham, Minh H., and Sombath Somphone. 2012. Draft Article: Listening to the People's Voice. Electronic document, www.sombath.org/en/who-is-sombath/sombaths-work/, accessed November 7, 2016.

Stuart-Fox, Martin. 1986. *Laos: Politics, Economics, and Society*. Boulder, CO: Lynne Rienner Publishers.

Transparency International. 2016. Corruption Perceptions Index 2016. Electronic document, www.transparency.org/news/feature/corruption_perceptions_index_2016, accessed November 7, 2016.

The 9th Asia-Europe People's Forum was held in Vientiane in October 2012, jointly organized by the AEPF's International Organizing Committee and the Lao National Organizing Committee. The latter was co-chaired by Somphone. The forum was, by far, the largest civil society event ever held in Laos, with around 1,000 Lao and international participants. "The Lao People's Vision" was presented and was referenced in the forum's closing declaration. Toward the end of the forum, security officials confiscated printed copies of the document that were to be distributed to participants, and plain-clothed security officials reportedly monitored and occasionally harassed some participants throughout the event.

Two months later, in December 2012, while driving home one evening along a busy street in Vientiane, Somphone's car was flagged over at a police kiosk. Footage from a CCTV traffic camera shows Somphone being escorted out of his car and into another vehicle. A short time later, unidentified men were observed driving Somphone and his car away.[6] Despite international condemnation, high-level inquiries, and bilateral offers of investigative assistance, the GOL reports that no progress has been made on identifying the people or cars in the video and Lao authorities continue to deny any involvement or knowledge. The campaign to uncover what happened to Somphone continues largely outside of Laos. Foreign embassies and multilateral organizations within the country do raise the issue regularly, but the civil society community within the country is cognizant of the risk of getting too publicly involved.

China's growing economic presence

For a complete understanding of the development and future prospects of civil society in Laos, a political economic examination of the international environment and its effects on the nation's economic development is important. The Lao economy is growing, and this development is squarely based on foreign direct investment, and often the investment in the exploitation of natural resources. Those who are negatively and directly affected by these projects, whether the dams or rubber plantations, have little or no say in their forced relocation, seized land, and the negative effects on their livelihoods, ranging from concerns over converting family rice fields into the production of commodity crops, to altered water quality or quantity that affects fish yields. In other countries, civil society groups or movements are often a means to provide input to the government policy or to seek recourse. At the same time, the main investor in the country and driving force of these industries is China, followed by Vietnam and Thailand; all countries with their own challenging records of human rights and civic participation. While Western governments and the UN can condemn particular actions of the Lao government, they do not provide either the foreign investment or the levels of aid that these three neighbors do, and, therefore, complying with their message holds less sway than continued economic growth. Furthermore, the aid from these neighbors does not come with conditionalities such as human rights or environmental standards.

Laos remains amongst the poorest countries in ASEAN, but in recent years, it has seen steady economic growth and increasing foreign direct investment. By December 2010, China surpassed Thailand as the single biggest investor in Laos. In 2010, the Lao Ministry of Planning and Investment reported that the Chinese investment from the years 2000 to 2010 reached about US$2.9 billion. Thailand has a total investment over the same period of about US$2.6 billion, and the third highest investment is by Vietnam, with a total of about US$2.2 billion. But what is more striking is the speed of the recent investment. In the first six months of 2010, Thai companies invested in four projects worth US$37 million. Chinese companies invested in sixteen projects amounting to US$344 million (Phoutonesy 2010). As for Chinese development aid, the figures are confidential and, at any rate, not clearly delineated from investment.

When Western donors or multilateral organizations that espouse human rights, civic participation, and civil society were the biggest contributors to Laos' international funding, they had more leverage to insist on certain levels of democratic norms. Access to Chinese investment (and aid), however, makes it possible for the Lao government to achieve economic growth and gain development resources without the complications of dealing with the conditions imposed by Western companies and aid agencies that might create, directly or indirectly, a more enabling environment for the development of civil society organizations.

Prospects for Lao civil society: what's to come next?

The one-party system in Laos is firmly in place and the LPRP faces no apparent internal or external threats. China's FDI in Laos will continue to be the most significant source of economic growth and it is benefitting those in power in Laos, and China's goals are furthered by minimizing citizen protest or advocacy. These factors point to a continuation of the status quo in Laos with respect to the development of civil society.

The motivation to permit some formal civil society continues to exist for the GOL in certain aspects such as assistance in meeting its development goals, building international legitimacy with Western democracies, and appearances of modernity and adherence to global norms. There are stronger motivations, however, for keeping it under tight control in order that civil society does not interfere with the state's stability or economic goals. As long as the LPRP continues to remain in power and view civil society as a threat to this power, the state will continue its heavy-handed approach toward civil society in the country.

In 2016, the Ministry of Foreign Affairs of the GOL stated that it will not approve any new Memoranda of Understanding with INGOs in Laos for projects that include working with NPAs.[7] The official explanation is that while INGOs and NPAs must provide financial reports to the government, there is no clear standardized system currently in place for NPAs to report the funds they receive from foreign sources and, thus, there is a risk of those funds being either miscounted or double counted. INGOs, therefore, have been informed that they should wait to pursue partnerships with NPAs until the amended Overseas Development Assistance Decree (Decree 075) is formally approved, which is scheduled for late 2016.[8] The Ministry of Foreign Affairs has not stated that it will resume approving MOUs that include partnerships with NPAs at that time, thus, for now, this freeze is in place and it is effectively halting new partnerships between INGOs and Lao NPAs. In doing so, it is also cutting off one of the primary means of funding for Lao NPAs.

Larry Diamond (1994) writes that pluralism, diversity, and partialness are distinguishing characteristics of civil society. In the context of Laos, where harmony, unity, and cohesion are amongst the highest ideals, this definition does not indicate much possibility for the development of Lao civil society (Kunze 2012). Rather than following the definitions prevalent in past literature, it appears more appropriate to consider this new and limited civil society as following a different path that is appropriate for the circumstances of Laos and a single-party state.

There is no indication that either the government or its international ties will change significantly in the near future, and, therefore, there are no strong indicators that formal civil society in Laos will change. The form of civil society that is permitted will likely continue to focus on service delivery provision and address the nation's development needs in line with the state's goals.

For the sector's survival, the development process of civil society will not be in opposition with the state, but it will progress in harmony with the state's interests and often in partnership with the state. If there is emerging space for civil society in Lao PDR, the process of increasing

the capacity and legal standing of civil society organizations will need to be carefully calibrated with building trust and understanding between the organizations, the government, and the larger society. Organizations that can successfully navigate effective ways to engage with the government in a positive and mutually supportive manner will be the ones to lead the way for other organizations to develop in the future.

The modest civil society sector in Laos will probably not adopt the Western role of advocacy, making demands, or building coalitions with foreign activist organizations. If the result, however, establishes a new route for opening paths of communication between citizens and government, more and better services for those who need them, and a freer flow of information and improved education, then this must not be considered as a failed project, even though it does not fit Western norms.

Notes

1 While the language is consistent with modern day constitutions, the final clause, "not contrary to the laws" refers to the Lao penal code, which can have a broad application, such as its prohibition of "undermining … the culture and society of Lao People's Democratic Republic" (Article 51) or "conducting propaganda activities against and slandering the Lao People's Democratic Republic" (Article 59).

2 Confirmed by the author's observation.

3 This is a reference to the slogan activists frequently use in their signs and banners at Lao embassies around the world. See www.sombath.org (accessed September 20, 2016) for further information.

4 Based on the author's conversation with a civil society leader, January 2013.

5 The text of the draft article states, "The people have spoken." The article is available in draft form, but was never published due to a request by Pham (Pham and Somphone 2012).

6 Sombath Somphone's wife filmed the video that she was shown by the police on her phone. It is now widely available on YouTube.com. This link is to the coverage of the story that includes the video being shown on Thai public television: www.youtube.com/watch?v=IKJEka6sov0 (accessed September 25, 2016).

7 Memoranda of Understanding, or MOUs, are legally required for INGOs to operate in Laos. The process of obtaining an MOU can be onerous and could take months or even years if the program is found to be questionable by the government. They must be in agreement with a relevant ministry (for example, the Ministry of Health for health-related programs) and approved by the Ministry of Foreign Affairs.

8 Interview with INGO staff in Laos, September 2016.

Suggested readings

Belloni, Roberto. 2014. Building Civil Society in Lao PDR: The Decree on Associations. *Development in Practice* 24(3): 353–365.

Evans, Grant. 1988. *The Politics of Ritual and Remembrance: Laos Since 1975*. Honolulu, HI: University of Hawai'i Press.

Evans, Grant. 2002. *A Short History of Laos: The Land In Between*. Crows Nest, NSW: Allen & Unwin.

Pholsena, Vatthana. 2006. *Postwar Laos: The Politics of Culture, History, and Identity*. Ithaca, NY: Cornell University Press.

Scott, James C. 2009. *The Art of Not Being Governed: An Anarchist History of Upland Southeast Asia*. New Haven, CT: Yale University Press.

Stuart-Fox, Martin. 1986. *Laos: Politics, Economics, and Society*. Boulder, CO: Lynne Rienner Publishers.

Websites

Learning House for Development, www.lao-cso-network.org.
A central network for civil society organizations in Laos, focusing on non-profit organizations working to alleviate poverty and aid disadvantaged communities.

14

THAILAND

Bencharat Sae Chua

Thai civil society at a crossroad

Since the start of its democratization process in the 1990s, Thailand has been known for its vibrant civil society, which constantly strives to expand the democratic space. The political conflicts of the last decade, however, have revealed a contentious side of Thai civil society, and they raise the question of the civil society's contribution to the development of democracy. In the movements aiming to overthrow the allegedly corrupt regime of former Prime Minister Thaksin Shinawatra, a number of Thai civil society actors called for the rejection of representative democracy and a turn toward military intervention and rule by seemingly morally superior people. This rejection of majority rule leads to the need to review both the concepts and practices of civil society and democracy in Thailand.

As part of the attempts to revisit the role and nature of civil society in Thailand, this chapter analyzes the development of Thai civil society in the context of the country's democratization. The chapter traces two key ideas of civil society operating in the Thai context, namely, the liberal conception of civil society as a space between the state and individuals working for the rights and freedoms of the people and the civic republicanism view focusing on spaces for the engagement and deliberation of active citizens. By showing how the supposedly independent civil society has evolved in close connection with the state, both in terms of its operations and in terms of ideology, the chapter revisits the role of Thai civil society in contemporary democratic consolidation. The first part of this chapter discusses the dynamics of democratization and the growth of civil society in Thailand since the 1970s. The second part revisits the understanding of civil society in the context of contemporary political conflicts and analyzes the current debates on civil society and democracy. The chapter ends by identifying the challenges faced by civil society during this return to authoritarian government.

Understanding Thai civil society in the context of democratization

The most common terms referring to civil society in Thai are *pracha sangkhom* and *pracha khom*. While they are very similar and sometimes used interchangeably, the two terms connote different understandings of civil society and its relationship with the state. The first term *pracha sangkhom* (*pracha*: people; *sangkom*: society) is usually used to refer to the civil society sector, in general, that operates outside the state and market. The term covers a range of organizational types from non-governmental organizations (NGOs) and community-based organizations (CBOs) to social movements. It also implies the liberal view of civil society, seeing it as being independent from the state with the roles of monitoring, questioning, and challenging the state to secure the people's interests. The latter term *pracha khom* (community of people) is formally recognized in the Thai state administrative terminology. It refers to the organized space of political deliberation and participation, especially in local administration. *Pracha khom*, unlike *pracha sangkhom*, does not imply a contentious relationship with the state. Instead, since the mid-1990s, the term has been used for collaborative forums, including state-organized ones, where the civil society sector could discuss and contribute to policy-making on different issues.

What is important to note here is that the civil society organizations operating under both concepts overlapped and shared more or less the same ground of development during the political liberalization of the late 1980s and the 1990s. Their contributions to grass-roots empowerment and democracy cannot be ignored. However, they have different implications for understanding civil society's role in Thai democratization, as revealed by the recent political conflicts. Through the discussion of political development, this section reviews how the changing democratic landscape has shaped the development of the concept and practice of civil society, and vice versa. It also introduces key civil society actors, in particular, NGOs and grass-roots social movements.

Opening the political space and the growth of civil society: cooperation and contention

During the first five decades after the Revolution of 1932, which transformed Thailand from an absolute monarchy to a constitutional democracy, the country was under military rule most of the time. Under such circumstances, the state was not open to people's claim-making. There was no development of large-scale social movements or civil society organizations to actively monitor or challenge the state. During the late 1950s and early 1970s, the situation got worse due to the active insurgency of the Communist Party of Thailand (CPT) and the expansion of the state's anti-communist responses. The urban opposition, left-wing intellectuals and activists, who were accused of being communists, often faced violent repression by the state. The regime's suppression forced many left-wing intellectuals and writers into exile or practicing self-censorship (Prajak 2005: 101).[1]

With a political atmosphere that did not allow public contention with the state, civil society organizations before the 1970s were limited to mainly philanthropic organizations acting as service providers, bringing resources to areas unfulfilled by the state (Shigetomi 2004: 46). Some oppositional groups and movements did emerge in the 1960s, but they tended to limit their protest tactics to peaceful, non-confrontational ones. This began to change, however, when the ongoing perceived threat of communism and economic inflation in the early 1970s led several sections of the public to question the government's promised political stability and economic development. Benedict Anderson (1977: 17) points out that the expansion of secondary and university education in the 1960s led to growing expectations of improved status in the society, whose failure to materialize further fueled the people's dissatisfaction with the government. The student protests of 1973 were evidence of this growing disaffection toward dictatorial rule and the influence of intellectuals exposed to discussions of the New Left and student power (Prajak 2005: 284–319).

People's dissatisfaction with the government and the lack of unity within the government itself led to a "snowballing mass demonstration," culminating in the October 1973 demonstrations demanding the adoption of a constitution (Anderson 1977: 17). These demonstrations, which were followed by a clash between the students and police on October 14, ended with the resignation of Prime Minister General Thanom Kittikachorn. A new government was then formed, marking the end of more than a decade of authoritarian military rule and the transition to a more democratic regime—though a brief one.

Democracy and political activity flourished in Thailand during the three years after October 14, 1973, before being crushed by the violent suppression of student protests on October 6, 1976. During these three years, university students were engaged in democracy promotion activities in rural areas, where they learned about the problems and hardships of these communities. Consequently, many students started working to improve rural livelihoods (Prudhisan and Maneerat 1997: 198). These student activists formed a close alliance with peasant/farmer organizations, which also became more active during the brief democratic period of 1973–1976. The first large-scale peasant organization in Thailand, the Farmers' Federation of Thailand (FFT), was formed in November 1974 in this relatively open environment. While there had been peasant rebellions up until the late 1950s, they were mainly "reactions against the process of integration and extension of [the] central power of Bangkok over the outer territories" (Kanoksak 1984: 13) and focused on issues pertaining to local identity and traditions. With the formation of the FFT, peasants and landless farmers started to change their tactics and organized marches, rallies, and demonstrations to demand governmental intervention to halt the decline in prices of agricultural products and assist in the problems of land rent (Luther 1978). By mid-1975, about 1,500,000 families had become members of the FFT (Kanoksak 1983: 26) despite the fact that many peasant leaders faced a violent backlash from the state and right-wing groups (see Haberkorn 2011; Luther 1978). Although the FFT stopped its operations after a few years, its activists and ideas continued to be influential in the movements that evolved later.

The violent suppression of the student demonstration on October 6, 1976, subsequent *coup d'état*, and exercise of strong state control in the name of suppressing the communists interrupted the growing civil society activities for another few years. The transition to democracy gradually progressed in the early 1980s with the weakening of the CPT and the change from a military government to one with a formal parliamentary structure, while other forms of popular political participation in the democratic system were still limited. This change in political structures created opportunities for civil society to increase its interaction with the state. In addition to the development of student activism and peasant mobilization, the open political atmosphere enabled the vigorous development of NGOs, which had slowly emerged as philanthropic organizations during the 1960s.

The lessening of the repressive nature of the regime and the recognition of formal democracy in the 1980s made the regime relatively more open for civil society to operate. This led to an increasing number of civil society organizations, in particular, NGOs and grass-roots social movement organizations. The NGOs were joined by social activists who had left the CPT and saw the NGOs as another means to exercise their sense of social commitment. In addition, a number of university graduates whose employment opportunities were limited by the economic problems of the time opted to join the NGOs (Quinn 1997). This development was facilitated by the expansion of international NGO activities in Thailand during the end of the 1970s and early 1980s, which partly aimed to provide assistance to Indo-Chinese refugees (Aphichat 2004: 156) and later expanded to rural development and provided funding to local NGOs. At the time, there was also an expansion of religious organizations, such as the Catholic Council of Thailand, whose mandate was partly rural development work. Altogether, these actors gradually formed a civil society that both cooperated with and challenged the state's development schemes.

This was also the period when the ideology of the NGOs was formed. While part of this ideology is rooted in anti-state ideas, the shared rural poverty work created more cooperation between the government and NGOs (Shigetomi 2004: 48) with a lasting effect on the nature of Thai civil society. On the one hand, the NGOs were actively engaged in rural grass-roots mobilization against the impacts of industrial and export-led development on rural livelihoods and natural resources (Kasian 2004; Prapart 1998). These grass-roots struggles were mainly active at the local level and received support from the NGOs who adopted community-centered and community empowerment approaches in their work and started building networks with potential allies in academia and the media in their policy advocacy (Prudhisan and Maneerat 1997: 201–203). Apart from the NGOs, local struggles during this period started to take more direct action against the state and led to the formation of more sustained social movements. These local-issues-based struggles were extended to a nationwide network for policy changes later, in the 1990s, when the political system accommodated more claims from actors outside the parliamentary system.

On the other hand, the NGOs were welcomed to work with the state by participating in development policy-making. Although the NGOs had started questioning the state on the impacts of development, their relationship with the state was not necessarily hostile. The National Economic and Social Development Board (NESDB) reached out to NGOs during the implementation of the fifth National Economic and Social Development Plan (1982–1986), which focused on community development. The NESDB organized several meetings on government and NGO cooperation (Shigetomi 2004: 48) and helped to found an NGO Coordinating Committee (NGO-Cord) by the end of 1985.[2]

Both approaches transformed the nature of NGOs from being service providers during the 1950s–1960s to becoming more politically engaged, although with different forms and levels of relationship with the state. The proliferation of the NGOs in the late 1970s and 1980s included both moderates and radical activists or former left activists. As Somchai Phatharathananunth (2006) observed, the inclusion of former leftist activists in NGOs since the mid-1980s led to the increased adoption of political mobilization strategies to empower affected villagers to negotiate with either the state or corporate interests. Other development NGOs continued to follow a non-political involvement strategy from the suppressive 1970s onward and concentrated on micro-issues like alternative livelihoods. These two approaches, adoption of political mobilization and non-political involvement strategies, often labeled as "cold" and "hot" issues, respectively, continue to be the two major streams of NGO activities even today. What they had in common were their doubts about the state-dominated development discourse and exploitation by businessmen. They also more or less share the community culture approach to development, which values the community's morality in self-management and sustainable environmental exploitation.

Such an approach manifests in how the emerging social movements, with support from NGOs, develop their claim-making strategies. Significantly, it also shapes how the civil society views politics, as discussed further below.

People's politics

The political reform of the 1990s marked a significant point in the development of democracy and growth of civil society, which by then included grass-roots social movements. After another violent crackdown against anti-military junta demonstrations in May 1992,[3] the urban middle-class activists launched efforts to liberalize the Thai state and entrench a parliamentary system. This liberal reform culminated in the drafting of the so-called People's Constitution in 1997.

With inputs from civil society and social movements,[4] the Constitution guaranteed a range of political and social rights and introduced several new rights, such as community rights to natural resource management. The Constitution also established some monitoring institutions, the National Human Rights Commission and Administrative Court, in particular, which became the tools of civil society for claims-making with respect to rights, despite the institutions' primary aim of limiting the power of politicians. They provided opportunities for civil society organizations and social movements to submit complaints and petitions for remedies and bring their causes to public attention. As such, civil society organizations and social movements could use both the formal political institutions and public spaces to campaign for their causes.

The political reform ran in parallel with growing rural mobilization, especially of those affected by state development schemes. Peasants and local communities impacted by these changes, together with their intellectual allies and NGOs, grasped the expanding political opportunities in the more relaxed political environment to stage protests and demand governmental intervention to defend their livelihoods. The repertoire of protests, which were formerly highly localized and involved mainly negotiations with local officials during the 1980s (Baker 2000: 13), was expanded to a national network and often included policy advocacy. The formation of the Assembly of the Poor in 1995 as a national network of movements and groups affected by government policies, including, for example, those on land and forests, mega-development projects, labor rights, and occupational health and housing rights, reflected this development (for details on the Assembly of the Poor, see Missingham 2003; Prapart 1998).[5] Aside from this nationwide network, local struggles pertaining to the environment and right to manage natural resources were also active, mostly in connection with the wider networks.

With the growth of people's politics, collaboration between NGOs and the state continued to the extent of the institutionalization of civil society engagement. In the late 1990s, international donor NGOs started to announce their withdrawal of support from Thailand (Gawin 2004: 76) due partly to the rapid economic development of the country and the increasing confrontation between social movements and the state. In the northeast, in particular, Somchai (2006: 79) documents that after the successful protest against the land redistribution scheme, which was implemented in a violent manner in the early 1990s,[6] foreign donors cut back their support for the seemingly aggressive political mobilization activities of the NGOs in this region. Similar to the situation in the 1980s, the need to avoid confrontation with the state forced NGOs to focus on non-political issues and limit their involvement in political campaigns.

More domestic support was offered by government agencies during this period. Examples include the Ministry of Public Health and its health-related NGO allies, and the Ministry of Science, Technology and Environment, which partnered with registered NGOs as required by the 1992 Enhancement and Conservation of National Environmental Quality Act. Other state-led or semi-state development organizations, some of which were formed as the result of civil society advocacy, also have mechanisms to work with NGOs or have key NGO activists joining them. Some examples are the Social Investment Fund, which is the loan that the Thai government got from World Bank after the 1997 economic crisis for distribution amongst communities as part of an attempt to boost the economy; the Community Organizations Development Institute (CODI), which provides the Urban Community Development Fund for the urban poor; and the Thai Health Promotion Foundation, which funds the NGOs and local initiatives that adopt a holistic health promotion approach.

While street activism and social movements become major forms of the civil society's interaction with the state, civil society participation is institutionalized in the form of *pracha khom*. As mentioned earlier, the Thai state invited civil society participation in the drafting of the fifth National Economic and Social Development Plan (1982–1986). This participation was later institutionalized during the drafting process of the eighth development plan through the formation of a public forum called *pracha khom*. With key civil society figures, including public intellectuals, academics, and leaders of the NGO-CORD, working with the NESDB, *pracha khom* forums at provincial and other levels were formalized for civil society to discuss proposals for the development plan (for more details, see Yutthadanai 2011). Similar forms of *pracha khom* were later organized by other ministries. Most notable is the *pracha khom changwat* (provincial civil community) supported by the Ministry of Interior. Another important *pracha khom* initiative is the *Pracha Khom Sukkaphab* or Health Civil Community, which was promoted through the cooperation between the Ministry of Public Health and Local Development Institute, a leading NGO following a community culture approach. The *Pracha Khom Sukkaphab* offered public forums to deliberate policy recommendations during the drafting process of the National Health Act (2007). The Act also includes provisions for establishing a National Health Assembly as a deliberative public forum to develop health-related policy recommendations. It is important to note here, however, that the participation of *pracha khom* in policy-making, though supported by the state, is informal and marginal (Shigetomi 2002: 138–139).

Despite some questions on whether the relationship between NGOs and local community members or community-based organizations is equal (Elinoff 2014; Missingham 2003), and whether the NGOs' ideology really represents the views and desires of the local communities (Atchara 2011; Vandergeest 1996; Walker 2001; Yukti 2005), the close collaboration between NGOs and grass-roots social movements is undeniable. In fact, NGOs play crucial roles in social movement activities, if not acting as an essential component of the movements themselves. Both become part of the so-called "people's politics" (*kan mueang phak prachachon*), which implies collective action taken by those who lack access to formal political channels and resort to their own initiatives to pressure the state and, therefore, includes both contentious and collaborative relationships with the state. The view that people's politics is non-homogeneous, however, is often understudied despite its significant implications in understanding civil society and democracy. It was only during the political conflicts of the last decade that the issue of civil society's different approach to politics was brought to the surface.

Civil society and democracy: a need to revisit

From November 2013 to May 2014, protesters who called themselves the People's Democratic Reform Committee (PDRC) rallied and later occupied major streets in Bangkok. They were protesting against the government's proposal for an amnesty bill that, if passed, would give amnesty to anyone accused of wrongdoing by the military coup government of September 19, 2006, including ex-Prime Minister Thaksin Shinawatra, who was ousted by the coup and was at the center of the PDRC protest. The bill would also give amnesty to anyone related to the 2010 Red Shirt demonstration, mostly supporters of Thaksin, including both the protesters and the state authorities involved in the violent use of force to crack down on the demonstrations. After the then government led by Yingluck Shinawatra, Thaksin's sister, dissolved the parliament to avoid the escalation of violent conflict, the PDRC extended its goal to call for "reform before election," arguing that only "moral" people should be allowed to govern and that rural Thai people are not capable of choosing moral people via the electoral system. On February 2, 2014, PDRC protesters disrupted the general election, in some cases with the support of election officials who supported the PDRC and boycotted the election. A total of 10,284 polling stations in eighteen provinces were barricaded or forcibly closed down. Further, twenty-eight out of 375 electoral constituencies were not able to hold elections anyway because there were no candidates, as opposition politicians boycotted the election or potential candidates were blocked by protesters from registering themselves as candidates (Matichon 2014).[7] Similar to the People's Alliance for Democracy (PAD), which launched the anti-Thaksin movement in the late 2000s, the PDRC also called for military intervention to break the political deadlock, and their wish came true when the military staged a *coup d'état* on May 22, 2014.

Given Thailand's experiences of democratization, with at least three mass demonstrations against military dictatorship taking place since the 1970s[8] and the growing participation of civil society in politics since the 1980s, such a rejection of democratic principles, the rule of law, and civil society's support for the military may seem surprising. A critical analysis of the inherent beliefs, ideology, and practices of Thai civil society in light of the recent political conflicts sheds some light on this divorce from democratic principles of people's sovereignty, which is discussed in the following section.

Politics of morality versus electoral politics

The middle class' call for the military to intervene in what the class perceived as failed democracy is not a rare occurrence in the last two decades (Kurlantzick 2013: 17–18). What makes Thailand's experience distinct is that civil society's objection to the elected government was not only due to the people's frustration with the failure of representative democracy or simply the co-optation between the elites and civil society actors (Kuhonta and Aim 2014; Thorn 2016) but also because of the underlying values that put perceived morality above basic democratic principles. Thaksin Shinawatra and his authoritative parliamentary regime brought this politics of morality to life.

In early 2001, Thaksin came to power with a majority of votes in the general election and became the first elected prime minister to complete a four-year term. His second term in power, which was also with a majority of votes in the 2005 election, did not last. He was overthrown by a military coup in September 2006, after a few months of demonstrations against him led by the PAD. Thaksin's personal qualities, policies, and mass-based legitimacy created a parliamentary regime with authoritarian tendencies.

Thaksin proposed a range of policies aiming to "eradicate poverty" and ensure the mass endorsement of his government. Some of these policies, for example, the Million Baht Village Fund and One *Tambon* (sub-district) One Product (OTOP) programs, brought rural communities in direct contact with the state and market. Other policies, including the universal healthcare scheme, the housing for the poor project, and universal education, expanded access to welfare rights of the poor. While these policies were arguably designed to attract public support (Pasuk and Baker 2008) and their implementation was far from perfect, they expanded the welfare rights available to a wider public. On the other hand, some of Thaksin's economic liberalization policies caused further encroachment on people's lives, especially in rural areas. Many such policies, for example, the Sea Food Bank, the New Forest Village program, and free trade agreements, had impacts on the natural resources on which rural people depended. The policy to "turn assets into capital," in particular, commercialized natural resources and resulted in increasing conflicts over natural resources between local communities and private businesses.

At the beginning of his regime, Thaksin showed sympathy toward rural social movements, which constituted the backbone of his constituency, and conceded to their demands. However, not long after coming to power, he started to become hostile toward NGOs and people's movements. Thaksin argued that NGOs were no longer needed because the government was already providing welfare and economic development to the poor (Pasuk and Baker 2004: 147). He also adopted a claim made by many different regimes that NGOs were the "poverty sales agents," who work merely to attract international financial support and launched an audit into the financial records of twenty leading Thai NGO workers (Pasuk and Baker 2004: 144–145). In addition, his government violently cracked down on some social movement demonstrations.

Thaksin not only confronted civil society but also rose to power in conflict with the old ruling elites, which led to protracted political conflicts from 2005 onward. In 2006, the PAD was formed as a national network of the movement against Thaksin. Contrary to previous mass demonstrations for democracy, the PAD made the undemocratic demand for the king to appoint a prime minister to replace Thaksin and also pressured for military intervention to oust the regime. The PAD was also joined in their demands by many leading civil society organizations, NGOs, and grass-roots social movements, who felt that Thaksin was a threat to the communities they were working with,[9] and, therefore, not moral enough to rule.

In September 2006, a military *coup d'état* overthrew the Thaksin government. Labeled "the coup for the Monarchy" (Kasian 2007), its leaders claimed a legitimate role in protecting the monarchy, perceiving it as being under threat from Thaksin. What followed the 2006 coup was a series of undemocratic removals of elected Thaksin-allied governments and mass anti-Thaksin demonstrations. As mentioned above, in late 2013, another mass demonstration led by the PDRC was mobilized against the Yingluck Shinawatra government. Once again, civil society's role as a democratic force was brought into question when it rejected representative democracy and called again for military intervention.

As Thongchai Winichakul (2008) shows, the PAD campaign and its support from the middle class (and civil society organizations) reflect one of the dominant discourses in Thai politics since the 1980s, namely, that of "clean politics," which portrayed politicians as playing "money politics." In line with the community culture approach adopted by most NGOs that resent modern capitalist life, the clean politics discourse rejected electoral democracy as a Western idea that lacks morality. Politics is seen as a corrupted space where immoral politicians seek personal gain. Kevin Hewison summarizes, "[P]oliticians were untrustworthy; voters are bought, duped or ignorant; and so electoral politics is the core of the corruption problem" (2015: 58). The discourse of dirty politics implies that democracy is unfit for Thai Buddhist communities, which should be best governed by morally superior leaders. The PAD's discourse on corruption led to the campaign for "righteousness" as it promoted the idea of having "good people" to rule and maintained that the majority of the people are incapable of choosing a good person (Aim 2014: 533). In a similar way, the PDRC proposed a People's Council, which was a body of selected professional representatives and PDRC-nominated people to act as a legislative body and select a "decent person" as an interim prime minister (Bangkok Post 2013). The council would also lead political reform and design a new electoral system. This type of moral value allows a section of civil society and the conservative ruling elites to connect and share the same political strategy (Thorn 2016: 530).

Apart from doubts about the community culture approach that became trapped in the politics of morality, the way NGOs operate in close connection with the state also needs to be re-examined. Despite their insistence on being independent from government funding, it is arguable that the NGO ideology is to a degree shared by the state and NGOs, therefore, are not independent ideologically. As shown throughout this chapter, the relationship between NGOs and the state is closer than one might expect. Some civil society organizations not only receive financial support from the government but also are institutionalized within the state structure without a substantive role or influence beyond marginal contributions. Atchara Rakyutitham, in her study on the relationship between NGOs and the state, argues that the shared idea of "people empowerment" is in fact the promotion of self-dependence to the extent that the poor accept their status without questioning the structural factors underlying poverty (2014: 156).

This, Atchara contends, "depoliticizes" development problems and people participation. Similarly, Eli Elinoff argues, in a study on the relationship between the CODI, NGOs, and the urban poor, that both the CODI and NGOs share the "project of governmentality" and try to govern the conduct of the urban poor in the name of their empowerment (2014: 359–360).

Even after another military coup in May 2014 and amid the junta's claim to be moral ruler, these questions and debates on the nature of Thai civil society continue. Some key civil society activists have joined the junta's "political reform" process and mechanisms, seeing this as a chance to get rid of immoral politics. Under the restricted political space allowed by the military regime and the ongoing contention over the meaning of democracy, the role of civil society in democratization needs to be re-examined now than ever before.

Looking ahead: the future of Thai civil society

The political conflicts that centered on the debate on politics and morality have revealed new faces of Thai civil society. Not only are the existing NGOs and social movements being questioned and re-examined for their role in promoting (or undermining) democracy but also a need is perceived to study the strategies and new forms of political expression and participation under this authoritarian regime.

The political movements of the last decade have brought more people into civil society activities. The PAD, PDRC, and Red Shirts have been able to mobilize the masses in large numbers, which has not been experienced in Thai politics for at least three decades. Civil society actors then expanded from the NGOs and grass-roots social movements to include more of the middle class and younger urban population on one side and the rural masses on the other. These political movements also actively use mass media and new methods of mobilization. Despite some challenges and controversy over their role in democracy and the use of violent tactics, it will be interesting to observe how civic engagement is maintained and strengthened in the future.

For the moment, what is at stake is the practice of civil society under the repressive regime led by the National Council for Peace and Order (NCPO), which came to power through a *coup d'état* on May 23, 2014. While the NCPO has been able to ensure consent to its rule from much of the middle class and civil society, the junta also exercises repressive power to control political stability. Unlike the period after the September 2006 coup, when the military-led government did not strictly control the opposition, the NCPO suppresses any dissident voice. Throughout its time in power, the junta has used intimidation, surveillance, legal control, and even force to prevent the rise of the opposition and contain public protest. As reported by iLaw, an NGO monitoring political rights after the coup, at least 1,319 people were summoned by the military or visited by soldiers (as of May 2017); this number also includes those with whom the military arranged informal meetings (iLaw 2017). The report on arrests and intimidation two years after the coup shows that 527 people have been arrested on political grounds. Of these, 225 people were arrested for peaceful association (iLaw 2016: 13). Symbolic resistance to the junta, which is the most viable method of opposition as it allows participants to disperse quickly and safely, is also strictly controlled.

Besides the authoritarian and coercive military rule, a political culture that is not conducive to democracy is another key challenge that will define its future. As shown by the evolution of civil society in Thailand, the development of democracy and that of civil society is interrelated. It is only by keeping the debates and practices on civil society and democracy alive that meaningful change will occur.

Notes

1 In Thailand, individuals are addressed and recognized using their first name. I have followed this convention when referring to individuals with Thai names in the text and in preparing the bibliography.
2 NGO-CORD, with no direct link to any government agency currently, still acts as the coordinating body of development NGOs throughout the country.
3 The military staged a *coup d'état* in February 1991.
4 For the experience of the Women and Constitution Network in the drafting process, see, for example, Ticha (2002).
5 See also the movement of the Small Scale Farmer Assembly of Isan (northeast), which preceded the Assembly of the Poor, in Somchai (2006).
6 For details regarding the struggles against the land allocations for the poor living under the degraded reserved forests scheme or *Khor Jor Kor*, see Pye (2005).
7 For accounts of the violence perpetrated during the anti-election movement in 2014 and the movement's exploitation of the democracy discourse, see Prajak (2016). The Constitutional Court later nullified the election on the grounds that, given that twenty-eight constituencies had no candidate, the general election could not be held on the same day throughout the country as required by the Constitution.
8 Namely, in October 1973, October 1976, and May 1992.
9 For further discussion on the anti-Thaksin movement's three discourses on nationalism, communitarianism, and anti-money politics, see Kengkij and Hewison (2009: 458–462).

Suggested readings

Connors, Michael Kelly. 2003. *Democracy and National Identity in Thailand*. New York: Routledge.
Veerayooth Kanchoochat, and Kevin Hewison. 2016. Understanding Thailand's Politics (Special Issue). *Journal of Contemporary Asia* 46(3).
Shigetomi, Shinichi. 2002. Thailand: A Crossing of Parallel Relationship. In *The State and NGOs: Perspective from Asia*. Shinichi Shigetomi, ed. Pp. 125–144. Singapore: Institute of Southeast Asia Studies.
Somchai Phatharathananunth. 2006. *Civil Society and Democratization: Social Movements in Northeast Thailand*. Copenhagen: Marston.

References

Aim Sinpeng. 2014. Corruption, Morality, and the Politics of Reform in Thailand. *Asian Politics & Polity* 6(4): 523–538.
Anderson, Benedict. 1977. Withdrawal Symptoms: Social and Cultural Aspects of the October 6, 1976 Coup in Siam. *Bulletin of Concerned Asian Scholars* 9(3): 13–18.
Aphichat Thongyou. 2004. Thai NGOs and Rural Development: Formation, Growth, and Branching Out. In *The NGO Way: Perspectives and Experiences from Thailand*. Shinichi Shigetomi, Kasian Techapira, and Aphichat Thnogyou, eds. Pp. 2–37. Chiba: Institute of Developing Economies.
Atchara Rakyutitham. 2004. Uppatham krobyam rue ruammue? En-gee-o nai prathet thai kab sammakngan kongtun sanabsanun kan sangserm sukaphab (sor sor sor) [Patronage, Domination of Cooperation? Thai NGOs and the Health Promotion Office]. *Fah Daew Kan* [*The Same Sky*] 12(2–3): 139–156 (in Thai).
Atchara Rakyutitham. 2011. Kan pattana tangluek krasaelak [Mainstream Alternative Development]. *Varasan Sangkhom Wittaya Manusaya Wittaya* [*Journal of Social Sciences and Anthropology*] 30(2): 13–43 (in Thai).
Baker, Chris. 2000. Thailand's Assembly of the Poor: Background, Drama, Reaction. *South East Asia Research* 8(1): 5–29.
Bangkok Post. 2013. Suthep Details Council Goals. *Bangkok Post*, December 4, 1.
Elinoff, Eli. 2014. Unmaking Civil Society: Activist Schisms and Autonomous Politics in Thailand. *Contemporary Southeast Asia* 6(3): 356–85.
Gawin Chutima. 2004. Funding for NGOs in Thailand: The Politics of Money in the Nonprofit Section. In *The NGO Way: Perspectives and Experiences from Thailand*. Shinigi Shigetomi, Kasian Techapira, and Aphichat Thongyou, eds. Pp. 61–98. Chiba: Institute of Developing Economies.

Haberkorn, Tyrell. 2011. *Revolution Interrupted: Farmers, Students, Law, and Violence in Northern Thailand.* Madison, WI: University of Wisconsin Press.

Hewison, Kevin. 2015. Thailand: Contestation Over Elections, Sovereignty and Representation. *Representation* 51: 51–62.

iLaw. 2016. *24 Months Under NCPO: When the Military is Above Justice.* Bangkok: ilaw.

iLaw. 2017. Latest Statistic. https://freedom.ilaw.or.th/en/content/latest-statistic, accessed August 6, 2017.

Kanoksak Kaewthep. 1983. *Prawat kan kluenwai kong chowna Thai jak adeet-pajjuban: bot wikroh tang settasat kan muang* [The History of Thai Peasant Movement: The Political Economic Analysis]. Bangkok: Social Sciences Association of Thailand (in Thai).

Kanoksak Kaewthep. 1984. *The Political Economy of Modern Thai Peasant Movement: A Case of the Farmers' Federation of Thailand (FFT), 1973–1976.* Bangkok: Faculty of Economics, Chulalongkorn University.

Kasian Techapira. 2004. The Emergence of NGO Movement in Thailand and the Sarit Regime. In *The NGO Way: Perspectives and Experiences from Thailand.* Shinigi Shigetomi, Kasian Techapira, and Aphichat Thongyou, eds. Pp. 2–37. Chiba: Institute of Developing Economies.

Kasian Techapira. 2007. *Rattaprahan 19 kanyayon por sor 2549 kab kan muang Thai* [The 19 September 2006 coup d'état and the Thai Politics]. Paper presented at the Eight National Political Sciences and Public Administration Academic Conference, Bangkok, December 13–14 (in Thai).

Kengkij Kittirianglap, and Kevin Hewison. 2009. Social Movements and Political Opposition in Contemporary Thailand. *Pacific Review* 22(4): 451–477.

Kuhonta, Erik K., and Aim Sinpeng. 2014. Democratic Regression in Thailand: The Ambivalent Role of Civil Society and Political Institutions. *Contemporary Southeast Asia* 36 (3): 333–355.

Kurlantzick, Joshua. 2013. *Democracy in Retreat: The Revolt of the Middle Class and the Worldwide Decline of Representative Government.* New Haven, CT and London: Yale University Press.

Luther, Hans U. 1978. Peasants and State in Contemporary Thailand. *International Journal of Politics* 8(4): 1–120.

Matichon. 2014. Long mati jud luangtungsom ko ko to lui toa perd ka bud nuai tuk pid [Decided to Run Another Election, Electoral Commission to Continue Voting in the Closed Down Voting Stations]. *Matichon*, 9 February, 1, 11 (in Thai).

Missingham, Bruce D. 2003. *The Assembly of the Poor in Thailand: From Local Struggles to National Protest Movement.* Chiang Mai: Silkworm Books.

Pasuk Phongpaichit, and Chris J. Baker. 2004. *Thaksin: The Business of Politics in Thailand.* Chang Mai: Silkworm Books.

Pasuk Phongpaichit, and Chris J. Baker. 2008. Thaksin's Populism. *Journal of Contemporary Asia* 38(1): 62–83.

Prajak Kongkitari. 2005. *Lae laew kwam kluenwai ko prakod: Kanmuang wattanatam kong naksuksa lae panyachon kon 14 tula* [Here Comes the Movement: Cultural Politics of the Students and Intellectual Before October 14]. Bangkok: Thammasart University Publishing House (in Thai).

Prajak Kongkirati. 2016. Thailand's Failed 2014 Election: The Anti-Election Movement, Violence and Democratic Breakdown. *Journal of Contemporary Asia* 46(3): 467–485.

Prapart Pintobtaeng. 1998. *Street Politics: 99 Days of the Assembly of the Poor and the History of Protest in Thailand.* Bangkok: Textbook Project, Krek University.

Prudhisan Jumbala, and Maneerat Mitprasad. 1997. Non-Governmental Development Organisations: Empowerment and Environment. In *Political Change in Thailand: Democracy and participation.* Kevin J. Hewison, ed. Pp. 195–216. New York: Routledge.

Pye, Oliver. 2005. *Khor Jor Kor: Forest Politics in Thailand.* Bangkok: White Lotus.

Quinn, Rapin. 1997. *NGOs, Peasants and the State: Transformation and Intervention in Rural Thailand, 1970–1990.* PhD thesis, Australian National University, Canberra.

Shigetomi, Shinichi. 2002. Thailand: A Crossing of Parallel Relationship. In *The State and NGOs: Perspective from Asia.* Shinichi Shigetomi, Tejapira Kasian, and Aphichat Thongyou, ed. Pp. 125–144. Singapore: Institute of Southeast Asia Studies.

Shigetomi, Shinichi. 2004. Spaces and Performance of NGOs in Thailand: Their Transformation in the Development Process. In *The NGO Way: Perspectives and Experiences from Thailand.* Shinichi Shigetomi, Tejapira Kasian, and Aphichat Thongyou, eds. Pp. 39–60. Chiba: Institute of Developing Economies.

Somchai Phatharathananunth. 2006. *Civil Society and Democratization: Social Movements in Northeast Thailand.* Copenhagen: Marston.

Thongchai Winichakul. 2008. Toppling Democracy. *Journal of Contemporary Asia* 38(1): 11–37.

Thorn Pitidol. 2016. Redefining Democratic Discourse in Thailand's Civil Society. *Journal of Contemporary Asia* 46(3): 520–537.

Ticha Na Nakorn, Ed. 2002. *phuying kab rattatammanoon: buntuk kan doentang su kwam samerpak* [*Women and Constitution: The Memoir of the Journey Toward Equality*]. Bangkok: Women and Constitution Network (in Thai).

Vandergeest, Peter. 1996. Property Rights in Protected Areas: Obstacles to Community Involvement as a Solution in Thailand. *Environmental Conservation* 23: 259–268.

Walker, Andrew. 2001. The "Karen Consensus": Ethnic Politics and Resource-Use Legitimacy in Northern Thailand. *Asian Ethnicity* 2(2): 145–162.

Yukti Mukdawichit. 2005. *Aan wattatham chumchon: vatasilp lae kanmuang khong wattanatham chumchon* [*Reading Community Culture: Rhetoric and Politics of Ethnography's Community Culture Approach*]. Bangkok: Fa Daew Kan (in Thai).

Yutthadanai Sidala. 2011. Vetee prachakhom paen 8: jud ruem ton suu kabuankan pracha sangkhom [*The Eight Plan Prachakhom: The Starting Point Towards Civil Society*]. In *Chumchon kemkaeng lae pracha sangkhom: 20 pee khong sathaban chumchon thongtin pattana* [*Strong Communities and Civil Society: Twenty Years of the Local Development Institute*]. Poldej Pinprateep, ed. Pp. 108–116. Bangkok: Local Development Institute (in Thai).

15

BURMA (MYANMAR)

Stephen McCarthy

The impact of military rule on civil society

For the past two decades, much of the scholarship and commentary on Southeast Asia's former hard authoritarian state, Burma (Myanmar), has been directed toward analyzing the prospects for the country's democratic transition. The role that civil society can play in that transition, however, requires further analysis. Theoretical generalizations regarding military rule have often been inappropriate and the nature of civil society varies considerably across Southeast Asia (Hughes 2009). Whether authoritarian or democratic, domestic variables such as traditional sources of power, political culture, and the strength of civil society are likely to remain critical to regime outcomes in the Asia-Pacific. This chapter examines the nature of civil society in Burma, a region where military rule had been entrenched, either directly or indirectly, for almost fifty years and where there exists a real potential for future military influence or domination of political society (the institutions of government, political parties, and political processes).

Research on civil society under military rule is limited, partly due to the assumption by many scholars that it does not exist. Yet history shows us that at times of crisis there is often a source of non-government local aid or a resurgence of critical voices that have hitherto been forced underground. The chapter will examine how the military in Burma co-opted civil society—in particular, important elements of traditional civil society that threatened its own position in political society. In the Asia-Pacific region, these elements tend to be associated with traditional, religious, customary, and indigenous sources of power and legitimacy that may lie outside of the normal democratic institutional framework. While civil society is not always directed toward democratic ends, these elements may adopt a democratic posture in opposition to military rule. The chapter will also discuss the steps that the military has taken to safeguard its role in political society during the transition away from direct military rule, and how transitional civil society in Burma today is influenced by the legacies of such rule.

Civil society under military rule

In most definitions, civil society is considered to be the space between the private and the public, the state and the individual, where public organizations or associations, independent of the state and the market, voluntarily conduct their activities toward public ends. Larry Diamond (1999: 222–223) believes that one of these ends is to improve the political system and make it more democratic, and that civil society is different from political society in that it does not seek control over the state as a political party would (Edwards 2004). This Tocquevillean or liberal-democratic (neo-Tocquevillean) view of civil society assumes that the state has a high degree of legitimacy and capacity for governance, and that civil society promotes democracy and builds trust (Tocqueville 1966). The major alternative Gramscian view sees civil society as a contested space where deeply divided factions dispute the legitimacy of the state and compete not only to overturn state policy but also for state power (Gramsci 1971). According to Muthiah Alagappa, although conceptually distinctive, in practice, there is normally much overlap between civil and political societies—the boundary separating them is porous, and in these (authoritarian) situations civil and political societies tend to fuse (2004: 11, 469).

Civil society therefore is not always liberal-democratic, or even civil, and its composition will reflect the nature of the political regime. Moreover, as Jasmin Lorch notes that vertically structured relationships or religious and ethnic cleavages in society as a whole are usually repeated in civil society (2008a: 153). In his study of civil society in Asia, Alagappa distinguished three kinds—legitimate, controlled and communalized, and repressed—and placed countries like Burma in the "repressed" category where the authoritarian state attempts to penetrate, co-opt, control, and manipulate civil society thus forcing independent voices underground (2004: 32). Political and civil societies merge when dissidents take refuge in civil society to survive and to construct counter-narratives and networks that can be deployed when the opportunity arises. One such example would be Aung San Suu Kyi's alliance with the *sangha* (Buddhist monks) in Burma upon her various releases from house arrest in the 1990s and 2000s.

The reasons some scholars claim that Burma was devoid of a civil society under military rule are obvious. Following their coup in 1962, the *Tatmadaw* (Burmese armed forces) clamped down on all social movements and introduced the National Solidarity Act prohibiting any political organizations apart from their own Burma Socialist Program Party (BSPP). This was reiterated in their 1974 constitution, which created the grounds for indirect military rule under the auspices of the BSPP. Under the BSPP, in David Steinberg's (1997) opinion, civil society was "murdered." The government created its own social organizations or government-organized non-governmental organizations (GONGOs) to counter the independent formation of social movements for workers, peasants, youth, veterans, literary workers, and artistic performers (Alagappa 2004: 475). In 1993, following their electoral loss in 1990, the *Tatmadaw* ruling directly as the State Law and Order Restoration Council (SLORC)[1] created the Union Solidarity and Development Association (USDA), a mass civil movement designed to foster patriotism and loyalty to the government. The USDA was the regime's attempt to recreate civil society in its own manner while suppressing alternative possibilities (Steinberg 2001: 110). Similar to the Golkar party in Indonesia, for the next seventeen years the USDA would play a pivotal role in securing the regime and harassing its opponents. Before the 2010 election, the USDA transformed into a political party (the Union Solidarity and Development Party—USDP) and went on to win 76.5 percent of the contested parliamentary seats nationwide (Thar Gyi 2010).

In their exploratory account of civil society, Kevin Hewison and Susanne Prager Nyein (2010: 13–16) further suggest that under military rule it was no longer possible to think of civil society in Burma as anything other than being politically organized, and that a "politicized" civil society is composed of organizations that seek to establish and expand the political space available for non-state actors. Because the state wields a powerful influence over the available political space for autonomous, but not necessarily independent, organizations, their narrower definition of civil society focuses on political oppositions. Hewison and Prager Nyein specifically note that many civil society organizations may exist that are not necessarily political in their orientation. However, under military rule and the restrictions imposed on political space, their analytical attention moves toward "non-violent political, advocacy, labor, and religious organizations and movements that seek to promote human rights and democratization in authoritarian states" (Hewison and Prager Nyein 2010: 16). They assert that their narrowed focus and attention is not natural in the sense that it is not predetermined by history or colonial legacy, nor is it culturally embedded. Rather, restricted political space and a "politicized" civil society only occur under these conditions. Moreover, like Lorch (2008a), they also reiterate that civil society is not necessarily liberal or democratic. Rather, it naturally reflects the variety of divisions in society (Hewison and Prager Nyein 2010: 15; see also Rodan 1996).

An alternative conception of civil society allows for further exploration. Based on Lorch's (2008a) adaptation of Marina Ottaway (2004), it involves the contextualization of civil society in terms of state weakness— that is, cases where states fail to deliver positive political goods like education, health, infrastructure, and the like. Ottaway (2004) notes that in weak states *modern civil society*—comprised secularized and formally organized groups such as non-government organizations (NGOs)—tends to be relatively weak; while *traditional civil society*—comprising mostly informal groups such as religious and ethnic organizations—can be relatively strong and provides a coping mechanism for state failure such as community-based schooling (Lorch 2008a: 154). Thus by separating modern civil society from traditional, we can see how civil society operates under military rule and subsequently how militaries have particularly tried to co-opt the traditional elements of civil society.

To be sure, the state's neglect of social welfare services in Burma, particularly under the rule of the SLORC-SPDC, created a space for local civil society organizations to operate. While relatively few of these organizations were formally registered as NGOs (Heidel 2006), many were informal (unregistered) community-based initiatives. Of these, we can distinguish modern civil society associations from traditional, and they may be both formally and informally organized. Amongst the *modern civil society* associations, we find community-based organizations (CBOs) and NGOs that blossomed in the 1990s. The size and scope of civil society space, or the freedom with which these organizations were permitted to operate, varied in accordance with the state's ability to extend its power over their territory.[2] Thus the space available for these groups to operate was far less in government-controlled areas than it was in the ceasefire areas, the latter having been dominated by ethnic civil wars since independence, quelled only through ceasefires negotiated by the military government after 1989.

In government-controlled areas, CBOs provided humanitarian relief (food and health care), small infrastructure projects, community-based schools and teachers, and funeral help associations at the local or village level funded through local community donations. Above the village level, organizations performing similar functions in towns and cities could be required to register as an NGO—an act that could attract foreign donations but also risked the possibility of being co-opted by the state. CBOs and NGOs operating in government-controlled areas focused on local welfare issues and remained apolitical partly to ensure their own survival. In the ceasefire areas, CBOs and NGOs focused on basic developmental needs and reconstruction of war-torn local ethnic minority communities. Some examples include the Development Support Programme in Mon State, and the Metta Development Foundation and Shalom Foundation that grew out of the Kachin ceasefire but extended their operations elsewhere. Their development programs included disaster relief and food assistance, health care, community hospitals and nursing schools, sustainable agriculture, and farmer education for increasing rice production (Lorch 2008b: 40–41). Almost half of the CBOs and over 60 percent of local NGOs were affiliated with religious groups, mostly Buddhist or Christian (South 2008; Heidel 2006).

By adopting the same typology for *traditional civil society*, we find that in government-controlled areas, it was the *sangha* that traditionally provided much of the welfare that the state neglected. The *sangha* operate Buddhist monastic schools and private education centers, providing free education for the poor, as well as basic literacy skills; some that teach the government curriculum were registered with the Ministry of Education. Monastic education centers also serve as orphanages, which are run by the *sangha*; these centers played a major relief role during the aftermath of Cyclone Nargis in 2008. Monasteries are also well integrated with the local community and the *sangha* have traditionally been involved with local development projects. In the ceasefire areas, Christian churches provided welfare services and education, and initiated development projects—responsibilities that the state neglected. Community-based schools and Christian colleges, often with linkages to international sources of funding, provide schooling in theology and some secular studies as well as English language. The state granted the churches a comparatively large degree of autonomy to operate in the ceasefire areas—possibly because church leaders also acted as mediators in ceasefire negotiations—but it limited any missionary efforts in Buddhist areas and, in any case, the churches were marginalized, being a minority amongst the Burmese population, and this limited their political potential as well (Lorch 2008b: 45–46). Moreover, the overwhelming majority of the civil society groups active in Burma's welfare sector were apolitical in nature (their survival required this), though some local NGOs had been co-opted by the regime (Lorch 2008b: 48).

Co-optation of traditional civil society

That militaries should pay particular attention to traditional civil society and attempt to either form alliances with or co-opt and suppress these organizations requires further investigation. Traditional civil society is the space occupied predominantly by religious or ethnic organizations and it is much stronger in weak states. Moreover, elements of traditional civil society may threaten the military's own position in political society. These groups manifest indigenous sources of power and legitimacy that under normal circumstances may lie outside the reach of the military. Furthermore, while not inherently democratic by nature, they may for various reasons adopt a "democratic" political posture in opposition to oppressive military rule. Their position in society is generally respected by the people and by the rank and file of the military itself. In Burma, the major group comprising this part of civil society is the *sangha*, whose influence extends predominantly over government-controlled areas. As noted above, Christian groups were too marginalized amongst the Buddhist population to pose a serious political threat.

In 1990, the SLORC's refusal to hand over power to the National League for Democracy (NLD) after the elections, as well as the *Tatmadaw*'s shooting of a monk and several students during a pro-democracy demonstration, triggered a rebellion in Mandalay, and the subsequent decision of *sayadaws* to invoke a religious boycott in monasteries across Burma—that is, the *sangha* refused to accept alms from the *Tatmadaw* or perform religious services for their families. Over 400 monks were arrested and monastery property was destroyed. The SLORC soon after issued the *Sangha Organization Act* stipulating the proper conduct for a Buddhist monk (including the avoidance of politics) and penalties for their violation by monks or monk organizations. The *Tatmadaw* then sought after the blessing and support of *sayadaws* with a carrot and stick—those who resisted cooperating had their monasteries placed under surveillance and were often arrested, while those who were compliant received donations, gifts, and elaborate ceremonies granting honors and titles.

In 2007, the All Burma Monks Alliance (ABMA—an organization formed by a group of senior monks in response to the severe economic and social problems existing at the time) threatened the military with another religious boycott and called for peaceful marches in Rangoon, Mandalay, and elsewhere. As in 1990, this threat was taken very seriously by the military since it had the potential to demoralize the *Tatmadaw* and questioned the loyalty of its rank and file soldiers and security forces, now almost entirely composed of Burman Buddhists. On the final days before the crackdown, an estimated 30,000 to 50,000 monks and nuns carrying overturned alms bowls were joined by the same number of civilians, many holding flags, including the NLD and the banned All Burma Buddhist Monks Union. The monks who took part in the so-called "Saffron Revolution" came predominantly from private monk schools and monasteries whose *sayadaws* had not been co-opted by the military. Their schools were abandoned following the crackdown and the monks fled to villages or across the border to avoid persecution. Although severely weakened since 2007, the *sangha*'s potential as a force for political opposition in Burma would remain and the military would continue to monitor their activities.

Safeguarding a role in political society

Militaries in the Asia-Pacific undertake the political steps needed to secure their reserve domains or at least their influence over political society. In Burma, a long drawn out and controlled process of constitutional drafting produced a document containing striking similarities to Indonesia's constitution under Suharto's New Order. The military's role in politics would be ensured through stronger amendment provisions, the military's control or support throughout the process, and success at subsequent elections. The military followed its own "roadmap to democracy" and, for over thirteen years, held a National Convention on a new constitution with hand-picked representatives from the ethnic minorities. It created its own social organization along the lines of Indonesia's Golkar, and also converted the USDA into a political party (the USDP). It held a referendum of sorts on their constitution, which secured a permanent role for the military in the national and regional legislatures—one-quarter of the seats in both the lower house (*Pyithu Hluttaw*, or the People's Assembly) and the upper house (*Amyotha Hluttaw*, or the House of Nationalities) were reserved for the military, in addition to one-quarter of the seats in the fourteen state and division assemblies. In November 2010, the military held its first general election in twenty years, securing a victory across the board and indirect rule until 2015. The election in 2010 was widely disputed on numerous grounds. The generals held Aung San Suu Kyi under house arrest (barring her from running as a candidate) until after the election. Her National League for Democracy boycotted the election on the grounds that the rules were too unfair—hundreds of its members and potential candidates were disqualified from running as they had served or were still serving prison sentences at the time of registration.

A Joint Parliamentary Committee for Reviewing the 2008 Constitution was created in July 2013 to conduct a nationwide consultation exercise on amending the Constitution. The Committee's findings were tabled in January 2014—Article 59(f) would remain, along with Articles 109 and 436, which together effectively barred Aung San Suu Kyi from becoming president, guaranteed the military one-quarter of the seats in parliament, and required three-quarters of the parliament (which includes the military) to approve amendments to the Constitution. A smaller Parliamentary Constitutional Amendment Implementation Committee and a joint sitting of parliament reaffirmed this in 2015 by rejecting any proposed changes to these articles. Later that year, Suu Kyi would claim to rule "above the president," if her party won the looming election. The NLD went on to win the general election in late 2015 in a landslide victory and, while not assuming the presidency in 2016, Suu Kyi claimed four cabinet positions in the new government as well as a newly created prime-minister-like role called "state counselor."

Civil society in transition

Civil society under military rule may be suppressed but it is never dead or "murdered." In order to examine how and where civil society operates under authoritarian conditions, it is useful to distinguish modern from traditional civil society and, if possible, also distinguish areas that are beyond the reach of the state from those that are within the state's control. When groups in traditional civil society threaten the monopoly held by militaries over political society, they are effectively silenced, as occurred in Burma. The militaries then move to secure their roles in political society in preparation for their transitions to post-military rule. While the nature of civil society in the post-military rule environment may appear diverse, there are also lasting legacies in terms of the military's influence over civil and political society.

The reforms introduced by Burmese President Thein Sein in 2011 created the impression amongst many observers that civil society was liberated, that civil liberties had returned, and that the country was well en route to a full democratic transition. To be sure, there had been substantial changes to everyday life compared to the days of direct military rule. Many political prisoners were released, the numbers of newspapers and magazines flourished, access to printing facilities and the Internet was no longer tightly controlled, and a tsunami of CBOs and international NGOs re-entered and explored in country possibilities. Even public demonstrations against electricity blackouts and media restrictions were tolerated in 2012. Moreover, new laws were enacted to provide easier access to registration and association for unions, employers, and NGOs/CBOs, including the Labor Organization Law (2012) and the Association Registration Law (2014). Some environmental NGOs also had some success in influencing the government to halt construction at controversial sites such as the Chinese-funded Myitsone dam project.

However, while media restrictions were eased somewhat with the removal of pre-publishing censorship by the government, this merely placed the onus of self-censorship on editors and publishers, who were still required to conform to the Printers and Publishers Registration Law of 1962. The Ministry of Information's censorship board, the Press Scrutiny and Registration Division (PSRD), continued to issue guidelines to journalists and monitor publications critical of the state. The PSRD retained substantial powers under the media laws, including the right to suspend publications or to revoke publishing licenses. A new Printers and Publishers Registration Law was passed in 2014, including a range of vague definitions, bureaucratic procedures, and registration requirements. Although there was a substantial increase in the number of publications covering political and social issues (including the NLD's own newspapers), various news journals were suspended in 2012, and there was a rise in criminal defamation actions launched against editors and journalists by members of the government. By 2014, scores of journalists and editors had been arrested and imprisoned under the criminal code or the 1950 Emergency Provisions Act for publishing defamatory, erroneous, or alarming stories, and one freelance journalist had died in custody. The number of political detainees and human rights activists held in custody also increased.

A series of major student protests against a new education law also ended with a violent police crackdown and subsequent arrests in Letpadan and Rangoon in 2015. Students and activists protested in early 2015 over the National Education Law passed in September 2014. Their demands for academic freedom included reversing the centralization of authority over universities, the prohibition of student unions, and the banning of teaching in ethnic minority languages. The protesters began marching from Mandalay and provincial towns to Yangon in January 2015—over 100 were dispersed outside the Yangon City Hall in March and eight were arrested. Another 200 protesters were dispersed when they attempted to break through a police blockade in the town of Letpadan, 145 km north of Yangon. Following negotiations with the police, the protesters continued to push back the blockade and were violently resisted, leading to the arrest and detention of over 100 people, including student leaders.

In the post-military-rule period, there has also been a rise in Buddhist nationalism and anti-Muslim violence spurred on by a small clique of the *sangha* led by the Mandalay-based monk U Wirathu and the 969 Movement—a religious-nationalist group encouraging Buddhists to boycott Muslim businesses and prohibit interfaith marriages. Throughout 2012 and 2013, violence occurred in Rakhine State and in pockets across the country where Muslim communities were targeted by Buddhists. The rape and killing of a Rakhine Buddhist woman by Muslim men in May 2012 was followed by the killing of ten Rakhine Muslim passengers on a bus. The subsequent rioting by thousands of Rohingya Muslims and communal violence led to the government imposing a curfew in May that same year, and the following month President Thein Sein declared a state of emergency. Approximately 140,000 Rohingya Muslims were displaced, fleeing to communities and camps across Myanmar, as well as to Bangladesh and Malaysia. The rioting and communal violence led to numerous presidential declarations of states of emergency. In most instances, the local police did not interfere and the military remained silent—their inaction fuelled speculation that hardliners used these incidents to showcase the need for a strong military presence.

Following violence in Meikhtila in March 2013, which was directed at local Muslims rather than the displaced Rohingyas, the president issued a statement emphasizing government support for the freedom of religion and the protection of citizens' rights. However, in May 2014, the parliament introduced four "Race and Religion Protection" bills for debate, drafted by the Ministry of Religious Affairs—including a bill on religious conversion, which would require local government approval and registration of people seeking to convert to another religion. Other proposed legislation involved restrictions on interfaith marriage (the Buddhist Women's Special Marriage Bill) and polygamy, as well as the Population Control Healthcare Bill (aimed at limiting the population growth of Rohingya Muslims). The proposed legislation drew criticism from local religious organizations and the UN Special Rapporteur on Freedom of Religion who condemned it as an organized attack on religious freedom. The four bills were promoted by Buddhist nationalist movements and in particular by the Organisation for the Protection of Race and Religion (also known as Ma Ba Tha), which collected over a million signatures supporting the draft legislation. These groups considered the laws necessary to protect Buddhism against a perceived Islamic threat.

By August 2015, the parliament had approved all four bills, and the Ma Ba Tha group held celebrations across the country and warned against voting for those who did not support the legislation. At the same time, the country suffered heavy monsoon rains, widespread flooding, and landslides following the development and passing of Cyclone Komen off the Arakan (Rakhine) coast in late July. The government declared Chin State, Rakhine State, Magwe Division, and Sagaing Division as disaster areas. Unlike the isolationist reaction of military authorities to Cyclone Nargis in 2008, President Thein Sein appealed directly for international assistance and called for residents in low-lying areas along the Irrawaddy River and the delta region to move to safer ground. In the wake of the flooding, many affected people again turned to local monasteries and community groups for assistance rather than relying on the limited government help.

The slow government response to the anti-Muslim violence across the country from 2012 to 2015 prompts us to question the extent such regimes become indebted to (or even captured by) the civil society organizations with which they look to develop relationships. Given the power and influence of the *sangha* in Burma, it is questionable as to whether the president or the armed forces could have confronted Buddhist extremists and challenged anti-Muslim sentiment without considerable cost to the country's stability and possibly even themselves. The political sensitivity of the anti-Muslim riots before the November 2015 election also placed the democratic opposition in an awkward position with their electorates—in the 2015 election, the NLD leadership chose not to pre-select any Muslim candidates. However, following their landslide election victory, the NLD would be in a better position to undermine the legitimacy of the Ma Ba Tha. The state Buddhist authority, the State Sangha Maha Nayaka Committee (Ma Ha Na), in July 2016 disowned the Ma Ba Tha, claiming that the latter was not a Buddhist organization formed in accordance with the basic *sangha* rules, regulations, and directives of the State Sangha. The action followed comments made by the NLD's chief minister of Yangon, U Phyo Min Thein, that Ma Ba Tha was not needed because the state already had a committee to oversee Buddhist religious life. The Ma Ha Na further stated that none of the Sangha conventions of all Buddhist orders from 1980 to 2014 had endorsed Ma Ba Tha's legitimacy; that such organizations may never deal in political affairs; and that the formation of a new Buddhist order was prohibited. Under the previous (Thein Sein) government, the Ma Ba Tha had been responsible for organizing anti-Muslim protests, instigating violent reprisals against Muslims across the country, and pushing controversial race and religion laws through parliament.

There are limits to the degree that civil society can develop and mature when there is a strong military presence or influence over political society following periods of direct military rule. In post-military rule environments, when civil society is still in its early stages of transformation and development, many freedoms remain undefined as groups explore and challenge the limits of boundaries set up by their former military rulers and their quasi-military contemporaries. These conditions existed under the Thein Sein government in Burma between 2011 and 2015, and they will continue to be challenged under the NLD-led government while the military maintains its reserve domains and position in parliament. While new freedoms created a sense of openness in society, unrestrained freedom also challenged conservative military thinking. However, practicing self-censorship and self-restraint is difficult in this context given the changes to public and social media and the arrival of new CSOs, NGOs, and international NGOs—many of whom are unaware of the deep-rooted interests and unstated limits that they may challenge. An independent civil society takes time to mature and levels of independence depend to a very large degree on the militaries' continued involvement in political society and the likelihood of any future intervention. Indeed, in any study of civil society in the Asia-Pacific region, it would be a mistake not to keep the interests of the military in mind. Understanding how militaries aim to preserve their rule provides a better understanding of authoritarian resilience—what tactics are used to resist democratic forces, how civil and political society are influenced by military rule, and how their legacies persist in transitional settings.

Notes

1 The SLORC changed its name to the State Peace and Development Council (SPDC) in 1997.
2 For a similar account of the limitations of state control and degrees of independence of upland peoples in Southeast Asia, see Scott (2009).

Suggested readings

Alagappa, Muthiah, ed. 2004. *Civil Society and Political Change in Asia: Expanding and Contracting Democratic Space*. Stanford, CA: Stanford University Press.
Heidel, Brian. 2006. *The Growth of Civil Society in Myanmar*. Bangalore: Books for Change.
Hewison, Kevin, and Susanne Prager Nyein. 2010. Civil Society and Political Oppositions in Burma. In *Myanmar: Prospect for Change*. Chenyang Li and Wilhelm Hofmeister, eds. Pp. 13–34. Singapore: Select Publishing.

Hughes, Caroline. 2009. Civil Society in Southeast Asia. In *Contemporary Southeast Asia*. 2nd Edn. Mark Beeson, ed. Pp. 125–142. New York: Palgrave Macmillan.

Lorch, Jasmin. 2008a. Stopgap or Change Agent?: The Role of Burma's Civil Society after the Crackdown. *Internationales Asienforum* 39(1–2): 21–54.

Lorch, Jasmin. 2008b. The (Re-) emergence of Civil Society in Areas of State Weakness: The Case of Education in Burma/Myanmar. In *Dictatorship, Disorder and Decline in Myanmar*. Monique Skidmore and Trevor Wilson, eds. Pp. 151–176. Canberra: ANU Press.

Rodan, Garry. 1997. Civil Society and other Political Possibilities in Southeast Asia. *Journal of Contemporary Asia* 27(2): 156–178.

South, Ashley. 2008. Civil Society in Burma: The Development of Democracy Amidst Conflict. *Policy Studies No. 51*. Washington DC: East-West Center.

Weiss, Meredith. 2015. Civil Society and Democratisation in Southeast Asia: What is the Connection?. In *Routledge Handbook of Southeast Asian Democratization*. William Case, ed. Pp. 135–146. London: Routledge.

Website

Online Burma/Myanmar Library, www.burmalibrary.org/.
Links to journals, articles, databases, and documents relating to Burma (Myanmar).

References

Alagappa, Muthiah, ed. 2004. *Civil Society and Political Change in Asia: Expanding and Contracting Democratic Space*. Stanford, CA: Stanford University Press.

Diamond, Larry. 1999. *Developing Democracy: Toward Consolidation*. Baltimore, MD: Johns Hopkins University Press.

Edwards, Michael. 2004. *Civil Society*. Cambridge: Polity Press.

Gramsci, Antonio. 1971. *Selections from the Prison Notebooks*. New York: International Publishers.

Heidel, Brian. 2006. *The Growth of Civil Society in Myanmar*. Bangalore: Books for Change.

Hewison, Kevin, and Susanne Prager Nyein. 2010. Civil Society and Political Oppositions in Burma. In *Myanmar: Prospect for Change*. Li Chenyang and Wilhelm Hofmeister, eds. Pp. 13–34. Singapore: Select Publishing.

Hughes, Caroline. 2009. Civil Society in Southeast Asia. In *Contemporary Southeast Asia*. 2nd Edn. Mark Beeson, ed. Pp. 125–142. New York: Palgrave Macmillan.

Lorch, Jasmin. 2008a. The (Re-) Emergence of Civil Society in Areas of State Weakness: The Case of Education in Burma/Myanmar. In *Dictatorship, Disorder and Decline in Myanmar*. Monique Skidmore and Trevor Wilson, eds. Pp. 151–176. Canberra: ANU Press.

Lorch, Jasmin. 2008b. Stopgap or Change Agent? The Role of Burma's Civil Society after the Crackdown. *Internationales Asienforum* 39(1–2): 21–54.

Ottaway, Marina. 2004. Civil Society. In *Politics in the Developing World*. Peter J. Burnell and Vicky Randall, eds. Pp. 120–135. Oxford: Oxford University Press.

Rodan, Garry. 1996. Theorising Political Opposition in East and Southeast Asia. In *Political Oppositions in Industrialising Asia*. Garry Rodan, ed. Pp. 1–39. London: Routledge.

Scott, James. 2009. *The Art of Not Being Governed: An Anarchist History of Upland Southeast Asia*. New Haven, CT: Yale University Press.

South, Ashley. 2008. Civil Society in Burma: The Development of Democracy Amidst Conflict. *Policy Studies 51*. Washington DC: East-West Center.

Steinberg, David. 1997. *A Void in Myanmar: Civil Society in Burma*. The Burma Library. Electronic document, www.burmalibrary.org, accessed November 19, 2016.

Steinberg, David. 2001. *Burma: The State of Myanmar*. Washington, DC: Georgetown University Press.

Tocqueville, Alexis de. 1966. *Democracy in America*. Jacob Peter Mayer and Max Lerner, eds. Translated by George Lawrence. New York: Harper and Row.

Thar Gyi. 2010. USDP Wins 76.5 Percent of Vote. *The Irrawaddy*, November 18. Electronic document, www.irrawaddy.org, accessed November 19, 2016.

16

INDIA

Pradeep Taneja and Salim Lakha

State and civil society in India: collaboration and contestation?

With its immense diversity and divisions along religious, caste, class, and a multitude of other lines, India is perhaps an unlikely place for democracy to take root. But the fact that it is one of the few post-colonial societies to have almost continually managed to elect its government and leaders through the ballot makes it a rare success story. Despite all its flaws and quirks, democracy in India could not have endured without the presence of a robust and sometimes raucous civil society.

Civil society in India is itself a product of the country's own pluralist traditions and its contacts with the outside world over the past several centuries, including the colonial experience. The anti-colonial movement led by Mahatma Gandhi, which was based on his philosophy of nonviolence, has also had a major impact on the character, substance, and style of civil society-led mass mobilization in India. Unsurprisingly, therefore, Gandhian civil society activists jostle for space with both the left-wing and the right-wing grass-roots organizations in India's already congested political and social milieu.

As is often the case, the state is usually the target of civil society activism in India, and the relationship between the two is the focus of much of the literature dealing with civil society in India. This relationship is complex since many actors and forces are involved in shaping it. Of these, changing government attitudes to civil society organizations (CSOs), the reliance of CSOs on funding from the state and international agencies, the rise of the neoliberal agenda, and attempts by CSOs to safeguard democratic rights and fight corruption are some of the important factors influencing the relationship between civil society and the state.

In this chapter, we aim to highlight the role of civil society in India and examine the relationship between the state and civil society through three case studies or examples. The first section of the chapter provides a brief overview of the evolution of civil society and the views of the scholars on the nature of civil society–state relations in India. The second section then presents three different examples of civil society activism in India, focusing on: (1) the Right to Information movement; (2) Mahatma Gandhi National Rural Employment Guarantee Scheme (MGNREGS); and (3) the Anti-Corruption Movement of 2011. These particular case studies were chosen because they are national in scope and impact; they have had a transformative impact on the nature of democracy; and, importantly, they demonstrate the vibrancy of civil society activism in India. The use of case studies is intended to draw on a range of examples to portray a complex picture of civil society in India that goes beyond simple classifications or binaries. Based on our case studies, the concluding section identifies a few necessary conditions under which CSOs can be effective in achieving transformational change.

Civil society state relations and the accountability of CSOs

Neera Chandhoke adopts a critical view of state-CSO collaboration in India by arguing that CSOs are legitimizing the state by collaborating with them (2012: 40). She takes a Gramscian approach to analyzing state–civil society relations and claims that civil society, according to Gramsci, "is the space where the state and dominant classes produce and reproduce projects of hegemony" (Chandhoke 2012: 39). Her position is in stark contrast to liberal theorists who believe civil society provides a check on the power of the state and is necessary for strengthening democracy (Berglund 2009: 11; Mercer 2002: 7). This liberal view is also espoused by international financial institutions like the World Bank, which regards civil society as critical to ensuring good governance (Berglund 2009: 12). In India in the post-independence period, CSOs established themselves to safeguard "democratic rights" and compensate for the state's shortcomings in delivering the benefits of development (Chandhoke 2012: 42). Some political scientists/public intellectuals even viewed CSOs as "an alternative to the state" (Chandhoke 2012: 42). Thus, liberal notions of state–society relations were important in shaping the outlook and activities of these intellectuals. However, their claims of CSOs representing "an alternative to the state" were unusual as historically no theorists of civil society took that view but instead posited the two as complementary to each other (Chandhoke 2007: 609).

In India, some CSOs like non-governmental organizations (NGOs) are increasingly receiving their funding from the state, and many CSOs are now involved in government-sponsored projects at all levels (Goswami, Rajesh, and Bandyopadhyay n.d.: 10). The provision in the guidelines for MGNREGS mentioned above is a case in point. The reliance on state funding has increased over time, especially with the onset of the new millennium, and as foreign funding for CSOs has diminished (Goswami *et al.* n.d.: 11). Suspicion of foreign funding on the part of past and present Indian governments and stricter guidelines for foreign donations may account for the reduced flow of foreign funding (Kumar 2015).

According to Chandhoke, the role of CSOs was transformed in India during the 1990s as the development narrative brought to the forefront notions of governance and accountability (2012: 43). An upshot of this was the greater professionalization of NGOs, especially as NGOs/CSOs began to play an active role in delivering services to the poor and low-income citizens who were bypassed in the development process. Referring to the broader landscape of developing countries, Mercer claims that under neoliberalism NGOs have emerged as "public service contractors" (2002: 11). It is performance of this role that has called into question, on the one hand, the relationship between the state, CSOs, and the poorer sections of the population and, on the other hand, those whom CSOs are accountable to. These issues have become pertinent to both India and other so-called developing countries. Importantly, these concerns raise the question whether CSOs are service providers for the state or a medium for societal transformation.[1]

Chandhoke claims that when CSOs engage in state initiated schemes they lose their credibility with the underprivileged and vulnerable segments of the population who are victims of these schemes (2012: 40). For example, the government mobilizes CSOs and NGOs as "partners" of the state when it wants to remove the urban poor from parts of the city that the government wants to reclaim for its own purposes. Through their role as service providers to the poor on behalf of the state and international donors, it is argued NGOs are bolstering the state and thus maintaining "the status quo" rather than contesting it (Mercer 2002: 17). In the process, their political impact is substantially diminished (Mercer 2002: 14).

As CSOs/NGOs assume the role of service providers and source funds from national and international donors, it raises the question of who are they accountable to? The nexus between CSOs and donors also raises the question as to what extent do they represent the interests of those who are vulnerable? Some argue that as a result of reliance on funds from the state and international agencies, CSOs/NGOs are forced into being more accountable to their donors instead of those they claim to represent, that is, the underprivileged (Goswami *et al.* n.d.: 18; Mercer 2002: 16). As a consequence of the compliance and reporting requirements set by the donors, the emphasis shifts to upward accountability to donors rather than downward accountability to those they claim to represent. Also, the status and influence of CSOs is reduced in aid programs channeled through multilateral agencies that loan funds to national and state governments that in turn merely use CSOs to implement projects at the local level (Goswami *et al.* n.d.: 18). Sometimes these programs create demands beyond the capabilities of CSOs, placing them in difficult circumstances with the local people they are serving and who also question their values.

The questions relating to accountability, representation, and the autonomy of CSOs raise substantial issues regarding state–civil society relations. While critics of neoliberalism have rightly drawn attention to the shifting roles of CSOs/NGOs under neoliberal policies and the compromises that they face, one needs to guard against generalizations. There are a multitude of civil society actors who are engaged in different roles. Some are more engaged with external donors and reliant upon government funding where their activities are defined by the requirements of foreign donors and the state. In other cases like *The Mazdoor Kisan Shakti Sangathan*[2] (MKSS) and the movement for Right to Information (RTI) discussed below, civil society actors are more engaged with the needs of ordinary citizens, where they demand transparency and accountability from state agencies. They contest the state and exert pressure upon the state to meet the needs of its citizens. It is, therefore, important and necessary to distinguish between different types of civil society actors and the types of activities they are involved in. The service providers need to be distinguished from those demanding respect for human rights and the need for livelihood security. Similarly, civil society groups that are socially inclusive have to be distinguished from those with exclusionary agendas.

Another significant area of debate pertains to the role of CSOs in policy-making and framing government legislation. When the National Advisory Council (NAC) was functional under the United Progressive Alliance (UPA) government's first term in office (2004–2009), several prominent civil society actors were represented on it and played an influential role in policy framing that ultimately shaped legislation. This role has invited criticism from some political scientists who argue that framing of legislation is "strictly a function" of those elected to parliament and CSOs should confine themselves to campaigning on issues of public interest (Varshney 2011). They argue that once this distinction is breached it subverts "the basic principle of a democratic society" (Varshney 2011). It is a pertinent criticism that raises a question about the autonomy of CSOs: To what extent can CSOs claim to be autonomous from the state once their representatives accept positions on government bodies like the NAC?

Chandhoke claims that the state sets the "boundaries" of what civil society can do and to that extent civil society is not completely autonomous (Chandhoke 2012: 40). While we concur with Chandhoke, we argue the "boundaries" are contested and the parameters do shift periodically. In India, some of the major achievements in recent times, like the RTI Act and MGNREGS (discussed below) have come about through the efforts of CSOs and in the process, they have expanded the economic and political space for ordinary citizens, though much remains yet to be achieved.

Examples of civil society movements

Right to information campaign and movement

The vibrant character of civil society in India is evident in the vast array of social movements active in the country. Some of these movements demonstrate both social and regional depth by their mobilization of diverse social groups and their spread over several or many regions. A clear example is the RTI campaign, which extended its influence over time to become a movement that was remarkable for mobilizing a wide range of social groups across the nation (Singh 2014). Its activities, which resulted in the passing of the RTI Act in 2005, empowered individuals and CSOs in their quest for transparency in public affairs. For a small sum of money, any person or organization can demand information from a government agency, which has to release it within thirty days of request, if it is submitted to the Central Public Information Officer (GoI 2011: 6). Through this process, the RTI Act has ensured some measure of transparency and accountability from state officials and, as a consequence, checked corruption in government agencies.

A significant feature of the RTI movement was its grass-roots origins in the state of Rajasthan. What distinguished Rajasthan from other states was a long-standing tradition of demanding government accountability with pressure emanating from civil society groups like MKSS, an organization of workers and farmers (Jenkins and Goetz 1999). MKSS, which was led by a renowned activist Aruna Roy (a former employee of the Indian Administrative Service or IAS), was founded formally in 1990 and since 1994, it had vigorously campaigned for both the right to obtain information from official sources (Chandhoke 2011) and the right to work (Afridi 2008). According to Jenkins and Goetz, the role of MKSS was vital in promoting accountability and transparency demands in Rajasthan (1999). They characterize MKSS as a "grassroots organisation" that eschewed political party affiliation (1999: 603). Neither was it an NGO, because it did not involve itself in distributing funds from outside sources or delivering services. Instead, its main aim was to deal with those matters that affected the living conditions of people who were economically deprived or underprivileged (Jenkins and Goetz 1999). Significantly, MKSS instituted an innovative mode of accountability through "collective" scrutiny of information that was followed by public hearings or *jan sunwais*, which were inclusive since they welcomed all stakeholders and did not exclude village officials who received invitations to be present at the hearings (Jenkins and Goetz 1999: 604). According to Chandhoke (2011), these public hearings represent what some political theorists refer to as deliberative democracy.

From the perspective of our discussion, what is significant is that a grass-roots movement that began as a campaign for work and the right to seek information transformed itself into a wider movement encompassing groups and individuals from many professional backgrounds and different social classes across the country (Singh 2014: 7–8). By drawing into its fold influential members of the urban middle class, it was able to both widen its support base and exert strategic influence over politicians and the government. The movement's success in getting the government to enact the right to information legislation is revealing of state–civil society relations in India. It demonstrated that while social and political mobilization across class and spatial boundaries was important, it also required a government that was sympathetic to the movement's demands, even if some of the government members resisted the proposal. While the previous BJP led government (1998–2004) was reluctant to adopt the proposal, the incoming UPA government led by an eminent economist, Manmohan Singh, was keen to show it wanted to make a difference and the proposal elicited decisive support from Sonia Gandhi, leader of the Congress Party, who was also the chair of the UPA (Singh 2014: 9). It is our contention that while CSOs play an important oppositional role through lobbying, campaigning, and mobilizing a range of social groups, their success rests ultimately upon effective negotiation with the government and an accommodative state that is willing to accept their demands as demonstrated by the achievement of the RTI Act. This dialectical relationship between the state and civil society is part of the democratic process in India which is marked by periodic setbacks and victories for ordinary citizens.

Since the passing of the RTI Act, it has been widely utilized by CSOs and individuals who have pressed government agencies to provide greater transparency in their functioning. In the space of two and a half years from implementing the scheme, there were around 2 million applications for information under the Act (Roberts and Roberts 2010: 927). The Act has been hailed as a great success by some CSOs and scholars, including Lord Meghnad Desai who referred to it as "a great and revolutionary act … another step further in the embedding of democracy" (quoted in Roberts and Roberts 2010: 926). While the Act has certainly emboldened CSOs and individuals demanding more transparency and accountability, a sober assessment reveals substantial obstacles in its effectiveness because of limited awareness (especially amongst the less literate and poorer sections of the population) of the Act, combined with insufficient guidelines for users, hostility on the part of public officials, the large number of applications, and limited infrastructure in government departments to adequately deal with requests for information (Roberts and Roberts 2010: 927–930).

Mahatma Gandhi National Rural Employment Guarantee Scheme (MGNREGS)

Despite these shortcomings, the significance of the RTI Act for transparency is well recognized by the government and its provisions have been incorporated into the Mahatma Gandhi National Rural Employment Guarantee Scheme (MGNREGS), which was implemented in 2006. The scheme is the largest rights-based employment program both nationally and at the international level. It offers 100 days of guaranteed employment to an adult member of a rural household as a means of ensuring livelihood security. To facilitate transparency and accountability in the implementation of the scheme, there is also a mandatory requirement for conducting social audits. According to the guidelines of MGNREGS,

> The Right to Information Act shall be followed both in letter and in spirit in all matters relating to Mahatma Gandhi NREGA. Section 4 of the Act, which concerns proactive disclosure of information, must be strictly complied with at all levels.
>
> *(MoRD 2013: 113)*

In order to ensure freer flow of information and transparency, there is even provision for the involvement of CSOs in the guidelines (MoRD 2013: 139). Their participation is welcomed at different levels of the implementation of the scheme such as raising awareness of workers' entitlements, training, monitoring, and conducting social audits (MoRD 2013: 140).

The participation of CSOs in MGNREGS is another example of the role that civil society institutions play in Indian society. In this case, it involves CSOs partnering government agencies in the development process. This partnership is marked by both mutual collaboration and tension between CSOs and government agencies. The source of tension is partly related to resistance on the part of government officials at both the *gram panchayat* (village council) level and those above to provide transparency in the implementation of MGNREGS.

Andhra Pradesh offers a case study in constructive collaboration between the state government and CSOs. It exemplifies a state that is amenable to accommodating the involvement of non-government organizations in order to promote workers' entitlements under MGNREGS.

One major obstacle to workers gaining the benefits of MGNREGS is their lack of awareness of their entitlements. To overcome this hurdle, both the state government and NGOs have made efforts to apprise workers of their entitlements. For example, NGOs have set up Wage Seeker's Associations at the local level to provide both information on their entitlements and improve their capacities to deal with officials who are sometimes reluctant to cooperate and divulge information to ordinary villagers (Galab and Revathi 2012: 150). This collaboration between the government and NGOs took a significant step forward in 2010 with the setting up of a formal partnership entitled the Andhra Pradesh NGO Alliance (APNA) for the implementation of MGNREGS. As a consequence of the state government's active promotion of MGNREGS and the engagement of concerned NGOs, Andhra Pradesh has gained a remarkable reputation for transparency and accountability in the implementation of MGNREGS. The state's favorable attitude toward the scheme and similar welfare programs has its roots in the competitive politics (Maiorano 2014).

The constructive engagement between CSOs and the state government in Andhra Pradesh is not characteristic of some other states in India. Even though in Rajasthan and Karnataka, for example, CSOs/NGOs are involved in MGNREGS, their experiences have not always been marked by constructive collaboration with local government and other state officials. Rajasthan's experience is revealing because it represents a case of accountability from the "bottom up," where civil society actors are very active in disseminating the information on rights to rural dwellers and aiding them to obtain their entitlements (Afridi 2008: 37–38). However, this involvement has been marked by both cooperation and conflict between CSOs and government officials. Conflict occurred when Aruna Roy and her group the *Rozgar Evum Suchana Ka Adhikar Abhiyan* (Campaign for Right to Work and Right to Information) were invited initially by the state government to conduct an audit in Banswara district in December 2007 (Indian Express 2007). Though the planned audit was to be conducted in cooperation with the state and district authorities, the government retreated on its initial commitment and ordered district officials to withhold the information required for the social audits. When members of the group requested the information from the authorities, they were physically assaulted. This was not an isolated case of violence, though on other occasions government officials have extended their cooperation in conducting social audits.

In Karnataka, CSOs/NGOs are also involved in conducting social audits and raising awareness amongst those working under MGNREGS, but interviews with NGO workers revealed resistance and hostility toward them from local level officials. According to an NGO worker from one of the districts, the social audit conducted by his NGO showed serious misuse of funds and corruption by officials implementing the scheme. It revealed fraudulent practices in the implementation of MGNREGS, such as fudging of work records, creating fictitious names of jobseekers, and inflating wages. But the government officials failed to take any firm action against the accused persons. The NGO worker stated that NGOs taking part in social audits are not free to submit an independent report, reflecting the reality of social audits on the ground.[3] The payment for audit services to NGOs is made by the *taluk panchayat*, and where office-bearers at the *taluk panchayat* are involved in corrupt practices, they can cause difficulties for the NGOs concerned if the social audit report provides a negative evaluation highlighting the misuse of funds and fraudulent practices. The NGOs are, therefore, forced to submit a moderate and partial report to the government. Under these conditions, it is arguable whether involving NGOs can lead to impartial presentation of social audit findings when their payment is at stake!

While the above example shows how NGO reporting may be compromised by reliance upon government funding, it is not universally representative of CSO involvement in

MGNREGS. However, it does reveal the problematic nature of CSO collaboration with government agencies. Further, it raises important questions about the constraints upon the independence of CSOs/NGOs and whom they are accountable to.

The anti-corruption movement of 2011

The second term (2009–2014) of Prime Minister Manmohan Singh's UPA government was marred not only by slower economic growth than its first term in office (2004–2009), but also by revelations of a number of corruption scandals. One of these scandals revolved around the awarding of construction and supply contracts and other irregularities related to the hosting of the 2010 Commonwealth Games in New Delhi. These scandals and the tardy progress toward the completion of the necessary infrastructure for the Games received widespread media coverage both at home and abroad. It was against this background, and feelings of hurt nationalist sentiments, that an anti-corruption movement began in April 2011 in the national capital, before spreading to other major cities across the country. Several high-profile politicians had already been arrested on suspicion of corruption in the Commonwealth Games-related cases, as well as another case involving the sale of the 2G mobile telecommunications spectrum. The unrelenting media and opposition attacks on the integrity of accused politicians and officials had quickly set the scene for a grass-roots campaign against corruption to break out.

Anna Hazare, a 74-year-old ex-soldier and social activist, emerged as the leader of a largely middle-class movement—India Against Corruption (IAC)—demanding the enactment of a new law to establish a powerful anti-corruption agency—the Lokpal (ombudsman). This was of course not the first time that the demand for a Lokpal was raised in India. The proposal for the establishment of a Lokpal had been debated in India since the 1960s without success. A Lokpal bill was passed by the lower house of India's Parliament in 1969, but it never got through the upper house. Hazare, a self-styled Gandhian, who had a reputation for running successful anti-corruption campaigns in his home state of Maharashtra, had written a number of letters to the prime minister demanding the enactment of a strong Lokpal law but did not receive a satisfactory response. Upset at government inaction, he staged a hunger strike in the center of New Delhi in April 2011, thus launching the movement.

As the movement unfolded, Hazare received support from a number of other civil society groups, including those that spearheaded the right to information campaign discussed above. His key advisers and supporters were drawn from a variety of personal and professional backgrounds, including a former senior civil servant, Arvind Kejriwal, who had quit his government job to pursue social causes. His other high-profile supporters included a well-known lawyer with reputation for pursuing governments, Shanti Bhushan, and a former senior female police officer known for fearlessly acting against powerful figures, Kiran Bedi. Another prominent face of the movement was a Yoga guru, Baba Ramdev, who had vowed to launch his own movement against corruption and black money earlier that year.[4]

Hazare ended his hunger strike when the government agreed to set up a joint committee, including him and his top advisers (known as Team Anna), as well as senior government ministers, to draft the new Lokpal bill. There were early signs that the work of the drafting committee was progressing well, but serious differences soon surfaced between the government and Team Anna over the scope of the Lokpal's powers. Team Anna demanded that the Lokpal should have sweeping powers to investigate anyone, even the prime minister and the members of the judiciary. The government disagreed, preferring to set up a separate body to investigate complaints of irregularities against the judiciary. There were also differences over the type of investigative powers the Lokpal could wield. For example, Team Anna wanted the Lokpal's investigators to have powers to use wiretaps, which the government opposed.

Ultimately, the two sides could not overcome their differences and each issued its own version of the Lokpal bill, with Team Anna calling its draft bill the Jan Lokpal Bill (Citizens' Ombudsman Bill). Anna Hazare declared that he would begin another hunger strike after Independence Day (August 15) to draw attention to his demand for their version of the bill to be passed by the parliament. He was denied permission to use the venue of his choice and the police arrested him on August 16 as he was preparing to begin the hunger strike. His arrest caused mass public outrage, leading to a massive social media campaign for his release (Rajagopal 2011). The calls for his release poured in from all corners of the country. The authorities ordered his release within twelve hours of his arrest but with conditions attached. Realizing the power of his movement, he refused to leave the notorious Tihar Jail until he was allowed to go unconditionally.

Hazare eventually left Tihar Jail on August 18 to continue his hunger strike at the city's Ramlila Grounds, where he was joined by thousands of his supporters. The venue was festooned with national flags and famous people took turns to wave the national flag on stage. Hazare was positioned in the middle of the stage against a huge picture of Mahatma Gandhi. After nearly two weeks of noisy but generally orderly protests, Anna Hazare agreed to "suspend" his hunger strike on August 28, following a parliamentary vote supporting most of his key demands. The "sense of the house" resolution, passed by the parliament with a voice vote, cleared the way for a standing committee of the parliament to redraft the bill incorporating Hazare's main demands.

Eventually, the Lokpal Act was passed by both houses of parliament in December 2013 and came into force on January 16, 2014. Anna Hazare now believes that the new law can only control "40 to 50 percent" of corruption and he wants effective enforcement of the law (Economic Times 2014). The enactment of the Lokpal Act met most of his demands, but there is no indication that it has had any significant impact on corruption. Most of the structural factors behind the prevalence of corruption in India remain unaddressed.[5] The movement eventually faded away. Some of its leaders formed a new political party called the Aam Aadmi Party (or common man party), which won the 2015 Delhi local assembly elections, while others joined the right-wing Bharatiya Janata Party. Hazare himself remains outside the formal political party system. As Rajagopal, quoting the social activist Aruna Roy, ruefully writes:

> the huge Lokpal mobilisation had a relatively small outcome. No corrupt politicians were pin-pointed, much less punished, although that was the stimulus for the movement. No relief was offered for the unaffordably high cost of living, although that was a major motivation for the agitation. Instead we were given the promise of a new bureaucracy to examine bureaucratic corruption.
>
> *(Rajagopal 2011: 20)*

Unanswered questions

The anti-corruption movement of 2011 raised a number of questions that continue to be debated by scholars. Why did the usually apathetic and complicit-in-corruption urban middle class lend its support to the anti-graft movement? Why did the movement by and large fail to attract the support of liberal and left-wing intellectuals in the country (Sengupta 2014)?

The answer to the first question can be linked to the market-friendly neoliberal economic policies that were introduced as part of the economic reforms in 1991. As a direct result of these policies, India became one of the world's fastest growing major economies, adding millions more to the growing ranks of the middle class. Indian consumers began to enjoy access to a range of new locally produced and imported products, bringing them closer to their counter-parts in the West. Since the early 1990s, the face of shopping for many urban Indians has changed dramatically, with air-conditioned shopping malls replacing the old poorly lit and family-run stores. In an open market economy, businesses vie with each other to offer com-petitive prices and friendly service to the consumer. India, for example, has some of the lowest mobile call charges in the world because of intense competition in the sector.

The Indian consumer today enjoys convenient market transactions and higher levels of service, with businesses willing to accommodate the demands of even the fussiest of customers. But the consumer as a citizen in her daily life still needs to navigate the large and generally unresponsive bureaucracy that prioritizes responding to the needs of the well-connected and wealthy individuals over the average middle-class citizen. In their normal lives, average Indians have to contend with lower-level government bureaucrats at various stages. These differences in what we call transactional experiences between a market economy and an insensitive and unresponsive government go some way toward explaining the middle-class support for the anti-corruption campaign.

Another possible explanation for the middle class's willingness to throw its weight behind a civil society-led anti-corruption campaign may lie in the resurgence of nationalism in India, which at least in part has been stoked by a rising economy. The global recognition of the coun-try's software sector and the elevation of a number of expatriate Indians to the helms of large multinational companies in the United States and elsewhere, have contributed to a new sense of self-assuredness and pride amongst young Indians. This upbeat narrative of India as a rising power does not sit easily with the older and gloomier narrative that showed India in a poor light as a corrupt and inefficient underdeveloped nation. The latter narrative was amply demonstrated in the lead-up to the 2010 Commonwealth Games when both the local and international media portrayed India's preparations for the Games as a disaster marked by incompetence and corrup-tion. It especially hurt the nationalist sentiments when contrasted with China's apparently flaw-less management of the 2008 Beijing Olympics.

The answer to the second question raised above, that is, the movement's failure to attract the support of progressive and liberal intellectuals, is more complex. Sengupta (2014: 407) argues that Indian progressives were from the beginning against Hazare. This was partly because of his dalliances with the right-wing Hindu nationalist groups, but also because of the "authoritarian" manner in which Hazare had presided over social and economic changes in his village of Ralegan Siddhi for years. A lack of support from the otherwise anti-establishment thinkers and activists may indeed have undermined the legitimacy of the anti-corruption movement to some extent. However, there is no doubt that the movement was a clear example of the potential of civil society to animate change at the grass-roots level.

Conclusion

As signaled in the introduction, this chapter emphasized the potential of civil society for trans-formational change. This was particularly evident in the enactment of the Right to Information legislation that facilitates greater transparency by empowering citizens with access to informa-tion. Similarly, the implementation of the MGNREGS has assured the delivery of income support and livelihood security to tens of millions of poor households in the country by guar-anteeing employment at the minimum wage for at least a part of each year. The anti-corruption movement may not have succeeded in removing structural sources of corruption but it too led to the passage of important legislation that has the potential to curb corruption given the right conditions.

In sum, this chapter has identified the following necessary conditions that are essential for civil society to effectively play its democratic role in bringing about transformational change:

1   The national ecosystem in which civil society organizations operate is an important determining factor in the impact the CSOs can have at the local and national level, particularly the degree to which the state is accommodative of their role in the social and economic development of the country.

2   The CSOs are more likely to succeed in achieving their objectives if their relationship with the state is not based solely on opposition but on finding complementary grounds for cooperation. Our intention here is not to suggest that CSOs should uncritically embrace the state's agenda or merely act as service providers for the government. To be effective, the CSOs must engage in contesting harmful policies with damaging effects on ordinary citizens, but they can and should also cooperate in strengthening democracy and enhancing the living conditions of citizens.

3   In all three case studies examined in this chapter, the success of the movement was predicated on the mobilization of a cross-section of social groups and organizations. The support of the middle class and the intelligentsia played a significant role in their success. In the third case study, the anti-corruption movement, where the support of the progressive intellectuals was not forthcoming, the movement failed to sustain itself as a transformative force, despite achieving its immediate objective.

Notes

1   See Edwards (2004) for an illuminating discussion on this topic.
2   Association for the Empowerment of Workers and Peasants.
3   We are grateful to Professor D. Rajasekhar at the Institute for Social and Economic Change, Bangalore, for sharing this information with us.
4   In June 2011, Ramdev did launch a protest against corruption and black money (income on which tax has not been paid or that has been earned through illegal activities such as drug trafficking or bribes and kickbacks) under the guise of a Yoga camp in Delhi's famous Ramlila Ground. But his protest was broken up by the police and he was briefly detained in Delhi before being sent off to his Ashram in the holy city of Haridwar.
5   There was a change of government in the May 2014 general elections. The centrist UPA government lost power to the right-wing Bharatiya Janata Party (BJP) led by a charismatic but divisive politician, Narendra Modi, who campaigned strongly against corruption and black money. The Modi government has so far avoided any large-scale revelations of corruption by the media.

Suggested readings

Chandhoke, Neera. 2002. *The Conceits of Civil Society.* New Delhi: Oxford University Press.
Chandhoke, Neeera. 2012. Whatever Has Happened to Civil Society? *Economic and Political Weekly* 47(23), June 9: 39–45.
Sahoo, Sarbeswar. 2013. *Civil Society and Democratization in India: Institutions, Ideologies and Interests.* London: Routledge.
Singh, Richa. 2014. Civil Society and Policy Making in India: In Search for Democratic Spaces A Case Study. In *Centre for Democracy and Social Action.* Electronic document, www.oxfamindia.org/sites/default/files/WP7-Civil-Scty-n-plcy-mkg-in-India.pdf, accessed September 22, 2016.
Tandon, Rajesh, and Ranjita Mohanty. 2003. *Does Civil Society Matter? Governance in Contemporary India.* Thousand Oaks, CA: Sage.

Websites

Centre for Civil Society. Social Change Through Public Policy, http://ccs.in.
A think-tank based in New Delhi, working to promote choice and accountability in public policy through education and social change.

Centre for Policy Research, www.cprindia.org.
A non-profit public policy think-tank based in New Delhi, dedicated to research, policy and freedom of public discourse.

References

Afridi, Farzana. 2008. Can Community Monitoring Improve the Accountability of Public Officials? *Economic and Political Weekly* 18: 35–40.

Berglund, Henrik. 2009. Civil Society in India: Democratic Space or the Extension of Elite Domination? *Working Papers 2009: 1*. Electronic document, www.socant.su.se/polopoly_fs/1.129706.1364285702!/menu/standard/file/berglund_civil_society_in_india_oct_2009.pdf, accessed September 22, 2016.

Chandhoke, Neera. 2007. Civil Society. *Development in Practice* 17(4/5): 607–614.

Chandhoke, Neera. 2011. Our Latest Democratic Predicament. *Economic and Political Weekly* 46(19): 17–21.

Chandhoke, Neera. 2012. Whatever Has Happened to Civil Society? *Economic and Political Weekly* 47(23): 39–45.

Economic Times. 2014. Effective Implementation of Lokpal Act Necessary: Anna Hazare. *Economic Times*, January 2. Electronic document, http://economictimes.indiatimes.com/news/politics-and-nation/effective-implementation-of-lokpal-act-necessary-anna-hazare/articleshow/28293485.cms, accessed January 2, 2017.

Edwards, Michael. 2004. *Civil Society*. Cambridge: Polity Press.

Galab, Shaik, and E. Revathi. 2012. MGNREGS in Andhra Pradesh: Examining the Role of State-Enabled Institutions. In *Right to Work and Rural India: Working of the Mahatma Gandhi National Rural Employment Guarantee Scheme (MGNREGS)*. Ashok K. Pankaj, ed. Pp. 149–168. New Delhi: Sage.

Goswami, Debika, Tandon Rajesh, and Bandyopadhyay. n.d. In *Civil Society in Changing India: Emerging Roles, Relationships and Strategies*. Electronic document, www.c2d2.ca/sites/default/files/Civil%20Society%20Study%20Report_India.pdf, accessed September 22, 2016.

GoI (Government of India). 2011. Right to Information Act, 2005 (Act No. 22 of 2005). *Ministry of Law and Justice*. Electronic document, http://righttoinformation.gov.in/rti-act.pdf, accessed September 13, 2016.

Indian Express. 2007. NREGA: Rajasthan Govt, Activists on Collision Course Over Social Audit. In *Indian Express*, December 26. Electronic document, www.indianexpress.com/news/nrega-rajasthan-govt-activists-on-collisio/254692/, accessed September 22, 2016.

Jenkins, Rob, and Anne Marie Goetz. 1999. Accounts and Accountability: Theoretical Implications of the Right-to-Information Movement in India. *Third World Quarterly* 20(3): 603–622.

Kumar, Sanjay. 2015. Modi's Systematic Clampdown on Indian Civil Society Must Stop. In *The Diplomat*, June 4. Electronic document, http://thediplomat.com/2015/06/modis-systematic-clampdown-on-indian-civil-society-must-stop/, accessed September 22, 2016.

Maiorano, Diego. 2014. The Politics of the Mahatma Gandhi National Rural Employment Guarantee Act in Andhra Pradesh. *World Development* 58: 95–105.

Mercer, Claire. 2002. NGOs, Civil Society and Democratisation: A Critical Review of the Literature. *Progress in Development Studies* 2(1): 5–22.

MoRD (Ministry of Rural Development). 2013. *Mahatma Gandhi National Rural Employment Guarantee Act 2005 (Mahatma Gandhi NREGA, Operational Guidelines 2013)*. 4th Edn. New Delhi: Department of Rural Development, Government of India.

Raj, Panchayat, and Rural Development (RD-II) Department. 2010. In *Government of Andhra Pradesh Abstract*. Electronic document, www.rd.ap.gov.in/EGS/GOMSNO_211_EGS_04062010.pdf, accessed September 13, 2016.

Rajagopal, Arvind. 2011. Visibility as a Trap in the Anna Hazare Campaign. *Economic and Political Weekly* (46–47): 19–21.

Roberts, Nancy, and Alasdair Roberts. 2010. A Great and Revolutionary Law? The First Four Years of India's Right to Information Act. *Public Administration Review* 70(6): 925–933.

Sengupta, Mitu. 2014. Anna Hazare's Anti-Corruption Movement and the Limits of Mass Mobilization in India. *Social Movement Studies* 13(3): 406–413.

Singh, Richa. 2014. Civil Society and Policy Making in India: In Search for Democratic Spaces. A Case Study. *Centre for Democracy and Social Action*. Electronic document, www.oxfamindia.org/sites/default/files/WP7-Civil-Scty-n-plcy-mkg-in-India.pdf, accessed September 22, 2016.

Varshney, Ashutosh. 2011. State of Civil Society: Why we Need to be Precise in How We Define Civil Society. In *The Indian Express*, June 14. Electronic document, http://indianexpress.com/article/opinion/columns/state-of-civil-society/, accessed September 22, 2016.

17

PAKISTAN

Nadeem Malik

The state of civil society in Pakistan—an overview

Though there is a strong history of citizens' action in Pakistan, the term civil society has only been in use since the late 1980s (Baig, Sattar, and Sattar 2001). Before the 1980s, the term civil society usually referred to civil bureaucracy and political parties in contrast to the military establishment. Voluntary organizations were mainly referred to as "welfare societies" or "welfare organizations." The tradition of welfare organizations existed even before the British colonial rule in the part of the Indian subcontinent that forms today's Pakistan. Before the colonial period, welfare activities were motivated primarily by religious beliefs, for example by Hindu concepts of *daana* (giving), *seva* (service), and the Islamic practices of *zakat* (offering to the poor), *khairat* (charity), and *haqooq-ul-ibad* (human rights).

During the British colonial period, foreign missionaries founded modern schools and convents in the provinces of Punjab, Sindh, and the North-West Frontier Province (now known as Pakhtunkhwa). The missionaries also established hospitals, dispensaries, orphanages, hostels, infirmaries, and seminaries (SPDC 2002). Following such trends in welfare, domestic religious movements also contributed to social welfare, for example, Zoroastrians established several schools in the city of Karachi (Iqbal, Khan, and Javed 2004), which are still considered to be most prestigious in Pakistan.

Later, in the second half of the nineteenth century, the colonial government introduced a legal framework for social welfare organizations, known as the Societies Registration Act (1860), and the Trust Act (1882) to monitor and regulate welfare organizations (Iqbal *et al.* 2004). These frameworks are still operative in Pakistan. After the independence of the country, these new welfare institutions played a significant role in the settlement of a massive number of refugees, who migrated from India (ADB 2009). A huge number of new hospitals, maternity homes, and dispensaries were also established, where doctors and nurses provided free medical aid. Later, several cooperatives such as the Family Welfare Cooperatives Housing Society, Lahore and the Social Welfare Society, Lahore were established that provided housing and dealt with issues such as poverty reduction, education, health care, and population control (Iqbal *et al.* 2004).

Civil society, in the way that it is understood today in Pakistan, emerged in the mid-1980s as a consequence of the end of the Cold War, after Soviet disintegration and the so-called triumph of neoliberalism on the one hand, and on the other, the failure of structural adjustment programs (SAPs) that were considered to be promoting development without a human face by the United Nations. This led to a reconfiguration of the aid agenda by the World Bank and the International Monetary Fund (IMF). SAP was replaced by the "good governance" agenda that espoused involvement of institutions, channels, and networks from outside the government in the provision of public goods (Malik 2016). Civil society in this picture of governance stood prominent. Its role was not merely to monitor state activities and act as a watchdog, but also to help create social capital, which was considered important for participation, empowerment, and economic growth (Malik 2014).

Several authorities on the subject variously define the concept of civil society. For the purposes of this chapter, I will follow the functions of civil society identified by Larry Diamond:

> civil society performs many … crucial functions for democratic development and consolidation: limiting the power of the state more generally, and challenging its abuses of authority; monitoring human rights and strengthening the rule of law; monitoring elections and enhancing the overall quality and credibility of the democratic process; educating citizens about their rights and responsibilities, and building a culture of tolerance and civic engagement; incorporating marginal groups into the political process and enhancing the latter's responsiveness to societal interests and needs; providing alternative means, outside the state, for communities to raise their level of material development; opening and pluralizing the flows of information; and building a constituency for economic as well as political reforms.
>
> *(Diamond 1997, 24, cited in Makumbe 1998: 306–307)*

The above functions emphasize the role of civil society in strengthening democracy and making the state accountable to people for their social, political, and economic rights. In the light of these functions, for most of Pakistan, civil society would include various types of non-governmental organizations (NGOs), trade unions, the media, and professional associations, and their role in economic development and strengthening democracy in Pakistan. This chapter provides an overview and analysis of civil society in Pakistan by providing a portrait of NGOs, trade unions, various Bar Councils and Bar Associations (particularly known for the Lawyers' Movement they initiated against General Musharraf) in Pakistan, and the media. However, in order to provide an overall political context to the above, a succinct socio-political profile of the country is in order.

Pakistan: an overall socio-political profile

Pakistan is in Southern Asia, bordering the Arabian Sea, between India in the east, Afghanistan in the northwest, and China in the north. The population is approximately 182 million. Pakistan is a parliamentary federal state with a three-tier governance structure. This consists of the central government (comprising the national parliament, also called national assembly and the senate), provincial governments, and local governments (Malik 2009a). The country is passing through a period where political, economic, and socio-cultural crisis and confusion are conspicuous everywhere.

Since its inception, politics in Pakistan has remained a powerful man's vocation. For most of the time, the country has been dominated by a political structure controlled by the military, and even during the times of a civilian government, the power is wielded by the military. This has resulted in constitutional development of Pakistan that is entangled in, and influenced by, an unstable political system. Pakistan has had three periods of military rule: 1958–1971, 1977–1988, and 1999–2008. Periods alternating between military regimes and democratic rule seem to replace each other with intervals of approximately ten years. Democracy was never given a chance to fully take root in the country. State institutions such as the judiciary system remain weak and democratic discourse has not been embedded. The civil political leadership of the country is tied to the traditional feudal power structure and the military, and the less privileged are not able to rise to political power.

Due to a protracted history of military domination in Pakistan, today the country faces multiple imbalances. The critical issues are an uncontrollable law and order situation, militarization of state and society, drug trafficking, ethnic and sectarian violence, religious extremism, and violence against women, minorities, and journalists and human rights activists. Poverty looms large, putting 60 million people below the poverty line (The Economic Times 2016). The continued denial of basic human rights, strengthening civil society institutions, and people's participation has considerably reduced the capacity of the state and civil society to effectively address these challenges (Malik 2009b). Though civil society in Pakistan is struggling to grapple with the above issues, it still has to cross several posts to achieve its goals. This would be explicitly demonstrated through the following analysis of the NGOs, trade unions, the media, and various Bar Councils and Bar Associations (and their movement against General Musharraf known as "the Lawyers' Movement") in strengthening human rights, rule of law, and democracy in Pakistan.

NGOs

NGOs known as "welfare societies" have been operative in Pakistan since Independence and a few (such as *Anjuman Hamayat-e-Islam*) even existed before the partition of the Indian subcontinent. These were mostly "non-political, private and voluntary organizations that worked either under the patronage or in close association with the government" (Jilani 1998: 100). Being mostly charitable and welfare organizations, they worked either for the general benefit of people or were related to some ethnic or religious groups and worked to fulfill the welfare aims of such organizations (Jilani 1998: 100). Though a few human rights and advocacy organizations were formed before the 1980s, such as the United Front for Women's Rights and the Pakistan Family Planning Association formed in 1953, and Shirkatgah in 1975, most human rights and advocacy NGOs that are active today have their origin in the 1980s (Iqbal *et al.* 2004).

In recent years, there has been an enormous growth of NGOs in Pakistan. Their outreach and resources are unprecedented, even by Pakistani standards. There is hardly any reliable data available on the number of NGOs (as several are not registered by the government), however, according to Faiza Shah (2014), the number of active NGOs in the country is between 100,000 and 150,000 groups. This is a significant increase compared to the figures provided by a report prepared by the Social Policy and Development Center Pakistan (SPDC; SPDC 2002), according to which there were 45,000 NGOs in Pakistan in 2002. An unprecedented rise in the number of NGOs can be linked to huge funding (donations, grants) provided by foreign donors. Shah argued that:

> A major part of this money came into Pakistan due to the peculiar political and economic situation in the country. We have been through multiple violent conflicts during the last decade and a half; we have been transitioning from a dictatorship to a controlled democracy to a fully functional democracy, and our economy has been undergoing massive liberalization. All this necessitated that foreigners came in to help with expertise and money to take Pakistan and Pakistanis through this troubled period of our history.
>
> *(Shah 2014: 1)*

The need for foreign aid was further compounded by natural disasters—an earthquake in 2005, floods in 2010–2011. Together, "these political, economic, and environmental issues have resulted in foreign money coming into Pakistan in buckets and leaving in its wake an NGO at every step" (Shah 2014: 1).

There is a dearth of studies that provide a comprehensive profile of NGOs in Pakistan. Only a few studies, such as those conducted by CIVICUS (World Alliance for Citizens' Participation) in collaboration with the Aga Khan Foundation (see Baig *et al.* 2001), and the SPDC in collaboration with Johns Hopkins University, USA (see SPDC 2002) provide a profile of the NGOs. The CIVICUS study also provides an overview of NGOs' political significance and contributions. Another study by Iqbal *et al.* (2004) provides the history of civil society organizations in Pakistan; Hina Jilani (1998) conducted a study that most explicitly (though briefly) addressed the history of development and human rights NGOs and their political significance in Pakistan. According to Jilani, there are two types of development NGOs in Pakistan. The first type is engaged in service-oriented work such as microfinance and infrastructural development (mostly in the health and education sectors), while the second type has adopted rights-based approaches to their work. I would add that many of those NGOs that are providing services have also included rights-based approaches in their work. For example, such NGOs have been incorporating gender equality as a cross-cutting theme in their service-oriented projects. Other NGOs are those that mainly do advocacy work, for example, on human rights, women's rights, and children's rights issues. It is these foreign-funded NGOs (development and advocacy or rights-based), as they are popularly known, are an essential part of civil society in Pakistan. They work in collaboration with transnational actors, such as the United Nations and its associated agencies, international financial institutions, and international donor countries.

Foreign funding has important implications for the sustainability of NGOs' projects, their accountability, and legitimacy (Malik 2014). Since these NGOs and their projects largely depend on the continuous flow of funds from foreign donors, it becomes difficult for them to sustain their projects once the funding is not available—at times, the organization itself discontinues once the flow of funds ceases. The other implication is for the organizational environment and the nature of NGO accountability. Claire Mercer (2002) noted that in the1980s, two sets of literature emerged about NGOs: one that praised them in strengthening democracy; and the second that accused NGOs of being "often fragmented, unorganized, uncooperative and weak" (Mercer 2002: 13). He further argued that NGOs are often "internally undemocratic; characterized by authoritarian or charismatic personalized leaderships; competitive; riven along class, gender, religious, regional, spatial and ethnic fault-lines; and steered by either the state or donors, or both" (Mercer 2002: 13). This seems true for the NGOs in Pakistan too. For example, during my study on corporate social responsibility (CSR) and development in Pakistan in 2012, many community members and NGO workers informed me that the decision-making in NGOs is usually a centralized process. It is usually the chief executive officers who take major decisions. This is because it is such executives and their assistants who typically do the major public relations work with international officials and foreign donors to get funds.

Several authors (see Bratton 1989; Hudock 1995; Mercer 2002; Najam 1996) argue that most NGOs are primarily accountable to the sources of their funding, and not to the local communities they work for. During my field research for the study on CSR mentioned above, most community-based organizations' (CBOs) activists complained that the national-level NGOs get foreign funding on their behalf, and when the funding is not available, these national NGOs discontinue CBO projects. There is no mechanism through which local communities can make them accountable when a certain project is discontinued. Since the national-level NGOs (having their base in major urban centers) are managing development projects through partner CBOs in rural areas, the ultimate pressure is placed on the latter, as they are in contact with local communities and are held responsible for the discontinuation of the project. The national-level NGOs, instead of facing this pressure, start making plans to solicit funds for new projects. These NGOs are, therefore, not accountable to CBOs. In this regard, Mubarak Ali noted that:

> These NGOs generally have no constitution and no system of election, therefore also no accountability. Structurally they are like corporations that sell their products on the basis of foreign funding; their potential buyers are the ordinary social workers who are persuaded and lured into participating in seminars, workshops, and brainstorming sessions.
>
> *(Ali 2003: 51)*

Another implication of foreign funding for NGOs is that it provides opportunities to potential detractors within the state and society (such as extremist religious groups and part of the conservative media) to discredit NGOs as foreign agents promoting Western agendas. In this context, Richard Holloway argued that:

> Foreign funding makes you politically vulnerable to accusations that you are only doing the work because you are paid to do so, or because you are obeying the instructions of some foreign power that may have some concealed motives to the detriment of your country. Development is a political process and foreign funding provides ammunition to detractors—especially those in government—that you are being used politically by foreigners.
>
> *(Holloway 2001, 8, cited in Malik 2014: 121)*

The validity of Holloway's argument in the case of Pakistan can be illustrated through the example of a series of attempts by the government, politically motivated religious groups, and a section of the state-manipulated media to discredit NGOs as foreign agents. For example, the government proposed a bill in the Senate called the Social Welfare Agencies (Registration & Regulation) Act in 1996. The bill proposed the elimination of civic education as an acceptable NGO activity, thus forbidding NGOs to perform their advocacy role (Baig *et al.* 2001: 13). While the bill could never become law, it did create a strong sense of fear and insecurity amongst NGOs. Further, an intense media campaign against NGOs was launched in late 1998–1999, resulting in deregistration of a huge number of NGOs by the government (around 2,500 just in the provinces of Punjab, Khyber Pakhtunkhwa, and Sindh). The bill aimed to restrict NGOs' activities, especially pertaining to advocacy, and social and political education. The accusation made by the government, the state media, the dominant section of the print media, and the extremist elements in the society was that NGOs (especially women's and human rights organizations) in Pakistan were promoting Western values and were pursuing a foreign agenda detrimental to the cultural fabric of Pakistani society. Recently, on a private television channel in December 2012, a prominent political leader accused NGOs of acting as intelligence agencies for foreign donors. Such campaigns and propaganda further erode people's confidence in development and rights-based NGOs and harm their credibility. Such detractors are successful because foreign-funded NGOs lack roots in the society.

NGOs (mainly rights-based and advocacy NGOs) have failed to develop an effective local base of supporters who would provide them with resources and genuine political support in their fight against repressive state laws, practices and policies that are in conflict with basic human rights, and the right to the freedom of speech. Masooda Bano (2008) noted that these

NGOs are not member-based organizations. This is probably the main reason for the failure of these NGOs to develop a local support base. Bano's (2008) study also found a strong correlation between the receipt of international aid and the absence of members that in turn impacts their organization performance negatively.

Moreover, with the change of foreign donors' priorities, NGOs' projects discontinue, leading to distrust that these NGOs would be around, interested in the same issues, and ready to take input from below. It is commonly observed that a small number of the same supporters (mainly NGO workers and some of their sympathizers who are already converted) participate in NGO processions. The awareness of such a precarious situation is gradually visible within foreign-funded NGOs, but not many of them have decided to find alternative local sources of funding and create a network of local members and friends/supporters necessary to acquire political legitimacy within the country. The reason is that NGOs are conditioned by the availability of funds from foreign donors. With the change in donor priorities, their projects are discontinued, which further harms the credibility of their work.

However, despite all this, it is an undeniable fact that rights-based and advocacy NGOs have created enormous awareness about human rights, women's rights, children's rights, minority rights, and ethnic and religious rights in Pakistan. Up to the mid-1980s, people in Pakistan were hardly aware of the meaning of human rights and the international debate on human rights issues. Leaving aside what NGOs could achieve in terms of actually empowering communities to gain such rights, it is because of their efforts that today human rights concepts are not unknown to the people in Pakistan. Given such an ability to create awareness, if an organic and sustained local support base is established, NGOs can be a vanguard force in strengthening democracy and democratic culture in Pakistan.

Trade unions, the media, and the lawyers' association of Pakistan

Trade unions

According to some estimates, there are 63.34 million workers in Pakistan and the country is considered to be tenth largest labor force in the world (Raza 2016). Besides federations and confederations, there are 945 trade unions currently active in Pakistan, with their combined membership standing at 1.8 million. In absolute terms, the number appears gigantic; in the larger picture, only 3 percent of the Pakistani labor force is unionized.

Trade unions in Pakistan are weak and there has been a significant decline in union membership because of massive privatization and downsizing, an anti-trade union drive by successive government regimes and anti-union laws, the collapse of the left-oriented trade unions and leadership, the policies of the IMF and World Bank, especially in the so-called structural adjustments, liberalization, and last, a series of capitulations by the leadership of the trade unions (Hashmi and Bawa 2010). Other crucial factors undermining the trade union movement in Pakistan include internal fragmentation within unions, lack of an educated cadre and committed leadership, ethnic and sectarian divide, and co-option by political governments.

While these issues have confronted the trade union movement, the foremost is the structure of economic activity itself in the country (Javed 2009). The informal sector extends well beyond family and affects the structure of the formal sector. Employers tend to pass a majority of work to subcontractors and daily wage earners, preventing workers from availing existing legal welfare provisions and making it difficult for them to register unions, as employers can simply disown non-permanent workers. Within the existing formal sector, unions have a certain degree of collective bargaining power and have been able to protect the wages and conditions of workers.

Nevertheless, as mentioned earlier, less than 3 percent of the workers in the formal sector are organized. Employers in Pakistan use several tactics, including harassment, threats, and the dismissal of workers to weaken or curb union activities.

In general, though industrial workers have been given the right to form trade unions, their activities are circumscribed by a variety of restrictions that allow them limited trade union rights—the right to strike is particularly circumscribed by excessive restrictions (Ahmad 2009). In particular, the Essential Services Maintenance Act of 1952 (ESMA) (which covers government services and state enterprises, such as energy production, power generation, and transmission) is usually invoked to limit or ban strikes, and is also used to severely curtail collective bargaining rights. The strikes are often broken up by the police and used by employers to justify the dismissal of workers. Trade union rights are often violated, and in the last few years, several trade union activists have been arrested and detained as well. Moreover, employers often create obstacles and strongly resist the unionization of workers by resorting to intimidation, dismissal, and blacklisting. If an employer is opposed to the formation of a union, the procedures for union registration and the appeals process can take many years. Sometimes the employers artificially promote workers to managerial status, usually without the concomitant salary increase, so that they no longer qualify for union membership (see also Shaheed 2007).

Workers' welfare is given some protection by the Factories Act of 1934 that requires inspection of enterprises, but this authority has been increasingly devolved to provincial and lower-level governments, with the net result that labor inspections are hardly ever performed, and that employers are able to violate key provisions of the law on wages and conditions of work with impunity (Shafi and Shafi 2005). The most disturbing aspect of Pakistani law is that it prevents agricultural workers from forming unions and they are thus prevented from organizing strikes, bargaining collectively, or making any demands on their employers. Consequently, rural workers and contract workers, in particular, face bad working conditions and almost no access to labor rights. Industrial workers having union membership could raise a voice for the urgent increase in the minimum wage to cope with the soaring prices resulting from an economic crisis, but rural and contract workers do not have any platform to raise their voices (Ahmad 2009). Many traditional labor problems abound outside the formal sector. The use of child labor and bonded labor is common (HRCP 2011). Working conditions are virtually non-regulated and the terms of employment are oppressive. Formal sector, and particularly government, employment comes to be regarded almost as a sinecure and the efforts of unions are largely limited to trying to contain the shrinkage of the traditionally unionized areas. A critical challenge confronted by the labor movement concerns its limited area of impact, which is further shrinking with the expansion of the informal sector and the emergence of new forms of employment at scattered and isolated workplaces. Though the number of women in the formal sector has increased significantly over the years in many cities, they remain largely outside the ambit of unionization (see also Javed 2009).

Overall, trade unions are weak and their activity is remote from the realities facing the overwhelming majority of the labor force. The effects of trade union movements in Pakistan have been less favorable, because organized labor was depoliticized from above through exogenously imposed factory-based labor policies. Trade unions in Pakistan, thus, could not play any significant role in making the state and corporate sector accountable for workers' economic or political rights, or more broadly in strengthening democracy in Pakistan.

The media

Media, especially electronic media, have considerably grown since 2002, as a result of the establishment of several private television and radio channels. Unlike in the past, when Pakistan had only one state-controlled television channel, today there are eighty-nine television channels (Eijaz *et al.* 2014) that air soap operas, satire, music programs, films, religious speech, political talk shows, and current news. Although at times criticized for being unprofessional and politically biased, the television channels have made a considerable contribution to the media landscape in Pakistan. Similarly, there are 155 radio channels, particularly popular in rural areas for providing entertainment and important information to their audiences. Apart from current news, the emphasis of private radio channels is on providing musical entertainment. Furthermore, there are hundreds of newspapers and sixty-eight weeklies and monthlies in Pakistan ranging from the large national Urdu and English newspapers to the small newspapers published in provincial languages such as Punjabi, Pashto, Sindhi, and Baluchi. Media on the whole as well are multi-linguistic and multi-ethnic—though the dominant language is Urdu and next is the English. The readers, listeners, and viewers of Urdu media are generally the rural population and the majority of those in urban areas who lack English language proficiency. Primarily, the urban elite and part of the rural gentry who know English consume the English media. Though much more professional and progressive, English newspapers, television, and radio channels have far smaller audiences compared to Urdu media. Any criticism against the government is, therefore, taken much more seriously by the government, if it is aired on Urdu television or radio networks or published in Urdu newspapers.

The media bears the brunt of political pressures exerted by the government. The media outlets disseminating critical reviews about the government are usually removed from the list of media outlets that receive advertisements provided by the government (Sabir 2011). The government's media regulatory authorities are used to curtail media freedom, for example, the Pakistan Electronic Media Regulatory Authority (PEMRA) has been used to silence the broadcast media either through direct bans or by simply threatening to impose such bans (Siraj 2009). Several prominent journalists have shown their concerns about the government's draconian laws and regulatory authorities such as PEMRA. Syed Abdul Siraj's account of such views is instructive:

> Mazhar Abbas, Secretary General PFUJ, said, "It was surprising that without mentioning names the PEMRA issued warning to channels for violating its rules and went to the [extent] of accusing them of inciting violence." Sohail Iqbal says, "The government wanted to impose complete ban on television channels before elections or convert [a] majority of them into state controlled media." Talat Hussain, director news, AAJ television, whose program "Live with Talat" had been shut down on the orders of the government, said, "The government through PEMRA is trying to create a scare among the journalists so that they resort to self-censorship." Hamid Mir, a senior anchor and Executive Editor of GEO television, whose program "Capital Talk" was forcibly shut down said, "It was an attempt to sabotage the struggle and movement of the press against black laws." He said the government as yet has not been able to prove that the reporting by television channels was damaging the interests of the State. However, the new government of the Pakistan People's Party has promised maximum press freedom and curtailing the stronghold of PEMRA on the private TV channels and cable networks.
>
> *(Siraj 2009: 45)*

In addition, the media are also exposed to propaganda from state agencies, pressured by powerful political elements and non-state actors involved in the current religious conflicts.

The private media are owned by large media groups and big businessmen (Sabir 2011). Their political and commercial interests dominate their decisions about media coverage. Mostly, the marketing managers of the media groups and the owners themselves decide on the space and coverage of news reports, influencing administrative and editorial policy matters with their own political and commercial interests (see also Mezzera and Safdar 2010).

Media owners have practically taken over the institution of professional editors. This has negatively impacted unbiased journalism due to the supremacy of owner's commercial interests over professional editorial decisions and policies. Increased importance given to commercial interest has led to disproportionate importance being given to advertisements and political news reports, where focus on social and human rights issues seems to be quite low on their agenda. Such commercial interests in the end serve more the political and military elites who patronize owners of different media groups in Pakistan, rather than the ordinary people. Journalists, especially those who aspire to provide unbiased objective news reports, face challenges of intimidation and control by the owners of the media groups.

Journalists in Pakistan face several other challenges as well—particularly, the security situation they face, which has deteriorated in the past few years. Threats and intimidation against journalists and media workers by state and non-state actors is widespread. On July 8, 2012, a workshop on "Media and Civil Society in Balochistan" was informed that the media in Balochistan were not free and journalists on professional duty often faced harassment from influential elements and different pressure groups active in the province; it was reported that twenty-two journalists were killed in the province during 2009–2012 (DAWN Pakistan 2012). Similar cases were found in other provinces as well.

There have been different alarming figures about the killings and deaths of journalists in Pakistan. According to the Friedrich-Ebert-Stiftung, out of seventeen journalists who were killed in South Asia in 2011, twelve were Pakistanis (Friedrich-Ebert-Stiftung 2012, as cited in Eijaz et al. 2014). The Committee to Protect Journalists report (CPJ 2016) has identified thirty-three journalists who were killed since 1992, due to suicide bombings, target killings, and the deteriorating law and order situation. Such security threats impede the functions of the media in acting as a watchdog.

Another challenge that the media in Pakistan frequently face is the interference of the government and the military. They use censorship and security threats to control the media. The fragile financial model of the media that prioritizes profits and political interests further makes it vulnerable to being dictated to by powerful state and private institutions. Journalists often complain about harassment and threats. A journalist of the Express Group was reported as saying: "Whenever journalists report something, pressure groups ask them to amend it and warn them of dire consequences if their 'orders' are not obeyed" (DAWN Pakistan 2012). Similarly, another journalist of ARY TV said the media face pressures from powerful institutions, political leaders, militants, and criminals. He added: "We get diktats from all stakeholders, so we cannot follow journalistic rules and face threats and censure," and "there are red lines and we cannot dare to be objective in reporting" (DAWN Pakistan 2012).

Huma Yusuf and Emrys Schoemaker produced a comprehensive briefing paper on media in Pakistan, according to which, "military and civilian governments alike have long influenced media content by bribing media houses and individual journalists through what is known colloquially as the *lifafa* (envelope) culture" (2013: 19). Cable operators have also been used by government institutions such as the media regulatory authority PEMRA to censor content on privately owned television channels. Cable operators are forced to block certain channels from broadcasting politically sensitive material. In 2010, for example, "PEMRA ordered cable operators to block the broadcasts of Geo News and ARY TV after they aired footage of a protester in Birmingham, UK throwing a shoe at President Asif Ali Zardari" (Yusuf and Schoemaker 2013: 19–20).

Since the military is the most influential political player in Pakistan, its influence on the media is most pronounced. Apart from bribing journalists and media houses, the military has also been accused of controlling the media through direct tactics, and their intelligence agencies have been accused of threatening and attacking journalists who cover topics and provide information that the military and intelligence agencies do not want to be made public. Walsh Declan noted that:

> Pakistan's media are on a "tight leash" when it comes to covering military and intelligence agencies, according to a 2011 report by Radio Free Europe/Radio Liberty. The coverage is "narrow, the reporting of sensitive security and human rights stories limited, and coverage in general tends to follow the official line … Pakistan's powerful army … still dictates the broader terms of what Pakistanis can read and watch."
>
> *(Walsh 2012)*

Pakistan's media landscape thus remains vulnerable to political influence, pressures, and harassment.

In sum, the media are expected to play several important roles in a democratic society—for example, boasting informational outflow; forming and influencing public opinion; and providing a platform that allows interaction between different segments of society (CCE Pakistan 2004). More importantly, they play a role of "creating a discursive public sphere that is so crucial to nurture participatory and functioning democracy" (CCE Pakistan 2004: 1). Though the media in Pakistan have seen unprecedented growth, they have yet to fully realize their role in developing and promoting an informed citizenry instrumental in achieving democratic goals. There is little doubt that the media in Pakistan have started to enjoy considerable freedom as compared to the past, but there still seems to be a long way to go for Pakistan's media to be able to be free from the interest groups within the state and society and play a more democratic role.

Pakistan Bar Council/Bar Associations and the Lawyers' Movement

Bar Councils in Pakistan are governed by the Pakistan Legal Practitioners and Bar Councils Act 1973. It recognizes two tiers of bar councils, the first being the Pakistan Bar Council, which is the parent body of lawyers' associations, and the second comprising the four provincial bar councils. Then there are district and high court bar associations functioning under the rules of the provincial bar councils.

The main functions of the Bar Councils under the act are to safeguard the rights, privileges, and interests of advocates (Hussain 2014). The Bar Councils promote and suggest law reforms, and take measures to ensure inexpensive and fair justice from the judiciary. Being the governing bodies of lawyers, they also organize examinations, tests, or interviews to admit new advocates on their rolls and to entertain and determine cases of misconduct, punish the advocates, and remove their names from the rolls, if guilt is proven. In recent history, during General Musharraf's regime, these Bar Councils and Bar Associations were praised for playing a significant role in the promotion of the rule of law and democracy and strengthening the civil society movement in Pakistan.

Since General Musharraf's takeover through a coup against Nawaz Sharif's government on October 12, 1999, there have been a large number of judicial casualties. The most prominent was the suspension of the Supreme Court Chief Justice Iftikhar Chaudhry. The Chief Justice refused to comply with General Musharraf's decision. Following the suspension of the Chief Justice, the Supreme Court Bar Association (SCBA) declared the judge's removal as an "assault on the independence of judiciary" (DAWN Pakistan 2007). Several political parties backed the SCBA's contestation against the government. This led to nationwide protests, inspiring a twenty-four-month movement led by the lawyers of Pakistan that successfully ousted Musharraf's regime in the long run, returned Chaudhry to his position as Chief Justice, and restored over fifty other judges, who had sided with Chaudhry, to their previous offices (Abbas and Saima 2009). For many Pakistanis, the movement's success represented an important sign of increasing judicial empowerment in a nation where courts had long followed the dictates of either the ruling civilian elite or the military. Any discussion on civil society, therefore, would be incomplete without discussing the Lawyers' Movement in Pakistan.

To begin with, Iftikhar Chaudhry was considered to be Musharraf's ally by Pakistani lawyers, as he was sworn in as Pakistan's Chief Justice in 2005 under Musharraf's Provisional Council Order (Zaidi 2008). The suspicion of lawyers in considering Chaudhry as Musharraf's man was not unfounded in light of the judicial history of Pakistan. Some historical background of judicial practices in enforcing dictatorial rule is therefore in order.

The establishment of democratic constitutional governance had a very weak beginning since the independence of Pakistan in 1947. In 1954, the Constituent Assembly agreed on the governing legal framework (Baxter 1974). However, later in the year, Governor-General Ghulam Muhammad dissolved the Assembly. He declared an emergency, arguing that the Constituent Assembly had lost the Pakistani people's confidence (Malik 2009b). The actual reason behind enforcing an emergency was that the new legislation would curtail his powers. In order to preserve his powers, Ghulam Muhammad invited the military's support, appointing the army chief General Ayub Khan as a minister in his new cabinet (Somjee 1984). This was an extra-constitutional act that cleared the way for military intervention in Pakistani politics in the long run.

In such a political scenario, the judiciary acted as the establishment's stooge, as the Federal Court upheld the legality of the Assembly's dissolution. A constitutional crisis ensued, which the court resolved by relying on the "doctrine of necessity" (Chaudhary 1993). According to this controversial principle, extra-constitutional actions can be legally justified under special circumstances. The man behind this legal maneuver was Chief Justice Muhammad Munir. His ruling justified Pakistan's first extra-constitutional coup that proved immensely damaging to the prospects of democracy and the rule of law in Pakistan in the long run.

Following the above legacy, General Ayub Khan suspended the constitution in 1958, and imposed the first martial law (Sayeed 1967). Again, it was Justice Munir who passed a judgment validating this military coup. This time, the coup was interpreted as a "revolution" by invoking the speculative theory of "revolutionary legality" developed by the Austrian jurist Hans Kelsen (Munir 2009). The court argued that since the "revolution" satisfied "the test of efficacy," it could thereby be deemed legitimate. In other words, the success of the military coup automatically furnished the justification for its legality.

The jurisprudence of the Munir court set the tone for constitutional reasoning in Pakistan. The doctrine of necessity, in particular, was used repeatedly to legitimate extra-legal usurpations of power. Both General Zia ul-Haq's and General Pervez Musharraf's military takeovers, in 1977 and 1999, respectively, were validated using this doctrine (Munir 2009). One of the members of the bench who reviewed and endorsed the legality of Musharraf's military *coup d'état* in May 2000 was Justice Iftikhar Chaudhry, and it is because of this that the lawyers' community was suspicious of him (Zaidi 2008). Soon after his appointment, however, Chaudhry began working to expand the role of Pakistan's judiciary. While reducing the case backlog, he simultaneously expanded the number of public interest cases accepted by the Supreme Court for review. During Chaudhry's first year, the Supreme Court disposed of over 30,000 cases—nearly a third of its docket. Most notably, the number of politically sensitive and contentious *suo moto* cases (cases seeking to check government power and authority) skyrocketed (Berkman 2010).

In 2006, in connection with one such case, Chaudhry took the unprecedented step of subpoenaing representatives of Pakistan's feared Inter-Services Intelligence Agency to account for its actions in connection with the "global war on terror" (Zaffar 2010). Musharraf balked at these reforms, perceiving them as direct challenges to his authority. In March 2007, Chaudhry, who had been bolstering the judiciary's independence and severing its traditionally close ties with the president, was removed from office by Musharraf, after resisting army pressure to resign (Mullally 2009). This led to a Long March initiated by lawyers that brought together a broad spectrum of civil society institutions, political parties and the media with an agenda of ensuring institutional supremacy and restoring democratic rule in Pakistan. The movement demanded the independence of the judiciary, parliamentary supremacy, free media, and free and fair elections (Khan, Islam, and Rizvi 2013).

For this purpose, the lawyers in Pakistan bore the brunt of the attacks of the Musharraf regime when protests were stifled. The protest led to the detainment of several lawyers and judges from 2007 onwards and several were severely injured. The state violence on lawyers in Karachi was particularly appalling, lasting several days. The Tahir Plaza building in Karachi containing 200 lawyers' offices were torched by unidentified attackers and many lawyers were incinerated. A proper investigation of the incident has never been held. Others lawyers from Karachi met by a delegation of lawyers in Lahore were arrested by police with charges of terrorism under the Anti-Terrorism Act. Being a large-scale grass-roots struggle, the Lawyers' Movement stands as a unique example of restoring the rule of law (Zaffar 2010).

Not many examples in modern history "can be found where lawyers expressed their opinions so forcefully and with such unbridled success" (Zaffar 2010: 1). By fighting for their cause on the "streets of Pakistan rather than in the courtrooms of Islamabad, Pakistan's lawyers demonstrated the power of popular movements to bring about judicial reform. The movement represents a unique moment in global legal history" (Zaffar 2010: 1).

Sheila Fruman identified a number of factors responsible for the success of the Lawyers' Movement. She noted that the movement was a success because of:

> A unified coalition of political parties and civil society with the common goal of defending the judiciary's independence; strong leadership from the lawyers and the judiciary itself; the return of influential political leaders from exile; the existence of private media that could contest the official version of events, promote an alternative narrative, and mobilize supporters; and an agreement between Pakistan's key political leaders on a charter of democracy setting out a plan for Pakistan's governance after the end of military rule.
>
> *(Fruman 2011: 5)*

Apart from the collaboration of various segments of civil society, the most prominent development that can be singled out is what Fruman called "a unified coalition of political parties" (2011: 5). Traditionally, the dominant political parties have been arch-rivals. Such rivalries had created a space for the military to intervene in politics. However, the Lawyers' Movement's success in bringing the dominant political parties together on an agenda of judicial independence and strengthening of democracy was considered a significant step forward. Such unity amongst rival political parties and their collaboration with civil society was rather unique in the Pakistani context. However, once the Musharraf government was ousted, the classic fragmentation between these political parties resurfaced. This again created a space for the military to dominate. The quest for the consolidation of democracy therefore remained fragile, and it becomes difficult to ascertain whether Pakistan can break its traditional cycle of military dominance.

As for the Lawyers' Bar Associations that mobilized tens of thousands of lawyers who formed the Lawyers' Movement and who were joined by thousands more from other civil society sectors, including students, women's groups, journalists, human rights activists, academics, trade unions, and professional groups, with some exceptions, they became much less visible than hoped. Since the elections in 2008 after Musharraf's ouster, they have generally failed to occupy the political space that they helped to create. In sum, the Lawyers' Movement created significant awareness in a particular moment in Pakistan's history for the restoration of democracy, rule of law, and judicial independence, however, it did not achieve any substantial success in the desired outcomes of establishing democracy or rule of law in the long run.

Conclusion

In the West, civil society grew with the rise of capitalism. More importantly, "it grew up around the free association of individuals in secularized, democratizing, pluralist capitalist states" (Sampson 1996: 141), most of which developed through a series of social revolutions that came in transnational waves. In countries like Pakistan, which are known to be semi-feudal, semi-industrial, with non-capitalist social relations in many of its tribal/rural areas, civil society concepts and models of organizations gained currency through the discourse of what Steven Sampson (1996) called "foreign-funded NGOs' projectisation." In most cases, these projects are unsustainable, because donor priorities keep changing and, more often, the NGOs either have to discontinue projects for which the funding is no longer available or close entirely. Their legitimacy is a big issue, because foreign-funded NGOs are ultimately not accountable to local communities, but to their donors. The nature of the relationship between NGOs and communities is finally that of patronage rather than of equal partnership. Nevertheless, advocacy and rights-based NGOs have created considerable awareness about human rights, women's rights, children's rights, and the rights of minorities, and ethnic, religious and linguistic rights of people in Pakistan. With more effort to develop a sound local resource base by soliciting the support of an army of local individuals and organizations, these NGOs can significantly contribute to protecting human rights and strengthening democracy in Pakistan. NGOs can also do a lot in strengthening trade union organizations in Pakistan that are appallingly weak and incapable of effectively fighting for workers' rights. On their own, it seems to be a daunting task for trade unions to achieve their desired goals in a society dominated by feudal lords, business elites, the military, and the anti-labor regimes in Pakistan.

The media in Pakistan also face several challenges, such as law and order, religious extremism, intimidation, coercion, bribery, threats, and pressures from the government, the military, and intelligence services, making it hard for journalists to work in a safe and secure environment. It is also because of these external challenges that the media content in Pakistan is significantly distorted and journalists are not able to provide objective news reports.

The proliferation of media since 2002 is often cited as a proof of the plurality and freedom of media in Pakistan. However, the evidence shows that it would be incorrect to correlate the expansion of media outlets with the degree of press freedom without taking into account the socio-economic and socio-political conditions in which the media operate. These overall conditions refer to the contractual nature of the jobs of many journalists that compels them to raise their income from sources other than their salaries, hidden state elements within the media organizations, the commercial and political interests of media houses, and the pervasive power and influence of the military.

Though the media have achieved more freedom due to a significant increase in private media outlets compared to the past when only state-owned television and radio channels were available, there are still many posts to cross to overcome the influence and pressures of state and non-state actors in Pakistan. If the Pakistani state and society want the media to play their due role in socio-economic and socio-political development, with the exception of regulations for professional and ethical practices, the media need to be left alone by the state, interest groups, and owners of media houses.

Finally, with regard to the Lawyers' Movement in Pakistan, it is beyond doubt that while it had a huge impact through media coverage and public participation and had a large political effect on Pakistanis, in the end, as was predicted by Zaidi in 2008, it failed to forge lasting ties with civil society in a more organic and sustained manner. It is also clear that it could not sustain any efforts to strengthen democracy in the long run. Overall, it can be argued that civil society in Pakistan is weak due to the particular socio-economic and socio-political history of the country dominated by the military establishment.

Suggested readings

Ali, Karamat. 1996. Social Clauses and Workers in Pakistan. *New Political Economy* 1(2): 269–273.

Candland, Christopher. 2001. The Cost of Incorporation: Labor Institutions, Industrial Restructuring, and New Trade Union Strategies in India and Pakistan. In *The Politics of Labor in a Global Age: Continuity and Change in Late-industrializing and Post-socialist Economies*. Christopher Candland and Rudra Sil, eds. Pp. 69–94. New York: Oxford University Press.

Malik, Muneer. 2008. *The Pakistan Lawyer's Movement: An Unfinished Agenda*. Karachi: Pakistan Law House.

Pasha, Aisha Ghaus, Muhammad Asif Iqbal, and Soofia Mumtaz. 2002. Non-profit Sector in Pakistan: Government Policy and Future Issues [with Comments]. *The Pakistan Development Review* 41(4): 879–908.

Ricchiardi, Sherry. 2012. *Challenges for Independent News Media in Pakistan*. Washington, DC: Center for International Media Assistance.

References

Abbas, Azmat, and Jasam Saima. 2009. A Ray of Hope: The Case of Lawyers' Movement in Pakistan. In *Pakistan: Reality, Denial and the Complexity of Its State*, Vol. 16 Democracy series. Jennifer Bennett, ed. Pp. 140–170. Berlin: Heinrich-Böll-Stiftung.

ADB (Asian Development Bank). 2009. Overview of Civil Society in Pakistan. Asian Development Bank. Electronic document, www.adb.org/publications/overview-civil-society-organizations-pakistan, accessed September 7, 2016.

Ahmad, Iftikhar. 2009. Labor and Employment Law: A Profile on Pakistan. Electronic document, www.wageindicator.org/main/documents/Labor_and_Employment_Law-A_Profile_on_Pakistan.pdf, accessed September 14, 2016.

Ali, Mubarak. 2003. NGOs in Pakistan. In *The NGOs Conspiracy in Pakistan*. Jalalzai Musa Khan, ed. Pp. 230–236. Lahore: Classic Publishers.

Baig, Adnan, Rabia Sattar, and Adnan Sattar. 2001. Civil Society in Pakistan: A Preliminary Report on the CIVICUS Index on Civil Society Project in Pakistan. *CIVICUS Index on Civil Society Occasional Paper Series* 1(11): 1–28.

Bano, Masooda. 2008. Dangerous Correlations: Aid's Impact on NGOs' Performance and Ability to Mobilize Members in Pakistan. *World Development* 36(11): 2297–2313.

Baxter, Craig. 1974. Constitution Making: The Development of Federalism in Pakistan. *Asian Survey* 14(12): 1074–1085.

Berkman, Toby. 2010. The Pakistani Lawyers' Movement and the Popular Currency of Judicial Power. *Harvard Law Review* 123(7): 1705–1726.

Bratton, Michael. 1989. The Politics of Government and NGO Relations in Africa. *World Development* 17(4): 569–587.

CCE Pakistan. 2004. *Window on Pakistan Media*. Islamabad: Center for Civic Education (CCE).

Chaudhary, Zahid. 1993. *Political History of Pakistan*. Lahore: Institute of Historical Studies Pakistan.

CPJ (Committee to Protect Journalists). 2016. 59 Journalists Killed in Pakistan Since 1992/Motive Confirmed. Committee to Protect Journalists (CPJ). Electronic document, https://cpj.org/killed/asia/pakistan/, accessed September 8, 2016.

DAWN Pakistan. 2007. SCBA Terms Removal Assault on Independence of Judiciary. *Dawn Pakistan*, March 10. Electronic document, www.dawn.com/news/236735/scba-terms-removal-assault-on-independence-of-judiciary, accessed January 25, 2017.

DAWN Pakistan. 2012. 22 Balochistan Journalists Killed in Four Years. *Dawn Pakistan*, July 9. Electronic document, www.dawn.com/news/732853/22-balochistan-journalists-killed-in-four-years, accessed January 25, 2017.

Diamond, Larry. 1997. Prospects for Democratic Development in Africa. Paper presented at the Department of Political and Administrative Studies, University of Zimbabwe, Democratic Governance Project. Harare, March.

The Economic Times. 2016. 60 Million Pakistanis Living Under Poverty Line. April 8. Electronic document, http://economictimes.indiatimes.com/news/international/world-news/60-million-pakistanis-living-under-poverty-line/articleshow/51741132.cms, accessed September 9, 2016.

Eijaz, Abida, Rahman Bushra Hameed, Ahmad Rana Eijaz, and Butt Jawad Ashraf. 2014. Challenges and Options for Pakistani Media in the 21st Century. *Journal of Political Studies* 21(1): 78–82.

Fruman, Sheila. 2011. *Will the Long March to Democracy in Pakistan Finally Succeed?* Washington, DC: United States Institute of Peace.

Hashmi, Waqar Haider, and Riffat Bawa. 2010. Labor Unionization in Pakistan: History & Trends. *Pakistaniaat: A Journal of Pakistan Studies* 2(2): 78–82.

Holloway, Richard. 2001. *Towards Financial Self-Reliance: A Handbook on Resource Mobilization for Civil Society Organizations in the South*. London: Earthscan.

HRCP. 2011. *State of Human Rights in Pakistan: Annual Report*. Lahore: Human Rights Commission of Pakistan.

Hudock, Ann. 1995. Sustaining Southern NGOs in Resource-Dependent Environments. *Journal of International Development* 7(4): 653–667.

Hussain, Faisal. 2014. Bar Councils' Decline. *Dawn Pakistan*, August 17. Electronic document, www.dawn.com/news/1125766, accessed on January 25, 2016.

Iqbal, Muhammad Asif, Hina Khan, and Surkhab Javed. 2004. Nonprofit Sector in Pakistan: Historical Background. *SPDC Working Paper: 4*. Karachi: Social Policy and Development Centre (SPDC).

Javed, Tazeen. 2009. Understanding Labor Issues in Pakistan. *Briefing Paper Series: 25*. Islamabad: Pakistan Institute of Legislative Development and Transparency (PILDAT).

Jilani, Hina. 1998. *Human Rights and Democratic Development in Pakistan*. Lahore: Human Rights Commission of Pakistan.

Khan, Faqir, Fakhrul Islam, and Shahid Hassan Rizvi. 2013. The Lawyers Movement for Judicial Independence in Pakistan: A Study of Musharraf Regime. *Asian Journal of Social Sciences & Humanities* 2(2): 345–357.

Makumbe, John Mw. 1998. Is There a Civil Society in Africa? *International Affairs* 74(2): 305–317.

Malik, Nadeem. 2009a. The Modern Face of Traditional Agrarian Rule: Local Government in Pakistan. *Development in Practice* 19(8): 997–1008.

Malik, Nadeem. 2009b. *Citizens and Governance in Pakistan: An Analysis of People's Voices*. Pakistan: Sanjh Publications.

Malik, Nadeem. 2014. *Corporate Social Responsibility and Development in Pakistan*. London and New York: Routledge.

Malik, Nadeem. 2016. Analyzing Good Governance and Decentralization in Developing Countries. *Journal of Political Science & Public Affairs* 4: 209.

Mercer, Claire. 2002. NGOs, Civil Society and Democratization: A Critical Review of the Literature. *Progress in Development Studies* 2(1): 5–22.

Mezzera, Marco, and Sial Safdar. 2010. *Media and Governance in Pakistan: A Controversial Yet Essential Relationship*. Initiative for Peace Building. Electronic document, www.clingendael.nl/sites/default/files/20101109_CRU_publicatie_mmezzera.pdf, accessed September 12, 2016.

Mullally, Siobhan. 2009. *A Long March to Justice: A Report on Judicial Independence and Integrity in Pakistan*. International Bar Association. Electronic document, file:///C:/Users/Nadeem/Downloads/Pakistan-Report_Sept09%20(2).pdf, accessed September 17, 2016.

Munir, Daud. 2009. Struggling for the Rule of Law: The Pakistani Lawyers' Movement. *Middle East Report* 251: 37–41.

Najam, Adil. 1996. NGO Accountability: A Conceptual Framework. *Development Policy Review* 14(4): 339–354.

Raza, Mansoor. 2016. On Death's Door: Trade Unions in Pakistan. *DAWN Sunday Magazine*, May 1. Electronic document, www.dawn.com/news/1255333/on-deaths-door-trade-unions-in-pakistan, accessed August 25, 2016.

Sabir, Munawar. 2011. The Role of Media in Creating Values of Nationalism in Pakistan. *Journal of Political Studies* 18(2): 17–36.

Sampson, Seven. 1996. The Social Life of Projects: Importing Civil Society to Albania. In *Civil Society: Challenging the Western Models*. Chris Hann and Elizabeth Dunn, eds. London and New York: Routledge.

Sayeed, Khalid B. 1967. *The Political System of Pakistan*. Boston, MA: Houghton Mifflin.

Shafi, Mohammad, and Pasha Shafi. 2005. *Labor Code of Pakistan*. Karachi: Bureau of Labor Publications.

Shah, Faiza. 2014. The Rise of NGO's and heir Harmful Impacts on Pakistan. *Herald Pakistan*, April issue. Electronic document, http://herald.dawn.com/news/1152863, accessed September 14, 2016.

Shaheed, Zafar. 2007. *The Labor Movement in Pakistan*. Oxford: Oxford University Press.

Siraj, Syed Abdul. 2009. Critical Analysis of Press Freedom in Pakistan. *Journal of Media and Communications* 1(3): 43–47.

Somjee, Abdulkarim H. 1984. *Political Society in Developing Countries*. London: Macmillan Press.

SPDC (Social Policy and Development Center). 2002. Dimensions of the Non-profit Sector in Pakistan: Preliminary Estimates. *Working Paper Series: 1*. Pakistan: Center for Civil Society of John Hopkins University and Social Policy and Development Center (SPDC).

Walsh, Declan. 2012. Reporter Dies in Pakistan, and Taliban Warns Others. *New York Times*, January 18. Electronic document, www.nytimes.com/2012/01/19/world/asia/reporter-dies-in-pakistan-and-taliban-warn-others.html?_r=1&pagewanted=print, accessed September 10, 2016.

Yusuf, Huma, and Emrys Schoemaker. 2013. The Media of Pakistan: Fostering Inclusion in a Fragile State. *BBC Media Action* Policy Briefing No. 9. Electronic document, http://downloads.bbc.co.uk/mediaaction/pdf/bbc_media_action_pakistan_policy_briefing.pdf, accessed September 15, 2016.

Zaffar, Ehsan. 2010. History and Continuing Influence of Pakistan Lawyer's Movement. Muftah. Electronic document, http://muftah.org/the-history-and-continuing-influence-of-pakistans-lawyers-movement-by-ehsan-zaffar/#.V_h_P499671, accessed September 10, 2016.

Zaidi, Syed Akbar. 2008. An Emerging Civil Society? *Journal of Democracy* 19(4): 38–40.

18

BANGLADESH

M. Anwar Hossen

A quest for civil society on environment and human rights

Bangladesh, which achieved independence from Pakistan in 1971, is surrounded on the western, northern, and eastern sides by India and on the southeast by Myanmar and has a parliamentary democratic system. It has an area of 56,990 square miles and more than 160 million people, 84 percent of whom earn less than US$2 a day (ADB 2008). The majority live in rural areas where the major basis for protecting human rights is agricultural production based on the ecological resources of the Ganges–Brahmaputra Basin. Here, "human rights" are defined as access to proper food, employment, health care, housing, and education. Due to climate change and inappropriate development programs, major environmental degradation causes human rights concerns for the marginalized, who historically depended on common property. In this context, I will define civil society, based on Jan Aart Scholte's definition, as "a political space where voluntary associations deliberately seek to shape the rules that govern one or the other aspect of social life" (2002: 283). These rules are described as laws, policies, and programs important for addressing local issues and concerns. Based on this institutional framework, non-governmental organizations (NGOs) focus on some specific programs like microcredit to empower local poor people. Three major NGOs—the Bangladesh Rural Advancement Committee (BRAC), Proshika, and Grameen Bank—are world renowned and are working for marginalized people in Bangladesh.

These NGOs represent a major component of the civil society organizations. In addition to these international organizations based in Dhaka, some others like the Landless Development Organization (LDO) and Uttaran originate locally and work for specific local issues and concerns. Here, the key question is whether these organizations represent local community voices related to local environmental issues and human rights concerns. To address this question, it is important to understand the nature of marginalized people's survival challenges in Bangladesh. For this purpose, I am sharing some Focus Group Discussion (FGD) notes from my PhD field-work observation in 2011 and 2012 in Bangladesh.

Most of the civil society organizations never address the structural context of environmental concerns and human rights problem, although they are supposed to find the root causes so as to promote sustainable development. In most cases, they follow a direction compatible with elite-centric globalization and unfavorable to local people, the environment, and development.

In their official pronouncements, most of them always talk about the issue of marginalized people's representation, but in reality, the practice is different. This critical contribution is visible in the different types of civil society organizations and members like academics, electronic and print media personalities, business sector representatives, development agencies, NGO executives, community leaders, human rights advocates, and women's rights activists. They perform significant roles, directly or indirectly, in the process of formulating and implementing new laws, policies, and programs related to environmental concerns and human rights even though marginalized people are increasingly encountering biodiversity losses, irregular floods and droughts, salinity intrusions, cyclones, and river bank erosion. These environmental issues are major causes of human rights violations in relation to food, employment, health care, education, and housing. For example, they discuss slum dwellers' human rights but do not address the ecological disasters as one major root cause of their displacement. In this context, it is important to understand this critical role of civil society in some of the important theoretical literature.

Theoretical orientation to civil society

Members of civil society develop their consciousness in relation to issues like respect, participation, inclusion, and good governance through their socialization process. Micha de Winter (2012) describes the beginning of this freedom of expression as starting at the early stage of childhood. Parents' roles in nurturing this freedom will decide a child's future direction. Children always want to try out every possible activity available to them, whereas parents forbid some of them and encourage others to promote the "proper" direction. In addition to parental guidelines, they learn from media outlets in this globalized world. Based on this background, a child develops into a mature adult and evaluates everything, like the environment and human rights.

Fahimul Quadir (1999: 7) focuses on the role of civil society in promoting liberal democracy and economic liberalization in Bangladesh. The guidelines of the World Bank (WB), the International Monetary Fund (IMF), and the Structural Adjustment Programs (SAPs) were the main drivers for this liberalization, which was pursued to develop market mechanisms and macroeconomic stabilization (Quadir 1999: 15). This economic development approach weakens state roles and promotes new civil society movements with NGOs as major development partners. The major logic of the donor agencies is that they want to liberate civil society from state control in order to promote liberal democracy and free markets. In this way, international donors provide support to expand civil society networks so that liberal democracy can function properly by removing authoritarian regimes. Fahimul Quadir and Jayant Lele (2004: 8) describe this linkage between liberal democracy and civil society from a Gramscian perspective and envision civil society as having less potential. This perspective focuses on a critical approach to direct the government system for the promotion of the human rights of local citizens, although some major civil society organizations currently support authoritarian regimes in order to benefit themselves.

Jean Cohen and Andrew Arato (1997: 3) describe how democracy theory discusses the different approaches of elitism and participation to operate the government and state system. The elitist approach follows market economic strategies in place of welfare systems. This approach believes in acquiring and exercising power in controlling resources and economic growth, which discourages the values of human rights and common property, and encourages efficiency and growth with consumerism and entrepreneurship. In opposition to this elitist model, rights-oriented liberalism describes normative forms of democratic justice based on the concepts of human rights that are specific to history and culture (Cohen and Arato 1997: 8). The major point here is how can the present world protect the freedom of individuals to secure these human rights that emphasize individual autonomy and moral egalitarianism in the context of historical and social identity. This process defines the values, duties, and virtues of individual rights and a shared understanding of communities and common good (Cohen and Arato 1997: 9). Civil society follows this liberal approach in addressing local environmental issues and human rights concerns.

Terje Tvedt (2002: 363) describes the internationalization of civil society based on aid systems that support development NGOs as a structural force to influence local organizations. The author describes two opposite examples of this NGO contribution: President Nelson Mandela rebuked NGOs as working at the behest of foreign interests in 1997, while Kofi Annan as the Secretary-General of the United Nations glorified NGOs as promoters of human rights. These two examples describe the two opposite scenarios of NGO contributions (Tvedt 2002: 368). Every year, the different gatherings—conferences, meetings, seminars, and summits all over the world—bring together the different NGO partners, government agencies, corporate houses, and business people from the South and North, and make decisions about global and local environmental issues and human rights concerns in a manner that favors corporate interests and not the local marginalized.

Consequently, Geof Wood (2014) argues, the traditional roles of states are increasingly getting fragile due to elite-centric approaches or coalitions of elites, where the rich get richer by depriving the poor. Since the birth of Bangladesh in 1971, major aid dependency established new civil society organizations that favor a Western normative discourse and discriminate against the local base. Here, the local institutional base is defined as rules, norms, conventions, and beliefs (Wood 2014: 3). The transformation of this base is guided by a civil society that ignores traditional local culture in favor of a corporate culture.

Nora McKeon (2009) describes these issues in the context of United Nations' roles related to current issues and concerns like globalization, migration, diaspora, private unilateralism, and ultra-nationalism to promote civil society voices. Since 1990, the United Nations Non-Governmental Liaison Service (UN-NGLS) has supported many of the civil society organizations (CSOs) with networking systems. However, the author cautions that the CSOs are not able to perform their proper roles due to the geopolitical domination of economic agendas like the neoliberal development approach. In this context, a strong linkage amongst development discourse, institutional change, and civil society has existed within the UN system. McKeon describes this linkage with an example from the Food and Agriculture Organization related to global governance of food security, which is connected with human rights. The idea of food as a human right is a major issue for civil society organizations in the global South.

Jose Harris (2001) describes the issue of food security according to two ideological lines of civil society, the market-oriented approach and the socialist or quasi-socialist approach, which describes the directions of individualism and collectivism respectively (Harris 2001: x–xiii). This dichotomy is described with Ferdinand Tönnies' text of *Gemeinschaft und Gesellschaft* (1887) in the context of small-scale communities and large-scale market-oriented civil societies. This text describes the social basis of will and pleasure based on Kant's ethical and cognitive theories, which can be described with two types of consciousness: natural and spontaneous versus artificial, deliberative, and rational calculation. The Gemeinschaft is associated with community-based kinship, authority, and ownership whereas the Gesellschaft is associated with individualism and state systems that are linked to with bureaucratic rationality and legislation (Harris 2001). This individualistic rationality focuses on some piecemeal issues like gender equality for accessing food rather than focusing on food rights for all.

Marjorie Lister and Maurizi Carbone (2006) describe this neoliberal empowerment approach in the context of the European Union's gender equality perspective since its inception in the

1950s. Based on this "Women in Development" (WID) approach, donor agencies like the World Bank, the UN, the Department For International Development (DFID) for the UK, the Danish International Development Agency (DANIDA), and the Swedish International Development Cooperation Agency (SIDA) are working for women's rights. On the other hand, the voices of women in the developing countries on issues like unemployment are termed as "women and development" (WAD). In the context of WID and WAD, new groups of women use the term "Gender and Development" (GAD) to describe gender and power relations rather than women in the context of development (Lister and Carbone 2006: 4). This linkage between power structures and gender can be described with the historically developed relationships between women and nature. These relationships can protect the environment and human rights based on natural resource management.

However, a patriarchal development approach creates ecocracies (defined by Wolfgang Sachs (1993) as the politics of global natural resource management with a modernization approach and its effects) that create multiple challenges for the relationship between women and nature. In this context, some major Environmental NGOs (ENGOs) after the Rio Earth Summit in 1992 have been actively contributing to this through research, advocacy, and awareness based on the active support of donor agencies like the World Bank, the United Nations Development Program (UNDP), the United States Agency for International Development (USAID), and DFID. D. A. Ahsan, T. A. Del Valls, and J. Blasco (2009) focus on the roles of NGOs in addressing environmental degradation like biodiversity degradation, loss of wetlands, and arsenic pollution. The authors list some of the factors responsible for these degradations as population growth, lack of good governance, and the capacity of government agencies like the Department of Environment (DoE) to protect the wetlands in Bangladesh. These degradations are closely connected with the dominant development approach that causes human rights concerns regarding the poor in Bangladesh.

Scholte (2002) describes the linkage between civil society and globalization related to the protest movements in different places like Seattle, Davos, Prague, Melbourne, Porto, and Genoa. This global nature of a local movement raises questions about the effectiveness of democracy and legitimacy in the context of global governance. For this purpose, the term "civil society" is defined differently based on time, place, theoretical perspective, and political ideology (Scholte 2002: 283). Hegel focuses on the market to describe civil society whereas the current dominant development discourse emphasizes a non-profit approach. This discourse, according to Gramsci, describes civil society as part of class hegemony to support their own agendas. This global nature of power structure was only possible with the promotion of public space as the major site for communication and social change.

Manual Castells (2008) takes a positive approach in describing this public space as the center of interaction for argument, debate, and new ideas that are helpful for communication between government and civil society to reshape local communities and promote social change. Globalization operates in this public space to address local environmental issues and human rights concerns that generate new aspects of global communication networks, information, public diplomacy, and global governance (Castells 2008: 78). Here, the different media like internet and wireless communication, as well as print media, perform major roles in this public diplomacy. Based on this type of socio-political organization, people nurture and promote their individual views to influence political institutions. Civil society as an organized force promotes these viewpoints as a foundation for democracy, inclusion, and participation. However, the poor find themselves excluded when power relations become dominated by a particular segment of society with their conflicting interests (Castells 2008: 80). This exclusion can be described in terms of three types of capacity: technological, institutional, and organizational, which can be helpful to describe the different issues and concerns like global warming, environmental degradation, terrorism, human rights, and social justice that have arisen as a result of the rise of global civil society (Castells 2008: 83). These issues and concerns encourage local public participation at the global level by using print and electronic media. All of these activities are a foundation for global governance despite facing major organizational, technical, and political coordination problems (Castells 2008: 88). This governance approach is exemplified by inter-government organizations like the United Nations. The role of civil society in this global governance is increasing in Bangladesh with the different policy documents like the Poverty Reduction Strategy Paper (PRSP) and the Sustainable Development Goals (SDGs).

Review of civil society in Bangladesh

The members of civil society receive their socialization from the very beginning of their lives as members of a family, community, and society. This process can produce enlightened people with proper educational and spiritual backgrounds to make rational judgments. The nature and roles of this civil society base in Bangladesh have changed over time due to major social transformations. In this context, NGOs appeared as a new civil society to promote democracy, inclusion, and participation for the goal of sustainable development in Bangladesh (Quadir 1999: 16).

David Lewis (2011) gives an overview of politics, economy, and civil society related to the historically developed and politically grounded development approach in Bangladesh. Since the 1980s, Bangladesh has continuously been pushed toward a liberalization and stabilization approach to economic development based on foreign aid. NGOs are major supporters of this approach to address the different concerns like climate change, ecological vulnerabilities, and human rights. Local people had enormous ecological resources like cropland siltation, wild fish, and vegetation within the Ganges–Brahmaputra Basin to protect their environment and human rights. However, they currently encounter environmental degradation, biodiversity loss, and human rights violations.

Continuous ecological vulnerabilities like irregular flooding, drought, salinity intrusion, and riverbank erosion reduce these resources and cause multiple socio-economic vulnerabilities. Many of the marginalized people suffer unemployment and become *mustaan* (musclemen) while the beneficiaries of the development programs like MDGs see themselves promoted to *bhadralok* (gentlemen). The *bhadralok* and *mustaan* create new forms of patron–client relationships with NGO activities in this new development discourse. Lewis (2011: 25) describes the civil society as being more than just these NGOs although this civil society does not have a proper definition in Bangladesh. The Islamic religion terms its followers *ashraf* and *ajlaf* families, which are described as "noble" and "commoner." Some male members of these *ashraf* families become *pirs* (holy men), while some others become *baul*, *sadhu*s, and *faqir*s (traditional philosophers: *baul* sing philosophical songs, *sadhu* and *faqir* spread educative words with their respective Hindu and Muslim religious approaches). Some of them can be described as civil society representatives in traditional Bangladesh and the *pir* and *baul* form part of the structure of secularism which, along with nationalism, democracy, and socialism, is one of the four pillars of the Bangladesh constitution.

Since the 1990s, the principle of socialism has diminished in importance and democracy has received more focus in the government system due to the reshaping of the global power structure (Lewis 2011: 30). This new power structure promotes structural adjustment, liberalization, privatization, and deregulation, which bring new types of civil society in Bangladesh, and transforms the understanding of environmental issues and human rights concerns from a collective to an individualistic approach. This transformation has increased agricultural production but with major ecological costs like environmental degradation, biodiversity loss, and salinity intrusion, which increase poverty, social inequality, and insecurity. Traditional civil society representatives like *pir* are replaced with NGOs that are currently addressing many of these socio-ecological concerns. Lewis (2011: 110) informs us that 206,000 "not-for-profit" organizations contribute 8 percent of annual GDP in Bangladesh. Of these, 54,536 and 1,925 were registered by the Ministry of Social Welfare and NGO Affairs Bureau respectively. As civil society representatives, these NGOs promote good governance, human rights, and land reforms. In this context, *sadhu*s and *faqir*s are described as the most vulnerable people in a local community and the frontline targets of NGOs. Three major globally known NGOs in Bangladesh are BRAC, Grameen Bank, and Proshika. They use villages, *samaj*, under the leadership of *mathbor*, a village leader, to address the different local issues like environmental and human rights concerns.

There is a major historical factor behind this boom in the NGO sector in Bangladesh. The War of Independence in 1971 caused 3 million deaths and another 3 million displacements. Again, natural disasters like flood and drought caused an average annual food crop loss of 1.7 million tons during the 1970s and 1.46 million tons during the 1980s (ADB 2008: 2). In response to these losses from natural disasters and war, some NGOs like the Bangladesh Rural Advancement Committee (BRAC) begun their activities based on relief and rehabilitation programs related to human rights like health and education with microfinance programs. With an annual budget of US$235 million, BRAC works in 68,408 villages with 4.8 million group members and 4.2 million borrowers (ADB 2008: 3). Proshika is another NGO, established in 1976, working in 23,475 villages and 2,101 urban slums for 2.75 million members on various issues like poverty alleviation, environmental protection, and people's participation. Another NGO, Grameen Bank, founded in 1976 by Nobel laureate Muhammed Yunus, focuses on women's empowerment with microcredit programs (ADB 2008).

Most local, national, and international NGOs are part of a common platform, the Association of Development Agencies in Bangladesh (ADAB), that has 1,071 members (ADB 2008: 6). ADB identified five basic points in Bangladesh—innovation, accountability, responsiveness, participation, and sustainability—to describe the major activities of civil society (2008: 8).

As mentioned earlier, NGOs began their tasks as promoters of relief and rehabilitation immediately after independence in 1971. This focus on relief and rehabilitation has changed to service delivery due to the changing paradigm of the global political economy of local development. In this context, local NGOs find out local people's issues and concerns, such as unemployment, illiteracy, maternal mortality, and malnutrition, to improve the human rights condition of the marginalized. They extend their roles to policy advocacy on local concerns like environmental conservation, gender equity, and good governance. Some NGOs like the Bangladesh Environmental Lawyers Association (BELA) and the Bangladesh Legal Aid and Services Trust (BLAST) contribute to environmental and human rights issues respectively. Most of these organizations emphasize the global understanding of environmental and human rights that are linked with the dominant development paradigm. In this context, Paul Henderson and Ilona Vercseg (2010: 5) describe the linkage between community and civil society to establish the effects of social change on local people.

The development of NGOs in the period 1947–1970 saw a transformation of cooperatives from village-based to union-based multipurpose cooperative societies (ADB 2008). Some major cooperative enterprises like the National Industrial Society, the National Fishermen's Society, and the Sugarcane Growers' Federation were established during this period (ADB 2008: 1). In 1959, the Bangladesh Academy for Rural Development (BARD), also known as the Comilla Cooperative Model, was established to carry out the different projects and plans in rural development. This model provided a major foundation for integrated rural development with the support of bilateral and multilateral partners like USAID and DFID (ADB 2008).

Based on this international involvement, local civil society in Bangladesh was established to follow a particular ideology in terms of development approach, democracy, and social change (Quadir 1999). The government in Bangladesh began this market-oriented reform in the 1970s with the Zia government's (1975–1981) privatization programs even before the SAPs (Quadir 1999: 17–18). The development partners encouraged these privatization programs with conditional aid that was also closely linked to the promotion of democracy. This donor-supported democracy can be termed as democratization from above, which is evident in other regimes like the Ershad Government (1982–1990). During this democratization process, the country encounters different challenges to inclusion, political stability, and election governance. The major political parties exploit violence in pursuit of their political goals (Quadir 1999: 20). Most civil society representatives are divided along political party lines about this violence and explain the different issues like ecological vulnerabilities, environmental degradation, and human rights violations based on their political ideology; this is a critical factor in trying to address local people's issues and concerns.

Contributions of civil society organizations to representing community voices

In general, civil society performs important roles on different issues like democracy and governance. It is in this context that I understand the roles of civil society organizations and members in addressing the environmental issues and human rights concerns faced by marginalized groups in Bangladesh. Most of these issues and concerns are related to local development promoted by external agencies using the buzzwords of social mobility, empowerment, and sustainability. Civil society can represent local voices and can address local concerns like biodiversity loss, irregular flooding, salinity intrusion, drought, and river bank erosion by challenging the dominant approach. They can also address these concerns by revealing corruption and malpractice related to development projects like the Flood Action Plan (FAP) and social services programs like the EGPP (Employment Generation Program for the Poorest). For this purpose, civil society organization follows different advocacy approaches like conformist, reformist, or transformist (Scholte 2002: 284). These contributions can be formal or informal based on their nature and responsibilities, such as academic institutions, business forums, consumer advocates, environmental movements, ethnic lobbies, faith-based associations, human rights promoters, labor unions, local community groups, peace movements, and women's networks.

Based on these contributions, civil society in Bangladesh guides social transformation that can be described in terms of Tönnies' Gemeinschaft and Gesellschaft. Rural villages and their traditional socio-economic and political practices have changed significantly in coordination with new development approaches. This transformation process sometimes carries some major risks of inequality, exploitation, and domination, which are regulated by public opinion, politeness, and good norms. The different civil society organizations like BRAC and the Grameen Bank are working to reduce these issues and concerns. For example, BRAC has three major sectors: well-being and resilience, economic development and social protection, and empowerment. Each of these sectors has expanded to other major areas like disaster management related to health, nutrition, water sanitation, and hygiene.

BRAC's report informs us that they provided relief to 1,200 flood victim families in Gaibandha, Lalmonirhat, Kurigram, and Sirajgonj with 1.4 tons of food supplies and US$9,758 in cash support in 2015 (2015: 6). In addition to these emergency supports, they operated some recovery programs with vegetable seed distribution to 20,000 households and mobile money to

3,000 marginal farmers so that they could overcome the impact of the floods. Based on these supports, BRAC is encouraging the generation of a resilience fund known as *Community-Level Disaster-Resilient Funds* (CLDRF) to deal with new disasters. For this purpose, BRAC uses its organization *Polli Samaj* (Village Society), a women's local community organization, to coordinate the CLDRF in the disaster-affected districts like Sirajgonj, Kurigram, Gaibandha, and Lalmonirhat. Additionally, BRAC provided support to form 764 groups with more than 19,000 women who live in disaster-vulnerable districts in Bangladesh (BRAC 2015: 14).

As part of economic development, BRAC focuses on agriculture and food security to fight against climate change effects, which is closely linked with the second of the UN's Sustainable Development Goals. For food and nutritional security in coordination with biodiversity conservation, BRAC promoted 117 aromatic and seventy-seven non-aromatic traditional rice varieties and connected 156,352 farmers in fifty-one sub-districts with these new agriculture and aquaculture technologies. In this context, BRAC introduced rice intensification programs to 6,693 farmers and 1,332 hectares of croplands in seventy-three drought-prone sub-districts. As part of this environmental focus, aquaculture was promoted in thirty seasonal floodplains to protect local fish in sixteen sub-districts (BRAC 2015: 27).

Through their program activities, the organization would like to reduce the socio-economic harm to children from the effects of disaster. At present, BRAC operates 14,153 primary schools for different groups of marginalized children in geographic regions like the *haor* or low-lying areas, the Chittagong Hill Tract, and urban slums. These schools have more than 396,595 students, 62 percent of them female. Up until 2015, more than 6 million children had completed pre-primary education in BRAC pre-primary schools with a 99.75 percent successful completion rate, 61 percent of them female. BRAC has reduced dropout rates by providing *Medhabikash Udyog* (Promoting Talent) since 2005. This talent scholarship program identifies poor yet high-performing students so that they get an opportunity for social mobility. Based on these activities, the BRAC schools and scholarship programs are helpful for coping with disaster effects. Moreover, they also provide other program supports to parents to reduce child marriage and to promote women's empowerment (BRAC 2015: 14). This approach is not only helpful for disaster risk reduction but also provides major scope for reducing violence against women and promoting gender equality and social justice (BRAC 2015: 26).

BRAC's programs are transforming the socio-economic and political structure from the Gemeinschaft to the Gesellschaft system. For example, BRAC's agricultural intensification based on the rational–legal authority of the state transforms traditional agricultural production with plough, oxen, and cow dung to the Green Revolution. This transformation encourages commercial agricultural production that promotes an international market for local crops. To overcome negative effects, BRAC simultaneously promotes equality, social justice, and good governance based on the different programs. These programs transform a community's values and its perception of what constitute appropriate duties and virtues in the development of women's identities in the social structure. This approach also replaces the shared understanding of communities and the common good with individual rights.

In addition to this civil society contribution at national level, some local organizations like Uttaran and the Landless Development Organization (LDO) are working to address community-specific issues and concerns. The Bengali term "uttaran" is defined as a transition from poverty to upward mobility. This organization was registered with the Department of Social Welfare on March 5, 1985 and works in five divisions: Khulna, Barisal, Chittagong, Rajshahi, and Dhaka. More than 181,710 marginalized people are getting direct benefits from Uttaran based on issues like human rights, agrarian reform and land rights, community-based river basin management, sustainable development, climate change adaptation, ecocentric agricultural production, and food security. For example, Uttaran supports a local civil society committee, the Paani (water) Committee, to promote drinking water free of salinity and local rainwater harvesting for local communities' sustainable water management. This committee works closely with local communities for Tidal River Management, a major effort to reduce waterlogging of the southwest region. As part of this process, Uttaran emphasizes the Multi-Stakeholder Forum (MSF) for regional river water resource management and for reducing ecological vulnerabilities. Moreover, the organization contributes to disaster risk reduction in terms of relief and rehabilitation with awareness raising, capacity building, and social mobilization as southwest Bangladesh encounters multiple disaster challenges like waterlogging, flooding, and cyclone.

In the context of land rights, Uttaran promotes the fair distribution of khasland, state-owned dry and wetland, to landless poor people in Satkhira and Khulna Districts by developing a governance approach known as the Tala Model. Based on this model, Uttaran recovered 3297 hectares of illegally occupied khasland and distributed them to 11,589 families.

In addition to Uttaran, another civil society organization, the Landless Development Organization (LDO), is working to address local community-specific issues and concerns. LDO was established in 1992 in the Chatmohor sub-district of Pabna District that is under Chalan Beel, the biggest wetland in Bangladesh. The LDO committee, composed of a chairman, a vice-chairman, six executive members, and one member secretary, who are local teachers, social workers, and housewives. As part of their organizational system, the LDO has 140 groups with 3,372 members. Its major objectives are to distribute local common property resources like khasland based on historical rights and to ensure the human rights of marginalized groups. Two major beel or wetlands in Chatmohor sub-district are Beelkurulia and Dischirbeel, which received ecological support from Chalan Beel. However, these wetlands were transformed into dry land, locally called khasland. Local poor people used these khaslands for protecting their human rights. However, these khaslands were encroached upon by the then government in the 1960s and were increasingly controlled by local elites for commercial interests. In combating this occupancy, there were bloody conflicts between the elites and the local landless farmers in 1961 that left one landless farmer dead and several wounded. This conflict and disorder has continued for around three decades.

The LDO fought these occupants by organizing local landless people under the land reform ordinance of 1987 and the leadership of K. M. Ataur Rahman Rana, a freedom fighter and local school teacher (ALRD 2012). On June 30, 1992, local poor people like landless farmers, day laborers, and fishermen organized a demonstration and announced that the khaslands were their own lands and the elites should not be allowed to control them. They also submitted a Memorandum of Understanding to the Upazila Nirbahi Officer, the head of local government at sub-district level, regarding this matter. Moreover, they established control over a significant amount of land and distributed it to 1,045 landless families for agricultural production on December 10, 1992. This khasland is very fertile and successfully produces two crops a year; each hectare produces 7,410 kilograms of HYV paddy a season, which is helpful for protecting human rights like food security, education, and employment. The LDO promoted legal steps against the rich people's occupancy; moreover, the Association for Land Reform and Development (ALRD), a national-level civil society organization based on the example of K. M. Ataur Rahman Rana, raised the issue through two Members of Parliament (MPs). The MPs brought the issue before the Jatiya Sangsad (the national parliament) and received a significant amount of support from the other MPs. This discussion motivated local governments to resolve the issue properly; therefore, 534 landless families were successful in getting 135 hectares of khaslands under the Bangladesh government legal system. Since 2005, the Bangladesh NGO Foundation has provided support to these landless people for agricultural production and food security. In this process, in

2015, the government approved 1,196 applications from landless people, 223 of them female-headed and widow households. Amongst them, 547 have taken control of the land and the others are in the process of completing the necessary formalities.

Here, the LDO approach to addressing local marginalized people's issues and concerns is very different from BRAC. The LDO emphasizes local movements to promote local voices, while BRAC is closely connected with the neoliberal development approach. Uttaran's approach can be described being between the two. Some other major civil society organizations like the Bangladesh Porinesh Andolon (BAPA, Bangladesh Environmental Movement), the Bangladesh Environmental Lawyers Association (BELA), the UBINIG (Policy Research for Development Alternatives), and SHUJAN or Citizens for Good Governance focus on poor people's empowerment related to environmental and human rights protection. However, the major question here is the long-term sustainability of this empowerment when local people in Bangladesh encounter increasing biodiversity loss, environmental degradation, and ecological vulnerabilities. Due to ecosystem failures and biodiversity loss, the Agro-Ecological Zone (AEZ) on the High Ganges River Floodplains (HGRF) in Bangladesh is currently encountering losses of soil fertility within a range of 20 to 45 percent (BARC 2006). Consequently, 35 percent of fish species encounter water pollution and 17 percent encounter habitat degradation (Afrose and Ahmed 2016). Currently, 10 percent of 260 fish species are facing survival challenges (Khan 2013). The overuse of TSP fertilizer for agricultural production generates an average of 0.099 milligrams of cadmium in one kilogram of rice in Kushtia and some other areas in Bangladesh (Bhuyan 2013). According to the Internal Displacement Monitoring Centre, for example, 531,000 people in Bangladesh encountered internal displacement in 2015. Civil society needs to address this displacement and the environmental concerns with locally embedded understanding to protect marginalized people's human rights.

Future direction of civil society to address environmental and human rights

In Bangladesh, the fact that there has been major aid dependency since independence has connected civil society with the Western ideology of local development. This ideology has transformed aspects of the local institutional base like norms, laws, policies, and programs to Western normative courses of action. The ruling government in Bangladesh and opposition political parties accept this transformation as part of the global governance system. In this context, the Jatiya Sangsad is dominated by people who believe in this development ideology of liberal democracy. Therefore, the parliament contains many business people and industrialists who are the major beneficiaries of the dominant development paradigm. This liberal democratic and market economy ideological standpoint has caused them to abandon their locally embedded understanding of environmental and human rights. Consequently, they focus less on the broader issues like the basin flow concerns, ecological vulnerabilities, and ecosystem protection, and focus more on issues like microcredit and flood control.

This new approach displaces community-based institutions of common property and replaces them with the new institutions of Union and Upazila councils compatible with the neoliberal approach. In this process, new political parties come to power but civil society movements are not supporting any significant efforts to provide Bangladesh's poor with opportunities for upward social mobility. Many of the organizations exploit the poor people's vulnerabilities to get grants or other funds and use them for the benefit of themselves and their organizations rather than the people themselves. Consequently, every street in Dhaka has homeless men, women, and children who do not have enough clothes on their bodies, have been starving for days, and are awaiting death; all this is happening because their social benefits are controlled by these people and organizations. This socio-economic condition of the homeless needs to be addressed under three major headings: root causes of the displacement, proper development policies, and social programs with accountability. Civil society organizations like BRAC, Uttaran, and the LDO have a major responsibility to address these points.

Castells (2008) describes the optimism to overcome the current challenges with new electronic media like Facebook, Viber, and YouTube to promote the views of the marginalized to influence opinions and political institutions. These media focus on new dialogues amongst civil society organizations, villagers, farmers, and state agencies to develop community-based resource management. This development approach begins with community movements in coordination with civic and non-government organizations. They work toward Ganges Basin ecological system conservation, democracy, bottom–up development approaches, and community participation. For example, Policy Research for Development Alternatives and New Agricultural Movements in Bangladesh represent local voices to promote bottom–up development approaches. Some local groups form transnational alliances based on their common grounds to promote these objectives.

This media-based representation reduces the roles of Gemeinschaft in the different issues like equality, human rights, and social justice based on the neoliberal approach. However, the problem in accessing new media is that the majority of people in Bangladesh live in rural areas and do not have basic services like electricity, internet, and literacy. Therefore, their voices are under the control of urban-based civil society representatives who describe these voices in the process of policy formulations and implementations. This representation favors deregulation, liberalization, and privatization, which cause social inequality and displacement for some of the marginalized.

The majority of local people fail to avail the new media to promote their issues and concerns. Therefore, their voices are excluded from the globalization process and they encounter elite domination of their lives, liberties, and freedoms in relation to different issues like global warning, environmental degradation, terrorism, human rights, and social justice. Again, the different civil society organizations and members describe these issues with some buzzwords compatible with the global power structures and extract benefits from the system.

In this process, civil society is promoting a neoliberal understanding of social service programs. In Bangladesh, the government provides authority to the civil society organizations like BRAC to operate the subsidy programs. This social service management approach is helpful in generating employment opportunities based on economic growth, new investment, and stabilization. To regulate new enterprises, national and international laws support labor unions to create a balance-of-power relationship between laborers and entrepreneurs in the hope of promoting social justice. However, the promotion of this balance is not successful in Bangladesh as the government is directly and indirectly in the hands of industrialists and the business class.

This power structure fails to protect the ecology-based livelihood practices of the marginalized. This failure to adopt an ecocentric development approach causes human rights challenges for the different groups of marginalized people like traditional farmers, fishermen, and boatmen. Therefore, the traditional agricultural practices of *Kharif*-I, *Kharif*-II, and *Robi* in coordination with the seasonal patterns of winter, summer, and rainy seasons are replaced with the Green Revolution. BRAC promotes hybrid seeds for commercial agricultural production by using their microcredit loan holders in Bangladesh. When their investments encounter damage and losses from ecological disasters, marginalized farmers are unable to recover. Many of them become displaced and suffer major human rights violations. The civil society organizations do not care much for these concerns. They are focused on getting back their investments and making profits.

Here I will describe the FGD viewpoints of one of my PhD respondents, Billal. He informed me that he had taken a loan from an NGO to buy a cow. Two weeks after receiving the loan, the NGO staff visited him to collect the installment although the cow is far from producing. If he had failed to pay the installment, the NGO would have taken away household assets to recover the loan. Another respondent, Joardar, encountered agricultural production failures in 2011 due to sudden floods and, finding no other alternatives, he received an NGO loan. Like Billal, he needed to pay the installment after two weeks, although he had not yet started agricultural production. He had no way to complete the agricultural tasks and pay installments, so he sold small household resources and timber to pay them.

The major reasons for loan default in most cases, according to Billal and Joardar, are crop production failures due to damage and losses from flood, drought, river bank erosion, or embankment failure. However, NGO staff do not address these causes and apply pressure for the installment to be paid. When people fail to pay the loan, the staff take household assets like domestic animals, ornaments, or land. Some people even sell their organs like a kidney or an eye to pay off this loan. Others borrow money from one NGO for investments, another NGO for loan payments, and a third for installment payments. In extreme cases, they surrender their last assets and are displaced from their ancestral home. The homeless people in Dhaka are some examples of this type of displacement.

According to Billal, one BRAC school is operated by a single teacher, who teaches every subject like English, Bengali, Math, Physics, Biology, and Social Sciences. This is not a teaching method that will provide quality education. The salary of a BRAC schoolteacher does not meet the minimum standard and they receive no other benefits like health care. Moreover, only BRAC loan subscribers are entitled to admission and other poor people are excluded from this school. This neoliberal approach to education fails to ensure equality and no civil society organization raises questions about it.

Recently, one group of civil society promoted a new argument in relation to development in Bangladesh that places less importance on democracy. Another group is keener to promote democracy and does not focus properly on the inclusion of the local poor in relation to environmental conservation and human rights protection. In this context, local elections are the bidding ground to win a specific constituency based on offering a better package for a particular time and geographic region. Here, voters are described as consumers while political parties are entrepreneurs. Civil society works to ensure transparency and accountability in the process of bidding, competition, accessibility, and representation so that everyone, voters and candidates, can get fair treatment. Civil society would like to ensure a peaceful environment and stability, and they do not tolerate any violence, vote-rigging, or ballot-box snatching in this process. The problem with this elitist form of democracy, however, is that voters are not able to raise their livelihood problems and encounter multiple survival challenges because of exclusion and misrepresentation. Here, "participation" and "representation" are buzzwords for poor voters and civil society is busier with their own interests. This democratic system fails to empower local groups of people leading to displacements and human rights violations. This cause needs to be addressed properly so that the marginalized can protect their standard of living.

NGOs as civil society representatives should maintain a major focus on marginalized women. Currently, this focus is divided into the empowerment discourse of developed and developing countries. Women of developed counties want equal rights while the developing countries' women place more emphasis on different issues like unemployment, low wages, and poor working conditions. Civil society in Bangladesh needs a specific focus based on the linkage between gender, power, and development. Some of them focus more on the developed countries' feminist approach and ignore local contexts. They also coordinate with various political regimes that may not be compatible with liberal democracy. They ensure their own benefit from the regimes and promote market economic systems in local resource management and fail to represent local environmental and human rights. This new approach has transformed Bangladesh from a pre-capitalist to a market economic system by displacing local livelihoods, values, and beliefs and civil society has failed to perform its proper role in addressing the transition. Here, the Gramscian critique of civil society fits as they support authoritarian regimes and fail to ensure de Tocqueville's free-standing independence.

Conclusion

In Bangladesh, civil society emphasizes the promotion of human rights and the conservation of the local environment although the marginalized are facing major survival challenges. The major reason for this gap is that the national parliament of Bangladesh is dominated by business people and industrialists, who make decisions for their own good that create major challenges to the protection of the human rights of the marginalized. Sometimes they make this decision in coordination with the global power structure and suppress local community voices. This power structure encourages global governance based on inter-government organizations like the United Nations, which follow the precepts of liberal democracy. In this context, local politics expand to international domains for environmental resource management and livelihood protection. The different development programs like the Millennium Development Goals (MDGs) focus on these issues based on their top-down understanding. In this context, the nature and roles of civil society organizations have changed over time in coordination with the MDGs. Therefore, socio-economic conditions in Bangladesh transform from a natural economy to a neoliberal approach and local social organizations like village- and network-like kinship are replaced by modern associations like farmers' cooperatives and networks. This new approach causes multiple problems like ecological vulnerabilities and human rights concerns, which create major threats to marginalized community livelihoods. Civil society needs to take on these challenges, reduce environmental degradation, biodiversity loss, and displacement, and promote ecosystems, equality, social justice, and human rights.

Suggested readings

Castells, Manual. 2008. Public Diplomacy in a Changing World. *The Annals of the American Academy of the Political and Social Science* 616: 78–93.

Harris, Jose, ed. 2001. *Ferdinand Tönnies: Community and Civil Society*. Translated by Jose Harris and Margaret Hollis. Cambridge: Cambridge University Press.

Lewis, David. 2011. *Bangladesh: Politics, Economy and Civil Society*. New York: Cambridge University Press.

Quadir, Fahimul. 1999. Democracy, Development and Civil Society in Bangladesh: The Quest for a New Praxis for Sustainability. PhD thesis, Dalhousie University.

Wood, Geof. 2014. Can Civil Society be Free of the Natural State?: Applying North to Bangladesh. *Working Paper* No. 33. Bath: The Centre for Development Studies.

References

Afrose, Sania, and Nesar Ahmed. 2016. Effects of Degraded Ecosystem on Fish Biodiversity in the Old Brahmaputra River, Bangladesh and Its Conservation Measures. *IOSR Journal of Environmental Science, Toxicology and Food Technology* 10(9): 37–43.

Ahsan, D. A., T. A. Del Valls, and J. Blasco. 2009. The Relationship of National and International Environmental NGOs in Bangladesh and Their Role in Wetland Conservation. *International Journal of Environmental Research* 3(1): 23–34.

ADB (Asian Development Bank). 2008. Overview of NGOs and Civil Society: Bangladesh. Electronic document, www.adb.org/publications/overview-ngos-and-civil-society-bangladesh, accessed February 24, 2017.

ALRD (Association for Land Reform and Development). 2012. Bilkuraya Manifests Demanding Land Rights/Bilkuralia and ALRD Demands to Establish the Right to Land. Dhaka.

BARC (Bangladesh Agriculture Research Council). 2006. Table 4.04: Losses of Fertility of Soil by Intensified Crop Cultivation from 1967–68 to 1997–98. Government of Bangladesh. Electronic document, www.moa.gov.bd/statistics/Table4.04.htm, accessed July 3, 2012.

BRAC (Bangladesh Rural Advancement Committee). 2015. BRAC 2015 Annual Report. Electronic document, www.brac.net/images/reports/BRAC-Bangladesh-Report-2015.pdf, accessed February 15, 2017.

Bhuyan, O. U. 2013. Study Finds Cadmium in Rice Samples. Dhaka: New Age. Electronic document, http://nagoriknews.org/index.php/bangladeshi-newspaper/english-newspaper/new-age.html, accessed June 15, 2013.

Castells, Manual. 2008. Public Diplomacy in a Changing World. *The Annals of the American Academy of the Political and Social Science* 616: 78–93.

Cohen, Jean L., and Andrew Arato. 1997. *Civil Society and Political Theory.* Cambridge: MIT Press.

Harris, Jose, ed. 2001. *Ferdinand Tönnies: Community and Civil Society.* Translated by Jose Harris and Margaret Hollis. Cambridge: Cambridge University Press.

Henderson, Paul, and Ilona Vercseg. 2010. *Community Development and Civil Society: Making Connections in the European Context.* Bristol: Policy Press.

Khan, A. R. 2013. Indigenous Species of Fish Die: Dhaka. *The Independent*, May 31.

Lewis, David. 2011. *Bangladesh: Politics, Economy and Civil Society.* New York: Cambridge University Press.

Lister, Marjorie, and Maurizi Carbone. 2006. *New Pathways in International Development: Gender and Civil Society in EU Policy.* Aldershot: Ashgate.

McKeon, Nora. 2009. *The United Nations and Civil Society: Legitimating Global Governance—Whose Voice?* London: Zed Books.

Quadir, Fahimul. 1999. *Democracy, Development and Civil Society in Bangladesh: The Quest for a New Praxis for Sustainability.* PhD thesis, Dalhousie University.

Quadir, Fahimul, and Jayant Lele, eds. 2004. *Democracy and Civil Society in Asia.* Vol. 1: *Globalization, Democracy and Civil Society in Asia.* New York: Palgrave Macmillan.

Sachs, Wolfgang, ed. 1993. *The Development Dictionary: A Guide to Knowledge as Power.* Johannesburg: Witwatersran University Press.

Scholte, Jan Aart. 2002. Civil Society and Democracy in Global Governance. *Global Governance* 8: 281–304.

Tvedt, Terje. 2002. Development NGOs: Actors in a Global Civil Society or in a New International Social System? *International Journal of Voluntary and Nonprofit Organizations* 13(4): 363–375.

de Winter, Micha. 2012. *Socialization and Civil Society: How Parents, Teachers, and Others Could Foster a Democratic Way of Life.* Rotterdam: Sense Publication.

Wood, Geof. 2014. Can Civil Society be Free of the Natural State?: Applying North to Bangladesh. *Working Paper* No. 33. Bath: The Centre for Development Studies.

19

NEPAL

Mukta S. Tamang

Citizen's society in democratic transitions

In Nepal, civil society is referred to as *nagarik samaj* or "citizen's society" in contemporary discourse. The current scholarship and debates surrounding civil society shows that the term accommodates a vast array of associations, public deliberation, and concepts. What this suggests is that, despite the Western pedigree of the idea, civil society in Nepal existed in particular forms in the past and has surfaced as a powerful phenomenon with an undeniable presence in recent decades as the country undergoes an exciting, yet troubling, process of democratization. In this chapter, I aim to offer a general introduction to the scholarship on civil society as well as civil society organizations and practices in Nepal. The review attempts to understand the civil society in its complexity of definitions, operations, and changes in the context of state functioning in Nepal and to assess the ways civil society has contributed or hindered the possibilities of an open, tolerant, and accountable society critical for fostering democracy in the country. I argue that civil society in Nepal is in the making and is in need of revolutionizing itself in terms of inclusion of wider sections of communities and functioning.

A diverse range of organizations and collective actions of non-state organizations evade a single definition of civil society in Nepal. In dominant discourse, while civil society in Nepal is more often than not equated with non-governmental organizations (NGOs) that are an offshoot of international donor funding, recent developments in civil society engagement in the public sphere have significantly expanded the idea of civil society. Studies on the topic show that a range of entities—from traditional, self-help groups, human rights and professional organizations, ethnic- and caste-based advocacy groups, to conglomeration of independent individuals at certain times for specific goals—have been considered as part of the civil society. Broadly, for the purpose of this chapter, I categorize the civil society in Nepal into three overlapping domains: non-state associations, public deliberation, and a concept linked to citizenship with equal rights and duties. In particular, I focus on the understanding of the civil society that plays a role in the struggle for expanding civic space, fundamental freedoms, and human rights for all.

In Nepal, a wide range of organizations are registered under the Social Welfare Act 1992, including NGOs, community-based organizations (CBOs), federations, networks, professional associations, clubs, and research organizations. These organizations differ in terms of their orientation, scope, and function. From the perspective of characteristics generally ascribed to civil society, based on the idea of Tocqueville that involves non-state actors coming together in some form of associative action at a level above family and kinship, but separate from market and the state, the associations and practices found in Nepal can well be regarded as part of civil society (Tocqueville 2000). Despite the range of different purposes and orientations, the fact that they are voluntary in spirit and non-profit in motive, as prescribed by the Social Welfare Act, provides a basis for identified as part of civil society.

Engagement in public deliberation is another characteristic for identifying civil society organizations. The phenomenon of active involvement of individuals belonging to different organizations coming together as citizens in the public sphere, particularly during the 2005 and 2006 citizen's movement, offers an avenue for understanding the civil society as public deliberation in Nepal. The movement known as "Citizens' Movement for Democracy and Peace" not only participated in the mass movements but also led political parties by bringing together cross-sectional population for regime change and state restructuring. As a civil society intervention, they aimed at curbing state arbitrariness and ensuring accountability of the state. This shows that the concept of civil society in Nepal has expanded beyond non-state and non-profit organizations, and encompasses public deliberation with explicit political agenda. The phenomenon offers a way to understand civil society as not simply a society in general nor as an interest group, but as an organized action of individuals who voice their concern as equals, or people coming together with a general concern for civil rights and empowerment.

Civil society, as a concept, is about promoting the rights of citizens inhabiting within a particular state as equals. The Nepali word *nagarik* denotes a citizen and is generally applied in opposition to the concept of *praja*, or subject, in Nepal. The notion of citizenship emerged in Nepal in conjunction with the emergence of the modern concept of welfare statehood in the 1990s, when it formally broke away from the feudal autocratic regime that considered its people as subjects rather than citizens. The citizen, therefore, is a label with legal status, which confers people equal rights and duties in the country. In this context, being part of civil society in Nepal is partly a movement toward becoming fuller citizens of the political system that ensures protection of human rights, fundamental freedom, and civil liberties. The civil society is, thus, also a part of the movement for civic culture in which the ideas and aspirations of ordinary citizens are taken into account through political equality and participation, and the state is seen as acting on behalf of the public interest (Cohen and Arato 1992). Given the history of discrimination based on ethnicity, caste, language, and religion, civil rights in Nepal, however, are not limited to an individual's political right but also extend to groups' rights.

The above conceptualization of civil society in Nepal is in line with civil society as a normative ideal of liberal democracy. In this formulation, civil society grows in parallel with democracy and acts to curb the tendencies of state monopoly and market exploitation that is against public interest (Chandhoke 2013; Edwards, Foley, and Diani 2001). Civil society in Nepal, however, also has another facet. It is not a homogenous entity pursuing the democratic ideal. Some exist for purposes that are quite opposite to what liberal democracy desires as they function to maintain status quo, or even perpetuate an existing inequality. Evangelical organizations, Hindu fundamentalist associations, and other conservative groups even resort to xenophobia and intolerance. In Nepal, all organizations, including those whose purpose may be contradictory to democracy, are registered as NGOs under the same umbrella law and operate in different garbs in civil society.

In addition, most civil society organizations in Nepal, especially NGOs, are formed by the urban, educated, upper-caste individuals who have access to language and power (Dilli Ram Dahal 2001). Critics have argued that NGOs in Nepal were born out of global expansion of neo-liberalism promoted by international donor regime and financial institutions. On the one hand, such a civil society, promoted by international donors, can be understood as undermining the state; on the other, NGOs formed and run by people close to national elites tend to work in complicity with the state. As suggested by Antonio Gramsci, Quintin Hoare, and Geoffrey Nowell-Smith (1971), NGOs that work in complicity with the state fulfill the purpose of manufacturing consensus for the hegemonic state. To bring about real change for the masses and for liberation of the historically excluded communities as envisioned by Gramsci, civil society must revolutionize itself (Quadir and Lele 2004). The limitation of civil society, in this context in particular, is stark, where a majority of ordinary people are yet to feel their status as citizens, and feel empowered to voice their concern collectively.

As suggested by scholars, civil society in Nepal and its dynamics should be analyzed in the context of the changing nature of the state and struggle for democracy in Nepal (Dilli Ram Dahal 2001; Hachhethu 2006; Tamang 2002). Since the formation of the Nepali state approximately two and a half centuries ago by the conquering power of the Gorkha Empire, it has undergone some major changes. Up until 1950, the state of Nepal functioned as a patrimonial, feudal regime that depended on the extortion of the meager surplus from poor peasants. Political struggle, along with the decolonizing movement across South Asia, ended the family autocracy in Nepal in 1950. However, unfortunately, soon after the installation of multi-party democracy by the national elite, it was replaced by autocratic monarchy. The feudal monarchy established a system of partyless Panchayat in which freedom of speech, association, and other fundamental rights were suspended. It was only in 1990 that monarchy was made constitutional by the peoples' movement and multi-party democracy was reinstalled. The growing discontent of the people over the misrule by the so-called democratic parties in the 1990s gave rise to armed rebellion for a period of about ten years between 1996 and 2005. Since then, the country has been undergoing a painful transition. With each struggle for regime shift, and under the subsequent political system adopted by the state, civil society's efforts and engagement were redefined and transformed.

I suggest that the people's movement in 1990 and 2005 were two defining moments for civil society in Nepal. Although some scholars, who insist on promoting civil society as a normative ideal, favor the idea of rooting civil society in Nepal to ancient times, I suggest that civil society, in relationship to the state, and the ideal of protecting rights of the people as equal citizens of the country emerged only with the struggle against the Panchayat system with an active monarch, which culminated in the change in 1990. The decade of 1990s witnessed a mushrooming of NGOs—self-fashioned civil society actors—in a plethora of activities. However, it was only during the movement to overcome the totalitarian regime of the last king returning to power as an absolute head and to end the violent conflict waged between the government security forces and Maoist rebels in 2005 through promulgation of new constitution in 2015 that civil society emerged as a powerful actor for voicing public concern.

Patrimonial state and embryonic civil society

In order to understand the evolution of civil society in Nepal in the historical context, I begin by presenting the genesis of state formation in brief. The state of Nepal, with the current territorial boundary, lying between two giant countries—China and India—came into existence in the middle of eighteenth century. The origin of the country goes back to the conquest of the small principality of Gorkha, west of the Kathmandu valley, by a chieftain, King Prithvi Narayan Shah, via a combined use of military force and diplomacy. After bringing multiple autonomous polities of various indigenous nationalities and others under effective control, a patrimonial state was established. The king considered the conquered territory primarily as private property and its people as his subjects. The king and the political leaders belonged to upper caste from Indian plains and were ideologically guided by the Hindu scriptures. The project of conquest and colonization, referred to as Gorkha imperialism, came to a halt after its defeat against British East India Company in 1816 (Regmi 1999). Thirty years later, through an infamous *coup d'état* remembered as the *Kot* massacre, Jung Bahadur Rana, a despot, emerged to rule the country in 1846. He declared himself as the supreme commander and made the prime ministership heredi-tary to his family. Under the patronage of the British Empire, the military rule of the Ranas lasted for more than a century, and they used Nepal as their fiefdom and legally reinforced seg-regatory caste practices (Whelpton 2005).

What would be the chances for the voice of civil society in a political system obsessed with exhortation of resources, forced labor of common people, and ruthless, violent suppression of any dissenting voices? Naturally, Nepali society succumbed to avoid the state as much as pos-sible and managed their affairs outside the state. Prior to the Gorkha conquest, indigenous peoples and local communities enjoyed political autonomy and had their systems of social organizations, cultural traditions and ethos, resource management arrangement, and customary laws. Non-state institutions or traditional self-help social organizations in this situation were a natural strategy for survival and mutual support. In the spirit of a symbiotic give-and-take rela-tionship and community self-organizing, as Lama *et al.* noted, "local disputes were redressed, utilities such as roads and irrigation canals were repaired, people were organized during festivals and agricultural seasons, and important information regarding the state and the people were dis-seminated" (Lama *et al.* 1992: 84). Significant examples of such organizations included *Guthi* amongst Newars, *Bhejas* amongst Magars, *Chumlung* amongst Rai and Limbus, *Nangkhor* amongst Tamangs, and *Nogar* amongst Gurungs. There were also a number of religious organizations that extended their agenda beyond religious activities to philanthropy to social reforms during the period.

These traditional self-help organizations are also characterized as NGOs and are part of civil society according to the studies on civil society in Nepal. Although, as non-state organizations, they may qualify as civil society organizations, the dimension of engagement with the state is critically absent in their functioning. They were largely self-help organizations supporting them-selves often outside the state. In this sense, I suggest that they should be regarded as social organizations rather than civil society. There was, however, an emerging prototype of civil society organizations, which aimed at resisting the tyranny of the rulers. Tulsi Mehar Gandhi Pracharak Mahaguthi, a nonviolent movement founded by Tulsi Mehar Shrestha in 1924, is one example. The Mahaguthi was inspired by a vision to free the people of Nepal from the mental and physical bondage of the Rana oligarchy, as much as it was established for social reform. There were other individuals who made efforts to build associations that combined the work of social welfare and public interest. Amongst them Shukra Raj Shastri was prominent. He founded Nepal *Nagarik Adhikar Samiti*, or the Nepal Citizen's Right Committee, together with Kedar Man Byathit, Ganga Lal Shrestha, and others in 1937. These associational initiatives, which raised their voice and consciousness for the rights and dignity of people, were the first amongst the early attempts on public deliberation (Dilli Ram Dahal 2001; Lama *et al.* 1992). In addition, a number of writers engaged in writing poetry and prose about the need for political change and a new vision for society free of oppression by the ruling class using the state as a tool (Hachhethu 2006). Collective organizations against the oligarchy were the beginning of the civil society engagement in Nepal, and this was the early embryonic period for civil society in Nepal.

Civil society of and against the neo-feudal regime

The next turning point for the growth of civil society organizations evolved around the peoples' movement in 1990. After the *coup d'état* in 1959, the king introduced a political system called partyless Panchayat, under which the civil society organizations were brutally suppressed or co-opted by the regime. King Mahendra, in contradiction to the ethnically diverse characteristic of the Nepali society, opted for violent homogenization. He derived his ideology of rule conveniently from a fusion of modernist notion of nationalism and Hindu divine kingship (Burghart 1984). In an attempt to homogenize, Nepal was declared "the only Hindu kingdom" where loyalty to the monarchy was the yardstick for measuring Nepaliness and national unity. This process of nation building was termed "Nepalization," in which language, cultural ethos, dress, festivals, and Hindu religion of the dominant, Hill, upper caste. The Brahman Chhetri community were officially promoted as the standard to become modern Nepali. The state promoted education and media, and engaged in propaganda through print media imagining a national community and for the assimilation of diverse ethnic groups. However, unlike the formulation by Benedict Anderson (1983), print media was not part of the capitalism to produce autonomous individuals for market. The print, in this particular era of Nepali history, was used to producing homogenized subjects, loyal to feudal crown, which I call "print feudalism," to achieve hegemony. The Panchayat regime was an experiment in neo-feudalism in which the aspirations of a modern life were entrusted to legitimize the power of the feudal lord.

Many intellectuals from amongst the elite complied with the king's rule and became part of the state's project of nation building. Through the 1970s, the state even created its own civil society branded as *bargiya sangathan*, or class organization, of peasants, women, ex-army, youth, and others. These organizations were devoted as much to producing consensus as to suppressing non-conformist expressions. When the hegemonic state was at its peak in around 1980, the civil society–state distinction almost ceased to exist. The dissolution of civil society is epitomized in the proverbial slogan of the state, which imagined "*sabai pancha Nepali, sabai Nepali pancha*," or all Nepalese are *pancha* and all *panchas* are Nepali.[1]

In order to bring other possible associations to life outside the state, which may speak back to the power, the government introduced the concept of "social service" and established Social Service National Coordination Council (SSNCC) through an Act in 1977 (Uprety 2011). The patron of this Council was the queen and it functioned under direct control of the palace. From community libraries to local sports clubs and religious assemblages to organizations involved in charity and philanthropy, they were all considered to fall under the rubric of "social service," and they were required to register with the Council. The state also prescribed that pure social service must be "apolitical." The idea of social service devoid of politics served a two-pronged purpose: expanding centralized control to the periphery, and monitoring the fermenting ground of resistance against the rule. The conditions for civil society, thus, were severely unfavorable, and thriving was extremely difficult, if not impossible, under the uncivil, religious state of the time.

The basic fact that the Nepali state was different from Nepali society became apparent. The Nepali state wanted to homogenize people, while the society resisted it. Despite such surveillance, both liberal and left-oriented groups were active underground. Civil society started to re-emerge in vibrant ways in the 1980s and joined the intensifying political struggle in the country. The revival of the peoples' movement in Nepal during this period coincides with the resistance movements in Eastern Europe against authoritarian regimes, which is often referred to as the third wave of democracy. As Dev Raj Dahal states,

The increasing resilience of the social and civic institutions and activities, such as literary societies, underground publications, students unions, teachers unions, human
rights organizations and social and cultural associations of citizens revived the power of
the public to a rich associational life.

(Dev Raj Dahal 2001: 18–19)

Krishna Hachhethu offers an account of five open forums—Democratic National Unity
Forum, National People's Forum, Civic Rights Forum, People's Right Protection Forum, and
Human Rights Protection Forum—in 1985 as key markers of development in this resistance
movement (Hachhethu 2006). These forums characterized the alliance of multiple actors
belonging to different walks of life and ideological orientations. They also overlap between
political and civic society. On the political front, these forums brought together various brands
of left-oriented communist parties and liberal democratic parties, such as the Nepali Congress.
Activism of various professional and occupational groups, including lawyers, doctors, engineers,
journalists, and artists, helped overcome the constraint imposed by the system on civil society.
The struggle to join the mass movement through a professional solidarity group in 1990 challenged the state-enforced vision of apolitical civil society that works in service of the system. At
the same time, many historically oppressed ethnic groups also came together to form the Nepal
Federation of Indigenous Nationalities (NEFIN), along with Dalit and women's movements, in
the stream of civic mobilization for ending discrimination based on ethnicity, caste, language,
religion, and gender. Ethnic organizations otherwise considered "communal," or ethno-
nationalist organizations, in the South Asian context of heterogeneity and hierarchy, also entered
into the public sphere with concerns about cultural preservation, identity, and group rights as
an equally important part of civil society in Nepal during this period (Gellner 2009; Oomen
2004; Tamang 2009). I suggest that this period is characterized by a play of contradictory forces
giving rise to a civil society that can engage with the state.

Growth and fragmentation of civil society

The year 1990 was a watershed in Nepal in terms of opening up of the civic space. The realization of freedom of expression and the right to association were two major achievements of the
1990 movement. With a widened civic space, Nepal of the 1990s witnessed bewildering arrays
of civil society organizations and activism. With multi-party system restored, political party
activities flourished and expanded to rural areas. Nepal took a stronger stance of a developmental state with promises of modernization and introduced policies guided by neoliberal ideologies. The arrival of a developmental state coincided with the onset of increased international
aid, donor funding, and the intervention of global financial institutions in Nepal. With these
developments, Nepal's exposure to the global discourse on human rights and advocacy networks was also effectively initiated. The period is characterized by both the growth and fragmentation of civil society in Nepal.

In this context, civil society in Nepal flourished in multiple directions. Growth of the civil
society, in general, was celebrated as a sign of progress in democratic practice. Academics, development practitioners, planners, and political analysts joined in the atmosphere of positivity in
the formation of the public sphere. For example, the Human Development Report 1998,
authored by well-known scholars, stated:

since 1990, the civil society is beginning to emerge into the mainstream of national
activities. The growth of civic associations and NGOs during this period has been

phenomenal. Occupational and professional associations have sprung up as never before. Trade unions have grown in size and diversity. Human rights groups taking special interest in the rights of women, children, the disabled and consumers have grown. Corruption, though growing rampantly, is being challenged.

(NESAC 1998: 139)

The post-1990 associational existence of civil society took the name and shape of NGOs, to the extent that civil society virtually became synonymous with NGOs. There was a dramatic rise in the number of NGOs in Nepal after 1990. For example, the number of NGOs registered in Social Welfare Council (SWC) in 1990 was only 219. However, by 1997, the numbers had reached 5,128 (Dahal 2001) and further to 15,520 by November 2003 (Hachhethu 2006). According to SWC records, the number of NGOs reached 39,717 in November 2016.[2] In addition to the above, there were several thousand registered in the Chief District Office.

Scholars have classified formally registered NGOs using different criteria. Some have categorized them in the chronological order of their emergence and logic of operation, while the majority tend to classify them based on their thematic involvement (Chand 2000; Shrestha 1998). SWC has its own classification system in which it categorizes affiliated organizations in eight different sectors. Of the total, 63.9 percent of the NGOs are categorized under the Community and Rural Development Sector, 13.6 percent in the Youth Service, and 7.4 percent in the Women Service. Other categories include Environmental Protection (3.7 percent), Child Welfare (2.9 percent), Moral Development (2.9 percent), Handicapped and Disabled Services (1.9 percent), Health Services (2.2 percent), Educational Development (1.3 percent), and AIDS and Abuse Control (0.2 percent).

These categories are elusive as they try to accommodate a myriad range of organizations at different levels, sometimes with contradictory purpose and functions, in eight boxes. The category of community and rural development, which lumps together more than 25,000 organizations, is an illustrative case for understanding the divergence and diversity of the associations under the rubric of NGO. The list of organizations in this category shows that they include sports clubs, neighborhood management committees, and voluntary philanthropic work, and associations of lawyers, teachers, doctors, artists, and literary societies, and organizations working on anti-trafficking, human rights, and cultural preservation. The majority of them, however, were those working on different fields of community or rural development. They may be termed as developmental NGOs that are involved in activities to promote literacy, education, agricultural improvements, health and sanitation, and income generation, amongst others. A bulk of these NGOs is expected to deliver services in areas where the government has failed to reach, or to complement the governmental goal of delivering development. Although SWC has a separate category for education, health, youth, and women services, they generally overlap in their operation of managing development services to the community. Developmental NGOs partnered with international development agencies that were often frustrated with the corrupt and inefficient government mechanism for extending their assistance. Developmental NGOs, thus, functioned as intermediary organizations, or even subcontractors, of technical-managerial teams of individuals in the post-1990 scenario.

The category of moral development is more puzzling than other categories. Organizations within this category range from Bishwo Hindu Mahasangh, Shiva Sena Nepal, meditation centers, clan and lineage organizations, temples, monasteries, mosque management committees, and Christian evangelical missionaries. While all have their constituencies to serve, the purpose of these organizations can also go contrary to the notion of civil society. Instead of promoting openness and values of equality amongst the individuals and the community, their activities could potentially also promote intolerance, xenophobia, and religious fundamentalism. This shows that the only commonality amongst the diverse range of organizations is merely the fact that they are registered under the same law in Nepal and are referred to as a "non-governmental organization."

If we take civil society as a normative ideal of civic sensibility, values, community solidarity, social space, or anti-hegemonic movement (Tamang 2002; Van Rooy 1998), it is clear from the nature of NGOs in Nepal that all of them cannot be taken as part of civil society. Further, the composition of NGOs shows that they do not have a membership structure to represent wider sections of people. For example, a minimum of seven persons are required to form an NGO in Nepal. NGOs often distinguish themselves from their stated target groups or beneficiaries, but, in practice, NGO members themselves become primary beneficiaries of the projects they implement (Heaton-Shrestha and Adhikari 2013). Similarly, NGOs in Nepal are not truly autonomous to take a stance to curb the power of arbitrariness of the state, as they must be affiliated to the Social Welfare Council, which functions as a government entity that coordinates and monitors their work. In this sense, NGOs in Nepal are expected to work under the surveillance of the state, and it is not necessarily easy to take a stance in opposition to the government policies. Even when they speak of rights, they can only do so by associating rights with development—as promoting rights-based development.

There are other limitations in thinking of NGOs as civil society. The concept of NGOs as civil society is of Western origin, and is promoted by international development agencies, donors, and global financial institutions in Nepal (Shah 2008). The motivation behind such support can be seen in two interrelated trends in the global North. The first is the extension of Western, Enlightenment optimism through development assistance to underdeveloped countries, and the second is the triumph of neoliberalism and the Western drive to expand this to global South. In this drive, the central idea is to reduce the role of the state to the bare minimum and replace it with the market. For promoters of neoliberal ideology, civil society is to society as market is to economy. In this sense, the way civil society has evolved in Nepal can be seen as being more in support of a neoliberal regime and as a downsizing of the state, rather than being an anti-hegemonic voice.

As critics have pointed out, NGOs in Nepal are also known for their middle- or upper-middle-class origin and upper-caste dominance in terms of its leadership and agenda (Bhattachan 2003). The conducive political environment for open space provided by the 1990 change was certainly the context for the mushrooming of NGOs in Nepal, but the opportunity was not necessarily open for all citizens. As Partha Chatterjee (2001) argued regarding the post-colonial situation in India, civil society in general, and NGOs in particular, was captured by the dominant section of national elites. Civil society in Nepal is still inaccessible to historically marginalized groups, as they lack the level of language proficiency and social capital necessary for accessing the network. Overt or tacit affiliation of NGOs with mainstream political parties in Nepal often makes them an association of party cadres who serve their own electorate in line with their party ideology. The Nepal Communist Party (UML), for example, is ironically referred to as the party of NGOs. As NGOs in Nepal become politically partisan with their interests overwhelmingly focused on the seat of state power, the greater the political agenda of cross-sectional relevance of civil rights gets overshadowed (Siwakoti 2000).

The disintegration of civil society into factions is compounded by the erosion of positive image and expectations of NGOs, as they become known more as avenues for jobs than service. Since the 1990s, NGOs have significantly absorbed the educated-unemployed with command over the Nepali and English languages, including college graduates, ex-bureaucrats, fringe political leaders, journalists, and intellectuals. The tarnished image of NGOs in Nepal is captured in the colloquial phrase for NGO jobs—"dollar farming"—as their existence relies on foreign funding (Heaton-Shrestha 2002).

The above critique of NGOs in Nepal, however, does not mean that all NGOs are devoid of any achievements toward societal good and irrelevant as civil society. NGOs in Nepal are also characterized as being part of the global expansion of discourse and activism on human rights and social justice through the United Nations agencies and international advocacy organizations. Activities carried out by some of the NGOs in rural communities, to increase literacy, awareness of legal rights, and capacity building for advocacy to free bonded laborers, oppressed women, the discriminated Dalit communities, marginalized indigenous peoples, and poor farmers, have, in some ways, contributed to expanding the democratic values in the country. Despite the fact that NGOs themselves are susceptible to authoritarian tendencies (Tamang 2002) and lack transparency, the public debates, in which some NGOs collaborated with other social movement actors, has heightened the general awareness on social inclusion, participatory development, social justice, and the empowerment of the communities (Tamang 2014). Many of the NGOs not only championed civil and political rights, but also supported social movements that advocated for economic, social, and cultural rights, deploying the United Nations human rights covenants and treaties. Besides general international human rights instruments, these instruments became important tools that could be deployed in the public sphere by social movements led by disenfranchised communities. The Convention on Elimination of all Forms of Racial Discrimination (CERD) by Dalit communities, the Convention on the Elimination of all Forms of Discrimination Against Women (CEDAW) by the Nepalese women's movement, and the International Labor Organization Convention 169 on Indigenous Peoples and the United Nations Declaration on Rights of Indigenous Peoples (UNDRIP) by indigenous ethnic groups, are noteworthy examples in terms of expanding the public debate on equality. In conclusion, although not all NGOs that have come into existence since 1990s can be considered as civil society in the strict sense of the term, some amongst them have contributed to make society more open and have worked as a part of the democratic struggle.

Civil society for democracy and peace

The years 2005 and 2006 were momentous for the civil society in Nepal to redefine its identity and to reinvigorate its public engagement. The movement termed *nagarik andolan*, or citizen's movement, undertaken by groups of individuals as autonomous citizens for inclusive democracy and peace became a new identity for civil society in Nepal that distinguished itself from donor funded, apolitical, service-delivering, technical NGOs, and rightist forces that advocated for the continuation of the old, feudal regime, values, and state structure. The transformed identity emerged out of the throes of political struggle involving the political parties, king, and Maoist rebels with contending agendas, interpretations, and interests.

The context for the emergence of citizen's movements is provided by the post–1990 political crisis in Nepal. The failure of political parties to make democracy meaningful to ordinary people, the eruption of countrywide violence in conflicts between Maoist rebels and the government security forces, and attempts of the old tyrannical monarchy to return are three key aspects that brought about such a crisis. The Nepali Congress, followed by the CPN-UML, came into power in a series of frequent changes after the first parliamentary elections in 1991. Due to internal feuds within and amongst the parties on running the government, the country experienced damaging instability. The political parties in power not only demonstrated their irresponsibility in making the welfare available to people, but also failed to ensure citizen participation in running the country. As a result of growing dissatisfaction, a splinter of one of the

Community Parties, the CPN-Maoist started an armed insurgency against the government in 1996. Instead of looking at the insurgency as a political issue, the government responded to it as a law and order problem and intensified the deployment of security forces. By the year 2000, insurgency had spread across the country, to the extent that large parts of the rural areas were under the control of rebels.

With slogans of the necessity of destroying the old to reconstruct the new, the Maoists wanted to destroy the base of the government at the local level. The Maoists took a hostile view toward NGOs and labeled them as agents of Western imperialism. Many NGO operations in rural areas were forced to close by the rebels. In this climate of violent clashes, NGO workers faced severe security threats, and it became virtually impossible to remain in the villages for their usual community development work. This situation led to a shift in donor agency priority to funding conflict resolution and peace building, from development and service delivery. NGOs and other civil society actors also gradually moved in this direction. The engagement of NGOs in mediating conflict for peace in the period after 2000 has substantially increased (Basnet 2012; Chand 2001).

The involvement of civil society in peace and democracy further heightened after the increased threat to liberal democracy from the resurgent feudal monarch. After the palace carnage in June 2001, when all the members of the royal families were brutally killed, Gyanendra declared himself as the king. In a series of developments after the event, the Nepali Congress leader and Prime Minister Sher Bahadur Deuba dissolved the parliament and declared an emergency in November 2001. However, in a dramatic move, the king dismissed Deuba and replaced him with a prime minister loyal to the palace in May 2002, just six months later. The climax was reached when Gyanendra dismissed the government in February 2005, restored absolute monarchy, mobilized the army citing the need to defeat Maoist rebels, and arrested the key party leaders.

The crackdown by the royal regime against democracy and censorship on freedom of speech and expression became a threat not only to the political parties but also to ordinary citizens. Although the political parties organized several street demonstrations demanding a return to democracy, they were not able to garner wider support from the disillusioned masses. The political parties and their various factions sent confusing messages, as some of them supported the king's move or were merely focused on obtaining political power. If the political parties were indifferent to the issues of the ordinary people, the king wanted the ordinary people to be Hindu subjects of a feudal *Kshatriya* crown, and the Maoists wanted to make the citizens their cadres, who subscribed to Maoist ideology.

The vacuum created by the political crisis provided the context for the re-emergence of civil society, reconstituted in a new form with a focus on democracy and peace. The constellation of different independent individuals for collective action first took concrete shape when the intellectuals, human rights activists, professionals, journalists, lawyers, and others came together in July 2005 to plan public meetings, sit-ins, public protests, and deliberations. Initially comprising approximately 100 individuals, it staged protests to oppose the prohibition imposed by the government for public meeting at the center of city, Ratnapark. With a series of such public events during July and August 2005, the support of the ordinary population to the movement substantially increased. A public meeting held in Baneshor on August 5 was one of the biggest after the king's takeover in February. The public deliberation and mass participation in subsequent rallies and meetings in Kathmandu was successful in making it clear that ordinary people in Nepal only support a democratic system and peace which secured their rights and dignity (Panday 2008). The public deliberation held in 2005 and early 2006 was the defining moment in terms of civil society identity, its central goal, and its impact on Nepal.

The public deliberation by independent individuals coming from different backgrounds was named the Citizen's Movement for Democracy and Peace (CMDP). The process of public engagement was also a part of getting civil society redefined in Nepal as a "movement" by a collectivity of "autonomous citizens." The new definition was partly a conscious strategy of the leaders and activists of the civil society to reclaim the lost credibility of the civil society in Nepal. The new definition attempted to distance the movement not only from political parties, NGOs, and funding agencies, but also from various kinds of professional groups that operated as trade unions or interest groups. The movement organization set the standard for identifying its members as "autonomous citizens" as opposed to a member representing a particular agency or party. The collective would also endeavor to raise their own funds through individual donations rather than seeking resources from foreign donor agencies. In terms of its goal, the CMDP stated that it is concerned with the nature of state and democracy and differentiated itself from political parties interested mainly in political power. The crystallization of its goal also triggered the need for revisiting its composition, as civil society in Nepal is a conglomeration of self-identified people who range from members of the aristocracy favoring a royal regime and the status quo to radical revolutionaries. In the process of its campaign, the CMDP also clarified that civil society cannot remain an assortment of people and associations with ideas, beliefs, and purposes incongruous to the democratic ideal. In its bid to bring the Maoist rebels into mainstream politics, the CMDP also advocated that peace built on equality and social justice must be the purpose of civil society public deliberation.

The CMDP's intervention in public deliberation, in terms of redefining some of the crucial concepts related to democracy, has been fundamental. For example, in a cacophony of multiple voices and contending the definition of what democracy is, the CMDP popularized the term *loktantra*, denoting the centrality of citizenship as opposed to the previous term *prajatantra* that links people as subjects to its rulers. In the new understanding of democracy, meaningful inclusion and participation of minorities and women was a key issue. The state restructuring, demanded by civil society joining with other social movements, advocated for an end of a centralized unitary system of rule and the adoption of a federal structure that respects autonomy and ethnic diversity. The pro-democracy civil society movement, according to Pandey,

> did not limit itself in safeguarding rights of their own professional community but also struggled to end the subjugation of tyrannical monarch once and for all but also for restructuring of the state for equitable social and economic development from the front line. It struggled for the end of feudalism. It worked for replacing old power base and existing discriminatory social relation with political system and culture in which all Nepalese can feel dignified.
>
> *(Panday 2008: 62)*

Moreover, the CMDP redefined nationalism so that it could overcome the parochial understanding of nationalism given by the conquering powers—as protection of the territory and harmony through coercion. The CMDP advocated for national unity based on socio-economic equality and the celebration of cultural diversity, rather than one sustained by the violence, myth, and discrimination in the past. As Devendra Raj Pandey, himself one of the prominent civil society activists, further wrote: "modern Nepal will not need king, but without wellbeing of the people, there can be no stable state or nation. In modern Nepal, all people will be equal citizen of the state and member of nation" (Panday 2008: 31).

The CMDP, thus, can be marked distinctly in the history of civil society in Nepal, both in terms of its constitution and its accomplishments. The CMDP was able to attract a range of people, including those from ethnic- and caste-based organizations, who were fighting for their linguistic and cultural rights and for the end of caste-based discrimination. The civil society involvement in the nineteen-day movement, popularly known as the April Awakening, was outstanding, which culminated in the Comprehensive Peace Agreement in April 2006. Despite numerous challenges, including its urban-based nature and being led by educated and often upper-caste males, and inaccessible to the rural and working classes and minorities, the citizen's movement, starting in 2005, has left a mark of clarity regarding what civil society can be and a legacy for future public deliberation for democracy.

Conclusion

Civil society in Nepal is viewed as part of the struggle for democracy. As has been argued by various scholars, the civil society in Nepal emerged and transformed itself in particular relationship to the state project. Although some scholars engaged in civil society development in the country have argued that civil society has ancient roots, contemporary discourse and practice exhibits that the meanings and practices of civil society are crystallizing around the struggle for realization of three fundamental rights: the right to association, the right to peaceful assembly, and the right to freedom of expression. This, however, does not mean that all actors of civil society are democratically oriented. Sectors of civil society actors in Nepal have opted to support the autocratic regime, status quo, and even the reactionary backlash.

Civil society in Nepal, like political party leadership, bureaucracy, media, and other state entities, is still controlled by upper-caste traditional elites and the dominant class, and is exclusionary in composition. After the people's movement in 2006, the political arena in the country entered into a long and painful transition. From the Comprehensive Peace Agreement in 2007, which ended the ten-year violent conflict, the two and a half century old institution of monarchy, and two Constituent Assembly elections, the country drafted a new constitution in 2015. A continuous bargaining and negotiation of divergent views amongst the dominant classes has characterized this process. Although the process has failed to promulgate a constitution that gained broader public ownership, at a surface level, such divergent views give a false appearance of democracy and disguise the exclusion of historically marginalized people, as in other Asian countries (Alagappa 2004). Civil society in Nepal, thus, has participated as an additional actor in an exercise of negotiation with the dominant elites, belonging to higher class and caste, for sharing the power and wealth of the country and is in need of revolutionizing itself.

Despite these limitations, civil space, acquired through a series of struggles by the people, offers a rich possibility for expanding and deepening democracy in Nepal. Whether it be functioning to counterbalance the state or as an instrument of the state for manufacturing public consensus, or to prepare citizens as consumers, liberal democrats or neoliberal thinkers believe that civil society discourse has helped create and expand the civic space. The available civic space, nevertheless, should also be occupied by ordinary people who have not yet become equal citizens of the country. All these indicate that civil society in Nepal is in the making, and is evolving as a part of a larger democratic struggle.

Notes

1 *Pancha* is an official title of the person who is part of the Panchayat system. In a broader sense, *pancha* refers to people who believe in that political system. The origin of the word goes back to the notion of a traditional council of five people who administer justice in the community.
2 Social Welfare Council, www.swc.org.np, accessed November 2, 2016.

Suggested readings

Bhattachan, Krishna B. 2003. Civil Society and Protection of Diversity in Nepal. In *Nepal Tomorrow: Voices and Visions*. D. B. Gurung, ed. Pp. 32–62. Kathmandu: Koselee Prakashan.

Dahal, Dev Raj. 2001. *Civil Society in Nepal: Opening the Ground for Questions*. Kathmandu: Center for Development & Governance.

Hachhethu, Krishna. 2006. Civil Society and Political Participation. In *Nepal: Quest for Participatory Democracy*. Lok Raj Baral, ed. Pp. 111–132. New Delhi: Adroit.

Heaton-Shrestha, Celayne, and Ramesh Adhikari. 2013. Struggling on Two Fronts During Nepal's Insurgency: The Citizens' Movement for Democracy and Peace and the Meanings of "Civil Society." *European Bulletin of Himalayan Research* 42: 39–74.

Lama, Mukta S, Rekh Blon, Narendra Gurung, and Deepak Tamang. 1992. Non-Governmental Organizations (NGOs) and Grassroots Development. *Administration and Management Review* 6: 81–101.

Panday, Devendra Raj. 2008. *Nagarik Andolan Ra Gantantrik Cetana* [*Citizen's Movement and Democratic Consciousness*]. Kathmandu: Fineprint. (in Nepali).

Websites

Social Welfare Council, Nepal, www.swc.org.np.
Operating under the Social Welfare Act 2049, and the Social Welfare Regulation.

NGO Federation of Nepal, www.ngofederation.org.
A national federation of non-governmental organizations based in Nepal, established in 1991 and working to promote human rights and social justice.

Nepal Federation of Indigenous Nationalities (NEFIN), www.nefin.org.np.
Formed in 1991, NEFIN is a non-partisan, umbrella organization of indigenous peoples in Nepal, working as a member of the United Nation's Working Group on Indigenous Populations.

Dalit NGO Federation (DNF), www.dnfnepal.org.
An umbrella organization of Dalit NGOs in Nepal, fighting caste-based discrimination.

Social Science Baha, www.soscbaha.org.
An independent, non-profit organization working to enhance the study of, and research in, social sciences in Nepal; focused primarily on establishing and maintaining a dedicated social science library with access to far-reaching information.

Martin Chautari, www.martinchautari.org.np.
A discussion group aiming to bring together professionals, social activists, and academics to share information relating to Nepali society and development; the organization also supports research projects and publishes books and journals.

Child NGO Federation-Nepal, www.cnfnepal.org.
An NGO with a specific focus on ensuring children across Nepal are provided with opportunities to become productive, educated, and responsible members of society.

Beyond Beijing Committee, www.beyondbeijing.org.
A network with the vision: "social, political, and economic empowerment of women and girls"; connecting likeminded individuals and groups to further awareness, education, and programs dedicated to gender equality.

National Indigenous Women's Federation (NIWF), www.niwf.org.np/.
An organization working to promote and protect indigenous women's rights and equality.

NGO-Federation of Nepalese Indigenous Nationalities, www.ngofonin.org.np.
A federation working to establish a network of organizations dedicated to ensuring indigenous rights in Nepal.

References

Alagappa, Muthiah. 2004. *Civil Society and Political Change in Asia: Expanding and Contracting Democratic Space*. Stanford, CA: Stanford University Press.

Anderson, Benedict R. O'G. 1983. *Imagined Communities: Reflections on the Origin and Spread of Nationalism.* London: Verso.

Basnet, Chudamani. 2012. Three Faces of Civil Society Activism in Nepal. In *New Angle: Nepal Journal of Social Science and Public Policy* 2(1). Electronic document, www.nepalpolicynet.com, accessed September 15, 2016.

Bhattachan, Krishna B. 2003. Civil Society and Protection of Diversity in Nepal. In *Nepal Tomorrow: Voices and Visions.* D. B. Gurung, ed. Pp. 32–62. Kathmandu: Koselee Prakashan.

Burghart, Richard. 1984. The Formation of the Concept of Nation-State in Nepal. *The Journal of Asian Studies* 44(1): 101–125.

Chand, Diwakar. 2000. Understanding Voluntary Action in Nepal. In *Development NGOs Facing the 21st Century—Perspectives from South Asia.* Farhad Hossain, JuhaVartola, Marko Ulvila, and Tek Nath Dhakal, eds. Pp. 65–73. Kathmandu: Institute for Human Development.

Chand, Diwakar. 2001. Peace Building Role of the Civil Society in Maoist Areas. In *Quest for Peace.* South Asia Partnership-Nepal, ed. Pp. 214–222. Kathmandu: SAP-Nepal.

Chandhoke, Neera. 2013. The Promises and the Limits of Civil Society. In *Expanding Civil Space: Building Democracy in South Asia.* Alliance for Social Dialogue, ed. Pp. 51–64. Kathmandu: Alliance for Social Dialogue.

Chatterjee, Partha. 2001. Civil and Political Socisties in Post-Colonial Democracies. In *Civil Society: History and Possibilities.* Kaviraj Sudipta and Sunil Khilnani, eds. Pp. 165–178. Cambridge: Cambridge University Press.

Cohen, Jean L., and Andrew Arato. 1992. *Civil Society and Political Theory.* Cambridge, MA: MIT Press.

Dahal, Dev Raj. 2001. *Civil Society in Nepal: Opening the Ground for Questions.* Kathmandu: Center for Development & Governance.

Dahal, Dilli Ram. 2001. Problems and Prospects of Relationship between Government Organizations and NGOs/INGOs in Nepal. In *NGO, Civil Society and Government in Nepal: Critical Examination of Their Roles and Responsibilities.* Krishna B. Bhattachan, Dev Raj Dahal, Sheetal Rana, Jyoti Gyawali, Min Bahadur Basnet, Kashi Ram Bhusal, and Ram Raj Pokharel, eds. Pp. 105–128. Kathmandu: Central Department of Sociology/Anthropology, Tribhuvan University.

Edwards, Bob, Michael W. Foley, and Mario Diani. 2001. *Beyond Tocqueville: Civil Society and the Social Capital Debate in Comparative Perspective.* Hanover, NH: University Press of New England.

Gellner, David N. 2009. Introduction: How Civil Are "Communal" and Ethno-Nationalist Movements? In *Ethnic Activism and Civil Society in South Asia.* David N. Gellner, ed. Pp. 1–24. New Delhi: SAGE.

Gramsci, Antonio, Quintin Hoare, and Geoffrey Nowell-Smith. 1971. *Selections from the Prison Notebooks of Antonio Gramsci.* London: Lawrence and Wishart.

Hachhethu, Krishna. 2006. Civil Society and Political Participation. In *Nepal: Quest for Participatory Democracy.* Lok Raj Baral, ed. Pp. 111–132. New Delhi: Adroit.

Heaton-Shrestha, Celayne. 2002. NGOs as Thekedar or Sevak: Identity Crisis in Nepal's Non-Governmental Sector. *European Bulletin of Himalayan Research* 22(2002): 5–36.

Heaton-Shrestha, Celayne, and Ramesh Adhikari. 2013. Struggling on Two Fronts During Nepal's Insurgency: The Citizens' Movement for Democracy and Peace and the Meanings of "Civil Society." *European Bulletin of Himalayan Research* 42: 39–74.

Lama, Mukta S., Rekh Blon, Narendra Gurung, and Deepak Tamang. 1992. Non-Governmental Organizations (NGOs) and Grassroots Development. *Administration and Management Review* 6: 81–101.

NESAC. 1998. *Nepal: Human Development Report.* Kathmandu: Nepal South Asia Center.

Oomen, T. K. 2004. State, Civil Society and Market in India: Gradual Autonomisation. In *Nation, Civil Society and the Social Movements: Essays in Political Sociology.* T. K. Oomen, ed. Pp. 107–127. New Delhi: Sage.

Panday, Devendra Raj. 2008. *Nagarik Andolan Ra Gantantrik Cetana* [*Citizen's Movement and Democratic Consciousness*]. Kathmandu: Fineprint. (in Nepali).

Quadir, Fahimul, and Jayant Lele. 2004. *Democracy and Civil Society in Asia.* New York: Palgrave Macmillan.

Regmi, Mahesh C. 1999. *Imperial Gorkha: An Account of Gorkhali Rule in Kumaun (1791–1815).* Delhi: Adroit Publishers.

Shah, Saubhagya. 2008. *Civil Society in Uncivil Places: Soft State and Regime Change in Nepal.* Washington, DC: East-West Center.

Shrestha, Ananda, ed. 1998. *The Role of Civil Society and Democratization in Nepal.* Kathmandu: Nepal Foundation for Advanced Studies.

Siwakoti, Gopal "Chintan." 2000. Foreign Intervention in Politics through Ngos: A Case of the Left in Nepal. In *Development NGOs Facing 21st Century—Perspectives from South Asia*. Farhad Hossain, JuhaVartola, Marko Ulvila, and Tek Nath Dhakal, eds. Pp. 134–143. Kathmandu: Institute for Human Development.

Tamang, Mukta S. 2009. Tamang Activism, History and Territorial Consciousness. In *Ethnic Activism and Civil Society in South Asia*. David N. Gellner, ed. Pp. 269–290. New Delhi: SAGE.

Tamang, Mukta S. 2014. Perspectives on Social Inclusion and Research in Nepal. In *Perspective on Social Exclusion and Inclusion in Nepal*. Gurung Om, Mukta Tamang, and Mark Turin, eds. Pp. 11–37. Katmandu: Central Department of Sociology/Anthropology, Tribhuvan University and Social Inclusion Research Fund (SIRF).

Tamang, Seira. 2002. Civilizing Civil Society: Donors and Democratic Space. *Studies in Nepali History and Society* 7(2): 309–353.

Tocqueville, Alexis de. 2000. *Democracy in America*. Translated, edited, and with an introduction by Harvey C. Mansfield and Delba Winthrop. Chicago, IL: Chicago University Press.

Uprety, Uttam. 2011. A Reflection on the Legal Framework for Civil Society in Nepal. *International Journal of Not-for-Profit Law* 13(3): 50–89.

Van Rooy, Alison. 1998. *Civil Society and the Aid Industry: The Politics and Promise*. London: Earthscan.

Whelpton, John. 2005. *A History of Nepal*. Cambridge and New York: Cambridge University Press.

20

BHUTAN

Michiyo Kiwako Okuma Nyström

Civil society in Bhutan and its national contexts

Civil society in Bhutan consists of institutions and organizations that have two fundamentally different characteristics in terms of formality, participants, and the nature of activities: (1) the traditional self-reliant civil society consisting of people in rural communities, where the operation of activities is regulated by unwritten customary norms and rules (Galay 2001); and (2) the formal and modernized organizations consisting of people who join them freely, where activities are regulated by written rules and acts. The latter are further grouped into organizations that are regulated by different acts: civil society organizations (CSOs) regulated by the Civil Society Organizations Act, cooperatives regulated by the Cooperatives Act, and religious organizations regulated by the Religious Organizations Act.[1]

The distinction between characteristics (1) and (2) is, however, not always self-evident. Owing to decentralization, which has reached the grass-roots level, the traditional civil society in rural communities is expected to play increasingly important roles in various programs. As a result, traditional civil society sometimes becomes the main implementing body of governmental policies and programs, and it has been transformed into a more formalized society that is regulated by written rules.

In Bhutan, civil society and governmental institutions have complementary relationships (Dorji 2005). For example, in the Tenth Five Year Plan (2008–2013), whose objective was poverty reduction, the government was to: (1) emphasize the development of strategic partnerships with various CSOs to implement poverty interventions and diversify sources of income in rural areas; (2) strengthen existing farmer cooperatives by providing assistance and support; and (3) stress the importance of involving rural civil society through, for example, the establishment of Community Forests (see the case presentation below) (Gross National Happiness Commission 2009). Likewise, the Eleventh Five Year Plan (2013–2018), which aims to realize "Self-reliance and Inclusive Green Socio-Economic Development," stresses collaborations with CSOs that have contributed to the empowerment of women and disadvantaged remote communities (Gross National Happiness Commission 2013).

The characteristics of civil society in Bhutan derive largely from the geographical, socio-cultural, historical, and political contexts of the country. Bhutan is a small, landlocked country situated on the eastern edge of the Himalayas between China and India; the country's capital is

Thimphu. The population in 2015 was approximately 774,830 on a surface area of 38,394 km², with 3.2 percent annual urban population growth (World Bank 2016a, 2016b). The altitude in the country varies from approximately 150 meters in the south to over 7,000 meters in the north and 1,500–2,500 meters in the central area (Miyashita 2009; Ueda 2011). While the Constitution of the country stipulates that at least 60 percent of the land shall be continuously maintained under forest cover, the coverage accounted for 70.5 percent in 2015 (World Bank 2016a).

The people primarily consist of three different groups: Scharchops (mainly in eastern Bhutan), Ngalongs (mainly in western Bhutan), and ethnic Nepalese. However, the historical backgrounds and settlements of these groups are complex (US Department of State 2008; T. Wangchuk 2001). Although the state religion is Mahayana Buddhism, freedom of religion is ensured by the Constitution. Ethnic Nepalese often practice Hinduism. While the national language is Dzongkha, English is used as the medium of instruction. Several ethnic languages are spoken, as well (National Assembly of Bhutan 2008; US Department of State 2008; T. Wangchuk 2001).

Life expectancy at birth has increased from 60.2 years in 2000 to 69.8 years in 2015 (WHO 2015). The modern education system in Bhutan benefiting ordinary people was implemented in the early 1950s (Hirayama 2016; Sugimoto 2000). After many years of effort toward increasing enrollment in primary education, the net enrollment in primary schools reached 89.3 percent in 2011, and the adult literacy rate was 52.8 percent in 2012 (UNICEF 2013).

Bhutan's economy is largely based on agriculture, forestry, tourism, and hydroelectricity and has shown strong economic performance (Country Watch 2015; US Department of State 2008). On the other hand, the gap in standards of living between rural and urban areas is still large. Rapid urbanization caused problems in the urban environment and restricted employment opportunities, as well as introducing vulnerabilities to the economic infrastructure (Japan International Cooperation Agency n.d.). The Gross National Income (GNI) per capita was US$2,370 in 2015 (World Bank 2016b). Despite the relatively high GNI, both the Human Assets Index and Economic Vulnerability Index reflect the weaknesses of the country (Gross National Happiness Commission 2013).

Bhutan experienced a major transformation from an absolute monarchy to a constitutional monarchy over the course of ten years. The Constitution of the Kingdom of Bhutan was formally promulgated in 2008 (Bertelsmann Stiftung's Transformation Index [BTI] 2014; Country Watch 2015). In December 2006, the fourth king, King Jigme Singye Wangchuck (r. 1972–2006), announced that the Crown Prince would become the king of the new democratic Bhutan. The fifth king, King Jigme Khesar Namgyel Wangchuck, thus took over the rule from his father immediately, although his coronation was delayed until November 2008 (Phuntsho 2013). Bhutan's case is seen as the "middle path to democracy," and its democratic transition does not comply with the conventional theories based on Western history (Masaki 2013a; Wangchuk 2004).

The general election of the National Council (upper house) took place in December 2007 and that of the National Assembly (lower house) in March 2008. Two political parties, the Druk Phuensum Tshogpa (DPT) and the People's Democratic Party (PDP), competed in the election. As a result, the DPT formed the first democratically elected government with Jigmi Thinley as the prime minister. In 2013, the PDP formed the second government following an election, with Tshering Tobgay as the prime minister. Today, there are five registered political parties (Office of the Prime Minister & Cabinet 2016; Royal Government of Bhutan 2013).

Bhutan was a closed country until the 1950s. It was King Jigme Dorji Wangchuck (r. 1952–1972), the third king, who opened the country to the international community, and the First Five Year Plan began in 1961 (Sugimoto 2000). The fourth king initiated the unique development philosophy of Bhutan, Gross National Happiness (GNH), in the 1970s. GNH challenged the conventional narrow interpretations of development, where economic development is strongly emphasized (GNH Centre Bhutan n.d.). Bhutan pursues a good balance between economic development, on the one hand, and the happiness and well-being of its citizens, on the other. The personal satisfaction prioritized by Buddhism is considered the ethical base for GNH (Ministry of Foreign Affairs of Denmark n.d.; Walcott 2011).

In the beginning, GNH was a rather abstract policy ideal. However, since the late 1990s, various policies and programs have started clearly describing how they can contribute to GNH (Ueda 2011). The four pillars of GNH were established as a more practical conceptualization of its guiding principles. They are:

1   Sustainable and equitable socio-economic development;
2   Conservation of the environment;
3   Preservation and promotion of culture; and
4   Promotion of good governance.

(Thinley 2005: 9)

It is clearly stated even in the Constitution that "[t]he State shall strive to promote those conditions that will enable the pursuit of Gross National Happiness" (The Kingdom of Bhutan 2008: 18). In 2008, the Planning Commission, which was responsible for the Five Year Plans and their evaluations, was reorganized and transformed into the GNH Commission. This Commission plays a crucial role in the pursuit of GNH in the operation, adjustment, and evaluation of policies in all sectors (Ueda 2011). In the Tenth Five Year Plan, compared with the previous plans, there are more concrete plans for achieving GNH, along with the four pillars (see Gross National Happiness Commission 2009).

The four pillars were further elaborated into the following nine domains that serve as measurement tools: (1) Living standards, (2) education, (3) health, (4) environment, (5) community vitality, (6) time-use, (7) psychological well-being, (8) good governance, and (9) cultural resilience and promotion. Based on these domains, thirty-eight subindexes, seventy-two indicators, and 151 variables are developed and used to measure and analyze the happiness of the people (GNH Centre Bhutan n.d.).

Today, Bhutan consists of twenty *Dzongkhags* (districts), 205 *Gewogs* (blocks) below the level of the districts, and four *Thromdes* (municipalities) (Gross National Happiness Commission 2013). A *Gewog* consists of a few *Chiwogs* (villages). In 1981, political, administrative, and financial decision-making power was decentralized to the district level through the establishment of *Dzongkhag Yargay Tshogdu*s (district development committees). A further decentralization to the grass-roots level took place with the establishment of *Gewog Yargay Tshogchung*s (block development committees) in 1991 (Gross National Happiness Commission 2007).

Different administrative levels are responsible for the monitoring and evaluation of GNH, and the following mechanism has been established: a GNH Commission at the national level; GNH Committees at the ministry and agency level; *Dzongkhag Tshogdu* (district development committees) at the district level; and *Gewog Tshogde* at the block level (Gross National Happiness Commission 2009). Thus, the pursuit of GNH encompasses every level of government, from the national to grassroots.

Traditional civil society in Bhutan

Grass-roots democracy and civil society

Katsu Masaki states, "In Bhutan, the term 'civil society' usually denotes leverage for maintaining and further developing a cohesive society, or congenial state–society relations" (Masaki 2013a: 65). According to Lham Dorji, civil society in Bhutan constitutes "social, cultural, and economic institutions of relational network and collective action—encompassing a wide range of local institutions" (2005: 11). In traditional civil society, volunteerism is deeply grounded in daily life, and egalitarianism deriving from Buddhism prevails in the community institutions and organizations in Bhutan (Choden 2003; Masaki 2013a). The democratic principles of justice, liberty, and equality are highly valued. Their philosophical basis lies in Buddhism and, thus, are different from the democratic principles found in the Western world (Wangchuk 2004). It is, therefore, insufficient to equate democracy with the modern institutional notions of politics (Masaki 2013a). Such democratic aspects prevailing in rural communities in Bhutan are conceptualized as "village-based participatory democracy" (Horgan 2015), "natural democracy" (Masaki 2013b), and "primary democracy" (Wangchuk 2004).

Several scholars (e.g., Choden 2003, 2005; Dorji 2005; Galay 2001; Horgan 2015; Kinga 2008; Masaki 2013a; Penjore 2008; S. Wangchuk 2001) state that the roots of civil society in Bhutan are based on the democratic values prevalent in rural villages and communities. Individuals share interests simply by virtue of the fact that they reside in the same village. In the difficult living conditions of rural communities, mutual help and self-reliance within the community are necessary practices that foster community vitality (Galay 2001; Kinga 2008).

On the other hand, it is wrong to believe that disputes based on individual interests are completely absent in the rural communities in Bhutan. Rather, there are local institutions with a consensual democratic framework that prevent and resolve conflicts and disputes within communities (Horgan 2015). In urban areas, kinship networks play important roles and maintain close interactions. The loose networks and activities based on kinship can be seen as a continuation of traditional volunteerism and community participation (BTI 2014; Choden 2003; Kinga 2008).

Traditional organizations and institutions

Civil society in rural Bhutan consists of community organizations and institutions having various purposes. Some examples of organized activities are cooperation for agricultural activities; mutual support and dependence in times of hardship, such as events of sickness and death in families; labor sharing for building houses; management of common resources and spiritual services; and cooperation for livelihood security. There are complex unwritten norms of mutual obligations. When a household does not comply with the social norm of a mutual obligation, it can be ostracized (BTI 2014; Masaki 2013a; Walcott 2011; Wangchuk 2004). In rural communities, decisions affecting local areas are mostly discussed in community meetings, in which at least one representative from each household participates. Both men and women can represent a household in such meetings (Masaki 2013a; Wangchuk 2004).

In subsistence livelihoods in rural Bhutan, labor is an important resource that has often been a scarce resource. According to Sonam Kinga (2008), a household is not able to complete agricultural activities within an appropriate period using the labor available within the household. In order to secure a subsistence livelihood, there are different forms of labor arrangements. One such arrangement is a reciprocal labor exchange that involves two or more households. It is not only the labor of humans but also that of animals, such as bulls and horses, that is exchanged. The exchange between households is not based on an exactly balanced reciprocity, but it is practiced in a flexible manner (Kinga 2008).

There are traditionally evolved local resource management institutions that have contributed to controlling resource usage, and ensuring the sustainability of the community resources. Some of these institutions have faded away, while others have further evolved and become institutionalized in accordance with the socio-economic changes taking place in the country. Table 20.1 shows some of the local resource management institutions that existed before modern institutionalization. However, there may be specific differences between different regions (see, e.g., Dorji 2005; Penjore 2008). In addition, institutions such as those presented in the table do not necessarily exist across the country, and the generalization of their effects must be avoided.[2]

As Table 20.1 shows, traditional institutions function through customary regulations and restrictions, and the purpose of the institutions is to ensure the democratic sharing and maintenance of local resources. In case of disputes and conflicts between households, people in small communities tend to avoid bringing their problems into the formal legal system. Instead, they first attempt to solve the problems within the community through arbitration by the responsible person in a relevant institution[3] (S. Wangchuk 2001).

Modern civil society organizations

Regulated civil society organizations

This section focuses on CSOs that are regulated by the Civil Society Organizations Act. The first modern type of CSO of Bhutanese origin, the National Youth Association of Bhutan, which was formed by young civil servants, came into existence in 1973. Since then, many new and modern associations have been established by educated people. Unlike the traditional institutions in rural communities, these modern CSOs operate on the basis of written rules and regulations[4] (Asian Development Bank 2013; Galay 2001). As mentioned above, cooperatives and

Table 20.1 Example of traditional local resource management institutions in Bhutan

Institution	Roles and functions
Reesup (Village Forest Guard)	• To ensure that everyone has adequate firewood and construction timber • To prohibit forestry activities at certain periods of time to ensure sustainability of the forest
Meesup (Forest Fire Watcher)	• To protect the forest from fires • To mobilize labor to fight forest fires • To detect the cause of the fire
Chusup (Drinking Water and Irrigation Water Watcher)	• To ensure traditionally established canals for drinking water are respected by households • To ensure proper distribution of irrigation water among households • To arbitrate minor disputes among households
Shingsungpa (Agricultural Crop Damage Arbitrator)	• To inspect crop damage • To settle disputes with regard to crop damage

Source: this table was created by the author based on S. Wangchuk (2001).

religious organizations are not regulated by the Civil Society Organizations Act and, thus, are not included in the CSOs.

The Civil Society Organizations Act was officially legislated in 2007 and, consequently, the Civil Society Organizations Authority was established in 2009. The purpose of the Act and Authority was to build a legal and regulatory framework for CSOs. Needless to say, the Authority does not supervise the traditional civil society in rural communities. The Authority is responsible for: (1) reviewing all applications and approving CSOs that meet the requirements in the Act for registration; (2) approving the accreditation of foreign CSOs according to the laws of Bhutan and the Act; and (3) monitoring the activities of CSOs that should follow the Act and their own aims and charters[5] (Civil Society Organizations Authority n.d.a).

All CSOs should register with the Authority under the Act (Civil Society Organizations Authority 2007). CSOs are categorized into two groups: (1) Public benefit organizations, and (2) mutual benefit organizations. The former are defined as organizations that were established in order to benefit a section of the society or the society as a whole, while the latter are defined as those that advance the shared interests of their members. As of June 2016, thirty-five public benefit organizations and twelve mutual benefit organizations were registered with the Authority (Civil Society Organizations Authority n.d.b).

The Authority receives many applications from CSOs to be approved and registered. Most of the registered CSOs are based in urban areas, although their activities and programs may reach out to rural areas. As indicated above, there were a few CSOs even before the Act was legislated in 2007, and their function was clearly recognized by the government despite the absence of a legal entity to regulate them. In the Authority, the board consists of five members: two representatives of the CSOs who are elected from the forty-seven CSOs; two members from the government (the Ministry of Finance and Ministry of Home and Cultural Affairs); and one legal expert. Thus, the Authority can be considered to be the interface between governmental institutions and the CSOs, where the government and the CSOs are equal partners, and the CSOs give various inputs to governmental policies.[6]

As presented above, GNH is deeply embedded in a web of institutions and networks that have various aims, missions, and operations in different sectors. Article 6, paragraph (g) in the Civil Society Organizations Act states that public benefit organizations shall serve to supplement or complement the efforts made by the government to promote social harmony and GNH (Civil Society Organizations Authority 2007). The government and civil society have a symbiotic relationship in Bhutan, and the four pillars of GNH are covered by various CSOs.

International civil society organizations

With respect to the accreditation of foreign CSOs, Section 48 in the Act states, "A Foreign CSO shall request a government agency in a relevant sector to act as a technical collaborator to implement the CSO's goals and activities in Bhutan" (Civil Society Organizations Authority 2007: 21). Consequently, Section 49 states, "A CSO registered as a non-governmental organization in a foreign country that is operating or intending to operate in Bhutan shall apply for accreditation with the Authority" (Civil Society Organizations Authority 2007: 21). As of July 2016, there was no foreign CSO accredited by the Authority. Foreign CSOs are currently categorized as development partners of the government, together with the institutions of Official Development Assistance (ODA) and institutions of the United Nations, such as UNICEF. As development partners, the foreign CSOs come under the direct supervision of the government without any involvement of the Authority.[7]

Challenges faced by CSOs

Funding is one of the major challenges that CSOs face, and many CSOs have to compete for funding. There have been mergers of CSOs with similar objectives. There have also been "natural deaths" of CSOs when organizations could not sustain their activities due to a lack of finances. There have been cases of voluntary dissolution of CSOs. Most of the activities of the CSOs take the form of projects that are funded by donors for limited periods and, therefore, CSOs constantly need to look for funds. When the donor withdraws, project funding also comes to an end, which threatens the sustainability of the CSOs. The fact that many CSOs are donor dependent is a major problem.[8]

Gross national happiness and changes in civil society

The pursuit of the four pillars of GNH is emphasized in the Tenth and Eleventh Five Year Plans, which is reflected in concrete programs. It was the fourth king who initiated the decentralization process, in order to promote local socio-economic development by empowering the people in decision-making concerning their own needs. It is believed that the pursuit of the four pillars of GNH is impossible without the empowerment and involvement of local people (Gross National Happiness Commission 2007, n.d.; National Assembly of Bhutan 2002a, 2002b).

In decentralization, traditional civil society has crucial roles to play. In order to pursue the self-reliance stated in the Eleventh Five Year Plan, rural communities need to remain vital. In order to keep young school-leavers within the agricultural community, the government offers various training programs (Ministry of Agriculture and Forests 2014). In pursuit of GNH, there are increasing interventions from the government and CSOs entering the territory of traditional civil society. As indicated above, informal organizations and institutions in traditional civil society are sometimes transformed into more formalized organizations.

Some of the modern CSOs have been expected to play important roles in the Tenth and Eleventh Five Year Plans in that they have the competence to eradicate poverty and build an inclusive and sustainable society in pursuit of equitable development. An encounter between CSOs and traditional civil society implies an encounter between different types of knowledge, as well, which may create certain tensions and friction.

In the sections that follow, there are presentations of cases that depict changes in traditional civil society and certain tensions that arise when different types of knowledge meet. It is not a question of whether these changes are positive or negative. Instead, these changes naturally follow the socio-economic changes in the country.

Changes in the concept of the community primary school

Voluntary labor and community ownership of the school

Owing to the country's mountainous geographical features and scattered human settlements, it has been a challenge for the Bhutanese government to increase school enrollment. To tackle this problem, the government has been building community primary schools (CPSs) to bring the schools closer, within an hour's walking distance, to the communities. CPSs are small schools with minimum facilities, and the average enrollment in one school can be between fifty and 120 students. In the Ninth Five Year Plan (2002–2007), the plan was to construct 119 new CPSs (Ministry of Education 2009; UNESCO 2004; World Bank 2003).

The civil society in rural communities has been playing a crucial role in the construction and maintenance of CPSs. In the Ninth Plan, owing to a rapidly increasing demand for education and the limited available resources, the government had to involve the rural communities and *Dzongkhag Tshogdus* in constructing CPSs. The government offered the design and materials, while the community supplied the manual labor and locally available materials, such as stones. Because communities were involved in the construction and maintenance of the schools by providing voluntary labor, those schools have been called "community primary schools." These communities have a sense of ownership toward their schools, as well as pride and satisfaction[9] (Gross National Happiness Commission 2007; Ministry of Education & Development Partners 2009; UNESCO 2004).

From voluntary labor to paid labor

During the period of the Ninth Five Year Plan, the Millennium Development Goal prevailed in development policies, which led to an effort to increase primary school enrollment rates. The Tenth Five Year Plan (2008–2013) proposed the building of a further forty-five CPSs in rural and remote communities[10] (Ministry of Education n.d.; Ministry of Education & Development Partners 2009). On the other hand, it was recognized that some CPSs faced a shortage of students due to migrations and that the expansion of CPSs had reached the point of saturation (Ministry of Education 2009, n.d.; Ministry of Education & Development Partners 2009).

In the Tenth Five Year Plan, there was a shift in policy, whereby the concept of CPSs in the sense of voluntary labor offered by the community was discontinued. Today, therefore, the CPS is simply called "primary school." Currently, the request for constructing a primary school is submitted by a *Gup* (an elected *Gewog* leader) at the district level, which is, in turn, submitted to the Ministry of Education. Once the request is approved, the district puts together a budget to construct the school. The district government fully finances the construction of schools in rural communities in several ways. For example, the district government signs a contract with the rural community and gives money as a lump sum to the community for the construction of the school. Then, the community decides how the money should be spent. The community people who are involved in the actual construction of the school building are paid from the lump-sum budget given by the district government. In the case where the construction of a school is beyond the capacity of a community, the district government outsources the work to a private contractor. With respect to school maintenance, the school currently receives a budget for maintenance from the district government. If local people wish to contribute to school maintenance, the school pays for the work done by the people and, thus, there is no free voluntary labor today[11] (Ministry of Education n.d.).

There are several reasons as to why there have been changes from free voluntary work to paid work by community members in the construction and maintenance of the school. The first is an issue of inequity. In urban areas, parents do not need to contribute their labor to school construction and maintenance and, therefore, requesting free labor from rural parents undermines equitable development, which is one of the four pillars of GNH. The second factor is the economic development in Bhutan that has enabled the government to offer full financial support to community school construction and maintenance. The third factor is that there are always a number of projects in different sectors in which community members are involved; this is a great burden for the community[12] (Ministry of Education n.d.).

The case of Bayta Primary School

The classroom building and administration building of Bayta Primary School in Phobjikha reflect two different ways of constructing buildings in two different policy periods. The classroom building was constructed in 2005, during the period of the Ninth Five Year Plan, in response to a request from the community. The government offered the construction materials, while the community provided voluntary labor. The administration building, with a library and teachers' office, was built in 2013 under the Tenth Five Year Plan. The request for this building came from the teachers, and the building was constructed by a contractor selected by the district government after tendering. No community labor was involved in the construction of the administration building. However, with respect to the maintenance of the classroom building, the community continuously offers labor, while the materials are offered by the district government.[13]

Gross National Happiness, new ideas, and community volunteerism

One of the four pillars of GNH, equitable development, has brought about the new idea that it is unfair if people in rural communities are required to supply free labor for the construction of schools. In the new system adopted in the Tenth Five Year Plan, the free labor supplied by the rural community was discontinued. On the other hand, communities that built CPSs literally by hand have a sense of ownership toward the schools, and there are cases in which the traditional civil society spirit of voluntary self-help in rural communities continues. In cases where there is an urgent need to repair a school building because of damage caused by a natural disaster, there are examples of communities where members mobilize resources, spontaneously collect money, and do repair works without payment from the government.[14]

Community forestry program

Background of the program

Prior to the enactment of the Forest Act in 1969, Bhutan had a long tradition whereby people in rural communities used and managed forest resources for fuel wood, housing materials, food, medicines, and religious purposes. It was not illegal to harvest forest resources for one's own use without obtaining formal permission from the state, with the exception of hunting endangered species. It was the informal self-evolved restrictions imposed by local institutions that ensured the sustainability of forest resources (Belsky 2015; S. Wangchuk 2001). In 1969, however, the forests in Bhutan were nationalized by the Forest Act and declared Government Reserved Forests with restricted community rights to use and manage them. There was no consideration given to the customary rights and practices of the communities over the forests, or to the traditional institutions that managed and guarded the forests. On the other hand, in reality, customary rights and practices sometimes continued because of the inadequacy of the resources of the government to implement the Act fully (Moktan, Norbu, and Choden 2016; Penjore 2008; S. Wangchuk 2001).

Under the Act, it became a time-consuming procedure for community members to obtain permits to get fuel wood, timber for houses, poles for prayer flags, and other forest products from Government Reserved Forests[15] (Penjore 2008). At the same time, the traditional guardianship system of the forests in rural communities, presented in Table 20.1, declined without the development of an alternative authority. As a result, the forests became accessible to outside communities, which led to unregulated forest product extraction (Belsky 2015; Wangdi and Tshering 2006).

Community forest management group

Having recognized the importance of the participation of community members in forest management, some of the forestry activities were decentralized from the central to district level. Community Forestry was introduced in 1992, and the Forest and Nature Conservation Act 1995 legalized the Community Forestry. The Act and the Nature Conservation Rules support the formation of the Community Forestry Management Group (CFMG), while the ownership of the forest remains with the central government[16] (Belsky 2015; Moktan et al. 2016; Temphel and Beukeboom 2006; Temphel and Lhendup 2007; Wangdi and Tshering 2006). This devolution of the power to manage the forest from the central government to the community is seen as a paradigm shift from a tree-centered approach to a people-centered approach (Phuntsho and Sangye 2006).

With the Community Forestry, interested communities, with help from the forester in the *Gewog* (who is a civil servant posted by the central government), submit an application to form a CFMG to the district government, and then the Divisional Forest Office. Once approval is given, the CFMG is formed. The members of the CFMG are households in the community who are interested in the group. As of July 2016, there were 655 CFMGs in Bhutan,[17] and the size of the groups varies significantly. The CFMG makes plans for the management of the community forest, again with help from the forester in the *Gewog*. The plan must be approved by the Department of Forests and Park Services in the Ministry of Agriculture[18] (Temphel and Lhendup 2007).

Membership in a CFMG is voluntary, although most of the households join the group. It is the CFMG that issues permits to the members who need forest products from the community forest. The Government Reserved Forests continue to exist and are clearly demarcated from the community forest. Those who are not members of the CFMG should continue to obtain permits from the government in order to obtain forest products from the Government Reserved Forests. However, obtaining permits from the CFMG is much less time-consuming and burdensome, which is the main reason why households join it[19] (Belsky 2015).

Regulation by the plan and rules

All activities in the Community Forestry must follow the community forest management plan made by the CFMG, and every CFMG has its own unique plan, depending on the characteristics of the forest, as well as the needs, demands, and interests of the members. As stated above, the ownership of the forests remains with the central government, and every community plan is evaluated after ten years of operation. If the evaluation result is poor and shows no room for improvement, the community forest is taken over by the central government. Otherwise, the CFMG can renew the Community Forestry with or without minor corrections advised by the *Gewog* forester.[20]

In Tangsibji *Gewog*, for example, if a household in a CFMG needs trees to build a house, it obtains a permit from the CFMG. It is then the *Gewog* forester, not the members of the CFMG, who selects the trees to be cut by the household. The household pays for the trees, and the money is saved in the bank account of the CFMG. The number of trees that can be cut is clearly defined in the plan made by the group, and it is the *Gewog* forester who decides which trees can be cut according to the silviculture system. In a case where there are no suitable trees within the community forest, the household receives a receipt from the CFMG, with which the former can obtain a permit to obtain trees from the Government Reserved Forests.[21]

GNH and the institutionalization of traditional civil society

With the entrance of Community Forestry, it is said that the forest is back in the community after decades of being controlled by the central government. The Community Forestry contributes to two pillars of GNH: conservation of the environment and promotion of good governance. After the introduction of the Community Forestry, community people generally manage the forest in a highly sustainable manner. The formation of a CFMG contributes to good governance and promotes transparency and the equitable sharing of resources.[22] On the other hand, the Community Forestry may be seen as the institutionalization of traditional civil society where the traditional informal forest management institution has very limited room, if any, to influence forest management. In the Eleventh Five Year Plan, people are encouraged to increase their income in a sustainable manner in rural communities using non-wood forest products, such as mushrooms. At the same time, unlike the traditional forest management institution, Community Forestry is linked with formal regulation.

Holistic environmental protection and different types of knowledge

The case of Phobjikha

The Royal Society for Protection of Nature (RSPN) is a CSO in Bhutan that was established in 1987. It is one of the oldest CSOs and the only one in Bhutan that focuses on environmental protection. One of the programs that the RSPN has been conducting is black-necked crane conservation in the Phobjikha Valley in Wangduephodrang District. This endangered species migrates from the Tibetan Plateau to Phobjikha, one of its major roosting grounds in Bhutan, every autumn and stays there until the spring[23] (RSPN 2016a, 2016b).

The habitat of the crane is used for agricultural and development activities that have both direct and indirect impacts on the wetland, forests, and watersheds, which, in turn, may threaten the survival of the crane and other species. One major problem in Phobjikha is that the conservation area has no special legal status. It is treated as a multiple-use forest area, which allows the people living within and outside the valley to exploit the forest products in the area. As Buddhists, people tend to feel that they are not harming living beings, without realizing the indirect impacts of their development aspirations on the environment. It is also unclear to the people whether the area should come under the protected area system. In such cases, the RSPN is often consulted. One positive change is that the conservation area is now registered in the Ramsar Convention[24] (RSPN 2016b).

The balance between development and the conservation of nature

For the RSPN, GNH is an inspiration, and one of the four pillars—conservation of the environment—is the major mission of this organization. It follows the middle-path policy in which development is not undermined by focusing on conservation, and it pursues sustainable development.

The presence of the crane in Phobjikha Valley attracts tourists. At the same time, the crane requires a suitable environment for its survival. Owing to a fear that electric poles would harm the crane, people in Phobjikha Valley did not prioritize having electricity, except for small-scale electricity produced by solar systems, and they did not gain it until relatively recently. In 2009, the underground electricity project was started at the suggestion of the RSPN, which led to the electrification of Phobjikha. Over the years, the RSPN has established the Integrated

Conservation and Development Program. This program encompasses the conservation of cranes, community-based sustainable wetland management, and the promotion of environmental sensitization in the community. In addition, since Phobjikha is a tourist destination, efforts have been made to establish community-based sustainable tourism to create alternative sources of income for the community[25] (RSPN 2016a, 2016b).

The encounter of different types of knowledge

Although the RSPN is widely supported by the community, certain tensions emerge amongst the people since there are different types of knowledge regarding the protection of cranes. For some farmers, protecting the cranes is not a new phenomenon. The cranes came to Phobjikha every year even before the RSPN appeared in the valley. At that time, the arrival of the cranes made the people happy. Even when the cranes destroyed the crops in fields, people did not chase them away. Since the coming of the RSPN to Phobjikha, people have had the same attitude toward the cranes, and they do not have any negative feelings about them.[26]

In the protected wetland area in the valley, it is forbidden to construct houses and extend agricultural fields toward the wetland. However, some farmers argue that the construction of houses does not impact the well-being of the cranes for the following reasons: (1) The cranes are not a new species in the area; (2) if houses disturb the roosting areas of the cranes, the cranes would not roost close to the houses; and (3) the cranes may feed near the houses, although they fly to other places to roost.[27]

GNH, local knowledge, and scientific knowledge

Traditional ways of thinking about and understanding the environment and nature in civil society are found in the rural areas of Bhutan, which may be termed "local knowledge" (Geertz 1983). When modern CSOs come to traditional civil society with more scientific knowledge, a tension between different types of knowledge can arise (see, e.g., Robles 2016). The RSPN came to Phobjikha in order to pursue one of the four pillars of GNH—conservation of the environment—equipped with modern scientific knowledge and methods. Some of the local farmers with traditional knowledge may not be able to understand or accept the activities of the RSPN.

Analyzing the fact that the community in Phobjikha did not prioritize electricity in order to protect the cranes, Hiroko Aoki, Hikari Ishido, and Kana Kawashima (2009) state that community members did not necessarily understand that the crane was an endangered species. Instead, they did not want to harm the crane, which was traditionally believed to be a sacred bird. They also state that for Bhutanese people who do not harm nature, nature is something to both protect and utilize.

With the conservation of the environment being one of the four pillars of GNH, new types of knowledge will increasingly be introduced to rural communities, in which local community people may feel a loss of ownership of their own environment. Although the majority of the people in Phobjikha have an aspiration to protect the cranes, the community does not feel a sense of ownership regarding certain aspects of the activities led by the RSPN. On the other hand, the crane festival, for example, which was originally initiated by the RSPN, is now in the hands of the community in a sustainable manner. It takes a long time before the community feels a sense of ownership toward the values brought from elsewhere.[28]

Conclusion

In general, civil society is an important factor of the democracy of a country. In this sense, Bhutan is a unique country where the development of democracy does not necessarily comply with conventional Western theories. To understand the civil society in Bhutan, it is crucial to understand the democracy that has been prevailing in the rural communities of Bhutan. With the evolution of the socio-political systems of the country, more modernized CSOs emerged. These organizations are similar to those found in Western countries in their characteristics, yet they are of Bhutanese origin. As observed in the philosophy of GNH and its four pillars, Bhutan tries to maintain its unique nature of economic and socio-cultural profiles, and recent policies emphasize the notion of self-reliance. Bhutan has been cautious in welcoming CSOs of foreign origin. Modern CSOs are highly regulated by the Civil Society Organizations Act and Civil Society Organizations Authority, which is necessary as Bhutan is a small country where an unnecessarily large number of CSOs with overlapping objectives and missions can easily create problems. The Authority also supervises the ethical and moral aspects of registered CSOs.

As this chapter demonstrates, both informal organizations of traditional civil society and modernized CSOs in Bhutan have had important roles to play in implementing policies aimed at GNH. The philosophy of GNH has gradually been changed from an abstract ideal to measurable forms of indexes and indicators. GNH emphasizes the importance of enlarging "opportunities for people at all levels to participate more fully and effectively in decisions that have a bearing on their lives and livelihoods and the future of their families, communities and the nation" (Royal Government of Bhutan 2011: 13). Accordingly, the decentralization of the governing system has been taking place, which requires increasing participation of people at the grass-roots level in decision-making. With the development of the decentralized system, certain traditional organizations in rural communities have come to be incorporated into the formal governing system, which has led to the institutionalization of informal organizations of traditional civil society. On the other hand, some traditional organizations in rural areas have faded away.

Compared with the long history of traditional informal organizations of civil society in rural Bhutan, the history of modernized CSOs is rather short; the first modernized CSO was established only in 1973. One of the characteristics of the civil society in Bhutan is the close collaboration between the government and CSOs based on equal partnership, which differs from some cases from other countries where civil society challenges the government or state institutions. The government of Bhutan recognizes the competencies that some CSOs have in areas such as sustainable rural development and nature conservation.[29] The modernized CSOs that work in rural communities may meet "local knowledge" that differs from the knowledge that the CSOs bring into rural communities. In such cases, negotiations between "local knowledge" and scientific knowledge may occur.

The political system of Bhutan was transformed from an absolute monarchy to a constitutional monarchy in 2008. The emergence of the new political system resulted in more policies being established in pursuit of GNH. Both informal organizations in traditional civil society and modernized CSOs will continue to play crucial roles in Bhutan. In order to further understand the civil society in Bhutan, one should observe how traditional informal organizations in rural communities are transformed and developed over time, as well as how CSOs tackle the problems identified by them.

Notes

1 Personal communication with the Program Coordinator, July 27, 2016, Civil Society Organizations Authority.
2 Personal communication with a Researcher, August 4, 2016, Center for Bhutan Studies.
3 Personal communication with the Leader of the Tangsibji Community Forestry Group, July 29, 2016, Tangsibji Gewog.
4 Personal communication with the Program Coordinator, July 27, 2016, Civil Society Organizations Authority.
5 Ibid.
6 Ibid.
7 Ibid.
8 Personal communication with the Program Coordinator, July 27, 2016, Civil Society Organizations Authority; Personal communication with the Project Officer, July 26, 2016, RSPN; Personal communication with the Program Officer, Senior Program Officer of the Tarayana Foundation, and Director of Bussi-en Group, July 26, 2016, Tarayana Foundation.
9 Personal communication with the Chief Planning Officer, Senior Planning Officer, and Chief Engineer, August 3, 2016, Ministry of Education.
10 Ibid.
11 Ibid
12 Ibid.
13 Personal communication with the Principal, August 1, 2016, Bayta Primary School, Phobjikha.
14 Personal communication with the Chief Planning Officer, Senior Planning Officer, and Chief Engineer, August 3, 2016, Ministry of Education.
15 Personal communication with the Deputy Chief of Forestry, July 26, 2016, Department of Forests and Park Services; Personal communication with the Park Ranger and Gewog Forester, July 29, 2016, Tangsibji Gewog.
16 Personal communication with the Deputy Chief of Forestry, July 26, 2016, Department of Forests and Park Services.
17 Ibid.
18 Personal communication with the Deputy Chief of Forestry, July 26, 2016, Department of Forests and Park Services; Personal communication with the Park Ranger and Gewog Forester, July 29, 2016, Tangsibji Gewog.
19 Personal communication with the Deputy Chief of Forestry, July 26, 2016, Department of Forests and Park Services; Personal communication with the Leader of the Tangsibji Community Forestry Group, July 29, 2016, Tangsibji Gewog; Personal communication with Park Ranger and Gewog Forester, July 29, 2016, Tangsibji Gewog.
20 Personal communication with Park Ranger and Gewog Forester, July 29, 2016, Tangsibji Gewog.
21 Personal communication with the Leader of the Tangsibji Community Forestry Group, July 29, 2016, Tangsibji Gewog; Personal communication with the Park Ranger and Gewog Forester, July 29, 2016, Tangsibji Gewog.
22 Personal communication with the Deputy Chief of Forestry, July 26, 2016, Department of Forests and Park Services.
23 Personal communication with the Project Officer, July 26, 2016, RSPN.
24 Ibid.
25 Ibid.
26 Personal communication with a farmer, July 31, 2016, Gangtey, Phopjikha.
27 Ibid.
28 Personal communication with the Project Officer, July 26, 2016, RSPN.
29 Personal communication with the Project Officer, July 26, 2016, RSPN; Personal communication with the Program Officer, Senior Program Officer of the Tarayana Foundation, and Director of Bussi-en Group, July 26, 2016, Tarayana Foundation.

Suggested readings

Choden, Tashi. 2005. Civil Society in Bhutan: Manifesting the Spirit Within. In *Understanding Civil Society in Bhutan*. Tashi Choden and Lham Dorji, eds. Pp. 1–110. Thimphu: The Centre for Bhutan Studies.

Dorji, Lham. 2005. Understanding the Concept of Civil Society in Bhutan. In *Understanding Civil Society in Bhutan*. Tashi Choden and Lham Dorji, eds. Pp. 1–107. Thimphu: The Centre for Bhutan Studies.

Horgan, Gerard W. 2015. The Role of Deliberative Mini-Publics in the Quest for Gross National Happiness. *Journal of Bhutan Studies* 32: 45–73.

Masaki, Katsu. 2013a. Exploring Bhutan's "Natural Democracy": In Search of an Alternative View of Democracy. *Journal of Bhutan Studies* 28: 47–72.

Masaki, Katsu. 2013b. A Proposition "Bhutan is a Democracy": Beyond the Constricted, Popular Wisdom of "Democracy". *Journal of Bhutan Studies* 29: 1–34.

Websites

Center for Bhutan Studies, www.bhutanstudies.org.bt.
Established in 1998, the objectives of the Center are to evaluate existing programs of the government, support research on socio-cultural and economic aspects of Bhutan and publish journals and research papers relating to studies in these areas.

Civil Society Organization Authority (CSOA), www.csoa.org.bt/content/index.php.
Working under the Civil Society Organizations Act of Bhutan (2007), the CSOA works to promote growth in CSOs focused on improving quality of life in Bhutan.

GNH Centre Bhutan, www.gnhcentrebhutan.org.
A center promoting the Gross National Happiness philosophy, which focuses on social and economic equality, environmental conservation and quality of life.

Gross National Happiness Commission (GNH Commission), www.gnhc.gov.bt.
The GNH Commission focuses on development plans and objectives (its work includes providing support services, allocation of resources, and monitoring existing programs) to promote the GNH philosophy.

National Assembly of Bhutan, www.nab.gov.bt/en/.
Information on Bhutan's democratically elected parliament, including mission and vision, members, library, and forum.

References

Aoki, Hiroko, Hikari Ishido, and Kana Kawashima. 2009. *In Search of Abundance: The Case of Bhutan's Gross National Happiness*. Electronic document, www.tci.ac.jp/smj/wp-content/uploads/Bhutan2.pdf, accessed August 13, 2016.

Asian Development Bank. 2013. *Civil Society Briefs: Bhutan*. Electronic document, www.adb.org/sites/default/files/publication/30296/csb-bhu.pdf, accessed April 30, 2016.

Belsky, Jill M. 2015. Community Forestry Engagement with Market Forces: A Comparative Perspective from Bhutan and Montana. *Forest Policy and Economics* 58: 29–36.

Bertelsmann Stiftung's Transformation Index (BTI). 2014. *BTI 2014 Bhutan Country Report*. Electronic document, www.bti-project.org/fileadmin/files/BTI/Downloads/Reports/2014/pdf/BTI_2014_Bhutan.pdf, accessed April 30, 2016.

Choden, Tashi. 2003. *Traditional Forms of Volunteerism in Bhutan*. Electronic document, www.bhutanstudies.org.bt/publicationFiles/Monograph/monoVolunteerism.pdf, accessed April 30, 2016.

Choden, Tashi. 2005. Civil Society in Bhutan: Manifesting the Spirit Within. In *Understanding Civil Society in Bhutan*. Tashi Choden and Lham Dorji, eds. Pp. 1–110. Thimphu: The Centre for Bhutan Studies.

Civil Society Organizations Authority. 2007. *The Civil Society Organizations Act of Bhutan*. Electronic document, www.csoa.org.bt/publication/files/pub6ud10589zr.pdf, accessed April 30, 2016.

Civil Society Organizations Authority. n.d.a. *Civil Society Organizations Authority*. Electronic document, www.csoa.org.bt/content/pageContent.php?id=8, accessed June 11, 2016.

Civil Society Organizations Authority. n.d.b. *Status of CSOs in Bhutan*. Electronic document, www.csoa.org.bt/content/pageContent.php?id=39, accessed June 11, 2016.

Country Watch. 2015. *2015 Country Review*. Electronic document, www.countrywatch.com/Content/pdfs/reviews/B35333Q4.01c.pdf, accessed May 26, 2016.

Dorji, Lham. 2005. Understanding the Concept of Civil Society in Bhutan. In *Understanding Civil Society in Bhutan*. Tashi Choden and Lham Dorji, eds. Pp. 1–107. Thimphu: The Centre for Bhutan Studies.

Galay, Karma. 2001. Bhutanese Context of Civil Society. *Journal of Bhutan Studies* 3: 199–218.

Geertz, Clifford. 1983. *Local Knowledge*. New York: Basic Books.

GNH Centre Bhutan. n.d. *Gross National Happiness in Action*. Electronic document, www.gnhcentre bhutan.org/what-is-gnh/the-story-of-gnh/, accessed June 4, 2016.

Gross National Happiness Commission. 2007. *Assignment of Functional and Financial Responsibilities to Local Governments*. Electronic document, www.gnhc.gov.bt/wp-content/uploads/2011/05/Assignment_of-Responsibilities_to_LGs-GNHC_Website.pdf, accessed September 1, 2016.

Gross National Happiness Commission. 2009. *Tenth Five Year Plan 2008–2013 Volume 1: Main Document*. Electronic document, www.gnhc.gov.bt/wp-content/uploads/2011/10thplan/TenthPlan_Vol.1_Web.pdf, accessed August 12, 2016.

Gross National Happiness Commission. 2013. *Eleventh Five Year Plan Volume 1: Main Document*. Electronic document, www.gnhc.gov.bt/wp-content/uploads/2011/04/Eleventh-Five-Year-Plan.pdf, accessed September 1, 2016.

Gross National Happiness Commission. n.d. *9th Five Year Plan (2003–2008)*. Electronic document, www.gnhc.gov.bt/wp-content/uploads/2011/04/5yp09_main.pdf, accessed June 22, 2016.

Hirayama, Takehiro. 2016. Bhutan ni okeru Shoki-kindai Kyoikujijo no Kaimei: Kindai-kyoiku 50 Nen-shi [Explication of the Modern Educational Situation in Bhutan: Fifty Years of the Modern Education]. *Himaraya Gakushi [Himalayan Study Monographs]* 17: 162–173 (in Japanese).

Horgan, Gerard W. 2015. The Role of Deliberative Mini-Publics in the Quest for Gross National Happiness. *Journal of Bhutan Studies* 32: 45–73.

Japan International Cooperation Agency. n.d. *Bhutan*. Electronic document, www.jica.go.jp/bhutan/, accessed May 19, 2016.

Kinga, Sonam. 2008. *Reciprocal Exchange and Community Vitality: The Case of Gortshom Village in Eastern Bhutan*. Electronic document, www.bhutanstudies.org.bt/publicationFiles/ConferenceProceedings/3r dGNH/5.3rdGNH.pdf, accessed January 10, 2016.

The Kingdom of Bhutan. 2008. *The Constitution of the Kingdom of Bhutan*. Electronic document, www.nationalcouncil.bt/assets/uploads/files/Constitution of Bhutan English.pdf, accessed July 26, 2016.

Masaki, Katsu. 2013a. Exploring Bhutan's "Natural Democracy": In Search of an Alternative View of Democracy. *Journal of Bhutan Studies* 28: 47–72.

Masaki, Katsu. 2013b. A proposition "Bhutan is a Democracy": Beyond the Constricted, Popular Wisdom of "Democracy". *Journal of Bhutan Studies* 29: 1–34.

Ministry of Agriculture and Forests. 2014. *Rural Development Training Center*. Electronic document, www.moaf.gov.bt/agencies/rural-development-training-centre/rtdc-about-us/, accessed August 13, 2016.

Ministry of Education. 2009. *A Study on Enrolment and Retentions Strategies in Bhutan*. Thimphu: Ministry of Education, Policy & Planning Division.

Ministry of Education. n.d. *10th Five Year Plan (2008–2013) Education Sector*. Electronic document, http://planipolis.iiep.unesco.org/upload/Bhutan/Bhutan_Tenth_Five_Year_Plan_2008-2013_Education_Sector.pdf, accessed June 26, 2016.

Ministry of Education & Development Partners. 2009. *Fast Track Initiative Appraisal Report: Education Sector Strategy*. Thimphu: Royal Government of Bhutan.

Ministry of Foreign Affairs of Denmark. n.d. *Denmark in Bhutan*. Electronic document, http://bhutan.um.dk/en/about-bhutan/, accessed May 19, 2016.

Miyashita, Fumiaki. 2009. GNH no Gainen to Bhutan Okoku no Shorai [The Concept of GNH and the Future of the Kingdom of Bhutan]. *Waseda Shogaku [Waseda University Journal of Commerce]* 420/421: 39–74 (in Japanese).

Moktan, Mani Ram, Lungten Norbu, and Kunzang Choden. 2016. Can Community Forestry Contribute to Household Income and Sustainable Forestry Practices in Rural Area? A Case Study from Tshapey and Zariphensum in Bhutan. *Forest Policy and Economics* 62: 149–157.

National Assembly of Bhutan. 2002a. *Dzongkhag Yargay Tshogdu Chathrim, 2002. [Rules and Regulations of District Development Committees, 2002]* Electronic document, www.nab.gov.bt/assets/uploads/docs/acts/2014/DYT_2002Eng.pdf, accessed August 30, 2016 (in English).

National Assembly of Bhutan. 2002b. *Geog Yargay Tshogchhung Chathrim, 2002* [*Rules and Regulations of Block Development Committees, 2002*]. Electronic document, www.nab.gov.bt/assets/uploads/docs/acts/2014/GYT_2002Eng.pdf, accessed September 1, 2016 (in English).

National Assembly of Bhutan. 2008. *The Constitution of the Kingdom of Bhutan*. Electronic document, www.nab.gov.bt/assets/templates/images/constitution-of-bhutan-2008.pdf, accessed May 29, 2016.

Office of the Prime Minister & Cabinet. 2016. *Prime Ministers of Bhutan since 1998*. Electronic document, www.cabinet.gov.bt/?page_id=34, accessed May 29, 2016.

Penjore, Dorji. 2008. Is National Environment Conservation Success a Rural Failure? The Other Side of Bhutan's Conservation Story. In *Towards Global Transformation*. The Centre for Bhutan Studies, ed. Pp. 66–87. Thimphu: The Centre for Bhutan Studies.

Phuntsho, Karma. 2013. *The History of Bhutan*. London: House Publishing.

Phuntsho, Sonam, and Mani Sangye. 2006. Entire Rural Wood Supply from Community Forests: A Challenging Mission. *A Series of Case Studies on Community-Based Forest and Natural Resource Management in Bhutan*. Thimphu: Ministry of Agriculture.

Robles, Chelsea M. 2016. *Education and Society in Bhutan: Tradition and Modernisation*. Abingdon: Routledge.

Royal Government of Bhutan. 2011. *Bhutan 2020: A Vision for Peace, Prosperity and Happiness, Part II*. Electronic document,www.gnhc.gov.bt/wp-content/uploads/2011/05/Bhutan2020_2.pdf, accessed May 29, 2016.

Royal Government of Bhutan. 2013. *The State of the Tsa-Wa-Sum*. Electronic document, www.cabinet.gov.bt/annual_report/Annual Report 2013 new gov.pdf, accessed May 29, 2016.

RSPN. 2016a. *Black-Necked Crane Conservation*. Electronic document, www.rspnbhutan.org/black-necked-crane-conservation/, accessed August 10, 2016.

RSPN. 2016b. *Phobjikha Conservation Area*. Electronic document, www.rspnbhutan.org/phobjikha-conservation-area/, accessed August 10, 2016.

Sugimoto, Hitoshi. 2000. Bhutan Okoku ni okeru Ko-kyoiku to Seinen no Ishiki: Dento to Kindai [Public Education and Consciousness of the Youth in the Kingdom of Bhutan]. *Himaraya Gakushi* [*Himalayan Study Monographs*] 7: 11–31 (in Japanese).

Temphel, Karma J., and Hans J. J. Beukeboom. 2006. Community Forestry Contributes to the National and Millennium Development Goals Without Compromising the Forestry Policy! *A Series of Case Studies on Community-Based Forest and Natural Resource Management in Bhutan*. Thimphu: Ministry of Agriculture.

Temphel, Karma J., and Tenzin Lhendup. 2007. Dynamics of Different Ethno-Linguistic Groups: A Case Study of Three Community Forests. *A Series of Case Studies on Community-Based Forest and Natural Resource Management in Bhutan*. Thimphu: Ministry of Agriculture.

Thinley, Jigmi Y. 2005. What is Gross National Happiness? In *Rethinking Development*. The Centre for Bhutan Studies, ed. Pp. 3–11. Thimphu: The Centre for Bhutan Studies.

US Department of State. 2008. *Background Note: Bhutan*. Electronic document, http://2001-2009.state.gov/r/pa/ei/bgn/35839.htm, accessed May 26, 2016.

Ueda, Akiko. 2011. *Relationship, Balance and Contentment: Perspective and Practice of Gross National Happiness*. Electronic document, www.glocol.osaka-u.ac.jp/staff/ueda/ueda_kagaku201106.pdf, accessed September 20, 2016.

UNESCO. 2004. *National Report on the Development of Education*. Electronic document, www.ibe.unesco.org/National_Reports/ICE_2004/bhutan.pdf, accessed October 15, 2015.

UNICEF. 2013. *Bhutan*. Electronic document, www.unicef.org/infobycountry/bhutan_statistics.html, accessed August 10, 2016.

Walcott, Susan M. 2011. One of a Kind: Bhutan and the Modernity Challenge. *National Identities* 13: 253–265.

Wangchuk, Sangay. 2001. Local Resource Management Institutions: A Case Study on Sokshing Management. *Journal of Bhutan Studies* 3: 1–44.

Wangchuk, Tashi. 2001. Changes in the Land Use System in Bhutan: Ecology, History, Culture, and Power. *Journal of Bhutan Studies* 2: 48–75.

Wangchuk, Tashi. 2004. The Middle Path to Democracy in the Kingdom of Bhutan. *Asian Survey* 44: 836–855.

Wangdi, Rinchen, and Nima Tshering. 2006. Is Community Forestry Making a Difference to Rural Communities?: A Comparative Study of Three Community Forests in Mongar Dzongkhag. *A Series of*

Case Study on Community-Bases Forestry and Natural Resources Management in Bhutan. Thimphu: Ministry of Agriculture.

WHO. 2015. *Life Expectancy at Birth (years), 2000–2015*. Electronic document, http://gamapserver.who. int/gho/interactive_charts/mbd/life_expectancy/atlas.html, accessed August 10, 2016.

World Bank. 2003. *Project Appraisal Document on a Proposed Credit in the Amount of SDR 22.0 Million (US$31.0 million equivalent) to the Kingdom of Bhutan Education Development Project*. Electronic document, www-wds.worldbank.org/external/default/WDSContentServer/WDSP/IB/2003/07/25/000090341 _20030725133340/Rendered/PDF/258020PAD.pdf, accessed June 26, 2016.

World Bank. 2016a. *Bhutan*. Electronic document, www.worldbank.org/en/country/bhutan, accessed May 19, 2016.

World Bank. 2016b. *World Development Indicators*. Electronic document, http://databank.worldbank.org/ data/reports.aspx?source=2&country=BTN, accessed May 29, 2016.

21

SRI LANKA

Udan Fernando

Sri Lankan civil society: roller coasters and a repeat of history?

In mid-2014, a Colombo-based country office of an international non-government organization (INGO) commissioned me to write a position paper on Civil Society and Non-Government
Organizations (NGOs) in Sri Lanka. The paper was to provide a basis for them to formulate a
new policy and strategy. This was at a time when a very strong but near-authoritarian government was ruling the country with a not-so-friendly attitude toward civil society actors clamoring for human rights, justice, rule of law, etc. The relationship between the government and
that section of civil society was characterized by deep distrust, suspicion, and antagonism. The
government took a hardline stance against this variety of civil society that was, according to the
government, working against the interests of the country; they were called "betrayers of moth-
erland," "traitors serving foreign interests," "conspirators undermining Buddhism," and "dollar-
vultures." The exchanges between both parties were acutely adversarial. The government was
led by a well-consolidated president, who was riding a political and popularity wave following
military victory over a separatist insurgency and a protracted war of nearly three decades. The
antagonism between the government and civil society heightened toward the end of 2015 when
the all-powerful president announced a Presidential Election in January 2015, two years before
the end of his term. I was expected to submit my paper by early December 2014 for feedback
from the relevant staff of the INGO. By the time I submitted my draft in mid-December, most
of the staff at the INGO had gone on their year-end vacation and their feedback was sent only
in mid-January 2016. By then, the Presidential Election had taken place—it was held in the first
week of January. The president, who claimed to be invincible, was defeated by a wildcard candidate representing the combined force of the opposition parties. This phenomenal political
transformation that took place in January 2015, popularly dubbed as "*venasa*" (Sinhala term for
"change") was followed by an equally important change of powers at the parliamentary elections in August. This changed the equation of civil society–government relations drastically.
The changes were so significant, to the extent that what I had written a few weeks back became
grossly obsolete and irrelevant, leaving me to rewrite the entire position paper. Such is the
roller-coaster nature of civil society dynamics in Sri Lanka.

In this chapter, I take a closer look at the so-called "*venasa*" ("change") described before.
However, before doing so, I briefly discuss the scholarship of Sri Lankan civil society and its

history and orientation, since the mid-1990s, with a commentary on civil society's interface with the government. I pay particular attention to the period that marks the run-up to the Presidential Election that was held in January 2015 and the General Election in August of the same year. The purpose of such close scrutiny is to understand the changing character of the civil society during that period and how it has configured itself vis-à-vis a changing political landscape since 2009, which coincides with the end of the civil war between the minority Tamils and the majority Sinhalese state.

The scholarship on civil society in Sri Lanka

Comprehensive studies on Sri Lankan CSOs/NGOs are carried out by a combination of Sri Lankan and non-Sri Lankan scholars such as Sunil Bastian (2003), Udan Fernando (2003, 2007), Peter Kloos (1999), Camilla Orjuela (2005), Jayadeva Uyangoda (2001), and Nira Wickramasinghe (2001). Though the emphasis was on the transformation of Buddhism, the work by Richard Gombrich and Gananath Obeyesekere (1988) sheds a great deal of light on the ideological currents of the voluntary organizations in the 1950s adapting to the transformation in society. Similarly, Uyangoda (2001) makes an in-depth analysis of the intrinsic relationship in the evolution of the Left and NGOs. Fernando (2007) documents and analyzes how NGOs and civil society strivings have become extensions or results of political persuasions and how political activists have become NGO/CSO leaders and vice versa.

Literature on Sri Lanka and by Sri Lankan authors uses terms such as voluntary organizations, civil society organizations (CSOs), non-governmental organizations (NGOs), and community-based organizations (CBOs) to denote various forms and manifestations of civil society actors. These terms are often used loosely and interchangeably. The terms gained currency in society, as well as in the academic sphere, at different stages of history. The early writings, that is, pre-1970s, used the term voluntary organizations to describe organizations that worked toward the well-being of a particular section of society pursuing a particular cause. The scope of such organizations is often limited in terms of work and working areas but could also be large and country wide. A *Wew Sabhaa*, a committee of farmers using water from a reservoir, is an example of the former, while examples of the latter are the Young Men's Buddhist Association (YMBA) or Young Men's Christian Association (YMCA).

The term NGO gained currency in the post-1977 period, coinciding with the phenomenal spread of a particular variety of organizations that were called NGOs. One of the main particularities of NGOs was the explicit "funding" and "donor" element, which was often connected to a source in a developed country. The term Community-Based Organizations (CBOs) became popular with the spread of the NGOs. CBOs in Sri Lankan parlance are organizations with members of a community in a relatively small geographical area who come together to work around a cause that concerns them and/or their area. Often, CBO members function on a voluntary basis and do not get paid—in contrast to NGOs—for the work they carry out. CBOs became a popular term to denote many such organizations that were recognized under the Janasaviya (the welfare scheme initiated by the United National Party [UNP] during the era of President R. Premadasa [1991–1994], coinciding with the Structural Adjustment Program—SAP) and Janasaviya Trust Fund. In fact, the Janasaviya scheme set a trend in poverty alleviation. Subsequent governments continued this model of poverty alleviation, but under different titles such as Samurdhi (Chandrika Bandaranaike governments from 1994) and Divineguma (Mahinda Rajapaksha governments from 2005). The CBO element was retained in these schemes as well. In general, civil society is denoted as the larger category and NGOs are considered a subcategory. This suggests that there is a civil society space that goes beyond that of the NGOs.

Often, CSOs/NGOs/CBOs are understood from an instrumentalist perspective, treating them as a means of achieving something. Hence, they are classified by what they do—gender, savings, good governance, health, income generation, etc. Such a treatment obscures the broader political role that these organizations might play in a particular historical moment. Even a seemingly small and insignificant CBO cannot be a neutral and apolitical entity. Alternative terminology that sheds more light on understanding the character and dynamics of civil society are Non-Party Political Formations (Kothari 1984) and Non-Party Left Formations (Kamat 2002). The substance of these types of groups is understood as transformatory politics,

> which do not necessarily require capturing or possessing state power in a traditional instrumentalist sense, but rebuilding spheres of social mobilization in such a way that democratic and progressive constituencies will once again begin to define the terms of political engagement in society.
>
> *(Uyangoda 2001: 189)*

Still, the terms can be misguiding and confusing. A way out of this is to focus on the "acquired meaning" of the term (Nauta 2001). Kloos, who is a pioneer scholar on Sri Lankan NGOs/CSOs, asserts that "an NGO is what is called an NGO in Sri Lanka" (1999). Hence, there is a need to position the CBO, NGO, or CSO in a historical and contextual canvas to understand the larger picture in which they play a particular role.

Orientation of civil society in Sri Lanka

Sri Lanka maintained a robust welfare system from pre-independence. The state was the custodian and deliverer of this welfare system and later it was closely linked to electoral politics through a system of patronage. This meant that successive governments could not afford to abandon their role as the deliverer of welfare and development. The experience of major poverty alleviation schemes since the 1990s—Janasaviya and Samurdhi (a scheme introduced in 1994 under the Peoples' Alliance [PA] government, which was established after a seventeen-year rule by the United National Party)—which changed the mode of delivery of the welfare system, showed the sheer reluctance of respective governments to allow the NGOs to get involved in the poverty-alleviation program funded by the World Bank. On the other hand, Sri Lanka's relatively satisfactory health and education systems required no additional players to run such services as in countries such as Bangladesh and Nepal, where NGOs played a major role. All these conditions and situations left a limited scope for non-state actors to enter the domain of development as deliverers or implementers. Even massive development initiatives such as Mahaweli[1] were the exclusive preserve of the state. Hence, development NGOs in Sri Lanka did not emerge as a major force compared to NGOs in the other South Asian countries mentioned above. This experience runs counter to the common argument that liberalization policies would diminish the welfare role of the state and NGOs would fill the void. The above characteristic of Sri Lankan NGOs suggests that they have very little control and influence over what is considered "development" work. Their scope of influence has been in the area of "rights."

The dominant civil society/NGO identity in Sri Lanka has been more closely connected to the political—in its wider meaning—domain. Social action and voluntary organizations have been at the forefront of social and political reforms since the pre-independence era. The Temperance Movement is a prominent example. These efforts were intensified when NGOs dealing with rights issues proliferated in the 1970s and 1980s. Thus the cutting edge of Sri Lankan NGOs is not so much "development" NGOs but "rights" NGOs. Arguably, the ethnic issue has been the area where Sri Lankan rights-oriented NGOs have made a lasting impact. Their impact has been high on the fronts of lobbying and advocacy, human rights issues, and the promotion of concepts such as pluralism, devolution, federalism, etc. The political orientation of Sri Lankan civil society organizations means that they invariably capture the political realm as part of their environment. This means that Sri Lankan civil society organizations are highly sensitive toward the shifts taking place in the political realm.

The link between Sri Lankan CSOs/NGOs and the Left is a special feature. The pioneer justice-oriented groups had close links with the old Left. The entrance of the New Left activists (JVP and others) to NGOs in the post-1977 period, and trade union activists in the post-1980 period, gave Sri Lankan NGOs a strong political identity. This generation of Left political activists dominated the NGO scene in the 1980s and the early 1990s. In a way, the NGO activism in the 1980s and the early 1990s partially replaced the void created by the decline of the Left and trade unionism. The Leftist parties suffered a massive defeat in the general election of 1977, which was won by the rightist United National Party (UNP) with an overwhelming 5/6 majority in the parliament. Such a working majority in the parliament and a newly created all-powerful executive presidential system gave the ruling party the upper hand to curb all forms of opposition and resistance for the liberal economic policies introduced. The government crushed a general strike in 1980, which marked the milestone of the further decline and weakening of the Left and trade unionism. In this regard, some NGOs have played the role of gap fillers for a moribund Left and trade unions. Hence, the terms Non-Party Political Formations (Kothari 1984) or Non-Party Left Formations (Kamat 2002) encapsulate the nature and character of the above cluster of Sri Lankan NGOs. However, the NGO sector in Sri Lanka should not be understood as an exclusive preserve of the Left. It is a much more diverse arena. For instance, NGOs such as the Civil Rights Movement (CRM), MARGA, International Center for Ethnic Studies (ICES), and Law and Society Trust (LST) had a largely liberal political orientation. There are also many NGOs whose leaders are closely linked to non-Left parties. Some examples are: the former UNP parliamentarian and current provincial council member S. Velayuthan runs an NGO called POWER in Uva Province; the late Buelah Munasinghe, director of Agro-mart Foundation, was a member of the UNP Working Committee; the late Nissanka Wijer-atne, a UNP stalwart and former Minister of Justice, was the patron of the Law & Society Trust; K.M. de Silva, who heads the Kandy branch of ICES, was an advisor to President Jayewardene; and the late Neelan Thiruchelvam, who headed ICES and LST represented the Tamil United Liberation Front (TULF) in parliament from 1994 to 1999 (Fernando 2007). The rights NGOs that became a vociferous force in the 1980s and early 1990s were dominated by Leftists but accommodated the liberals. However, later on, this balance tilted toward a liberal political orientation.

A reversal of this trend in civil society and NGOs was witnessed from the mid-1990s. This trend became established firmly in the post-2002 period. The key staff and leaders who entered NGOs in the mid-1990s and beyond came from professional and academic backgrounds with little or no background in political activism (Fernando 2007). Their political sympathies were mostly with liberal thinking (Uyangoda 2001). Though this new breed of NGO leaders and functionaries have been able to make an impact in high-level advocacy-type interventions, the popular base and mobilization capacity that NGOs had in the 1980s and early 1990s have been drastically eroded. Uyangoda goes further on the issues of these "new kids on the block," stating that: "the politics of the Left has been appropriated—or hijacked—by a new elite of middle-class, urban, Western-educated professionals whose commitment to the goals of anti-systemic politics is non-existent, or even dubious" (Uyangoda 2001: 187). The mass base and engagement at the grass-roots level was part of the environment enacted by the old generation. Another addition in the new environment was the business sector, as the new NGOs seemed to explore possibilities of collaboration with the sector. During the same period, microcredit and small and medium enterprises (SMEs) were embraced by the NGOs. Sarvodaya's microcredit arm SEEDS (now called Deshodaya Finance) expanded the scope of their work and outreach at this time. The Federation of Thrift and Credit Cooperative Societies (FTCCS, better known as "Sanasa," the Sinhala abbreviation), which was the largest network of savings and credit groups (organized under the Cooperative Ordinance), formed a Development Bank in 2001. At present, it is a well-established bank with a network of branches. Both the Sarvodaya-affiliated microfinance operation, as well as Sanasa Development Bank, are self-sustained and generating profits.

Civil society and government relations

For the greater part of its history and particularly from the 1990s, Sri Lankan civil society has experienced confrontational and antagonistic relations with successive governments. This has been the case particularly for those organizations addressing issues of human rights, ethnic conflict, devolution of power, etc. Development NGOs were spared this trend to a certain extent. Civil society character was dominated by NGOs from the 1980s and the latter became the face of civil society. NGOs were largely tolerated by the United National Party (UNP) governments that were in power from 1977 to 1994. NGOs were in fact accommodated as collaborators of the Janasaviya Trust Fund (JTF), which was part of the then World Bank-supported island-wide welfare scheme called Janasaviya. However, a major fallout with the NGOs took place during the last phase of the government of President Premadasa, who also championed the Janasaviya welfare system. The Presidential Commission on NGOs and the Monitoring of Receipts and Disbursements of Non-Governmental Organizations (Regulation No. 1 of 1993) came about as a result. The above regulation defined NGOs as organizations that are dependent upon public or government grants for funds and that are engaged in social welfare, development, empowerment, research, and environmental protection activities. Those NGOs with annual budgets less than Rs.50,000 (approximately US$860, according to the exchange rate at that time) and cooperatives were excluded from the above definition. All other organizations were required to register with the Director of Social Services, submitting information regarding receipts and disbursements, including the sources of receipts and the receipts of funds and goods and services. Heavy penalties for non-compliance were incorporated into the regulation, with fines and prison sentences of up to five years for officers concerned. This regulation, however, lapsed in the following year (Fernando 2003).

The People's Alliance (PA) government coming to power in 1994 marked another phase for NGO–government relations. The constituent parties of the PA were the Sri Lanka Freedom Party (SLFP), the Lanka Sama Samaja Party (LSSP), the Communist Party (CP), and the Sri Lanka Mahajana Party (SLMP). The latter three were Leftist parties with very little clout, while the bigger player was the SLFP, an erstwhile center-left party that embraced a reformist liberal economic policy in 1994. A large number of NGOs advocated a change of government after the seventeen-year rule by the UNP. Many NGOs openly campaigned for the PA. The PA's pledge to introduce a political solution to the ethnic problem attracted the support of NGOs. Upon forming the new government, many NGOs actively supported the government's efforts to restore peace. The peace talks held in 1994 under the PA government included two prominent NGO personalities—Dr. Jayadeva Uyangoda and Charles Abeysekera. Neelan Thiruchelvam, a constitutional expert and the head of the International Center for Ethnic Studies (ICES) and the Law & Society Trust (LST), was closely engaged in drafting the proposals for devolution as part of the PA government's peace efforts. Arguably, it was the PA government that co-opted the largest number of leaders and activists from NGOs to take responsible positions on government bodies, ministries, and various government-sponsored projects and programs. Many NGO staff persons were hired as consultants and staff for the government's peace propaganda programs, such as *Sudu Nelum Viyaparaya* and *Saama Thawalama*. An initiative called the National Integration and Planning Unit (an independent unit formed under the Ministry of Constitutional Affairs and Ethnic Integration with the assistance of Norwegian bilateral aid) made available large amounts of funds for NGOs. Many existing NGOs diverted their attention to peace-related work, while a new breed of peace NGOs proliferated, largely due to the availability of funds. However, the honeymoon of collaboration was short-lived. Relations became strained with the PA government's shift to the "War for Peace" (late 1995), and were finally broken with the infamous Wayamba Election (March 1999). In the run-up to the election in December 2001, the PA government took an antagonistic and confrontationist stance against CSOs/NGOs. State media was used to discredit the work of the NGOs and defame many NGO leaders. They were branded as "rogues," "pro-UNP," and "pro-Liberation Tigers of Tamil Eelam (LTTE)."

Other than those who were engaged in election monitoring and related activities, NGOs in general maintained a low profile in the December 2001 elections. PAFFREL (People's Action for Free and Fair Elections) and the Center for Monitoring Election Violence monitored the elections, while the Institute of Human Rights (IHR) monitored the misuse of public property for the election campaign. Soon after the formation of a government led by the United National Party (UNP), in 2002, it tried to collaborate with the development-oriented NGOs. In January 2002 Charitha Ratwatte, secretary of the Ministry of Finance & Planning and the Treasury, addressed a group of representatives of NGOs and reiterated the above position. Ratwatte invited the NGOs to actively participate in the government's 100-day accelerated development program. Commenting on the role of the national NGO Secretariat, Ratwatte pledged that it would shift its role from a regulator to that of a coordinator. The secretariat would conduct a series of capacity-building programs for NGOs (Fernando 2003). Some NGOs saw this as an opportunity to forge a working relationship with the government so that NGOs could perform their role without being harassed by the government. These NGOs emphasized the need to pressurize the government to recognize the legitimate right of the NGOs to be active in their respective fields. In this connection, some NGOs presented a proposal at the above meeting requesting the government to repeal Section 14.1 of the Voluntary Social Service Organizations (Registration and Supervision) Act of 1980 (VSSO Act). (Fernando 2003: 71). The large amount of funds that was made available under the "peace and development" banner resulted in an "NGO boom." This trend brought in many international agencies working on issues such as good governance, anti-corruption, and democracy. In April 2004, the SLFP-led United People's Freedom Alliance (UPFA) government came into power. In the run-up to the elections, the JVP, which was a constituent party of the UPFA, as well the Jathika Hela Urumaya (JHU), which extended its support to the government, made severe attacks on NGOs for being the "agents" of donors who have vested interests and are biased toward the LTTE. The NGOs, in general, did not take any special interest in the election. The election monitoring organizations came under heavy criticism by the UPFA alleging that they were biased toward the UNP.

Heightened civil society–government relations

Government–NGO relations were severely strained during the period 2005–2014. Anti-NGO sentiment and civil society phobia were promoted by governments, as well as various political forces that supported the governments. Civil society groups, NGOs, and individuals who held a critical view of the government became the target of government-owned media. Ideologically, the role and legitimacy of civil society organizations was contested by the government and the pro-government lobby, especially in the last couple of years before the end of the war in May 2009. Practically, the government restricted these organizations from functioning and carrying out their work and activities by using red tape and allowing the police and the military to threaten, arrest, and conduct surveillance and intelligence operations. However, the government welcomed engagements with civil society when their work was non-controversial, such as in the delivery of hardware-type development interventions.

The discourse on Sri Lankan civil society during the period of 2005–2014 is best reflected through posters pasted on walls and newspaper headlines. One poster, apparently put up by a pro-government group, posed this question when the UNHCR Sessions were being convened in Geneva, Switzerland, in October 2014: "*NGO nadaya mahindata ochchara baya eyi*" (why is the NGO bunch so scared of Mahinda?). Two days before the appearance of this poster, a group of NGOs revealed plans to commemorate the Day of the Disappeared (October 27, 2014) in Seeduwa. In response, colored posters were pasted on walls in Seeduwa and surrounding areas; but obviously not by the organizers of the commemoration. The posters, which included photographs of the organizers of the event, were titled "*Raakshayo—Duka Vikunan Kanno*" (*Demons—Those Who Sell Others' Misery*). The organizers in turn, convened a press conference under the banner: "Why so scared of NGOs—stop hide and seek—come clean."

The attempt to form a coalition of opposition political parties and trade unions to field a common candidate for the presidential elections in January 2015, as a strategy to abolish the Executive Presidency, was dubbed as an "NGO conspiracy" (Fernando 2014). The resignation of a minister and a Provincial Council Minister belonging to the JHU from the government was dubbed as an act funded by NGOs (Fernando 2014). A surprise defection of a group of government ministers took place on October 21, 2014 and one of the defectors was announced as the candidate for the presidential election. (He won the elections and was installed as president in January 2015.) This surprise move, too, was "credited" to the conspiracy of the NGOs, the Tamil diaspora, and the West; and diplomatic missions of Western nations in Colombo were accused of supplying satellite telephones to those who were behind the above "conspiracy" (Daily Mirror 2014).

With state patronage, as well as extensive coverage by state-owned print and electronic media, civil society and NGOs were painted as a dangerous and conspiratorial force supported by the West and the Tamil Diaspora (linked to the LTTE) to destabilize Sri Lanka. Over time, particularly during the last decade of the war between the LTTE and the Sri Lankan Armed Forces, the anti-NGO/civil society rhetoric was well rooted in Sri Lanka. The anti-NGO/civil society lobby was initially represented by only a few individuals, but subsequently gathered the support of other individuals and groups. By the mid-1990s, some political groups and parties took an explicit stance against NGOs/CSOs. This trend culminated in 2005, when a then JVP member, who later became a leader of a breakaway political party (National Freedom Front) and a government minister, pleaded that the public should "spit on NGOs and stop them from walking on streets" (Tamilnet 2005).

Within the same period, Sri Lankan society saw the ascendency of a few new religious-nationalist, mainly Sinhala-Buddhist, groups such as *Ravana Balakaaya*, *Sinhala Ravaya*, and *Bodu Bala Sena* (BBS). With a great deal of importance attached to media publicity, these groups attracted a substantial degree of popular support. The groups received a new lease of life after the end of the war in 2009, due to the relative stability in the country. Though formal ties were absent, the confrontational position on NGOs/CSOs taken by the political parties within the ruling coalition, such as the Jathika Hela Urumaya (JHU) and Jathika Nidahas Peramuna

(National Freedom Front), and their respective constituencies, provided the ideological fodder for these new groups. The new ethno-religio-nationalist groups followed unconventional strategies, such as hate speech, verbal threats, intimidation, and at times physical threats/assaults.

The NGO Secretariat, the government body that played a coordinating and regulatory role, came under the Minister of Defence during this period. Both Sri Lankan NGOs and international NGOs found it difficult to work because of administrative red-tape directives by the NGO Secretariat (Dbsjeyaraj.com 2014). The Ministry of Defence took over the governance and management of a Northern-based NGO called the Community Trust Fund (CTF) on charges of financial mismanagement. An amendment to the VSSO in 1998 gave the Registrar of the NGO Secretariat the power of interim management, if a registered NGO is suspected of fraud or misappropriation. This discretionary power is used only in a few instances. The other instance was when a similar action was taken on the Sri Lanka Red Cross Society (SLRC) in 1998. A civil society study carried out during this period noted thus:

> In July 2014, the Ministry of Defence issued a letter instructing all CSOs to refrain from holding press conferences, workshops, and training for journalists, and disseminating press releases. Prior to the letter, workshops for investigative journalists organized by Transparency International Sri Lanka were called off after being disrupted by organized mobs. While the Ministry of Defence's letter does not have the force of law, it sanctioned previous disruptions and overtly intimidated CSOs. It also prevented a number of CSOs from conducting programs. Around the same time, the Ministry of Finance and Planning issued a public notice to all government officials, CSOs, and the general public to exercise due diligence on the utilization of foreign funds received by CSOs.
>
> *(The Sunday Times 2016)*

Indications were made to introduce new legislation to strictly regulate the work of NGOs (ColomboPage 2014). This situation drastically shrank the space for such civil society organizations and groups. The space for engagement and collaboration between the two parties was very limited.

Civil society's contribution to the "change" in 2015

As the previous section explained, the civil society groups functioned under very difficult circumstances. The space for the kind of civil society that pursued particular political values and virtues shrank drastically, especially since the end of the war in 2009. The anti-NGO environment, particularly in the period of 2005–2014, compelled certain INGOs to withdraw or phase out from Sri Lanka. The strict control and surveillance paralyzed many local NGOs. Sri Lanka achieving the Middle Income Country (MIC) status in 2010 also resulted in a gradual drop in donor support to NGOs. However, one can see an emergence of a new wave of civil society activism, coalescing with a variety of actors, ranging from political parties to trade unions with political agendas that were based on the discontent with the then government and a clamor for a political transformation. Some of these forces are summarized below.

1   *Platform for Freedom* (PFF): This was formed in early 2009 in the immediate aftermath of the killing of Lasantha Wickramatunga, a well-known editor of an English weekly, which often criticized the then government. PFF is an interesting political experiment where a section of civil society actors have made an alliance with the United National Party, Tamil

National Alliance, other opposition parties, and trade unions. The collaboration with the political parties, particularly with the main opposition party, the UNP, took place openly. The PFF played an explicit political role with political parties in the opposition and established an agenda for what was commonly called a "regime change." The PFF did not follow a traditional NGO "work-shopping strategy." They did not mince their words—they boldly and fearlessly voiced their concerns on corruption, impunity, militarization, and rule of law and vehemently advocated a regime change.

2   *Saadhaarana Samaajayak Sandahaa Vyaapaaraya* (The Movement for a Just Society): The Movement for a Just Society mooted the idea of a Common Presidential Candidate and initially rallied around Rev. Maduluwave Sobitha, a prominent Buddhist clergyman. This movement was not a typical NGO-led coalition. It included political parties and broad civil society groups such as trade unions, academics, and political activists. This group's work gathered momentum and created not only a ground swell for a change but also generated some fresh ideas for a broader political agenda. The charismatic leader of this group, Rev. Sobitha, later signed an Memorandum of Understanding, representing a group of civil society groups, with the presidential candidate in December 2014.

3   *Pivithuru Hetak* (Just and Fair Society for a Better Tomorrow): *Pivithuru Hetak* was another novel experiment by a political party—the JHU, led by Rev. Athuraliye Rathana—to mobilize civil society perhaps *a la* Anna Hazare and Arvind Kejriwal in India. Initially, there was some enthusiasm from civil society groups toward this initiative. But it didn't gather momentum, perhaps due to the fact that Rev. Rathana found himself more at home with a political party than in civil society.

4   *Purawesi Balaya* (Citizens' Power): *Purawesi Balaya* is a coalition initiated by what can be called Left-leaning or progressive artistes, authors, academics, and professionals with little or no NGO elements in it. This group successfully organized a rally on December 2, 2015 in Colombo, which was attended by a large crowd. Other groups called the Artists for Democracy and *Aluth Paraoura* (New Generation) emerged as offshoots of *Purawesi Balaya*. This group showed a great deal of potential as a broad-based citizens' movement.

5   Professional Organizations/Trade Unions: The Bar Association of Sri Lanka (BASL), Free Media Movement (FMM), and the Federation of University Teachers' Associations (FUTA) have been active in voicing their concerns on the general crisis of the country, as well as particular concerns on their respective sectors—legal, media, and education. The FMM pledged their support to the Common Presidential candidate. Subsequently, the FMM submitted their proposals to the Common Candidate to voice their concern on the Right to Information, Impunity, Independence of Media and Censorships (Free Media Sri Lanka 2014).

These different strands of broader civil society formations finally coalesced with the political parties that worked toward a regime change in general and in the run-up to the presidential election that was held in January 2015. The presidential contender, who represented the opposition political parties, signed a Memorandum of Understanding (MoU) with a coalition of thirty-six organizations, including political parties, civil society groups, and trade unions, that pledged their conditional support to the candidate (Lanka Business Online 2014). The overarching slogan of the political campaign of the opposition candidate was "*yahapalanaya*" ("good governance" in Sinhala), which was hitherto raised by civil society. Similarly, the "*yahapalanaya*" coalition signed an MoU with forty-nine civil society organizations in the run-up to the general elections (Ceylon Today 2015). The broad coalition of "*yahapalanaya*" won both the presidential election (January 2015) and the general election (August 2015). The prime minister himself assured freedom for NGOs soon after assuming duties (The Sunday Leader 2015). Some civil society activists have been mobilized by the government for various areas of work, such as the Task Force on Reconciliation. The Secretary of the Task Force in Reconciliation, under the Ministry of Foreign Affairs, is Dr. Pakiasothy Saravanamuttu, the Executive Director of the Center for Policy Alternatives (CPA), a Colombo-based think-tank that was a vociferous critic of the governments during 2005–2015. Dr. Saravanamuttu was a co-convener of the Platform for Freedom, referred to earlier. The NGO Secretariat, which was under the Ministry of Defence, was shifted to the Ministry of National Dialogue, Co-Existence and Languages by the new government that came to power in 2015. The minister in charge, Hon. Mano Ganesan, MP, was a prolific speaker of the Platform for Freedom (PFF), a civil society–opposition political party alliance founded in 2009. Some of the advisors appointed to the NGO Secretariat include two co-conveners of the PFF. Two prominent conveners of the PFF, Sudarshana Gunawardena and Dr. Nimalka Fernando, were appointed as advisors to the NGO Secretariat. It is still premature to predict the direction of government–civil society relations, as the government is still finding its way to establish itself as a coalition government with a constellation that is new to Sri Lanka, in the sense that the two main political parties have come together to form a government for the first time in history. However, the anti-NGO/civil society sentiment is kept alive by a group of MPs who are loyal to the defeated president who is also a member of parliament. Such sentiments are also subscribed to by the ethno-religio-nationalist groups that thrived during the period of 2005–2014.

Conclusion

The foregoing sections on the history of civil society–government relations show an almost identical and repetitive pattern of their relational dynamics. This is particularly the case since 1994. Civil society has played an active role in voting out two different authoritative and repressive governments, in 1994 and 2015, which had remained in power for long periods of seventeen years and ten years, respectively. Civil society organizations and groups have worked in tandem with different opposition parties that have been languishing out of power for long periods. Upon the formation of the new governments, civil society members have been mobilized and co-opted by the government for various areas of work that require the expertise civil society members possess. Such collaborations can be observed in the immediate aftermath of 1994 and 2015. However, the collaboration in 1994 was short-lived. It is premature at the time of writing (September 2016) to comment on the direction and sustainability of collaborations between the Good Governance Government and civil society following the political changes in 2015.

While a great deal of parallels can be observed in the patterns of relational dynamics between civil society organizations and the government, a phenomenal change in the character of the civil society itself can also be observed. Such changes compel the scholarship on civil society to reconsider the conceptual and definitional frameworks of understanding civil society. How can one understand the Sri Lankan civil society? Are we talking about NGO-type organizations? Or are we talking about the informal, non-institutionalized, spontaneous, ad hoc citizen groups or civic groups that are relatively independent? The foregoing sections suggest that civil society is a vague and often loosely understood concept. The main point of departure toward reaching a reasonable and realistic understanding is to avoid the slip of treating civil society as a homogenous entity. On the contrary, it is a domain where there is a plethora of strands of ideologies, strategies, and activisms at play. At times, these strands contradict each other. As such, civil society is not a harmonious site; often it is a contradictory and conflict-ridden site. Therefore, in order to have a holistic idea, one should see many strands of civil societies—underlining their plurality and diversity—within the broader domain of what lies outside the market and state. But then, the boundaries are fluid and blurred; they overlap. The Sri Lankan civil society canvas, particularly since 2005, displayed this messy, blurry, and conflictual character.

On one hand, the new ethno-religio-nationalist groups defamed, threatened, and challenged the so-called civil society groups. On the other hand, these new groups carved out a niche for themselves in civil society itself. Some would not see these groups as part of "civil" society due to their apparent "uncivil" behavior. However, leaving aside the normative dimension of the term "civil society," these groups indeed function in the realm of society that is beyond the state, market, and family, commonly defined as civil society. Such a phenomenon infused an element of messiness to the hitherto neatly and normatively defined civil society. The ascendancy of these new groups, therefore, compels us to recognize the diverse and at times contradictory and even conflict-ridden nature of civil society. One therefore needs to move away from treating civil society as a homogenous and harmonious entity. In other words, what is manifested today in Sri Lanka is the presence of multiple and contradictory forms of civil societies, rather than a single, monolithic, and homogenous civil society.

The various forms of civil society alliances that emerged when civil society groups existed under trying circumstances (in 2005–2014) have added new dimensions as well as some challenges to understanding civil society as a neat scheme. Some such formations, such as the Platform for Freedom, were alliances between civil society groups, oppositional political parties, and trade unions. An initiative such as *Pivithuru Hetak* was led by a political party, JHU, which strived to form a "civil society wing" of a political party. Other initiatives such as *Purawesi Balaya* and *Saadhaarana Samaajayak Sandahaa Vyaapaaraya* showed the form of a "mass-movement" character and mobilized sections of society that were not hitherto engaged actively in civic action aimed toward the change of governments. These two movements kept a distance, to a great extent, from the NGO-type civil society groups, thus giving it a mass character. However, both these movements maintained a constant dialogue with the oppositional political parties and included their demands as conditions to support the political campaigns to oust the president/ government that was in power. Overall, these different formations of civil society compel us to revisit the narrow understanding of civil society that lies outside the state and market. The emergence of such diverse formations of civil society persuasions toward explicit political changes suggests a distinguishing character of the Sri Lankan civil society, which is the primacy of the political.

Note

1 The Mahaweli Development Program (MDP) is considered the most ambitious development initiative undertaken in Sri Lanka in the recent past. Five major dams constructed on the largest river, "Mahaweli," supplied irrigation water to an area of 144,000 ha, deemed unproductive due to lack of water. Nearly 125,000 families were settled in the downstream areas during the early and mid-1980s— many of them poor, landless peasants who left their homelands and journeyed to the "promised land" with the dream of becoming proud owners of a plot of irrigated paddy land. Each settler family was entitled to 1 ha of irrigated lowland and 0.2 ha of rain-fed highland for a homestead; see Wettasinha (2001).

Suggested readings

Fernando, Udan. 2003. *NGOs in Sri Lanka: Past and Present Trends.* Kohuwala: Wasala Publishers.
Fernando, Udan. 2007. *Uneasy Encounters, Relationship between Dutch Donors and Sri Lankan NGOs.* PhD thesis, Amsterdam: AMIDST.

Fernando, Udan. 2016. New MIC in the Block: Middle Income Country Status and Civil Society in Sri Lanka. In *Development Cooperation, Policy Advice and Middle Income Countries.* UN Reflection Series 2016. Berlin: United Nations System Staff College and Hertie Schools of Governance.

Uyangoda, Jayadeva. 2001. From Class and Trade Unions to NGOs: Sri Lanka's Left. In *Sri Lanka: Global Challenges and National Crisis, Proceedings of the Hector Abhayawardhana Felicitation Symposium.* Rajan Philips, Kumar David, and Seelan Kadirgamar, eds. Pp. 187–216. Colombo: Ecumenical Institute and Social Scientists Association.

Wickramasinghe, Nira. 2001. *Civil Society in Sri Lanka: New Circles of Power.* London: Sage.

References

Bastian, Sunil. 2003. Foreign Aid, Globalisation and Conflict in Sri Lanka. In *Building Local Capacities for Future Peace: Rethinking Conflict and Development in Sri Lanka.* 1st Edn. Markus Mayer, Darini Rajasinghe-Senanayake, and Yuvi Thangarajah, eds. Pp. 132–151. New Delhi: Macmillan.

Ceylon Today. 2015. MOU With Ranil 49 Civil Society Orgs to Sign. *Ceylon Today.* Electronic document, www.ceylontoday.lk/51-98156-news-detail-mou-with-ranil-49-civil-society-orgs-to-sign.html, accessed May 16, 2016.

ColomboPage. 2014. All NGOs in Sri Lanka are Required to Work Within Their Annual Action Plan—External Affairs Ministry. *ColomboPage*, July 11. Electronic document, www.colombopage.com/archive_14B/Jul11_1405061280CH.php, accessed May 16, 2016.

Daily Mirror. 2014. Common Candidate is a Foreign Conspiracy. *Daily Mirror*, November 22. Electronic document, www.dailymirror.lk/57147/common-candidate-is-a-foreign-conspiracy-slfp, accessed May 16, 2016.

Dbsjeyaraj.com. 2014. Non-Governmental Organizations in Sri Lanka Warned by Defence Ministry not to Hold Press Conferences, Workshops, Journalist Training Courses and Issue Press Releases. *Dbsjeyaraj. com*, July 8. Electronic document, dbsjeyaraj.com/dbsj/archives/31637, accessed May 16, 2016.

Fernando, Udan. 2003. *NGOs in Sri Lanka: Past and Present Trends.* Kohuwala: Wasala Publishers.

Fernando, Udan. 2007. *Uneasy Encounters: Relationship between Dutch Donors and Sri Lankan NGOs.* PhD thesis, Amsterdam: AMIDST.

Fernando, Udan. 2014. The Role of Civil Society in Sri Lanka. Report of the Study Commissioned by Oxfam-Australia, Colombo, December 2014.

Free Media Sri Lanka. 2014. Media Reform Proposals to Common Presidential Candidate. *Free Media Sri Lanka*, December 17. Electronic document, https://freemediasrilanka.wordpress.com/2014/12/17/media-reform-proposals-to-common-presidential-candidate/, accessed May 16, 2016.

Gombrich, Richard, and Gananath Obeysekere. 1988. *Buddhism Transformed: Religious Change in Sri Lanka.* Princeton, NJ: Princeton University Press.

Kamat, Sangita. 2002. *Development Hegemony: NGOs and the State in India.* New Delhi: Oxford University Press.

Kloos, Peter. 1999. *The Sri Lankan Government and the NGOs. An Ambivalent Relationship.* Anthropologische Bijdragen, 8 VU Amsterdam: Free University.

Kothari, Rajani. 1984. The Non Party Political Processes. *Economic and Political Weekly* 19(5): 216–224.

Lanka Business Online. 2014. Opposition Presidential candidate Maithripala Sirisena Signs MoU. *Lanka Business Online.* Electronic document, http://ftp.lankabusinessonline.com/news/opposition-presidential-candidate-maithripala-sirisena-signs-mou/1574168170, accessed May 16, 2016.

Nauta, Wiebe. 2001. *The Implications of Freedom: The Changing Role of Land Sector NGOs in a Transforming South Africa.* PhD thesis, Amsterdam Free University.

Orjuela, Camilla. 2005. *Civil Society in Civil War: Peace Work and Identity Politics in Sri Lanka.* PhD thesis, Goteburg University.

Tamilnet. 2005. JVP Slams NGOs, Western Countries For Meddling. *Tamilnet*, April 6. Electronic document, www.tamilnet.com/art.html?catid=79&artid=14625cr, accessed May 16, 2016.

The Sunday Leader. 2015. No Restrictions on NGOs. *The Sunday Leader*, February 1. Electronic document, www.thesundayleader.lk/2015/02/01/no-restrictions-on-ngos/, accessed May 16, 2016.

The Sunday Times. 2016. Few NGOs Implement Good Governance Practice Verite Research Says. *The Sunday Times*, February 28. Electronic document, www.sundaytimes.lk/160228/business-times/few-ngos-implement-good-governance-practices-verite-research-says-184414.html, accessed May 16, 2016.

Uyangoda, Jayadeva. 2001. From Class and Trade Unions to NGOs: Sri Lanka's Left. In *Sri Lanka: Global Challenges and National Crisis, Proceedings of the Hector Abhayawardhana Felicitation Symposium.* Rajan

Philips, Kumar David, and Seelan Kadirgamar, eds. Pp. 187–216. Colombo: Ecumenical Institute and Social Scientists Association.

Wettasinha, Chesa. 2001. Scaling Up Participatory Development in Agricultural Settlements. *Agricultures Network*. Electronic document, www.agriculturesnetwork.org/magazines/global/lessons-in-scaling-up/scaling-up-participatory-development-in, accessed June 3, 2016.

Wickramasinghe, Nira. 2001. *Civil Society in Sri Lanka: New Circles of Power*. London: Sage.

PART II

Thematic review

22

DEMOCRATIZATION

Apichai W. Shipper[1]

Civil society and democratization in Asia

As military-led authoritarian governments in Asia and Soviet-style communist regimes in Eastern and Central Europe started declining during the late 1980s and early 1990s, the impact of civil society on democratization began to attract increased scholarly interest. Scholars searched for intellectual tools to understand this phenomenon and found them in modernization theory, which provided a basic foundation to interpret the linkages between civil society and democratization. That is, economic growth fosters the emergence of the *bourgeoisie* (middle and business classes), which inevitably leads to the development of a vibrant civil society. This development often results in an increase in discontentment amongst these classes, unavoidable conflict with authoritarian states, and an eventual transition to democracy (Moore 1966). Therefore, numerous scholars, especially labor scholars and constructivist international relations theorists, have tried to interpret democratization through the lens of civil society. They view civil society as a force of counter-elites that often seeks to reduce the political weight of the state. In their theoretical framework, they assume a zero-sum relationship between the state and society: A strong state entails a weak society (as observed in authoritarian regimes), and a weak state implies a strong society (as evident in many democracies).

As Table 22.1 indicates, countries in Asia have not provided support for the modernization theory. After almost two decades of double-digit economic growth, China remains an authoritarian communist state. While Singapore and Brunei can boast the highest per capita income in the region, neither can claim to have produced a strong civil society and/or full democracy. In fact, Brunei is best characterized as an absolute monarchy. Moreover, Table 22.1 also shows that a strong civil society can coexist with authoritarian states such as China and Vietnam. From this contrary evidence, many democratic theorists and comparative political scientists have argued that the presence of a vibrant civil society does not necessarily enhance democratization and/or that a strong state and a strong society may coexist in a given country.

Understanding democracy through the lens of civil society has been a well-established research tool since Robert Putnam's 1993 classic, *Making Democracy Work: Civic Traditions in Modern Italy*. In this seminal work, Putnam specifically chooses to examine how effectively local governments deliver services to their citizens, and he developed a measurement of trust based on social capital to evaluate good governance. For Putnam, social capital and networks are

Table 22.1 Indexes of demography, income, democracy, and civil society in Asia

	Total population (CIA world factbook 2016)/ foreigners in country	GDP/capita (IMF, 2015) Amount (US$)	Rank	Political system (CIA world factbook 2016)	Democracy index category (EIU 2016)	Democracy index score (EIU 2016)	Civil society index (Civicus 2016)
Northeast Asia							
China	1,373,541,278 1,020,145	14,340	84	Communist State	Authoritarian	3.14	5.5
Japan	126,702,133 2,230,000	38,142	28	Parliamentary Constitutional Monarchy	Flawed Democracy	7.96	
Mongolia	3,031,330 282,398	12,178	91	Semi-Presidential Republic	Flawed Democracy	6.62	5.4
North Korea	25,115,311 N/A	N/A	N/A	Communist State	Authoritarian	1.08	
South Korea	50,924,172 2,034,878	36,612	29	Presidential Republic	Flawed Democracy	7.97	7.6
Taiwan	23,464,787 562,233	46,833	18	Semi-Presidential Republic	Flawed Democracy	7.83	8

Mainland Southeast Asia

Burma (Myanmar)	56,890,418	5,480	126	Parliamentary Republic	Hybrid Regime	4.14	
Cambodia	15,957,223 80,000	3,498	140	Parliamentary Constitutional Monarchy	Hybrid Regime	4.27	
Laos	7,019,073 49,134 53,589	5,351	127	Communist State	Authoritarian	2.21	
Thailand	68,200,824 3,514,831	16,130	74	Constitutional Monarchy (Military-Run)	Hybrid Regime	5.09	
Vietnam	95,261,021 75,000	6,037	125	Communist State	Authoritarian	3.53	5.9

Maritime Southeast Asia

Brunei	436,620 87,867	79,508	4	Absolute Monarchy			
Indonesia	258,356,051 912,947	11,149	99	Presidential Republic	Flawed Democracy	7.03	6.5
Malaysia	30,949,962 3,265,100	26,211	47	Federal Constitutional Monarchy	Flawed Democracy	6.43	
Philippines	102,624,209 177,365	7,282	117	Presidential Republic	Flawed Democracy	6.84	
Singapore	5,781,728 541,002	85,382	3	Parliamentary Republic	Flawed Democracy	6.14	
Timor Leste (East Timor)	1,261,072 10,983	4,715	134	Semi-Presidential Republic	Flawed Democracy	7.24	

Key (Bad → Good)			185 → 1			1 → 10	1 → 10

Source: CIA (2016); CIVICUS (2016); EIU (2016); IMF (2015).

prerequisites to improving trust and, ultimately, civil society organizations (CSOs). Lily Tsai (2007) further develops the idea of social capital in non-democratic societies such as China. She studies why some villages in China have paved roads, good schools, and running water, while others do not. She finds that it has nothing to do with elections (liberal democracy), sanctions from above, or wealth, but it has to do mostly with social capital developed through solidarity groups, including temples, churches, and lineages. These institutions enmesh local officials in norms, expectations, and moral obligations that motivate them to provide villagers with public goods and services. In essence, Tsai sees no correlation between civil society and democracy.

How, then, do we understand the role of civil society in democratization or democracy, in general? This chapter discusses the relationship between civil society and democratization in the context of Asia. Civil society consists of organized groups whose members are bonded together for a common purpose or purposes, including democratization and/or democratic deepening. Student groups and organized labor constitute important civil society actors for democratic transitions (Lipset 1968; Valenzuela 1989). Civil society generally exists outside of the state, but it can also be politically organized. I interpret political democracy in classic procedural terms to include free and fair elections to government offices, accountability through the rule of law, and freedoms of association and expressions. I define democratization as the process of movement from authoritarianism toward these conditions.

Democratic deepening is understood as the further fulfillment of democratic ideals such as inclusive diversity, transparency of governance, and political and economic decentralization. In general, CSOs can deepen democracy by demanding that the state protect human rights, encourage political participation, promote civic engagement, enhance multicultural understanding, lessen social, economic, and gender differences, broaden citizenship rules, and extend social and welfare services to its members. Students of corporatism have cautioned that "associations do not just make demands on the public authorities, they also perform a quasi-public role of regulating their members on behalf of the state" (Williamson 1989: 3). Rather than becoming a pluralist state like the United States, societies with certain associational characteristics and specific institutional structure can become corporatist states, where CSOs:

> are organized into a limited number of singular, compulsory, non-competitive, hierarchically ordered or licensed (if not created) by the state and granted a deliberative representational monopoly within their respective categories in exchange for observing certain controls on their selection of leaders and articulation of demands and supports.
>
> *(Schmitter 1974: 93–94)*

This corporatist framework, which links the associationally organized interests of civil society with the decisional structures of the state, can help us conceptualize democratic deepening in Asian societies. In contrast, democratic retrenchment refers to the process of moving toward greater state control and/or less inclusivity. Moreover, growth of hate groups and accompanying violence can put a society on a dangerous path toward democratic retrenchment.

This chapter examines the role of civil society in democratic transition by first focusing on student groups and organized labor in challenging authoritarian regimes and subsequently reviewing how local CSOs utilize transnational advocacy networks (TANs) to push for democratic transition overseas. It also discusses the contribution of CSOs in democratic deepening/consolidation in advanced industrialized economies in Asia. It then explores the negative role of certain CSOs in reinforcing the status quo, as well as in contributing to democratic retrenchment. The chapter ends with general concluding remarks on civil society and democratization.

Civil society and democratic transitions

Student and labor activism

In the authoritarian states in Asia, students constitute an effective oppositional force, as their moral positions are often endorsed and magnified by other frustrated, but more constrained and less privileged, segments of the society. Because higher education in Asia is expected to provide a form of social mobility, particularly in a country's bureaucracy, it is seen that university graduates, who face limited job opportunities under an authoritarian regime, have turned to street protests. When labor unions join such protests by making demands to authoritarian regimes for democratic transitions, they further bring to the democratic movement their organizational and mass mobilization skills and "can contribute to a climate of ungovernability and deligitimation that leads directly to a general destabilization of authoritarian regimes" (Neureiter 2013: 1066). Such a destabilizing political environment created by student movements and uprisings effectively questions the legitimacy of authoritarian regimes and often calls for new leadership.

Indeed, student groups and/or labor unions played key roles in bringing about democratic transitions in Thailand (1973), the Philippines (1986), South Korea (1987), Mongolia (1990), and Indonesia (1998). During the 1960s and early 1970s, young Thais from diverse backgrounds entered universities, where norms advocating progress and individual achievement were espoused. They then grew frustrated by their inability either to secure prized civil service positions or to advance political democratization (Darling 1974). They started out as discussion groups with high-quality critical analyses of the society and government and initiated summer work camps in rural areas, which gave them experience with rural life (Morell and Chai-Anan 1981). They also launched a successful Anti-Japanese Goods Campaign, gaining popularity and legitimization as an important extra-bureaucratic force as a result. In October 1973, they campaigned directly against the military regime, which brought hundreds of thousands of Thais onto Bangkok streets. This student-led movement, which was joined by organized labor and farmers' organizations, resulted in the dissolution of the Thanom-Praphat military government and led to a brief period (1973–1976) that was characterized as Thailand's first democratic experimentation.[2] During this period, labor pressed successfully for the enactment of new legislation that provided for union recognition and collective bargaining rights. The newly elected civilian government established a minimum wage and required employers to provide a number of new benefits, including workers' compensation.

In the Philippines, student groups, organized labor, and organizations representing farmers, women, and ethnic minorities played important roles in the resistance against the Marcos dictatorship. Following his declaration of martial law in 1972, Ferdinand Marcos outlawed strikes and forcefully repressed union militancy in export processing zones as part of his efforts to attract foreign investors and institute "crony capitalism" (Kang 2002). In 1973, Marcos called for a parliamentary form of government and issued a new constitution that allowed him to make and execute all laws until he convened the assembly. On convening the assembly, an authoritarian party, the Kilusang Bagong Lipunan (or the New Society Movement), was established with the mission of keeping him in power indefinitely. When Marcos tried to steal electoral victory from Corazon Aquino in 1986, civil society groups joined forces with the Catholic Church and Aquino's LABAN Party in the famous "People's Power" Revolution, which ended the Marcos dictatorship. Once Aquino entered office, civil society "organizers and activists developed demands for deep structural change" (Boudreau 2013: 61), including the passage of the Freedom Constitution of 1987. The constitution was the most democratic one in all of Southeast Asia at the time, since it imposed the subordination of the military under civilian rule and protected the citizens' civil liberties and rights of participation in choosing government representatives. CSOs also successfully demanded that in the first three terms of the Congress, laborers, the peasantry, the urban poor, women, youth, and other underrepresented groups must comprise half of the representatives. In summary, the People's Power Movement triggered a series of institutional reforms that transformed the Philippines' political system.

Likewise in South Korea, student groups and labor unions played significant roles in democratic transitions. Between the early 1950s and late 1980s, Korean military regimes treated all forms of political dissidence as pro-communist and dissidents were harshly prosecuted under the National Security Law. Military leaders imposed strict labor laws on industrial laborers, who worked under deplorable conditions, as the country underwent rapid industrialization. However, President Chun Doo-hwan, who came to power after a military coup in 1979 and was blamed for his use of elite paratroopers from the Special Forces to contain demonstrators during the 1980 Gwangju Uprising that resulted in at least 600 deaths, decided to increase the number of students in order to improve his legitimacy.[3] He also granted greater freedom to students, allowing them to grow long hair and drink alcohol. Moreover, the Chun Doo-hwan administration left churches relatively free from government scrutiny during this period. These churches, including the Myongdong Catholic Cathedral in downtown Seoul, where students established small reading groups and educational activities, became the gathering grounds for democratic movements. The turning point for Korea's democratic movements occurred in June 1987, when news broke about of the death of a student demonstrator from torture while in police custody and the sexual assault of a female student labor activist by a police interrogator. Student groups led massive street protests, which were joined by white-collar workers and other citizens, who were becoming increasingly distrustful of the Chun Doo-hwan administration (Kim 2000). This massive mobilization of anti-government protests involving more than 1 million people forced the government to revise the constitution and implement a direct presidential election. Soon after announcing their demands for greater democratization, trade unions throughout the country launched strikes, demanding better pay and working conditions. After two months of labor strikes, street protests, and violent clashes, companies conceded to the workers' demands. The "Great Workers' Struggle" paved the way for an independent and more democratic trade union movement.

Student and labor activism was also central to the democratic transition of a communist government. In 1990, Mongolia became the first Asian country to successfully transition itself from communist rule to democracy. A small group of young, like-minded people, led by Mongolia National University lecturer Sanjaasürengiin Zorig (and journalist Tsakhiagiin Elbegdorj), secretly met at Zorig's apartment to discuss various topics, including democracy, free market economic policy, and other prohibited subjects at the time (Rossabi 2005). These youths, many of whom were recent returnees from the USSR or Eastern Europe, where they had been influenced intellectually by Gorbachev's ideas of *glasnost* and *perestroika*, began to draft a plan to organize a democratic movement. On December 10, 1989, the first open, pro-democracy demonstration, which consisted of approximately 200 activists, was held in front of the Youth Cultural Center in Ulaanbataar, where Elbegdorj announced the creation of the Mongolian Democratic Union (MDU), the country's first popular mass movement organization. The MDU founders publicly petitioned the government to implement perestroika, including demands for a free market economy and free elections. In January 1990, the group began weekend protests in Sükhbaatar Square in the center of Ulaanbaatar. As the group's demands resonated with many other Mongolians, more than 100,000 people participated in these protests. Even teachers and workers, who typically aligned themselves with socialist ideals, joined in these strikes. In March 1990, the politburo resigned and the one-party rule ended in Mongolia. Thereafter, the 1992 constitution guaranteed democracy and a free market economy.

In Indonesia, student activism also contributed to the fall of Gen. Soeharto's three decades of authoritarian rule. When the International Monetary Fund (IMF) rescued Indonesia during the Asian Financial Crisis, it demanded the establishment of government measures that cut deeply into Soeharto's patronage networks (Haggard 2000). During the 1998 general election, Soeharto talked nationalistically against the IMF, which responded by withholding further disbursement of funds. Meanwhile, opposition groups, including the Indonesian Democratic Party (led by Megawati Sukarnoputri) and the modernist Islamic Muhammadiyah organization (led by Amien Rais), openly criticized Soeharto for his management of the economic crisis, as well as his authoritarianism, corruption, and lack of attention to social justice. However, students led the *Reformasi* Movement, demanding that Soeharto step down. This democratic movement turned violent in May 1998 following the killing of four students outside Trisakti University. Between March 13 and 15, 1998, riots and social violence erupted in Jakarta, resulting in the death of approximately 1,200 people, mostly ethnic Chinese who radical Islamic groups and individuals blamed for the financial crisis. After the Speaker of the Parliament called for Soeharto to step down or face impeachment, Soeharto resigned on May 21, 1998 and handed the government over to his protégé B. J. Habibie. Habibie then launched sweeping reforms, including, most fundamentally, the freedom of association and expression. These reforms guaranteed press freedom and removed the restrictions placed on the formation of political parties, unions, and other associations. The government also released political detainees and prisoners and set a timetable for elections. His economic reforms were equally comprehensive, including promoting transparency, strengthening the independence of bank authorities, and improving economic redistribution amongst ethnic minorities. In particular, he worked to restore the confidence of the Chinese business community. In summary, Habibie's reforms ultimately led to Indonesia's democratization.

Transnational advocacy networks

When channels between democratic groups and their governments are blocked, students and/ or business people living abroad in more democratic societies form CSOs and establish networks of transnational activists. In some cases, local CSOs establish TANs with CSOs in other more developed states. Working through TANs, transnational activists lobby their host government (as well as intergovernmental organizations) to pressure their authoritarian home government to undergo democratization (or simply protect human rights). Margaret Keck and Kathryn Sikkink (1998) metaphorically called this transnational process of democratic transformation through TANs the "boomerang effect."

The democratization processes that took place in Taiwan in 1996 and Burma (Myanmar) in 2016 illustrate the important role that TANs have played in democratic transitions. Long before the founding of the Democratic Progressive Party (DPP) in 1986 to compete against the ruling Kuomintang (KMT) and the lifting of martial law in 1987, civil society had been making invaluable contributions to Taiwan's democratic transition (Fan 2004). CSOs collectively mobilized political resistance and social protests, advanced counter-narratives and ideologies in newspapers and magazines, and secured international support from organizations like the Amnesty International and individuals in Western governments. For example, overseas Taiwan students (and business people) in the United States founded the Formosan Association for Public Affairs (FAPA). FAPA lobbied the US Congress through the Congressional Taiwan Caucus to pressure the KMT regime into releasing political prisoners and respecting human rights. Yun Fan affirms,

"The international mobilization of overseas Taiwan associations has encouraged the opposition and indirectly promoted the growth of political resistance, thus furthering Taiwan's transition to democracy" (Fan 2004: 176).

Meanwhile, student groups in Taiwan provided new ideas and helped guide the transition. In March 1990, students from the National Taiwan University organized a sit-in at the Memorial Square (known today as Liberty Square) in Taipei, which grew to include 22,000 participants. Demonstrators of the so-called "Wild Lily Student Movement" pushed for direct elections of the president and vice-president of Taiwan, as well as new popular elections of all representatives in the National Assembly to replace those elected in Mainland China prior to the mass migration to Taiwan following the end of the Chinese Civil War in 1949. Although members of the National Assembly elected Lee Ten-hui to become president without competing candidates in 1990, President Lee invited fifty students to meet with him on his first day and expressed support for implementing immediate democratic reforms. Six years later, Lee became Taiwan's first popularly elected leader. Thereafter, regular elections were firmly institutionalized as a political process by which the KMT and DPP competed peacefully for control of the Taiwan authorities. As authoritarian rule eased, an array of CSOs emerged, encompassing a wide range of issues including consumer protection, pollution, nuclear power, protection of the disadvantaged, workers' rights, women's rights, and minority rights, amongst others (So and Hua 1992).

The democratic transition in Myanmar similarly exemplifies the boomerang pattern. In March 1988, students in Myanmar led nationwide protests, which resulted in the resignation of Gen. Ne Win and eventually a democratic transition two decades later. Min Ko Naing (alias for Paw Oo Tun), who was the head of the All Burma Federation of Student Unions (ABFSU) (a successor of the historically famous Rangoon University Students' Union, which the independence movement leaders Aung San and U Nu helped found in the 1930s), initially organized a student rally on a Yangon university campus. During a march to the Yangon Institute of Technology, riot police attacked these students. Several died, and many others were arrested. On August 8, 1988 (or 8–8–88), Min Ko Naing called for a general strike, which drew hundreds of thousands of people to the streets of Yangon demanding democratic change. The protests lasted until September 18, when soldiers violently cracked down the participants and opened fire on the crowds, killing at least 3,000 people. Gen. Saw Muang, who took control of the government and tried to appease the protestors, made a surprising announcement that the military would hold multi-party elections. In May 1990, although national elections took place, the junta refused to hand over control of the government to the victorious National League for Democracy (NLD), claiming that the general election was invalid without a constitution.

Protestors returned to the streets, and the military launched an aggressive campaign against the dissidents. The junta restricted university life and halted new admissions of undergraduates into universities in Yangon and Mandalay. The ABFSU-Foreign Affairs Committee (ABFSU-FAC) then began to intensify its work outside Myanmar. It provided to the outside world reliable information on the violations of rights, including attempts by the junta to intimidate and silence those involved in the pro-democracy movement. Many student groups and labor unions, which could not operate freely inside the country, joined this international effort. These groups included the All Burma Students' Democratic Front (a militant student group based along the Thai-Burmese borders) and the Federation Trade Union of Burma—Japan (a labor group with institutional support from Japan's largest labor union Rengo). These transnational advocacy groups formed alliances with transnational activists in Japan and Western countries, who then lobbied their governments to impose economic sanctions/pressure on Myanmar. The military junta finally completed the drafting of the constitution and introduced a referendum in 2008. Without being asked to offer input to the draft, the NLD initially decided to boycott the general election in 2010. After realizing the disadvantages of not being a part of Myanmar's political reforms and institutional building process, the NLD later decided to participate in the 2012 by-elections and the 2015 general election, in which it won an absolute majority, with a few members of the 8–8–88 Movement being elected to the parliament. In 2016, Myanmar witnessed a peaceful transfer of power, with the NLD forming a new cabinet. CSOs with links to foreign entities continue to promote Myanmar's democratization process, as exemplified by their recent efforts to influence policy decisions to halt the construction of the Myitsone Dam as well as other dams.

Civil society and democratic deepening

In addition to promoting democratic transitions in authoritarian states, CSOs continue to deepen democracy in newly formed democratic societies by pressuring the governments for additional political reforms. These reforms include creating new democratic institutions (e.g., competitive political parties and democratic labor unions), improving democratic processes (e.g., political decentralization, personal freedoms, and deliberative schemes), increasing economic/social equality (e.g., inclusive diversity in terms of gender, race, and ethnicity), and promoting social justice (e.g., problems solved and needs met). CSOs work to ensure that these reforms occur and can be sustained in their newly formed democratic societies.

After Korea's democratic transition in 1987, the civilian governments maintained a relatively amicable relationship with civil society (Koo 2002). During the early 1990s, there were two types of Korean CSOs: people's movement organizations and citizens' movement organizations (Kim 2000). The former continued their militant pro-democracy movement for greater democratization, while the latter, which eventually came to dominate, peacefully focused on economic equality, political reforms (to curb corruption), and environmental issues. In response to the financial crisis that occurred in 1997–1998, CSOs expanded their activities to include corporate restructuring, demanding the facilitation of corporate reforms to make the governance structure of major industrial conglomerates more transparent and efficient.

During the 1990s and 2000s, CSOs continued to campaign for political reforms and played a crucial role in consolidating democracy and promoting political, economic, and social reforms in Korea (Bae and Kim 2013). These CSOs include the Citizens' Coalition for Economic Justice (CCEJ), the People's Solidarity for Participatory Democracy (PSPD), and the Civic Movement for Decentralization (CMD). The CCEJ, established in 1989, originally focused on the issues of economic justice, economic inequality, business–labor relations, and poverty; however, lately, it has expanded its interest to cover a broader range of policy and governance issues. The PSPD, established in 1994, tended to lean toward issues of substantive democracy and citizen participation. The CMD, established in 2000, advanced decentralization reform by cooperating with local governments and their associations to put pressure on politicians and central bureaucrats. Members of the CMD personally lobbied National Assembly members to support decentralization. Bae Yooil and Kim Sun-hyuk (2013) argue that these CSOs emerged as "policy competitors" with professional knowledge to produce better policy alternatives.

One interesting factor about Korea is that activists can find elite allies to their causes amongst judges (Shipper 2012). The president, who appoints the chief justices to the Supreme Court, can potentially influence the ideological nature of the judicial system. This was particularly important for activism during the presidencies of Kim Dae-jung (1998–2003) and Roh Moo-hyun (2003–2008), both of whom had backgrounds in national democratic movements and civic activism before being elected to office. During the Roh administration, for example, Roh Moo-hyun appointed Park Si-hwan and Kang Kum-sil as Supreme Court Chief Justice and

Justice Minister, respectively. These individuals were pro-democracy activists within the judicial system during the late 1980s and founding members of the Society for Research on Our Law. This Society was established in 1988 when some 430 judges protested the reappointment of the conservative and controversial Supreme Court Justice Kim Yong-chul. During the Roh administration, the Society enhanced its status as the "386-generation" aides to the president, recognized and facilitated the judiciary branch's capacity to change society.[4] These aides and judges believed that they could change society with a court ruling. Indeed, most progressive policies were passed during the Roh administration. In her comparative study on victim redress movements and government accountability in Korea and Japan, Celeste Arrington (2016) cautions that gaining an elite ally too early can reduce incentives for CSOs to mobilize fellow claimants and sympathetic citizens to follow a common cause. The importance of such potential allies can be undermined by the presence of elite allies.

In October and November 2016, Korea's civil society again displayed its vitality when the PSPD and the Korean Confederation of Trade Unions (KCTU) helped to organize through social media nationwide "candle light protests," bringing hundreds of thousands of people from all walks of life to the streets demanding the resignation of President Park Geun-hye. The protestors, many of whom are children of the 386 generation, accused President Park of illegally allowing her long-time friend Choi Soon-sil, who did not hold a government position, to edit her speeches and thereby manipulate government affairs. Moreover, they suspected that the president colluded with Choi to extort money and favors from *chaebol* (big businesses, including Samsung), which was a common practice during her father's dictatorship. These revelations reinforced the growing concern regarding President Park's undemocratic tendencies and aloofness toward government affairs. They caused the protestors to demand accountability for corrupt politicians and their relatives and friends as well as a halt to *chaebol*'s collusive practices that have worsened economic inequality. On December 9, 2016, the National Assembly impeached President Park, and on March 11, 2017, the country's Constitutional Court confirmed the impeachment.

In Taiwan, workers and students continued to pressure the Taiwan authorities to strengthen democracy after the transition. As the economic growth and diversification of Taiwan attracts foreign workers, workers' organizations, such as the Taiwan International Workers Association (TIWA) and Labor Rights Association, started addressing the concerns of the growing number of foreign workers and hoped that their activities would lead to larger movements aimed at realizing social justice and upholding social rights. For example, TIWA supported the 300 Thai workers who rioted and set fire to management property in Kaohsiung City on August 21, 2005, protesting against their ill treatment and poor living conditions. The management company had been cutting costs by providing substandard food and cramped living conditions to these workers and paying for only forty-six hours out of every 100 hours of their overtime labor. TIWA's efforts to mobilize public opinion and official sentiments in favor of Thai workers resulted in a policy shift aimed at lessening the unequal relationship between employer and employee. In December 2005, the government increased the number of times that foreign workers can change their employment from two to three. Similarly, activism by the Alliance for Human Rights Legislation for Immigrants and Migrants (AHRLIM) has contributed to the improvement of Taiwan's inclusive democracy (Hsia 2013). The AHRLIM spearheaded the amendments of the Immigration Act in 2007, which allowed marriage migrants, who were the victims of domestic violence, to remain in Taiwan even after divorce and secured the im/migrants' rights to assembly and rally.

After the "Sunflower Movement" of March 2014, Taiwan's democracy further deepened. Students and civic groups organized to protest the allegedly unconstitutional passing of the

Cross-Strait Service Trade Agreement (CSSTA) by the ruling KMT party in the Legislative Yuan. The trade pact with China had not undergone a clause-by-clause review and the full screening of public hearings in the presence of non-governmental organizations (NGOs) and industry representatives. Moreover, protestors perceived that the trade pact would hurt Taiwan's economy and make it vulnerable to political pressure from Beijing. The protestors occupied the legislature between March 18 and April 10, 2014, before reaching an agreement with the government. Some protest leaders of the Sunflower Movement went on to form the Taiwan March organization, which aims to reform Taiwan's referendum laws and push for legislative review of the CSSTA, along with other cross-strait pacts and economic bills. Other activist leaders went on to establish the National Power Party (NPP), which has become the "Third Force" in Taiwan's politics after winning five seats in the 2016 general election (Wang 2016). With its roots in the civil society movement, the NPP pursues progressive social justice, human rights, and democratic values in the Legislative Yuan.

Japan, which is a more developed democracy compared to the other Asian countries mentioned earlier, has a robust civil society (Kingston 2004). Robert Pekkanen (2006) characterized Japan's civil society as being dualistic, consisting of a few large CSOs and numerous small ones. Pekkanen explains that the Japanese state provides preferential treatment to those civic organizations that are useful to the state, such as neighborhood associations, and promotes their growth before eventually exerting influence over them. In contrast, the government makes it difficult for issue-oriented organizations, such as environmental NGOs, to expand, because it fears that these organizations may undermine its power. In summary, the state shapes civil society by selectively promoting certain organizations and allowing them to expand, while regulating others and making it difficult for them to survive or flourish. Pekkanen interprets the impressive increase in CSOs in Japan during the past few decades and passage of the Non-Profit Organization (NPO) Law in 1998 as continued efforts by the state to control and shape CSOs.

Akihiro Ogawa (2009), who employs an action research methodology at an NGO that he calls SLG, concurs with Pekkanen's findings. Ogawa observes at SLG that its top leadership comprised mostly "invited" volunteers, its funding came mainly from the government, and nearly all its activities were conducted in a government facility. He interprets this trend of allowing private organizations to incorporate and take over the provision of services formerly offered by the government as a wider spread of global neoliberalism. Unlike Pekkanen, who sees little meaningful impact of CSOs on Japan's democracy, Ogawa argues that this neoliberal development is transforming the "practices of citizenship," where CSOs are promoting a new image of an ideal citizen, one who actively volunteers to help his or her community in cooperation with the government.

Both Pekkanen and Ogawa highlight the dominant role of the state and, consequently, portray Japan as having a dependent civil society. In contrast, Mary Alice Haddad (2007) observes that Japan has a strong state and a vibrant civil society. She characterizes CSOs with close relations with the state as "embedded organizations." These organizations enjoy high rates of participation from citizens who voluntarily cooperate with the government in supporting community goals. She explains that the state helps nurture civil society, while civil society helps perform state functions for the sake of the community. For Haddad, embedded organizations can perform vital functions for a democratic society while keeping the government accountable to the people. She observes that Japan's vibrant civil society comprises new generations of citizens who are better educated in democratic values compared to older generations (Haddad 2015). They incorporate traditions and political culture into their efforts to tinker with new democratic values, institutions, and practices. For her, this group progressively leads Japan's democratic transformation.

Pekkanen assumes that meaningful policy change requires large groups or large-scale mass mobilization. Therefore, small, issue-oriented advocacy groups are not expected to have an important democratic impact on public policies. Several scholars have vigorously argued otherwise that small CSOs have brought about favorable policy changes and contributed to the deepening of Japan's democracy (Chung 2010; Shibuichi 2016; Shipper 2008; Steinhoff 2015). Apichai Shipper (2008) details how Japanese citizens have established a variety of local advocacy groups to help immigrants secure access to social services, economic equity, and political rights. Shipper asserts that small CSOs that support undocumented foreigners make dramatic contributions to democratic multiculturalism by improving the quality of deliberative democracy in Japan. Using "associative activism" (in contrast to mass movement mobilization), he explains how local activists in the course of solving practical problems influence local and national governments and, thereby, have a transformative effect on otherwise inflexible political institutions.

Whereas immigrant communities are believed to be less active in the political process, Erin Aeran Chung (2010) demonstrates that non-citizens without voting rights have engaged "in a wide range of extra-electoral political activities in order to voice their concerns and shape public debate and policy" (Chung 2010: 12). In her detailed examination of post-war Korean activism in Japan, Chung keenly observes that a change occurred during the early 1970s, when activism moved away from the two large centralized national organizations—Chongryun and Mindan— toward more decentralized grass-roots organizations, such as Mintōren and Zenchōkyō. These grass-roots CSOs have campaigned successfully to end employment and housing discrimination, remove nationality requirement in public sector employment, and facilitate access to various social welfare benefits. More recently, they have been engaging in a politics of ideas, as they seek to gain political visibility and power in order to diversify the meaning of Japanese citizenship. They hope that such efforts would result in Japan becoming more inclusive of other ethnic groups in its society. These activisms, Chung argues, have laid institutionalized paths for foreigners other than Koreans to attain political empowerment at the levels of policies, local institutions, and ideas. For Chung, these multi-generational Korean activists, who engage in a wide range of extra-electoral political activities, contribute to the democratization of the Japanese society.

Unlike the above scholars, who opine that a significant upsurge in civic engagement occurred after the 1995 Kobe earthquake and the passage of the 1998 NPO Law, Patricia Steinhoff (2015) notes that several members of small advocacy CSOs gained experience by participating in Japan's New Left Movement during the 1960s and 1970s. She argues that these small but vibrant civic groups constitute Japan's "invisible civil society," because they simultaneously produce advocacy and social capital. Similarly, Daiki Shibuichi (2016) has found that anti-racism groups, which tap the resources of certain social elites and fight against anti-democratic ideals and xenophobic groups, also constitute a part of Japan's invisible civil society. In essence, this invisible civil society, comprising small CSOs, has deepened Japan's democracy over the previous two decades or so.

Small CSOs can also work with international organizations to deepen democracy. As political leaders try to reshape the national identity of Japan as one of the world's economic powers and developed democracies, they seek international legitimacy by adopting certain global norms and signing international treaties (Flowers 2009). Domestic advocates assist in the adoption of norms with their role of socializing Japan into the international community. By signing an international treaty, the government must change some domestic policies in order to fulfill the duties and obligations that accompany the treaty. Civil society actors then mobilize around a widely accepted global norm by pressuring their government to enact numerous political reforms to comply with international norms. In other words, a certain level of domestic advocacy remains necessary to maintain at least a moderate level of compliance after Japan's adoption of an international norm. Sidney Tarrow (2005) calls this process "internationalization," whereby external pressures influence domestic politics and the triangular relationship created by this process amongst citizens/activists, their governments, and international institutions.

Civil society and the status quo or democratic retrenchment

Much of the scholarship on modernization begins with the misconception that all civil society organizations enhance democracy or challenge undemocratic governments. We often forget that some CSOs function to reinforce the status quo or to reflect the power struggles between competing societal factions (Alagappa 2004: 40–50). They can also represent the unequal power relations prevalent within the wider society, thereby reproducing inequalities of society at large. In places where civil society is divided, not all CSOs will seek to advance democratic political positions (Rodan 1996). Dietrich Rueschemeyer, Evelyne Stephens, and John Stephens (1992) note that where powerful and cohesive upper classes dominate CSOs, these CSOs may "serve as conduits of authoritarian ideologies, thus weakening democracy." Kevin Hewison and Garry Rodan aptly describes, "The emergence of 'civil society' cannot be understood as a natural opposite to an authoritarian state or as being separated from capitalist relations of exploitation and domination" (Hewison and Rodan 2014: 28).

In Thailand and the Philippines, two societal camps with their own supporting CSOs have emerged to play important roles in the political scenes of these countries. Their power struggles reflect a conflict amongst different networks containing parties and political officials, factions of the military, activist organizations, and mass organizations (Boudreau 2013). One camp, comprising rural people and the urban poor, supports the idea of procedural democracy as fidelity to an *electoral mandate* and the empowerment of new, populist forces. In Thailand, these populist supporters, who are known as the "Red Shirts," back Thaksin Shinawatra, Yingluck Shinawatra, and various pro-Thaksin forces. In the Philippines, they back Joseph Estrada and Rodrigo Duterte. The other camp, comprising traditional elites and the urban middle class, supports the idea of democracy as *good governance* (e.g., transparency, accountability, and low levels of corruption). This affluent and urban camp tries to adhere to the global norms of neoliberalism. In Thailand, they are known as the "Yellow Shirts," and they consistently back candidates from the Democratic Party. In the Philippines, they are political elites backed by the oligarchy.

Many CSOs from the latter camp do not necessarily support political democracy in classic procedural terms. Interestingly, some of these CSOs have joined forces with the elite and urban middle class in mounting street protests to topple elected leaders and their popular policies. In the Philippines, the Arroyo oligarch family led street protests and successfully brought down the elected and populist leader Joseph Estrada in 2001. In Thailand, the Yellow Shirts organized street protests, creating an unstable political condition that was ripe for military coups in 2006 and 2014. Some Yellow Shirts' CSOs in Thailand even espoused elitist and anti-democratic ideals and argue against popular elections. They reasoned that rural people lack intelligence/education and, therefore, good judgment on political matters. Meanwhile, the populist camp in the Philippines strongly supports President Duterte's anti-drug policy of extra-judiciary killings, which took thousands of lives within the first few months of Duterte's presidency.

In fact, certain CSOs, such as xenophobic or racist groups, may hinder democratization by inciting hatred and/or violence against minority groups. In Myanmar, the radical Buddhist group Ma Ba Tha, which has garnered members/followers at around 20 percent of the nation's total population, has been engaging in controversial political activities, including hate speeches against Muslims. Since the passing of the Race and Religion Protection Laws, which restrict the influence and expansion of Islam in Myanmar, in 2015, the government has turned a blind eye toward Ma Ba Tha's undemocratic ideals and destructive activities. Meanwhile, the government is taking action against those who dare to speak against the "969 Buddhist Movement." In effect, the Ma Ba Tha serves as a tool for the government and the Movement, since the people cannot criticize the Buddhist group. Ashley South keenly observes that: "civil society in Burma [Myanmar] tends to be determined by elites" (South 2009: 174).

Even in democratic Japan, the country has witnessed a growth of xenophobic groups that oppose, at times violently, the ideal of inclusive diversity/democracy. In recent years, a prominent xenophobic group has emerged to specifically challenge the "special privileges" granted to *zainichi* (Japan-born) Koreans called the Citizens against the Special Privilege of Zainichi (*Zainichi token o yursusanai shimin no kai* or Zaitokukai, hereafter). Zaitokukai, which was founded in 2007 by a 35-year-old tax accountant, who uses the assumed name Sakurai Makoto, is a "Net-Far-Right" (*netto uyoku*) group with approximately 12,000 "supporters"—comprising mostly young men with low-paying, part-time jobs who read/contribute to Sakurai's blog. Group leaders use the Internet to organize and gather for demonstrations alone, where approximately 200–300 people show up and display racist placards like "Koreans get out," "Korean return home," and even "Go hang yourselves" (Shipper 2017). In December 2009, for example, nearly a dozen Zaitokukai members organized a protest at the Kyoto No. 1 Korean Elementary School, where they gathered in front of the school gate and used megaphones to call the students "cockroaches" and "Korean spies."

Xenophobic activism in Japan also includes violent acts conducted by small, armed vigilante groups. Certain members of ultra-nationalist vigilante groups have attacked Chongryun and its members, who are seen by the vigilantes as representatives of the North Korean communist regime. They have targeted Chongryun's headquarters and affiliated regional offices with numerous threats (Shipper 2008). These threats include phone threats, envelopes containing bullets, gunshots fired inside its offices, and bomb threats. For instance, the ultra-rightist group called the "Nation-Building Volunteer Corps to Punish Korea" (*Kenkoku giyūgun chōsen seibatsu-tai*) orchestrated numerous incidents of intimidation against Chongryun and its affiliated organizations between November 2002 and August 2003. They included sending a threatening letter with bullets inside to Chongryun's Tokyo headquarters in November 2002, firing shots at the Nagoya branch of the Chongryun-affiliated Chōgin Chobu Credit Union in January 2003, firing shots at Chongryun's Niigata office and leaving a home-made bomb near the Korean-operated Hana Credit Union in July 2003, leaving a home-made bomb near the Chongryun-affiliated Chōgin-nishi Shinkumi Bank in Fukuoka and another near Chongryun's Fukuoka office in August 2003, and firing shots at Chōgin-nishi Shinkumi headquarters in Okayama Prefecture in August 2003. The group also claimed responsibility for placing a bomb on September 10, 2003 in the garage of the Ministry of Foreign Affairs Director General Tanaka Hitoshi, who was considered to favor North Korea. In addition, eleven members of the group were arrested for other related crimes. Because Japan did not have a law against racist criminal acts or hate crimes at the time, they were charged simply with twenty-three incidents of intimidation acts, violation of firearms laws, and damaging property, which carry a sentence of no more than three years in prison (Shipper 2008).

This vigilante group can be considered to be a right-wing political organization, whose members comprise company employees, antique dealers, a teacher, a dentist, and a Buddhist priest, all in their forties and fifties. All were members of the *Token-tomo-no-kai* or enthusiasts and collectors of Japanese swords. The leader of the group, Murakami Ichiro, yearned for the "pure" Japan of the samurai age (Shipper 2008). In September 2003, another ultra-rightist group, the *Nippon Kōfugun* or Japan Imperial Grace Army, poured gasoline on a car in the parking lot of Chongryun's Oita office and set it ablaze (Shipper 2008). Members of these vigilante groups were reacting to the actions by the North Korean government that were considered a threat to Japan's national security, and they considered Chongryun's facilities approachable targets of intimidation and violence for venting their anger, as well as promoting their cause for a stronger and more militant Japan.

Conclusion

During the last few decades, several Asian societies have undergone democratization. In explaining the process of democratic transitions, democratic deepening, and democratic retrenchment, I have focused on the role of CSOs. In particular, I have emphasized the ways in which student groups and labor activism have challenged authoritarianism. More specifically, some activists operate within their existing political opportunity structure to democratize their societies, while others must utilize transnational actors/institutions from abroad to pressure their home governments to implement political/structural reforms. Overall, I have provided a description of how CSOs have affected democratic transitions, democratic deepening/consolidation, and even democratic retrenchment. The interplay between state and societal actors in shaping the direction of democratization is of particular importance to my analysis.

Although I have focused on the democratization of selected Asian societies where CSOs have played a significant role, it is important to emphasize that democracy/democratization is a function of many variables other than CSOs. Socialist societies such as China, North Korea, Vietnam, and Laos, where CSOs have had little/no impact on democratization, are absent from my analysis. The Communist Party in all these societies is deeply uneasy about civil society or any form of organization that operates outside the state or ruling party structure. Further, I have not analyzed the economically rich societies of Singapore and Brunei, where the development of a viable opposition party and CSOs takes place under the control of the government. Therefore, we should not expect to witness democratization in these societies any time in the near future, as predicted by the modernization theory. In contrast, Malaysia and Cambodia, which recently saw the emergence of a strong opposition political party, as well as CSOs (especially student and labor organizations), are ripe for democratic transitions. In certain societies where xenophobic or racist groups have joined forces with conservative political elites, CSOs can hinder democratization by inciting undemocratic ideals and ethnic violence against minority groups. In summary, I hope to have improved our understanding on democratization in Asia by exploring the varieties of roles that CSOs can play in bringing about democratic transitions, deepening, and retrenchment.

Notes

1 For their helpful comments of the paper and/or assistance with the research, I thank Alasdair Bowie, Euisuok Han, Brian Moser, Akihiro Ogawa, Hae-Ran Shin, Myint Soe, Kazuto Tsuchiya, and Bob Wang. An earlier version of this chapter was presented at the University of Melbourne. The views expressed in this chapter are those of the author and do not necessarily reflect the views of the US Department of State or the US Government.

2 A coup in 1976 ended this democratic experimentation. An election took place in 1988; however, a coup in 1991 shortened the term of the elected Chartichai government. The 1992 Democratic Movement (popularly known as "Black May") led to the demise of a military-based government and placed Thailand on the path to democracy again. This path ended in successive military coups in 2006 and 2014 (Interview with Charnvit Kasetsiri, January 15, 2017).

3 Interview with a former democratic activist and current mayor of the Seongbuk-gu, Seoul, Young-bae Kim, January 10, 2017.
4 The "386-generation" refers to people who were in their thirties during the early 1990s (when the term was first coined), attended university during the 1980s (and, therefore, were politically active in the democracy movement), and were born in the 1960s.

Suggested readings

Alagappa, Muthiah. ed. 2004. *Civil Society and Political Change in Asia: Expanding and Contracting Democratic Space*. Stanford, CA: Stanford University Press.
Ford, Michele. ed. 2013. *Social Activism in Southeast Asia*. New York: Routledge.
Kim, Sun-hyuk. 2000. *The Politics of Democratization in Korea: The Role of Civil Society*. Philadelphia, PA: Temple University Press.
Pekkanen, Robert. 2006. *Japan's Dual Civil Society: Members without Advocates*. Stanford, CA: Stanford University Press.
Tsai, Lily L. 2007. *Accountability without Democracy: Solidarity Groups and Public Goods Provision in Rural China*. New York: Cambridge University Press.

References

Arrington, Celeste L. 2016. *Accidental Activists: Victim Movements and Government Accountability in Japan and South Korea*. Ithaca, NY: Cornell University Press.
Alagappa, Muthiah. 2004. Civil Society and Political Change: An Analytical Framework. In *Civil Society and Political Change in Asia: Expanding and Contracting Democratic Space*. Muthiah Alagappa, ed. Pp. 25–57. Stanford, CA: Stanford University Press.
Bae, Yooil, and Sunhyuk Kim. 2013. Civil Society and Local Activism in South Korea's Local Democratization. *Democratization* 20(2): 260–286.
Boudreau, Vincent. 2013. Philippine Contention in the Democratic "Transitions." In *Social Activism in Southeast Asia*. Michele Ford, ed. Pp. 56–71. New York: Routledge.
Chung, Erin Aeran. 2010. *Immigration and Citizenship in Japan*. New York: Cambridge University Press.
CIA (Central Intelligence Agency). 2016. The World Factbook. Electronic document, www.cia.gov/library/publications/the-world-factbook, accessed April 10, 2017.
CIVICUS. 2016. CIVICUS Civil Society Index. Electronic document, http://csi.civicus.org, accessed April 10, 2017.
Darling, Frank C. 1974. Student Protest and Political Change in Thailand. *Pacific Affairs* 47(1): 6–8.
EIU (Economist Intelligence Unit). 2016. Democracy Index 2016. Electronic document, www.eiu.com/public/topical_report.aspx?campaignid=DemocracyIndex2016, accessed April 10, 2017.
Fan, Yun. 2004. Taiwan: No Civil Society, No Democracy. In *Civil Society and Political Change in Asia: Expanding and Contracting Democratic Space*. Muthiah Alagappa, ed. Pp. 164–190. Stanford, CA: Stanford University Press.
Flowers, Petrice R. 2009. *Refugees, Women, and Weapons: International Norm Adoption and Compliance in Japan*. Stanford, CA: Stanford University Press.
Haddad, Mary Alice. 2007. *Politics and Volunteering in Japan: A Global Perspective*. New York: Cambridge University Press.
Haddad, Mary Alice. 2015. *Building Democracy in Japan*. New York: Cambridge University Press.
Haggard, Stephen. 2000. *The Political Economy of the Asian Financial Crisis*. Washington, DC: Institute for International Economics.
Hewison, Kevin, and Garry Rodan. 2014. Southeast Asia: The Left and the Rise of Bourgeois Opposition. In *Routledge Handbook of Southeast Asian Politics*. Richard Robison, ed. Pp. 25–39. New York: Routledge.
Hsia, Hsiao-Chuan. 2013. The Tug of War over Multiculturalism: Contesting between Governing and Empowering Immigrants in Taiwan. In *Migration and Diversity in Asian Contexts*. Lai Ah Eng, Francis L. Collins, and Brenda S. A. Yeoh, eds. Pp. 130–159. Singapore: Institute of Southeast Asian Studies.
IMF (International Monetary Fund). 2015. World Economic Outlook Database, October 2015. Electronic document, www.imf.org/external/pubs/ft/weo/2015/02/weodata/weoselgr.aspx, accessed April 10, 2017.

Kang, David. 2002. *Crony Capitalism: Corruption and Development in South Korea and the Philippines.* New York: Cambridge University Press.

Keck, Margaret, and Kathryn Sikkink. 1998. *Activists Beyond Borders: Advocacy Networks in International Politics.* Ithaca, NY: Cornell University Press.

Kim, Sunhyuk. 2000. *The Politics of Democratization in Korea: The Role of Civil Society.* Philadelphia, PA: Temple University Press.

Kingston, Jeff. 2004. *Japan's Quite Transformation: Social Change and Civil Society in the Twenty-First Century.* New York: RoutledgeCurzon.

Koo, Hagen. 2002. Civil Society and Democracy in South Korea. *The Good Society* 11(2): 40–45.

Lipset, Seymour Martin. 1968. Students and Politics in Comparative Perspective. *Daedalus* 97(1): 1–20.

Moore, Barrington. 1966. *Social Origins of Dictatorship and Democracy: Lord and Peasant in the Making of the Modern World.* Boston, MA: Beacon Press.

Morell, David, and Samudavanija Chai-Anan. 1981. *Political Conflict in Thailand: Reform, Reaction, Revolution.* Cambridge: Oelgeschalager, Gunn & Hain.

Neureiter, Michael. 2013. Organized Labor and Democratization in Southeast Asia. *Asian Survey* 53(6): 1063–1086.

Ogawa, Akihiro. 2009. *The Failure of Civil Society? The Third Sector and the State in Contemporary Japan.* Albany, NY: SUNY Press.

Pekkanen, Robert. 2006. *Japan's Dual Civil Society: Members without Advocates.* Stanford, CA: Stanford University Press.

Putnam, Robert. 1993. *Making Democracy Work: Civic Traditions in Modern Italy.* Princeton, NJ: Princeton University Press.

Rodan, Garry. 1996. Theorising Political Opposition in East and Southeast Asia. In *Political Oppositions in Industrialising Asia.* Garry Rodan, ed. Pp. 1–39. London: Routledge.

Rossabi, Morris. 2005. *Modern Mongolia: From Khans to Commissars to Capitalists.* Berkeley, CA: University of California Press.

Rueschemeyer, Dietrich, Evelyne Stephens, and John Stephens. 1992. *Capitalist Development and Democracy.* Cambridge: Polity Press.

Schmitter, Philippe C. 1974. Still the Century of Corporatism? *The Review of Politics* 36(1): 85–131.

Shibuichi, Daiki. 2016. The Struggle Against Hate Groups in Japan: The Invisible Civil Society, Leftist Elites and Anti-Racism Groups. *Social Science Japan Journal* 19(1): 71–83.

Shipper, Apichai W. 2008. *Fighting for Foreigners: Immigration and Its Impact on Japanese Democracy.* Ithaca, NY: Cornell University Press.

Shipper, Apichai W. 2012. Influence of the Weak: The Role of Foreigners, Activism, and NGO Networks in Democratizing Northeast Asia. *International Studies Quarterly* 56(4): 689–703.

Shipper, Apichai W. 2017. Activism for Harmony? Immigrants' Rights Activism and Xenophobic Activism in Japan. In *Activism in Contemporary Japan: New Ideas, Players and Arenas?* David Chiavacci and Julia Obinger, eds. Forthcoming. London: Routledge.

So, Alvin Y., and Shiping Hua. 1992. Democracy as an Antisystemic Movement in Taiwan, Hong Kong, and China: A World Systems Analysis. *Sociological Perspectives* 35(2): 385–404.

South, Ashley. 2009. *Ethnic Politics in Burma: States of Conflict.* New York: Routledge.

Steinhoff, Patricia G. 2015. Finding Happiness in Japan's Invisible Civil Society. *Voluntas: International Journal of Voluntary and Nonprofit Organizations* 26: 98–120.

Tarrow, Sidney. 2005. *The New Transnational Activism.* New York: Cambridge University Press.

Tsai, Lily L. 2007. *Accountability without Democracy: Solidarity Groups and Public Goods Provision in Rural China.* New York: Cambridge University Press.

Valenzuela, Samuel J. 1989. Labor Movements in Transitions to Democracy: a Framework for Analysis. *Comparative Politics* 21(4): 445–472.

Wang, Robert. 2016. *Taiwan's Vibrant Democracy and Beleaguered Economy.* Washington, DC: Center for Strategic & International Studies.

Williamson, Peter J. 1989. *Corporatism in Perspective: An Introductory Guide to Corporatist Theory.* Thousand Oaks, CA: Sage.

23

AUTHORITARIAN RULE

Jörg Wischermann

Authoritarian rule and civil society: a difficult, but not necessarily hostile, relationship

Civil society, civil society organizations (CSOs), and authoritarian regimes are sworn enemies. This is, at least, the view shared by important mainstream political science protagonists and many development practitioners. Both use simplified, schematic, and realm-based definitions (viz., implying separate social layers or spheres) of civil society, which indicate a certain affinity to neoliberal ideas. These definitions assume that civil society organizations need to be autonomous from and act as counterweights to the state (see Diamond's 1999 widely used definition).[1] Additionally, many protagonists of such a concept assume that "real" civil society is a force of democratization and that civil society organizations are "schools of democracy" (in the sense expressed by Tocqueville). However, autocratic rulers and politicians from parties ruling a polity in an authoritarian manner (such as the Communist Party of Vietnam [CPV]) are supposed to strictly negate any autonomy of civil society and civil society organizations; to oppose any counterweight to the state that they are in control of; and, finally, to keep the forces of democratization from having their way. An unavoidable conclusion of these assumptions is that under authoritarian rule there can be no, or only a very weak, civil society and there can be no, or only a few, civil society organizations.

Yet, historical reality and practical experience show us different and changing situations. In many, if not most, polities under authoritarian rule, we find a more or less thriving field of associations. This should not cause one to wonder. Research on authoritarian regimes indicates that these polities are different from totalitarian regimes. The former, unlike the latter, give civil society, civil society organizations, and other political and economic actors at least some space and room to maneuver, although the particular regimes vary significantly in the actual manner in which they allow space for these actors.[2] Moreover, in polities under authoritarian rule, the existence of civil society, civil society organizations, political parties, and other organizations and institutions (such as national parliaments and the elections to such bodies) is not mere window dressing. Rather, research results suggest that these organizations and institutions play a decisive role in enabling the persistence of authoritarian regimes. More specifically, research on civil society under authoritarian rule in various regions of the world shows that civil society organizations can even be obstacles to democratization and be supporters of and important to

344

the perseverance of different types of authoritarian regimes, although such support varies amongst countries according to policy areas, types of authoritarian regimes and civil society organizations, etc. Finally, research shows that civil society is not always and everywhere a haven of democracy and suggests that not all civil society organizations are "schools of democracy."

Thus, research on civil society under authoritarian rule reveals that the interpretation of civil society and civil society organizations as "the realm of organized social life autonomous from the state" implies a theoretical idealization that does not work well in empirical research. Other approaches show a greater variety of concepts and are much more accepting toward the various ideas and practices of civil society and civil society organizations. One difference is that these alternative approaches examine how civil society and civil society organizations and the authoritarian state are related to one another, instead of claiming their separateness and strict opposition to one another. Another difference is that they focus on what civil society and civil society organizations are *doing* instead of what following certain definitions civil society organizations are thought to *be*. Thereby, such alternative approaches also take into account the actors' views of civil society and civil society organizations. More often than not, these differ significantly from various civil society theoreticians' views. Last but not least, such less rigid concepts and approaches allow us to deal better with the cognitive problems that civil society research is confronted with, thus enabling us to connect the three different forms of knowledge generation through empirical research, theoretical codification, and critical reflection of normative assumptions that guide the research process, and the ways of practice and action of CS and CSOs.

In this chapter, I offer theoretical and empirical insights into various ways of understanding, conceptualizing, and examining empirically authoritarian regimes and authoritarianism, civil society and civil society organizations, and their relationships. To this end, in the next section, I first delve into various ways of understanding, defining, and classifying authoritarian regimes and authoritarianism. Subsequently, I describe in detail the most important theoretical problems that come with the use of a simplified, schematic, and realm-based understanding of civil society. Thereafter, I examine alternative ways of conceptualizing civil society and civil society organizations: here, I refer to an actor- and action-centered understanding of civil society; concepts based on functionalist and relational assumptions; and, finally, a Gramsci-inspired perspective on civil society. In the following section, I present the results from some Vietnam-related studies. It was there that researchers first made use of the cited simplified and realms-based approach to civil society. However, in an impressive turnaround between 2005 and 2016 researchers started using alternative approaches. In the conclusion section, I summarize what civil society theory and research on civil society organizations can learn from these Vietnam-related analyses using alternative approaches to examine civil society and civil society organizations under authoritarian rule.

Theoretical problems and potential solutions

What are authoritarian regimes and what is authoritarianism?

Authoritarian regimes are different from totalitarian regimes in that the former give civil society, civil society organizations, and other political and economic actors at least some space and room to maneuver (although the regimes may vary depending on the respective regime subtype, the country and region, and other conditions).[3] In his widely cited definition, Juan Linz defines authoritarian regimes as:

political systems with limited, not responsible, political pluralism, without elaborate and guiding ideology, but with distinctive mentalities, without extensive nor (sic) political mobilization, except at some points in their development, and in which a leader or occasionally a small group exercises power within formally ill-defined limits but actually predictable ones.

(Linz 2000: 159)

Critics point out that this definition is very broad and "says little more than that relevant systems of political rule are non-totalitarian non-democracies. This problem might have contributed to the fact that Linz's elaborate, if rather historically grounded typology of authoritarian regimes has hardly been used in empirical studies" (Croissant *et al.* 2015: 4). However, the disadvantages of Linz's definition are shared by other definitions of authoritarianism.[4] To date, research on authoritarianism has not come up with a substantive definition of authoritarianism: "The most common, and little debated, definition of authoritarianism remains 'a national regime type that fails to organize free and fair elections.' And (…) 'that fails to guarantee the rights necessary to enable elections to be free and fair'," as noted by Marlies Glasius (2015: 5). Based on Schumpeter's understanding of democracy, in many, if not most, definitions of authoritarian regimes, elections have been reified, and made the "sole touchstone to arbitrate the division between authoritarian and democratic systems" (Glasius 2015: 5).

Instead of substantiating the concept of authoritarianism and "focusing on what authoritarianism *is* and *does*, rather than what it lacks and falls short of" (Glasius 2015: 7, emphasis by the author), over the last fifteen years, research on authoritarian regimes has turned its attention to the development of narrow, brief, and sharp typologies of authoritarian regimes. Here, Barbara Geddes' (1999) typology of autocracies stands out.[5] Such typologies suited the intentions of political scientists who aimed at testing hypotheses related to, for example, the varying longevity of various subtypes of authoritarian regimes by means of analyzing huge data sets. In an interesting institutionalist turn, various scholars made use of these and other classifications (or added even new subtypes) and examined the significance of various institutions and organizations (e.g., parliaments, elections, parties, and mass organizations more or less closely related to the regime, etc.), which helped them explain the durability of authoritarian regimes (see, e.g., Brownlee 2007; Gandhi 2008; Levitzky and Way 2002; Schedler 2009).[6] Unfortunately, organizations such as civil society organizations have not played a prominent role in these analyses. Thus, leaving aside the discovery, which is without any doubt important, that various institutions and organizations are of enormous, though varying, use for autocrats (the "institutional ambivalence," as Andreas Schedler [2009: 337f.] calls this phenomenon), I conclude that those who want to explore empirically the relationship between civil society, civil society organizations, and authoritarian regimes might not gain much from mainstream research in political science and its efforts to create various typologies of authoritarianism and identify varying subtypes of this regime.

Somewhat external to the mainstream political science research on authoritarian regimes, I find an understanding and a definition of authoritarianism that, meanwhile, have proven useful for research on civil society and civil society organizations (see, e.g., Wischermann *et al.* 2016a, 2016b). Karen Stenner (2005), in her actor-centered and action-based definition of authoritarianism, offers research on civil society and civil society organizations under authoritarian rule a more substantial understanding of such a rule. From her perspective, authoritarianism and democratic rule are not mutually exclusive. Authoritarianism can also be found under democratic rule and in organizations that are deemed to be structured democratically. Basically, Stenner argues that authoritarianism repudiates collective and individual self-determination and autonomy and strictly negates the supremacy of the individual over a group or system. More concretely, according to Stenner (2005), authoritarianism consists of an ensemble of attitudes and ways of acting that link the uncompromising denial of difference and diversity with an unconditioned demand for homogeneity and uniformity. This, in turn, leads to coercive action toward and suppression of people who are "different." According to Stenner, authoritarianism involves:

- a lack of tolerance of others and of views that diverge from one's and the group's own, as well as a strict rejection of pluralism;
- the rejection of difference and an insistence on sameness and the prioritization of the group over the individual, as well as of the group's interests over those of the individual ("groupiness");
- the personal coercion of and bias against people who are (ethnically, politically, and morally) "different," as well as political demands for placing authoritative constraints on their behavior (i.e., forms of state coercion);
- structures and mechanisms that ensure the prioritization of the group over the individual, as well as the group's interests over those of the individual.

(Stenner 2005: 14–20)

Thus, the literature and research on authoritarianism shows that approaches originating from the assumption that civil society, civil society organizations, and authoritarianism are mutually exclusive are misleading. Civil society and civil society organizations seem to be compatible with authoritarian rule, at least in a certain sense and to a certain degree and extent. Furthermore, authoritarianism can be found in democratic regimes, as well, and even in organizations that are considered the protagonists of democracy (such as civil society organizations). These insights pose a major problem at least for the widespread understanding and definition of civil society cited in the introduction. Moreover, these problems have to do with some, more fundamental, problems of a specific understanding of CS and CSOs, which we will now discuss.

Civil society: theoretical understandings and problems[7]

Realm-based definitions of civil society and their problems

Many, if not most, analyses of civil society in Asia are based on the premises of variations of a realm-based approach. Following such an understanding, civil society is a realm that is separate and distinct from the state, economy, and private sphere, in which associations of various sorts are active.[8] More often than not, such a way of understanding civil society is based on a variety of normative assumptions, for example, the assumption that civil society stands in opposition to the state and civil society organizations are the protagonists of democracy.

From a theoretical point of view, nothing is wrong with the assumption of various realms or layers of society. However, it is important to examine how the relationships between these realms are theoretically understood and conceptualized, who is seen as a member of a particular social sphere, what specifics the members of a sphere are assumed to have, and what reasons are given for the above specifics. Furthermore, it should be asked which normative assumptions are implied in the conceptualizations and how these assumptions can be justified.

A closer look at the implications of Larry Diamond's definition (see Note 1) and a concomitant understanding of civil society unveil several theoretical and practical problems:

- First, the concept assumes clear-cut boundaries between the state and CS. Furthermore, civil society is thought to be (completely) "autonomous from the state." The latter is considered necessary, because otherwise civil society cannot fulfill its tasks, for example, that of limiting the power of the state. However, even Diamond (1999: 224) admits that the boundaries between the state and civil society are always blurred and are thus a matter of degree, rather than an either/or view. Furthermore, there are good reasons to assume that the relationship between the state and civil society in any type of regime is based on "interrelatedness rather than separateness" and is thus "more complex and reciprocal than the state–society dichotomy depicts" (Beckmann 2001: 55). It would be even more difficult to assume that the entirety of civil society is opposed to the state:

    > Civil societies elsewhere include both those associations that strive to limit state power or even change the regime and those who cooperate with the state in achieving their goals. The interaction between the two realms thus includes conflict, compromise and cooperation at the same time.
    >
    > *(Perinova 2005: 7)*

- Second, civil society is depicted as being separate from the economy, as well. However, the boundaries between civil society and the economy are also blurred. John Keane, referring to similar discussions on global civil society and their relationship with the capitalist economy, criticizes that:

    > the dualism between market and global civil society (…) is (…) a bad abstraction, for in reality markets are always a particular form of socially and politically mediated interaction structured by money, production, exchange, and consumption. Global civil society (…) could not survive for a day without the market forces unleashed by turbo-capitalism. The converse rule also applies.
    >
    > *(Keane 2001: 31)*

    As a result, theoretically, it might be more fruitful to assume different varieties of relationships, forms, and contents of interaction between civil society, the state, and the economy; empirically, it would be more useful to explore these varieties instead of presuming and focusing on the separation between civil society, the state, and the economy.
- Third, there is the problem of deciding who should be seen as actors within this realm. In the case that all the actors in this realm are automatically included, then even hate groups and criminal gangs could be considered as civil society actors. Thus, in many analyses based on a realm-based approach, specific types of associations are introduced and specified as "civil-society-like organizations" (especially non-governmental organizations [NGOs]) and/or normative criteria such as tolerance, adherence to nonviolent behavior, and so on are used in order to differentiate between civil and "uncivil" actors and behaviors. Such classifications based on fixed (Western) norms more often than not lead to assessments concluding that CS civil society in the South is "weak," not (yet) "fully developed," and the like.
- Fourth, this understanding is based on the assumption that all civil societies and civil society organizations strive for democracy and to facilitate processes of democratization or at least strengthen the development of democratic virtues. However, if not for theoretical reasons (presented in Warren 2001) then for empirical reasons, it must be concluded that not all associations are democratic, virtuous, or trustful (see, e.g., Wischermann et al. 2016a, 2016b), let alone always and exclusively nonviolent as far as the means they apply to achieve their aims are concerned.

Other realm-based definitions and concepts of civil society besides the one suggested by Diamond (e.g., the definition by the LSE Centre for Civil Society 2009; see Note 1) offer ways to alleviate the first and address the second problem. However, then, those definitions still face the third and fourth problems: They have to build on a couple of normative assumptions that imply further cognitive problems, both empirical (e.g., not all civil society organizations act in a "civil" way) and theoretical (e.g., the depiction of a state–society dichotomy in which an "evil state" confronts a basically "good society") ones.

One solution to these problems offer concepts of civil society that:

- operate with an action-centered understanding of civil society,
- make use of functionalist and relational approaches, or
- are founded on Gramsci's idea of civil society.

Such approaches are based on theoretically founded assumptions that say how and why certain realms interact with each other; they give reasons why certain actors are assumed to be in their respective realms; and, finally, these approaches imply that hypotheses are empirically tested and assumed norms are empirically verifiable. We now turn to these approaches.

An action- and actor-centered understanding of civil society

According to a view of civil society based on the logic of action rather than a conceptualization based on the logic of realms, civil society is a particular mode and interaction within a given society and, hence, not a fixed entity. It manifests itself in these concrete actions and also in social institutions. Authors such as Jörg Wischermann (2010, 2011) understand civil society not as a noun but as an adjective, which describes a certain kind of action (Uphoff and Krishna 2004: 358). Moreover, civil society action (CSA) is seen as a relationship (between people; between people and the state and/or the economy; between various actors' practices and what constitutes these practices, values and/or norms, etc.).

Theoretically, authors like Wischermann (2010, 2011) proceed from the assumption that CSA differs from other types of actions and interactions, namely, from power and rule, with concomitant hierarchical relationships; exchange and other market-related activities; family and kinship, which is based on closeness and personal relations; and, last but not least, fighting wars and other acts of unrestrained and indiscriminate use of force.[9] CSA comes into being by way of the discourse on dealing with force, power, and social exclusion.

Based on such a general description and the delimitation of CSA vis-à-vis action in the sphere of the economy, state, and community ("Gemeinschaft"), it is possible to define CSA as a specific type of interaction that takes place in not only the public sphere but also other spheres, for example, within state institutions. "Mutual recognition" is at the core of CSA, and "the empirical validation of the principle of 'mutual recognition' is the central criterion of civil society" (Gosewinkel 2003: 5, n. 13, translation by the author). Thus, such an understanding of civil society is not normative by itself but "raises the empirical validity of certain norms to a criterion. In this way, it is possible to come to a decision regarding whether and to what degree one can speak of a civil society" (Gosewinkel and Rucht 2004: 49, translation by the author).

For heuristic purposes, Gosewinkel and Rucht describe CSA as follows: "Civil society relations imply respect, but not like-mindedness and social closeness; a recognition of procedural rules, but not a commonality of world vision; the readiness to compromise, but not a convergence of interest; empathy, but not unconditional identification" (Gosewinkel and Rucht 2004: 50, translation by the author). From an operational point of view, CSA has four aspects: respect, empathy/sympathy, willingness to compromise, and sticking to rules once agreed upon (for a detailed description of the operational form of these aspects, see Wischermann 2010: 12). Wischermann (2010, 2011) and his Vietnamese colleagues applied these aspects and character-istics to four continua, each of which ranges from "less and somewhat civil society like" to "more civil society like." These continua accord with their assumption that civil society only exists in a "more-or-less-like" way; it never exists in a "completed" or an "achieved" way. These continua serve as an instrument that allows us to assess whether, in which sense, and to what extent we can speak of civil society and CSA in a given country and/or polity. Further, the category of gender is integral to the analysis of CSA (Howell 2007: 428). CSA not only is constituted by gender relations but also shapes them in diverse ways (Howell 2007: 427). CSA is "gendered" in nature.

A relational perspective on civil society

Suited for a combination with an action- and actor-centered understanding of CS are approaches drawing on functionalist and relational theoretical concepts. Like the former, the latter seem suited to solve problems entailed by simplified and realm-based definitions of and ways to understand CS. How a relational perspective on CS addresses such problems should become clear from the following short list of basic assumptions that Wischermann *et al.*'s (2016a, 2016b) approach is based upon:

- Civil society, civil society organizations, and the state are not opposites. Rather, they form an overall whole; influence one another; are dependent on one another; and take part, in different forms and functions, in the societal exertion of power and in power structures. The state is seen as a relatively autonomous actor in relation to civil society and civil society organizations, which follows its own interests and strategies; at the same time, the state as a discursive construct needs the interpretation of civil society, civil society organizations, and individuals, out of whose interpretations it comes into being.
- Civil society organizations are part of the whole societal–political complex and of societal conflicts, all of which constitute the state. CSOs are thus themselves the sites of societal conflicts, are part of specific practices of state power exertion, and can also contribute to the maintenance of state power. However, they can also change these practices, insofar as their actions are not one-sidedly and mechanistically determined by the economic base, because states are "constantly contested projects" and a "state per se is characterized by compromise" (Sauer 2011: 134, translation by the author).
- Civil society and civil society organizations can be both: the supporters of democracy *and* organizations that help to maintain authoritarian rule. Sometimes, they can be both at the same time: Civil society organizations are "polyvalent" (Kössler 1994).

Most recently, Wischermann and his colleagues have applied this approach and explored the role played by civil society organizations in three post-socialist countries, namely, Algeria, Mozambique, and Vietnam. They gave tentative answers to the question of whether CS supports and/or weakens authoritarian regimes.

When exploring the roles of civil society organizations as supporters and/or weakening forces of the authoritarian state, Wischermann *et al.* (2016a, 2016b) analyze what impact the state—as the most important conditioning factor—has on civil society organizations and what impact civil society organizations have on the state. More concretely, they examine what impact two forms of state power have on civil society organizations and what impact civil society organizations have on these forms of state power. The first form of state power that they address is infrastructural power, which denotes the "logistics of political control" (Mann 1984: 192). It includes two specific forms of such control, namely, "control through welfare provision" and "control through limited participation."[10] The second form of state power with which they are concerned is discursive power, that is, the "power employed by agents of the state through/on discourse" (Göbel 2011: 188, n. 7). Discursive power denotes the state's control of societal discourse and the shaping of understandings of political issues, historical events, etc.

A "weakening" of the infrastructural or discursive power of the authoritarian state occurs when associations' actions support the development of citizens' individual and collective self-determination and autonomy. Such forms of state power are, on the other hand, "maintained" when the associations' actions negate and deny such self-determination and when autonomy is denied and negated—a negation that is at the core of authoritarianism (for an operational, detailed description of both the terms, see Wischermann *et al.* 2016b: 7f.). The results of this survey are to be found at the end of the next section of this chapter.

A Gramsci-inspired understanding of civil society

In a similar way to that of a functionalist and relational approach, a Gramsci-inspired view on civil society overcomes the problems of the widely quoted, but simplified, understanding of civil society. Like the relational approach, a Gramsci-inspired approach focuses on the relationships between civil society and the authoritarian state, not its separation, and on the contributions made by civil society to varying forms of domination prevalent in modern (capitalist) societies.

From a Gramscian perspective, civil society and civil society organizations are considered part of the whole economic-political complex and a site of societal conflicts. Gramsci understood civil society as a contested terrain where hegemonic and counter-hegemonic forces are fighting each other, and where hegemony and counter-hegemony can be achieved. Thus, he understood civil society as a field that is permeated by and reflects power relations.

Civil society's function is to help maintain and/or change existing power positions and power relations of classes and social groups. As part of the practices of the state, civil society and civil society organizations can contribute to the maintenance of state power. On the other hand, they have a transformative capacity to change power, economic, and socio-cultural relations. This perspective, which leaves behind a simple economic determinism, implies a view of economic and political (power) relations where the state appears as a constantly contested project, characterized by conflict and compromise.[11]

In Gramsci's view, civil society, the state, and the economy complement each other, with each having specific tasks in the modes of domination. There is no primacy of politics, the economic realm, or civil society: rather, they depend on one another, are reciprocally interlocked, and influence each other, forming a complex unity of economic structures, functional mechanisms of civil society, and institutions of the state (Votsos 2001: 120). In the following section, we show how Thiem Hai Bui (2013) applied Gramsci's idea of civil society to the case of Vietnam.

In summary, simplified and realm-based civil society approaches, especially those following Diamond's definition (see Note 1), create difficult theoretical problems. They are based on presumptions that:

> create together an image of state–society dichotomy in which the state is associated
> with coercion and civil society with freedom, and in which these two realms are

opposed to each other. This view (...) tends to preclude that civil society can exist only under more or less democratic regimes, because it is obvious that under authoritarian rule no organization can be wholly autonomous and separate from the state.

(Perinova 2005: 7)[12]

Following approaches based on such assumptions makes it very difficult, at the very least, to analyze civil society under authoritarian rule.

Meanwhile, an action-centered functional and relational approach or an approach applying Gramsci's ideas of civil society helps to get out of most of the theoretical and operational problems, when analyzing civil society under authoritarian rule:

- An actor- and action-centered approach starts from the assumption that civil society action (CSA) exists not only in civil society but also in the state and other layers of the society. The empirical examination of this assumption (see the next section) suggests that CSA exists even in the realm of the authoritarian state. Research can identify the patterns of change caused by these forms of action.
- Relational and Gramsci-inspired approaches assume the relatedness and interaction of various societal layers; they aim at exploring the relations between the state and civil society and, finally, they aim at analyzing the roles of CS, CSOs, and the state in various forms and patterns of domination and/or liberation thereof.
- All these approaches imply a critical reflection on the theoretical and normative assumptions that guide research, and they offer empirical validation for the most important normative assumptions.

In the next section, I show how various civil-society-related approaches have been applied to the specific case of civil society under authoritarian rule in Vietnam and the results that they have yielded.

Research on civil society under authoritarian rule: examples from Vietnam-related research

Following Vietnam's re-unification 1975–1976 and until the mid-1990s, the Vietnamese state was considered as being almighty and strictly negating civil society. This was the perspective of not only local politicians but also foreign scholars. Many, if not most, scholars analyzing Vietnam's political regime used Thomas Henry Rigby's (1990) term "mono-organizational socialism." This term implies that there is no space and no need, at least none in the eyes of the rulers, for any other societal organizations besides mass organizations and some other regime-related organizations (such as hand-picked professionals' organizations) working as "transmission-belts" in Lenin's sense (i.e., transmitting the policies from the CPV to the societal and grass-roots level). Using Linz's typology, "mono-organizational socialism" could be considered more closely related to totalitarian than authoritarian regimes.

Scholars could not ignore the "mushrooming" of a variety of new associations during the 1990s and the "noughties" (see Chapter 8: Vietnam). However, whether this development and the spread of various new types of associations bespoke the existence of civil society, and whether (and if so, which of) these associations should be called civil society organizations, remained heavily contested. David Marr, for example, stated that what he observed developing in the 1990s was more:

an expansion of the "public sphere" in Vietnam, rather than civil society in the tradition of Hegel, de Tocqueville and Habermas. Public sphere (cong) is a well understood term going back centuries in Vietnam, representing the space in which people conduct affairs beyond the family or private sector (tu), but not specifically under the jurisdiction of government officials (quan). Unlike most conceptions of civil society, Vietnamese active in the public sphere do not generally see themselves as asserting civic power against state power. Rather, they prefer to infiltrate the state, find informal allies, and build networks that may conceivably be seen as fulfilling state, public and private objectives simultaneously. Most of this accomplished at a personal rather than institutional level, without legal guarantees, and subject to ambush other such alliances. This way of operations is inherently elitist, though public sphere activists usually believe what they are doing is altruistic and good for their constituents.

(Marr 1994: 13f)

However, only a few years later, Ben Kerkvliet ascertained that:

numerous (…) groups have emerged that are clearly part of a widening civil society. Through their actions, meetings, conferences, and printed and verbal statements, they advance arguments and propose courses of action about rural development, ethnic relations, workers' rights, relations between communities and the state, poverty, land use and distribution, corruption, and other major issues … [However], civil society activities are still significantly constrained.

(Kerkvliet 2003: 16)

Amongst scholars, skepticism regarding the existence of civil society and civil society organizations lasted until the end of the "noughties." Carlyle Thayer's article from 2009 serves as an example. In this article, he rates Vietnamese associations, especially local NGOs, as "extensions of, if not agents of, the state" (Thayer 2009: 6). In his view, only political organizations such as the network "8406" (dissolved by the Vietnamese security apparatus in 2006–2007, with many of its members and activists being incarcerated for many years) deserve to be called *political* civil society organizations (because they were opposed to the CPV). In Thayer's view, all other associations are apolitical and, in one way or the other, supporters of the CPV's authoritarian regime. In stark contrast to Thayer, Irene Norlund's (2006) CIVICUS study describes and analyzes a weak, but existing, civil society, with a variety of civil society organizations developing within the framework of a still pretty much authoritarian environment.

Despite the apparent discrepancies, what Thayer, Norlund, Kerkvliet, and even Marr have in common is that their approaches are based on an understanding of civil society that sees it as an entity or realm with fixed boundaries vis-à-vis the state, economy, and family. Moreover, their understanding of civil society has at its core a fixed set of normative assumptions against which the civil society and civil society organizations in Vietnam are measured. Due to these (and other) presumptions that this approach is built on, authors following these assumptions could only come to the conclusion that in an authoritarian environment civil society is either non-existent or, at best, weak.

Against the view of civil society as a separate entity and civil society organizations as a type of association embodying at least a minimum of democratic norms, between 2005 and 2016, a process of reorientation with respect to research on civil society and civil society organizations in Vietnam took place. Resorting to various theoretical foundations from different strands of social science theory, scholars no longer asked what Vietnamese civil society *was*, what

Vietnamese civil society organizations *were*, which associations could be called civil society organizations and which did not "deserve" this name, etc. Instead, in empirically rich studies, various scholars turned to an actor- and action-centered understanding of civil society. They explored Vietnamese *actors' views* of civil society and civil society organizations and analyzed what Vietnamese civil society was and civil society organizations were *doing*; what *roles* the civil society organizations played; what their *function* was; what changes they helped to achieve or prevent from happening; and, finally, how civil society organizations functioned *inside*.

These scholars suggested that what civil society organizations were *doing*, which roles they played, and what functions they had should be "measured" on continua. This idea was brought up by Norman Uphoff and Anirudh Krishna (2004), who suggested that civil society, civil society organizations, and civil-society-like action should always be seen as "more or less civil-society-like" and that civil society should be understood as something that can never be realized completely. The terms civil society and civil society organizations became increasingly understood as being in a constant flux and having a fluid and localized character, their respective senses different (at least to a certain extent) for different actors and according to the context against which the actors apply these terms (Wischermann 2010: 11, n. 9). Moreover, instead of focusing on the separation of civil society, the state, and the economy, researchers began to explore the multiplicity of relationships between these different societal layers. Resorting to functionalist theoretical approaches, drawing on the fundamentals of relational sociology, and applying Gramsci's idea of civil society, Vietnamese and foreign scholars very recently explored the role of Vietnamese civil society organizations as supporters of or obstacles to the processes of democratization.

Joseph Hannah, one of the first scholars who applied an actor- and action-centered understanding of civil society and civil society organizations, defined civil society "in terms of the activities and roles of various social actors, rather than in terms of specific forms of organizations, associations, and institutions" (Hannah 2007: 6). He argued:

> against limiting the idea of civil society to only autonomous, intermediate organizations, which is common in writings on civil society, an approach that I believe limits our ability to observe civil society in non-Western contexts. I argue instead for looking for civil society activities and functions—civil society *process*—wherever it can be found in a society, even if that means looking in state or quasi-state organizations. By doing so, we become much more open to the possible forms civil society can take.
>
> *(Hannah 2007: 6)*

Moreover, Hannah has argued:

> that looking at civil society process as a continuum of possible roles in society allows us to capture both the mundane and the dramatic instances of civil society. (…) Such a continuum, based on civil society process (actions and roles) rather than institutions and organizations, illustrates how civil society can exist in a variety of forms simultaneously in any given society. (…) It also gives us a heuristic for describing contestation over what types of civil society activities are possible or "appropriate" in a given place.
>
> *(Hannah 2007: 7–8)*

In the empirical part of his oeuvre, Hannah (2007) analyzed the various roles played by CSOs in Vietnam's political system. Following his assessment, in 2005–2006, most, if not all, Vietnamese

CSOs could be found on the right side of the continuum; there were a few in the middle and very few on the left (see Figure 23.1).

In a similar action- and actor-centered way of understanding civil society, Wischermann (2010, 2011) and his Vietnamese colleagues analyzed the specifics of civil society action (CSA) in Vietnam and its impact on the state. In one of the only two representative surveys on civil society organizations and civil society in Vietnam (though the survey was confined to CSOs in Hanoi and Ho Chi Minh City), Wischermann (2010) comes up with the result that there is strong and solid empirical evidence for CSA in Vietnam. Such kind of action exists in many of the forms of social action and interaction of civil society organizations' representatives, albeit this happens to varying extents and degrees. More specifically, the data analysis unveils the existence of respect and empathy/sympathy, willingness to compromise, and sticking to rules once agreed upon, though the respective values of these dimensions of CSA vary strongly. Aside from these characteristics, the survey finds elements inseparably linked with CSA "in Vietnamese colors": "Consensus-seeking, an aversion to conflicts and an affinity to synthesis. They represent elements of authoritarian political thinking in Civic Organizations' leaders' mindsets" (Wischermann 2010: 33).

Furthermore, Wischermann finds that:

> (t)here is CSA *within* the state apparatus *and* this specific mode of action and interaction effects changes in governance. Patterns of change precipitated by such mode of action and interaction vary from moderate changes in the governance area of security to more substantial changes in the governance area of welfare. In both areas problems of mis-representation and mis-recognition to a certain degree have been successfully addressed. (…) In the area of legitimate rule, however, CSA seems to have interesting limits. (…) In this area of governance the powerful seem to see any further change to the formal governance architecture as implying fundamental questions of their own political power, and thus reject it.
>
> *(Wischermann 2011: 406, emphasis in original)*

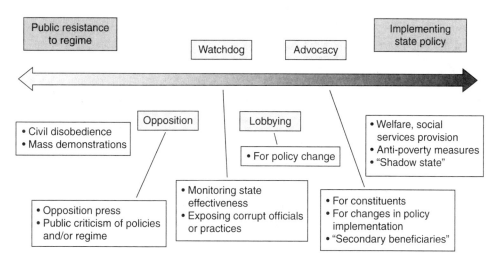

Figure 23.1 Civil society roles.

Source: Hannah (2007: 209).

In a further step away from a simplified and realm-based understanding of CS and toward an actor- and action-centered understanding of civil society and civil society organizations, Andrew Wells-Dang conceptualized civil society organizations:

> as a process of collective action that occurs and develops when organizations and individuals join together to influence power and promote positive, nonviolent social change. The basic units that comprise civil society in this analysis are networks of organizations, informal groups and individual activists, rather than non-governmental organizations alone. (…) One subset of networks consists of *civil society networks*, which engage in advocacy in pursuit of a shared agenda for social change.
>
> *(Wells-Dang 2011: 24, emphasis by the author)*

In his combination of network and social movement theory, networks, campaigns, and movements are forms of CS, and "differences among networks, campaigns and movements are not fixed but are rather a question of perspective, size, and degree" (Wells-Dang 2011: 50). Wells-Dang anticipated a relational perspective on civil society in that his theoretical understanding differs from traditional depictions of civil society and "describes the relationships among the components, showing that social movements and campaigns are sub-sets of the broader phenomenon of civil society networks, and that all forms of networks are based on underlying social relations" (Wells-Dang 2011: 51).

In the empirical parts of his dissertation, Wells-Dang analyzes how the CPV uses NGOs in trying out development policies or for environmental policy-making. He explicitly questions the tendency of considering civil society in Vietnam as weak. Through case studies, Wells-Dang makes the point that Vietnam has a civil society that exercises significant political influence and that this strong position of the civil society has been achieved through or in spite of the formal political system.

Bui applied Gramsci's idea of civil society to the case of Vietnam. Analyzing the impact of civil society in the areas of environmental governance, constitutional amendments, and anti-China demonstrations. He found that:

> (t)he development of civil society is now coming to the fore of Vietnam's politics. It has become the space for counter-hegemonic discourse and for intellectuals to mobilize support. (…) Power has been increasingly contested throughout civil society. They represent ideas and values in governance about democratic freedoms, transparency, accountability, and meaningful participation. These critical issues in governance keep being highlighted throughout different areas and times, revealing increasingly complex aspects of struggles of ideas and values in state–civil society relations. They serve as fundamental platforms for the changing dynamics of governance in Vietnam.
>
> *(Bui 2013: 93)*

Between 2013 and 2016, Wischermann and his Vietnamese colleagues carried out another study on Vietnamese civil society organizations in Hanoi and Ho Chi Minh City (Wischermann *et al.* 2016a). In their strictly exploratory study, they asked whether civil society and civil society organizations are supporters of or obstacles to the processes of democratization in Vietnam. To answer this question, they applied a functionalist and relational approach that has key characteristics in common with Bui Hai Thiem's Gramsci-inspired understanding of civil society and civil society organizations.

Since the results from this survey are laid out in Chapter 8: Vietnam, here, it will suffice to add a very brief summary of the most important results from this survey:

- Seen from the perspective of intra-organizational decision-making processes, most Vietnamese civil society organizations are hierarchically structured, if not organized in an authoritarian way. In the sense of Tocqueville, they are not "schools of democracy."
- Most Vietnamese civil society organizations engaged in the welfare provision sector, either willingly or unwillingly, helped foster the foundations of authoritarianism. They could be called obstacles to further democratization. Some NGOs can be called *potential* supporters of further democratization.
- The interviewed business and professionals' organizations are not agents of further democratization. These organizations help to secure existing power structures and those in power and can be assessed as being obstacles to further democratization.
- In the policy field of gender equality, women's rights, and the rights of sexual minorities, the interviewed mass organization can be called an obstacle to further democratization. By contrast, some NGOs that are active in this policy field can be considered supporters of further democratization.

Overall, there is no *one* type of civil society organization that, without further qualification, can be called a supporter of *or* an obstacle to further democratization.

In summary, from a theoretical point of view, the studies for which the most important results have been described above show that civil society and civil society organizations are better understood from an action- and actor-related perspective. In such approaches, what civil society *is* and what civil society organizations are *doing* are not determined beforehand with misleading normative definitions and assumptions. In analyses of civil society and civil society organizations, there are additional advantages to a relational understanding, as well as the application of Gramsci's idea of civil society. Varying relationships between the state and civil society are empirically explored, and various contributions of civil society and civil society organizations toward supporting and/or weakening authoritarian state power and hindering and/or furthering the processes of democratizations are empirically examined. There is much more to explore than merely a state–civil society dichotomy, and not all civil society organizations are forces of democratization. Insofar as these analyses imply normative assumptions, these are reflected critically as part of the theory and verified in empirical research.

Conclusion

The history of civil society theory shows that theoretical and research-related problems accompany its development and application. The application of a simplified and realm-based definition and understanding of civil society applied to civil society and civil society operating under authoritarian rule indicates such theoretical and research-related problems. Theoretically, well-informed empirical research on civil society under authoritarian rule offers the advantage of being able to address and solve at least some of these problems.

As the Vietnam-related studies on civil society under authoritarian rule suggest, there are some alternative approaches that have demonstrated their theoretical soundness and research-related viability. We can learn from such approaches and case studies, respectively, that it is reasonable to take a relational perspective and to start from the assumption that civil society and civil society organizations are "polyvalent" (Kössler 1994). We agree with Berman, who suggests that civil society and civil society organizations should not be considered "an undisputed good, but a politically neutral multiplier—neither inherently 'good' nor 'bad,' but dependent on the wider political environment and the values of those who control it" (Berman 2003: 266). Furthermore, we can learn from these studies that civil society and civil society organizations can be not only supporters of but also forces that weaken such regimes and that they can even be both at the same time. Moreover, civil society theory and research will benefit from considering the perspectives of various actors on civil society and civil society organizations operating under such difficult conditions. Actors' understanding of civil society and civil society organizations corrects and, in many ways, enriches the understanding of researchers. In the given case of Vietnam, actors prefer ways other than a simplified and realm-based understanding of civil society and civil society organizations (see Chapter 8: Vietnam). This suggests that civil society and civil society organizations exist only in the sense of a plurality of historically and societally varying forms and contents.

Finally, though we criticize specific definitions of civil society and various concepts of civil society that are closely related to liberal or neoliberal ideas, we do not argue that the research on civil society in Vietnam has shown that civil society theory has to be stripped of its liberal or neoliberal sources. The individual and collective self-determination and autonomy of civil society actors can form a substantial presumption of civil society-related research, though within a set of changed theoretical assumptions that form the bedrock of an empirically well-informed and theoretically sound theory of civil society. In such a theory, theoretical concepts and normative assumptions should be reflected on critically and verified through empirical research.

Notes

1 Diamond characterizes civil society as:

> the realm of organized social life that is open, voluntary, self-generating, at least partially self-supporting, autonomous from the state, and bound by a legal order or a set of shared rules. It is distinct from "society" in that it involves citizens acting collectively in a public sphere to express their interests, passions, preferences, and ideas, to exchange information, to achieve collective goals, to make demands on the state, to improve the structure and functioning of the state and to hold state officials accountable. Civil society is an intermediary phenomenon, standing between the private sphere and the state.
>
> *(Diamond 1999: 221)*

Other definitions, for example, the one used by the London School of Economics Centre for Civil Society (2009), agree with Diamond in that civil society is "an arena of un-coerced collective action around shared interests, purposes and values"; "in theory, its institutional forms are distinct from those of state, family and market"; and, finally, civil society is populated by a variety of organizations. However, the Centre's obviously purposeful definition leaves out the assumption that civil society should be considered autonomous of the state, and it stresses that "in practice" the boundaries between the state, family, and economy are at least "complex, blurred and negotiated." Though this definition suits better the specifics of authoritarian regimes, it does not solve all the problems that come with a realm-based definition of civil society. I address these problems in the second section of this chapter.

2 In this chapter, I use the terms authoritarian regimes, authoritarian rule, autocracies, autocrats, and autocratic rulers interchangeably.

3 For an introduction to political science's debate on authoritarian regimes, see, for example, the introduction by and contributions to Croissant *et al.* (2015) and Brooker (2009) and contributions to APSA Comparative Democratization (2015).

4 Prezworski *et al.* (2000: 15), for example, conceive democracies as "regimes in which those who govern are selected through contested elections," whereas autocracies are "not democracies" (2000: 18).

5 Geddes differentiates between three forms of authoritarian rule (based on the question "Who rules?" rather than formal institutional characteristics): military rule, single-party rule, and personalist regimes; these forms can manifest themselves in combinations, as well (Geddes 1999: 121). Later, she added

monarchies and differentiations in military and party regime types. Others have built on her classification. Hadenius and Teorell (2007), for example, differentiate between monarchies, military regimes, and party regimes (although they leave out personalistic autocracies).

6 Levitzky and Way, for example, coined the term "competitive authoritarianism" for regimes in which "formal democratic institutions are (…) the principal means of obtaining and exercising political power," but where incumbents violate those rules so often and to an extent that those regimes fail minimum standards for democracy (Levitzky and Way 2002: 52).

7 This section draws on the research by Wischermann (2010: 5–12).

8 Here, I refer to not only Diamond's (1999) widely used definition but also the LSE Centre for Civil Society's definition cited above (see Note 1).

9 This understanding of specifics of civil society action (CSA) derives from not only various sociologists' (such as Parsons and Giddens) works but also many political scientists' (such as Offe) and philosophers' (e.g., Habermas) analyses of modern capitalist and other societies. For details, see Gosewinkel and Rucht (2004: 41–48) and Wischermann (2010: 10, n. 8).

10 With respect to the former, Wischermann *et al.* assume that the state aims to exert control over the society by providing welfare services and, in this respect, the state utilizes civil society organizations (e.g., in order to reach specific groups of people living in urban "problem areas"). With respect to the latter, the authors assume that the state invites carefully selected civil society organizations representing specific social strata to participate in policy formulation and decision-making processes, while it keeps those civil society organizations away from the places where the "real" decisions are made (Wischermann *et al.* 2016a: 61f.).

11 More specifically, Gramsci, in contrast to Marx, stressed the role and function of specific parts of the superstructure for maintaining and/or changing existing power positions and power relations of classes and social groups. With respect to civil society, his intention was to analyze the role and function of private organizations and the political society (=state); its contribution to and role in achieving, preserving, and eventually changing forms of domination (here, Gramsci's famous dictum of "hegemony armored with coercion" crosses one's mind); and how all these are closely related to the economic structure as the final determining instance, though this structure may assert its influence in different ways at various times in history.

12 This argument mirrors Walzer's "paradox of the civil-society argument," which says, "that a democratic civil society seems to require a democratic state, and a strong civil society seems to require a strong and responsive state" (Foley and Edwards 1996: 48).

Suggested readings

APSA Comparative Democratization. 2015. Reconzeptualizing Authoritarianism, online. Electronic document, www.ned.org/apsa-cd-newsletter-reconceptualizing-authoritarianism/, accessed November 14, 2016.

Croissant, Aurel, Steffen Kailitz, Patrick Koellner, and Stefan Wurster, eds. 2015. *Comparing Autocracies in the Early Twenty-first Century, Volume 1: Unpacking Autocracies—Explaining Similarity and Difference.* London and New York: Routledge.

Croissant, Aurel, Steffen Kailitz, Patrick Koellner, and Stefan Wurster, eds. 2015. *Comparing Autocracies in the Early Twenty-first Century, Volume 2: The Performance and Persistence of Autocracies.* London and New York: Routledge.

Perinova, Marie. 2005. *Civil Society in Authoritarian Regimes: The Analysis of China, Burma and Vietnam.* Thesis, Department of Political Science, Lund University. Electronic document, https://lup.lub.lu.se/luur/download?func=downloadFile&recordOId=1330580&fileOId=1330581, accessed December 28, 2016.

Stenner, Karen. 2005. *The Authoritarian Dynamic.* Cambridge: Cambridge University Press.

Warren, Mark. 2001. *Democracy and Association.* Princeton, NJ: Princeton University Press.

Wischermann, Jörg, Bettina Bunk, Jasmin Lorch, and Patrick Köllner. 2016b. Do Associations Support Authoritarian Rule? Tentative Answers from Algeria, Mozambique, and Vietnam. *GIGA Working Paper* No. 295, November 2016. Hamburg: GIGA. Electronic document, www.giga-hamburg.de/en/publication/do-associations-support-authoritarian-rule-algeria-mozambique-vietnam, accessed December 27, 2016.

Website

IDCAR: International Diffusion and Cooperation of Authoritarian Regimes, https://idcar.giga-hamburg.de/network.

A research network of scholars investigating authoritarian regimes; promoting exchange of ideas, analysis of methodological approach, and establishing a research agenda.

References

APSA Comparative Democratization. 2015. Reconzeptualizing Authoritarianism, online. Electronic document, www.ned.org/apsa-cd-newsletter-reconceptualizing-authoritarianism/, accessed November 14, 2016.

Beckman, Björn. 2001. Civil Society and Alliance Politics. In *Civil Society and Authoritarianism in the Third World: A Conference Book*. Björn Beckman, Eva Hansson, and Anders Sjögren, eds. Pp. 49–68. Stockholm: Department of Political Science, Stockholm University.

Berman, Sheri. 2003. Islamism, Revolution, and Civil Society. *Perspectives on Politics* 2: 257–72. Electronic document, www.carnegieendowment.org/pdf/files/berman.pdf, accessed December 28, 2016.

Brownlee, Jason. 2007. *Authoritarianism in the Age of Democratization*. New York: Cambridge University Press.

Brooker, Paul. 2009. *Non-Democratic Regimes*. New York: Palgrave Macmillan.

Bui, Hai Thiem. 2013. The Development of Civil Society and Dynamics of Governance in Vietnam's One Party Rule. *Global Change, Peace & Security* 25(1): 77–93.

Croissant, Aurel, Steffen Kailitz, Patrick Koellner, and Stefan Wurster. 2015. Introduction: The Performance and Persistence of Autocracies. In *Comparing Autocracies in the Early Twenty-first Century, Volume 2: The Performance and Persistence of Autocracies*. Aurel Croissant, Steffen Kailitz, Patrick Koellner, and Stefan Wurster, eds. Pp. 1–18. London and New York: Routledge.

Diamond, Larry. 1999. *Developing Democracy: Toward Consolidation*. Baltimore, MD: Johns Hopkins University Press.

Foley, Michael, and Bob Edwards. 1996. The Paradox of Civil Society. *The Journal of Democracy* 7(3): 38–52.

Gandhi, Jennifer. 2008. *Political Institutions under Dictatorship*. Cambridge and New York: Cambridge University Press.

Geddes, Barbara. 1999. What Do We Know About Democratization After Twenty Years? *Annual Review of Political Science* 2: 115–144.

Glasius, Marlies. 2015. Introducing The Symposium and a Research Agenda. *Comparative Democratization* 13(2): 1–8.

Göbel, Christian. 2011. Authoritarian Consolidation. *European Political Science* 11: 176–190.

Gosewinkel, Dieter, and Dieter Rucht. 2004. "History Meets Sociology": Zivilgesellschaft als Prozess ["History Meets Sociology": Civil Society as Process]. In *Zivilgesellschaft—National und Transnational, WZB-Jahrbuch 2003 [Civil Society—National and Transnational, Berlin Social Science Center Yearbook 2003]*. Dieter Gosewinkel, Dieter Rucht, Wolfgang van den Daele, and Jürgen Kocka, eds. Pp. 29–60. Berlin: Sigma Verlag (in German).

Gosewinkel, Dieter. 2003. Zivilgesellschaft—eine Erschließung des Themas von den Grenzen her [*Civil Society—Developing the Topic from its Boundaries*]. Discussion Paper Nr. SP IV 2003–505. Berlin: Wissenschaftszentrum Berlin (in German).

Hadenius, Axel, and Jan Teorell. 2007. Pathways from Authoritarianism. *Journal of Democracy* 18(1): 143–157.

Hannah, Joseph. 2007. *Local Non-Government Organizations in Vietnam: Development, Civil Society and State–Society Relations*. PhD thesis, University of Washington.

Howell, Judith. 2007. Gender and Civil Society: Time for Cross-Border Dialogue. *Social Politics: International Studies in Gender, State & Society* 14(4): 415–436.

Keane, John. 2001. Global Civil Society?. In *Global Civil Society*. Helmut Anheier, Marlies Glasius, and Mary Kaldor, eds. Pp. 23–47. Oxford: Oxford University Press.

Kerkvliet, Ben T. 2003. Introduction: Grappling with Organizations and the State in Contemporary Vietnam. In *Getting Organized in Vietnam. Moving in and Around the Socialist State*. Benedict J. Kerkvliet, Russell Heng Hiang-Khng, David Koh Wee Hock, eds. Pp. 1–24. Singapore: Institute of Southeast Asian Studies.

Kössler, Reinhardt. 1994. *Postkoloniale Staaten: Elemente eines Bezugsrahmens* [*Post-Colonial States: A Conceptual Framework*]. Hamburg: Deutsches Übersee Institut (in German).

Levitzky, Steven, and Lucan A. Way 2002. The Rise of Competitive Authoritarianism. *Journal of Democracy* 13(2): 51–65.

Linz, Juan J. 2000. *Totalitarian and Authoritarian Regimes: With a New Introduction*. Boulder, CO: Lynne Rienner Publishers.

London School of Economics Centre for Civil Society. 2009. *What is Civil Society?* Electronic document, www.webarchive.org.uk/wayback/archive/20100820110531/www.lse.ac.uk/collections/CCS/introduction/what_is_civil_society.htm, accessed November 14, 2016.

Mann, Michael. 1984. The Autonomous Power of the State: Its Origins, Mechanisms and Results. *Archives européennes de sociologie* [*European Archives of Sociology*] 25: 185–213.

Marr, David. 1994. *The Vietnam Communist Party and Civil Society*. Paper presented at the Vietnam Update conference: Doi Moi, The State and Civil Society, Australian National University, November 10–11.

Norlund, Irene, ed. 2006. *The Emerging Civil Society: An Initial Assessment of Civil Society in Vietnam*. Hanoi: CIVICUS, VIDS, SNV, UNDP. Electronic document, www.undp.org/content/dam/vietnam/docs/.../22110_3202_Civicuc_report__E_.pdf, accessed December 28, 2016.

Perinova, Marie. 2005. *Civil Society in Authoritarian Regimes: The Analysis of China, Burma and Vietnam*. Thesis, Department of Political Science, Lund University. Electronic document, https://lup.lub.lu.se/luur/download?func=downloadFile&recordOId=1330580&fileOId=1330581, accessed December 28, 2016.

Przeworski, Adam, Michael E. Alvarez, Jose A. Cheibub, and Fernando Limongi. 2000. *Democracy and Development: Political Institutions and Well-Being in the World, 1950–1990*. Cambridge: Cambridge University Press.

Rigby, Thomas Henry. 1990. *The Changing Soviet System: Mono-Organizational Socialism from its Origins to Gorbachev's Restructuring*. Aldershot: Edward Elgar Publishing.

Sauer, Brigitte. 2011. "Only paradoxes to offer?" Feministische Demokratie- und Repräsentationstheorie in der "Postdemokratie" ["Only Paradoxes to Offer?" Feminist Democracy and Representation Theory in the Era of Post-Democracy]. *Österreichische Zeitschrift für Politikwissenschaft* [*Austrian Journal of Political Science*] 40 (2): 125–138 (in German).

Schedler, Andreas. 2009. The New Institutionalism in the Study of Authoritarian Regimes. *Totalitarismus und Demokratie* [*Totalitarianism and Democracy*] 6: 323–340.

Stenner, Karen. 2005. *The Authoritarian Dynamic*. Cambridge: Cambridge University Press.

Uphoff, Norman, and Anirudh Krishna. 2004. Civil Society and Public Sector Institutions: More than a Zero-Sum Relationship. *Public Administration and Development* 24(4): 357–372.

Thayer, Carlyle A. 2009. Vietnam and the Challenge of Political Civil Society. *Contemporary Southeast Asia* 31(1): 1–27.

Votsos, Theo. 2001. *Der Begriff der Zivilgesellschaft bei Antonio Gramsci* [*Gramsci's Concept of Civil Society*]. Hamburg: Argument Verlag (in German).

Warren, Mark. 2001. *Democracy and Association*. Princeton, NJ: Princeton University Press.

Wells-Dang, Andrew. 2011. *Informal Pathbreakers: Civil Society Networks in China and Vietnam*. PhD thesis, University of Birmingham.

Wischermann, Jörg. 2010. Civil Society Action and Governance in Vietnam. Selected Findings from an Empirical Survey. *Journal of Current Southeast Asian Affairs* 2: 3–40. Electronic document, www.giga-hamburg.de/en/publication/civil-society-action-and-governance-in-vietnam-selected-findings-from-an-empirical, accessed December 27, 2016.

Wischermann, Jörg. 2011. Governance and Civil Society Action in Vietnam: Changing the Rules form Within—Potentials and Limits. *Asian Politics & Policy* 3(3): 383–411.

Wischermann, Jörg, The Cuong Bui, and Thi Viet Dang Phuong, 2016a. Vietnamese Civic Organisations: Supporters of or Obstacles to Further Democratisation? Results from an Empirical Survey. *Journal of Current Southeast Asian Affairs* 35(2): 57–88. Electronic document, https://journals.sub.uni-hamburg.de/giga/jsaa/article/view/954/961, accessed December 27, 2016.

Wischermann, Jörg, Bettina Bunk, Jasmin Lorch, and Patrick Köllner. 2016b. Do Associations Support Authoritarian Rule? Tentative Answers from Algeria, Mozambique, and Vietnam. *GIGA Working Paper* No. 295 November 2016. Hamburg: GIGA. Electronic document, www.giga-hamburg.de/en/publication/do-associations-support-authoritarian-rule-algeria-mozambique-vietnam, accessed December 27, 2016.

24

THE THIRD SECTOR

Ruth Phillips

Diversity and distinctiveness: positioning the third sector in Asia

Given that two-thirds of the world's population is in Asia, to generalize about it in any way will result in an inadequate analysis and will produce claims of such breadth that it will fail to represent the extensive cultural, geographical, political, and economic diversity that exists in the collection of regions described as Asia. Therefore, in this chapter, rather than attempting to discuss all of Asia, specific Asian countries will be the focus in the hope that it will at least provide some insight into the presence and role of the third sector and the kind of research that has been conducted in this field. This chapter will aim to provide an overview of the wide literature and research on the third sector, which has mostly been conducted in South Asia, South East Asia, and East Asia. It will also recognize that the functions of the third sector operate on three distinct levels, at a grass-roots community level, at a national level, and at an international level. The international level can, like many groups of actors, be viewed as operating regionally or globally, and often there are extensive overlapping boundaries amongst these actors.

By writing "the third sector in Asia," an implicit binary is established between the East and West or North and South, suggesting a possible orientalist perspective of "the Other" (Connell 2007; Said 1978). It is not the intention of this chapter to view or even construct the third sector in Asia as a curiosity that is distinct from that in more familiar Western research and understandings of the third sector, but rather to build knowledge about a less referenced domain within the Western literature. I, therefore, wish to acknowledge my perspective as that of a white, Euro-centric (albeit from the South, geographically) scholar, who has simply had the privilege to be engaged with and become more knowledgeable about the third sector in Asia through my own research and academic role and as part of a network of researchers in the Asia-Pacific region. As an academic in Sydney, Australia, I have had the privilege of supervising many research students from countries in Asia, including Japan, Taiwan, South Korea, Thailand, and Indonesia. This research relationship allows particular insight into the operation of the third sector in those various countries that have allowed me deeper insight into the social and political interests of emerging and well-developed civil societies in the Asian region. My own third sector research, beginning with my PhD nearly twenty years ago, has also facilitated continued knowledge building about our geographic neighbors. My research has been related to three areas of third sector organizations: welfare, women, and environment. This has included interest in organizations that provide social or welfare services and those engaged in advocacy and social and environmental change.

My wider association with the third sector in Asia has been mostly under the auspices of the International Society for Third Sector Research (ISTR), which holds a large international conference every two years, mostly in the Northern hemisphere, and an Asia-Pacific ISTR Conference held in the region. Through attending and participating in the academic committees of these conferences, I have witnessed some significant developments in third sector research, particularly in China, Japan, Indonesia, South Korea, and Taiwan, and I have also had the opportunity to gather information about third sector research in India, Nepal, Malaysia, Thailand, Bangladesh, and the Philippines. Asian countries that have been less visible in these arenas are Vietnam, Cambodia, North Korea, Myanmar, Sri Lanka, Pakistan, Mongolia, smaller countries such as Brunei and Singapore, and South Asian countries such as Afghanistan, Iraq, and the countries of the Middle East that are technically in Asia. This does not mean of course that there is an absence of a third sector or third sector researchers in these countries, and some of that research will be acknowledged in this chapter. Although generalizations about Asia will be avoided, there can be some distinctions and parallels made on the basis of how the state relates to the third sector and the third sector to the state, and therefore, due to my deeper familiarity with pluralistic democracy, some comparisons will be made in terms of how the state has exercised power over and power with the third sector. This relates particularly to states that have undergone substantial transformations in governance and shifted toward more open, freer, social and/or economic structures.

What is the third sector?

Although not universally used and a highly debated term, the "third sector" (or as it is increasingly termed, civil society) is generally understood to be not-for-profit, often largely voluntary, entities that are not part of the state and not part of the market; in relative terms the state is seen as the first sector and the market as the second sector, and the third sector is made of "intermediate organizations" (Bransden, van de Donk, and Putters 2005; Najam 2000; Wagner 2012). Many may object to such a hierarchy that places at a lower level the thousands of organizations and services that function in non-state and non-profit ways to advocate, protect, and provide services to address the entire range of human needs, as well as act as guardians and advocates for animals and the natural environment. However, what is useful about the third sector paradigm is that it is placed between the market (the individual) and the state (the collective) and adds depth and significance to the relationship between the state and a sense of holistic rather that technical citizenship (Bransden *et al.* 2005; Najam 2000; Wagner 2012). What is also very evident across all societies with the third sector is that there is much blurring of boundaries between the state, the third sector, and the market, particularly in relation to any form of service delivery. Although, if the wider relationship to large business corporations and their corporate social responsibility (CSR) is taken into account, the blurring of the market boundary can be seen to apply in a more political and resources related sense than in service delivery. This has been an increasing complication for the third sector since the rise and dominance of neo-liberalism that has encouraged and even demanded a shift away from reliance on the state for welfare and other human services and a greater role for the market in the delivery of all services (Goodwin and Phillips 2015). It has also demanded the adoption of market-oriented managerialism and the rise of market-oriented mechanisms for self-funding of third sector organizations such as social enterprise and microfinancing—two areas of significant growth in poverty programs within the third sector across Asia.

Given the scope of what it does, the third sector is extremely diverse and, depending on the context, can include major players in the politics, economy, and society in which they exist. The increasingly major role that third sector organizations play in the global context sees them contributing to global social, labor, and environmental policies and acting as key vehicles for social change through social movement networks that have a wide diversity of agendas and causes. They also work in partnerships with states, corporations, and international institutions such as the United Nations (UN), the World Health Organisation (WHO), and the United Nations Environmental Program (UNEP). The international dimension of the third sector has been a powerful contemporary influence on what third sector organizations are able to do in Asia, as they are linked to social change and developmental and environmental movements that provide both a global mission and greater access to resources through global networks of international non-governmental organizations (NGOs). This has been particularly important for countries that have endured autocratic state regimes in the last half century, where a less than democratic form of governance would not allow public participation, the influence of individuals, the third sector in the development of policy, advocacy for change, nor unfettered access by international NGOs to carry out development and humanitarian activities. South Korea, Indonesia, Vietnam, and China, although at very different stages of democratic development, are good examples of recently evolving political environments where a third sector has become more evident and active (Schak and Hudson 2003). This evolution of freedoms for citizens has been linked to a characterization of an Asian third sector by some researchers. For example, David Schak and Wayne Hudson observed:

> East Asian states were sufficiently strong and centralized that no group in society could challenge their hegemony. In South-East Asia there was only a series of weak, short-lived city-states, and the transitory nature of states prevent the creation of a civil society. Equally, traditional Asian states often did not undertake roles undertaken by states in Europe. For example, they never implemented or seldom attempted a general provision of public welfare ... with the exception of Japan.
>
> *(Schak and Hudson 2003: 3)*

A growing number of researchers from Asian countries also argue for a unique understanding of the third sector in their countries, to see it as reflective of the political, social, and economic transformations the country has been through in recent history (Azra 2003; Choi and Yang 2011; Kim 2003). For example, Sang Ok Choi and Seung-Bum Yang (2011) put a strong case that third sector organizations in South Korea should not be compared with their European counterparts due to particular characteristics of rapid growth and strong links to the relatively recent development of a democratic society. They argued that, "nonprofit organizations in Korea have developed so much faster than those in other countries that they became core players to substantially influence Korean society" (Choi and Yang 2011: 52). They then proceeded to develop a typology of Korean third sector organizations that seem to be comparable to US-based state/third sector relations. For example, compared to the USA's hierarchical integration, Korean third sector organizations are of a small size, have limited organizational capacity, and are concerned with civil society, social services, culture, economy, and environmental issues (Choi and Yang 2011: 57). They also point out the unique role of the third sector in South Korea in challenging the dominant state-market relationship that had emerged under prior military regimes. For example, the Citizens' Coalition for Economic Justice forced the issue of real estate speculation onto the public agenda and challenged public support for "chaebols (large, conglomerate, family-controlled firms ... characterized by strong ties with government agencies) reform," a movement initiated by the People's Solidarity for Participatory Democracy in response to the government's relatively weak action during the Asian financial crisis in the late 1990s (Choi and Yang 2011: 58). South Korea's third sector grew organically, although heavily influenced by external, international social movements such as human rights, the women's movements, and environmental movements. As Kyungja Jung (2014) points out, South Korea had a clearly identifiable national women's movement that was not seen as an imposition by the West (as has been claimed in other Asian countries), and that was rooted in community-based third sector organizations formed by women in response to domestic and sexual violence against women.

However, in post-colonial states (meaning those colonized by Western countries rather than Asian neighbors) in Asia, the international connections to third sector organizations, particularly international NGOs that are based in their prior colonizer states, raise complex questions related to the deep impact of prior colonization (Choudry 2013). Aziz Choudry clearly articulated this analysis when he observed that:

> While numerous scholars and political commentators celebrated the ascendancy of NGOs and the rise of "global civil society," more radical critiques charged that the environmental, aid, and development, and advocacy NGOs, which dominated this milieu and their campaigns were attempting to humanize capitalist exploitation. Some take the critique further, arguing that through their refusal to confront ongoing colonial practices, these NGOs are themselves behaving as colonizers.
>
> *(Choudry 2013: 25)*

This points to an increasing post-colonial analysis of how international NGOs perpetuate colonial impositions on cultures and economies that have been particularly evident in third sector research in African states, and also in Asia (Bernal and Grewal 2014), which should be acknowledged in this discussion. However, because there is not an even spread of post-colonial resistance or experience across Asia, this will not be a specific focus in this chapter. The main focus of this chapter will therefore be on research about the role of national or local organizations, networks with international NGOs, and the recognition that the third sector, particularly in the delivery of social provision or human services via charitable organizations, has a long and deeply entwined history and presence in some countries in Asia. According to Samuil Hasan (2008), two of the largest countries in Asia, India and China, have histories of third sector organizations going back a thousand years or so. Thomas Davies (2013), in his history of transnational civil society, has also documented historical records of countries such as Egypt, India, Japan and, collectively, East Asia establishing and forming transnational third sector networks since the mid- to late nineteenth century.

Research on the third sector in Asia

Due to its Eurocentric and North American origins as a research field, third sector studies have been slower to give prominence to research in Asia, particularly to research done by Asian researchers. This is not to suggest that there has not been a history of research on what NGOs and volunteer or charitable organizations have been doing or have contributed throughout Asia; rather, due to the highly interdisciplinary range of research interests in this field, it does not compare with the history of more focused explorations of the third sector in Europe and the USA. English language third sector research centers and organizations that have promoted this field have produced significant research on other parts of the world such as Latin America and

Africa and local scholars publishing in English emerged in those continents due to that focus. A similar process has been evident in the last two decades in Asian countries.

There have been diverse edited volumes in English about civil society or the third sector in Asia, particularly since the early 2000s. For example, sponsored by the Griffith University's key Centre for Ethics, Law, Justice and Governance, David Schak and Wayne Hudson (2003) edited a volume titled *Civil Society in Asia: In Search of Democracy and Development in Bangladesh*. The research published in this volume represents the wide interdisciplinarity of this field of research and, due to the Australian editors, it has a focus on Southeast and East Asia. As Schak and Hudson (2003) point out in the first chapter, this research focuses on the emergence of a more visible and important civil society in light of the impact of the Asian financial crisis and its impact on politics across the region. The collection includes researchers from the disciplines of politics, sociology, anthropology, and business in Taiwan, Malaysia, Thailand, South Korea, Indonesia, Singapore, the Philippines, Australia, and the USA. The key themes in the research are based around the relatively recent development of civil society in Asia, the impact that civil society organizations had on processes of democratization, the nature of "Asian" civil society, and whether there is a contrast to European civil society.

An important book produced by the third sector field, Samiul Hasan and Jenny Onyx's (2008) edited volume *Comparative Third Sector Governance in Asia: Structure Process and Political Economy* was the result of a research project funded by the Ford Foundation and supported by the Asia Pacific Philanthropy Information Network. The research project had a key objective of extending and consolidating "a network of scholars in Asian countries with an interest in the third sector so that they can act as advisers and offer training programs in governance to third sector organizations in their countries" (Hasan and Onyx 2008: vi). The research project not only provided an opportunity for overviews of the state of the third sector in several Asian countries such as China, India, Indonesia, and Vietnam from local third sector researchers, but it also presented research on historical, legal, social, and organizational understandings and theorizations of the third sector across Asia. Since this wave of research, there has been rapid growth in the breadth of third sector research in Asia, particularly in China.

Owing to its reputation of having one of the largest populations of NGOs in the world, research on the third sector in the Philippines has been a focus of many non-Philippine scholars. According to Gerald Clarke (1998), NGOs proliferated in the Philippines in the late 1980s through to the late 1990s and they had a crucial role in wider Philippine politics as well as in resistance to state policies and objectives, however, the proliferation related primarily to the burst of development activity across the country at that time. Typical of third sector research in the Philippines two decades ago was a focus on activist NGOs against mining and for Indigenous rights. A significant amount of research in the Philippines focused on the core issue of mining and minerals exploration, as this area brought key activist groups together, those representing Indigenous people's rights and protection of traditional lands and sites and environmentalist organizations. This is well represented in Raymond Bryant's (2005) study on environmental NGOs of the late 1990s, where he conducted cases studies on two core Philippine NGOs—the Haribon Foundation and the Philippine Association for Intercultural Development (PAFID)—both renowned for their work on environmental and indigenous rights. The Haribon Foundation was established in 1972 and continues to be a core conservation and environmental protection NGO in the Philippines. PAFID was established in 1967 but does not currently have an active profile. However, more recent research about environmental NGOs and activism in the Philippines is concerned with the powerful impact of climate change and consequent disaster management (Brower, Magno, and Dilling 2014; Gera 2016). In an exploration of the key role of environmental NGOs in relation to climate change and disasters work together with the state, Weena Gera argues:

> that the country's institutional framework for public participation is decisively under-
> mined by the lack of systematic public deliberation and consolidation among civil
> society groups. This renders them overwhelmed by patrimonial power structures pre-
> dominating in decisions over the boundaries of involvement in environmental
> governance.
>
> *(Gera 2016: 502)*

Gera's core argument is toward strengthening and consolidating the role of Philippine NGOs in environmental governance. This is a key theme in third sector research in the Philippines due to the critical role third sector organizations play in representing the complex diversity of a country made up of some 14,000 islands and extremely diverse social and cultural communities. A body of research about the human service third sector organizations in the Philippines that reflects a unique focus is Ledivina Cariño and Dolores Gaffud's (2007) edited collection on the third sector in the Philippines. This publication presents findings of local researchers on the role and operation of third sector organizations in the Philippines and their long history and deep involvement in filling the gaps of a very limited welfare state. Third sector research interests in the Philippines represents a general profile of key areas that are central to the Asian third sector development and the role of and relationship with the state and environmental and social welfare governance, as can be seen in the discussion below in relation to other Asian countries.

One of the first English language collections of third sector research in China by Chinese scholars was published in Yuwen Li's edited volume *NGOs in China and Europe: Comparisons and Contrasts* (2011). The China-based research in this book was supported via the Netherlands Embassy in Beijing in its project supporting a study and promotion of social organization development in China (Li 2011). The China research in this volume covers a wide breadth of legal, state, international, and community based NGO relations and demonstrates the early stages of growth in scholarship based on third sector research in China. However, wider third sector scholarship in China is increasingly evident in peer-reviewed journals. For example, in 2016, the first special issue of the journal *VOLUNTAS* was entirely dedicated to China-based research. This issue mostly focuses on citizenship and civil society in China, but includes other research papers that report research on issues such as the growth and status of grass-roots organizations (Zhou 2016); NGO service contracting and development; organization and growth of HIV/AIDS organizations; student volunteering in Hong Kong; faith based organizations; foundations; and strategic alliances with cooperatives (Brandsen and Simsa 2016).

It is arguable that in some Asian countries, the rise of social enterprise has been seen as a solution to the failure of market mechanisms such as employment and has been fully supported by states as a means of addressing areas of social policy failure, particularly as regards to employment and training policies and poverty alleviation. For example, although initially an initiative of third sector organizations in South Korea, the government instituted social enterprise into law in 2006 to facilitate it as a system of addressing unemployment and social exclusion of "specific categories of persons such as women, older workers, low-skilled workers and migrants" by creating a social services market where social enterprises became a key delivery mechanism (Bidet and Eum 2011: 75–76). Another dominant market orientation of the third sector in Asia is microfinance; as a means of alleviating poverty, it has become a highly favored form of "empowerment" and has been focused primarily on women in development and gender equality programs. This has been a particularly big program in India and other South Asian states and has therefore been subject to extensive third sector research (Hunt and Kasynathan 2001; Karim 2014; Salam and Naher 2014). Juliette Hunt and Nalini Kasynathan (2001) found in their research on India that such a deep association between microcredit/microfinance and development programs had emerged that:

> communities have come to expect to be offered credit as an essential part of the development package. Some NGOs in South Asia find it difficult to sustain group-based development programmes without the provision of credit, and some large NGOs have at times deliberately tried to encroach on community groups set up by smaller NGOs, by offering them loans.
>
> *(Hunt and Kasynathan 2001: 43)*

From a broader perspective, Durgam Rajasekhar (2000) had documented a history of "NGOs" in India, which is an overview of the interests, political engagement, and role and nature of the third sector from before the end of colonization up to the late 1990s. He points out that in India, the early beginnings of the third sector saw a focus on charitable poverty work and partnerships with Christian missionaries and the state, with a rapid growth in the number of organizations in the 1970s associated particularly with development programs in partnership with the state that then, the 1980s, saw a distinction between charitable approaches and those with a more political structural agenda and the growth of a strong grass-roots NGO movement (Rajasekhar 2000: 6–7). More recent research on NGOs in India has been mostly related to their role in development and to the rapid and massive growth in the number NGOs. Debiprasad Mishra, Saswata Biswas, and Shiladitya Roy (2005) indicated that the best estimates within India suggest that there were between 25,000 and 30,000 in 2005 and that most of those emerged between 1985 and 1995.

The widespread growth in local third sector researchers conducting research within their own country contexts in Asia has produced a profoundly important body of knowledge of the roles, functions, and impact of third sector organizations. This is, in part, due to the growth of the role of the third sector in relation to the state, particularly in the participation in human services. In reference to China, for example, Lester Salamon, a world leader in third sector research, observed that: "nonprofits are occupying sizable arenas in which government action has been lagging and where nonprofits are finding space to operate" (Salamon 2015: 2153). Third sector/state relations is also the focus of Chinese scholars, particularly in relation to transformations in active citizenship via the third sector (Yuanfeng 2015; Zhou 2016) and the impact of external international NGOs (Junkui 2011).

However, explorations of the less than independent status of third sector organizations have also been an important topic of inquiry. For example, Akihiro Ogawa's (2009) in-depth action research study on third sector organizations in Tokyo demonstrated a lack of distinction between third sector organizations and the state, and how the values of the state governed the institutional and social operations of third sector organizations. Therefore, he described civil society in Japan in the twenty first century as having failed due to its lack of independence from national state agendas. Moreover, Minho Lee, in research conducted under a research branch of the national South Korean government, found that the funding of and administrative relationships with local third sector organizations by local government was stifling the growth of the nonprofit sector in South Korea due to a form of resource co-dependency (Lee 2008: 112). In contrast, more recent research by Millie Creighton (2015) explores how a grass-roots movement of third sector organizations against the state's desire to delete Japan's important post-war Article 9 renunciation of war and militarism, organized and fought to maintain the status quo.

This included extending membership and new networks of organizations beyond Japanese shores within and beyond their Asian neighbors (Creighton 2015: 139–140). Creighton observed that these groups were also highly active and mobilized around the earthquake of 2011 and noted that:

> Save Article 9 groups were pivotal as already existing civil society groups of networking members that became immediate foci for discussion on the issues and enactment of citizen's benkyo-kaior "study groups" about the potential problems and hazards of nuclear energy usage.
>
> *(Creighton 2015: 138)*

Creighton's research demonstrated that a highly independent and activist third sector has also emerged in Japan.

Due to the dramatic shifts in the nature of the state in Indonesia from autocracy to democracy, there has been significant research on Indonesian NGOs and their relationship to the state. Yumasdaleni and Tanya Jakimow (2016) see this as an important context for contemporary research on the relationship between NGOs and what they describe as straddler organizations that are half state and half non-government agencies that operate as a means to extending development policies of the state. They made the following observation about the historical relationship between NGOs and the state in Indonesia:

> the last two decades has seen a radical shift from an authoritative regime that suppressed uncomfortable elements of civil society, to a democratic decentralized polity and a burgeoning NGO sector. The heyday of the Suharto regime in the 1970s was a time of proliferation of NGOs, … Suharto's initial hesitations with the sector, which he viewed as "latent elements of instability" … were quelled when he recognized the potential of NGOs to assist the state in the delivery of services. Select NGOs became partners in government development projects … The space afforded to NGOs did not, however, extend to the ability to criticize public policy or the government, and there remained … This started to change in the 1990s, which saw an increase in the number of NGOs … Many argue that the efforts of civil society actors' (including NGOs) promoting democratic values played an important role in the downfall of the Suharto government in 1998. Once the authoritarian government was removed, so too were the restrictions on citizen participation and free speech, enabling … NGOs' role in national development was further enhanced through government reforms of decentralization.
>
> *(Yumasdaleni and Jakimow 2016: 4–5)*

The narrative of the growth of evolving freedom of the third sector in Indonesia was also somewhat reflected in the research of Anthony Spires, Lin Tao, and Kin-man Chan on the growth of grass-roots organizations in three regions of China, where they found a strong preference of personal donors to support more politically radical groups that were not registered and were able to attract local volunteers and were seen by the researchers as "probably the single most unpredictable development factor for contemporary Chinese civil society" (Spires *et al.* 2014: 90) at a still nascent stage of China's third sector development.

Women and the third sector in Asia: research

In most Asian countries' policy agendas, strategies and services for women have been hard fought for, to achieve results from the work of third sector organizations. As the key focus of my own third sector research has been on women's NGOs, I would like to conclude this chapter with a discussion of research on the role of women's third sector organizations in Asia. In a global study of how gender equality was understood by women's NGOs, I found that there was a very lively and diverse group of organizations dedicated to addressing gender inequality and women's emancipation in Asia. This finding was based on survey responses from women's organizations across the breadth of Asia, including Israel, Lebanon, Palestine, Bangladesh, Cambodia, China, India, Indonesia, Japan, Malaysia, Nepal, the Philippines, Thailand, and South Korea (Phillips 2016). Although often supported by and networked with international women's NGOs or institutions such as the United Nations, the majority of women's NGOs are grassroots local or national organizations (Phillips 2015, 2016).

Research on third sector organizations that focus on women and services for women in Asia have been intensified by a global acceptance that to tackle many of the world's social problems, particularly those related to poverty, women must be the focus in both action and policy. This has been exemplified by the United Nations Millennium Development Goals (2000–2015) and the more recently announced Sustainable Development Goals that have specific goals on gender equality and maternal health and rely primarily on women's NGOs to implement the agendas of the goals (UNDP 2016).

Moreover, due to the essentially collectivist nature of women's movements, third sector organizations have been important vehicles for social change toward gender equality throughout Asia. This means that much of the research on women's movements has in fact been third sector research. For example, Jung's (2014) research on "Practicing Feminism in South Korea: The Women's Movement Against Sexual Violence" is essentially a study of voluntary women's organizations that developed services and performed advocacy for social policy change in South Korea. This is also the case in chapters of feminist research books on Japan by authors such as Nicola Piper (2001), Vera Mackie (2003), and Nami Otsuki (2011), where the role of women's third sector organizations as part of the women's movements is explored. Similarly, Paola Cagna and Nitya Rao (2016), in a cross-national study of the women's movement against violence toward women in China, India, and Indonesia, focused on the important role of third sector organizations in activism for legislative and social change. They concluded that:

> A strategy adopted across the three countries was channeling claims to the state through women's national machineries or commissions, which proved effective in building bridges between women's organisations and the executive and legislative bodies of the state.
>
> *(Cagna and Rao 2016: 284)*

Stephanie Bräuer's (2016) research on women's performance art and public interest advocacy organizations involved in anti-domestic violence campaigns in China is highly significant due to the activism being a tactical strategy for political protest in the oppressive political environment of the Chinese state. The activist performance art groups are a far cry from the kinds of more formal NGOs that often have some sort of state relationships, researched by Shen Guoqin (2011), where she traced the evolution of women's NGOs in China though three stages of development from the earliest period of 1978 to 1995, the second stage from 1995 to 2004, and the third from 2004 to 2011. The Beijing World Conference on Women in 1995 was a significant launch pad for women's NGOs in China and other parts of Asia, particularly given the substantial engagement with outside, international NGOs and feminist theories that enabled theoretical expansion beyond Marxist ideas of gender equality in China (Guoqin 2011: 101; Howell 2007: 20). Guoqin (2011) reported that after the Beijing conference, different types of women's NGOs began to emerge, including organizations involved in research, service, and advocacy, which were not related to state structures. Such NGOs reflected similar foci to those everywhere else in the world: women and work, women's health, women's legal centers, domestic violence shelters, and so on. She also noted that by the twenty-first century, relative to other NGOs in China, women's NGOs had undergone a relatively smooth process of development as their goals for gender equality and protection of women were in keeping with the state's objectives and also due to well established connections to international women's organizations (Guoqin 2011: 113). However, according to Guoqin, research within China has found at least two significant problems with Chinese women's NGOs. The first is that they tend to cater to advantaged groups of women and disadvantaged women rarely benefit from their activities, and the second is that they also struggle to gain legitimization with the state despite being tolerated by the government (Guoqin 2011: 115–116). Bräuer's (2016) more recent research confirms the lack of legitimization by the state, as despite twenty years of NGO activities raising the problem of domestic violence, the cause has not been supported by protective legislation by the state, resulting in the growth of a more radical protest movement in China organized by anti-domestic violence organizations.

The majority of third sector research about women's organizations relates to development and poverty and has focused on South Asian countries (Handy, Kassam, and Renade 2002; Hunt and Kasynathan 2001; Kabeer, Mahmud, and Isaza Castro 2012; Khan and Rahman 2016; Panday and Feldman 2015; Weiss 2014). Patrick Kilby, an Australian, has been a long-time development NGO researcher with a strong focus on women's NGOs in India and his book *NGOs in India: The Challenge of Women's Empowerment and Accountability* (2010) includes a report on detailed research on rural women's NGOs in India and their "empowerment programs." As with much research on Indian NGOs, the ever-changing and often intervening state has a very strong presence in Kilby's (2010) research. In particular, funding arrangements of rural women's NGOs were greatly affected by state policies to exclude external funding from international NGOs and directly fund programs as part of the government's poverty program albeit primarily to achieve better political support from rural voters (Kilby 2010: 46).

More recently, published feminist third sector research on NGOs in South Asia comes from key post-colonial analysis of imposed developmental systems such as microcredit. Lamia Karim's (2014) research on NGOs engaged in microcredit schemes targeting women in Bangladesh delivers three key analyses. They are that: "NGOs working with microcredit manipulate existing notions of Bangladeshi rural women's honor and shame" and via the pursuit of capitalist gains "violate local norms of cohesion and community"; microcredit has produced "unanticipated neoliberal subjects" such as the "female petty moneylender" and; that the development NGO as a "shadow state in Bangladesh is able to exercise tremendous control over the lives of the poor" including the neutralizing of dissenting voices (Karim 2014: 195). This analysis gets to the heart of a wider critique of how NGOs carry neoliberal agendas propagated by international institutions such as the International Monetary Fund and the UN to the detriment of local communities that would benefit much more from support of their own grass-roots organizations to ensure deep social and economic changes toward equality. This echoes the sentiments of the women's NGOs that were part of my research mentioned above that pinpointed the lack of progress toward genuine gender equality outcomes (Phillips 2015, 2016).

Conclusion

Despite a reluctance to generalize, there are some observations about the third sector in Asia that can be highlighted. The first is that the roles that third sector organizations play across Asia are not that different from the roles they play in other parts of the world. They are similarly engaged with social welfare services—some on behalf of the state and others due to the failure of the state. They are advocates for social change and the disadvantaged or excluded peoples, they fight for and educate on issues such as gender equality, indigenous rights, or social legal rights, they work toward saving and preserving the environment and threatened species, they are networked from the grass-roots to the global level, they engage and rely on volunteers, they are also engaged in and depend on philanthropy, and so on.

What is distinct perhaps from the Northern third sector is that they have often complex relations with the state, which have been heavily influenced by colonization, prevailing politics, or recent political history, and have had varying degrees of legitimacy in relation to the state. Post-colonial Asian countries colonized by Northern states have mostly experienced autocratic rule in the post-colonial period and this has imposed very clear constraints on the political freedom of the third sector in different periods of time. This has also been the case in countries such as China, South Korea, and Thailand, which had different types of major disruptions and historical continuities that have caused autocratic governance. The various types of state relations imply that there are trends across much of Asia of rapid growth in the number of NGOs or third sector organizations from the 1980s through to the 1990s, which has taken place due to two major factors: the first is the opening of doors to international NGOs in development or disaster responses and the second relates to processes of democratization or political and economic shifts that have created a more pluralistic society. It is also observable that even more recently, there has been a rapid growth in home-grown scholarship and research on the third sector, rather than the dominance of research on the third sector in Asia held by external scholars from the North.

Suggested readings

Brandsen, Taco, and Ruth Simsa. 2016. Civil Society, Nonprofit Organizations, and Citizenship in China: An Editorial Introduction to the China Issue. *VOLUNTAS: International Journal of Voluntary and Non-profit Organizations* 27(5): 2011–2020.
Hasan, Samuil, and Jenny Onyx. eds. 2008. *Comparative Third Sector Governance in Asia: Structure, Process, and Political Economy.* New York: Springer.
Ogawa, Akihiro. 2009. *The Failure of Civil Society? The Third Sector and the State in Contemporary Japan.* Albany, NY: State University of New York Press.
Schak, David C., and Wayne Hudson, eds. 2003. *Civil Society in Asia: In Search of Democracy and Development in Bangladesh.* Burlington, VT: Ashgate.

References

Azra, Azyumardi. 2003. Civil Society and Democratization in Indonesia: The Transition under President Wahid and Beyond. In *Civil Society in Asia: In Search of Democracy and Development in Bangladesh.* David C. Schak and Wayne Hudson, eds. Pp. 73–86. Burlington, VT: Ashgate.
Bernal, Victoria, and Inderpal Grewal, eds. 2014. Introduction. In *Theorizing NGOs: States, Feminisms, and Neoliberalism.* Victoria Bernal and Inderpal Grewal, eds. Pp. 1–18. Durham, NC: Duke University Press.
Bidet, Eric, and Hyung-sik Eum. 2011. Social Enterprise in South Korea: History and Diversity. *Social Enterprise Journal* 7(1): 69–85.
Brandsen, Taco, and Ruth Simsa. 2016. Civil Society, Nonprofit Organizations, and Citizenship in China: An Editorial Introduction to the China Issue. *VOLUNTAS: International Journal of Voluntary and Non-profit Organizations* 27(5): 2011–2020.

Bransden, Taco, Wim van de Donk, and Kim Putters. 2005. Griffins or Chameleons?: Hybridity as a Permanent and Inevitable Characteristic of the Third Sector. *International Journal of Public Administration* 28(3): 749–765.

Bräuer, Stephanie. 2016. Becoming Public: Tactical Innovation in the Beijing Anti-domestic Violence Movement. *VOLUNTAS: International Journal of Voluntary and Nonprofit Organizations* 27(5): 2106–2130.

Brower, Ralph, Francisco Magno, and Janet Dilling. 2014. Evolving and Implementing a New Disaster Management Paradigm: The Case of the Philippines. In *Disaster and Development, Examining Global Issues and Cases*. Naim Kapucu and Kuotsai Tom Liou, eds. Pp. 289–315. New York: Springer.

Bryant, Raymond. 2005. Nongovernment Organizations in Environmental Struggle, Politics and the Making of Moral Capital in the Philippines. New Haven, CT: Yale University Press.

Cagna, Paola, and Nitya Rao. 2016. Feminist Mobilisation for Policy Change on Violence against Women: Insights from Asia. *Gender & Development* 24(2): 277–290.

Cariño, Ledivina V., and Dolores D. Gaffud, eds. 2007. *What they Contribute, Case Studies on the Impact of Nonprofit Organizations*. Quezon City: Center for leadership, Citizenship and Democracy, National College of Public Administration and Governance, University of the Philippines.

Choi, Sang Ok, and Seung-Bum Yang. 2011. Understanding Challenges and Opportunities in the Nonprofit Sector in Korea. *International Review of Public Administration* 16(1): 51–70.

Choudry, Aziz. 2013. Saving Biodiversity, for Whom and for What?: Conservation NGOs, Complicity, Colonialism and Conquest in an Era of Capitalist Globalization. In *NGOization Complicity, Contradictions and Prospects*. Aziz Choudry and Dip Kapoor, eds. Pp. 25–44. London: Zed Books.

Clarke, Gerard. 1998. *The Politics of NGOs in South-East Asia, Participation and Protest in the Philippines*. London: Routledge.

Connell, Raewyn. 2007. *Southern Theory: The Global Dynamics of Knowledge in Social Science*. Sydney: Allen & Unwin.

Creighton, Millie. 2015. Civil Society Volunteers Supporting Japan's Constitution, Article 9 and Associated Peace, Diversity, and Post-3.11 Environmental Issues, *VOLUNTAS: International Journal of Voluntary and Nonprofit Organizations* 26 (1): 121–143.

Davies, Thomas. 2013. *NGOs: A New History of Transnational Civil Society*. London: C. Hurst & Co.

Gera, Weena. 2016. Public Participation in Environmental Governance in the Philippines: The Challenge of Consolidation in Engaging the State. *Land Use Policy* 52: 501–510.

Goodwin, Susan, and Ruth Phillips. 2015. Policy Capacity in the Community Sector. In *Policy Analysis in Australia*. Brian Head and Kate Crowley, eds. Pp. 245–258. Sydney: Policy Press Australia.

Guoqin, Shen. 2011. The Development of Women's NGOs in China. In *NGOs in China and Europe, Comparisons and Contrasts*. Yuwen Li, ed. Pp. 95–116. Burlington, VT: Ashgate.

Handy, Femida, Meenaz Kassam, and Shree Renade. 2002. Factors Influencing Women Entrepreneurs of NGOs in India. *Nonprofit Management and Leadership* 13(2): 139–154.

Hasan, Samuil. 2008. Third Sector Growth and Governance: Contexts and Traditions in Asia. In. *Comparative Third Sector Governance in Asia: Structure, Process, and Political Economy*. Samuil Hasan and Jenny Onyx, eds. Pp. 19–38. New York: Springer.

Hasan, Samiul, and Jenny Onyx, eds. 2008. *Comparative Third Sector Governance in Asia: Structure, Process, and Political Economy*. New York: Springer.

Howell, Jude. 2007. Civil Society in China: Chipping Away at the Edges. *Development* 50(3): 17–23.

Hunt, Juliette, and Nalini Kasynathan. 2001. Pathways to Empowerment?: Reflections on Microfinance and Transformation in Gender Relations in South Asia. *Gender & Development* 9(1): 42–52.

Jakimow, Tanya. 2012. *Peddlers of Information: Indian Non-Government Organizations in the Information Age*. Sterling, VA: Kumarian Press.

Jung, Kyungja. 2014. *Practicing Feminism in South Korea: The Women's Movement against Sexual Violence*. Routledge: London.

Junkui, Han. 2011. International NGOs in China: Current Situation, Impacts and Response of the Chinese Government. In *NGOs in China and Europe, Comparisons and Contrasts*. Yuwen Li, ed. Pp. 23–52. Burlington, VT: Ashgate.

Kabeer, Naila, Simeen Mahmud, and, Jairo G. Isaza Castro. 2012. NGOs and the Political Empowerment of Poor People in Rural Bangladesh: Cultivating the Habits of Democracy? *World Development* 40(10): 2044–2062.

Karim, Lamia. 2014. Demystifying Microcredit: The Grameen Bank, NGOs and Neoliberalism in Bangladesh. In *Theorizing NGOs, States Feminisms, and Neoliberalism*, Victoria Bernal and Inderpal Grewal, eds. Pp. 193–217. Durham, NC: Duke University Press.

Khan, Hafiz, and Twyeafur Rahman. 2016. Women's Participations in Economic and NGO Activities in Bangladesh. *International Journal of Sociology and Social Policy* 36(7/8): 491–515.

Kilby, Patrick. 2010. *NGOs in India: The Challenge of Women's Empowerment and Accountability*. London: Routledge.

Kim, Hyuk-Rae. 2003. Unraveling Civil Society in South Korea: Old Discourses and New Divisions. In *Civil Society in Asia: In Search of Democracy and Development in Bangladesh*. David C. Schak and Wayne Hudson, eds. Pp. 1–8. Burlington, VT: Ashgate.

Lee, Minho. 2008. Government Influence on the Formation of Nonprofits: A Dual Relationship between Local Government and Local Nonprofits. *International Review of Public Administration* 13(2): 97–115.

Li, Yuwen, ed. 2011. *NGOs in China and Europe, Comparisons and Contrasts*. Burlington, VT: Ashgate.

Mackie, Vera. 2003. *Feminism in Modern Japan: Citizenship, Embodiment and Sexuality*. Cambridge: Cambridge University Press.

Mishra, Debiprasad, Saswata N. Biswas, and Shiladitya Roy. 2005. Governance of NGOs: Contextualising in Indian Experience. *International Journal of Rural Management* 1(2): 185–201.

Najam, Adil. 2000. The Four-C's of Third Sector–Government Relations Cooperation, Confrontation, Complementarity, and Co-optation. *Nonprofit Management & Leadership* 10(4): 375–396.

Ogawa, Akihiro. 2009. *The Failure of Civil Society? The Third Sector and the State in Contemporary Japan*. Albany, NY: State University of New York Press.

Otsuki, Nami. 2011. The Nonprofit Sector. In *Transforming Japan: How Feminism and Diversity are Making a Difference*. Kumiko Fujimura-Faneslow, ed. Pp. 302–313. New York: Feminist Press.

Panday, Pranab Kumar, and Shelley Feldman. 2015. Mainstreaming Gender in Politics in Bangladesh: Role of NGOs. *Asian Journal of Political Science* 23(3): 301–320.

Phillips, Ruth. 2015. How "Empowerment" May Miss Its Mark: Gender Equality Policies and How They are Understood in Women's NGOs. *VOLUNTAS: International Journal of Voluntary and Nonprofit Organizations* 26(4): 1122–1142.

Phillips, Ruth. 2016. A Global Analysis of the Empowerment Paradigm and the Influence of Feminism in Women's NGOs. In *Women's Emancipation and Civil Society Organisations Challenging or Maintaining the Status Quo?* Christina Schwabenland, Chris Lange, Jenny Onyx, and Sachiko Nakagawa, eds. Pp. 21–48. Bristol: Policy Press.

Piper, Nicola. 2001. Transnational Women's Activism in Japan and Korea: The Unresolved Issue of Military Sexual Slavery. *Global Networks* 1(2): 155–170.

Rajasekha, Durgam. 2000. Non-governmental Organisations in India: Opportunities and Challenges. *Working Paper 66*. Bangalore: The Institute for Social and Economic Change. Electronic document, http://203.200.22.249:8080/jspui/bitstream/2014/7180/1/ISEC-WP-66.pdf, accessed October 25, 2016.

Said, Edward. 1978. *Orientalism*. London: Routledge & Kegan Paul.

Salamon, Lester. 2015. Introduction: The Nonprofitization of the Welfare State. *VOLUNTAS: International Journal of Voluntary and Nonprofit Organizations* 26 (6): 2147–2154.

Salam, Sha Abdus, and Ainoon Naher. 2014. Research on Poverty Reduction and Women Economic Leadership in Asia: Roles, Potentials and Challenges of Social Enterprises. Development Wheel (DEW), Dhaka, Bangladesh. In *Final Report*. Electronic document, http://dewbd.org/dew/images/Social_Enterprise_Study-Bangladesh-Final_Report.pdf, accessed October 21, 2016.

Schak, David C., and Wayne Hudson. 2003. *Civil Society in Asia: In Search of Democracy and Development in Bangladesh*. David C. Schak, and Wayne Hudson, eds. Pp. 1–8. Burlington, VT: Ashgate.

Spires, Anthony J., Lin Tao, and Kin-man Chan. 2014. Societal Support for China's Grassroots NGOs: Evidence from Ynnan, Guangdong and Beijing. *The China Journal* 71 (January): 65–90.

UNDP. 2016. Goal 5: Gender Equality. United Nations Development Programme. In *Sustainable Development Goals*. Electronic document, www.undp.org/content/undp/en/home/sustainable-development-goals/goal-5-gender-equality.html, accessed October 11, 2016.

Wagner, Antonin. 2012. "Third Sector" and/or "Civil Society": A Critical Discourse about Scholarship Relating to Intermediate Organisations. *Voluntary Sector Review* 3(3): 299–328.

Weiss, Anita. 2014. Progressive Women's NGOs. In *Interpreting Islam, Modernity, and Women's Rights in Pakistan*. Anita Weiss, ed. Pp. 75–99. New York: Palgrave Macmillan.

Yuanfeng, Zhang. 2015. Dependent Interdependence: The Complicated Dance of Government–Nonprofit Relations in China. *VOLUNTAS: International Journal of Voluntary and Nonprofit Organizations* 26(6): 2395–2423.

Yumasdaleni, and Jakimow Tanya. 2016. NGOs, "Straddler" Organisations and the Possibilities of "Channelling" in Indonesia: New Possibilities for State–NGO Collaboration? *VOLUNTAS: International Journal of Voluntary and Nonprofit Organizations.* DOI: 10.1007/s11266-016-9719-y.

Zhou, Huiquan. 2016. Mapping the Level of Development of Grassroots NPOs in China. *VOLUNTAS: International Journal of Voluntary and Nonprofit Organizations* 27(5): 2199–2228.

25

SOCIAL ENTERPRISES

Rosario Laratta

Emergence and diffusion of social enterprise

Social enterprises are increasingly mentioned and used as promising tools to address some of the current economic, social, and environmental challenges. Social entrepreneurship has received growing attention from practitioners, academics, and governments, all of whom regard it as a possible answer to the challenges and aspirations of our age: the transformation of social protection and solidarity systems; the need for greater ethics and transparency in the economic system; the desire for sense and motivation in the workplace, etc.

Existing scholarship (Borzaga and Defourny 2001; Laratta, Nakagawa, and Sakurai 2011; Nyssens 2006) has defined social enterprises as collective public-benefit organizations that pursue the satisfaction of social needs through the provision of general interest services. Social enterprises are characterized by the imposition of at least a partial non-profit constraint and the obligation to devote most of their positive residuals to the accumulation of asset locks. Moreover, social enterprises are frequently found to have multi-stakeholder membership because their governance structures involve diverse types of stakeholder (Laratta *et al.* 2011). However, depending upon a country's incorporation laws, social enterprises can be created by non-profit, for-profit, or government host organizations. Social enterprises can also have bureaucratic or participatory governance structures. The resources created by social enterprises, profits, for example, can be distributed to owners, investors, consumers, the community in which the social enterprises are embedded, or recipient groups outside the social enterprises. Alternatively, the resources can be returned to the operations of the host organizations. This range of structural options allows social enterprises to tailor their operations to the particular social purposes of their businesses (Laratta *et al.* 2011).

One option for social enterprises is to utilize a cooperative form of organization.[1] Common types of cooperative include a workers' cooperative, where the workers in the enterprise jointly own and benefit from the business; a consumers' cooperative, where the customers of a business jointly own the enterprise and benefit from its lower prices and profits; a farm cooperative, where independent farmers collaborate to own equipment, supply and distribution channels, and, in some cases, brands and products; and a housing cooperative, where the housing needs of individuals and families are organized collectively, with members owning rights to the use of housing through shares in the cooperative. The cooperative form of business is quite flexible and diverse, and can be adapted to the requirements/needs of many of the groups and organizations that form social enterprises.

Social enterprises and social entrepreneurship can be observed in various economic sectors (health care, recycling, renewable energy, fair trade, microfinance, personal services, integration of low-skilled workers, etc.). While observing that most of these organizations actually belong to what has been called the "third sector" (neither for-profit nor state), it should be kept in mind that recently established social enterprises highlight the blurred frontiers between sectors. Moreover, opportunities also exist for social entrepreneurship within the private for-profit sector and the public sphere (Austin, Stevenson, and Wei-Skillern 2006; Nicholls 2010). In addition, social enterprises have existed since well before the mid-1990s, when the term began to be increasingly used in both Western Europe and the United States. Indeed, the third sector in which most social enterprises are found, be it called the non-profit sector, the voluntary sector, or the social economy (Defourny and Monzón Campos 1992; Evers and Laville 2004), has long witnessed entrepreneurial dynamics that resulted in innovative solutions for providing services or goods to persons or communities whose needs were neither met by private companies nor by public providers (Defourny 2001). However, for reasons that vary according to the specificities of national or regional contexts, the concept of social enterprise is now attracting fast-growing interest worldwide along with two closely related terms, namely, "social entrepreneur" and "social entrepreneurship" (Bacq and Janssen 2011; Mair and Marti 2006; Nicholls 2010).

Nonetheless, a broad and precise view of most social enterprise models as they are emerging worldwide is still lacking. In addition to the fact that research on social enterprises is rather recent, at least two major reasons explain the absence of such an overall view. First, as explained in the prior section, the concepts of social enterprise and social entrepreneurship can have different meanings in different contexts or for different schools of thought (Laratta and Nakagawa 2016; Laratta *et al.* 2011). Second, much of the literature has relied so far on case studies, especially to highlight the achievements of outstanding social entrepreneurs, who are presented as heroes (Bornstein 2004, amongst many other authors). As a consequence, only a few countries have witnessed attempts to delimit, describe, and analyze the whole landscape (or a great deal) of the social enterprise field at national level. Because they have experienced specific and strong public or private strategies promoting social enterprise and social entrepreneurship, some countries have been studied to a greater extent. For example, in the USA, Ashoka, various foundations, and numerous consulting companies have provided a range of support to innovative social entrepreneurs and to non-profit-pursuing earned-income strategies (Boschee 2006); in the UK, the Blair government promoted the establishment of a wide spectrum of tools to foster social enterprise (Mulgan 2006); and in Italy, social cooperatives have received similar support since the early 1990s (Borzaga and Santuari 2001; Laratta and Nakagawa 2016).

Although it is less documented compared with Western countries, the Asia-Pacific Region is also experiencing very rapid growth in the social enterprise sector (Defourny and Kuan 2011). According to Chi-Hing Kee (2015), in 2014, the total revenue of the 457 social enterprises operating in Hong Kong was HK$1.1 billion, which was equivalent to 0.05 percent of Hong Kong's GDP. Moreover, 62.9 percent of these social enterprises were found to be either at break-even or profitable. These figures show that Hong Kong is quite successful in the marketization of social enterprises. The situation in Taiwan seems very different. Here, the social enterprise sector is growing because of significant dependency upon government subsides (Kuan *et al.* 2015). Since 2014, the Taiwanese Ministry of Economic Affairs has promoted the "Action Plans for Social Enterprises," encompassing tasks ranging from adjustments to relevant regulations to the generation of more funding for social enterprises. A total of NT$161 million

(US$5.4 million) has been allocated for 2014–2016 (Hsiao 2015). The situation in South Korea is similar. Here, civil society's initiatives for the development of a social economy and the government's policy of active promotion in the face of social–economic challenges, such as unemployment and no increase in jobs, have produced an incredible growth of social enterprises (Chung, Han, and Park 2015). Further, South Korea is the only country in the region to have a specific legal context: the Law on the Promotion of Social Enterprise. This law was enacted in 2007 and has enabled the government to subsidize the labor costs of certified social enterprises, producing a rapid increase in these organizations. Despite the sector's growth, when we compare such countries with Japan, we notice some clear differences in attitude in and toward the sector. For example, Japanese social enterprises do not follow market mechanisms in order to maintain their operations, as is the case in Hong Kong. Moreover, the Japanese government is less supportive of the sector compared with the Taiwanese government. In addition, Japan lacks a legal framework that properly regulates and supports social enterprises. Although South Korea has its 2007 Law on the Promotion of Social Enterprise, Japan's Bill on Social Enterprises, which was about to be submitted in 2010, failed to be approved because of a lack of support. Further, a lack of discussion amongst the public and a vague understanding of the role of social enterprises at the institutional level make the notion of these organizations ambiguous and lead to an underestimation of their social, economic, and political contributions, thereby hindering their development (Laratta *et al.* 2011). Japan is one of the developed countries where the social enterprise field has yet to be delimited and analyzed (Laratta *et al.* 2011).

Thus, in the last five years, the objectives of my academic research have been as follows.

1 To identify and characterize major models of social enterprise in Japan in accordance with such organizations' fields of activity, social missions, target groups, operational models, stakeholders, legal frameworks, etc.
2 To analyze the relations between these models and major external drivers or supporting forces that are likely to explain and shape the development of social enterprises. Such drivers and forces include public policies fighting unemployment or promoting social services through quasi-markets, foundations establishing new philanthropic tools, incubators and development agencies, and supporting structures.
3 To examine the specific roles and contributions of such social enterprises in the overall socio-economic landscape of Japan.

In order to characterize major social enterprise models (objective 1, on which I am still working), I have been relying on the hypothesis that data on three major dimensions would particularly inform the diversity of such models. These dimensions are the nature of the social missions or social aims, the types of economic model, and the governance structures. Some of the questions with which I am capturing these three dimensions in my recent qualitative and quantitative studies are as follows.

Social mission. What is the explicit social aim of the social enterprise? Who are the users or customers of the social enterprise? What kind of profit distribution is allowed, if any? Who launched the social enterprise?

Economic projects. What types of goods or services does the social enterprise produce or provide? What are the proportions of paid staff and volunteers in the social enterprise labor force? What kind of economic risk does the social enterprise bear? What are the main resources sustaining the production of goods and services? What are the shares of market resources, public grants, and voluntary resources (giving, volunteering)? Where do these resources come from (private customers, public contracts, foundations, etc.)?

Specific governance. Who is the main manager of the social enterprise? Does the board have the right to adopt its own position ("voice") and terminate the activity of the social enterprise ("exit")? Has any external body (public authorities, a for-profit company, etc.) a right to be involved in such decisions? What types of stakeholder are involved in the activities and governance of the social enterprise, especially in the general assembly, the board, or through other channels? How is the decision-making power allocated in the general assembly and the board?

My research projects are trying to build a body of knowledge about emerging or already well-established social enterprise models in Japan. This, in turn, will foster international comparative analysis between Japan and other developed countries such as the UK, Italy, South Korea, and Taiwan, where scholars have already delimited and analyzed the social enterprise field following very similar research guidelines. Further, my research aims to build a database of social enterprise models in Japan, including case studies for each identified model. This database could be used by the Japanese government to develop a regulatory framework that would support a sector that is considered to be expanding (Laratta and Nakagawa 2016). Indeed, many "hybrid organizations" (i.e., organizations that engage in selling goods and/or services, an approach that is typical of enterprises with social missions/aims and typical of non-profit organizations and charities) often end up registering as non-profit organizations or small/medium enterprises. Such legal forms do not actually reflect the hybrid nature of these organizations; consequently, they have to operate in a less supportive regulatory environment compared with their non-profit or for-profit counterparts.

In this chapter, I focus on the predominant type of social enterprises that we have found in Asia, known as "work integration social enterprises" (WISEs). As my research has been focused mostly on Japan, I will investigate WISEs in a specific region of Japan, Hokkaido.

WISEs concentrate on the employment of disadvantaged people. Such people include those with mental disabilities and, to a lesser extent, those with physical disabilities and the long-term unemployed.[2] WISEs act as cooperatives, with the aim of integrating disadvantaged people into society by providing them with work opportunities.[3]

The number of Japanese social enterprises is increasing (Laratta *et al.* 2011). As of May 2012, it was estimated that over 1,900 WISEs provided work and vocational training to the disabled. Many WISEs are located in rural Hokkaido (Welfare and Medical Service Agency 2012). In Hokkaido, WISEs perform a vanguard role in promoting long-lasting partnerships with local governments and for-profit partners. Moreover, they are recognized as a successful business model, particularly in times of fiscal restraint (Nakagawa and Laratta 2012). WISEs in Hokkaido are regarded as economically and socially sustainable. From 2008 to 2011, SORA (a pseudonym for a well-known WISE in rural Hokkaido) increased its number of disabled workers. Moreover, the number of trained disabled workers who left the organization because they had found an occupation in local companies increased (Laratta 2013). The same research also showed that WISEs in rural Hokkaido have evolved in terms of organizational goals, repertoires, support structures, and networks.

This current study is based on a secondary data set regarding WISEs (Laratta 2011–2014) that describes the development of these organizations as a result of three different typologies of policy. In addition, a qualitative study of ten WISEs in rural Hokkaido reveals their role in community development regarding the social inclusion of disadvantaged people. The study also identifies major factors that make WISEs a sustainable business model. One case study of a WISE includes interviews of its members, supplemented with observations of the facility (Laratta 2013).

I argue that three factors account for the sustainability and growth of this social business model: (1) a supportive infrastructure system in the form of cooperative banks that promote the activities of social enterprises; (2) a willingness to promote partnerships with other sectors in the local community; and (3) democratic operational governance, where transparency and cooperation amongst stakeholders give cohesion to effective performance.

The development of Japanese WISEs

This section highlights the background and development of WISEs. It also considers the situation of disabled people and the legal frameworks that support and enable them to integrate into society and the general workforce. Three typologies of policy have impacted the development of WISEs (Laratta *et al.* 2011). These policies have different targets: (A) service providers, (B) work integration, and (C) mentally disabled people.

Typology A—"service providers" as a target

Since 1951, local governments and social welfare corporations have monopolized services related to the welfare and human rights of the disabled in Japan. However, these services did not always achieve social integration of the disabled. The number of vocational support centers was limited and only disabled people who had a viable chance to return to a normal life benefited from them. Besides, these centers were established in remote places (Nishio 1986). Most disabled people remained at home. It was against this background that in the 1960s, WISEs emerged. Their objective was to provide vocational training and work for the disabled in local communities and encourage disabled people to interact with other people in their hometowns. In 1977, the Association for Small Workshops (*Kyosaren*) was established. This organization organized sixteen workshops on an exchange basis with local communities. In 1981, the Association for Tackling Exclusion (*Kyodoren*) was founded. Its purpose was to build new social and economic systems and to spread social cooperatives in Japan. Such action triggered the development of a remarkable number of Japanese WISEs after the 1980s. We believe that there were around 800 WISEs in 1981, which is double the vocational support centers operated by governments and social welfare corporations in the same year (Ministry of Health and Welfare 1981). Some local governments offered subsidies to these WISEs. However, despite this financial help, many WISEs were not able to pay their disabled workers enough to make a living. According to a member of the Research Committee for Systems and Support for Work Integration of the Elderly and the Disabled, some WISEs that managed small workshops paid their workers no more than JPY14,548 (US$125) a month. However, this situation changed when a need for services, government financial difficulties, and the need to improve the quality of services combined with the public expectation of the third sector as a new provider. In 2006, the government promulgated the Act on Services and Support for the Disabled (*Shōgaisha jiritsu shien hō*), which enables WISEs to engage in the following two categories of service. The first category is called the Transitional Support for Work. This service is twofold: (1) for disabled people who hope to work in for-profit companies; and (2) for disabled people who acquire a qualification to start a new business or to work from home. These transitional services are limited to disabled people under sixty-five years old. Moreover, integration into the mainstream labor market must be completed within two years. The second category of services is named Continuative Support for Work. Unlike Transitional Support for Work, there are no time limits. The Act distinguishes two types of disabled person: (1) the A type targets disabled people under sixty-five years old and stipulates an employment contract with them; and (2) the B type provides a service for all disabled people regardless of age and does not demand an employment contract.

Typology B—"work integration" as a target

The Japanese government established the Act on Employment Promotion of the Physically Disabled (*Shōgaisha koyō sokushin hō*) in 1960. The Act introduced the first quota system in Japan. However, it had some defects. First, it only applied to the physically disabled. Second, the achievement of a specific quota was not binding. Third, the quota system was complex and difficult to understand. Fourth, the lowest wage defined by the Act on Minimum Wages did not apply to physically disabled employees, which made integration difficult. In 1976, the government revised the Act on Employment Promotion of the Physically Disabled. Meeting the quota of employees with disabilities in the workforce in national and local governments and for-profit companies was now mandatory. Originally, the target of the quota system was limited to the physically disabled, however, in 1987, people with learning difficulties were also included. The mentally disabled have long been excluded from the Act; only in 2006 did an amendment to the Act obligate employers to hire people with mental disabilities. Non-compliance with the law leads to the publication of the companies' names on a black list as "non-cooperators for work integration." In 1977, a System of Payment for the Employment of the Disabled was enforced that imposed a penalty of JPY70,000 (US$595) per month on for-profit companies that did not meet the quota. Companies that achieved the quota were awarded a sum of JPY40,000 (US$337) a month. The System of Payment for Employment of the Disabled was extended to for-profit companies with more than 201 employees. The government also introduced Employment Support in 2003 whereby job coaches help disabled employees to develop communication and work skills. Such coaches also advise employers on the effects of mental disorders on work. In 2009, 1,061 job coaches worked with 3,100 disabled persons (Ministry of Health, Labor, and Welfare 2009). Disabled workers also benefit from a System of Special Subsidiaries (*Tokurei kogaisha no shisutemu*) that was established by the government in 1976. The system consists of a number of limited companies with an overall workforce of more than 20 percent disabled. These companies have special facilities for disabled employees such as barrier-free buildings and highly trained instructors. Companies can establish special subsidiary companies as their affiliates by obtaining authorization from the Ministry of Health, Labor, and Welfare. The number of special subsidiaries has since increased. In 2013, there were 378 special subsidiaries nationwide (Ministry of Health, Labor, and Welfare 2013).

Typology C—"mentally disabled people" as a target

Before World War II, mentally disabled people were mostly kept at home. With the establishment of the new constitution, the national government promoted public health, and in 1950 the Mental Hygiene Law (*Seishin eisei hō*) was enacted. Public mental hospitals were established in each prefecture. In addition, the government subsidized mental hospitals operated by the third sector. In 1987, the Mental Hygiene Law was revised and changed to the Mental Health Law (*Seishinhoken fukushi hō*). The purpose of this new law was to protect the human rights of the mentally disabled and promote their reintegration. In 1993, group homes were recognized in legislation and the "Center for Promoting the Return of the Mentally Disabled to Society" was established. In 1995, the name of the law was changed again to the Law Related to Mental Health and Welfare of People with Mental Disorders (*SeishinHoken oyobi SeisinshogaishaFukusi ni kansuru hō*). Under the new law, vocational support centers and centers to support the community life of the mentally disabled were advanced. Further, the home service for the mentally disabled was expanded.

WISEs' evolution: organizational goals, repertoires, support structure, and networks

Hokkaido WISEs evolved from "vocational support centers," whose purpose was the integration of all psychiatric patients. However, in reality these centers benefited only disabled people who had a viable chance of returning to a normal life in society. This goal has gradually moved toward the inclusion of mentally ill people. Japanese WISEs aim to increase employment opportunities for disadvantaged workers outside the WISE organizations through on-the-job training. This change of objective has also altered the type of market contracts that WISEs embrace. Previously, when the integration of disadvantaged workers was the primary objective, open-ended contracts were the norm, however, under the new strategy, temporary contracts are more common.

WISEs in rural Hokkaido have also developed organizational repertoires, which Elisabeth Clemens describes as models that: "comprise both templates for arranging relationships within an organization and scripts for action culturally associated with that type of organization; they carry cultural expectations about who can organize and for what purposes" (1999: 62). When vocational support centers were first created, many of them were dominated by a professional–psychiatric approach. Disadvantaged workers were seen in terms of their needs and conditions, which usually provided the basis for professional schemes and employment plans. The disadvantaged were essentially dependent and had little opportunity to contribute to an organization; they were simply viewed as a different type of worker compared with other employees and volunteers. The relationship between the professional and the disadvantaged was effectively contractual, with the former being expected to follow ethical standards of professional practice, even though these were often constrained by funding limitations or other accountability issues. However, today, WISEs in rural Hokkaido follow a different approach. For example, relationships are supposed to be egalitarian and based on personal dignity rather than on hierarchical relations. Moreover, WISEs empower workers, rather than diminish them, and focus on workers' strengths, rather than on their pathology or diagnosis. Anyone can be a member, co-owning a WISE, participating in its management, and partaking in all its decision-making processes.

Finally, WISEs have been able to create a strong supportive network through "cooperative banks" that focus on specific requirements. In May 2002, the Center for Supporting Social Enterprises in Hokkaido, an intermediary non-profit organization, conducted a survey of 120 social enterprises in order to assess their financial situation and hear their opinions on potential loan programs in terms of amounts, target usage, credit limits, and rates of interest. The main finding of this survey was that many social enterprises were struggling to survive the strong competition for funding and the pressure of accountability from public administrations and foundations. In August 2002, the first general meeting of the Hokkaido Cooperative Bank was held, and in October of the same year the bank started its work. The mission of cooperative banks is to help social enterprises expand their activities by lending them the money that local residents invest. These "alternative" banks help local social enterprises financially so that these, in turn, create new jobs for local residents. Cooperative banks have a social vision for local community development, and it is exactly this vision that distinguishes them from conventional banks. Cooperative banks act as umbrella organizations for WISEs. They provide services such as the preparation of joint tenders, fundraising for bigger projects, and payroll administration. Municipal contracts enable cooperative banks to subcontract work related to their WISE affiliates and monitor the activities of their members through audit processes. This facilitates a better distribution of funds and fewer funding pressures. In addition, WISEs can borrow from cooperative banks at lower interest rates with negotiated arrangements and guaranteed loans.

WISEs also enjoy a good relationship with local industries and governments as a result of fostering numerous long-term partnerships. WISEs show governments and for-profit companies what can be done to integrate marginalized people. They act as initiators of partnership development by making governments and for-profit companies aware of their responsibilities for social exclusion issues. WISEs have moved away from the concept of a competing service that is provider-oriented toward a vanguard role as part of civil society's infrastructure. By so doing, they are able to motivate governments and for-profit companies to eliminate social exclusion and build an inclusive society in partnership.

A case study: SORA

SORA is one of the ten WISEs that the author investigated. It is located in northern Hokkaido and is part of a regional network of social enterprises. It originated in 1998 through efforts made by parents and friends of mentally disabled people, who believed that a PC was a powerful tool to eliminate the barriers that disabled people were facing and promote participation of these people in society. SORA now provides on-the-job training for mentally disabled and other disadvantaged workers and employs them in key sectors such as web design and data input. Currently, SORA employs forty-three people, compared with five when it started, and has a turnover of approximately JPY200 million (approximately US$1.7 million). All workers are also SORA members. They include twenty-three mentally disabled people and ten people who were long-term unemployed. Before joining SORA, applicants must be assessed to determine what tasks they can undertake. This process starts with an evaluation of the compatibility of an applicant's abilities with the work of the WISE and then develops into a personally tailored employment-training program. As part of this training, workers' individual goals are identified through one-to-one interviews with other workers. Goals are broken down into manageable steps and a trainee's progress is reviewed regularly. The goal is to create career paths for disadvantaged workers to enable them to move beyond entry-level jobs. This allows each worker to gain a level of self-respect and experience a sense of inclusion in the community.

Members work side by side without assistance from either professional or non-professional workers. Everyone helps and encourages each other, an approach that has proven to be more effective than receiving support from "professionals." The central task of former workers is to engage new workers in meaningful work and to facilitate peer support. When visiting this organization, it is almost impossible to distinguish the disadvantaged workers from the others. Indeed, because the workers all undertake useful activities for the community, even local residents may not realize that the person who designs a website is a mentally disabled person.

SORA recognizes the importance of collaboration with the local government and other institutions. Hokkaido's local government has had a close working relationship with SORA, contracting more than 50 percent of its IT work to the WISE. SORA could also not survive without the support of the Hokkaido Cooperative Bank. This bank was established in October 2002 as a specified non-profit corporation. The bank only provides loans to social enterprises whose social mission must be to benefit the development of the entire community. The bank excludes governmental organizations, for-profit companies, and individual citizens. The Hokkaido Cooperative Bank has a credit line of approximately JPY2.6 million (US$22,000) and a low interest rate of 2 percent. SORA has used the bank not only for borrowing money but also as a forum to advance the promotion of its own brand identity. The Hokkaido Cooperative Bank imposes a limit on the number of loans that its affiliate social enterprises, such as SORA, are able to have. The reason is to ensure that all affiliates develop along equal lines, thereby avoiding the possibility that one may expand to the detriment of another.

Until 2000, SORA had only one for-profit partner but, following the enactment of long-term national insurance, the number of for-profit partners rose to seventeen. This development contributed to SORA's increase in turnover and consistently positive balances. SORA is now able to make an untaxed annual contribution to a fund that helps to finance the establishment of new social enterprises in other parts of Hokkaido.

The chief director of SORA described how he initiated a partnership with a for-profit company. He said:

> When I first met the director of the company, I told him that I had taught IT skills to the disabled, so I was trying to help qualified people to find jobs related to IT, such as making illustrations, producing websites and inputting data. I also expressed my sincere wish to have some of these skilled disabled employed in his company. A deal with this company did not start immediately. It took about two years before we received an offer from the company. During these years, we continuously reminded them of our mission and emphasized how our partnership could yield opportunities for the disabled.[4]

This first initiative led SORA to establish other partnerships. For example, following an informal talk on disabled employees by staff and volunteers of SORA, an Internet service provider company named *Hokuden Jōhō Technology* developed a plan to help disabled people obtain jobs. In 2004, *Hokuden Jōhō Technology* launched a new service named the SORA Setup Course, which enables SORA's disabled workers to visit new customers' homes and help set up Internet connections and email. Wages for these services are paid by *Hokuden Jōhō Technology*. In order to encourage new customers to apply for this service and provide wages for disabled workers, *Hokuden Jōhō Technology* offers free services and discounts to applicants. Currently, seven or eight for-profit companies are collaborating in similar ways with SORA. In September 2002, after being informed that the Ministry of Health, Labor, and Welfare demanded a budget for an IT Support Center for the Disabled, SORA quickly submitted a proposal in less than a week for such a center in Hokkaido and suggested a partnership with the ministry's center. The municipal government cooperated with SORA regarding the establishment of an IT Support Center for the Disabled but requested SORA not to mention disabled providers in the organization's pamphlet. SORA insisted that publishing the names of disabled providers in the pamphlet was positive because it encourages such providers. SORA realized that it was essential to provide places where social enterprises and the government exchange ideas and understanding about disabled people, their potential abilities, and their limitations, and where it was possible to reflect upon the roles that social enterprises and government must fulfill to solve problems together. Between April and August 2004, SORA organized a roundtable with different departments of the municipal government, other social enterprises, and an association of small workshops, in order to launch the first organized joint study on this topic. As a result, the municipal government established the Committee for Supporting the Disabled Working at Home through IT and asked social enterprises, including SORA, to participate. The municipal government also introduced a subsidy for all social enterprises that support disabled people who work at home through IT and that promote related activities.

Sustainability of rural Hokkaido WISEs

Japanese WISEs face many challenges in sustaining the employment of the disabled, with surprisingly few differences between rural and urban areas (Laratta and Nakagawa 2016). Some of the challenges are as follows.

a   *Absence of a legal framework.* There is no specific legal framework for social enterprises. WISEs are not yet sufficiently valued by the public and policy makers. Further, the existence of different interpretations of what a social enterprise is or should be contributes to misunderstandings that often jeopardize social enterprises' real contributions in the social, economic, and political spheres.

b   *Competition for funds.* The Special Nonprofit Organization Promotion Law (*Tokutei hi-eiri katsudō sokushin hō*), also known as the New NPO Law, was enacted in 1998. This was followed two years later by the Long Term Care Insurance (LTCI) system. The 1998 Law enabled many previously unincorporated associations, such as WISEs (which had no legal status), to be incorporated as specified non-profit corporations. In 2000, all these corporations became eligible for financial support under the LTCI system as providers in the "quasi-market." From 2000 onwards, WISEs began to compete for funds not only with organizations that shared their legal status but also with for-profit organizations that were considered eligible for financial support under the LTCI system.

c   *A low level of financial independence and a high level of accountability.* Over half of WISEs' annual revenue comes from governments (Laratta 2013), a situation that puts them under government accountability pressure in the form of audits and monitoring visits. These pressures often prompt organizations to count members rather than focus on the quality of training that they should provide to members. This financial dependence also negatively impacts on WISEs' level of independence regarding the choices they make as well as on their advocacy roles.

d   *Conventional banks versus cooperative banks.* WISEs have had a difficult time borrowing funds from conventional banks because they lack collateral. Conventional banks are often willing to lend money to big companies that can offer protection for such loans. Cooperative banks play a decisive role in the sustainability of WISEs. However, there are only thirteen cooperative banks in Japan. This number is not enough to support the nearly 2,000 WISEs currently operating in the country. In addition, not all cooperative banks are as supportive as the Hokkaido Cooperative Bank described in this study; in fact, some cooperative banks in Japan misunderstand their social role and act exactly as conventional banks.

Rural Hokkaido WISEs set themselves apart. They represent a sustainable social business model of working with disadvantaged workers, especially the mentally disabled, and reuniting them with the community. WISEs have created jobs and career paths for people for whom moving beyond entry-level jobs would have been previously unthinkable. Through careful consideration of suitable and innovative economic activities designed to fit mentally disabled workers' abilities, WISEs have been able to address the stigma associated with many disadvantaged people.

What this study has shown is that beyond this success, a model of public service co-production has emerged. By building on each other's assets, experiences, and expertise, WISEs, public administration, and for-profit enterprises have shown that local services can be delivered more efficiently by disadvantaged workers who gain self-respect and feel part of the community through their employment. This co-production model (e.g., Brandsen and Honingh 2015; Osborne, Radnor, and Strokosch 2016) is supported by three factors as follows.

1   An infrastructure support system that includes elements such as cooperative banks and funding schemes. The system promotes the activities of social enterprises, monitors these activities by placing accountability demands on such enterprises, and prevents the over-expansion of one social enterprise at the expense of others. The Hokkaido Cooperative

Bank starts by identifying all possible assets—organizational, individual, and physical—that are present in the community. Then, the bank mobilizes local assets by directly involving WISEs and other social enterprises in the development of their communities. Finally, it fulfills the role of a coordinator by: (a) putting local residents with similar skills in touch with each other; (b) helping local residents who have a similar vision for the development of their communities to share their visions; and (c) providing the organizational and physical means to help local residents realize these visions and collaborate with local social enterprises and local governments.

2   *Cross-sector partnerships*, which are a means of achieving social inclusion. As part of the infrastructure of civil society, social enterprises should ideally consider innovative ideas based on solidarity and share these ideas with other sectors such as the government and the market. Social enterprises should also work to create an environment where such ideas can be freely and fully explored and, if collectively agreed, make the current community governance and management systems more effective. By taking a vanguard role, social enterprises have the unique opportunity to motivate governments and for-profit companies to reduce social exclusion in partnerships and to involve these partners in their conventional civil attempts toward an inclusive society.

3   *Democratic operational governance*, whereby transparency amongst stakeholders and peer support between members give cohesion to effective performance. The WISE model embeds a rehabilitation program in its philosophy. Participants support one another on their paths to recovery through work integration. WISEs have professionals at their senior levels of governance where all strategic planning and project implementation usually take place, however, this approach is not an obstacle to behaving as self-help organizations where all members (including those who are disadvantaged) have operational-level control. In fact, in these organizations, relationships are found to be egalitarian and based on personal dignity rather than on a hierarchical structure. Anyone can be a member and thereby co-own a WISE, participate in its management, and partake in all the decision-making processes.

Notes

1   The International Co-operative Alliance defines cooperatives as an autonomous association of persons united voluntarily to meet their common economic, social, and cultural needs and aspirations through a jointly owned and democratically controlled enterprise.

2   Disabled people in Japan represent the most excluded group, and many WISEs act to promote their social inclusion. Only 5.4 percent of the 7.4 million disabled are employed in the mainstream labor market (Ministry of Health, Labor, and Welfare 2009). As of May 2012, there were approximately 2,000 WISEs that were working on this issue (Welfare and Medical Service Agency 2012). This is why Japanese WISEs have mainly disabled people as their employees. The situation seems to be different for EU WISEs: over 40 percent of employees in these organizations are long-term unemployed who struggle to find work. Multiple studies show that long-term unemployed applicants are only half as likely to be considered for hiring compared with others with identical education and experience, even though evidence demonstrates that they perform just as well when in work (Borzaga and Defourny 2001).

3   This form of organization can also be found in other countries. For example, in Italy a WISE is known as a *B-type social cooperative*; in Portugal it is called a *cooperativa de solidariedade social*; in Spain it is named a *cooperativa de iniciativa social*; in Greece it is called a *Koinonikos Syneterismos Periorismenis Eufthinis*, or KoiSPE; and in France it is known as a *société coopérative d'intérêt collectif*, or SCIC (Defourny and Nyssens 2008). All these forms are incorporated in their respective countries' laws.

4   Interview with the director of SORA, October 11, 2013.

Suggested readings

Bidet, Eric, and Hyung Sik Eum. 2011. Social Enterprise in South Korea: History and Diversity. *Social Enterprise Journal* 7(1): 69–85.

Chan, Kam Tong, Yu Yuan Kuan, and Shu Twu Wang. 2011. Similarities and Divergences: Comparison of Social Enterprises in Hong Kong and Taiwan. *Social Enterprise Journal* 7(1): 33–49.

Defourny, Jacques, and Shin Yang Kim. 2011. Emerging Models of Social Enterprise in Eastern Asia: A Cross Country Analysis. *Social Enterprise Journal* 7(1): 86–111.

Xiaomin, Yu. 2011. Social Enterprise in China: Driving Forces, Development Patterns and Legal Framework. *Social Enterprise Journal* 7(1): 9–32.

Websites

Institute for Social Entrepreneurship in Asia, www.isea-group.net.
A "learning and action" network established by social enterprises to promote and support social entrepreneurship in Asia, and exchange information relating to the theory and practice of transforming markets.

Asia Centre for Social Entrepreneurship & Philanthropy, www.bschool.nus.edu/acsep.
A school within the National University of Singapore, the Asia Centre aims to advance understanding and practice of philanthropy and social entrepreneurship in Asia, through education and support in research.

Asian Venture Philanthropy Network, https://avpn.asia/.
A funder's network based in Singapore, dedicated to establishing and supporting a high impact social investment community in Asia, increasing financial and intellectual capital in the social sector.

Asia Impact Exchange, www.asiaiix.com.
A social stock exchange: "the world's first public trading platform dedicated to connecting Social Enterprises with mission-aligned investment."

EMES International Research Network, http://emes.net/.
The EMES research network connects university research centers and aims to build up theoretical and empirical knowledge regarding social enterprise, social entrepreneurship, and solidarity economy.

CIRIEC INTERNATIONAL, www.ciriec.ulg.ac.be/en/.
The International Centre of Research and Information on the Public, Social and Cooperative Economy is a non-governmental international scientific organization with the objective to promote the collection of information and research on economic sectors in the service of the collective interest.

Global Social Entrepreneurship Network, www.gsen.global/.
In collaboration with social enterprises internationally, GSEN aims to build "the foundations for a high-impact social entrepreneurship ecosystem."

NESsT, www.nesst.org/social-enterprise/.
An organization which invests and support social enterprise in many countries around the world.

Inwork Project, www.inworkproject.eu.
A European project aiming to improve participation of marginalized groups on the labor market; promoting education, self-reliance and integration.

Governance International, www.govint.org/our-services/co-production/.
Working with organizations to provide tools, resources, and information to promote international good practice within public services.

References

Austin, James, Howard Stevenson, and Jane Wei-Skillern. 2006. Social and Commercial Entrepreneurship: Same, Different, or Both? *Entrepreneurship: Theory & Practice* 30(1): 1–22.

Bacq, Sophie, and Frank Janssen. 2011. The Multiple Faces of Social Entrepreneurship: A Review of Definitional Issues Based on Geographical and Thematic Criteria. *Entrepreneurship & Regional Development* 23(5–6): 373–403.

Bornstein, David. 2004. *How To Change The World: Social Entrepreneurs and the Power of New Ideas*. Oxford: Oxford University Press.

Borzaga, Carlo, and Jacques Defourny, eds. 2001. *The Emergency of Social Enterprises*. Trento: Edizioni 31.

Borzaga, Carlo, and Andrea Santuari. 2001. Italy: From Traditional Co-operatives to Innovative Social Enterprises. In *The Emergence of Social Enterprise*. Carlo Borzaga and Jacques Defourny, eds. Pp. 166–181. London: Routledge.

Boschee, Jerr. 2006. Social Entrepreneurship: The Promise and the Perils. In *Social Entrepreneurship. New Models of Sustainable Social Change*. Alex Nicholls, ed. Pp. 356–390. Oxford: Oxford University Press.

Brandsen, Taco, and Marlies Honingh. 2015. Distinguishing Different Types of Coproduction: A Conceptual Analysis Based on the Classical Definitions. *Public Administration Review* 76(3): 427–435.

Chung, Moo-Kwon, Sang-il Han, and Mingjeong Park. 2015. Government's Financial Support and Social Performance of Social Enterprises: Lessons and Policy Implications from the Korean Case. Keynote speech, The 2015 International Conference on Social Enterprise: Innovation, Cultivation and Social Impact, Taiwan, September 2–3.

Clemens, Elisabeth. 1999. Politics and Institutionalism: Explaining Durability and Change. *Annual Review of Sociology* 25(1): 441–466.

Defourny, Jacques. 2001. From Third Sector to Social Enterprise. In *The Emergence of Social Enterprise*. Carlo Borzaga and Jacques Defourny, eds. Pp. 1–28. London: Routledge.

Defourny, Jacques, and Yu-Yuan Kuan. 2011. Guest Editorial: Are there Specific Models of Social Enterprise in Eastern Asia? *Social Enterprise Journal* 7(1): 1–9.

Defourny, Jacques, and José Luis Monzón Campos, eds. 1992. *The Third Sector. Cooperative, Mutual and Non-Profit Organizations*. Brussels: De Boeck.

Defourny, Jacques, and Marthe Nyssens, eds. 2008. Social Enterprises in Europe: Recent trends and developments. *EMES Working Papers 08/01*. Electronic document, https://orbi.ulg.ac.be/bitstream/2268/11568/1/WP_08_01_SE_WEB.pdf, accessed January 17, 2017.

Evers, Adalbert, and Jean-Louis Laville. 2004. Defining the Third Sector in Europe. In *The Third Sector in Europe*. Evers Adalbert and Laville Jean-Louis, eds. Pp. 11–42. Cheltenham: Edward Elgar.

Hsiao, Hsin-Huang Michael. 2015. Social Enterprise Development in Taiwan: Profile and Assessment. Keynote speech, The 2015 International Conference on Social Enterprise: Innovation, Cultivation and Social Impact, Taiwan, September 2–3.

Kee, Chi-Hing. 2015. Assessing the Social Enterprise Sector: The Case of Hong Kong. Keynote speech, The 2015 International Conference on Social Enterprise: Innovation, Cultivation and Social Impact, Taiwan, September 2–3.

Kuan, Yu-Yuan, Kam-tong Chan, Shu-twu Wang, and Cherng-rong Duh. 2015. Mixed Financial Resource Strategies Adopted by Work Integration Social Enterprises in Taiwan and Hong Kong: A Comparison. Keynote speech, The 2015 International Conference on Social Enterprise: Innovation, Cultivation and Social Impact, Taiwan, September 2–3.

Laratta, Rosario. 2013. The Integration of Marginalised People in Times of Fiscal Restraint: An Examination of the Role of Japanese Social Enterprises. *Journal of Governance* 9(1): 73–108.

Laratta, Rosario, and Sachiko Nakagawa. 2016. Shedding Light on the Japanese Social Enterprise Sector: Concepts, Policies and Models. *Psychosociological Issues in Human Resource Management* 4(1): 115–142.

Laratta, Rosario, Sachiko Nakagawa, and Masanari Sakurai. 2011. Japanese Social Enterprises: Major Contemporary Issues and Key Challenges. *Social Enterprise Journal* 7(1): 50–68.

Mair, Johanna, and Ignasi Marti. 2006. Social Entrepreneurship Research: A Source of Explanation, Prediction, and Delight. *Journal of World Business* 41(1): 36–44.

Ministry of Health and Welfare. 1981. *Shōkibo Tsūsho Shisetsu no Chōsa Kekka ni tsuite* [*The Results of the Survey for WISEs*]. Tokyo: Ministry of Health and Welfare.

Ministry of Health, Labour, and Welfare. 2009. *Shokuba Tekiou Enjyosha (Jyobu Kochi) niyoru Shien* [*Employment Supported by the Job Couch System*]. Tokyo: Ministry of Health, Labour, and Welfare. Electronic document, www.mhlw.go.jp/bunya/koyou/shougaisha02/pdf/13.pdf, accessed March 23, 2011.

Ministry of Health, Labour, and Welfare. 2013. *Tokurei Kogaisha Ichiran* [*List on the Special Subsidiary*]. Tokyo: Ministry of Health, Labour, and Welfare. Electronic document, www.mhlw.go.jp/bunya/koyou/shougaisha/dl/20.pdf, accessed October 24, 2013.

Mulgan, Geoff. 2006. Cultivating the Other Invisible Hand of Social Entrepreneurship: Comparative Advantage, Public Policy, and Future Research Priorities. In *Social Entrepreneurship: New Models of Sustainable Social Change*. Alex Nicholls, ed. Pp:74–95. Oxford: Oxford University Press.

Nakagawa, Sachiko, and Rosario Laratta. 2012. Public Policy and Social Innovation: A Study of Work Integration Social Enterprises (WISEs) in Japan. *Leadership and Policy Quarterly* 1(1): 13–34.

Nicholls, Alex. 2010. The Legitimacy of Social Entrepreneurship: Reflexive Isomorphism in a Pre-Paradigmatic Field. *Entrepreneurship Theory and Practice* 34(4): 611–633.

Nishio, Suehiro. 1986. Yutaka Fukushi Kai no Jigyō to Jissen [Activities and Practice of Yutaka Fukushi Kai]. *Chingin to Shakai Hoshō* [*Wages and Social Security*] 945: 42–52.

Nyssens, Marthe, ed. 2006. *Social Enterprise*. London: Routledge.

Osborne, Stephen P., Zoe Radnor, and Kirsty Strokosch. 2016. Co-Production and the Co-Creation of Value in Public Services: A Suitable Case for Treatment? *Public Management Review* 18(5): 639–653.

Welfare and Medical Service Agency. 2012. *Fukushi, Hoken, Iryō Jōhō—WAMNET—*[*Welfare and Medical Service Network System*]. Tokyo: Welfare and Medical Agency. Electronic document, www.wam.go.jp/content/wamnet/pcpub/top/, accessed May 2, 2012.

26

PHILANTHROPY

Masayuki Deguchi

Definition in the Asian context

Philanthropy has been defined in several different ways within academia (Sulek 2010). Consistent with Robert Payton (1988), Theo Schuyt (2010) defined philanthropy as voluntary action for the public good. Another definition, proposed by Lester Salamon describes philanthropy as "the private giving of time or valuables (money, security, property) for public purposes" (1999: 10). One implication of these definitions is that philanthropy can be thought of as a universal concept, and one that can be found in a number of contexts. Giving, the provision of alms, and manifest benevolence occur in many Asian countries characterized by a variety of languages and religions. *Bhiksha* in Buddhism, *daana* and *dakshina* in Hinduism, *zakat* and *sadaqat* in Islam, and *jen* and *yi* in Confucianism represent just a few examples of philanthropic activity in Asian countries (Kassam, Handy, and Jansons 2016; Viswanath and Dadrawala 2004; Young 2004).

Philanthropy dates back several centuries. Some researchers have explored these activities in their proper historical contexts (Imada 2010; Wang *et al.* 2015). However, the lack of a common ontology amongst Asian languages and cultures makes an academic cross-culture comparison of philanthropic activities difficult. María Olivia Domingo (2010) offered a broad definition that circumvents this issue. She argued that "philanthropy" is often associated with the wealthy, the elite, and the West (Domingo 2010: 121). This definition for philanthropy has been adopted by many Asian scholars.

The term "philanthropy" is derived from Greek. Its prefix, *phil-*, means "to love." The term's suffix, *-anthropos*, relates to mankind. Etymologically, philanthropy is the "love of mankind" and "benevolence to humanity" (Anheier 2014). In the American context, the basic concept of philanthropy has been extended to include the benevolent activities of large foundations and organizations. To illustrate, John D. Rockefeller used the term in the early twentieth century to describe his foundation's activities as "scientific philanthropy." Rockefeller and his adviser, Frederic Gates, emphasized the transition from "retail charity" to "wholesale philanthropy." At that time, most wealthy individuals gave money directly to the needy so they could purchase food. However, Rockefeller and his advisor considered this to be a stopgap measure, dubbing it "retail charity." In contrast to the temporary solutions provided by "retail charity," they geared their giving practices toward researching medicine that could provide more permanent possibilities for recovery to the sick, thereby supporting medical advancements and public health to improve the human condition (Anheier and Leat 2006; Bremner 1988; Bulmer 1995; Deguchi 1993; Neilson 1972). They called this style of giving "wholesale philanthropy." Domingo's assertion that "philanthropy is often associated with the wealthy, the elite, and the West" (2010: 121) simultaneously epitomizes the influence of Rockefeller's definition of philanthropy while illustrating the difficulty associated with defining it in the Asian academic context. Further complicating matters, the term "philanthropy" has no direct Japanese translation. Instead, the word is transliterated to *firansoropi or firansuropi* (Deguchi 1993; Hayashi and Yamaoka 1993; Watanabe 1992). Still, empirical studies of philanthropy broadly associated the concept with charitable acts, like giving and volunteering (Brown and Ferris 2007; Lyons, McGregor-Lowndes, and Philip O'Donoghue 2006; Salamon 1999).

Keeping in mind the issues above, there are two definitions for "philanthropy" in the Asian context. The first (which is influenced by the American concept) argues that philanthropy is narrowly related to institutional giving. The broader definition, which is utilized more pervasively in Asia, claims that philanthropy is concerned with all forms of giving and volunteering. Although both definitions have some validity, this chapter adopts the first definition to: (a) examine how the American concept of philanthropy permeates Asian society; and (b) identify the carriers of this type of philanthropy.

Due to limitations in economic power following World War II, there have historically been few large organizations in Asia. One exception has been Japan, which has been successful in its economic expansion, largely due to being one of the first countries to join the Organisation for Economic Co-operation and Development (OECD) in 1964. Since then, Asian corporations have become more powerful and have come to engage in "corporate philanthropy," as modeled in the Unites States. Barnett Baron described philanthropy as it relates to Asian corporations:

> There is great diversity in the types of philanthropic institutions and foundation-like entities in East Asia. Unlike the U.S., however, there are still very few private foundations based on individual or family wealth … Most philanthropic entities in the region are corporate foundations or, even more commonly, corporate giving programs funded on an annual basis rather than endowed.
>
> *(Baron 1997: 1)*

In addition to Japan, Korea and other countries have developed notions of "corporate philanthropy." With corporate philanthropy's growing popularity and pervasiveness in Asia, this chapter considers corporate activities to be concept carriers of philanthropy. Corporate philanthropy is more easily identified and analyzed than Domingo's (2010) conceptualization of "philanthropy."

Corporate philanthropy is active in China and India as well. As unique practitioners of philanthropy, however, there are notable factors related to philanthropy that are specifically applicable in these two countries. These differences (relative to philanthropy in Japan and Korea) are associated with the fact that many Chinese and Indian citizens live outside their home countries (many have made homes in the United States). Some individuals and organizations in these diasporas send money back to their home countries as an institutional form of philanthropy (Dekkers and Rutten 2011; Johnson 2007; Newland, Terrazas, and Munster 2010). In addition to examining corporate philanthropy as modeled by American philanthropic activities, this chapter also addresses "diaspora philanthropy" as a second carrier of American-style philanthropy in Asia.

People in several developing countries understand philanthropic activities to take the form of development programs performed by large, foreign foundations. To wit, many large American foundations have launched local offices in Asia that engage in philanthropy. With this tendency in mind, this chapter discusses the presence of large American foundations and their philanthropic activities in Asia as a third carrier of American-style philanthropy.[1] Last, this chapter features a discussion of how philanthropic organizations are networked, new trends in philanthropy, and future issues facing philanthropic activity.

Corporate philanthropic activities as concept carriers: Japan

Corporate philanthropy refers to business activities through which company-sponsored foundations or employees provide resources to those in need as a form of corporate citizenship or corporate social responsibility (CSR). At present, Asia represents the most rapidly expanding economic region. As a result, many corporations in Asian countries have begun to engage in corporate philanthropy.

Given its economic growth in the 1960s and 1970s, Japan is a prime example of this expansion.[2] As a function of this growth, many Japanese corporations have established company-sponsored foundations (Hashimoto, Furuta, and Homma 1986). The most influential company-sponsored foundation in Japan is the Toyota Foundation, which was established to celebrate the fifty-year anniversary of the founder's first invention and the merger between Toyota Motor and Toyota Motor Sales in 1974 (Deguchi 1993; Onishi 2016). As the largest foundation at the time of its inception, the Toyota Foundation learned both the concepts of "philanthropy" and "independent foundation" from the Ford Foundation (The Toyota Foundation 2007). The Toyota Foundation describes its origins:

> Sitting around the giant boardroom table were President Eiji Toyoda and directors of Toyota Motor and Toyota Sales. Also in attendance was Yujiro Hayashi, executive director of the new foundation … Hayashi stood and citing the work of the giant American foundation—the Ford Foundation (est. 1936), Carnegie Corporation of New York (est. 1911), and the Rockefeller Foundation (est. 1913)—passionately articulated his desire that the Toyota Foundation join their ranks. The Ford Foundation, the largest in the world and associated with the Ford Motor Company, was the perfect analogue for Hayashi as he presented his vision to the directors of Toyota Motor. Moreover, the Ford Foundation's activities were entirely separate from the commercial activities of the company.
>
> *(The Toyota Foundation 2007: 25)*

After being appointed as executive director of the Toyota Foundation, Yujiro Hayashi visited large, private foundations in the United States. During this trip, Hayashi met with Waldemar Nielsen, a former staff member of the Ford Foundation and researcher of philanthropy in the United States. It was interesting that the Toyota Foundation did not model company-sponsored foundations like the Ford Motor Company Fund, but instead independent foundations like the Ford Foundation. This is likely due to the fact that only the Ford Foundation was famous in Japan.[3] Hayashi translated Nielsen's book *Big Foundations* (which did not describe any company-sponsored foundations) into Japanese, thereby bringing concepts related to large American "independent" foundations to a Japanese audience (Hayashi 1984). Following the publication of this book in Japanese, nearly all Japanese corporate foundations became "independent" of their parent companies. The widespread establishment of these "independent" corporate foundations negatively affected neither businesspeople nor Japanese society. As such, this tendency confirmed the utility of the closed foundation community.

At the same time, the Japan Center for International Exchange (JCIE), an operating foundation, introduced the concept of philanthropy to Japan. After sending several missions to the USA and Europe to study philanthropy, the JCIE held an international symposium on philanthropy in Tokyo titled "The Role of Philanthropy in the Advanced Societies" in 1975. High-ranking specialists in philanthropy were invited, including the president of the Ford Foundation. This symposium featured the first appearance of the word "*firansopopii*" as the Japanese transliteration of the term "philanthropy" (JCIE 2016; Onishi 2016). In addition to this initial symposium, the JCIE (headed by Tadashi Yamamoto) held many other symposia related to philanthropy throughout the 1980s.

Although these activities expanded the network of people in Japanese foundations, the philanthropic community remained relatively small. This was due to the symposia being closed, with only those who had already been part of a foundation able to attend. Independent foundations of sponsoring companies were often physically separated from their head offices. As a result, company-sponsored foundations often failed to exert any effects on their parent companies, and were often forgotten by them. Therefore, the concept of philanthropy did not pervade Japanese society when it was initially instituted. Instead, it was popular only within the foundation community.

After the 1985 Plaza Accord, however, some companies expanded the concept of philanthropy due to an increase in direct foreign investment (DFI). The Plaza Accord is an agreement between G5 governments to depreciate the US dollar in relation to the Japanese yen and German Deutsche Mark by intervening in currency markets. As the result of the Accord, the Japanese yen appreciated very quickly, and many Japanese corporations were forced to purchase lands and build factories in the United States. As another form of FDI, many Japanese companies purchased other properties in the USA. For example, Sony purchased Colombia Pictures and Mitsubishi Group purchased the Rockefeller Center in New York City. The Japanese referred to this trend as "Buying America" (Felsenthal 1990; Sato 1994). Upon expanding into American markets, Japanese companies came to learn about philanthropy as a result of pressure from local communities in the USA (Bob 1990). Japanese corporations in the USA were flooded with requests for donations, teaching a number of Japanese CEOs about the importance of corporate philanthropy. The concept of corporate philanthropy gained such momentum amongst Japanese corporations in the USA that publications on the topic became popular. For example, *Joining-in!: A Handbook for Better Corporate Citizenship in the United States* is a typical guidebook of corporate citizenship (Japanese Chamber of Commerce and Industry of New York Inc. 1990). In short, the Japanese business sector learned about philanthropy directly from American businesses and their philanthropic practices.[4]

Head offices in Tokyo became aware of the importance of corporate donations. After this realization, the head offices became willing to give money to their US-based affiliated companies. One obstacle, however, was the tax levied on such provisions. To circumvent this problem, the Keidanren Japanese Business Federation established the Council for Better Corporate Citizenship (CBCC) in 1989. The CBCC operates as a pass-through foundation through which Japanese companies can receive tax benefits on donations from Japan to the USA. Donations from Japanese parent companies to the CBCC can be deductible from pre-tax profits, and the CBCC would provide money to the local affiliated companies in the USA for philanthropic activities. This funding stream was fundamentally different from one in which funds move through the peripheral third sector.

Most businesspersons returned to Japan to become influential there. One of these influential businessmen is Kazuo Watanabe, who served as CEO of Mitsubishi Electronic Ltd. in the USA. Once back in Japan, Watanabe was the first to transliterate philanthropy to *firansuropii* rather than *firansopoii* (Watanabe 1992). These expressions are evident of the distinction between the two streams through which the American concept of philanthropy was imported to Japan. In Japan, the business world is much more influential than the foundation world. As such, Watanabe's activities were more visible in Japanese society than the Toyota Foundation's or JCIE's.

In 1989, the foundation community and business community merged. The JCIE and the Keidanren (which is the symbol of the Japanese business sector) collaborated to hold a symposium that included Akio Morita from Sony and David Rockefeller from Chase Manhattan Bank. The inclusion of these panelists was symbolic of the friction caused by the "Buying American" stance and ongoing economic conflict between the two countries. As the result of the high-profile nature of the symposium, many newspapers reported on it, bringing the concept of philanthropy to the fore in Japanese society. In addition, the Keidanren established the "One Percent Club" in 1990. This club is a corporate donors' club whose member corporations pledge to donate at least 1 percent of their pre-tax profits. This idea was derived from the "The Five Percent Club" established in Minnesota in 1976. Throughout the 1970s and 1980s, many corporations in the USA established 2 percent or 5 percent clubs to signal their intentions to donate these respective portions of the pre-tax profits to their communities. These figures were used because the national average of community donations was less than 2 percent.

Historically, Japanese companies have given money to festivals and cultural events in local communities as well as national projects (e.g., the Olympic Games). The latter donations were initially collected by the Keidanren, which allocates the money to industrial federations of which corporations are a part. Each federation then allocates money to member corporations. Dubbed "Keidanren-style" philanthropy, this method spurred some Japanese corporations to give more than their 1 percent pretax benefit, even before 1990. Based on its efficacy, it seems that the notion of the "One Percent Club" is useful for encouraging philanthropy. Moreover, it represents a simple criterion with which Japanese corporations can judge their philanthropic efforts (Deguchi 1995; Homma and Deguchi 1996). Many Japanese corporations established philanthropy departments in their head offices in 1990. As a consequence of these developments, newspapers and other media began reporting on the corporations' philanthropic activities to a substantial extent in that year. Thus, 1990 is often referred to as *firansoropii gannen* or "the epoch-making year of Japanese philanthropy" (Homma and Deguchi 1996: 1).

Diaspora activities as concept carriers: China and India

A second type of philanthropy relates to activities performed by Asians who live overseas, especially in the USA (i.e., Asian *diasporas*). Originally, the term *diaspora* was meant to relate to communities of Jewish settlers that had left Israel after the Babylonian exile. Now, however, the term is used to describe all types of population dispersions. In many cases, members of diasporas give money to their home countries. Some donations are limited to the providers' family networks, but others send money for the general public good of their communities. This kind of philanthropy is called "diaspora philanthropy" (Johnson 2007; Young and Shih 2004). It is important to note that diaspora philanthropy relates not only to individual remittance, but also to philanthropic activities undertaken through hometown associations (HTAs; Dunn 2004; Newland *et al.* 2010). Whereas corporate philanthropy (in Asia) originally developed in Japan and Korea, diaspora philanthropy is more popular in China and India (Geithner, Johnson, and Chen 2004).

Chinese-American diaspora philanthropy

About 35 million people of Chinese heritage live in countries other than China (Newland and Patrick 2004). The Chinese-American population, in particular, has grown rapidly in the last few decades. According to the US Census Bureau (as cited in Yin and Lan 2004: 91), in 1950, there were 150,000 Chinese-Americans. By 1970, this number had grown to 435,000. By 2000, the number of Chinese-Americans had grown to 2,870,000. These growing numbers of Chinese-Americans have engaged in philanthropic activities for some time.

After the People's Republic of China was founded in 1949, philanthropy was considered an unnecessary component of a foregone Republican Era (Wang *et al.* 2015). However, in 1979, the Chinese government changed several of its policies. Xiao-huang Yin and Zhiyong Lan (2004: 87) highlight two important policy changes: (a) normalization of the relationship between China and the USA, and (b) holding conferences to facilitate contributions from Chinese citizens overseas. As a result of these policy changes, the *Qiaoban* (Overseas Chinese Affairs Office) system, which develops relationships with Chinese living overseas, was fully restored. Since these policy changes in the 1970s, donations from Chinese-Americans have increased, and the methods by which they donate have diversified. According to the typology proposed by Yin and Lan (2004: 94), Chinese diaspora philanthropy in the USA can categorized as one of five types: traditional philanthropy, mainstream US institutions, ethnic American transnational non-governmental organizations (NGOs), "New Players," and Chinese-American Transnational Academic Societies.

First, traditional philanthropy is based on the HTAs (Newland *et al.* 2010; Yin and Lan 2004). For example, the *Sanri* Association in San Francisco's Chinatown district collects donations for the Chinese Government, particularly for the purpose of disaster relief (Yin and Lan 2004: 94). Donations made at HTAs are "not directed exclusively to the donor's own family and friends, are not intended to generate direct commercial gain for the donor, and are not primarily for the purpose of achieving political power" (Newland *et al.* 2010: 3).

Second, Yin and Lan (2004: 96) argue that American non-profit organizations collect donations and engage in other types of philanthropy to serve China-related projects. One illustrative example is the philanthropy conducted through Johns Hopkins University. Many Chinese-Americans have donated to the Hopkins-Nanjing Center in China. It is important to note that this kind of philanthropy may be rare; very few researchers have discussed this kind of giving as diaspora philanthropy.

Third, many Chinese-American transnational NGOs, including professional organizations established by Chinese-Americans, engage in some form of philanthropy. Founded by a group of Chinese-Americans influenced by the Tiananmen Incident in 1989, the 1990 Institute in San Francisco pursues philanthropic activities to support China (Yin and Lan 2004: 100). The Institute is supported not only by Chinese-Americans, but also by more traditional American organizations, like the Gates Foundation and Facebook (The 1990 Institute 2016).

Fourth, "New Players" are organizations founded by recent Chinese immigrants. These organizations include transnational alumni associations or fraternities with hometown networks. In contrast to more traditional diaspora philanthropy, recent immigrants who have graduated from elite Chinese universities often organize foundations in the USA to support scholarship programs and research. One example is the University of Science and Technology of China (USTC) Alumni Foundation, which is a 501(c)(3) (tax-exempt) organization in the USA (Yin and Lan 2004: 103). The foundation's dual mission is to promote the work of USTC personnel (including students, teachers, and alumni) in the USA and elsewhere, and to encourage cultural exchange between Chinese and American researchers (USTC Alumni Foundation 2016). The

Peking University Education Foundation is another example of this "New Player" philanthropy (Peking University Education Foundation 2016). This "New Player" philanthropy has become more popular due to the increasing mobility of talent and widespread changes in communication technologies. In addition, successful immigrants with access to Internet technology can more easily maintain personal relationships with individuals in their home countries over distance and time (Newland *et al.* 2010).

Last, Chinese-American Transnational Academic Societies are scholarly organizations that volunteer to teach and work in China for virtually no financial compensation. According to Yin and Lan (2004: 107), this type of philanthropy has gained in popularity, resulting in the foundation of multiple Chinese academic societies, including the Chinese Economists Society in 1985, the Association of Chinese Political Studies in 1986, the Association of Chinese Historians in the United States in 1987, the Association of Chinese Professors of Social Sciences in 1995, the Association of Chinese Scientists and Engineers in 1996, and the Overseas Young Chinese Forum in 1999. Each of these foundations is registered as a non-profit organization in the USA.

Indian-American diaspora philanthropy

Although Yin and Lan's (2004) typology was designed to apply to types of Chinese philanthropic efforts, it can also be applied to Indian philanthropy. Indian citizens engage in diaspora philanthropy to a substantial extent; India is currently the largest recipient of remittances (Shiveshwarkar 2008: 132). Indian diasporas are thought to include non-resident Indians (NRIs) and Persons of Indian Origin (PIOs). NRIs are citizens of India (who possess an Indian passport), and PIOs are individuals of Indian origin, but do not have an Indian passport. In September 2000, the Indian government created a High Committee on the Indian Diaspora. This committee estimated that around the world, there were about 20 million NRIs and PIOs in total (Newland and Patrick 2004). Although Indian corporate philanthropy is extensive, Indian diaspora philanthropy is a key component of Indian philanthropy on the whole. Moreover, there have been two key phases of migration from India—from the nineteenth century to the 1950s and from 1959 forward (Shiveshwarkar 2008). This chapter focuses on the latter.

Owing to the Immigration Act of 1965, Indian immigration to the USA accelerated in the late 1960s. Consider that there were 380,000 Indians living in the USA in 1980, over 800,000 in 1990, and more than 1.6 million by 2001 (Sidel 2004). Many of these immigrants engaged in philanthropy designed to help others in their home countries. Yin and Lan's (2004) taxonomy for identifying types of Chinese diaspora philanthropy can be applied to the Indian context. This is particularly true of professional organizations established by Indian-Americans. More than 1,000 Indian American organizations engage in philanthropy geared toward helping the NRI community in the USA. Many of these organizations are "umbrella" organizations, which include the American Hotel Owners Association (AAHO) and the National Federation of Indian American Associations (NFIA; Sidel 2004). These organizations encourage networking and look to connect Indians in the USA with citizens of their homeland. For example, the NFIA's mission statement explicitly refers to the people of India:

> The NFIA is committed to promoting and fostering goodwill between the people of the United States and the people of India.
>
> *(NFIA 2016)*

Ethnic transnational academic societies comprised citizens of Indian heritage (e.g., the American Association of Physicians of Indian Origin [AAPI]) also engage in philanthropic activities.

The AAPI, which represents over 60,000 practicing physicians and over 20,000 medical students, residents, and fellows, established the Charitable Foundation (AAPI-CF). This foundation operates seventeen free clinics in different Indian states in an effort to assist the poorest of the poor (American Association of Physicians of Indian Origin Charitable Foundation 2016).

Unfortunately, most philanthropy is encouraged by tragedy. For example, the 2001 Gujarat earthquake, which killed around 20,000 Indian citizens, was a catalyst for diaspora philanthropy. As a result of the earthquake, the Federation of Gujarati Associations in North America (FOGANA) emerged as a strong supporter for developing projects Gujarat (Sidel 2004). This is an illustrative example of transnational NGOs engaging in philanthropy.

Following the Gujarat earthquake in 2001, U.S. President Bill Clinton and Indian Prime Minister Atal Bihari Vajpayee recognized the need for a cross-national philanthropy platform. This vision resulted in the American–Indian Foundation. This foundation is dedicated to promoting social and economic change in India and building a lasting connection between the USA and India (The American–Indian Foundation 2016).

As in China, "new players" are critical contributors to Indian–American philanthropy. As many members of the Indian diaspora in the United States have become entrepreneurs, venture capitalists, and top executives, they have supported the development of Indian IT experts. In 1992, a group of successful Indians, many of them engineers living in the San Francisco Bay Area, founded The Indus Entrepreneurs (TIE) to support and mentor promising Indian entrepreneurs in Silicon Valley (Newland and Tanaka 2010: 6). There are currently 13,000 members of TIE Global, including over 2,500 charter members in sixty-one chapters across eighteen countries. TIE Global has catalyzed the liberalization of key economic sectors in India and Pakistan (The Indus Entrepreneurs Global 2016). Relative to Japanese corporate foundations—which often serve as grant-makers in the USA—both the Chinese and Indian diasporas are powerful fundraisers in the USA.

US foundations in Asia as concept carriers

American foundations in Asian countries are visible philanthropic organizations that originated in the USA. For example, the Ford Foundation established a local office in New Delhi in 1950. This office was the first Ford office to be located outside the USA. Over the past sixty years, the Ford Foundation has written more than 3,500 grants in the region, totaling more than $508 million. This money has been distributed to over 1,200 institutions in India, Nepal, and Sri Lanka. In 1988, the Ford Foundation also established a local office in China. Since that time, the Foundation has worked with Chinese partners to support many aspects of economic and social development, including equitable, sustainable urbanization (The Ford Foundation 2016). Kathleen McCarthy (1995) showed how the Ford Foundation transitioned from large-scale technical assistance programs rooted in government and academia to assisting grass-roots women's groups and community-based NGOs. In this way, the Foundation moved from "disinterested expertise" to "self-interested expertise" in relation to local populations (McCarthy 1995). These efforts are a form of local "empowerment."

The Rockefeller Foundation similarly established an office in Bangkok in 1964 (The Rockefeller Foundation 2016), and the MacArthur Foundation opened an office in New Delhi in 1994. The MacArthur Foundation primarily designs and implements programs related to population and reproductive health (MacArthur Foundation 2016). In 1954, a group of twenty-one forward-thinking citizens from business and academics established a private, non-governmental organization devoted to promoting democracy, rule of law, and market-based development in post-war Asia. This organization—The Asia Foundation—is headquartered in San Francisco, and works through a network of offices in eighteen Asian countries: Afghanistan, Bangladesh, Cambodia, China, India, Indonesia, Japan, Korea, Laos, Malaysia, Mongolia, Myanmar, Nepal, Pacific Island Nations, Pakistan, Philippines, Singapore, Sri Lanka, Thailand, Timor-Leste, and Vietnam (The Asia Foundation 2016). The Asia Foundation not only promotes development, but also spreading the concept of philanthropy throughout Asia and beyond.

The trend of US foundations establishing local offices in Asia has been passed on to the more contemporary foundations, including the Bill & Melinda Gates Foundation, the Ford Foundation, and the Rockefeller Foundation. These foundations tend to focus on innovation rather than grants and emphasize the impact they have rather than their output. The Gates Foundation has offices in both New Delhi and Beijing (Bill & Melinda Gates Foundation 2016). In addition to American foundations, international NGOs (e.g., CARE, OXFAM, MSF, and Save the Children) are also active in Asia. In total, there are between 3,000 and 6,000 foreign NGOs based in China, including about 2,000 foundations (Chen 2006).

Forming philanthropy networks in Asia

This chapter has thus far demonstrated how the American concept of philanthropy has come to Asia. It is also important to examine how these philanthropic organizations network within Asia.

Domestic networks

Philanthropic efforts by individual organizations rarely make a significant impact on Asian society. However, by developing networks of philanthropic organizations, it is possible to more effectively illustrate the sorts of problems that can benefit from philanthropy.

In Asia, the Philippines were one of the first to engage in networking to this end. In 1970, fifty Filipino corporations came together to form a business-led social development foundation called the Philippine Business for Social Progress (PBSP). This foundation has grown to include more than 160 member organizations, has worked with about 2,500 partner organizations, and has provided over PhP4.6 billion (US$84 million) in financial assistance to over 5,000 projects. The PBSP is the first of its kind in Asia, to promote corporate social responsibility in the form of philanthropy (Amott 2007).

In addition to the PBSP, the Association of Foundations (AF) was created in the Philippines in 1972. The AF is the country's first network of NGOs and foundations (The Association of Foundations 2016). Also in 1972, the Japan Association of Charitable Organizations (JACO) was established (Japan Association of Charitable Organizations 2016). Member organizations of JACO are both grant-making foundations and operating foundations and associations. In 1985, the Japan Foundation Center (JFC) was created to imitate the Foundation Center in the USA (Japan Foundation Center 2016; The Toyota Foundation 2007).

Similarly, the China Foundation Center (CFC) was created in China in 2008, and includes a number of global foundations. These foundations include the Bill & Melinda Gates Foundation, the Ford Foundation, the Asia Foundation, the Rockefeller Brothers Fund, Give2Asia, Stiftung Mercator, Robert Bosch Stiftung, and many Chinese foundations. The CFC is an independent non-governmental information disclosure platform of foundations, and represents a historic milestone in China's philanthropic development (China Foundation Center 2017).

The creation of the Asian Pacific Philanthropy Consortium (APPC)

In December 1994, a symposium was held in Osaka, Japan, called "Developing Nongovern-mental Underpinnings of the Emerging Asia Pacific Community." This symposium was attended by fifty leaders of philanthropic foundations, corporate foundations, NGOs, and academics came together to discuss philanthropic issues. In total, fourteen countries were represented at the symposium. At the conference, The Asia Foundation and the JCIE proposed the develop-ment of the APPC. Designed to be an informal association of "like-minded institutions, each independent, but jointly pursuing a common objective" (Yamamoto and Hubbard 1995: 65), the APPC was formally launched in May 1995. The APPC—which is the first transnational network of philanthropic organizations in Asia—encourages supply-side methods to strengthen philanthropy in the Asia-Pacific region (Yamamoto and Hubbard 1995).

By networking philanthropic foundations, the APPC can support research teams working in twelve countries as part of the Asia Pacific Philanthropy Information Network (APPIN; Lyons and Hasan 2002). In addition, since 2002, the APPC has worked with the Asian Institute of Management's RVR Center to organize the annual Asian Forum on Corporate Social Respons-ibility (Biggers 2010). By 2010, the APPC faced a serious lack of funding, and began to seek funds to continue its operations. As a result, the APPC was absorbed by Give2Asia in 2010. As such, Give2Asia (which was founded in 2001 by the Asia Foundation) currently serves as a cata-lyst for philanthropic investment in Asia (Give2Asia 2016).

New trends

The twenty-first century has seen the emergence of a new level of wealth amongst some indi-viduals and organizations. Moreover, Internet technology has expanded the means through which these individuals and organizations can engage in fundraising and other philanthropic efforts. Taken together, the development of exceptional wealth and new technologies represent new trends in philanthropy. Acknowledging these benefits, the current period is often referred to as "the new golden age of philanthropy" (Ferris 2016; Havens and Schervish 2014).

As outlined above, traditional philanthropy spread to Asia in the twentieth century. However, substantial economic growth in Asia has allowed some Asian citizens and organizations to become native philanthropists. These wealthy entities do not need American avenues for phi-lanthropy. For example, Samuel (Yen-Liang) Yin in Taiwan, current chairman of Ruentex Group and of Ruentex Construction Group, established the Tang Prize Foundation December 2012. This prize (which can be awarded to an individual of any race or nationality) is meant to encourage sustainable development, develop biotechnology medicine, promote Sinology, and maintain the rule of law. This award is the largest in the world, exceeding even those provided to Nobel laureates (The Tang Prize Foundation 2016).

In addition, the quality of philanthropic efforts has begun to change. Philanthropic efforts have changed from the old-fashioned Rockefeller model of scientific philanthropy to "creative philanthropy" (Anheier and Leat 2006) and "new frontiers" (Salamon 2014) models. One cata-lyst for this change is that venture entrepreneurs have become philanthropists, and seek to improve the world around them rather than just profit from it. In April 2001, the Rockefeller Foundation, the Cisco Systems Foundation, and three individual philanthropists formed Acumen. As a new type of philanthropic organization, Acumen emphasizes social entrepreneur-ship, which dictates that: "small amounts of philanthropic capital, combined with large doses of business acumen, can build thriving enterprises that serve vast numbers of the poor" (Ebraham and Rangan 2009: 1–2) The purpose of Acumen is to transform the world of philanthropy by perceiving all human beings not as distant strangers, but as members of a single, global community where everyone has the opportunity to build a life of dignity (Acumen 2016).

Although Acumen engages in philanthropic activities in countries in all parts of the world, it is most active India and Pakistan, where it utilizes a business model based on "patient capital." This model emphasizes debt or equity investment in early-stage enterprises that provide low-income consumers with access to health care, water, housing, alternative energy, or agricultural inputs. As a function of these efforts, Acumen seeks to have a significant impact on target regions. Acumen opened offices in India and Pakistan in 2006 (Acumen 2016).

In this way, the concept of venture philanthropy has come to penetrate Asian countries in recent years. The Asia Venture Philanthropy Network (AVPN), which is a membership organization based in Asia, includes organizations from sixteen countries. This network was modeled on the European Venture Philanthropy network (EVPN; AVPN 2016). Venture philanthropy is not a traditional form of philanthropy, but instead follows the venture capital funding model associated with entrepreneurship (Anheir and Leat 2006; Moody 2008; Porter and Kramer 1999).

Future concerns: new regulatory movement

Even if we are currently living in a "new golden age of philanthropy" (Ferris 2016; Havens and Schervish 2014), there are two major concerns regarding the future of philanthropy in Asia. One concern relates to philanthropy within Asia, and the other relates to the West (including the USA). The philanthropic activities described above disseminate not only monetary resources, but also American values, including human rights, democracy, gender roles, and animal ethics. However, some Asian states in which religion plays a key societal role are not always amenable to accepting American values. Many of these states have begun to regulate philanthropic organizations within them (Breen, Dunn, and Sidel 2016).

Douglas Rutzen described several tendencies of regulatory frameworks regarding philanthropic organizations, a trend he dubbed "philanthropic protectionism." Rutzen argued that an increasing number of countries constrain the ability of CSOs to receive international funding, including cross-border philanthropy. Common constraints include:

1 requiring prior government approval to receive international funding;
2 enacting "foreign agents" legislation to stigmatize foreign funded CSOs;
3 capping the amount of international funding that a CSO may receive;
4 requiring that international funding be routed through government-controlled entities;
5 restricting activities that can be undertaken with international funding;
6 prohibiting CSOs from receiving international funding from specific donors;
7 constraining international funding through the overly broad application of counter-terrorism and anti-money laundering measures;
8 taxing the receipt of international funding, including cross-border philanthropy;
9 imposing onerous reporting requirements on the receipt of international funding; and
10 using defamation laws, treason laws, and other laws to bring criminal charges against recipients of international funding.

(Rutzen 2015: 6)

China is an illustrative example of one of the states that has begun to regulate the philanthropic activities that occur within its boundaries. Although many foreign NGOs operate within China, the 2016 PRC Law on the Management of Foreign Non-Governmental Organizations'

Activities Within Mainland China (i.e., "China's Foreign NGO Law"), which began being enforced on January 1, 2017, requires foreign NGOs to register with Chinese police and the Ministry of Public Security before beginning operations. Moreover, it may result in foreign NGOs coming under police investigation. Foreign NGOs operating within mainland China must not endanger China's national or ethnic unity or its security, nor must they harm China's national interests (Article 5 of China's Foreign NGO Law). These stipulations have resulted in substantial international criticism (BBC 2016; Buckley 2016; Tiezzi 2016; Yu and Marro 2016). In India, meanwhile, NGOs must receive permission to receive foreign money. NGOs that meet certain requirements[5] for three years are eligible to register under the Foreign Contribution (Regulation) Act (FCRA) of 2010. If this registration is approved, the organization is authorized to receive foreign contributions for up to five years (Rutzen 2015: 8).

These laws regulate diaspora philanthropy from the receiver-side. This is not to say that Western culture (as a sender of diaspora philanthropy) has not changed as well. To illustrate, the United States has changed its philanthropic activities in recent years. The terror attacks of September 11, 2001 have resulted in anti-terrorism policies (including the USA PATRIOT Act) that may limit the degree to which international philanthropy can be exercised. Included in the PATRIOT Act are guidelines for best practices related to US-based charities (Sidel 2004). For example, as part of the PATRIOT Act, the transfer of money from the USA to Asia is sometimes regulated, making it more difficult. Counter-terrorism regulations like the PATRIOT Act are crucially important for Western governments. Used for security and counter-terrorism, these regulations deprive NGOs of civic space (Bloodgood and Tremblay-Boire 2011; Sidel 2006). As such, these "risk-based regulations" (Atkinson 2008) can affect new regulating agencies in Asia, including Japan's Public Interest Corporation Commission (PICC) in 2007 and The Singaporean Charity Council in 2007 (Cordery 2013: Deguchi 2016). The respective influences of these new regulators remains to be seen, but will become clear in the coming years.

Notes

1 Tamaki Onishi (2016) also provides a historical account of Japanese philanthropy (including corporate philanthropy) between the 1970s and 1990s. This period is a particularly important one in the historical development of Japanese philanthropy.

2 Ku-Hyun Jung (1994) described the general landscape of philanthropy in the Asia-Pacific region in the 1980s and the early 1990s. More specifically, Jung explored philanthropic efforts in Japan, Korea, Taiwan, Hong Kong, Indonesia, Malaysia, the Philippines and Thailand, most of which are home to companies that engage in corporate philanthropy.

3 The Ford Foundation was established by Henry Ford and his son Edsel Ford. It is independent of the Ford Motor Company. In contrast, the Ford Motor Fund was established and completely advised by the Ford Motor Company. The Toyota Foundation was established by the Toyota Motor Company, and is modeled from the Ford Motor Fund rather than the Ford Foundation (Deguchi 1993).

4 Japanese corporations have also established company-sponsored foundations in the USA. As noted above, Japanese company-sponsored philanthropy initiatives often serve as foundations independent of their home offices. For example, the first Japanese corporate foundation in the USA was the Hitachi Foundation, located in Washington, DC. Interestingly, Hitachi has no offices or factories in Washington. Hitachi's establishment of the foundation was criticized by American communities that suspected Hitachi of seeking political benefits. However, this is an illustrative example of an "independent" company-sponsored foundation. The Hitachi Foundation appointed Delwin Roy, the former Program Officer of the Ford Foundation, as President and CEO. After fulfilling its role, the Hitachi Foundation ended its activities at the end of 2016 (The Hitachi Foundation 2016).

5 FCRA Article 12 indicates totally twenty-eight requirements. For example, the person making an application for registration under sub-section (1) has undertaken reasonable activity in its chosen filed for the benefit of the society for which the foreign contribution is proposed to be utilized (Article 12 4b). The person making an application for giving prior permission under sub-section (1) has prepared a

reasonable project for the benefit of the society for which the foreign contribution is proposed to be utilized (Article 12 4c), in case the person being other than an individual, any of its directors or office bearers has neither been convicted under any law for the time being in force nor any prosecution for any offence is pending against him. (Article 12 4e).

Suggested readings

Geithner, Peter F., Paula D. Johnson, and Lincoln C. Chen, eds. 2004. *Diaspora Philanthropy to India: A Perspective from the United States*. Cambridge: Global Equity Initiative, Asia Center, Harvard University.

Jung, Ku-Hyung, ed. 1994. *Evolving Patterns of Asia Pacific Philanthropy*. Seoul: Institute of East and West Studies, Yonsei University.

Websites

Asia Foundation, http://asiafoundation.org/.
A non-profit international development organization working throughout Asia to strengthen governance, empower women, improve economies, and promote environmental awareness.

Asia Venture Philanthropy Network, https://avpn.asia/.
A funders' network based in Singapore, working with the social investment community across Asia to advocate high impact philanthropy.

Give2Asia, www.give2asia.org/.
An extensive team of local staff across Asia, connecting support with local organizations to address critical progress in health care, education, economy, and environment.

References

The 1990 Institute. 2016. 1990 Homepage. Electronic document, www.1990institute.org/donate/, accessed December 1, 2016.

Acumen. 2016. Acumen. Electronic document, http://Acumen.Org/, accessed December 1, 2016.

American Association of Physicians of Indian Origin Charitable Foundation. 2016. Electronic document, http://aapicharitablefoundation.org/, accessed December 1, 2016.

The American Indian Foundation. 2016. Electronic document, http://aif.org/, accessed December 1, 2016.

Amott, Natasha. 2007. Cases from the Philippines in Innovative Philanthropy: An Overview of the Philippines. In *Innovation in Strategic Philanthropy: Local and Global Perspectives*. Helmut K. Anheier, Adele Simmons, and David Winder, eds. Pp. 61–78. Boston, MA: Springer.

Anheier, Helmut K. 2014. *Nonprofit Organizations: Theory, Management, and Policy*. 2nd Edn. Abingdon: Routledge.

Anheier, Helmut K., and Diana Leat. 2006. *Creative Philanthropy: Toward a New Philanthropy for the Twenty-First Century*. London and New York: Routledge.

The Asia Foundation. 2016. The Asia Foundation. Electronic document, http://asiafoundation.org/, accessed November 11 2016.

Asian Venture Philanthropy Network (AVPN). 2016. AVPN Annual Report 2016: April 2015 through March 2016 features Singapore. Electronic document, https://avpn.asia/wp-content/uploads/2016/10/annual-report-2016.pdf, accessed January 16, 2017.

The Association of Foundations. 2016. Association of Foundations. Electronic document, http://afonline.org/, accessed December 1, 2016.

Atkinson, Karen. 2008 Charities and Political Campaigning: The Impact of Risk-Based Regulation. *Liverpool Law Review* 29(2): 143–163.

Baron, Barnett F. 1997. Funding Civil Society in Asia. *The Asia Foundation Working Paper Series* 3. Pp. 1–33. Philippines Asia Pacific Philanthropy Consortium.

BBC. 2016. China Passes New Laws on Foreign NGOs Amid International Criticism. Electronic document, www.bbc.com/news/world-asia-china-36157052, accessed December 1, 2016.

Biggers, Christopher S. 2010. Asia Pacific Philanthropy Consortium (Appc). In *International Encyclopedia of Civil Society*. Helmut K. Anheier and Stefan Toepler, eds. Pp. 34–35. New York: Springer.

Bill & Melinda Gates Foundation. 2016. Electronic document, www.gatesfoundation.org/, accessed December 1, 2016.

Bloodgood, Elizabeth A., and Joannie Tremblay-Boire. 2011. International NGOs and National Regulation in an Age of Terrorism. *VOLUNTAS: International Journal of Voluntary and Nonprofit Organizations* 22(1): 142–173.

Bob, Daniel E. 1990. *Japanese Companies in American Communities: Cooperation, Conflict & the Role of Corporate Citizenship*. New York: Japan Society.

Breen, Oonagh B., Alison Dunn, and Mark Sidel, eds. 2016. *Regulatory Waves: Comparative Perspectives on State Regulation and Self-Regulation Policies in the Nonprofit Sector*. Cambridge: Cambridge University Press.

Bremner, Robert. H. 1988. *American Philanthropy*. 2nd Edn. Chicago, IL: University of Chicago Press.

Brown, Eleanor, and James M. Ferris. 2007. Social Capital and Philanthropy: An Analysis of the Impact of Social Capital on Individual Giving and Volunteering. *Nonprofit and Voluntary Sector Quarterly* 36(1): 85–99.

Buckley, Chris. 2016. Uncertainty Over New Chinese Law Rattles Foreign Nonprofits, *New York Times*, December 29. Electronic Document www.nytimes.com/2016/12/29/world/asia/china-foreign-ngo.html?_r=0, accessed January 29, 2017.

Bulmer, Martin. 1995. Observations on the History of Large Philanthropic Foundations in Britain and the United States. *Voluntas: International Journal of Voluntary and Nonprofit Organizations* 6(3): 275–291.

Chen, Jie. 2006. The NGO Community in China: Expanding Linkages with Transnational Civil Society and Their Democratic Implications. *China Perspectives* 68: 29–40.

China Foundation Center. 2017 Donor & Partnership. Electronic document, http://en.foundationcenter.org.cn/donor.html, accessed February 21, 2017.

Cordery, Carolyn. 2013. Regulating Small and Medium Charities: Does it Improve Transparency and Accountability?. *Voluntas: International Journal of Voluntary and Nonprofit Organizations* 24(3): 831–851.

Deguchi, Masayuki. 1993. *Firansoropi; Kigyō to hito no syakai kōken* [*Philanthropy: Social Contribution by Business and Individuals*]. Tokyo: Marzen (in Japanese).

Deguchi, Masayuki. 1995. Suiito kappuru—Hanshin daishinsai ni mirareta kigyō to NPO no atarasii kankei [*Sweet Couple—New Relations Between Business and Non-Profit Organizations after the Great Hansin Awaji Earthquake*]. *Economy Society Policy* 281: 69–73 (in Japanese).

Deguchi, Masayuki. 2016. Globalization, Globalization, and Galapagos Syndrome: Public Interest Corporations in Japan. *International Journal for Not-for-Profit Law* 18(1): 5–14.

Dekkers, Natascha, and Mario Rutten. 2011. Diaspora Philanthropy from a Homeland Perspective: Reciprocity and Contestation over Donations in Central Gujarat, India. *ProGlo Working paper* No. 2. Bangalore and Amsterdam: National Institute of Advanced Studies and Amsterdam Institute for Social Science Research.

Domingo, Ma. Oliva Z. 2010. Philanthropy in South East Asia. In *International Encyclopedia of Civil Society*. Helmut K. Anheier and Stefan Toepler, eds. Pp. 1221–1226. New York: Springer.

Dunn, Kathleen. 2004. Diaspora Giving and the Future of Philanthropy. *White paper, The Philanthropic Initiative*. Electronic document, www.tpi.org/downloads/pdfs/whitepaper-diaspora_giving.pdf, accessed December 1, 2016.

Ebraham, Alnoor, and V. Kasturi Rangan. 2009. Acumen Fund: Measurement in Venture Philanthropy (A). Harvard Business Case N9–310–011. Electronic document, www.hbs.edu/faculty/Pages/item.aspx?num=37915, accessed March 6, 2017.

Felsenthal, Edward. 1990. Threat to the Republic?: The Politics of Foreign Direct Investment in the United States. *The Fletcher Forum of World Affairs* 14(2): 354–371.

Ferris, James M. 2016. Is This a New Golden Age of Philanthropy?: An Assessment of the Changing Landscape. *Voluntary Sector Review* 7(3): 315–324.

The Ford Foundation. 2016. China Overview. Electronic document, www.fordfound.org/regions/china/, accessed November 11, 2016.

Geithner, Peter F., Paula D. Johnson, and Lincoln C. Chen, eds. 2004. *Diaspora Philanthropy to India: A Perspective from the United States*. Cambridge: Global Equity Initiative, Asia Center, Harvard University.

Giving2Asia. 2016. Give2Asia Local Knowledge Counts. Electric document, www.give2asia.org/, accessed December 1, 2016.

Hashimoto, Toru, Seiji Furuta, and Masaaki Homma, eds. 1986. *Koekihojin no Katsudō to Zeisei* [*Activities and Tax System of Public Interest Corporations*]. Osaka: Seibunsya (in Japanese).

Havens, John J., and Paul G. Schervish. 2014. A Golden Age of Philanthropy Still Beckons: National Wealth Transfer and Potential for Philanthropy: Technical Report. Boston, MA: Center on Wealth and Philanthropy, Boston College. Electronic document, www.bc.edu/content/dam/files/research_sites/cwp/pdf/A%20Golden%20Age%20of%20Philanthropy%20Still%20Bekons.pdf, accessed March 3, 2017.

Hayashi, Yujiro. 1984. *Amerika no Ogata Zaidan: Kigyō to Syakai*. Tokyo: Kawade shobo shinsha. A Japanese translation of *The Big Foundations in the United States: Corporations and Society*. 1972. Waldemar A. Neilsen. New York: Columbia University Press.

Hayashi, Yujiro, and Yoshinori Yamaoka. 1993. *Firansoropi to Shakai* [*Philanthropy and Society*]. Tokyo: Diamond (in Japanese).

The Hitachi Foundation. 2016. The Hitachi Foundation 30 Years. Electronic document, www.hitachi-foundation.org/, accessed January 29, 2017.

Homma, Masaaki, and Masayuki Deguchi, eds. 1996. *Borantexia Kakumei* [*Volunteer Revolution*]. Tokyo: Toyo Keizai (in Japanese).

Imada, Makoto. 2010. Civil Society in Japan: Democracy, Voluntary Action, and Philanthropy. In *Civic Engagement in Contemporary Japan: Established and Emerging Repertoires*. Henk Vinken, Yuko Nishimura, Yuko, Bruce. L. White, and Masayuki Deguchi, eds. Pp. 21–40. New York: Springer.

The Indus Entrepreneurs Global. 2016. Electronic document, http://tie.org/, accessed December 1, 2016.

Japan Association of Charitable Organizations. 2016. Electronic document, www.kohokyo.or.jp/index.html, accessed December 1, 2016.

Japan Center for International Exchange (JCIE). 2016. A Historical Chronology of JCIE. Electronic document, www.jcie.or.jp/jcie/chrono2.html, accessed December 1, 2016.

Japanese Chamber of Commerce and Industry of New York Inc. 1990. *Joining-In!: A Handbook for Better Corporate Citizenship in the United States*. New York: Japanese Chamber of Commerce and Industry of New York Inc.

Japan Foundation Center. 2016. Japan Foundation Center. Electronic document, www.jfc.or.jp/, accessed December 1, 2016.

Johnson, Paula Doherty. 2007. Diaspora Philanthropy: Influences, Initiatives, and Issues. *The Philanthropic Initiative*. Boston and Cambridge, MA. The Philanthropic Initiative, Inc. And the Global Equity Initiative, Harvard University, Electronic document, www.cbd.int/financial/charity/usa-diaspora philanthropy.pdf, accessed March 1 2017.

Jung, Ku-Hyung. ed. 1994. *Evolving Patterns of Asia Pacific Philanthropy*. Seoul: Institute of East and West Studies, Yonsei University.

Kassam, Meenaz, Femida Handy, and Emily Jansons. 2016. *Philanthropy in India*. New Delhi: SAGE Publications India.

Lyons, Mark, and Samiul Hasan. 2002. Researching Asia's Third Sector. *Voluntas: International Journal of Voluntary and Nonprofit Organizations* 13(2): 107–112.

Lyons, Mark, Myles McGregor-Lowndes, and Philip O'Donoghue. 2006. Researching Giving and Volunteering in Australia. *The Australian Journal of Social Issues* 41(4): 385–397.

MacArthur Foundation. 2016. India. Electronic document, www.macfound.org/tags/india/, accessed November 11, 2016.

McCarthy, Kathleen D. 1995. From Government to Grass-Roots Reform: The Ford Foundation's Population Programmes in South Asia, 1959–1981. *Voluntas: International Journal of Voluntary and Nonprofit Organizations* 6(3): 292–316.

Moody, Michael. 2008. "Building a culture": The Construction and Evolution of Venture Philanthropy as a New Organizational Field. *Nonprofit and Voluntary Sector Quarterly* 37(2): 324–352.

Neilson, Waldemar A. 1972. *The Big Foundations*. New York: Columbia University Press.

Newland, Kathleen, and Erin Patrick. 2004. *Beyond Remittances: The Role of Diaspora in Poverty Reduction in Their Countries of Origin*. Washington, DC: Migration Policy Institute. Electronic document, www.migrationpolicy.org/research/beyond-remittances_0704pdf, accessed March 1, 2017.

Newland, Kathleen, and Hiroyuki Tanaka. 2010. Mobilizing Diaspora Entrepreneurship for Development. Washington, DC: Migration Policy Institute Electronic document, www.migrationpolicy.org/article/mobilizing-diaspora-entrepreneurship-development, accessed March 1, 2017.

Newland, Kathleen, Aaron Terrazas, and Roberto Munster. 2010. *Diaspora Philanthropy: Private Giving and Public Policy*. Washington, DC: Migration Policy Institute. Electronic document, www.migration policy.org/research/diaspora-philanthropy.pdf, accessed March 1, 2017.

(NFIA) National Federation of Indian–American Associations. 2016. Who We Are. Electronic document, www.nfia.net/who-we-are, accessed December 1, 2016.

Onishi, Tamaki. 2016. Institutionalizing Japanese Philanthropy Beyond National and Sectoral Borders: Coevolution of Philanthropy and Corporate Philanthropy from the 1970s to 1990s. *Voluntas: International Journal of Voluntary and Nonprofit Organizations*. DOI: 10.1007/s11266-016-9809-x.

Payton, Robert L. 1988. *Philanthropy: Voluntary Action for the Public Good*. New York: American Council on Education/Macmillan.

Peking University Education Foundation. 2016. Peking University Education Foundation. Electronic document, www.pkuf.org/, accessed December 1, 2016.

Porter, Michael E., and Mark R. Kramer. 1999. Philanthropy's New Agenda: Creating Value. *Harvard Business Review* 77: 121–131.

The Rockefeller Foundation. 2016. Bangkok, Thailand. Electronic document, www.rockefeller foundation.org/about-us/offices-contact-us/bangkok-thailand/, accessed November 11, 2016.

Rutzen, Douglas. 2015. Aid Barriers and the Rise of Philanthropic Protectionism. *International Journal of Not-for-Profit Law* 17(1), March 2015. Electronic document, www.icnl.org/research/journal/vol.17/ss1/Rutzen.pdf, accessed March 6, 2017.

Salamon, Lester M. 1999. *America's Nonprofit Sector: A Primer Second Edition*. New York: Foundation Center.

Salamon, Lester M., ed. 2014. *New Frontiers of Philanthropy: A Guide to the New Tools and New Actors that are Reshaping Global Philanthropy and Social Investing*. New York. Oxford University Press.

Sato, Ryuzo. 1994. The Chrysanthemum and the Eagle: The Future of US–Japan Relations. New York: New York University Press.

Schuyt, Theo N. M. 2010. Philanthropy in European Welfare States: A Challenging Promise? *International Review of Administrative Sciences* 76(4): 774–789.

Shiveshwarkar, Shyamala. 2008. Diaspora Giving: An Agent of Change in the Asia Pacific Communities? India. *Asia Pacific Philanthropy Consortium*. Electronic document, http://asianphilanthropy.org/APPC/DiasporaGiving-conference-2008/DiasporaGiving-India-2008.pdf, accessed January 15, 2017.

Sidel, Mark. 2004. *Diaspora Philanthropy to India: A Perspective from the United States*. In *Diaspora Philanthropy and Equitable Development in China and India*. Peter F. Geithner, Paula D. Johnson, Lincoln C. Chen, eds. Pp. 215–257. Cambridge: Global Equity Initiative, Asia Center, Harvard University.

Sidel, Mark. 2006. The Third Sector, Human Security, and Anti-terrorism: The United States and Beyond. *Voluntas: International Journal of Voluntary and Nonprofit Organizations* 17(3): 199–210.

Sulek, Marty. 2010. On the Modern Meaning of Philanthropy. *Nonprofit and Voluntary Sector Quarterly* 39(2): 193–212.

The Tang Prize Foundation. 2016. The Tang Prize Foundation. Electronic document, www.tang-prize.org/first.php, accessed December 1, 2016.

Tiezzi, Shannon. 2016. China Passes Foreign NGO Law Amid National Security Push. *The Diplomat*, April 29. Electronic document, http://thediplomat.com/2016/04/china-passes-foreign-ngo-law-amid-national-security-push/, accessed January 29, 2017.

The Toyota Foundation. 2007. *The Toyota Foundation: 30 Years of History 1974–2004*. Tokyo: The Toyota Foundation.

USTC Alumni Foundation. 2016. USTC Almini Foundation. Electronic document, www.ustcaf.org/en/home, accessed December 1, 2016.

Viswanath, Priya, and Noshir Dadrawala. 2004. Philanthropic Investment and Equitable Development: The Case of India. In *Diaspora Philanthropy and Equitable Development in China and India*. Peter Geithner, Paula D. Johnson, and Lincoln C. Chen, eds. Pp. 259–289. Cambridge: Global Equity Initiative, Asia Center, Harvard University.

Wang, Xinsong, Liu Fengqin, Nan Fang, Zhao Xiaoping, and Zhang Xiulan. 2015. Giving in China: An Emerging Nonprofit Sector Embedded within a Strong State. In *The Palgrave Handbook of Global Philanthropy*. Pamela Wiepking and Femida Handy, eds. Pp. 354–368. Hampshire and New York: Springer.

Watanabe, Kazuo. 1992 *Taikenteki firansuropii* [*Philanthropy as Experience*]. Tokyo: Soryu Shuppan (in Japanese).

Yamamoto, Tadashi, and Susan Hubbard. 1995. Conference Report. In *Emerging Civil Society in the Asia Pacific Community: Integrative Survey Report and Conference Report of the Osaka Symposium*. Japan Center for International Exchange, ed. Pp. 49–67. Tokyo: Japan Center for International Exchange (JCIE).

Yin, Xiao-huang, and Zhiyong Lan. 2004. Why Do They Give?: Chinese American Transnational Philanthropy since 1970s. In *Diaspora Philanthropy and Equitable Development in China and India*. Peter F. Geithner, Paula D. Johnson, Lincoln C. Chen, eds. Pp. 79–127. Cambridge: Global Equity Initiative, Asia Center, Harvard University.

Young, Nick. 2004. Richesse Oblige, and So Does the State; Philanthropy and Equity in China. In *Diaspora Philanthropy and Equitable Development in China and India*. Peter F. Geithner, Paula D. Johnson, Lincoln C. Chen, eds. Pp. 29–77. Cambridge: Global Equity Initiative, Asia Center, Harvard University.

Young, Nick, and June Shih. 2004. In *Diaspora Philanthropy and Equitable Development in China and India*. Peter F. Geithner, Paula D. Johnson, Lincoln C. Chen, eds. Pp. 129–175. Cambridge: Global Equity Initiative, Asia Center, Harvard University.

Yu, Yan, and Nick Marro. 2016. Concerns Linger about Final NGO Law Provisions, *China Business Review*. July 4, 2016. Electronic document, www.chinabusinessreview.com/concerns-linger-about-final-ngo-law-provisions/, accessed January 29 2017.

27

DEVELOPMENT

Chika Watanabe

Changing paradigms of aid

In 2011, the Fourth High Level Forum on Aid Effectiveness took place in Busan, Korea. Approximately 3,000 delegates gathered from around the world to discuss how to formulate a global partnership on aid effectiveness. As Emma Mawdsley, Laura Savage, and Sung-Mi Kim (2013) explain, the forum in Busan was the culmination of international discussions that aimed to address the shortcomings of the Washington Consensus of the 1980s and 1990s, and push the global aid agenda toward improving the effective delivery of aid. The agenda included stipulations that recipient countries should take greater ownership for their own development efforts, employ strategies based on targets such as all-round well-being that go beyond poverty reduction, and a shift in aid paradigms due to the growing participation of non-traditional donors. This last characteristic is noteworthy, as commentators increasingly point to so-called "emerging donors," such as China, India, and Brazil, which are shifting the balance of power away from "Western" countries and introducing new foci in the development agenda (DeHart 2012; Mawdsley 2012; Tan-Mullins, Mohan, and Power 2010). These trends arguably take development efforts beyond "aid," foregrounding interests around trade, finance, large infrastructural projects, and technical assistance that are undertaken by corporations and other "new" actors. We are increasingly witnessing an era of multiple actors, interests, and approaches in development interventions.

As the terrain of development actors changes, so does the understanding and role of civil society. The Busan forum in 2011 was the first time that civil society groups were officially acknowledged in discussions on development effectiveness with the establishment of the Global Partnership for Effective Development Cooperation (GPEDC) (Poskitt, Shankland, and Taela 2016: 28). In development and humanitarian activities, "civil society" includes an array of groups, but generally refers to local associations and non-governmental organizations (NGOs) or non-profit organizations that engage in poverty alleviation, environmental activities, emergency relief, social service provision, and other related efforts (Poskitt *et al.* 2016). In "emerging" donor countries, civil society organizations (CSOs) often exist in political and economic environments that differ from Euro-American contexts. For example, new donor countries such as BRIC (Brazil, Russia, India, and China) tend to operate on ideologies of a strong and benevolent state, making it difficult for CSOs to gain legitimacy in activities outside of state interests

(Poskitt *et al.* 2016: 11; see also Hirono 2013). This is also the understanding in Asia, where the strong "developmental state," based on the Japanese model, has often been invoked to describe "Asian approaches" to development (Johnson 1982). In short, Asian leaders have often referenced a growth-oriented, state-led, and bilateral model of development, as seen in Japan, in contrast to "Western" neoliberal approaches, as "the Asian way" to development. Although the theory of the developmental state has lost its analytical edge and relevance over time, especially with the neoliberalization of development systems in the 1990s and 2000s (Hirata 2002), it appears to be resurfacing in light of "emerging" Asian donors (e.g., Kim and Kim 2014). However, in other aspects, CSOs in these countries have also had the space to develop innovative approaches to tackle issues of poverty and social enterprise beyond an authoritative, developmental state. The degrees of freedom vary greatly from country to country, and observers and aid practitioners debate whether CSOs are public service providers or activist movements (Shigetomi 2002). Despite these contestations, we can now see a burgeoning interest amongst state and international aid officials in the role of civil society in achieving the goals of development effectiveness, including in Asia (Lu and Mulakala 2016; Sukma and Gannon 2013).

So then, how are we to understand civil society organizations in light of this changing landscape of development assistance? In this chapter, I offer a number of possible perspectives for studying civil society—specifically, NGOs—in the context of development aid efforts in Asia, through the case study of an organization in Japan.[1] To provide a comprehensive overview of the situation of development NGOs in different Asian societies is beyond the scope of this chapter and other works that collate regional expertise already exist (Farrington and Lewis 1993; Shigetomi 2002; Yamamoto 1995). As such, my aims, in this chapter, are ethnographic, specific, and conceptual, rather than informative and expansive.[2] In particular, I examine the history and characteristics of one of the oldest NGOs in Japan, the Organization for Industrial, Spiritual, and Cultural Advancement (OISCA), to argue that relationships between NGOs and the state in Asia cannot be understood through "a strong state" or state-driven developmentalist theories that often mark analyses in the region. What we need are perspectives that allow us to look at the micro-level interactions between NGO and state actors. In the case of OISCA, the lens of religion will illustrate ethnographically how fine-grained and multifaceted historical, political, economic, and social processes and relations coalesce around NGOs as nodes of aspirations and "development imaginaries" (Mawdsley 2012: 13). Important to note here is that this perspective does not preclude the political in Chantal Mouffe's (2005) sense, that is, in terms of agonistic struggles and contestations over established orders, even if these are not about state-led or even governmental forces. Thus, the ethnographic sections below depict the politics of establishing a development regime in Japan without necessarily assuming that these are about a "top-down" or developmentalist structure.

Readers might be puzzled that this is a chapter on a Japanese NGO, following an introduction that focused on "emerging donors." Japan has been an early member of the Development Assistance Committee (DAC) of the Organisation for Economic Co-operation and Development (OECD), groups in charge of setting the global aid agenda, thereby taking part in strategic global discussions about development and foreign aid policies with Euro-American countries since the 1960s. As such, Japan is usually seen as a "traditional donor." Nevertheless, with the emergence of new donor countries, especially in Asia, observers have pointed out that more careful analysis should be directed toward Japan, which has too easily been glossed over to be the same as "Western" actors (see, e.g., Mawdsley 2012: 9). In fact, historical Japanese approaches to development resonate with current "new" paradigms amongst emerging donors, such as the active participation of the private sector, the emphasis on infrastructural projects and human resource development activities, and the language of mutuality rather than charity. Scholars have proposed that, perhaps, Japanese forms of development can serve as lessons and models for emerging donors, particularly in Asia (Kato, Page, and Shimomura 2016).

At the same time, if Japan's historical trajectory and characteristics as a donor can inform our understandings of emerging donors today, it can be an opportunity to rethink Japan's history of development itself. In other words, the current juncture can be a time to reflect on how "Japanese characteristics" could be understood differently from the usual narrative of the developmental state. Specifically, I am concerned with destabilizing the prevailing understanding that civil society and NGOs in Japan operate according to a top-down framework in which the state dictates civic activities, or conversely, civic groups are seen to present an anti-state "grass-roots" politics. My ethnographic research shows that various actors in Japan have interacted with each other in contingent and horizontal ways, mutually shaping "development" as a governmental system, moral concept, and political ambition, touching on questions of the state but not necessarily confined to them or tied to top-down views of state–society relations. Enabled by the insights from OISCA's history, this alternative reading of Japanese development shows that civil society, and specifically NGOs in Asia, might be working in parallel with state actors, mutually engaged in aspirational as well as political constructions of "development," and not in a hierarchical relationship.

Rethinking NGOs

OISCA is an apt case study for rethinking development aid and NGOs in Japan because it is one of the oldest of such organizations in the country. It was established in 1961 to provide agricultural assistance and training activities mainly in Asia-Pacific countries, with its own training centers around the region. Over time, it has expanded its projects to environmental education and reforestation activities, becoming one of the most established sustainable-development and environmental NGOs in Japan. When OISCA staff members began their agricultural and training activities, the Japanese government had only just begun to formulate its own development aid system. In 1961, developed countries from Europe and the United States established the OECD and DAC to discuss issues of international development and poverty reduction, which Japan joined in 1964. In Japan, the precursor to the Japan International Cooperation Agency (JICA)—the Overseas Technical Cooperation Agency (OTCA)—was established in 1962, and the Japanese version of the Peace Corp—Japan Overseas Cooperation Volunteers (JOCV)—began in 1965. NGOs were unheard of in Japan during this time, with only a couple of civic groups engaged in international development or humanitarian projects, one of which was OISCA. Even though there would be no clear laws for such groups to register officially with state bodies, and thus, receive favorable tax exemptions and funds until 1998, OISCA, along with a few other NGO-type groups, was able to become an incorporated foundation (*zaidan hōjin*) relatively quickly, in 1969. It also began to receive government subsidies from the Ministry of Foreign Affairs (MOFA) in 1972.

How can we understand OISCA's early rise to prominence and what might it tell us about how we can understand development NGOs in Asia? At first glance, the story might fit the usual framework that scholars employ when talking about civil society and especially NGOs. From Hegel to Marx and Engels, Western philosophers have defined "civil society" in a framework of opposition between the state and society. Civil society, then, has been imagined as "an amorphous space that lies somewhere between the state and society and mediates between the two" (Coombe 1997: 3; see also Comaroff and Comaroff 1999). NGOs in development (and humanitarian aid) have been conceptualized along these lines as well. This space of mediation can be taken in different ways. On the one hand, several scholars and commentators alike have tended to see NGOs as harbingers of an anti-state civil society, especially in "developing" and nascent democratic countries (Schuller 2007: 69). On the other hand, often the most common approach to NGOs amongst anthropologists has been to frame them in the context of neoliberalization, in which civic groups like NGOs exist largely as extensions of a state that exerts its governance via voluntary and entrepreneurial subjects (Kamat 2002; Ogawa 2009; Sharma 2006).

In countries like Japan, the prevailing theory of the developmental state predetermines understandings of civic groups and NGOs within a top-down imaginary hierarchy of state and society (Schwartz and Pharr 2003; Reimann 2010). Some studies have begun to point to other dynamics at play that complicate the picture (Hirata 2002; Leheny and Warren 2010). However, a general understanding remains that Japanese development and NGOs are ultimately state-led. Despite the recent rise of corporations and their social responsibility schemes, and the growth of NGOs and non-profits in the past two decades, observers continue to explain that a strong state restricts Japanese civil society and international aid efforts. To a certain extent, this is true. Until the late 1990s, legal restrictions and unfavorable taxation systems constrained the operation of civic groups, including NGOs. The majority of organizations could only register as a public interest corporation (*kōeki hōjin*) in the form of either an incorporated association (*shadan hōjin*) or an incorporated foundation (*zaidan hōjin*), as defined by the Japanese Civil Code of 1896.[3] In order to do this, groups such as OISCA needed the permission of relevant bureaucratic agencies that would oversee the organization after incorporation. Moreover, most ministries required an endowment of at least 3 million yen (about US$300,000) for associations and 300 million yen (about US$3 million) for foundations—a major hurdle for most groups in Japan, which do not have the backing of philanthropists and large donors like in Euro-American countries (Reimann 2010: 36–37). Thus, observers have understood civic groups including NGOs to exist largely within the confines of a state-controlled structure for most of Japan's post-war history. Additionally, if organizations succeeded in establishing themselves in these early years, like OISCA, commentators and scholars have tended to see them as extensions of the Japanese developmental state.

The situation seemed to change after the 1995 Great Hanshin Earthquake in Kobe City and Awaji Island, when the Japanese public saw unprecedented numbers of volunteers arrive in the devastated city to help with relief efforts. In 1998, the Law to Promote Specified Nonprofit Activities ("NPO Law"), the first legal framework for non-profits in Japan, was created. This new law enabled groups to register as formal organizations more easily than before, which facilitated their cooperation with other organizations and government agencies, and the expansion of funding possibilities (Pekkanen 2003). Thus, while civic actors tended to take an anti-state stance in the 1960s, the 1990s saw a culmination of a different approach in which civil society actors and activists saw the benefit in cooperating with the state. Conversely, state actors regarded civic groups and NGOs as helpful collaborators in welfare provision, international aid, and other activities (Avenell 2010; see also Hirata 2004).

Despite the changes in the relationship between NGOs and the state throughout Japan's post-war history, the narrative follows understandings of civil society outlined above: that of NGOs as existing in a middle ground between "the state" (up above) and "the community" (from below). Whether this was a relationship of opposition, co-optation from above, or strategic participation from below, the dyad of state and society has generally remained the same in these analyses. However, in recent years, a number of anthropologists have proposed that NGOs should be seen not so much in the state–society hierarchy, but as nodes of broader, parallel, and more fluid sets of relations (Leve and Karim 2001). Even in Japan, there are contexts where state and society might not be in (vertical) opposition, or where these are not the main or only relevant players, or where international forces cut across multiple types of social actors (cf. Schuller 2007).

James Ferguson and Akhil Gupta's (2002) classic essay in rethinking analyses of the state strikes at the heart of the challenge here. They argue that, in the context of transnational forces and actors such as NGOs, the fallacy of a hierarchical state–society relationship becomes evident. Rather than assume, from the beginning of our analyses, that there is a top-down structure, they submit that we attend to the spatial imaginaries that underlie our approaches to the state and NGOs in the first place, namely, that of "verticality" and "encompassment." They explain:

> *Verticality* refers to the central and pervasive idea of the state as an institution somehow "above" civil society, community, and family. Thus, state planning is inherently "top down" and state actions are efforts to manipulate and plan "from above," while "the grassroots" contrasts with the state precisely in that it is "below," closer to the ground, more authentic, and more "rooted." The second image is that of *encompassment*. Here, the state (conceptually fused with the nation) is located within an ever widening series of circles that begins with family and local community and ends with the system of nation-states … These two metaphors work together to produce a taken-for-granted spatial and scalar image of a state that both sits above and contains its localities, regions, and communities.
>
> *(Ferguson and Gupta 2002: 982; emphasis in the original)*

Ferguson and Gupta, thus, warn us away from preconceived definitions of "the state" and "civil society," and guide us toward a perspective that attends to the imaginaries and social practices that constitute something to appear "state-like." The notion of state–civil society relations as "top-down," and the categories of "the state" and "civil society" themselves, are not givens but contingent achievements of social imagination and action.

Considering how different actors produce effects of vertical encompassment, and therefore "state-like-ness," with various degrees of success, enables us to look at government officials, NGO workers, villagers, and other people side-by-side, as they craft a politics of scale in practices of governance. Thus, the hierarchical relationship between "the state" and "the NGO" should not be the assumption of analyses but the object of ethnographic inquiry itself. I take inspiration from this perspective to study the interactions between NGO workers, politicians, government officials, and others involved in OISCA's activities without assuming a vertical topography—that is, in the context of Japan, without assuming a top-down structure between the state and NGOs in a developmentalist paradigm. In fact, it is not even helpful to think of "the state" and "the NGO" as entities that exist a priori. Instead, I will concentrate on a handful of specific characters in an ethnographic narrative, and trace the historical, political, and aspirational trajectories and relationships that have constituted one slice of the story of development aid and NGOs in Japan. Ultimately, tracing these specific relations, without assumptions of scale, takes us to understandings of NGOs that do not fit into concerns of the state, or even state-like effects of governmentality. What NGOs can reveal are not only how imaginations of "the state" are constructed, but other religious, political, and personal aspirations generated around conceptions of "doing good" that development work promises to deliver, not always in the presumed field of poverty alleviation.

In the ethnographic section that follows, I use OISCA as a way to understand NGOs and their connections to state actors through particular personal relationships. Methodologically focusing on specific relationships, rather than starting with sociological categories, such as "the state" or "civil society" or even "NGO," can take us to new ways of analyzing NGOs beyond concerns of government, without writing out politics from the analysis. In other words, if we eschew a hermeneutics of suspicion and "take seriously" people's reasoning for supporting an NGO, we could come to understand how different actors might find moral meaning in supporting and participating in an NGO, and the political implications and historical situated-ness of these moral commitments without assuming a top-down and state-led framework.

A perspective of religion

In May 2010, I was rushing to the opening ceremony for the election campaign office of a Liberal Democratic Party (LDP) politician in Tokyo, Hosaka Sanzō. The LDP is the dominant, conservative party that has ruled for most of Japan's post-war history and Hosaka Sanzō was a prominent party member. Shiraki-san, a senior OISCA staffer in his mid-seventies, had told me about it, and asked me to join him so that I could experience another aspect of his work. A couple of days earlier, I had helped Shiraki-san and other OISCA staffers send out postcards showing support for Hosaka-sensei's upcoming House of Councillors (*sangiin*) elections.[4] A seasoned politician in his seventies, Hosaka-sensei was aiming to return to a seat in the Diet three years after his last defeat. As we sorted the colorful and glossy postcards with Hosaka-sensei's smiling face on the front, a staff member told me that OISCA does not usually get involved in political activities such as this, but Hosaka-sensei had been helping OISCA for many years, and so this was their way of giving back. They were sending the postcards to long-time OISCA donors and supporters to ask that they distribute them to their acquaintances. Shiraki-san was going to call each of them in order to make the request over the phone as well.

Shiraki-san's participation in the ceremony for Hosaka-sensei's new campaign office was an extension of this expression of gratitude, both from OISCA as an organization and from Shiraki-san himself, in a personal capacity. Shiraki-san had been with the OISCA for over half a century and the way he spoke of his work there often made me think that this was not simply a profession for him, but a way of life. As soon as I arrived, I gave him a call and he told me to sign my name at the reception tent set up on the street outside the small office building. I was surprised to see that the campaign office for this senior politician existed in such a small structure, wedged between a narrow five- or six-storied apartment building and a shop. There were several important-looking people in suits, both men and women, lining up at the tent to give their names to the young, female receptionist. I signed my name like everybody else but felt acutely out of place, being, by far, one of the youngest people there, without looking like one of the elegant, politicians' female secretaries. When I entered the narrow building, I saw that the elevator was packed and so I made myself to the emergency stairs. I gingerly opened the door to the fifth floor into a room overflowing with people. I squeezed myself through the door and saw Shiraki-san a few steps ahead. He saw me and motioned for me to stand next to him.

Through the crowd, I saw one of the senior staff members from OISCA walking toward the main seating area at the front of the room. Shiraki-san whispered to me to move forward into the seating area as well, but there were too many people for me to move more than a few steps. Besides, there was clearly a hierarchy in the seating as well as the standing arrangements. Most people who were sitting were in their sixties or seventies, and the youngest people, in their late thirties and early forties, were standing at the back. As a thirty-year-old graduate student, I wanted to stand as far back as I could.

My watch ticked past the 10.30am mark, and even though there were still people streaming out of the tiny elevator, the ceremony began. A Shinto priest (*kannushi*) appeared at the front of the room and began reciting prayers in a deep and booming voice. He took a long stick with white streams of paper at the end and waved it above our heads to "cleanse" the space. Next came the offerings (*otamagushi*) from the audience. One by one, people walked up to the front of the room, holding leafy branches. They would put it down at the makeshift altar, clap twice, bow, and walk back to their seats. This continued for a long time. When the last person had walked back to his seat, the priest chanted another prayer and the ceremony was over. A man stood up to thank the priest. He then turned to the audience and asked us to move outside to the street for the rest of the event.

The crowd of politicians and supporters took up the entire sidewalk and spilled out onto the road. There was a microphone on a raised platform that was connected to speakers on a truck with signs for the LDP. People walked up to the microphone to say a few words of encouragement to Hosaka-sensei. Their voices were amplified out onto the street through the speakers and passers-by looked on with curiosity. After what felt like an endless stream of speeches, Hosaka-sensei took the microphone. This was the first time that I had clearly seen him. He energetically took the microphone out of the stand and jumped onto the metal rail that lined the sidewalk. He gave his speech from that higher but awkward position. After he finished and everyone clapped enthusiastically, a woman in her fifties announced that they were now going to give a toast. Young women in their twenties and early thirties had been preparing small paper cups filled with green tea and they began to hand them out. Once we each had a cup in our hands, someone called out "*gambarō!*" (Let's work hard!). Everyone shouted back, "*Ou!*" (Yes!). We all took a swig of our green tea.

This event highlights two intersecting issues: the question of religion, especially Shinto, and conservative politics in Japan and the relationship between politics and NGOs. Topics of religion are rare in the study of NGOs in Japan, much less, those relating to Shinto, but it is a fruitful line of inquiry in understanding the development of international NGOs in Japan. Observers usually tell the history of NGOs in Japan from the late 1970s, when groups emerged to respond to the crises of Indo-Chinese refugees in Southeast Asia (JANIC 2007). This history is not wrong, but it omits the role that earlier organizations, such as OISCA, played, save for a passing mention of them in the context of the origins of NGOs today. However, when we look at OISCA closely, we see that it reveals a history that does not easily link to subsequent NGOs or to established interpretations of top-down or anti-state structures. To understand this account, we need to know more about OISCA's beginnings.

The history that most casual observers do not know is that the founder of OISCA, Nakano Yonosuke, was also the founder of a Shinto-based new religion called Ananaikyō.[5] I have argued elsewhere that, despite this history, OISCA staff members assert that the organization is not religious (*shūkyō ja nai*) and taking such claims seriously are important in understanding the politics and moral imaginaries of development aid in Japan (Watanabe 2015a, 2015b). In short, OISCA staffers and supporters interpreted the links with Ananaikyō as links to Shinto, and therefore, to Japanese cultural values, especially those of ecological harmony ("living in harmony with nature") and a collectivist ethos, ideas that appear, in one way or another, in OISCA's activities. They obfuscate the categories of religion and secularity by referencing Shinto values as cultural ("Japanese").

Yonosuke's role as a leader of Ananaikyō facilitated the political support that OISCA received in later years from conservative LDP politicians. As Nakano Tsuyoshi (2003) shows, when the LDP was still in its nascent stages in the 1960s, politicians sought the support of leaders of new religions as a way to strengthen their electoral base. As new religious groups such as Sōka Gakkai, and more precisely, its political party, Kōmeitō, gained political prominence in elections throughout the 1950s and 1960s, politicians at the time considered these groups as helpful allies in consolidating the LDP monopoly of politics. This favorable link between new religions and politicians, especially in the case of Sōka Gakkai, came to an abrupt and scandalous halt in

1970, and the story has not been the same since (McLaughlin 2014). However, the era before 1970 is still relevant in understanding OISCA's prominence and the long-term political support it has enjoyed from LDP politicians ever since.

Political actors in the 1950s and 1960s approached Yonosuke, just as they did with other leaders of new religions. One man's name came up several times in interviews with the older OISCA staff members in their seventies and eighties: Furuta Jūjirō. He was the chairperson of Nihon University from 1958 to 1969, and a prominent figure in right-wing politics. He became infamous for violently suppressing student protests from 1968 to 1969. He was a good friend and supporter of Satō Eisaku, a powerful LDP prime minister who governed from 1964 to 1972. In order to boost Satō's influence, Furuta mobilized business, religious, and other leaders. Senior OISCA staffers said that Furuta was the one who introduced Yonosuke to Satō. In 1967, Satō led a number of LDP politicians in establishing the National Diet League to Promote OISCA's International Activities (*OISCA kokusai undō sokushin giinrenmei*, "OISCA Diet League"). The group has remained strong over the decades (with approximate fifty LDP members as of 2011), helping promote OISCA amongst politicians, bureaucrats, and business leaders in Japan, and other prominent government and other actors in the countries where OISCA operates. Amongst members of the OISCA Diet League, we find the names of politicians such as Ōhira Masayoshi and Fukuda Takeo, both former prime ministers (OISCA 1967; OISCA 1973).

Evaluating the role of religion in the rise and development of NGOs takes us to the untold story that connects one of the earliest NGOs with powerful politicians and right-wing public figures. One could interpret this history as, once again, evidence of state actors' co-option of NGOs in a top-down imaginary of a form of government, or perhaps as inconsequential in that we cannot say for certain that these individual links had any influence on the making of Japan's development aid systems. Nevertheless, tracing specific interactions and histories can gives us insight into processes that are more multifaceted and contingent than usual accounts of NGOs in Japan. For example, even though powerful LDP politicians embraced OISCA by the late 1960s, this was not an automatic relationship. Archival material and senior OISCA staffers' narratives suggest that, at first, politicians and bureaucrats in the 1960s and even early 1970s did not embrace OISCA, since it seemed to pose a threat as a "competitor" for the newborn development system of the government. One senior OISCA staff member, who went with the first team to India in the early 1960s, explained to me that, when the OISCA team first visited the Japanese embassy in Delhi, the ambassador and embassy officials told them that they were being a nuisance (*meiwaku*)—that agricultural aid was difficult even for government agencies, and thus, impossible for civic groups such as OISCA. These bureaucrats told the OISCA staffers (unpaid volunteers at the time, to be specific) to return to Japan because they would be a national embarrassment.

Despite such discouragement, the OISCA staffers continued their agricultural activities in India; after all, they relied mainly on the financial and moral support of Ananaikyō members, and thus, did not need embassy support to conduct their activities. After a couple of years, OISCA succeeded in increasing agricultural production at their project sites and in introducing new farming techniques amongst villagers there. Even embassy officials could not ignore these achievements. Ban Shōichi, who was a diplomat in India and subsequently became one of the founders of JOCV, describes how he came to admire the OISCA staff members for their full commitment to their work, a commitment of such degree that they would devote their lives living alongside local villagers for decades (Ban 1974). Stories from overseas traveled back to Japan through such state officials and others, gradually bolstering OISCA's reputation amongst bureaucrats, politicians, and other aid agencies. By 1987, the then Prime Minister Nakasone Yasuhiro could talk about OISCA as an exemplary "civic group" (*minkan dantai*) that he wanted to support as a government and for which he wished to develop a financial support system, without any questioning or challenges from other politicians and bureaucrats present at the meeting (Sangi-in 1987).

This small window into OISCA's progression from a "nuisance" to "an exemplary civic group" for state actors suggests a narrative that complicates the top-down understanding of NGOs. We cannot comprehend NGOs as simple handmaidens of governmental forces, whether they are neoliberal, developmentalist, or otherwise—nor can we conclude that they are anti-state movements. The relationships between NGO workers and various political actors unfold contingently along different lines—in the case of OISCA, along questions of religion, secularity, Shinto, and politics, as well as along historical memories of Japanese colonialism in Asia (see Watanabe 2014).

On another level, these relationships also hinge on factors that seem highly personal, which constitute an important part of the politics underlying the growth and success of OISCA. Take, for instance, the experiences of Matsui-sensei. In August 2010, Shiraki-san took me to meet this senior LDP politician, a man in his seventies who had been a member of the OISCA Diet League for decades. When we arrived at his office in central Tokyo, his secretary showed us to a room occupied mainly by a large oval table made of dark wood. We sat at one end of this centerpiece, with Matsui-sensei at the other end. Shiraki-san pointed to the painting above my head and asked me if I recognized the man's outfit. I turned my head to look at the portrait but I shook my head. Matsui-sensei told me that these were the clothes that Mito Kōmon wore, the vice-shogun Tokugawa Mitsukuni as portrayed in the popular, fictional, period drama series that lasted from 1969 to 2011. He explained that this was a portrait of former Prime Minister Fukuda Takeo, another OISCA Diet League member. Apparently, other politicians called him Mito Kōmon because of their physical resemblance. We laughed. The elderly politician then added that it was, in fact, Fukuda Takeo and Abe Shinzō who encouraged him to join politics. Given that, Abe is the current prime minister of Japan (as of 2017), we can see how well-connected Matsui-sensei was.

We talked about Matsui-sensei's experiences as a member of the OISCA Diet League, including his trips to Myanmar and other countries to visit OISCA's project sites. At one point, I asked him why he had joined and continued to participate in the OISCA Diet League. He thought for a while and answered,

> Probably because it is fun. OISCA has no interest in things like profit or other "gross" things related to money. It is pure. There is a little bit of benefit in terms of votes but not much … There are so many serious (*majimena*) people in OISCA. OISCA has particularly good people.

I asked him what he thought was the best way for members of the OISCA Diet League to support OISCA. He replied that whenever he visited OISCA's project sites, he saw how local communities took note that people from other countries were interested in them, and that was valuable. For him, visiting overseas project sites was an important aspect of being an OISCA Diet League member.

Later, on our way back, I asked Shiraki-san what Matsui-sensei might have meant when he said, "it was fun" being in the OISCA Diet League. Shiraki-san explained to me that, in the case of this politician, his local district was in a city where there is an OISCA training center, and thus, many OISCA supporters. "And so Matsui-sensei can connect with many people in his area through OISCA, and that is probably a lot of fun for him." As important as it was that OISCA helped politicians secure votes, part of the reason that politicians joined the OISCA Diet League was based on other factors such as personal relationships with other politicians and members of the general public, and the experiences of visiting the NGO's projects overseas. It is easy to dismiss these statements as mere propaganda that mask the fact that the relationships afforded by Diet Leagues are entangled in political interests and calculations. Nevertheless, there is value in considering such claims of "pure relations" and of being in touch with "the field," thanks to OISCA, as windows into dynamics that are often overlooked in the study of NGOs. Specifically, in this case, OISCA's establishment and growth have depended greatly on the ways that questions of religion, secularity, Shinto, and politics have intersected in post-war Japan, and on the affective and ideological appeal of factors such as "personal relationships" and "the field." NGOs in development aid can be framed in relation to state actors, but these perspectives show that the interaction is not simply a top-down process. We need to devise new ways to understand civil society players in Asia so that we can analyze how historical trajectories, political contexts, and aspirations coalesce around NGOs, and most significantly, why people continue to participate in them in this era of "emerging" aid regimes.

A methodological conclusion

In 1997, William F. Fisher began his overview of the burgeoning study of NGOs amongst anthropologists in terms of the impetus of "doing good" (Fisher 1997). The question mark at the end of the title of the article—"Doing Good?: The Politics and Antipolitics of NGO Practices"—highlights the debates over whether NGOs were the answer to neo-imperialist development regimes or part of the problem. Subsequently, anthropological scholarship on NGOs has continued to grow and the general tendency has been to frame them as extensions of the state, whatever form that might take. A side effect of this trend has been that the "development imaginaries" of aid actors have been under-examined, as if the motivations of "doing good" did not matter for critical analysis. However, what if we returned to the old formulation of NGOs as "doing good," and not simply as a mask for a continuation of politics by other means? Such a perspective could help us understand the history and role of NGOs doing development work in Asia beyond a simple slotting of Asian organizations into existing theorizations of state–society relations. There are continuities, certainly, but we must also entertain the possibility of other perspectives.

In order to explore alternative avenues for understanding NGOs in Asia, in this chapter, I proposed to begin our studies by strategically *not* using the categories of "the state" or "civil society" as our analytical tools. Instead, starting with specific actors and tracing particular relationships can lead us to alternative narratives about the development and characteristics of NGOs. In studying NGOs in Asia, it is easy to begin with the assumption that they operate under the purview of a developmental state, or within a top-down structure—or conversely, that they signal the emergence of a democratic society. However, when we track the specific relationships that interlink, in the case of OISCA, aid workers with politicians, and bureaucrats with leaders of new religions, we find that the trajectories of NGOs are contingent and multi-layered. Questions of the state and civil society are not irrelevant here, but if we were to turn to these issues after following the paths that specific and personal relationships take, we might begin to see what other factors might be at play in shaping, what is considered to be, "civil society." As "new" and emerging aid actors appear on the global scene today, we need to explore avenues of analysis that might not fit into existing paradigms. Following specific and individual relationships around questions of religion and the concerns that this inquiry lead us to, such as "pure relations" and contact with "the field" of development, could be one possible line of analysis. To understand NGOs in the "new" context of a world of emerging and non-Western donors, we might need to start with an ethnographic character and follow the histories, politics, and relations to which this particular actor takes us. This trajectory might illustrate a more complex relationship between "state" and "society" than we anticipated.

Notes

1 Civil society would also include neighborhood organizations, kinship-based groups, and other non-formalized associations and relations of gift giving and philanthropy that also have a role to play in poverty alleviation and welfare provision (Bornstein 2012; Shigetomi 2002: 5). Nevertheless, I focus here on non-governmental organizations officially registered with the government.
2 My focus is also on development in terms of aid provision, not on issues of poverty and livelihood improvement from the perspective of aid recipients.
3 Some organizations that conduct NGO-like activities have also registered as religious organizations (*shûkyô hôjin*) or educational foundations (*gakkô hôjin*).
4 Politicians were called "*sensei*" (teacher) instead of the more common honorifics of "*san*" or "*sama*" that go at the end of names in Japan.
5 Yonosuke was a member of Ōmoto before and during World War II, and thus, the worldview underlying Ananaikyō resonates with this Shinto-based new religion.

Suggested readings

Edelman, Marc, and Angelique Haugerud, eds. 2005. *The Anthropology of Development and Globalization: From Classical Political Economy to Contemporary Neoliberalism.* Malden, MA: Blackwell Publishing.

Ferguson, James, and Akhil Gupta. 2002 Spatializing States: Toward an Ethnography of Neoliberal Governmentality. *American Ethnologist* 29(4): 981–1002.

Fisher, William F. 1997. Doing Good?: The Politics and Antipolitics of NGO Practices. *Annual Review of Anthropology* 26: 439–464.

Gardner, Katy, and David Lewis. 2015. *Anthropology and Development: Challenges for the Twenty-First Century.* London: Pluto Press.

Lewis, David, and David Mosse. 2006. Encountering Order and Disjuncture: Contemporary Anthropological Perspectives on the Organization of Development. *Oxford Development Studies* 34(1): 1–13.

Markowitz, Lisa. 2001 Finding the Field: Notes on the Ethnography of NGOs. *Human Organization* 60(1): 40–46.

Mosse, David, and David Lewis. 2005. *The Aid Effect: Giving and Governing in International Development.* London: Pluto Press.

Venkatesan, Soumhya, and Thomas Yarrow, eds. 2012. *Differentiating Development: Beyond an Anthropology of Critique.* Oxford: Berghahn Books.

Watanabe, Chika. 2015. The Politics of Nonreligious Aid: A Japanese Environmental Ethic in Myanmar. In *Religion and the Politics of Development.* Robin Bush, Michael Feener, and Philip Fountain, eds. Pp. 225–242. London: Palgrave Macmillan.

Websites

Japan International Cooperation Agency (JICA), www.jica.go.jp/index.html.
A governmental agency that coordinates official development assistance for the government of Japan.

JICA volunteers (including the Japan Overseas Cooperation Volunteers), www.jica.go.jp/volunteer/application/seinen/.
A link to volunteer opportunities within the JICA.

Japan's Official Development Assistance (ODA), www.mofa.go.jp/policy/oda/index.html.
ODA works to provide financial aid, emergency assistance, and facilities to underdeveloped nations.

Organization for Industrial, Spiritual and Cultural Advancement (OISCA), http://oisca.org/.
OISCA International focuses on community and resource growth through environmentally sustainable development; in particular, they support programs worldwide to transmit knowledge and skills.

References

Avenell, Simon A. 2010. *Making Japanese Citizens: Civil Society and the Mythology of the Shimin in Postwar Japan*. Berkeley, CA: University of California Press.

Ban, Shōichi. 1974. OISCA to no shimai kankei [Sisterly Relationship with OISCA]. In *Making Tomorrow: OISCA's Action and Principles*. OISCA, ed. P. 90. Tokyo: Japan Life (in Japanese).

Bornstein, Erica. 2012. *Disquieting Gifts: Humanitarianism in New Delhi*. Stanford, CA: Stanford University Press.

Comaroff, John, and Jean Comaroff. 1999. *Civil Society and the Political Imagination in Africa: Critical Perspectives*. Chicago, IL: University of Chicago Press.

Coombe, Rosemary. 1997. Identifying and Engendering the Forms of Emergent Civil Societies: New Directions in Political Anthropology. Special Issue: The Forms of Civil Society in Postcolonial Contexts. *Political and Legal Anthropology Review (PoLAR)* 20(1): 1–12.

DeHart, Monica. 2012. Remodelling the Global Development Landscape: The China Model and South–South Cooperation in Latin America. *Third World Quarterly* 33(7): 1359–1375.

Farrington, John, and David Lewis. 1993. *Non-Governmental Organizations and the State in Asia: Rethinking Roles in Sustainable Agricultural Development*. London: Routledge.

Ferguson, James, and Akhil Gupta. 2002. Spatializing States: Toward an Ethnography of Neoliberal Governmentality. *American Ethnologist* 29(4): 981–1002.

Fisher, William F. 1997. Doing Good?: The Politics and Antipolitics of NGO Practices. *Annual Review of Anthropology* 26: 439–464.

Hirata, Keiko. 2002. *Civil Society in Japan: The Growing Influence of NGOs over Tokyo's Aid and Development Policy*. New York: Palgrave.

Hirata, Keiko. 2004. Civil Society and Japan's Dysfunctional Democracy. *Journal of Developing Societies* 20(1–2): 107–124.

Hirono, Miwa. 2013. Three Legacies of Humanitarianism in China. *Disasters* 37(2): 202–220.

JANIC (Japan NGO Center for International Cooperation). 2007. *NGO dçta book 2006: sûji de miru nihon no NGO [Data Book on NGOs 2006: Japanese NGOs Seen Through Numbers]*. Tokyo: JANIC (in Japanese).

Johnson, Chalmers. 1982. *MITI and the Japanese Miracle: The Growth of Industrial Policy, 1925–1975*. Stanford, CA: Stanford University Press.

Kamat, Sangeeta. 2002. *Development Hegemony: NGOs and the State in India*. Delhi: Oxford University Press.

Kato, Hitoshi, John Page, and Yasutami Shimomura, eds. 2016. *Japan's Development Assistance: Foreign Aid and the Post-2015 Agenda*. New York: Palgrave Macmillan.

Kim, Eun Mee, and Phil Ho Kim. 2014. From Development to Development Cooperation: Foreign Aid, Country Ownership, and the Developmental State in South Korea. In *The South Korean Development Experience: Beyond Aid*. Eun Mee Kim and Phil Ho Kim, eds. Pp. 7–25. London: Palgrave Macmillan.

Leheny, David, and Kay Warren, eds. 2010. *Japanese Aid and the Construction of Global Development*. New York: Routledge.

Leve, Lauren and Lamia Karim. 2001. Privatizing the State: Ethnography of Development, Transnational Capital, and NGOs. *Political and Legal Anthropology Review (PoLAR)* 24(1): 53–58.

Lu, Zeng, and Anthea Mulakala. 2016. Asian NGOs Expand Global Influence: The Asia Foundation. In *Asia: Weekly Insights and Analysis*. Electronic document, http://asiafoundation.org/2016/05/04/asian-ngos-expand-global-influence/, accessed August 30, 2016.

McLaughlin, Levi. 2014. Electioneering as Religious Practice: A History of Sōka Gakkai's Political Activities to 1970. In *Kōmeitō: Religion and Politics in Japan*. George Ehrhardt, Axel Klein, Levi McLaughlin, and Steven S. Reed, eds. Pp. 51–82. Berkeley, CA: Institute of East Asian Studies.

Mawdsley, Emma. 2012. *From Recipients to Donors: Emerging Powers and the Changing Development Landscape*. London: Zed Books.

Mawdsley, Emma, Laura Savage, and Sung-Mi Kim. 2013. A 'Post-Aid World'? Paradigm Shift in Foreign Aid and Development Cooperation at the 2011 Busan High Level Forum. *The Geographical Journal* 180(1): 27–38.

Mouffe, Chantal. 2005. *On the Political*. New York: Routledge.

Nakano, Tsuyoshi. 2003. *Sengo nihon no shūkyō to seiji [Religion and Politics in Post-War Japan]*. Tokyo: Daimeido (in Japanese).

Ogawa, Akihiro. 2009. *The Failure of Civil Society?: The Third Sector and the State in Contemporary Japan.* Albany, NY: SUNY Press.

OISCA. 1967. OISCA Kokusai undō sokushin giinrenmei sōkai hirakaru [National Diet League to Promote OISCA's International Activities General Meeting Takes Place]. *OISCA Magazine*, April, 32–33 (in Japanese).

OISCA.1973. Shukuga taikai zenkoku kakuchi de kaisai [Celebratory Congresses Held Nationwide]. *OISCA Magazine*, July, 4–5, 10–11.

Pekkanen, Robert. 2003. Molding Japanese Civil Society: State-Structured Incentives and the Patterning of Civil Society. In *The State of Civil Society in Japan.* Frank J. Schwartz and Susan J. Pharr, eds. Pp. 116–134. Cambridge: Cambridge University Press.

Poskitt, Adele, Alex Shankland, and Katia Taela. 2016. Civil Society from the BRICS: Emerging Roles in the New International Development Landscape. *Rising Powers in International Development, Evidence Report No. 173.* London: Institute of Development Studies.

Reimann, Kim. 2010. *The Rise of Japanese NGOs: Activism from Above.* New York: Routledge.

Sangi-in [House of Councillors]. 1987. Yosan i-inkai [Budget Committee]. 108th session. Part 10. May 12, 1987 (in Japanese).

Schuller, Mark. 2007. Seeing Like a "Failed" NGO: Globalization's Impacts on State and Civil Society in Haiti. *Political and Legal Anthropology Review (PoLAR)* 30(1): 67–89.

Schwartz, Frank J., and Susan J. Pharr, eds. 2003. *The State of Civil Society in Japan.* Cambridge: Cambridge University Press.

Sharma, Aradhana. 2006. Crossbreeding Institutions, Breeding Struggle: Women's Empowerment, Neoliberal Governmentality, and State (Re)Formation in India. *Cultural Anthropology* 21(1): 60–95.

Shigetomi, Shinichi. 2002. *The State and NGOs: Perspectives from Asia.* Singapore: Institute of Southeast Asian Studies.

Sukma, Rizal, and James Gannon, eds. 2013. *A Growing Force: Civil Society's Role in Asian Regional Security.* Tokyo: Japan Center for International Exchange.

Tan-Mullins, May, Giles Mohan, and Marcus Power. 2010. Redefining "Aid" in the China–Africa Context. *Development and Change* 41(5): 857–881.

Watanabe, Chika. 2014. Muddy Labor: A Japanese Aid Ethic of Collective Intimacy in Myanmar. *Cultural Anthropology* 29(4): 648–671.

Watanabe, Chika. 2015a. The Politics of Nonreligious Aid: A Japanese Environmental Ethic in Myanmar. In *Religion and the Politics of Development.* Robin Bush, Michael Feener, and Philip Fountain, eds. Pp. 225–242. London: Palgrave Macmillan.

Watanabe, Chika. 2015b. Porous Persons: The Politics of a Nonreligious Japanese NGO. In *Global Secularisms in a Post-Secular Age.* Michael Rectenwald, Rochelle Almeida, and George Levine, eds. Pp. 271–285. Berlin: De Gruyter.

Yamamoto, Tadashi, ed. 1995. *Emerging Civil Society in the Asia Pacific Community: Nongovernmental Underpinnings of the Emerging Asia Pacific Regional Community.* Singapore: Institute of Southeast Asian Studies.

28

MEDIA

Claudia Astarita

Civil society and social media: a powerful relationship

A thriving civil society has always been dependent on free, strong and critical media.
They enable us to know, to imagine and to organize to make the world better.

(Mulgan 2010: 9)

When new media began to reveal its potential for global outreach and accessibility, the Internet was promoted as a powerful defender of civil societies and their values. However, after confirming the difficulty of measuring the media's role in engaging the civil society, this chapter evaluates the benefits and the risks that the widespread use of social media carries for contemporary societies. It is argued that when media are too free, they can become a double-edged sword for civil societies.

The limited number of studies testing the relationship between new media and civil society has influenced this chapter to focus on social media platforms rather than on the Internet in general. The diversity of the new media spectrum has forced this research to narrow its scope in order to provide relevant insights and interpretations on how new media can (or cannot) effectively promote citizen engagement and participation. This analysis is a first attempt at untangling the dynamics of a powerful yet problematic relationship between social media and civil society.

The chapter begins with a review of the limited existing literature in the field, followed by a section on the importance of studying the dynamics of people-to-people and organization-to-people interactions on social media, in order to understand the power and perils social media use poses for civil society actors. Case studies on China and India are introduced to explain the role social media play in these two countries and why it is crucial to regulate media and the massive flow of information spread through them, in order to improve their relationship with civil society.

Civic engagement in a digital era

Although it is a known fact that digital technologies have facilitated new forms of civic engagement, it remains difficult to quantify what kind of impact these new forms have on civil society.

Research on the Internet, social networks, and political activism and participation has developed substantially during the last few decades, as has the recognition that: "citizen engagement can have a range of differing impacts, in multifaced forms" (Koc-Michalska, Lilleker, and Vedel 2016: 1807). Further, more recent research on social networks has found that these impacts may not always be positive for the broader society (Koc-Michalska *et al.* 2016).

The importance of evaluating the impact of new media on civil society comes from three different research perspectives. First, digital media have significantly broadened the spectrum of participation, offering more and more people the ability to access information and actively participate in public debates. Second, it is much harder to weight the influence of the so-called "Internet-mediated issue generalists" within societies than it was to evaluate and monitor that of traditional forms (Karpf 2012). These figures, who regularly populate forums, comment on social networks accounts, have blogs, initiate petitions, and often post their views in different online platforms, cannot necessarily be identified as activists in the traditional sense (Koc-Michalska *et al.* 2016). On the contrary, data suggest that the majority of them are simply "extremely active online users," whose opinions may become more relevant thanks to the amount of time that the users themselves spend in disseminating their opinions (Karpf 2012). Third, other sets of data also suggest that: "the mechanisms for facilitating political participation are evolving alongside technological innovation," making it extremely hard to keep research findings in the field updated and relevant for future studies (Koc-Michalska *et al.* 2016: 1807).

New Media and Social Media have taken on such a powerful and widespread role in contemporary society that it would be short-sighted, if not dangerous, not to support further studies in this field. This chapter argues that future research efforts should focus on three different areas. First, on social networks themselves, considering both their empowering impact on engagement and the way in which civil society movements could or should rely on them to support campaigns. Second, identifying and defining the new roles and figures that have emerged on the Internet and investigating how these roles and figures favor (or limit) engagement. Third, given how rapidly new technologies are spreading in Asia as well as the lack of quantitative and qualitative studies covering this region, it is recommended that researchers concentrate new studies on Asian nations.

The importance of studying social networks

Everywhere in the world, social networks have emerged as people's favorite platforms for staying in touch with relatives and friends. The extreme popularity that some of these platforms have gained through years has transformed them into powerful tools for achieving other aims, from reconnecting with colleagues to engaging with citizens users would not otherwise be able to approach. Following this evolution, already-existing networks have started being used for an increasingly broader range of activities, and new platforms have been launched to offer online users new experiences of virtual interactions.

Social networks are usually defined as online platforms supporting three different kinds of activities: gathering information, networking, and active interaction amongst users. All these activities can be considered to be expressions of online civic engagement, which usually materialize outside traditional political institutions and channels but can still have an impact on them. Marina Svensson defines civic engagement as a:

> range of increasingly diverse ways of expressing concern on social issues. This includes personal engagement with peer networks on social media, that is, clicking, liking, and sharing views and offering support. It also includes involvement in civic activities both

online and offline, ranging from online petitions to participation in loose networks and communities to joining social and issue-based campaigns, to donating money, to volunteering and working for NGOs [non-governmental organizations].

(Svensson 2016: 51–52)

Although scholars agree on the fact that civic engagement can be facilitated and expanded online, they offer different interpretations about how social media can support and stimulate connectivity, civic engagement, social change, and political mobilization. Some scholars have welcomed new technologies, online media, and social media for their empowering potential, which offers both ordinary and marginalized people a platform from which to express their own views of and challenges to entrenched visions and institutions (Dahlgren 2013; Diamond 2010). Augusto Valeriani and Cristian Vaccari, after recognizing that: "the Internet has enhanced choice opportunities in individualized media diets" (2016: 1858), note that new technologies have made it easier for citizens to select the information they want, and also decide whether they want to be informed or not. Valeriani and Vaccari's findings, taken in conjunction with those of other authors (see Bimber and Davis 2003; Brundidge and Rice 2009; Prior 2007), implies that the Internet is not necessarily spreading new information to everybody, but rather it can easily leave "the politically uninterested or uninformed trapped in such condition" (Valeriani and Vaccari 2016: 1858).

Other researchers have emphasized the difficulty of calculating the effects of the exposure to information Internet users gain not through autonomous searches, but rather through content shared by other users (Tewksbury, Weaver, and Maddex 2001). Traditional media offer a specific set of information that is pre-arranged by media editors. People watching television news or reading newspapers have the option of skipping an article or not following a piece of news they are not interested in, but their relationship with media is passive, as they are not playing any role in selecting the topics and the news that are offered to them. New media has partially changed this approach, allowing users to be exposed to "an array of information choices that extend far beyond what he or she intentionally seeks" (Tewksbury *et al.* 2001: 534). This happens for two main reasons: many more sources are accessible online than are in offline platforms. By browsing the web pages of several newspapers, Internet users can be confronted with a broader and more diverse set of information than they might otherwise be able to. In this way, the chances that users will be accidentally exposed to news they were not looking for increase as well. "This may in turn enhance political learning and participation, perhaps especially among those who, being less politically interested and involved, are more likely to stumble on political news online than to actually seek it" (Valeriani and Vaccari 2016: 1858).

If the development of online media has made the relationship amongst media editors and consumers slightly less passive, the success of social media has transformed this connection into an active one, by both increasing the number of sources regular users can be exposed to and by giving users the chance to play a powerful role in contributing to the further spread of the content that is relevant to them.

Although the Internet has been broadly recognized as a new platform with the potential to increase users' knowledge of current and political affairs, it remains debated whether the Internet has increased the likelihood that most individuals will be confronted with alternative sets of news, or if broad access will be limited to a cohort of educated users that are by definition more informed than average Internet users, confirming the "rich get richer" paradigm (Norris 2003; Scheufele and Nisbet 2002; Xenos and Moy 2007; Yoo and Gil de Zúñiga 2014). Unfortunately, few studies so far have explored these dynamics. Researchers such as Andrew Chadwick (2009), Shelley Boulianne (2009), David Tewksury *et al.* (2001), and Homero Gil de Zúñiga and Sebastián Valenzuela (2011) have become more optimistic about the positive impacts of the current "information exuberance" (Chadwick 2009). "Web 2.0 platforms have lowered the threshold for producing, distributing, and engaging with political information on the web, [increasing] the likelihood that citizens are accidentally exposed to news online, which in turn may affect patterns of political engagement" (Valeriani and Vaccari 2016: 1858).

Research seems to suggest that web portals, defined as online platforms where news is offered together with specific online services (email, search engines, stock quotes, etc.) as well as entertainment content (Tewksbury *et al.* 2001; Tewksbury and Rittenberg 2012) have significantly increased the possibility that citizens are inadvertently exposed to political content they were not necessarily seeking (Valeriani and Vaccari 2016), and that the emergence of social networking platforms has further increased the outreach of this phenomenon by creating new platforms that allow users to take a more active role in them by deciding what kind of information to access and share with other users. Last but not least, the continual presence of social media in people's lives has progressively transformed them into extremely powerful tools for spreading and sharing ideas and information (Chadwick 2009; Wright 2012).

The sense of empowerment associated with social media is linked to two main factors. First, they have shaped new hybrid spaces where public discourses (either political or non-political) can coexist with private information and entertainment news. Second, they have created new forms of participation amongst online users, allowing them to get in touch with their peers and to mobilize consensus on a particular cause. These new patterns of direct participation tend to be considered by some scholars as more effective than traditional ones, due to their ability to bypass more institutionalized organizations and traditional media. However, although social media have already proved to be an effective platform for rapidly mobilizing consensus and support for a specific event (from a street protest to a pro-democracy mass-mobilization), how useful social media can be in strengthening a civil society movement remains a contentious issue.

Similar doubts are held by numerous groups of scholars that paint a more negative picture of the impact that social media can have on civil society and civic engagement. Christian Fuchs (2014) describes the broad fragmentation of the virtual sphere in which online users interact with each other as a disruptive environment where no proper engagement can ever materialize. Additionally, a series of studies conducted in Western countries have confirmed the existence of a digital divide in modern societies that is perpetrating the dominance of so-called privileged actors on social media (Sloam 2014; Sloan 2014).

Another major concern with online civic engagement is related to the fact that, despite their effectiveness in spreading information and mobilizing consensus, it is hard to affirm that social media can "lead to sustained commitment and real social and political changes" (Svensson 2016: 52). On the contrary, online support for real causes appears to be volatile and keen to embrace extreme tones. Some critics describe engagement on social media as clicktivism or slacktivism because people's engagement is limited to clicking, sharing, and liking on Twitter and Facebook. Evgeny Morozov is often quoted as one of the strongest critics of techno-optimism and clicktivism (Morozov 2011, 2013). According to Morozov, the problem with online activism is that it seldom, if ever, goes beyond virtual reality. More and more people have become interested in signing online petitions, donating money, condemning new laws and political initiatives, giving voice to people experiencing discrimination, violence or other forms of abuses, but their engagement is limited to clicking, sharing, and liking "illusionary quick fixes and easy-to-do activities that do not involve any sustained efforts or offline activities" (Svensson 2016: 53). As long as online and offline realities remain separate, virtual activists can claim to be engaged even while their contribution to the cause they are trying to support fails to move beyond a mere forwarding of information. "They make people feel good about themselves but prevent in-depth analysis of more complex social and political problems and political organizing" (Svensson 2016: 53). Finally, activities labeled as "clicktivism" or "slacktivism" are seen with increased skepticism by a growing number of scholars, who criticize them as a "lazy, light-hearted, low-cost, and low-risk, maybe even selfish, form of commitment that builds on the false belief that posting, liking, and sharing will change the world" (Svensson 2016: 53). At the same time, it is important to remember that "clicktivism" is perceived by some Internet users as an "ad hoc and reflexive act that does not aim to further any ideological or political cause" (Svensson 2016: 53). With social media platforms as hybrid zones where the borders between the private and the public spheres are blurred, the idea that a click may imply active political engagement might be far beyond the original intention of the Internet user. At the same time, there are studies proving that a click can be classified as one of the possible actions leading to more sustained activism. Finally, in a set of specific social contexts, such as authoritarian societies, a click could be the only strategy to raise "awareness on hidden or suppressed issues" (Svensson 2016: 53).

Such skeptical, imbalanced and insufficiently nuanced attitudes are not shared by all studies focusing on social media. There are researchers emphasizing that: "in the past ten years, the proliferation of affordable Internet devices and the rise of social media platforms has enabled highly decentralized (co)production and dissemination of ideas, public discussion and deliberation, and allowed new forms of network organization" (Skoric *et al.* 2016: 1819; see also Bennett 2008). Research does seem to confirm the pivotal role that social media have played in transforming the nature of online interaction, "enabling new forms of personalized public engagement that no longer require significant organizational resources nor common identity or ideology" (Skoric *et al.* 2016: 1819; see also Bennett and Segerberg 2012). Some scholars argue that the new opportunities for discussion, debate, and deliberation created by social media can lead to specific and unexpected behavioral outcomes (Skoric *et al.* 2016). However, there is no consolidated research proving that activism on social networks can strengthen civil society movements. Skoric *et al.*'s review is one of the few studies that have tried to fill this research gap and have examined all the empirical research studies published from 2007 to 2013, with an aim of evaluating the relationship between social media use and citizen engagement. The review includes twenty-two studies that used self-reported measures of social media use and participation, with a total of 116 relationships and effects explored. The findings seem to suggest a positive relationship between social media use and citizen engagement. In particular, more support was provided to previous studies' findings that: "easy and expanded access to diverse political information might reinvigorate citizen participation by improving political knowledge and stimulating political discussion" (Skoric *et al.* 2016: 1833; see also Boulianne 2009). The Internet appears as a powerful platform offering "new opportunities for citizen networking and open[ing] up new venues for political expression, potentially activating those previously disengaged citizens" (Skoric *et al.* 2016: 1833). As opposed to what used to happen in the pre-social network era, when the Internet was mainly used for social and recreational purposes that were not positively correlated with social participation, the growth of interactions on identity-centric networks with non-anonymous or pseudonymous settings represents an intrinsic change in the nature of online interaction. Recent studies (Gil de Zúñiga, Molyneux, and Zheng 2014) seem to suggest that:

> the exposure to political information and social interactions on social media steers citizens on a path of political expression which may lead to political participation. The acts of political expression on social media are personalized and identity-focused and

may be aimed at different audiences depending on a specific context. Given the number of potential social settings and overlapping audiences on egocentric networks, citizens engaging in political expression need to develop a broader repertoire of political selves which triggers a process of inadvertent civic learning and may lead to spillover effects on real-world political action.

(Skoric et al. 2016: 1834)

More research on the nature of the connection between social media use and civil society engagement is needed to understand other powerful dynamics that appear to be emerging on online platforms. First, the role of "senders"— users who are either posting or sharing messages online—should be better explored. Empirical studies have already confirmed that senders can have both a direct and mediating role in stimulating and predicting users' engagements on social media; however, not enough research has been conducted to measure and rationalize their role, or to understand how and under which circumstances "senders" becomes "influencers" (Gil de Zúñiga *et al.* 2014; Pingree 2007; Rojas and Puig-i-Abril 2009). Second, new theoretical models are needed to clarify how to measure the expressive uses of social media, including their discussion- and deliberation-inducing properties, as well as, "the conditions and social context under which political expression is most likely to be followed by political action (e.g. non-anonymous vs. pseudonymous platforms; voting vs. protest participation)" (Skoric *et al.* 2016: 1834).

The urgency of filling this gap in social media research is further confirmed by numbers. Shelley Boulianne has recently published an interesting study on social networks, civic awareness, and engagement in which she discovered that: "approximately half of Facebook users follow traditional news sources through Facebook, [and] 78 percent [of them] report being exposed to the news incidentally through social network ties" (Boulianne 2016: 1841). Engagement growth on social media comes from at least three different dynamics: first, sharing news amongst network members is a very easy process (Boulianne 2016). Second, thanks to incidental learning, news sharing from well-informed users can easily reach less-informed ones (Tang and Lee 2013). Third, "senders" tend to be more influential within their network than they are outside it because they are perceived as a "trusted" source from their family and friends (Bode *et al.* 2014). Fourth, once "senders" become "influencers," their messages remain strong and valid even outside their networks.

If research should be oriented at understanding the mechanisms through which social media affects engagement, rather than limiting its focus to the direct link between the two variables, more effort should be devoted to disclose how social media affects engagement. Boulianne's work hypothesizes that online news can increase civic awareness, which, in turn, can increase engagement in civic and political life (Boulianne 2016). She argues that: "the more a citizen knows about the world, the more likely the citizen will find something that interests them enough to become engaged in the political process" (Boulianne 2016: 1843). At the same time, the understanding of engagement cannot be reduced to "campaign participation," as several other forms of engagement can take place in civil society. Unfortunately, much of the existing studies investigating social media and engagement are campaign-focused, and this approach is misleading as both trends and results may be campaign-specific (Boulianne 2016).

This literature review confirms that no clear or univocal relationship can be identified between the broader media accessibility the Internet can guarantee and engagement in civil society movements. This lack of consensus does not imply a negative correlation between the two variables, but rather that more studies have to be conducted to untangle the dynamics of their interactions as well as the factors that influence them. This need is perceived as even more urgent considering that not only have the Internet and social media already changed the nature of everyday interactions and thereby enabled personalized public engagement, but also that their outreach is expected to expand, as new technologies develop, Internet-accessible devices become more affordable, and social media platforms continue to spread.

More studies are also recommended to promote the responsible use of social media, by bolstering their assets and controlling the risks embedded in the currently unrestrained use of these platforms. By proposing a review of how social media are used in Asia, this chapter attempts to further elucidate three concepts: First, that social media are a powerful tool for spreading awareness about social and political events, and that this awareness can lead to engagement. Second, the power of accidental exposures to information and the persuasiveness of discussion disagreement (by making users' social context more heterogeneous, social media can boost flexibility, tolerance, and intellectual stimulation). Third, the conditions under which virtual communities can stimulate civic engagement. The following sections of this chapter will also emphasize the risks connected with the easy creation and dissemination of individual political content, which may create a dangerous sense of empowerment linked to a more and more popular and firmly held belief that everybody can "do" politics in some form. These dynamics are creating confusion, facilitating the spread of fake news, and nurturing a dangerous wave of cynicism, and protests, as well aggressiveness from the so-called social networks' "trolls," all of which demands a prompt response. It is suggested that an effort to re-emphasize integrity—defined as the promotion of values such as truthfulness and accuracy—is key to facing this threat.

Social networks in Asia: a preliminary case study on the Chinese and Indian experiences

The urgency of reducing the current absence of studies exploring the impact of digital technologies and social media in Asia becomes even more pressing after recognizing the popularity of online platforms in this region. According to data published by Miniwatts Marketing Group, an American organization famous for collecting and analyzing Internet-related data, Asia already hosts 50.2 percent of global Internet users. The significance of this quota becomes even more relevant when compared to the online populations of other world regions: 8.7 percent of virtual users are in North America, 10.5 percent in Latin America, and 16.7 percent in Europe (Miniwatts Marketing Group n.d.b). To fully understand the potential outreach of digital technologies and new media in Asia, it is important to link these numbers to the ones emerging from another dataset, the one ranking connection rates, or "Internet penetration," defined as the portion of the population that has access to the Internet. From this perspective, North America stands out, with 89 percent Internet penetration, followed by Europe (73.5 percent), Latin America (59.4 percent), and Asia (45.6 percent) (Miniwatts Marketing Group n.d.b). The huge digital divide that currently characterizes Asian societies, together with a generalized preference in the region for accessing news and any other information through mobile technologies, further speaks to the necessity for better analyzing the dynamics of online interactions. In societies in which online access is guaranteed by the use of smartphones, their increased affordability offers the chance to significantly expand the outreach of messages distributed online.

Unfortunately, the most relevant studies on digital media and political engagement (of which there are still very few), have been conducted in the United States (Kim, Hsu, and Gil de Zúñiga 2013; Tewksbury et al. 2001; Tewksbury and Rittenberg 2012). Although the number of studies investigating the impact and power of social media in Europe is increasing (Boulianne 2016; Valeriani and Vaccari 2016), there are still few concentrating on Asia. The Internet already plays a major role in a region in which the number of Internet users is expected to register an exponential growth in the near future. It is all the more urgent to study these areas because of the difficulty of generalizing the findings of social media studies focusing on other regions with specific political, economic, and social features.

Online media in China

Analyzing the impact of new media in China is a difficult task. With nearly half of the population accessing the Internet, particularly through portable technologies, the enormous influence of these media is undeniable, and new media are emerging as useful and friendly platforms for ordinary people "to express and share opinions and information" (DeLisle, Goldstein, and Yang 2016: 1). Moreover, they

> have changed the way the Chinese authorities communicate with the people they rule. China's party state now invests heavily in speaking to Chinese citizens through the Internet and social media, as well as controlling the speech that occurs in that space.
>
> *(DeLisle et al. 2016: 1)*

This double use of online media is common in liberal and democratic societies as well, although at a lower scale. What makes China a unique case is the power of censorship, which significantly impedes the reliability of any attempt to critically analyze the impact of new media and social platforms in the country. This awareness, together with the limited transparency of information collection and dissemination in China and the poverty of existing studies conducted in this field, is de facto reducing the ability of existing studies to be accurately applied to the situation in China. At the same time, the latter remain a useful starting point for understanding the impact of new technologies and media in China, as well as a warning sign about the urgency of deepening research in this area.

Consolidated studies have proved that: "expectations that the Internet would quickly become an overwhelmingly positive and transformative force in China" are misplaced, as the Chinese government has rapidly "adapted and developed new means of limiting and controlling speech in cyberspace, including mechanisms of participation, monitoring, regulating, censoring and sanctioning" (DeLisle *et al.* 2016: 4).

In China, "the coevolution of digital activism and authoritarianism does not pronounce immediate winners and losers. However, it has become increasingly clear that the Internet is not necessarily an insurmountable threat to capable illiberal regimes" (Jiang 2016: 30). The case in China then, confirms the idea that the Internet is a powerful tool to spread the awareness on specific events leading to engagement. However, what is unique in China is that this awareness is strongly mediated by the Communist Government. In a cat-and-mouse game, the Communist Party of China (CPC) has succeeded in promoting a select use of the Internet, allowing people to use it as a "means for socioeconomic development while successfully minimizing its political impact" (Jiang 2016: 30). According to Min Jiang, to understand the role of the Internet in China, it is important to accept the existence of an implicit state–society pact that includes "the political status-quo, a one-party system monopolized by a small group of élites with the assurance of reasonable performance social stability, and continued economic growth, shall remain unchallenged" (Jiang 2016: 30). If this is the case, it is impossible to argue that grass-roots empowerment is either wholly manipulated by the CPC or that it is not happening. Rather, social activism is spreading online, but following rules and dynamics decided by the government.

During the last few decades, and thanks to the Internet, civil society organizations in China have registered a dramatic growth (Yang 2009). However, the major limitation of any attempt to evaluate the impact of the Internet on civic engagement is the reliability of studies' collected data. Some studies argue that many Chinese citizens exhibit low levels of trust and interest in official organizations, implying they might prefer to be in touch with informal online communities (Svensson 2016). There are other studies claiming that certain groups are more active than others online. Amongst the more active groups are the youth (for being digital natives and individualistic), the growing middle class (as more interested in safeguarding its interests without opposing the party-state), and professional groups such as lawyers and journalists (as more inclined to spread and support sensitive and highly politicized campaigns) (Svensson 2016). Other researchers argue that the reliability of collected data in China can be compromised by the active role the government plays, as it employs intimidating measures ranging from information filtering and hiring pro-state commentators to supporting official views, to more contemporary initiatives such as the Real Name Registration Policy and anti-rumor campaigns (Creemers 2012). Finally, there are studies claiming that China has a problem with "uncivil society virtual groups" (Simon 2013; Zheng 2007), a term used to "capture the extreme incivility of online exchanges between individuals and groups over public issues, which not only fail to produce solutions to problems, but also accentuate group identities and widen the ideological chasms between them" (Jiang 2016: 46). Although this disruptive phenomenon is a problem for many countries, in a nation like China, the non-existence of adequate mechanisms to channel online exchanges to build constructive dialogue can further limit the positive and powerful role the Internet and social networks can play in promoting engagement.

That being said, it is important to keep in mind that, in China, individuals, networks, and organizations that are critical of the government continue to be prosecuted by it. However, any campaign able to successfully deal with censorship and repression is de facto spreading the positive effects of accidental exposure to information and creating conditions for the empowerment of online discourse. If, in the authoritarian context, a click is the only strategy to raise awareness on hidden or suppressed issues, all new forms of social activism, either censored or self-censored, may favor the opening of new spaces for the emergence of civil society movements, even in non-democratic countries like China. At the same time, promoting social activism in areas that are not discouraged by the government may indeed consolidate the idea that activism is not always dangerous, but rather can achieve limited successes. Only time will tell whether, in the long run, civil society or the party will win this still unbalanced game of cat-and-mouse.

The power of social media in India

India is another relevant case study emphasizing the urgency of deepening research on the impact of social media for information dissemination and civic engagement. According to a recent report published by the marketing agency We Are Social (Kemp 2015), India has 462 million active Internet users (out of a global total of 3.63 billion), and this number is growing at a rate of 90 percent per year (the global average is 19 percent). India also counts 153 million active social media users, of which 130 million operate on mobile devices. Considering that the country has 1,012 million mobile connections registered, their actual penetration rate is limited to a mere 10 percent, but this value is growing at a rate of 20 percent per year (Kemp 2015).

These numbers can confirm two trends: First, 65 percent of India is still far from having access to the Internet, but the country is catching up increasingly quickly. Second, the Internet is the only platform in the county available for engaging and mobilizing people, and both politicians and civil society activists have started regularly using it to expand their outreach in the country.

As was the case in China, the lack of quantitative studies on how social media are used in India makes it impossible to evaluate their impact on local civil society. However, the exponential growth in the use of social media confirms the urgency of gaining better understanding of what kind of roles these new platforms play in society.

The number of mobile Internet users has been growing hand in hand with politicians' online activism. In particular, it is claimed that: "the incorporation of politics into social networking sites has made it impossible for political parties to ignore social media" (Neyazi 2013). Although some scholars have argued that voters' changing expectations toward their elected representatives have given social media disproportionate power compared to their real coverage and representation of countries' preferences, when a group of researchers attempted to measure the impact of social networks on political engagement in India, mixed findings were collected. It has been confirmed that social networks are part of the daily routine amongst urban Indian youth, but their use is seldom associated with political engagement.

> Youth feel that politics can be discussed in social media. However, they limit their political participation to giving likes to others' posts/tweets/videos and so on. If and when they post political content, it is mostly in the form of status updates/tweets and memes. Youth, by and large, do not use social networks to propagate political ideologies or support/criticize political parties and movements. They also feel that social networks do not really connect them with political leaders. Very few of the youth feel that social networks are an effective tool for political engagement.
>
> *(Rupa and Karnamaharajan 2015: 220)*

If we think about how people usually form their ideas, although we tend to assume that no external influence will interfere with the way in which we see things, it has been proved that: "citizens are often influenced by messages filtered through the news media, the social context of their peer group, or both" (Diehl, Weeks, and Gil de Zúñiga 2016: 1875). The reason why social media have emerged as the best social environment for shaping ideas is linked to the fact that these platforms offer a unique environment in which users can be simultaneously exposed to news and to the views of the people that are part of their social network (Diehl *et al.* 2016: 1875).

The case of India is useful for validating the idea that social media can facilitate political persuasion. Literature has already confirmed that political persuasion can occur through conversation and constant exposure to diverse opinions (Gastil 1993; Ryfe 2005). According to Trevor Diehl, Brian E. Weeks, and Homero Gil de Zúñiga, "both basic social interaction and use of news within social media are directly related to persuasion on social media." In particular, they claim that: "news and social interaction behaviors indirectly facilitate political persuasion, by increasing the diversity of individuals' networks, which subsequently increases their exposure to political views that differ from their own" (Diehl *et al.* 2016: 1876–1877), and that this can lead to political persuasion.

Although Diehl *et al.* do not refer directly to "influencers," their analysis confirms research findings that people that are used to interacting in large and diverse cohorts are more likely to be exposed to alternative views (Huckfeldt, Johnson, and Sprague 2004; Mutz 2002), and can become more tolerant of those views (Mutz 2002) and even more likely to change their own perspectives over time (Levitan and Visser 2009).

> At the heart of this literature is a fairly simple idea: individuals' opinions and attitudes are contingent upon characteristics imbedded in their social connections. Since the

Internet and social media make it much easier to access and build diverse networks, it stands to reason that persuasion on social media happens through connections in heterogeneous networks.

(Diehl et al. 2016: 1877)

There are three major dynamics that can transform social media into extremely persuasive tools. The first is accidental exposure to news, a phenomenon that is broadening the number and type of sources that online users are confronted with. Second is the "discussion disagreement" process, which, by exposing individuals to dissenting views, can force them to seek more information, reflect on their own opinions, and ultimately even increase their willingness to reconsider their views (Mutz 2002; Mutz and Martin 2001). Third, the informal setting constituted by social media has increased the opportunities for traditional users to get in touch with "influencers." Traditionally understood as people who are highly active on social media and blogs and who can influence consumers through recommendations or stories about their direct experiences, influencers are becoming more and more popular and powerful in political arenas as well.

With Internet users looking for direct and authentic rather than media-mediated connections with their favorite opinion leaders, the latter have realized the potential of the Internet to raise consensus on specific causes. In particular, it has been argued that, as individuals encounter messages on social media from other users that they know or trust (at least to some extent, which makes this condition applicable to public figures as well), they are likely to process what they are saying in a more positive and unbiased way compared to their interpretation of messages from impersonal sources such as the mass media (Valeriani and Vaccari 2016: 1861).

The Indian anti-corruption leader Anna Hazare effectively used social media to mobilize Indian people over the issue of the Jan Lokpal Bill in 2011. "The effective use of social media not only brought the issue into cyber space and made it more global, but also garnered huge support for the anti-corruption campaign" (Neyazi 2013), a statement reinforced by the fact that Anna Hazare and the Jan Lokpal Bill were the most popular topic of Facebook status updates in India throughout 2011.

The role of political influencers can become particularly strong in countries where the government is delegitimized. While looking for reliable leaders, data, and opinions, Internet users may end up trusting their online networks more than traditional media, and start regularly approaching influencers to follow their perspectives and insights on specific issues. This practice gives political influencers more and more power, but it also favors the proliferation of less qualified figures interested in spreading negative, cynical, and biased views online.

In India, social media again became a prominent political platform when the current Premier Narendra Modi decided to use it to connect with the national population. The way in which the Indian leader has been able to build a better image for himself, gain people's trust and support, and create a special relationship with his supporters has no precedent in India, or anywhere else in the world, and is the result of a successful campaign conducted on social media (Ramalingegowda 2014). On September 2014, Twitter decided to release a special blog on the 100 days of Twitter diplomacy by Narendra Modi. In particular, it was highlighted that the Indian premier was using both his personal handle (@NarendraModi) and his official handle (@PMOIndia) to give live updates to his cohort of 8.5 million followers, which has since expanded to 44.6 million people. His election victory Tweet from @NarendraModi was the most-retweeted Tweet of all time from India. A look at the geo-tagged Tweets of the first 100 days of Government about @NarendraModi suggests that he was and likely continues to engage with users all over the world who are interested in Indian politics and his administration (Khursheed 2014).

Narendra Modi is not the only politician who has decided to use social media to engage his supporters. However, no matter how much online users enjoy this idea of feeling directly in touch with their leaders, more research is needed to verify whether political leaders can be classified as influencers. The role of influencers should be to mediate harsh and biased political views that circulate online, and to offer users a more solid and accurate perspective on specific topics under discussion. Considering that political leaders' views are not always moderate and well articulated, they will not all fall into the category of "influencers." Rather than trying to become influencers themselves, using social networks to be perceived as being closer to people, it is suggested that politicians may become more powerful on social media by relying on influencers' support.

Conclusion

It is clear from this review on how new media and social media work in Asia and elsewhere that more empirical studies are needed to understand the role these new platforms are playing in contemporary societies and the way in which civil society movements may use them to promote engagement.

That said, social media seems to be emerging as a double-edged sword, able, on the one hand, to create and consolidate a dangerous trade-off between the freedom to access news, valuable opinions, public officers and influencers, and on the other, to spread cynicism, fake news, biased perspectives, and aggressive messages.

At the same time, consolidated research has proven that online activism can not only promote engagement, but also have a "real-world" impact when a critical mass of users is involved in a concerted action. This finding is enough to suggest that social media may be used to promote support for civil society campaigns.

However, to foster a mutually supportive relationship between civil society actors and social media, new rules should be created to avoid having the Internet become an uncontrollable "Far West." An effort to re-emphasize integrity—the promotion of values such as truthfulness and accuracy—which can be made by strengthening the synergy between social networks and traditional media and by promoting the role of influencers, is a key element in reshaping the Internet as a more trustable, safer, and less aggressive space. However, more research is needed to understand who is expected to discuss, define, and implement these new rules for our virtual reality. In particular, it is important that future studies concentrate on identifying legislators whose decisions can be easily accepted by Internet users. Valid and reliable influencers could play an important role in this process as well.

Finally, it is important to always keep in mind that rapid and unexpected changes in technologies will continue to reshape the relationship between Internet use and civil and political engagement, creating more pressure on scholars researching in this field to keep their findings up to date.

Suggested readings

Boulianne, Shelley. 2009. Does Internet Use Affect Engagement? A Meta-Analysis of Research. *Political Communication* 26(2): 193–211.

Boulianne, Shelley. 2016. Online News, Civic Awareness, and Engagement in Civic and Political Life. *New Media & Society* 18(9): 1840–1856.

Chadwick, Andrew. 2009. Web 2.0: New Challenges for the Study of E-Democracy in an Era of Informational Exuberance. *I/S: A Journal of Law and Policy for the Information Society* 5(1): 9–41.

Gil de Zúñiga, Homero, and Sebastián Valenzuela. 2011. The Mediating Path to a Stronger Citizenship: Online and Offline Networks, Weak Ties, and Civic Engagement. *Communication Research* 38(3): 397–421.

Koc-Michalska, Karolina, Darren G. Lilleker, and Thierry Vedel. 2016. Civic Political Engagement and Social Change in the New Digital Age. *New Media and Society* 18(9): 1807–1816.

Tewksbury, David, Andrew Weaver, and Brett D. Maddex. 2001. Accidentally Informed: Incidental News Exposure on the World Wide Web. *Journalism and Mass Communication Quarterly* 78(3): 533–554.

Tewksbury, David, and Jason Rittenberg. 2012. *News on the Internet: Information and Citizenship in the 21st Century.* Oxford: Oxford University Press.

References

Bennett, W. Lance. 2008. Changing Citizenship in the Digital Age. In *Civic Life Online: Learning How Digital Media Can Engage Youth.* W. Lance Bennett, ed. Pp. 1–24. Cambridge, MA: MIT Press.

Bennett, W. Lance, and Alexandra Segerberg. 2012. The Logic of Connective Action. *Information, Communication & Society* 15: 1–30.

Bimber, Bruce, and Richard Davis. 2003. *Campaigning Online: The Internet in US Elections.* New York: Oxford University Press.

Bode, Leticia, Emily K. Vraga, Porismita Borah, and Dhavan V. Shah. 2014. A New Space for Political Behavior: Political Social Networking and Its Democratic Consequences. *Journal of Computer-Mediated Communication* 19(3): 414–429.

Boulianne, Shelley. 2009. Does Internet Use Affect Engagement? A Meta-Analysis of Research. *Political Communication* 26(2): 193–211.

Boulianne, Shelley. 2016. Online News, Civic Awareness, and Engagement in Civic and Political Life. *New Media & Society* 18(9): 1840–1856.

Brundidge, Jennifer, and Ronald E. Rice. 2009. Political Engagement Online: Do the Information Rich Get Richer and the Like-minded More Similar? In *Routledge Handbook of Internet Politics.* Andrew Chadwick and Phillip N. Howard, eds. Pp. 144–156. New York: Routledge.

Chadwick, Andrew. 2009. Web 2.0: New Challenges for the Study of E-Democracy in an Era of Informational Exuberance. *I/S: A Journal of Law and Policy for the Information Society* 5(1): 9–41.

Creemers, Roger. 2012. Some Beijing Municipal Provisions on Microblog Development and Management. China Copyright and Media. Electronic document, https://chinacopyrightandmedia.wordpress.com/2011/12/16/some-beijing-municipal-provisions-on-microblog-development-and-management/, accessed March 15, 2017.

Dahlgren, Peter. 2013. *The Political Web: Media Participation and Alternative Democracy.* Basingstoke: Palgrave Macmillan.

DeLisle, Jacques, Avery Goldstein, and Guobin Yang. 2016. Introduction: The Internet, Social Media, and a Changing China. In *The Internet, Social Media, and a Changing China.* Jacques deLisle, Avery Goldstein, and Guobin Yang, eds. Pp. 1–27. Philadelphia, PA: University of Pennsylvania Press.

Diamond, Larry. 2010. Liberation Technology. *Journal of Democracy* 21(3): 69–83.

Diehl, Trevor, Brian E. Weeks, and Homero Gil de Zúñiga. 2016. Political Persuasion on Social Media: Tracing Direct and Indirect Effects of News Use and Social Interaction. *New Media and Society* 18(9): 1875–1895.

Fuchs, Christian. 2014. *Social Media: A Critical Introduction.* London: Sage.

Gastil, John. 1993. *Democracy in Small Groups: Participation, Decision Making, and Communication.* Philadelphia, PA: New Society Publishers.

Gil de Zúñiga, Homero, and Sebastián Valenzuela. 2011. The Mediating Path to a Stronger Citizenship: Online and Offline Networks, Weak Ties, and Civic Engagement. *Communication Research* 38(3): 397–421.

Gil de Zúñiga, Homero, Logan Molyneux, and Pei Zheng. 2014. Social Media, Political Expression and Political Participation: Panel Analysis of Lagged and Concurrent Relationships. *Journal of Communication* 64(4): 612–634.

Huckfeldt, Robert, Paul E. Johnson, and John Sprague. 2004. *Political Disagreement: The Survival of Diverse Opinions Within Communication Networks.* New York: Cambridge University Press.

Jiang, Min. 2016. The Coevolution of the Internet, (Un)Civil Society, and Authoritarianism in China. In *The Internet, Social Media, and a Changing China.* Jacques deLisle, Avery Goldstein, and Guobin Yang, eds. Pp. 28–48. Philadelphia, PA: University of Pennsylvania Press.

Karpf, David. 2012. *The MoveOn Effect: The Unexpected Transformation of American Political Advocacy*. Oxford: Oxford University Press.

Kemp, Simon. 2015. Digital StatShot India. We Are Social. Electronic document, http://wearesocial.com/sg/special-reports/digital-social-mobile-india-2015, accessed February 12, 2017.

Khursheed, Raheel. 2014. #NaMo100days Sets New Standard for Indian diplomacy on Twitter. Electronic document, https://blog.twitter.com/2014/namo100days-sets-new-standard-for-indian-diplomacy-on-twitter, accessed March 16, 2017.

Kim, Yonghwan, Shih-Hsien Hsu, and Homero Gil de Zúñiga. 2013. Influence of Social Media Use on Discussion Network Heterogeneity and Civic Engagement: The Moderating Role of Personality Traits. *Journal of Communication* 63(3): 498–516.

Koc-Michalska, Karolina, Darren G. Lilleker, and Thierry Vedel. 2016. Civic Political Engagement and Social Change in the New Digital Age. *New Media and Society* 18(9): 1807–1816.

Levitan, Lindsey Clark, and Penny S. Visser. 2009. Social Network Composition and Attitude Strength: Exploring the Dynamics within Newly Formed Social Networks. *Journal of Experimental Social Psychology* 44(3): 640–649.

Miniwatts Marketing Group. n.d.a. Internet Usage in Asia. Electronic document, www.internetworldstats.com/stats3.htm, accessed January 7, 2017.

Miniwatts Marketing Group. n.d.b. Internet Users in the World by Region. Electronic document, www.internetworldstats.com/stats.htm, accessed January 7, 2017.

Morozov, Evgeny. 2011. *The Net Delusion: How Not to Liberate the World*. London: Allen Lane.

Morozov, Evgeny. 2013. *To Save Everything, Click Here: Technology, Solutionism and the Urge to Fix Problems that Don't Exist*. London: Allen Lane.

Mulgan, Geoff. 2010. Making Good Society: Final report of the Commission of Inquiry into the Future of Civil Society in the UK and Ireland. Electronic document, www.futuresforcivilsociety.org, accessed December 2, 2016.

Mutz, Diana C. 2002. The Consequences of Cross-cutting Networks for Political Participation. *American Journal of Political Science* 46(4): 838–855.

Mutz, Diana C., and Paul S. Martin. 2001. Facilitating Communication across Lines of Political Difference: The Role of Mass Media. *American Political Science Review* 95(1): 97–114.

Neyazi, Taberez Ahmed. 2013. Social Media and Political Communication in India. In *The Indian Medialogue*. Electronic document, https://indianmedialogue.com/2013/05/07/social-media-and-political-communication-in-india/, accessed February 14, 2017.

Norris, Pippa. 2003. Preaching to the Converted?: Pluralism, Participation and Party Websites. *Party Politics* 9(1): 21–45.

Pingree, Raymond J. 2007. How Messages Affect their Senders: A More General Model of Message Effects and Implications for Deliberation. *Communication Theory* 17(4): 439–461.

Prior, Markus. 2007. *Post-Broadcast Democracy: How Media Choice Increases Inequality in Political Involvement and Polarizes Elections*. Cambridge: Cambridge University Press.

Ramalingegowda, Chaitanya. 2014. *How Indian Politicians are Using Social Media to Build Personal Brands*. Electronic document, https://yourstory.com/2014/09/politicians-social-media/, accessed March 16, 2017.

Rojas, Hernando, and Eulalia Puig-i-Abril. 2009. Mobilizers Mobilized: Information, Expression, Mobilization and Participation in the Digital Age. *Journal of Computer-Mediated Communication* 14(4): 902–927.

Rupa, P. and K. Karnamaharajan. 2015. The Use of Social Networks for Political Engagement by Indian Youth. *Indian Journal of Applied Research* 5(6): 218–220.

Ryfe, David M. 2005. Does Deliberative Democracy Work? *Annual Review Political Science* 8(1): 49–71.

Scheufele, Dietram A., and Matthew C. Nisbet. 2002. Being a Citizen Online. New Opportunities and Dead Ends. *The Harvard International Journal of Press/Politics* 7(3): 55–75.

Simon, Karla. 2013. *Civil Society in China: A Legal Framework from Ancient Times to the "New Reform Era."* Oxford: Oxford University Press.

Skoric, Marko, Qinfeng Zhu, Debbie Goh, and Natalie Pang. 2016. Social Media and Citizen Engagement: A Meta-Analytic Review. *New Media & Society* 18(9): 1817–1839.

Sloam, James. 2014. New Voice, Less Equal: The Civic and Political Engagement of Young People in the United States and Europe. *Comparative Political Studies* 47(5): 663–688.

Sloan, James. 2014. The Outraged Young: Young Europeans, Civic Engagement and the New Media in a Time of Crisis. *Information, Communication & Society* 17(2): 217–223.

Svensson, Marina. 2016. Connectivity, Engagement, and Witnessing on China's Weibo. In *The Internet, Social Media, and a Changing China*. Jacques deLisle, Avery Goldstein, and Guobin Yang, eds. Pp 49–70. Philadelphia, PA: University of Pennsylvania Press.

Tang, Gary K. Y., and Francis L. F. Lee. 2013. Facebook Use and Political Participation: The Impact of Exposure to Shared Political Information, Connections with Public Political Actors, and Network Structural Heterogeneity. *Social Science Computer Review* 31(6): 763–773.

Tewksbury, David, Andrew Weaver, and Brett D. Maddex. 2001. Accidentally Informed: Incidental News Exposure on the World Wide Web. *Journalism and Mass Communication Quarterly* 78(3): 533–554.

Tewksbury, David, and Jason Rittenberg. 2012. *News on the Internet: Information and Citizenship in the 21st Century*. Oxford: Oxford University Press.

Valeriani, Augusto, and Cristian Vaccari. 2016. Accidental Exposure to Politics on Social Media as Online Participation Equalizer in Germany, Italy, and the United Kingdom. *New Media and Society* 18(9): 1857–1874.

Wright, Scott. 2012. Politics as Usual? Revolution, Normalization and a New Agenda for Online Deliberation. *New Media & Society* 14(2): 244–261.

Xenos, Michael, and Patricia Moy. 2007. Direct and Differential Effects of the Internet on Political and Civic Engagement. *Journal of Communication* 57(4): 704–718.

Yang, Guobin. 2009. *The Power of the Internet in China: Citizen Activism Online*. New York: Columbia University Press.

Yoo, Sung Woo, and Homero Gil de Zúñiga. 2014. Connecting Blog, Twitter and Facebook Use with Gaps in Knowledge and Participation. *Communication & Society* 27(4): 33–48.

Zheng, Yongnian. 2007. *Technological Empowerment: The Internet, State, and Society in China*. Stanford, CA: Stanford University Press.

29

HUMAN RIGHTS

Jennifer Chan

Competing rights discourses in Asia

"I think of it often and imagine the scene clearly. Even if they come to kill me, I will tell them what they are trying to do is wrong, that education is our basic right," says Malala Yousafzai, the youngest Nobel Peace Prize awardee (Peer 2012). One may not associate human rights in Asia with Malala, a petite Muslim girl who defends girls' right to education; or the unknown Indian activist Kailash Satyarthi, whose campaigns led to the adoption of the International Labor Organization Convention No. 182 on the worst forms of child labor; or with the Chinese writer Liu Xiaobo, who has been imprisoned since 2008 for demanding political reforms; the Bangladeshi economist and founder of the revolutionary Grameen Bank for the poor in 1983, Muhammad Yunus; the South Korea President, Kim Dae-jung, for his work on peace and reconciliation with North Korea; Bishop Carlos Belo and José Ramos-Horta, who fearlessly defended the independence of East Timor; Aung San Suu Kyi, the indefatigable Burmese democracy fighter, who was under house arrest for fifteen out of the twenty-one years from 1989 to 2010; the Dalai Lama, spiritual leader and Tibetan independence advocate; and Eisaku Sato, the Japanese politician, who signed the Nuclear Non-Proliferation Treaty in 1970.

Beginning a book chapter on human rights and civil society in Asia with luminary Nobel laureates risks giving the readers an illusion of a rights haven in this most populous region. Behind these inspiring figures loom some of the most repressive governments in the world, under which the exercise of freedom of expression, media, assembly, association, labor organizing, religion, and sexuality routinely comes with the price of arbitrary arrest, disappearance, torture, long imprisonment, and death. Such is the complex reality of human rights and civil society mobilization in Asia. Given the historical, geographical, conceptual, and thematic scope of the task at hand, this chapter is necessarily only a modest introduction.

Before I proceed, let me offer my working definitions and conceptual boundaries of human rights, civil society, and Asia. While the literature on human rights in Asia has traditionally been dominated by a legal approach (e.g., looking at state ratification of international conventions and compliance issues), I am more interested in how grass-roots groups produce competing rights knowledge to counter-hegemonic statist discourses (Chan 2008, 2015). While the term "civil society" originates in Europe, as an intermediate sphere between family and the state in which actors pursue neither profit within the market nor power within the state, my concern is less about whether Asian human rights and civil society are viable cultural and political concepts/ projects, and more about how Asian civil society is part and parcel of global civil society. I pay particular attention to Asef Bayat's (2009) concept of the rise of "social nonmovements"—how non-collective actors such as bloggers, netizens, and spontaneous protestors/occupiers express and organize themselves in creative and strategic ways in a region where traditional repertoires of contentious actions, such as demonstrations and protests, are often banned or repressed. Finally, I take Pheng Cheah's (2001) post-colonial approach to Asia to examine it less as a carto-graphically delimited region or a static object of inquiry (in contrast to the universal, non-bounded West), but more as spheres of power. "Asian values," "Asian solutions," and Asian multilateralism, etc., I argue, should be read as narratives in flux and techniques of power by a myriad set of actors with their own interests, values, and claims. To limit the discussions on human rights in Asia to the region is to ignore the global scale of mobilizations surrounding numerous rights issues and the important question of Asia's role in the world.

This chapter is structured in four sections. Part I introduces the major developments and scholarship on human rights in Asia in three historical periods since 1989. Part II then uses spe-cific examples of civil society actors in five major clusters of rights: political liberalization, accountability for past abuses, minority rights, socio-economic rights, and women's human rights. Part III traces my own work under four themes: grass-roots mobilization of rights dis-courses and advocacy education; intersectionality; the post-structuralist turn and rights as com-peting narratives; and beyond the state and the civil society strengthening imperative. I conclude by projecting a few key challenges concerning human rights and civil society in Asia: demo-cratic reforms, accountability for past abuses, minority rights, socio-economic rights, and women's human rights.

Competing narratives on human rights, civil society, and Asia: conceptual fuzziness or political manipulation?

Major scholarship on human rights in Asia in the past twenty-five years largely reflects the historical currents in three main periods: (1) 1989–1997, (2) 1998–2008, and (3) 2009–2015.

1989–1997: From Tiananmen to the Asian financial crisis

1989 was no doubt a watershed year in human rights in Asia. Not that human rights violations did not exist before: the Cambodian genocide under the Pol Pot regime between 1975 and 1979, and the subsequent Vietnamese invasion; the corrupt Marcos and Suharto governments in the Philippines and Indonesia; autocratic and paternalistic one-party rule in Singapore and Malaysia; Indonesian occupation of East Timor; military dictatorship in Burma; and the ongoing repression of independence movements in Tibet, Xinjiang, Inner Mongolia within China, and in Punjab, Jammu and Kashmir in India, just to name a few. In the shadow of the dramatic fall of the Berlin Wall in 1989, however, the harsh repression of the pro-democracy Tiananmen protests in China stood as a reminder that it was too early to proclaim any "end of history." Tiananmen was pivotal. It brought global attention to civil and political rights in China and spearheaded local, regional, and international civil society organizing, first on the release of Tiananmen political prisoners and later on a wider spectrum of rights issues across Asia. Although human rights liter-ature on Asia existed prior to 1989 (Asian Coalition of Human Rights Organizations 1984; Asia Watch Committee 1985; Gelatt 1987; Hsiung 1985), the painstaking 1990 Human Rights Watch report, *Repression in China since June 4, 1989*, documenting the arrests and detention of over 900 Tiananmen activists, signaled a new era of human rights monitoring and research in Asia.

Then followed an unexpected turn that skewed human rights debates in Asia until today: the 1993 UN World Conference on Human Rights in Vienna, where regional preparatory negotiations turned into a heavily politicized discursive battlefield. Two years prior, China had issued its first White Paper on human rights, arguing that the right to subsistence and collective interests, as well as national independence, take precedence over the so-called inalienable, indivisible, and universalist human rights. This particular reading of human rights echoed well amongst other Asian leaders from Singapore, Malaysia, Indonesia, and Vietnam. As a result, the final regional declaration officialized "Asian values" in international human rights politics, a debate that has dominated literature ever since. The "Asian values" camp congregates around a cluster of ideas: i) states have the right to determine their political systems and development; ii) Asia has no history of human rights as understood in its Western context; iii) the rights of the community come before individual rights; iv) socio-economic rights take precedence and, if necessary, subsume civil and political rights; v) national sovereignty is a legitimate defense against rights interference, vi) Asian people prefer order and harmony to freedom; and vii) the Asian miracle (South Korea, Singapore, Malaysia, Taiwan, colonial Hong Kong, and later China) is the best empirical proof of efficient economic growth under authoritarian regimes (Le 2012). Scholarly works by Ann Kent (1999) and Daniel Bell (2000), for example, try to search for historical and cultural roots of "Asian values" and propose a democratic regime that combines elements of traditional Confucianism. "The current West-centric human rights regime needs to be modified with input from East Asian voices," Bell (2000: 13) argues. The skeptical rights camp argues that displacing civil and political rights with socio-economic rights is little more than a diversionary tactic to deflect criticism for the most egregious human rights violations by these Asian governments. Research by Uyen Le (2012), Kenneth Christie and Denny Roy (2001), and Marina Svensson (2002), however, deconstructs "Asian values" as political manipulation. Le writes:

> In the NGOs' Declaration, the Asian NGOs confirmed that the human rights violations in their countries were not the result of cultural differences, but rather of the specific political interests of the ruling elites in their states. These human rights groups reiterated that the "pretext for constraining the channels of freedom of expression is often internal or national security and law and order; this is a facade for authoritarianism and for the suppression of democratic aspirations and institutions.
>
> *(Le 2012: 493)*

The Fourth World Conference on Women in Beijing that followed in 1995, which put women's human rights on the global and regional maps, was a game-changer. The twelve critical areas of action in the Platform for Action—on poverty, education, health, violence against women, armed conflict, the economy, power and decision-making, institutional mechanisms for the advancement of women, human rights of women, the media, the environment, and rights of the girl-child—resonated strongly in Asia. From military base violence and the "comfort women" issue to honor killing, trafficking, political representation, religion, labor market participation, education, and the girl-child, Beijing generated a flurry of mobilization and marked the entry of gender research in the largely gender-blind scholarly work and an irreversible engendering of human rights mobilization in Asia (Chan-Tiberghien 2004a; Enloe 2000; Hilsdon *et al.* 2000; Human Rights Watch *et al.* 1994; Murthy and Sankaran 2001; Schellstede and Yu 2000; Tinker and Summerfield 1999).

The Hong Kong handover to China and the Asian financial crisis in 1997 spurred many subsequent civil and political rights debates, including on the right to vote, the freedom of media and assembly, and the "Asian values" myth. The Asian financial crisis that began with the collapse of the Thai baht eroded the economic benefits of double-digit growth for millions of Asians, brought down the Suharto regime in Indonesia and the Thai government under General Chavalit Yongchaiyudh, and exposed the myth that authoritarianism created growth. When their currencies and stock markets came crumbling down, Asian leaders tempered their reified discourse by offering a milder version of "Asian solutions" (Human Rights Watch 1998).

Two important regime changes happened in Asia during this period. After much violence, Nepal became a constitutional monarchy in 1990, and the Paris Peace Agreement signed in 1991 marked the end of a long bloody civil war in Cambodia. Human rights research remains dominated by a focus on political detention and other areas of civil and political rights, as repression in China, Burma, Indonesia and East Timor, Singapore, Malaysia, India, and Pakistan continues (see, e.g., Acharya 1995 and Asia Watch 1990).

1998–2008: From past abuses to the Beijing Olympics

The adoption of the Rome Statute of the International Criminal Court (ICC) in 1998, allowing for the prosecution of crimes of genocide, crimes against humanity, and war crimes, provided a legal frame for the pursuit of war crime responsibility in Asia. When General Augusto Pinochet was indicted by a Spanish judge and later arrested in London for war crimes committed in Chile, Asian governments might have trembled. From slave labor to military sexual slavery, war crime accountability remains outstanding in Japan (see Chan-Tiberghien 2004a; Chang and Barker 2003; Yoshimi 2002). Despite funding crises and political setbacks, the establishment of a special panel in Dili, East Timor, to try those responsible for crimes against humanity and serious crimes committed in 1999 and the Extraordinary Chambers in the Courts of Cambodia (ECCC), commonly known as the Khmer Rouge Tribunal, in 2007 to prosecute crimes committed during the Cambodian genocide from 1975 to 1979 were two human rights victories in Asia (Documentation Center of Cambodia 2007; Human Rights Watch 2000; Ratner, Abrams, and Bischoff 2001).

This period was also characterized by heightened attention to rights abuses of marginalized populations, including laborers and migrants; children; ethnic, religious, and sexual minorities; AIDS patients, sex workers, and drug users. China's rise—economically, politically, and militarily—has caused much concern both in and outside the region. Despite the official reassurance of "China's peaceful rise" by the Hu Jintao government, there is much documentation on labor abuses and crackdown on pro-democracy activists, especially during sensitive periods such as the 15th anniversary of Tiananmen in 2004 (Chan 2001; China Labour Bulletin 2007, 2009; Human Rights Watch 2005; Santoro 2000). More research on these rights in Southeast Asian countries also began to emerge (Gurowitz 2000; Human Rights Watch 2002a; Piper n.d., 2008; Rahman and Lian 2005; Singapore National Trades Union Congress 2005). Religious persecution continues to attract scholarly as well as activist attention, while health activism helped bring forth the rights abuses of sex workers, sexual minorities, and drug users (Cohen and Amon 2008; Misra and Chandiramani 2005; Tong 2005).

The period 1998–2008 ended with a severe repression of the monk-led Saffron Revolution in Burma (Human Rights Watch 2009c) and the Beijing Olympics. The mega sport event once again spurred international discussions on the relevance of human rights standards in site decision by the International Olympic Committee (IOC) and on whether the IOC abets censorship through its inaction. It also brought attention to conditions of migrant construction workers, forced disappearance and/or detention of Olympics dissenters and other pro-democracy activists, and the harassment and restriction of foreign media. Amongst others, human rights lawyer Teng Biao was abducted by Beijing security agents in March 2008 and detained for two days.

The AIDS activist Hu Jia, who co-signed an open letter with Teng and forty other human rights defenders, "One World, One Dream: Universal Human Rights," was arrested and later sentenced to three and a half years in prison for "inciting subversion of state power (Human Rights Watch 2008a)." In the open letter, they wrote, "When you come to the Olympic Games in Beijing ... you may not know that the flowers, smiles, harmony and prosperity are built on a base of grievances, tears, imprisonment, torture and blood (Human Rights Watch 2008a)." Unrests in Lhasa began in March 2008 and the torch relay/"Journey of Harmony" across North America and Europe turned into pro-Tibet independence global protests. Beijing reacted heavy-handedly, causing over eighty deaths and 2,300 subsequent arrests in Tibet and sparking a wave of Tibetan self-immolation, with 143 deaths from 2009 to 2015 (Human Rights Watch 2008b; International Campaign to Save Tibet 2015; Tibetan Centre for Human Rights and Democracy 2009).

2009–2015: from regional institutional building to China in Africa

Political rights, past abuses, national security "crimes," police brutality, torture in custody, death penalty, minority rights, women's rights, and labor rights, etc. did not fade away (Arifin 2012; de Varennes and Gardiner 2016; Ding 2012; Fincher 2014; Hood and Deva 2014; Human Rights Watch 2009a-b, 2010a-b, 2011a-e, 2012a-b, 2013a-b, 2014a-c, 2015a-d; Johnson and Zimring 2009; Lintner 2014; Mackie 2014; Maglipon 2013; Mohan and Morel 2014; Nielsen 2014; Offord 2013; Schroeter 2016; South Asia Human Rights Documentation Centre 2014; Streckfuss 2011; UNESCO 2011). But the past few years saw several important new developments: the establishment of an ASEAN Intergovernmental Commission on Human Rights (AICHR) in 2009, Arab-Spring- and Occupy-inspired protests in Tibet, China, Malaysia, Burma, Vietnam, and Hong Kong, the "Snowden effect" and the tug of war between online dissent and Internet surveillance, "counter-terrorism" measures, and a whole range of issues pertaining to sustainability, the role of extractive industries, and the role of China in Africa.

After the 1993 World Conference on Human Rights in Vienna, Asian activists put the creation of a regional human rights body as a priority. Until the formation of AICHR in 2009, Asia was the only area in the world that did not have one. The 2012 ASEAN Human Rights Declaration affirms: "[T]he rights of women, children, the elderly, persons with disabilities, migrant workers, and vulnerable and marginalised groups are an inalienable, integral, and indivisible part of human rights and fundamental freedoms." The emergent literature on Asian human rights institution-building is roughly divided into a "functionalist" camp, focusing on rule-making of an emerging human rights system (Baik 2012; Nasu and Saul 2013), and a skeptical camp that critiques the lack of transparency and inclusion for meaningful engagement of civil society in Asia (Gomez and Ramcharan 2012).

Arab-Spring-inspired protests in Asia caught some governments in the region off guard and the response was swift and severe. In China, several hundred human rights lawyers and activists were arrested and convicted in the aftermath of the 2011 Chinese pro-democracy protests. In Malaysia, the Bersih (Coalition for Clean and Fair Elections) rallies in 2011, 2012, and 2015 were promptly dispersed with detentions and arrests (The Economist 2011). In Myanmar, activists started "Just Do It Against Military Dictatorship" Facebook campaign (Allgee 2011; Kaung 2011). In Vietnam, one of the most prominent dissidents, Nguyen Dan Que, was arrested after he called for the overthrow of the government in a Middle-East-style uprising (Amnesty International 2011). Inspired by the Occupy movement, tens of thousands of students and citizens in Hong Kong staged their own largest occupation, dubbed the Umbrella Movement, in September 2014 against Beijing's intervention on its 2017 election.

State surveillance and censorship of the Internet and social media in Asia has attracted a lot of scholarly attention in the past few years, especially after the dramatic flight of Edward Snowden from Hong Kong (Diamond and Plattner 2012; Epstein 2013; MacKinnon 2012; Qiang 2012; Yang 2011; Zheng 2007). During the Umbrella Movement in Hong Kong, the Chinese government authorities issued a clear censorship directive: "All websites must immediately clear away information about Hong Kong students violently assaulting the government and about 'Occupy Central.' Promptly report any issues" (Rudolph 2014). The Chinese government clearly stipulated the "seven bottom lines"—legal, socialism, national interest, legitimate interest of citizens, public order, moral, and authentic information—and uses a range of measures, from the Great Fire Wall to arrests, to censor any information deemed subversive, including political reform, rule of law, Taiwan and Tibet independence, transparency, police brutality, forced evictions, Falun Gong, Tiananmen, environment, food safety, labor rights, and Western media, including BBC, YouTube, and Twitter. In 2013, China passed the "online rumor" law that prosecutes those who disseminate false information on social media or other media platforms, with up to three years' imprisonment if their actions result in social disorder. The sentence was increased to seven years in 2015 (Mozur 2013). Since the law was passed, hundreds of thousands of *weibo* accounts have been deleted and hundreds of arrests have been made. In December 2015, human rights lawyer Pu Zhiqiang was given a suspended three-year prison sentence for "inciting ethnic hatred" for his social media posts questioning the government's policies toward Uighurs and Tibetans. Bloggers in Burma, Malaysia, Vietnam, Singapore, Indonesia, India, Nepal, and Pakistan are subject to similar scrutiny and penalty (BBC 2008; Bland 2010; Ramzy 2015; Reporters Without Borders 2015).[1]

In the name of "counter-terrorism," several Asian governments either use existing national security laws liberally or pass more restrictive counter-terrorism measures. China's continuous crackdown on separatist movements or the Indonesian government's treatment of terrorist suspects are prime examples (Human Rights Watch 2010d; Istiqomah 2015; Terricabras 2014). The harsh life imprisonment of Uighur professor, Ilham Tohti, in 2014 for his research on regional autonomy of Xinjiang has caused much concern over how the Chinese government defines terrorism. Following the Urumqi attack that same year, the Chinese government carried out a year-long anti-terrorism crackdown in Xinjiang, with over 300 arrests for terror-related offenses. Finally, issues pertaining to sustainability and the role of extractive and other industries (e.g., seafood farms in Thailand and Vietnam; "blood jade" in Burma; palm oil plantations in Malaysia and Indonesia, to name just a few) have given rise to a whole new range of human rights research (Hanlon 2014; Human Rights Watch 2012b; Mohan and Morel 2014). An emergent literature specifically focuses on the role of Chinese aid, trade, and investment in Africa, including corruption, substandard labor practices in Africa, environmental destruction, and aiding and abetting dictatorial regimes (Brautigam 2011; Power, Mohan, and Tan-Mullins 2012; Rotberg 2008; Taylor 2010).

(Re)narrating human rights: the role of civil society in Asia

Apart from the threat of exclusionary ideologies, civil society is also endangered by attacks on the very nature of democracy. Although most governments today claim to be democratic, an increasing number have sought to redefine the term as a form of narrow electoralism, with periodic balloting but without the independent institutions of civil society—a free and robust press, outspoken bar associations and religious institutions, freely organized labor unions and uninhibited grass-roots organizations—that permit people to debate issues of importance and to organize and petition their governments in a manner that permits them to be heard.

(Human Rights Watch 1992)

It is disheartening to read this Human Rights Watch comment from over twenty years ago that unfortunately still rings true in Asia today. Despite significant gains since the late 1980s—regime changes in South Korea, Nepal, the Philippines, and Indonesia, and greater recognition of women's and children's rights—the region faces old and new challenges alike. In this section, I showcase a few key human rights movements in the region on five major clusters of rights: (1) political liberalization; (2) accountability for past abuses; (3) minority rights; (4) socio-economic rights; and (5) women's rights that cut across these areas.

"Asking the Tiger for His Skin"²: political liberalization

The bulk of civil society attention on Asian human rights is on first-generation civil and political rights: the right to life, equality before the law, the right to a fair trial, freedom of information and expression, freedom of assembly and association, right to privacy, freedom of religion, and voting rights. In these areas, China crowns it all, whether they pertain to torture, police brutality, disappearance and arbitrary detention, house arrests, politically motivated sentencing with trumped-up charges, death penalty, information and media censorship, or the repression of religious freedoms and minority rights. The Chinese democracy movement is really a movement of movements, campaigns, petitions, and ad hoc grouping of like-minded writers, lawyers, artists, labor activists, and bloggers. One can trace its roots to the "Beijing Spring" in 1978 with the famous manifesto "Fifth Modernization" (to add democracy to the four official modernizations of industry, agriculture, science and technology, and national defense) by the electrician Wei Jingsheng, who was sentenced to fifteen years in prison before being deported to the USA in 1997. The Tiananmen crackdown spurred the creation of many non-governmental groups and networks: the China Support Network, Human Rights In China, and the Independent Federation of Chinese Students and Scholars, all formed by overseas Chinese student activists; China Support Network, established by US activists; the Free China Movement, led by a Tiananmen activist, Lian Shengde; and the Overseas Chinese Democracy Coalition, founded by Wei Jingsheng. On June 28, 1998, when US President Bill Clinton was visiting China, human rights activists Wang Youcai, Wang Donghai, and Lin Hui tried to register the China Democracy Party that advocated direct elections and the formation of a multi-party system in China. The founders and members were promptly arrested the following day and quickly sentenced for subversion, harming state security, and overthrowing the CCP (Human Rights Watch 2000).

In the early 2000s, the *Weiquan* (rights defense) movement was formed by a group of lawyers who took up cases of forced evictions, property rights, AIDS compensation, religious freedom, and freedom of speech and the press. In 2003, four amongst them—Xu Zhiyong, Teng Biao, Yu Jiang, and Zhang Xingshui—from the Peking University Law School formed the Open Constitution Initiative to advocate greater rule of law and constitutional protections. Its website was shut down within a year, and the group was declared illegal and fined RMB1 million, while Xu Zhiyong was arrested on charges of tax evasion in 2009.

Modeled after Charter 77 by anti-Soviet Czech dissidents, the Charter 08 manifesto was signed by over 350 Chinese intellectuals in 2008, demanding wholesale reforms in China in nineteen areas from legislative democracy to an independent judiciary, guarantee of human rights, public official election, abolition of the *hukou* (household registration) system; freedom of association, assembly, expression, and religion; civic education; protection of private property; financial and tax reform; and the protection of the environment (Human Rights in China 2008). The leading author, Liu Xiaobo, was honored with the Nobel Peace Prize, but was handed an eleven-year sentence in 2009. The following year, a group of lawyers, journalists, and activists drafted an open letter called "The Citizens' Pledge," beginning the New Citizens'

Movement. Its financial supporter, Wang Gongquan, spearheaded the "equal rights for education" campaign to advocate successfully for the abolition of the *hukou* system that discriminates against migrant children's education. A few activists followed the wealth disclosure campaigns in Europe by staging demonstrations in Beijing and Jiangxi in April 2013, but were promptly arrested. *Weiquan* lawyers and activists also defended the freedom of religion, Tibetan and Uighurs' rights, reproductive rights against the one-child policy, AIDS justice, food safety, labor rights, and environmental concerns.[3] Since Xi Jinping came to power in 2013, the pro-democracy movement in China has encountered one of the harshest crackdowns. In 2014 alone, over 280 human rights lawyers and activists were detained, many in secret with no information and access to lawyers.[4]

Across Asia, new forms of national, regional, and global organizing for political liberalization have emerged. Heavily constrained by structural legal and political barriers, civil society has to find strategic ways to organize itself and push for political reforms. In Singapore, censorship of political expression is achieved through a web of means, including quasi-exclusive state ownership, legislation, defamation suits, harassment, and self-censorship (Article 19 2005; Seow 1998). Singaporeans for Democracy, a nascent human rights NGO founded in 2010 to advocate political and social reforms, for instance, had to dissolve itself as a political organization two years later because it was constantly being investigated and denied permits under myriad laws, including the Societies Act, Political Donations Act, Broadcasting Act, the Employment of Foreign Manpower Act, Films Act, Penal Code, and Public Order Act (Online Citizen 2012). One of the most prominent new social movements in Asia, Bersih (meaning clean in Malay) skillfully framed its demands around the *rakyat* (people in Malay) to appeal to the mass, in great contrast to the previous smaller, middle-class, and issue-based civil society organizations (Höller-Fam 2015). Formed by a coalition of over sixty NGOs in 2006, advocating free, clean, and fair elections in Malaysia, its first rally in 2007 successfully shifted the political landscape in the 2008 general election.[5] Bersih 2.0 enjoyed even wider support and its 2011 rally forced the government to organize a committee to look into electoral reforms and subsequently included seven of the eight demands by the Bersih.[6] Bersih 3.0 in 2012, organized in conjunction with Global Bersih in thirty-five other countries, was the largest democratic protest in Malaysia, drawing a crowd of 300,000 before it was dispersed by the police with tear gas and water cannons (Malaysiakini 2012). While Bersih managed to carve out an unprecedented socio-political space by mobilizing on existing political party structures and focusing on processes and institutions rather than directly challenging the ruling party (Höller-Fam 2015), other structural barriers such as the broadly used Sedition Act remain. In 2014 alone, fifteen bloggers and activists were charged with sedition for blogging, posting on Facebook, and making comments at rallies. Finally, one should not forget, amidst these newer, highly mediatized rallies and campaigns, a smaller dedicated group of human rights activists has been working tirelessly for the less known and less popular death penalty abolition movement across Asia. The Anti-Death Penalty Asia Network was formed in 2006 with twenty-two members in the region where more people are executed than in the rest of the world combined.[7]

Minority rights

In one of the most linguistically, culturally, ethnically, and sexually diverse regions in the world, the challenge of minority rights in Asia is immense. The scope of this chapter does not allow a full discussion of these movements. A few examples illustrate their long history and strong regional and international linkages. The Tibet independence movement, a loose collection of Tibetans in exile, legal professionals, students, youth, nuns, and journalists, advocates Tibetans' right to self-determination through lobbying the UN and national governments for dialogue with China, refugee protection, improving the self-governance and economic welfare of Tibetans in exile, and environmental monitoring (e.g., International Campaign for Tibet, Tibet Justice Center, Students for a Free Tibet, Tibetan Women's Association, Tibetan Youth Congress, Tibetan Nuns Project, and Association of Tibetan Journalists). In 2000, the International Tibet Network, a global coalition of over 180 Tibet-related NGOs from fifty different countries, was formed to increase the capacity of individual member organizations and to develop coordinated strategic campaigns.[8] NGOs in other countries such as Delhi-based Act Now for Harmony and Democracy (ANHAD) also advocate ethnic and religious rights.[9]

Another long-standing movement in Asia pertains to migrant rights. With hundreds of millions of internal, regional, and cross-regional migrants, migration in Asia is characterized by a high number of unskilled, irregular or undocumented, and women laborers, with female migration concentrated in service industries such as domestic help (Singapore, Hong Kong) and the entertainment industry (Japan), while male workers are found in construction (Singapore), plantation work (Malaysia), fishing industry (Thailand), and manufacturing (Japan, Taiwan, Malaysia, and South Korea) (Wickramasekera 2002). Two of the earliest action research and advocacy networks include the Asia Pacific Mission for Migrants and the Asian Migrant Center (AMC), created in Hong Kong in 1984 and 1991 respectively. The AMC then helped to establish many migrant grass-roots groups in Hong Kong, as well as the Asian Migrant Credit Union. It also helped create the Migrant Forum of Asia in 1994, which publishes the bi-annual Asian Migrant Yearbook and partners with the Diplomacy Training Program, an independent Australian NGO founded in 1989 by Nobel Peace Laureate José Ramos-Horta, to train community advocates In 2001, AMC brought together over twenty project partners to initiate the Mekong Migration Network to conduct research to map out migration policies, issues, and responses in the subregion.[10] Further, in 2011, the Migrant Forum of Asia created Lawyers Beyond Borders, a transnational network that focuses on legal redress mechanisms for migrants (International Labour Organization 2015). Finally, a relatively new social movement in Asia relates to sexual minorities. The Asia and Pacific Transgender Network, for example, was launched in 2009, when fifteen transgender women from ten Asia and Pacific countries came together to advocate the health, legal, and social rights of transgender women.[11]

Accountability for past abuses

The International Military Tribunal for the Far East left out many war crimes issues and subsequent atrocities in Cambodia, East Timor, and Burma, meaning that accountability for past abuses is another strong focus for civil society in Asia. Civil society drove the adoption of the ICC Statute in 1998 and continues to be a leading force in its ratification. The Asian International Justice Initiative (AIJI) and the International Center for Transitional Justice work (ICTJ) advocate fair trials, reparation, apology, and education against genocide, war crimes, and crimes against humanity. The Khmer Rouge Tribunal, established in 2007 to try the most senior responsible members of the Khmer Rouge for serious crimes perpetrated during the Cambodian genocide, has been criticized for corruption, political interference, and inefficiency (having indicted only five and convicted one), and has suffered repeated funding crises. AIJI monitors and disseminates trial proceedings, facilitates community dialogues, and partners with local universities to integrate a fair-trial-rights curriculum into Cambodian legal education women (AIJI 2015). Since 2005, the ICTJ has worked with the ECCC and local civil society partners on outreach, victim participation, and other initiatives, including reparation programs, institutional reform, and truth-seeking to fill the "impunity gap."[12] In Burma, the ICTJ trained local activists to document abuses and helped the Burmese Network for Human Rights Documentation to build a database of over 3,000 records of human rights violations. In East Timor, human rights activists successfully lobbied for the creation of the Commission for Reception, Truth, and Reconciliation (CAVR) in 2002 and the bilateral Commission for Truth and Friendship (CTF) in 2005 to investigate crimes committed between 1974 and 1999 during the Indonesian occupation. Although both the CAVR and CTF recommended reparations and a mechanism to search for disappeared persons, there has been little progress to date.[13]

Socio-economic and sustainable development rights

Poverty, unemployment, underemployment, child and slave labor, and feminization of work, lack of schooling, unaffordable health care, slums and poor sanitation, ecological disasters … Asia suffers from these all, and in frightening numbers. Thousands of local, national, regional, and international community-based organizations (CBOs), non-profits, NGOs, coalitions, and networks work on labor rights, children's rights, the right to education and health, access to water and sanitation, and sustainable development. As the manufacturing base for the world's technology, apparel, sports, and retail giants, China alone is a mecca of labor and environmental exploitation, much of which would have remained undocumented without civil society monitoring. China Labour Bulletin, an early NGO founded by labor organizer and Tiananmen activist Han Dongfan in Hong Kong in 1994, conducts research on work conditions, trains independent workers organizations on collective bargaining and labor rights litigation, works with law firms to provide legal assistance, and hosts the most extensive database of labor cases in China (China Labour Movement 2013). Regional networks such as the Asia Monitor Resource Centre (founded in Hong Kong in 1976) support independent labour movements in Asia.

In the area of educational access, early local efforts were charity-based and organized by church denominations in Asia. In the mobilization leading up to the adoption of the Convention of the Rights of the Child in 1989, NGOs began to adopt a rights framework. The movement by the Nobel Peace laureate, Kailash Satyarthi, *Bachpan Bachao Andolan* (Save Childhood Movement), for instance, is an India-based global movement campaigning for the rights of children, focusing on child labor, trafficking, and education. Two global coalitions in the late 1990s—the Global March Against Child Labor and the Global Campaign for Education—transformed the children's rights movement in Asia. In 1998, Satyarthi organized the global march against child labor, ending in the headquarters of the International Labour Organization (ILO) in Geneva. The coalition's work became the blueprint for the ILO Convention against the Worst Forms of Child Labor (No. 182), the fastest ratified convention in the history of ILO, with adoption by 150 countries. The Global Campaign for Education, with its roots in the Education for All movement since the 1990 Jomtien conference and the 2000 Dakar conference, lobbied for free, universal early childhood education, elimination of gender disparities, skills training, and adult literacy (Education for All n.d.). The movement goals have been adopted as part of the Millennium Development Goals (2000–2015) and Sustainable Development Goals (2015–2030).

Health activism has a long history in a region where the majority of people have neither health insurance nor access to basic health care. Although the right to health was clearly stipulated in the World Health Organization constitution, it was not until the Alma-Ata Declaration at the International Conference on Primary Health Care in 1978, affirming health as a fundamental human right and the government's responsibility for primary health, that grass-roots groups found a people's centered approach to health (Declaration of Alma-Ata. 1978). Out of

Alma Ata emerged a rights-based grass-roots global initiative called the People's Health Movement that conducts research and educates people to demand public health care.

Then the AIDS epidemic occurred. Three milestone developments—the declaration of the "Greater Involvement with People Living with HIV/AIDS" (GIPA) principle in 1994, the *Médecins Sans Frontières* (MSF) Access to Essential Medicines Campaign in 1999, and the creation of the Global Fund to Fight AIDS, Malaria, and Tuberculosis in 2002—transformed health activism (Chan 2015). In Asia, national networks such as the Delhi Network of Positive People and the Thai Network of People Living with HIV/AIDS were formed to provide a stronger voice and platform. The Asia Pacific Network of People Living with HIV/AIDS was established in 1994 at a meeting in Kuala Lumpur with forty-two members from eight countries. With little government funding and recognition, however, early AIDS CBOs and NGOs were confined to their service provision role in supporting AIDS patients in medical care, housing, and nutrition. After treatment became available in 1996, AIDS activism centered on exposing pharma greed and finding creative legal and political ways to bypass expensive patents. MSF's Access Campaign for affordable AIDS medicines since 1999 became a turning point. Many AIDS groups adopted a rights-based approach to advocate treatment and other rights. Further, the creation of the Global Fund to Fight AIDS, Malaria, and Tuberculosis in 2002 spurred the formation of thousands of local and regional CBO and NGO AIDS networks such as the Beijing Aizhixing Institute of Health Education led by Chinese dissident Hu Jia and the Malaysian AIDS Council, a network of eighteen NGOs. Global Fund funding has also helped the creation of sex worker, drug use, and gay and transgender activist networks, such as the China Sex Worker Organization Network Forum, the Asia Pacific Network of Sex Workers, and the Asian Network of People Who Use Drugs.

Finally, new groups and movements have sprung up in the past few years to mobilize around third-generation rights on development, healthy environment, natural resources, intergenerational equity, and sustainability. While there is a history of ecological activism in Asia, such as the Narmada dam protests throughout the 1980s and 1990s and forest monitoring in Laos, Indonesia, Malaysia, and Vietnam, global attention to climate change since the Kyoto Protocol and on human rights issues arising from extractive industries have given civil society more legitimacy. In 2015, a documentary, *Under the Dome*, by a former Chinese television journalist, Chai Jing, on air pollution in China took the nation by storm, enjoying 15 million views over three days before it was promptly removed. In Burma, activists formed the Myanmar Alliance for Transparency and Accountability to use the Extractive Industries Transparency Initiative, an international guideline, to monitor corporate and government management of revenues from natural resources. And the question of the Chinese government's management of revenues from natural resources is likely to receive more attention in the coming years.

Women's rights are human rights

The women's movement works across all the above areas. The precursors of contemporary women's movements in Asia in the early twentieth century mirrored developments elsewhere in the world: suffrage, labor rights, and the temperance movement, etc. National in scale and largely sidelined by male-dominated nationalist and decolonization movements, women's movements in Asia did not take off until the first UN Decade for Women (1975–1985) and the adoption of the Convention on the Elimination of All Forms of Discrimination against Women in 1979. New networks such as the International Womens' Rights Action Watch Asia Pacific were established to mobilize for CEDAW ratification and the creation of national machineries on the status of women. The 1990s saw an unprecedented level of participation of women's groups in various world conferences: the World Conference on Human Rights in Vienna in 1993; the Cairo Conference on Population and Development in 1994; the Social Summit in Copenhagen in 1995; the Beijing Conference on Women in 1995; the UN Conference on Human Settlements in Istanbul in 1996; the first World Congress against Commercial Sexual Exploitation of Children in Stockholm in 1996; the adoption of the ICC Statute in 1998; and the World Conference against Racism in Durban in 2001. Asian feminist groups were part and parcel of transnational feminist organizing that took the global human rights stage by storm. They proclaimed "women's rights are human rights," redefined population issues as reproductive health and rights, drafted a comprehensive twelve-item action plan encompassing all critical areas of women's rights, pushed to outlaw child pornography and prostitution, successfully lobbied for the inclusion of rape and other sexual violence as acts of genocide under the ICC Statute, and challenged gender-blind minority movements, as well as race-blind feminist hegemony. The impact of this abundant mobilization by women's groups and networks is evident throughout Asia. In Japan, the low-dose pill was at long last legalized in 1999 after the Japan's Network for Women and Health shamed their government in front of the world at the Cairo Conference and demanded their reproductive rights. At the Beijing conference, women from Okinawa, the Philippines, Taiwan, and Indonesia denounced structural sexual violence in US military bases across the Asia-Pacific. The World Conference against Racism further brought the attention of intersectional discrimination faced by minority women in Asia to the forefront. The NGO, End Child Prostitution in Asian Tourism, was a lead organizer of the 1996 first World Congress against Commercial Sexual Exploitation of Children in Stockholm and successfully lobbied for the law banning child prostitution and child pornography in Japan in 1999. After the Statute, three Asian women's networks—the Violence Against Women in War Network Japan, the Korean Council for the Women Drafted for Military Sexual Slavery by Japan, and the Philippine-based Asian Center for Women's Human Rights—organized a people's tribunal, the Women's International War Crimes Tribunal on Japan's Military Sexual Slavery, in which four judges found Emperor Hirohito criminally responsible for crimes against humanity ... and that the state of Japan has acted in violation of both its treaty obligations and obligations under customary international law and that "rape and sexual slavery, when committed on a widespread, systematic or large-scale basis, constitute crimes against humanity."[14]

Grass-roots mobilization and advocacy education

> Resistance lies in self-conscious engagement with dominant, normative discourses and representations and in the active creation of oppositional analytic and cultural spaces. Resistance that is random and isolated is clearly not effective as that which is mobilized through *systemic politicized practices of teaching and learning*. Uncovering and reclaiming subjugated knowledge is one way to lay claim to alternative histories.
>
> *(Chandra Mohanty, quoted in bell hooks 1994: 32 [italics author])*

Nothing in my colonial Hong Kong upbringing prepared me for human rights research. My own foray into this challenging work began with an empirical puzzle while living in Japan: in a country not known for a strong human rights tradition, high representation of women in politics, strong women's movements, or speedy political change, why has the Japanese government suddenly taken elaborate measures to affirm the human rights of women during the "lost decade" of the 1990s? My conceptual quest was to understand how human rights ideas travel and take root to the point of causing socio-political changes. My conceptual findings based on a wide range of rights issues throughout Asia can be summarized in four themes: (1) grass-roots mobilization of rights discourses and advocacy education; (2) intersectionality; (3) the post-structuralist turn and rights as competing narratives; and (4) beyond the state and the civil society strengthening imperative.

Grass-roots mobilization of rights discourses and advocacy education

My research on sexuality in Japan—the pill, sexual harassment, military sexual slavery, domestic violence, and child prostitution—helped me spot a few key omissions in the predominant literature on human rights in Asia at the time. A legal focus on state ratification of international human rights laws has largely left sub-state actors out of scholarly attention. Gender was largely absent as any sort of variable or lens to understand human rights in Asia, and the disciplinary domination of law and political science meant that other angles were either ignored or sidelined (Chan-Tiberghien 2004a). My research attempts to address all three issues by focusing on the role of grass-roots feminist mobilization of human rights norms through advocacy education.

The changes in Japan regarding women's and children's human rights at the turn of the twenty-first century were nothing short of extraordinary: the amendment of the Equal Employment Opportunity Law in 1997 mandating workplace sexual harassment prevention; the legalization of the pill, the passage of the Basic Law on Gender Equality, and the Child Prostitution and Pornography Prohibition Law, all in 1999; and the passage of the Anti-Stalking Law in 2000 and the Anti-Domestic Violence law in 2001. Japanese NGOs used global rights discourses to reframe formerly separate and illegitimate concerns of reproductive freedom, *seku hara*, (sexual harassment) "comfort women," "marital disputes," and "assisted entertainment," and successfully lobbied for legal and political change. By focusing on human rights and feminism in Japan, I had to engage in the universalism versus cultural relativism debate. Are human rights concepts and feminism Western? Who is authorized to speak on behalf of human rights and gender in Japan? There are few better ways to challenge a reified dichotomy than a detailed study of local negotiations of human rights. Every day in Japan and in Asia, local NGOs engage in and educate about a wide range of human rights ideas.

Intersectionality

The World Conference against Racism in Durban, South Africa, in 2001 was an educational moment, and a serendipitous lunch encounter with a Japanese labor rights activist at the World Social Forum in Mumbai in 2004 highlighted my own feminist blind spots. Donning an intersectional lens opens up new human rights landscapes. The accountability movement for the "comfort women" issue did not take shape until the late 1980s, due to the male-dominated pro-democracy movement in Korea and the race-blind Japanese women's movement. Okinawan feminists have to press fellow Okinawan anti-war activists to go beyond a security frame to include issues of gender-based violence on the one hand and convince mainland Japanese feminists to go beyond a gender equality approach to recognize intersectional forms of discrimination experienced by Okinawan women on the other (Chan-Tiberghien 2004a, 2004b). My subsequent research on labor rights, sustainability, and access to essential medicines looks at how gender, sexuality, ethnicity, race, class, mobility, nationality, and disability interact to shape the situated experiences and rights claims of diverse populations in Asia (Chan 2008, 2015).

The post-structuralist turn and rights as competing narratives

My third conceptual concern is how alternative human rights discourses challenge the meaning and boundary of citizenship. The works of Foucault and Rorty help me reconceptualize human rights as techniques of power and competing narratives. My research on activism as the production of alternative cultural meanings and knowledge reframes citizenship as a process, a becoming, rather than a status. I am interested in documenting how civil society provides cultural and political space for the right to narrate counter-hegemonic stories that challenge statist and corporatist definitions of rights, justice, and citizenship.

Beyond the state and the civil society strengthening imperative

With my classic Western political science training, I was slow to recognize and shake off the hegemonic state referent in the study of civil society. It was a humbling lesson from a young Japanese woman activist that expanded my re-imagination of Asian civil society beyond the realm of statist political changes. Extending the definition of "change" methodologically opens up new territories to examine creative pedagogies, empowerment, and capacity building. Throughout Asia, activists use creative ways to play tongue-in-cheek to subvert state control of dissent expressions.[15] Last, my latest research on AIDS and human rights in Asia taught me an important lesson: civil society itself does not equate democracy or progress. AIDS has helped to develop not only communities, but also a community development industry. The co-optation of civil society calls for greater self-reflection and scrutiny. For civil society to exercise its role properly, many changes need to happen. Donors need to reflect on the changing civil society dynamic, including new movement forms and actors beyond large, established, and well-known groups, and consider changing funding priorities accordingly. Funding long-term political liberalization and the removal of structural barriers such as civil society registration and funding laws is also vital. Civil society actors themselves need to be held accountable by the same stringent principles of democratic governance and diversity.

Conclusion

This chapter provided an overview of major human rights developments and scholarships in Asia in the past twenty-five years. From Tiananmen to counter-terrorism, human rights debates closely followed local and regional developments, while being shaped by global events and discourses. Issues of political liberalization—democratic transition; political reforms; freedom of information, expression, media, assembly, association, conscience, and religion; and the right to life, etc.—are present throughout the region. Accountability for past abuses, gender-based violence and other women's rights, children's rights, minority rights, and sustainability have also become an integral part of the human rights landscapes in Asia.

Through specific examples in five clusters of rights on political liberalization, war crimes, minority rights, socio-economic rights, and women's rights, I tried to showcase the work of a few leading NGO networks focusing on human rights in Asia. In each case, human rights activists produce alternative framing and knowledge on citizenship, justice, and rights to counter statist and corporate meta-narratives about national security, terrorism, work, migration, gender, AIDS, environment, and "Asian values." In this light, human rights activism engages in cultural struggles, in redefining socio-political meanings through their pedagogic and advocacy practices.

Projecting forward, five issues are likely to dominate human rights discussions in Asia: democratic reforms, the "multicultural challenge," Internet surveillance, counter-terrorism, and the

China in Africa question. Finding creative and strategic ways to fight against structural legal and political barriers such as NGO registration and funding laws or new counter-terrorism measures and cyber-crime laws on the one hand and strengthening its own capacity and governance on the other become an urgent agenda for Asian civil society.

Notes

1 ASEAN Human Rights Declaration. 2012. ASEAN Intergovernmental Commission on Human Rights, Electronic document, http://aichr.org/documents/, accessed January 21, 2016.

1 A young Burmese blogger, Nay Phone Latt, was sentenced to twenty years in jail for posting a cartoon of the military leader Than Shwe. Malaysia's best-known blogger, Raja Petra Kamarudin, who edits the *Malaysia Today* website, fled to the UK in 2010 after hearing that he would be detained without trial for the third time. In Singapore, a 16-year-old blogger, Amos Yee, was convicted of hurting religious feelings for comparing Mr. Lee's supporters unfavorably to Christians, and of obscenity for posting an image that depicted Mr. Lee and Margaret Thatcher, the former British prime minister, engaged in a sex act on YouTube. Though subsequently released after a brief detention, a judge ordered him to have a psychiatric examination after a doctor's report suggested he had autism spectrum disorder.

2 Pils (2006).

3 See the memoirs by Chen (2015) and Gao (2007). Barefoot lawyer Chen Guangcheng filed a landmark class-action lawsuit on the excessive enforcement of the one-child policy in 2005, for which he was imprisoned for four years and put under house arrest before making a dramatic escape to the USA in 2012. Gao Zhisheng, one of the founding members of the *Weiquan* movement, for instance, wrote a series of letters to the Chinese leadership on the torture and sexual abuse against Falun Gong practitioners, for which he was detained, tortured, and lost his legal license.

4 On January 16, 2016, an international group of prominent judges and jurists wrote an open letter to the Chinese government appealing for the information and due process for at least twelve Chinese lawyers, www.abc.net.au/news/2016-01-14/china-charges-human-rights-lawyers-subversion/7088348, accessed January 21, 2016.

5 Bersih 2.0, www.bersih.org/, accessed January 21, 2016.

6 For "Our 8 Demands," see www.bersih.org/about-bersih/bersihs-8-points/, accessed January 21, 2016.

7 Anti-Death Penalty Asia Network, http://adpan.org/aboutus/, accessed January 21, 2016.

8 Its two notable campaigns include the 2008 Beijing Olympics and the 2011 "Stand Up for Tibet" campaign in response to the wave of Tibetan self-immolations, http://tibetnetwork.org/about-us/history-of-the-network/, accessed January 21, 2016.

9 Proposed Amendments to the Communal Violence (Prevention, Control And Rehabilitation Of Victims) Bill, 2005, submitted June 24, 2010, www.countercurrents.org/hashmi260610.htm, accessed January 21, 2016.

10 They include the Asian Domestic Workers Union, Filipino Migrant Workers Union, Indonesian Migrant Workers Union, Thai Women Association, Thai Migrant Workers Union, Federation of Asian Domestic Workers Unions, Coalition of Migrants' Rights, and The Hong Kong Coalition of Indonesian Migrant Workers Organisations, www.asianmigrantcentre.org/#!about-us/cchl, accessed January 21, 2016.

11 Asia and Pacific Transgender Network, www.weareaptn.org/, accessed January 21, 2016.

12 International Center for Transitional Justice, www.ictj.org/our-work/transitional-justice-issues/criminal-justice, accessed January 21, 2016.

13 International Center for Transitional Justice, Timor-Leste, www.ictj.org/our-work/regions-and-countries/timor-leste, accessed January 21, 2016.

14 The Women's International War Crimes Tribunal for the Trial of Japan's Miliary Sexual Slavery, Case No. PT-2000-1-T, corrected January 31, 2002, www.asser.nl/upload/documents/DomCLIC/Docs/NLP/Japan/Comfort_Women_Judgement_04-12-2001_part_1.pdf, accessed January 21, 2016.

15 See the online *China Digital Times*' compilation of the Grass-Mud Horse (the homophone of a profane expression in Chinese) Lexicon, a glossary of terms created by Chinese netizens and frequently used in online political discussions, http://chinadigitaltimes.net/space/The_Grass-Mud_Horse_Lexicon, accessed January 21, 2016.

Suggested readings

Article 19. 2005. *Freedom of Expression and media in Singapore*. London: Article 19, Electronic document, www.article19.org/data/files/pdfs/publications/singapore-baseline-study.pdf, accessed January 21, 2017.

Chan-Tiberghien, Jennifer. 2004a. *Gender and Human Rights Politics in Japan: Global Norms and Domestic Networks*. Stanford, CA: Stanford University Press.

Chan-Tiberghien, Jennifer. 2004b. Gender as Intersectionality: Multiple Discrimination against Minority Women in Japan. In *Comparative International Studies of Social Cohesion and Globalization in Asia: Japan*. Masaya Nakamura and Pitman Potter, eds. Pp. 158–181. New York: Palgrave Macmillan.

Chan, Anita. 2001. *China's Workers Under Assault: Exploitation and Abuse in a Globalizing Economy*. New York: Routledge.

Chan, Jennifer, ed. 2008. *Another Japan is Possible: New Social Movements and Global Citizenship Education*. Stanford, CA: Stanford University Press.

Chan, Jennifer. 2015. *Politics in the Corridor of Dying: AIDS Activism and Global Health Governance*. Baltimore, MD: Johns Hopkins University Press.

Hanlon, Robert J. 2014. *Corporate Social Responsibility and Human Rights in Asia*. New York: Routledge.

Hilsdon, Anne-Marie, Martha Macintyre, Vera Mackie, and Maila Stivens, eds. 2000. *Human Rights and Gender Politics: Asia Pacific Perspectives*. New York: Routledge.

Höller-Fam, Manuel. 2015. Malaysia's Civil Society in light of the Bersih Movement. Electronic document, https://th.boell.org/en/2015/12/16/malaysias-civil-society-light-bersih-movement, accessed November 12, 2016.

Human Rights Watch (see References).

Websites

Asian Migrant Center, www.asianmigrantcentre.org/.
A regional NGO based in Hong Kong, focusing on promoting human rights and conducting action research relating to protecting the rights of migrants to Asia.

Bersih 2.0, www.bersih.org/.
Previously known as NET, the Coalition for Clean and Fair Elections became Bersih 2.0 in 2010. It comprises civil society organizations dedicated to ensuring clean and fair elections, and effectively monitoring the political situation in Malaysia.

China Digital Times, http://chinadigitaltimes.net/.
An independent, bilingual media organization delivering news from China to the wider world.

China Labour Bulletin, www.clb.org.hk.
Working with individual labor activists, lawyers, and civil society organizations to ensure resource allocation and support in reflecting the rights of workers across China.

Human Rights in China, www.hrichina.org/en.
An NGO comprising human rights activists and scholars in China; supporting research, discussion and targeting issues of human rights across China.

Human Rights Watch, www.hrw.org/.
A non-profit, non-governmental organization with staff members around the world, dedicated to enforcing the rights of people worldwide.

References

Acharya, Amitav. 1995. *Human Rights in Southeast Asia: Dilemmas for Foreign Policy*. North York, ON: University of Toronto-York University Joint Centre for Asia Pacific Studies.

Allgee, Alex. 2011. Burmese Activists Launch Facebook Group. *Time*, March 12.

Amnesty International. 2011. Vietnamese Authorities Must Release Dr. Nguyen Dan Que. Electronic document, www.amnesty.org/en/press-releases/2011/02/vietnamese-authoritiesmust-release-dr-nguyen-dan-que/, accessed November 11, 2016.

Arifin, Syamsul. 2012. Indonesian Discourse on Human Rights and Freedom of Religion or Belief: Muslim Perspectives. *Brigham Young University Law Review* l(3): 775–808.

Article 19. 2005. *Freedom of Expression and media in Singapore*. London: Article 19, Electronic document, www.article19.org/data/files/pdfs/publications/singapore-baseline-study.pdf, accessed January 21, 2017.

ASEAN Human Rights Declaration. 2012. ASEAN Intergovernmental Commission on Human Rights, Electronic document, http://aichr.org/documents/, accessed January 21, 2016.

Asian Coalition of Human Rights Organizations. 1984. *Human Rights Activism in Asia: Some Perspectives, Problems, and Approaches*. New York: Council on International and Public Affairs.

Asian International Justice Initiative (AIJI) 2015. East-West Center. Electronic document, www.eastwest center.org/research/asian-international-justice-initiative, accessed January 21, 2016.

Asia Monitor Resource Centre. n.d. What We Do. Electronic document, www.amrc.org.hk/content/what-we-do, accessed January 21, 2016.

Asia Watch. 1990. *Injustice, Persecution, Eviction: A Human Rights Update on Indonesia and East Timor*. New York: Human Rights Watch.

Asia Watch Committee. 1985. *Human Rights in Korea*. New York: Asia Watch Committee.

Baik, Tae-Ung. 2012. *Emerging Regional Human Rights Systems in Asia*. Cambridge: Cambridge University Press.

Bayat, Asef. 2009. *Life as Politics: How Ordinary People Change the Middle East*. Stanford, CA: Stanford University Press.

BBC. 2008. Burma Blogger Jailed for 20 Years. *BBC*, November 11. Electronic document, http://news.bbc.co.uk/2/hi/asia-pacific/7721271.stm, accessed November 11, 2016.

Bell, Daniel A. 2000. *East Meets West: Human Rights and Democracy in East Asia*. Princeton, NJ: Princeton University Press.

Bland, Ben. 2010. Malaysian Blogger Continues Attacks from his UK Base. *Guardian*, August 9. Electronic document, www.theguardian.com/media/2010/aug/09/raja-petra-malaysia-today-blogger, accessed November 11, 2016.

Brautigam, Deborah. 2011. *The Dragon's Gift: The Real Story of China in Africa*. Oxford: Oxford University Press.

Chan, Anita. 2001. *China's Workers Under Assault: Exploitation and Abuse in a Globalizing Economy*. New York: Routledge.

Chan, Jennifer, ed. 2008. *Another Japan is Possible: New Social Movements and Global Citizenship Education*. Stanford, CA: Stanford University Press.

Chan, Jennifer. 2015. *Politics in the Corridor of Dying: AIDS Activism and Global Health Governance*. Baltimore, MD: Johns Hopkins University Press.

Chang, Maria Hsia, and Robert P. Barker. 2003. Victor's Justice and Japan's Amnesia. *East Asia: An International Quarterly* 19(4): 55–86.

Chan-Tiberghien, Jennifer. 2004a. *Gender and Human Rights Politics in Japan: Global Norms and Domestic Networks*. Stanford, CA: Stanford University Press.

Chan-Tiberghien, Jennifer. 2004b. Gender as Intersectionality: Multiple Discrimination against Minority Women in Japan. In *Comparative International Studies of Social Cohesion and Globalization in Asia: Japan*. Masaya Nakamura and Pitman Potter, eds. Pp. 158–181. New York: Palgrave Macmillan.

Cheah, Pheng. 2001. Universal Areas: Asian Studies in a World in Motion. *Traces, A Multilingual Journal of Theory and Translation* 1: 37–94.

Chen, Guangcheng. 2015. *The Barefoot Lawyer: A Blind Man's Fight for Justice and Freedom in China*. New York: Henry Holt and Co.

China Labour Bulletin. 2007. *Speaking Out: The Workers' Movement in China, 2005–2006*. Electronic document, www.clb.org.hk/sites/default/files/archive/en/File/research_reports/Worker_Movement_Report_final.pdf, accessed November 12, 2016.

China Labour Bulletin. 2009. *Going it Alone: The Workers' Movement in China (2007–2008)*. Electronic document, www.clb.org.hk/en/files/share/File/research_reports/workers_movement_07-08_print_final.pdf, accessed November 12, 2016.

China Labour Movement. 2013. What We Do. Electronic document, www.clb.org.hk/en/content/what-we-do, accessed January 21, 2016.

Christie, Kenneth, and Denny Roy. 2001. *The Politics of Human Rights in East Asia*. London: Pluto Press.

Cohen, J. Elizabeth, and Joseph J. Amon. 2008. Health and Human Rights Concerns of Drug Users in Detention in Guangxi Province, China. *PLOS Medicine* 5(12): 234.

Declaration of Alma-Ata. 1978. International Conference on Primary Health Care, Alma-Ata, USSR, September 6–12. Electronic document, www.who.int/hpr/NPH/docs/declaration_almaata.pdf, accessed January 21, 2016.

de Varennes, Fernand, and Christie May Gardiner, eds. 2016. *Routledge Handbook of Human Rights in Asia*. New York: Routledge.

Diamond, Larry, and Marc Plattner, eds. 2012. *Liberation Technology: Social Media and the Struggle for Democracy*. Baltimore, MD: Johns Hopkins University Press.

Ding, Sheng. 2012. Is Human Rights the Achilles' Heel of Chinese Soft Power? A New Perspective on Its Appeal. *Asian Perspective* 36(4): 641–665.

Documentation Center of Cambodia. 2007. *A History of Democratic Kampuchea 1975–1979*. Phnom Penh: Documentation Center of Cambodia.

The Economist. 2011. Crackdown in KL. *The Economist*, www.economist.com/blogs/banyan/2011/07/political-demonstration-malaysia, accessed January 21, 2016.

Education for All. n.d. Global Campaign for Education. Electronic document, www.campaignforeducation.org/en/about-us/about-education-for-all, accessed January 21, 2016.

Enloe, Cynthia. 2000. *Bananas, Beaches and Bases: Making Feminist Sense of International Politics*. Berkeley, CA: University of California Press.

Epstein, Gady. 2013. China's Internet: A Giant Cage. *The Economist*, April 6.

Fincher, Leta Hong. 2014. *Leftover Women: The Resurgence of Gender Inequality in China*. London: Zed Books.

Gao, Zhisheng. 2007. *A China More Just*. Flusing: Broad Press.

Gelatt, Timothy A. 1987. *Human Rights in Taiwan, 1986–1987*. Washington, DC: Asia Watch.

Gomez, James, and Robin Ramcharan. 2012. The Protection Of Human Rights In Southeast Asia: Improving the Effectiveness of Civil Society. *Asia-Pacific Journal on Human Rights and the Law* 13(2): 27–43.

Gurowitz, Amy. 2000. Migrant Rights and Activism in Malaysia: Opportunities and Constraints. *The Journal of Asian Studies* 59(4): 863–888.

Hanlon, Robert J. 2014. *Corporate Social Responsibility and Human Rights in Asia*. New York: Routledge.

Hilsdon, Anne-Marie, Martha Macintyre, Vera Mackie, and Maila Stivens, eds. 2000. *Human Rights and Gender Politics: Asia Pacific Perspectives*. New York: Routledge.

Höller-Fam, Manuel. 2015. Malaysia's Civil Society in Light of the Bersih Movement. Electronic document, https://th.boell.org/en/2015/12/16/malaysias-civil-society-light-bersih-movement, accessed November 12, 2016.

Hood, Roger, and Surya Deva. 2014. *Confronting Capital Punishment in Asia: Human Rights, Politics and Public Opinion*. Oxford: Oxford University Press.

hooks, bell. 1994. *Teaching to Transgress: Education as the Practice of Freedom*. London and New York: Routledge.

Hsiung, James Chieh, ed. 1985. *Human Rights in East Asia: A Cultural Perspective*. New York: Paragon House Publishers.

Human Rights in China. 2008. Charter 08, December 9, www.hrichina.org/en/content/238, accessed January 21, 2016.

Human Rights Watch. 1990, 1992, 1998, 2000, 2002a, 2005, 2009a. *Human Rights Watch Report*. New York: Human Rights Watch.

Human Rights Watch. 2008a. *China: Olympics Harm Key Human Rights Chinese Government, IOC Wasted Historic Opportunity for Reform*. August 6. Electronic document, www.hrw.org/news/2008/08/06/china-olympics-harm-key-human-rights, accessed November 12, 2016.

Human Rights Watch. 2008b. *Forbidden Zone: Shutting The Media Out of Tibet and Other "Sensitive" Stories*. New York: Human Rights Watch. Electronic document, www.hrw.org/reports/2008/china0708/china0708web.pdf, accessed November 12, 2016.

Human Rights Watch. 2009b. *No Tally of the Anguish: Accountability in Maternal Health Care in India*. Electronic document, www.hrw.org/sites/default/files/reports/india1009web_0.pdf, accessed November 12, 2016.

Human Rights Watch. 2009c. *Burma: End Repression of Buddhist Monks Intimidation Intensifies Ahead of Second Anniversary of Crackdown*. September 22. Electronic document, www.hrw.org/news/2009/09/22/burma-end-repression-buddhist-monks, accessed November 12, 2016.

Human Rights Watch. 2010a. *"Skin on the Cable": The Illegal Arrest, Arbitrary Detention and Torture of People who use Drugs in Cambodia*. Electronic document, www.hrw.org/sites/default/files/reports/cambodia0110webwcover.pdf, accessed November 12, 2016.

Human Rights Watch. 2010b. *Turning Critics into Criminals: The Human Rights Consequences of Criminal Defamation Law in Indonesia*. Electronic document, www.hrw.org/report/2010/05/03/turning-critics-criminals/human-rights-consequences-criminal-defamation-law, accessed November 12, 2016.

Human Rights Watch. 2010d. *Analysis: Inside Perspective on Uighurs.* Electronic document, www.hrw.org/news/2010/12/20/analysis-inside-perspective-uighurs, accessed November 12, 2016.

Human Rights Watch. 2011a. *The Party vs. Legal Activist Cu Huy Ha Vu.* Electronic document, www.hrw.org/report/2011/05/26/vietnam-party-vs-legal-activist-cu-huy-ha-vu, accessed November 12, 2016.

Human Rights Watch. 2011b. *You'll Be Fired if You Refuse: Labor Abuses in Zambia's Chinese State-Owned Copper Mines.* Electronic document, www.hrw.org/sites/default/files/reports/zambia1111ForWeb Upload.pdf, accessed November 12, 2016.

Human Rights Watch. 2011c. *They Deceived us at Every Step, Abuse of Cambodian Domestic Workers Migrating to Malaysia.* Electronic document, www.hrw.org/report/2011/10/31/they-deceived-us-every-step/abuse-cambodian-domestic-workers-migrating-malaysia, accessed November 12, 2016.

Human Rights Watch. 2011d. *The Rehab Archipelago: Forced Labor and Other Abuses in Drug Detention Centers in Southern Vietnam.* Electronic document, www.hrw.org/report/2011/09/07/rehab-archipelago/forced-labor-and-other-abuses-drug-detention-centers-southern, accessed November 12, 2016.

Human Rights Watch. 2011e. *My Children Have Been Poisoned: A Public Health Crisis in Four Chinese Provinces.* Electronic document, www.hrw.org/report/2011/06/15/my-children-have-been-poisoned/public-health-crisis-four-chinese-provinces, accessed November 12, 2016.

Human Rights Watch. 2012a. *Tell Them That I Want to Kill Them: Two Decades of Impunity in Hun Sen's Cambodia.* Electronic document, www.hrw.org/report/2012/11/13/tell-them-i-want-kill-them/two-decades-impunity-hun-sens-cambodia, accessed November 12, 2016.

Human Rights Watch. 2012b. *Out of Control: Mining, Regulatory Failure, and Human Rights in India.* Electronic document, www.hrw.org/sites/default/files/reports/india0612ForUpload_0.pdf, accessed November 12, 2016.

Human Rights Watch. 2013a. *Breaking the Silence: Child Sexual Abuse in India.* Electronic document, www.hrw.org/report/2013/02/07/breaking-silence/child-sexual-abuse-india, accessed November 12, 2016.

Human Rights Watch. 2013b. *In Religion's Name: Abuses against Religious Minorities in Indonesia.* Electronic document, www.hrw.org/report/2013/02/28/religions-name/abuses-against-religious-minorities-indonesia, accessed November 12, 2016.

Human Rights Watch. 2014a. *"No Answers, No Apology": Police Abuses and Accountability in Malaysia.* Electronic document, www.hrw.org/report/2014/04/01/no-answers-no-apology/police-abuses-and-accountability-malaysia, accessed November 12, 2016.

Human Rights Watch. 2014b. *Public Insecurity: Deaths in Custody and Police Brutality in Vietnam.* Electronic document, www.hrw.org/report/2014/09/16/public-insecurity/deaths-custody-and-police-brutality-vietnam, accessed November 12, 2016.

Human Rights Watch. 2014c. *"I'm Scared to Be a Woman": Human Rights Abuses Against Transgender People in Malaysia.* Electronic document, www.hrw.org/sites/default/files/reports/malaysia0914_ForUpload.pdf, accessed November 12, 2016.

Human Rights Watch. 2015a. *30 Years of Hun Sen: Violence, Repression, and Corruption in Cambodia.* Electronic document, www.hrw.org/sites/default/files/reports/cambodia0115_ForUpload.pdf, accessed November 12, 2016.

Human Rights Watch. 2015b. *Work Faster or Get Out": Labor Rights Abuses in Cambodia's Garment Industry.* Electronic document, www.hrw.org/report/2015/03/11/work-faster-or-get-out/labor-rights-abuses-cambodias-garment-industry, accessed November 12, 2016.

Human Rights Watch. 2015c. *Toxic Water, Tainted Justice: Thailand's Delays in Cleaning Up Klity Creek.* Electronic document, www.hrw.org/sites/default/files/reports/thailand1214_web.pdf, accessed November 12, 2016.

Human Rights Watch. 2015d. *"Will I Get My Dues … Before I Die?": Harm to Women from Bangladesh's Discriminatory Laws on Marriage, Separation, and Divorce.* Electronic document, www.hrw.org/sites/default/files/reports/bangladesh0912ForUpload.pdf, accessed November 12, 2016.

Human Rights Watch (Women's Rights Project), Asia Watch Committee, Dorothy Q. Thomas, and Sidney Jones. 1994. *A Modern Form of Slavery: Trafficking of Burmese Women and Girls into Brothels in Thailand.* New York: Human Rights Watch.

International Campaign to Save Tibet. 2015. *Self-Immolations by Tibetans.* September 4. Electronic document, www.savetibet.org/resources/fact-sheets/self-immolations-by-tibetans/, accessed November 12, 2016.

International Labour Organization. 2015. Migrant Forum in Asia (MFA). May 5, www.ilo.org/dyn/migpractice/migmain.showPractice?p_lang=en&p_practice_id=58, accessed January 21, 2016.

Istiqomah, Milda. 2015. In the Name of Counter-Terrorism: Human Rights Abuses in Indonesia. Paper presented at the First Asia Pacific Conference on Advanced Research. Electronic document, http://apiar.org.au/wp-content/uploads/2015/08/APCAR_BRR742.pdf, accessed November 12, 2016.

Johnson, David T., and Franklin E. Zimring. 2009. *The Next Frontier: National Development, Political Change, and the Death Penalty in Asia.* Oxford: Oxford University Press.

Kaung, Ba. 2011. Burmese Attempt Own "Facebook Revolution." *The Irrawaddy*, March 2. Electronic document, www.dejunterlabirmanie.fr/?p=1589, accessed November 12, 2016.

Kent, Ann. 1999. *China, The United Nations, and Human Rights: The Limits of Compliance.* Philadelphia, PA: University of Pennsylvania Press.

Le, Uyen P. 2012. A Culture of Human Rights in East Asia: Deconstructing "Asian values" Claims. *Journal of International Law & Policy* 18(2): 469–504.

Lintner, Bertil. 2014. *Outrage: Burma's Struggle for Democracy.* Collingdale, PA: Diane Pub Co.

Mackie, Vera, ed. 2014. *Ways of Knowing about Human Rights in Asia.* New York: Routledge.

MacKinnon, Rebecca. 2012. China's Networked Authoritarianism. In *Liberation Technology: Social Media and the Struggle for Democracy.* Larry Diamond and Marc Plattner, eds. Pp. 78–92. Baltimore, MD: Johns Hopkins University Press.

Maglipon, Jo-Ann.Q., ed. 2013. *Not On Our Watch: Martial Law Really Happened. We Were There.* Manila: LEADS-CEGP.

Malaysiakini. 2012. 300,000 at Bersih 3.0, Ambiga Claims Success. April 28. Electronic document, www.malaysiakini.com/news/196344, accessed January 21, 2016.

Misra, Geetanjali, and Radhika Chandiramani. 2005. *Sexuality, Gender and Rights: Exploring Theory and Practice in South and Southeast Asia.* New York: SAGE Publications.

Mohan, Mahdev, and Cynthia Morel, eds. 2014. *Business and Human Rights in Southeast Asia: Risk and the Regulatory Turn.* New York: Routledge.

Mozur, Paul. 2013. Crossing Lines: Sina Punishes More Than 100,000 Weibo Accounts. *Wall Street Journal,* November 13. Electronic document, http://blogs.wsj.com/chinarealtime/2013/11/13/following-7-bottom-lines-sina-strikes-at-weibo-accounts/, accessed January 21, 2017.

Murthy, Ranjani K., and Lakshmi Sankaran. 2001. *Denial and Distress: Gender, Poverty, and Human Rights in Asia.* London: Zed Books.

Nasu, Hitoshi, and Ben Saul, eds. 2013. *Human Rights in the Asia-Pacific Region: Towards Institution Building.* New York: Routledge.

Nielsen, Gert Holmgaard. 2014. *Walking a Tightrope: Defending Human Rights in China.* Honolulu, HI: University of Hawai'i Press.

Offord, Baden. 2013. Queer Activist Intersections in Southeast Asia: Human Rights and Cultural Studies. *Asian Studies Review* 37(3): 335–349.

The Online Citizen. 2012. Singaporeans For Democracy (SFD) to de-register from Registrar of Society (ROS). June 12, www.theonlinecitizen.com/2012/06/singaporeans-for-democracy-sfd-to-de-register-from-registrar-of-society-ros/, accessed January 21, 2016.

Peer, Basharat. 2012. The Girl Who Wanted to Go to School. New Yorker. *The New Yorker*, October 10. Electronic document, www.newyorker.com/news/news-desk/the-girl-who-wanted-to-go-to-school, accessed January 21, 2017.

Pils, Eva. 2006. Asking the Tiger for his Skin: Rights Activism in China. *Fordham International Law Journal* 30(4): 1209–1287.

Piper, Nicola. n.d. Migrant Labor in Southeast Asia: Country Study: Singapore. Electronic document, www.fes.de/aktuell/focus_interkulturelles/focus_1/documents/8_000.pdf, accessed November 12, 2016.

Piper, Nicola. 2008. *New Perspectives on Gender and Migration—Livelihood, Rights and Entitlements.* New York: Routledge.

Power, Marcus, Giles Mohan, and May Tan-Mullins. 2012. *China's Resource Diplomacy in Africa: Powering Development?* London: Palgrave Macmillan.

Qiang, Xiao. 2012. The Battle for the Chinese Internet. *Journal of Democracy* 22(2): 47–61.

Rahman, Mizanur M., and Kwen Fee Lian. 2005. Bangladeshi Migrant Workers in Singapore: The View from Inside. *Asia-Pacific Population Journal* 20(1): 63–87.

Ramzy, Austin. 2015. Singapore Frees Amos Yee, 16, Blogger who Criticized Lee Kuan Yew. *New York Times*, 6 July. Electronic document, www.nytimes.com/2015/07/07/world/asia/singapore-amos-yee-lee-kuan-yew.html?_r=0, accessed January 21, 2017.

Ratner, Steven R., Jason S. Abrams, and James L. Bischoff. 2001. *Accountability for Human Rights Atrocities in International Law: Beyond the Nuremberg Legacy.* Oxford: Oxford University Press.

Reporters Without Borders. 2015. Three Bloggers Get Jail Terms For "Abusing Democratic Freedoms." *Reporters Without Borders*, February 17. Electronic document, http://en.rsf.org/vietnam-three-bloggers-get-jail-terms-for-17-02-2015,47588.html, accessed November 12, 2016.

Rotberg, Robert I. 2008. *China into Africa: Trade, Aid, and Influence*. Washington, DC: Brookings Institution Press.

Rudolph, Josh. 2014. Minitrue: Delete Harmful Information on Hong Kong. *China Digital Times*, September 28. Electronic document, http://chinadigitaltimes.net/2014/09/minitrue-delete-harmful-information-hong-kong/, accessed January 21, 2017.

Santoro, Michael. 2000. *Profits and Principles: Global Capitalism and Human Rights in China*. Ithaca, NY: Cornell University Press.

Schellstede, Sangmie Choi, and Soon Mi Yu, eds. 2000. *Comfort Women Speak: Testimony by Sex Slaves of the Japanese Military*. New York: Holmes & Meier.

Schroeter, Susanne. 2016. *Gender and Islam in Southeast Asia: Women S Rights Movements, Religious Resurgence and Local Traditions*. Leiden: Brill.

Seow, Francis. 1998. *The Media Enthralled: Singapore Revisited*. Boulder, CO: Lynne Rienner Publishers.

Singapore National Trades Union Congress. 2005. Background Paper on Migrant Workers in Singapore. June 15, Singapore: National Trades Union Congress.

South Asia Human Rights Documentation Centre. 2014. *Handbook of Human Rights and Criminal Justice in India*. New Delhi: Oxford India Handbooks.

Streckfuss, David. 2011. *Truth on Trial in Thailand: Defamation, Treason, and Lèse-Majesté*. New York: Routledge.

Svensson, Marina. 2002. *Debating Human Rights in China: A Conceptual and Political History*. New York: Rowman & Littlefield Publishers.

Taylor, Ian. 2010. *China's New Role in Africa*. Boulder, CO: Lynne Rienner Publishers.

Terricabras, Josep-Maria. 2014. China's Crackdown on Uighurs Requires EU Response. *Parliament Magazine*. 20 October. Electronic document, www.theparliamentmagazine.eu/articles/opinion/chinas-crackdown-uighurs-requires-eu-response, accessed January 21, 2017.

Tibetan Centre for Human Rights and Democracy. 2009. *Annual Report*. Electronic document, www.tchrd.org/annual-report-2009/, accessed November 12, 2016.

Tinker, Irene, and Gale Summerfield, eds. 1999. *Women's Rights to House and Land: China, Laos, Vietnam*. Boulder, CO: Lynne Rienner Publishers.

Tong, James W. 2005. *Revenge of the Forbidden City: The Suppression of the Falungong in China, 1999–2005*. Oxford: Oxford University Press.

UNESCO. 2011. *Human Rights Protections for Sexual Minorities in Insular Southeast Asia: Issues and Implications for Effective HIV Prevention*. Paris: UNESCO.

Wickramasekera, Piyasiri. 2002. Asian Labour Migration: Issues and Challenges in an Era of Globalization, ILO. Electronic document, www.ilo.org/wcmsp5/groups/public/--asia/--ro-bangkok/documents/publication/wcms_160632.pdf, accessed November 12, 2016.

Yang, Guobin. 2011. *The Power of the Internet in China: Citizen Activism Online*. New York: Columbia University Press.

Yoshimi, Yoshiaki. 2002. *Comfort Women*. Suzanne O'Brien, trans. New York: Columbia University Press.

Zheng, Yongnian. 2007. *Technological Empowerment: The Internet, State, and Society in China*. Stanford, CA: Stanford University Press.

30

FAMILY

Allison Alexy

Entering civil society through family life

Most common definitions of "civil society" posit it as fundamentally exterior to family life. Muthiah Alagappa (2004: 28), for instance, traces civil society as existing "between the family and the state" and Robert Pekkanen defines it as "the organized non-state, nonmarket sector [...] exclud[ing] government bureaucracies, parastatal organizations, and political parties, as well as the family" (2004: 224). Across scholarship, family is frequently used to define the outer edge of civil society, suggesting that family lives and civil society are non-overlapping, separate spheres (Hagemann 2008; Kocka 2006). In this chapter, I argue that despite such common definitional exclusions, in practice civil society and family membership intertwine to a substantial degree. Primarily drawing from scholarship about Asia, I posit that this interrelationship occurs through three overlapping dynamics: first, family membership regularly motivates or is used to legitimize civil society participation; second, many civil society groups are organized specifically around family issues and concerns; third, boundaries between civil society, the public sphere, and families are fundamentally blurred. In practice, scholarship reveals that civil society and families often operate in conjunction with each other, and are not as fundamentally isolated as common definitions suggest. Artificially excluding civic participation motivated by or responding to familial topics therefore ignores the powerful familial connections, identities, and perspectives that draw people into civil society. By paying attention to these overlaps, we can better theorize the processes that pull people into civic engagement or refuse them entry.

This chapter begins by analyzing various definitions of civil society to trace how scholars have located it exterior to family lives. I use theorizations of gender and public space to re-situate the common separation of family and civil society. Rather than reproducing the notion that civic engagement is impossible in domestic spaces, or that civil sociality must be understood exterior to familial relationships, I argue instead that discursive constructions of private, domestic spaces have rendered the civic engagements happening there as largely illegible. Next, I describe three dynamics visible in scholarship that link families and civil society, before I offer a short example from my own ethnographic work about parental abduction and activism around it in contemporary Japan.

Defining "civil society" in relation to families

Despite ubiquity in scholarship, or perhaps because of it, definitions of "civil society" vary over time and context. In most scholarly definitions now operable, civil society describes a network of potentially productive relations extant between the state and private spheres; there remains debate over the possible inclusion of market or corporate actors (Kocka 2006). Traceable back to Greek, Roman, and Ottoman thinkers (Islamoglu 2015), the concept's "Western pedigree" (Alagappa 2004: 2) seemed for a time to restrict its use to only Western cultures as a "normative ideal" (Anderson 2011: 317; Comaroff and Comaroff 1999; Ehrenberg 1999: Keane 1998). While scholars have challenged the Eurocentrism previously implied in the term by elucidating the potential for, and importance of, civil society around the globe (Anderson 2011; Johnson 2003; K. Kumar 1993) and in Asia specifically (Bandyopadhyay 2013; D. Kumar 1993; Ma 1994; Pekkanen 2004; Qiu 2008; Schwartz and Pharr 2003), the concept retains cultural odors (Hann and Dunn 1996; Iwabuchi 2002).

Within these variable definitions, civil society is almost universally categorized as exterior to families. For instance, Yuko Kawato, Robert Pekkanen, and Hidehiro Yamamoto (2011: 117) concisely define civil society as "the organized non-state, non-market sector that exists above the family and individual."[1] Craig Calhoun (2001: 702), tracing notions of "civility" in Europe, suggests that it was "a normative order facilitating amicable or at least reliable and nonthreatening relationships amongst strangers and in general all those who were not bound together by deep private relations like kinship." This phrasing suggests reasons why familial bonds might be antithetical in most definitions of civil society; because family members are assumed to be tightly and uniquely bonded with each other, such relationships must be categorized separately from other bonds of civil engagement. By this logic, if we want to explore how people come together to protest the government, build democratic associations, or organize their communities, including familial ties would undermine our analysis. These common definitions of civil society mistakenly assume that family ties are too automatic or natural to compare with civil ties, which instead must be consciously created. Challenging the "distinction between private and public spheres of interest and sociation" (Anderson 2011: 321), and building on previous calls to understand family as a "core component" to civil society (Cohen and Arato 1992), I argue that refusing to see the overlaps between civil society and family membership mischaracterizes the ongoing, and simultaneous, processes of creating civil society and creating family bonds. In practice, as this chapter demonstrates, civil society frequently melds with family membership.

Gender, civil society, and the public sphere

From the beginning, conceptions of civil society have rested on deeply gendered but unstated assumptions about the public sphere. Although the public sphere and civil society are not identical, most common definitions of civil society describe it as fundamentally *public*, a category that explicitly excludes families and implicitly excludes the actions of many women and other minoritized persons. Scholars have long described how the Western model of the public sphere relies on a gendered dichotomy that contrasts male, public, sociality with female, private, domesticity (Benhabib 1992; Boyd 1997; Elshtain 1981; Rosaldo 1974; Tester 1992: 135). While historians have recuperated otherwise muted voices in a challenge to this dichotomy (for instance, Davis 1987), theorizations of civil society that restrict its possibility to the public sphere continue to reproduce these exclusions. Karen Hagemann states this problematic relationship clearly: "The enlightened distinction between public and private helped to define civil society, like politics in general, as an exclusively male sphere, with the family as the female 'other' complementing the state and civil society" (2008: 24). Simply put, when we imagine civil society as only possible in public, we unwittingly sustain the biases that have long determined who is allowed to participate in public life.

For decades, scholars have been working to reject such flawed associations between civil society and the public sphere, specifically highlighting how families are always already hotbeds of civic engagement. Jean Cohen and Andrew Arato (1992) carefully pull apart Hegel's adamant refusal to include families in his understandings of civil society. Despite Hegel's repeated use of "family" as a positive metaphor for other types of civic engagement and solidarity, he refuses to see actual families "as the voluntary association par excellence" and instead "exclude[s them] from civil society altogether" (Cohen and Arato 1992: 629). With convincing clarity, Cohen and Arato argue that Hegel, and the concept of civil society he was building, could only exclude families from civil society if he imagined them to be a "natural community" with "no conflict or even difference of interests among family members" (Cohen and Arato 1992: 629). One only need remember the stress of discussing politics over a holiday meal to understand this as absurd. Of course family members disagree, and of course kinship ties are not so natural as to make a family act like a single person with uniform opinions. Uncritical definitions of civil society that automatically exclude families have, at root, precisely these assumptions.

Family membership motivating and justifying civil society participation

Although civil society and family are often understood as categorically separate from each other, in practice many activists are motivated to participate in civil society specifically because of their family membership. In these cases, being a mother, father, or grandparent and *consciously identifying as such* offers both a reason to enter civic protest and a justifiable rationale that supports such a decision. For instance, Japanese women who are actively involved in political discourse and protest explain their participation through their identities as "housewives" (LeBlanc 1999). Labeling these activists "bicycle citizens" after their modest mode of transport and local engagement with national issues, Robin LeBlanc describes housewives as an effective political force precisely because they are mothers and housewives who identify as such. In this case, housewives work through a well-organized community co-op (*seikatsu kurābu*) to "consciously seek a voice in political arenas" (LeBlanc 1999: 123). Parallel examples abound, including mothers who become activists for their disabled children (Chang 2009), young women who advocate class mobility (Ram 2008), parents who bring lawsuits on behalf of their hemophiliac children with AIDS contracted through blood transfusions (Kingston 2004), mothers involved in schools through the PTA (Nakano 2005), and mothers loudly protesting government responses and environmental risks after the 3/11 disasters in Japan (Freiner 2013; Slater, Morioka, and Danzuka 2014). Such civic engagement literally depends, and draws rhetorical and social strength from, the activists' familial relationships and status.

Family relationships further provide justifiable explanations for activists whose social identities might otherwise mute their civil society participation. Stephanie Strulik (2010: 119) offers the example of a woman in Utter Pradesh, who very rarely left her marital home because her in-laws observe *purdah* (gendered segregation). Despite her initial reluctance, she eventually agreed to be nominated for a local governance council (*panchayat*), explaining her participation by suggesting it would contribute to "her husband's 'happiness' and 'her family's status'" (Strulik 2010: 119). In this case, as in many others, specific family relationships can be convincingly used to support civic involvement that would otherwise be foreclosed. Rhetorically, in many different cultural contexts, family membership can be used to justify participation in civil society for people who are otherwise structurally marginalized, what Lynn Stephen (1997) calls "power from below." Rather than arguing that such justifications necessarily represent either a true reason or a mere excuse to be part of civil society, I am highlighting the ways in which family membership is often a powerful and effective explanation for civic engagement for people who might otherwise be excluded.

At the same time, family relationships also motivate civic participation for people whose social identities more closely align with those holding structural power. In Taiwan, for instance, fathers' rights groups have grown partially in response to changing family law. As Chao-ju Chen (2016: 123) describes, patriarchy was a legal standard and, until 1996, manifested in a categorical preference for fathers to have custody of all children after divorce. Since that time, unlike in other countries where mothers are more likely to get custody, fathers' rights groups in Taiwan have focused on advocating improved social welfare systems instead of presenting explicitly anti-feminist, anti-mother arguments. Rather than suggesting that women should not be granted custody of children after divorce, or demanding child support from mothers, activists in these groups are working to increase the likelihood that single fathers have access to social welfare. As Chen narrates, fathers in this broad movement are using their identities as fathers—at least implicitly acknowledging the relative privilege that this category held historically—to bring attention and weight to their calls for welfare and legal reforms. In other cultural contexts, too, activists who might otherwise have access to civil society highlight their family relationships as explanations of, and justifications for, their civic engagement (Crowley 2008).

Civil society groups focused on "fixing" families or using families to "fix" society

Although civil society is frequently defined as exterior to family lives, substantial civic engagement targets families as the ultimate object for reform. Many civil society organizations are designed specifically to address problems, issues, or concerns within families. Further blurring the lines between civil society and family life, these groups organize people—many of whom justify participation through their status as family members, as explained above—to lobby for changes to family norms, laws, and practices. For instance, substantial civic protest surrounded Nepal's new Constitution, promulgated in 2015, seven years after the nation's monarchy was dissolved. A particular point of protest concerned women's capacity to pass their citizenship status to their children. In the midst of larger protests and activism around new possibilities for government, these protestors focused on a contradiction embedded within the Constitution draft: one section stated that anyone whose "father or mother" was a citizen would acquire citizenship at birth, but another section stated that a child born to a Nepali mother and foreign father could only acquire citizenship through a naturalization process. In practice, many (male) government bureaucrats refuse citizenship to children of Nepali mothers who can't prove paternity. Grossman-Thompson and Dennis narrate public protests by women attempting to convince the public that a small word—"father *or* mother" versus "father *and* mother"—would make a tremendous difference. Their activism, which highlighted their identities as mothers and citizens, demonstrates how civil society forms and practices can be directed at improving family lives.

Parallel cases in which civil society groups organize protest to target changes in families occur throughout Asia and beyond. In Japan and South Korea, generations of activists have focused on reforming the family law systems and, in particular, reducing or removing patriarchy enshrined in the law. For decades, South Korean activists were focused on removing the legal requirement that all households have a singular, male head (*hoju chedo*), a structure that had been promulgated by Japanese colonizers and then sustained in the South Korean Civil Code after independence

(Kim and Kim 2011; Kim 2014; Nam 2010; Yang 2007). By the time the Civil Code was eventually revised to remove the most patriarchal requirements—including the family head system, the family registry, children receiving only their father's surname, and a ban on so-called "same name" spouses[2]—a network of at least 355 civil society organizations had organized together to release a new demand for family law reform every day of the year (Shin 2006: 114). Changes were passed in 2005 and went into effect in 2008, at the same time Japanese activists were unsuccessfully lobbying for similar reforms. Post-war revisions to the Japanese Civil Code removed the requirement that household heads be male, but the household system remained a legal requirement and forced all family members to have the same surname. In practice, because the vast majority of household heads are male, over 96 percent of women must change their surname when they get married (Shin 2008; White 2014). Despite a number of prominent cases attempting to challenge this requirement, the Japanese Supreme Court has repeatedly refused to change the Civil Code (White 2014). Activism in Japan has also targeted a gender inequity surrounding divorce law. Until 2015, a woman was legally unable to remarry after a divorce for 180 days, whereas men could remarry immediately. In theory, this law was in place to determine paternity: by preventing a divorced woman from remarrying, the state could declare that any children born during that period were legally her ex-husband's.[3] Of course, in an age with medical paternity tests, such a waiting period is no longer necessary to determine genetic paternity. As suggested by Susan Burns (2009), "genetics" as an *idea* rather than a biological reality is extremely important in the Japanese family court system. Legally constructed paternity, defined by whom a woman is married to and when, continues to be given priority over genetic, biological, and testable paternity. Generations of activists have been engaged in civil society protests calling for family law reform (Boling 1998; White 2014). Although in 2015 the waiting period for women to remarry was reduced from 180 days to 100 days, the gender inequity remains and continues to be a focus of civil society groups.

Blurring the lines between family and civil society

Challenging problematic definitions of civil society, scholars working in Asia provide key examples of fundamental overlaps between families and the civic engagement. Yunxiang Yan (2003) describes domestic lives, and increasingly popular ideologies of companionate romance, as key manifestations of civil society in rural China. Although, he states, scholarship on Chinese families has long seen them as "corporate" entities, in fact domestic relationships and private performances of intimacy have tremendous ramifications for civil society. Most obviously, perhaps, individual preferences for children generally, and sons specifically, induce engagement with local politicians and agents of the state. Motivated by their preferences to build families in contrast to those officially sanctioned, the villagers described by Yan assert themselves in civic arenas (Yan 2003).

Female factory workers in South Korea, as examined by Seung-kyung Kim (1997), similarly blur boundaries between civil society and family membership. Exploring female employment and labor organizing in the 1980s, Kim found that employers relied upon the workers' family relationships to induce young women to work in difficult positions for relatively low wages. Kim explains that: "[w]omen workers were encouraged to behave as dutiful daughters toward their families, their employers, and the state" (1997: 8). By leveraging metaphoric familial and filial relationships, employers attempted to build a more loyal and willing workforce, ensuring activists also had to address such powerful symbolic links in their union organizing. This example demonstrates how any lines between civil society and family are further blurred through extensive metaphorical and symbolic cross-fertilization.

Research on microfinance offers another powerful example of the constant, if hidden, intersections of civil society and family lives. Microfinance or microcredit is a business model that offers small loans to poor women to simultaneously provide them opportunities to start small businesses, reduce gendered inequities and poverty, and make profit for the lender. As described by Lamia Karim (2011), these ideal outcomes diverge substantially from the practices that actually allow microfinance to function. In her ethnographic analysis focused on Bangladesh, Karim finds that microcredit lending is entangled in "relationships of power, inequality, and obligation," many of which reflect family networks and kinship ties (Karim 2011: 192). Contrary to the expectation that such loans would allow women to escape from family obligations into civil society, in practice the money ties women more tightly to family members. For instance, because the microcredit business model requires loan repayment (i.e., these are loans, not grants or donations), lenders often force women to repay, regularly putting pressure on family members to lean on the borrowers. Women with outstanding loans might be harassed by in-laws, cousins, or their siblings, who in turn are being pressured by lenders. Far from offering an escape into a civil society full of possibilities, these loans often impoverish women while reinforcing structures of power within extended family networks. Most important for our purposes, this example makes clear that actions in civil society are always already linked with, and supported by, family relationships.

Case study: parental abduction and activism in contemporary Japan

In order to describe parental abduction and the activism that surrounds it in contemporary Japan, I will begin with three short examples that represent relatively common patterns.[4]

Case 1—International abduction within an international family

Michael last saw his daughter in Texas, six years before he told me about his experiences. Michael had met and married Yoko, a Japanese women who had been living in the United States. After they had their daughter, Anna, problems had begun to appear in their marriage. Ultimately, they mutually decided to separate and worked out a functioning plan to share custody. Their attempt at co-parenting was mostly smooth, until one day, when it was Michael's turn to pick up Anna, Yoko called and said Anna was suddenly sick and couldn't meet her father. Yoko didn't contact Michael again for days. It turned out that, without Michael's knowledge or permission, and against orders from the judge presiding over their divorce case in the United States, Yoko had illegally brought Anna to Japan with plans to remain there. Although Anna was eventually enrolled in Japanese elementary school, and their location was therefore possible to apprehend, Yoko never faced criminal charges or any action from Japanese police or law enforcement. As far as Michael knows, Yoko and Anna remain living in Japan and as long as they don't try to enter the United States, there appear to be no legal consequences for Yoko. Michael still lives in the United States and has become highly active in an NGO focused specifically on combating parental abduction in Japan. He lobbies American politicians to put pressure on Japan to "return children" and helps provide support for other "left-behind fathers."

Case 2—Domestic abduction within an international family

Margaret is a British woman living in Japan who is now divorced from Kohei, her Japanese ex-husband. They have a son, Ben, who was eight when his parents got divorced. Because there is no legal joint or shared custody in Japan, Margaret and Kohei split Ben's custody by dividing two types of legal responsibilities between them: Margaret holds Ben's "custody and care rights"

461

(*kangoken*), which includes the right to take care of him on a daily basis, and Kohei holds Ben's "legal parental rights" (*shinken*), which includes making legal decisions for the children, for instance where they live or go to school.[5] When Ben was twelve, he lived with his mother, but regularly spent weekends with his father. Once, during one of these visits, Kohei suddenly announced to Ben that he would no longer live with his mother. Without informing Margaret or Ben, Kohei had switched Ben's school registration and legal address, keeping him against his will, and moving him in the middle of the school year. Kohei refused to let him visit Margaret and she had little recourse through the law or criminal justice systems. She began intensive mediations with Kohei, trying to figure out how to convince him that he was causing harm to their son. For more than a year, Ben lived with Kohei and attended the new school, only seeing Margaret occasionally in public at school functions. Finally, for no particular reason that Margaret could discern, Kohei told Ben he could leave. He did, and returned home to live with his mother. In the years since his abduction, Ben has tried to rebuild a relationship with his father and has returned to visiting him on many weekends. During Ben's ordeal Margaret was extremely involved with "left-behind" parents' non-governmental organizations (NGOs) in Japan. Now, although she remains in contact with some members, she has less time to devote to activism, but is happy to share her story and experiences with those who ask.

Case 3—Domestic abduction within a Japanese family

Hideki is a Japanese man involved in an NGO focused on reforming Japanese family law. He is now divorced from a Japanese women, Megumi, with whom he has a daughter, Maki. When Maki was five years old, Hideki and Megumi discussed divorce. They had many serious conflicts, specifically over their daughter's education. Suddenly, while they were still legally married, Hideki came home one day to find his wife and daughter gone. Megumi had moved them both to another part of the same city. Although Hideki and Megumi were still legally married and therefore shared custody of their daughter, Megumi refused any contact between Maki and her father. Moreover, Megumi submitted a divorce notification to the local government office. Because Hideki would not agree to the divorce, he was required to begin mediation sessions with Megumi. Eventually, after many months of mediation, he said he would agree to the divorce if she permitted him regular contact with Maki. Megumi refused this stipulation and their mediation was at an impasse for months. Finally, one of the mediators suggested to Hideki that his daughter would benefit from the relative clarity that would come from the divorce. Rather than continue to fight for the possibility of seeing his daughter, Hideki decided to sign the divorce agreement and work hard to be the best person he could be, including setting aside money each month in his daughter's name. That way, he figured, if Maki was interested in contacting him when she was older, he would be prepared to support her. He now volunteers with a Japanese NGO focused on publicizing problems within the Japanese family law system and working to induce change. He hasn't seen his daughter for years.

Discussion: family and civil society

The constant, if largely downplayed, interrelationships between civil society and family lives find purchase in contemporary cases surrounding "parental abduction" in Japan. These highly controversial cases involve one parent taking their own child/ren and restricting access to the other, "left-behind" parent, often for many years. These cases can be international abductions, involving one parent taking their child over international borders into Japan, or domestic abductions, involving one parent removing their child from the other parent entirely within Japan. In

Japan, police and law enforcement agents have refused to punish the taking parent, or assist in returning the child, but often do punish a left-behind parent who tries to recover their child (Lee 2010). Although, as I will explain below, this policy has shifted since 2014 for international cases, in domestic cases Japanese law enforcement remain extremely unlikely to assist. In recent years, international cases have garnered more attention, both in Japanese media and elsewhere, and typically involve a Japanese mother taking children from a non-Japanese father. For this reason, most, but certainly not all, activists are men, both from Japan and elsewhere, although they are joined by left-behind mothers, grandparents who have lost grandchildren, and a few young adults who were formerly abducted by a parent themselves. Activists have organized themselves in a number of different civil society groups with overlapping, but not identical, goals. Groups located outside of Japan, for instance, are more focused on using diplomatic pressure to force changes in the Japanese family court system, while groups in Japan seem more intent on informing the Japanese public of what is occurring. Many, if not all, groups offer triage, legal advice, and support for frantic parents whose children were just taken. Among this diverse population of activists, widely diverging cultural perspectives, preferences, and access to power mean that activists do not always share the same motivations, methods, or desired outcomes.

Although some people label these cases "abductions," others understand these as "rescues," and there is tremendous debate about how to label such actions. Accusations of domestic violence abound, and many so-called "taking" parents accuse the "left-behind" parent of abuse. In Japan, such accusations are especially hard to analyze, because the family court system holds a low standard for evidence in divorce or child custody cases. If a spouse makes an accusation of domestic violence during a child custody negotiation, for instance, the court system is not required to conduct a criminal investigation of the evidence supplied (Jones 2007). Therefore, although domestic violence is certainly a real and substantial problem in Japan (Kuwajima, forthcoming), it is difficult to ascertain the validity of any particular claim when articulated as justification for removing a child from contact with one parent. Moreover, because there is no joint or shared custody option for children after a divorce, the family court system tends to adjudicate disagreements that parents cannot solve by granting sole custody, and severely restricting the non-custodial parent's contact. In this way, results from custody disputes settled within the Japanese family court system often include substantially curtailed contact between a child and their non-custodial parent.

Parental abduction is a controversial topic in contemporary Japan partially because of the gap between experiences based on nationality and citizenship. Before Japan's accession in 2014 to the Hague Convention on the Civil Aspects of International Child Abduction, an international agreement designed to ameliorate such cases, domestic cases in and international abductions to Japan had more in common. The Hague Convention is designed to work outside local court systems to determine quickly if an abduction has taken place and then return any children to their "habitual place of residence" (Hague Convention 1980). Rather than determining guilt or deciding which parent should have custody, the Hague Convention relocates a child back to wherever they were taken from, and relies on that local court system to determine how custody, and the possible abduction, should be treated. The Convention does not hold retroactively, which means that many activists who worked to get it passed in Japan do not receive any relief in their own particular cases. In practice, since Japan's accession to the Hague Convention, this means that left-behind parents in new *international* cases have at least a possibility that their children will be returned. This legal change, which pertains only to new cases in which children were brought over international borders, varies substantially from standard practices within the Japanese family court system to address such abductions. As described by scholars and in the brief examples narrated above, parents whose contact with their children is being restricted rarely find assistance from formal legal mechanisms. If a child is taken while their parents are still married, the parent without de facto custody is often pressured to agree to a divorce by the lawyers or court mediators.

Before the Japanese government agreed to accede to the Hague Convention, the diverse ecosystem of activist groups regularly articulated that as a primary goal. Groups organized within Japan, either of Japanese or foreign parents, as well as groups organized outside Japan, situated Japan's accession as a step in the right direction. Now, however, with the Hague Convention's passage and the first international cases adjudicated under it, activists in different groups articulated diverse goals to me. Many foreign parents, most commonly left-behind fathers, still sought assistance for their particular cases, which had been grandfathered out of the Hague Convention's purview. While Japanese father-activists also wanted assistance for their particular cases, they tended to describe the need to change popular perceptions around what is good for children after parental divorce, and were organizing to legalize joint or shared custody as an option. Many of the foreign parents came from countries like the United States, where shared custody is an ideal after divorce, and were therefore incredulous that the Japanese family court system didn't recognize the harm it was causing by allowing the separation of children and their non-custodial parents.

While all parent-activists were working to change the Japanese family law system, individuals described to me how cultural differences were manifested in styles of protest. For instance, some majority Japanese groups held small rallies in public places (like busy train stations), handing out balloons to children and information to parents about the need for family law reform. Certainly, many foreign parents in Japan participate in these events as well. Outside Japan, activists meet in Washington, DC to lobby American politicians, their staff, and members of the diplomatic corps, but the geographic distance also make face-to-face meetings less common. Instead, members of these groups spent substantial time talking to each other online (Google Hangouts, email, and instant messages) and developed elaborate websites packed with information. In contrast, in Japan, a number of foreigner fathers began particularly public demonstrations and protests after they found no assistance from Japanese courts. Some foreign fathers, for instance, made signs (in Japanese) and stood outside their children's schools. Some American fathers described such protests as powerful ways to demonstrate a continued commitment to children you aren't allowed to visit. But some Japanese fathers instead found those displays embarrassing for the children, and worried that the father's good intent would nevertheless cause anxiety for his children. For these fathers, much as Hideki described above, it might be better to demonstrate paternal commitment by dropping out, refusing to fight publicly, and letting your child grow up with as little conflict as possible. For the most part, I did not see such disagreements about methods or means directly inhibit shared goals around this issue; instead, linguistic abilities seem to divide parent-activists into groups who speak Japanese and those who don't. A number of foreign, English-speaking parents did not speak Japanese despite living in Japan for many years, and some foreign parents didn't trust me because I speak Japanese, even though I am a white American. Such linguistic delineations suggest ongoing fault lines for at least a few members in these diverse groups of activists.

Conclusion

In this chapter, I have argued that, despite popular definitions to the contrary, families are always already involved in civil society. Many people are motivated to participate in civil society through their identities as family members, and otherwise excluded persons might be able to justify their engagement by suggesting its benefit for their families. People of all ages similarly participate in civil society directly to improve family lives or laws governing families. Despite such long-standing patterns, extant across cultures, many scholars automatically exclude families from civil society. Following the scholarships outlined above, I understand this exclusion to reflect deeply gendered hierarchies built into distinctions between "public" and "private," which implicitly imagine certain people and certain spaces as more engaged with civil society. Echoing Chris Hann (1996: 3), I suggest that the "informal, interpersonal" and, indeed, familial practices that significantly contribute to the creation and maintenance of civil society need to be recognized. As suggested by the wide range of people—mostly fathers—protesting in response to domestic and international parental abductions in Japan, the relationship between family and civil society is neither hermetic nor waning. It is up to scholars to continue to pay attention.

Notes

1 Many scholars explicitly exclude "family" from their definitions of civil society. Diamond (1999: 221) describes civil society as "an intermediary phenomenon, standing between the private sphere and the state" that excludes "individual and family life." Pérez-Daíz defines it as "a type of society that combines, to one degree or another, markets, voluntary associations, and the public sphere (Pérez-Daíz 1993: 3). While arguing that civil society in Asia necessitates reconsideration of basic definitions of the Eurocentric term, Schak and Hudson (2003: 4) challenge the requirement that civil society be a "distinctive sphere," but do not challenge the exclusion of family.

2 Until 1997, people who have the same surname and the same ancestral seat were prohibited from getting married. Because some surnames are extremely common, this prohibition had a real impact, although it utterly ignored any possibly shared lineage through the mother's line (Shin 2006).

3 Before December 2015, the law required that all divorced women wait 180 days before they could remarry. Moreover any child born within 300 days of a divorce would legally be the child of her former husband. In 2015, the Supreme Court reduced the required waiting time for a divorced woman to remarry to 100 days.

4 I share my gratitude with all the men and women who were kind enough to share their extremely difficult stories with me in the course of this research. The research described in this chapter was funded by the Abe Fellowship, and administered by the SSRC; I thank these organizations for their generous support. My thanks to Akihiro Ogawa for inviting me to consider these topics, and to Madeline Kahl and Zari Smith for their research assistance.

5 For more on the legal structures of child custody in Japan, see Jones (2007).

Suggested readings

Elshtain, Jean Bethke. 1981. *Public Man, Private Woman: Women in Social and Political Thought*. Princeton, NJ: Princeton University Press.

Hague Convention on the Civil Aspects of International Child Abduction. 1980. Electronic document, https://assets.hcch.net/docs/e86d9f72-dc8d-46f3-b3bf-e102911c8532.pdf, accessed January 29, 2017.

Karim, Lamia. 2011. *Microfinance and its Discontents: Women in Debt in Bangladesh*. Minneapolis, MN: University of Minnesota Press.

Nautz, Jürgen, Paul Ginsborg, and Ton Nijhuis, eds. 2013. *The Golden Chain: Family, Civil Society, and the State*. New York: Berghahn Books.

References

Alagappa, Muthiah. 2004. Civil Society and Political Change: An Analytical Framework. In *Civil Society and Political Change in Asia: Expanding and Contracting Democratic Space*. Muthiah Alagappa, ed. Pp. 25–57. Stanford, CA: Stanford University Press.

Anderson, Sally. 2011. Civil Sociality and Childhood Education. In *A Companion to the Anthropology of Education*. Bradley Levinson and Mica Pollack, eds. Pp. 316–332. Oxford: Wiley Blackwell.

Bandyopadhyay, Kaustuv Kanti. 2013. Civil Society at Multiple Crossroads in Asia. *Development in Practice* 23(5–6): 644–652.

Benhabib, Seyla. 1992. *Situating the Self: Gender, Community and Postmodernism in Contemporary Ethics*. Cambridge: Polity Press.

Boling, Patricia. 1998. Family Policy in Japan. *Journal of Social Policy* 27(2): 173–190.

Boyd, Susan B., ed. 1997. *Challenging the Public/Private Divide: Feminism, Law, and Public Policy*. Toronto: University of Toronto Press.

Burns, Susan. 2009. Local Courts, National Laws, and the Problem of Patriarchy in Meiji Japan: Reading "Records of Civil Rulings" from the Perspective of Gender History in Interdisciplinary Studies on the Taiwan Colonial Court Records Archives. In *Interdisciplinary Studies on the Taiwan Colonial Court Records Archives*. Tay-sheng Wang, ed. Pp. 285–309. Taipei: Angle Publishing Company.

Calhoun, Craig. 2001. Civil Society and the Public Sphere: History of the Concept. In *International Encyclopedia of the Social & Behavioral Sciences*. 2nd Edn, Vol. 3. James D. Wright, ed. Pp. 701–706. Amsterdam: Elsevier.

Chang, Heng-hao. 2009. From Housewives to Activists: Lived Experiences of Mothers for Disability Rights in Taiwan. *Asian Journal of Women's Studies* 15(3): 34–59.

Chen, Chao-ju. 2016. The Chorus of Formal Equality: Feminist Custody Law Reform and Fathers' Rights Advocacy in Taiwan. *Canadian Journal of Women and the Law* 28(1): 116–151.

Cohen, Jean L., and Andrew Arato. 1992. *Civil Society and Political Theory*. Cambridge, MA: MIT Press.

Comaroff, John L., and Jean Comaroff. 1999. Introduction In *Civil Society and the Political Imagination in Africa: Critical Perspectives*. John L. Comaroff and Jean Comaroff, eds. Pp. 1–43. Chicago, IL: University of Chicago Press.

Crowley, Jocelyn Elise. 2008. *Defiant Dads: Fathers' Rights Activists in America*. Ithaca, NY: Cornell University Press.

Davis, Natalie Zemon. 1987. *Fiction in the Archives: Pardon Tales and Their Tellers in Sixteenth-century France*. Stanford, CA: Stanford University Press.

Diamond, Larry. 1999. *Developing Democracy: Toward Consolidation*. Baltimore, MD: Johns Hopkins University Press.

Ehrenberg, John. 1999. *Civil Society: The Critical History of an Idea*. New York: New York University Press.

Elshtain, Jean Bethke. 1981. *Public Man, Private Woman: Women in Social and Political Thought*. Princeton, NJ: Princeton University Press.

Freiner, Nicole. 2013. Mobilizing Mothers: The Fukushima Daiichi Nuclear Catastrophe and Environmental Activism in Japan. *ASIANetwork Exchange* 21(1): 1–15.

Hagemann, Karen. 2008. Civil Society Gendered: Rethinking Theories and Practices. In *Civil Society and Gender Justice: Historical and Comparative Perspectives*. Karen Hagemann, Sonya Michel, and Gunilla-Friederike Budde, eds. Pp. 1–16. New York: Berghahn Books.

Hague Convention on the Civil Aspects of International Child Abduction. 1980. Electronic document, https://assets.hcch.net/docs/e86d9f72-dc8d-46f3-b3bf-e102911c8532.pdf, accessed January 29, 2017.

Hann, Chris. 1996. Political Society and Civil Anthropology. In *Civil Society: Challenging Western Models*. Chris Hann and Elizabeth Dunn, eds. Pp. 1–26. London: Routledge.

Hann, Chris, and Elizabeth Dunn, eds. 1996. *Civil Society: Challenging Western Models*. London: Routledge.

Islamoglu, H. 2015. Concept and History of Civil Society. In *International Encyclopedia of the Social & Behavioral Sciences*. 2nd Edn, Vol. 3. James D. Wright, ed. Pp. 707–712. Amsterdam: Elsevier.

Iwabuchi, Kōichi. 2002. *Recentering Globalization: Popular Culture and Japanese Transnationalism*. Durham, NC: Duke University Press.

Johnson, Ian. 2003. The Death and Life of China's Civil Society. *Perspectives on Politics* 1(3): 551–554.

Jones, Colin. P.A. 2007. In the Best Interests of the Court: What American Lawyers Need to Know About Child Custody and Visitation in Japan. *Asian-Pacific Law and Policy Journal* 8(2): 167–269.

Karim, Lamia. 2011. *Microfinance and its Discontents: Women in Debt in Bangladesh*. Minneapolis, MN: University of Minnesota Press.

Kawato, Yuko, Robert J. Pekkanen, and Hidehiro Yamamoto. 2011. State and Civil Society in Japan. In *Routledge Handbook of Japanese Politics*. Alisa Gaunder, ed. Pp. 117–129. London: Routledge.

Keane, John. 1998. *Civil Society: Old Images, New Visions*. Stanford, CA: Stanford University Press.

Kim, Seung-kyung. 1997. *Class Struggle Or Family Struggle?: The Lives of Women Factory Workers in South Korea*. Cambridge: Cambridge University Press.

Kim, Seung-kyung, and Kyounghee Kim. 2011. Gender Mainstreaming and the Institutionalization of the Women's Movement in South Korea. *Women's Studies International Forum* 34: 390–400.

Kim, Seung-kyung with Kyounghee Kim. 2014. *The Korean Women's Movement and the State: Bargaining for Change*. London and New York: Routledge.

Kingston, Jeff. 2004. *Japan's Quiet Transformation: Social Change and Civil Society in the 21st Century*. New York: Routledge.

Kocka, Jurgen. 2006. Civil Society in Historical Perspective. In *Civil Society: Berlin Perspectives*. John Keane, ed. Pp. 37–50. New York: Berghahn Books.

Kumar, Dharma. 1993. States and Civil Societies in Modern Asia. *Economic and Political Weekly* 28(42): 2266–2269.

Kumar, Krishan. 1993. Civil Society: An Inquiry into the Usefulness of an Historical Term. *The British Journal of Sociology* 44(3): 375–395.

Kuwajima, Kaoru. Forthcoming (2017). My Husband is a Good Man When He Doesn't Hit Me: Redefining Intimacy among Victims of Domestic Violence. In *Intimate Japan*. Allison Alexy and Emma E. Cook, eds. Honolulu, HI: University of Hawai'i Press.

LeBlanc, Robin. 1999. *Bicycle Citizens: The Political World of the Japanese Housewife*. Berkeley, CA: University of California Press.

Lee, Robin S. 2010. Bringing Our Kids Home: International Parental Child Abduction and Japan's Refusal to Return Our Children. *Cardozo Journal of Law and Gender* 17: 109–137.

Ma, Shu-Yu. 1994. The Chinese Discourse on Civil Society. *The China Quarterly* 137: 180–193.

Nakano, Lynne. 2005. *Community Volunteers in Japan: Everyday Stories of Social Change*. London: Routledge.

Nam, Sanghui. 2010. The Women's Movement and the Transformation of the Family Law in South Korea: Interactions Between Local, National and Global Structures. *European Journal of East Asian Studies* 9(1): 67–86.

Pekkanen, Robert. 2004. After the Developmental State: Civil Society in Japan. *Journal of East Asian Studies* 4(3): 363–388.

Pérez-Daíz, Victor M. 1993. *The Return of Civil Society: The Emergence of Democratic Spain*. Cambridge, MA: Harvard University Press.

Qiu, Jack Linchuan. 2008. Mobile Civil Society in Asia: A Comparative Study of People Power II and the Nosamo Movement. *Javnost—The Public Journal of the European Institute for Communication and Culture* 3: 39–58.

Ram, Kalpana. 2008. A New Consciousness Must Come: Affectivity and Movement in Tamil Dalit Women's Activist Engagement with Cosmopolitan Modernity. In *Anthropology and the New Cosmopolitanism: Rooted, Feminist and Vernacular Perspectives*. Pnina Werbner, ed. Pp. 135–155. Oxford: Berg.

Rosaldo, Michelle Zimbalist. 1974. Women, Culture, and Society: A Theoretical Overview. In *Women, Culture, and Society*. Michelle Zimbalist Rosaldo and Louise Lamphere, eds. Pp. 17–43. Stanford, CA: Stanford University Press.

Schak, David C., and Wayne Hudson. 2003. Civil Society in Asia. In *Civil Society in Asia: In Search of Democracy and Development in Bangladesh*. David C. Schak and Wayne Hudson, eds. Pp. 1–8. Burlington, VT: Ashgate.

Schwartz, Frank J., and Susan J. Pharr, eds. 2003. *The State of Civil Society in Japan*. Cambridge: Cambridge University Press.

Shin, Ki-young. 2006. The Politics of the Family Law Reform Movement in Contemporary Korea: A Contentious Space for Gender and the Nation. *The Journal of Korean Studies* 11(1): 93–125.

Shin, Ki-young. 2008. The Personal is the Political: Women's Surname Change in Japan. *Journal of Korean Law* 8: 161–179.

Slater, David H., Rika Morioka, and Haruka Danzuka. 2014. Micro-Politics of Radiation. *Critical Asian Studies* 46(3): 485–508.

Stephen, Lynn. 1997. *Women and Social Movements in Latin America: Power from Below*. Austin, TX: University of Texas Press.

Strulik, Stephanie. 2010. Can Women be Mobilized to Participate in Indian Local Politics? In *Varieties of Activist Experience: Civil Society in South Asia: In Search of Democracy and Development in Bangladesh*. David Gellner, ed. Pp. 103–130. New Delhi: Sage Publications.

Tester, Keith. 1992. *Civil Society*. London: Routledge.

White, Linda E. 2014. Challenging the Heteronormative Family in the Koseki: Surname, Legitimacy and Unmarried Mothers. In *Japan's Household Registration System and Citizenship: Koseki, Identification and Documentation*. David Chapman and Karl Jakob Krogness, eds. Pp. 239–256. London: Routledge.

Yan, Yunxiang. 2003. *Private Life Under Socialism: Love, Intimacy, and Family Change in a Chinese Village 1949–1999*. Stanford, CA: Stanford University Press.

Yang, Hyunah. 2007. Changing Position of Women in Korean Family Law. *Gender and Society* 6(2): 45–62.

31

QUEER

Claire Maree

LGBT civil society

The Asian region is witnessing a surge in the visibility of and organization around LGBTI (lesbian, gay, bisexual, transgender, and intersex) and/or SOGI (sexual orientation and gender identity) related rights and advocacy. Activism, networking, and community building around sexuality and/ or sexual orientation and gender identity related rights and issues have a long history at the local, national, and transnational levels within the Asian region (see, e.g., Engebretsen and Schroeder 2015; Huang 2011; Mackie and McLelland 2015). At the global level, use of the term "LGBT civil society" in key reports and documents appears to represent a shift in global human rights discourse and civil society organization around the legal, social, and cultural barriers experienced by peoples of diverse sexualities and gender identities. This is in part propelled by the adoption of the Sustainable Development Goals (SDGs) by 193 United Nations (UN) member countries in 2015.

Preceded by groundbreaking initiatives such as the Declaration of Montreal (2006; Swiebel 2009), which was endorsed by the International Conference on LGBT Human Rights, and the Yogyakarta Principles (2007), which were drafted by a panel of human rights and SOGI advocacy experts, the SDGs guiding principle to "leave no one behind" encompasses the vision of reaching "all people regardless of their sexual orientation or gender identity" (Ban 2015). Initiatives such as the *Being LGBT in Asia*[1] project encapsulate this vision. One of the stated objectives of the second three-year phase of the project is enabling a "[g]reater understanding and knowledge base from which future LGBT-inclusive development programming and targeted support to LGBT civil society can be planned and initiated" (2015). Similarly, the third recommendation of *Investing in a Research Revolution of LGBTI Inclusion* (Badgett and Crehan 2016) directly calls for funding for research priorities "identified by LGBTI civil society":

> *Recommendation 3*. Fund existing, new, or future research priorities identified by LGBTI civil society, whether related to local, national, regional, or global issues. Civil society has already identified and embarked on some essential projects that will need funding. Other important initiatives to fund would expand the knowledge base on under-researched groups, particularly intersex people, transgender people, low-income LGBTI people, and LGBTI people in ethnic minority groups.
>
> *(Badgett and Crehan 2016)*

The use of the term "LGBTI civil society" here is instructive, as it implies an already existing collective presence in LGBT and SOGI advocacy, and through the use of the acronym LGBTI, also references intersex peoples, issues, and rights. Modifying the term "civil society" with the acronym "LGBTI" and thereby distinguishing it from the more general "civil society," which appears in the sentence that follows it, highlights the possible limitations apparent within wider communities and movements when civil society organizations are tasked with addressing LGBTI[2] issues.

Judith Butler notes in *Undoing Gender* (2004) that the task of international lesbian and gay politics is "a remaking of reality" wherein the "very public assertion of gayness calls into question what counts as reality and what counts as a human life" (Butler 2004: 30). Furthermore, that discussion of the concept of "lesbian and gay human rights" "performs the human as contingent, a category that has in the past, and continues in the present, to define a variable and restricted population, which may or may not include lesbians and gays" (Butler 2004: 38). The concept of "human rights," therefore, is capable of encompassing more than what it is currently posited to include. Using Butler's notion of "cultural translation" (Butler 2004; Butler, Laclau, and Slavoj 2000), Kathryn McNeilly argues that: "(c)laiming rights as human even though excluded from the current articulation of this concept begins with re-reading human rights and their current limits in contexts of power" (McNeilly 2016: 283). Use of the term "LGBT/I civil society" in UN-related documents and reports could be understood as one form of rereading in which existing networks of advocacy around LGBTI rights, and the limitations of civil society that have previously precluded attention to LGBTI peoples and issues are simultaneously made visible.

In her writing on gender and civil society, Jude Howell notes that although civil society provides "a site for organizing around feminist issues, for articulating counter-hegemonic discourses, for experimenting with alternate lifestyles and for envisioning other less sexist and more just worlds," it is potentially a space in which "gendered behaviors, norms and practices are acted out and reproduced" (Howell 2005: 39–40). Following on from Howell's observation, we can say that in terms of issues and rights in relation to sexuality, sexual orientation, and gender identity, civil society can at once be a site in which counter-heteronormative discourse may be voiced, yet at the same time an arena in which some issues are included to the exclusion of others. Josephine Ho's critique of global governance, or "global civil society" (Ho 2015: 123), in relation to conservative Christian groups' campaigns against sex-positive advocacy in Taiwan is illustrative. It has also shown that one possible downside of the increased activity of non-governmental organizations (NGOs) is the weakening of connections amidst a proliferation of groups. The term "LGBT/I civil society," therefore, invokes both the potential for change and the ongoing challenges of advocating for LGBTI and SOGI rights within civil society organizations and within the contested space of sexual expression, LGBTI rights, and SOGI recognition.

This chapter draws on the work on the critical deployment of queer theories from the contested locales of "Japan" and "Asia" to critically engage with the concepts of "civil society" and "LGBT/I civil society." David Eng, Judith Halberstam, and José Esteban Muñoz (2005) remind us that in any discussion of queer studies today, questions of empire, globalization, neoliberalism, sovereignty, terrorism, and I would add able-bodiedness, trouble localized demands for rights. This can be said of the so-called "Asian region," too, where the term "queer" has a different history and trajectory in the diverse languages and history of activism within the region. In her introduction to *Queer Singapore*, Audrey Yue uses the term both as a referent for "the diverse LGBT community" and as "a critical tool to unsettle heteronormativity" (Yue 2012b: 4). In relation to Taiwan, however, Ho notes that the term *queer* has been mobilized in resistance to "homonormativity and feminist gender doctrines" (Ho 2015: 123). This includes collaborative resistance in regards to sex work, participation in the movement campaigning against the eviction of Hansen's disease patients, as well as opposition to investment in marriage rights (Ho 2015: 125).

There are points of intersecting advocacy and activism within specific localized movements. Indeed, as research on the *tongzhi*[3] movement in China has underlined, exactly what constitutes activism or political engagement has different permutations in localized contexts (see, for example, Schoeder 2015). In this chapter, to explore this further, I begin by highlighting the tensions between a critical questioning of "norms" and discussions of universalistic "rights." I then critique discourses of "norm entrepreneurship" that have been mobilized to explain recent global positioning toward LGBTI peoples and SOGI issues. Following that, I look at two examples of the complex intersections of the global, local, and regional in relation to rights, advocacy, and activism.

Entrepreneurial tipping points and homonational modernities

In contemporary reports, international human rights organizations call for greater understanding of the issues faced by LGBTI peoples, and LGBTI rights "whether related to local, national, regional, or global issues" (Badgett and Crehan 2016). This call invokes existing networks at the local, national, regional, and global levels. In an article that traces this history, Elizabeth Baisley (2016) argues that contrary to assumptions about social movement actors being the major influencers on advancing LGBTI and SOGI rights at the global level, civil society organizations and experts, such as the International Gay and Lesbian Organization (ILGA),[4] and NGOs and activists at the Fourth World Conference on Women held in Beijing in 1995,[5] have had limited success. Historically speaking, state-advanced norms have been relatively more effective, and most recently, high-ranking UN officials have been the most influential in this area (Baisley 2016). Baisley argues that due to their ability to "make universalistic claims, emphasize violations of civil and political rights (especially among 'vulnerable' or 'innocent' populations)," high-ranking UN officials have successfully operated as "norm entrepreneurs" (2016). Due to the recent success of these norm changers, we are currently at a point that will potentially result in pro-SOGI norms becoming broadly accepted (Baisley 2016: 163), or internalized (Finnemore and Sikkink 1998: 895) in the not-too-distant future.

The term "norm entrepreneurs" emerges from the work on the life cycle of norms in legal and international relations studies (Finnemore and Sikkink 1998; Sunstein 1996). It refers to those people and groups, including religious, environmental, and civil society organizations (Sunstein 1996: 947), who are "interested in changing social norms" and who can exploit the fact that others may adhere to social norms to which they do not necessarily have a strong allegiance (Sunstein 1996: 909). Accordingly, local and global norms can be shaped through the actions of groups and individuals advocating for change. A "norm cascade," or possible "rapid shifts in norms" (Sunstein 1996: 909) occur when "norm entrepreneurs" have provoked a "tipping point," or a threshold of change (Finnemore and Sikkink 1998), that sparks broader acceptance of the norm. Circa 2015 and the adoption of the SDGs, it would indeed appear that there has been a shift in the normative thinking toward LGBT rights and SOGI issues at the global level. According to Baisley's analysis, this has been facilitated not because of advocacy by "LGBT/I civil society," but because influential international norm leaders have been successful in appealing to universalistic values.

The mobilization of the norm life cycle paradigm in Baisley's analysis alerts us to the rhetoric of entrepreneurship. The notion of entrepreneurial risk-taking and innovation is common to neoliberal discourses that encourage individualized innovation for personal economic advancement. Jasbir Puar's influential work on "homonationalism" offers a critical tool to unraveling the ways in which LGBT identities are imbricated in configurations of citizenship in neoliberal societies (Puar 2007). Arguing from the analytical space of post 9/11 USA, Puar notes that benevolence toward lesbian, gay, and bisexual citizens is contingent on "white racial privilege, consumption capabilities, gender and kinship normativity, and bodily integrity" (Puar 2007: xii). Normative gay and lesbian identities and normative rights such as marriage equality are co-opted into the machinations of the states through "multicultural tolerance and diversity" (Puar 2007: xii). As global discourses increasingly posit LGBTI and SOGI rights as markers of progressive democracies, Puar's analysis remains a strong critique of normative civil society discourses that impinge on intersectionalities of sexualized and racialized bodies.

Although we cannot directly map neoliberalism onto all of Asia, the ways in which neoliberal discourses impinge on sexualities in the contest locale of Asia has been taken up by those writing on localized contexts within the region. The concept of homonationalism has also been influential in thinking through the intersections of nationalism, sexuality, and normative gender and sexual identities in social, cultural, and political domains in the context of LGBT rights in Asia (Tan 2015; Treat 2015; Yue 2012a; Yue and Zubillaga-Pow 2012). Recent scholarship, however, has also cautioned over privileging discourses that imply a teological and/or geospatial movement from regression to liberty (Chiang and Wong 2016; Huang 2011). This progressive approach is often referred to as a "Western post-Stonewall" approach to LGBTI rights. And, although the shift to frame LGBTI rights as human rights is facilitated by *transnational* movements (Kollman and Waites 2009: 4–5), queer research situated in and around Asia critically highlights the complex interrelationship of the local, regional, and global.

In the so-called Asia region, local movements intersect with regional and global discourses of gender and sexuality. Such processes have been referred to as "queer modernity" (Jackson 2009) in relation to Thailand, "homonational modernity" (Yue 2012a) in relation to Australia, "sexual modernity" (Huang 2011) in relation to Taiwan, and glocalqueering (Lim 2005) in relation to Singapore. In the case of Singapore, for example, Audrey Yue argues that "illiberal pragmatics" is crucial to understanding how queer creative industries in Singapore have been allowed to flourish alongside state-sanctioned criminalization of homosexual acts. What Yue terms the "illiberal pragmatics of survival" differs significantly from a "Western post-Stonewall emancipation discourse of rights" (Yue 2007: 151). In the Singaporean case, local pragmatic actions have resulted in unexpected consequences that enable specific queer practices to be tolerated.

One example Yue discusses is the opening of the property market for cheaper subsidized government housing to people of the same-sex. This has allowed heteronormative sexual norms to be maintained at the same time as it enables same-sex couples the opportunity to engage in new domestic arrangements. In another example, Yue discusses the success of the multilingual and multimodal online corporate entity Fridae. The largest operation of its kind in the region, Fridae combines services such as online LGBT dating services with platforms for HIV/AIDS research and education. An environment of "unofficial tolerance" (Yue 2012c: 197) that rewards innovative corporate initiatives enables this openly LGBT-oriented social enterprise to flourish. That Fridae's offices were used by activists to coordinate the campaign to overturn Section 377a of the Penal Code that criminalizes acts of "gross indecency" between males[6] is further evidence of the complex environment (Yue 2012c: 209). The campaign was ultimately unsuccessful, yet the Fridae case illustrates how support for local LGBT activism is facilitated via innovative business practices that align with national economic guidelines

Whilst illiberal pragmatism might be the best way of understanding the intersections of the governing of homosexuality within neoliberal Singapore, in the case of Japan, the in/visibility of LGBT people, that is a media produced hypervisibility that relies on a making certain histories and issues invisible, is juxtaposed within the operations of what might best be called "pressure from the outside (*gaiatsu*)." In the contemporary period, Japan has witnessed several booms of interest in gay, lesbian, and transgender culture and issues (see, e.g., Mackie and McLelland 2015). Most recently, this has manifested in the form of an "LGBT" boom (Maree in press). Media visibility for the so-called "LGBT" markets has been celebrated via discourses of "diversity" within corporate social responsibility paradigms. Calls for greater understanding of workplace diversity are situated alongside corporate generated interest in so-called "LGBT markets" purported to be worth over 5.7 billion yen. Media coverage has also been afforded to the struggles of same-sex couples to gain family acceptance, as local government ordinances to recognize same-sex partners registered as couples at the municipal level have been introduced, for example, in the Shibuya and Setagaya wards of Tokyo. Within greater media visibility, however, a history of activism and advocacy around issues such as same-sex partnerships is rendered invisible.

Community networking around same-sex partnership issues stretches back to at least the women's organizations and gay subcultures of the 1970s, and work at the community level on raising awareness of issues to do with partnership rights in Japan has been ongoing since at least the 1990s in both feminist and queer arenas. When the politician Otsuji Kanako came out during her campaign for a seat in the national elections in 2007[7] and held a public wedding ceremony at a regional LGBT pride event, the media also briefly covered this topic. It was not until the 2010s, however, that a significant inroad into mainstream political discourse has been made. Whilst the work of LGBT activists and advocacy groups must not be denied, this sudden change at the mainstream political level needs be contextualized by the inclusion of sexual orientation in Principle 6 of the Fundamental Principles of Olympism in the *Olympic Charter* (International Olympic Committee 2015) and its impact on the forthcoming 2020 Olympic and Paralympic Games to be held in Tokyo.

Headed by the Liberal Democratic Party (LDP) member, Hase Hiroshi, a multiparty caucus to examine discrimination against sexual minorities was formed in March 2015. At a press conference held after the first gathering of the caucus, Hase explained that its aim is to illustrate "that there is no discrimination against LGBT peoples in the run up to the 2020 Olympics and Paralympics" (NTV News 24 2015). Positioning LGBT rights and issues in the context of the Olympics effectively renders invisible a history of action at the local level.

A document released by the LDP Special Committee on Sexual Orientation and Gender Identity that describes the party's "foundational thoughts on sexual orientation/gender identity" (LDP 2016) is an example of the ways in which a return to "traditional" formulations of diverse gender and sexual identities decontextualizes contemporary realities. The preamble contains a section stating that "since the Middle Ages (*chūsei*) our nation (*wagakuni*) is said to have been tolerant (*kanyō*)" of diverse gender identifications and sexual orientations. While the expectation might be for a plan to acknowledge this diversity, the document goes on to state hopes for a society in which there is no need to "come out" and in which "we each accept each other naturally" (*tagai ni shizen ni ukeirerareru*).

The examples from Singapore and Japan alert us to the complex "flows of queer realities" within the Asian region that are inflected by, at the least, "inter-Asian diasporic circuits and exchanges" (Lim 2005: 384). Inflections of the queer are also heavily impacted by global movements in late modern capitalism such that calls to return to "traditional" formulations of diverse gender and sexual identities often decontextualize or elide localized contemporary realities (Boellstorff 2007; Jackson 2009). In the case of Tokyo, therefore, the application of global norms to facilitate obligations in the staging of a global mega-event such as the Olympics reinstates a "traditional" interpretation of SOGI issues. This political process elides continued advocacy by queer and LGBT groups at the local level, and impacts the implementation of LGBT/I policies beyond those constraints.

LGBT civil society as contested space

This chapter has drawn on collaborative transnational work on the critical deployment of queer theories from the contested locales of "Japan" and "Asia" to critically engage with civil society. Given the linguistic, social, cultural, and political diversity within the Asian region, it is impossible to generalize about what precisely constitutes LGBTI and/or queer activism and advocacy, or what shape the contested locale of "LGBT/I civil society" might take. In this chapter, therefore, I make no claims to do so. My aim is to conceptualize the possible tensions in the framing of "LGBT/I civil society" within overlapping histories of queer activism in the Asian region.

As was noted in the introduction, the term "LGBT/I civil society" invokes already existing networks of advocacy and activism around issues and rights of a diversity of gender and sexual orientations. At the same time, the term alerts us to how these issues are often precluded from mainstream civil society. For those working within "queer studies" or "queer theory," the term "LGBT civil society," therefore, represents a space that is contested, and critiqued. Within the contested locale of the Asian region, global contexts both shape and trouble localized demands for rights in response to the operation of mainstream political powers. Any call for global initiatives to dialogue with "LGBT/I civil society" at the local level needs to be contextualized in the history of repeated efforts of LGBTI activists and civil rights groups to gain an audience for their concerns where the push and pull of local and global discourses of sexuality, desire, and the body intersect with those of family, religion, and culture.

Notes

1 The first phase, 2012–2015, was known as *Being LGBT in Asia*. The second phase, 2015–2017, is called *Being LGBTI in Asia*. Since December 2015, the United Nations Development Programme (UNDP) has worked with partners such as the United States Agency for International Development (USAID) and produced resulting country reports that are based largely on community dialogues with LGBT groups.
2 As some of the documents refer to "LGBT" and other "LGBTI," in this chapter I will use the acronym LGBT/I when invoking those documents, and LGBTI in all other instances.
3 For a brief outline of the term *tongzhi*, see Engebretsen and Schoeder (2015) and Liu (2010).
4 First known as the International Gay Association, ILGA was formed in 1978 in the UK. It was renamed the International Gay and Lesbian Society in 1986, the same year as its first conference in Asia was held in Tokyo. The organization still goes by the acronym ILGA, despite renaming itself as the International Lesbian, Gay, Bisexual, Trans and Intersex Association in 2008.
5 The actions of women's groups and lesbian groups to include "lesbian rights as human rights" are well documented. See, for example, Wilson (1996).
6 See Hor (2012) for further discussion of the enforcement of 377A.
7 A member of the Osaka Prefectural Assembly from 2003 to 2007, Otsuji was unsuccessful in her bid for a seat in the 2007 elections, but later took up a seat in the House of Councillors (May–July 2013) that was vacated due to a resignation. She is the first openly lesbian politician in the National Diet in Japan.

Suggested readings

Engebretsen, Elisabeth L., and William F. Schroeder, eds. 2015. *Queer/Tongzhi China New Perspectives on Research, Activism and Media Cultures*. Copenhagen: NIAS Press.

Huang, Hans Tao-Ming. 2011. *Queer Politics and Sexual Modernity in Taiwan*. Hong Kong: Hong Kong University Press.

Mackie, Vera, and Mark McLelland, eds. 2015. *Routledge Handbook of Sexuality Studies in East Asia*. Abingdon: Routledge.

Yue, Audrey, and Jun Zubillaga-Pow. 2012. *Queer Singapore: Illiberal Citizenship and Mediated Cultures*. Hong Kong: Hong Kong University Press.

References

Badgett, Mary Virginia Lee, and Philip Robert Crehan. 2016. Investing in a Research Revolution for LGBTI Inclusion. Washington, DC: World Bank Group.

Baisley, Elizabeth. 2016. Reaching the Tipping Point?: Emerging International Human Rights Norms Pertaining to Sexual Orientation and Gender Identity. *Human Rights Quarterly* 38(1): 134–163.

Ban, Ki-moon. 2015. Secretary-General's remarks at the High Level LGBT Core Group Event "Leaving No One Behind: Equality & Inclusion in the Post-2015 Development Agenda." September 29. Electronic document, www.un.org/sg/en/content/sg/statement/2015-09-29/secretary-generals-remarks-high-level-lgbt-core-group-event-leaving, accessed November 30, 2016.

Boellstorff, Tom. 2007. *A Coincidence of Desires: Anthropology, Queer Studies, Indonesia.* Durham, NC and London: Duke University Press.

Butler, Judith. 2004. *Undoing Gender.* New York and London: Routledge.

Butler, Judith, Ernesto Laclau, and Žižek. Slavoj. 2000. *Contingency, Hegemony, Universality: Contemporary Dialogues on the Left.* London: Verso.

Chiang, Howard, and Alvin K. Wong. 2016. Queering the Transnational Turn: Regionalism and Queer Asias. *Gender, Place & Culture* 23(11): 1643–1656.

Declaration of Montreal. 2006. [endorsed by the] International Conference on LGBT Human Rights [of the] 1st World Outgames Montreal 2006. Electronic document, www.declarationofmontreal.org, accessed August 20, 2016.

Eng, David L., Judith Halberstam, and José Esteban Muñoz. 2005. Introduction: What's Queer About Queer Studies Now? *Social Text* 23(3–4): 1–17.

Engebretsen, Elisabesth L., and William F. Schoeder, eds. 2015. *Queer/Tongzhi China: New Perspectives on Research, Activism and Media Cultures.* Copenhagen: NIAS Press.

Finnemore, Martha, and Kathryn Sikkink. 1998. International Norm Dynamics and Political Change. *International Organization* 52(4): 887–917.

Ho, Josephine. 2015. Localized Trajectories of Queerness and Activism under Global Governance. In *The Global Trajectories of Queerness: Re-thinking Same-Sex Politics in the Global South.* Ashley Tellis and Sruti Bala, eds. Pp. 121–136. Amsterdam: Rodopi.

Hor, Michael. 2012. Enforcement of 377A: Entering the Twilight Zone. In *Queer Singapore: Illiberal Citizenship and Mediate Cultures.* Audrey Yue and Jun Zubillaga-Pow, eds. Pp. 45–58. Aberdeen and Hong Kong: University of Hong Kong Press.

Howell, Jude. 2005. Gender and Civil Society. In *Global Civil Society 2005/6.* Helmut K. Anheier, Mary Kaldor, and Marlies Glasius, eds. Pp. 38–63. London: Sage.

Huang, Hans Tao-Ming. 2011. *Queer Politics and Sexual Modernity in Taiwan.* Hong Kong: Hong Kong University Press.

International Olympic Committee. 2015. Olympic Charter. Lausanne : International Olympic Committee.

Jackson, Peter A. 2009. Capitalism and Global Queering: National Markets, Parallels Among Sexual Cultures, and Multiple Queer Modernities. *GLQ: A Journal of Lesbian and Gay Studies* 15(3): 357–395.

Kollman, Kelly, and Matthew Waites. 2009. The Global Politics of Lesbian, Gay, Bisexual and Transgender Human Rights: An Introduction. *Contemporary Politics* 15(1): 1–17.

LDP. 2016. Jiyuminshutō Seimuchōsakai Seitekishikō/seijinin ni kansuru tokumei iinnkai [*Liberal Democratic Party Special Committee on Sexual Orientation and Gender Identity*]. 2016. Giron Matome [*Collection of Discussion*]. Tokyo (in Japanese).

Lim, Eng-Beng. 2005. Glocalqueering in New Asia: The Politics of Performing Gay in Singapore. *Theatre Journal* 57(3): 383–405.

Liu, Petrus. 2010. Why Does Queer Theory Need China? *Positions: East Asia Cultures Critique* 18(2): 291–320.

Mackie, Vera, and Mark McLelland. 2015. *Routledge Handbook of Sexuality Studies in East Asia.* Abingdon: Routledge.

Maree, Claire. (In press). Writing Sexual Identity onto the Small Screen: *Seitekishōsū-sha* (sexual minorities) in Japan. In *Routledge Handbook of Japanese Media.* Fabienne Darling-Wolf, ed. Abingdon: Routledge.

McNeilly, Kathryn. 2016. After the Critique of Rights: For a Radical Democratic Theory and Practice of Human Rights. *Law and Critique* 27(3): 269–288.

NTV News 24. Nippon Hōsō Online, March 17, 2015. Electronic document, www.news24.jp/articles/2015/03/17/04271175.html, accessed March 28, 2015.

Puar, Jasbir K. 2007. *Terrorist Assemblages: Homonationalism in Queer Times*. Durham, NC: Duke University Press.

Schoeder, William. 2015. Research, Activism, and Activist Research in Tongzhi China. In *Queer/Tongzhi China: New Perspectives on Resarch, Activism and Media Cultures*. Elisabesth L. Engebretsen and William F. Schroeder, eds. Pp. 57–80. Copenhagen: NIAS Press.

Sunstein, Cass R. 1996. Social Norms and Social Roles. *Columbia Law Review* 96(4): 903–968.

Swiebel, Joke. 2009. Lesbian, Gay, Bisexual and Transgender Human Rights: The Search for an International Strategy. *Contemporary Politics* 15(1): 19–35.

Tan, Chris K. K. 2015. Rainbow Belt: Singapore's Gay Chinatown as a Lefebvrian Space. *Urban Studies* 52(12): 2203–2218.

Treat, John Whittier. 2015. The Rise and Fall of Homonationalism in Singapore. *Positions: East Asia Cultures Critique* 23(2): 349–365.

United Nations Development Programme (UNDP). 2015. Being LGBT in Asia: A Participatory Review and Analysis of the Legal and Social Environment for Lesbian, Gay, Bisexual and Transgender (LGBT) Persons and Civil Society. Electronic document, www.asia-pacific.undp.org/content/rbap/en/home/operations/projects/overview/being-lgbt-in-asia.html, accessed November 30, 2016.

Wilson, Ara. 1996. Lesbian Visibility and Sexual Rights at Beijing. *Signs: Journal of Women in Culture & Society* 22(1): 214–218.

Yogyakarta Principles on the Application of International Human Rights Law in Relation to Sexual Orientation and Gender Identity. 2007. Electronic document, www.yogyakartaprinciples.org, accessed November 30, 2016.

Yue, Audrey. 2007. Creative Queer Singapore: The Illiberal Pragamtics of Cultural Production. *Gay & Lesbian Issues & Psychology Review* 3(3): 149–160.

Yue, Audrey. 2012a. Queer Asian Mobility and Homonational Modernity: Marriage Equality, Indian Students in Australia and Malaysian Transgender Refugees in the Media. *Global Media & Communication* 8(3): 269–287.

Yue, Audrey. 2012b. Introduction: Queer Singapore: A Critical Introduction. In *Queer Singapore: Illiberal Citizenship and Mediated Cultures*. Audrey Yue and Jun Zubillaga-Pow, eds. Pp. 1–26. Aberdeen and Hong Kong: Hong Kong University Press.

Yue, Audrey. 2012c. "We're the Gay Company, as Gay as it Gets": The Social Enterprise of Fridae. In *Queer Singapore: Illiberal Citizenship and Mediated Cultures*. Audrey Yue and Jun Zubillaga-Pow, eds. Pp. 195–212. Aberdeen and Hong Kong: Hong Kong University Press.

Yue, Audrey, and Jun Zubillaga-Pow. 2012. *Queer Singapore: Illiberal Citizenship and Mediated Cultures*. Aberdeen and Hong Kong: Hong Kong University Press.

32

YOUTH ACTIVISM

Ian Rowen

The East Asian Youth Movement resurgence of 2014 and 2015

Youth activism has been a major mode of social and political change in East Asia. Young activists have driven a number of the most significant reforms and revolutions in the region, including modernization campaigns, environmental protection, democratization, and anti-militarization advocacy. Such activism has not only affected government policy and structure, but has also cultivated new generations of political and intellectual leaders.

In general, youth-led movements have made greater impact when they are able to draw support from a wide swath of civil society. This observation presents an epistemological and methodological question for any account of such activism—although a number of well-known movements have been led by youth, because many of them positioned themselves as part of broader-based movements, it is not immediately obvious which movements may qualify specifically as "youth activism." For the sake of temporal, regional, and analytical coherence, this chapter focuses specifically on the 2014 Taiwan Sunflower Movement, the Hong Kong Umbrella Movement, and Japan's SEALDs. These examples were chosen not only because they were nominally youth or student-led, but also due to their regional proximity, mutual awareness and even collaboration, and continued contemporary relevance.

These movements followed the "Arab Spring" of major uprisings and regime change that swept the Middle East in 2011, prompting some observers to speculate that the region may be undergoing its own kind of "Asian Spring." While such speculation turned out to be premature, the Sunflower Movement transformed Taiwan's society and politics, the Umbrella Movement riveted Hong Kong and captured global attention, and SEALDs renewed the vigor and spontaneity of student organizations in Japan. Together, these movements demonstrate the key role played by youth in coordinating civil society groups and driving social and political change in East Asia.

Taiwan Sunflower Movement

What started as a youth-led protest against the near passage of a trade deal between Taiwan and China ultimately led to a twenty-four-day occupation of Taiwan's parliament and the biggest pro-democracy protest rally in the island's history. Taiwan's Sunflower Movement reset discussion about the island's political and social trajectory, precipitated the electoral defeat of the ruling party, prompted the creation of a new political party that won several national seats, and revitalized Taiwan's civil society.

While Taiwan has a history of youth-led movements that have driven major democratic reform, such as the 1990 Wild Lily Movement (Ho 2010; Wright 1999), the Sunflower Movement's more recent roots were a series of protests against the 2008 visit of Chinese representative Chen Yunlin and the attempted buyout of major media assets by a conglomerate with close ties to the irredentist Beijing leadership (Cole 2015; Harrison 2012; Ho 2014b). These movements were driven by and cultivated student activists, such as Lin Fei-fan and Chen Wei-ting, and connected youth activist and civil society groups, such as Black Island Nation Youth and the Defend Democracy Platform, that would go on to play key roles in the Sunflower Movement.

The Sunflower Movement was nominally a response to the botched near-passage of a trade deal negotiated in secret by representatives from Taiwan and China. Critics alleged that the Cross-Strait Services Trade Agreement (CSSTA), championed by Taiwan President Ma Ying-jeou and submitted for passage in the Legislative Yuan, would threaten Taiwan's sovereignty by opening up sensitive sectors, including media, health care, and tourism. Activists argued that Taiwan's free press would be threatened by collusion between oligarchs on both sides of the Taiwan Strait, and that other industries would be co-opted by state-owned investors from China, a hostile power that threatens military invasion should Taiwan declare de jure independence.

To assuage such concerns, the Chinese Nationalist Party (KMT), which then held both Taiwan's presidency and a legislative majority, had promised a line-by-line review of the controversial agreement. However, on March 17, 2014, the committee convener declared that the review period was over after only thirty seconds and that the bill would be sent to a plenary session for a vote, where it almost certainly would have been approved. Claiming that the refusal to conduct the promised review was an affront to legislative due process, an ad hoc group led by the "Black Island Nation Youth," an amorphous youth-led activist group, stormed the back of the Legislative Yuan, while their allies staged a decoy incursion at the front gate. After entering the building, they carried out the few police officers who were guarding the Assembly Hall, barricaded the doors with rope, and repelled subsequent attempts to remove them.

Sympathetic opposition legislators, many of them past activists themselves, arrived on the scene to serve as human shields against possible state violence. An executive order to send in riot police was ignored by Wang Jin-pyng, the long-serving speaker of the Legislative Yuan, who was at the time facing expulsion from the KMT due to a dispute with President Ma Ying-jeou. Wang, the man legally responsible for the daily operation of the Legislative Yuan, ignored Ma's call for an emergency meeting and promised the protesters that they would not be removed by force.

The movement found its moniker after a local florist donated a case of fresh sunflowers to the front lines of the protest, meant metaphorically to cast light on the opaque "black box" trade deal negotiations. Some activists welcomed the flower symbolism, which recalled the "Wild Lily Movement" of 1990, a six-day movement that ultimately led to direct presidential elections. Others found the Sunflower imagery a bit too twee, but were forced to go along with it as soon as the mass media picked up on the name (Rowen 2015).

Activists continued entering the building through windows and ladders before developing an ID system with serialized badges to bring in trusted people at the door, which was guarded by legislators, who had the legal right to admit aides or guests, and followed directions from activists. Occupiers formed increasingly cohesive work units with an emergent division of labor, including teams for security, information and technical support, media and translation, and even curating for the proliferating political poster art adorning the walls of the chamber. These teams ultimately reported to a council of nine decision makers (Beckershoff 2017), composed of five students and four non-governmental organization (NGO) representatives. These included prominent activists such as Lin Fei-fan and Chen Wei-ting, graduate students who had gained wide exposure during the Wild Strawberry and anti-Media Monopoly Movement. In heated strategy sessions, Lin Fei-fan advocated for the inclusion of representatives from NGOs and other civil society groups, such as the Taiwan Association of Human Rights, the Taiwan Professors Association, and others. While some radical students disputed this apparent cession of authority to non-students, this tactic helped consolidate wider support and build logistical capacity for what turned into a surprisingly lengthy occupation of the government building and its surrounding streets.

As the Legislative Yuan became an administrative center with an evolving division of labor, so too did the growing tent city outside subdivide into zones and districts with distinct characters and organizing bodies, including university student groups, NGOs, and ad hoc collectives. Support for these temporary communities was provided by expanding security, supply, and waste disposal teams who maintained uneven and occasionally strained communications and coordination with each other and with their counterparts inside the Legislative Yuan, who were insulated behind rows of police and volunteer security teams.

Emboldened by growing popular support and joined by scholars and civil activists, occupation leaders soon expanded their demands. With legal scholar Huang Kuo-chang and representatives from NGOs taking increasingly assertive strategic and logistical roles, the demand for a review of the CSSTA instead became a demand for the government to create an oversight body for the review of cross-strait agreements. Huang argued that because existing law, based on the Republic of China constitution adopted in 1949, still treated the "Mainland Area" and "Taiwan Area" as separate jurisdictions within the same country, there was no proper legal procedure for a review of an agreement like the CSSTA. Supporters argued that short of drafting a new constitution—no easy task—an oversight body would at least increase public input into the drafting and passage of cross-strait agreements.

Students demanded a public meeting with the president, which was rebuffed, leading to an increasingly desperate mood within the occupied chamber. On Sunday night, March 23, a group of students and activists stormed the Executive Yuan, Taiwan's cabinet building. Their connection to the occupation's core leadership was unclear even to people on the front lines of the campaign. As with the initial occupation, the participants joined in an ad hoc fashion, loosely coordinated via online platforms and hasty face-to-face meetings. The premier ordered riot police to remove the protesters, and the televised state violence elevated the situation into a national crisis. Over 150 activists were injured and many hospitalized. Despite the failure to hold the building, vivid images of bloodied students appeared on television and in newspapers, raising public attention and protestor passions.

To build wider support, Sunflower leaders announced there would be a rally in front of the Presidential Office on March 30. An estimated 350,000 to 500,000 people joined the throngs, making it the largest non-partisan rally in Taiwan's history. Still, with the president and activists unwilling to compromise, no end was in sight until April 6 when Legislative Speaker Wang entered the assembly hall with several other legislators and promised that the CSSTA would not be passed before the establishment of a supervisory mechanism for cross-Strait agreements. Sunflower leaders decided in secret that this was a sufficient concession, and declared that they would retreat on April 10. The announcement took many activists by surprise, but they had little choice and few resources to continue an indefinite occupation with broader goals. In the next few days, activists cleaned up the building and the surrounding streets, assessed property damages and promised to pay them back in full, and exited as promised on April 10 in a choreo-graphed march carrying real-life sunflowers and culminating in a stage show of tearful speeches and public recollections.

Although the controversial trade deal was placed on ice, Taipei continued to be rocked by protests for weeks after the occupation ended. Activists, still mobilized, quickly turned to the unsettled issue of Taiwan's fourth nuclear power plant, a KMT-driven project that had been under construction for decades. After Japan's 2011 Fukushima disaster, Taiwanese public opinion turned against the opening of the reactor—regular protest events had in fact preceded and helped provide social capacity for the Sunflower Movement itself.

Seizing the momentum, senior democracy activist and past DPP co-founder Lin Yi-hsiung announced an indefinite hunger strike against the plant, starting on April 22. In solidarity with Lin, young activists occupied the street in front of the Taipei Train Station on the night of April 27. Echoing the state violence of several weeks prior at the Executive Yuan, protesters were dispersed by water cannons and riot police on the order of Taipei Mayor Hau Lung-Bin. However, the following day, the Ma administration capitulated and announced a temporary halt to construction. Lin soon ended his hunger strike.

While direct action seems to have quickly achieved the initial objectives of both the Sun-flowers and the overlapping anti-nuclear movement, the centralization and unity of purpose maintained inside the Legislative Yuan occupation and outside during the anti-nuclear street occupation proved difficult to maintain. The broad base splintered into several groups, includ-ing Taiwan March, led by the most visible Sunflower activists like Lin Fei-fan and Huang Kuo-chang, and advocating primarily to lower the voting thresholds for national referendums. Not long after that, Huang Kuo-chang announced the establishment of the New Power Party, a pro-independence, generally left-wing party that would both collaborate with and pressure the DPP in the upcoming elections. Other spin-off groups included Democracy Tautin, which focused on wider grass-roots action, and Democracy Kuroshio, a student alliance. Strikingly, none of these groups chose to maintain the "Sunflower" moniker, despite the symbol's wide appeal and high profile.

Although the integration of the Sunflower activists proved difficult to maintain, the move-ment handily demonstrated its alignment with the electorate when the KMT lost key mayor-ships in the midterm local elections in November 2014. Smaller Sunflower-affiliated parties, including the Green Party of Taiwan and the Tree Party, also won their first local seats. This gave the DPP and Huang's New Power Party considerable momentum for the 2016 presidential and legislative elections, which proved even more devastating for the KMT, which lost not only the presidency but also, for the first time, a legislative majority.

The geopolitical impact of the Sunflower Movement is significant. Following wide public support for the movement and the electoral collapse of the KMT, any prospect of Taiwan and China's "peaceful unification" appears to have vanished. Especially in light of later unrest in Hong Kong, the showcase of the supposedly successful "One Country, Two Systems" scheme originally designed for Taiwan by China's leadership, Taiwan and its youth activists appear set to pursue greater international space and autonomy.

Hong Kong Umbrella Movement

Hong Kong's Umbrella Movement began as a call for "genuine universal suffrage," meaning the right to freely choose and directly elect the territory's Chief Executive. Like the Sunflower Movement, Hong Kong's Umbrella Movement was propelled by seasoned youth activists, accelerated in unpredictable ways and received a name not of its choosing. Unlike the Sunflower

Movement, it began as a protest not against an opaque trade deal, but against the deferral of democratic elections. While the Chinese leadership was implicated in both this case and the Sunflower Movement, their role was different, as Hong Kong is administered as a Special Administrative Region (SAR) of the People's Republic of China and Taiwan is a de facto independent contested state with limited international recognition. While the scale, duration, and activation of Hong Kong civil society astonished even the movement's most ardent supporters, it ended without any concrete policy achievements. It did, however, consolidate a new generation of activists, several of whom won elected office in the following years.

Hong Kong's capacity for youth activism had rapidly accelerated over the years prior to 2014, most notably in the movement against the Moral and National Education (MNE) compulsory curriculum. Part of a "nation-building program" (Morris and Vickers 2015: 305) to inculcate Chinese national identities, the Moral and National Education curriculum was announced in 2010 and withdrawn in 2012 after a movement led by high school students, including Joshua Wong, successfully rallied public sentiment and cultivated a new generation of youth activists.

As Paul Morris and Edward Vickers write:

> The MNE controversy was significant in that it: dominated public discourse for nearly 18 months; involved numerous marches, public protests and strikes; prompted the creation of over 24 civic groups dedicated to opposing the new subject; witnessed the emergence of secondary school students as leaders of the opposition movement; severely challenged the legitimacy of the government; and contributed significantly to the subsequent pro-democracy "Occupy Central/Umbrella Movement" of 2014.
>
> *(Morris and Vickers 2015: 306)*

Hong Kong's path to democracy has been partly determined by the Beijing leadership's interpretation of the Basic Law, a mini-constitution drafted in the 1980s by Chinese and Hong Kong elites to govern the territory following the 1997 handover from the United Kingdom to the People's Republic of China. Article 45 of the Basic Law states that: "The ultimate aim is the selection of the Chief Executive by universal suffrage, upon nomination by a broadly representative nominating committee in accordance with democratic procedures." Based on this, Hong Kong's pan-democratic political and social activist camps pushed for years for a gradual move toward formal procedural direct democracy. In response, China's National People's Congress Standing Committee (NPC-SC) issued a decision in 2007 promising universal suffrage by 2017.

During subsequent consultations between Hong Kong and Beijing agencies, Hong Kong's pan-democratic lawmakers pushed for "civil nominations" open to a wide variety of possible candidates. A civil society group called "Occupy Central with Peace and Love" (OCLP), formed by two professors, Benny Tai and Chan Kin-Man, and the Reverend Chu Yiu-ming, held unofficial referendums in which a majority of participants indicated support for civil nominations (K. Chan 2016). However, on August 31, 2014, the NPC-SC issued a legal decision that although candidates could be submitted through civil nominations, the two or three candidates who would be permitted to stand in the general election must be approved in advance by half of the 1,200 members of an elite elections committee (J. Chan 2014). It was a vote of 689 members of a similar committee that had brought Chief Executive C. Y. Leung, the target of much activist ire, to power in 2012.

Democracy activists denounced this move as a form of non-genuine "universal suffrage." However, they were clearly unsurprised, having laid the groundwork for a public demonstration well in advance of its announcement. The OCLP had prepared a plan to occupy the central business district as early as 2013. Following the NPC-SC decision, they indicated it would begin on October 1, 2014, the Chinese national holiday, and held advance promotional and training meetings.

Student activists, while generally supportive of the OCLP's goals, had different ideas about tactics and representation. Scholarism, a high school student group led by Joshua Wong, and Hong Kong Federation of Students (HKFS), a university group, announced class boycotts to begin on September 22 and a sit-in on September 26 at Civic Square, the public space in front of the Legislative Council that had been blocked off due to government security concerns. Joshua Wong and several fellow students were arrested that day for entering the square, leading to the arrival of more protesters. OCLP leaders noted that the students were already well ahead of their own October 1 start date, and urged their supporters to begin the campaign early and join the students. By September 28, the police reacted to the swelling crowds by firing eighty-seven rounds of tear gas, a heavy-handed miscalculation that shocked the public and provoked tens of thousands of Hong Kongers to flood the streets in support of demonstrators. The crowds ended up spilling over to Causeway Bay, a shopping district, and ill-considered police-implemented mass transit shutdowns led protestors to cross into Mong Kok, a working-class district across Victoria Bay in Kowloon.

The three different occupation sites quickly developed different characters. Civic Square in Admiralty, adjoining Hong Kong's Government and the People's Liberation Army offices, was the closest thing to the movement's spatial center. The first-aid station of that initial protest site, later dispersed by the notorious police attack, was reclaimed to sport a makeshift Umbrella Shrine. This center, unlike Sunflower Movement's Legislative Yuan, however, was not an occupied building that could be held as a bargaining chip. Counter-intuitively for a student encampment, the mood, while inspired and idealistic, was generally more severe, reflecting the higher strategic stakes of the site as well as the memory of recent violence. The Mong Kok site, while smaller than the island-side encampment, immediately drew a wider range of ages and social classes and featured a more expressive, even chaotic atmosphere. By October 3, waves of blue ribbon-wearing counter-demonstrators began flooding into the area and verbally and even physically attacking student demonstrators. Demonstrators and supportive legislators complained about a slow and passive police response that further polarized society (Branigan and Batty 2014). Still, the protestors defied the "blue ribbons" and stayed until forcible police clearance over two months later. The Causeway Bay encampment was the most compact and smoothly managed of all—a veritable civil society showcase, said some activists, in part meant as a display for the many Chinese tourists who frequented the busy shopping district (Rowen 2016). Coordination proved extremely difficult not only between the different occupation sites, but within them, due to leadership struggles and philosophical differences about the nature of demo-cracy and collective decision-making (Liu and Lin 2016).

Slogans with uncanny parallels to those of Taiwan Sunflower proliferated in the sprawling on and offline spaces. "We are all Hong Kong People," "Save your own Hong Kong." After seeing the now-iconic photo of a protestor holding up an umbrella in the face of tear gas, a British Twitter user dubbed the uprising, the "Umbrella Movement." The name was quickly picked up by the protesters themselves, who began using it to withstand not only tear gas but also the sweltering sun and pounding rain. International media extensively covered the early weeks of the movement, and Joshua Wong even appeared on the cover of *TIME* magazine.

Public support was strongest during the early weeks of the movement, with HKFS briefly becoming the most popular political group in all of Hong Kong, according to the University of Hong Kong public opinion research center. The possibility of a breakthrough appeared briefly with a televised live debate between government leaders (excluding C. Y. Leung) and representatives from Scholarism and HKFS, who performed confidently but were still unable to win any concessions (Veg 2015). After several weeks of traffic disruptions and no compromise in sight, public support gradually eroded. By early December, based on civil court injunctions, the government ordered clearances of all of the occupation zones. Prominent pan-democratic lawmakers joined the sit-in and were removed and arrested along with other activists.

In the following months, student activists such as Joshua Wong and Nathan Law defended themselves in court while simultaneously forming Demosisto, a new political party. Other "localist," or Hong Kong-centric groups, including Youngspiration and Civic Passion, also ran their own candidates in the 2016 Legislative Council elections. Several, including Nathan Law, won seats, only to be challenged in court by the central government, based on the elected candidates' reading of the oath of office, which was accused of being insufficiently patriotic. Further electoral fallout from Hong Kong's largest-ever protest movement included C. Y. Leung's decision to not seek re-election, making him the first Chief Executive to step down after one term.

SEALDs and contemporary Japanese youth anti-war activism

The Students' Emergency Action for Liberal Democracy (SEALDs) was a student-led movement against the Japanese Prime Minister Shinzo Abe's proposed security laws. Abe championed legal amendments and constitutional reinterpretations that would allow Japan to participate in international military campaigns in the name of "collective self-defense." Youth activists criticized such maneuvers as not only a violation of constitutional due process, but also as a potentially fascist turn that threatened to derail Japan's future as a democratic and peaceful nation. Although SEALDs only functioned for over a year, having been established on May 3, 2015 and disbanded on August 15, 2016, it provided an important gathering point for a variety of Japanese activists of all generations.

SEALDs, while nominally a response to militarization, was the most significant recent renewal of Japanese youth activism, which had been relatively stagnant under the long shadow of the sometimes-violent 1960s-era opposition movement to the Anpo US base treaty. The past ideological stances and militant tactics of past movements had grown unappealing to contemporary students (Slater *et al.* 2015). Explicitly recognizing the need for a new approach, the SEALDs' savvy use of social media and self-presentation as ideologically "regular" and non-radical attracted a new generation of participants, while also garnering the support of more senior activists.

SEALDs itself was formed by the core members of an earlier group, Students Against the Secret Protection Law (SASPL), including Aki Okuda, who had gathered to protest this Abe-led (and US-supported) bill that criminalized public reporting of vaguely defined, mostly military-related "state secrets." Although activists suffered a major setback after the smooth passage of the Secrecy Law in 2015, they quickly reconstituted as SEALDs to drive the next iteration of a broader campaign. They were helped along by the renewed anti-nuclear movement, which had picked up steam and staged regular protests following the March 11, 2011 disaster at Fukushima. This momentum "paved the way" for SEALDs, which had broader ambitions and more international inclinations, as demonstrated by the choice of a name resembling the English word, "shields" (Slater *et al.* 2015).

Abe's push to amend Article 9 of Japan's constitution, which guaranteed Japan's legal obligations as a peaceful nation, was, as he explained in an address to the US Congress, intended to "make the cooperation between the US military and Japan's SDF (Self-Defense Forces) even stronger, and the alliance still more solid, providing credible deterrence for peace in the region" (Japanese Cabinet Office 2015). Although Abe's moves came in part as a response to the changed security environment brought by China's rise, student activists argued that Abe's policies risked a return to the militarism of the past and posed an existential threat to a "free and democratic Japan." They argued that Abe's tactics, which included passing the bills through cabinet review instead of full parliamentary deliberation, were autocratic and in violation of democratic due process. By framing themselves as defenders of the constitutional order, SEALDs presented their position as one of moderation rather than as a radical challenge to the national order.

While anti-nuclear activists had been protesting weekly outside the prime minister's office since 2011, SEALDs and affiliated groups chose instead to protest in front of the Diet, Japan's parliament, every Friday evening starting June 5, 2015. Popular chants included "Kenpō Mamore" [Defend the Constitution], "Abe wa yamero!" [Let's get rid of Abe], and "Tell me what democracy looks like, this is what democracy looks like!" Although they received limited coverage from mainstream news outlets, their persistence and carefully calibrated online presence earned them a crowd of approximately 120,000 at their peak on August 30, 2015, placing them amongst Japan's largest-ever protest movements (Kingston 2015). Satellite demonstrations also took place in other cities including Sapporo, Fukushima, Kyoto, Osaka, and Nagasaki.

Despite this up-swell of support, the SEALDs was ultimately unable to block the security bills and disbanded on August 15, 2016. Although Okuda, the most visible face of the movement, said, "We have to admit that we did lose" (Kikuchi 2016), SEALDs has secured its legacy not only by reinvigorating Japanese youth and civil society, but also by provoking cooperation between opposition parties with the formation of Shimin Rengō (Civil Alliance for Peace and Constitutionalism), an alliance between the Democratic Party of Japan, the Japan Innovation Party, the Social Democratic Party, and the Japanese Communist Party, which won eleven seats—nine more than were won in the last such election in 2013. While Abe's Liberal Democratic Party maintained the executive branch and a two-thirds parliamentary majority, at least the SEALDs showed the potency of new cultural and technological forms for future Japanese activism.

Continuity, contrast, and inspirational relationships

All three of these movements had been preceded by years of capacity building amongst a diverse and often fractious set of constituencies from a wide variety of civil society groups. They spatially targeted centers of legislative power. They also positioned themselves as unaffiliated with any pre-existing political parties, or even traditional left or right-wing ideology, even if they informally communicated or collaborated with opposition parties and ultimately helped sway later elections.

Comparisons between the Sunflower and Umbrella Movements were common not only amongst protesters, but also amongst prominent government figures in both Taiwan and Hong Kong. In Taiwan, Ma Ying-jeou simultaneously praised the Hong Kong Umbrella and criticized the Taiwan Sunflowers as "violent" (Bradsher and Ramzy 2014). Given Ma's questionable logical consistency, such a statement was perhaps intended to score the KMT some political points in advance of elections. In Hong Kong, pro-government legislator Regina Ip, who had championed the failed passage of an "anti-subversion" bill ten years prior to the movement, which ultimately triggered the national patriotic education debate, reflected on the "inspirational relationship" between the Sunflowers and the Umbrellas in a newspaper editorial about how best to "counter pernicious external influences" (Ip 2014). Such "pernicious influences" included not only the Taiwanese activists and academics who visited the occupation sites in

Hong Kong, but also the very idea of public nomination, which is "much harder to eradicate." Ip's article reflected the government's broader efforts to paint the protests as the product of "foreign forces" and thereby disclaim responsibility for listening to the demands of its own well-educated youth.

Although the USA has frequently been accused by Chinese leaders of domestic meddling or fomenting "color revolutions" in Central and Eastern Europe via the National Endowment for Democracy and other state and quasi-state organs, activists in all three polities in fact expressed distress about being geopolitically trapped between self-interested superpowers. While Sunflower and Umbrella gave voice to fears about China's economic and political influence on Taiwan and Hong Kong, SEALDs was driven more by Japan's changing military alliance with the USA. All three movements generally espoused self-determination and advocated adherence to legal, democratic processes.

Other civil society groups, particularly labor and environmental, shared affiliation and support with these movements. While the Hong Kong movement did not directly address environmental issues, the Sunflowers and SEALDs share a synergistic relationship with anti-nuclear movements. Both of them were enabled and in turn re-energized nuclear movements in both polities. Moreover, inasmuch as the Sunflowers inspired the Umbrellas, the Taiwan anti-nuclear movement gained new focus after the Fukushima nuclear disaster (Ho 2014a).

Media, both online and offline, and domestic and international, played important roles in these movements. Both the Taiwan Sunflower and Hong Kong Umbrella Movements earned their monikers externally, either from mass or social media, while SEALDS at least was self-chosen. SEALDs received little media attention and the Sunflower Movement received perhaps even less international attention, especially compared to coverage of the Umbrella Movement. Loathe to miss the largest protest on Chinese soil since the Tiananmen Square protests in 1989, foreign correspondents arrived in droves to cover the story. Reporters could also easily utilize Hong Kong's relatively proficient English-language resources.

Although movement names and other forms of representation often proliferated beyond central control, all three movements deliberately used art and other creative techniques to shape and transmit their messages. Although the following observation was made about Japan, it could have been applied to all three of the movements: "For SEALDs, the cultural coding is not to demonstrate subversiveness but normality, that being involved in politics is neither dark and dangerous, but neither are their members odd and out of step with the mainstream" (O'Day 2015: 4). As André Beckershoff, following Bourdieu's concept of "synchronization," wrote of the Sunflower Movement's "integration" rather than simple "addition" of protest groups (2017), all three movements provided public platforms for other issues beyond the immediate targets of discontent. In so doing, they brought together a variety of groups to shared and often festive protest spaces, and built capacity for new forms of collaboration.

Conclusion: not quite an Asian Spring, but at least not an Asian Winter

Questions of success and failure have dogged all three of these movements, amongst both activists and outside commentators. The Taiwan Sunflower Movement's blockage of the disputed services trade deal and the decision by its leaders to retreat at a time and on terms of their choosing makes it probably the most successful of these movements, if the metric is policy achievements. Hong Kong's Umbrella Movement did not fold by choice and, unlike the Sunflowers, they achieved no short-term political concessions. It would be misleading to pin this entirely on the activists themselves. Up against a more intransigent opponent in the form of the Chinese Communist Party and the Hong Kong administration than the Sunflowers were in the form of an internally divided KMT, the movement performed far above expectations. It augured a cultural shift that Beijing may find difficult to contain, and led to the formation of several new political parties that won seats in subsequent elections. As for SEALDs, although they failed to prevent Abe's security bills, they awoke a long-dormant segment of Japanese civil society and likely influenced subsequent elections.

Maintaining and widening their circles, youth activists have since set up regional associations, including the Network of Young Democratic Asians, led by Lin Fei-fan, who held a 2016 meeting in Manila that was joined by Umbrella leaders Alex Chow and Nathan Law, SEALDs leaders Aki Okuda and Chiharu Takano, Taiwan Black Island Youth Front's Fi Tseng, as well as activists from Myanmar and Thailand. Follow-up meetings are planned for Korea and other regional centers. Another follow-up event was a December 2016 forum between Taiwan's New Power Party and pro-democracy Hong Kong activists and politicians, which earned even more press attention after being targeted by pro-Beijing groups with underworld ties, who attacked the guests upon arrival in Taipei and targeted Nathan Law in particular on his return at the Hong Kong airport.

Given their scale, logistical extent, and use of communication tools, the 2014 Asian protests were amongst the most sophisticated social movements the world has ever seen. Yet, even at their peaks of mobilization and public support, youth activists and sympathetic civil society groups were too savvy and reserved to call for regime change or other radical measures that, even in the unlikely event of success, may have allowed military or religious groups to fill a power vacuum, or lead to civil war, as in Egypt or Libya. They were, in the words of Sebastian Veg, simultaneously "legalistic" and "utopian" (Veg 2015). While 2014 will not be remembered as the beginning of an "Asian Spring" or new wave of "Color Revolutions," at least it did not prompt an "Asian Winter," and laid new groundwork for social movements yet to come.

Suggested readings

Broadbent, Jeffrey, and Vicky Brockman, eds. 2011. *East Asian Social Movements: Power, Protest, and Change in a Dynamic Region.* New York: Springer.

Rowen, Ian. 2015. Inside Taiwan's Sunflower Movement: Twenty-Four Days in a Student-Occupied Parliament, and the Future of the Region. *The Journal of Asian Studies* 74(1): 1–15.

Slater, David, Robin O'Day, Satsuki Uno, Love Kindstrand, and Chiharu Takano. 2015. SEALDs (Students Emergency Action for Liberal Democracy): Research Note on Contemporary Youth Politics in Japan. *The Asia-Pacific Journal* 13 37(1).

Veg, Sebastian. 2015. Legalistic and Utopian: Hong Kong's Umbrella Movement. *New Left Review* 92: 55–73.

Websites

Sunflower Movement Facebook group, www.facebook.com/sunflowermovement.
This multi-lingual Facebook group connected the Sunflower Movement with the world.
SEALDS website, http://sealdseng.strikingly.com/.
A platform for students to support the freedom and democracy campaigns of the SHIELDS movement.
Hong Kong Free Press, www.hongkongfp.com/.
Independent, non-profit Hong Kong-focused news and commentary.
New Bloom, http://newbloommag.net/.
This is an online bilingual magazine covering activism and youth politics in Taiwan and the Asia Pacific.

References

Beckershoff, André. 2017. The Sunflower Movement: Origins, Structures, and Strategies of Taiwan's Resistance against the "Black Box." In *Taiwan's Social Movements under Ma Ying-Jeou*. Dafydd Fell, ed. Pp. 113–133. London and New York: Routledge.

Bradsher, Keith, and Austin Ramzy. 2014. Taiwan Leader Stresses Support for Hong Kong Protests. *New York Times*, November 1.

Branigan, Tania, and David Batty. 2014. Hong Kong Legislator Says Government Using Triads against Protesters. *Guardian*, October 4.

Chan, Johannes. 2014. Hong Kong's Umbrella Movement. *The Round Table: The Commonwealth Journal of International Affairs* 103(6): 571–580.

Chan, Kin-man. 2016. Occupying Hong Kong. *Sur Journal* 12(21).

Cole, J. Michael. 2015. *Black Island: Two Years of Activism in Taiwan: Essays from the Frontlines*. Seattle, WA: CreateSpace Independent Publishing Platform.

Harrison, Mark. 2012. The Anti-Media Monopoly Movement 反媒體壟斷運動 in Taiwan. *The China Story*, December 20. Electronic document, www.thechinastory.org/2012/12/the-anti-media-monopoly-movement-反媒體壟斷運動-in-taiwan/, accessed March 10, 2017.

Ho, Ming-sho. 2010. Understanding the Trajectory of Social Movements in Taiwan (1980–2010). *Journal of Current Chinese Affairs* 39(3): 3–22.

Ho, Ming-sho. 2014a. The Fukushima Effect: Explaining the Resurgence of the Anti-Nuclear Movement in Taiwan. *Environmental Politics* 23(6): 965–983.

Ho, Ming-sho. 2014b. The Resurgence of Social Movement under the Ma Ying-Jeou Government: A Political Opportunity Structure. In *Political Changes in Taiwan under Ma Ying-Jeou*. Jacques deLisle and Jean-Pierre Cabestan, eds. Pp. 100–119. New York and London: Routledge.

Ip, Regina. 2014. How Hong Kong Can Best Counter Pernicious External Influences. *South China Morning Post*, November 23.

Japanese Cabinet Office. 2015. Toward an Alliance of Hope. *Address to a Joint Meeting of the US Congress by Prime Minister Shinzo Abe, April 29, 2015*. Electronic document, http://japan.kantei.go.jp/97_abe/statement/201504/uscongress.html, accessed March 10, 2017.

Kikuchi, Daisuke. 2016. SEALDs to Disband but Founder Says Political Activism Just Beginning. *Japan Times*, August 14.

Kingston, Jeff. 2015. SEALDs : Students Slam Abe's Assault on Japan's Constitution. *The Asia-Pacific Journal* 13 36(1).

Liu, Zhongxuan, and Shih-Diing Lin. 2016. Occupation as Prefiguration? The Emergence of a New Political Form in the Occupy Central Movement. *Contemporary Chinese Political Economy and Strategic Relations: An International Journal* 2(2): 775–794.

Morris, Paul, and Edward Vickers. 2015. Schooling, Politics and the Construction of Identity in Hong Kong: The 2012 "Moral and National Education" Crisis in Historical Context. *Comparative Education* May 2015: 1–22.

O'Day, Robin. 2015. Differentiating SEALDs from Freeters, and Precariats: The Politics of Youth Movements in Contemporary Japan. *The Asia-Pacific Journal* 13 37(2).

Rowen, Ian. 2015. Inside Taiwan's Sunflower Movement: Twenty-Four Days in a Student-Occupied Parliament, and the Future of the Region. *The Journal of Asian Studies* 74(1): 1–15.

Rowen, Ian. 2016. The Geopolitics of Tourism: Mobilities, Territory and Protest in China, Taiwan, and Hong Kong. *Annals of the American Association of Geographers* 106(2): 385–393.

Slater, David, Robin O'Day, Satsuki Uno, Love Kindstrand, and Chiharu Takano. 2015. SEALDs (Students Emergency Action for Liberal Democracy): Research Note on Contemporary Youth Politics in Japan. *The Asia-Pacific Journal* 13 37(1).

Veg, Sebastian. 2015. Legalistic and Utopian: Hong Kong's Umbrella Movement. *New Left Review* 92: 55–73.

Wright, Teresa. 1999. Student Mobilization in Taiwan: Civil Society and Its Discontents. *Asian Survey* 39(6): 986–1008.

33

MIGRATION

Daniel Kremers and Stefan Rother

We are living in an "Age of Migration" (Castles and Miller 2014). Economic disparities, combined with better and more affordable mobility and communication opportunities, have led to an increase in movements within and across borders. As elsewhere in the world, migration flows in Asia are highly complex, and often, temporary or circular in nature. A migrant in Asia might be an internal Chinese migrant moving to the big city, a Vietnamese marriage migrant to Taiwan, or an undocumented Indonesian plantation worker in Malaysia. Thus, it is very hard to find common characteristics, with one notable exception—migrants, particularly in the so-called *low-skilled* sector, rarely have a lobby or significant government support in their countries of destination. They also, naturally, cannot look to their countries of origin for support, since bad governance there might have been the reason why they had left in the first place.

This gap in support can be filled by civil society actors, including various non-governmental organizations (NGOs), labor unions, church groups, and individual citizens, that provide services or advocacy—sometimes accompanied or induced by political activism of migrants themselves. The focus of this chapter is on civil society organizations that support, organize, represent, or advocate for cross-border migrant workers. Our main case studies are from Japan and Hong Kong, which we compare with other destinations in East Asia. We are pointing out the differences in the backgrounds of these organizations but also observe emerging similarities when it comes to transnational migrant advocacy.

Large-scale international migration in Asia is a relatively new phenomenon that is closely linked to the emergence of nation states; and in Asia, the majority of nation states are a product of decolonization in the second half of the twentieth century. Though post-colonial migration out of Asia began in the late 1960s, it was not until the 1980s that Asia became a region of significant international migration. This is why post-war industrialization in Japan, Taiwan, and the Republic of Korea (ROK) happened without large-scale international labor migration (Chiavacci 2011: 87). However, urban economies lacking a rural work force, such as Singapore and Hong Kong, depended on international migrants much earlier (Athukorala 2006: 33–34; Chiavacci 2011: 87–88).

Several violent events, such as wars in Vietnam, Cambodia, and Laos, ethnic and religious conflicts, political oppression and persecution, natural disasters, and social inequality have *pushed* people from their home countries to seek peace and livelihood somewhere else. Meanwhile, in the 1960s, the USA, Canada, and Australia gave up their anti-Asian immigration policies, which resulted in a sharp increase of migration out of Asia and toward these destinations (Chiavacci 2011: 88). Furthermore, globalized markets and monetary flows resulting in increased international, socio-economic inequality, and mobility have *pulled* migrants toward the faster industrializing sub-centers of Asia.

Asian governments have, in general, engaged in very restrictive immigration policies that became known as the "East Asian model." Only migrants with certain qualifications were legally permitted to engage in work temporarily. This resulted in social exclusion of the majority of migrant workers. Rather than coordinated policies, it was mostly socio-economic, push-and-pull factors[1] that fostered international migration in East Asia (Chiavacci 2011: 91). As a result, labor migration is often temporary, contract-based, and into so-called "low-skilled" jobs with no option of obtaining the right to abode, even in the case of long-term, repeated migration. Some migrant workers, like trainees in Japan and South Korea, and domestic workers in Singapore, have been excluded from labor laws. Migrant domestic workers—almost exclusively female—are a particularly restricted group since their work is often not considered *work*, and thus, lack standards and protection. Hiring is often through agencies—the "migration industry"—which are often insufficiently regulated and accused of exploitative practices such as underpayment and overcharging (Rother and Piper 2015: 42). In light of the high fees extracted by private and government actors and an often-bureaucratic process, it might seem an almost rational choice for migrants to cross the border undocumented or seek employment illegally outside the job assigned to them. This further increases the risk of abuse and exploitation by employers—and sometimes also the governments of the destination countries.

Prominent labor migration destinations in Asia today are Malaysia, Hong Kong, the Republic of Korea (ROK), Taiwan, and Japan. Prominent countries of origin are Bangladesh, Cambodia, China, Indonesia, Myanmar, Nepal, the Philippines, and Vietnam.[2] Besides these, because of its size, the People's Republic of China (PRC) displays an internal labor migration that most likely outnumbers international migration in East Asia. However different these countries might be, similar patterns can be seen in labor migration policies, and in the way that civil society has reacted.

Civil society and migration

The relationship between migration and civil society can be studied from a variety of viewpoints and with numerous questions of interest. We will be focusing on representation and advocacy for migrant workers in East Asia. Construing a path-dependent model of migration-related civil society, our analysis tries to answer the following questions: (1) How have the economy and policies shaped migration patterns?; (2) How have migrants shaped and transnationalized the civil societies in their respective countries of origin and destination?; and (3) How has a transnationalized civil society influenced immigration policies? We understand civil society, broadly, as a set of actors, institutions, and practices within a complex community (e.g., a nation state) through which opinions, norms, and values are formulated and are put into practice without coercion, that is, without the threat of legal sanctions (cf. Buttigieg 2005).

Forms of migrant interest organizations, networks, and alliances

When looking at an NGO, the first crucial differentiation to make is whether it is an organization that provides services and support to individuals, or an organization whose main activity is representation, raising awareness, or political influence. We will refer to the first spectrum of activities as *migrant support* and to the second as *migrant advocacy* (cf. Reimann 2010: 12). Another important variety of migrant support and advocacy is whether it is initiated and carried out by citizens of the destination country or the result of migrants' self-organization. Concerning the outreach of organizations, we differentiate between local, national, and transnational organizations.

Our categorization of civil society organizations combines models from three previous studies on the topic, by Natalia Banulescu-Bogdan (2011), Daniel Kremers (2014), and Apichai Shipper (2006). Studying the role of civil society in the European Union's (EU) migration policy, Banulescu-Bogdan, has chosen five categories: "service provision, advocacy, policy formulation, implementation and monitoring, umbrella groups" (Banulescu-Bogdan 2011: 4). These categorizations do not seem to be sufficiently practical, as we understand "policy formulation" and "monitoring" as aspects of advocacy, and we also find organizations engaging in advocacy to be "umbrella groups."

Looking at the scene in Japan, Kremers (2014) and Shipper (2006) have developed more detailed categories. In a study for the *Japan Institute of Labor Policy and Training* (JILPT), Shipper conducted a survey on "immigrant rights NGOs" in Japan and came up with six categories: Christian NGOs, unions, women's support groups, medical NGOs, lawyer support groups, and concerned citizen groups (Shipper 2006: 47–52). In a study on the political influence of migrant interest organizations (MIOs), Kremers differentiated between nationality based organizations (NBO), local resident organizations (LRO), migrant support organizations (MSO), cause lawyering organizations (CLO), and migrant advocacy organizations (MAO) (Kremers 2014: 728).

The outlook of MIO differs considerably whether these are based in countries of origin or destination. This is because, in destination countries, MIOs are not only affected by political regulations regarding associations, but more so, they are preconditioned by the effects of national immigration policies on the immigrant population. In countries whose policies have recently, or in the past, preferred a single nationality of migrants, it is more likely to find strong migrant interest organizations formed along the lines of nationality. In countries that rely on immigration in feminized jobs such as in food production, the textile industry, as well as domestic services, care, and sex work, there is a stronger presence of organizations focusing on the rights and interests of migrant women. Countries that focus on temporary migration in manufacturing, construction, and farm work display a tendency to develop migrant interest organizations that have strong ties with unions and a labor movement background. Finally, the religious orientation of a country's demographic has an impact on how migrants are received and what kind of civil society organizations prosper. Approaching civil society from the viewpoint of migration, thus, makes it necessary to also consider the effects that ethnicity, beliefs, gender, and class have on civil society.

However, there is no country with a migration policy that prefers migrants of only one ethnicity, gender, and class, and therefore, we find similar MIOs in many countries, although with a difference in density, size, and outreach. Another effect that we can observe is that, through transnational networks and learning effects, migrant interest organizations either transform from support organizations into advocacy organizations or unite and form umbrellas that specialize in networking and advocacy. This is why, in the course of forty years of continuing international migration in Asia, migrant organizations in different countries start to display similar characteristics, which can further contribute to the emergence of networks and processes of learning and diffusion. The current stage of development is characterized by the presence of transnational advocacy organizations, networks, and alliances, which unite migrant workers and activists from various backgrounds and nationalities, and have started to address, inform, pressure, and cooperate with national governments and international organizations.

The research on civil society in the context of migration

While "only a small body of studies […] takes migrant rights activism as the starting point with civil society," migrant support and advocacy organizations have been a prominent topic of research on international migration (Rother and Piper 2015: 36). Three major approaches have been observed: "(1) a microsociological approach focusing on group formation and local impacts, (2) a micropolitical approach interested in intragroup democratization and empowerment and (3) a macropolitical approach testing the impact of migrant interest organizations on policy making" (Kremers 2014: 720).[3] The following overview on previous studies is structured by focus on local support for migrants, advocacy, self-organization, and transnationalization—though these fields often overlap or are in a process of development from one stage to another.

From support to advocacy for migrants—the local and national level

One of the first Asian countries to be studied as a migration destination was Japan, and as civil society organizations supporting migrants have formed on the local level, this is also where research started (Herbert 1996; Komai 1993; Nimura 1992). These works, especially that of Komai, are characterized by a criticism of the role and attitude of the national government, employers, and the majority of the Japanese public, and a sympathetic view for MSOs, nonetheless, with a pessimistic outlook on their political impact. This changed by the late 1990s. In 2000, Glenda Roberts observed that activists in local unions and women's shelters had become "knowledgeable in working the system" and had built networks to "lobby the national government" (Roberts 2000: 294–295).

Nevertheless, research was struggling to understand these newly formed organizations. One author labeled them "support activity groups" (*shien katsudō dantai*), while others highlighted their networking activities (Takao 2003: 551; Tsukada 2001: 139). Masataka Okamoto even coined the term "network-movement" (Okamoto 2004: 203). While Roberts and Takao already hinted at the micropolitics of these organizations, this becomes more prominent in the works of Apichai Shipper, who was interested in their potential for deliberative democracy, and Jennifer Chan, who also observed global citizenship education within some of these groups (Chan 2008; Shipper 2008).

However, the majority of studies focused on the local aspects of civil society when discussing international migration. Important questions in this field are voting rights and local citizenship (Han 2004; Harada 2004; Itoi 2004; Kim 1994; Minegishi 2004), long-term residence, denizenship, social integration, and naturalization (Du 2015; Kempka 2012; Morris-Suzuki 2010), as well as identity, culture, ethnicity, and experiences of discrimination, xenophobia, and racism (Arudou 2015). In the Japanese case, this strand of research focuses mainly on migrant settlers, for example the North and South Korean minorities (*zainichi chōsenjin kankokujin*), and immigrants of Japanese ancestries (the so-called *Nikkeijin*) or mixed-nationality couples and their children.

Just like in Japan, in other countries, migrant support often starts from the local level. Vipul Mudgal has investigated the formation and activity of Ajeevika, an organization that supports seasonal migrant workers in India (Mugdal 2016). NGOs supporting migrant workers in China were discussed in John Tai's study on civil society in the PRC (Tai 2015).

Since migrants are not allowed to form their own political associations in Singapore, they rely on support networks such as Transient Workers Count Too (TWC2) and the Humanitarian Organization for Migration Economics (HOME) that perform their humanitarian work within an illiberal political terrain (Yee 2009). These alliances can reach beyond the support of "concerned citizens": Nicola Piper has pointed out that despite government repression in Singapore and Malaysia, migrant workers were "reinvigorating the labor movement," but that levels of organization varied depending on job type and nationality. Unlike in Hong Kong, and similar to Japan and ROK, migrant workers did not organize by themselves but had received support and advocacy from local NGOs and national trade unions such as the Singapore National Trade Union Congress (SNTUC) and Malaysian Trade Union Council MTUC (Piper 2006: 376–377). The link between trade unions, NGOs, and migrant labor has also been explored by Michele Ford as "organizing the unorganizable" (Ford 2004). In South Korea, NGOs and unions have played an important role in supporting and organizing migrant workers as well as in protesting and abolishing the Industrial Training System (ITS) (Lee 2015; Lim 2006: 245; Park 2008: 10).

In Japan, since the late 1990s, local MSOs have established national networks that seek to connect with international partners and lobby the government. Gabriele Vogt and Christoph Lersch observed that: "most migrant support organizations" are service providers that act locally, except for the *Solidarity Network with Migrants Japan* (SMJ), which they describe as an "informal network" and "one of the largest migrant support organizations in Japan" (Vogt and Lersch 2007: 265, 277). Ryoko Yamamoto pointed out that SMJ was a national umbrella of local NGOs (Yamamoto 2010). Migrant advocacy had, by the late 2000s, achieved only minor political success, for example, in promoting stricter anti-trafficking regulations and in individual amnesties for migrant families without legal status (Chiavacci 2011: 192). Thus, authors tried to explain its lack of influence. Erin Aeran Chung argued that: "pro-immigrant advocacy in Japan" had "failed to generate structural reforms regarding migrant labour rights" because of the dominance of Korean permanent residents' interest groups, a conservative ruling party, the lack of mass mobilization, and an emphasis on local citizenship (Chung 2010: 677, 688). David Chiavacci, on the other hand, came to the conclusion that an "ideological fragmentation" of political institutions concerning immigration had curbed the influence of "civil society" (Chiavacci 2011: 192, 275).

Comparing the rights of migrants in Malaysia and Spain, Blanca Garcés-Mascareñas concluded that while, in Spain, "civil society and the opposition parties have played a highly significant role in the legal inclusion of immigrants," this was not the case in Malaysia, where migrants' rights were even less robust than in Europe (Garcés-Mascareñas 2012: 186). On the other hand, Nana Oishi acknowledged that civil society organizations have improved the situations for female migrants in several Asian countries, such as the Philippines, where they pressured the government to "repeal the ban on the emigration of domestic workers" (2005). Oishi also pointed out that transnational migrant advocacy can be difficult because labor and migrants' rights do not rank very high on the agenda of civil society and philanthropists in rich nation states, which are the source of financial support for many of the civil society organizations active in poor countries. That was why, in Bangladesh, another emigration country with a strong civil society, the "majority of its NGOs do not work on migration issues because those issues do not appear on the radar of western donors" (Oishi 2005: 172).

Transnationalization and advocacy beyond the local and national level

Even if the focus of support groups is at the local or national level, they often have to reach out beyond the nation state in order to further their advocacy. Migrant advocacy in Japan has become better organized and more influential than previous studies have suggested. Apichai Shipper has observed close cooperation between local governments and NGOs in offering service and support for migrants (Shipper 2011: 546). Furthermore, MAOs emerging as networks of local support groups have used transnational networks of human rights organizations, the UN, and the US government to pressure the Japanese government for immigration reforms that protect migrants' rights (Kremers 2014; Shipper 2011).

However, migrant self-organization is also often transnational in outlook, particularly when it brings together temporary, contract-based migrants. Nicola Piper sees this activism as the source of "political remittances" and argues that: "taking a transnational perspective that links origin and destination countries is paramount, as the [...] issues these contract migrants face occur at both 'ends' of the migration journey, often simultaneously" (Piper 2009: 215). In a case study on migrant organizations formed by migrant domestic workers in Hong Kong, Stefan Rother has argued that these operate in "transnational political space," linking not only the countries of origin and destination, but also bringing together migrants from different origins for advocacy work (Rother 2009). Hong Kong has probably received the most scholarly attention on migrant organizing due to the density of organizations and networks there (cf. Hsia 2009; Wee and Sim 2004).

This political space can be created not only horizontally, but also vertically, reaching up to the regional level. The spreading of digital communication technologies led Lisa Law (2003) to observe "transnational cyberpublics" created by the media activism of the Migrant Forum in Asia (MFA), an umbrella organization or network of networks based in Manila (cf. Piper and Rother 2011).

Most of the literature on migration in Asia has used a state-centric and top-down perspective, discussing how states can "manage" migration (cf. Chanda and Gopalan 2011). This ignores the fact that, for well over a decade, the MFA has employed a multilevel approach to promoting Asian workers' rights (Alcid 2004). In the case of the Association of Southeast Asian Nations (ASEAN), Rother and Piper (2015) argue that such civil society interactions on the regional level can be a building block for "alternative regionalism from below." Furthermore, civil society organizes around migration issues in countries of origin. Looking at a region of out-migration, Azis (2015) has attributed three main functions of civil society organizations (CSOs) in Indonesia: services for migrants such as assistance, information, and training often carried out by labor unions; advocacy; and research, adding that organizing migrants was rather difficult (Azis 2015: 112). Indonesia is also an example for the organizing of migrant families at the local level (Ford and Susilo 2010).

Case studies from two migrant destinations in East Asia: Hong Kong and Japan

In this section, we will review the different origins and processes of transnationalization of MIOs in Hong Kong and Japan. We believe that these two destinations make for a good comparison due to the scope of activism and the composition of migrant groups. Overseas Filipino Workers (OFW) and Indonesian-based NGOs are prominent in Hong Kong, and civic activism rooted in Korean and Chinese minorities as well as in Catholicism and the labor movement characterizes migration and civil society in Japan.

Migrant interest organizations in Japan: from local support to transnational advocacy

In Japan, MIOs are mostly organized by Japanese citizens and have their roots in the labor movement or Christian belief. The most prominent migrant populations are the Korean minorities that have lived in Japan since its colonial encroachment on Asia, migrants of Japanese descent (or so-called *Nikkeijin*) from Brazil and other Latin American countries that started to settle in Japan from the late 1980s, as well as temporary migrant workers from Asia, mostly the PRC, Vietnam, Cambodia, Indonesia, and the Philippines, whose numbers have grown significantly since the second half of the 1990s. Several CSOs have tried to represent and organize these migrants. The post-war era has seen two large opposing Korean organizations in Japan, the *Mindan*, representing South Korea and *Chōsen Sōren*, representing North Korea (Shipper 2008: 62). Shipper argued that, far from promoting social integration, these organizations have tried to uphold the migrants' ties to their country of nationality by cultivating "long distance nationalism" (Shipper 2008: 59).

Foreign nationals with Japanese family backgrounds are privileged when it comes to immigration, but their legal and social status in Japan is often precarious. According to the Immigration Bureau of Japan (IBJ), their number decreased from over 500,000 in 2006 to *circa* 300,000 in 2014 (IBJ 2015).[4] Since 1991, they can prolong their visas and receive a default work permit in Japan. Most of them work in the automotive industries, and though many have become permanent residents, their degree of social integration and upward mobility is low, the working environment is unstable, and their incomes are small. They also have not developed huge interest groups. Their interests are sometimes represented by Christian organizations or local labor unions (Roberts 2000: 278). Another set of residence permissions that gave rise to the number of temporary workers in Japan were *training* and *designated activities*, which, until 2009, were mainly used for the Industrial Training and Internship Program (IT-TIP), as well as *entertainment*, which became widely used by migrant women engaging in adult entertainment and sex work.

While most MSOs in Japan are run by Japanese citizens, few are based on migrant self-help. One such exemption is Kalakasan (Tagalog for "strength") Migrant Women Empowerment Center in Kawasaki, which was founded in 2002 by Philippine women to support victims of domestic violence in mixed nationality couples (Tolentino 2008: 21). But already in the early 1990s, the change in the composition of the workforce has been recognized by Japanese labor activists. In 1992, the Zentōitsu Workers Union (ZWU), a small union for workers in small- and medium-sized enterprises (SME) in Tokyo, reacted by establishing a section for migrant workers (Roberts 2000). Initially, the ZWU cooperated with other unions such as the Tokyo Nambu FWC, a subsection of another local union that mainly organizes foreign English teachers, and the Kanagawa City Union, a local union with many Korean and Latin American members (Roberts 2000). During the 1990s, they gradually expanded their cooperation to women's shelters, offering help to migrant women and other NGOs concerned with migrant rights all over Japan. In 1997, the ZWU joined with 200 members of several migrant interest organizations, such as the women's shelter House of Emergency in Love and Peace (HELP), *Karabao no kai* (or Kalabaw, Tagalog for "water buffalo"), and *Arusu no Kai*, at the second migrant workers issue forum in Aichi, to establish the Solidarity Network With Migrants Japan (SMJ)[5] (SMJ 2014). The same year, the organization submitted its first set of demands to the Japanese Ministry of Labor (SMJ 2006: 187). While working as an organization without legal form for most of its activity, in October 2015, the SMJ finally became legally incorporated as a Specified Non-Profit Activity Corporation (confirmed through participant observation by the authors). It is an advocacy organization that also acts as an umbrella and information hub for *circa* 100 local groups and organizations from all over Japan.

Amongst the fourteen residence permissions that the Japanese government designated for the "purpose of labor" in 2004, the second most frequently used was *entertainment* (*kōgyō*), with 64,742 registered migrant residents. Looking only at immigration, it accounted for 80 percent (134,859) of all entries to Japan for the purpose of work that year. From 2005, this number decreased significantly (IBJ 2015). This change can be attributed to transnational campaigning by the SMJ (cf. Chiavacci 2011: 254).

The entertainment visa is given to foreigners seeking income in the entertainment sector (music, dance, sport, etc.) in Japan. More than 80 percent of the migrant entertainers are women from the Philippines (IBJ 2015). Japan displays a vibrant sex industry, mainly catering to hetero-sexual men, and many migrants are engaging in sex work as hostesses, dancers, and masseuses (Chiavacci 2011: 92; Roberts 2000: 294). A number of young women, though, were lured to Japan by criminals who forced them into sexual servitude through debt bondage and physical violence (Roberts 2000: 296). As prostitution is not covered by the work permit related to the entertainment visa, foreign women offering sexual services are engaging in *illegal work*. Thus, even though there were victims of trafficking amongst them, they were prosecuted by the Police and Immigration Control, which increased their vulnerability and dependency on pimps and traffickers. To support these migrant women, Japanese Christian and feminist organizations established shelters (Roberts 2000: 284).

In September 2000, the international NGO Human Rights Watch (HRW) published an extensive survey on debt bondage and trafficking of migrant women in Japan (HRW 2000). The report was mainly based on information gathered by Japanese MSOs such as *Mizura*, HELP, Kalabaw, Immigration Review Task Force, Japan Civil Liberties Union (JCLU), the YWCA in Kyoto, and Minatomachi Medical Clinic—some of these being SMJ member organizations (HRW 2000). HRW demanded the Japanese government to sign several human rights cove-nants and end the criminalization of foreign sex workers and trafficking victims by reforming its immigration and penal codes (HRW 2000). In 2002, the SMJ demanded to protect the rights of migrants in gastronomy and sex work under the labor laws, regardless of the residence per-mission, and asked the government to prosecute traffickers and prostitution managers of migrant women and children. At the same time, the organization proposed a system of medical and psychological services for victims in Japan (SMJ 2002). In October, MSOs founded a single-issue-advocacy-organization for trafficking victims, named Japan Network Against Trafficking in Persons (JNATIP) (Chiavacci 2011: 255; Shipper 2011: 542).

Two years later, diplomatic pressure from the US government increased. The US Depart-ment of State (DOS) put Japan on the watch list of its *Trafficking in Persons Report* (DOS 2004: 28). The responsible diplomat, John R. Miller, had consulted Japanese NGOs (Chiavacci 2011: 256; Shipper 2011: 541). The Japanese government reacted immediately. In April, the Cabinet Secretariat (CAS) established a desk against human trafficking, and in December, the govern-ment announced concrete measures (CAS 2009; cf. ILO 2005). One measure was to monitor the issuing of the entertainment visa more strictly. As a result, entries of entertainers decreased by 50 percent between 2004 and 2006. However, the government did not comply with most of the other measures that had been proposed by the SMJ. Other residence permissions, such as spouse visas, can also be used for bringing sex workers to Japan (Cameron and Newman 2002: 6). Thus, migrant sex workers and trafficking victims are still lacking fundamental legal protec-tion and support. Their vulnerability has recently been taken advantage of by the international evangelical group Not For Sale, who, under the pretense of protecting trafficking victims, is recruiting members for its cult.

Another partial success was achieved by Japanese MAOs, who demanded an abolition of temporary labor migration in the form of training and internship programs. In 1993, the Immi-gration Control and Refugee Recognition Act (ICRRA) was amended to allow migrants, who had completed a one-year Industrial Training Program (ITP) in Japan, to stay and work in the same company for another year as technical interns. In 1997, the ITP was expanded to two years. Thus, the consecutive programs allowed for three years of work in Japan: the first year as trainees without work permit and worker rights, and the second and third years as formal workers (Kremers 2014). The program was reformed in 2009 and expanded to a maximum of five years in 2017.

Following the recession of the early 1990s, there was a high demand for labor in small- and medium-sized enterprises (SME), especially in Japan's semi-urban periphery, where the Japanese had left and where few migrants went to seek employment. Not being free to choose their site of occupation, program participants were dispatched in large numbers to these SME, which form the backbone of Japan's domestic, industrial supply chain. The number of migrant trainees and interns rose from *circa* 47,000 in 1998 to *circa* 200,000 in 2008. In 2014, 167,626 foreign interns were registered, and another 99,157 entered Japan in 2015 (IBJ 2015; MOJ 2016). In 2015, 66 percent of migrant interns came from the PRC, where labor dispatch businesses worked closely with Japanese employers, 16 percent were from Vietnam, and 7 percent were from Indonesia and the Philippines. Others came from Thailand, Cambodia, Nepal, Laos, and other Asian countries—as participation is limited to those nationalities that receive official development assistance (ODA) from Japan. Most of the trainees worked in machinery and metal manufacturing, textiles, agriculture, food processing, and construction (JITCO 2015).

During the years prior to revision of the ICRRA in 2009, the IT-TIP became a scandal-tainted and contested human rights issue for Japanese MAO (Kremers 2014). Due to insufficient legal protection, their lack of knowledge of Japanese laws, the dire situation of SMEs, and supervisors that encouraged migrants to follow any order given at the job, trainees and interns suffered serious human rights abuses, in some cases resulting in accidents, deaths, and suicides. Participants also found themselves in a double bind, as many of them had taken loans to pay the brokers who arranged for their internship in Japan, where they realized they could not make enough money to pay back their debt. Thus, a small number of trainees left their companies to illegally seek better conditions elsewhere. Meanwhile, Japanese employers tried to restrict their freedom of movement further, by confiscating passports and cell phones (GKMN 2006; Kremers 2014).

In reaction, members of the SMJ set up a single-issue advocacy organization called Advocacy Network for Foreign Trainees (GKMN), through which they published several books and informed the media and foreign governments (GKMN 2000; GKMN 2006; SMJ 2006). This way the organization was able to contribute to a public opinion that was more aware and critical of the program (Kremers 2014: 725; Shipper 2011: 545). In due course, the Ministry of Justice (MOJ) and the Ministry of Health, Labor and Welfare (MHLW), backed by large labor union federations as well as the members of large political parties such as LDP and DPJ, began to propose reforms to the program (Kremers 2014: 726). By 2007, the only actors unambiguously supporting the program and even demanding its expansion were the Ministry of Economy, Trade and Industry (METI) and the large employer interest organizations, *Nippon Keidanren* and the Japanese Chamber of Commerce and Industry (JCCI) (Kremers 2014: 740).

Meanwhile, the US government started to pay more attention to human trafficking for labor purposes unrelated to the sex industry. Thus, Japanese migrant interest organizations managed to get their reports on human rights violations within the IT-TIP to be mentioned in the DOS's reports from 2007 onward, linking the program to "forced labor" (DOS 2007: 124). As a result, in 2009, the program was reformed to grant the protection of labor laws—including minimum wages—to migrant participants from the first year on (Kremers 2014: 726). Since then, however, reconstruction in the areas struck by the tsunami of March 2011 and preparations for the Olympic games in Tokyo in 2020 have spurred the demand for labor, especially in the construction sector. The government thus decided to expand the program to a maximum of five years to supply the domestic manufacturing and construction sector with temporary workhands (Kremers 2014: 741).

In both campaigns described here, Japanese NGOs went to the US government in order to increase the pressure on their own government. They were thus able to initiate "boomerang patterns" by reaching out to "transnational advocacy networks" (Keck and Sikkink 1998: 13; Vogt and Lersch 2007: 269). The role played by the US government in Japan's immigration policies on the other hand resembles what Salvatore Babones called "monitory empire" (Babones 2014). A very similar migration scheme existed in South Korea between 1991 and 2007. Here too, labor conditions were bad, human rights violations occurred, migrants fled their jobs, and NGOs and labor unions such as JCMK, MTU, and KCTU started to support and organize migrant workers and launched protests. This resulted in the internship program to be abolished and replaced with an employment permit system (EPS) (Lee 2015; Lim 2006). Interestingly however, this was achieved without the US government or international organizations ever paying attention to Korea's program. This can be explained by a lack of pro-program interest groups within Korea. While, in Korea, the program was supervised by an existing agency, the Small and Medium Business Administration (SMBA), in Japan, the government, together with interest groups, established a foundation named Japan International Training Cooperation Organization (JITCO) with the sole purpose of promoting and supervising the program (Hurights Osaka 2007; Kremers 2014). Thus, vested interest became institutionally linked to the program, making it harder to abolish.

Hong Kong—a hot spot for transnational migrant activism

In the research on migrant activism and advocacy, Hong Kong has gained particular prominence, and for good reason. The Special Administrative Region has been the nucleus of the formation of transethnic-transnational, regional, and global migrant civil society organizations. There are numerous support groups, such as Friends of Domestic Helpers (FDH), who offer legal support, and faith-based organizations such as Christian Action. However, the most remarkable characteristic of Hong Kong is the large degree of migrant self-organizing in a sector that is seen as particularly vulnerable: domestic work.

Hong Kong households started hiring "foreign domestic helpers" in the 1970s, when married women and mothers increasingly joined the workforce and local *amah* (Chinese for domestic servants) were hard to come by and were considered too dominant by younger couples (Constable 2007). These so-called *maids*[6] were mostly recruited from the Philippines, due to its geographic proximity, high level of English proficiency, and a strong surplus in the labor workforce of their country, which initiated its labor export program at that time. While they may have lived up to the gendered image of being caring and emphatic, the Filipinas brought with them also another quality: experience in organizing. During the 1970s, the mass movement against the Philippine dictator Ferdinand Marcos began to form across the country and, in particular, on university campuses. Since the comparatively good payment in Hong Kong and poor job prospects back home attracted university graduates to seek employment as domestic workers in Hong Kong, they applied their organizing strategies to the new settings as well and started to form organizations. The granting of certain liberties, such as freedom of organization, by the colonial administration made these formations possible, unlike, for example, in Singapore, where migrant domestic workers are, until today, banned from forming any kind of advocacy organization.

Its first success came in the early 1980s, when the Marcos administration announced plans to force migrants to send at least half of their remittances through Philippine banks back to the country. As a result, a loose alliance—the United Filipinos Against Forced Remittances (UNFARE)—was formed and started to protest on Sundays (their one day off) at Statue Square, in front of the Philippine consulate. Their advocacy work led to the plans being scratched, and as a result, the United Filipinos in Hong Kong network (UNIFIL-HK) was formed. It still exists, and is closely connected to organizations such as Migrante International, a "global alliance of overseas Filipinos and their families," which was founded in 1996, as a reaction to the execution of the Philippine domestic worker, Flor Contemplacion, in Singapore, with the goal to defend the rights and welfare of OFWs. Church-based groups such as the Mission for Filipino Migrant Workers (now renamed Mission for Migrant Workers) also played an important supportive role and provided office space and logistics.

The advocacy work, thus, was transnational right from the beginning, targeting the Philippine government and its ongoing labor export policy, while advocating for better working conditions in Hong Kong and blaming and shaming exploitative recruitment agencies. In the 1990s, in cooperation with the independent Hong Kong Central Trade Union (HKCTU), the first migrant domestic worker unions were started.

Filipinas, thus, were an already well-established group when the number of Indonesian migrant domestic workers started to rise dramatically, from almost zero to more than 150,000, from the mid-1990s. The Filipinos' success in organizing may, in fact, have been one explanation for the increasing recruitment of Indonesians, who were marketed as being more docile, and thus, easier to exploit. Underpayment and overcharging were rampant amongst Indonesians and the mandatory day off was rarely granted. Their response lay in organizing—with more than just a little help from the Filipinas. When the Indonesian domestic worker, Eni Lestari, ran away from the unbearable circumstances of her employer's family, she found refuge in a Filipina-run shelter. There, she was politicized and received training and support in organizing (Rother 2017).

As a result, she formed issue-based Indonesian organizations such as United Indonesians Against Overcharging (PILAR) that conducted research and advocacy, and the Association of Indonesian Migrant Workers (ATKI-HK), which has, by now, branched out to other destinations for Indonesians as well. Lestari later became a spokesperson for a transethnic-transnational alliance, the Asian Migrant Coordinating Body (AMCB), which brings together Indonesian, Philippine, Thai, Sri Lankan, and Nepalese domestic workers. In this function, Eni Lestari spoke at the United Nations Summit for Refugees and Migrants in September 2016 about the plights and rights of migrant workers. In 2008, Hong Kong was also the founding place of the International Migrants Alliance (IMA).

Thus, Hong Kong can be seen as the basis for a truly multilevel civil society engagement for migrant rights. However, there is also a deep ideological divide amongst migrant organizations that can be traced back to a split in the Philippines left after the fall of Marcos, which also split the Hong Kong organizers into two camps. This has resulted in many splits and changed allegiances, particularly in the various migrant unions in the SAR, but also, viewed from a more positive perspective, in a lively and pluralistic civil society landscape. For example, the Migrant Forum in Asia (MFA), the largest network of migrant rights organizations in the region, was founded in Hong Kong before moving to the Philippines. It has also been instrumental in the establishment of a second global migrant's rights umbrella organization, the Global Coalition on Migration (GCM), which was also present during the UN summit, organizing speakers and side events.

Asian, and in particular Southeast Asian, migrant activism has, thus, truly gone global, and activists from the region are very visible in international fora such as the Global Forum on Migration and Development (or protesting against it) and the International Labour Conference of the ILO, where they supported the decent work for domestic workers' convention, C189. In recent years, they have also started to address the regional level, through participation in the

ASEAN Civil Society Conference (ACSC) (Rother and Piper 2015). There are also cross sectoral alliances with organizations working on issues such as women's rights, labor rights, climate change, or the peasant movement.

It must be stated, however, that governments in the region remain very unresponsive to the demands of migrant workers, and even in Hong Kong, many of them remain unfulfilled, such as the abolition of the two-week rule, which grants the migrants only this short period to find employment after a contract has been terminated.

Conclusion

Organizations defending the rights and promoting the interests of migrant workers have played an important role in improving the situation for migrants in Asia through self-organization and self-help, support, education, as well as advocacy and raising awareness. Migrant communities and migration policies are diverse, and so are the organizations representing them. The more industrialized Asian countries have a high demand for highly qualified work, which they often satisfy by trying to attract workers from outside the region. However, there is even more demand for cheap and flexible temporary labor without any prospects of gaining a long-term status. Countries of origin, on the other hand, often promote out-migration, but in the trade-off between remittances and rights, the well-being of their citizens abroad often falls short.

This has left migrants vulnerable to exploitation and human rights violations, and often civil society stepped in to provide migrants with a minimum of social safety and political voice. On the other hand, the lack of protection of migrants makes them an easy target, not just for profit-seeking employers, but also for religious cults and the rescue industry. Victims of trafficking and sexual exploitation easily fall prey to evangelical groups, who are more interested in their moral conformity than in their well-being.

The scope of civil society formation and activity also differs significantly due to different political systems with different levels of civic freedoms in Asia. This has a significant impact on the services they can offer and the political space for their advocacy. Transnational organizing can address these shortcomings. If the government in the destination country is not responsive, migrants might pressure their country of origin and its embassy staff abroad, or they might form trans-sectoral and transnational alliances with trade unions, and women's or broader human rights organizations.

Our two case studies have revealed such processes of transnationalization on various levels. While civil society organizations representing migrant interests in Hong Kong are characterized by a high level of self-organization of migrants of various ethnic backgrounds that have established offices of their organizations in various countries and transnationalized their organization from within, Japan's most active advocacy organization, though actively seeking cooperation and exchange with migrants, is dominated by activists of Japanese nationality. Rather than expanding their presence to the regions of origin of the migrants they represent, these activists have built loose networks with MIOs in other destination regions, such as Korea, while they came in close contact with parts of the national and international media, lawyers, academics, the US Government and the UN.

Our overview has shown that, while transnational networking and activism might be important for many social movements, it is of particular relevance in the case of migrants' rights. For one, the transnational nature of migration subjects migrants to the policies of at least two nation states. While migrant support organizations focus on the situation in the destination, migrant self-organizing often targets both countries with their advocacy. This is also due to the temporary nature of most migration in Asia—since most migrants in low-skilled jobs have to face return, their advocacy focuses less on integration and more on transnational rights. The establishment of very active networks at the regional and global level also adds *vertical spaces* for advocacy, which could be helpful if the local and national levels are unresponsive. In global migrants' rights advocacy, Asian activists have become particularly involved and visible, and their goals can be illustrated by the speech of Hong Kong domestic worker activist Eni Lestari in front of the UN General assembly:

> We have a clear message: listen to us. Don't talk about us without us. You want us to remit but what we need is for you to commit. To justice, to a development that does not tear our families apart, to a future that relies on the strength of its own people and not on the constant export and exploitation of our labor.
>
> *(South–South News 2016)*

Notes

1 In migration research, unfavorable situations in regions of origin that motivate out-migration, such as poverty, inequality, unemployment, epidemics, famine, persecution or war, are referred to as push factors, while favorable conditions in destination areas that attract migrants, such as a demand for labor, higher wages, and peace, are called pull factors (Brettel and Hollifield 2000: 3).
2 In our definition, a destination country can, at the same time, be a country of origin and transit.
3 Macro-sociological migration studies have, so far, shown little interest in civil society and migrant interest organizations.
4 This number refers to foreign nationals registered in Japan as either long-term resident (*teijūsha*) or the child or spouse of Japanese national (*Nihonjin no haigūsha*). A vast majority of them are migrants of Japanese descent.
5 In Japan, the organization is better known by its Japanese name, *Ijūsha to rentai suru zenkoku nettowāku* (Nationwide Network for Solidarity with Migrants) or *Ijūren* for short.
6 Activists refuse the term and use "domestic workers" instead to highlight the aspect that domestic work is indeed work.

Suggested readings

Caballero-Anthony, Mely, and Toshihiro Menju, eds. 2015. *Asia on the Move: Regional Migration and the Role of Civil Society*. Tokyo: Japan Center for International Exchange.

Constable, Nicole. 2007. *Maid to Order in Hong Kong. Stories of Migrant Workers*. 2nd Edn. Ithaca, NY: Cornell University Press.

Fielding, Tony. 2016. *Asian Migrations: Social and Geographical Mobilities in Southeast, East, and Northeast Asia*. Abingdon and New York: Routledge.

Sakanaka, Hidenori. 2014. *Japan as a Nation for Immigrants—A Proposal for a Global Community of Humankind*. Japan Immigration Policy Institute. Electronic document, http://jipi.or.jp/wp-content/uploads/2013/04/20150515.pdf, accessed December 16, 2016.

Solidarity Network with Migrants Japan. 2014. *Solidarity Network with Migrants Japan (SMJ)'s Views on "Panel Report and Recommendations on Technical Intern Training Program (TITP)."* Electronic document, http://migrants.jp/archives/news/20140616policyview, accessed December 16, 2016.

Solidarity Network with Migrants Japan. 2014. *Joint Statement Protesting the Government's Hasty Decision to Introduce "Foreign Human Resources for Domestic Work Support" and Demanding the Ratification of ILO Domestic Workers Convention (C189)*, Electronic document, http://migrants.jp/archives/news/20140627 domestic-work, accessed December 16, 2016.

Solidarity Network with Migrants Japan. 2014. *NGO Report Regarding the Rights of Non-Japanese Nationals, Minorities of Foreign Origins, Migrants, and Refugees in Japan—Prepared for the 111th Session of the Human Rights Committee*. Electronic document, http://tbinternet.ohchr.org/Treaties/CCPR/Shared%20 Documents/JPN/INT_CCPR_CSS_JPN_17462_E.pdf, accessed December 16, 2016.

Websites

Asia-Japan Women's Resource Center, www.ajwrc.org.
An organization working to end gender-oriented violence and discrimination.

Asia-Pacific Migration Network, http://apmigration.ilo.org.
Part of the International Labour Organization, the Asia-Pacific Migration Network is a regional online community providing access to resources and information relating to migration in Asia-Pacific.

Asian Migrant Center (AMC), www.asianmigrantcentre.org.
A regional NGO based in Hong Kong, focusing on promoting human rights and conducting action research relating to protecting the rights of migrants to Asia.

Asia-Pacific Mission for Migrants, www.apmigrants.org.
A non-profit organization founded in 1984, focused on helping those who migrate to other countries.

International Migrants Alliance (IMA), https://wearemigrants.net/about.
A global alliance of organizations of "grassroots migrants, refugees, and displaced peoples."

Japan Immigration Policy Institute, http://jipi.or.jp.
A think-tank led by former immigrant chief Hidenori Sakanaka, emphasizing Japan's need for a revised immigration policy.

Migrant Forum in Asia (MFA), www.mfasia.org.
A regional network of NGOs, trade unions and advocates and organizations dedicated to representing the rights of all migrants in Asia.

Migrante International, https://migranteinternational.org.
A global alliance of Filipino migrants, working to actively defend the rights and welfare of overseas Filipino workers.

Solidarity Network with Migrants Japan, http://migrants.jp.
A network in Japan, dedicated to protecting the rights and welfare of migrants.

US Department of State: *Trafficking in Persons Report Heroes*, www.tipheroes.org.
Required by law under the Trafficking Victims Protection Act, the report provides as assessment of the actions taken by foreign governments to end human trafficking.

References

Alcid, Mary Lou L. 2004. The Multilevel Approach to Promoting Asian Migrant Workers' Rights: The MFA Experience. *International Migration* 42(5): 169–176.

Arudou, Debito. 2015. Japan's Under Researched Visible Minorities: Applying Critical Race Theory to Racialization Dynamics in a Non-White Society. *Washington University Global Studies Law Review* 14: 695–723.

Azis, Avyanthi. 2015. Indonesia and Labor Outmigration: The Role of Civil Society. In *Asia on the Move— Regional Migration and the Role of Civil Society*. Mely Cabalero-Anthony and Toshihiro Menju, eds. Pp. 103–119. Tokyo and New York: Japan Center For International Exchange.

Athukorala, Prema-Chandra. 2006. International Labour Migration in East Asia: Trends, Patterns and Policy Issues. *Asian-Pacific Economic Literature* 20(1): 18–39.

Babones, Salvatore. 2014. From Monitory Democracy to Monitory Empire: Social Movements after Capitalism. *Oriental Institute Journal* 24(2): 62–71.

Banulescu-Bogdan, Natalia. 2011. *The Role of Civil Society in EU Migration Policy: Perspectives on the European Union's Engagement in its Neighborhood*. Washington, DC: Migration Policy Institute.

Brettel, Caroline B., and James F. Hollifield, eds. 2000. *Migration Theory—Talking Across Disciplines*. New York: Routledge.

Buttigieg, Joseph A. 2005. The Contemporary Discourse on Civil Society: A Gramscian Critique. *Boundary 2* 32(1): 33–52.

Cameron, Sally, and Edward Newman. 2002. *Trafficking of Filipino Women to Japan: Examining the Experiences and Perspectives of Victims and Government Experts*. Tokyo: United Nations University. Electronic document, www.unodc.org/pdf/crime/human_trafficking/Exec_summary_UNU.pdf, accessed September 29, 2016.

CAS (Cabinet Secretariat). 2009. Jinshin Torihiki Taisaku ni Kansuru Kankei Shōchō Renraku Kaigi [Conference Connecting Relevant Ministries and Offices on Measures against Human Trafficking].

Electronic document, www.cas.go.jp/jp/seisaku/jinsin/index.html, accessed December 16, 2016 (in Japanese).

Castles, Stephen, and Mark J. Miller. 2014. *The Age of Migration: International Population Movements in the Modern World*. New York: Guilford Press.

Chan, Jennifer. 2008. *Another Japan is Possible: New Social Movements and Global Citizenship Education*. Stanford, CA: Stanford University Press.

Chanda, Rupa and Sasidaran Gopalan. 2011. Managing Migration in Asia: The Role of Interstate Cooperation. In *Migration, Nation States, and International Cooperation*. Hansen Randall, Jobst Koehler, and Jeanette Money, eds. Pp. 170–210. London: Routledge.

Chiavacci, David. 2011. *Japans neue Immigrationspolitik: Ostasiatisches Umfeld, ideelle Diversität und institutionelle Fragmentierung [Japan's New Immigration Policies: East Asian Environment, Ideological Diversity and Institutional Fragmentation]*. Wiesbaden: VS Verlag für Sozialwissenschaften (in German).

Chung, Erin Aeran. 2010. Workers or Residents? Diverging Patterns of Immigrant Incorporation in Korea and Japan. *Pacific Affairs* 83(4): 675–696.

Constable, Nicole. 2007. *Maid to Order in Hong Kong: Stories of Migrant Workers*. Ithaca, NY: Cornell University Press.

DOS (US Department of State). 2004. Trafficking in Persons Report. Electronic document, www.state.gov/j/tip/rls/tiprpt/2004/index.htm, accessed December 16, 2016.

DOS (US Department of State). 2007. Trafficking in Persons Report. Electronic document, www.state.gov/j/tip/rls/tiprpt/2007/index.htm, accessed December 16, 2016.

Du, Guojing. 2015. Spatiotemporal Analysis of Naturalization in Japan. In *International Migrants in Japan*. Yoshitaka Ishikawa, ed. Pp. 74–93. Melbourne: Transpacific Press.

Ford, Michele. 2004. Organizing the Unorganizable—Unions, NGOs, and Indonesian Migrant Labour. *International Migration* 42(5): 99–119.

Ford, Michel, and Wahyu Susilo. 2010. *Organising for Migrant Worker Rights. Inside Indonesia*. Electronic document, www.insideindonesia.org/organising-for-migrant-worker-rights-2, accessed October 1, 2016.

Garcés-Mascareñas, Blanca. 2012. *Labour Migration in Malaysia and Spain—Markets, Citizenship and Rights*. Amsterdam: Amsterdam University Press.

GKMN (Gaikokujin Kenshūsei Mondai Nettowāku), ed. 2000. *Mayakashi no Gaikokujin Kenshū Seido* [The Fraudulent Training Program for Foreigners]. Tokyo: Gendai Jinbunsha (in Japanese).

GKMN (Gaikokujin Kenshūsei Mondai Nettowāku), ed. 2006. *Gaikokujin Kenshūsei: Jikyū 300 en no Rōdōsha—Kowareru Jinken to Rōdō Kijun [Foreign Trainees: Workers for 300 Yen Hourly Wage—Violated Human Rights and Labor Standards]*. Tokyo: Akashi Shoten (in Japanese).

Han, Seung-Mi. 2004. From the Communitarian Ideal to the Public Sphere—The Making of Foreigners' Assemblies in Kawasaki City and Kanagawa Prefecture. *Social Science Japan Journal* 7(1): 41–60.

Harada, Nahomi. 2004. Gaikokujin Shūchū Toshi Hamamatsu ni okeru Chiiki Kyōsei no Tori kumi [Struggling for Living Together Regionally in Hamamatsu, a City with a Concentration of Foreigners]. In *Imin wo Meguru Jichitai no Seisaku to Shakai Undō [Local Government Politics and Social Movements Directed at Immigrants]*. Hiroshi Komai, ed. Pp. 45–67. Tokyo: Akashi Shoten (in Japanese).

Herbert, Wolfgang. 1996. *Foreign Workers and Law Enforcement in Japan*. London: Paul Kegan.

Hsia, Hsiao-Chuan. 2009. The Making of a Transnational Grassroots Migrant Movement in Hong Kong. A Case Study of Hong Kong's Asian Migrants' Coordinating Body. *Critical Asian Studies* 41(1): 113–141.

Hurights Osaka—Ajia-Taiheiyō Jinken Jōhō Sentā. 2007. *South Korea: Constitutional Court Recognized Equal Labour Rights for "Industrial Trainees."* Electronic document, www.hurights.or.jp/archives/news inbrief-en/section1/2007/09/south-korea-constitutional-court-recognized-equal-labour-rights-for-industrial-trainees.html, accessed October 5, 2011.

HRW (Human Rights Watch). 2000. *Owed Justice—Thai Women Trafficked into Debt Bondage in Japan*. Electronic document, www.hrw.org/reports/2000/japan/, accessed November 8, 2016.

IBJ (Immigration Bureau of Japan). 2015. *Immigration Control Report*. Electronic document, www.immi-moj.go.jp/english/seisaku/index.html#sec_02, accessed October 1, 2016.

ILO (International Labour Organization). 2005. Human Trafficking for Sexual Exploitation in Japan. Electronic document, www.ilo.org/global/topics/forced-labour/publications/WCMS_143044/lang-en/index.htm, accessed December 16, 2016.

Itoi, Masanobu. 2004. Ōizumi Machi no Gaikokujin Shimin Seisaku [Ōizumi town's foreign citizens policies]. In *Imin wo Meguru Jichitai no Seisaku to Shakai Undō* [*Local Government Politics and Social Movements Directed at Immigrants*]. Hiroshi Komai, ed. Pp. 69–93. Tokyo: Akashi Shoten (in Japanese).

JITCO (Japan International Training Cooperation Organization). 2015. *Kenshū Ginō Jisshū ni Kansuru JITCO Gyōmu Tōkei* [*Operational Statistics of JITCO Concerning Training and Technical Internship*]. Electronic document, www.jitco.or.jp/about/statistics.html, accessed January 25, 2016 (in Japanese).

Keck, Margaret E., and Kathryn Sikkink. 1998. *Activists Beyond Borders: Advocacy Networks in International Politics*. Ithaca, NY: Cornell University Press.

Kempka, Frauke. 2012. *Vertraute Fremde—Akzeptanz in der Integrationsförderung von MigrantInnen in Japan und Deutschland* [*Familiar strangers—Accepting in Integration Support for Migrants in Japan and Germany*]. Wiesbaden: Springer VS (in German).

Kim, Donghun. 1994. *Gaikokujin Jūmin no Sanseiken* [Political Participation Rights of Foreign Residents]. Tokyo: Akashi Shoten (in Japanese).

Komai, Hiroshi. 1993. *Gaikokujin Rōdōsha—Teijū ye no Michi* [Foreign workers—The Path Toward Long Term Residence]. Tokyo: Akashi Shoten (in Japanese).

Kremers, Daniel. 2014. Transnational Migrant Advocacy From Japan: Tipping the Scales in the Policy-Making Process. *Pacific Affairs* 87(4): 715–741.

Law, Lisa. 2003. Transnational Cyberpublics: New Political Spaces for Labour Migrants in Asia. *Ethnic and Racial Studies* 26(2): 234–252.

Lee, Hyejin. 2015. Challenges of and Coping with Immigration in Korea: The State, Civil Society, and Migrant Workers. In *Asia on the Move—Regional Migration and the Role of Civil Society*. Mely Cabalero-Anthony and Toshihiro Menju, eds. Pp. 44–64. Tokyo; New York: Japan Center For International Exchange.

Lim, Timothy C. 2006. NGOs, Transnational Migrants, and the Promotion of Rights in South Korea. In *Local Citizenship in Recent Countries of Immigration: Japan in Comparative Perspective*. Takeyuki Tsuda, ed. Pp. 235–269. Lanham, MD: Lexington Books.

Minegishi, Yoshio. 2004. Kawasaki-shi no Gaikokujin Shimin Seisaku to NPO [Kawasaki City's Foreign Citizens Policies and NPOs]. In *Imin wo Meguru Jichitai no Seisaku to Shakai Undō* [*Local Government Politics and Social Movements Directed At Immigrants*]. Hiroshi Komai, ed. Pp. 95–124. Tokyo: Akashi Shoten (in Japanese).

MOJ (Ministry of Justice). 2016. Zairyū Gaikokujin Tōkei (Kyū Tōroku Gaikokujin Tōkei) Tōkeihyō [Statistic on Residing Foreign Nationals (Formerly Statistic on Registered Foreign Nationals) Statistic Tables]. Electronic document, www.moj.go.jp/housei/toukei/toukei_ichiran_touroku.html, accessed December 16, 2016 (in Japanese).

Morris-Suzuki, Tessa. 2010. *Borderline Japan: Foreigners and Frontier Controls in the Postwar Era*. Cambridge: Cambridge University Press.

Mugdal, Vipul. 2016. *Claiming India from Below: Activism and Democratic Transformation*. Abingdon and New York: Routledge.

Nimura, Kazuo. 1992. The Trade Union Response to Migrant Workers. In *The Internationalization of Japan*. Glenn D. Hook and Michael A. Weiner, eds. Pp. 246–266. London: Routledge.

Oishi, Nana. 2005. *Women in Motion—Globalization, State Policies, and Labor Migration in Asia*. Stanford, CA: Stanford University Press.

Okamoto, Masataka. 2004. Ijūsha no Kenri wo Mamoru Nettowāku Undō no Kiseki to Kadai [Track and Challenge of a Network-Movement Protecting the Rights of Immigrants]. In *Imin wo Meguru Jichitai no Seisaku to Shakai Undō* [*Local Government Politics and Social Movements Directed at Immigrants*]. Hiroshi Komai, ed. Pp. 203–239. Tokyo: Akashi Shoten (in Japanese).

Park, Young-bum. 2008. Admission of Foreign Workers as Trainees in Korea. *ILO Asian Regional Programme on Governance of Labour Migration Working Paper* No. 9. Bangkok: International Labour Office.

Piper, Nicola. 2006. Migrant Worker Activism in Singapore and Malaysia: Freedom of Association and the Role of the State. *Asian and Pacific Migration Journal* 15(3): 359–380.

Piper, Nicola. 2009. Temporary Migration and Political Remittances: The Role of Organisational Networks in the Transnationalisation of Human Rights. *European Journal of East Asian Studies* 8(2): 215–243.

Piper, Nicola, and Stefan Rother. 2011. Transnational Inequalities, Transnational Responses: The Politicization of Migrant Rights in Asia. In *Globalization and Inequality in Emerging Societies*. Boike Rehbein, ed. Pp. 235–255. Basingstoke: Palgrave Macmillan.

Reimann, Kim D. 2010. *The Rise of Japanese NGOs: Activism from Above*. London: Routledge.

Roberts, Glenda S. 2000. NGO Support for Migrant Labor in Japan. In *Japan and Global Migration: Foreign Workers and the Advent of a Multicultural Society*. Mike Douglass and Glenda S. Roberts, eds. Pp. 273–300. New York: Routledge.

Rother, Stefan. 2009. Transnational Political Spaces: Political Activism of Philippine Labor Migrants in Hong Kong. In *Changing Dynamics in Filipino Overseas Migration: Nationalism, Transnationalism, Regionalism and the State*. Jorge V. Tigno, ed. Pp. 109–140. Quezon City: Philippine Migration Research Network and Philippine Social Science Council Publishing.

Rother, Stefan. 2017. Indonesian Migrant Domestic Workers in Transnational Political Spaces: Agency, Gender Roles and Social Class Formation. *Journal of Ethnic and Migration Studies* 43(6): 956–973.

Rother, Stefan, and Nicola Piper. 2015. Alternative Regionalism from Below: Democratizing ASEAN's Migration Governance. *International Migration* 53(3): 36–49.

Shipper, Apichai W. 2006. *Illegal Democrats: Immigrant Rights NGOs in Contemporary Japan*. Tokyo: Japan Institute of Labour Policy and Training Research.

Shipper, Apichai W. 2008. *Fighting for Foreigners—Immigration and Its Impact on Japanese Democracy*. Ithaca, NY: Cornell University Press.

Shipper, Apichai W. 2011. Contesting Foreigners' Rights in Contemporary Japan. *North Carolina Journal of International Law and Commercial Regulation* 36(3): 505–555.

SMJ (Solidarity Network with Migrants Japan). 2002. *Hōkatsuteki gaikokujin seisaku teigenshū [Comprehensive Foreigner Policies—A Collection of Proposals]*. Tokyo: Solidarity Network with Migrants Japan (in Japanese). Electronic document, www.g-jinkenho.net/modules/sections/index.php?op=viewarticle&artid=15, accessed July 18, 2017.

SMJ (Solidarity Network with Migrants Japan), ed. 2006. *Gaikokuseki Jūmin to no Kyōsei ni Mukete—NGO kara no Seisaku Teigen [On Living Together with Residents of Foreign Nationality—Policy Proposals from NGOs]*. Tokyo: Solidarity Network with Migrants Japan (in Japanese).

SMJ (Solidarity Network with Migrants Japan). 2014. *Ijūren to wa [About SMJ]*. Electronic document, http://migrants.jp/about, accessed August 12, 2016 (in Japanese).

South–South News. 2016. *UN's First Refugee Summit*. September 19. Electronic Document, www.south-southnews.com/south-south-news/ssn-features/448-un-coverage/un-main-bodies/112354-un-s-first-refugee-summit, accessed January 25, 2017.

Tai, John W. 2015. *Building Civil Society in Authoritarian China: Importance of Leadership Connections for Establishing Effective Nongovernmental Organizations in a Non-Democracy*. Cham: Springer.

Takao, Yasuo. 2003. Foreigners' Rights in Japan: Beneficiaries to Participants. *Asian Survey* 43(3): 527–552.

Tolentino, Leny. 2008. Migrant Women as Working Subjects—A Conversation with Leny Tolentino, Kalakasan—Migrant Women Empowerment Center. *Women's Asia 21—Voices from Japan* 20: 20–21. Electronic document, www.ajwrc.org/english/sub/voice/20-1-6.pdf, accessed January 25, 2017.

Tsukada, Mamoru. 2001. Shien Soshiki to Gaikokujin Rōdōsha [Help Organizations and Foreign Workers]. In *Gaikokujin Rōdōsha no Jinken to Chiiki Shakai—Nihon no Gendai to Shimin no Ishiki Katsudō [Human Rights of Foreign Workers and Regional Society—Japan's Present and the Consciousness and Activity of Citizens]*. Haruhiko Kanegae, ed. Pp. 138–190. Tokyo: Akashi Shoten (in Japanese).

Vogt, Gabriele, and Philipp Lersch. 2007. Migrant Support Organizations in Japan: A Mixed-Method Approach. In *Japan 2007: Politik, Wirtschaft und Gesellschaft [Japan 2007: Politics, Economy and Society]*. Manfred Pohl and Iris Wieczorek, eds. Pp. 265–285. Berlin: Vereinigung für sozialwissenschaftliche Japanforschung (in German).

Wee, Vivienne, and Amy Sim. 2004. Transnational Networks in Female Labour Migration. In *International Migration in Southeast Asia*. Aris Ananta and Evi Nurvidya Arifin, eds. Pp. 166–198. Singapore: Institute of Southeast Asian Studies.

Yamamoto, Ryoko. 2010. Migrant-support NGOs and the Challenge to the Discourse on Foreign Criminality in Japan. *The Asia-Pacific Journal—Japan Focus* (2010). Electronic document, http://apjjf.org/-Ryoko-YAMAMOTO/2521/article.html, accessed December 16, 2016.

Yee, Yeong Chong. 2009. Migrant Rights in Singapore. Political Claims and Strategies in Human Rights Struggles in Singapore. A Reply to Lenore Lyons. *Critical Asian Studies* 41(4): 575–604.

34

BASE PROTEST

Yuko Kawato

Recurring protests against the US military base policy in Asia

On the evening of April 28, 2016, a 20-year-old woman disappeared while taking a walk in Okinawa, Japan. Four weeks later, a veteran of the United States (US) Marines admitted that he killed her and provided the police with the location of her body. He was initially arrested for illegal disposal of a body, and was re-arrested for murder and rape resulting in death. The suspect was a contractor at Kadena Air Base, a major American military installation in Okinawa. Civil society organizations in Okinawa quickly mobilized to protest against the murder, arguing that this crime occurred because of the US military presence there. Organizations held demonstrations in front of US military installations, and press conferences and other events in protest. On June 19, approximately 65,000 people participated in the Okinawan Citizens' Rally (*kenmin taikai*), a demonstration organized by an umbrella group, All Okinawa Conference (*All Okinawa Kaigi*), which included civil society organizations of various types (women's, peace, youth, labor associations, etc.) as members. The participants of these protests made four main demands. First, they demanded an apology, compensation, and "care" for the victim's family. Second, protesters demanded a reduction of military bases and personnel in Okinawa, for example, through a closure of the Marine Corps' Futenma Air Station without its relocation to Henoko in northeastern Okinawa. Sixteen women's organizations protesting together went further and called for a closure of all military bases and the withdrawal of troops. The organizers of the Okinawan Citizens' Rally also demanded that the US Marines withdraw from Okinawa. Third, protesters demanded effective measures to prevent crimes by US military personnel and the civilian component of the US military (*gunzoku*). Fourth, protesters demanded a revision of the Status of Forces Agreement (SOFA), which establishes the rights, privileges, and obligations of the US military, military personnel, their family members, and the civilian component.

In Okinawa, protests like this one have recurred since the 1950s. Protests against US military base policy have also occurred in South Korea since the 1990s and in the Philippines from the 1960s, until the US military withdrawal in 1992. Mobilizations have addressed many types of base policy. Protesters have advocated base closure and opposed base construction through land expropriation. They have demanded more jurisdiction and the right of custody for host countries when American military personnel commit crimes. There have been protests against the storage and transit of American nuclear weapons in host countries. People mobilized against environmental problems in and around military bases as well. In the 1990s and the 2000s, protesters urged the USA to prohibit American military personnel's involvement in prostitution as customers. Civil society organizations led the protest mobilization in most cases. This chapter presents why civil society groups organize protests against US military base policy, when and how they mobilize citizens to protest, and the policy consequences of these protests.

Challenging decisions made in "high politics"

US military base policy deals with various issues related to the US military presence in host states. It specifies the land, sea, and air space provided by host countries to the USA, how the USA may use these areas (i.e., environmental agreements, whether the USA may bring in nuclear weapons, construction and closure of military facilities, and the division of costs between the USA and host states), and the rights and privileges of US military personnel in host states. Government representatives from the USA and host states conduct negotiations on base policy. Officials participating in policy-making include executive leaders, ministers, and bureaucrats in foreign affairs, defense, and other relevant ministries depending on the policy issue involved (e.g., environment, justice). US embassy and military officials stationed in host states, and legislators can also have a role in decision-making. Officials often believe that the US military presence in host countries reinforces alliances, which contribute to US strategic goals and the host countries' security. Officials also tend to believe that military bases help maintain regional stability, which promotes trade and economic development.

US military base policy is a part of international security policy that governments normally handle without significant participation by the public. In this "high politics," well-established channels for policy participation by the public do not exist. However, US military base policy can have important impact on local citizens' day-to-day life. For example, the USA and Japan agreed that US forces in Okinawa limit aircraft take-off and landing between 10 pm and 6 am in two major installations surrounded by residential areas, but flights during this time remain frequent and cause a problem for local citizens wishing to have quiet nights. In fact, the US military presence creates various problems for local citizens, such as military aircraft and vehicle accidents, environmental problems including soil and noise pollution, and the criminal conduct of US military personnel. Many local citizens and others living outside of host communities also believe that the presence of US forces in their countries creates tension in the region, by unnecessarily provoking other countries, and worry that bases might become targets of external attack. Some citizens also argue that basing agreements violate host states' sovereignty. For example, they complain about host states' lack of the primary right to exercise jurisdiction over offenses involving local victims and US military perpetrators in the performance of their official duty. Civil society groups organize protests against US military base policy because citizens wish to communicate their objections to the policy, but there is no direct access to policy-making. Protesters challenge not only the content of base policy, but also the fact that government officials make policy without their participation or consent.

Sources of outrage

Why do civil society groups organize protests, and why do ordinary citizens participate in them, when these actions require much time, energy, and resources that could be spent on other activities? Analysis of past protests against US military base policy shows that large protests occur when there is a broadly shared perception that a policy violates important principles (Kawato 2015). These principles, or norms, specify what ought and ought not to be done. When people think that military base policy violates norms, they demand a change in policy in accordance with the norms (Benford and Snow 2000; Finnemore and Sikkink 1998; Price 1998; Tarrow 1998). Protest organizers create norm-based policy demands, which I call "normative arguments." A normative argument looks like this: policy X violates a norm so it needs to be replaced by policy Y, which is in accordance with the norm.

Protests against base policy have emphasized one or more of the following norms: anti-war, anti-militarism, sovereignty, human rights, anti-nuclear, and environmental. First, many protests have emphasized anti-war and anti-militarism norms. Protesters wish to voice their opposition to war and other use of force (or threat to use force) as a means to settle international disputes. They see military bases and personnel as instruments of war and militarism, and demand base closure and withdrawal of troops (Arasaki 1996; Yonakuni 2005).

Second, many protesters seek to protect host states' sovereignty. For example, they complain that the USA curtails host states' sovereignty when it limits jurisdiction over crimes committed by US military personnel. Furthermore, when the USA administered host communities (e.g., Okinawa, 1945–1972) or were perceived as wielding great influence upon host governments to maintain military bases (e.g., Philippines 1945–1991), protesters criticized the violation of democratic principles (Garcia and Nemenzo 1988; Simbulan 1991). Related concepts such as nationalism and anti-imperialism have also appeared in protests against base policy.

Third, protesters emphasize environmental norms to draw attention to the soil, water, and noise pollution that military activities generate (Urashima 2005). US forces abroad adhere to the environmental governing standards in the Department of Defense's Overseas Environmental Baseline Guidance Document and host states' laws that are "uniformly applied and enforced" (i.e., application and enforcement not limited to US forces). However, many citizens in host countries think these environmental measures are inadequate. For example, US forces remedy environmental contamination that causes "known, imminent, and substantial endangerment to human health and safety."[1] Remedying contamination below this level is at the base commanders' discretion and is not guaranteed. How the USA remedies contamination is another important issue. It could be removal of a toxic substance or simply a fence built around a contaminated site with a warning posted. Protesters have demanded bilateral agreements to oblige the USA to follow (and not just "respect") host states' environmental laws, and clean up (and not just "remedy") environmental contamination.

Fourth, human rights norms are important in many protests (Fukuchi 1999). For example, women's organizations refer to "women's human rights" to protest against American sexual crimes and involvement in prostitution as customers (Francis 1999; Mikanagi 2004; Moon 1999, 2007; Takazato 1996). In addition, protesters argue that land expropriation without the owners' consent is a violation of property rights (Yeo 2011: 118–148). Furthermore, protesters highlighted human rights where the USA supported or appeared to support repressive governments. The anti-base movement in the Philippines, under Ferdinand Marcos's dictatorship, alleged that the USA violated human rights by providing Marcos with military assistance—which he used to repress his political adversaries—in return for military bases (Bonner 1988).

Finally, a norm against nuclear weapons has appeared in some protests. Protesters demand the prohibition of nuclear transit and storage in US military bases. For example, anti-base activists in the Philippines claimed that the USA stored nuclear weapons on military bases and that this could invite external attack (Simbulan 1989).

Mobilizing protests

A variety of civil society groups organize and join protests against US military base policy. Some organizations, such as the Okinawan Women Act against Military Violence (*Kichi, Guntai wo Yurusanai Kōdōsuru Onnatachi no Kai*), focus exclusively on military base issues. Other organizations work more broadly on issues related to military bases, such as the environment and women's rights. There are still others who work on issues not necessarily related to military bases but organize or join protests against base policy. Okinawa Teachers' Association (*Okinawa Kyōshokuin Kai*) for example, played a central role in mobilizing protests against US military base policy in the 1950s and 1960s. University student organizations have actively participated in protests against base policy, as well.

Organizations often build a coalition to coordinate their demands and actions as well as to maximize resources and the size of mobilization. Protest organizers create policy demands that are most likely to attract public support, even if this might moderate the demands of some of the organizations in the coalition. There are three ways in which protest organizers use norms to create policy demands. First, protest organizers can match their grievances about base policy with norms that directly address those issues. Norms against nuclear weapons and environmental damage are two examples. Second, protest organizers can apply a broader international norm to a grievance. For example, women's organizations in Okinawa condemned the rape of a 12-year-old girl by three US military personnel in 1995 as a violation of "women's human rights." The organizations had just attended the Fourth World Conference on Women in Beijing, where they started to conceptualize "military violence against women" as a human rights violation. Third, protest organizers choose norms according to historical legacy. For example, anti-war and anti-militarism norms are potent in Okinawa given the memory of the Battle of Okinawa. Sovereignty and democratic norms are also powerful in the Philippines, South Korea, and Okinawa given their colonial experiences.

Protest mobilization has often occurred in response to trigger events, such as accidents and crimes that US military personnel commit against local victims. Protesters also react to the states' announcement of a new base policy. Some protests occur pre-emptively to influence impending bilateral negotiations on base policy. Civil society organizations publicize their plans for demonstrations through their networks and the press in order to encourage citizens to join them.

Protests' impact on policy

Protests against US military base policy have recurred in Okinawa since the 1950s, in the Philippines since the 1960s (until the US withdrawal in 1992), and in South Korea since the 1990s. Despite the long history of protests, research about how these protests influence policy is relatively new. Publications on protests against US military base policy have mostly been single-case, descriptive studies (Lutz 2009; McCormack and Norimatsu 2012; Moon 1997; Simbulan 1985; Smith 2000). Kent Calder's *Embattled Garrisons* (2007) and Alexander Cooley's *Base Politics* (2008) are path-breaking volumes that explored base politics theoretically using comparative research methods. However, their volumes examine the influence of host countries' regime type on US military base policy, and the authors agree that protests and their normative arguments have very limited—if any—influence on base policy. Andrew Yeo's *Activists, Alliances, and Anti-U.S. Base Protests* (2011) is the first research work to explore the influence of protests on base policy. Yeo argues that protests can influence military base policy when host states' policy makers do not strongly concur that a positive relationship with the USA is critical to national security. A weak security consensus opens up a political opportunity for anti-base movements, and a strong security consensus closes it. My review of protests in Asia suggests that policy makers respond to different normative arguments in different ways under a given security consensus. My research focuses on normative arguments to explore that variation, and explain when, how, and to what extent protesters' normative arguments matter.

My analysis of past protests shows that there are four categories of policy outcomes. First, a protest leads to a fundamental change in base policy. Second, a protest results in a limited policy change. Third, a protest does not result in any change in policy. Fourth, a protest does not lead to policy change but states' decision makers nevertheless decide to offer symbolic concessions to protesters. Symbolic concessions are gestures to create a public image that governments pay attention to citizens' grievances. These four policy outcomes raise some questions: Why do some protests lead to change in base policy while others do not? When states decide to change base policy, what influences the extent of change? When states decide not to change base policy, why do they sometimes offer symbolic concessions? Below, I briefly answer these questions by focusing on policy makers' perceptions of protesting organizations and normative arguments against base policy. A more detailed discussion of the theory, methodology, and cases are available in my book *Protests against U.S. Military Base Policy in Asia: Persuasion and Its Limits* (Kawato 2015).

When protests lead to a fundamental change in base policy

Protesters' normative arguments can persuade policy makers to change a policy in a fundamental way. According to social psychologists, persuasion is a process in which a communicator transmits a message to change the attitude of another person in a context in which the person has some degree of free choice (Perloff 1993: 14). Attitude change includes the adoption of a new attitude and of an attitude opposite to the initial one.[2] Social psychologists have developed a vast number of hypotheses on persuasion (Petty and Wegener 1998). I highlight two as the most important in base politics. First, protesters' normative arguments are more likely to persuade policy makers when they fit in with policy makers' knowledge and beliefs. Second, persuasion is more likely when policy makers think that protest leaders and organizations are credible. Persuasion leads to policy change under domestic institutional settings that allow persuaded policy makers to shape policy.

There are several means through which leaders of protesting civil society organizations can try to persuade policy makers to change policy in accordance with norms. First, protest leaders can visit policy makers to submit petitions and other statements of protest. Second, protesters rely on media coverage of mobilizations that includes explanations of protesters' arguments. Some protest organizations inform academics, analysts, and other commentators who discuss base policy in the media. Third, protest organizations ask local elected officials, such as governors and mayors, to communicate their arguments to national policy makers. Finally, in some rare instances, policy makers and protest leaders are friends, colleagues, or family members, making communication of normative arguments more direct and intimate.

In base politics, policy change through persuasion is rare. In fact, my analysis of twelve major protests against US military base policy in Asia since the end of World War II shows that normative arguments persuaded policy makers only in two cases. Policy change occurred in just one of these two cases in which domestic institutions permitted persuaded policy makers to change policy. This case is from the Philippines where a twelve to eleven vote in the twenty-three-person Senate in 1991 defeated a treaty with the USA that would have extended the American military presence in the Philippines after the expiration of the Military Bases Agreement. The rejection of the new treaty in the Senate led to a closure of all US military bases in the country in 1992.

I argue, based on interviews with many of the senators, their memoires, and other sources, that normative arguments against military bases persuaded ten out of the twelve senators who voted against continued US military presence (Guingona 2008; Pimentel 2006; Salonga 1995, 2001). Two remaining senators had other reasons for voting against the treaty. Many of the anti-base senators shared a historic understanding that the relationship between the Philippines and the USA had been unequal, mostly benefiting the USA to the detriment of the Philippines. Protesters' normative argument that the US military bases were instruments of American neo-colonialism and they should be closed for true Philippine sovereignty and independence, fit with their nationalist belief. In addition, most of the persuaded senators actively participated in the campaign against President Ferdinand Marcos's dictatorship, founding and/or joining civil society organizations that demanded democratic rule. The future senators were persuaded that US military bases must close for democracy in the Philippines, because they believed that the USA was giving economic and military support to Marcos in exchange for military bases. Even after Marcos's fall, the senators believed that the American interest in securing military bases made American interference in Philippine politics likely. Next, during Marcos's era, many of the senators defended political prisoners as lawyers and/or suffered imprisonment and exile. To those who fought against Marcos's human rights violations, anti-base arguments referring to human rights—such as to protect the rights of Filipino victims of American crimes, to oppose military prostitution around bases, and so on—were persuasive. Finally, some of the senators opposed construction of a nuclear plant in the Philippines in the 1980s. This experience led them to accept protesters' anti-nuclear argument against military bases, that US military bases should close because the USA stored nuclear weapons and this infringed on Philippine sovereignty (Philippine constitution and legislation declare "freedom from nuclear weapons"). Furthermore, people with credibility influenced the senators' thinking about military bases. They included the senators' family members, friends, colleagues, advisors, and respected others, whom the senators trusted and thought were experts on the military base issue. Some of these people led civil society organizations, making their organizations credible as well.

Whether persuaded policy makers can change base policy depends on the domestic institutions within which they operate. Important domestic institutional factors include formal rules that allocate decision-making authority, the balance of power amongst policy makers in different domestic institutions, and laws that policy makers can rely on to defend their position. In the Philippines, the Constitution of 1987, which was created after the ouster of Marcos through the People's Power Revolution, curtailed presidential power and gave the Senate the final authority to decide whether US military bases would be allowed to remain in the Philippines after the expiration of the Military Bases Agreement in 1991. The Senate's decision to close the US military bases was, therefore, more important than President Corazon Aquino's preference to keep them open. Other provisions in the constitution—at least two-thirds of the Senate must support ratification of a treaty, pursuit of an independent foreign policy, freedom from nuclear weapons, renunciation of war as an instrument of national policy, and independent national economy—and a series of anti-nuclear resolutions in the Senate also offered the anti-base senators legal arguments to defend their position.

The role of civil society organizations varied over time and they had different influence on different senators. During the Marcos era, nationalist and anti-Marcos organizations that many of the senators created and joined embraced an anti-base position. These organizations served as important venues in which future senators exchanged views on US military bases and were persuaded that the US supported Marcos for military bases and that the bases must close for true Philippine sovereignty. In the post-Marcos period, civil society organizations played a supporting role for the persuaded senators, making the senators' position against military bases more defensible. Civil society organizations did this by informing representatives of a commission that drafted the new constitution so that the new constitution included the aforementioned provisions and transferred the power to decide on the future of US military bases from the president to the Senate. Civil society organizations also informed the public about problems related to the US military bases so that vocal and well-informed supporters for the anti-base senators could be mobilized to mitigate the fact that the broader public preferred the retention of military bases (Coronel Ferrer 1994). Persuasion of senators, together with the favorable domestic institutional setting, led to the closure of all US military bases in the Philippines—a fundamental change in policy.

When protests lead to limited change in policy

Even when normative persuasion fails, protest leaders and organizations are still able to change base policy in a limited way by mobilizing large protests and generating important political and military incentives for policy makers. In this process, which I call "compromise," normative arguments help mobilize large protests but do not have a persuasive impact on policy makers. Policy makers' decision to change policy is due to their rational calculation of costs and benefits in the face of large protests. The type of incentives varies across cases. Policy makers in host states may become concerned that protests might reduce public support for their government (Ripsman 2009: 188; Schweller 2006: 49–50). Policy makers in the USA and host states may worry about diminishing support for the security alliance and a reduction of US military effectiveness. Policy makers try to eliminate these political and military concerns by changing base policy. However, policy makers' security, political, and economic interests prevent a fundamental change in policy according to normative prescriptions. Policy makers offer compromise solutions, which are limited changes in policy, in order to calm public outrage while protecting their own interests.

For example, Japanese and American policy makers responded to a large protest mobilization in Okinawa during 1995 and 1996 with a limited policy change. The mobilization occurred after three US marines abducted and raped a 12-year-old girl in Okinawa in September 1995. Soon after the local media reported the crime, various organizations held protest rallies and street demonstrations, and issued statements of protest. On October 21, 1995, about 85,000 people participated in the Okinawan Citizen's Rally, which eighteen groups organized with support from some 300 other groups. At the rally, protesters made four demands: 1) an expeditious revision of the SOFA; 2) a reduction in the number and size of US military bases in Okinawa; 3) eradication of crimes by US military personnel and the strict enforcement of discipline; and 4) apologies and payment of compensation to victims of crimes committed by US military personnel.

Protest organizers argued that existing base policy violated several norms. First, in the mobilization following the rape, women's organizations referred to "human rights of women" in demanding change in base policy. Takazato Suzuyo, the leader of the Okinawan Women Act against Military Violence, demanded that the US military in Okinawa establish a prevention program to address crimes against women, and the US military withdraw from Okinawa (Francis 1999: 190). She also argued that militaries train people to become violent, and that military prostitution and other types of sexual violence would continue as long as bases remained in Okinawa (Takazato 1996).

Second, protesters in Okinawa argued that the SOFA curtailed Japanese sovereignty, and that the two governments must revise it. According to SOFA's Article 17, Section 5c, Japanese authorities could not take custody of the US military suspects before an indictment, and in 1995, the US military resorted to this provision in refusing to transfer the rape suspects to Japanese authorities. Protesters saw this as the curtailment of the Japanese power to investigate, and demanded a SOFA revision that would enable US military suspects' transfer before indictment.

Third, Okinawan protesters argued that the USA should consolidate and reduce the number and size of its bases in Okinawa because various base-related problems violated the Okinawans' "right to live in peace," a right specified in the preamble of the Japanese constitution. This argument reflected many Okinawans' belief that a reduction in the number and size of bases would help decrease base-related problems, such as accidents during military exercises, environmental problems (e.g., noise and soil pollution), and crimes committed by US military personnel.

Finally, landowners, whose land was in "mandatory use" (*kyōsei shiyō*) without their consent, demanded a reduction in the number and size of bases. They had refused to lease their land to the Japanese government for US military use due to their anti-war and anti-military beliefs (Arasaki 1996). They also argued that the expropriation of their land violated their constitutional right of private ownership.

These normative arguments failed to persuade Japanese or US policy makers to change base policy because the arguments did not fit policy makers' beliefs, and policy makers did not find the leading protest organizations credible. First, Okinawan women's organizations argued that the US military should withdraw because it trains its personnel to be violent and this makes them more likely to commit violent crimes in host communities. However, US policy makers rejected this argument. In an interview with me, a US military public affairs officer in Okinawa stressed that the total number of crimes committed by US military personnel, US civilians working for the US military in Okinawa, and their family members comprised only a small percentage of all crimes in Okinawa between 1990 and 1995, but protest organizations politicized the crimes.[3] Second, US and Japanese policy makers did not agree with protesters that a SOFA revision was necessary to protect Japanese sovereignty. Japan's Foreign Minister, Kōno Yōhei, for example, thought, "all this talk about revising SOFA is going too far," claiming that the investigation of the rape was proceeding unhindered (Funabashi 1999: 303). Third, protesters argued that the various base-related problems violated their constitutional right to live in peace, so that the number and size of bases should be reduced. This argument did not persuade policy makers who considered base-related problems as unfortunate side effects of maintaining military bases, which they believed were important for Japanese security and US military effectiveness. As will be discussed later in this chapter, Japanese and US policy makers decided to reduce the number and size of military bases to save the security alliance in response to declining public support for the alliance, rather than implement a norm-driven base policy.

As for property rights, Japanese policy makers rejected protesters' arguments and prioritized the stable provision of base land to the US military. The Japanese government sued the Okinawan Governor, ōta Masahide, who refused to participate in the procedure to expropriate some of the land against the landowners' will. The government also passed laws to be able to continue using the base land during procedures to renew expired leases.

US and Japanese policy makers did not find protesting organizations credible. They claimed that "anti-US" and "anti-military" groups were behind the protests in Okinawa, and insisted that these groups were only using the rape to manipulate public opinion to serve their policy preference of eliminating military bases (Funabashi 1999: 302; Vogel and Giarra 2002: 129).

Protesters' normative arguments did not persuade policy makers, but the protests generated incentives for policy change by fostering the perception amongst policy makers that the USA–Japan alliance was in crisis. The protests occurred while Japan and the USA engaged in efforts to redefine and strengthen their security alliance for the post-Cold War era. As the protests continued, Japanese public support for the alliance fell dramatically. According to *The Yomiuri*

Shimbun and the US Gallup's joint survey between October and November 1995, the number of Japanese citing "good" bilateral relations fell to just over 20 percent, the lowest figure since the survey started in 1978. Although 60 percent of the respondents said that the bilateral security treaty was "beneficial," that figure was fourteen points lower than in 1998 and five points lower than in 1994 (Funabashi 1999: 70). Policy makers in both states worried that Japanese public support for the security alliance was at risk, precisely when they needed that support to strengthen the alliance.

The two governments, therefore, decided to return some base land, most importantly the Futenma Air Station, after relocating its facilities and functions mostly within Okinawa. The Okinawan public welcomed the announcement regarding the return of the land, but strongly opposed the requirement to relocate facilities within the prefecture. Tokyo and Washington also decided to improve some of the SOFA procedures. Their plan included improvements on various issues such as accident notification to local communities and supplemental automobile insurance for US military personnel, but the most important was the agreement that the USA would consider transferring its military suspects of heinous crimes (rape and murder) to Japanese authorities before indictment. However, this was an agreement to improve the implementation of the existing SOFA, not a revision of its text that the Okinawan protesters had demanded. Tokyo and Washington tried to address some of the local grievances while ensuring US military effectiveness, with a limited policy change.

When protests do not change base policy

Base policy does not change when protests fail to persuade policy makers or generate significant incentives for them. Base policy also does not change when protesters generate incentives for policy makers to change policy but other factors, such as lobbying by actors that support the policy that protesters seek to change and the states' capacity, under law, to impose their will, reduce or eliminate these incentives. Furthermore, my case studies show that policy does not change when protesters generate incentives for host-state governments, but the USA opposes the change.

For example, civil society organizations in South Korea tried to stop Seoul and Washington's plan to expropriate farmland to expand a US military base in Pyeongtaek. In March 2005, Pyeongtaek residents opposing the expropriation formed protest groups, and organizations from outside Pyeongtaek joined them to form the Pan-South Korean Solution Committee against Base Extension in Pyeongtaek (KCPT). KCPT organized daily candlelight vigils, marches, press conferences, fund-raisers, and other activities.

The protesters advanced two normative arguments against base expansion, but these arguments did not persuade policy makers. First, the KCPT argued that Pyeongtaek farmers needed their land to survive, and expropriation would violate their human rights by taking away their livelihood. This argument did not persuade policy makers because they believed that the Korean government offered adequate monetary compensation and relocation aid, such as alternative land to farm or places to live. Some US officials believed that the residents who continued to protest did so, not out of any principle, but for the sake of obtaining more compensation.[4] In addition, the fact that the land expropriation was legal added an obstacle to normative persuasion. Article 23 of the Korean constitution guarantees the right of property, but it also enables "expropriation, use, or restriction of private property from public necessity" with compensation. An official from the National Human Rights Commission of Korea confirmed that: "NGOs tend to think in terms of justice and moral rightness, but the commission must think in terms of legality. The government is carrying out the relocation legally."[5]

Second, the KCPT used anti-war and anti-militarism norms to argue that base expansion threatened peace and stability in the Korean Peninsula. They contended that the planned relocation of the US forces from the North Korean border and Seoul to Pyeongtaek was a force protection measure in preparation for a pre-emptive US attack on North Korea (Nam 2006: 626). KCPT also argued that base expansion would make Pyeongtaek a giant hub that would allow the USA to deploy its forces to regional conflicts more easily, even if involvement in these conflicts may not serve Korean interests. This argument did not persuade policy makers either. In fact, they believed the opposite, that advancing base consolidation in South Korea, through the base expansion in Pyeongtaek, would enhance the US forces' military effectiveness and deterrent capabilities, and would contribute toward security on the peninsula and in the region.[6]

Policy makers did not consider many organizations that joined the KCPT from outside of Pyeongtaek to be credible. The lack of credibility is likely to have created an additional barrier to normative persuasion. Both Korean and US policy makers believed that national protest organizations—which mobilized or joined other protests regarding US military bases—latched onto the Pyeongtaek case, dramatizing the plight of the farmers to create a negative image of the US forces and further the ultimate cause of prompting a US withdrawal from South Korea.[7]

Even when protest organizations fail to persuade policy makers, policy change is possible if they generate important incentives for policy makers to change policy. Although KCPT organized some large demonstrations, there is no evidence that policy makers felt that protests created significant incentives to cancel the base expansion in Pyeongtaek. The two governments maintained the policy of land expropriation and base expansion in Pyeongtaek.

When protests do not change policy but policy makers offer symbolic concessions

When policy does not change, policy makers can nevertheless offer symbolic concessions for three reasons. First, policy makers wish to show that the USA and host-state governments are norm abiding, even if they do not change policy in response to protests. Second, symbolic concessions allow states to save face. When policy makers reject policy change, symbolic concessions help host-state governments appear effective, and help prevent the USA from appearing like a bully. Finally, policy makers decide to make symbolic concessions to enable a smoother implementation of the policy that protesters oppose.

There is an example of this from South Korea: environmental consciousness developed in South Korea in the 1990s. Two major environmental organizations, Green Korea United (*Nogsaeg Yeonhab*) and the Korea Federation of Environmental Movements (*Hwangyeong Undong Yeonhab*), were established in 1991 and 1993, respectively. In cooperation with organizations around US bases and some local residents, these environmental organizations started to assess the environmental impact of US military bases in 1996. Based on their research, environmental organizations charged that the US forces caused oil leakages and noise pollution, as well as water and soil contamination with heavy metals and other hazardous wastes. They demanded that South Korea and the USA insert environmental provisions into the SOFA, obligating the USA to publicly disclose all cases of pollution and conduct thorough clean-ups using its own funds to restore affected land to its "original" state. They also asked for specific measures to prevent base pollution. Finally, they demanded their participation in environmental decision-making and implementation.

In spring 2000, Green Korea United received information that a large amount of formaldehyde, a toxic chemical commonly used to preserve corpses, was inappropriately disposed of in the Yongsan Army Garrison in Seoul. After three months of evidence gathering, Green Korea

United announced, in a press conference in July 2000, that a deputy director of the Eighth Army's mortuary ordered his subordinates to pour 480 bottles (228 liters) of fluid containing formaldehyde down the drain on February 9, 2000. Green Korea United charged that this toxin, which flowed into the Han River that supplies water to Seoul, was strong enough to kill 8,000 people (Ryukyu Shimpo Sha 2003: 172). Korean environmental groups publicized the issue widely and organized protests with other types of civil society groups. Environmental organizations also lobbied the Ministry of Environment to include environmental provisions in the SOFA.

The United States Forces Korea (USFK) admitted that the deputy director of the mortuary, a civilian employed by the USFK, ordered two subordinates to dispose of a formaldehyde mixture (Choe 2003). The USFK said that the disposal violated both US and Korean laws, and that it punished the deputy director with a one-month suspension without pay. The USFK emphasized, however, that the disposal did not pollute the Han River, because the formalde-hyde mixture was diluted in about 1.9 million gallons of other wastewater and went through three treatment processes (Kirk 2001). Despite the USFK's announcement that the toxin did not pollute the Han River, the protest organizations' arguments raised fear and suspicion amongst the public.

USFK officials agreed that they should prevent and remedy serious environmental pollution that harmed people's health. However, environmental organizations failed to persuade them about the need to strengthen their environmental policy and accept new obligations such as restoring polluted land to its original state.[8] First, since USFK officials adhered to the US environmental policy to remedy "known, imminent, and substantial endangerment to human health and safety," they did not think that they were violating environmental norms. Second, Article IV of the US–ROK SOFA states that the USA is not obliged to restore military facilities to their original state, or to compensate South Korea for restoration. Environmental organiza-tions' "polluter pays" principle, which demanded that USFK pay for clean-ups, sounded unfair to USFK officials given the SOFA. Officials also believed that their presence significantly con-tributed to Korean security and that South Korea should share the alliance's financial burden.

Third, environmental organizations' argument that the USFK must clean up all pollution sounded unworkable to many officials. A USFK official, for example, said "it does not make sense" to clean up a bombing range used for fifty years to the standards required for building parks and residential areas.[9] Such a clean-up would require decades and be extremely expensive. Protest organizations' arguments did not fit the knowledge and beliefs of US policy makers, and moreover, policy makers considered protesters' arguments to be unrealistic and unfair. As a result, persuasion failed.

Furthermore, many USFK officials did not find South Korea's environmental organizations credible. They wondered how these organizations could evaluate pollution on bases without having access to the bases. In questioning environmental groups' findings that US military bases were highly contaminated, a USFK official said that if there were significant environmental problems on the base, the USFK would fix them for the sake of the health of the Americans and Koreans who worked and lived there.[10] In addition, many USFK officials considered environ-mental organizations a part of the anti-base coalition that "picked on" and "went after" the USFK to damage the US–ROK alliance.[11] For all these reasons, many officials did not consider environmental organizations to be credible, and the organizations' normative arguments were not persuasive.

However, given the increasing environmental consciousness in South Korea and the protest organizations' efforts in publicizing the environmental problems associated with military bases, the USA decided to include environmental provisions in the SOFA in 2001. The environmental provisions did not change existing policy, however. The new Agreed Minute to the SOFA read in part that the USA confirms its policy to respect relevant Republic of Korea Government environmental laws, regulations, and standards. The US obligation to *respect* Korean domestic laws was not new, as it had already been codified in the SOFA (Article VII, Respect for Local Law). The Ministry of Environment's position that the USFK *complies with* Korean laws was rejected by the Ministry of Foreign Affairs and Trade, the Ministry of National Defense, and the USA. The two governments also signed the Memorandum of Special Understandings on Environmental Protection, which included four sections: environmental governing standards, information sharing and access, environmental performance, and environmental consultation. These sections, however, reiterated the existing USFK policy and did not offer anything new. Moreover, the USA considered the memorandum to be a declaration of intent, and therefore, not binding.

The US policy makers decided against changing the environmental policy because they believed existing policy was already adequate to protect the environment on bases. In addition, policy change would have entailed relaxing the principle of remedying "known, imminent, and substantial endangerment to human health and safety," and this would have created expensive obligations that the USA was unwilling to assume.[12] Furthermore, base commanders already had the authority to remedy pollution below the recommended level of environmental damage at their discretion, based on expert advice. Given this, the US policy makers believed that the USA was not in violation of environmental norms and that a change in policy was not necessary.[13]

Policy change also did not occur because adding environmental provisions to the SOFA appeared sufficient to create a public impression that the USA cared about the environment. Environmental provisions were not a part of the SOFA, and US officials hoped that the addition—even if they only reiterated the existing policy—would generate a public image that progress had been made on this issue.[14] As such, the environmental provisions in the SOFA were symbolic concessions that signaled the US adherence to environmental norms. The symbolic gesture was also a face-saving measure, which allowed Seoul to claim credit for some progress on the issue.

Conclusion

When some aspects of the US military base policy outrage citizens of Asian host countries, civil society groups have been successful in organizing large protests with normative arguments for policy change. However, not all protests have policy impact. In fact, my analysis of twelve large protests in Asia since the end of World War II has shown that protests failed to bring about policy change more often than not (seven cases without policy change, five with policy change). When policy change did occur, it was more often due to large protests pressuring policy makers to change policy through a rational calculation of political and military costs and benefits (four cases), than due to protesters' normative arguments persuading them (one case).

Nevertheless, when I set aside my snapshot case studies and look at the evolution of base policy and related practices over the years, there have been significant changes in the direction of normative prescriptions. For example, today, the US military has procedures for discarding toxic wastewater instead of releasing it directly into the soil and rivers. The US military no longer condones its personnel's involvement in prostitution. Host states can try US military personnel suspected of crimes against host-state citizens if the suspects were off-duty when they committed the crimes. It appears that precedents play an important role in norm internalization in base politics. Once policy makers who carry out rational, cost-benefit calculations in response to protests create new laws, policy, or practice in the direction that the norms recommend, these laws, policy, or practices become authoritative precedents that shape policy makers' behavior and beliefs. Over time, precedence-following and incremental changes may lead to full acceptance of norms. Protests by civil society organizations that repeatedly forced policy makers to think about normative resolution to base problems appear to have been important in the evolution of state behavior.

Notes

1 This phrase comes from Secretary of the Defense, Leslie Aspen, Jr., "DOD Policy and Procedures for the Realignment of Overseas Sites" MSG142159Z, December 1993.
2 Social psychologists assume that persuasion has occurred when a person's attitude shifts in the direction of the message. This includes the two persuasion outcomes which I focus on: adoption of a new attitude and adoption of an attitude opposite to the initial one. However, persuasion can also: 1) reinforce an existing attitude that the message promotes; and 2) weaken an attitude that the message opposes without the recipient being won over by the position that the messenger promotes. I do not examine these outcomes but acknowledge that they are possible.
3 Interview, July 3, 2007.
4 Interview with a USFK official, November 27, 2006.
5 Interview, December 5, 2006.
6 Interview with a USFK official, November 15, 2006.
7 Interviews with a USFK official, November 27, 2006, and a former Korean Ministry of National Defense official, December 13, 2006.
8 The evidence that follows comes from my interviews with multiple US officials in November and December 2006.
9 Interview, November 27, 2006.
10 Interview, November 27, 2006.
11 Interviews with USFK officials, November and December 2006.
12 Interview, November 27, 2006.
13 Interview, December 11, 2006.
14 Interview, March 9, 2011.

Suggested readings

Bengzon, Alfredo R. A., and Raul Rodrigo. 1998. *A Matter of Honor: The Story of the 1990–91 RP-US Bases Talks.* Manila: Anvil.
Center for Strategic and International Studies, eds. 2001. *Path to an Agreement: The U.S.-Republic of Korea Status of Forces Agreement Revision Process.* Washington DC.
Coronel Ferrer, Miriam. 1992. The Dynamics of the Opposition to the US Bases in the Philippines. *Kasarinlan* 7(4): 62–87.
Durant, Robert F. 2007. *The Greening of the U.S. Military: Environmental Policy, National Security, and Organizational Change.* Washington, DC: Georgetown University Press.
Feinerman, James V. 2005. The U.S.–Korean Status of Forces Agreement as a Source of Continuing Korean Anti-American Attitudes. In *Korean Attitudes toward the United States: Changing Dynamics.* David I. Steinberg, ed. Pp. 196–219. Armonk, NY: M. E. Sharpe.
Moon, Katharine H.S. 2002. Korean Democracy, Civil Society Activism, and Anti-Americanism. *Korean Studies Forum* 1: 53–72.
Moon, Katharine H.S. 2012. *Protesting America: Democracy and the U.S.–Korea Alliance.* Berkeley, CA: University of California Press.
Smith, Sheila A. 2006. *Shifting Terrain: The Domestic Politics of the U.S. Military Presence in Asia.* Honolulu: East-West Center.
Sturdevant, Saundra Pollock, and Brenda Stoltzfus. 1992. *Let the Good Times Roll: Prostitution and the U.S. Military in Asia.* New York: The New Press.
Tanji, Miyume. 2006. *Myth, Protest and Struggle in Okinawa.* London: Routledge.
Yeo, Andrew. 2006. Local–National Dynamics and Framing in South Korean Anti-Base Movements. *Kasarinlan: Philippine Journal of Third World Studies* 21(2): 34–60.

Websites

Focus on the Global South, http://focusweb.org/.
A transnational alternative policy group, which focuses on producing tools for the enhancement of social and ecological sustainability, primarily in South Asia.

Green Korea United, http://green-korea.tistory.com/.
An environmentally oriented group based in Seoul.

Ministry of Foreign Affairs of Japan www.mofa.go.jp/region/n-america/us/q&a/index.html.
A Q&A on the relations between Japan and the USA, published through the Ministry of Foreign Affairs.

National Campaign for Eradication of Crimes by US Troops in Korea, http://usacrime.or.kr/doku/doku.
php.
The homepage of the "USFK Crime Exercise Headquarters," a Wiki-site that summarizes issues with the United States Forces Korea.

Okinawa Prefecture, Military Base Affairs Division, www.pref.okinawa.jp/site/chijiko/kichitai/25185.
html.
Information relating to the US military base in Okinawa.

Ryukyu Simpo (Daily Newspaper in Okinawa), http://english.ryukyushimpo.jp/.
Special topic news article relating to the protests associated with the US military base in Okinawa.

Stars and Stripes, Pacific Edition, www.stripes.com/news/pacific.
News articles relating to the US relations with Asia.

United States Forces Korea (USFK), www.usfk.mil/.
The official site of the USFK, including history, information about the organization and media relations, and philosophy.

References

Arasaki, Moriteru. 1996. *Okinawa: Hansen Jinushi* [*Okinawa: Anti-War Landowners*]. Tokyo: Koubunken (in Japanese).

Benford, Robert D., and David A. Snow. 2000. Framing Processes and Social Movements: An Overview and Assessment. *Annual Review of Sociology* 26: 611–39.

Bonner, Raymond. 1988. *Waltzing with a Dictator: The Marcoses and the Making of American Policy*. New York: Vintage Books.

Calder, Kent E. 2007. *Embattled Garrisons: Comparative Base Politics and American Globalism*. Princeton, NJ: Princeton University Press.

Choe, Song-won. 2003. Army Civilian Still Could Be Tried in Formaldehyde Case. *Starts and Stripes*, October 25. Electronic document, www.stripes.com/news/army-civilian-still-could-be-tried-in-formaldehyde-case-1.12952, accessed November 22, 2016.

Cooley, Alexander. 2008. *Base Politics: Democratic Change and the U.S. Military Overseas*. Ithaca, NY: Cornell University Press.

Coronel Ferrer, Miriam. 1994. Anti-Bases Coalitions. In *Studies on Coalition Experiences in the Philippines*. Cesar P. Cala and Jose Z. Grageda, eds. Pp. 4–27. Manila: Bookmark.

Finnemore, Martha, and Kathryn Sikkink. 1998. International Norm Dynamics and Political Change. *International Organization* 52(4): 887–917.

Francis, Carolyn Bowen. 1999. Women and Military Violence. In *Okinawa: Cold War Island*. Chalmers Johnson, ed. Pp. 189–203. Cardiff, CA: Japan Policy Research Institute.

Fukuchi, Hiroaki. 1999. *Kichi to Jinken: Okinawa No Sentaku* [*Bases and Human Rights: The Choice for Okinawa*]. Tokyo: Doujidai Sha (in Japanese).

Funabashi, Yoichi. 1999. *Alliance Adrift*. New York: Council on Foreign Relations Press.

Garcia, Ed, and Francisco Nemenzo. 1988. *The Sovereign Quest: Freedom from Foreign Military Bases*. Quezon City: Claretian Publications.

Guingona, Tito. 2008. *Fight for the Filipino*. Quezon City: Academic Publishing Corporation.

Kawato, Yuko. 2015. *Protests against U.S. Military Base Policy in Asia: Persuasion and Its Limits*. Stanford, CA: Stanford University Press.

Kirk, Jeremy. 2001. USFK Negotiates with S. Korea on Punishment in Formaldehyde Dumping. *Stars and Stripes*, May 24.

Lutz, Catherine, ed. 2009. *The Bases of Empire: The Global Struggle against U.S. Military Posts.* New York: New York University Press.

McCormack, Gavan, and Satoko Oka Norimatsu. 2012. *Resistant Islands: Okinawa Confronts Japan and the United States.* Lanham, MD: Rowman & Littlefield.

Mikanagi, Yumiko. 2004. Okinawa: Women, Bases and US-Japan Relations. *International Relations of the Asia-Pacific* 4(1): 97–111.

Moon, Katharine H.S. 1997. *Sex among Allies: Military Prostitution in U.S.–Korea Relations.* New York: Columbia University Press.

Moon, Katharine H.S. 1999. South Korean Movements against Militarized Sexual Labor. *Asian Survey* 39(2): 310–327.

Moon, Katharine H.S. 2007. Resurrecting Prostitutes and Overturning Treaties: Gender Politics in the "Anti-American" Movement in South Korea. *The Journal of Asian Studies* 66(1): 129–157.

Nam, Chang-hee. 2006. Relocating the U.S. Forces in South Korea: Strained Alliance, Emerging Partnership in the Changing Defense Posture. *Asian Survey* 46(4): 615–631.

Perloff, Richard M. 1993. *The Dynamics of Persuasion.* Hillsdale, NJ: Erlbaum Associates.

Petty, Richard E., and Duane T. Wegener 1998. Attitude Change: Multiple Roles for Persuasion Variables. In *The Handbook of Social Psychology.* Daniel T. Gilbert, Susan T. Fiske, and Gardner Lindzey, eds. Pp. 323–390. New York: McGraw-Hill.

Pimentel, Aquilino Q. Jr. 2006. *Martial Law in the Philippines: My Story.* Mandaluyong: Cacho Publishing House.

Price, Richard. 1998. Reversing the Gun Sights: Transnational Civil Society Targets Land Mines. *International Organization* 52(3): 613–644.

Ripsman, Norrin M. 2009. Neoclassical Realism and Domestic Interest Groups. In *Neoclassical Realism, the State, and Foreign Policy.* Steven E. Lobell, Norrin M. Ripsman, and Jeffrey W. Taliaferro, eds. Pp. 170–193. Cambridge: Cambridge University Press.

Ryukyu Shimpo Sha. 2003. *Rupo: Gunjikichi to Tatakau Jyuumin Tachi: Nihon, Kaigai No Genba Kara* [*Reportage: Local Residents Who Fight Against Military Bases in Japan and Abroad*]. Tokyo: NHK Shuppan (in Japanese).

Salonga, Jovito R. 1995. *The Senate That Said No: A Four-Year Record of the First Post-EDSA Senate.* Manila: University of the Philippines Press.

Salonga, Jovito R. 2001. *A Journey of Struggle & Hope.* Quezon City: University of the Philippines and Regina Publishing.

Schweller, Randall. 2006. *Unanswered Threats: Political Constraints on the Balance of Power.* Princeton, NJ: Princeton University Press.

Simbulan, Roland G. 1985. *The Bases of Our Insecurity: A Study of the US Military Bases in the Philippines.* 2nd Edn. Manila: BALAI Fellowship, Inc.

Simbulan, Roland G. 1989. *A Guide to Nuclear Philippines: A Guide to the US Military Bases, Nuclear Weapons and What the Filipino People are Doing About These.* Manila: IBON Databank Philippines Inc.

Simbulan, Roland G. 1991. *The Continuing Struggle for an Independent Philippine Foreign Policy.* Philippines: Nuclear Free Philippines Coalition.

Smith, Sheila A. 2000. Challenging National Authority: Okinawa Prefecture and the U.S. Military Bases. In *Local Voices, National Issues: The Impact of Local Initiative in Japanese Policy-Making.* Sheila A. Smith, ed. Pp. 75–114. Ann Arbor, MI: University of Michigan.

Takazato, Suzuyo. 1996. *Okinawa No Onnatachi: Jyosei No Jinken to Kichi, Guntai* [*Women of Okinawa: Human Rights of Women and Bases, Military*]. Tokyo: Akashi Shoten (in Japanese).

Tarrow, Sidney. 1998. *Power in Movement: Social Movements and Contentious Politics.* Cambridge: Cambridge University Press.

Urashima, Etsuko. 2005. *Henoko: Umi No Tatakai* [*Henoko: Struggles in the Sea*]. Tokyo: Impact Shuppan Kai (in Japanese).

Vogel, Ezra F., and Paul Giarra. 2002. Renegotiating the U.S.–Japan Security Relationship, 1991–96. In *Case Studies in Japanese Negotiating Behavior.* Michael Blaker, Paul Giarra, and Ezra Vogel, eds. Pp. 93–146. Washington DC: United States Institute of Peace.

Yeo, Andrew. 2001. *Activists, Alliances, and Anti-U.S. Base Protests.* New York: Cambridge University Press.

Yonakuni, Noboru. 2005. *Okinawa: Hansen Heiwa Ishiki No Keisei* [*Okinawa: How Antiwar Peace Consciousness Was Formed*]. Tokyo: Shinsensha (in Japanese).

35

SUSTAINABILITY AND CLIMATE GOVERNANCE

Janelle Knox-Hayes

Civil society at the interface of global and local initiatives

Since the negotiation of the Kyoto Protocol, market mechanisms have been the global prescription for addressing climate change. Yet, while market mechanisms are universal in their underlying logics, they are enacted in very different political economics. Thus, market governance of climate change is situated at the interface of two competing logics: universalistic governance predicated on technocratic norms, and the particularities of politics embedded in local cultures. Here, "local" refers to sub-global (region, state, city) political units that are internally constructed as political entities. Because civil societies play a pivotal role in the construction and enactment of local political economies, civil society is central to the translation of global-level ideational frameworks into local contexts. Non-governmental organizations help broader society to understand the issues at play and the appropriate responses derived from socio-economic norms. Businesses and other economic actors shape formal and practiced climate policy in line with their understanding of standard economic practice.

The role of civil society in climate policy is at once obvious and obscure. Civil society plays a clear role in awareness raising, as evidenced in climate marches and other profile-building activities. But civil society's role in economic practice of climate policy is far less obvious. This is because markets represent a universalistic or technocratic logic that contends that global problems can be solved with the application of one-size-fits-all solutions derived from science and economics (Bailey and Wilson 2009). Interwoven into this logic is the idea that markets can be made to work more effectively for environmental and social equity through the recalibration of economic valuations aimed at making environmental investments more desirable, not just on moral grounds or as responses to practical problems, but also because they offer profitable investment options (Newell and Paterson 2010). This logic is reductionist, operates at scale, and is built from codified knowledge that exists independent of the particularities of location.

The universalistic assumptions underlying global climate policy are similar to the high-modernist logics in centrally planned state projects (Scott 1998). These projects often fail because they are based on presumptions about the effectiveness of state coordination and do not take into account local or practical knowledge (*metis*) that arises from everyday life and are grounded within civil society. The application of technocratic approaches to climate governance highlights both the universalistic assumptions about market financialization and how these fail to appreciate the ways scale and place impact political and economic behavior. The Kyoto Protocol's use of certified emissions reductions as a principal policy response to climate change (United Nations 1998), along with the accompanying requirements for commoditization, standardization of measurement, and homogenization, matches well with high-modernist ideology.

However, by focusing on market mechanisms, the Protocol marginalizes other policies (taxation, command-and-control, and technology transfer) that may be more effective in some political economies (Knox-Hayes 2012). While governments have mobilized a primarily techno-economic fix to address climate change, this is not necessarily indicative of the solutions desired by various societal stakeholders (Owens and Cowell 2011).

The tensions between the universalist logics underpinning carbon markets and the perspectives of local civil society come to the fore when governments translate global policy prescriptions into the particularities of each operating jurisdiction. Here, the universalistic logic encounters different socio-political and cultural governance logics and values operating through civil society on the ground. Variations in political-economic cultural contexts—understood as socially established norms, rules, and expectations that define how social actors operate and interact (Katzenstein 1996)—play a key role in shaping how societies respond to global imperatives. Culture influences the conduct of economic interactions within specific societies, as well as the role of economic processes in policy and society. As the markets are constructed, everything, from the nature of the legislation that is developed, to the organizations used to operationalize the markets, to the ways in which various polities respond to the idea of market-based governance, is affected. The dynamics on the ground shape the markets and affect the ways in which they perform.

Another important point of analytical concern for understanding the role of civil society in climate policy is the issue of scale. Non-governmental organizations (NGOs), corporations, and government agencies in "hybrid" (combining state and non-state actors) and transnational environmental governance networks play an increasingly important role in climate governance (Andonova, Betsill, and Bulkeley 2009; Betsill and Bulkeley 2007). One of the effects of this dispersal of governance is a resistance to efforts to establish environmental governance arrangements, because regional/local governments, businesses, and communities reinterpret governance concepts through the particular lenses of their beliefs, traditions, circumstances, and dilemmas (Krueger and Gibbs 2010). The creation of standards and agreements through which carbon management occurs can similarly vary (Ocampo 2011).

As a consequence, the institutional landscape of carbon governance is highly variegated across initiatives, actors, and countries. The translation of international commitments into action remains reliant on and imbued within territorially bound politics (While, Jonas, and Gibbs 2010), giving a substantial role to civil society. Thus, this plurality of approaches can in part be seen as a response by the various actors involved in promoting and implementing the carbon governance to integrate—and potentially challenge—neoliberal capitalist attempts to fit environmental problems within prevailing political-economic paradigms (Pattberg 2007; Redclift 2012).

Examining the governance structure of carbon markets—the organizations and mechanisms of generating and enforcing legislation—provides one avenue for understanding how governance is achieved across the global-local and technocratic-political spectrums, as well as the role of civil society. In this chapter, I construct a case history of carbon market development in Japan and examine the unique socio-political and cultural context that has shaped the development of emissions markets in the various jurisdictions. Interviews conducted with a range of government, industry and civil society actors (see Table 35.1) were used to inform this analysis.[1]

Cultural norms mediated through crisis and environmental context

The case of Japan highlights the dynamics of culture and civil society that are central to this chapter. While Japan has experimented with emissions trading systems at the regional scale, it has yet to develop a national emissions trading system. Moreover, Japan is increasingly reliant on bilateral technology exchange programs that have relatively little engagement with markets.

In some ways, market-based governance is a poor fit for Japan. Japan's political and cultural history is as an old empire with roots in Confucian-based governance. The Confucian system—attributed to its fifth-century BC Chinese namesake—emphasizes mutual obligation and hierarchical submission to leaders and elites as the bearers of moral authority, education and institutions crucial to shaping character, and hierarchy and obligation in governance (Kaufman 2007). Perhaps as a reflection of this heritage, Japan maintains strong state involvement in the economy and direct relationships between the government and industry. For example, there is still a system of *amakudari* (literally translated, "descent from heaven"), in which retiring senior government officials take executive positions in Japan's largest companies (Colignon and Usui 2003). This dynamic creates strong but informal ties and cooperation between government and industry. In addition to these strong ties between national ministries and industry, the Japanese political economy is defined by a strong role for powerful industry associations like the *Keidanren* (Japan Business Federation). Thus, economic elements of Japanese civil society are able to exercise profound influence over climate policy.

Having hosted the 1997 United Nations Framework Convention on Climate Change (UNFCCC) Conference of Parties (COP) that led to the Kyoto Protocol, Japan has strong connections to the international system that gave rise to international emissions trading. As a consequence, Japan has been experimenting with the development of an emissions trading system since the ratification of the Kyoto Protocol in 1998. Not surprisingly, competition between the ministries has been a recurrent issue in Japan. The Ministry of Environment is responsible for environmental policy and has some natural jurisdiction over climate change, but is a relatively new ministry—upgraded to a ministry from an agency only in 2001. It has limited regulatory authority over energy policy, which is the traditional purview of the Ministry of Economy, Trade and Industry (METI). METI and Japan's powerful industry association, the *Keidanren*, generally oppose all forms of emissions regulation that could harm the competitiveness of Japan's industry. However, strong pressure at the international level created the impetus first at the Tokyo Municipal Level in 2007 (Bureau of Environment 2015), and eventually at the national level (although those plans would be cancelled) for emissions trading to be developed by the Ministry of Environment (Sharp 2010).

The Fukushima crisis, also referred to as the Fukushima Daiichi nuclear disaster, in which a magnitude 9.0 earthquake triggered a tsunami that devastated eastern Japan and led to the meltdown of three nuclear reactors in 2011, disrupted the development of Japan's climate policy. In the aftermath of the accident, which was the worst nuclear incident since the Chernobyl disaster, the elements of Japanese civil society rallied the public to put strong pressure on the Japanese government to abandon nuclear power. Considering the high proportion of nuclear energy in Japan's energy mix before Fukushima (30 percent), the country has had few options but to increase its use of fossil fuels (Lesbirel 2004; World Nuclear Association 2015). The Fukushima crisis highlighted the possible overreliance on nuclear power as a semi-indigenous source of energy, as well as a breakdown in the implicit arrangement between the government and the public to ensure energy stability, albeit at high prices (Knox-Hayes, Brown, Sovacool, and Wang 2013).

As the subsequent discussion explores, these energy constraints combined with concerns over the possibility that emissions trading may affect innovation in the context of underlying Japanese values of materiality and technological innovation to allow the *Keidanren*, in conjunction with METI, to be successful in sidelining an emissions trading scheme. In its place, they have proposed a Joint Crediting Mechanism, through which Japan exchanges its technology with developing countries for emissions offsets. The scheme is innovative and harmonizes with Japanese political economic culture, but has raised questions about whether or not it and Japan's overall climate policy are sufficient to meet international reduction targets (Obayashi and Sheldrick 2015).

Balance amongst policy, ministries, and industry

The process of legislation in Japan is relatively complicated and highlights the importance of the bureaucracy. While both the Diet (parliament) and the cabinet can submit bills for consideration, in practice the vast majority of bills come from the cabinet (Fujikura 2011). For legislation introduced by the cabinet, the process starts in the most relevant ministry, which produces a first draft of the bill. In the process of producing the draft, ministries often call together *shingikai* (advisory councils) in the drafting of legislation, typically comprised members of civil society coming from academia, NGOs, and industry. The *shingikai* are one of the important channels through which civil society—including powerful industry associations such as the *Keidanren*—exerts its influence:

> In the case of the bill submitted by the government, the *shingikai* will discuss it, and then the ruling party like LDP authorizes it. Then, the government submits that bill to the parliament … We usually recommend the [association's] members to the *shingikai*. From his or her mouthpiece we present our voice in the policy making process. Usually, the *shingikai*'s members are from business committees and the labor unions and academics, or sometimes, a representative from the consumer organization or something like that. In the case of environmental issues, of course, the environmental NGO would be a member of the shingikai, which means the government collects many voices from many stakeholders.
>
> *(Industry Association, Senior Manager of Environment, Tokyo, Japan, July 24, 2013)*

Japan's system of government has been described as a "ruling triad" (*sei kan zai*) of conservative politicians, elite bureaucrats, and leading businessmen (Carpenter 2003). This triad is perpetuated in part through the unique bureaucratic structure in Japan and the central importance of the ministries in policy-making. Much of the strength of Japan's ministries can be traced to the aftermath of the World War II, when the Japanese government established special corporations linking ministries and industry in foundational ways to aid in reconstruction of infrastructure and to resuscitate Japan's industry. For example, in 1956 the Ministry of Construction established the Japan Highway Corporation (which managed Japan's national highway system until 2005, when it was privatized), while METI established the Japan Finance Corporation (wide-ranging financial services to the private sector) in 1955. These protected corporations served as extensions of the ministries and were used to promote the interests of elite officials (Carpenter 2003). Thus, at least in economic policy, there is no clear line distinguishing ministries from the industries they oversee and regulate.

Not surprisingly, in light of the direct linkages between ministries and the broader society, considerable authority for policy rests with the ministries who draft virtually all laws, ordinances, regulations, and licenses that govern society (Johnson 1995). This authority is bolstered by the prestige accorded to ministry employment, which is in turn derived from the traditional roots of modern government structures (Wilks 1990). For example, government positions are considered highly desirable, and bureaucrats are recruited exclusively from elite universities, primarily the University of Tokyo. Once in the ministries, civil servants compete for promotion through an age-driven system to increasingly fewer spots of leadership. This intense competition results in a meritocratic bureaucratic elite forced to retire by their mid-fifties, and through *amakudari*, to move to the boards of directors of public and private sector corporations, or to political office (Carlile and Tilton 1998).

The re-employment of high-level officials in the firms and industries they once regulated generates pervasive interpersonal networks amongst numerous elements of Japanese business, politics, and the bureaucracy. The transfer of personnel and knowledge maintains smooth relations between the ministries and industry. While these smooth relations can be useful, they can also be problematic. Some scholars have pointed to problems arising in the nuclear sector due to the blurred lines between ministry and industry before the disaster at Fukushima, where regulatory failure was prominent (Clenfield and Sato 2007; Onishi and Belson 2011). Calmers Johnson (1995) contends that the line between bureaucracy and industry is incredibly thin; it exists, but it is a legal formality. From the standpoint of industry, the formal and informal ties with the ministry maintain an important line of communication through which the real-world experience of industry is brought into consideration in the policy-making process:

> We are representing our business and the knowledge of the business like what happens in the real business activities. Bureaucrats or lawmakers, and also the social scientists don't know about it. Only the business people know about business activities in my opinion. But, real policy making has to be based on the fact of real business activities or real people's lives.
> *(Industry Association, Senior Manager of Environment, Tokyo, Japan, July 24, 1013)*

These strong interpersonal connections between ministries, government, and industry are the legacy of Japan's rapid development in the nineteenth century—spurred in part by fear of colonial conquest after US Admiral Perry sailed into Tokyo Bay in 1853 demanding trade concessions. Susan Carpenter (2003) suggests that the seeds of the modern bureaucracy were sown a few years later at the beginning of the Meiji restoration in 1868, when the government charged the bureaucracy with converting feudal Japan into an industrialized country. To muster sufficient political and societal authority for the monumental task, prominent members of civil society—samurai families, who as a class topped the feudal socio-political hierarchy—staffed the bureaucracy (Mosk 2008). Although Japan would eventually evolve into an industrialized nation with Western institutions, the legacy and the values of these ruling families remain.

While the strong linkages between bureaucracy and industry were founded in the state-driven process of modernization, they were reinforced by the unique nature of corporate structure that emerged in Japan at the end of the nineteenth century: the *zaibatsu* (Mosk 2008). *Zaibatsu* were large family-owned combines, with a holding company on top, a banking subsidiary providing finance, and several industrial subsidiaries controlling specific sectors of the economy. Four of the largest were Sumitomo, Mitsui, Mitsubishi, and Yasuda. The integrated, centralized structure of *zaibatsu* helped the government manage modernization and industrialization through a few corporate nodes (Carpenter 2003).

After the war, the hierarchical order of the *zaibatsu*, with a chain of command ending with a single family, was formally dismantled, although they were subsequently reconstituted in a similar form through informal, interlocking linkages between nominally independent corporations (Morikawa 1992). These business groups, called *keiretsu*, allowed the core of many of the *zaibatsu* to remain active, even maintaining their original family names: Mitsui, Mitsubishi, and Sumitomo (Yafeh 2000). The *keiretsu*, like the *zaibatsu* before them, play an important role in regulating and guiding the Japanese economy. They offer stability to the economy and facilitate the effectiveness and survival of corporations (Dore 2000). They also provide a foundation for *amakudari*—thus perpetuating linkages between the ministry and industry that would be difficult in a fragmented economic landscape.

Japan's large *keiretsu* formally collaborate with other industries through the comprehensive economic organization of the *Keidanren*. Information sharing within the *Keidanren* binds government and private interests and accounts for the tenacity and adaptability of the political bureaucratic business (Carlile and Tilton 1998). One of the tasks of the *keiretsu*—which typically have financial services at their core to provide support to manufacturing and service sector elements of the business group—is to serve as intermediaries between global initiatives and Japanese companies, translating (linguistically and culturally) these initiatives into a format that is more comfortable for Japanese companies. For example, the *keiretsu* create counterparts for initiatives such as the United Nations Environment Program (UNEP) Finance Initiative (a platform associating the UN and the financial sector), or the United Nations Global Compact (a global corporate sustainability initiative):

> The Global Compact has more than ten thousand signatories. It's the biggest CSR initiative in the world. But as far as I know, there are only about roughly 100 Japanese signatories of the Global Compact. There are a small number of Japanese companies, not only financial institutions but Japanese companies that joined the Global Compact proactively. Japanese companies are too serious about jumping into those global initiatives. Whereas with the U.S. or European companies, they might feel they can join one year and drop out, then join again, there is a strong commitment and a very strict obligation with the Japanese companies. We can make a win–win situation between global initiatives and our domestic initiatives. Japanese intermediaries are set up and they help acclimate the companies into trading or into meeting their obligation. But they're structured in a very Japanese way.
>
> *(Managing Director, Financial Services Company, Tokyo, Japan, August 5, 2012)*

This interlocutor highlights the need for political-economic cultural translation between Japanese economic actors and global initiatives. In this case, the strong cultural expectation in Japan that participating in a voluntary program creates a binding commitment can make the initiatives daunting for these companies and thus preclude Japanese participation. A sense of strong commitment to obligations is one of the traditional values that permeate Japanese climate governance. Language also has an effect; without the *keiretsu*, small to medium Japanese companies would not join these initiatives, in part because of language barrier. The initiatives tend to be mediated in English, which creates a significant disadvantage for Japanese companies. This was also an oft-cited complaint amongst interview respondents regarding their interactions with the UNFCCC's Clean Development Mechanism (CDM) executive board.

As a result, for global finance initiatives, as well as policies like the CDM or even the creation of emissions trading, the *keiretsu* serve to insulate the economic elements of Japanese civil society by creating services that mimic the intent and function of their global counterparts but without forcing the small to medium industries to interact and participate on the international level. For some emissions trading programs, the *keiretsu* also provided intermediary services, allowing companies to avoid trading allowances or offsets on a market platform and instead acquire credits in line with other goods and services they regularly purchase from the *keiretsu*.

Trial emissions trading programs

The relationship between elected policy makers, the bureaucracy, and industry has shaped Japan's response to emissions trading in important ways. Japan's initial response was to follow the emissions trading agenda established by the Kyoto Protocol and to emulate the European Union's Emissions Trading System (EU ETS). Despite Japan's early international declarations, the country's climate policy struggled to gel, as competition between the ministries resulted in several competing proposed emissions reduction systems. Much of this discord traces back to a stark division in perspective between the Ministry of Environment, which supported emissions trading, and the Ministry of Economy Trade and Industry, which joined with the *Keidanren* in opposing emissions trading. Of particular significance is the emphasis on materiality in the Japanese economy, and the importance of manufacturing and the weakness of finance (the latter being central to emissions trading):

> In Japan there is always a conflict between the Ministry of the Environment and METI. The *Keidanren*, Japanese Business Federation Committee, is working very closely with METI. METI's priority is to help those Japanese big companies. There was a very strong debate between the Ministry of Environment and METI. Of course the Ministry of Environment would like to establish a carbon market, but METI doesn't like it, and the Nippon *Keidanren* also doesn't like it ... Heavy industry companies such as Toyota, Nihon Steel, or Tokyo Electric Power or many chemical companies in these industries are the key players among the Nippon *Keidanren*. The financial sector is very weak in the Nippon *Keidanren* Business Federation.
> *(Chief CSR Officer, Insurance Company, Tokyo, Japan, July 31, 2012)*

As a consequence of the structure of the organization, the traditional values of heavy industry, such as materiality, technological development, and hierarchic order, have played an important role in structuring Japan's response to emissions trading. Another interlocutor highlighted the relationship between scope of economic operation and receptivity to emissions trading.

> Companies who do not emit CO_2 or more advanced companies who work globally not just domestically, those companies are more flexible and more understanding on these market mechanisms because they are doing business in Europe and they're more flexible to the new era. But still Japanese discussion is dominated by these kinds of heavy industry or chemical, steel or car companies, and they have a very big impact on the policy.
> *(Senior Researcher, Energy Foundation, Tokyo, Japan, August 16, 2012)*

These interlocutors suggest dual dynamics at play. First, there is a power asymmetry in the representation of the *Keidanren*, which leads to an emphasis on the values of material production embodied in Japan's heavy industry groups. Second, there is an issue of domestic versus international representation. The few companies that engage in business abroad are more likely to support the idea of emissions trading, because they recognize it as an important international standard. However, most companies are domestically oriented, and are guided in their limited interaction with international initiatives by larger companies such as the *keiretsu*. These large companies play an important role in mediating the flow of not only products but also ideas and institutional structures into Japan's economy.

Despite resistance from METI and the *Keidanren*, Japanese policy makers initially decided to pursue emissions trading to meet its international obligations under the Kyoto Protocol. The decision was outward facing, primarily concerned with linking Japan to the international initiative that bore the name of its former imperial capital, and vesting its trust in partners such as the United States that had pushed for emission trading as the basis of a global response. To that end, the Tokyo Metropolitan Government worked to develop a voluntary ETS initially planned to operate in two phases, 2002–2004 and 2005–2009 (Environmental Defense Fund and International Emissions Trading Association 2012). The program missed those initial targets and only in 2008 was the program (now mandatory rather than voluntary) formalized through legislation at the municipal level to reduce emissions from large-scale emitters using a cap and trade system (Bureau of Environment 2015). The Tokyo cap and trade system came into force April 2010 and in the first compliance period (2010–2015) functioned with the goal of a 6 percent reduction in emissions from the year 2000.

In the context of efforts by the Tokyo government to introduce emissions trading and following the launch of the ETS in Europe, the Ministry of Environment introduced a national Japanese Voluntary Emissions Trading Scheme (JVETS) in September 2005 to support greenhouse gas reductions by Japanese companies. JVETS is a voluntary cap and trade system, under which participants adopt emission reduction targets and receive Japanese Emission Allowances (JPAs) from the government (Industrial Efficiency Policy Database 2015b).

Not surprisingly, civil society, through the *Keidanren*, was very active on the issue. As an alternative JVETS, the *Keidanren* also created an emissions reduction program—Voluntary Action Plan (VAP)—that was adopted by the government as part of the Kyoto Protocol Target Achievement Plan (Industrial Efficiency Policy Database 2015a). It included a non-binding target to reduce CO_2 emissions in industry and the energy sector below their 1990 levels by 2010. As with JVETS, companies could use offsets from the CDM or a domestic program to offset their emissions, but the VAP did not seek to implement an emissions trading program. Rather, the VAP sought commitments from industrial groups to environmental targets and checked on a periodic basis to review progress toward those targets. The VAP ended after Japan announced its decision to pull out of the second commitment period of the Kyoto Protocol. The 2012 withdrawal announcement suggests tensions within government and between government and civil society regarding the social, political, and economic foundations of climate policy. As the subsequent discussion explores, a substantial contributing factor is the mismatch between the norms of global market-based governance and Japanese political economic culture.

Resistance to cap and trade: the money game and materiality

Efforts by METI and the *Keidanren* to establish emissions reductions programs in competition with emissions trading demonstrate a pervasive resistance to these systems. Notable in the Japanese case are the values expressed to justify that resistance. While METI and the *Keidanren* in large part simply opposed the idea of regulation that would affect the competitiveness of Japanese industry, the idea of trading was *more offensive* than alternatives such as a carbon tax:

> Of course we oppose everything, but I think a tax is better. Many business people would agree that a carbon tax is better than the emission trading system because we can predict the tax better. It is very difficult to predict the market of the emission rights.
>
> *(Industry Association, Senior Manager of Environment, Tokyo, Japan, July 13, 2014)*

The sentiment expressed by the interlocutor is certainly a powerful one for Japan's policy makers. In 2012, Japan implemented a carbon tax leveraged through energy use that affects all consumers and helps to raise revenue for initiatives to combat climate change (Japan for Sustainability 2013). Yet, the interlocutor raises a puzzle: why is it that Japanese businesses—some of the most successful and advanced in the world—find the "unpredictability" of the carbon price so challenging, when economic actors in systems where emissions trading has been introduced do not express similar concerns? Put another way, why is pricing a liability for major elements of Japan's economic civil society but an opportunity for corporations in other political economic contexts?

In part, the curious difficulty of Japanese companies coming to terms with carbon pricing is grounded in the role of culturally specific discourses referencing values of techno-materiality. These values are perhaps most obvious in the remarkable consistency with which carbon trading was labeled as a money game, the creation of value from financial processes without material substance. One interlocutor explained:

> Industry members think that allowance trading is just trading, not the reduction of emissions. They say the trading of allowances is only for the benefit of the traders, banks, and financial sectors. The trading is not beneficial to the industries.
>
> *(Senior Fellow, Trading Company and Think Tank, Tokyo, Japan, July 24, 2012)*

The idea that the pursuit of profit for profit's sake is not acceptable references Japanese cultural values. This is not to say that profit is not important in Japan, merely that profit is grounded in assessments of techno-material advancement rather than financial gain. This valuation in the Japanese context is transmitted through the language of honor. Thus, when several respondents suggested that companies should pursue profit, but should do so in a way that is honorable, they are appealing to a techno-material conception of profit. The sense that emission trading creates value out of something that is artificial is at odds with these cultural norms.

> The money is not so powerful in society. They always respect the people, but money is not such an objective of the respect. I think that is historical. These days young people change but my father's generation or old generation when you … for example my father was a government official they don't like to say "I want to earn money a lot." It's a very cultural thing and … when the carbon markets are developed then people say that that's the money game so, that's why the money game.
>
> *(Senior Consultant, Securities Exchange, Tokyo, Japan, August 14, 2012)*

The way in which companies traditionally create honorable profit is through manufacturing, or the creation of material products and services that bring tangible value to society:

> Our slogan of country is *monozukuri* [literally translated, thing and process of making]. Monozukuri means manufacture. They are respected a lot so that's why the voice from manufacturers like steel company or Toyota or … they have a very strong voice, but not financial companies.
>
> *(Senior Consultant, Securities Exchange, Tokyo, Japan, August 14, 2012)*

The strength of the *keiretsu* lies not just in their historicity or their size, but in the fact that they are situated at the heart of a material economy, they trade commodities, heavy equipment, and manufacturing technology. As such, they are seen to fulfill the core principles and values upon which the Japanese economy is founded. Materiality is not just about physical impact—that value is created from the manufacture of a product rather than the trade of an emissions credit. In the Japanese context, the concept of materiality also reflects the idea that the action taken should be integral to the function of a company or what an industry does. In this way, material actions are embodied in the intent and function of an industry.

> CSR should be connected with the corporate value. That's why the materiality is important. The company could say so many great things; they plant trees in Papua New Guinea or whatever but that doesn't have any value for the company. Does it strengthen the corporate value? Business should improve their behavior or improve their environmental burden within *their main business*. That's materiality attitude. If a financial institution like us plants trees in Papua New Guinea or wherever, it's not material. But if a company like Tsumitomo Housing, they plant trees and use those lumber for their house making, then that's materiality. So if within their main business they use a sustainable tree then that's materiality because the volume they use is so huge because they are doing it for their business. But in case of us, if we plant trees, it's very tiny. It's not really material. If you are doing the housing business, why don't you build a more green house and if you're an automobile maker, you have to make more electric vehicles or other low emission cars.
>
> *(Managing Director, Financial Services Research Institute, Tokyo, Japan, August 15, 2012)*

From this perspective, materiality in terms of environmental impact lies in actual changes in industrial or corporate practice central to the corporate value added. Toyota cannot have a material impact by planting trees, because trees have nothing to do with manufacturing automobiles. Conversely, using a new manufacturing process that results in lower energy requirements per finished automobile would produce a material impact for Toyota. Thus, for emissions credits to be material, they must reflect a tangible impact relative to what a company is or does.

> In our group there is a company that announced that they were the first Japanese financial institution to be carbon neutral. So they claim that they are very advanced. But I don't think so. Because for the insurance companies to be carbon neutral is rather an easy task with not very much money. But for the Japanese big companies like Hitachi or Toyota, carbon neutral is not possible. So it's a kind of corporate image strategy or propaganda. I don't like that kind of thing … As an insurance company, we should focus on providing our main products and services to our customers and by doing so, we should contribute to help those environmental businesses or actual progress for the business.
>
> *(Chief CSR Officer, Insurance Company, Tokyo, Japan, July 31, 2012)*

These responses suggest that there are widely shared, culturally grounded doubts in major elements of economic civil society regarding what emissions trading can accomplish. Whereas technological innovation and energy efficiency are seen to have a material impact, emissions credits are structured from the absence of greenhouse gas emissions. In this regard, they are completely intangible and lack materiality. Continuing with the cultural significance of materiality, interviewees raise doubts about the ability of short-term pricing to effect long-term changes and technology development. Thus, assessment of success is not in terms of relatively abstract carbon emissions, but rather in terms of observable techno-material changes. It is not a market per se that Japanese interlocutors opposed, but rather the idea that the market should create a form of value that is purely financial, with merely assumed links to technological or material outcomes.

> What the government has to do is not create the market but support the R&D and the target shouldn't be mandatory but voluntary because the Japanese company's custom is not to try to make money from the market, but even though they don't have any mandatory target, Japanese companies would do what they have to do. There are a lot of companies who still believe in that [material] kind of value ... It is very different from the European or American [system].
>
> *(Analyst, Regulatory Body, Tokyo, August 1, 2012)*

Consistently in the interviews conducted across civil society and government in Japan, concerns with materiality manifested time and again, a finding echoed in the statistical analysis of interview responses. Participants show considerable skepticism about the absence of tangibility in emissions markets that are central to global emissions reductions under the Kyoto Protocol. The tension between the culturally grounded desire for material outcomes, and the need to meet international obligations driven by a different market culture led at first to the creation of the voluntary carbon reduction scheme. For a time, as evidenced by the voluntary market set up by the Ministry of Environment, Japanese policy makers made some effort to accommodate the norms of the globalized market approach.

Two factors contributed to the end of that policy and a shift to an approach more in line with Japanese market culture. First, the voluntary system was not effective. Japanese society views "voluntary" as binding once a company signs on, creating challenges for Japanese companies in the context of American and European companies that view "voluntary" in far less binding terms. Japanese policy makers pursued the approach anyway in the hope that voluntary markets would provide greater flexibility for the companies to try to achieve their targets, but to do so in a way that would allow them to focus on technology development and material outcomes, rather than just adjusting their manufacturing process year by year. A second, more potent, factor that redirected Japanese policy makers to refocus on harmonizing policy with domestic market culture was the Fukushima crisis. In the aftermath of the Fukushima crisis, the civil society driven concern with material outcomes led to the abandonment of emissions trading altogether and the creation of the Bilateral/Joint Crediting Mechanism.

Civil society and policy in the aftermath of the Fukushima crisis

On March 11, 2011, Japan was devastated by the Tohoku, or Great East Japan, earthquake, the most powerful earthquake ever recorded in Japan. The earthquake triggered powerful tsunami waves that reached heights of up to 133 feet and traveled up to six miles inland (BBC News 2011). The quake led to massive destruction of coastal towns across the Sendai region of eastern Japan, including the Fukushima Daiichi nuclear power plant, leading to the meltdown of three reactors. Given serious safety concerns and the public shock of the event, the Japanese government shut down nuclear reactors across Japan (Deutsche Welle 2015).

Japan is relatively energy resource-poor and relied on nuclear energy for a substantial portion of its energy portfolio. Before the crisis, nuclear energy provided up to 30 percent of Japan's electricity (World Nuclear Association 2015). The crisis following the Fukushima Daiichi meltdown, the worst nuclear incident since Chernobyl, pushed up Japan's carbon emissions through greater fossil fuel imports and exacerbated energy insecurity concerns. Indeed, the post-Fukushima energy mix, in many ways, was a reversal of decades of policy shaped by Japan's concern over petroleum reliance and various efforts to diversify its supply (Toichi 2003).

After the 1970s oil shocks, the government promoted a two-pronged approach to energy security; they diversified energy resources away from petroleum and reduced energy intensity by implementing rigorous energy efficiency standards across all sectors of the economy (Lesbirel 2004). As a consequence, Japan has become increasingly reliant on nuclear energy, and the technologies that are central to nuclear energy and energy efficiency have taken on increased symbolic and practical significance. The Fukushima disaster was thus double-pronged: it undermined Japanese energy stability and, through the manifest failure of technology, struck at a core totem of Japanese culture. In combination with existing resistance to the idea of emissions trading, the crisis halted Japan's development of climate policy.

> One reason is probably Japanese custom; people are very skeptical of the market mechanism to apply for these kinds of issues. More engineer-oriented is preferable for the people. The second reason is that I think the momentum of the climate change issue is very low internationally and in Japan. Internationally, it might be, we couldn't agree the international target. Domestically, it is because of the Fukushima accident; it is more the serious issue for the Japan to deal with because climate change is a little bit longer time issue, but energy issues are very, very short time issues … It seems that for a while we leave global warming issue aside. We first try to fix our energy policy and then global warming issue. For those three reasons, the artificial [carbon] market seems very, very low at this moment.
>
> *(Senior Researcher, Energy Foundation, Tokyo, Japan, August 16, 2012)*

In the wake of Fukushima, efforts to scale up the emissions trading system to a national mandatory program died. In addition, realizing that it would be impossible for Japan to meet its Kyoto targets without the use of nuclear energy, Japan pulled out of the second phase of the Kyoto Protocol. With climate policy pushed to the back burner, METI and the *Keidanren* were able to push forward an alternative to emissions trading.

In response to the energy crisis that resulted from the Fukushima disaster, the Japanese government turned to a proposal from METI and the *Keidanren* that also meshed well with Japanese cultural emphasis on materiality. In 2011, Japan announced the launch of the Joint Crediting Mechanism/Bilateral Offset Credit Mechanism (JCM/BOCM). In its essence, the JCM/BOCM is a low-carbon technology dissemination program, taking advantage of Japan's advanced position in energy efficiency technology.

The JCM/BOCM is intended to facilitate the transfer of low carbon technology and infrastructure to developing countries. Projects developed to take advantage of the technology transfer are assessed through jointly agreed measurement, reporting, and verification methodologies for greenhouse-gas emissions or removal (Government of Japan 2013). While the JCM/BOCM borrowed many features of the CDM and to some extent functions as a market mechanism, it critically allows Japan to focus on the development and exchange of technology:

> Actually, I cannot imagine the advantage of the cap and trade system. We are strongly opposing introducing the cap and trade emissions trading system. We should focus on the market, of course, but we should focus on good market, or technological market. In order to reduce the CO_2 emissions, we have to improve the energy efficiency or we have to reduce the carbon intensity to the energy: only two things. Then, in order to realize it we need technologies. Technologies are really the key to saving this planet.

Now, halving the CO_2 emissions by 2050, we are saying that we agreed. Even if Annex I countries reduce the 100 percent, which means zero emissions, and the developing countries have to reduce from their business as usual by 65 percent in order to realize halving the global share by 2050. In order to realize this, we need innovative technologies, so we really should focus on technologies, especially innovative technologies.

(Industry Association, Senior Manager of Environment, Tokyo, Japan, July 24, 2013)

The Japanese Joint Crediting Mechanism expresses and harmonizes with Japanese materiality values by providing a mechanism for Japanese companies to exchange clean energy technologies for offset credits from developing countries. Whereas a cap is seen to penalize industry, the JCM creates opportunities for industries and market development in line with core economic activities, tapping into materiality values.

Of course we started with CSR activities but definitely we also contribute something material to Japan, because we are Japanese company now. That's why our expertise can contribute now to be BOCM because BOCM also try to promote the Japanese technology. The BOCM works very well for technology transfers.

(Senior Consultant, Securities Exchange, Tokyo, Japan, August 14, 2012)

The JCM/BOCM provides the additional advantage of making it easier for Japan to reduce emissions overseas, not only because Japan is already very energy efficient, but also because climate policy competes directly with energy policy. Finally, the JCM/BOCM aligns internationally with Japan's understanding of itself post-World War II as a civilian and trading nation and with beliefs about the role of technology in preserving Japanese security (Samuels 1994). Japan has already developed partnerships with thirteen developing countries, including many partners in Southeast Asia (Ministry of the Environment 2015).

Whether the JCM/BOCM will be sufficient for Japan to achieve the domestic emissions reductions required to reach a binding international target remains to be seen. Nevertheless, from the standpoint of economic civil society, the JCM/BOCM confers many advantages in the Japanese political and cultural context beyond what a traditional emissions trading system would provide. The Japanese case, particularly the concern with materiality and the eventual policy harmonization with core elements of market culture, highlight the importance of local political economic culture and the civil society actors that inhabit and enact it in shaping responses to climate change.

Conclusion

There can be little doubt that civil society, particularly organized economic actors like the *Keidanren*, has had a substantial impact on Japan's climate policy. In general, civil society is explicitly integrated into Japanese policy making through *shingikai* (advisory councils). In the case of climate change, the ministry most connected to economic civil society actors—the Ministry of Trade Economy and Industry—as well as the *Keidanren* itself, opposed the markets because of the perceived effect they would have on the competition and technological innovation of industry, and advocated voluntary commitment programs. The Fukushima crisis raised the importance of energy policy, shifted the balance of authority between the ministries, and created space for an alternative approach advocated by organized elements of economic civil society. Moreover, by emphasizing Japanese traditional values of materiality and manufacturing, Japan's Joint Crediting Mechanism aligns policy with a broad swath of Japan's civil society.

Table 35.1 Interview subject list

No.	Date	Entity	Role	Place
1	July 13, 2012	Trading Company	Assistant General Manager, New Energy and Power	Tokyo
2	July 24, 2012	Think Tank and Trading Company	Senior Fellow, Green Innovation Department	Tokyo
3	July 25, 2012	Manager of Information Services	Manager of Information Services	Tokyo
4	July 25, 2012	Manager of Information Services	Information Services Department	Tokyo
5	July 26, 2012	Development Bank	Associate, Environmental Initiative and Corporate Social Responsibility Support Department	Tokyo
6	July 31, 2012	Insurance Company	Associate Director, Chief CSR Officer	Tokyo
7	August 1, 2012	Regulatory Body	Analyst	Tokyo
8	August 8, 2012	Trading Company	Chair of Principle Working Group	Tokyo
9	August 8, 2012	Government Affiliated Research Organization	Manager Market Mechanism Group	Tokyo
10	August 9, 2012	Bank	Head, Sustainable Development Department	Tokyo
11	August 9, 2012	Legal Firm	Director, Business Development and Marketing, Tokyo	Tokyo
12	August 9, 2012	Legal Firm	Lawyer	Tokyo
13	August 14, 2012	Securities Exchange	CDM/JI Senior Consultant Deputy Chairman Clean Energy Finance Committee	Tokyo
14	August 15, 2012	News Company	Reporter	Tokyo
15	August 15, 2012	Financial Services Research Institute	Research Division Managing Director	Tokyo
16	August 16, 2012	Regulatory Body	Analyst	Tokyo
17	August 16, 2012	Energy Foundation	Senior Researcher for Policy Innovation	Tokyo
18	August 22, 2012	Think Tank	Government Consultant and Associate Professor	Tokyo
19	July 24, 2013	Industry Association	Vice Chairman, Director General	Tokyo
20	July 24, 2013	Industry Association	Senior Manager, Environmental Policy Bureau	Tokyo
21	August 14, 2013	Nonprofit	Researcher	Tokyo
22	August 14, 2013	Nonprofit	Assistant General Manager, Principal Researcher	Tokyo
23	August 14, 2013	Project Developer	Director, Japan	Tokyo
24	August 16, 2013	Regulatory Body	Deputy Director, Environment and Economy Division	Tokyo
25	August 20, 2013	Federation	Deputy General Manager, General Planning Department	Tokyo
26	August 20, 2013	Federation	Manager International Affairs	Tokyo
27	August 20, 2013	Steel	General Manager, Climate Change Policy Group, Technology Planning Department	Tokyo
28	August 22, 2013	Automobile Manufacturer	Project General Manager, Environment Group, Environmental Affairs Division	Tokyo
29	August 22, 2013	Automobile Manufacturer	Project General Manager, Environment Group, Environmental Affairs Division	Tokyo
30	August 26, 2013	Accountancy	Senior Manager PPP and Infrastructure	Tokyo
31	August 28, 2013	Government Agency	Director, Bilateral/Joint Credit Office	Tokyo

While Japan's approach engages Japan's financial institutions (in the operation of the scheme) and civil society (NGO consultation in design), policy makers in Japan have often underappreciated the importance of civil society for policy stability. The Fukushima crisis exposed this fault line and disrupted the tenuous balance between global economic norms (market mechanisms) and local market culture (materiality and opposition to the money game). As a result, Japanese policy makers were forced to rethink and remake its energy and climate policies. Looking forward, Japan can build better support for its Joint Crediting Mechanism, and associated climate change policies like the carbon tax, by directly attaching the policies to core values of environmental protection, material manufacturing, and energy security. This would build a broader base support for policies that are otherwise discussed and debated outside the public domain.

To this end, the Japanese case also demonstrates the importance of civil society as carrier and enactor of cultural norms. In Japan, there is a strong cultural belief in the materiality of economic processes. Finance as a basis of economic practice for its own end is treated with skepticism if not outright suspicion, and as a result, carbon markets face substantial challenges from civil society actors and their government allies who are able to draw on the norms of materiality to make their case. The end result, the Joint Crediting Mechanism/Bilateral Offsetting Credit Mechanism, in which Japan effects carbon emissions reductions through technology transfers negotiated amongst bureaucratic elites, is a clear manifestation of Japanese political economic culture.

Note

1 Due to anonymity guarantees required to gain access to interview subjects, neither the individual nor organization names are listed. Rather the interlocutor's type of occupation and type of organization are listed in Table 35.1 with the date and location of the interview.

Suggested readings

Kuramochi, Takeshi. 2015. Review of Energy and Climate Policy Developments in Japan before and after Fukushima. *Renewable and Sustainable Energy Reviews* 43: 1320–1332.

Le, Hanh, and Anaïs Delbosc. 2012. Japan's Bilateral Offset Crediting Mechanism: A Bilateral Solution to a Global Issue. *Climate Brief* 11.

Poortinga, Wouter, Midori Aoyagi, and Nick Pideeon. 2013. Public Perception of Climate Change and Energy Futures Before and After the Fukushima Accident: A Comparison Between Britain and Japan. *Energy Policy* 62: 1204–1211.

Van Asselt, Harro, Norichika Kanie, and Masahiko Iguchi. 2009. Japan's Position in International Climate Policy: Navigating between Kyoto and the APP. *International Environmental Agreements: Politics, Law and Economics* 9(3): 319–336.

References

Andonova, Liliana B., Michele M. Betsill, and Harriet Bulkeley. 2009. Transnational Climate Governance. *Global Environmental Politics* 9(2): 52–73.

Bailey, Ian, and Geoff A. Wilson. 2009. Theorising Transitional Pathways in Response to Climate Change: Technocentrism, Ecocentrism, and the Carbon Economy. *Environment and Planning A* 41(10): 2324–2341.

Betsill, Michele, and Harriet Bulkeley, 2007. Looking Back and Thinking Ahead: A Decade of Cities and Climate Change Research. *Local Environment* 12(5): 447–456.

BBC News. 2011. Japan Earthquake: Tsunami Hits North-East. *BBC News*, March 11. Electronic document, www.bbc.com/news/world-asia-pacific-12709598, accessed August 11, 2015.

Bureau of Environment. 2015. Tokyo Cap and Trade. *Tokyo Metropolitan Government*. Electronic document, www.kankyo.metro.tokyo.jp/en/climate/cap_and_trade.html, accessed August 8, 2015.

Carlile, Lonny E., and Mark Tilton. 1998. Regulatory Reform and the Developmental State. In *Is Japan Really Changing Its Ways? Regulatory Reform and the Japanese Economy*. Lonny E. Carlile and Mark Tilton, eds. Pp. 423–425. Washington, DC: Brookings Institution Press.

Carpenter, Susan M. 2003. *Special Corporations and the Bureaucracy: Why Japan Can't Reform*. Basingstoke: Palgrave Macmillan.

Clenfield, Jason, and Shigeru Sato. 2007. Japan Nuclear Energy Drive Compromised by Conflicts of Interest. *Bloomberg*. Electronic document, www.bloomberg.com/apps/news?pid=newsarchive&sid=awR8KsLlAcSo, accessed August 10, 2015.

Colignon, Richard A., and Chikako Usui. 2003. *Amakudari: the Hidden Fabric of Japan's Economy*. Ithaca, NY: ILR Press.

Deutsche Welle. 2015. Japan Ends Two-Year Nuclear Shutdown by Restarting Reactor. *Deutsche Welle*, August 11. Electronic document, www.dw.com/en/japan-ends-two-year-nuclear-shutdown-by-restarting-reactor/a-18639756, accessed August 11, 2015.

Dore, Ronald Philip. 2000. *Stock Market Capitalism: Welfare Capitalism: Japan and Germany Versus the Anglo-Saxons*. Oxford and New York: Oxford University Press.

Environmental Defense Fund and International Emissions Trading Association. 2012. *Tokyo: A Case Study*. Washington DC: Development of Emissions Trading Around the World.

Fujikura, Ryo. 2011. Law Making in Japan. *USJI Seminar*. Electronic document, www.us-jpri.org/en/reports/seminar/fujikura_20111103.pdf, accessed August 10, 2015.

Government of Japan. 2013. *Recent Development of the Joint Crediting Mechanism (JCM)/Bilateral Offset Credit Mechanism (BOCM)*. Electronic document, www.mmechanisms.org/document/20130523_JCMBOCM_goj.pdf, accessed August 11, 2015.

Industrial Efficiency Policy Database. 2015a. JP-1: Keidanren Voluntary Action Plan (VAP) (ENDED). *Institute of Industrial Productivity*. Electronic document, http://iepd.iipnetwork.org/policy/keidanren-voluntary-action-plan-vap-ended, accessed August 11, 2015.

Industrial Efficiency Policy Database. 2015b. JP-2: Japanese Voluntary Emissions Trading Scheme (JVETS). *Institute of Industrial Productivity*. Electronic document, http://iepd.iipnetwork.org/policy/japanese-voluntary-emissions-trading-scheme-jvets, accessed August 11, 2015.

Japan for Sustainability. 2013. *Japan Introduces New Tax on Carbon Emissions*. Electronic document, www.japanfs.org/en/news/archives/news_id032490.html, accessed August 11, 2015.

Johnson, Calmers. 1995. *Japan, Who Governs?: The Rise of the Developmental State*. New York: W.W. Norton & Company.

Katzenstein, Peter J. 1996. Introduction: Alternative Perspectives on National Security. In *The Culture of National Security*. Peter J. Katzenstein, ed. Pp. 1–32. New York: Columbia University Press.

Kaufman, Alison Adcock. 2007. Confucian Governance. In *Encyclopedia of Governance*. Mark Bevir, ed. P. 140. Thousand Oaks, CA: SAGE Publications.

Knox-Hayes, Janelle. 2012. Negotiating Climate Legislation: Policy Path Dependence and Coalition Stabilization. *Regulation & Governance* 6: 545–567.

Knox-Hayes, Janelle, Marilyn A. Brown, Benjamin K. Sovacool, and Yu Wang. 2013. Understanding Attitudes Toward Energy Security: Results of a Cross-National Survey. *Global Environmental Change* 23: 609–622.

Krueger, Rob, and David Gibbs. 2010. Competitive Global City Regions and "Sustainable Development": An Interpretive Institutionalist Account in the South East of England. *Environment and Planning A* 42: 821–837.

Lesbirel, S. Hayden. 2004. Diversification and Energy Security Risks: The Japanese Case. *Japanese Journal of Political Science* 5: 1–22.

Ministry of the Environment. 2015. Joint Crediting Mechanism. In *New Mechanisms Information Platform*. Electronic document, www.mmechanisms.org/e/initiatives, accessed August 11, 2015.

Morikawa, Hidemasa. 1992. *Zaibatsu: The Rise and Fall of Family Enterprise Groups in Japan*. Tokyo: University of Tokyo Press.

Mosk, Carl. 2008. *Japanese Economic Development: Markets, Norms, Structures*. London: Routledge.

Newell, Peter, and Matthew Paterson. 2010. *Climate Capitalism: Global Warming and the Transformation of the Global Economy*. Cambridge: Cambridge University Press.

Obayashi, Yuka, and Aaron Sheldrick. 2015. Japan's Emissions Target, Relying On Nuclear, Seen As Unrealistic. *Reuters*. Electronic document, http://uk.reuters.com/article/2015/06/03/japan-carbon-idUKL3N0YH1BT20150603, accessed August 8, 2015.

Ocampo, José. 2011. The Transition to a Green Economy: Benefits, Challenges and Risks from a Sustainable Development Perspective: Summary of Background Papers. Prepared under direction of UN-DESA and UNEP. Paper presented at the UN Conference on Trade and Development, New York, 2011.

Onishi, Norimitsu, and Ken Belson. 2011. Culture of Complicity Ties to Stricken Nuclear Plant. *New York Times*, April 27. Electronic document, www.nytimes.com/2011/04/27/world/asia/27collusion.html, accessed August 10, 2015.

Owens, Susan E., and Richard Cowell. 2011. *Land and Limits: Interpreting Sustainability in the Planning Process*. London: Routledge.

Pattberg, Philipp H. 2007. *Private Institutions and Global Governance: The New Politics of Environmental Sustainability*. Cheltenham: Edward Elgar.

Redclift, Michael R. 2012. Living with a New Crisis: Climate Change and Transitions Out of Carbon Dependency. In *Climate Change and The Crisis of Capitalism: A Chance to Reclaim Self, Society, and Nature*. Mark Pelling, David Manuel-Navarrete, and Michael Redclift, eds. Pp. 1–26. London: Routledge.

Samuels, Richard J. 1994. *Rich Nation, Strong Army: National Security and the Technological Transformation of Japan*. Ithaca, NY: Cornell University Press.

Scott, James C. 1998. *Seeing Like a State: How Certain Schemes to Improve the Human Condition Have Failed*. New Haven, CT and London: Yale University Press.

Sharp, Andy. 2010. Japan Drops Cap and Trade. *The Diplomat* December. Electronic document, http://thediplomat.com/2010/12/japan-drops-cap-and-trade/, accessed August 8, 2015.

Toichi, Tsutomu. 2003. Energy Security in Asia and Japanese Policy. *Asia-Pacific Review* 10: 44–51.

United Nations. 1998. Kyoto Protocol to the United Nations Framework Convention on Climate Change.

While, Aidan, Andrew E. G. Jonas, and David Gibbs. 2010. From Sustainable Development to Carbon Control: Eco-State Restructuring and the Politics of Urban and Regional Development. *Transactions of the Institute of British Geographers* 35: 76–93.

Wilks, Stephen. 1990. The Embodiment of Industrial Culture in Bureaucracy and Management. In *Capitalism in Contrasting Cultures*. Stewart Clegg, S. Gordon Redding, and Monica Cartner, eds. Pp. 131–152. Berlin and New York: W. de Gruyter.

World Nuclear Association. 2015. *Nuclear Power in Japan*. Electronic document, www.world-nuclear.org/info/Country-Profiles/Countries-G-N/Japan/, accessed August 8, 2015.

Yafeh, Yishay. 2000. Corporate Governance in Japan: Past Performance and Future Prospects. *Oxford Review of Economic Policy* 16: 74–84.

INDEX

Page numbers in *italics* denote tables, those in **bold** denote figures.

abductions 462–3, 465
ABFSU 334; *see also* All Burma Federation of
  Student Unions
abolition 23, 441–2, 495, 499; and the abolition of
  the two-week rule 499; of the death penalty
  movement 442; of the *hukou* (household
  registration) system 441–2; of temporary labor
  migration 495
abuses 10, 162, 249, 423, 436, 438–9, 441, 443,
  448, 463; of authority 249; human rights 60,
  438, 496; of labor 438; sexual 151
academics 89, 196, 206, 260, 265, 319, 397, 399,
  499, 509
accountability 237–41, 251–2, 274–5, 336, 339,
  382, 436, 441, 443, 445; of CSOs (India) 237;
  political 110; promoting 239; war crime 438
accusations 152, 252, 463; of domestic violence
  463; relating to foreign funding 252; of theft
  152
ACFTU 50; *see also* All-China Federation of
  Trade Unions
activism 8–11, 164–5, 283, 335–6, 338, 370,
  459–62, 469–71, 473–4, 477; and advocacy
  473; anti-war 28; and civil society 153;
  consumer 24; contentious 25; creative 26;
  democratic 34; digital 427; ecological 445;
  eradicating leftist 24; on human rights and social
  justice 160, 286; independent grass-roots citizen
  24; in Japan 460; local LGBT 472; migrant
  497–8; migrant worker 166; non-violent 38;
  political 314, 421, 488; in Singapore 162; street
  219
activists 25–8, 60–1, 168–9, 439, 441–2, 458–60,
  463–4, 478–83, 485–6, 498–9; anti-
  government 38; anti-nuclear 28; civil society

223, 288, 320, 428; grass-roots 80–1, 83–4,
  89–90; Hong Kong 486; human rights 232,
  250, 260, 287, 442, 444, 448; Japanese 334,
  460, 483, 499; LGBT 473; political 312, 319;
  pro-democracy 36, 336, 438; student 79, 83,
  217, 482–4; youth 480–1, 483, 486
ADPAN 169, 442; *see also* Anti-Death Penalty
  Asia Network
advocacy 54, 67–8, 103–6, 166–9, 210, 212–13,
  469–71, 473–4, 488–93, 497–500; anti-
  militarization 477; foreign 102–3, 105–6; on
  gender rights 167; initiatives 28; of migrant
  worker groups 166; mobilization 68;
  professional 103–4; by queer and LGBT groups
  473; and rights-based NGOs 260; and social
  capital 338; and support 168; and welfare
  service delivery 5
advocacy groups 18–19, 24–5, 81, 147, 166, 278,
  334, 338, 473; caste-based 278; issue-oriented
  338; large professionalized 19; local women's
  147
advocacy organizations 67, 106, 250, 490–1,
  494–5, 497; active 499; international 286;
  single-issue 496
AEPF's International Organizing Committee 211
AEZ (Agro-Ecological Zone) 273
Africa 13, 96, 133, 366, 439–40
agencies 7, 19, 21, 114, 121–2, 161–2, 193, 198,
  489, 497; international 4, 195, 236, 238, 316;
  marketing 428; non-government 118; powerful
  anti-corruption 242
agendas 175, 181, 191, 196, 256, 259–60, 281,
  285, 364, 370; contending 286; economic 266;
  national state 368; political 368; socio-
  economic 34, 41

agreements 37, 130, 259, 337, 393, 479, 506, 513, 521; bilateral 507; controversial 478; cross-Strait 479; environmental 506; international 463
agricultural activities 296, 414; complete 296
agricultural production 264, 271–3; commercial 271, 274; increasing 269, 414; traditional 271
agriculture 87, 121, 207, 271, 294, 299, 302, 441, 496; new 271; organic 84; subsistence 207; sustainable 28, 229
aid 95, 151, 195, 211–12, 284, 365, 407, 448, 523; agenda 407–8; agricultural 414; conditional 270; contracted 458; dependence 196; donors 195; effectiveness 407; workers 416
AIDS 12, 52–3, 137, 170, 284, 438–9, 441–2, 445, 448, 458; activism 445; activist Hu Jia 439; groups 445; and human rights in Asia 448; organizations 367
Akihiro Ogawa 1, 14
Alagappa, Muthiah 110, 124–5, 163, 180, 228, 289, 339, 457
Aldrich, Daniel 20
Alexander, Jeffrey 145, 152
Alexy, Allison 456–65
All Burma Students' Democratic Front 334
All-China Federation of Trade Unions 50
alliances 36, 185, 187, 484, 489–90, 492, 506, 508, 512–13, 515; anti-state 35; changing military 485; cross-sectoral 135; student 480; umbrella 36
Allied Occupation of Japan, The 24
Alma-Ata Declaration 444–5
AMC (Asian Migrant Center) 443
AMCB (Asian Migrant Coordinating Body) 498
American foundations 392, 397–8; The Ford Foundation 51, 55, 366, 392–3, 397–8; The Rockefeller Foundation 392; Toyota Foundation 26, 392, 394, 398
American military 11, 505–6, 509
American non-profit organizations 395
American policy makers 511
American politicians 461, 464
American-style philanthropy 391–2
Amnesty International 150, 169, 333, 439
Ananaikyō (religion) 413–14
Anderson, Benedict 125, 216–17, 282, 457
Andhra Pradesh 240–1
Angkatan Belia Islam Malaysia 146
anti-corruption movements 4, 236, 242–5
Anti-Death Penalty Asia Network 169, 442
anti-government activists 38
approval rating of government institutions, 2003–2014 **39**
Aquino 115, 117, 331
Arab Spring 439, 477
Arato, Andrew 95, 265–6, 279, 457–8
Arrington, Celeste 33, 39, 336
Asia Foundation, The 103–5, 397–9

Asian civil society 1–2, 4–6, 9, 12, 180, 366, 436, 448–9; distinctive characteristics of 1; frameworks for understanding 2; scholarship 6, 12–13; society relations in 6; understanding 2; values in 2
Asian countries 2, 6–7, 362–7, 370, 390, 392, 397–8, 400, 491–2, 496; examples of philanthropic activity in 390; industrialized 499
Asian Financial Crisis 42, 333, 365–6, 436–7
Asian human rights 441; and civil society 436; institution-building 439
Asian societies 1–2, 10, 330, 341, 391, 398, 408, 426; democratic deepening in 330; democratization of 341; social movements in 10
"Asian values" 147, 178, 180, 436–7, 448
Aspinall, Edward 152
Association of Indonesian Migrant Workers 498
Astarita, Claudia 420–31
AusAID 103
authoritarian rule 1–2, 6, 9, 35–6, 110, 333–4, 344–7, 349–53, 355, 357; and civil society 344; nexus of 13; specifics of 132; state maintenance of 59
authoritarian state power 136–7
authoritarian states 49, 52, 56, 87, 228–9, 327, 331, 335, 339, 350–2
Avenell 17, 29; Simon 17–29

Babones, Salvatore 497
Bae, Yooil 3, 33–45, 335
Baisley, Elizabeth 471
Baker, Chris 219, 221–2
Bangladesh 4, 13, 28, 233, 264–76, 363, 366, 370–1, 489, 492; and agricultural production based on the ecological resources of the Ganges–Brahmaputra Basin 264; assistance to communities in 28; civil society in 4, 268, 275; and the civil society organizations 264–5; communities in 28; constitution 268; and deregulation 268, 274; goal of sustainable development in 268; government of 272; and Malaysia 233; marginalized groups in 270; nature of poor people's survival challenges in 264; and Nepal 313; and the parliamentary democratic system 264; poor people's survival challenges in 264; promoting liberal democracy and economic liberalization in 265; and the role of civil society in promoting liberal democracy and economic liberalization in 265; and the role of the NGOs 264; sustainable development in 268; and the theoretical orientation to civil society 265; traditional 268; transformed 276
Bangladesh Academy for Rural Development 269
Bangladesh Legal Aid and Services Trust 269
Bangladesh NGO Foundation 272–3
Bangladesh Rural Advancement Committee 264, 269–71, 273–4

Bankoff, Greg 112–15
Banulescu-Bogdan, Natalia 490
Bar Association of Sri Lanka (BASL) 319
Barr, Michael D. 163–5
base protests 11, 505, 507–9, 511, 513, 515, 517
Bay, Victoria 482
Bedi, Kiran 242
Beittinger-Lee, Verena 181–4, 186
Bell, Daniel 437
Berman, Sheri 183, 357–8
Betsill, Michele 521
Bhushan, Shanti 242
Bhutan 4–5, 293–305; and the capital Thimphu
    294; and the complementary relationships of
    civil society and governmental institutions 293;
    consisting of three different groups of people
    294; and King Jigme Dorji Wangchuck 294;
    and King Jigme Singye Wangchuck 294; new
    democratic 294; and the philosophy of "Gross
    National Happiness" 5; resource management
    institutions in 297; situated between China and
    India 293; transformed from an absolute
    monarchy to a constitutional monarchy 294
Bhutanese, economy 294
Bhutanese government 299
Bhutanese people 304
bloggers 148, 170, 436, 440–2
Borzaga, Carlo 376–7
Bouliannne, Shelley 422, 424–6
BRAC 264, 269–71, 273–4; *see also* Bangladesh
    Rural Advancement Committee
Bräuer, Stephanie 370–1
Brillantes, Alex 123
Broadbent, Jeffrey 21, 25
Bryant, Raymond 366
Bumochir, Dulam 95–106
Burma 6, 9, 13, 227–34, 329, 333–4, 436, 438–40,
    443, 445; and the All Burma Federation of
    Student Unions 334; force for political
    opposition in 231; government in 234; military
    dictatorship in 227, 436; nature of civil society
    in 227; political society in 9; Saffron
    Revolution in 438; social welfare services in
    229–30; transitional civil society in 227; *see also*
    Myanmar
Burma *see* Myanmar
Burma Buddhist Monks Union 230–1
Burma Socialist Program Party (BSPP) 228
Burns, Susan 460
Bush, George W. 43, 184
business groups 23, 524–5

Cagna, Paola 370
Calder, Kent 508
Calhoun, Craig 50, 179, 457
Cambodia 6, 191–200, 329, 363, 370, 438, 443,
    488–9, 494, 496; atrocities in 443; and civil

society 8, 191–3, 195–6, 198–200, 443; civil
    war in 438; democracy of 196; grass-roots 198;
    and Malaysia 341; natural resources in 200; and
    ODA & NGO Databases 195; and Vietnam
    207; watchers 200
Cambodian 8, 191–200, 436, 438, 443; Buddhism
    197, 199; CSOs 191, 195; genocide 436, 438,
    443; government values the resources and
    services NGOs provide 193; NGOs 191, 195;
    society 197–9; sovereignty 198; state and civil
    society 194
Carlile, Lonny E. 524–5
Carpenter, Susan 523–4
CBOs 67, 191, 194, 199, 216, 229, 232, 251–2,
    278, 312–13; *see also* community-based
    organizations
CGs 68, 169; *see also* conservation groups
Chadwick, Andrew 422–3
Chan, Anita 10, 12, 14, 49–51, 53, 435–6, 438,
    440, 444–8, 481
Chan, Jennifer 435–49
Chang, Peter T.C. 167, 438, 458
Chen, Fu-wei 81–2, 88–9, 394, 398, 459
Chiavacci, David 488–9, 492, 495
China 6–8, 49–61, 69–70, 72–3, 327–8, 363–72,
    395–8, 400–1, 427–9, 436–45; active foreign
    grantmakers in 55; air pollution in 445;
    analyses of 51; and the anti- China
    demonstrations 356; anti-domestic violence
    campaigns in 370; billionaires from 58; civil
    society organizations in 135, 356, 427;
    communist 72; compromising of collected data
    in 428; constitution of 479; cultural 81; FDI in
    Laos 212; GONGOs examples of state-led
    "corporatism" 51; and Hong Kong 6; and the
    Hong Kong handover to 437; human rights in
    441; impact of new media in 427; and India 6,
    280, 293, 365, 391, 394; influence on civil
    society in Laos 13; internet in 427; leadership
    of 480; and the limited transparency of
    information collected and disseminated 427;
    market economy and democratic politics 51;
    and the party state 427; philanthropic
    development 398; programs 55; and South
    Korea 195; southern 58; unified 81; and
    Vietnam 327
China Democracy Party 441
Chinese government 50–1, 57, 395, 427, 440;
    authorities 440; management of revenues 445;
    management of revenues from natural resources
    445; ministries 56
Chinese Malaysians 150, 152
Chinese state 7, 49–50, 53, 55, 59–60, 370
Chong, Gladys, P.L. 58, 161, 163, 167
Chosun Ilbo, Dong-A Ilbo 42
Christie, Kenneth 437
Chua, Bencharat Sae 215–23

Chua, Beng Huat 163–4, 166–8, 170, 216, 218, 220, 222, 224
Citizens' Forums for Community Empowerment 90
civic groups 18–20, 23, 26–7, 41, 43, 320, 336, 338, 409–10, 414; Japanese 26–9, 464; new 25; and NGOs 410; and students 336
civic organizations 33, 37, 40–2, 67, 122–3, 337, 355
CIVICUS Civil Society Index report for Mongolia 97
civil society 1–14, 17–29, 33–45, 129–39, 175–83, 191–200, 264–76, 278–89, 311–21, 344–58; activism 4, 36–8, 40–1, 43, 153, 167, 236, 318; activist citizens 143; activists 223, 288, 320, 428; activities 59, 163, 194–5, 223, 353–4; advocacy approach in Japan 21; advocates fuel the movement for the NPO Law 21; in Asia 1–2, 10, 12, 328, 366, 435–6, 439, 443; in Bangladesh 4, 268, 275; campaigns 431; capacity building 181; in China 7, 49–50, 54, 57, 61; and citizenship from queer theory perspectives 11; and civic engagement with social media 423; and civil society groups and actors 2; and civil society organizations 129–30, 132, 137–9, 344–5, 347, 350–1, 354, 356–8; contributions at national level 271; and CSA 350; definitions of 99, 192, 228, 347, 358, 456–7, 460; and democracy 102, 215, 220, 223, 286, 330; and democratization 124, 327, 330–1, 335; development 2–3, 8, 17, 20, 79, 181, 183, 187, 205, 212; dichotomy 357; dynamics 311, 313; in early Soviet Mongolia 98; engagement in Nepal 281; and family life 10, 456–62, 465; forms and practices 459; functions as a counter-image of the state 66; Gandhian activists jostle with left-wing and the right-wing grass-roots organizations in India 236; and globalization 267; and governmental institutions 293, 315, 530; guides social transformation in Bangladesh 270; in Hong Kong 68; human rights and the environment 264; independent 215, 234; and independent social organizations 37; in Indonesia 175; institutions 240, 250, 259; interactions on the regional level 493; interests through the use of the narrative of "Asian communitarianism" 161, 163; international 436; involvement in peace and democracy 287; in Japan 19–22, 26–7, 368; large-scale market-oriented 266; in Latin America 17; and migration 489; migration-related 489; mobilization in Asia 435; in Mongolia 97, 105; movements 120; in Nepal 4–5, 278–83, 285–6, 288–9; and networking 13; and NGOs 100, 105, 314, 317; and NGOs in Japan 409; non-partisan 151; in non-Western contexts 354; organizations in capitalist societies 139;

polarized 41; and policy in the aftermath of the Fukushima crisis 530; politicized 228–9; politics 34, 42; in post-colonial Hong Kong 69; pragmatic 169–70; progressive 23, 35; promoting as a normative ideal 280; protesters 75; protests 460; relations 6, 163, 237–9, 320, 349, 356, 411; research 345; and the role in economic practice of climate policy 520; and the role in Thai democratization 216; roles **355**; rural 293; in rural Bhutan 296, 305; in rural communities 300; scholars 10, 111; sector in Japan 18; sector in Laos 204–5, 209, 212–13; and social media 420; and social movements 219; in South Korea 33, 44; suppressed 164; and Taiwan's state-society dynamics 87; in Thailand 215, 223; and the threat to authoritarian regimes 57; threatened 35; for transformational change 244; in transition 232; and transitional justice 8; transnationalized 489
civil society action 191–2, 349–50, 352, 355
civil society actors 7, 9–10, 12, 130, 138, 215–16, 221, 223, 238, 289; clamoring for human rights 311; local 196; in Nepal 289; self-fashioned 280; and social media 431
civil society associations 229; in China 52
Civil Society Diamond 67
civil society groups 35–6, 115–16, 124–5, 162, 238–9, 318–19, 321, 459–60, 477–9, 506
Civil Society Index (CSI) 97, 99, 103, 124, 328
civil society organizations 2–10, 67–71, 110–12, 119–24, 129–39, 236–41, 297–9, 332–7, 341, 344–58; and aid dependency in Bangladesh 266; conceptualized as a process of collective action 356; developing in rural areas 210; and engagement in public deliberation 279; and governmental organizations 136; issue-based 442; in Japan 19–20; and members 265, 274; mobilizing their participants 71; national-level 272; in Nepal 279; in Okinawa 505; and other groups 318, 320; and practices in Nepal 278; pro-conservative 42; professional 204; publicizing their plans for demonstrations 508; regulated in China 54; and social movements 219; in South Korea 37, 513; and state relationships 136; in Vietnam 130, 134, 355
Civil Society Organizations Act 305
civil society organizations in China 135, 356, 427
Clarke, Gerard 110–13, 115–16, 120, 122–5, 366
Clemens, Elisabeth 382
climate change: and carbon governance 521–2; and the development of an emissions trading system in Japan since the ratification of the Kyoto Protocol in 1998. 522; and the issue of scale in the role of civil society 521; and the Kyoto Protocol's use of certified emissions reductions as a principal policy response to 521; market governance of 520–1; and the

resistance to establishing environmental governance arrangements 521; and the role of civil society 520; and the role of industry associations like the *Keidanren* (Japan Business Federation) 522

climate governance: and the balance between policy, ministries, and industry in Japan 523; effected by concerns over energy constraints and emissions trading 522; and the Fukushima Daiichi nuclear disaster 522; and the pressure on the Japanese government to abandon nuclear power 522; and the underlying Japanese values of materiality and technological innovation 522–3

Cohen, Jean 265, 438, 458

Collins, William 197

Comaroff, John 95, 409, 457

Communist Party of China 72, 427

Communist Party of Thailand (CPT) 216–17

Communist Party of Vietnam 129–33, 138, 344, 352–3, 356

community-based organizations 67, 191, 194, 199, 216, 229, 232, 251–2, 278, 312–13

community empowerment 85, 87, 89–90; approaches 218; projects 3, 84, 91

community movements 80–1, 83, 89, 274; conflates with the government's place-making effort 88; depicts Taiwan's relationship with the state 86; in Taiwan 83; urban 88

companies 99, 101, 160–1, 163, 377, 381, 384–5, 392–3, 495–6, 524–30; chemical 526; Chinese 211; financial 528; for-profit 379–81, 383–4, 386; governments and for-profit 383, 386; heavy industry 526; Hong Kong 67; independent drama 161; insurance 529; Japanese 393–4, 525, 527–8, 530, 532; largest listed 67; local affiliated 379, 393; mining 101–2, 105; newspaper 162; parent 392–3; private 377; special subsidiary 381; work in for-profit 380

conservation groups 68, 169

Constantino-David, Karina 122–3

Contemplacion, Flor 498

Cooley, Alexander 508

corporate philanthropy 6, 391–4, 396

corporate social responsibility 27, 251, 363, 392, 398–9, 529

Coventry, Louise 199

CPV 129–33, 138, 344, 352–3, 356; *see also* Communist Party of Vietnam

Creighton, Millie 368–9

CSA 191–2, 349–50, 352, 355; *see also* civil society action

CSOs 2–10, 67–71, 110–12, 119–24, 129–39, 236–41, 297–9, 332–7, 341, 344–58; and NGOs 238, 241–2, 316; *see also* civil society organizations

CSR 27, 251, 363, 392, 398–9, 529; *see also* corporate social responsibility

Dae-jung, Kim 34, 40, 42, 335, 435

Dahlin, Peter 57

Dakar Conference 2000 444

Dalai Lama 435

Dali Community, Taiwan 88–9

damage 274–5, 301, 480, 515; crop 297; environmental 508, 516

dams 83–4, 207, 211, 335; hydropower 207

Darkhad Depression 100–1

Darkhads 101–2; fighting for their territory *gazar* and homeland *nutag* 102; patrols 102; people's homeland 101; setting up small wooden sheds 101

Davies, Thomas 365

death penalty 170, 439, 441

death threats 152

deaths 113, 151, 186, 269, 274, 332–3, 435, 439, 496, 505; custodial 149; natural 299

debt 400, 495–6

debt collection 186

decentralization 33, 293, 295, 299, 305, 369; authorities 194; democratic 194; economic 330; political 335; process 299; reform 40, 335

defamation 163, 442

definitions 54, 59–60, 212, 227, 232, 344–6, 349, 390–1, 448, 457; action-based 346; common 10, 456; and conceptual boundaries of human rights 435; conservative 55; consistent 95; core 180; corporatist 448; narrow 54; normative 357; popular 464; preconceived 411; scholarly 457; substantive 346; unidimensional 60; variable 457

Defourny, Jacques 376–7

Deguchi, Masayuki 5–6, 22–3, 390–401

Delhi 243, 414

Delnoye, Rik 205–6

democracy 3–5, 33–8, 95–100, 151–3, 215–18, 222–3, 267–8, 278–80, 286–9, 345–8; activists 481; and censorship 287; and civil society 60, 95, 102, 215, 220, 223, 330; competitive 175; consolidating 335; constitutional 216; controlled 250; deliberative 239, 338, 491; development of 34, 45, 215, 218, 223, 305; donor-supported 270; establishing 260; failed 221; formal 217, 481; functional 250; global 96; grass-roots 74, 84; inclusive 4, 286, 336; Indonesian 8, 175, 186–7; internal 52; legislative 441; liberal 11–12, 22, 69, 144, 165, 265, 273, 276, 279, 287; movement 72, 74–5; multi-party 55, 280; natural 296; pluralistic 363; political 330, 339; primary 296; procedural 339; progressive 472; promoting 397; roadmap to 231; schools of 137, 344–5, 357; in South Korea 3, 34; strengthening 237, 245, 249, 251, 253–4, 260–1, 336; substantive 37, 335; vibrant 115; weakening 339 democratic 129, 137, 265; change 124, 138, 196, 334; claims 53; consolidation 3, 111, 116, 124–5, 165, 215; development 3, 125, 249, 364; elections 37, 69, 481; experimentation 331; governance 111, 448; governments 35–6; impact on public policies 338

democratic institutions 3, 60, 110, 112, 115, 183, 186; effective 112; new 335; working effectively 178

democratic movements 21, 37, 97, 100, 181, 331–3, 335

Democratic Party (Mongolia) 95–6, 98–100, 102, 339

Democratic Party of Japan 25, 484

Democratic Progressive Party (Taiwan) 333–4, 480

democratic retrenchment 330, 339, 341

democratic transitions 5, 13, 35, 164, 227, 232, 278, 294, 330–5, 341; impacted 5; promoting in authoritarian states 335

democratic values 13, 68, 113, 286, 296, 337; new 337; promoting of 369

democratization 5, 7–8, 36–8, 137–8, 327, 330–3, 337–9, 341, 344, 356–7; and citizenship 5; and civil society 36; and empowerment 134; hindering of 5, 339, 341; and human rights 229; in Indonesia 333; intragrouping 491; in Korea 37; movement 3, 36–8; in Myanmar 335; obstacles to 137–8, 344; political 81, 331; processes of 3, 7, 33, 36–7, 110–11, 130, 133, 137–8, 354, 356–7; of South Korea 44

demonstrations 49, 70, 74, 90, 106, 149, 216–17, 220–1, 505, 508; anti-military junta 218; large 24, 514; mass anti-Thaksin 222; and protests 436; social movement 222; staging of 442; student 217

demonstrators 332, 334, 482; anti-American 42; anti-regime 185; attacking student 482

depoliticizing 60, 195; of civil society 59; development problems 223

detention, political 145–6, 164, 233, 436, 438–9, 441

developing countries 27–8, 84, 181, 237, 267, 275, 391, 523, 531–2

development 27–8, 175–7, 211–12, 215–19, 251–2, 283–5, 363–8, 370–2, 378–80, 407–9; activities 303, 366; aid in Japan 409, 411, 413; of civil society in Hong Kong 69; of civil society in South Korea 34; of civil society organizations 212; constitutional 249; of democracy and growth of civil society 218; equitable 299–301; historical 17, 19, 66, 180; international 27, 267, 409; of Japanese civil society 26, 28; major human rights 448; and management of civil society 133; and NGOs 6, 218, 251, 313, 315, 371, 408–9; of NGOs in Asia 371, 409; organizational 209; of Philippine

civil society 124; projects 28, 96, 151, 270; regime in Japan 408; socioeconomic 131, 427; state-led 6; of Thai civil society 215; women in 267, 367

development approaches 270, 274; dominant 267; ecocentric 274; economic 265; grounded 268; new 270; patriarchal 267

Diamond, Larry 66, 110, 143, 160, 163, 212, 228, 249, 344, 348–9

diaspora 266, 391, 394; activities 394; philanthropy 6

diaspora philanthropy 6, 391, 394–7, 401

dictatorial rule 110, 216, 258

dictators 114–15, 117

dictatorships 35, 37, 114, 116, 132, 250, 336

Diehl, Trevor 429–30

digital technologies, and new media 426

diplomatic corps 464

diplomatic missions 317

diplomats 196, 414; in india 414; responsible 495

disabilities 121, 169, 381, 439, 447; mental 379, 381; physical 379

disabled people 5, 380–4

disabled workers 379–81, 384–5

disasters 244, 271, 367, 458, 483, 524; ecological 265, 274, 444; in Japan 458; nuclear 485, 522

discrimination 71, 99, 175, 279, 283, 286, 288, 445, 447, 473; caste-based 289; intersectional 446

discriminatory policies 149, 288

disputes 176, 296–7, 478; divided factions 228; international 507; marital 447; minor 297

dissidents 198, 228, 332, 334, 439; anti-Soviet Czech 441; and the Roh regime 38

divorce 105, 221, 336, 459–60, 462–4; agreements 462; notifications 462; parental 464

document abuses 444

domestic workers 11, 166, 489, 492–3, 497–8

dominance 37, 116, 363, 372, 423, 492; one-party 160; state's 9; upper-caste 285

donations 18, 26, 68, 105, 250, 288, 393–5, 461; anonymous 162; commercial 68; corporate 393; foreign 162, 229, 237; received 230

donor agencies 265, 267; aid 100; foreign 288; priority 287

donors 14, 18, 191, 195–6, 205–6, 208, 238, 285–6, 299, 395; corporate 394; emerging Asian 6, 407–9; external 238; foreign 105, 195, 219, 238, 250–3; interests and strategies 196; long-time OISCA 412; multilateral 195; non-traditional 407; non-Western 417; personal 369; traditional 408; western 210, 212, 492

Druk Phuensum Tshogpa (DPT) 294

Dunn, Elizabeth 193, 394, 400, 457

Duterte, Rodrigo 339

East Asia 2, 11, 362, 365–6, 391, 477, 488–9, 493

ECCC 196, 438; *see also* Extraordinary Chambers in the Courts of Cambodia
Economy, Elizabeth 51
Edwards, Michael 1, 17, 228, 279
Ehlert, Judith 192, 197
Elinoff, Eli 220, 223
empowerment, and democratization 134
Eng, David 199, 470
environmental movements 9, 25, 84, 104–5, 270, 364–5, 514
environmental NGOs 103, 232, 267, 337, 366–7, 409
Estrada, Joseph 115–16, 125, 339
Extraordinary Chambers in the Courts of Cambodia 196, 438

Faludi, Laura 135
family 10, 147–8, 152, 279–81, 353, 394–5, 456–65, 505, 509–10, 524–5; autocracy 280; bonds 457; and civil society 456, 458, 460–2, 465; court systems 463; foundations 58; law 148; law reform 460, 464; law systems 459; life 10, 456, 459; membership 10, 456; networks 394, 461; obligations 461; wealth 391
family membership 10, 456–61, 464, 505, 509–10, 512
family relationships 458–61
Farmers' Federation of Thailand 217
female factory workers in South Korea 460
Ferguson, James 95–6, 411
Fernando, Udan 311–21
Ferris, James M. 391, 399–400
FFT 217; *see also* Farmers' Federation of Thailand
Fisher, William F. 416
focus groups 54, 56
Food and Agriculture Organization 266
Ford, Michele 492
Forest Act 1969 301
Forthcoming, Dennis 459
Francesch-Huidobro, Maria 164, 169
Fruman, Sheila 259
Fu, Diana 60
Fulda, Andreas 52

Gaffud, Dolores 367
Gandhi, Sonia 239
Ganesan, Mano 320
Garcés-Mascareñas, Blanca 492
Gates, Frederic 390
GCM 498; *see also* Global Coalition on Migration
Geddes, Barbara 346
Gee, John 165–6
Gellner, Ernest 283
Glasius, Marlies 346
global civil society 55, 106, 198, 268, 348, 365, 436, 470
Global Coalition on Migration 498

Global Fund for Women 103
Goh, Daniel 144
Golkar Party 228
Gombrich, Richard 312, 427
GONGOs 7, 49–52, 57, 59–60, 228; *see also* government-organized non-governmental organizations
Gosewinkel, Dieter 349
government, central 56, 82, 85, 249, 302–3, 483
government agencies 51–3, 56, 59, 114, 120, 239–40, 242, 266–7, 410, 414; and CSOs 240; single designated 208
government officials 21, 53, 56, 80, 149, 196, 206, 240–1, 318, 411
government-organized non-governmental organizations 7, 49–52, 57, 59–60, 228
grass-roots organizations 52, 111–12, 117, 195, 367, 369, 371, 415
GROs 52, 111–12, 117, 195, 367, 369, 371, 415; *see also* grass-roots organizations
Grossman-Thompson, Barbara 459
groups 18–21, 23–6, 35–8, 50–7, 59–60, 161–2, 164–70, 316–21, 407–10, 463–4; animal welfare 162; anti-democratic 180, 183; business 23, 524–5; civic 18–20, 23, 26–7, 41, 43, 320, 336, 338, 409–10, 414; civil society 35–6, 115–16, 124–5, 162, 238–9, 318–19, 321, 459–60, 477–9, 506; in civil society 20; democratic 333; disadvantaged 5; disaster response 27; ethno-religio-nationalist 318, 321; focus 54, 56; grass-roots 52–3, 55–7, 60, 435, 444; interest 34, 38, 44, 257, 261, 279, 288, 492, 494, 497; international 209; in Japan 410, 463; LGBT 54, 473; marginalized 27, 117, 270, 272, 285; media 256; migrant worker 166; minority 5, 23, 207, 339, 341; and movements of workers and students 114; non-government 114, 122, 441; pan-democratic 74; people's 170; political 67, 317; pressure 4, 256; pro-government 317; racist 339, 341; religious 36–7, 110, 162, 167, 229, 250, 252, 486, 499; social 34, 41, 139, 239–40, 245, 351; in South Korea 28; student 24, 35–6, 330–2, 334, 341; in Thailand 28; ultra-rightist 340–1; women's 19, 23–4, 82, 144, 147, 260, 446; xenophobic 338, 340
growth 37–8, 40, 148, 180, 205, 207, 282–3, 367–9, 371, 415–16; of civic associations and NGOs 283; of civil society 40, 51, 216, 218; of CSOs 116; double-digit 438; exponential 91, 427, 429; and fragmentation of civil society 283; historical-cultural 86; massive 368; of NGOs 250, 410; of political resistance 334; of registered NGOs in the 2000s **40**; sector's 378; and success of OISCA 415; unprecedented 257

Hadiz, Vedi R. 175–87

Halberstam, Judith 470
Hall, John A. 95–6, 106
Hann, Chris 95, 193, 457, 465
Hannah, Joseph 354–5
Harris, Ian 198, 266
Harris, Jose 266
Hazare, Anna 4, 242–4, 319, 430
Henderson, Paul 269
Hewison, Kevin 144, 180, 222, 228–9, 339
Ho, Josephine 70, 79, 87, 91, 131, 133–6, 355–6,
    470–1, 478, 485
Hoare, Quintin 280
Holloway, Richard 252
Hong Kong 6–7, 11–12, 66–76, 377–8, 439–40,
    443–4, 480–5, 488–9, 492–3, 497–500; activists
    486; administration 485; airport 486; and
    Beijing agencies 481; characteristics of civil
    society in 69, 72, 75; and China 6; colonial
    437; domestic workers in 489, 493, 497; elites
    481; Gini coefficient 73; government 67–8,
    73–4, 76; hospitals 73; households 497;
    integration 72; and Japan 11, 488, 493;
    literature 66; maids in 12; on official tours 72;
    organizers 498; permanent residents in 73;
    police 71; politics 75–6; population 76; poverty
    in 73; social mobility in 73; sovereignty of 69;
    urban 71
Hong Kong activists 486
Hong Kong Umbrella Movement 11, 74–5,
    439–40, 477, 480–2, 484–5
Hossen, M. Anwar 264–76
Howell, Jude 51, 350, 371, 470
Hsia, Chu-joe 88–9, 336, 493
Hudson, Wayne 364, 366
Hughes, Caroline 193–5, 199, 227
human rights 10–12, 98–100, 210–12, 248–51,
    264–74, 276, 278–9, 435–7, 439, 445–9;
    activists 232, 250, 260, 287, 442, 444, 448; and
    advocacy organizations 250; in Asia 435–6,
    447–8; and civil society in Asia 10, 435–6; and
    civil society mobilization 435; concepts 253,
    447; covenants 286, 495; and democratization
    229; and the environment 265, 267–8; and
    feminism 447; and gender 447; and labor union
    movements 12; landscapes in Asia 448;
    literature 436; of marginalized groups 272;
    movements 441; organizations 95, 252, 283,
    436, 493, 499; and professional organizations
    278; promoters 266, 270; promotion of 276;
    protecting 260, 272; research 438, 440, 446;
    standards 166, 438; violations 265, 268, 270,
    275, 436–7, 444, 496–7, 499, 508, 510; of
    women 437, 446, 511
Human Rights Abuses 60, 438, 496
Human Rights Watch Report 436–41, 495
Hunt, Juliette 368, 371
hydropower dams 207

Ibrahim, Anwar (Deputy Prime Minister) 146–8,
    151
ILO 192, 443–4, 495, 498; *see also* International
    Labour Organization
immigration 75, 165, 490, 492, 494–5; Indian 396
Immigration Act 336, 396
Immigration Bureau of Japan 494–6
Immigration Control and Refugee Recognition
    Act 495–6
immigration policies 166; anti-Asian 488;
    influences 489; restrictive 489
indexes of demography, income, democracy, and
    civil society in Asia *328*
India 4, 236–45, 248–9, 365–8, 370–1, 394,
    396–8, 400–1, 414, 428–30; anti-corruption
    leader Anna Hazare 430; and China 6, 365;
    civil society activism in 236; civil society in 4,
    236–7, 239; complex picture of civil society in
    237; corruption in 243; democracy in 236, 240;
    entrepreneurs in Silicon Valley 397; and
    Mahatma Gandhi National Rural Employment
    Guarantee Scheme 4, 236–8, 240–2, 244; and
    the Muslim population 184; NGOs in 371; and
    Pakistan 400; power of social media in 428; role
    of civil society in 236; state and civil society in
    236
Indian 6, 237, 239–41, 244, 248, 250, 391, 396–7,
    429–30, 435; and American organizations
    engaged in philanthropy 396–7; citizens 6, 391,
    396–7; consumers 244; diasporas 396–7;
    governments 237, 396; passports 396; states 397
Indonesia 5–6, 8, 13, 175–9, 181–7, 362–4,
    369–70, 436–8, 440–1, 493–4; Association of
    Indonesian Islamic Intellectuals 182; Association
    of Indonesian Migrant Workers 498; and
    Canada 28; civil society in 175; colonizing of
    democratic institutions 183; conducting tests on
    communities where waterways had been
    contaminated with mercury 28; Constitution
    231; democratization 333; intellectual life in
    177; and the interests of youths 186; labor
    movement 177; and the Philippines 436; and
    President Soeharto 176, 182, 185, 333; rescued
    by the International Monetary Fund (IMF)
    during the Asian Financial Crisis 333
Indonesian 175–8, 181–3, 187, 498; applicability
    of the concept of civil society 181; based NGOs
    493; contemporary civil society 175; debates
    181; government's treatment of terrorist
    suspects 440; Islamic intellectuals 182; middle
    classes 176; migrants 11, 498; military and
    police forces 184; NGO movement 181–2,
    369; occupation of East Timor 436, 438, 444;
    politics and society 177, 186
Indonesian Communist Party 186
Indonesian Democratic Party 333
INGOs 49, 55–7, 68, 134, 196, 205–6, 208, 212,

media 3–4, 6, 13, 53, 207, 249–50, 255–7, 259–61, 420–3, 427; editors 422; groups 256; new 6, 170, 274, 420–2, 426–7, 431; in Pakistan 256–7, 260; restrictions 232; role of 13, 420; state 55, 252, 316; traditional 422–3, 430–1; visibility 473

media platforms (social) 54, 74, 420, 424, 426

Meiroku Zasshi 23

Mercer, Claire 110–11, 237–8, 251

METI 496, 520, 522–3, 526–7, 531; *see also* Ministry of Economy, Trade and Industry (Japan)

MGNREGS 4, 236–8, 240–2, 244; *see also* Mahatma Gandhi National Rural Employment Guarantee Scheme

migrant advocacy organizations 490, 493

Migrant interest organizations 11, 489–91, 493–4, 496, 499

migrant workers 165–6, 439, 489, 491–2, 494, 497–9

migration 8, 11, 104, 165, 443, 448, 488–91, 493, 495, 497–9; and civil society 489; and civil society in Japan 489, 493; female 443; flows 488; industry 489; mass 334; patterns 489; policies 443, 490, 499; post-colonial 488; repeated 489; schemes 497; temporary 490; varied transnational 11

military base protests 11, 505, 507–9, 511, 513, 515, 517

military bases 11, 505–8, 510–12, 515

Miller, John R. 488, 495

mining companies 101–2, 105

Ministry of Economy, Trade and Industry (Japan) 496, 520, 522–3, 526–7, 531

MIOs 11, 489–91, 493–4, 496, 499; *see also* Migrant interest organizations

Mir, Hamid 255

Mohamed, Tun Dr. Mahathir 143, 148

Mongolia 5, 9, 95–106, 328, 331–3, 363, 398; and civil society 96–9; democracy in 99–100; early Soviet 98; environmental movements in 105; environmental protestors in 106; media and public discourses in 96; nongovernmental organizations import foreign culture 51, 96; protest movements 100; state of civil society in 97, 105; and Western democrcy 97

Mongolian 9, 12, 97, 100, 332; civil society 9; democracy 99; democracy and civil society 96; democrats 98, 100; gold-mining companies 100–1, 104; history and tradition 10; understanding of democracy 98–9

Mongolian Democratic Union 332

Mongolian People's Republic 98–9, 182

monikers 478, 485

Morris, Paul 481

MPR 98–9, 182; *see also* Mongolian People's Republic

Musharraf, General Pervez 249–50, 257–60

Myanmar 5–6, 9, 13, 227, 229, 231, 233, 333–5, 339–40, 486

Myung-ja, Kim 40

Nakamura, Karen 20

Napal: and the Rana oligarchy 281; and Tulsi Mehar Gandhi Pracharak Mahaguthi (nonviolent movement) 281

National League for Democracy 230–2, 234, 334–5

National Taiwan University 88, 334

NED 103

NEFIN 283; *see also* Nepal Federation of Indigenous Nationalities

Nepal 4–5, 278–89, 313, 363, 370, 397–8, 438, 440–1, 489, 496; and Bangladesh 313; civil rights in 279; civil society in 4–5, 278–83, 285–6, 288–9; civil society organizations and practices in 278; deepening democracy in 289; defining moments for civil society in 280; definition of civil society inngo 278; fragmentation of civil society in 283; global financial institutions in 283, 285; growth and fragmentation of civil society in 283; history of civil society in 288; nature of NGOs in 285; new identity for civil society in 286; political crisis in 286; political parties in 285; public deliberation in 279; the state and struggle for democracy in 280; studies on civil society in 281; and substantial civic protest surrounding the new constitution of 459

Nepal Communist Party 285

Nepal Federation of Indigenous Nationalities 283

new media 6, 170, 274, 420–2, 426–7, 431

New People's Army 114, 204, 206, 209–10, 212

New Power Party 480

Ng, Cecilia 144, 161–2

NGOs 49–55, 120–5, 134–8, 143–54, 191–6, 216–23, 249–53, 283–8, 311–18, 364–9, 407–16; business-organized 122; and civil society 314, 317; community-based 397; contemporary 60; and CSOs 238, 241–2, 316; development 6, 218, 251, 313, 315, 371, 408–9; environmental protection 366; foreign-funded 4, 55–6, 191, 198, 251, 253, 260, 398, 400–1; in Japan 6, 27–9, 408–9, 411, 413–14, 447, 462, 497; in Nepal 279, 284–6; in Pakistan 250–1; and POs 112, 115, 119–20, 123, 125; in rural communities 286; in Sri Lanka 313–14; and the state 222, 313, 411; and women 147, 370–1; workers 196, 241, 251, 253, 287, 411, 415; *see also* non-governmental organizations

Nicholls, Alex 377

NLD 230–2, 234, 334–5; *see also* National League for Democracy

non-government organizations 79, 167, 229, 240,
   274, 311, 488; *see also* NGOs
non-governmental organizations 49–55, 120–5,
   134–8, 191–6, 216–23, 249–53, 283–8,
   311–18, 364–9, 407–16
non-profit organizations 2–3, 17–18, 42, 44, 122,
   279, 337, 379, 396, 407
non-resident Indians 396
Norén-Nilsson, Astrid 191–200
Norlund, Irene 134, 353
Norman, David 194–5
Nowell-Smith, Geoffrey 280
NPAs 114, 204, 206, 209–10, 212; *see also* New
   People's Army
NPOs 2–3, 17–18, 42, 44, 122, 279, 337, 379,
   396, 407; *see also* non-profit organizations
Nyström, Michiyo Kiwako Okuma 293–305

O'Day, Robin 485
O'Donoghue, Philip 391
Ogawa, Akihiro 1–14
Oh, Jennifer 34
OISCA 408–16; activities 411, 413; reputation
   414; staff members 409, 412–14; supporters
   415; *see also* Organization for Industrial,
   Spiritual, and Cultural Advancement
OISCA Diet League 414–15
Okinawa 18, 25, 446, 505–8, 511–13
Okinawan Citizens' Rally 505
Okinawan Women Act against Military Violence
   508, 511
Onyx, Jenny 366
Organization for Industrial, Spiritual, and Cultural
   Advancement 408–16
organizations 51, 90, 204, 284, 296, 340; anti-
   domestic violence 60, 371; anti-Marcos 510;
   anti-nuclear 24; civil-society-like 348;
   collective public-benefit 376; comprehensive
   economic 525; ethnic 229–30, 283; faith-based
   114, 130, 135, 497; illegal 52–3; Okinawan
   Women Act against Military Violence 508,
   511; philanthropic 6, 216–17, 392, 397–400;
   professional 129, 134, 138, 278, 395–6;
   voluntary 120, 131, 248, 250, 312–13
Orjuela, Camilla 312
Ottaway, Marina 229
Ovesen, Jan 197, 199

PAD campaign 222
Pakistan 4, 248–61, 264, 363, 397–8, 400, 438,
   440; analysis of civil society in 249, 257; anti-
   labor regimes in 260; civil society in 250–1,
   261; constitutional development of 249;
   constitutional reasoning in 258; deaths of
   journalists in 256; democracy in 250;
   democratic culture in 253; economic
   development and strengthening democracy in

249; employers in 254; and General Pervez
   Musharraf 249–50, 257–60; growth of NGOs
   in 250; history of civil society organizations in
   251; independence of 258; and India 400;
   institutional supremacy and restoring
   democratic rule in 259; journalists in 256;
   judicial history of 258; and the judiciary 259;
   killings and deaths of journalists in 256; lawyers
   in 258–9; linguistic rights of people in 260;
   non-state actors in 261; profile of NGOs in
   251; state and society 261; strengthening
   democracy in 249, 254, 260; trade union
   movements in 253–4
Pakistan Electronic Media Regulatory Authority
   255, 257
Pakistan media, groups in 256–7, 260
Pakistan People's Party 255
Park Chung-hee 34
patterns of social group participation in South
   Korea **41**
Payton, Robert 390
Pekkanen, Robert 17–19, 21, 27, 337–8, 410,
   456–7
people power 74, 110–11, 115, 117
people's organizations 111–12, 114–15, 117–20,
   122–3, 125
"People's Power" Revolution 331
People's Republic of China 51, 57, 395, 481, 489,
   491, 494, 496; *see also* China
People's Solidarity for Participatory Democracy
   39, 42, 335–6, 365; *see* PSPD
philanthropic activities 6, 390–6, 400–1
philanthropy 5–6, 27, 58, 281–2, 372, 390–401;
   American concept of 391, 394, 398; Chinese
   diaspora 395–6; corporate 6, 391–4, 396; cross-
   border 400; defined 390; diaspora 6, 391,
   394–7, 401; empirical studies of 391; and the
   Ford Foundation 392; Indian 396; Indian–
   American 397; institutionalized 58;
   international 401; in Japan 391; Japanese 394;
   Keidanren-style 394; networks in Asia 398;
   new trends in 6, 392, 399; private 58, 61;
   scientific 390, 399; in South Korea 391;
   traditional 395, 399; transliterate 393; wholesale
   390–1
Philippine 3, 11–13, 110–25, 331–2, 339, 366–7,
   398, 446, 494–8, 507–11; banks 497; civil
   society and CSOs 112; consulate 498; corporate
   law 113; CSOs 123–4; government 498; NGOs
   120, 123, 125, 367; politics 366, 510; women
   to support victims of domestic violence 494
Philippine-based Asian Center for Women's
   Human Rights 446
Philippine Business for Social Progress (PBSP) 398
Philippine Constitution 510
Philippine Health Insurance Corporation (PHIC)
   121

Philippine Partnership for the Development of
Human Resources in Rural Areas 123
Philippines 3, 5, 11–13, 110–25, 331–2, 339,
366–7, 398, 494–8, 507–11; and the distinction
between "stock" and "non-stock" corporations
122; and Ferdinand Marcos 110, 114–16, 331,
436, 497–8, 507, 510; and Indonesia 436;
sovereignty and independence 510; and women
494
Phillips, Ruth 5, 12, 362–72
Phnom Penh 191
Phuong, Dang Thi Viet 129–39
Piper, Nicola 165, 370, 438, 489, 491–3, 499
Poethig, Kathryn 198
Pol Pot 436
police 70–1, 75, 233, 243, 254, 259, 479, 482,
495, 505; brutality 439–41; cooperation 149;
custody 148, 332; enforcement 149; entrapment
161; investigations 401; local 233; and military
185; required 147
Police Act 145, 147
policy 11–12, 135–7, 221, 338–9, 506–9, 511,
513–14, 516–17, 523, 530–1; advocacy 38, 68,
119, 122, 124–5, 135, 218–19, 269; agendas 37,
370; changes 27, 338, 355, 509, 511–14, 516;
new 311; and politics 115; and society 521
policy makers 12, 52, 161, 164, 385, 508–17; to
change policy 509, 513–14; elected 526; large
protests pressuring 516; national 509; persuaded
509–10
political detention 145–6, 164, 233, 436, 438–9,
441
political parties: Burma Socialist Program Party
(BSPP) 228; China Democracy Party 441;
Communist Party of China 427; Communist
Party of Thailand (CPT) 216–17; Communist
Party of Vietnam 129–33, 138, 344, 352–3, 356;
Democratic Party (Mongolia) 95–6, 98–100,
102, 339; Democratic Party of Japan 25, 484;
Democratic Party of Mongolia 95; Democratic
Progressive Party (Taiwan) 333–4, 480;
Indonesian Communist Party 186; Indonesian
Democratic Party 333; LABAN Party 331;
Liberal Democratic Party (Japan) 412; Mongolian
Democratic Union 332; Nepal Communist Party
285; New Power Party 480; New Power Party
(Taiwan) 486; Pakistan People's Party 255; Sri
Lanka Freedom Party (SLFP) 315; Sri Lanka
Mahajana Party (SLMP) 315; and the Vietnam
Communist Party 129, 344
political society 9, 43, 66–7, 124, 143, 179, 227–8,
230–2, 234; in Burma 9; and civil society 43;
domination of 9, 227; elite-dominated 125;
traditional 124; under-developed 67
POs 111–12, 114–15, 117–20, 122–3, 125; and
NGOs 112, 115, 119–20, 123, 125; *see also*
people's organizations

President Chun Doo-hwan 34–5, 332
pressure groups 4, 256
Printing Presses Act (Malaysia) 146
Printing Presses and Publications Act (Malaysia)
147
pro-democracy: activists 36, 336, 438; advocates
36; demands 35; demonstrations 230, 332;
mass-mobilization 423; Mongols claiming
Genghis (Chinggis) Khan as a symbol 98;
protests 35, 436
pro-democracy movements 35–7, 334, 442; in
China 436, 439, 442; in Korea 447
protest movements 25, 97, 100, 102, 104, 267;
environmental 103; historical 100; largest-ever
483–4; radical 371
protesters 12, 70–1, 74, 220–1, 232–3, 257,
478–80, 482, 484, 505–16
protestors 10, 102, 104, 150, 166, 334, 336–7,
459, 482; environmental 10, 96, 100, 103,
105–6; nationalists 104; spontaneous 436
protests, pro-democracy 35, 436
PSPD 39, 42, 335–6, 365; *see also* People's
Solidarity for Participatory Democracy
Putnam, Robert 164, 178, 327

queer 11, 14, 469–73; activism 474; critical
deployment of 11, 470, 474; practices 472;
research 472; studies 470, 474; theorists 11;
theory 474

Rahman, Tunku Abdul 147, 371, 438
Ramzy, Austin 440, 484
Razak, Najib (Prime Minister) 150
Red Shirts Movement 152
registration/accreditation of non-governmental
entities in the Philippines *121*
Reimann, Kim 27, 410, 489
religious groups 36–7, 110, 162, 167, 229, 250,
252, 486, 499
repression: in China 438; of civil society 56
Repression in China since June 4, 1989 436
Republic of China *see* China
Republic of Singapore *see* Singapore
resource management institutions in Bhutan *297*
Rhee, Syngman (1948–1960) 34–5
Right to Information 4, 236, 238–42, 244, 319
Roberts, Glenda 491
Robison, Richard 175–7, 183
Rockefeller, David 394
Rockefeller, John D. 390
The Rockefeller Foundation 392, 397–9
Rodan, Garry 144, 163–4, 180, 229, 339
role of civil society 181, 249, 265, 268, 330,
407–8, 490, 520–1
Rother, Stefan 488–500
Rowen, Ian 477–86
Roy, Aruna 241

Roy, Denny 437
RTI 4, 236, 238–42, 244, 319; *see also* Right to
    Information
rural communities 85, 221, 286, 293, 296–301,
    303–5; of Bhutan 296, 305; civil society in 300;
    construction of schools in 300; NGOs in 286;
    people in 293, 301; work in 305
Rutzen, Douglas 400–1

Sabloff, Paula 97–8
Saich, Tony 51–2
Salamon, Lester 2, 53, 368, 390–1, 399
Sampson, Steven 95–6, 260
SAR 7, 66, 69, 72, 481, 497–8; *see also* Special
    Administrative Region
Schak, David 364, 366
Schedler, Andreas 346
Schoeder, William 471
Schroeder, F. 469
Schuyt, Theo 390
Schwartz, Frank J. 410, 457
SDGs 268, 271, 370, 444, 469, 471; *see also*
    Sustainable Development Goals
seafood farms in Vietnam 440
SEALDs 477, 483–6; *see also* Students' Emergency
    Action for Liberal Democracy
Shah, Faiza 250–1, 285
Shengde, Lian 441
Shinzō, Abe 415, 483–4
Shipper, Apichai W. 327–41
Shrestha, Tulsi Mehar 281
Sikkink, Kathryn 333, 471, 497, 499, 507
Singapore 6–7, 160, 162–6, 168–70, 327, 436–8,
    442–3, 472–3, 491–2, 497–8; and the Anti-
    Death Penalty Campaign 169; attractive to
    migrant labor and good for business
    interests166; and Brunei 327, 341; citizens and
    residents 162; and the civil society in 8; as a
    competitive authoritarian regime 163; and the
    Constitution prioritizing public order and
    security 162; an electoral authoritarian regime
    160; and the evolution of civil society in 160;
    and the freedom of association, assembly, and
    speech 162; and Hong Kong 488; and issues of
    gay rights 170; and Japan 473; neoliberal 472;
    religion, secularism, and morality 167; and the
    role of *Thev Straits Times* in causing unease
    among policymakers 161; the shaping of 167;
    state 8, 161
Singapore Constitution 162
Singapore National Employers Federation 165–6
Singapore National Trades Union Congress 438,
    492
Singaporean Charity Council 401
Singaporeans 8, 160, 162, 165, 167, 442, 472;
    leaders 164; residents 166
Singaporeans for Democracy (NGO) 442

Sneath, David 97
Snow, Keith Harmon 104, 507
Snowden, Edward 440
So, Alvin Y. 66–76
social enterprises 5, 17–18, 363, 367, 376–86, 408;
    activities of 5, 380, 385; certified 378; defined
    376; and government 384; instituted 367; legal
    framework for 385; local 382, 386; new 384;
    promoting 377; regional network of 383;
    research on 377; role of 378; and social
    entrepreneurship 17, 377
social groups 34, 41, 139, 239–40, 245, 351
social media 13, 42, 44, 234, 420–31, 440, 483,
    485; and digital technologies 426; engagements
    on 423, 425; and the internet 425, 427, 430;
    platforms 54, 74, 420, 424, 426
social networks 87, 90, 187, 421, 424–6, 428–9,
    431; activism on 424; in Asia 426; impact on
    political engagement 429; and the internet 428;
    to propagate political ideologies 429; recent
    research on 421; and traditional media 431;
    webs of 87
Socialist Republic of Vietnam *see* Vietnam
Societies Act (Malaysia) 146, 162, 442
Societies Registration Act (India) 248
Soeharto, President 176, 182, 185, 333
SOFA 43, 505, 511, 513–16; *see also* Status of
    Forces Agreement
Soon, Carol 170
Soon, Debbie 160–70
South, Ashley 340
South Korea 2–3, 33–7, 41, 43–5, 331–2, 362–8,
    370, 378–9, 508, 513–15; and the authoratarian
    regime of President Park Chung-hee 34; and
    the authoriarina reign of President Chun Doo-
    hwan 34–5, 332; and the authoritarian regime
    of Park Chung-hee (1963–1979) 34; "before
    and after" democratization 34; and challenges
    to civil society activism in contemporary Korea
    41–3; and China 195; citizens of 36; civil
    society actors, including laborers, journalists,
    university professors joined pro-democracy
    movements 35; and civil society after
    democratization 37; civil society and the
    transition to democracy 36–7; civil society in
    33, 44; and the development of civil society in
    34; and the disobedience movement 35; and
    the growth in the number of civil society
    organizations 33–4; and Japan 459, 489; and
    The Korean Central Intelligence Agency
    (KCIA) 35; and the Korean War 34–5; mass
    mobilizations over various political and socio-
    economic issues 43–4; and the notion of a
    "strong state and contentious society" 34; and
    the pro-democracy struggle against the new
    regime 35; and the right-wing conservative
    organizations ("New Right") 34; and the rise of

new citizens' movement group under the civilian governments 37–8; and the short period of democratic transition was crushed by a military coup in May 1961 35; social group participation in41; under the control of the military regime for more than two decades 35

SPDC 248, 250–1; *see also* State Peace and Development Council

Special Administrative Region 7, 66, 69, 72, 481, 497–8

Spires, Anthony J. 6–7, 49–61, 369

Sri Lanka 13, 311–13, 315, 317–21, 363, 397–8; and the anti-NGO/civil society lobby 317; and the ascendency of a few new religious-nationalist Sinhala-Buddhist groups 317; and the Bar Association of Sri Lanka (BASL) 319; CBOs in 312; civil society in 313, 321; and the development of NGOs in 313–14; and the dynamics of civil society in 311; NGOs in 313–14; and the orientation of civil society in 313; satisfactory health and education systems 313; and the war between the LTTE and the Sri Lankan Armed Force 317

Sri Lanka Freedom Party (SLFP) 315

Sri Lanka Mahajana Party (SLMP) 315

state media 55, 252, 316

State Peace and Development Council 248, 250–1

state power 66, 137, 228, 285, 313, 348, 350–1, 353, 439; authoritarian 136–7; maintenance of 350–1; practices of 350

Status of Forces Agreement 43, 505, 511, 513–16

Steinberg, David 228

Steinhoff, Patricia 338

Stenner, Karen 346–7

Stephen, Lynn 59, 458

Stephens, Evelyne 339

Stephens, John 339

Strulik, Stephanie 458

student activists 79, 83, 217, 482–4

student groups 24, 35–6, 330–2, 334, 341

Students' Emergency Action for Liberal Democracy 477, 483–6

Sukarnoputri, Megawati 333

Sun-hyuk, Kim 335

Sunflower 484

Sunflower Movement (Taiwan) 79, 336–7, 477–8, 480–2, 485

sustainability 269–70, 297, 299, 301, 384–5, 439–40, 445, 447–8, 520–1, 527–9; environmental 84, 86, 144; global corporate iniatives 525; long-term 273; of WISEs 385

Sustainable Development Goals 268, 271, 370, 444, 469, 471

Syngman Rhee (1948–1960) 34–5

TAF 103–5, 397–9; *see also* The Asia Foundation

Tai, Benny 481, 491

Taiwan 2–3, 5, 79–91, 333–4, 336, 362–3, 470, 477–8, 480–1, 488–9; authoritarian state of 87; cabinet building 479; central government of 85; and China 477–8; community activists 90; community-building in 3; community movement in relation to the state 86; constitution 82; and the controversial trade deal 480; and the Dali Community 88–9; democracy 336; government 79, 83–4, 378; and the government's agenda 84; history of 479; and Hong Kong 484–5; and Lin Yi-hsiung announced an indefinite hunger strike against the plant 480; and Ma Ying-jeou (President) 478; and the New Power Party 486; and the political influence of China 485; politics of 337; post-authoritarian 3, 79; post-authoritarian citizenship in 87; presidency of 478; process of democratization in 91; public opinion turned against the opening of the reactor 480; revitalized 478; sugar industry 88–9; and the Sunflower Movement 79, 336–7, 477–8, 480–2, 485; trajectory of civil society in 87; transition to democracy 334; urban 87

Taiwan Association of Human Rights 479

Taiwan International Workers Association 336

Taiwan Sugar Corporation 88–9

Tamang, Mukta S. 278–89

Tan, Alvin 53, 144, 153, 161–4, 168, 330, 333, 472

Tan, Kevin 164

Taneja, Pradee 236–45

Taneja, Pradeep 236–45

Tarrow, Sidney 339, 507

Tay, Simon 162, 164

Taylor, William 133–6, 440

Tewksury, David 422

Thailand 5–6, 9, 207–8, 215, 217, 219, 221, 223, 331, 339; democratic transitions in 331; evolution of civil society in 215, 223; expansion of international NGO activities in 217; growth of civil society in 215; nature of civil society in 215; recent political conflicts in 9; seafood farms in 440; surpassed by China as the biggest imnvestor in Laos 211; transformed from an absolute monarchy to a constitutional democracy 216; Yellow Shirts' CSOs in 339

third sector 1, 5, 12, 67, 362–72, 377, 380–1; in China 367; entities that are not part of the state and not part of the market 363; in Hong Kong 67; in India 363; made up of not-for-profit, often voluntary entities 363; organizations 5, 12, 67, 362–8, 370, 372; research 5, 362–3, 365–8, 370–1; in South Korea 364, 367; studies and research in he field of the 365–7; that are not part of the state and not part of the market 365; in Tokyo 368

Thompson, Mark 179, 197

Tigno 110–25; Jorge V. 110–25
TIWA 336; *see also* Taiwan International Workers
  Association
Tohti, Ilham 440
Tong, Irene 67, 438
Toyota Foundation 26, 392, 394, 398
Trade Unions Act (Malaysia) 146
Tria Kerkvliet, Ben 136
Tsai, Lily 330
Tsing, Anna 106
Tuaño, Phillip 123

UBINIG 273
UNDP (United National Development
  Programme) 11, 103, 210, 267, 370
Unger, Jonathan 50–1
United Sikhs 151
University and University Colleges Act (Malaysia)
  146
Uphoff, Norman 349, 354
Upton, Caroline 97, 105
US government 43, 493, 495–7, 499
US military personnel 11, 505–8, 510–13, 516
USAID (United States Agency for International
  Development) 11, 103, 267, 270

Vala, Carsten 60
Vanna, Nil 195
Veg, Sebastian 483, 486
Vercseg, Ilona 269
Vickers, Edward 481
Vientiane 206–7, 210–11
Viet Nam Farmers' Association 131
Viet Nam Fatherland Front 131
Viet Nam Veterans Association 131
Viet Nam Women's Union 131
Vietnam 129–35, 137, 142, 192–3, 206–7, 211,
  350–8, 363–4, 439–40, 488–9; case studies in 9;
  and the Citizens Committee for Peace in 24;
  civil society in 7; civil society organizations in
  130; and the issuing of legal documents 130;
  seafood farms in 440; and the spread of many
  new formal and informal associations 129; and
  Thailand 211; and the Viet Nam Fatherland
  Front 131; and the voices against nuclear
  energy 12
Vietnam Communist Party 129, 344
Vietnam War 24, 35, 206
Vietnamese 7, 130–1, 133, 137–9, 353–4, 356–7;
  authoritarian political regime 138; communists
  206; constitutions 130; CSOs 7; government

132; invasion 436; NGOs 134, 138; officials
  132; security apparatus 353
Vogel, Ezra F. 512

Wangchuck, King Jigme Dorji 294
Wangchuck, King Jigme Singye 294
Warren, Mark 348, 410
Watanabe, Chika 407–17
Wedel, Janine 96
Weeks, Brian E. 429
Weiss, Meredith L. 143–6, 148, 151, 371
Wells-Dang, Andrew 135, 192, 356
Welsh, Bridget 146, 149
Western democracies 33, 96, 98–9, 206, 212
White, Gordon 51, 66, 175–6, 179, 460
Wijeysingha, Vincent 165
Wilson, Ian 178, 184–6, 520
Wischermann, Jörg 129–39, 344–58
WISEs 5, 379–80, 382–3, 385–6; *see also* Work
  Integration Social Enterprises
women, and NGOs 147, 370–1
women's groups 19, 23–4, 82, 144, 147, 260, 446
women's movements 283, 365, 370, 445; in Asia
  445; contemporary 445; identifiable national
  365; strong 446; transnational 147
women's organizations 18, 370–1, 473, 507–8,
  511; international 371; in Okinawa 508, 512;
  protesting 505; voluntary 370
Wong, Joshua 74, 153–4, 162, 472, 481–3
Work Integration Social Enterprises 5, 379–80,
  382–3, 385–6
Wright, Scott 423, 478

Xiaoping, Deng 49

Yamamoto, Tadashi 18, 21, 26, 28, 399, 408, 492
Yang, Guobin 51, 82–4, 364–5, 427, 440, 460
Yangon 232, 234, 334
Yee, Yeong Chong 492
Yellow Butterfly Festival 83
Yeo, Andrew 36, 41–2, 507–8
Ying-jeou, Ma (President) 478
youth activism 1, 11, 477, 479, 481, 483, 485; and
  the "Arab Spring" 477; capacity for 481;
  histories of Asian 11; and the Hong Kong
  Umbrella Movement 11, 74–5, 439–40, 477,
  480–2, 484–5; Japanese 483; and Japan's
  SEALDs 477; and the Sunflower Movement
  79, 336–7, 477–8, 480–2, 485
youth activists 480–1, 483, 486
Yue, Audrey 470, 472